Introduction to the Science of Mental Health

Fr. Chad Ripperger, F.S.S.P., Ph.D.

Table of Contents

Vol. 1: Philosophical Psychology

Dedicated in Honor of
the Blessed Virgin Mary, Health of the Sick,
St. Thomas Aquinas
and
to St. Dymphna, Patroness of the Mentally Ill

Abbreviations

The following abbreviations are used in this text along with those abbreviations in use in standard English. Texts of Saint Thomas:[1]

Comm. de anima	*In Aristotelis Librum de Anima Commentarium*
Comp. Theol.	*Compendium Theologiae*
De anima	*Quaestiones Disputatae de Anima*
De causis	*In Librum de Causis*
De malo	*Quaestiones Disputatae de Malo*
De memoria	*In Libros de Memoria et Reminiscentia*
De Pot.	*Quaestiones Disputatae de Potentia*
De Spe	*Quaestiones Disputatae de Spe*
De spiritualibus creaturis	*Quaestiones Disputatae de Spiritualibus Creaturis*
De Ver.	*Quaestiones Disputatae de Veritate*
De Vir.	*Quaestiones Disputatae de Virtutibus*
In Ethic.	*In Decem Libros Ethicorum Aristotelis ad Nicomachum Expositio*
Meta.	*In Libros Metaphysicorum*
Quod.	*Quaestiones Quodlibetales*
Sent.	*In Quatuor Libros Sententiarum*[2]
SCG	*Summa Contra Gentiles*
ST	*Summa Theologiae*

Other texts:

CCC	*Catechism of the Catholic Church*[3]
CE	*Catholic Encyclopedia*[4]
CED	*Catholic Encyclopedia Dictionary*[5]
CIC/83	*Codex Iuris Canonici*[6]
SSP	*Summary of Scholastic Principles*[7]

---

[1] All citations from the works of St. Thomas are from *Thomae Aquinatis Opera Omnia*, Issu Impensaque Leonis XIII, edita, Roma: ex Typographia Polyglotta et al., 1882. All translations of St. Thomas are the author's own unless otherwise noted.

[2] Citations from the *Sentences* contain first the book number, then the abbreviation, followed by location within the book.

[3] Editio typica, Libreria Editrice Vaticana, 1997.

[4] The Gilmary Society, New York, 1913.

[5] The Gilmary Society, New York, 1941.

[6] *Code of Canon Law Annotated,* as edited by E. Cparros, M. Thériault and J. Thorn. Wilson & Lafleur Limitée, Montreal, 1993.

[7] Loyola University, 1951.

Acknowledgments

During my undergraduate years at the St. Ignatius Institute at the University of San Francisco, I began to reflect on the fact that modern psychology does not take into account the immaterial aspect of man. Much thought went into the various problems posed by the psychologists and a great deal of what is present in this text I realized almost twenty years ago. But at some point I decided not to write on the problems due to a lack of interest. While in the seminary, I provided a directed reading where the basic outline of the course ended up being remarkably similar to the outline of this text. Again, not much was done on the topic until almost ten years later. While meeting for the first time with Dr. John Thornbrugh, the Academic Dean of St. Gregory the Great Seminary, he asked if I had ever thought of doing a class on psychology in the modern sense. It was from that moment on that I began the process which eventually led to this text. It is for this reason that I have a profound gratitude to Dr. Thornbrugh whose encouragement, clarification during the review of the text and the disposition of my course work made it possible to complete this text.

I also have a profound gratitude to Bishop Fabian Bruskewitz for taking the time to write the foreword for the text and for arranging for a timely completion of the requirements for gaining the *imprimatur*. I also greatly appreciate the time and effort that Dr. Dennis McInerny expended to help clean up the text and to provide points of clarification which aided the readability of the text. Considering his course load and the other works which he has edited for me, this acknowledgment comes with profound gratitude. I thank John Saward whose close reading of the text provided very useful observations upon which important modifications were made to the text, resulting in a more accurate expression of my thought and reality itself. I also thank Keith Fick for the preparation of the diagram at the end of the text as well as for his review of the text. I am also indebted to Penny Thornbrugh who aided in the grammatical aspects of the text. I also thank Dr. Patrick DiVietri for reviewing the text as well as providing helpful information pertaining to the issues of music, the subconscious and the practical aspects of psychology. I am indebted to additional reviewers not yet mentioned who helped to provide import points of improvement for the text, viz. Sandra Fick, Luke Niewald Anthony Alt and John Belmont.

Lastly, as an act of devotion, I thank St. Thomas Aquinas whose writing and clarity of thought have proven to be a great source of joy in my pursuit of the virtue of science.

Foreword

Our Lord and Savior Jesus Christ warned us about what would happen if we do not base our endeavors on Him and His Eternal Truth. It will be "like a fool who built his house on sand. The rain fall, the floods came, and the winds blew and buffeted the house. And it collapsed and was completely ruined " (Matthew 7:26-27).

This applies especially to the science of modern psychology. Since it does not have a solid foundation in an authentic view of man, modern psychology is doomed to be "swept away" to the scrap heap of futility. As Fr. Ripperger argues in his book, modern psychology has made little real progress in helping the mentally ill because it has no true understanding of the immaterial, spiritual dimension of man's nature. Since the science of psychology starts with faulty premises about what constitutes mental health, it cannot help but produce useless and sometimes even harmful theories and remedies for mental illness. "Garbage in, garbage out" as the expression goes. In his book *Introduction to the Sciences of Mental Health and Illness, Volume 1: Philosophical Psychology*, Fr. Ripperger lays a foundation for the integration of principles of philosophical realism into the science of psychology. What he has done in his book is to give somewhat of a "primer" on basic philosophical principles of St. Thomas Aquinas with regards to the nature of the mind and soul of man. Fr. Ripperger's work explains the design of man's spiritual nature, and how a true understanding of it can provide valuable insights into psychological care, as well as illuminate potential pitfalls. He explains the various powers and faculties of man and provides clues for the psychologist that will help him as he renders care to his patient.

While the book is not an exhaustive treatment of the subject of the philosophy of man, it does a good job of tying together various parts of St. Thomas' thought and shows how necessary it is as a proper foundation for the science of psychology. Fr. Ripperger's book is very scholarly with extensive footnotes, showing the psychologist where to go for further exploration of the topics contained. In his work, Fr. Ripperger has provided an excellent starting point for the building of the science of psychology on a solid foundation. We should hope and pray that psychologists will listen.

Most Reverend Fabian W. Bruskewitz
Bishop of Lincoln

William Kirk Kilpatrick, in his book *Psychological Seduction,* addresses the problem of the failure of modern psychology to effect mental health. He is not the only one who is testifying to the failure of modern psychology; the books and articles supporting the same thesis tend to increase by the year. Yet, amongst all the criticism, there is a certain segment of the psychological community which seems to recognize there is a problem and they are addressing it. For instance, Conrad Baars and Anna Terruwe have published a great deal in trying to bring a more Thomistic approach to the science of psychology. However, their use of Thomistic anthropology is less than systematic and their actual use of Thomistic principles seems to be lacking in their practical applications as written in their texts, perhaps due to an incomplete explication of Thomistic principles. The work is important and valuable, however, because it is a good attempt to found a psychological praxis in a sound anthropology and, in that sense, it has helped the psychological community to begin seeking a proper direction in their science.

Yet, psychology did not start down the road which led it to a view which is incompatible with any sound understanding of man. Franz Brentano, who is considered by some to be the father of modern psychology, used Aristotle as the basis of his psychology.[1] However, shortly after Brentano did his work, the psychological community went another direction by embracing an anthropology and method which had a very different view of the nature of man. The psychological community embraced writers such as Freud, Jung and Watson whose view of man was not much more than materialistic and whose theories, even though often touted as "scientific," had very little basis in an empirical method or in sound philosophy.

Later, in the Catholic community, writers began addressing certain issues brought up by the modern psychological schools. Writers such as Rudolf Allers, Robert Brennan, James Royce and others began working on psychology in a way that was compatible with an authentic philosophical anthropology. Yet, none ever completed a systematic look at the very nature of psychology. One of Brennan's primary contributions was to show how modern science regarding the brain was compatible with Thomistic understanding of the various cognitive faculties of man. However, Brennan, as well as some of the other Catholics working in the area of psychology, was too quick to adopt the terminology of modern psychology. There appears among these writers a preoccupation to address modern psychologists on their own terms rather than seeking to transform modern psychology into a science compatible with an authentic view of man. It almost appears as if there is an attempt to justify the realist view of man to those who hold modern psychological theories. His work, nevertheless, is exceedingly important, even today as most of his conclusions are still accurate. His works should be

[1] It is unfortunate that Franz Brentano lapsed into heresy. This may be why, in the Catholic community, his psychological works were not studied with any seriousness. While his psychology is incomplete and problematic in points, it was a good start, despite his theological errors.

necessary reading in any psychology curriculum.

Rudolf Allers' work was also of great value. His work, primarily on character, provided a valuable look at the volitional building of character in order to act well (i.e. to avoid psychological problems and bad behavior). While not all of his conclusions are acceptable in a more systematic and Thomistic approach to man, his work provided a direction for psychology which, with some modification, could have provided a sound basis for psychological counseling. One thing that is apparent in his writing is that his work presumes a philosophical knowledge not had by most psychologists. Many of his works are being republished, some of them not requiring a philosophical foundation, yet there are others which require a great deal of philosophical background. To the philosophically unknowledgeable reader, his appears to be a system without a foundation. Part of the reason for this method of writing appears to be historical, insofar as he wrote his works in a period in which educated Catholics had enough philosophical background to understand the source of his conclusions.

The difficulty was, particularly in the Catholic community, a lack of a systematic approach to a fully developed science of mental health. The historical result of this, in the Catholic community, was a later invasion of modern psychologies into virtually every area of Catholic life, which were at variance with an authentic Catholic anthropology. While there are some Catholic psychologists working on a psychology which is compatible with an authentic view of man, the work seems to be progressing very slowly, if at all, even though the desire to advance the science of mental health is not lacking.

This book does not claim to answer all of the questions about psychology. Nor does it claim even to treat adequately the topics it does present. Its goal is to provide an initial impetus to founding a science of mental health on Thomistic philosophy, both in theory and in practice. This book should not be seen as a substitute for an in-depth formal education in philosophy, rather it is meant primarily as a pointer toward those things which must be studied by any serious psychologist.[2] It is, moreover, designed to provide an initial understanding of basic philosophical tenets in order to provide a direction for further study and development of the field.

---

[2]This is why the footnotes are somewhat extensive and numerous. They are intended as a guide for those who wish to investigate in greater depth the various topics covered.

Part I: The Proper Understanding of a Valid Psychology

Chapter 1: The Nature of the Science of Psychology

If a science is defined as an organized body of knowledge of things through their causes,[1] then the goal of any science of psychology must, by its very nature, be to arrive at the causes of mental health and illness. But this presupposes knowledge of the intellect itself as well as those faculties which may have some influence on the intellect. Moreover, it is apparent that modern psychology has not fully grasped the nature of the intellect itself since it has not been able to provide an accurate or complete definition of mental illness. Before any science engages in an investigation of its proper object, it is necessary to know those things which constitute each science in general in order to be certain that one's science is engaging its object properly. In other words, one must know those things which are required for each science to be certain that the particular science under question fulfills the requirements necessary to comprise any valid science. Given the aforesaid, this chapter will consider the following: 1) what comprises each science; 2) what principles must be accepted in any valid science of psychology and finally 3) what things comprise a valid science of psychology and some subsequent distinctions in order to limit the scope of this book.

I. The Constituents of Every Science

The intellect of man is fundamentally designed to know the truth and knowledge of the truth either pertains to his practical intellect or his speculative intellect.[2] "The speculative has for an end the truth which it considers, while the practical directs the truth considered to an activity as to an end."[3] The practical intellect seeks knowledge for the sake of action whereas the speculative intellect considers truth for its own sake. Thus, the science of metaphysics studies the existences of things for the sake of the knowledge itself. Ethics or morals, on the other hand, seeks knowledge for the sake of acting in accordance with the knowledge it grasps.

When considering the objects of the practical and speculative intellects, we see that every valid science has three constituents, viz. the material object, the formal object and the method. The material object of a science is the subject matter or the thing the science studies. Hence, one science is different from another insofar as its object of study differs from the other sciences,[4] e.g. biology studies living things and chemistry studies chemical reactions. Since the sciences are divided according to their objects,

---

[1] See SCG I, c. 94, n. 3 and Aristotle, *Posterior Analytics* (as found in *The Basic Works of Aristotle*, ed. by Richard McKeon, Random House, New York, 1941), I, 2 (71b10).

[2] These are not two different faculties in man, but the same intellect considered from the point of view of its different objects of consideration.

[3] *De trinitate*, p. 3, q. 5, a. 1: "speculativus habet pro fine veritatem quam considerat, practicus vero veritatem consideratam ordinat in operationem tamquam in finem."

[4] Ibid.: "et ideo oportet scientias speculativas dividi per differentias speculabilium, in quantum speculabilia sunt."

there are practical sciences, such as ethics, ergonomics, etc., and there are speculative[5] sciences, such as philosophy and astrophysics. The various speculative sciences are therefore based on their different objects or subject matters.

It may happen that one science studies something from another science and regarding this St. Thomas makes the following observation:

> One science is contained under another in two ways, in one way, as its part, because its subject is part of the subject of that other science, as plant is a certain part of natural body. Hence the science of plants is also contained under the natural science as a part. In another way, one science is contained under another as subalternated to it, when, namely, in a higher science there is given the reason for what a lower science only knows as fact, as music is contained under arithmetic.[6]

Here St. Thomas is noting that a science is under another in two ways. The first is when one science is a branch of another broader science, since it only studies a part of the other science, e.g. inorganic chemistry is a branch of the broader science of chemistry. The second way is when one science is subalternated to another science and by this St. Thomas means that the one science receives its principles from another science, e.g., the science of epistemology receives its principles from philosophical anthropology, logic and metaphysics. Therefore, in the consideration of the subject matter of the science, one must also consider if it is a branch of a broader science, i.e. if a science studies a subject matter which is covered at least in part by another science which considers the object of study more absolutely. In this case, the higher science[7] will supply the lower

---

[5]The term speculative is not to be understood as it is in modern parlance, viz. something of opinion or which is not based on fact or systematic investigation. Speculation is a philosophical term which refers to the process of reasoning by which we arrive at the knowledge of the truth about something. It is based on experience of reality and employs rules of reasoning (logic) in order to arrive at certain knowledge of its object. Outside the philosophical sciences, this term usually refers to formulating a theory or opinion based on uncertain facts or lacking all of the facts and therefore reaches a conclusion which is uncertain. This is not the case in scholastic philosophy.

[6]Ibid., ad 5:"aliqua scientia continetur sub alia dupliciter, uno modo ut pars ipsius, quia scilicet subiectum eius est pars aliqua subiecti illius, sicut planta est quaedam pars corporis naturalis; unde et scientia de plantis continetur sub scientia naturali ut pars. Alio modo continetur una scientia sub alia ut ei subalternata, quando scilicet in superiori scientia assignatur propter quid eorum, de quibus scitur in scientia inferiori solum quia, sicut musica ponitur sub arithmetica."

[7]A science is a higher science the more abstractly or the more completely it considers its subject matter in comparison to another. So, for instance, philosophy of man is a higher science than epistemology since it studies man in a more complete and abstract manner than epistemology, which only studies a part of man, viz. how his intellect comes to true knowledge.

science with conclusions about the object of study and that science assumes those conclusions as principles in its reasoning.[8] The subject matter in philosophy is called the material object.

The second of the three constituents of every science is the formal object. The question of the formal object arose because some sciences study the same thing and so the question is what makes them different. St. Thomas makes the following observation:

> Although the subjects of the other sciences are parts of being, which is the subject of metaphysics, nevertheless, it is not necessary that the other sciences are its parts. For each of the sciences treats one part of being according to a special mode of consideration other than the way in which it is considered in metaphysics. Hence, properly speaking, its subject is not part of the subject of metaphysics; for it is not part of being according to that point of view from which being is the subject of metaphysics, but considered from this point of view, it is a special science distinct from the others.[9]

St. Thomas is noting two things of importance: the first is that one science can differ from another science by the point of view (*ratio*) the respective sciences take. Hence, the philosophical science of nature differs from the empirical sciences of natural things by virtue of the fact that they look at the same things from different points of view. The philosophical science of nature considers physical things from the point of view of their

---

[8]St. Thomas observes that the division of sciences is threefold. The first division treats what is in matter and in motion and this pertains to physics. Here, physics is to be understood according to its Greek derivation, i.e. it studies those things which are part of nature. Hence, in a modern context, this would include all of the empirical sciences and the philosophy of nature. The second division of the sciences is that which treats of what is without matter or motion of that which is in matter, i.e. mathematics. For Aquinas, mathematics would be what is called today geometry insofar as geometry considers things which exist in reality but is not concerned with the actually existing thing as such, e.g. it considers how one can calculate angles based on knowledge of the length of the sides of a triangle, even though it is not looking at a specific triangular thing, like a child's building block. Modern mathematics actually employs both geometry and aspects of the empirical science of physics. The last division of the sciences is that which considers those things that are neither in matter nor in motion and this pertains to the science of metaphysics which considers the nature of being as such. These three divisions are seen in *De trinitate*.

[9]Ibid., ad 6: "quamvis subiecta aliarum scientiarum sint partes entis, quod est subiectum metaphysicae, non tamen oportet quod aliae scientiae sint partes ipsius. Accipit enim unaquaeque scientiarum unam partem entis secundum specialem modum considerandi alium a modo, quo consideratur ens in metaphysica. Unde proprie loquendo subiectum illius non est pars subiecti metaphysicae; non enim est pars entis secundum illam rationem, qua ens est subiectum metaphysicae, sed hac ratione considerata ipsa est specialis scientia aliis condivisa."

essences whereas the empirical sciences are not interested in the essences of things as such, but some part of the things, e.g. chemistry studies the various elements and how they react, biology considers cellular structures and their interrelations, etc. The perspective or point of view (*ratio*) taken within each science is called the formal object.[10]

The second thing of importance is regarding the method. St. Thomas notes that each science treats a thing in a special way which means that each science has a different method of proceeding which is proper to that science.[11] Moreover, it also means that the way we look at the subject matter, i.e. formal object, determines the method of proceeding, e.g. philosophy does not proceed in the same manner as empirical sciences which use physical tests to arrive at its conclusions. Rather, its method is proportionate to its object, e.g. the objects of metaphysics do not admit of an empirical method and therefore demand a different method.[12] Therefore, we must be clear that the method must be proportionate to the perspective or subject matter and this is likewise dependent upon the point of view taken. We must also clearly understand that the formal object,

---

[10]Here an observation must be made regarding the prejudice of the empirical sciences in reference to the philosophical sciences. Since a science is defined as an organized body of knowledge of things through their causes, then philosophy which studies the essences and causes of things is just as much a science as the empirical sciences. In fact, it is more of a science because it studies the essence and nature of causality as such which is completely beyond the scope of the empirical sciences. Moreover, since philosophy studies the nature of causes, the empirical sciences are dependent upon philosophy to tell them the nature of causality. Without a working presupposition about what causality is, the empirical sciences are incapable of engaging their proper method. Therefore, just because philosophy uses a different method and takes a different point of view to the objects which empirical sciences study does not make it any less of a science.

[11]Ergo, it must *not* be assumed that the empirical method is the only valid scientific method. While it may be used in all of the empirical sciences adjusted to each subject matter, nevertheless, philosophy is a science which proceeds in a different manner than the empirical sciences, but that does not make it any less accurate or inferior. In fact, it is the opposite since the more abstract and therefore universal one considers an object, the more noble that consideration will be and therefore the method of philosophy is more noble than the method of the empirical sciences.

[12]Empirical scientists should also avoid assuming that the empirical method is the only valid method of proceeding for any science whatsoever. While the empirical method is proper to its own material object, it is not proper to philosophy which is also a valid science. Very often, empirical sciences try to reformulate the definition of a science in order to exclude philosophy (and theology) from being considered sciences. However, such a motion on their part is inherently contradictory, for the formulation of the definition of a science is not open to the empirical method and therefore to give a true formal definition requires one to engage in philosophy. So either empirical scientists accept that philosophy is a science or they are left with the unseemly prospect of not having a "scientific" definition of science itself.

the point of view, must be proportionate to the subject matter which ultimately determines the proportionality of the method to the object.

Considering the aforesaid, we can now move to the third constituent of a science and that is the method. The method is defined as the mode of proceeding within a given science; it answers the question "how" (*quomodo* in Latin) the science investigates the object under consideration. Since the method is governed or determined by the object, both formal and material, there will be different methods of proceeding based upon the different objects of consideration. The empirical sciences begin with an induction[13] (formulation of a hypothesis), deduce certain things from the hypothesis, confirm or deny the hypothesis based on experimentation and then reformulate the hypothesis, if need be, based on data received from the confirmation stage of the method. The philosophical method varies with the material object but it does not contain the confirmation stage even though its knowledge of the object is drawn from things as they exist in reality and its conclusions can be judged to be true or not by looking at the object in reality.[14] Therefore, each science will have a method proper to its object.

II. The Principles of a Valid Psychology

A. Material Object, Formal Object and Method

One of the fundamental misunderstandings of modern psychology relates to its material object. Since the Thomistic/realist understanding of man is that man is a composite of body and soul,[15] we have reached our first fundamental difference with the way modern psychology views man. Modern psychology views man as nothing more

---

[13]By virtue of the fact that empirical sciences begin with an induction, they can never have absolute certitude in their conclusions. This follows from the fact that the conclusions are drawn from the premises, and one of the premises, which is the hypothesis, is not absolutely certain. Therefore, since one cannot assert in a conclusion what is denied or lacking in the premises, one cannot make absolutely certain assertions or conclusions when the premises do not provide it.

[14]The various philosophical methods are explicated by St. Thomas in *De trinitate*, p. 3, q. 6, a. 1.

[15]Aquinas discusses this in ST I, q. 76; SCG II, c. 56; *De anima* a. 1 and 2. Also, the Council of Vienne formally condemns the position that: "substantia animae rationalis seu intellectivae vere ac per se humani corporis non sit forma" ("the substance of the rational or intellective soul truly and per se is not the form of the human body" -- Henricus Denzinger and Adulfus Schönmetzer, *Enchridion Symbolorum Definitionum et Declarationum de rebus Fidei et Morum*, [Herder, Friburgus, 1976, henceforth, Denz.] 902 [481]). Essentially speaking a Catholic must hold that the soul is the substantial form of the body and that man is a composite of body and soul. See also Ludwig Ott, *Fundamentals of Catholic Dogma* (TAN Books and Publishers, Inc., Rockford, Illinois, 1974), p. 97.

than a physical or material thing.[16] However, since the faculties of man reside in the body and soul composite or in the soul alone, and since the intellect is one of these faculties, any valid psychology must recognize that its object of study is not merely material. Rather, man's intellect has three parts, two of which are immaterial and perform their functions independently of the body. Psychology has for its primary material object the intellect of man, for the science of mental health essentially studies the human intellect. But since the human intellect depends on other faculties for its knowledge and since other faculties can have a direct and indirect effect on the intellect, psychology studies secondarily those things and faculties of man which affect the human intellect. Some of those faculties are likewise immaterial (e.g. the will) and this must also be kept in mind regarding the material object of psychology. It is because modern psychology has departed from a proper understanding of man's ontological constitution that it has not had much success in curing modern man's psychological illnesses.

The formal object is the point of view taken toward the material object and since psychology has as its primary concern mental health, then its point of view or *ratio* will be from the perspective of health. Therefore, in a secondary fashion, psychology will look at those faculties and things which affect the health of the intellect. This is what essentially separates it from epistemology, for epistemology studies the human intellect from the point of view of how it knows rather than from the point of view of its health. Moreover, psychology also differs from the philosophy of man insofar as it considers only a part of man, i.e. the intellect and those things which affect the intellect, as well as things outside of man which affect the intellect.[17]

The method will essentially be philosophical. For since the method must be proportionate to the material object as governed by the formal object, then psychology must be a philosophical science. This follows from the fact that only a philosophical science is capable of addressing immaterial entities. The empirical sciences by their

---

[16]Consider the following passage of John Watson (*Psychology as the Behaviorist Views It* as found in *Classics in Psychology*, ed. By Thorne Shiply, Philosophical Library, Inc., New York, 1961, p. 798): "Psychology as the behaviorist views it is a purely objective experimental branch of natural science. Its theoretical goal is the prediction and control of behavior. Introspection forms no essential part of its methods, nor is the scientific value of its data dependent upon the readiness with which they lend themselves to interpretation in terms of consciousness. The behaviorist, in his efforts to get a unitary scheme of animal response, recognizes no dividing line between man and brute. The behavior of man, with all of its refinement and complexity, forms only a part of the behaviorist's total scheme of investigation." Modern psychology which had its beginnings with Franz Brentano did not begin with this conception of man. It originally began with the conception that man was a composite of body and soul and later psychologists began the move away from this notion until recently man is viewed as a purely material being no different from an animal.

[17]This qualification helps to avoid the problem in many modern empirical sciences which seek to make their own science the explanation for all things. Since psychology only covers a part of man, it does not discuss the whole of man and therefore is not as noble a science as the philosophy of man, nor does it explain everything about man.

very nature require that their objects be physical or material since they must, during the confirmation stage, perform some sort of test or experiment which can only be done on material things. Since the intellect of man is both material and immaterial, psychology can only legitimately employ a philosophical method, for only a philosophical method is proportionate to the material and formal objects of psychology. The method, therefore, proceeds essentially by induction[18] and deduction[19] which are the proper methods of philosophy. It is inductive because, in order to discuss mental health, one must first understand the nature of man and his faculties, which are apprehended through induction. Moreover, certain aspects of man are understood or reasoned out by deduction as well. Therefore, psychology will essentially employ a philosophical method by which it reasons to the nature of mental health, mental illness, the proper relationships of the faculties of man to the intellect, those things which affect mental health and illness outside of man, as well as how mental health will be gained or lost.

B. Additional Principles of the Science of Psychology

To fill out our understanding of how psychology proceeds, we must remember what goes into each science. Since a science is an organized body of knowledge of a thing through its causes, psychology will have as its primary task the understanding of the intellect of man from the point of view of its health and illness and the causes of that health or illness. However, before one can adequately discuss the proper subject matter of this science, he must have the prerequisite knowledge of those things which can affect the intellect. Psychology is a subalternated science since it receives its first principles as conclusions (facts) from other sciences. Psychology is subalternated first and foremost to the philosophy of man since it receives its understanding about man's nature and the nature of man's faculties from this science. This is perhaps modern psychology's most notable failing, for it has proceeded in its science by rejecting those principles which are proper to a Thomistic/realist philosophy of man.[20] Since it did not

---

[18]Induction is defined as a form of philosophical reasoning in which the conclusion does not necessarily follow from the premises and the certainty of the conclusion is based upon the amount of support provided by the premises; it is a form of argumentation in which one proceeds from the particular to the general.

[19]Deduction is defined as a form of logical reasoning in which the conclusion necessarily follows from the premises; it is a form of argumentation in which one proceeds from the general to the particular.

[20]The Church has repeatedly pointed philosophers in the direction of Thomism, e.g. see: Leo XIII, *Aeterni Patris*, passim, but especially paras. 21, 25 and 33; Pope St. Pius X, *Pascendi Dominici Gregis*, para. 45; CIC/83 can. 252, §3 and Sacred Congregation For Catholic Education, *Ratio Fundamentalis*, paras. 79 and 86. One can safely assume that by basing a psychology on the principles and teachings of St. Thomas one is not going to go too far afield. In considering the various philosophers, Aquinas seems to provide the best understanding and penetration into the nature of man, his faculties and their actions and objects.

begin with a clear philosophical understanding of the nature of man and his faculties, it was bound to err. Since psychology is a subalternated science, it must assume its first principles from other sciences and modern psychologists assumed the wrong principles. For that reason, the method of modern psychology was not proportionate to its object because it did not understand the object of its inquiry. Moreover, it assumed an empiricist conception of man without giving sufficient reason for doing so and these presumptions led to its errors.[21]

Moreover, while modern psychology erroneously thought that, by aligning itself with the empirical method, it would have a respectability in the scientific community since it was an empirical science, nevertheless, it constantly made philosophical statements about the nature of man and his faculties. For example, Freud and Jung's theories of the unconscious or subconscious are incapable of being proven empirically and yet to discuss the nature of the subconscious or unconscious required inductions and deductions without a confirmatory stage and that is nothing other than the philosophical method. To make the statements many psychologists did about man requires philosophical training and knowledge of the method which they neither had nor employed properly.

In addition to being subalternated to the philosophy of man, psychology is also subalternated to metaphysics, for it is proper to metaphysics to discuss what is not in matter nor in motion.[22] Since the intellect, will and other faculties in man are spiritual, at least *in radice* if not entirely, then only metaphysics can adequately discuss their nature. Moreover, concepts and volitional movements are immaterial entities which can only be addressed by the science of metaphysics. Since God and angels can have an effect on the operations of the intellect and other faculties which can be known through the natural light of reason,[23] then only metaphysics can draw the proper conclusions which are used as principles in psychology.

Psychology is subalternate to logic insofar as logic is the art and science of right reasoning and in order for the intellect to be healthy, it will have to comply with the principles of logic. Moreover, psychology will be subalternated to epistemology since that science tells us the nature of man's knowledge, his intellect and how he knows.

---

[21]Modern psychology is proof of the Aristotelian dictum: "A small error in the beginning becomes great in the end" (*De caelo* I, 5 [271b8-13]). Since they assumed the wrong principles which were their premises, they could only draw the wrong conclusions.

[22]See *De trinitate*, p. 3, q. 5, a. 4.

[23]The fact that man can arrive at knowledge of God by the natural light of reason is formally defined at Vatican I (*Filius Deus*, chap. 2 [Denz. 3004 (1785)]): "Eadem sancta Ecclesia tenet et docet, Deum, rerum omnium principium et finem, naturali humanae rationis lumine e rebus creatis certo cognosci possi" and (Ibid. canons 2. De revelatione, n. 1 (Denz. 3026 [1806])): "Si quis dixerit, Deum unum et verum, creatorem et Dominum nostrum, per ea, quae facta sunt, naturali rationis humanae lumine certo cognosci no posse: anathema sit." Aquinas argues to the existence of God, His attributes and His being a Creator through the natural light of reason in SCG I & II.

It will be subalternated to ethics insofar as ethics treats of the appetites and their right ordering and how they affect morally right or wrong behavior.

Finally, a full understanding of how man can gain and lose mental health cannot be understood without a serious consideration of how spiritual realities affect the operation of the faculties. While these can be considered in general in metaphysics, the actual operations of things like grace, the sacraments, the demonic, etc. can only be understood in light of revealed theology. We come to an important point in understanding, therefore, what a full psychology will entail. A complete science of psychology will include both what is known through the natural light of reason as well as what is known through the light of faith. While the natural[24] science of psychology can define mental illness and health and their causes, a full understanding of those causes can only be grasped when theological principles are likewise accepted. While there is not and cannot be a theological science of mental health,[25] nevertheless the material object of the natural science of psychology will not be fully grasped without an understanding of theological principles. While psychology is essentially a natural science and as a natural science is a science in its own right, the full understanding of psychology will not be achieved without theology playing a part.

C. Modern Psychiatry

Modern psychiatry has a valid basis for its method. While modern psychology is akin to alchemy in that it is not a valid science because it does not understand its object properly, modern psychiatry does have a sound basis as a science. As a subalternated science to psychology, it must accept the valid conclusions of psychology regarding what the faculties are, what their proper actions are and how they are composed. But part of psychology is a clear recognition that there is a material part of man's intellect and, as material, it can be affected by the various physical agents, such as chemicals, physical damage caused by pathological and non-pathological causes, etc. Since the study of these things is proper to an empirical science, it is not proper to psychology as such to investigate them. Therefore, there must be a science which does investigate the material operations of the brain as such.

This means that what is natural and proper to the material intellect will come generically from psychology, whereas how that works itself out chemically or biologically comes from psychiatry. For example, what the emotions are is properly and universally grasped by psychology (or more properly the philosophy of man), yet psychiatry can help us a great deal in understanding the chemical processes which accompany and affect the emotions. Moreover, while philosophy may discuss the acts of the passive intellect, since the faculty is partly material, it pertains to psychiatry to localize the parts of the passive intellect. Once psychology determines which activities

---

[24]The term natural here does not refer to an empirical science but a natural science as counter distinguished from a supernatural science.

[25]Why this is the case will be discussed at the beginning of Volume II.

of the passive intellect are appropriate, modern psychiatry can set about determining what chemical and biological dispositions are necessary for those functions to occur on a physical level. It pertains, however, to psychology to determine what is proper to the various physical faculties in general, although not chemically or biologically, since the faculties of man which are physical are part of a faculty which is both material and immaterial. Therefore, only psychology can grasp the whole nature of the faculty and that understanding is to be passed on to psychiatry which can then set about determining what is normal on a purely physical level.

Finally, psychology is much like ethics in that ethics, for Aquinas, is essentially a practical science. Nevertheless, there are certain speculative aspects to ethics, and this is true of psychology as well. Psychology is also analogous to the science and art of medicine. One must first study one's object scientifically before one practices medicine. Psychology, therefore, is both speculative and practical. It is speculative insofar as it strives for the knowledge of what mental health and illness and their causes are. While possessing this knowledge is a perfection in itself, nevertheless, psychology also has a practical role since the conclusions in the speculative part are applied in the practical part in order to achieve three things: 1) to provide the knowledge necessary to help those who have mental health maintain it; 2) to understand mental illness and its causes so as to be able to diagnose mental illness in those who have it and to determine what are the causes of those mental illnesses; 3) to provide the knowledge and other forms of help to aid those who are mentally ill, once properly diagnosed, to achieve mental health.

D. Modern Psychology

What then of all the work of modern psychology? Is it all to be considered for nought? The answer is obviously in the negative; even St. Thomas observed that no man is completely devoid of the truth and so the question shifts to what good things has modern psychology accomplished? Clearly, one of the achievements of modern psychology has been the classification of symptoms as demonstrated in the current text DSM IV.[26] Moreover, modern psychology has told us a great deal about what most people think and do by means of statistical analysis and this has its place in psychology.

However, before we can fully grasp the symptoms which are the effects of mental illness, we must first grasp what mental illness is, but that has been completely wanting in modern psychology. Because modern psychology does not understand its material object, psychology has not made much sense in its classification of all the psychological disorders. Moreover, it has failed to arrive at what mental health actually is and this makes it impossible really to know if the average man is doing what is right. Just because everyone in a society is engaging in certain types of behavior does not make those behaviors psychologically good. Here, psychology, assuming that man was purely physical and therefore was just a product of physical laws, failed to recognize

---

[26]The assertion here is that modern psychology has had some success in the area of diagnosis. It should not be assumed, however, that every form of classification of symptoms and causes is accurate.

than man can act contrary to his nature. And even if an entire society is engaging in a behavior which is not in congruity with man's nature, that behavior is not normal. While statistics can tell me what the *average* or *majority of people* are doing, it does not provide the *norm*.

It is only within the context of understanding the nature of Original Sin grasped through revealed theology, and the nature of man as such grasped by philosophy, that we arrive at the explanation of the difference between what the average man does and what constitutes the norm. Since man is affected by Original Sin, most men commit sins, but that does not mean that sins are natural. If they are not natural, how can they be the norm for psychologically good behavior? How can they be a sign of mental health? While these questions will be discussed, nevertheless, modern psychology has not been successful because it did not understand its object and therefore what is proper to it. We should not conclude, however, that everything modern psychology did was wrong or of no benefit. However, we must judge the conclusions and work of modern psychology only after we have grasped the conclusions of a valid psychology and are thereby able to use those conclusions as principles to judge modern psychology

III. The Scope of the Current Volume

Considering the aforesaid, this volume will have as its scope the following. It will first discuss in detail the subalternate principles accepted from other philosophical sciences. It will then discuss the relationship of the various faculties and how they affect one another. It will discuss the nature of mental health and mental illness in themselves. Finally, it will draw some conclusions about how one loses and gains mental health in light of the discussion on how the various faculties affect one another as well as a threefold division of causes of mental health and illness. Since psychiatry is a subalternated science to psychology and therefore operates on its own and since the author is not competent in that field, psychiatry will not be a formal part of this study.[27] Given the scope of this volume, a subsequent volume will cover the theological principles which affect psychology. Moreover, since psychology also has a practical aspect to it, a final volume will consider certain applications of the principles in the previous two volumes as well as other questions not addressed in the first two volumes, thereby completing an introductory look into psychology.

---

[27]Since it is not the competence of the author to discuss in detail psychiatric aspects of mental health, it will not be the proper scope of this text. Nevertheless, examples will be employed throughout the book from psychiatry when they properly apply.

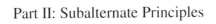

Part II: Subalternate Principles

Chapter 2: Ontological Structure of Man and His Acts

I. The Body/Soul Composite

The human supposit, viz. man, is composed of body and soul.[1] The body is the material element[2] in the composite and it individuates one person from another.[3] The soul is immaterial[4] and, consequently, immortal.[5] Soul is defined as " the first principle of life in those things which live among us"[6] and in the case of man who is a rational animal,[7] the soul is the substantial form of the body,[8] making the body to be a human body rather than some other thing. As the substantial form of the body, it has its own existence which it communicates to the body.[9]

II. Faculties

While the substance of man is a body/soul composite, man does not act through his substance[10] but through proper accidents[11] called faculties[12] and so the faculties are

---

[1]ST I, q. 76, a. 1; SCG II, cc. 56, 57, 59, 68, and 70; *Comm. de anima*, II, l. 4; ibid., III, l. 7; *De spiritualibus creaturis*, a. 2 and *De anima*, a. 1 and 2.

[2]*De ente et essentia*, c. 2, n. 6.

[3]Ibid., n. 11 and ST I, q. 76, a. 2.

[4]ST I, q. 75, a. 5; SCG II, c. 50; *De spiritualibus creaturis*, a. 1-3; *De anima*, a. 6 and Quod. III, q. 8, a. un.

[5]*De anima*, a. 14; ST I, q. 75, a. 6; II Sent., d. 19, a. 1; IV Sent., d. 50, q. 1, a. 1; SCG II, c. 75; Quod. X, q. 3, a. 2 and *Comp. Theol.* 84. Immortality is a proper conclusion to something being immaterial.

[6]ST I, q. 75, a. 1: "primum principium vitae in his quae apud nos vivunt."

[7]The definition of man as a rational animal is common to the school of philosophy. For an example of the discussion of man as an animal which is rational see Aristotle, *Politics*, l. 7, c. 13 (1332a42-1332b7).

[8]See references in footnote #1 of this chapter. Moreover, for Catholics, one cannot hold a position which rejects that the soul is the substantial form of the body as was noted in the prior chapter.

[9]ST I, q. 75, a.2; De Pot., q. 3, aa. 9 and 11; *Comm. de anima*, III, l. 7; *De spiritualibus creaturis*, a. 2 and *De anima*, a. 1 and 14.

[10]ST I, q. 77, a. 1; I Sent., d. 3, q. 4, a. 2; Quod. X, q. 3, a. 1; *De spiritualibus creaturis*, a. 11 and *De anima*, a. 12.

[11]A proper accident is an accident which always accompanies a given substance. Whenever a given substance exists, the accident is likewise present.

[12]See references to footnote #10 of this chapter. Faculties are also called powers or potencies.

those by which man acts. These proper accidents or faculties flow from the essence of the soul,[13] i.e. they are always present actually or at least *in principe vel radice*[14] as long as the soul exists. There are two kinds of faculties, those which are purely immaterial and therefore act independently of the body,[15] viz. the agent intellect, the possible intellect and the will, and those which are composed of a material element and an immaterial element,[16] e.g. sight, hearing, etc. Hence, faculties reside either in the body/soul composite or only in the soul.[17]

III. Specification of the Faculties

The faculties are ordered to and specified by their proper objects,[18] for a faculty is not ordered to every kind of object but "to that which the power essentially considers."[19] So the will is ordered to the good while the intellect is ordered to truth. All of the faculties are distinguishable from one another by virtue of their respective objects, e.g. the faculty of sight is ordered to the visible or colored while the concupiscible appetite is ordered toward the possession of bodily goods.

IV. Disposition

While each faculty has its proper object, sometimes the faculty relates to its object well and sometimes it does not. A disposition in a faculty occurs when the "matter is disposed to the reception of form"[20] or when "some agent is disposed to acting."[21] A disposition resides in the faculty and determines whether the faculty will act or be acted upon by its object well or poorly. So, for instance, some people have a concupiscible appetite that is more disposed towards its operation or towards its object than others. As a result, one man is more disposed than another toward eating excessively. The disposition affects the relationship the particular faculty has to its object and as a result

---

[13]ST I, q. 77, a. 6 and I Sent., d. 3, q. 4, a. 2.

[14]ST I, q. 77, a. 5, ad 1 and ibid., q. 77, a. 8. Those which are always actual are those which are purely spiritual, whereas those which are not always existing are those which while the supposit is whole, i.e. as long as man is alive and the material dimension of the faculties are whole, they are complete. Otherwise, they reside in the soul as a principle, unable to act due to something lacking in the material element by which they perform their functions, if the material element was present.

[15]ST I, q. 77, a. 6 and I Sent., d. 3, q. 4, a. 2.

[16]Ibid.

[17]Ibid.

[18]ST I, q. 77, a. 3; *Comm. de anima*, II, l. 6 and *De Anima*, a. 13.

[19]ST I, q. 77, a. 3: "ad quod per se potentia respicit."

[20]De Vir., q. 1, a. 1, ad 9: "materia disponitur ad formae receptionem."

[21]Ibid.: "aliquod agens disponitur ad agendum."

someone who has a bad disposition in the irascible appetite is more inclined to grow angry than someone who does not.

A disposition is the ability to effect or suffer something according to an innate readiness of something for certain kinds of activity. When a faculty is an active potency,[22] if it is disposed well, then it acts well and with facility; if the faculty is disposed poorly, that type of action is difficult even though it is able to perform it. For instance, someone with brain damage has a poorly disposed passive intellect and so his cogitative power does not associate well. Moreover, if the faculty is a passive potency, if it is disposed well, it will readily undergo the action proper to it. Whereas if it is disposed poorly, then it will find the action difficult or painful. For example, when one's finger tips are burned, they do not sense as well as when they are properly disposed.

V. Habits

A man can increase (or perfect) or decrease the inclination of some of his faculties towards certain objects by the actions he performs. When a disposition or quality[23] is increased or decreased by action, it is called a habit. A habit is an inclination towards a specific form of action and it aids the faculty in acting well or poorly in a given action.[24]

Habits are increased or decreased by action itself.[25] If the action is of the same species or form as the habit, then the habit increases in the faculty. If the action is contrary to the species or form of the habit[26] or if the action proper to the habit is

---

[22]A passive potency is one which has the capacity to undergo some form of change, whereas an active potency is one which has the capacity to perform some action or to place another thing in act.

[23]Aquinas refers to a habit as a quality primarily because there is a difference between a habit and a disposition (ST I-II, q. 49, 2, ad 3): "ex quo patet quod nomen habitus diuturnitatem quandam importat; non autem nomen dispositionis" ("from which it is clear that the name habit implies a certain long duration; not however the name of disposition"). Moreover, (ibid., q. 50, a. 6) "habitus...qui sunt dispositiones ad esse naturale, non sunt in angelis, cum sint immateriales" (habits which are dispositions to natural being, are not in angels, since they are immaterial"). While habit can be a disposition in things which have parts, viz. those things which are material, it is not a disposition in those things which do not have parts but is a quality. Hence, a habit in immaterial faculties is a quality rather than a disposition.

[24]De Ver., q. 20, a. 2 and ST I-II, q. 51, a. 1.

[25]ST I-II, q. 52, a. 3. This means that through one's actions one can ontologically change the disposition of the faculty. Hence, one can actually change oneself contrary to the position of the determinist schools of psychology. See Rudolf Allers, *The Psychology of Character* (Sheed and Ward, London, 1931), p. 10-21.

[26]ST I-II, q. 53, a. 1-3; ST I, q. 89, a. 5 and In Ethic. II, l. 2 and 3.

ceased,[27] then the habit is decreased or corrupted (i.e. lost). The increase and decrease of the habit is proportionate to the vehemence of the action performed.[28] If the vehemence of the action is less than the actualization of the habit in the faculty, then the habit will begin to decrease. If the habit is equal to the degree of act of the habit in the faculty, then the habit is maintained. If the action exceeds the act of the habit in the faculty, then it is increased. The habits correspond to a specific object as well[29] and so if the object is opposite in species to the habit present in the faculty, then the habit decreases. The amount of augmentation or diminution of the habit is proportionate to the vehemence of the action. For example, the concupiscible appetite can have a habit of inclining strongly towards the pleasures of sex and if the person engages in it repeatedly, the concupiscibile appetite grows in its disposition or "strength" in its movement in relation to that object. On the other hand, mortification is the opposite of bodily pleasure and so it can quiet the appetite's inclination, i.e. it can change its disposition. The faculty, therefore, resides in the soul, but the faculty can have a natural disposition towards its operation with respect to a specific object. The disposition or quality can be increased or decreased (at times, completely wiped away) by action which is the same in species or contrary in species to the disposition or quality.

VI. Virtues and Vices

Habits are distinguished between virtues and vices. A good habit is one which disposes the faculty towards a good action in relation to the faculty's proper object or action in congruity with the nature of the faculty,[30] and a good habit is called a virtue.[31] A bad habit is one which disposes the faculty towards a bad action in relation to the faculty's proper object, and this bad habit is called a vice.[32] There are as many virtues and vices as their active potencies. Therefore, there are physical, intellectual and moral vices and virtues which correspond to the physical faculties, intellectual faculties and appetitive faculties (i.e. will and appetite which encompass the moral sphere).

---

[27]ST I-II, q. 53., a. 3; ST II-II, q. 24, a. 10 and I Sent., d. 17, q. 2, a. 5.

[28]ST I-II, q. 52, a. 3: "si vero intensio actus proportionaliter deficiat ab intensione habitus, talis actus non disponit ad augmentum habitus, sed magis ad diminutionem ipsius."

[29]ST I-II, q. 54, a. 2; ibid., q. 60, a. 1; ibid., q. 63, a. 4 and III Sent., d. 33, q. 1., a. 1., qu. 1.

[30]ST I-II, q. 54, a. 3 and III Sent., d. 33, q. 1, a. 1, qu. 1.

[31]Ibid. Virtue comes from the Latin word *vis* which means power. A virtue is called a virtue because it gives the person or faculty the power or capacity to act well and with ease.

[32]Ibid. Vice comes from the Latin word *vitium* which means fault or defect. A faculty which has a vice lacks the power or facility with respect to its proper object and therefore is bound or restricted from moving freely due to the lack of virtue resident in the faculty.

VII. Actions

Every faculty performs or undergoes some form of action, for faculties are for the sake of action. This action is specified by the object toward which the faculty is ordered. The faculties are designed to perform certain kinds of actions and not others in relation to certain objects.[33] So, for example, sight is designed to see visible objects, whereas the auditory faculty is designed for hearing sound. The action is either done easily or with difficulty depending on the disposition, if it is a passive potency or faculty. If it is an active potency, then the action is done well or poorly based on the disposition and/or habit (virtue or vice).

Therefore, the faculties reside in the soul or the body/soul composite. The faculties, their actions, dispositions and habits are specified by their objects. The faculty, if it be an active potency, can undergo a dispositional change by the actions performed. This being the case, we must now delineate the various faculties.

---

[33]Ibid.

Chapter 3: The Cognitive Faculties - Section I

The faculties of man are classified into five genera based upon the types of objects the faculties consider, viz. the vegetative, the sensitive, the appetitive, locomotive and intellective. Those faculties contained under the genus of vegetative do not directly concern the topic of this book and therefore will not be discussed.[1] The sensitive faculties of import are the five exterior senses and the four interior senses which will be covered in this chapter. The appetitive and intellective faculties will be discussed at length. The locomotive faculty will not be discussed as such, since locomotion is not a cause of mental illness.[2]

I. The Five Exterior Senses

The five exterior senses are part of the knowing faculties in man because they do form a type of knowledge of the particular.[3] The exterior senses are passive potencies because they are acted upon and distinguished by their respective objects.[4] Sensation occurs when the proper object of the sense faculty causes a change in the faculty,[5] i.e. when the *species expressa* is impressed upon the faculty the *species impressa* is formed.[6] All sense faculties make use of a medium which is proper to the

---

[1] The species of vegetative faculties are the nutritive, the augmentative (growth) and the generative. The augmentative and the nutritive power could affect mental health if an improper diet or ingestion of foreign substances could cause imbalances in the chemical operations of the passive intellect. However, since that discussion pertains to the forum of psychiatry, it will not be discussed here. It is possible that problems in one of these faculties could lead to mental difficulties, but this is not due to the difficulties themselves but how one reacts to it, i.e. the appetitive or intellectual reaction to it. Thus, in themselves, they do not lead to mental difficulties except psychiatrically.

[2] Since the cause is somehow in the effect, mental health and illness will sometimes be manifest through the actions of the individual. So the forms of locomotion can sometimes give one knowledge of what is happening interiorly. However, locomotion as such does not tell us anything about mental illness or health in themselves and so it will not be treated here.

[3] SCG II, c. 66.

[4] ST I, q. 78, a. 3.

[5] Ibid.

[6] The *species expressa* is the species which expresses or causes the change in the faculty to which it relates. The *species impressa* refers to the species as it exists in the knowing faculty. The mode of existence of the species changes from object to faculty or from faculty to faculty. In other words, with exterior sensation, the object has accidental qualities which relate essentially to the sense faculty. As these accidental qualities act upon the sense faculty they constitute the expressed species. Once the accidental species has passed over into the sense faculty, it becomes the impressed species. The mode of existence changes from existence as an accident in the object to existence as an accident in the sense

type of accidental species communicated through that medium, e.g. surfaces which have the accident of color make use of the medium of the diaphanous which is capable of "transporting" that species from the object to the sense organ.

Truth is said to be in the senses but not properly speaking. Truth requires a judgment of a knowing power which has the capacity for self-reflection and since the senses are incapable of self-reflection, they are not said to have truth properly speaking.[7] However, truth is in the senses insofar as sense knowledge constitutes a form of knowledge of the particular. Sense knowledge is a form of knowledge insofar as the thing known (i.e. the object) is in the knower (i.e. the senses). But since the senses do not have the capacity for self-reflection, they do not know that they are knowing and therefore cannot judge whether the species in them congrues with its object.

Sensation is also true in another way, insofar as the senses always report what is there. A sense tells the knower what it is undergoing and unless there is some defect in the faculty of sensation, then the sense gives the knower true sense knowledge of the thing.[8] For instance, normal skin will communicate the sense species in a way that is in congruity with the thing whereas burned skin will not communicate it without alteration. For example, if a man has burned skin and he feels something that is ninety degrees, the senses will indicate that it is very hot. What this indicates is that the sense of touch is telling the person that it is in an altered state and, as a result, the thing is acting upon it more than normally. However, someone whose skin is normal, will feel the thing that is ninety degrees, and note that it is a bit warm but not hot. Nevertheless, the senses are reliable insofar as they always report their state which may be normal or they may indicate that it is not normal.

The five exterior senses are touch, taste, smell, hearing and sight; all of the senses are in a hierarchy depending upon how spiritual they are.[9] The sense of touch

---

faculty. But the species, aside from its mode of existence, is formally the same in both, e.g. in touch, the senses sense the heat which is passed from the object to the faculty of sense.

[7]De Ver., q. 1, a. 9 and ST I, q. 16, a. 2.

[8]Clearly, if the medium has affected the accidental species from the object, then the senses do report that as well. In other words, they report as they are acted upon and it pertains to the other powers of the soul to sort out whether the medium has affected the species of the object or whether the faculty of sense is defective or altered from its normal operation.

[9]St. Thomas says in ST I, q. 78, q. 3 that sight is the most spiritual sense and this has caused more speculation on the matter than is necessary. Two possible meanings are that sight takes more act on the side of the soul than other senses or it could mean that its object is more universal than touch. In other words, if I see something green, it tells me less specific information than touch which puts me in contact with the thing and is therefore more individual. While sight gives the most information in a universal sense, it gives less information on a particular level.

communicates two things, viz. pressure and temperature[10] and its medium is the skin or some other organ.[11] The sense of taste has as its object the humid flavored.[12] The sense of smell has as its object the odored[13] and its medium is the air. The auditory sense has as its object the "natural change according to place in sound"[14] or sound and its medium is air.[15] Finally, the last exterior sense is sight and it has as its object the visible or colored. The medium for sight is the diaphanous.[16]

II. The Four Interior Senses or the Passive Intellect

Once the different species in the various senses are received, they are then expressed to the passive intellect or the four interior senses. The interior senses, which are the material part[17] of the intellect, comprise four faculties; they are the common sense power, the memory, imagination and the cogitative power. Since the proper object of consideration of the four interior senses is the accidental qualities of some particular thing exterior to it, then their operations always consider particulars. This is one of the

---

[10]Both of these aspects of touch are necessary. For if something is the same temperature as the skin, one cannot sense it unless by pressure and if there is no pressure put on the organ of sense, one can only sense it by change of temperature.

[11]Normally speaking, we tend to think of touch as something exterior but it is also interior in the sense that it also tells us about other organs in our body. So, for example, if one has arthritis, his sense of touch tells him that there is something in his knee joint that should not be there. It should be noted that when Aquinas talks about the interior senses (see below), he uses the term interior as interior to the passive intellect and not interior in the sense of physically interior to the body.

[12]Aquinas calls the object of taste the humid flavored or flavor and he does this since two things are necessary for one to taste. The first is that it must be moist, for we cannot taste something that is completely dry. Second, the thing must be flavored, as a result, pure water does not have a taste to us. Also touch is required for taste, so if we cannot touch something, we cannot taste it.

[13]The five senses and their objects are delineated in ST I, q. 78, a. 3; II Sent, q. 2, q. 2, a. 2, ad 5; *Comm. de anima* II, l. 14; ibid., III, l. 1 and *De Anima*, a. 13.

[14]Ibid.: "transmutatio naturalis, secundum locum quidem, in sono." Aquinas means by this that sound is the result of locomotion of a natural body which causes some change in the air.

[15]The normal medium is air, but it would include virtually any physical substance that is capable of transmitting sound waves.

[16]The term diaphanous refers to anything that has the capacity to transmit light and color, therefore, air, certain liquids and solids would be included.

[17]Since the passive intellect is material, it is capable of being affected by material causes, e.g. lack of oxygen, bad diet, physical incursions and damage through contusions, etc. This conclusion follows from the fact that the passive intellect is corruptible, see *Comm. de anima* III, l. 10 and ST I, q. 79, q. 2, ad 2 and In Meta. VII, l. 10.

primary differences between man and animals, in that animals which also have particular reason,[18] can only deal with particulars and not universals.[19] Since the four interior senses operate through a bodily organ (viz. the brain), their activities will be localized.[20]

A. *Sensus Communis* or Common Sense Power

The first of the four faculties[21] is called the common sense power.[22] The proper function of the common sense power is to unify the various sense species from the five senses[23] and as a result its species extends to the five senses.[24] It is the medium between the five exterior senses and the other interior sensitive powers,[25] i.e. it is that which lies between exterior sensation and the other three interior senses as well as the other sensitive powers such as the appetites. Since it lies between the various powers and since it is the proper function of the common sense power to unify the five exterior sense species, it has the function of expressing that unified species into the imagination and memory.[26] For this reason, St. Thomas calls the common sense power the root of

---

[18]See below regarding the estimative power in animals.

[19]This means that studying animals will not tell us a great deal about man. It can give us some insights to man, but because man has an immaterial part of the intellect, his actions will be fundamentally different than animals.

[20]IV Sent., d. 50, q. 1, a. 1, ad 3. Modern science has been very successful in localizing the various functions of the passive intellect.

[21]These four faculties might only constitute part of the brain while other aspects of the brain may be used for other things, e.g. speech, etc. However, these other things while called faculties are more a result of a division within given faculties. For example speech is the product of memory, locomotion and the movements of the possible intellect and will on the passive intellect. So they are not separate faculties but constitute the specialized use of other faculties.

[22]In modern parlance, "common sense" refers to the innate capacity of a person to grasp the nature of things and the application of their use (i.e. exhibiting native good judgment or having sound practical judgment). However, the scholastic or philosophical understanding of the term is different.

[23]SCG II, c. 100, n. 3; Quod. VII, q. 1, a. 2, ad 1 and *Comm. de anima* II, l. 13, n. 8.

[24]ST I, q. 1, a. 3, ad 2. By extending to the five senses, it means that it unifies the sense species from all five senses (presuming one of the five has not been corrupted, then it would extend to all of the remaining senses).

[25]*Comm. de anima* III, l. 12, n. 4.

[26]The *species expressa* of the five exterior senses are received by the common sense power in its *species impressa*. Then the five species are unified and the common sense power expresses its unified sense species (phantasm) into the imagination and memory.

imagination and memory.[27] Since it unifies the sense data into a single species or phantasm,[28] it provides a coherent species for the other powers.

St. Thomas sometimes notes that the common sense power has the power of judgment[29] and this refers to the common sense's capacity to discern or distinguish among the various types of sensation.[30] In other words, it pertains to the common sense power to distinguish, e.g. between white and sweet, i.e. between the species proper to one sense faculty and that proper to another. This also means that when one discerns some sense data proper to a specific sense, one does so through the common sense power. Moreover, when one discerns the fact that a thing is hot and sharp, it is done through the common sense power as well as when one discerns that something is warm and blue. Since the five exterior senses cannot judge[31] their species in comparison to the species of other exterior senses, the common sense power which is the terminus of the five senses, does have this capacity since all five senses lie before it. As the common sense power has the power to unify and distinguish the various five senses, if something is wrong with the common sense power, then its function will break down, e.g. St. Thomas makes the observation that, when we think we see double, it is the result of a bad disposition in the common sense power resulting in its inability to unify the species.[32] Moreover, it means that if there is something wrong with the common sense power, the data from the five senses will not be unified properly and will make their way into the other interior senses as such, resulting in confusion.[33]

B. Memory
    1. The faculty itself

    "To conserve the species of things which are not apprehended in act is of the

---

[27]*De memoria*, l. 2, n. 12.

[28]"Phantasm" is a term used in scholastic parlance which refers to the image or sense data as it resides in the "phantasy" which also has the name imagination.

[29]For example, see IV Sent., d. 4, q. 2, a. 1c, ad 3 and De Ver., q. 15, a. 1.

[30]ST I, q. 78, a. 4, ad 2; Quod. VII, q. 1, a. 2, ad 1; *Comm. de anima* II, l. 13, n. 8; ibid., III, l. 12, nn. 10 & 11 and *Comm. de Sensu*, l. 19, n. 13.

[31]The term "judge" does not imply rational or intellectual judgment since they are very different. See below on the acts of the possible intellect.

[32]Meta. XI, l. 6, n. 7.

[33]This is borne out when one thinks one sees something happen at a different time from when they hear it. It means that the common sense power has as its function to ensure the proper time sequencing of data as it enters into the other interior senses.

notion of memory."[34] The very nature of memory is to preserve the sensitive species.[35] Memory retains[36] or reserves[37] the sensitive species and for this reason it is sometimes called the treasury[38] or storehouse[39] of the sensible species. Memory, insofar as it pertains to a species received,[40] concerns the past[41] and not the present. Insofar as memory concerns the past, it concerns that which is not present, i.e. absent,[42] to the knower. The thing remembered is not present before the knower here and now.[43] Memory, therefore, makes it possible for one to know something and to think about it even though it is not present.[44] By virtue of the fact that memory concerns the past, it is that by which one distinguishes between past and present.[45] Because the memory makes it possible for one to know something from the past and compare it with the same thing in the present, man is able to distinguish between his past and present experiences of a thing[46] as well as making it possible for one to estimate the lapse or passage of time.

---

[34]ST I, q. 79, a. 6: "de ratione memoriae sit conservare species rerum quae actu non apprehenduntur."

[35]St. Thomas makes a distinction between intellective and sensitive memory. Intellective memory will be discussed later; for references regarding this distinction, see ibid.; ibid., a. 7 and De Ver., q. 10, aa. 2 & 3. Also, since the sensitive memory concerns sensitive species, it concerns the singular or particular rather than the universal which is proper to intellective memory.

[36]See III Sent., d. 33, q. 3, a. 1a; SCG II, c. 73, n. 32; ibid., c. 74, n. 2; *De memoria* l. 1 (307) and ST I, q. 79, a. 6.

[37]ST I, q. 93, a. 6, ad 4.

[38]SCG II, c. 74, n. 2 and ibid., IV, c. 111, n. 4.

[39]This is the word used to translate the Latin "thesaurus" in the Notre Dame edition of SCG.

[40]II Sent., d. 17, a. 2, a. 1. In this passage St. Thomas makes the distinction between memory which concerns a received species as opposed to the senses which concern the species to be received.

[41]III Sent., d. 33, q. 3, a. 1; IV Sent., d. 14, q. 1, a. 3a; ST I, q. 22, a. 1; ibid., I-II, q. 30, a. 2 ad 1 and De Ver., q. 10, a. 2.

[42]ST I-II, q. 32, a. 3, ad 1 and ST I, q. 79, a. 6.

[43]While someone may close their eyes, and think of the person presently before them based upon memory, the memory does not concern the individual at the current moment because he is cut off from the thing known because his eyes are closed. Therefore, even his memory of the person immediately present to him, is based upon the past sense experience.

[44]*De memoria* l. 2 (311).

[45]De Ver. q. 10, a. 2; ibid., ad 2 and *De memoria* l. 2 (320).

[46]It also means that if the memory fails, one will not find past things familiar. This is what is experienced by those with Alzheimer's.

The first act of memory is retention or preservation of the species which indicates that the memory is at first a passive power. However, memory also can perform a second act, viz. recall,[47] i.e. it has the capacity to bring back to the imagination a species or image[48] previously stored and in that respect it is an active power. As an active power, its conservation or retaining of species is ordered toward the operations of the imagination,[49] i.e. it does not recall the image for its own sake but for the operations of imagination and the cognitive power.

The content which it stores pertains to all of the senses,[50] even though they are impressed as a single unified species. This follows from the fact that memory has as its root the common sense power.[51] As was mentioned, the common sense power after it has unified the sense data from the five exterior senses, impresses the unified species into the imagination and the memory simultaneously.[52] In addition to storing the sense species as such, it also stores our actions.[53] This can be verified on two levels, viz. every person experiences remembering his own actions as well as the fact that our actions likewise become part of the sense data of the five exterior senses. In other words, one can remember seeing oneself performing actions.

Memory is also a habit[54] as understood in two different ways which pertain to the two different ways the term "habitus" is used by Aristotle[55] and St. Thomas.[56] The

---

[47]*De perfectione spiritualis vitae*, c. 18. Another phrase St. Thomas uses for recall is "an act of remembering;" see *De memoria* l. 3 (343).

[48]Acts of memory pertain to the image (III Sent., d. 17, q. 1, a. 1a and IV Sent., d. 4, q. 1, a. 3c) or sensible species and is therefore ordered to it as its object.

[49]ST I, q. 78, a. 4.

[50]This is inferred from two statements of St. Thomas. The first is what follows after this footnote in the body of the text. Secondly, because St. Thomas says that from many senses come one memory and from many memories one experience, see III Sent., d. 14, q. 1, a. 3; ibid., d. 34, q. 1, a. 2 and SCG II, c. 83, n. 25.

[51]*De memoria*, l. 2 (322).

[52]This helps us to understand certain experiences which are proper to man, viz. how one can think about one thing and yet have memories of the thing which one was not concentrating on. In other words, since the common sense power impresses in the memory all the data from the five senses, and yet, one may be concentrating on only one sense or part of the sense data, the other sense data is stored though not at first recognized by the person. This is why in later recall, people can remember things which might not have been the primary object of concern at the time. Unfortunately, it is also one of the causes of many modern psychological misinterpretations on the operations of the intellect.

[53]This is understood by virtue of the fact that St. Thomas says that we retain our past transgressions; see II Sent., d. 21, q. 2, a. 1, ad 5 and IV Sent., d. 17, q. 2, a. 1a, ad 1.

[54]*De memoria*, l. 3 (349).

[55]Aristotle, *Metaphysics*, V, c. 20.

[56]*De memoria*, l. 3 (349).

first is that the term "habitus" is similar to a word which has it as its root, viz. habit in the religious sense, i.e. something worn. In this sense, it indicates that it is something "had" by the possessor. The second way "habitus" is used is in the sense of a disposition which can be changed in an active or passive power by its activity. Hence, the memory can be something which is habituated through its activity. This is why some can improve their memory by use or training.

Memory can be affected by several things in addition to habit and training.[57] The proper bodily disposition of the faculty can often determine whether something is remembered well or not.[58] The bodily disposition can be affected by several things: 1) age (both in the case of the young or old);[59] 2) the suffering of passions or emotions;[60] 3) chemical variances in the bodily organ of memory itself;[61] and 4) physical actions upon the organ.[62]

---

[57]What is clearly implied by saying that habit can affect the disposition of the faculty is that if the faculty has a material element, the actions of the agent causing the habit actually have a physical, chemical or biological effect on the faculties. It therefore follows that if one does not use one's memory then it could suffer chemical or biological change. This would also apply to the rest of the passive intellect in that if it is used contrary to its nature, it can actually cause chemical imbalances. The operative principle working in the background is that God designed our faculties to perform certain actions and He designed the material element in those faculties in a specific chemical way which is conducive to the action of the faculty. Therefore, if one abuses the faculty, it follows that one is acting contrary to the nature of the faculty and one will therefore suffer chemical changes. Moreover, it also means that if one acts in accordance with the nature of the corporeal faculty, one will actually improve or maintain its chemical balance to the degree that those actions are capable.

[58]*De memoria* l. 3 (330-2).

[59]The following list is contained in ibid.

[60]The passions and emotions will be discussed in a later chapter. However, experience bears this out, e.g. when someone is very frightened, they do not remember a great deal about an experience. In fact, if the occurrence is vehement enough, it can even cause the complete loss of memory regarding an experience. This could be the result of a mechanism in memory itself placed there by Divine Providence to soften extreme experiences, or the overwhelming motion of the passion itself or both.

[61]Here we are talking about bodily disposition in a more direct way. However, sometimes ingestion of chemicals and nutrition affected by diet can enhance or degrade the disposition of the bodily organ and thereby either improve or degrade the operations of the faculty (i.e. memory) since every faculty which is composed of a spiritual and a material element (or merely material as in the case of animals) acts according to the disposition of the bodily organ.

[62]When someone suffers physical abuse or contusions, it can affect memory. In fact, this is the argument used by the scholastics to prove that memory acts through a physical organ and is not purely spiritual since one can get hit on the head and forget (i.e. suffer amnesia).

Man's memory, however, differs from animals' memory in several different ways. The first is that it is a faculty having both spiritual and material elements, whereas, in animals, it is merely material. Secondly, man is capable of confirming or affirming his memory by thinking or meditating upon the memory.[63] In other words, man can maintain something in memory by thinking of it often, whereas an animal only remembers something as result of an exterior sensation[64], dreaming or training of estimative sense and if that is lacking, then the animal does not have the capacity to remember. Thirdly, man's memory is open to the process of reminiscence[65] whereas an animal's is not. Fourthly, man's memory has a *per accidens* relationship with rational judgment, i.e. reason and will.[66] Memory can be acted upon by reason and will in man but since these faculties are lacking in animals, their memories cannot be acted upon in this way. Finally, man's memory has the capacity to be false, whereas an animal's does not. This is for three reasons:[67] 1) we may not be sure if we had a previous experience (i.e. we cannot recall something) and as a result we may not remember that something that we experienced did actually occur. As a result, a man concludes from memory that it did not occur, whereas an animal does not conclude (since it does not have reason) that something did not happen due to a lack of memory. 2) Sometimes man understands or reminisces that in a previous instance he heard or saw something which is actually the image of some other thing. If one saw a man and remembered him and then saw another man who looked like him, he might consider himself to have seen the current man previously. St. Thomas says this is because the present phantasm is considered to be the thing which he thought he experienced. 3) Lastly, an occurrence can arise contrary to the first kind of error, viz. one can think one remembers something which in fact he did not experience in any way. For example, one may meet someone and think he has met him before even though there is nothing in his past experience which is even remotely like the person. Another example would be when we tend to think there was something accompanying an experience which was not really there.

2. Forgetfulness

The common experience of men is that they forget, i.e. that their memory is not perfect and not always perduring. Forgetfulness is the incapacity to recall a previously stored sense species and it has several causes. One of the most obvious causes of forgetfulness is time. St. Thomas notes that "time is the cause of forgetting *per*

---

[63]*De memoria* l. 3 (348). This mechanism has extreme importance regarding the maintenance, loss and regaining of mental health.

[64]While the exterior sensation prompts memory, it does so by entering into the imagination and the estimative power associates the image in the imagination with the memory.

[65] ST I, q. 78, a. 4.

[66] *De memoria*, l. 2 (320) and ibid., l. 3 (343).

[67]The three reasons are delineated by St. Thomas in *De memoria*, l. 3 (345-347).

accidens, insofar as motion of which it is the measure, is the cause of change."[68] Since material things are in motion which is measured by time, then man's body which is material is subject to change (e.g. the aging process itself). Hence, time measures the motion which is the actual change occurring to the corporeal organ of memory. Hence, time is not the cause of forgetting *per se,* but *per accidens.*

It can, likewise, be caused by passion,[69] e.g. if a man suffers rage, he may forget the fact that if he physically hurts someone he may go to jail. Another example is a man who is an alcoholic and who suffers the movement of the concupiscible appetite to drink, and so he may forget all the evil effects his drinking may cause and, as a result, there is less to inhibit him from drinking. Memory can also be lost due to some form of physical damage, e.g. if a man takes a blow to the head, he may suffer amnesia.[70]

In addition to being caused, memory is also a cause. It is the cause of the corruption of knowledge[71] in that one forgets what he once knew.[72] It can cause confusion[73] and motions of the irascible appetite.[74] Forgetfulness impedes prudence[75] insofar as prudence is built upon past experience and if it cannot be remembered, one cannot act according to one's experience. It can also cause the cessation of appetitive inclinations[76] insofar as the objects which move the appetites which may be stored in memory are lost and, as a result, the appetites are not moved by the recalled object.

---

[68]IV Sent., d. 50, q. 2, a. 2a, ad 3: "tempus est causa oblivionis per accidens, inquantum motus, cujus est mensura, est causa transmutationis." See also ST I-II, q. 48, a. 2, ad 2; ST I-II, q. 53, a. 3, ad 3; *In physicorum* IV, l. 20, n. 5 and ibid., IV, l. 22, n. 2.

[69]III Sent., d. 33, q. 1, a. 4, ad 2.

[70]Memory is localized just as all acts which occur through a bodily organ are localized. However, it may happen that if one part of the brain suffers damage, those things which pertain to specific kinds of memory may migrate to a different location of the brain. Speech is the result of several faculties, viz. the possible intellect, the will, the cogitative power, memory, imagination and the voice itself. If the memory is destroyed, the other faculties remain intact and so memory could be moved to another location to allow the speech faculty to operate. However, some faculties appear not to be able to migrate, e.g. when the cogitative power is destroyed by lobotomy or other physical causes, the person never seems to regain the actions of the cogitative power. Migration may occur if another organ or part of an organ is disposed to the operations of the other faculty.

[71]ST I, q. 89, a. 5 and ibid., q. 47, a. 16.

[72]Just as memory has to do with the past, forgetfulness has to do with what occurred in the past, see *Contra doctrinam retrahentium,* c. 9.

[73]*In Isaiam,* c. 54.

[74]This is known through common experience, i.e. when someone cannot remember something one suffers frustration.

[75]ST II-II, q. 47, a. 16.

[76]In Ethic. I, l. 16, n. 4.

3. Reminiscence

Reminiscence is "as it were, a syllogistic inquiring into memory of the past according to individual intentions,"[77] i.e. "a certain re-finding of what was received previously but not retained."[78] Reminiscence is a process by which one reconstructs what happened in the past. It is not the resumption of memory[79] in which the memory comes back to the individual. Rather, it is a reconstruction of the past events experienced, i.e. it is a process or motion. It is the result of man's capacity for interior self movement[80] and therefore is proper to man alone.[81]

St. Thomas describes the way in which the intellect reminisces in the following passage:

> one motion is followed by another either out of necessity or out of custom. It is necessary that when we reminisce, we move according to something of these motions until we come upon that to which we are moved apprehending that motion, which is accustomed to be after the first, which, namely, through the motion we intend to rediscover by reminiscing, since reminiscence is nothing other than the inquiry into something which was lost from memory. And therefore by reminiscing, we find, i.e. we seek that which is consequent from something prior, which in memory we have. For as he who seeks by demonstration, procedes from something prior, which is known, from which something posterior is come upon, which is unknown: so all reminiscing, from something prior, which is had in memory, procedes to re-finding that which was lost from memory.[82]

---

[77]ST I, q. 78, a. 4: "quasi syllogistice inquirendo praeteritorum memoriam, secundum individuales intentiones."

[78]*De memoria*, l. 1 (302): "quaedam reinventio prius acceptorum non conservatorum." Clearly, reminiscence in modern parlance tends to imply remembering things that occurred in the past which are actually remembered but often in a romantic way or by romanticizing about the good things in the past. However, in scholastic usage, it does not refer to things remembered but to things which are not remembered and it does not have a romanticized connotation.

[79]Ibid., l. 4 (355f).

[80]Ibid., l. 6 (375).

[81]It is proper to man alone since angels do not have sensitive memory. Moreover, animals cannot reason syllogistically (ibid., l. 8 [399]) and therefore cannot reconstruct the past based on what they know. Once an animal forgets some event in the past, it is permanently lost.

[82]Ibid., l. 5 (362): "motus sequitur post alterum vel ex necessitate vel ex consuetudine, oportet quod quando reminiscimur, moveamur secundum aliquem horum motuum quousque veniamus ad hoc quod moveamur apprehendendo illo motu, qui consuevit

Reminiscence is the process by which one goes from what is prior and known to what is posterior and unknown. The syllogistic motion or process proceeds according to necessity or custom, i.e. if one thing must logically follow another, then it is out of necessity. If it follows from the accustomed way in which things happen, or if one thinks according to the way he normally thinks, then that can be used to derive what happened. St. Thomas then states where one starts.[83] In syllogistic reasoning, one starts with principles which are known; in reminiscence one starts with something that is known. Sometimes we start with some *thing* which is known, e.g a person, animal or object and sometimes we start with some *time* which is known, e.g. one's wedding day.

Next, St. Thomas notes when one starts with a specific time, there are several ways of going about it.[84] One could start with the present and work one's way back according to the sequence of events. One could start at a time remembered which was prior to that and work one's way to the event. When one starts with the specific thing, he says that there are three ways in which this is done.[85] (1) Sometimes one proceeds by a similar notion, e.g. if one remembers Socrates and one therefore can reminisce to what happened to Plato. (2) Sometimes one proceeds by a contrary notion, e.g. one remembers that the South stood for slavery and since there is no slavery, the North must have won the Civil War. (3) Sometimes, one proceeds by things close to something, i.e. one remembers one thing and then by the closeness that thing has to another thing, one reminisces about what happened, e.g. one may forget the name of a man's wife, but remembering that their daughter took the mother's name as a middle name, and knowing that middle name, one can arrive at the conclusion that the mother's name is Mary.

Reminiscence, however, is not infallible and those things which can affect the way in which it can go awry are either intrinsic or extrinsic to the person. With respect to the intrinsic, one of the ways reminiscence can be affected is through passion,[86] e.g. if someone is scared about some event that happened in the past, their judgment in the process of reminiscing may be affected and therefore they may arrive at the wrong conclusion. Moreover, bodily disposition can affect how one reminisces,[87] e.g. if one is ill, it may be difficult to figure out what happened from what little one knows. Finally, how well one is accustomed through habits and virtues which may aid the process of

---

esse post primum, quem scilicet motum intendimus reinvenire reminiscendo, quia reminiscentia nil est aliud quam inquisitio alicuius quod a memoria excidit. Et ideo reminiscendo venamur, id est inquirimus id quod consequenter est ab aliquo priori, quod in memoria tenemus. Sicut enim ille qui inquirit per demonstrationem, procedit ex aliquo priori, quod est notum, ex quo venatur aliquid posterius, quod est ignotum; ita etiam reminiscens, ex aliquo priori, quod in memoria habetur, procedit ad reinveniendum id quod ex memoria excidit."

[83] Ibid. (363).

[84] Ibid.

[85] Ibid. (364).

[86] Ibid., l. 8 (401).

[87] Ibid (402).

reminiscing can affect how one reminisces.[88]

The extrinsic causes of false reminisce are several. The first can arise out of a false memory. Aquinas notes that memory occurs when the time and the thing are recalled together.[89] When someone thinks that these two are related but they are not related in memory either because there is lacking the motion of thing in the process of remembering or the motion of the time, then the thing is not remembered. Nothing prohibits falsity from being in memory, i.e. someone remembers something inaccurately. Sometimes, someone remembers something, even though he does not think he remembers it. In these two cases, the intellect may think that the current image was remembered, when in fact it was not, or the image may be stored in memory, even though the person does not realize its source. When one begins the process of reminiscence not thinking he knows something, it can lead to something contrary to his memory. Since reminiscence begins with partial memory, if that memory is in any way inaccurate, it can lead to false conclusions in the reminiscence.

The first way in which reminiscences can go awry is in the principles[90] but the second is the process of reminiscence itself, i.e. if the syllogistic process is not done properly. This can occur in different ways. The first is when one reminisces in a way contrary to the accustomed way of reminiscing. This can be the result of an exterior cause or happening which may affect the accustomed way one normally reminisces and, in this case, the exterior thing impedes the proper reminiscing process. St. Thomas gives the example of someone trying to draw the memory out of the person or draw the reminiscence process along in a way that is contrary to the person's accustomed way.[91] This becomes a distraction and draws the reminiscent process in the wrong direction.[92]

---

[88]St. Thomas does not seem to mention this one. However, it logically follows since there are several faculties involved in the process, and as a result, how they are habituated will determine how they proceed.

[89]Ibid., l. 7 (396).

[90]By principles here is meant that with which the process of reminiscence begins, viz. the premises, e.g. if one begins with memories that are flawed, then the whole reminiscence process will end in the wrong conclusion.

[91]Ibid., l. 6 (384).

[92]This observation of St. Thomas was in place long before modern psychologists realized that their influencing of patient's reminiscing process may be deluding him about the actual conclusions about what happened to him. Nowhere is this more poignantly seen than in the cases in which "by the help of a psychologist" some were led to believe that they had been sexually abused, when in fact, they were not. This ultimately means that if psychologists are going to have any role in the reminiscence process they must have a complete understanding of the nature of reminiscence as well as a profound knowledge of the directee and the directee's accustomed ways of reminiscing. Until objective principles are derived to govern the psychologist's involvement in this process, engagement in it should be avoided. The author writes this with full knowledge that this will impede the methods of several schools of contemporary psychology.

C. Imagination
    1. The Power Itself and Its Operations

The imagination[93] is the material faculty or interior sense which maintains the presence of the image[94] in the knower, i.e. it retains or keeps present in the knower the sensible species.[95] This sensible species or accidental similitude[96] to the exterior thing contains all of the perceivable material or bodily accidents[97] and therefore extends to all of the information given by the five senses.[98] While the initial image may come directly from the common sense power,[99] from common experience we know that an image can later be introduced into the imagination from memory.[100] When the imagination receives that image from memory, it is able to represent[101] the object of previous knowledge to the agent and possible intellects[102] and in so doing enables the person to know something which is absent to it exteriorly.[103]

----

[93]The imagination is sometimes referred to as the phantasy by Aquinas, i.e the power which corresponds to the phantasm.

[94]The image should not be confused with the concept. The distinction between the two is that the image concerns the sensible species whereas the concept is the intelligible species. This will become clear in the discussion of the agent and possible intellects.

[95]De Ver., q. 15, a. 1; ibid., q. 15, a. 2, ad 7; ibid., q. 19, a. 1 and ST I, q. 78, a. 4.

[96]Quod. VIII, q. 2, a. 2.

[97]I Sent., d. 3, q. 4, a. 3; III Sent., d. 35, q. 2, a. 2a; IV Sent., d. 49, q. 2, a. 7, ad 6; De Ver., q. 8, a 7, ad sed contra 8; ibid q. 10, a 4, ad 1; ibid., q. 15, a. 1, ad 1 and Quod. VIII, q. 2, a. 2.

[98]SCG I, c. 65, n. 6.

[99]St. Thomas notes that the imagination is the power which conserves the received accidental forms (in a different manner from memory): see ST I, q. 78, a. 4.

[100]See ST I, q. 78, a. 4 and ibid., q. 111, a. 3, ad 1.

[101]I Sent., d. 3, q. 4, a. 3.

[102]See below.

[103]De Ver. q. 1, a. 11; ibid. and q. 10, a. 4, ad 1. It is by virtue of the fact that the image contains its source or cause that the person is able to be in contact with reality. It is because the image in the imagination contains the fact that it came from the five exterior senses through the common sense power either now or in the past by means of memory, that one knows whether the thing exists or existed in reality or not. Moreover, if the image does not correspond to any thing existing outside of the knower, this is also provided making it possible for one to know if something is real or not. Because of the causal relations between the exterior and interior senses, one is able to have true knowledge of reality. This will be addressed again below regarding the reformulation of the image.

2. Its Relation to Other Powers

The imagination is not a power for its own sake but has a fundamental relationship to other powers which makes it highly important, e.g. as the imagination makes it possible to know something which is absent, it also makes possible the continual use of knowledge,[104] i.e. without it we cannot use our previous knowledge. Even more to the point is the fact that it is necessary for any knowledge whatsoever, insofar as one is not able to know anything[105] without it first being in the imagination, since it is that from which the agent intellect abstracts the concept and it is that to which the intellect turns in order to make a judgment.[106]

Moreover, the disposition of the bodily organ is determinative of the right functioning of the interior senses[107] and consequently of all of those other powers that depend on or relate to them in any way. This we know by virtue of the fact that those who suffer some lesion or brain damage are often impeded in their intellectual operations.[108] Another indication of this is that if one is intoxicated, the alcohol affects the brain, and therefore the person is not able to think or talk clearly. Since the imagination is that from which speech flows,[109] if the imagination is impaired, so will speech be impaired.

In addition to a relationship with the agent and possible intellects, the imagination also has a relationship to the will.[110] It has a relationship to memory insofar as memory can cause a previous image to be present in the imagination by virtue of its capacity to recall it. The image which is considered is often stored in memory, e.g. if one imagines himself somewhere, a little later he is able to remember himself daydreaming or imagining it.

In addition to the aforesaid relationships, the imagination has a fundamental relationship to instincts. For we know in ourselves and in animals that instinct is moved by the presence of something in the imagination[111] which comes to us from the exterior

---

[104]ST I, q. 84, a. 7.

[105]That the imagination is necessary for knowledge, see IV Sent., d. 17, q. 1, a. 3c, ad 1.

[106]This will be discussed in detail in the section on the second act of the possible intellect; see II Sent., d. 3, q. 3, a. 3 and ST I, q. 84, a. 7

[107]*De anima*, q. 8.

[108]See II Sent., d. 20, q. 2, a. 2, ad 3 and ST I, q. 84, a. 7.

[109]III Sent., d. 14, q. 1, a. 1d, ad 3; ST I, q. 34, a. 1; *In libros perihermenias* I, l. 4, n. 3 and *Comm. de anima* II, l. 18, n. 12. Speech is the result of a complex process of several faculties, viz. the possible intellect, will, imagination, memory, the cogitative power and the voice box or actual speech organs.

[110]This will be seen more clearly in relation to appetites and the reformulation of the image.

[111]ST I, q. 46, a. 7, ad 1.

senses either present now or in the past. Moreover, according to St. Thomas and common experience, the appetites, like the will, are blind faculties in that they are incapable of movement without an object for that would imply the possession of the object. Rather the appetites are moved by the image[112] in the imagination[113] and principally so. Even though it was noted earlier that the common sense power can move the appetites, nevertheless the primary way the appetites are moved is by the imagination. This follows from the fact that with a concentration on an image in the imagination one can override the movements of the appetites by the common sense power.

This capacity to move the appetites makes the imagination a pivotal faculty in relation to the various faculties. Since the imagination obeys reason,[114] reason is able to affect or move the appetites by means of it.[115] This means that the appetites can be taught, trained or ordered and it also means that they can be disordered since the imagination is also the cause of inordinate appetites.[116] The disordered appetites are not only the result of the movement of reason with respect to the imagination but can also be the result of those things which reach the imagination from the senses prior to the involvement of reason.[117] Since the appetites are moved by the image in the imagination, it means that the image can determine how much the appetites[118] are moved and in which direction.[119]

3. Effects Caused by the Imagination

In addition to its effects caused in the aforementioned powers, the imagination has other effects which are important for the study of psychology. St. Thomas observes that the imagination can cause bodily changes:

---

[112]This makes the image or the phantasm the object of the appetites.

[113]II Sent., d. 7, q. 3, a. 1; ibid., d. 24, q. 2, a. 1, ad 2; ibid., d. 24, q. 3, a. 1; III Sent., d. 15, q. 2, a. 2c, ad 3; IV Sent., d. 7, q. 3, a. 3b; ST I-II, q. 13, a. 2, ad 2; ibid., q. 77, a. 1 and ST III, q. 13, a. 3, ad 3.

[114]II Sent., d. 7, q. 2, a. 2, ad 6 and ST I-II, q. 17, a. 7.

[115]III Sent., d. 17, q. 1, a. 4, ad 4; ST I-II, q. 30, a. 3, ad 3 and De Ver., q. 25, a. 4, ad 5. This is why St. Thomas notes that we have political not tyrannical control over the appetites.

[116]II Sent., d. 39, q. 1, a. 1, ad 5.

[117]St. Thomas notes that the imagination can move the appetites prior to reason (later this will be discussed regarding antecedent and consequent passion) in ST I-II, q. 17, a. 7. This does not deny that the appetites can be trained even in this regard.

[118]ST I-II, q. 33, a. 1 ad 2.

[119]How the imagination moves the appetites will be discussed in the section on the appetites.

The body naturally obeys the imagination, if it would be strong, as to other things. For example so far as the case of the plank in a high place; since the imagination is born to be the principle of locomotion, as is said in the third book of *De Anima*. Similarly also as to the alteration which is according to hot or cold, as other consequences, because from the imagination are consequently born the consequent passions so far as the heart which is moved and thus by the commotion of the whole spirit the body is changed.[120]

St. Thomas is making two observations. The first is that the body is moved by the imagination insofar as the imagination is the natural principle of local motion with respect to the body. In other words, one moves oneself by means of the imagination. St. Thomas does not seem to indicate how this is to be understood, for there are two possible interpretations of this passage. The first is that the will moves the body mediated by the imagination, i.e. the will does not act directly on our limbs, etc. but acts upon the imagination which in turn moves the limbs, etc. The second possible interpretation is that the imagination acts as a guide to the other powers which actually move the individual. The person forms what he wants to do in the imagination and then the limbs are guided according to the sensible species in the imagination. While these two interpretations are possible, they do not necessarily exclude each other and in fact both seem to be the case. It is possible that the person moves the other limbs through the imagination and concomitantly forms the sensible species in the imagination which directs the motion.[121]

The second part of this passage is that St. Thomas is noting that the imagination can cause dispositional changes in the body by what it imagines. Certain images can cause bodily changes, e.g. an image may move a bodily appetite. This clearly implies that the imagination can aid or deteriorate bodily

---

[120]ST III, q. 13, a. 3, ad 3: "imaginationi, si fortis fuerit, naturaliter obedit corpus quantum ad aliqua. Puta quantum ad casum de trabe in alto posita; quia imaginatio nata est esse principium motus localis, ut dicitur in III de anima. Similiter etiam quantum ad alterationem quae est secundum calorem et frigus, et alia consequentia, eo quod ex imaginatione consequenter natae sunt consequi passiones animae, secundum quas movetur cor, et sic per commotionem spirituum totum corpus alteratur." See also II Sent., d. 20, q. 2, a. 1, ad 2 and De Pot., q. 6, a. 3.

[121]The fact that the imagination is the motive power of the limbs as a mediary between the will and the limbs seems to have support from the fact that if one suffers a fracture or break in the spine, even though he will the motion he cannot move his limbs. There must be some intermediary between the will and limbs, since if one breaks one's back, he cannot move his limbs. St. Thomas indicates that the imagination is an intermediary, and given the discussion that is to follow, we are inclined to agree with him.

dispositions, such as chemical dispositions, etc.[122]

To return to the fact that the imagination is naturally ordered toward moving locomotive powers, St. Thomas observes that the imagination can cause unreflected bodily actions.[123] For example, someone may be startled and the cogitative power may perceive some harm prior to the judgment of reason (reflection) and thus the imagination may move the locomotive powers to react. St. Thomas also notes that the imagination can move the locomotive powers in unreflected ways other than the aforementioned. One of the examples he often gives is the imagination moving one to scratch one's beard unreflectedly.[124]

St. Thomas also notes that the imagination can affect the organ of sensation:

> Some say that the sense comes into act not from the exterior sensible but from an effluence from the superior powers; as now the superior powers receive from the inferior powers as from the converse the inferior powers receive from the superior. But that motion of reception does not make a true sensation; since all passive powers are determined according to the nature of their species to some specific act: since a power, insofar as it is like this, has an order with respect to that which is said: hence when the proper act in the exterior sense is the thing existing outside the soul and not its intention in the imagination or reason; if the organ of sensing is not moved by some exterior thing, but the imagination or another superior power, it is not a true sensation.[125]

---

[122]It would seem that this is not only the case because it can move other powers which result in a bodily dispositional change, but certain images may actually result in chemical and subsequent biological changes in the passive intellect itself. This would follow from the fact that if a person habitually thinks of sad things, it can lead to a chemical imbalance associated with depression.

[123]II Sent., d. 40, q. 1, a. 5; ST I-II, q. 18, a. 9 and *De malo* q. 2, a. 5.

[124]This observation will have a great deal of import in the discussion of the subconscious or unconscious.

[125]IV Sent., d. 44, q. 2, a. 1c: "alii dicunt, quod sensus in actu fiet per susceptionem non quidem ab exterioribus sensibilibus, sed per effluxum a superioribus viribus; ut sicut nunc superiores vires accipiunt ab inferioribus, ita tunc e converso inferiores accipient a superioribus. Sed ille motus receptionis non facit vere sentire: quia omnis potentia passiva secundum suae speciei rationem determinatur ad aliquod speciale activum: quia potentia, inquantum hujusmodi, habet ordinem ad illud respectu cujus dicitur; unde cum proprium activum in sensu exteriori sit res existens extra animam, et non intentio ejus existens in imaginatione vel ratione; si organum sentiendi non moveatur a rebus extra, sed ex imaginatione, vel aliis superioribus viribus, non erit vere sentire."

St. Thomas is noting that a superior power cannot move the sense itself since the sense is by nature a passive power moved by an exterior thing. However, he seems to indicate that the imagination can cause a change in the bodily organ and someone can sense that change. But this is not a true sensation, in the sense that it proceeds from something outside of the person but it is a sensation of the change of the bodily organ caused by imagination. However, this can lead to a false interpretation on the side of the individual as to thinking that there is something outside of him when, in fact, it has proceeded from the imagination causing a change in the bodily organ.

St. Thomas also notes that a vehemence in the imagination can make someone think he sees or hears something which is actually not there.[126] For example, someone, whose passive intellect is not functioning properly or is affected by some strong memory besetting the imagination, may become so engrossed in the image that he is incapable of distinguishing between the image and reality. Moreover, it is possible that the image itself does not contain the necessary information to indicate to the person that the thing is not real. For example, someone who wakes up and has a very strong and vivid dream may, for a short time, suffer confusion about the reality of the dream and may actually think it is real. This occurs when the memory is strong enough or if the imagination and cogitative powers form the image and place in the image a sensation of it being real. As a result, when the person wakes up, it takes a certain amount of time for the senses to override the imagination as to what is really present. In some of those suffering psychological disorders, the imagination may be so strong or be suffering some indisposition, or the senses may not be strong enough to overcome the imagination and as a result the person does not act according to reality.[127]

4. General Observations

Some of the observations which St. Thomas makes throughout the corpus of his writings are of importance in relation to the science of psychology but do not pertain to the actual acts of the faculty as such but to kinds of acts of the faculty. Among those are the fact that the intellect judges time by means of changes in the phantasm.[128] As one can judge time in the imagination, one can also imagine the future by means of the imagination.[129] Moreover, since the sense species pertains to the singular existing outside of the intellect and also the phantasm,[130] the singular is known by means of the

---

[126]III Sent., d. 21, q. 2, a. 4b.

[127]These mechanisms may explain why amputees have phantom sense experiences.

[128]SCG II, c. 36, n. 7; ST I, q. 46, a. 1, ad 6; and *In libros physicorum* VIII, l. 2, n. 20.

[129]III Sent., d. 26, q. 1, a. 1, ad 5.

[130]SCG II, c. 67, n. 3; De Ver., q. 8, a. 11 and *De anima* q. 4, ad 3 and ad 5.

image in the imagination.[131] As it is that to which we convert to know the singular, it is also that to which we convert to judge the existence of a thing. The imagination plays an integral part in dreaming but it is not the only faculty involved.[132]

While the right order of operation of the various faculties allows the imagination to play its important role in the aforementioned activities, nevertheless its improper functioning can lead to difficulties. Since speech flows from the imagination, if the imagination becomes distracted, the person forgets what they should have said or what they were saying. This implies that there are several powers acting on the imagination, viz. the common sense power, the memory, cogitative power and the will, and any one of these can cause distraction from the current object under consideration by moving it in another direction. But on the other side of the coin, the imagination when it is under the control of the will, e.g. during meditation[133] or deep thought, may not be subject to the senses. For if the imagination is under the control of the will, the other powers may not be able to act upon it. For example, one can keep an image in the imagination and block memory from introducing something into the imagination or one can keep the cogitative power from changing the image through association.[134] This also holds true when the appetites through passion hold the imagination captive and resist the imagination being acted upon by other powers, making it difficult for the person to move the imagination by an act of the will.[135] Moreover, it means that if the imagination is held by passion, the senses may not act upon it as well.[136]

---

[131]SCG I, c. 65, n. 6 and ibid., II, c. 74, n. 6. St. Thomas also observes that the singular is known by means of the senses (see *Comm. de anima* III, l. 8, n. 17), however, this should be understood in light of his teaching on the other faculties. The singular is known by means of the senses because they provide the phantasm in the imagination which is the proper object of conversion. However, even though the image in the imagination is that to which the intellect converts, man can still distinguish between something in his imagination alone and something coming from the senses, otherwise man would not know whether something was imaginary or real (see SCG III, c. 104, n. 4).

[132]Dreaming involves directly the imagination, memory and cogitative power. It also involves indirectly the appetites and the habituation caused by the higher powers even though they are not operative when the lower powers are engaging in dreaming.

[133]*De causis*, l. 6.

[134]This will be discussed below.

[135]ST I-II, q. 17, a. 1. This is one of the reasons St. Thomas observes that animal imaginations are more quiet than human (I Sent d. 7, q. 2, a. 2 ad 6) because the animal's imagination is not moved by the intellect (and will) and as a result it reduces the number of powers which move it. Moreover, it means that animals are more moved by sensation than volitional recall (memory) or volition association (cogitative power) since they do not have these capabilities. This is largely due to the fact that an animal does not have a self-moving principle (the will).

[136]When the image in the imagination is powerful and the movement of the passion is extreme, a person can lose contact with reality since the imagination is held captive.

St. Thomas observes that the imagination can suffer confusion as a result of a lack of a proper disposition.[137] For example, if someone was to drink excessively or take drugs, the chemical indisposition in the brain may result in confusion. Confusion can also come from what St. Thomas calls indeterminate phantasy[138] or an indeterminate phantasm. He notes that sometimes something in the imagination is determined as suitable but "not, however, this or that, here or there."[139] In other words, the phantasm may not contain determinate information and this leads to a confusion on the side of the imagination, e.g. if one walks into a room and commotion in the room comes from several sources moving quickly resulting in the person not knowing exactly where the things causing the commotion are, the imagination will contain indeterminate information. Confusion is ultimately the result of placing two things next to each other which tend to be at odds with each other, contradict each other or which mix together in an indeterminate fashion.[140]

The imagination can become confused, therefore, when two things come together in the image which contradict or are at odds with each other, e.g. when people are in love, they will tend to see the faults of the person and become concerned with them; they also imagine the pleasure or good times derived in the person's presence. This results in confusion as to what course of action should be taken in a relationship. Moreover, the person can become confused when there is simply not enough sensory information about the thing and the image remains indeterminate. Finally, the person can become confused when there is conflicting input from the various sources which affect the imagination, viz. the possible intellect, will, memory, cogitative power and the senses. For example, one may hear that a particular person is dangerous and harmful and then meet the person in real life, portraying himself as concerned with one's safety, with being nice, etc. All of the information comes into the imagination and is there for the intellect or exterior factors to sort out.[141] Moreover, one may suffer confused images

---

[137]In II Sent., d. 20, q. 2, a. 2, ad 4, St. Thomas observes that a child can become confused as a result of excessive cerebral humidity which corresponds to the science of the day. Even if the science is not perfect, we know that people can become confused when the brain is ill disposed.

[138]*Comm. de anima* III, l. 16, n. 4.

[139]Ibid.: "non autem ut hoc aut illud, hic aut ibi."

[140]The term confusion comes from the two Latin words "cum" meaning with and "fundere" meaning pour forth or pour. Confusion then is when two elements come together and mix (whence the phrase "mixed up" referring to confused).

[141]This is one of the biggest differences between humans and animals. An animal's images get sorted out by events which happen to them and circumstances, e.g. a person may present two snacks of equal tastiness to a dog and the dog may for a bit not know which direction to go. Often the circumstances will determine it, e.g. which is easier to acquire or if the dog is pushed by the owner in one direction it will move toward one snack. The point is that the dog in these cases is determined by exterior sense data whereas human beings can be affected by the exterior sense data but they also have reason which is capable of clearing

when the intellect either fails to sort things out or if the intellect itself introduces into the phantasm conflicting or disordered information.[142]

5. Forming a New Image

While it is a commonly accepted fact that certain people are more creative than others and that we can imagine things the way we want, very few know the actual mechanism behind reformulating or creating an image. There are several passages in St. Thomas' corpus where he talks about this process and each has its points to contribute to the discussion. In the *Summa Contra Gentiles*, St. Thomas makes the following observation:

> But after the [intelligible] species is received in it [i.e. the possible intellect], [the possible intellect] needs [the intelligible species] as an instrument or foundation of its species: hence, it relates to the phantasms as the efficient cause; for according to the command of the intellect a suitable phantasm is formed in the imagination to such an intelligible species in which shines the intelligible species as an exemplar in the example or in the image.[143]

The possible intellect by means of a command forms an image in the imagination and is thereby the efficient cause of the phantasm. This indicates that there are several efficient causes of a phantasm, viz. the primary efficient cause which are the senses, the memory, the cogitative power and the possible intellect (presupposing the act of use on the side of the will). Second, the image is an example of the exemplar which is in the possible intellect so that the possible intellect is also the formal cause of the image. This indicates that the image can actually contain more information than what can come from

---

out the confusion in the phantasm, provided it has some principles upon which it will judge the various sources of sense data. It is often when the principles or habits in the possible intellect are not strong enough or present that the confusion in the imagination becomes difficult to sort out.

[142]From the aforesaid, it is evident that what is contained in the imagination may be false. While the senses always report what is there, if the imagination is confused or if the image changed by reason is not in congruity with reality then we can have a false image. It should be noted, however, that falsity for St. Thomas resides, properly speaking, only in judgment (i.e. the mind of the knower), yet there can be a sense in which what is in the imagination is false.

[143]SCG II, c. 73, n. 36: "sed post speciem in eo receptam, indiget eo quasi instrumento sive fundamento suae speciei: unde se habet ad phantasmata sicut causa efficiens; secundum enim imperium intellectus formatur in imaginatione phantasma conveniens tali speciei intelligibili, in quo resplendet species intelligibilis sicut exemplar in exemplato sive in imagine." See also II Sent., d. 7, q. 2, a. 2, ad 6 and III Sent., d. 15, q. 2, a. 2c, ad 3.

the senses alone as well as the fact that a rational structure (or irrational if the person is mentally ill, succumbing to error or evil) finds itself in the new image.

Aquinas states in another place that:

> there are some cognitive powers which are able to form others first from species of concepts. As the imagination from the species previously conceived mountain and gold, forms the species of gold mountain, and the intellect from the species preconceived of the genus and difference, forms the rational species. And similarly from the similitude of the image, we are able to form in us its similitude which is the image.[144]

Not only can the intellect be the formal cause of the image, but it can also compose different sensible species in the imagination. The intellect can place two or more things together in the imagination which it retrieved from memory.[145] But just as it can compose the two things in the imagination, it can also divide them, for that also is an act of the possible intellect which is able to impose its formality on the image in the imagination. So, one could have the image of a gold mountain and just imagine gold or mountain by separating what is proper to those respective species. Finally, it would appear that one can modify the species, retaining what is in it by replacing one of the accidents with another, e.g. the accident of disposition or position could be altered in one's image of Socrates. One can imagine Socrates sitting and merely change the accident of position to standing while retaining all of the rest. This means that anything that is a sensible accident can be taken away, added or modified by the intellect in the image in the imagination.[146]

Another passage of import to the discussion is found in the *Secunda Secundae*:

> In the imagination alone are the forms of sensible things insofar as

---

[144]ST I, q. 12, a. 9, ad 2: "aliquae potentiae cognoscitivae sunt, quae ex speciebus primo conceptis alias formare possunt. Sicut imaginatio ex praeconceptis speciebus montis et auri, format speciem montis aurei, et intellectus ex praeconceptis speciebus generis et differentiae, format rationem speciei. Et similiter ex similitudine imaginis formare possumus in nobis similitudinem eius cuius est imago." See also De Ver. q. 8, a. 5 and ibid., q. 8, a. 9.

[145]St. Thomas is very clear to note that this form of a new image is the result of previously known images (see De Ver., q. 19, a. 1). The material or sensible species used must be previously experienced. Even when the image has very little or virtually no relation to anything that could possible exist, the raw data or material is still taken from memory. This can be as remote as merely color, shapes, etc. and not actually things. But all has to come from memory regardless of how much the sensible species is reduced down to its basic elements of the proper objects of the individual five senses.

[146]The power of the imagination and memory (and cogitative power) to undergo these actions determines one's "creativity" as understood in the modern sense.

they are received from the senses, but it is changed in diverse ways, either because of some bodily change as it happens in those sleeping or the insane; or also according to the command of reason the phantasms are disposed in an ordering toward that which is understood. For as from diverse orderings of the same letters are taken diverse understandings, so also according to a diverse disposition of the phantasm in the intellect diverse intelligible species result.[147]

St. Thomas is observing that the possible intellect can move the imagination in different ways in order to reformulate the sensible species, image or phantasm so that it can understand it differently; just as we rearrange different letters in different ways to spell different words and thereby understand something different, so too can the intellect reformulate the image to understand something differently.

What Aquinas is really observing is that we can come to the understanding of something better by modifying the image from which we abstract and thereby modify our understanding. While every true understanding is that which congrues with reality, if there is to be true understanding, the image must produce the right concept in abstraction. We cannot rewrite reality the way we want, rather we work with the image by adding to it, taking away from it, and modifying it in ways which are in congruity with reality so that we can better understand reality.

This also implies that the possible intellect affects the associations made by the cogitative power. While in this section we have focused on the possible intellect's capacity to move the imagination, the possible intellect will also sometimes form an image in the imagination and then move the cogitative power to perform acts proper to itself with respect to the new image adding even more to our understanding. Therefore, the possible intellect can actually help itself by moving the lower powers in their operations.

St. Thomas also notes that the possible intellect can reformulate the image[148] and thereby affect the motions of the appetites.[149] The possible intellect can cause changes in the image in the various ways described and thereby formulate a phantasm which will affect the appetites according to its intentions. As can be imagined, this will

---

[147]ST II-II, q. 173, a. 2: "in imaginatione autem non solum sunt formae rerum sensibilium secundum quod accipiuntur a sensu, sed transmutatur diversimode, vel propter aliquam transmutationem corporalem, sicut accidit in dormientibus et furiosis; vel etiam secundum imperium rationis disponuntur phantasmata in ordine ad id quod est intelligendum. Sicut enim ex diversa ordinatione earundem litterarum accipiuntur diversi intellectus, ita etiam secundum diversam dispositionem phantasmatum resultant in intellectu diversae species intelligibiles."

[148]This ability of the intellect to reformulate an image in the imagination is done via the will, i.e. the possible intellect and will act together to change the image.

[149]De Ver., q. 26, a. 3, ad 13.

have a grave import regarding mental health, but that topic cannot be broached until we have completed our discussion of other subalternate principles.

D. The Cogitative Power

1. Its Acts

The last and highest[150] of the interior senses is the cogitative power. The essential activity of the cogitative power is, according to St. Thomas, as follows:

> Since the operations of the cogitative power concern only particulars, of which it composes and divides intentions and it has a corporeal organ through which it acts, it does not transcend the genus of the sensitive soul. Man, moreover, is not a man from a sensitive soul, but because he is an animal.[151]

The cogitative power is proper to man insofar as he is a (rational) animal. The cogitative power acts through a corporal organ and it is for this reason that it concerns singulars or particulars[152] and not universal concepts or species.[153]

St. Thomas then makes the observation that the cogitative power composes and divides intentions. Here we see why he also calls the cogitative power particular reason[154] and the passive intellect,[155] viz. because the cogitative power composes and divides, it acts much like the possible intellect. However, unlike the possible intellect which works with universals, the cogitative power composes and divides particulars. This composition and division is not the same as the composition or division of the possible intellect which is proper to judgment in the strictest sense. Rather, it is a type of physical or natural judgment[156] in which the cogitative power places two things side

---

[150]De Ver., q. 14, a. 1, ad 9.

[151]SCG II, l. 73, n. 14: "quia, cum virtus cogitativa habeat operationem solum circa particularia, quorum intentiones dividit et componit, et habeat organum corporale per quod agit, non transcendit genus animae sensitivae. Homo autem ex anima sensitiva non habet quod sit Homo, sed quod sit animal."

[152]See also III Sent., d. 23, q. 2, a. 2, ad 3.

[153]This follows from the fact that for St. Thomas the principle of individuation is matter and anything that acts through matter will therefore concern the particular, singular or individual and not the universal.

[154]See IV Sent., d. 50, q. 1, a. 1, ad 3; ST I, q. 81, a. 3; ST I-II, q. 51, a. 3 and De Ver., q. 14, a. 1, ad 9.

[155]IV Sent., d. 50, q. 1, a. 1, ad 3; SCG II, l. 60, n. 1; ST I, q. 79, a. 2, ad 2 and ST I-II, q. 53, a. 1. The various names given to this power find their place in SCG II, l. 73, n. 14. St. Thomas often notes that Aristotle called this power the passive intellect.

[156]St. Thomas uses this phrase in De Ver., q. 1, a. 11.

by side and compares them. St. Thomas uses the term *collatio*[157] in reference to this activity, which is often translated as comparison, which is a suitable translation since the term *collatio* comes from the Latin words *cum* and *latus* which means with the side or on the side of, or perhaps more appropriately it means to place side by side. The cogitative power takes the phantasm present in the imagination and compares it with another phantasm, either from the senses or from memory or as formulated by reason, etc. (i.e. from some other source) and then declares something about the two. It either composes them, i.e. it declares they are the same or similar or it divides them,[158] i.e. it denies that they are the same or similar. This is its primary function and all other acts it performs are specifications of this kind of action.

The next thing St. Thomas observes is that it concerns intentions. Now "intention" has two connotations, the first is that it refers to an intentional species, i.e. a species interior to man. Normally, this is associated with the universal species of the possible intellect, but here St. Thomas seems to be indicating that it is like the possible intellect in that it works with species, albeit particular sensible species. The second connotation of "intention" indicates a type of finality; in other words, St. Thomas is noting that the cogitative power has the capacity to ascertain whether a given sensible species is harmful or suitable[159] for a thing. It is for this reason that St. Thomas makes the following observation:

> Other intentions are sought which a sense does not apprehend, such
> as harmful and useful and others of this kind. And indeed, man
> arrives at this knowing by inquiring and conferring; other animals,
> truly by a certain natural instinct, as the sheep naturally flees the wolf
> as harmful. Whence in other animals the natural estimation is ordered
> to this; in man, however, it is the cogitative power, which is the
> comparison of particular intentions: hence it is called particular
> reason and the passive intellect.[160]

---

[157]For example, see *De anima*, q. 13.

[158]Composition can, at times, be a form of merging the two images and division can be a form of dissecting or dividing an image. Composition is sometimes a form of association because it associates something from memory with the image. This results in two important things: 1) it is the basis of familiarity insofar as we are familiar with an object because the cogitative power associates the image with past experience; and 2) it is how we make connections between different sense data.

[159]By the term suitable, it should not be taken as morally suitable but as appropriate or good for the person on a sensory level.

[160]*De anima*, q. 13: "quarto autem, requiruntur intentiones aliquae quas sensus non apprehendit, sicut nocivum et utile et alia huiusmodi. Et ad haec quidem cognoscenda pervenit homo inquirendo et conferendo; alia vero animalia quodam naturali instinctu, sicut ovis naturaliter fugit lupum tamquam nocivum. Unde ad hoc in aliis animalibus ordinatur aestimativa naturalis; in homine autem vis cogitativa, quae est collativa intentionum

The intentions, which the cogitative power is able to grasp, pertain to particular, i.e. material things as to whether they are harmful, useful, good or things of this kind which is something that is not, strictly speaking, sensible.[161] St. Thomas observes that this knowledge is arrived at in man by means of inquiring and conferring and here we understand why it is called particular reason. For the cogitative power not only composes and divides, but it can do so in several steps, i.e. through the comparison of one species with another, it may also associate with the conclusion from that comparison some other species. This process constitutes a type of syllogizing although this is not a formal kind of syllogizing as is the case with the possible intellect, but the cogitative power does piece together various things.

Two of the three fundamental activities of the cogitative power have thus been discussed, viz. 1) composition and division and 2) assessment of harmfulness, goodness or usefulness of some thing. The last act[162] the cogitative power performs is the following:

> The cogitative power does not have an order to the possible intellect,
> by which man understands, except through its act by which phantasms
> are prepared so that by the agent intellect the intelligibles and the
> performances of the possible intellect are made in act.[163]

This last activity is of extreme importance. The cogitative power, by means of associating previous memories with the current sensible species and making comparisons, prepares the phantasm for abstraction and is therefore pivotal for immaterial intellectual activities.[164] This means that a person's understanding is

---

particularium: unde et ratio particularis dicitur, et intellectus passivus."

[161]By this St. Thomas indicates that finalities and intentions are not properly sensibles, i.e. they are not the proper objects of any one of the senses, but that the cogitative power is able to make that assessment on the sense data and arrive at new knowledge.

[162]All other things which the cogitative power does are some form of these three.

[163]SCG II, l. 73, n. 16: "virtus cogitativa non habet ordinem ad intellectum possibilem, quo intelligit homo, nisi per suum actum quo praeparantur phantasmata ut per intellectum agentem fiant intelligibilia actu et perficientia intellectum possibilem." See also ibid., II, l. 60, n. 1.

[164]It has been wrongly assumed by modern psychology, psychiatry and medicine, that abstract thought is the product of the frontal lobes of the human brain. While this is the locus of the actions of the cogitative power, it is not that which performs abstract thinking, but it is that upon which abstract thinking is based. Certain kinds of frontal lobotomies may destroy the capacity for abstract thought, not because the cogitative power performs these actions, but that these acts depend on the cogitative power to derive their formal content. Moreover, since volition results from the possible intellect presenting to the will something under the notion of the good, there is also no volition since the will depends on the possible

dependent upon the cogitative power's capacity to perform its functions, although not entirely, for it is also dependent upon memory, imagination and its own virtues.[165]

2. The *Vis Aestimativa* and the *Vis Cogitativa*

In the previous quotes, St. Thomas noted that the cogitative power and estimative power,[166] which is in animals, differ. In man, the cogitative power proceeds by inquiring and conferring, whereas in animals the estimative sense proceeds by instinct. While in man this too will have a role, it is less predominant. The primary difference is, of course, that the cogitative power prepares the phantasm for abstraction. Since animals do not have immaterial faculties, this activity will be completely missing from the estimative power.

However, St. Thomas makes a further observation about their differences in his commentary on Aristotle's *De Anima*:

> The cogitative and the estimative relate differently to this for the cogitative apprehends the individual, as existent under the common nature; which befalls it insofar as it is united to the intellective in the same subject; hence, it knows this man as this man, and this wood as this wood. The estimative, however, does not apprehend some individual, insofar as it is under the common nature, but only insofar as it is the terminus or principle of some actions or passion; as the sheep knows the lamb, not insofar as it is this lamb, but insofar as it nurses it; and this grass is its food. Hence, to another individual to which its action or passion does not extend, in no way does its natural estimation apprehend it. Natural estimation is given to animals so that through it they are ordered in their proper actions, or passion,

intellect. This is why to perform a full frontal lobotomy can have no justification insofar as it destroys one's moral agency.

[165]Aquinas notes that the cogitative power is not ordered to the possible intellect except insofar as it prepares the phantasms. This indicates that the cogitative power has its ordering toward sensible species as its proper object and that its ordering to the possible intellect is really an ordering to the sensible species in a specific way, i.e. its task is really to prepare phantasms and not to act upon the possible intellect (it is not possible for a material faculty to act upon an immaterial one). So its ordering is really to phantasms immediately, and indirectly it is ordered to the possible intellect but insofar as it prepares phantasms.

[166]See *Comm. de anima* II, l. 13, n. 13.; IV Sent., d. 49, q. 2, a. 2 and De Ver., q. 14, a. 1, ad 9.

tending toward or fleeing.[167]

The cogitative power differs from the estimative power in that its acts can consider the individual under some common notion, not as a universal but *qua* individual. Whereas in animals, their estimative power is fundamentally ordered to action or passion and does not consider the thing insofar as it is an individual, but insofar as it is the terminus of their action or passion. This indicates that the cogitative power has the capacity to engage an object impartially,[168] whereas the estimative power does not. In other words, the cogitative power is able to perform its actions on the sensible object without having motion as its end which makes it capable of disinterested actions. While it can judge something as harmful and good, etc., it does not always engage its object that way but can do so impartially. While an animal may recognize its young, i.e. the individual, it does not do so insofar as it is a particular thing but as the terminus of its action. The cogitative power must be able to compare individual sensible species impartially in order to make it possible for man to engage in abstract thinking, i.e. for man to engage in a speculative science rather than practical science. If the cogitative power was always looking at something as the terminus of the man's action, he would have a hard time engaging in abstract, purely intellectual pursuits.

3. Further Observations

Since the cogitative power is a faculty which acts through a corporeal organ,[169] it can be affected by disposition. If the disposition is good then the person is apt mentally,[170] but if the corporeal organ is ill disposed then the cogitative power can be

---

[167]*Comm. de anima* II, l. 13, n. 16: "differenter tamen circa hoc se habet cogitativa, et aestimativa. Nam cogitativa apprehendit individuum, ut existens sub natura communi; quod contingit ei, inquantum unitur intellectivae in eodem subiecto; unde cognoscit hunc hominem prout est hic Homo, et hoc lignum prout est hoc lignum. Aestimativa autem non apprehendit aliquod individuum, secundum quod est sub natura communi, sed solum secundum quod est terminus aut principium alicuius actionis vel passionis; sicut ovis cognoscit hunc agnum, non inquantum est hic agnus, sed inquantum est ab ea lactabilis; et hanc herbam, inquantum est eius cibus. unde alia individua ad quae se non extendit eius actio vel passio, nullo modo apprehendit sua aestimativa naturali. Naturalis enim aestimativa datur animalibus, ut per eam ordinentur in actiones proprias, vel passiones, prosequendas, vel fugiendas."

[168]See L.M. Regis, O.P, *Epistemology* (MacMillan Company, New York, 1959), p. 272f.

[169]The actual location in modern science is rather clear, i.e. at the frontal lobes. St. Thomas notes that doctors of his time situated it in a different location and he himself observes that it is in the middle of the head (e.g., see IV Sent., d. 50, q. 1, a. 1, ad 3). Even though the medieval medical knowledge may have been wanting in this regard, the fact that it operates through the bodily organ does not take away the subsequent observations.

[170]SCG II, c. 73, n. 25.

impeded in its operations.[171] Moreover, the general capacity for understanding is based upon the disposition of the cogitative power; as a result, one's raw intelligence is based upon the disposition of the brain.[172] This necessarily follows from the fact that in different men, the possible and agent intellects do not differ in capacities but according to the disposition of the corporeal organ of the brain. This tends to be confirmed by common experience insofar as those who suffer brain damage are less capable of understanding certain things than others whose brains are well disposed. If disposition is important in the operations of the intellect, then the operations of the intellect can be affected by those things which increase or decrease right disposition in the brain.[173]

If the cogitative power has a disposition, it would seem that it is also capable of habituation. In other words, the cogitative power composes and divides in certain ways: in some men, it associates one thing with another and in other men it associates differently. This means that the cogitative power is capable of being trained. This would follow from what St. Thomas notes about the relationship between the cogitative power and the possible intellect. For the possible intellect not only moves the imagination but it also directs the cogitative power.[174] This means that it is able to be habituated in specific ways by the actions which the possible intellect commands. If the possible intellect and will move the cogitative power in one way repeatedly, it is disposed toward that kind of action. Hence, how we associate by means of the cogitative power can often be the result of our own command and volition. Moreover, it was noted above that in the process of reformulating an image, the possible intellect moves not only the imagination but also the cogitative power to help it reformulate the image based on past experience. If the possible intellect does not have the species it needs in order to grasp something, it moves the cogitative power to make comparisons and associations in order to get the phantasm it needs.[175] This means that the actions of the cogitative power are permeated by the species of the possible intellect which helps its considerations as well as its preparations for abstraction.

While the cogitative power has the capacity to make its own comparisons, nevertheless, it can be moved to compare something in a certain way by the forms or species from the possible intellect, i.e. the possible intellect moves it to consider something in a specific way. This is why St. Thomas notes that the cogitative power is

---

[171]SCG III, c. 84, n. 14.

[172]ST I, q. 85, a. 7. The raw intelligence would be based not only on disposition of the cogitative power but the whole brain, for if the cogitative power is well disposed but the imagination or memory are poor, this will impede one's capacity to grasp things quickly, easily and in depth.

[173]This is clear from the fact that diet, nutrition and different drugs can drastically affect the brain in its biological electrochemical operations.

[174]ST I, q. 81, 3, ad 2.

[175]See SCG II, c. 73, n. 36 and n. 39.

pivotal for prudence[176] and election[177] because the cogitative power is moved to consider particulars according to a certain light, i.e. a certain species or form from the possible intellect. For example, if one wants to know the most prudent way to obtain the money necessary to pay his bills, he does not let the cogitative power go off on its own. Rather, he forms the image in the imagination and then moves the cogitative power to consider particulars in light of a goal imposed on the cogitative power by the possible intellect. It is precisely because the cogitative power works with particulars and can be guided by the possible intellect, that it makes it possible for man to consider various ways of moral and non-moral action.

Finally, St. Thomas makes an observation in addition to the foregoing which is very significant for psychology. He makes the observation that the cogitative power in man and the estimative power in animals are able to move the appetites.[178] This follows from the fact that the appetites are moved by the phantasm in the imagination and since the cogitative power can make assessments about the goodness and badness of a sensible thing, that goodness or harmfulness is associated or merged with the image in the phantasm and as a result moves the appetites. Therefore, the cogitative power is exceedingly important in the appetitive life. While the appetites may be moved merely by the image in the imagination, nevertheless, a phantasm can be altered to increase or decrease the movement of the appetites based on the assessment of the cogitative power.[179] For example, if one sees a man, when his phantasm is first in the imagination, the appetite may not be moved, but then the cogitative power could see something in the man's phantasm which is a cause for alarm, and fear could rise. Conversely, if a person has suffered injury from a person of a specific gender, that person may react to others of that gender due to the association made by the cogitative power, but since the cogitative power can assess the phantasms of individuals, it could assess that a specific person of the same gender is not to be feared.

A further consideration is the fact that since the cogitative power is capable of being moved by the possible intellect and will, it means that one can lessen or increase one's appetitive movements by means of control of the image and the cogitative power. In a word, the appetites are within the indirect control of the possible intellect and will and, therefore, one does not have to accept the idea that one is at the whim of one's emotions, for the possible intellect can move the cogitative power with a specific motion or form and change its assessment of the phantasm, thereby affecting the appetites. This means that the appetitive life is heavily dependent upon the intellectual life.

Moreover, since the reformulated image is pressed back into memory, we can actually have an indirect control over certain aspects of memory. For one can confuse oneself by reformulating the phantasm in a way contrary to the way something was

---

[176]In Ethic. VI, l. 9 (1255) and De Ver. q. 10, a. 5, ad 2.

[177]De Ver., q. 10, a. 5.

[178]ST I, q. 81, a. 3.

[179]Ibid., I, q. 81, a. 2.

remembered.[180] On the other hand, if one has a false or bad memory, reformulating the phantasm can actually be curative of memory.

Conclusion

The exterior senses and the interior senses are extremely important regarding their impact on one's psychological health. While the full implications of this will be discussed later, we must now move to the second section on the cognitive faculties. In this section we considered the cognitive faculties which operate through a bodily organ; so now we move to the consideration of the cognitive faculties which do not depend on a bodily organ for their operations.

---

[180]Common experience shows us that those who lie (and thereby change their image) sometimes become confused as to what actually happened and lying can therefore erode one's grasp of the truth.

Due to a completely inadequate anthropology, modern psychology has failed to grasp that man and animals differ by virtue of the fact that man performs immaterial actions or operations while animals do not. Often it is asserted that the difference between animals and man is merely a matter of degree of intelligence rather than a matter of kind. However, the mere fact that man contemplates the nature of truth is a sign that he is different from animals according to kind. For one cannot point to a physical instance of truth, for truth is not a material thing and therefore cannot be grasped by a material thing. This is why man, not animals, discusses truth. Therefore, to have a complete picture of the cognitive faculties of man, we must discuss those cognitive faculties and operations which do not occur through a bodily organ, viz. the agent and possible intellects.[1]

I. The Agent Intellect

A. The Faculty Itself

The agent intellect, which is an immaterial[2] faculty,[3] like the other faculties, is an accident,[4] by which the soul acts. The primary function of the agent intellect is to abstract[5] the concept out of the phantasm in the imagination and press it into the possible intellect.[6] Hence, the agent intellect is proportionate to the possible intellect[7] since it produces intelligibles which are proportionate[8] to the possible intellect. This proportion reflects that both faculties are immaterial and that the agent intellect has the capacity to

---

[1] In one sense, the intellect is a single faculty comprising the four interior senses, agent and possible intellects since it is that by which the soul understands. However, each of these are ontologically distinct even though each is a part of the whole intellect. It is because they are ontologically distinct and perform essentially different operations that they are sometimes referred to as separate faculties.

[2] We know that the agent intellect is immaterial by virtue of the subsequent considerations of its actions and the fact that it is proportioned to the possible intellect. Since the effect cannot be greater than the cause, the effects which it produces in the possible intellect are immaterial and therefore the agent intellect must likewise be immaterial. Ontologically, a material thing does not have enough act to be able to affect an immaterial thing which is much greater in act.

[3] SCG II, c. 78, n. 3 and 5; ibid., II, c. 96, n. 8 and *Comp. Theo.* I, c. 87.

[4] SCG III, c. 42, n. 7.

[5] SCG II, c. 82, n. 3; ST I, q. 79, a. 3, ad 3; ibid., q. 79., a. 4, ad 4; ibid., q. 85, a. 1, ad 4; ibid., q. 87, a. 1, ad 2; De Ver., q. 10, a. 8, ad sed contra 11; *De anima*, q. 5.

[6] De Ver., q. 11, a. 1, ad 16.

[7] Ibid., II, c. 76, n. 3.

[8] SCG II, c. 77, n. 5.

act upon the possible intellect, which is why St. Thomas calls it a light[9] since it has the capacity to enlightened the possible intellect.

While man is not able to understand without the agent intellect,[10] it itself does not understand what it makes in act.[11] It is the principle of action in the intellect[12] since it makes the intelligibles to be in act, yet, it is not the form of the possible intellect,[13] but it places intelligible forms in the possible intellect[14] which understands. Since it makes the intelligibles[15] in act, it is the efficient cause of the intelligibles[16] while the formal content is abstracted from the phantasm. As it produces diverse forms in the possible intellect[17] according to the various phantasms, the agent intellect relates to the possible intellect as artifex to matter.[18] In other words, just as an artist causes the accidental forms in the stone, which already exists and has its own substantial form, so the agent intellect causes the intelligible forms in the possible intellect which already exists and has its own accidental form.[19] Since the agent intellect makes the sensible species (i.e. the phantasm) intelligible,[20] the phantasm is the instrumental and secondary cause while the agent intellect is the principal and first cause of the intelligible species in the possible intellect.[21] This ensures that our knowledge is founded in the phantasm which has a causal connection to the object exterior to the individual. This ultimately means that man's knowledge is founded in reality and therefore only realism is an adequate epistemology. Moreover, no psychology can treat the individual without recognizing

---

[9]III Sent., d. 14, q. 1, a. 1b; SCG II, c. 79, n. 9; ibid., III, c. 53, n. 6; ST I, q. 79, a. 3, ad 2; De malo, q. 16, a. 12, ad 1; De spiritualibus creaturis, q. 10 and De anima, q. 4, ad 4.

[10]SCG II, c. 76, n. 17 and De anima, q. 4, ad 4.

[11]SCG II, c. 76, n. 31 and De Ver., q. 10, a. 8, ad sed contra 11.

[12]De Pot., q. 8, a. 1.

[13]II Sent., d. 17, q. 2, a. 1.

[14]II Sent., d. 17, q. 2, a. 1 and SCG III, c. 42, n. 4.

[15]II Sent., d. 17, ., 2, a. 1; III Sent., d. 23, q. 1, a. 1; SCG II, c. 76, n. 4 and 20 and ibid., II, c. 77, n. 5.

[16]SCG II, c. 78, n. 4.

[17]ST I, q. 76, a. 2.

[18]II Sent., d. 17, q. 2, a. 1; SCG II, c. 60, n. 14; ibid., II, c. 76, n. 19 and De spiritualibus creaturis, q. 10, ad 11.

[19]The possible intellect is also an accident which makes the intelligible form as existing in the possible intellect a modification of a pre-existing accident, i.e. it is an accident of an accident. But since it has its own existence and nature, it has its own structure and determinations in its own acts.

[20]II Sent., d, 17, q. 2, a. 1; SCG II, c. 60, n. 19; ibid., II, c. 77, n. 2; ibid., II, c. 96, n. 8 and De anima, q. 15.

[21]De Ver., q. 10, a. 6, ad 7.

that he gains his knowledge by means of reality.

The agent intellect is not the subject of habits[22] since it is determined in its act.[23] The agent intellect always abstracts from the same source (a phantasm in the imagination) and expresses the intelligible species in the same possible intellect provided the conditions are present for its operations.[24] Therefore, its activity cannot be enhanced or altered by different actions and so it cannot be the subject of habits. Because it performs the same function each time the phantasm is prepared, it has the capacity to abstract the form from any material thing which is knowable by the senses and it is for this reason that the agent intellect is said to make all things intelligibile.[25]

B. The Process of Abstraction

From the previous discussion, it has already been mentioned that abstraction is a process of the agent intellect. Abstraction comes from the two Latin words "ab" and "trahere" which mean to draw out of. Abstraction is the process by which the agent intellect draws the intelligible species out of the phantasm[26] present in the imagination. This implies that the phantasm contains in some way the intelligible species,[27] although not explicitly, otherwise it would not have to be drawn out. Abstraction is the process by which the intelligible species is drawn out of the material conditions of the

---

[22]III Sent., d. 14, q. 1, a. 1b, ad 2 and De Ver., q. 16, a. 1, ad 13.

[23]III Sent., d. 23, q. 1, a. 1. As it is determined in its act, it is not in potentiality to different kinds of act. Nor is it in potentiality to any other faculty. For even the imagination from which it abstracts does not act upon the agent intellect but merely provides the phantasm from which the agent intellect abstracts. Therefore, St. Thomas observes that the agent intellect is in act and not in potency. See SCG II, c. 78, n. 2 and ST I-II, q. 50, a. 5, ad 2.

[24]What this essentially means is that the phantasm has to be prepared for abstraction which requires that the cogitative power prepare it. This is why people are not volitional agents during sleep; for in order for the will to will something it must be in the possible intellect. But since the possible intellect is made in act only by the agent intellect, then only when the phantasm is ready for abstraction does the agent intellect actually abstract. During sleep, the imagination and cogitative powers are not disposed to preparing the image for abstraction and, therefore, no abstraction occurs. This appears to be based on the fact that during sleep the brain does not function the same way as it does awake and so disposition in the passive intellect is also determinative of abstraction. It would also appear, then, that those whose intellects are not disposed, such as those who suffer certain degrees of brain damage, etc., do not perform abstractions.

[25]SCG II, c. 78, n. 6; ST I, q. 79, a. 4, ad 3; ibid., I, q. 88, a. 1 and De Ver., q. 10, a. 6.

[26]ST I, q. 86, a. 2, ad 2; ibid., q. 89, a. 4 and ibid., II-II- q. 15, a. 3.

[27]How this is the case will be discussed below.

phantasm.[28] Since something is intelligible insofar as it is separated from matter,[29] the intelligible species is drawn out of the matter. This also means it is drawn out of the concrete, singular and particular.[30] The phantasm which represents the concrete individual is a unified sensible species and it is from that sensible species[31] that the intelligible species is abstracted. These sensible species are the sensed accidents[32] of the exterior object. As a result, abstraction is a process of induction[33] in which one goes from the particular accidental qualities of a thing to an intelligible species which is universal[34] since it is separated from matter which is the principle of individuation.[35] Abstraction results in an intelligible form which is drawn out of accidents and pressed into the possible intellect, thereby putting the possible intellect into act.

C. The Ontological Basis of Abstraction

If the agent intellect abstracts a form from a set of accidents existing as a sensible species in the intellect, it would appear as if it is getting something out of nothing. However, there is an ontological basis for abstraction and the abstraction cannot be fully understood without a grasp of this ontological order. In the ontological order, material things are composed of substance and accidents. The substance is sometimes referred to as the first act of a thing and the accidents are referred to as the second act of a thing[36] because they are as second forms of actualization of some thing.[37] For example, an individual person is a substance and has substantial existence, but he can have different types of secondary actualizations, e.g. the existence of blond hair is a secondary form of existence, since blondness exists in the hair rather than brownness.

Operations of a substance, such as thinking, talking, etc, are likewise called

---

[28]II Sent., d. 3, q. 1, a. 1; IV Sent., d. 49, q. 2, a. 2, ad 4; SCG II, c. 82, n. 12; ST I, q. 40, a. 3; ibid., q. 55, a. 2, ad 2; ibid., q. 57, a. 2, ad 1; ibid., q. 79, a. 3; ibid., I-II, q. 29, a. 6; *De anima*, q. 2, ad 5; ibid., q. 4; ibid., q. 14 and Quod. XII, n. 12, q. 8.

[29]SCG II, c. 82, n. 3.

[30]ST I, q. 12, a. 4, ad 3; ibid., q. 13, a. 9; *De unitate intellectus*, c. 5 and *Post. Anal.* II, c. 20, n. 12.

[31]ST I, q. 89, a. 7.

[32]*De trinitate*, p. 3, q. 5, a. 3, c. 4.

[33]Post. Anal. I, l. 30, n. 5.

[34]II Sent., d. 40, q. 1, a. 5; ST I, q. 40, a. 3; ibid., q. 57, a.2, ad 1; ibid., q. 85, a. 3, ad 4; *De anima*, q. 2, ad 5; ibid., q. 4, ad 3 and ibid., q. 14.

[35]*De ente et essentia*, c. 2, nn. 4-5.

[36]I Sent., d. 7, q. 1, a. 1, ad 2; ibid., d. 33, q. 1, a. 1, ad 1; II Sent., d. 35, q. 1, a. 1; IV Sent., d. 4, q. 2, a. 2a, ad 3; ibid., d. 49, q. 3, a. 2; ST I, q. 48, a. 5; ibid., q. 76, a. 4, ad 1; ibid., q. 105, a. 5; De Ver., q. 27, a. 3, ad 25; De Pot., q. 1, a. 1; De Vir., q. 1, a.9, ad 11 and *De caelo et mundo* II, l. 4, n. 5.

[37]II Sent., d. 26, q. 1, a. 2, ad 3; *Comp. Theol.* I, c. 23 and ST I, q. 3, a. 6.

second acts since they are accidents[38] or modifications in the already existing substance. One of the ways this can be seen is that the substance or essence of a thing does not change in itself when it acts. For example, a human being is a person and is an individual substance of rational nature,[39] but when a person talks, the person does not change into a dog. Therefore, the existence of the substance is distinct from the existence of the accidents,[40] for the existence of thought in a person does not change the person into another substance but is merely a modification of the already existing substance.

However, not any accident can exist in any substance, e.g. thought cannot exist in a stone because the substance of a stone does not have enough act to cause the act of existence of thought. St. Thomas makes the following observations about the relationship of substances and accidents:

> As the essence of some universal species is related to its per se accidents of the species, so the essence of the singular is related to all the proper accidents of that singular; all the accidents found in it are of such a kind: since those are made proper to things by virtue of that in which things are individuated. Moreover, the intellect knowing the essence of the species, through it comprehends all the per se accidents of that species: since, according to the Philosopher [i.e. Aristotle], of every demonstration which arrives at a conclusion about the proper accidents of a subject, the principle [i.e. premise] is that which is.[41]

St. Thomas is noting that the intellect knows the accidents which relate per se (i.e. essentially) to a specific kind of essence. In other words, certain kinds of accidents reside in certain kinds of substances. Not every accident can reside in every kind of substance. For example, accidents of lead, such as its color, texture, density, etc. cannot be the same as the accidents of a human being. Each have different accidents. Since the substance can only cause certain accidents, only certain accidents can exist in it. The

---

[38]IV Sent., d. 50, q. 1, a 4, ad 5.

[39]St. Thomas accepted Boethius' definition of a person, see III Sent., d. 2, q. 1, a. 1a; SCG IV, c. 38, n. 2 and ST I, q. 40, a 3.

[40]De ente et essentia, c. 6, n.2.

[41]De Ver., q. 2, a. 7: "sicut se habet essentia universalis alicuius speciei ad omnia per se accidentia illius speciei, ita se habet essentia singularis ad omnia accidentia propria illius singularis, cuiusmodi sunt omnia accidentia in eo inventa: quia per hoc quod in ipso individuantur, efficiuntur ei propria. intellectus autem cognoscens essentiam speciei, per eam comprehendit omnia per se accidentia speciei illius: quia, secundum philosophum, omnis demonstrationis, per quam accidentia propria de subiecto concluduntur, principium est quod quid est." The Latin phrase "quod quid est," translated as "that which is," is a technical Latin idiom in the medieval period referring to the essence of a thing.

different kinds of accidents relate to the different kinds of substance.[42] This essentially means that a specific set of accidents actually reveals the nature of the substance. For instance, when we observe a stone, we do not observe rational behavior; we do not observe free acts of the will; we do not observe speech coming from the stone because these types of accidents cannot exist in a stone. However, the stone does reveal its substance through its accidents, i.e. by virtue of the fact that it has certain colors and textures and consistencies, it reveals that it has the essence of stoneness and not the essence of dogness. The fact that it lies motionless unless it is acted upon from outside indicates that it is not alive nor possesses a faculty of locomotion. Its rest reveals that it is a stone and not an animal.[43]

---

[42]In De Ver., q. 27, a. 2, ad 7, St. Thomas makes the observation that the accidents of the soul are proportionate to the soul. This is a sign that there is a fundamental relationship between the kinds of accidents that can exist in certain kinds of substances.

[43]This also implies that two essentially different substances are incapable of having the same accidents. For instance lead and gold cannot have the same accidents since they are essentially different. However, this is not to deny that some categories of accidents cannot be shared by two essentially different substances, e.g. a man with black hair has the same quality of color of hair as a black bear. However, while they may have some accidents in common they do not have all the same accidents in common, i.e. a man and bear do not have the exact same set of accidents, for a man is bipedal while a black bear is quadrupedal. Moreover, even the hair that might have the same color will reveal that it comes from a bear by virtue of its coarseness, consistency, etc., so that even among accidents which are shared, they are joined to accidents which differentiate the thing which they affect, e.g. even though a bear and a man may have the same hair color, the hair of a bear is accidentally different in other ways from the hair of a man. Hence, the various accidents come together collectively to reveal the essence of a thing. There appear to be three kinds of accidents in relation to essences. 1) There are those kinds of accidents which are per se accidents and always accompany a given essence, sometimes called proper accidents since they are proper to an essence as such, e.g. whenever one finds a human essence, one also finds a possible intellect and will. 2) Then there are those accidents which are common to many in a species but not necessarily to all, e.g. man, generally speaking, has hair on his head, but some men are bald. Even these accidents reveal the nature, for as was shown in the example, a bear's hair and man's hair are different. Moreover, the fact that one finds a biped which is bald on the head but has hair elsewhere is found only in men, even though it is not a proper accident. 3) Then there are those accidents which are not common or found in the most part in men, but in a few, e.g. red haired people are not that common in comparison to black or blond haired people. But even the scarcity of the red-hairedness reveals man's nature to a degree because, again, it is coupled with other qualities which other animals do not have and the accidents are a part of the total number of possible types of accidents in relation to the human essence. In other words, even though two substances have the same essence, their accidents may vary, but even those accidents which vary are limited by the nature of the thing. It is not possible for a human essence to have the accidental qualities of hair which are proper to a goat. What this means is that even though a given essence can reveal itself in a variety of accidental variations, those variations are always within a given set of possibilities and the agent

Since there is a specific kind of relation between the accidents and the substance, the essence of a thing is implicitly contained in the accidents, for only certain accidents can reside in certain substances. This fact is expressed in the principle of operation, which is expressed as *agere sequitur esse* (action follows upon being) or *operatio sequitur esse* (operation follows upon being). This principle essentially states that the nature of the being determines the nature of the operation or act. In this case, a substance determines the types of accidents or actions.

The reversal of this principle expresses the basis of the cognitive order. While in the ontological order the type of being determines the actions, in the cognitive order, the actions reveal the substance. This is because the human intellect is a mirror image[44] of the ontological order. The ontological order starts first with existence of some thing (essence) in which adhere accidents (existence-essence-accidents) whereas the human cognitive powers first know the accidents, then the essence, then the existence. Abstraction is the process by which the agent intellect draws out the essence which is revealed in the accidents which are contained in the phantasm in the imagination. Therefore, the agent intellect is able to derive the intelligible species by means of induction, i.e. by separating the form which is implicit in the particular accidents of a thing to derive the universal nature or essence of the thing which corresponds to those accidents. It is precisely because the substance expresses or reveals itself through its accidents, that the agent intellect is able to derive the essence from those revealing accidents. The process of abstraction which is the process of drawing the essence out of the accidents is analogous to the putting together of the pieces of a jigsaw puzzle. If one took a box containing the pieces of the puzzle which was not yet constructed, one could not see the picture, even though the entire picture was contained in the pieces. Analogically, the agent intellect is able to "see" the picture (essence) in the pieces (accidents) which contain the picture. The agent intellect is an important faculty. It makes it possible for man to keep in contact with reality since it abstracts the essences of real things from their accidents. It makes it possible for man to have true intellectual knowledge of things by means of his senses.

---

intellect is able to abstract a given essence which can have a variety of accidents but always within a given set of limits determined by that essence. But those various accidents in themselves reveal something about the nature, but in different ways, e.g. one person's speech which is an accident may contain a southern drawl but another's may reflect a different accent and yet the agent intellect knows that those two accidents are possible modifications of speech.

[44]St. Thomas observes that the concept in the possible intellect is like a mirror image with respect to the thing itself, see SCG II, c. 74, n. 2. While this is observed in respect to the possible intellect, it can be applied to the entire intellect, including the possible intellect, agent intellect, four interior senses and the five exterior senses.

II. The Possible Intellect

A. The Faculty Itself

In the treatment of the agent intellect, it has already been seen that the possible intellect is an immaterial power[45] which receives its intelligible species or object from the agent intellect.[46] The possible intellect is really distinct from the agent intellect[47] and the agent intellect is a light with respect to the possible intellect[48] and, as a light, the agent intellect puts the possible intellect into act.[49] Insofar as the agent intellect acts upon the possible intellect, the possible intellect is a passive power.[50] As a passive power, the possible intellect initially starts out as a *tabula rasa*,[51] i.e. it lacks all conceptual knowledge. While initially it may lack any conceptual knowledge, nevertheless it is a certain infinite power[52] in the sense that it is in potency with respect to all forms.[53] As it receives its form, the possible intellect is perfected or made in act by the intelligible species.[54] While the agent intellect is said to put the possible intellect into act, it does so by the concept, which is the actualization of the possible intellect.

---

[45]See SCG II, c. 59, n. 6; ibid., c. 60, n. 16; ibid., c. 62, n. 2; ibid., c. 62, n. 11 and ibid., c. 75, n. 10. Insofar as the faculty is immaterial, it is also subsistent, i.e. it does not lose its existence at death but continues to exist after death; see SCG II, c. 60, n. 23.

[46]II Sent., d. 17, q. 2, a. 1 and ibid., d. 20, q. 2, a. 2, ad 2.

[47]II Sent., d. 17, q. 2, a. 1; SCG II, c. 78, n. 3 and ST I, q. 79, a. 10.

[48]I Sent., d. 32, a. 2, a. 1, ad 3; II Sent., d. 20, q. 2, a. 2, ad 2; IV Sent., d. 49, q. 2, a. 4 and De Ver., q. 9, a. 1, ad 12.

[49]II Sent., d. 17, q. 2, a. 1 and SCG II, c. 73, n. 30.

[50]De Ver., q. 16, a. 1, ad 13. In relation to the agent intellect, the possible intellect is a passive power, but it is also an active power which will be seen with respect to the three acts of the possible intellect.

[51]I Sent., d. 40, q. 1, a. 2, ad 5. The possible intellect, while being a "blank slate" that lacks any conceptual knowledge, does possess what St. Thomas calls connatural knowledge which will be discussed below.

[52]SCG II, c. 59, n. 6. By "infinite" is not implied that it is actually infinite like the intellect of God, but that there is no limit to what it can know regarding that which is in its natural capacity to know.

[53]II Sent., d. 3, q. 3, a. 3, ad 4; ibid., d. 17, q. 2, a. 1; II Sent., d. 14, q. 1, a. 1e and ST I, q. 79, a. 7. The terms used in reference to the object of the possible intellect, viz. intelligible species, form, etc., also go by the name of universal, essence, concept, idea, etc. While each name refers to the same thing, often their connotation is slightly different, in order to emphasize some aspect of the intelligible species; nevertheless, they are the same object.

[54]SCG II, c. 59, n. 8 and 10; ibid., c. 73, n. 39 and ibid., c. 74, n. 4 and n. 16.

The possible intellect is the highest cognitive power in man.[55] It is not the same thing as the imagination[56] or the cogitative power[57] since their objects are essentially different, for one is material and particular, the other universal and immaterial. This observation is of importance for several reasons. First, it rejects the rationalist position that the image and idea are the same. Moreover, it rejects the modern psychological position which asserts that the frontal lobes are where abstract thought occurs. As was mentioned, even though the cogitative power may be located in the frontal lobes and without it the possible intellect cannot perform its operations, that does not mean that the possible intellect is not distinct from the cogitative power. Since their objects are ontologically different, they cannot be the same power; conversely, if they cannot be the same power, there must be two distinct powers performing very different acts since acts are also specified by the objects of the faculties.

The possible intellect is that by which man or the soul knows.[58] While the passive intellect is said to have a type of sensitive knowledge, true intellectual knowledge does not occur except in the possible intellect. This is knowledge in the fullest sense since it grasps the essence of a thing as well as its existence, which cannot occur at the sensitive level. The possible intellect is also the subject of habits and virtues.[59] It is the power which moves the will[60] and is therefore important in the moral life. It is the faculty of self-knowledge, in that it is not only the faculty by which man knows himself; it is also the faculty which has the capacity to know itself by means of an intelligible species[61] and reflexive act.

B. The Operations of the Possible Intellect
1. Understanding or Simple Apprehension

St. Thomas observes that the possible intellect performs three distinct acts, viz. understanding or simple apprehension, judgment and ratiocination.[62] Understanding is the act of the possible intellect by which one apprehends the essence or quiddity of a thing.[63] Understanding is either of a simple concept, i.e. one which has just been abstracted or a complex concept, i.e. one which is the product of judgment or

---

[55]SCG II, c. 62, n. 7.

[56]II Sent., d. 17, q. 2, a. 1 and SCG II, c. 67, n. 4.

[57]IV Sent., d. 50, q. 1, a. 1, ad 3.

[58]SCG II, c. 73, n. 17 and n. 37.

[59]SCG II, c. 73, n. 21 and ST I, q. 50, a. 4, ad 1.

[60]SCG II, c.76, n. 20.

[61]SCG II, c. 98, n. 2. The topic of self-knowledge which is pivotal to psychology, will be discussed in volume III.

[62]For a listing of the three see In Peri., l. 1, n. 1. See also ST I, q. 79, a. 8; ibid., q. 85, a. 5 and De Ver., q. 15, a. 1 ad 5.

[63]*In libros perihermenias*, l. 1, n. 1; De Ver., q. 15, a. 1, ad 5 and ST I, q. 85, a. 5.

ratiocination. Once judgment or ratiocination occurs, the complex concept at times may be re-grasped by the intellect in an act of understanding.[64]

Understanding is the first level in intellectual knowledge, i.e. it is an act of knowing a thing in which the thing is in the knower according to the mode of the knower. St. Thomas observes that to understand (*intellectus*) comes from the two Latin words *intus* and *legere* which means to read into, i.e. by an act of understanding the intellect is able to penetrate the interior or essence of the thing and see what it is.[65]

2. Judgment

The second act of the possible intellect is judgment. Judgment is an act of the intellect by which two terms are either affirmed of each other or denied of each other. When the two terms are affirmed of each other, they are placed together, which is called affirmation or composition, i.e. one thing is made of two. When the two terms are denied of each other, it is called negation or division.[66] Composition and division, i.e. judgment, always results in a proposition[67] which is composed of the two terms, viz. subject and predicate.[68] An example of composition would be the following proposition: Socrates is mortal; where the predicate "is mortal" is affirmed of the subject "Socrates." An example of division would be the following proposition: Socrates is not immortal; where the predicate "is immortal" is denied of the subject "Socrates."

Judgment is a form of knowledge in which we know something by means of

---

[64]There are two different kinds of grasping a complex concept. The first which is understood is when the complex concept is grasped as a unified whole in which the intellect does not consider the subject and the predicate of a proposition, i.e. the two or more aspects in the complex concept distinctly, e.g. one can simply understand "healthy food" under a unified or whole notion. That is different when the two or more aspects of the concept are considered distinctly, e.g. in the proposition "the food is healthy," one is applying one thing to another and, in this case, the complex concept or proposition is grasped through judgment with two distinct aspects making a single proposition. In the first case, one may grasp immediately "healthy food" as a whole in which neither part of the complex concept is considered in particular but as a whole, i.e. there is no assertion made regarding the complex concept. The second is grasped only through judgment when the parts are grasped as constituting a unity, but the terms of the position are grasped distinctly or the parts of the complex concept are asserted of each other.

[65]ST II-II, q. 8, a. 1; De Ver., q. 1, a. 12 and In Ethic., IV, l. 5, n. 5.

[66]See ST I q. 58, a. 4; ibid., q. 85, a. 5; In Peri., I, l. 3, nn. 3 and 9; SCG II, q. 76, a. 9; ST I, q. 14, a. 15, ad 3; ibid., q. 58, a. 5; Meta., V, l. 9, n. 11; *Comm. de anima* I, l. 10, n. 19.

[67]I Sent., d. 33, q. 1, a. 1, ad 1; SCG I, c. 58, n. 6; De Ver., q. 2, a. 7, ad 3; Quod., n. 5, q. 5, a. 2 and *De trinitate*, p. 3, q. 5, a. 3. Propositions are sometimes referred to as enunciables.

[68]ST I, q. 58, a. 4.

composition and division.[69] For instance it is one thing to know or grasp the concept of "health" and the concept of "food" independently of each other; it is another to compose the two concepts and arrive at the knowledge of "healthy food." Judgment helps us to gain further knowledge of a thing than what is gained merely by simple apprehension. It helps us to know differences between things as well as differences within a thing; moreover, it helps us to know the similarities of things.[70] For instance, by composition, we can know that "house cats are like lions" and through further judgments we can assert how they are alike. As was mentioned in the previous chapter, we can reformulate the image to come to a better understanding of something, so composition and division can be used to formulate different images in order to better understand something.[71]

As every composition and division results in a proposition, there are three kinds of propositions produced by the possible intellect by means of judgment. The first is complex concepts,[72] i.e. the possible intellect is able to form different concepts by using other concepts. The example above regarding health and food shows that through an act of judgment one can produce the complex concept of healthy food. The concepts can be very complicated due to the fact that even the complex concept can then be composed and divided, e.g. one can assert "healthy food is good tasting," thereby adding more to the concept of food.

The second product of judgment or the second kind of proposition is an existential proposition in which through an act of judgment the existence of a thing is either affirmed or denied.[73] In this act, the intellect is able to know whether something exists or not in reality, i.e. it concerns the existence of a thing in reality.[74] For instance,

---

[69]ST I, q. 85, a. 5.

[70]ST I, q. 85, a. 5, ad 1 and *De trinitate* p. 3, q. 5, a. 3.

[71]ST I, q. 84, a. 6, ad 2. It should be noted that it was said that the cogitative power performs a type of composition or division. While the cogitative power composes and divides sensible species, the cogitative power does not understand the content of the sensible species and therefore it is not true composition since it does not truly understand or know whether one sensible species goes with another except by similarity or dissimilarity of the species themselves. However, the possible intellect understands the intrinsic content of the essences and can assess whether the two terms should really be composed or divided. On the other hand, the cogitative power can be trained to compose things in a false fashion and continue to do so since it does not understand what it does. Moreover, judgment is a form of knowledge and so the composition and division performed by the possible intellect is essentially different from the composition of the cogitative power which does not understand or know what it produces by combining and separating sensible species.

[72]III Sent., d. 24, q. 1, a. 1b, ad 1; ST I, q. 58, a. 5; De Ver., q. 1, a. 3 and ibid., q. 3, a. 2.

[73]I Sent., d. 33, q. 1, a. 1, ad 1; II Sent., d. 34, q. 1, a. 1; III Sent., d. 24, q. 1, a. 1b; *De malo* q. 16, a. 6, ad sed contra 1; Quod. IX, q. 2, a. 2 and *In libros perihermenias* I, l. 3, n. 9.

[74]I Sent., d. 19, q. 5, a. 1, ad 7.

by means of judgment, one can look at the book in front of him and assert "this book exists." On the other hand, one can know that the image of unicorn in one's imagination does not correspond to anything in reality and therefore he can deny existence of the unicorn: the unicorn is not.[75]

The third kind of proposition is the judgment of the truth of a thing.[76] Through an act of judgment, one is able to look at the concept in one's intellect and look at reality and see whether the concept in one's intellect is in conformity with the way the thing exists in reality. This is one of the acts which separates man from animals, in that animals cannot judge whether their sensible species in their interior senses conforms to reality.[77]

The judgment of the truth of a proposition or concept[78] as well as the judgment of the existence of a thing is a reflexive act. While the initial concept which results from the agent intellect is simple, nevertheless, the subsequent concepts are done by reflexion,[79] i.e. by the intellect considering something which is in itself. Moreover, it is by reflexion that one knows oneself,[80] i.e. one reflects upon oneself by one's knowledge of oneself.[81] Again, this is where animals and man differ. Reflexive knowledge is not proper to the sensitive powers because they are not able to reflect upon themselves.[82] Material things are unable to reflect upon themselves, i.e. a material thing cannot both be the thing which reflects and that upon which it reflects, e.g. a steel beam cannot turn in upon itself. Material things are not capable of reflexive actions and therefore neither are the sensitive powers which are material and so animals cannot reflect upon themselves. St. Thomas observes that only immaterial things can reflect upon

---

[75]How this is done will be discussed below. If one examines the three kinds of propositions, all are based on the affirmation or denial of existence. For example, one can say "the food *is* healthy." The complex concept of healthy food is a form of asserting the healthy quality of the food in reality. While each form of proposition is based on the assertion or denial of existence in something in some way, the existential proposition focuses on the existence strictly speaking. In the other forms of proposition, existence *per se* is not the focus, but, in an existential proposition, it is.

[76]III Sent., d. 23, q. 2, a. 2a; ST I, q. 16, proem.; ibid., q. 16, a. 2; ST II-II, q. 1, a. 2; De Ver., q. 1, a. 3; ibid., q. 1, a. 11 and *In libros perihermenias* I, l. 3, n. 9.

[77]Actually, all the kinds of judgment show that man is essentially different from other animals. The fact that he can consider the lack of existence of a thing – i.e. he can consider whether a unicorn exists or not – makes him very different from animals which cannot perform these functions.

[78]De Ver., q. 1, a. 9.

[79]ST I, q. 76, a. 2, ad 4 and *Comm. de anima* III, l. 8, n. 19.

[80]SCG II, c. 75, n. 13 and ST I, q. 85, a. 2.

[81]III Sent., d. 23, q. 1, a. 2, ad 3.

[82]SCG IV, c. 11, n. 4 and *De unitate intellectus*, c. 5.

themselves.[83] This is due to the fact that immaterial substances are not bound by material or physical laws and so they are able to reflect upon themselves, whereas material things cannot do so since physical laws prohibit it.

When the possible intellect makes an act of judgment, it ascertains whether the content of the judgment is true in a specific way. St. Thomas observes that in judging the existence of a thing, the possible intellect "converts back to the phantasm."[84] What this means is that the possible intellect looks at the concept or proposition in the intellect and then looks back to the phantasm to see whether the thing to which the concept or proposition corresponds actually exists or not. The phantasm contains within it whether the phantasm was caused by some real thing present to the person outside of himself in reality or whether it actually existed in the past by means of memory. Moreover, it contains whether the phantasm is reformulated or "created" by the intellect and therefore does not correspond to something in reality.[85]

St. Thomas also notes that through converting back to the phantasm, one is able to judge time.[86] Since the possible intellect is immaterial and since time is the measurement of motion of a physical thing, then the acts of the possible intellect occur outside of time. Therefore, it must convert back to the phantasm which is in time in order to judge time.[87] St. Thomas observes that one judges time by means of composition and division[88] and this occurs by judging the differences in the phantasm. For example, someone who is sitting outside may see the sun at a certain position and then a little later, he sees the sun at a different location and judges the differences in the location in order to judge the lapse of time. In modern life, the watch or clock is virtually everywhere and so a person can look at the clock at one point and that image is stored in memory. Then a little later the person looks at the clock again and by an act of division determines that 15 minutes have lapsed due to the differences in the two phantasms of the clock. Hence, without the phantasm in the imagination and memory,

---

[83]De Ver., q. 22, a. 12.

[84]*De trinitate*, p. 3, q. 5, a. 1.

[85]We know that the possible intellect converts back to the phantasm to make its judgment, however, how it does so is a natural mystery. It is like the agent intellect in which we know that it abstracts and we know something about abstraction and we know the effect of the agent intellect, since we do not have an immediate grasp or vision of that faculty, we do not possess the knowledge of how it does its function. Even though we know that the agent intellect abstracts and that the possible intellect converts back to the phantasm, we do not know how the agent intellect is able to do what it does nor are we able to know how the possible intellect in converting back to the phantasm is able to judge the existence of the thing. This also applies to any time the possible intellect converts back to the phantasm. It seems that whenever the gap between the material and the immaterial is bridged, man is left with a natural mystery.

[86]ST I, q. 85, a. 5, ad 2; De Ver., q. 1, a. 5 and ibid., q. 14, a. 12.

[87]Ibid.

[88]Ibid.

it would be impossible to judge time (including dates, etc.). Moreover, if the phantasm is corrupted or if the imagination or memory are corrupted in their function, this results in a disorientation or inability to judge time properly.

Since the possible intellect performs its functions outside of time, its acts coincide with time when they are dependent upon the phantasm in any way. However, someone can experience a type of disorientation even though there is, strictly speaking, nothing wrong with the phantasm. When a person engages in abstract thought, the judging of time is left behind or simply not performed. The person may focus on aspects of the phantasm or have a phantasm which does not contain explicit time information and, as a result, when the person engages in abstract thought for a long time, he may not know how much time has lapsed during his abstract thinking. For example, someone may engage in thought about the nature of truth which is timeless and if he thinks about it for a long period of time, when he finally does judge time, he may be surprised at the amount of time which has lapsed.[89] Moreover, if one is thinking about an abstract concept, which is done outside of time, the body continues in time and the person may actually contemplate the thought outside of time in such a way that the lapse of time for the body is great. As a result, the person is not really certain of the amount of time that passes since the act he engaged in is "timeless."[90]

Finally, it is by converting back to the phantasm that the person knows the individual, particular and concrete.[91] Since in the process of abstraction one leaves behind the particular conditions of the thing and arrives at a universal concept, the only way to determine whether what one knows universally pertains to the singular or to know the thing *qua* particular is by looking back at the phantasm which contains the sensible species which contains those accidents which pertain to the singular. This is very important since it is the only thing that keeps a person in contact with reality. If judgment is compromised in any way, the person loses contact with reality.[92] While the concept comes from the sensible species which may be caused by some real object outside of the individual, all the things which tell the possible intellect that the thing corresponds to reality are left behind in the process of abstraction. The possible intellect is designed to reconnect to reality by means of converting back to the phantasm which has a causal link to reality by means of the senses. As a result, if any faculty upon which

---

[89]The converse can actually be the case as well. For example, if someone thinks of some abstract thought, the absence of judging time or thinking about a phantasm that is laden with time information may lead the person to thinking he has been engaging in the thought for a very long period of time when in fact it has only been briefly.

[90]While the possible intellect depends on the phantasm which is time laden for its initial concept, the accident of time is left behind and so the possible intellect in contemplating the concept for a long duration can pass a lot of time without knowing it. As will be seen, the possible intellect can maintain the concept without the need of the agent intellect once the concept is obtained.

[91]ST I, q. 84, a. 7.

[92]The precipitation of judgment will be treated in greater detail in a later chapter.

the possible intellect depends in order to judge reality is corrupted or if the possible intellect fails in its operations, then contact with reality is compromised. This is why those who suffer from brain damage, delirium caused by material indisposition or by the precipitation of judgment, do things or say things which have no correspondence to reality. In effect, they are not in contact with reality.[93]

3. Ratiocination

The third act of the possible intellect is ratiocination or reasoning.[94] Ratiocination, which is proper to man alone,[95] is discursive,[96] i.e. a form of motion[97] of the intellect. The term ratiocination comes from the two Latin words "ratio" and "cursus" which literally means running reason. It is the process by which one goes from judgment to judgment, i.e. it proceeds by composition and division[98] and finally ends with a conclusion.[99] This form of inquiry,[100] or seeking after understanding of a thing, is syllogistic in form.[101] Therefore, it starts with a previous understanding of some thing,[102] i.e. premises (known through judgment), and proceeds from premise to premise and ends in a conclusion by which it arrives at new knowledge or ends in knowing.[103] This process is governed by operative as well as ontological principles[104] and so it cannot proceed in any fashion it deems fit. When it does deviate from these principles and since it is based on judgment, which can err,[105] it can be false or end in falsity.[106]

Ratiocination or reason can also be a process by which the possible intellect

---

[93]The particulars of this statement will be drawn out later, but the maintenance of mental health consist in maintaining contact with reality and the recovery of mental health consist in reconnecting with reality.

[94]II Sent., d. 3, q. 1, a. 2; ST I, q. 79, a. 8; SCG I, c. 57, nn. 3 and 7 and *De trinitate*, p. 3, q, 6, a. 1 ad 21.

[95]III Sent., d. 10, q. 1, a. 1b and SCG II, c. 60, n.2. This is the case since in God there is no motion; an angel's knowledge of an essence is fully exhausted instantaneously and animals do not engage in immaterial acts of thought or knowledge.

[96]SCG I, c. 57, n. 2.

[97]ST I, q. 79, a. 12.

[98]ST I, q. 85, a. 5.

[99]II Sent., d. 24, q. 3, a. 3, ad 5.

[100]De Ver., q. 15, a. 1.

[101]ST I, q. 58, a. 4

[102]ST II-II, q. 8, a. 1, ad 2.

[103]ST I, q. 85, a. 5.

[104]See ST I-II, q. 91, a. 2, ad 2.

[105]See below.

[106]*Post. Anal.*, II, l. 20, n. 15; ST I, q. 89, a. 5 and ST II-II, q. 51, a. 1, ad 1.

compares the conclusions and the premises.[107] Once the conclusion is reached, the intellect can go back and consider whether the conclusion does in fact follow from the premises. Moreover, the process ends with a complex concept, i.e. a conclusion and so the conclusion is grasped by another act of understanding or judgment, i.e. ratiocination ends in consideration[108] or a pondering of the conclusion. While the ratiocinative process can end in error, by virtue of the fact that it can compare the conclusion with the premises as well as compare a certain conclusion as a premise to a second syllogism, it is actually capable of taking away error.[109] For example, a teacher can dispel error by getting a student to accept certain premises and then draw a conclusion which contradicts the previous opinion of the student. Yet, man's reasoning process can be inadequate if it does not end in perfect knowledge of a thing.[110] Someone can begin the process of reasoning and not arrive at a firm or adequate conclusion due to the lack of information in the premises or due to a lack of intellectual capacities on the side of the intellect. However, even though the conclusion may not represent full knowledge of a thing, that does not make the reasoning process or even the conclusion false. For example, in mystery novels, the detective often concludes that various characters were not involved in a murder. While those conclusions are not adequate to know who the murderer is, the conclusion that the others are not the murderer is not false, provided it is based on sufficient evidence.

The syllogistic process depends on various faculties, and not just the possible intellect. While it is a process proper to the possible intellect, the possible intellect itself depends on various faculties, such as memory,[111] imagination, the cogitative power, etc. and so error can occur in the reasoning process if there is any defect in those faculties or their objects. Moreover, sometimes the objects of consideration can lend themselves to uncertainty. Since the ratiocinative process can concern not only the speculative but practical knowledge,[112] it is easily prone to error and uncertainty. For example, in practical matters when there is no certainty about the facts (premises), there will not be certitude in the conclusion.

C. Intellective Memory

St. Thomas makes a distinction between sensitive memory and intellective memory, where sensitive memory pertains to the sensible species and intellective

---

[107]ST I, q. 58, a. 4.

[108]*De trinitate*, p. 3, q. 6, a. 1, c. 22.

[109]De Ver., q. 24, a. 10 and Meta., XI, l. 6, n. 17.

[110]De Ver., q. 14, a. 6.

[111]*Post. Anal.*, II, l. 20, n. 10.

[112]II Sent., d. 24, q. 2, a. 2; ST I, q. 79, a. 12; De Ver., q. 5, a. 1 and *In VIII libros physicorum*, II, l. 15, n. 5.

memory pertains to the intelligible species. Memory, in its normal connotation,[113] pertains to the sensitive part and when one refers to memory, one refers to the conservation of species pertaining to the past[114] and so memory in the proper sense refers to sensitive memory.[115] This follows from the fact that since the possible intellect operates outside of time, it does not consider, properly speaking, things of the past. Moreover, time, being an accident, is left behind in the process of abstraction. Therefore, intellective memory pertains only to something present.[116] What this means is that intellective memory pertains to the conservation of the intelligible species[117] but it is not time laden.

The question remaining is how the possible intellect is said to conserve the species. The possible intellect when it is not actually understanding or performing an operation is said to be in potency and when it is understanding or knowing, it is said to be in act. St. Thomas observes that intellective memory is the possible intellect neither in potency nor in act but *in habitu*.[118] When the possible intellect is put in act by an intelligible species, there is an "impression" or "habit" left in the possible intellect according to the form of that species. The retention of the intelligible species in the possible intellect by habit is ordered toward the habits of science.[119] The form of the habit which pertains to the previously known intelligible species remains in the possible intellect and that is what is referred to as intellective memory. Since species of habits are determined by their respective objects, the species of the habit corresponds to the species of the object.

It is the common experience of man to have experienced knowing that he previously knew a particular concept or idea, i.e. the intellect knows itself to have known.[120] It appears that when the possible intellect acts according to a specific habit, the object which pertains to that habit is understood as being previously known. Since the thing previously known is not received anew, i.e. it is not relearned but is immediately grasped as having been grasped before, for this reason, the possible intellect is said to have memory.[121] Moreover, St. Thomas observes that the will can move the possible intellect into act and thereby reduce it to knowing a previously known concept

---

[113]De Ver., q. 10, a. 2.

[114]ST I, q. 79, a. 6 and ibid., ad 2.

[115]De Ver., q. 10, a. 2.

[116]IV Sent., d. 44, q. 3, a. 3, qu. 2, ad 4. In this passage, St. Thomas observes that it also pertains to the imagination to have memory of the present.

[117]ST I, q. 79, a. 6 and ST I-II, q. 67, a. 2.

[118]ST I, 79, 6, ad 3.

[119]De Ver., q. 10, a. 2.

[120]ST I, q. 79, a. 6 and De Ver., q. 10, a. 2.

[121]De Ver., q. 10, a. 2.

according to habit present in the possible intellect.[122]

D. Error

The human intellect is not infallible and so the question which remains to be discussed is: from whence does error in the intellect come? Error does not occur, strictly speaking, in the senses,[123] since the senses merely report what is there. As an exterior object acts upon the senses, the senses report the sensible species. Even if the faculty is impaired, the senses report their state as being acted upon by the exterior object. So, for instance, if the skin is burned, the senses may touch an object which is not very hot, but the senses report a burning sensation. They are, in fact, simply reporting what is their state, viz. the burned skin is more sensitive, so they will report that the object acts upon them with more vehemence because of the skin's indisposition. Another example is the sensible species in the eye. When the eye is not capable of focusing, it is in fact reporting the sensible species as it acts upon the eyeball which may have a disfigured shape and as a result does not focus properly. Hence, the eye is reporting its state of being incapable of focusing on the object.

Nor is falsity, strictly speaking, in the interior senses, as what is in the interior senses is first in the senses. Moreover, in order for falsity or error in the strict sense to be in the five exterior senses or the four interior senses, they would have to have the capacity for self-reflection. Truth, which is the adequation of the thing and the knower, occurs when the knower can look upon the thing known in reality and upon the species of the thing in the knower and determine that they congrue. Falsity occurs when the knower assesses that the thing known in reality does congrue with the species in the knower when in fact it does not.[124] Since the five interior senses and the four interior senses do not have the capacity for reflecting both on their sensible species and the thing outside at the same time, truth or falsity is not said to be in them, *properly speaking*. As a result, they do not err in the proper sense since they merely act according to their object, nature and disposition.

Therefore, error in the proper sense must occur in the possible intellect since it alone has the capacity for self-reflection. But error is not in the first act of the

---

[122]Ibid. St. Thomas observes that in this life, the will moves the possible intellect to convert to the phantasm (by means of the agent intellect) to know that which corresponds to the intellective memory (habit); see ST I, q. 89, a. 1. However, in the next life, the will is able to move the possible intellect directly to knowing and therefore the intellect can actually understand a previously known concept by being moved directly by the will according to the habit in the possible intellect which persists after death; see De Ver., q. 19, a. 1 and Quod. III, q. 9, a. 1.

[123]De Ver., q. 1, a. 11 and ST I, q. 85, a. 6.

[124]The exact nature of truth and falsity will be seen in greater detail in another chapter.

intellect,[125] since judgment of the truth, which is done by an act of reflexion, does not occur in the first act of the intellect. Rather, error in the proper sense in human knowledge occurs in the second act of the intellect, i.e. error lies in judgment.[126] Since judgment results in a proposition, then error occurs when something is composed when it should not be or something is divided when it should be united.[127] For example, if one were to compose the proposition: man is an ass, then the composition would be in error or if one were to divide two terms, as in the following proposition: dogs are not animals. Moreover, since the ratiocination process depends upon judgment, then reasoning can go awry if error occurs in one of the propositions or in the forming of the conclusion which is likewise a proposition.

In the previous chapter, it was mentioned that the possible intellect guides and is able to determine the reformulation of the image in the imagination. This means the error that occurs in the possible intellect is able to flow over into the image or phantasm. Error of the possible intellect is able to affect the imagination and therefore can disorder the appetites which have as their object the image in the imagination. Since what is in the imagination is also pressed into memory, one can actually have false memory. In addition to false memory, when the possible intellect reformulates the image by moving the cogitative power, the cogitative power is trained or habituated in the error. As a result, in the future when those types of sensible species occur which are similar or the same as the sensible species formulated erroneously by the possible intellect, then the cogitative power will associate erroneously according to its habituation. This is why certain people have a hard time thinking about something in a different fashion than they are normally habituated because each time the cogitative power sees a sensible species it associates according to its previous habituation. Finally, since the will is moved by the possible intellect, error in the possible intellect can result in the volition of evil.[128]

On the other hand, this also means that if judgment is correct, one can use the correct judgment to correct (heal) memory, order the appetites, correct wrong phantasms which have been stored from the past, correct the cogitative power and re-direct it according to right order. Moreover, through right judgment, one can correct the will or help it to choose what is right. Finally, the possible intellect can help itself to judge rightly by formulating phantasms which help it think rightly. On the other hand, if the possible intellect confuses or causes error in the phantasm, then when it converts to the phantasm to make a judgment, it will be adversely affected and as a result will find it more difficult to judge rightly since there is error or disorder in the phantasm.

---

[125]I Sent., d. 19, q. 5, a. 1, ad 7; ST I, q. 17, a. 3, ad 1; ibid., q. 58, a. 6 and ibid., q. 85, a. 6.

[126]I Sent., q. 19, q. 5, a. 1, ad 7; ST I, q. 85, a. 6; ST I, q. 85, a. 6 and De Ver., q. 1, a. 12.

[127]ST I, q. 85, a. 6 and SCG II, c. 76, n. 9.

[128]This topic will be discussed in a subsequent chapter on the will.

E. Self- Knowledge

Maintaining and recovering mental health is dependent upon self knowledge. While all of the different aspects of self-knowledge shall be covered at another time,[129] the basics of self-knowledge on a strictly cognitive level shall be treated here. It should be recalled that the possible intellect performs three acts, one of which, viz. judgment, at times is reflexive, i.e. by an act of judgment the possible intellect can reflect upon itself. We know that through an act of reflexion, when we reflect upon ourselves, we know ourselves. While our knowledge is first of things, then of ourselves, we are able to reflect on ourselves by means of our knowledge of ourselves. The concept and image we have of ourselves is that by which we know ourselves. We understand several things by means of reflection regarding ourselves. We know by means of our intellect that our intellect understands,[130] i.e. we can reflect upon our act of understanding, e.g. one can reflect upon his act of understanding a tree and "see" himself understanding the tree. It is for this reason that St. Thomas observes that we know ourselves to be intellectual.[131] Unlike Descartes, Aquinas maintains that our first knowledge is of things extrinsic to ourselves[132] and then we know ourselves subsequently. Moreover, we know ourselves by means of sensibles,[133] e.g. one knows one's race, gender and a variety of other physical characteristics by means of the sensible species, i.e. man senses himself.

While only that which is subsistent knows itself,[134] nevertheless unlike God, we know ourselves, not essentially[135] but as an object of knowledge.[136] What this means is that we do not see our essence directly, but only know it and ourselves by means of an intelligible object (i.e. a concept) abstracted from the sensible species we have of ourselves. Therefore, we do not see our souls directly but can only reason to knowledge of the soul by means of our knowledge of ourselves gained through sensible species, reasoning regarding the intelligible species known in understanding and judgment as well as the immaterial acts we perform.

Because our knowledge of ourselves is an act of judgment, i.e. reflexion, it is prone to error and since we are often influenced by our appetites regarding ourselves, our judgment is often blind and easily moved to falsity regarding ourselves. We also know ourselves by means of our conscience, knowing that we are thieves, liars or good in certain respects. The image we have of ourselves which is in our imagination is often

---

[129]That is, in volume three.

[130]SCG II, c. 66, n. 5.

[131]SCG III, c. 46, n. 9.

[132]SCG IV, c. 11, n. 5.

[133]SCG III, c. 47, n. 8.

[134]ST I, q. 14, a. 2, ad 1. Only that which can bend back or reflect upon itself is subsistent since it is immaterial and therefore incorruptible.

[135]SCG III, c. 46, nn. 2-6.

[136]III Sent., d. 23, q. 1, a. 2, ad 3 and SCG II, c. 98, n. 2.

distorted by means of the possible intellect's false judgment and the reformulating of the image of ourselves in ways which do not congrue with reality. Moreover, the concept and image we have of ourselves is built up by means of several sources and tends, therefore, to be very complex.

Chapter 5: Truth

Truth is the foundation of every science insofar as no science can proceed which does not strive to arrive at the truth regarding its object of inquiry. In this respect, psychology is no exception for two reasons. The first is that psychology must strive to know the truth about mental health and illness. Secondly, the study of mental health includes in its very *ratio* or notion the necessity of the mind to attain the truth in order to have mental health. Conversely, we know that those who suffer from mental illness often do not possess the truth about the thing(s) which troubles them. Therefore, it is of the utmost importance that the science of mental health and illness grasp the nature of truth so as to be able to foster it in those under its care.

I. The Nature of Truth

Truth is defined as "the adequation of intellect and thing."[1] Truth occurs when the intellect is able to see that what it understands congrues with the thing. In places, St. Thomas modifies the definition slightly to "the adequation of intellect *to* the thing."[2] The first definition indicates the nature of truth in general while the second indicates the requirement of the created intellect to congrue or adequate itself to the thing.[3] Truth in the created intellect is a conformity,[4] i.e. the created intellect conforms itself to the thing. This clearly indicates that truth for the created intellect is therefore founded in the thing[5] and not in the mind of the knower. The human intellect, in order to know the truth, must conform or adequate itself to the thing.

---

[1]De Ver., q.1, a. 1 (adaequatio intellectus et rei); ST I, q. 16, a. 1; SCG I, c. 59, n. 2; De Pot., q, 3, a. 17, ad 27; *De anima*, q. 3, ad 1 and *Super Ad Thim.* I, c. 6, l. 1.

[2]See De Pot., q, 3, a. 17, ad 27 and *De anima* q. 3, ad 1 (adaequatio intellects ad rem).

[3]St. Thomas in a variety of places (among which see De Ver. q. 1) notes that there are three kinds of truth, viz. divine truth which exists in the divine mind, the truth of the created intellect in which the created intellect congrues to the thing, and the truth of things which is two fold. The first is that things congrue with the divine mind and the second is in artifacts or human actions: the thing congrues with the image that the artist has in his mind in making a thing or an action actually expresses a formulated intention. However, truth in the created intellect must congrue itself with the thing even in the latter cases to know whether the things made or intended congrue with the thought or image.

[4]De Ver., q. 1, a. 1; ST I, q. 16, aa. 1 and 2 and ibid., I-II, q. 57, a. 5, ad 3.

[5]De Ver., q. 1, a. 1, ad 1; ST I, q. 16, a. 3 ad 2; I Sent., d. 19, q. 5, a. 1 and ibid., ad 7. In the later quote, Aquinas observes that the intellect conforms itself or is founded in being.

II. Truth as the Good of the Intellect

Part of the scourge of modern philosophy and its effect on modern society is that people expect reality or things to congrue to them: this is prime material for mental illness. We know based on our experience, that it is necessary for someone to congrue their thought to the thing in order for them to know the truth. For example, if someone asserted that the sky was green, we would immediately assess that he does not have the truth regarding the actual color of the sky. While he may *want* the sky to be green, nevertheless reality dictates that it is actually blue. If the individual is to have the truth about the actual color of the sky, he is required to conform his intellect to the thing regardless of what he wants. People who suffer from a grave psychological illness make assertions which do not congrue with reality and it is precisely because the individual's intellect is not functioning properly that he states what is false.[6] From this observation, we can see that rationalism and empiricism are incapable of contributing anything of value to the science of mental health. Rationalism cuts itself off from reality by denying sense knowledge.[7] Empiricism does not help since it rejects knowledge of anything beyond sense knowledge, which means that part of the intellect lies beyond its purview. Therefore it cannot give an adequate understanding of subalternate principles of psychology and, consequently, of psychology itself. In effect, only a realist epistemology can be the basis of true psychology.

The human intellect, in conforming itself to material things, has an intrinsic ordering to material reality[8] from which it derives its knowledge of not only material things but also immaterial things.[9] Hence, the good of the intellect consists in the truth,[10]

---

[6]When people do not *want* something to be true and act as if it is not true, they are in fact beginning the first step toward mental illness. If they are unwilling to conform to reality, they have already begun the process which will result in causing mental illness. As will be seen, sometimes mental illness is the result of someone's unwillingness to accept reality while at other times mental illness causes the person not to be able to recognize the truth about things.

[7]Ironically, civil authorities place in mental institutions people who do not have any contact with their senses, and yet modern philosophy and civilization have given great honors to the names of those who espoused this in a formal structured way in a systematic philosophy.

[8]ST I, q. 85, a. 1.

[9]There are two ways the human intellect derives knowledge of the immaterial, viz. by remotion from material things, e.g. when one arrives at the conclusion that there is order in the universe caused by an exterior agent by looking at material things and realizing they cannot account for their own order. The second is by one's own interior acts of the possible intellect and will.

[10]II Sent., d. 3, q, 3, a. 1; ibid., d. 39, q. 1, a. 2; III Sent., d. 23, q. 2, a. 3; ibid., d. 26, q. 2, a.1; SCG I, c. 59, n. 5; ibid., c. 61, n. 8; ibid., c. 71, a. 4; SCG II, c. 84, n. 4; SCG III, c. 25, n. 10; ibid., c. 106, n. 7; ibid., c. 118, n. 5; ST I, q. 94, n. 4; ST I-II, q. 5, a. 4; ibid.,

for an ordering implies finality[11] and finality implies goodness.[12] Since the truth or the thing is the good of the intellect, then it follows that suitability of being or the thing to the intellect indicates the name or nature of truth.[13] It is proper to the nature of the intellect to congrue itself with the thing and so the rectitude[14] of the intellect consists in truth, i.e. in congruing itself with reality.

Consequently, it is clear that truth is objective for two reasons. St. Thomas observes that truth is convertible with being and insofar as a thing is, it is true.[15] Secondly, truth is objective insofar as the intellect must conform itself to the object of knowledge. If a notion in the intellect does not congrue with reality, then it is simply not true. Therefore, the subjective factor in knowing a thing is precisely to arrive at what the object is, i.e. a subject is to strive for knowledge of the object and once one reaches the truth, one's knowledge is objective.

Modern civilization as well as psychology has succumbed to the facile and yet completely erroneous notion that truth is relative. St. Thomas would assert that truth is a relation insofar as one thing is related to another, viz. the intellect of man congrues or relates to the thing. However, to say that truth itself is relative in the sense that what is true for one individual may not be true for another falls prey to the weakest form of thinking. First, to say "All truth is relative" is inherently contradictory, for a relative predicate is asserted of an absolute subject.

Moreover, truth is objective from the point of first principles, particularly that

---

q. 57, a. 2, ad 3; ST II-II, q. 1, a. 3, ad 1; ibid., q. 60, a. 4, ad 2; De Ver., q. 1, a. 10, ad sed contra 4; ibid., q. 18, a. 6; De Vir., q. 1, a. 7, ad 5; ibid., q. 1, a. 13 and Quod., IV, q. 9, a. 1, ad 1.

[11]In SCG III, c. 107, n. 8, St. Thomas makes the observation that the knowledge of the truth and the thing is the good or natural end of the intellect. In other words, truth is that to which the intellect is fundamentally ordered.

[12]At times, St. Thomas observes that the good of the intellect is also virtue, e.g. see III Sent., d. 23, q, 1, a. 4a, ad 3. However, virtues are determined by the objects (see below) and therefore nothing prohibits both being the good of the intellect since the virtue is a mean between the intellect and the thing and virtues are specified according to their objects, which in this case is the truth. As will be seen later, virtue is a perfection of the intellect and in that sense it is the good of the intellect.

[13]De Ver., q. 1, a. 1.

[14]Ibid.

[15]Ibid. and I Sent., d. 19, q. 5, a. 1, ad 3. The complexity of this statement prohibits a full exposition of the notion here. Those interested in convertibility of the transcendentals and how truth is convertible with being can read De Ver., q. 1, a. 1 in conjunction with any sound modern Thomistic ontology text which deals with it.

of non-contradiction and the excluded middle.[16] In other words, either an intellect congrues with reality or it does not. One cannot assert that two intellects have contradictory congruities with the same object because then one would violate the principle of non-contradiction.[17] With respect to the principle of the excluded middle, we can assert with absolute certitude that either a thing is or it is not, there is no middle between being and non-being. Therefore, either one's intellect is adequated to the thing or it is not.

III. The Nature of Knowledge

If truth is the congruity of intellect with the thing, how does one know the thing? We have already discussed in detail the ontological structure of knowing, but a further clarification is needed, since rationalism has introduced into philosophy the notion that we know our concepts of things and not things themselves.[18] However, the some of the scholastics had already dealt with the issue long before rationalism made its appearance. St. Thomas observes that the concept is not that which (*quod*) we know, but that by which (*quo*) we know the thing.[19] The concept is a medium between the intellect and thing,[20] i.e. an individual understands some thing by means of the concept (the concept is a means).[21] Our own experience tends to bear this out. When we first come

---

[16]In a subsequent chapter, these two principles will be discussed.

[17]For example, if a cow in reality is black, two individuals in order for what they hold to be true, must hold the cow is black. It is not possible for one to hold the cow is white and the other to hold that the cow is black and both be true. Since truth requires that the intellect congrue with reality, then if the intellects of two people congrue with reality, there will be agreement in their respective understandings.

[18]This assertion with proper qualifications could also be made of Platonism in its various forms.

[19]III Sent., d. 14, q. 1, a. 2a; De Pot., q. 8, a. 1; ibid., q. 9, a. 5; *Comm. de anima* III, l. 4, n. 10 and ibid., l. 8, n. 19.

[20]De Ver., q. 4, a. 2, ad 3.

[21]St. Thomas observes in I Sent., d. 2, q. 1, a. 3 a three fold relation of the concept to the thing: "Unde sciendum, quod ipsa conceptio intellectus tripliciter se habet ad rem quae est extra animam. Aliquando enim hoc quod intellectus concipit, est similitudo rei existentis extra animam, sicut hoc quod concipitur de hoc nomine homo; et talis conceptio intellectus habet fundamentum in re immediate, inquantum res ipsa, ex sua conformitate ad intellectum, facit quod intellectus sit verus, et quod nomen significans illum intellectum, proprie de re dicatur. Aliquando autem hoc quod significat nomen non est similitudo rei existentis extra animam, sed est aliquid quod consequitur ex modo intelligendi rem quae est extra animam: et hujusmodi sunt intentiones quas intellectus noster adinvenit; sicut significatum hujus nominis genus non est similitudo alicujus rei extra animam existentis; sed ex hoc quod

into contact with a thing, we tend to study it and then we know it and only later do we reflect upon the concept in order to look at it as it resides in our intellect, i.e. as to its formal content.[22]

       This distinction between the concept by which a thing is understood and that which is understood is of extreme importance. If the concept is that which is understood, then we really do not know the thing but merely the similitude of the thing which resides in our intellect. Whereas if the concept is that by which we understand the thing, then it is the thing which is understood. In the latter case, we can also say that

---

intellectus intelligit animal ut in pluribus speciebus, attribuit ei intentionem generis; et hujusmodi intentionis licet proximum fundamentum non sit in re sed in intellectu, tamen remotum fundamentum est res ipsa. Unde intellectus non est falsus, qui has intentiones adinvenit. Et simile est de omnibus aliis qui consequuntur ex modo intelligendi, sicut est abstractio mathematicorum et hujusmodi. Aliquando vero id quod significatur per nomen, non habet fundamentum in re, neque proximum neque remotum, sicut conceptio chimerae: quia neque est similitudo alicujus rei extra animam, neque consequitur ex modo intelligendi rem aliquam naturae: et ideo ista conceptio est falsa." ("Hence it is known that the very concept of the intellect has a threefold relation to the thing which is outside the soul. For sometimes that which the intellect conceives is the similitude of the thing existing outside the soul, as that which is conceived by the name man; and such a concept of the intellect has a foundation in the immediate thing, insofar as the thing itself, from its conformity to the intellect, makes what is understood be true, and which the name signifying that which is understood is properly said of the thing. Sometimes, moreover, that which the name signifies is not the similitude of the thing existing outside the soul, but as something which follows from the mode of understanding the thing which is outside the soul: and in this way intentions are found in our intellect; as signified by the name of the genus it is not the similitude of some thing existing outside the soul; but from this that the intellect understands the animal as in many species attributes to it an intention of the genus; and in this way of intention, although the proximate foundation is not in the thing but in the intellect, nevertheless the remote foundation is the thing itself. Hence the intellect is not false which has these intentions. And similarly it is of other things which follow from the mode of understanding, as the abstraction of mathematicals and things of this kind. Sometimes, truly, that which is signified by the name does not have a foundation in the thing, neither proximate nor remote, as the concept of a chimera: since neither is it a similitude of something existing outside the soul, nor does it follow from the mode of understanding some natural thing: and therefore this concept is false.")

[22]Clearly children who engage in fewer acts of reflexion than adults are seen to operate as not knowing the concept but knowing the thing. In fact, they tend not to reflect upon their knowledge of the thing, but tend to engage the object as they understand it. This is why children tend less to engage in dialogues where there is reflexion upon one's own knowledge of something. Whereas adults, who engage in more second operations of the possible intellect are more likely to discuss the various concepts they and other people have of different things.

the concept is that which is understood but only in a secondary reflection upon the concept itself. In most instances, one reflects upon the thing by means of the concept, not the concept itself.[23] Moreover, our contact with reality is twofold, viz. the first is the process from sensation of a thing, which puts us in immediate contact with it, to abstraction and the pressing of its likeness on the possible intellect. Hence, the thing is the cause of one's knowledge. Secondly, we can perform a two-fold reflection which helps us to know the thing by means of the essence or concept. The first is by means of the judgment of the truth of the concept. In other words, one can look at the concept and look at the thing and see that they congrue. In this case, one actually looks at the concept itself and the thing. Another operation can be done which is actually performed in the first operation of the intellect in knowing a thing. A later motion of the will focuses the intellect on a particular object, to view the object with the senses and, at the same time, with the intellect to see the essence of the thing in the object. This later act is in fact a species of the judgment of the truth of the thing, but the finality is somewhat different. In the judgment of the truth, one's finality in the action is to assess the congruity of the concept and the thing, whereas, in the latter case, one's finality is to see the universal in the particular thing, i.e. to see it outside of oneself as existing according to the mode of the essence which corresponds to what is understood.

Since knowledge of the thing is achieved by means of a concept, this means that knowledge consists in the assimilation of the thing by the knower.[24] For man, this means there are two types of knowledge, viz. sense knowledge which is of the accidents of a thing and intellectual knowledge which is of the essence of the thing. Yet, the assimilation of the known by the knower is always done according to the mode of the knower.[25] The process of sensation, the actual object of sense, is left behind while the species or its likeness is impressed into the senses. The senses, having their own existence and nature, receive the impressed species according to the way they were designed to receive that species. The species passes through the various sensitive powers. The agent intellect then abstracts the concept or intelligible species from the sensible species and expresses it in the possible intellect. The possible intellect is an accident which, when knowing, receives the intelligible species as a modification of it, so one has a further modification of an accident.

The mode of existing of the intelligible species is different from the mode of the existing thing, i.e. the essence exists in the thing and in the intellect but in different ways. However, the intelligible species contains the formal content of the essence of the thing existing outside of the knower. This is why knowledge is called an assimilation, i.e. a likeness of thing is held according to an intentional mode of existing in the knower. Moreover, truth is not defined as the *equation* but the *adequation* of the intellect and

---

[23]This distinction is what separates realism from rationalism.

[24]De Ver., q. 1, a. 1; ibid., q. 2, a. 1; De Pot., q. 7, a. 5 and ST I, q. 16, a. 1.

[25]De Ver. q. 1., a. 2.

thing. This definition contains not only the fact that the formal content of the intelligible species conforms to the essence of the thing, but also the prefix of "ad" in adequation indicates that the essence of the thing and the essence in the intellect do not possess the same mode of existence, even though they do possess the same formal content. It is precisely because it contains the same formal content that the intelligible species is not a falsification of the essence of the thing as it exists in reality. Rather, it recognizes the distinct modes of existing of the two essences.

IV. The Locus of Truth

The question that remains to be discussed is where truth actually resides. St. Thomas notes that truth is not, strictly speaking, in the senses.[26] While the sense species has a congruity with the accidental species in the thing, nevertheless, the senses are incapable of reflecting upon the species residing in them and thereby determining whether there is a congruity or not. Truth is precisely the adequation, or knowledge of the adequation, that can only be known by a reflexive power that has the capacity to reflect upon its own act of knowing. Therefore, none of the sensitive knowing powers have truth in them in the proper sense.

Consequently, the imagination, memory, etc. do not know the truth. While their species may or may not congrue with reality, the passive intellect, being a material thing, cannot reflect upon itself and, therefore, truth does not exist, properly speaking, in the imagination, cogitative power or memory. However, this does not deny that their images or phantasms cannot be falsified by the possible intellect and will. While an image may be false, truth consists in knowledge of the congruity between two things and none of the sensitive powers have that capacity. To actually know whether a phantasm or image is false as it is located either in the imagination or memory, one must have a power which has the capacity to reflect on it as well as the thing and this pertains only to the possible intellect.

As was seen in the previous chapter, the knowledge of truth is known in the second operation of the possible intellect.[27] It does not lie in the first operation[28] for the same reasons truth does not lie in the operations of the sensitive powers. Since in the first operation of the possible intellect only the knowledge of the essence of the thing is attained, the intellect is not reflecting upon itself in simply knowing an essence. Rather that pertains to the second operation, called judgment, in which the intellect turns in upon itself and views its own action. In the judgment in which truth is the product, the possible intellect turns and views what is contained in its first operation, i.e. it looks at the understood concept. It then turns, by means of a judgment, to the phantasm and sees

---

[26]ST I, q. 16, a. 2 and De Ver., q. 1, a. 9.

[27]That is judgment. See De Ver., q. 1, a. 3 and ST I, q. 16, a. 2.

[28]I Sent., d. 19, q. 5, a. 1, ad 7.

whether the concept congrues with the way the thing exists in reality. Since the possible intellect is put in contact with reality, not immediately, but by means of the phantasm which has a causal connection to the thing existing outside of it, it must turn to the phantasm to make judgments of the truth of its knowledge.[29] As can be seen, the judgment of truth, like all products of judgments, results in a proposition, i.e. truth is known by composition and division.[30] The product of a judgment of truth is: X (concept) is in conformity with Y (thing).

V. Falsity

If truth is the adequation of the intellect and thing, then falsity is the inadequation or lack of conformity of one's concept to the thing.[31] Insofar as it is an incongruity, it is a lack of being,[32] i.e. it lacks the being of congruity. Hence, falsity occurs when one understands one thing and the reality is another. Falsity is the result of a false composition or division,[33] in which one asserts something which in fact is not the case or one denies something which is the case. For example, if one is to assert "the sky is green" and one judges it to be so, then falsity exists in the intellect since the sky is not green but blue. Consequently, it is not difficult to see that falsity is the evil or bad of the intellect[34] for if the intellect is by nature designed to know the truth, then falsity militates against that nature.

From the previous section and the previous chapter, we see that just as truth occurs in the possible intellect in its second operation, so also falsity occurs in the same place. Falsity does not lie in the thing itself since the thing itself always congrues with the divine intellect. However, falsity can be said to be in the thing, but only in a certain respect (*secundum quid*) and not properly speaking (*secundum se*). It can be said to be in a thing in a certain respect insofar as certain things are more likely to give rise to false

---

[29]At times, the thing is not actually present outside of it here and now. Memory can provide the phantasm necessary to make the judgment of truth. However, judgments of truth based on memory are more prone to error since the memory can be falsified or inadequate in comparison to the thing actually present to the knower.

[30]ST I, q. 16, a. 2 and *Comm. de anima* III, l. 11, n. 5.

[31]De Ver., q. 1, a. 10.

[32]Ibid., ad 1.

[33]De Ver., q. 1, a. 12; I Sent., d. 14, q. 1, a. 1, ad 5; ST I, q. 17, a. 3; ST I, q. 85, a. 6 and *Comm. de anima* III, l. 11, n. 15.

[34]ST I, q. 94, a. 4; ST I-II, q. 5, a. 4; ST II-II, q. 60, a. 4, ad 2 and De Ver., q. 18, a. 6. Falsity is not, strictly speaking, an illness of the intellect. Rather, falsity is either the cause of illness in the intellect and/or caused by illness in the intellect.

judgments in the possible intellect.[35]

Moreover, just as truth is not in the senses, neither is falsity in the strict sense.[36] However, in one respect, falsity can be said to be in the senses. This occurs when the intellect actually judges falsely something in the senses. The classic example is a stick in water. As one views the stick before it is placed in the water, one sees that it is straight. Then one puts the stick in the water and it appears bent. However, the senses are not false in the strict sense since they are actually reporting the refraction of light caused by the water on the sensible species of the stick. It is because of a false judgment that one actually thinks the stick is bent.

Another way in which the senses can be false, although not strictly speaking, is when they report that something is when it is not or, when it is not, that it is.[37] This occurs in two ways. The first is from an extrinsic cause, e.g. something in the medium distorts the sensible species. The second is from an intrinsic cause[38] and that is when there is some bad disposition in the organ of sense or when the senses fail to operate properly on their own. However, even in this case, the senses are not false since they actually report what the truth of the matter is, viz. this object is acting upon the ill-disposed organ in this way. Senses not only tell us about what they sense outside of themselves but also their state, e.g. when someone who has blurred vision looks at something, it appears blurred. The eye is reporting that it is not functioning properly and so the image, which it reports, tells us that the eye did not receive it well. Conversely, a common experience to all modern men is the seeing of a picture (object) which is blurred. When the eye looks at it, one knows that the picture is blurred since one knows that one's eye is working properly by looking at something else which one sees clearly or by remembering seeing other things clearly. Therefore, falsity exists properly speaking in judgment and is commonly called error.

---

[35]ST I, q. 17, a. 1; ibid., ad 2 and I Sent., d. 19, q. 5, a. 1.

[36]De Ver., q. 1, a. 11 and ST I, q. 17, a. 2.

[37]De Ver., q. 1, a. 11. This case and the previous case of falsity are different according to the perspective but are the same materially. In the first case, emphasis is placed on the falsity in the judgment. The second sense emphasizes the complexity of difficulties in the sensible species themselves which are true but which are judged falsely. Thus one emphasizes judgment; the other the source of the wrong judgment, viz. the senses.

[38]De Ver., q. 1, a. 11 and ST I, q. 85, a. 6.

Chapter 6: Selected Principles of Logic, First Philosophy and Connatural Principles

This chapter will be viewed by many as perhaps the least applicable to the subject of mental health.[1] However, before the issues of logic, first philosophy and other aspects of Thomistic anthropology are dismissed, the reader is asked to consider one's own experience of someone who has a mental illness. Do not those who are mentally ill act contrary to logical and ontological principles?[2] As a general rule, when socially engaging normal people, i.e. people who are mentally healthy, we do not explicitly think to ourselves "this person is acting and talking according to rational principles." Yet, the principles are present, though not explicitly. Moreover, if lack of employment of logical reasoning is indicative of those who are mentally ill, it will be necessary to know what the logical and ontological principles are in order to be sure that a psychologist, who has someone under his care, is able to be certain whether there is actually a problem or not in the person's reasoning. Teaching those, who suffer from some forms of mental illness the principles which affect human thought and existence, can be an aid in leading them out of their mental illness. By acting according to rational principles, one ensures the maintenance of mental health. While it is not possible to go into all the principles here, any psychologist of worth should have a very clear grasp of the art and science of logic and the principles of ontology and anthropology long before he counsels anyone. This chapter, however, shall be limited to some of those issues of greater importance in this field in regard to mental health and illness and shall provide as well indications of the requisite knowledge in these fields in order to engage in counseling the mentally ill.

I. Logic and Logical Principles

A. Some General Observations

The human intellect is structured and designed in a specific way. It is ordered toward specific ways of reasoning which are proper to its nature. The right functioning of the human intellect is based upon its operating within a given set of parameters which

---

[1] The reader may be left with a sense of dissatisfaction at the end of this chapter due to the lack of depth in the coverage of some of the issues. To cover all aspects of this chapter in detail would constitute several books on their own. Therefore, the issues shall be addressed in sufficient depth to draw the attention of the reader to the requisite knowledge which should be possessed before proceeding any further.

[2] A logical principle is one which governs the process of reasoning whereas an ontological principle is one which is intrinsic to the nature of being as such. Some ontological principles are also logical principles, i.e. the principles, sometimes formulated slightly differently, apply both to being as such as well as to the structure of man's reasoning.

are determined by the ontological structure of the intellect. These parameters or guidelines, which set the limits of right reasoning and functioning of the intellect, are the logical, ontological and connatural principles latent in the intellect and other faculties which affect the operations of the intellect.

The intellect, so far as it is an existing thing, is governed by the same principles as all other beings. However, above and beyond those principles of ontology, which apply to the intellect insofar as it is a being, are logical principles which are an integral part of the structure and nature of human reasoning itself. In other words, when God designed the human intellect, He designed it to act not only according to ontological principles, but logical principles as well, which means that man's intellect must proceed in a specific way in order that it may act according to its nature and thereby arrive at its inherent finality, viz. the truth.[3] In addition to logical principles, God also added certain connatural principles which are above the process of reasoning and the grasping of the essences and natures of things. He placed them in the intellect and other faculties so that man could conduct his life according to the finalities of other faculties as well as in accordance with the very nature of being human, in all that entails.

The principles with which we shall concern ourselves here are primarily those which belong to the operative principles, i.e. those principles which affect the operations of the soul, and thereby affect mental health and illness. Operative principles are determinations in the structure of the intellect which help it to reason according to the way things are in reality. For example, operative in the human intellect is the principle of sufficient reason,[4] so that when someone sees something happening which is unexplained, the human intellect automatically seeks to find a sufficient explanation for why it happened or is the case. For instance, if one sees a piece of matter floating over a surface without any strings from which it is suspended and nothing underneath is holding it up, the intellect would automatically begin looking for the reason why the material is floating in mid-air. After the explanation is found that superconducting materials can float over certain kinds of surfaces under certain conditions, the intellect would find rest in the sufficient explanation. The intellect thereby comes to rest. But if there is not a sufficient reason, the intellect seeks to find the answer unless, on an appetitive level, the energy expended does not seem proportionate to the desire to know and so the person remains content in his ignorance. Yet, he still knows there must be some explanation for the occurrence but he simply does not find it important enough for his life.

---

[3]It should be recalled that the human intellect is a "mirror" of material reality and so it must adhere to the ontological principles in the possible intellect itself and reality as well as act the way a "mirror" should. In other words, the intellect must act according to its latent principles so as to be able truly to "reflect" reality.

[4]See below for the delineation of this principle.

B. The Nature of Language

Language consists of a set of signs or words by which people are able to communicate. A word is a sign, either audible or written,[5] which has a significance beyond itself. A word is something which is a sign or a reference to some thing and so each word has a meaning or significance; significance comes from the two Latin words *signum* and *facere* which literally mean to make a sign. Reality is full of things and man has the capacity to use words (signs) by which he communicates his knowledge of things[6] to another. Words or signs, which are associated with the things, make it possible for man to communicate his thought to another.

There are, therefore, several things which must be in place in order for there to be communication between two knowing powers. There must be a set of signs which they have in common which refer to the same things. It is possible to have several languages in which different words in the different languages refer to the same thing. However, their formal content must be the same for there to be any real communication. For example, in English we refer to that in which we sleep as a "bed" whereas in Italian it is called a "letto," in Latin, a "lectus", etc. Therefore different signs can be used by different languages. However, when one communicates in a specific language, it is understood that a set group of signs which comprise that language is to be employed. When one speaks in a given language, one is able to communicate because the word "lectus", for example, has the same formal meaning or refers to the same concept to the two people speaking. When one shifts to another language, such as English, one uses the word "bed" and yet in both instances the same concept or conceptual content is grasped.

This brings out two aspects of language which have caused a great deal of difficulty for philosophers over the years, viz. the natural and conventional aspects of a language. There are some aspects to language which are natural and some which are based upon convention. Without dwelling on it too much, we can say that certain aspects of language are natural to every language, e.g. every language has substantives and predicates; every language has tenses, etc. It would seem therefore that there are a few things which are natural to every language and those things are grouped into two categories, viz. the structure of reality and the structure of the human mind and its possible modes of expression. Anything outside of those two is capable of being subject to convention. Therefore, things such as expression of time, singularity, plurality of things, the structure of the intellect regarding judgment which has a subject and a predicate, these things are natural and cannot change from language to language. However, the actual audible signs which we attach to specific concepts and by which we

---

[5]A sign can also be in other forms, such as in sign language, etc.

[6]Sometimes the spoken or written word is called the material sign whereas the concept in the intellect is called the formal sign. See Oesterle, *Logic*, p. 6.

express those things which are natural are open to change. Therefore, two languages are bound to the same cognitive structures, while the modes of expression and the words themselves can vary. For example, in English we may say "the bed was good" and in Latin we would say "lectus bonus erat." In this case, the mode of expression which indicates word placement and the actual signs differ. Yet, in both sentences, the formal content must express the time reference, the quality and the thing.[7]

Therefore, when a person expresses himself, there are in fact three things with which the psychologist must be concerned. The first is the thing to which the person is referring in his language, i.e. he must concern himself with the sign. Sometimes people employ words in ways which are not according to standard usage. Secondly and related to the first, he must be concerned with not only the thing to which it refers but also the concept or image the person is trying to express. In other words, the person may be using words to refer to things but may not understand them the way they exist in reality or the way they are normally understood. Thirdly, he must observe the mode of expression which can be the vehicle by which the person expresses more fully what he means. For example, take the sentence "I am angry." This sentence conveys two things initially; the first is the person is making a reference to himself and secondly to his state, viz. he is experiencing the passion of anger. However, the mode or way in which the person expresses it can indicate the degree or quality of the anger, e.g. if someone yells the sentence or pounds the table when he is angry, then it can indicate that the anger is of higher intensity. On the other hand, if the person says it quietly then it indicates that he has rational control over it or that it is more of an irritation than full-fledged anger.

However, at times, people are not able to communicate properly. This can occur for several reasons. The first reason is that the person may not adequately apprehend the thing he is trying to communicate, i.e. he does not understand the thing, lacks an adequate grasp of it or has a false understanding of the thing. Second, it may be that the words or signs which he has attached to his concepts are not clear when expressed. We can see this in the three following sentences: 1) "I am angry with my brother"; 2) "I am having severe motions of my irascible appetites while I am talking to my brother;" 3) "I hate my brother." Sometimes people substitute words which do not have the exact same meaning, e.g. sometimes people will say, "I hate you", when in fact they mean "I am angry with you." Anger and hate are two entirely different passions and yet sometimes the person does not express precisely what they are going through. Third, sometimes people can express themselves very clearly, which can be a great aid to communication. On the other hand, sometimes people are able to couch their intentions in words which do not really reflect the interior or exterior reality. Other times, people simply lie.

---

[7] It is not possible to go too far in depth on this discussion since it is not the scope of this book to do so. The point is to give the reader a general notion of the nature and function of language so as to discuss it within a psychological framework.

At issue in all this discussion is the necessity for the psychologist to have a twofold knowledge. First he must understand how language functions and how it corresponds to thought and to things in order to be able to determine clearly whether a person under his care is employing it properly. A great deal can be learned not so much by what people say, but how they say it or what they are not saying. However, the psychologist must at first be willing to take what a person says on face value. Unfortunately, some overanalyze and end up twisting what the person says. Moreover, the psychologist should be aware of how he himself uses language so as to be sure not to mislead the directee.

The second thing is that a psychologist must have a certain amount of practical prudence or wisdom based upon experience in order to know how to understand what a person is conveying. Unfortunately, modern psychology has substituted the empirical method for actual experience. Since it is possible for someone to engage in the empirical method without experience, it became possible for the very young as well as the mentally ill or imprudent to engage in the science. However, psychology is both a speculative science and a practical science. It is a speculative science insofar as it has principles and an organized body of knowledge. But it is also a practical science by virtue of the fact that its application deals with contingencies and comes through experience, not through techniques developed from an empirical method. This is why some psychologists who have difficulties themselves have not been very successful in the field. Also, psychologists tend to forget the principle of resemblance (to be discussed later), viz. like begets like. A psychologist must have a sound philosophical grasp of language and human nature as well as be mentally healthy himself if he is to guide his directee to mental health. This is perhaps where the method is determinative of its effects, viz. if one uses an empirical method, then even the insane can be psychologists as long as they employ the method; whereas if psychology is a philosophical/speculative science and a practical science, then method is not enough; one must possess what one begets. It will take a mentally healthy individual to beget a mentally healthy directee.

C. The Structure of Logic

The science and art of logic provide a clear view into the structure of the acts of the intellect. The right use of terms and how different terms (such as univocal, equivocal and analogical) are understood provide a grasp of the structure of the first operation of the intellect.[8] As to the structure of the second operation of the intellect in reasoning, the various methods of formulating statements and propositions and their

---

[8]Again, the details of logic shall not be broached here. Those who lack a sufficient training in logic should spend the time either taking a class in logic, particularly Aristotelian logic, or simply do the reading necessary to fill out that lacuna in their knowledge.

values and applicability to their matter help to regulate initial judgments. For example, if one were to assert: All A are B, he would be governed by the principles delineated in logic to know the truth value of the statement, its applicability, and whether the predicate can actually be asserted of the subject. The principles governing the third act of the intellect, viz. ratiocination, are all those principles governing syllogistic reasoning as well as informal argumentation. Logic in this sense is very useful for helping one arrive at the conclusion which is to be drawn from the premises as well as helping one to make the proper inductions. Moreover, the principles governing conditional statements, etc. can help one to see how the intellect must proceed if it is to function according to its nature; for logical principles are merely the delineation of the structure of the proper acts of intellect, the nature of things and the relationship of the two.

All of these aspects of the science of logic when applied to actual argumentation build the art of logic and train the intellect to act according to its structure and the principles innate in it. One of the difficulties of modern life is that the principles innate in the intellect are being denied and so people who are trained to think contrary to right reasoning have difficulties working their way through life's normal problems. In the past, common sense, which is the ability to grasp the natures of things, tended to be a guiding light. Moreover, by the physical toil involved in the average person's life, one learned how reality functioned and so between common sense and experience, people could work their way out of difficult situations. However, in a technocratic culture which pervades society today, less contact is had with reality as the technology becomes the prism by which a technocratic generation views reality. The technology stands between the knower and reality and thereby the knower is distanced from reality and loses the opportunity to gain the necessary experience in order to live life according to reason (rather than depending on technology and science always to solve the problem in a mechanistic or artificial way). Moreover, excessive use of technology[9] tends to strip one of common sense because it keeps a person from being in direct contact, either physically or psychologically, with reality and therefore the person loses his capacity to grasp the nature of things and how they are to be treated.[10]

The structure of induction and deduction gained in logic is necessary for

---

[9]Technology is a useful good (*bonum utile*). When it is made into an end in itself (*bonum honestum*), when its use is applied to things to which it should not be or when it is overused (i.e. when it becomes the *summum bonum*), the user's view of reality becomes distorted. We should mention that those who hold the position that technology is evil are incapable of distinguishing between man's overuse or abuse of it and the effects thereof from the reality that it is a good but its use should be limited.

[10]A clear sign of this is that only in a technocratic society could people seek to give animals the same rights as people. As man grew less dependent on animals and technology tended to intervene between man and the remaining use of animals, man lost sight of the proper relation between man and animals.

psychology. Induction presents particular difficulties for those who suffer psychological illness, since they tend to engage in induction in ways which are not rational. For example, a woman who has been raped may find it difficult to make proper distinctions and thereby induce from a single experience a generalization about all men, making it difficult for her to engage in a normal social life. Psychologists, in knowing what constitutes legitimate deductions according to Aristotelian and conditional logic, can employ logic themselves in their own science as well as ascertain the reasoning process of a particular individual and where it is going wrong. Moreover, the psychologist can instruct the person in their formal logical error so that they can begin the process of correcting it. A psychologist should know that a sound argument is one in which the premises are true and the argumentation or syllogism is valid in form. In other words, the psychologist should have a clear grasp of what constitutes sound argumentation.

In relation to this, psychologists should have a clear grasp of enthymemes. An enthymeme is an argument in which one or more of the premises is missing. The person arguing enthymematically assumes on the side of the hearer knowledge of the principle or premise and the hearer supplies the premise himself to fill out the argument. Enthymematic arguments are useful but they can also be dangerous for a few reasons. The first is that the hearer may or may not know the premise which the arguer presumes he knows. Secondly, the hearer may not agree with the unstated premise. Third, sometimes the enthymematic argument is used so that the hearer automatically supplies the premise but does not pay attention to what the premise really entails.

A psychologist, by knowing these difficulties, can sort out many things regarding the person he counsels. First, sometimes when a directee explains his difficulties, he may state conclusions and some premises but leave others unsaid. A psychologist can reconstruct the premise by knowing the conclusion and other premises or statements of the directee, and then ask him if that is how or what he is thinking. This can help the psychologist to know the things which the directee either does not want to state, does not explicitly grasp himself, or presumes everyone thinks are the case when in fact they are not. Moreover, sometimes the situation with which a directee comes into contact is "enthymematic." The term, being applied analogically to a situation, means that there could be things happening in the life of a directee which are not explicitly grasped by the directee or others who are affecting the directee. Analyzing the situation or the directee's reaction to it can help to flush out reasons which are operative but not clearly grasped. This can then provide the directee with the requisite knowledge to be able to deal with the situation.

An example of an enthymematic situation would be the following. A woman comes to a psychologist very distraught and tells the psychologist that her husband came home drunk when he was out with his friends. The women then tells the psychologist that she could not deal with living with another alcoholic since her childhood experience of living with an alcoholic father was nightmarish. Of course, the missing premise which is causing her fear is that "all drunks are alcoholics" leading to the following syllogism: "All drunks are alcoholics; my husband is drunk, therefore my husband is an alcoholic."

Being drunk once does not constitute being an alcoholic. Moreover, if a person enjoys having a glass of wine at dinner each night, that should not be confused with being an alcoholic, in which there is a dependency on or addiction to the alcohol. Therefore, someone may tell the psychologist that her husband has a beer every night when he comes home from work and she cannot stand living in the same house as an alcoholic, as when she was a child. Therefore, she does not know how to deal with her husband's drinking problem. The missing premise is: everyone who drinks every day is an alcoholic. However, this is not necessarily the case if the person demonstrates moderation and if he does not have the alcohol for some time, he does not think about it, then there is no dependency. Therefore, the wife can be assured that as long as the husband demonstrates moderation and does not suffer mood swings from the alcohol, she does not have anything to be concerned about. That defuses one aspect of the problem; the other is how she will deal with having grown up in an alcoholic environment.

At times, situations become very complex, as do the particular psychological difficulties of an individual. Logic can help by training one to break down the problems into the fundamental premises, ideas or difficulties in order to reconstruct the overall complexity. Once this is done, the source of the problem can be addressed and thereby resolved. This occurs when one problem is merely the cause of the whole difficulty even though there are a variety of complex effects from the one problem. Other times, there are several problems causing complex difficulties and at still other times a single problem causes other problems and, while they may be addressed, the root problem is not addressed.

Within any situation, there is often a question of when a given idea or principle applies. Often people tend to think somewhat logically about a situation, but if they do not know when something formally applies or is inherent to a given sphere of life or reality, they may draw the wrong conclusions. In logic, this is called distribution, i.e. when a term "occurs in a position in a categorical statement such that every term which appears in that position in every statement of that form refers to all the members of a class named by the term."[11] Different rules apply for the distribution of terms in a syllogism, but an example can show the importance of distribution, which is a way of seeing when something applies and when it does not. Take the following syllogism: All alcoholics drink liquor; John drinks liquor; therefore John is an alcoholic. The formal fallacy in this argument is the implication that all those who drink liquor are contained with the group of alcoholics. The fallacy of this syllogism is the fallacy of the undistributed middle, since the subject of the major premise is distributed but the predicate of the subject is not distributed and therefore does not apply to the predicate of the minor premise. The point is that the understanding of logical principles can aid the process of determining the error or difficulty under which a directee may labor.

---

[11]Robert Baum, *Logic* (Holt, Rinehart and Winston, New York, 1981), p. 218.

D. Informal Fallacies

In the art and science of logic, there are two types of fallacies. Formal fallacies are those committed while reasoning syllogistically. Informal fallacies are those types of fallacies which do not pertain necessarily to the rules of a syllogism, but which can be committed due to an error in judgment. The informal fallacies are numerous, and like other aspects of logic, a psychologist should have a thorough grasp of the different forms of informal fallacies so as to be able not only to detect them in his own work and reasoning, but also in those under his care. However, since the number of informal fallacies is large,[12] we shall concern ourselves only with a few in order to draw out their importance in the science of psychology. Informal fallacies can be committed by the agent of the communication or by the receiver of the communication.

One type of fallacy concerns those errors committed in relation to language or linguistic confusion. The fallacy of semantical ambiguity occurs when the word in a discussion or argument is unclear in its meaning throughout the course of the discussion, e.g. consider the following discussion between a psychologist and a directee:
Psychologist: "Tell me about your childhood. Did you and your father have any interaction when you were young, e.g. did you ever play games?"
Directee: "Yes, we played games and he also beat me often."
Psychologist: "Your father beat you?"
Directee: "Yes it was terrible and I felt humiliated when he beat me."
The term "beat" can have different meanings and in the case above the meaning shifted from the winning of a game to physical abuse as understood by the psychologist. The point is that when a psychologist discusses anything with a directee, he must be certain that they are using the same meanings for the same terms.

Another type of fallacy is called the fallacy of accent and it occurs when improper or unusual emphasis is placed on a word or phrase, which leads one to conclude something false even though the person states what is materially true. For example, if a directee were to say "I often saw my father in public, but never with *my* mother." The directee could mean that his mother was bed ridden most of her life and never could go out in public, but the psychologist could take it as the directee saw his father in public with other women.

Another fallacy is called the fallacy of wishful thinking. This fallacy consists in the assertion that because one wants something to be the case, it is the case or it will be the case. For example, a mother says to her husband, "that boy of yours is never going to amount to anything." If the mother has a particular dislike of the child and wishes that he will never amount to anything as "his just deserts" then her wanting him not to succeed in life moves her to state that the boy will never amount to anything.

---

[12]Different texts on informal fallacies tend to call the fallacies by different names, usually as a way of stressing some aspect of the fallacy.

Another fallacy that is plaguing our society is the fallacy of the golden mean. This fallacy consists in assuming that the mean or the middle view between two extremes is where the truth lies. Sometimes the truth does lie in the mean between two positions, but more often than not, it does not. For instance, in political matters, people are often caught committing the fallacy of the golden mean, e.g. pro-abortionists will insist that abortion on demand be part of the American legal system. Pro-life people insist that direct abortion should not be legal under any circumstances. Then a politician will assert that perhaps we need to curtail the number of abortions and allow them under certain circumstances, considering himself to have struck a mean between the two extremes. The problem is that this example also begs the question as to whether the unborn are persons; if they are, then striking a mean is not sufficient to protect them; only reasoned principle is sufficient.

The last example of a fallacy which shall be given here is the *ad hominem* fallacy. This fallacy occurs when, during a discussion, one of the parties attacks the character of his opponent in some way rather than addressing the issue. For example, a wife may say to her husband, "perhaps you need to re-think the punishment you have given to Johnny since it is having a bad effect on the child." The husband then retorts, "You are only saying that because all our married life you have been soft on disciplining the children. If you weren't such a pushover, I wouldn't have to be so harsh." Psychologists must be careful not to allow the directee to use this fallacy against them in light of some reasonable proposed course of action. Moreover, sometimes directees use the fallacy against themselves by unduly attacking their own character when discussing some course of action they took. Rather than discussing the course of action and learning from it, they will wallow in verbal self abuse. This is often a tactic used in order not to deal with the point at hand. People often fall into *ad hominem* argumentation in order to commit the fallacy of *non ad rem*, i.e. they do not want to deal with the point at hand.

Informal fallacies are very important for understanding the directee's *modus cogitandi* because when he commits the fallacies, one can ascertain what the directee is actually doing. If the directee does not want to deal with a particular problem, he may resort to informal fallacies in order to avoid the discussion. At any rate, any psychologist of any merit must have a clear grasp of the nature of informal fallacies and how people are prone to commit them.

II. Principles from First Philosophy

First philosophy is the branch of metaphysics which treats the first causes and principles of things. While the causes of mental health and illness shall not be discussed at this time, it is important to discuss those first principles which are of particular importance to the matter at hand. A principle is defined as that from which any thing in any way proceeds; the starting point of being, change or thought. A first principle is a principle which does not proceed from a prior principle in its own series. This indicates that a principle is some truth or thing from which being, change, knowledge or discussion starts. There are four types of principles which are of importance in our discussion of mental health and illness, viz. logical, ontological, practical and operative. A logical principle is a truth from which other truths proceeds, i.e. a principle of knowledge. A logical principle may be expressed in an ontological formula, then a general truth or a definition is expressed in terms of being. A logical principle may also be expressed in a logical formula, then a general truth or proposition is expressed in terms of thought or speech (that is, of affirmation, negation, or predication). The logical principles in scholasticism are usually principles about real things or being. An ontological principle is a being from which another proceeds or which refers to some aspect of the nature of being. A practical principle is a principle concerned with activity, whether doing or making. An operative principle is one which governs the actions of a faculty or thing. Many of the ontological, logical and practical principles are also operative principles in that they are latent in the very structure and nature of the faculty and govern its activity.

Most principles are self-evident, i.e. once the meaning of the terms is known, the truth of the principle becomes immediately known. This is important to keep in mind as some people will deny the truth of first principles.[13] However, if someone denies a first principle it is due to one of three reasons. The first is that they understand different things about the terms than the principle actually expresses. The second is that they have fallen into absurdity or foolishness. The third is that the person refuses to give assent to a principle which may militate against his own opinion or against his own code of conduct which he has chosen for himself.

Again, as with logic, not every principle can be discussed in detail here. However, there are some principles which should be discussed because of their importance in the field of psychology. The first logical as well as ontological principle is the principle of non-contradiction.[14] The principle of non-contradiction states "a thing cannot both be and not be in the same time and in the same respect."[15] This principle essentially states that things cannot exist in a contradictory fashion, e.g. the grass outside cannot be both brown and green (not brown) at the same time and in the same respect. One of the variants of this principle is "the same judgment cannot at the same time and in the same meaning be both true and false." What this indicates is that either one's judgment congrues with the thing, i.e. with reality or it does not. One cannot have two contradictory judgments of a thing at the same time and in the same respect and both be

---

[13]In fact, the history of philosophy is replete with examples.

[14]At times, authors will refer to this as the principle of contradiction. However, it is a misnomer since the name expresses the essence or nature of the principle; the principle is not that things contradict themselves, but that they do not contradict themselves; therefore the proper name of this principle is the principle of non-contradiction.

[15]SSP, p. 15.

true.

Contradictory speech is a sign of one of three things. At times a person is dishonest or disingenuous. Sometimes it is a sign of real confusion in the mind of the individual. In the former case, it is a matter of the will or a spirit of falsity, whereas in the latter case, people of good will can be confused about something either due to their lack of understanding or due to the difficulty of the object of knowledge in relation to the limits of the human intellect, either of a specific individual or in general. The third cause of contradictory speech is that the person can be mentally ill; in fact, contradictory speech is a clear sign of mental illness. When people talk incoherently, they will often say contradictory things without being aware of the fact that they are being contradictory.

A closely related principle to the principle of non-contradiction is the principle of excluded middle. This principle states: "A thing must either be or not be at the same time and in the same respect."[16] This principle differs from non-contradiction in that non-contradiction states a thing *cannot* both be and not be, where as the principle of excluded middle states that a thing *must* either be or not be. The variant formulation of this principle is "there is no intermediate between being and non-being or between any pair of contradictories."[17] An example may help to make this clearer; grass must be either green or not green. This principle states something positive about the nature of being, viz. either it is or it is not. It is that simple. One of the logical formulations of this principle is "an attribute must be either affirmed or denied of a subject. A proposition must either be true or false."[18]

We saw above regarding the nature of truth that truth is a congruity of the intellect with the thing. Either the intellect congrues with reality or it does not. The intellect cannot both not congrue and congrue at the same time and in the same respect, as in the case of non-contradiction. On the other hand, from the point of view of the principle of excluded middle, there is no mean between truth and falsity, i.e. either what one understands is the truth or it is not. The definition of truth coupled with these two principles excludes any possibility of relativism, either intellectual or moral. Psychology must admit this and recognize that it is actually harmful to the intellect (i.e. to mental health) to foster a relativism in the minds of directees. First, it militates against the good of the intellect by teaching them falsity and it also militates against the intellect by short-circuiting these principles as operative in the intellect. These principles are not only ontological or logical, they are also operative in that they determine or order the intellect toward a mode of operation which is natural to the intellect, not only because it is a being itself and therefore subject to the principles but also because it has been designed to grasp things according to the first principles.

---

[16]SSP, p. 15.

[17]Ibid.

[18]ibid.

One of the most important first principles for psychology is the principle of sufficient reason. The formulation of the principle of sufficient reason varies and each variation brings out different aspects of the same principle which are of importance. The first formulation is "the existence of a thing is accountable either in itself or in another." This indicates that a thing's existence is explained either by the very thing itself or it is explained in reference to another thing. Usually this involves some form of causality, e.g. the computer on my desk does not account for why it is there, one must look to another reason as to how the computer got there in the first place. Sometimes, this principle is formulated as "you cannot give what you do not have." For instance, we observe billiard balls on a pool table; they do not have within themselves the capacity to start moving on their own because there is no principle of motion in them. However, if someone hits a ball and then we see the motion of the ball going from one ball to another, we know that the movement of the one ball is accountable by means of the movement in another. For the one ball simply cannot begin moving on its own since it does not have the motion, and therefore it cannot give it to itself.[19] If someone denies this principle, it is easy to reduce them to absurdity. If he asserts that one can give what one does not have, then simply ask him for a million dollars (assuming he is not a millionaire). Of course, he will insist that he cannot give it since he does not have it.

The principle of sufficient reason is important for psychology since those who suffer from delusions often are not operating according to this principle. They tend to think that certain things are causing their problems when those things (or people) are not capable of it. Moreover, the principle of sufficient reason has taken a beating in the field of parapsychology, in that parapsychologists have been asserting the mind's capacities for things (while still holding the intellect to be purely material) which by nature it is completely incapable of doing.[20]

Another formulation of the principle of sufficient reason is "every judgment (affirmative or negative) about a being should have a sufficient reason (i.e. sufficient evidence)."[21] This is perhaps one of the most systematically abused principles in psychology. For example, as will be discussed at another time,[22] the theories of the subconscious and unconscious have no scientific foundation or evidence and yet the insistence on existence of the subconscious is almost at the level of the irrational. Rather than seeking true scientific explanations for the occurrences explained in terms of the subconscious, in a *deus ex machina* fashion, the subconscious was dreamed up to be able to explain that which was beyond the explanation of certain psychologists. Every valid science must respect the principle of sufficient reason if it is to proceed in an

---

[19]David Hume's critique of causality is a failure to understand the principle of sufficient reason.

[20]This shall be discussed more at length in volume III.

[21]SSP, p. 15.

[22]The topic will be discussed at length in volume III.

authentically scientific fashion.[23]

The next principle is the principle of resemblance. The principle of resemblance states, "Every agent produces a thing that is in some degree similar to itself."[24] In colloquial terms, this principle is formulated as "like begets like." Any time something causes or begets another thing, that thing is in some way like its cause. A clear example is a cow which, when it has offspring, has a calf of the same species.[25] This principle is important for psychology because sometimes the mentally ill think one thing is the cause of another when it is not reflective of that cause in any way.

Moreover, psychologists need to be aware of the operative aspects of this principle. First, if like begets like, then being around the mentally ill a great deal and trying to think the way they do in order to understand them can lead to the psychologist's own mental illness.[26] Second, a psychologist himself must have mental health if he is to beget it in the directee. Unfortunately, since modern psychology has wrongfully claimed for itself the empirical method, the impression is given that one can merely employ the method and get the results necessary. While this may apply to psychiatry, it does not apply to a true psychology. Since the science of psychology is a philosophical science, then its application in regards to those under one's care requires all those things which a practical science will entail, one of which is prudence. If he has mental problems himself, the psychologist will not possess the prudence necessary to guide the directee.

The next principle is the principle of economy which states that "distinctions must not be multiplied without good reason."[27] This principle has two applications. The directee should not be allowed to complicate his situation with unnecessary distinctions. Secondly, the psychologists and psychology as a science must not be too quick to make distinctions regarding mental illness where there is no merit.

Perhaps one of the most important principles of all of philosophy with respect to psychology is the principle of operation. It has several formulations, all of which express the same thing. The principle of operation is formulated as "operatio sequitur

---

[23]Here again, the reader should keep in mind that the object of each science determines the method.

[24]SSP, p. 15.

[25]Here we are prescinding from the condition that modern science often causes through manipulation, various animals begetting offspring not of their species. However, here the principle still applies, for instead of the animal being the cause of its progeny, the altered species is caused by man's reason.

[26]How this is avoided shall be discussed in another volume on the practical aspects of psychology.

[27]SSP, p. 20.

esse"[28] or "agere sequitur esse."[29] This principle essentially states that the nature of a thing's being determines the types of action or operation it is able to perform.[30] For example, a rock which has a material non-living existence is not capable of locomotion (except by an exterior force), whereas an animal which has a living existence is. Moreover, neither a rock nor animal is capable of immaterial acts of intellection because they do not have an immaterial existence.

This principle is not only operative regarding the relation of first to second act, i.e. between the existence/essence of a thing and the secondary operations it performs, like walking, eating, etc., it also refers to the types of actions which flow from the second act themselves.[31] Therefore, anything that is present or resident in the faculty, will affect its operation. For example, if someone suffers from the vice of anger, the vice will affect the irascible appetite when it acts. This observation is pivotal for a clear understanding of the nature of psychology. It has a twofold significance; the first is that when there is some psychological defect, it will affect the person's behavior.[32] The second is on a cognitive order, viz. while the principle states that the actions follow on the type of being, it conversely means that one can know something about the being of a thing by the way it acts. In fact this is the entire basis of the cognition of the essences of things. For the accidents (second act - sometimes refers to operations, etc.) reveal the essence (which is that which has first act), as was seen in the section regarding the agent intellect.

It is also very important regarding what we can know about people psychologically. For instance, Skinner asserted that one cannot know anything about what is going on inside a person, and so psychology has to content itself with discussing

---

[28]Operation follows upon being. See SSP, p. 22.

[29]Action follows upon being. St. Thomas tends to use the previous phraseology, however, in modern philosophical circles the later formulation tends to be more dominate.

[30]The interpretation of this principle pivots on how one understands the Latin word *esse*. If the word is interpreted as referring not just to the mode of existence but to "being" in general as inclusive of the existence and essence of a thing, then the principle needs no further distinctions in order to apply it to various beings. However, if *esse* is interpreted in the strict sense as existence, then a distinction must be made between unmediated operation and act and mediated operation and act. Unmediated operation is one which would flow immediately from the mode of existence as such whereas some operations of a thing would occur as flowing from the essence of a thing and thus the essence would mediate the operation and the existence. Nevertheless, the conclusions drawn from the principle, regardless of interpretation, would be the same.

[31]Action in a thing is actually an accident of an accident, i.e. it is a further modification of a faculty which is already an accident modifying the essence of a thing.

[32]At the moment we are prescinding from the consideration of freewill and how it can affect the operations of other faculties.

behavior only. Skinner and others have denied that you can really know what is going on in the individual because they have effectively denied the cognitive aspect of this principle. For a realist, the interior activities are revealed (although in some cases not fully) by means of the exterior activity. This means that psychologists can come to an understanding of the state of the directees' faculties and thereby know their mental condition. The problem in the past was that there was an incomplete and inadequate anthropology used by the psychologists which did not provide them with the capacities to properly interpret the exterior activities and thereby know the state of the interior faculties. Granted that some interior activities may not be fully revealed, nevertheless, the directee can discuss his state if properly guided and therefore the psychologist can come to a true knowledge of the person's mental condition. This is why an adequate anthropology is absolutely necessary to be a good psychologist, not only in the sense of being a (philosophical) scientist but in the sense of being able to ascertain a directee's condition and thereby know how to direct him.

Another aspect of this is that the psychologist can help people to learn to appropriate their problems. Just as in the case of an alcoholic who cannot begin the process of overcoming his problem until he admits he has one, a psychologist can aid the directee in coming to a knowledge of his difficulty and thereby accept the fact (reality) that he has a specific problem and so begin to work on it. Psychology has caused an enormous amount of damage by preventing people from appropriating their problems. This occurs when someone commits a horrific act which later affects them mentally. The psychologist comes to knowledge of it but tries to assure the person that he is "OK" and that he should not concern himself with it. Often this is done in order to avoid causing emotional disturbances. The problem is that it is a denial of reality and denying reality has never helped any mental patient. One should not necessarily conclude that one should rudely point out a directee's faults. Sometimes because of his state the psychologist must lead him slowly, but the process should lead him to a recognition of the problem and not away from the problem.

The principle of operation coupled with the principle of resemblance indicates that a person or faculty will operate according to its nature, i.e. the faculties beget actions which are like unto them. For example, the possible intellect is capable of reflexion because its immaterial nature allows it to reflect upon itself. Therefore, psychologists can be reassured that when ascertaining the state of a directee, the directee will reveal his state, but this requires that the psychologist be properly trained to interpret the directee's words and actions.[33]

Another area of psychology in which this principle has been absent is that of parapsychology. Part of the principle of operation is that the second acts or operations cannot exceed or surpass the perfection of the nature or powers which are principles

---

[33]This applies to whether the directee is being truthful or not since a good psychologist would be able to judge the veracity of a directee.

from which those operations proceed. In other words, "every agent acts in proportion to its activities."[34] There are certain acts attributed to people which they are incapable of doing on their own because of the limitations of man's faculties.

Another principle of importance is that of finality, viz. "every agent or nature in acting must act for an end."[35] Anything that anyone ever does has some end toward which the action finds its completion. This principle is important because what a person does (the means) very often implicitly contains the end, since it is directed toward that end. Hence, a psychologist can know for what a person is striving, what things are important to that person by the ends revealed in his actions.

Another principle closely related to the above is the principle of specification. This principle states "the particular end (good or formal object) determines and specifies the type of nature. Specific natures determine or define intrinsic ends."[36] The nature of a thing determines the ends for which it was made. This must be understood in light of the previous principle of operation, viz. the operations of various faculties have different ends or objects for which they strive or act upon. It is a thing's nature which determines, 1) which faculties the thing will have and 2) the finalities for which the faculties will be designed or ordered.[37] Moreover, the very nature of a thing itself reveals some aspects of its finality. This is the entire basis of the Natural Law which will be discussed at another time. However, suffice it to say that faculties are ordered toward specific things by virtue of the nature of the thing. For example, the generative faculty does not have *any* end whatsoever. For instance the generative faculty does not have as its end food and its assimilation. There is another faculty for that (i.e. the nutritive faculty). Rather the generative faculty has as its embodied finality, the begetting of children (proximate end) and their rearing (the remote end).

To deny the proper ends of the given faculties can cause a great deal of moral, physical and, consequently, psychological damage. Psychologists who put patients on contraception, for example, are not only short-circuiting the generative faculty, but they are short-circuiting the cognitive faculty which learns that the generative faculty is not ordered to what, in fact, it actually is. In other words, it breeds error in the intellect. Therefore, psychologists must have a clear grasp of the faculties and their finalities

---

[34]SSP, p. 22.

[35]SSP, p. 25.

[36]SSP, p. 25.

[37]See SSP, p. 26 regarding the principle of *a posteriori* knowledge of intrinsic ends: "The intrinsic natural purpose of a nature is learned from the powers, constant and universal tendencies, and the constant and common needs of the nature whose end is being sought. These in turn are known from the activities of the nature."

before they engage in any counseling.[38]

III. Things Which Are Connatural to Human Nature

A. Connatural in General

Something is connatural which belongs "to a nature and exist[s] in it from its beginning; congenital or innate; not acquired; present in and operating by natural endowment, tendency or need of nature."[39] Something is connatural which is in the very nature of the thing; it is innate or had from its beginning and it is not acquired or added.[40] Some of the principles which we have discussed are connatural in one sense, i.e. some of the logical and ontological principles. For instance, we know it is connatural to the intellect to perform its operations according to the first principles, e.g. it is contrary to the nature of the intellect to violate the principle of non-contradiction.

In previous chapters, some things were discussed that indicate a connatural aspect, e.g. the ordering of the intellect to knowledge of the essences of material things.[41] This essentially means that man is by nature ordered toward knowing reality. It also indicates that the intellect is naturally ordered toward converting back to the phantasm for its knowledge.[42] We also know that the intellect is ordered toward the truth and the good.[43] The ordering and following of the Natural Law in all its aspects and precepts is connatural. Moreover, there are certain things which are connatural according to

---

[38]This topic shall be discussed again with respect to the Natural Law but not in full detail. This is one of the reasons why a full knowledge of anthropology is needed. This text will only provide some of that knowledge since its primary focus is to provide a basic understanding of the nature of psychology. Psychologists must have a great deal of philosophical training in order to understand fully all the subalternate principles necessary. While many of them will be discussed here, it simply is not possible to cover them all in a single text and therefore a psychologist must have a great deal of philosophical background before engaging this science. Moreover, while only some of the more important first principles are covered here, a psychologist should have a thorough knowledge of all first principles.

[39]Bernard Wuellner, S.J., *A Dictionary of Scholastic Philosophy* (Bruce Publishing Company, Milwaukee, 1966), p. 59.

[40]Sometimes acquired habits and virtues are called connatural as if to indicate that they constitute a second nature. However, they are not connatural in the proper sense since they are not innate.

[41]ST I, q. 12, a. 4; ibid., q. 87, a. 1; ST II-II, q. 84, a. 2; ST III, q. 60, a. 4 and SCG III, c. 119, n. 1.

[42]See ST I, q. 111, a. 1.

[43]III Sent., d. 33, q. 1, a. 2c.

specific qualities of the individual and here we call to mind the fundamental ordering (and therefore intrinsic finalities) regarding masculinity and femininity.[44]

B. *Intellectus Principiorum*

St. Thomas and the scholastics often talk about the difference between the practical and the speculative intellect. They are, in fact, not separate faculties but the distinction is made according to the objects of consideration of the intellect. The first kind of object of consideration is that object which is known for its own sake, i.e. one simply wants to know the truth about that object and this pertains to the speculative intellect which concerns itself with truth. The second kind of object of consideration is something seen as related to action, i.e. one wants to know something in order to produce action and this pertains to the practical intellect. In the writings of St. Thomas, we see that regarding the speculative intellect and the practical intellect there are natural habits regarding the first principles of the respective intellects. These habits are connatural or natural in the sense that they are not acquired but are in the intellect from the beginning.

Regarding the speculative intellect, St. Thomas discusses what he calls the natural habit[45] of *intellectus principiorum* or understanding of the [first] principles. It is a natural or innate[46] habit by which we are able to understand the first principles and insofar as it is innate it is found equally in all men.[47] We have already discussed many of the first principles, such as non-contradiction, sufficient reason, etc. and this habit helps one to grasp or understand those first principles without inquisition or motion of the intellect,[48] i.e. once the terms are grasped and the formulation of the first principle is heard or thought, one immediately knows or understands the meaning and truth of the principle. This natural habit moves the intellect to grasp the first principles immediately, without ratiocination. This means that one does not grasp the first principles as in a conclusion[49] but they are grasped immediately as self-evident.[50]

---

[44]Unfortunately, modern man has been militating against the intrinsic finalities of the two genders for some time now and it is causing a great deal of psychological damage.

[45]See III Sent., d. 23, q. 3, a. 2, ad 1; ST I, q. 58, a. 3; ibid., q. 79, a. 12; ST I-II, q. 51, a. 1 and ibid., q. 57, a. 2 and De Ver., q. 1, a. 12.

[46]II Sent., d. 24, q. 2, a. 3.

[47]ST II-II, q. 5, a. 4, ad 3.

[48]II Sent., d. 3, q. 1, a. 6, ad 2; ibid., d. 24, q. 3, a. 3, ad 2; III Sent., d. 27, q. 1, a. 3, ad 1 and *De malo* q. 16, a. 5.

[49]ST I-II, q. 65, a. 1, ad 3. This would indicate that the Cartesian mentality that one must be able to prove something for it to be true cannot stand for two reasons. The first is the first principles from which all other conclusions are drawn are self-evident, i.e. grasped

This means that since they are self-evident, one must give assent to the first principles[51] as moved by this natural habit. Moreover, it means that one cannot err regarding the first principles,[52] i.e. reason is always right when it grasps the first principles. However, the history of philosophy, the history of man, as well as common sense experience have shown that man does not always act according to these principles or he does not understand them. Some philosophers have denied implicitly the first principles of the speculative intellect in their philosophical discourses.[53] However, there are two reasons for the repudiation of first principles. The first is that the person does not understand the terms of the principle and therefore cannot give assent to it because he cannot understand the formulation of the principle since it is composed of terms not understood. The second is that there is something impeding the use of reason. For example the young cannot make use of the habit[54] because they have not reached sufficient maturity to think abstractly enough to grasp the principles fully. The gravely mentally ill cannot make use of the habit because of reason's inability to function properly. In fact, one of the ways we know someone is mentally ill is by virtue of the fact that they do not act according to first principles, e.g. they contradict themselves or assert things which violate the principle of sufficient reason. Another impediment the foolishness of the person, i.e. as Aristotle observes, it pertains to the fool to deny what is self-evident.

Again, this is why modern philosophy can contribute very little to a valid

---

immediately without proof. One can only show that, if one rejects a first principle, one is left in absurdity. The second is if everything must be proven, the first principles must be proven by syllogistic reasoning and the premises of that syllogism must be proven, etc. *ad infinitum*. The problem is that there would never be a first principle and subsequently never anything after it. The impossibility of an infinite regress regarding principles militates against the Cartesian notion of everything having to be proven.

[50]I Sent., d. 3, q. 1, a. 4, ad 3; ST I, q. 17, a. 3, ad 2; SCG II, c. 47, n. 3 and De Ver., q. 10, a. 11, ad 12.

[51]ST I, q. 82, a. 2. See also De Ver., q. 15, a. 1.

[52]ST I, q. 17, a. 3, ad 2.

[53]For example, Hume in his critique of causality not only denies the principle of causality which is self-evident but he must also deny the principle of sufficient reason and non-contradiction as a result of his rejection of the principle of causality. Hegel, in his dialectic, holds that in the synthesis both contradictories are contained in the synthesis together, thereby indicating that reason gives assent to two things which are contradictory.

[54]ST I-II, q. 94, a. 1, ad 4.

psychology. When the "father" of modern philosophy[55] denies the senses, which is to deny what is self-evident, one cannot build a psychology on his philosophy since it is not proceeding rationally. In fact, to act contrary to the nature of reason or to connatural principles can actually lead to mental illness. If that is the case, employment of modern philosophy in psychology will only lead to more error regarding mental health and illness.[56]

C. Synderesis

Shifting attention to the practical intellect, St. Thomas discusses the natural habit which guides the practical intellect called synderesis. Synderesis is "the natural habitual knowledge of the basic principles of the natural law; the common human knowledge of the universal first principles of the practical order."[57] Synderesis is divided or distinguished from the first principles of speculative reason[58] in that its end is not truth but action. It is the natural habit of the first principles of the practical intellect,[59] i.e. it is the habit by which we understand the principles of acting.[60] This means that in synderesis are the universal principles of the Natural Law,[61] i.e. it contains the first precepts of the Natural Law.[62] Synderesis is a natural habit by which we know the first precepts of the Natural Law and it relates to reason insofar as it is the understanding of the first principles used in ratiocinating about practical conclusions[63] and hence it moves prudence.[64] For example, the first principle of practical reason is "do

---

[55]Some might deny that Descartes is the father of modern philosophy by arguing to those before him or after him but regardless of who one asserts is the father of modern philosophy, Descartes is nonetheless pivotal.

[56]Obviously, not all modern philosophy is bad and some philosophies in comparison to others are more dangerous. Nevertheless, if one is to progress seriously in the science and art of psychology, one must begin with realism. Denying reality or what is self-evident cannot lead to mental health when the intellect is designed to give assent and be in contact with reality.

[57]Wuellner, *A Dictionary of Scholastic Philosophy*, p. 300.

[58]II Sent., d. 24, q. 2, a. 3, ad 1.

[59]ST I, q. 79, a. 12; ibid., q. 79, a. 13, ad 3 and De Ver., q. 16, a. 1.

[60]II Sent., d. 39, q. 3, a. 2 and De Malo, q. 16, a. 6, ad sed contra 5.

[61]II Sent., d. 7, q. 1, a. 2, ad 3; ibid., d. 24, q. 2, a. 3 and De Ver., q. 16, a. 1, ad 9.

[62]ST I-II, q. 94, a. 1, ad 2; *De malo*, q. 3, a. 12, ad 13. Compare with II Sent., d. 24, q. 2, a. 3, ad 4.

[63]II Sent., d. 24, q. 3, a. 3, ad 5 and ST I, q. 79, a. 12.

[64]ST II-II, q. 47, a. 6, ad 3.

good and avoid evil" and in reasoning about what should be done, synderesis moves prudence to judge based on whether something is morally right or wrong and therefore should or should not be done. In this respect, it is called the law of the intellect[65] insofar as it ordains reason toward the good.[66]

Synderesis instigates or prompts one to the good[67] and rumors against evil in general.[68] Since it is a natural habit, it cannot be extinguished or lost.[69] It cannot fail regarding the universal first principles of practical reason, but the applications to particular actions can fail.[70] Moreover, it can fail if the use of reason is impeded in some way,[71] e.g. by a lesion or something of this sort. Insofar as it instigates or prompts one to the good, it opposes sensuality[72] and one could also say the law of the flesh.[73]

Conclusion

While the intellect is a *tabula rasa* in the sense that it does not contain innate

---

[65]ST I-II, q. 94, a. 1, ad 2.

[66]It should be noted that synderesis concerns the first precepts or principles of the Natural Law, such as do good, avoid evil, obey God etc. However, these are distinct from the secondary precepts or principles of the Natural Law which are connatural to us in the sense that the Natural Law is connatural, but synderesis does not concern the secondary principles of the Natural Law as such. An example of a secondary precept of the Natural Law would be "Thou shalt not steal."

[67]ST I, q. 79, a. 12; De Ver., q. 16, a. 1, ad 12 and ibid., q. 16, a. 2. The difference between synderesis and the conscience is that conscience is an act in which one judges whether a particular action is good or not, whereas synderesis is natural habit affecting acts of the intellect regarding the first principles of practical reason.

[68]II Sent., d. 39, q. 3, a. 1, ad 3; ST I, q. 79, a. 12; De Ver., q. 16, a. 1, ad 12 and ibid., q. 16, a. 2.

[69]II Sent., d. 24, q. 2, a. 3, ad 5; ibid., d. 39, q. 3, a. 1, ad 1 and De Ver., q. 16, a. 3. Since synderesis cannot be lost and it prompts one to the good, St. Thomas observes that it is a perpetual rectitude, i.e. it is something in man's intellect always inclining him toward performing the good, even if it be apparently and not really good; see II Sent., d. 24, q. 3, a. 3, ad 5 and De Ver., q. 16, a. 2.

[70]De Ver., q. 16, a. 3.

[71]Ibid.

[72]ST I, q. 79, a. 12, ad 3.

[73]The *lex fomitis* or law of the flesh is that inclination which resulted from Original Sin by which man is inclined by his flesh to disordered living, i.e. it is movement of the appetites and those things which pertain to the flesh or body contrary to the judgment of reason and intention of the will.

conceptual knowledge, it is not entirely free of habit or orientation. Even though man is not born with innate conceptual knowledge, his intellect is designed and structured a certain way by its nature as well as by natural habits which orient him toward reality and reasoning about reality in a manner consistent with its own functions. Therefore, psychology must be sure never to counsel contrary to that natural structure and those things which are connatural to the intellect, lest contradiction arise in the intellect.

Chapter 7: The Will

As modern science finds many similarities between man and animals, it has on occasion asserted that man is not fundamentally different from animals but that man is merely an advanced animal. While it has already been indicated that man not only has an immaterial soul as well as immaterial faculties of the agent and possible intellects, man has another faculty which is likewise immaterial, viz the will. Even in modern society, one of the fundamental ways which man is treated differently from animals is the fact that he is responsible for the actions which he does voluntarily. The fact that we incarcerate and punish human beings for their behavior indicates that man is essentially different from others in the genus of animals. No other animals incarcerate members of their own group. No other animals make distinctions between felonies and misdemeanors based upon the different kinds of transactions against society and engage in trials and execute punishments, both of which are carried out by those who were not directly transgressed.[1] One of the greatest differences between man and animals is the fact that he has freewill and therefore is responsible for his actions. Since freewill is integral to man, the power of the will is deserving of treatment as a sub-alternate principle which is necessary to know in order to proceed in psychology.

Many psychologists deny that man has freewill. However, the common experience of every individual in making choices regarding his life as well as the experience we have of other people making choices, often contrary to reason as well as appetite, indicates that he has freewill. Moreover, since one makes choices in one's life, the choices he makes can affect one's emotional well being as well as mental health. Therefore, any sound psychology must have a clear grasp of the nature of the will, freedom and the nature of voluntariness.

I. The Faculty of the Will

The will is an immaterial[2] faculty sometimes called intellective appetite.[3] Insofar as it is an immaterial faculty it does not use a bodily organ[4] and is thereby a

---

[1]Ironically, even in Protestant cultures, the distinction between a serious offense against the laws of society and a slight offense is maintained, even when in religious matters, they do not hold to serious and slight transgressions against another form of law, viz. divine laws. While Catholics have always maintained the distinction between mortal and venial sin which is implied by the very nature of moral matter either being serious or slight, Protestants, who maintain that same distinction in civil law, disallow it in relation to divine laws.

[2]*De malo*, q. 6, a. un.

[3]De Ver., q. 22, a. 4.

[4]De Ver., q. 22, a. 4.

distinct power from the sensitive appetites.[5] Since it is an appetite,[6] it is a blind faculty insofar as it does not know its object, for that pertains to a knowing power. Rather, like all appetite, some knowing power must apprehend the object proper to the appetite which is moved by that apprehensive power. The will, being an immaterial appetitive power, must have a proportionate apprehensive power which grasps its object and moves it. Since the possible intellect is the only immaterial knowing power in the soul, it is that which moves the will, i.e. the will is moved by the apprehension of reason or the possible intellect.[7] Since the will is moved by the intellect,[8] the good as grasped by the intellect, i.e. the understood good,[9] moves the will. Since the will is moved by a universal power,[10] i.e. the possible intellect grasps universals, the object it presents to the will is the end or good *in general*.[11] For this reason, it is a universal appetite[12] and not a particular appetite[13] and, therefore, it differs from the lower appetites according to its mode of desiring.[14]

The good which is the object of the will is grasped by the intellect in an act of judgment,[15] which is why St. Thomas notes that the object of the will is presented by the intellect under the *ratio boni*,[16] i.e. the notion or aspect of the good. When the intellect judges something, it judges it as good and presents that object to the will with the aspect which results from its judgment. Yet, St. Thomas goes on to note that the will is moved not just by the *ratio boni* but the *ratio boni* under the aspect of being suitable (*conveniens*).[17] This indicates that the will does not incline to the good in the sense that it is good for any man, but for oneself here and now. For example, one may judge that marriage is good for man in general, but it may not be good for one here and now. So the intellect must judge that the good under consideration is not only good for all men

---

[5]De Ver., 22, a. 4 and ST I, q. 82, a. 5.

[6]ST I, q. 83, a. 3.

[7]De Ver., q. 22, a. 4; ST I, q. 82, a. 4 and *De malo*, q. 6, a. un.

[8]De Ver., q. 22, a. 12; ibid., q. 24, a. 7, ad 5 and ST I, q. 82, a. 4.

[9]De Malo, q. 6, a. un.

[10]ST I, q. 82, a. 4.

[11]ST I, q. 82, aa. 4 and 5.

[12]De Ver., q. 22, a. 4 and ibid., ad 4.

[13]De Ver., q. 22, a. 4, ad 2 and ibid., ad 4.

[14]Its mode of desiring is different since its mode of being and therefore operation is different, i.e. it is immaterial and differs from sensitive appetite which is material.

[15]*De Malo*, q. 3, a. 9, ad 3 and In Ethic. III, l. 13, n. 6.

[16]ST I, q. 82, a. 5.

[17]De Malo, q. 6, a. un.

but good for oneself here and now and then the good under consideration becomes an end for one here and now.

In addition to the will being passive with respect to the intellect when it proposes the good, the will is also an active power[18] insofar as it moves the intellect and other powers.[19] Once the intellect proposes some good to the will, the will inclines toward the good proposed and moves the other powers to pursue the good.[20] Therefore, if the will desires some good, it moves the intellect to the consideration of the means or to those things which will lead to the end. When the will moves the other powers, it moves them to the exercising of their acts[21] or operations and, for this reason, the other faculties are compared to it as its property.[22] Insofar as it uses the other faculties, it means that the will has the capacity to move not only the immaterial power of the possible intellect, but it also has a capacity to move material powers. This means that the will has power over the faculties of the body.

Even though the intellect proposes the will its object, it does not mean that the intellect is ignorant of the acts of the will. The intellect not only knows the object which the will wills, since it proposes that object; the intellect also knows the will itself and its acts.[23] Consequently, the intellect knows what the will chooses, because it can know not only when the other faculties and itself are moved, but also the actual choice itself. Moreover, the intellect must know the will in order to be able to propose its object to it. If the intellect did not know about the will, it could never present the will its object. This is the basis for how the intellect can know when the will has chosen what is right and wrong.[24]

II. Freewill

Liberty or freedom with respect to the will refers to the power[25] or capacity of the will to choose. It is a capacity or power of the will in the sense that it is proper to

---

[18]De Malo, q. 6, a. un.

[19]De Ver., q. 22, a. 12 and ST I, q. 82, a. 4.

[20]St. Thomas calls this movement of the other powers "use" as the will uses the powers to obtain its end.

[21]*De malo*, q. 6, a. un.

[22]De Ver., q. 22, a. 12. By "property" is meant that the other faculties are disposed to be used by the will.

[23]ST I, q. 82, a. 4, ad 1.

[24]This is the basis for the conscience, which is an act of the possible intellect and which stings the individual when he has chosen something bad and which "nags" him for what he has chosen.

[25]De Ver., q. 24, a. 4 and ST I, q. 83, a. 2.

the will to have the ability to choose. It is not a habit of the will[26] in the sense that it can be increased or decreased, nor is it a habit in the sense of a habitude, i.e. it is not a condition of the will but refers to the very nature of the faculty itself insofar as it has the capacity to choose. This freedom to choose indicates that the will is not determined out of necessity[27] but is indeterminate to many things.[28] Unlike other faculties which are determined to one thing, the will by virtue of the fact that it has the capacity for choice, is not determined to any one thing but is indeterminate to the many things which it could choose.

This means that it cannot be coerced[29] or suffer violence. In modern philosophy, freewill is often defined in terms of lack of exterior coercion. While this is true in that the will cannot be coerced, nevertheless, that definition is an extrinsic definition and does not actually define the intrinsic power for choice. Since the will is not determined out of necessity to any one thing, it has the capacity to incline toward some good or not,[30] and so it has the capacity for self-determination,[31] i.e. it moves itself. Hence, freewill refers to the fact the will is the principle of its own motion.[32]

Animals do not have freewill,[33] since they are material and therefore are subject to the determinations of physical laws. But the will, being an immaterial power, is not subject to physical laws with respect to its own actions. This also means that it differs from sensitive appetite, since the sensitive appetite is determined by some sensible nature (object) to which it is inclined. The will is not determined like the sensitive appetite,[34] since it is not physical like the sensitive appetites.[35]

---

[26]De Ver., q. 24, a. 4; ST I, q. 83, a. 2 and II Sent., d. 24, q. 1, a. 1.

[27]De Ver., q. 22, a. 4 and *De malo*, q. 6, a. un.

[28]De Ver., q. 22, a. 6 and ST I, q. 83, a. 1.

[29]De Ver., q. 22, a. 5; ibid., ad sed contra 1-3; ibid., q. 22, aa. 8 and 9 and ST I, q. 82, a. 1.

[30]De Ver., q. 22, a. 4.

[31]ST I, q. 83, a. 1, ad 3; De Ver., q. 22, a. 4; ibid., ad 4; ibid., q. 22, a. 6 ad 1 and *De malo*, q. 6, a. un.

[32]De Ver., q. 24, a. 1.

[33]ST I, q. 83, a. 1 and De Ver., q. 24, a. 2.

[34]De Ver., q. 22, a. 4 and ibid., ad 1.

[35]This is one of the reasons why man must have an immaterial soul. For if he performs operations which are not proper to a physical power, then they must be proper to an immaterial power. Consequently, since a power cannot exist except in some substance, then the substance of the soul in which the power resides must be immaterial as well. This follows from the fact that something cannot give what it does not have, i.e. if the substance was material, it could not provide the act (existence) of an immaterial faculty which is beyond the material. Rather, if the faculty or power is immaterial, it must receive its

While the will is indeterminate to many things, it is not indeterminate with respect to everything. There are some things which the will wills out of necessity. The first is that since its object is the universal good, then it cannot help but will that thing which is good in every respect. For this reason, it wills God out of the necessity of its nature[36] since God is good in every respect, i.e. He is perfect in every way.[37] Since the proper object of the will is the good universally considered, then the will cannot help but to incline toward the object which is universally good, i.e. not just under the notion of the good, but actually good in every way. Moreover, since its proper object is the good, then it must will the good out of necessity.[38] In other words, it is of the very nature of the will to will the good and it cannot help but will the good.

However, other than the *summum bonum* or the good which has every perfection, the will does not will other things out of necessity.[39] This follows from the fact that something which is grasped as good may not possess every perfection and therefore the will does not have to will it. The will may choose not to will the thing since it would be a good not to will it, i.e. the will simply does not choose that good since it lacks some perfection which the will may want. Consequently, while the will naturally wills the good, it does not have to will this or that particular good[40] since it may lack something the will wants. Then again the will could choose a particular good precisely because it contains some good that it wants, but it does not have to choose it out of necessity since that particular limited thing does not possess every perfection.

For this reason, St. Thomas observes that the will is indeterminate with respect to three things. The first is the object[41] or some thing which is a means to one's end, e.g. if one wants to hit a baseball around a park: if there is more than one ball, one can choose one out of the many balls available. The second is actions,[42] i.e. one is not determined with respect to acts which make use of objects. For example, one is free to choose to hit the baseball, throw it or even simply not even do anything with the baseball at all. Finally, the will is free with respect to the order to the end,[43] i.e. one can will actions and things as they are ordered to some end. For example, one can will all the

---

existence (since it is an accident residing in the substance) from a substance which is likewise immaterial.

[36]ST I, q. 82, a. 1; De Ver., q. 22, a. 5 and *De malo*, q. 6, a. un.

[37]ST I, q. 4 (entirety).

[38]De Ver., q. 22, a. 5, ad 12.

[39]ST I, q. 82, a. 2; De Ver., q. 22, a. 5 and ibid., q. 22, a. 6.

[40]De Ver., q. 22, a. 6, ad 5 and *De malo*, q. 6, a. un.

[41]De Ver., q. 22, a. 6.

[42]Ibid.

[43]Ibid. and ibid., q. 24, a. 7, ad 5.

actions and objects which are necessary to become a major league baseball player. On the other hand, one could play baseball for the sake of developing the virtue of sportsmanship. Hence, one can order one's actions and things towards various ends.

Within the metaphysics of St. Thomas, we find the teaching that all actions are done for the sake of the good,[44] since all actions are done in order to arrive at some end.[45] Consequently, all actions are done, either directly (explicitly) or indirectly (implicitly) for the sake of the ultimate end. While actions may strive for particular goods, all particular goods are said to be good by virtue of the fact that they participate in goodness itself, i.e. the goodness of God.[46] For every good sought is in some way like God and so when one pursues some good, he is in fact pursuing God, either directly as when God is the end of our actions, or indirectly, when some created good which is in the image of God (by virtue of the fact that it is good by participating in the goodness of God) is the end of our actions. Therefore, everything created has God as its end according to its mode of being.[47] For example, when the cow pursues sensible goods and arrives at them, she strives for God implicitly, though unknowingly.[48] Whereas, those with immaterial intelligence can have God as their end either directly, such as in prayer, or indirectly, such as in pursuing marriage which is a good ordered toward the majesty of God. That to which the will is determined (the ultimate end) is the principle of desiring those which are to the end, which are not determined.[49] Since everything which one chooses is either God or in His image by virtue of its goodness, God becomes the principle by which one chooses, either implicitly or explicitly. Consequently, God is the end of the created will[50] and so man ought to choose among those things which aid him in arriving at his ultimate end. Freewill is ultimately for choosing God, either by choosing the means which lead to Him or in willing Him directly, i.e. by love. Nevertheless, while man cannot help but will God directly or indirectly, he is free with respect to the objects,[51] his acts[52] in relation to those objects and the ordering[53] which

---

[44]How this is reconcilable with choosing evil, see below.

[45]ST I-II, q. 1, a. 1.

[46]SCG I, c. 38, n. 4.

[47]SCG III, c. 18; ST I-II, q. 1, a. 8 and De Ver., q. 22, a. 2.

[48]De Ver., q. 22, a. 2.

[49]De Ver., q. 22, a. 6. This is the difference between the Latin "finis" and "ea quae sunt ad finem." One is the end explicitly, the other contains the end as that to which the action is ordered.

[50]SCG III, c. 8, n. 3.

[51]De Ver., q. 22, 6.

[52]Ibid.

[53]Ibid.

those acts bring about.

The will has the capacity for election[54] and election is "the ultimate acceptance by which something is received to be pursued."[55] Choice or election is an act of the will which has the capacity to accept or not accept the (various) means judged by reason. In order fully to grasp free choice and the various acts of the will in relation to its objects, a digression into the psychology of human action according to St. Thomas must be made.[56]

The psychology of moral action is that process by which a person goes from perceiving an end to arriving at the end through a means. This process begins in the apprehension of the intellect of a particular good or end. An end may be a thing, such as someone else's property as in the case of stealing, or it may be an action such as committing adultery. In Aquinas' psychology of action, for each act of the will, there corresponds an act of reason in a particular way.[57] Therefore, prior to the will act of *velle*, there is an apprehension of the particular good: "so to intend (*intendere*) differs from to will (*velle*), in that to will tends to the end absolutely; but to intend calls for an order to the end, insofar as the end is that to which the means are ordered."[58] The term *velle* or "to will" may appear to be very difficult to pin down. However, elsewhere in his work he provides more information on what *velle* consists in.

> The will is not always of the impossible, but only sometimes; and it suffices, according to the intention of the Philosopher, to show the difference between will and election, which is always of the possible, and so that to elect is not entirely the same as to will; and similarly

---

[54]II Sent., d. 24, q. 1, a. 1; ST I, q. 83, aa. 3 and 4 and De Ver q. 22, a. 15. Election is often translated into English as "choice."

[55]De Ver., q. 22, a. 15: "ultima acceptio qua aliquid accipitur ad prosequendum."

[56]The treatment of the psychology of human action by St. Thomas comes in large part from the unpublished doctoral dissertation of the author *The Morality of the Exterior Act in the Writings of St. Thomas Aquinas*.

[57]What is not implied here is the idea that there are distinct kinds of acts of the intellect for each step in the decision-making process which are different in some way than the standard three acts of the intellect understood epistemologically. The three acts of the intellect of simple apprehension, judgment and ratiocination are *the* three acts of the intellect. However, these can be specified by their particular object and this is what is meant by saying there is a different kind of act of the intellect for each act of the will. For instance, counsel is actually an act of ratiocination because reason is judging and considering various ways of getting to the end.

[58]De Ver. q. 22, a. 13: "ita intendere in hoc differt a velle, quod velle tendit in finem absolute; sed intendere dicit ordinem in finem, secundum quod finis est in quem ordinantur ea quae sunt ad finem."

neither is to intend the same as to will.[59]

Velle, as it is described here, seems to include both those ends which are possible and those which are not possible, which makes it distinct from the act of *intendere* in that *intendere* is only of that which is possible to attain. A little later on in the same tract, he says that:

> thus, it is clear that an act of the will is to will (*velle*) and to intend.
> But with *velle*, reason proposes to the will something good absolutely,
> either it is worth electing for its own sake, as an end, or for the sake
> of another, as that which is for the end. But *eligere* is an act of the
> will in that reason proposes the good as more useful to the end. It is
> to intend, however, insofar as reason proposes to it a good to be
> attained from that which is to the end.[60]

From these passages, one can envision what Aquinas has in mind with respect to the difference between *velle* and *intendere*. "To will" (*velle*) is to desire or will something in the absolute sense, and by absolute is meant two things. The first is that it is not subject to the boundaries of being attainable and this is why some commentators have translated it as "to wish."[61] For wishing does not imply that it is possible to attain it. The second thing which is meant by the term *velle* is that there is no implication that it is that toward which means are being directed. That is why Saint Thomas asserts that intention somehow implies that something is being directed to the end.[62]

An example may make this clearer. A man looks up at the stars and wishes that he could board a spaceship and travel to the nearest star. Although he "wishes" he could go, which is an act of the will, he is not capable of going because his end is impossible

---

[59]Ibid., ad 12: "voluntas non semper est impossibilium, sed aliquando; et hoc sufficit, secundum intentionem philosophi, ad ostendendum differentiam inter voluntatem et electionem, quae semper est possibilium, ut scilicet eligere non sit omnino idem quod velle; et similiter nec intendere est omnino idem quod velle."

[60]Ibid., q. 22, a. 15: "sic ergo patet quod voluntatis actus est velle et intendere. Sed velle prout ratio proponit voluntati aliquid bonum absolute, sive sit propter se eligendum, ut finis, sive propter aliud, ut quod est ad finem: utrumque enim velle dicimur. Sed eligere est actus voluntatis, secundum quod ratio proponit ei bonum ut utilius ad finem. Intendere vero, secundum quod ratio proponit ei bonum ut finem consequendum ex eo quod est ad finem."

[61]For example see Vernon J. Bourke, *Ethics: A Text Book in Moral Philosophy* (New York, Macmillan Co., 1963), p. 59. Saint Thomas himself uses the word *velleitas* which is "wish" in ST I-II, q. 13, a. 5, ad 1.

[62]See De Ver. q. 22, a. 13 and ibid., q. 22, a. 15.

to attain. Hence, no means are even considered because the end is not even intended. If it was possible, he could intend it and consequently set about finding the means to attain his end. In other words, one cannot deliberate about the means to something which is impossible to obtain.

The point to draw out here is that there are two acts of the intellect and two acts of the will which have ends as their objects. The first act of the intellect apprehends something as good, presents it to the will as good[63] and the will wills it in an absolute sense. Next the intellect judges the end's attainability[64] and then if it is attainable presents the good to the will as attainable and the will may intend to obtain the object or the end. The object of *velle* may or may not become the object of intention. If the object is not attainable, then the object of *velle* never becomes an object of intention. However, the object of intention does not differ from the object of *velle* except to the extent that reason has added to that object the notion of being attainable. Moreover, freewill must likewise not be forgotten. A man may apprehend some thing as attainable, but he may not will it. For instance, space flight may actually be possible to the moon and the man may wish to go, but he may decide that he would rather do something else than go on a trip to the moon. Even though it is attainable, it does not necessarily follow that he will will it, even if it is wished for.[65]

The next step in the moral process is counsel, which is an act of the intellect whereby one considers the various means to the end intended.[66] When counsel is finished, the act of the will of consent takes place with respect to the various means proposed.[67] Then there is a judgment by the intellect with respect to the various means consented to as to which should be the one to be used.[68] The next act of the will in the moral process is *eligere* or election, also called choice. With respect to choice, he says that:

---

[63]See De Ver. q. 22, a. 12 and ST I-II, q. 13, a. 5, ad 1.

[64]See ST I-II, q. 12, a. 1, ad 1 and ad 3 and ibid., q. 12, a. 3, ad 2.

[65]This statement is made with the awareness that some have maintained that intention is not free or at least not a moral act (for instance the author of this text asserted that in his article "The Species and the Unity of the Moral Act," p. 82). However, if intention is an act of the will which is voluntary (it would be strange to assert that intending something is not in some way voluntary), then in some way it must be free. This is the case with all ends or objects of intention except the ultimate end. See below for a further discussion of freedom with respect to ends.

[66]See ST I-II, q. 14 (entirety).

[67]See ibid., q. 15 (entirety).

[68]See ibid., q. 13, a. 3: "electio consequitur sententiam vel iudicium." See also ibid., q. 13, a. 1, ad 2.

the proper object of election is that which is to the end, which pertains to the notion of the good, which is the object of the will; for the good is called the end, as honest or pleasurable, and that which is to the end, as useful.[69]

Here, Aquinas refers to those which are for the end as the "object" of election. Yet, the objects of election are exterior actions.[70] This is what divides the act of intention from the act of election, viz. they have different objects about which their actions are concerned. The object of the act of intention is the end and the object of the act of election is an exterior action or that which is to the end.[71] The actual shift in objects of the will occurs between the act of intention and the act of counsel.

The object of counsel, consent, judgment (of those which are to the end which should not be confused with judgment of the end), election, command and use is the same.[72] The difference is that the object is under a different notion or aspect in each act. For instance, in counsel the *ratio* of the object is its conduciveness to the end, whereas the *ratio* of the object with respect to judgment is whether it is the most suitable. Moreover, each object of the act of the will determines the character of the act of the will. This is precisely why Saint Thomas says that sin essentially resides in the will. For if the object of intention, i.e. the end, is bad, then the will will be bad for intending it. Moreover, if the will elects or chooses a bad means, then again, the will will be bad because it willed it.

The last two acts in the psychology of moral action are command and use. Command refers to that act of the intellect which guides and orders the exterior act in execution.[73] Use is an act of the will by which the exterior powers, i.e. those powers other than the will which are capable of being moved by the will, are moved to bring about the end.[74] Therefore, the final analysis of the moral process leaves the following depiction of moral objects and their acts:

---

[69]De Ver. q. 22, a. 15: "proprium obiectum electionis est id quod est ad finem, quod pertinet ad rationem boni, quod est obiectum voluntatis; nam bonum dicitur et finis, ut honestum vel delectabile, et quod est ad finem, ut utile."

[70]See ibid., ad 3 and ST I-II, q. 13 (entirety), *Veritatis Splendor* (#67) and CCC (1752) likewise discuss this.

[71]Cf. VS #77-80.

[72]For the fact that the object of use and command is the same as election see ST I-II, q. 17, a. 4, ad 2.

[73]See ST I-II, q. 17, a. 1.

[74]See ST I-II, q. 16, a. 1.

Act of the Intellect	Act of the Will		Their Object
Apprehension	*Velle*		End
Judgment	Intention	End	
- -	- -	-	-
Counsel	Consent		Means
Judgment	Election		Means
Command	Active Use		Means
Passive Use[75]			

In the psychology of moral action, there are two primary objects, viz. the end and the means or those which are to the end. In each act of the intellect and will, these two objects take on a different aspect or *ratio*. With the apprehension of the end and *velle* the end is considered absolutely, i.e. the notion of attainability is not considered part of it. Moreover, at that stage there is no consideration of ordering means to it. With respect to judgment of the end and intention, the notion of attainability is considered part of it and once it is intended, consideration of the means follow, for intention implies that one desires to arrive at the end intended which indicates that means are necessary. The primary difference between the means in counsel, consent, judgment and election and the means in command and use is that the former is part of the elective order, whereas the latter is part of the executive order. In other words, the means which is chosen is then executed so the moral psychology is not complete until fruition takes place which is the effect of command and use.[76]

---

[75]Active use refers to the act of the will of use, while passive use refers to powers other than the will, one of which is the intellect.

[76]See ST I-II, q. 16, a. 3. Some observations should be made regarding this overall psychology of moral action. The first observation one can offer is that this psychology of the human act is pieced together from Aquinas' discussion of them in various places which presents the problem of the certainty of this corresponding to his actual thought. While one can strive for as much clarity as possible regarding this process, the complete thought of Saint Thomas regarding these steps is not present because he did not deal with the process systematically, i.e. step by step. Rather some steps have been dealt with directly while others have only been mentioned in a few places or in passing. Recently, there has been some debate about certain steps in the decision-making process. The acts of the intellect and will as they have been delineated here tend to be, in substance, that which has traditionally been given. The second observation has to do with the completion of the process. Part of the problem in any human process is the possibility of it being cut short, i.e. it may not run its full course. So it may happen that one thinks that something is attainable, so he intends it, but he cannot arrive at the best means or any possible means to arriving at his end, which originally was judged to be obtainable. The point in all of this is that the process is not something perfectly packaged both in the writings of Aquinas and in real life. The various

At this point, we can now return to the discussion of freewill and the fact that St. Thomas discusses freedom often in relation to the act of the will of election. While each of the acts of the will in the decision-making process has a degree of freedom, in some respect they do not have the fullness of freedom that election has. *Velle* is restricted by the fact that the object may not be attainable. While one is free to wish for something or not, nevertheless, there is a lack of freedom from the fact that the object includes those things which cannot be obtained. With intention,[77] St. Thomas observes that one is not free with respect to the end.[78] However, this needs clarification so as not to be misunderstood. We have already seen that the will wills out of necessity the

---

steps in the concrete may not follow one after the other. As in the previous example, because the exterior act or object of the moral act of adultery could not be executed (i.e. command and use at the time were not possible), the process was cut short. Moreover, because human reason is fallible, one may judge the end to be attainable and intend it, and then as counsel begins to take place it becomes apparent that the end is, in fact, not attainable. Hence, just because something is intended does not necessarily mean a means will be chosen. This does not contradict what Saint Thomas was saying earlier, viz. the object of intention is that toward which the means is ordered. In the normal playing out of this process, that is true, but circumstances can interrupt the normal process. Moreover, because each volitional step in the process is in some way free, since it is based in a will that is free, the will can cut the process off at any step. The final observation is that each step is not necessary for a complete moral act. What is necessary for a complete moral act is an intended end, a chosen means and their execution. So, while each end is apprehended and judged, it may never be an object of *velle* in the sense that it could always be seen as attainable. Moreover, sometimes counsel is not taken regarding the means because the only means possible is proposed immediately by the judgment of the means to the will for election, which may or may not be chosen. For instance, a virtuous married man may intend to have a child. His only moral means is conjugal relations with his wife, so he may not spend any time taking counsel about the means because there is only one set of means available to him (qua virtuous man). Hence, no counsel is necessary. In the order of intention and the order of election it is possible to skip steps in the process, but not however in the order of execution. This is the case by virtue of the fact that in order to bring about the exterior act it has to be ordered and commanded by the intellect, and the other powers must be moved by the will.

[77]This observation would also apply to "wish."

[78]For example, see II Sent., d. 24, q. 1, a. 3 and De Ver., q. 24, a. 6. Moreover, when St. Thomas discusses freedom, it is often in terms of election of the means, e.g. see *De malo*, q. 6, a. un. St. Thomas notes that man wills the ultimate end and the good in general out of necessity and it may be wrongly concluded that he held that one is not free with respect to the end. The texts, though few, are not wanting in St. Thomas where he indicates the end falls under the voluntary, e.g. see III Sent., d. 27, q. 1, a 2 and especially IV Sent., d. 16, q. 3, a. 2b, ad 4.

ultimate end (God). Moreover, we have seen that the will wills the good out of necessity but not this or that good. So, in one sense, the will is not free with respect to the end, in that the good which is one's end must be willed. However, the will is indeterminate with respect to this or that end unless it contain every perfection. Moreover, the finalities to which man and his faculties are ordered are limited, i.e. those things which a person can intend are limited, e.g. one can either marry, become a priest (or become a religious) or stay single and these are the only ends with respect to the marital state. Consequently, the ends toward which man and his faculties are ordered are already predetermined. For example, the concupiscible appetite is ordered toward bodily goods and it cannot decide to cease being ordered towards its ends, i.e. bodily goods. This is why at times one is said not to be free with respect to one's ends since they have been predetermined by man's nature and the finalities of the faculties. One is not completely free with respect to the objects of intention. While there is some voluntariness regarding the object of intention in that one can intend or not intend an end and thereby either order a means to the end or not, nevertheless one is not completely free with respect to the ends since they have been predetermined.

As a result, St. Thomas tends to discuss freedom in the context of election or choice,[79] since the means to an end are virtually unlimited. Even if there is a given end which has only one means, one is still completely free to will the means or not. Whereas, even if one does not intend to pursue an end, it still remains an end to one's nature or faculties. In the decision-making process, voluntariness is part of each act of the will, but it is only in election where there is no preset determination and the will is completely free either to accept or reject the means. While one is free to intend an end, one does not "choose" the end since it is already predetermined. All one can do regarding the end is intend it and thereby set about ordering a means to that end.

St. Thomas uses various words for freedom, but he retains a phrase from St. Augustine as the primary expression of freewill, viz. *liberum arbitrium*[80] which is translated into English as "free judgment" or "free choice." *Arbitrium* is the sentence of an arbiter or judge when presented with two or more options. In the case of freewill with man, his freedom of choice is always between two goods, either two actual goods or the will is presented with either choosing a good or not choosing a good, which is likewise viewed as a good.[81]

Regarding what "free judgment" actually is, St. Thomas makes the following observation:

> Man, indeed, by the power of reason judging about actions, is to

---

[79]These interpretations regarding being free with respect to the means and not the end are the author's own interpretation of St. Thomas.

[80]See De Ver. q. 24, a. 1; ibid., ad 1; ibid., ad 20 and ST I, q. 83, a. 3, ad 2.

[81]Sometimes not to choose is a good.

judge from his own judgment [*arbitrium*] insofar as he knows the nature of the end and that which is to the end, and the habitude and order of one to the other. And therefore he is his own cause not only of motion, but of judging; and therefore he has free judgment and free judgment of acting or not acting.[82]

What St. Thomas seems to be saying is that man is not only the cause of his own motion or action, but of judging the action. What this judgment actually is, St. Thomas clarifies in a response to an objection in the *Summa Theologiae*:

judgment is as a conclusion or determination of counsel. Moreover, counsel may be determined, first by the sentence of reason and second by the acceptance of appetite, hence the Philosopher says in III Ethic. that judging from counsel we desire according to counsel. And in this way election itself is said to be a judgment, from which free judgment (*arbitrium*) is named.[83]

Judgment indicates two things, viz. something on the side of reason and something on the side of the will. On the side of reason, there is counsel taken about the means by which, as was seen above, a judgment about the means to be used is made by the intellect prior to proposing the means to the will for choice. Second, as the quote of St. Thomas here points out, through choice, the counsel about the means is determined (specified) and brought to a conclusion. In that sense, the will can be said to "judge" in that what was indeterminate with respect to the judgment of the intellect, is determined by the act of the will.

In his commentary on the *Sentences*,[84] St. Thomas tends to discuss free judgment primarily in terms of the intellect and in the later works, while the intellectual aspect is there, it is less dominant. Freedom can be said to be in the intellect insofar as it is not impeded in its operations. In the moral sphere, this would mean primarily that

---

[82]De Ver., q. 24, a. 1: "homo vero per virtutem rationis iudicans de agendis, potest de suo arbitrio iudicare, in quantum cognoscit rationem finis et eius quod est ad finem, et habitudinem et ordinem unius ad alterum: et ideo non est solum causa sui ipsius in movendo, sed in iudicando; et ideo est liberi arbitrii, ac si diceretur liberi iudicii de agendo vel non agendo."

[83]ST I, q. 83, a. 3, ad 2: "iudicium est quasi conclusio et determinatio consilii. Determinatur autem consilium, primo quidem per sententiam rationis, et secundo per acceptationem appetitus, unde philosophus dicit, in iii Ethic., quod ex consiliari iudicantes desideramus secundum consilium. Et hoc modo ipsa electio dicitur quoddam iudicium, a quo nominatur liberum arbitrium."

[84]See II Sent., d. 24, q. 1.

the intellect not be impeded in making its judgments about ends and means, otherwise, freedom is compromised. Since the will only wills that which is proposed to it by the intellect, the will will be debilitated in its freedom if the intellect is impeded in its operations. This is why St. Thomas tends to discuss free judgment in terms of both the intellect and the will. While freedom is really proper to the will, it cannot act according to its free capacity if the intellect is impeded in its operation and thereby affects the object as it is presented to the will. Therefore, both the operations of the intellect and will are implied.

This is also why St. Thomas notes that the root of freedom is constituted in reason,[85] for without reason, the will cannot perform its operations. It also means that free choice of the will ultimately has its root in the truth, for if the intellect fails in its operation to judge rightly about something, the object presented to the will will be affected. Consequently, true freedom for man consists not only in the capacity of the will to choose or "judge for itself" but also in the intellect's right operation which consists in knowing the truth.[86]

III. Choice of Evil

It is the common experience of all men that some people choose what is in fact evil. How does one reconcile that with St. Thomas' observation that one wills the good out of necessity? St. Thomas notes that when one wills the evil, one does not will the evil *per se*,[87] i.e. one does not will the evil for itself. The will which has as its proper object the good, cannot incline to something insofar as it is evil. Rather, one wills evil *secundum quid* (in a certain respect).[88] The will wills whatever it wills under the *ratio boni*[89] and so when it wills evil, it wills it under the notion of the good.[90] This indicates that when the object is presented by the intellect to the will, the intellect judges it as good, even though it is bad.[91] This can happen in two ways. The first is if the intellect is unaware or impeded in making a proper judgment about the evil of the thing and presents it to the will as good simply speaking. The second is when the intellect judges the object as good in one respect but bad in another, e.g. when a person sees some thing that he would like to own, he may think of stealing the object. In that case, he sees the

---

[85]See De Ver., q. 24, a. 2.

[86]This is why, in *Veritatis Splendor*, the Holy Father emphasizes the fact that true freedom cannot be had without the truth. See VS, intro and chapter 1.

[87]II Sent., d. 41, q. 2, a.1, ad 1.

[88]Ibid.

[89]ST I, q. 82, a. 2, ad 1.

[90]De Ver., q. 22, a. 6, ad 6.

[91]II Sent., d. 41, q. 2, a. 1, ad 1.

object as good, i.e. as something desirable to possess, even though he knows stealing is wrong. Hence, even the act of stealing in that case is presented according to the good of possession of the object. Consequently, the will is in fact presented something under the notion of the good, even though contained in that intelligible species is the fact that it is morally bad. The will, then, chooses to perform the action as choosing the good of obtaining the possession of the object. Before it actually wills the object which is under the notion of the good but is actually bad, it must do one of two things. Either it must ignore that aspect of the evil in the object and focus only on the good or it must move the intellect to separate out or to judge the intelligible species in such a way as to exclude the evil from the intelligible species or to minimize it so that it is easier to choose.[92]

When choosing evil, the intellect and will undergo a change. The definition of love is "willing the good of another."[93] When one wills something, it is actually an act of love in which the will goes out of itself to have union with the thing that it loves since the proper effect of love is union.[94] As it wills the object, it itself becomes a faculty which has willed that object and so the species of the object becomes present in the faculty of the will and it thereby changes accidentally. In other words, the will becomes a lover of God, people, houses, cars as well as a lover of theft, killing, etc. While it does not love the evil of the thing, it nevertheless loves the thing and is willing to accept the evil in order to obtain the good. It must accept the evil in its willing if it is to have the good thing and when it does so, the evil also becomes part of the will.[95] Consequently, psychologists who say that when a person does an evil thing, he does not become evil, simply cannot rationally sustain that position. The notion that "I'm OK, You're OK" is true only when both are really OK. People who choose evil are not OK.

The second aspect of this issue is that the intellect is forced to act contrary to its very nature. Perhaps the most obvious way to point this out is by the consideration

---

[92]This why when people commit evils, over time they habituate their intellect not to look at the evil of it. Later, they begin to "change their mind" about whether the action is actually evil at all, e.g. the cultural milieu in the Unites States in the past did not tolerate fornication. This is evidenced from the fact that there were fornication laws in many states. Yet, over time, fornication became so widespread, that now the cultural atmosphere actually encourages sexual activity outside of marriage.

[93]See Aristotle, *Rhetoric*, II, c. 4 (1380b35); ST I-II, q. 26, a. 4 and SCG I, c. 91, nn. 2 and 3.

[94]III Sent., d. 27, q. 1, a. 1, ad 5; ibid., d. 29, q. 1, a. 3, ad 1; ST I-II, q. 25, a. 2, ad 2; ibid., q. 28, a. 1 and ad 2; ibid., q. 32, a. 3 ad 3; De Ver., q. 26, a. 4 and Meta. I, l. 5, n. 10.

[95]This notion coupled with the notion that man has freewill is why sin is, properly speaking, in the will, see ST I-II, 74, 1.

of lying. When one lies, one says the false in order to deceive.[96] Yet, in order for a statement to have the true nature of a lie, one must know the truth about something but be unwilling to speak what the intellect knows. Now it is the nature of the faculty of speech to convey that which is known in the intellect,[97] so that in order to commit a lie, one must first know the truth, but the will chooses not to speak the truth. Second, before the lie can be stated, the will moves the intellect to reformulate the truth into falsity and to judge the falsity (or evil) as good and thus moves the intellect actually to judge something contrary to the way in which the intellect knows it is. So first the will moves the intellect to act contrary to its nature and then the intellect commands that the lie be said. Hence the intellect commands to be done what it knows to be false, which militates against the nature of the intellect which is designed to operate according to the principle of non-contradiction.

Choosing evil is somewhat the same thing. The intellect is often moved by the will to command something under the notion of the good which the intellect knows to be evil. Each time one chooses something evil, he militates against the intellect itself, which is why sin is said not to be rational and so any good psychology can never be indifferent to evil choices,[98] since they militate against the good of the intellect whose purpose is to know and command the truly good.

The ability to choose evil is seen by modern society as the hallmark of what it means to be human. Nothing could be further from the truth. If the structure of the intellect as such is to arrive at the truth, then it is not good for man to give assent to what is false. In fact, it is actually contrary to his nature in that the intellect is fundamentally ordered to the truth. Before one can will evil, one must hold that what is really only apparently good is to be pursued, i.e. something which is evil is presented under the notion of the good even though the intellect knows that it is not really good.[99] The will then wills something which is presented to it as only apparently good, and yet the will accepts it. This is not properly human; for the will is ordered by nature to the real good, not the apparent good. Hence, real freedom is ultimately for choosing among real goods since the will is ordered toward the real good and not the apparent good.

This is why St. Thomas says that willing evil is not freedom, nor a part of freedom, but merely a sign of freedom.[100] In other words, freedom is fundamentally designed for choosing among real goods and the choice of evil is in fact a case in which

---

[96]See ST II-II, q. 110.

[97]See ST II-II, q. 110, a. 3.

[98]As will be seen later, choosing evil is actually a way in which someone can voluntarily cause their own mental illness.

[99]This is why the conscience is so important and why it should not be ignored when one chooses one's action or in psychology.

[100]De Ver., q. 22, a. 6.

man is engaging in an action which is not proper to his human nature. It is unnatural.[101]

To return to the discussion of love, something should be said about the distinction between the passion of love and the act of the will of love.[102] Love is not merely a sensitive passion as its connotation is taken today.[103] Rather love is found in both the intellective appetite (will) and in the sensitive appetite,[104] but they are distinct. Love is the first act of the will,[105] insofar as anything that it wills, it wills under the notion of the good and the good is the object of love.[106] So, any time someone wills something, they are in fact loving the thing. Love is a motion or act of the will[107] in which the love or the will seeks union with the loved.[108] Insofar as the will loves that which it wills, the act of the will is rooted in love[109] and consequently, by the will and love, man is drawn to the thing that he wills and loves.[110] Hate also being an act of the will is the contrary of love and whatever is said of love can, in an opposite fashion, be said of hate, e.g hate does not seek union but aversion from the evil which is the object of hate.[111]

The primary definition of love is the willing of the good of another.[112] This definition has two aspects to it. The first is that one wills the good of some other thing

---

[101]It is interesting to note that St. Thomas notes that the *flexibility* (note the word is not capacity which implies a natural power) is a result of the fact that the will is not from God but is made out of nothing (see De Ver., q. 22, a. 6, ad 3). It is because of the fact that man is made out of nothing, that he has a "flexibility" to go back to nothing, since evil is actually the lack of the being of a due good. Moreover, it is because of Original Sin and man's seemingly never-ending slip into a life imbued with Actual Sin that it seems "natural" for man to choose evil. Rather, the fact that man is choosing evil is a sign that he is not functioning according to the natural state in which he was intended to thrive.

[102]St. Thomas actually observes that "love" is used in reference to three things, 1) love as an act of the will, 2) love as a passion of the concupiscible appetite and 3) love as a virtue in the will.

[103]The passion of love will be discussed later.

[104]III Sent., d. 27, q. 2, a. 1.

[105]ST I, q. 20, a.1; ST I-II, q. 4, a. 3 and *De divinis nominibus*, c. 4, l. 12.

[106]ST I-II, q. 29, a. 1.

[107]I Sent., d. 13, q. 1, a. 3, ad 4; II Sent., d. 41, q. 1, a. 1 and ST I, q. 20, a. 1.

[108]SCG IV, c. 23, n. 7.

[109]SCG IV, c. 19, n. 6.

[110]III Sent., d. 27, q. 1, a. 4 and ST I, q. 36, a. 1.

[111]ST I-II, q. 29, a. 1.

[112]Aristotle, *Rhetoric*, II, c. 4 (1380b35); ST I-II, q. 26, a. 4 and SCG I, c. 91, nn. 2 and 3.

or person for one's own sake.[113] This is proper to both sensitive and volitional love. The second aspect is that one wills the good of another for the sake of the other and not necessarily for oneself.[114] Sensitive love does not seek the good of another for his own sake, strictly speaking, but merely seeks its own fulfillment, whereas volitional love can terminate simply in seeing another attain his own good. This is why, for example, a parent wills good things for the child, even though he (the parent) does not benefit from it. This is also why married people will go without things for the sake of the spouse whom they love.[115]

IV. Voluntariness

Since the science of mental health wants to know how to direct those under its care to mental health, the will's involvement in that process will be of prime importance. For in some cases, one must want to become mentally healthy in order to be mentally healthy, just as an alcoholic must want to overcome his addiction and until he chooses to do so, no one can help him. Therefore, it is important to understand not only the nature of the will and free choice, but also what constitutes voluntariness.

When St. Thomas talks about the relation of the will to a given action, he makes a threefold distinction between the voluntary, involuntary and the non-voluntary. For an act of the will to be voluntary there must be two things, i.e. full (perfect) knowledge regarding the thing proposed and the motion of the will itself to the object.[116] In order for one to do something voluntarily, one must have a perfect grasp of what one is willing.[117] Moreover, the motion of the will and its act must be from its own inclination,[118] i.e. coming from itself as from an intrinsic principle.[119] Therefore, the voluntary is that which is in the power[120] of the will to act or not to act.[121]

---

[113]ST I-II, q. 26,a. 4.

[114]Ibid.

[115]One of the remarkable traits of modern man is that his love is degenerating into a strictly sensitive love. It seems that due to societal and environmental factors, he has not been trained or has willed not to love in the volitional sense, which is why this society is becoming so disordered. Natural volitional love is actually a good thing in that it is the foundation of the proper upbringing of children by the parents and, along with truth, is the sole basis of any society's existence beyond the mere material existence of man.

[116]ST I-II, q. 6, a. 1 and In Ethic. III, l. 1, n. 5.

[117]ST I-II, q. 6, a. 2 and ibid., q. 6, a. 3, ad 3.

[118]ST I-II, q. 6, a. 1.

[119]II Sent., d. 25, q. 1, a. 1, ad 6; ST I-II, q. 6, a. 1, ad 1 and ibid., q. 6, a. 5.

[120]De malo, q. 2, a. 1, ad 2.

[121]ST I-II, q. 6, a. 7, ad 3 and ibid., q. 71, a. 5, ad 2.

The involuntary occurs when full knowledge is absent, i.e. when ignorance occurs in the intellect, the voluntariness is diminished.[122] However, several distinctions must be made. Since the will is moved only by the possible intellect, only that which affects the possible intellect can affect the voluntariness of an act of the will, other than the will itself. Consequently, the will cannot be coerced from an exterior principle[123] even though the man can suffer bodily coercion. As a result a twofold distinction regarding the voluntary must be made. Regarding acts of the will, there are those which are elicited[124] (i.e. they pertain to the act of free choice) and these are voluntary and cannot be affected by any exterior agent. However, there are those which are commanded,[125] i.e. once one has made a decision to perform some action in choice (election), then the intellect commands the act to be done and the will exercises use over the exterior faculties. Consequently, man can suffer coercion regarding an act of the will of use when the act is commanded but the will is impeded in exercising the act commanded due to some impediment in the exterior faculties.[126] Yet, the will itself, properly speaking, cannot suffer violence or coercion since it is a certain inclination proceeding from an interior knowing principle.[127] Moreover, the will cannot be coerced from outside since that is contrary to its nature as a self-moving principle[128] and therefore it cannot suffer violence.[129] Man can suffer violence only outside the will[130] and this suffering violence is not a violence contrary to the will, simply speaking, since one does not act as an exterior agent directly on the will. Since the will is not a bodily organ nor exercises its act in a bodily organ,[131] it cannot be coerced from without.

The necessity of willing God and the good in general is not coercive since the will moves by its own inner nature to these things.[132] Other spiritual substances cannot

---

[122]ST I-II, q. 76, aa. 3 and 4.

[123]Motion from an exterior principle is in another genus than the voluntary since it is outside the will, see ST I-II, q. 6, a. 1, ad 2. Moreover, since animals do not have a will, the voluntary does not apply to them (ST I, q. 6, a. 2) and they can be coerced. Put plainly, animals are not the masters of their own acts and so the voluntary is not predicated of animals (ST I-II, q. 6, a. 2, ad 2).

[124]ST I-II, q. 6, a. 4.

[125]Ibid.

[126]ST I-II, q. 6, a. 4 and ibid., q. 6, a. 5, ad 1.

[127]ST I-II, q. 6, a. 4 and ST I, q. 82, a. 1.

[128]ST I-II, q. 6, a. 4.

[129]Violence is defined as action contrary to the nature of a thing.

[130]IV Sent., d. 29, q. 1, a. 1; ST I-II, q. 6, a. 4; ibid., q. 5, a. 5 ad 2 and ad 3.

[131]II Sent., d. 25, q. 1, a. 2.

[132]De Ver., q. 22, a. 5.

coerce the will[133] since they are not its proper moving agent; only the intellect is the proper exterior agent which moves the will. God can move the will[134] but only because He does so as acting in the will as an interior principle of motion.[135]

Other outside factors, such as fear do not cause the involuntary *per se* but *secundum quid*.[136] In other words, the passion of fear of the irascible appetite, which is a physical thing, cannot act upon the will directly and so it cannot cause the involuntary *per se*. However, insofar as it affects knowledge in the intellect[137] it can affect the voluntary. Hence it affects the voluntary not essentially, but only in a certain respect, i.e. insofar as it affects the intellect. Moreover, if the motion of the irascible appetite does not cause the involuntary *per se*, then neither does concupiscence[138] which is from the concupiscible appetite. However, like fear, it can affect the judgment of the intellect and thereby affect the voluntariness of the action indirectly. So only those things which affect the judgment of the intellect can affect the voluntariness. Consequently, things such as fear, concupiscence, weakness, illness, bodily violence and the like diminish the judgment of reason[139] and thereby cause the involuntary.

Yet, while all these affect the operations of the intellect and therefore cause ignorance in some fashion, a few distinctions must be made regarding the involuntary. The first is that not everything which affects the judgment will cause an action to be involuntary. If the will would have carried on in the act even though the intellect was affected, then the action would remain voluntary. However, if the presence of the knowledge would have moved the will contrary to the way in which it was moved by the ignorance,[140] then the involuntary would have truly occurred. Not everything reduces the voluntariness of what someone does, but only that which would make him act contrary to the way he would act with knowledge. The involuntary is caused by ignorance in the intellect: not just any form of ignorance, but ignorance which moves one to act contrary to the way he would if he were not ignorant. It is involuntary

---

[133]II Sent., d. 8, a. 5; SCG III, c. 88; ST I, q. 106, a. 2; ibid., q. 111, a. 2; ST I-II, q. 80, a. 1; *De malo*, q.3, aa. 3 and 4 and ibid., q. 22, a. 9.

[134]ST I, q. 105, a. 4; ibid., q. 106, a. 2, ibid., q. 111, a. 2; ST I-II, q. 9, a. 6, SCG III, c. 88 and De Ver., q. 22, a. 8.

[135]ST I, q. 103, a. 5, ad 2; ibid., q. 105, a. 4; ST I-II, q. 75, a. 3; ibid., q. 80, a. 1, ad 2; ibid., q. 111, a. 4; ST III, q. 18, a. 1, ad 1; *De malo* q. 6, a. un., ad 1 and ibid., q. 16, a. 11, ad 3.

[136]ST I-II, q. 6, a. 6.

[137]See ST I-II, q. 73, a. 6.

[138]ST I-II, q. 6, a. 6.

[139]ST I-II, q. 73, a. 6.

[140]ST I-II, q. 76, aa. 3 and 4 and *De malo*, q. 3, a. 8.

because, even though there is something willed,[141] it is contrary to that toward which the will would normally incline itself. The action of the will is not really free (voluntary) because it was done unknowingly. When one does not know what one is doing, he cannot be culpable since he cannot give full consent to something about which he is ignorant.[142]

Two further distinctions must be made. The first is regarding the degree of the voluntary. St. Thomas observes that when someone is completely ignorant of what he is doing, the act of the will is totally involuntary.[143] He also discusses how ignorance diminishes the voluntary[144] and so the voluntariness of an action can either be complete or incomplete depending upon one's knowledge. This leads to the conclusion that some actions are completely voluntary while other actions are mixed since they are a mix of the voluntary and the involuntary as a result of and to the degree of the ignorance. Consequently, passion may take away some, all or none of one's knowledge. Since the voluntary is not only a matter of the intellect but principally of the will, it may occur at times that the intellect clearly grasps something and the will does not carry on it fully, which likewise diminishes the voluntariness of the action.

The second distinction which is important has to do with the responsibility regarding the ignorance. Sometimes the ignorance is antecedent, i.e. sometimes the ignorance about something is voluntary, i.e. one wills to be ignorant.[145] For example, a ruler may choose not to know what is necessary regarding the status of poverty of his subjects because he knows that if he finds out that they are poor, it would prevent him from enacting a tax. In that case, the ignorance is voluntary and therefore the person is responsible for what follows from the ignorance.

Another form of ignorance is one in which one should have known.[146] The difference between this and the preceding form of ignorance is that in the former case one chose specifically to be ignorant, whereas in this case one did not choose to be ignorant but he should have known that upon which the ignorance touches. The second

---

[141]Prummer makes a distinction which is fully founded in a Thomistic understanding of the voluntary and involuntary, viz. between what is voluntary (*voluntarium*) and what is willed (*volitum*). Just because one has a motion of the will, it does not mean that it is voluntary. See Prummer, *Manuale Theologiae Moralis*, vol. 1, p.40 (para. 48).

[142]St. Thomas observes that the "amentes" i.e. those who are insane, do not have the use of reason and therefore whatever acts of the will they may make are not voluntary, see ST I-II, q. 6, a. 7, ad 3.

[143]ST I-II, q. 76, a. 4.

[144]For example, see ibid. and *De malo*, q. 3, a. 8.

[145]ST I-II, q. 6, a. 8 and *De malo*, q. 3, a. 8.

[146]ST I-II, q. 6, a. 8.

case is also culpable. Therefore, when the ignorance is voluntary, i.e. one chooses to be ignorant or one should have known because he did not take reasonable means to secure the knowledge, then the involuntary is not present, simply speaking,[147] i.e. that act of the will is voluntary. However, when the ignorance is concomitant with the act and there is no antecedent responsibility to know (i.e. when the ignorance is invincible or not able to be reasonably overcome), then the act of the will is involuntary, simply speaking.[148]

The last category which St. Thomas discusses is the non-voluntary. The non-voluntary occurs when one is ignorant of what he is doing, but what one is actually doing is in congruity with one's will, if he were to know.[149] This differs from the involuntary, for the involuntary occurs when one is ignorant of what one is doing and, if he knows, he would not have willed it. Whereas the non-voluntary occurs when one is ignorant about what one is doing, but what he is doing is not contrary to his will. For example, suppose a soldier during war time went into a field to go deer hunting. While hunting, he shot what he thought was a deer, but it is, in fact, the enemy. The killing of the enemy was not contrary to his will and so it was non-voluntary since he did it in ignorance but it was in congruity with his will to win the war. Whereas if he had killed a member of his own army, it would have been involuntary since it would have been contrary to his will. Acts which are non-voluntary are not voluntary, because even though they are in congruity with the will, they are done in ignorance.

Conclusion

The science of mental health and illness, while being essentially a study of the health of the intellect, also must take account of the acts of the will. This is especially important since the will can move the intellect as well as affect other faculties which could have an influence on the intellect. In this vein, it means that the choices one makes can actually lead to one's own health or mental illness. This can occur either directly by the will voluntarily choosing to be mentally ill or indirectly,[150] by choosing actions or things which affect the intellect, e.g. if one were to choose a course of action which actually led to a greater fear and consequently cause difficulties in the intellect when it is under the influence of the fear. What remains is to complete the discussion of those things that can influence the intellect and one's mental health.

---

[147]ST I-II, q. 6, a. 8 and *De malo*, q. 3, a. 8.

[148]ST I-II, q. 6, a. 8 and *De malo*, q. 3, a. 8.

[149]ST I-II, q. 6, a. 8; *De malo*, q. 3, a. 8 and In Ethic. III, l. 3, n. 1.

[150]St. Thomas does make the distinction between the direct and indirect voluntary and involuntary. See ST I, q. 76, a. 4; ibid., q. 77, a. 7 and *De malo*, q. 3, a. 8.

Chapter 8: The Sensitive Appetites and Passions

Since the science of mental health is about the intellect and its acts, then it is necessary to have a complete understanding of all those things which affect those acts. Now the average man from his common experience of himself knows that at times his passions or emotions affect the way he thinks. It is necessary, then, to have a grasp of the appetites and passions themselves and then to discuss their relationship with reason.[1]
So this chapter will discuss the appetites in general and specifically as well as the passions in general and specifically.

I. The Appetites in General

In the previous chapter, we saw that the will is sometimes called intellective appetite and this is because the will is moved by the intellect. But the intellective appetite is not the only kind of appetite, for in man there are two kinds of appetites, viz. the sensitive and the intellective.[2] The intellective appetite is an immaterial faculty which distinguishes it from the sensitive appetites which operate through the body or through a bodily organ.[3] The sensitive appetites pertain to those faculties which are composed both of an immaterial element and a material element, i.e. they are a joint physical and spiritual faculty.

Animals also have sensitive appetites and passions[4] as we know from our common experience of their desire for food, for example. But they are merely material things, i.e. they do not have a spiritual substance nor are their faculties immaterial. Since the senses move the appetites, as was seen earlier, and since animals have senses, their appetites can be moved by the senses just as man's can be moved by the senses. However, an animal's appetites can also be moved by the estimative power[5] as it associates the good or previous pleasure with some object.

Man, on the other hand, does not have an estimative power but a cogitative power, which performs the functions that are proper to animals in general but also performs actions which are proper to man, e.g. preparing an image in the imagination for abstraction. While the cogitative power does perform some properly human functions, it still performs the functions that are common to other animals. Since the cogitative power can associate or assess whether something is physically good or

---

[1] The latter topic will be discussed in the next chapter.

[2] IV Sent., d. 49, q. 3, a. 1, qu.1; ST I, q. 80, a. 2; ibid., ad 2; ibid., q. 82, a. 5; De Ver., q. 22, a. 4 and ibid., q. 25, aa. 1-3.

[3] ST I-II, q. 17, a. 7 and De Ver., q. 25, a. 3.

[4] ST I, q. 81, a. 2, ad 2 and De Vir., a. 4.

[5] ST I, q. 81, a. 2, ad 2; ibid., q. 81, a. 4 and De Ver., q. 25, a. 2.

harmful, it has the capacity to move the appetites and so in man the appetites are moved by the cogitative power.[6] We have also seen that the cogitative power is moved by reason[7] and so indirectly reason can move the appetites by moving the cogitative power to associate the good or harmful with some image. We also saw in a previous chapter that the appetites in man can be moved by the senses.[8] At times, the senses move the appetite without the sense data from the senses really making its way into the imagination, e.g. someone may experience a sweet aroma and one is moved to a physical longing for it even though he may have his imagination under the control of reason which is thinking about something abstractly. Once the sensible species of the aroma makes its way into the imagination, the individual then recognizes the odor and realizes that he is desiring the freshly baked pie. However, as a general rule, the sensitive appetites are moved by the imagination.[9]

We also know that every appetitive power is moved by some apprehensive power. This is derived from the knowledge that the will is moved by the intellect and the sensitive appetites are moved by the imagination. Since the appetites are passive powers,[10] they must be moved by an apprehensive power[11] and in man there are three apprehensive powers, viz. the senses, the imagination and the possible intellect. We have already seen that the appetites can be moved by all three, yet it is proper to the imagination to be the principal moving power of the sensitive appetites for the following reason. Since the senses can move the appetites not only without the imagination but with the imagination and since reason cannot move the appetites directly but does so indirectly by moving the cogitative power to change the image or by re-formulating the image directly, the sensitive appetites have as their principal moving power the imagination. Moreover, the imagination is more principal than the senses because of the fact that it has the capacity to contain the object more fully and therefore move the appetites more.

Yet, they are called *sensitive* appetites because the object to which the appetites correspond is something sensible, i.e. something material. The appetites concern the sensible nature or good[12] which is beneficial to an animal[13] or man who is a rational

---

[6]ST I, q. 81, a. 3.

[7]See discussion in previous chapters as well as ST I, q. 81, a. 3.

[8]See discussion in previous chapters as well as ST I, q. 81, a. 3, ad 2 and ST I-II, q. 17, a. 7.

[9]III Sent., d. 26, q. 1, a. 1; ST I, q. 81, a. 3, ad. 2; ST I-II, q. 17, a. 7 and *Comm. de anima* III, l. 15.

[10]ST I-II, q. 80, a. 2 and De Ver., q. 25, a. 1.

[11]ST I, q. 81, aa. 2 and 3 and De Ver., q. 25, a. 1.

[12]De Malo, q. 8, a. 3.

[13]De Ver., q. 25, a. 3.

animal[14] and these goods are particular, i.e. they are moved by this or that physical thing,[15] e.g. this apple or this pie. The appetites are not universally moved because that pertains to a universal power, viz. the will. Consequently, while the will may will some particular thing, it always does so under the universal notion of the good, whereas the sensitive appetites are always moved by this or that particular good.

The sensitive appetite has a sensible, i.e. physical or material, object and since it is ordered toward that object, it is *per se* ordered to a bodily transmutation or change,[16] i.e. it is ordered toward being acted upon physically by something. Sometimes the thing merely needs to be in the imagination to move the appetite and therefore it is not necessary that the thing be really present in order for the appetites to have a movement since memory can recall some previous sensible species into the imagination. Moreover, the sensitive appetites can be affected by one's bodily disposition[17] or conversely some appetible sensible object can move the appetite and cause a bodily change and thereby change one's disposition. For example, one may be "in the mood" for a steak rather than chicken and by this is meant that the appetites are more disposed at a given time toward being moved by one object rather than another. On the other hand, sometimes the object affects the disposition, e.g. someone may have the experience of not being inclined toward one food more than another. Yet, once the person starts eating the steak, the appetite is moved and his disposition changes. This occurs sometimes when one does not "feel like eating", but once he sits down and starts eating the steak, then his appetites rise and he eats more than he thought he would have eaten. Lastly, sometimes a person has a natural disposition toward one kind of motion of an appetite more than toward another, e.g. someone may be more inclined to eating rather than getting angry while another person finds himself very prone to getting angry but does not seem to be affected too much by food.

II. The Appetites in Particular

"An appetite is nothing other than an inclination of the desiring in something."[18] An inclination is an ordering of a faculty towards something, i.e. it is the

---

[14]This is the classical definition of man which can be seen throughout St. Thomas' writings. By this is understood that the goods towards which the appetites are ordered are those which are beneficial to him insofar as he is an animal.

[15]De Ver., q. 25, a. 1; ibid., ad 3 and ibid., q. 25, a. 3.

[16]ST I-II, q. 22, a. 2, ad 3.

[17]ST I-II, q. 17, a. 7.

[18]ST I-II, q. 8, a. 1: "appetitus nihil aliud est quam inclinatio appetentis in aliquid." The difference between an apprehensive power and an appetitive power is that with an apprehensive power, the end of the act terminates in the knower, i.e. in the apprehensive power. In an appetitive power, the action terminates in the thing. The difference lies in that

capacity of a faculty to be moved toward a specific object. The inclination indicates that the faculty is designed to be moved by its proper object which distinguishes that faculty from the others. As the appetite is moved by the presence of its object,[19] then the motions it has as well as the different appetites will be distinguished according to their proper objects. As a result, the sensitive appetites are divided into the irascible and the concupiscible.[20]

A. The Concupiscible Appetite

The concupiscible appetite takes its name from the Latin word "concupiscentia" which means desire. The concupiscible appetite is inclined "simply" toward that which suits sense and it flees what is harmful.[21] By "simply" is meant that it considers the sensible object without complexity under the notion of the good or evil, i.e. without further specification. This is how the concupiscible appetite differs from the irascible appetite which considers not the good or evil simply but the good or evil as arduous and so the irascible appetite requires a further specification to the good or evil thing. The concupiscible appetite is that appetite which concerns the suitability or unsuitability of

---

fact that in one action the motion is inward, the other is outward to the thing.

[19]This is a scholastic principle which is very important for the science of psychology. Modern man's relationship to this principle has been contradictory to say the least. On the one hand, modern advertising is based entirely upon this principle. Not only do advertisers try to move the appetite regarding their specific product, they adjoin to it the satiation of another appetite by presenting its object which may or may not have any connection to their product, e.g. a beautiful woman virtually unclothed is placed next to a beer product. The implication is that this product not only fulfills the appetite for food but also can lead to reproduction. On the other hand, women appear in public virtually unclothed and they expect men's appetites not to be moved, or do they? It seems as if they want to move the appetite of the male while being unwilling to accept the consequences of moving that appetite. In the past, women dressed modestly because it was understood that while the male is responsible for maintaining control of his appetite, all men and women suffer from disordered appetites and one did not want to arouse them due to the bad consequences that follow. Modern man uses principles but at the same time does not want to accept the conclusions or consequences of using the principles. Sex education is a classic example demonstrating a complete lack of prudence regarding this principle.

[20]ST I, q. 81, a. 2 and De Ver., q. 25, a. 2.

[21]ST I, q. 80, a. 2 and ST I-II, q. 23, aa. 1 and 2.

some thing[22] and the appetite considers some thing suitable because it is delectable.[23] Insofar as an object is delectable it is considered suitable and insofar as it is not delectable; it is not suitable. This appetite takes its name from the Latin word desire, and desire is about the obtaining of something, i.e. one desires something because one wants to have it or receive it. Consequently, this appetite is fundamentally ordered to receiving,[24] which makes it different from the irascible appetite.

B. The Irascible Appetite

The irascible appetite does not engage the good simply, but is inclined to the arduous good,[25] i.e it is inclined to overcome contraries and rise above obstacles.[26] The irascible appetite is ordered toward action,[27] rather than receiving, as is the concupiscible appetite. It is ordered toward engaging in actions or things which may be difficult in order to arrive at some good. The irascible passions (appetite) begin or are started by the concupiscible appetite,[28] i.e. when the concupiscible appetite sees something it loves or hates,[29] it moves the irascible appetite to fighting for or against or defending what the concupiscible appetite desires or flees.[30] Consequently, the irascible appetite is ordered toward the concupiscible appetite,[31] both as that which moves the irascible appetite to action as well as the end toward which it strives.[32] In other words, the concupiscible appetite sees something that it loves (or hates) which may be arduous to obtain; the irascible appetite is then moved to engage in action which is difficult; finally the irascible appetite comes to rest once the concupiscible appetite gets what it wants.

Even though the irascible appetite begins and terminates in the concupiscible appetite, St. Thomas notes that it is higher and closer to reason than the concupiscible

---

[22]ST I, q. 81, a. 2, ad 1 and De Ver., q. 25, a. 2, ad 3.

[23]ST I-II, q. 23, a. 1, ad 3 and De Ver., q. 25, a. 2. Here "delectable" does not merely refer to the sense of taste as the English connotation is understood. It refers to anything that can give pleasure or delight.

[24]De Ver., q. 25, a. 2.

[25]III Sent., d. 26, q. 1, a. 2; ST I, q. 81, a. 2; ST I-II, q. 23, a. 1 and De Ver., q. 25, a. 2.

[26]ST I, q. 81, a. 2.

[27]De Ver., q. 25, a. 2.

[28]ST I, q. 81, a. 2 and De Ver., q. 25, a. 2.

[29]ST I, q. 81, a. 2, ad 1 and ST I-II, q. 25, a. 3.

[30]ST I, q. 1, a. 2 and ST I-II, q. 23, a. 4.

[31]De Ver., q. 25, a. 2.

[32]ST I, q. 81, a. 2; ST I-II, q. 23, a. 1, ad 1 and De Ver., q. 25, a. 2.

appetite.[33] This follows from the fact that the concupiscible appetite is moved by the good simply, whereas the irascible appetite is moved not by the good simply, but the arduous good. Now for something to be under the notion of the arduous takes a knowing power to add that notion to the image in order for it to move the irascible appetite, e.g. a child may act up, but if the parent is distracted or thinking about something else, he may not discipline the child until he reflects on what the child is doing. The notion of the arduous good is beyond the mere consideration of a thing as good or evil without any further qualifications. Consequently, the irascible appetite is higher than the concupiscible appetite and closer to reason because its object is more complex and requires greater knowledge than the consideration of something which is good simply.[34]

III. The Passions in General

A passion is a motion of an appetitive power[35] and something is called a passion because its name is derived from the Latin word "pati" which means to suffer[36] or undergo.[37] Passion refers to an appetite's reception of something in some way[38] and the reception is an actual inclining or motion toward or away from some object. Passions occur with a bodily transmutation,[39] i.e. the sensitive object causes some bodily change in the one undergoing the action.

A passion is the same thing as a feeling[40] or emotion. A passion is called a feeling because it arises out of sensation or "feeling" and so it has a connotative connection to sensation since it pertains to the sensitive part (rather than to some other part, e.g. to the intellective part). It has the name of passion, not only because it refers to a "suffering" or undergoing in some sense, but also because it pertains to a passive

---

[33]III Sent., d. 26, q. 1, a. 2.

[34]Ibid.

[35]III Sent., d. 26, q. 1, a. 1 and *De malo*, q. 10, a. 1, ad 1.

[36]To suffer in the philosophical sense does not have the same connotation as the colloquial use of the term. While it includes that use, it refers to a broader category of the capacity for something to undergo some change. Suffer comes from the two Latin words "sub" and "ferre" which means literally to bear under. It means that something stands under while the process is going on over it or in it. Consequently, it can refer not just to some painful event someone happens to undergo, but the undergoing of any process whatever insofar as the thing is receptive to that process.

[37]ST I-II, q. 22, a. 1 and De Ver., q. 26, a. 1.

[38]De Ver., q. 26, a. 1.

[39]ST I-II, q. 22, aa. 1 and 3 and ibid., q. 37, a. 4, ad 1.

[40]The English connotation of the term "feeling" can refer to the act of sensation or the motion of an appetite. Here its meaning refers to the latter.

power. The term emotion refers to a passion from the point of view of motion, i.e. it is the moving[41] of an appetitive power. As the appetite is moved by the presence of its object, a passion refers to the form of motion caused in the appetite by the object and for this reason passions are also called emotions.

The forms of motion or passions are distinguished according to their objects.[42] Since powers are distinguished by different objects and since a passion is a motion of an appetitive power, then the passions are distinguished according to the same objects that distinguish the appetites. For this reason, the passions of the concupiscible and irascible appetites differ[43] since their objects differ. There are six passions of the concupiscible appetite and five of the irascible appetite. The passions are different not only because they occur in different powers, but they are different even within the specific appetite due to further qualifications of their objects. As there are different faculties, different passions and different objects, there are also different dispositions due to the fact that they occur in a bodily organ. Hence, one can have a disposition towards a particular passion[44] or passions, while not having a disposition towards other passions. Yet, a passion is strong or weak due to three things. The first, again, is the disposition of the bodily organ to undergo a specific type of action, e.g. some people have more of a bodily disposition to becoming angry as opposed to eating excessively. The second concerns whether the object which moves the passion is either really present to the senses (real union) or whether it is merely in apprehension but absent from sense. The common experience of man is that seeing someone who makes you angry is more likely to move one to anger as well as cause stronger anger than merely by imagining the person. The last has to do with the object's capacity to act upon the faculty, e.g. we are more likely to get angry with someone whom we consider beneath us, who causes some injustice towards us than with someone who is our superior. We have already seen that the appetites are moved, i.e. passion occurs in them, when their object is present in the imagination. Consequently, reason can affect not only the actual motions of the passions, but also their strength, depending on its operations on the image in the imagination.

IV. The Passions in Particular

The passions are divided into those of the concupiscible appetite and those of

---

[41] St. Thomas notes that a passion is a motion throughout the corpus of his writings. However, for examples, see II Sent., d. 24, q. 2, a. 1, ad 4; III Sent., d. 26, passim.; ibid., d. 34, q. 2, a. 1; ST I, q. 5, a. 4, ad 1; ibid., q. 5, a. 6; ibid., q. 81, a. 3; ST I-II, aa. 24-48, passim; De Ver., q. 15, a. 3 and ibid., q. 26, passim.

[42] S I-II, q. 23, a. 1.

[43] Ibid.

[44] ST I-II, q. 17, a. 7, ad 2.

the irascible appetite. It has already been noted that the irascible passions start and end in the concupiscible appetite. For that reason, the passions of the concupiscible appetite shall be treated first. The passion pertaining to the concupiscible part are love, hate, desire, flight, delight and sorrow and the passions pertaining to the irascible part are hope, despair, audacity, fear and anger. All of the passions in the concupiscible part have contraries, which is why there are six, while anger in the irascible part does not have a contrary and so there are only five in the irascible part.

A. Love

Love, which is a passion of the concupiscible appetite,[45] whose contrary is hate,[46] is the first of all the passions.[47] It is the first of all the passions since everything one does is done out of a movement to some end, i.e. the good or thing loved,[48] and the object of the passion[49] of love is the sensible good absolutely.[50] Love is an inclination, aptitude or connaturality with respect to the good[51] which indicates that it is the passion which occurs when some good object which suits or is in congruity with the appetite's nature moves that appetite. For this reason, St. Thomas calls love the *complacentia boni*[52] *aut appetibilis*,[53] i.e. that which is pleased with the good or the appetibile.

Love causes all of the other passions[54] and so it is the principle or beginning of motion to the end loved.[55] Love, which is caused by the apprehension of the good,[56] moves the irascible passions to obtain the good should it be difficult. It moves hope, insofar as one hopes for the loved not yet had; it causes despair when the loved cannot

---

[45]III Sent., d. 27, q. 1, a. 2 and ST I-II, q. 26, a. 1.

[46]ST I-II, q. 23, a. 4.

[47]III Sent., d. 27, q. 1, a. 3; ST I-II, q. 25, a. 2 and ibid., q. 46, a. 1.

[48]ST I-II, q. 28, a. 6.

[49]Since there is a passion of love, there are, in fact, two kinds of love, viz. volitional (which St. Thomas calls *dilectio* indicating that it proceeds from free choice -- *electio*) and sensitive.

[50]ST I-II, q. 26, a. 1; ibid., q. 27, a. 1 and ibid., q. 28, a. 6. What is indicated by the term absolutely is that this passion concerns the sensible good without qualification.

[51]III Sent., d. 26, q. 1, a. 3; ibid., d. 27, q. 1, a. 3, ad 2; ST I-II, q. 23, a. 4; ibid., q. 26, a. 1; ibid., q. 27, a. 1 and ibid., q. 29, a. 1.

[52]ST I-II, q. 25, a. 2 and ibid., q. 26, a. 1.

[53]ST I-II, q. 26, a. 2.

[54]ST I-II, q. 26, a. 1, ad 2.

[55]ST I-II, q. 26, a. 1.

[56]ST I-II, q. 27, a. 2; ibid., q. 28, aa. 1 and 2.

be had; it causes audacity by moving one to obtain the good; it causes fear when the thing loved may be subject to some future evil unable to be avoided and it causes anger when the good one loves suffers harm and it seeks to vindicate the harm done. It is also the cause of the other concupiscible appetites. It is the cause of hate in that one hates that which corrupts the thing loved. It causes desire in that one seeks to obtain the thing loved not yet had; it causes flight since it moves one to secure one's own good by fleeing that which is contrary to it; it is the cause of delight insofar as one takes delight in the possession of the loved as well as causing the other passions which move one to obtain the thing delighted in. Finally, it is the cause of sorrow since if one does not obtain the good loved, one sorrows.

While love causes the other passions, properly speaking no passion causes love,[57] since it is the first of the passions. However, in one sense, another passion may cause the passion of love in that the good of one passion may be the cause of the passion of love,[58] but the passion itself is not the cause. For example, hope is the cause of love or increases love insofar as one sees the good is possible,[59] but it is still the good as such which causes love. Delight also causes love in that the delight of the thing loved is prior in intention,[60] i.e. one loves a thing because it gives delight.

Love is defined as *the willing of the good of another*.[61] However, willing the good of another can be understood in two ways: the first is when one loves something for one's own sake or for oneself and this is called *amor simpliciter* (love simply) or *amor concupiscibile*[62] (concupiscible love). Concupiscible love moves one to go outside of oneself to enjoy the good loved for oneself.[63] The second form of love is *amor secundum quid* (love in a certain respect) or *amor amicitiae* (love of friendship).[64] This form of love is the love of the good for another as one would will it for oneself.[65] Love of concupiscence is love simply speaking because love seeks union with the thing loved and does not rest until it has union whereas love of friendship is love in a certain respect, since when another receives some good, it is the good of the lover in some way. Yet, the love of concupiscence is imperfect[66] because the lover considers only his own good,

---

[57]ST I-II, q. 27, a. 4.

[58]Ibid.

[59]ST I-II, q. 27, a. 4, ad 3.

[60]ST I-II, q. 25, a. 2, ad 3.

[61]ST I, q. 20, a. 1, ad 3 and ST I-II, q. 26, a. 4.

[62]ST I-II, q. 26, a. 4.

[63]ST I-II, q. 82, a. 3.

[64]ST I-II, q. 26, a. 4.

[65]ST I-II, q. 28, aa. 1 and 4.

[66]ST II-II, q. 17, a. 8.

whereas love of friendship is a perfect[67] love, because one wills not only the good of oneself but the good of the other for his own sake, which is a more complete form of love since it concerns not just oneself but both.

With love of friendship, the loved is in the lover when the good or bad of the loved is seen as one's own and what the loved wills is what the lover wills, so the lover can enjoy the good through the friend (the loved). Consequently, the lover wills and acts for the friend as for himself.[68] Hence, the love of friendship goes outside of oneself simply speaking[69] and terminates in the good of the other. So this form of love has a zeal for gaining the good of one's friend[70] as well as warding off evil from the friend.[71]

Even though one loves oneself out of necessity[72] since one naturally loves something only under the notion of the good,[73] one can still love what is good for another in that love sees the good of the loved as his own good, i.e. as a good for himself.[74] This is why St. Thomas remarks that love is caused by similitude.[75] With concupiscible love, one loves oneself and other things when one wants to participate in their form, i.e. one wants their form in oneself, e.g. one desires to eat food because one wants the good of the food within oneself. With love of friendship, we are of the same species (similitude) and so one participates in the good by virtue of the thing loved having some good, e.g. a father sees the good which he wills for his son as his (i.e. the father's) own good. So when a father provides for his family, he wills that they have the good of food and he wants it for their sake. Yet, he sees giving them food as good for himself because he wants the good for his family, for this makes him a good father and husband.

---

[67]Ibid.

[68]ST I-II, q. 82, a. 2. As mentioned in the previous chapter, the modern view of love has slowly degenerated into being solely associated with the sensitive love of concupiscence. Yet, it is imperfect and it too easily degenerates into selfishness. Moreover, since it is imperfect, psychologists must lead directees to all forms of love according to their priorities, i.e. the highest form of love is volitional love of friendship. While the other forms are not necessarily bad even though they have the capacity of being bad, the higher forms of love should be stressed as a form of perfection of the directee.

[69]ST I-II, q. 82, a. 3.

[70]ST I-II, q. 28, a. 4.

[71]Ibid.

[72]ST I-II, q. 29, a. 4.

[73]One loves the good for oneself even when it is, in fact, evil, for even the evil is viewed under the notion of the good in some way.

[74]III Sent., d. 27, q. 1, a. 1.

[75]ST I-II, q. 27, a. 3.

While the effects of love are manifold, its principal effect is union.[76] There are two kinds of union, one in apprehension alone which is called affective union which implies an already grasped good and the other is real union which results with the passion of delight.[77] While one can receive delight in the thing loved merely by reflecting upon it,[78] nevertheless love is not satisfied with the superficial apprehension of the thing loved,[79] but love causes the seeking of real union,[80] i.e. the real presence of the thing loved to the lover and not merely in the imagination.

Since love seeks union, the proper effect of love is mutual inhesion of the lover and the loved[81] and this is had in three ways. The first is through concupiscible love in which the love or being pleased with the thing occurs since the thing is present either in the intellect, the imagination, the sense or by desire.[82] The second is by love of friendship in which the good of one friend is present to the lover, as was previously discussed. The third is the mutual love of two friends for each other. The distinction between the second form and the third form is that the second form concerns only the presence of the good of the friend to the one lover rather than the two friends in mutual love.

One seeks union according to the suitability between the lover and the thing loved,[83] i.e. one does not love and consequently seek union with the loved unless there is some congruity or suitability between the lover and the loved. This union occurs in three ways.[84] The first occurs as the lover becomes one with the loved; the lover is transformed into the loved, since by the union, the loved penetrates into the lover and, for this reason, this union is called acute. The second occurs when, by becoming the loved, the lover is separated from himself, i.e. he goes outside of himself and this is called ecstasy.[85] The third occurs when, in going out of oneself, one cannot be contained and this is called liquefaction as "to liquify the heart", since it is not contained.[86]

---

[76]III Sent., d. 27, q. 1, a. 1; ST I, q. 20, a. 1, ad 3 and ST I-II, q. 28, a. 1.

[77]ST I-II, q. 25, a. 2, ad 2.

[78]See below.

[79]ST I-II, q. 28, a. 2.

[80]ST I-II, q. 26, a. 2, ad 2 and ST I-II, q. 28, a. 1, ad 2.

[81]ST I-II, q. 82, a. 2.

[82]Ibid.

[83]ST I-II, q. 28, a. 1, ad 2.

[84]These three ways are delineated by St. Thomas in III Sent., d. 27, q. 1, a. 1.

[85]It is called ecstacy from two Greek words which mean to stand outside of oneself.

[86]This is also why one is said to be hard of heart, i.e. when the heart is contained, one does not go out to the loved.

Related to these three are the four effects the loved causes on or to the lover.[87] The first is liquefaction, which is not only the lack of containment of the heart, but is the causing in the lover by the loved the capacity to go (flow) out of oneself and adapt oneself to the reception of the loved. Its opposite is congealing, which occurs when the heart becomes hard and bound into itself. The second is fruition which occurs when the loved is present to lover. Its opposite is the following last two effects. The first is languor which is sorrow at the absence of the loved, and the second is fervor which is the movement or drive to come to or strive for the loved.

Finally, not everything is good for the one that loves. The love of the good that is really good for the lover heals and perfects the person.[88] For instance, someone who is hungry sees food and the concupiscible appetite is moved to the passion of love for the food which will fulfill his hunger.[89] On the other hand, the love of that which is, in fact, bad for the lover wounds him and makes him worse.

B. Hate

Hate, which is the contrary of love,[90] is a passion of the concupiscible appetite[91] which has as its object evil.[92] Hate is a certain dissonance of the appetite of that which is apprehended as repugnant or harmful,[93] i.e. it refers to the concupiscible appetite, not only not being pleased with the object but actually having a dissonance, incongruity or unsuitability with the object to the appetite. As was mentioned, love is the cause of hate in that hate concerns the corruption or impediment of the good loved.[94] When the thing loved and hated is the same, then the love and hate are contraries in themselves, whereas when one thing is loved only, that thing's contrary is hated.[95] For example, at one time in a person's life he may love a particular friend, but when an injury or injustice occurs in the friendship, then the person is later hated. Consequently, the same object can be the subject of love and hate. On the other hand, one may have a child which one loves

---

[87]These four are delineated in ST I-II, q. 28, a. 5, ad 1.

[88]ST I-II, q. 28, a. 5.

[89]The truly good is that which fulfills something lacking in the lover and so someone who is in need of healing is lacking some good and so the truly good will heal or fulfill that thing lacking in the person.

[90]ST I-II, q. 23, a. 4; ibid., q. 29, a. 2 and ibid., ad 2.

[91]ST I, q. 82, a. 2, ad 3.

[92]ST I-II, q. 29, a. 1.

[93]ST I-II, q. 29, a. 2.

[94]ST I-II, q. 29, a. 2. See also the passion of love.

[95]ST I-II, q. 29, a. 2, ad 2.

and one wills the good of that child and so anything that is contrary to the good of the child, one hates.

Since love is the first of the passions, love is prior to hate[96] and yet like love, hate causes the motion of the irascible appetite[97] as well as subsequent concupiscible passions. It moves hope insofar as one hopes for something bad for someone, which is seen as the good of self or even the good of the person, e.g. one may wish that a child is spanked, which is a physical evil for the child but it is a moral corrective which is good. It also causes despair when the thing hated cannot be avoided. It causes fear, for example, when one fears that he will be subject to something he hates, like getting spanked. It causes audacity since one will go to great lengths to avoid some evil in which the avoidance is seen as a good in itself. Finally, it causes anger when the evil is present and the person seeks to vindicate the evil done, e.g. if someone sees someone whom he considers evil doing something bad against his friend, he is moved to anger to vindicate the wrong done.

Regarding the concupiscible appetite, it moves desire in that hate desires to avoid evil or moves one to obtain the good so as to avoid the evil. It moves flight as one tries to flee the thing hated. It causes delight, as when vindication through anger is obtained, the thing hated suffers some evil which is perceived as a good and so it causes delight in seeing someone get "his just deserts." It is the cause of sorrow, as when the thing hated is present and there is no way of getting away from it, e.g. when the evil of death befalls a friend, one sorrows.

As one naturally wills the good for oneself, one cannot *per se* hate oneself.[98] Yet, one can hate oneself *per accidens*,[99] since one can will for oneself what is good only in a certain respect (*secundum quid*) but which is really (*secundum se*) evil. For instance, one can commit suicide as a way of wanting the good of freedom from pain but which is really willing oneself evil.[100] One can love one's estimation of oneself while hating what one really is, [101] i.e. one may, due to an error in judgment, think that he is better than he actually is or is something which actually he is not and in reality he hates what he really is. This is very common for man in that one very often hates in his neighbor that of which he himself is quite guilty, e.g. one may hate others who treat him badly, while he himself does not recognize that he himself does not treat people well.

He who loves iniquity hates himself,[102] even though the evil is seen as good in

---

[96]ST I-II, q. 29, a. 2 and ibid., ad 3.

[97]ST I, q. 81, a. 2, ad 3.

[98]ST I-II, q. 29, a. 4.

[99]Ibid.

[100]See ST I-II, q. 29, a. 4, ad 2.

[101]ST I-II, q. 29, a. 4.

[102]Ibid.

a certain respect. Since one cannot will or do evil except under the notion of the good, one can only will oneself evil under the notion of the good.[103] One may avoid pain and misery which are actually for one's moral benefit, as when those who fight in battle gain the virtue of fortitude by doing so. Whereas if one avoids a battle because one flees pain and misery, he, in fact, becomes a coward. Consequently, he actually wills himself evil, i.e. he hates himself, even though he wills it under the notion of the good of avoiding pain and misery, which is done out of a disordered self-love.[104]

Just as one cannot hate oneself, strictly speaking, i.e. one cannot will something as evil for oneself but only that which is under the notion of the good (which can include the real good or the apparent good, i.e. that which is good in a certain respect), one cannot hate the truth,[105] which is the good of the intellect.[106] Yet, St. Thomas observes that the truth can be hated for three reasons. The first is that one can hate the truth when he wills some *thing* to be true which is not.[107] The second is that the truth impedes coming to the thing loved and this is regarding man's knowledge, e.g. one would not want to know the truth about the moral code so one could continue doing things which are evil. The last is when one hates the truth in another intellect. The former refers to the truth in one's own intellect which one does not want to know, whereas the latter refers to truth in someone else's intellect, e.g. one wishes that the police did not know where he lives because he does not want to get caught taking drugs.

C. Desire

Love and hate pertain to good and evil, whether they are past, present or future. Desire is a passion of the concupiscible appetite[108] which is a motion or inclination towards acquiring a loved thing *not yet had*.[109] Sometimes called concupiscence,[110]

---

[103]Ibid., ad 2.

[104]What constitutes ordered self love is that which seeks what is truly good for oneself and what constitutes what is truly good for oneself is known through the natural law, which will be discussed in a later chapter.

[105]ST I-II, q. 29, a. 4, ad 2.

[106]This is where the transcendentals play a crucial role since everything that is a being, is true, is good, etc. Yet, being in the intellect is good, i.e. the truth which is the due being in the intellect is the good of the intellect. But it is also the good of the whole person as will be seen in the discussion of the natural law.

[107]These three reasons can be found in ST I-II, q. 29, a. 5.

[108]ST I-II, q. 30, a. 1.

[109]ST I-II, q. 23, a. 4; ibid., q. 30, a. 2 and ibid., ad 1.

[110]ST I-II, q. 23, a. 4 and ibid., q. 30, a. 1.

desire occurs because of the real absence of the loved[111] and so it is caused by love. It was also observed that hate can cause desire in the way mentioned. Delight can cause desire not directly, but indirectly, i.e. once one has the thing loved, desire comes to rest, yet it can be the cause of desire indirectly by the memory of something in which one took delight in the past. So one may be inclined toward pursuit of something out of desire of the delight.

On the other hand, one can say that desire causes delight, not simply since the object of delight is the good possessed, but because it inclines one to obtain the good which gives delight. Desire can be the cause of flight as one flees to arrive at safety which is the good. It can also be the cause of the sorrow since one desires something which one does not receive, the desire is not fulfilled and sorrow ensues. Moreover, the desire can increase or decrease sorrow and delight depending on how much one desires the thing sought. The more one desires it, the more sorrow will arise if it is not obtained. Desire is also the cause of the irascible passions in that it is the cause of hope, for when one desires something, one hopes that it is obtainable. It is the cause of despair if one desires something but one knows it is unobtainable. It is the cause of audacity in that if one wants something enough, he will go to great lengths to obtain it. Sometimes it is the cause of fear, as when one desires something but it looks like he may not be able to obtain it. If he did not desire it, he would not fear not getting it. Finally, desire can be the cause of anger insofar as, if one does not get what one desires, he may become angry.

Love and desire differ, not only in the sense that love concerns the good absolutely and desire considers it as the good not yet had, but love is merely the passion which arises out of the fact that the appetite is pleased with the thing. It does not necessarily imply that the person wants it here and now, e.g. someone may have eaten a large meal consisting of turkey and all the trimmings. But if asked, "do you like steak" which means, "does steak cause the passion of love in your sensitive appetite," the person may respond, "yes." Yet, he may not desire the steak here and now, even though as a general rule he likes steak. The two English words "like" and "want" often display this difference in these two passions.

Desire, strictly speaking, does not have a contrary,[112] for desire is about the good not yet obtained, i.e. it is an inclination toward some good, but its contrary would be an inclination toward some evil, and there is no passion inclining us toward the evil as such. Yet, sometimes the passion of flight is called its contrary[113] insofar as desire is about inclining toward the good and flight is about receding from evil. Sometimes fear is said to be the contrary of desire,[114] insofar as fear concerns the future evil whereas

---

[111]ST I-II, q. 28, a. 1, ad 1 and ibid., q. 30, a. 1.

[112]ST I-II, q. 30, a. 1, ad 3.

[113]ST I-II, q. 30, a. 2.

[114]Ibid.

desire concerns the future good.[115]

One last observation St. Thomas makes regarding this passion which is of importance to the science of psychology has to do with natural and non-natural or unnatural desires.[116] Natural desires are those desires about things which are proper to man and to animals,[117] such as food, reproduction, etc.[118] Other desires are proper to man and not to animals because they arise from the process of thought,[119] i.e. some material (bodily) thing can be seen as good and so one can have the passion of desire for it, e.g. a car is a physical thing, but as such, the physical faculties of man do not need a car for their fulfillment and we do not have a faculty ordered towards "cars" as such, as we do with food. But reason can see that a car is a good thing and thereby cause the image to take on the notion of suitability and thereby move the appetite. Within these types of desires, there are some that are natural, i.e. proper or in accordance with man's nature and some that are not. Since reason can move the appetites by manipulating the image, he can associate something that is contrary to his nature with the notion of it being suitable or good and thereby move his appetite to desiring something that is in fact contrary to his nature in some way.[120] For example, reason may know that by taking some drug, the person will experience some pleasure and even though the drug is actually harmful to him, he can develop a desire for it by including in its image the pleasure to be obtained. There are other desires which do not fulfill some physical need or desire of man but which reason can see the good pertaining to them. Our previous example was with respect to cars. While there is no physical fulfillment *per se* by owning a car, nevertheless, reason knows that in owning a car, an avenue is opened up toward arriving at other goods, e.g. freedom, the ability to go to the grocery store to get what one needs, the ability to go to work in a different location to make more money,

---

[115]Sometimes today we say hate is the contrary of desire in that if one hates something, he does not desire to have it. However, they are not contraries, strictly speaking, since hate concerns the consideration of the object absolutely whereas desire considers it as not yet had, so they are not in the same genus in that respect.

[116]These observations can also be made regarding any of the passions, viz. any of them can be natural or unnatural. Yet, they tend to apply more fittingly to not just desire, but to love and delight, in that what one loves and delights may be unnatural. This topic will be revisited in the section on the passion of delight.

[117]ST I-II, q. 30, a. 3.

[118]This follows from the fact that man, while being rational, is an animal and so he has the same needs as other animals, i.e. all those things relating to bodily or physical well-being.

[119]ST I-II, q. 30, a. 3.

[120]What constitutes suitable and unsuitable to a nature will be delineated in the section on the natural law.

etc. As a result, anything physical which does not necessarily fulfill our material appetitive faculties can be the object of desire for man. In fact, one can actually have the passion of desire[121] for immaterial things provided reason creates an image which can move one to desiring them physically, e.g. one may think of the intellectual virtues and associate desirability with the phantasms that we use to think of the intellectual virtues. Hence, one's appetites can even be moved to desire immaterial goods.[122]

D. Flight

The passion of flight is a passion of the concupiscible appetite[123] which concerns evil.[124] It is a passion which follows upon or is caused by the passion of hate.[125] As one hates some evil, the passion of flight is a certain inclination in which one flees evil in order to follow or arrive at the good.[126] For this reason it is sometimes called aversion,[127] coming from the Latin word "to turn away from"[128] and at other times it is called abomination.[129] Yet, insofar as it turns from evil to the good, flight arises out of a desire for the good.[130] The causes of flight therefore are the passion of hate, desire and indirectly love, insofar as one flees the evil in order to pursue the good which is loved. It is also caused by sorrow, since when one sorrows one may also have the inclination to flee the thing that is causing the sorrow.

---

[121]This also applies to the other passions as well.

[122]While natural desires are finite in number due to the fact that the particular faculties are ordered toward specific goods; nevertheless, those desires which can arise from reason, either natural, i.e. proper to man such as the intellectual virtues etc., and those not proper to man, i.e. contrary to his nature or unnatural, can be infinite since they are not restricted by the specification of the physical appetites themselves but by the movements of reason which are virtually unlimited. St. Thomas observes this in ST I-II, q. 30, a. 4. The point is that, since reason is a certain "infinite" power in the sense that it can know all things, it can thereby move the appetite to desire all things. This is precisely why the reflection on the natural law is so crucial for man to know what he should and should not desire.

[123]ST I-II, q. 23, a. 2 and De Ver., q. 26, a. 5.

[124]ST I-II, q. 23, aa. 2 and 4.

[125]ST I-II, q. 60 a. 4. See also, In Ethic. II, l. 8, n. 4.

[126]ST I-II, q. 41, a. 3 and ibid., q. 77, a. 5, ad 4.

[127]In Ethic. II, l. 5, n. 5.

[128]Sometimes the word aversion in the corpus of Aquinas' writing refers also to hate in the sense that hate is a retraction or a turning away from some evil. However, in this case, it refers to the passion which seeks to get away from the evil that is hated.

[129]ST I-II, q. 23, a. 4.

[130]II Sent., d. 42, q. 2, a. 1 and ST I-II, q. 41, a. 2, ad 3.

Flight differs from hate since hate concerns the evil absolutely, while flight concerns the evil not yet present, i.e. one wants to avoid or get away from a situation which could lead to the evil. Yet, it is not sorrow because flight occurs when one wants to avoid the presence of evil, whereas sorrow is the passion which arises out of the actual presence of the evil. Consequently, flight has an antecedent and a consequent relationship to sorrow, i.e. it occurs before sorrow since it is the moving of the individual to get away from a situation which could result in suffering evil. Yet it is consequent to the presence of some evil, in that it still retains its inclination to avoid an evil not present, i.e. the evil not present is the future or continued presence of the evil. So the passion of flight moves us to get away from the present evil experienced in the passion of sorrow so as not to continue to experience it in the future.

As it is a movement of the appetite away from something not yet suffered, its opposite is desire[131] which is movement toward something not yet obtained. While desire concerns the good, flight concerns the evil, i.e. the thing under the notion of difficulty.[132] This is why, when something is difficult or will cause difficulties for the individual, the passion of flight arises so as to avoid it.[133] Flight moves the irascible passions of fear and audacity,[134] since when one sees some evil to be avoided, one seeks to flee from it and if one cannot flee it, then fear arises about its coming presence. It moves audacity in that, while it moves one to flee, sometimes one must lack the fear so as to do what is necessary in order to get away. It can also cause anger indirectly, insofar as one cannot actually flee the evil not present, then when it does come, the fact that it could not be avoided moves one to grow angry with the thing causing difficulty.

E. Delight

Delight is a passion[135] of the concupiscible appetite[136] which pertains to the

---

[131]III Sent., d. 26, q. 1, a. 3; ST I-II, q. 25, a. 3; De Ver., q. 26, a. 4 and In Ethic. II, l. 5, n. 5.

[132]III Sent., d. 26, q. 1, a. 1, ad 1.

[133]This passion can be a good sign and a bad sign. It is a good sign if the difficulties of the thing do not produce a good effect or which are not proportionate to some end sought, e.g. if one realizes that doing something one way will reduce the amount of effort he needs, this passion will move him to the easier, more efficient path. Yet, it can also be a bad sign if it is a sign of undue weakness or laziness on the side of the agent.

[134]See III Sent., d. 33, q. 3, a. 2a and ST II-II, q. 141, a. 3.

[135]The passion of delight should not be confused with pleasure. Pleasure is instantaneous, differs from motion, complete and whole, accompanies motion, admits of degrees, occurs when there is a well conditioned faculty to a fine or good object, varies based on faculty and condition, completes the activity, is a supervening good or end, and intensifies activity (See Aristotle, *Nicomachean Ethics*, chap. 10). Passions are not

good already possessed,[137] i.e. the presence of some good. Sometimes it is called joy[138] but joy can also pertain to reason[139] rather than the sensitive appetite. One can have joy in the intellect and not necessarily have it in the concupiscible appetite as well as one can have delight in the appetite while not having it in the intellect or will.[140] This is why St. Thomas observes that delight is said both of that about which the will and the appetite concern themselves, but joy is delight in the will, whereas delight in the body is not joy.[141] So one can have delight in either appetite but not joy,[142] since that pertains to the will. Delight is the passion of quieting or rest in the good present[143] as the good, and in a sense the delight itself, satisfies the appetite.[144] Therefore, once the thing is had, there is a cessation or termination of motion.[145] It is an operation of the connatural or the presence of the connatural good,[146] i.e. the good which is connatural[147] to the appetite causes delight when it is present.

The contrary to delight is sorrow[148] and yet two delights may be contraries,[149] e.g. one can delight both in virtue and in vice. There are three things required for delight, viz. 1) the good possessed; 2) that to which the good is joined and 3) the union of these

---

necessarily instantaneous, a passion is a motion and therefore does not complete an activity, nor is it a supervening good or end which accompanies the motion but is the motion itself.

[136]Like the other passions, it occurs with a bodily change; see ST I-II, q. 31, a. 4 and ibid., ad 2.

[137]ST I-II, q. 23, a. 4; ibid., q. 31, aa. 1 and 2 and ibid., q. 32, a. 1.

[138]ST I-II, q. 23, a. 4.

[139]ST I-II, q. 31, a. 3.

[140]ST I-II, q. 31, a. 3. See also SCG I, c. 91. Strictly speaking delight is the movement of an appetitive power and so, in the strictest sense, it is either in the will or in the concupiscible appetite. St. Thomas observes that it pertains to reason because the object is present in reason and judged as good by reason and then presented to the will.

[141]ST I-II, q. 31, a. 4.

[142]ST I-II, q. 31, a. 3.

[143]IV Sent., d. 49, q. 3, a. 2; ST I-II, q. 32, a. 4; ibid., q. 25, a. 1; ibid., q. 31, a. 1, ad 2 and ibid., q. 33, a. 4.

[144]ST I-II, q. 31, a. 1, ad 2.

[145]ST I-II, q. 31, a. 1, ad 2 and ibid., q. 31, a. 2.

[146]ST I-II, q. 31, a. 1, ad 1.

[147]What it means to be connatural will have a fuller meaning once the natural law is discussed.

[148]IV Sent., d. 49, q. 3, a. 3, qu. 1 and 2 and ST I-II, q. 23, a. 4.

[149]ST I-II, q. 31, a. 8.

two.[150] Delight is the end of desire[151] and delight can also cause desire when the whole thing is not had, i.e. when it is not complete or in memory only.[152]

Like desire, there are delights which are natural and those which are unnatural.[153] Natural delights are those proper to our animal nature and those which are proper to reason, which are the most properly human. Unnatural desires are those which are unnatural to human nature due to some corruption of nature. There are those which are unnatural or contrary to reason, such as taking delight in another's misfortune or those which are contrary to the conservation of his being, e.g. bestiality and cannibalism.

St. Thomas gives eight causes of delight. The first and primary is sense or sensation, i.e. the actual presence of the thing to sense.[154] While sight gives the greatest delight of the senses,[155] those pertaining to touch are most useful since they are ordered to conservation of the animal nature.[156] Touch is more ordered toward natural (physical) desires and sight being more spiritual[157] is more ordered toward intellectual delights, e.g. we see that touch is more ordered to things such as food and reproduction whereas sight can cause intellectual delight as when one obtains delight in the contemplation of the beauty of a sunset. This also indicates a difference between man and animals since only man takes delight in a particular sense for its own sake whereas an animal's delight is always referred in some way to touch.[158] For example, man can ignore the other senses in order to take delight in something seen, whereas an animal, even when it sees something, the sight is referred back either to its self-preservation, to food or to reproduction, all of which involve touch in some way. Common experience shows us that animals do not stop to contemplate the beauty of a sunset.

The second cause of delight is memory, since one can remember something or make it present by memory in the imagination[159] and so delight can be caused by apprehension even though it is absent from sense.[160] For instance, a man may love his wife, and while he is at work, his wife may not be present to the senses, but he can get

---

[150]ST I-II, q. 31, a. 5 and ibid., q. 32, a. 2.

[151]ST I-II, q. 33, a.1 ad 2.

[152]ST I-II, q. 33, a. 2.

[153]These two kinds of delight are discussed in ST I-II, q. 31, a. 7.

[154]ST I-II, q. 31, a. 1 and ibid., q. 35, a. 1.

[155]ST I-II, q. 31, a. 6.

[156]Ibid.

[157]ST I, q. 78, a. 3.

[158]ST I-II, q. 35, a. 2, ad 3.

[159]ST I-II, q. 32, a. 3.

[160]ST I-II, q. 35, a. 2.

delight by imagining her. The third cause is hope[161] since the thing which is desired is seen as obtainable and so hope causes delight both by having the thing present in the imagination and in the hope of fulfilment, i.e. of arriving at the thing desired. The fourth cause is love[162] insofar as love is a certain union of the lover and the thing loved and so since there is union, even if only in apprehension, love can cause delight. The fifth cause is desire[163] which has already had sufficient coverage. We have also seen how hate can be the cause of delight,[164] i.e. one estimates the good of another to be his contrary, and so the evil operation against the enemy is seen as good. St. Thomas says that even the contrary of delight, viz. sorrow, can be the cause of delight.[165] This occurs when in sorrow one thinks of the thing absent and insofar as one thinks or imagines it, the thing is present and so it can cause delight. When an evil is avoided or perceived as avoided, that is a good and so one can have delight, but this again is in apprehension.[166]

From the aforesaid, we can see that there are three grades of delight.[167] The highest grade of delight is that which is really present by sense. The second is hope and the third is by memory. Hope is greater than mere memory because hope includes not only that which is in the imagination, which comes from memory, but it also includes the fact that the good is expected to be obtained. Considering these three grades, we can see that joy is greater than the passion of delight.[168] Since the object of joy is an immaterial good, and since the will is an immaterial power and immaterial powers are greater than material ones, then joy of the will is greater than the passion of delight. While joy is greater than the passion of delight, with man, corporal delights are more vehement[169] and this is for three reasons. First, sensibles are more known than intelligibles to man. Second, they cause a bodily change and therefore have a greater impact on the individual. Lastly, sensible delights fulfill some lack or defect, e.g. those who lack

---

[161]ST I-II, q. 32, aa. 6 and 7.

[162]ST I-II, q. 32, a. 2, ad 3 and ibid., q. 32, a. 6.

[163]ST I-II, q. 32, a. 2, ad 3 and ibid., q. 32, a. 8.

[164]ST I-II, q. 33, a. 5.

[165]ST I-II, q. 33, a. 4; ibid., ad 1 and ibid., q. 35, a. 3, ad 1.

[166]Here the term apprehension is being used to refer to imagination and the possible intellect, even though the senses are said to be a kind of apprehension. When the proper object of a faculty is present to the faculty which is disposed toward receiving that object well, then pleasure can arise from it. If someone has a disposition to depression, i.e. recurrent or continuous sorrow, it can be the result of an attachment to the pleasure gained in thinking about the thing that makes one sad. Consequently, depression can have its cause in delight and pleasure.

[167]ST I-II, q. 32, a. 3.

[168]ST I-II, q. 31, a. 5.

[169]Ibid. See also IV Sent., d. 49, q. 3, a. 4.

delights suffer sorrow.[170]

While one cannot live entirely without delight,[171] many men cannot attain spiritual delights[172] and man in the current state[173] is inclined to pursue corporal over spiritual delights. While the aforesaid is true, it does not mean that the sensitive delight is the basis of something being morally good or bad.[174] One should not conclude that all delight is bad,[175] nor is all delight good.[176]

F. Sorrow

Sorrow, whose contrary is delight,[177] is the passion of the concupiscible appetite which occurs at the presence of some conjoined evil or lost good.[178] There are two things required for sorrow, which is sometimes called pain,[179] viz. the presence of some

---

[170]ST I-II, q. 31, a. 5. Since they fulfill some lack in us, St. Thomas says they are like medicines.

[171]ST I-II, q. 34, a. 1. This follows from the fact that any time someone would eat, they would get some delight, even if it is minimal, and if one never had delights, one would never eat.

[172]ST I-II, q. 31, a. 5. What Aquinas has in mind is that those who live an active life rather than a contemplative life are less capable, due to the material needs of the active life, to pursuing the intellectual virtues which give delight. However, they can pursue moral virtues which can give spiritual delight but they are not as great as the delights from intellectual virtues. This would also apply to pursuing strictly spiritual goods, such as prayer, etc., which can be restricted by the active life. Moreover, some do not have the intelligence to develop all of the intellectual virtues.

[173]That is in the state of Original Sin which will be discussed in volume two.

[174]ST I-II, q.34, a. 4. In the chapter on the natural law, it will be established that right reason is the basis of determining whether something is moral or not. Consequently, it is right reason, not sensitive delight or pleasure, which is the basis for determining whether something is moral or not.

[175]ST I-II, q. 34, a. 1. St. Thomas observes that without giving someone delight, he will tend toward bad teaching and action since the teaching would accompany evil rather than the good. See ibid.

[176]ST I-II, q. 34, a. 2.

[177]IV Sent., d. 49, q. 3, a. 3, qu. 1 and 2; ST I-II, q. 23, a. 4 and ibid., q. 35, aa. 3 and 4.

[178]ST I-II, q. 23, a. 4; ibid., q. 35, aa. 1 and 3; ibid., q. 36, a. 1 and ST III, q. 15, a. 7.

[179]ST I-II, q. 23, a. 4.

evil and the apprehension or perception of the evil.[180] There are two types of sorrow or pain, i.e. intellective and sensitive[181] and the passion refers to the sensitive sorrow or pain. Given the two types of sorrow or pain, there can be two ways it is caused, i.e. by sense, which is more properly called pain,[182] and by apprehension,[183] either intellectual or by imagination, which is more properly called sorrow.[184] Just as joy is a species of delight, so sorrow is a species of pain,[185] which is why sometimes sorrow is called interior pain.[186] While sorrow in the will is caused by the intellect, the passion of sorrow is caused both by the imagination and by the senses.[187] One of the differences between pain and sorrow is that pain is of the present,[188] since the senses are moved by that which is present, whereas sorrow can be of the past, present or future.[189]

Yet, sorrow can come from pain since it is the bad or the evil of the body[190] and since the concupiscible passion of sorrow is moved by the presence of some evil, one can also have the passion of sorrow when one experiences pain. Sometimes, one merely feels pain without sorrow, sometimes sorrow without pain and sometimes sorrow is accompanied by pain and therefore the sorrow is increased.[191] For example, when a friend physically causes someone pain, the pain can cause sorrow. Furthermore, the offense taken by the friend causing it can cause more sorrow. Yet, one does not necessarily follow upon the other, for one endures pain, at times, in order to avoid sorrow,[192] e.g. sometimes a husband will do painful things so as to avoid making his wife sad. Another example is that sometimes someone will endure hardships or mortifications to arrive at a virtue in order not to be saddened by the presence of the evil of vice. Yet, sorrow is stronger than pain since sorrow is the presence of some evil in

---

[180]ST I-II, q. 35, a. 1.

[181]Ibid. Clearly if there is delight in the will from the presence of the good, then there can be sorrow from the presence of some evil.

[182]ST I-II, q. 35, a. 2.

[183]ST I-II, q. 35, aa. 2 and 7.

[184]ST I-II, q. 35, a. 2.

[185]Ibid.

[186]ST I-II, q. 35, a. 7 and ST III, q. 46, a. 6.

[187]This follows from the fact that the passions can be caused by either something we sense which is different from pain, e.g. seeing one's child die, or by the imagination, by recalling something and thinking about it which is a sorrowful event.

[188]ST I-II, q. 35, a. 2, ad 1.

[189]Ibid.

[190]ST I-II, q. 35, a. 7.

[191]Ibid.

[192]Ibid.

apprehension rather than in sense.[193] While pain may move the appetite to sorrow, it does so either directly or indirectly. If it does so directly, it is not as great as apprehension since apprehension is a higher power; if it does so indirectly then it does so mediated by apprehension, i.e. through the image, and is therefore lower. Consequently, one sorrows greater at what is in apprehension rather than sense. This is why people would rather suffer all sorts of painful things than to see their child suffer. This is also why people would rather suffer pain and know the truth, or even suffer the passion of sorrow and know the truth, than be in falsity and endure no pain or sorrow.[194]

Sorrow is the *per accidens* cause of delight,[195] since when one sorrows at the loss of something, once it is recovered or possessed, the delight is greater. Sometimes sorrow moves one to obtain the presence of the lost good. From another perspective, the matter of sorrow and delight may be the same, if looked at differently,[196] e.g. a man may take delight in his wife because she has the ability to cook well, but suffer sorrow when she mistreats him. In another sense, sorrow is able to be delectable *per accidens*.

> Sorrow[197] itself can be pleasurable *per accidens* insofar as it has wonder joined to it, as in stage-plays; or insofar as it recalls a loved thing to one's memory, and makes one perceive his love of which its absence causes sorrow. Hence, since love is delectable, both sorrow and all things which follow from love, insofar as love is sensed in them, are delectable. And for this reason, sorrows in stage-plays are able to cause delight, insofar as in them, some concept of love is sensed in those which the stage-play commemorates.[198]

---

[193]Ibid.

[194]Here what is implied is that the normal man would prefer to know the truth. Only he who is disordered would prefer ignorance and falsity so that he can be without sensitive pain or sorrow.

[195]ST I-II, q. 35, a. 3, ad 1.

[196]The thing is one materially but two different things formally, i.e. looked at from different points of view.

[197]The word St. Thomas uses here is normally associated with pain, but it is more aptly translated, given the context, as sorrow; moreover, interior pain is sorrow.

[198]ST I-II, q. 35, 3, ad 2: "dolor ipse potest esse delectabilis per accidens, inquantum scilicet habet adiunctam admirationem, ut in spectaculis; vel inquantum facit recordationem rei amatae, et facit percipere amorem eius, de cuius absentia doletur. unde, cum amor sit delectabilis, et dolor et omnia quae ex amore consequuntur, inquantum in eis sentitur amor, sunt delectabilia. Et propter hoc etiam dolores in spectaculis possunt esse delectabiles, inquantum in eis sentitur aliquis amor conceptus ad illos qui in spectaculis commemorantur."

St. Thomas notes that there are two ways in which sorrow can bring delight. The first is when admiration or wonder is associated with the sorrowful thing. The second is that when one sorrows, he does so at the absence of the loved which is in apprehension and, since the loved is in apprehension, it can bring delight.

Some of the other passions are the cause of sorrow. Love is the cause of sorrow[199] insofar as one loves something and when it is absent, that is an evil and so sorrow ensues. Hate is the cause of sorrow as when something that is hated (seen as evil) is present. Desire is the cause of sorrow,[200] insofar as if we do not get the good we desire, we sorrow at the evil of "not obtaining the good loved." Flight is not the cause of sorrow, since it seeks to avoid the presence of evil and therefore actually takes away sorrow. In this respect, flight mitigates sorrow, i.e. it is the cause of the cessation of sorrow. It has already been mentioned that delight is the cause of sorrow, insofar as, if one does not get something which he has taken delight in or which he thinks he will take delight in, then he sorrows.

Hope is not the cause of sorrow, but the cause of delight, whereas despair is a cause of sorrow once one realizes he cannot obtain the good (which is a kind of evil) or avoid the evil, then one sorrows, not necessarily in sense but through apprehension, at least. Audacity is not the cause of sorrow insofar as it includes a notion of being secure from danger and seeks the good. Fear is the cause of sorrow, for if the evil feared comes to be, then one sorrows. All of the passions which pertain to evil as their objects can be the cause of sorrow insofar as the evil is present for they can give way to sorrow which considers the presence of the evil *per se*.

There are several things which mitigate sorrow. Flight has already been mentioned, i.e. if one sorrows in some evil present, then if one is moved to flee it, i.e. if the passion of flight arises, then the person can get away from the evil. St. Thomas observes that the more one sorrows in something, the more one struggles to shake off the sorrow, as long as there remains hope of expelling it, otherwise no motion or operation is caused by sorrow.[201] Delights mitigate sorrow, insofar as any sensitive good[202] can cause a motion of delight in the appetite which is the contrary of sorrow.[203] This is why wives will kiss their husbands when their husbands are sad in order to "cheer them up."

---

[199]ST I-II, q. 35, a. 6 and ibid., q. 36, aa. 1-3.

[200]ST I-II, q. 36, aa. 2-3.

[201]ST I-II, q. 37, a. 3.

[202]Here, the one sensing or apprehending must view it as good. It is not enough for the thing to be good for man in general, but here and now to this particular individual.

[203]ST I-II, q. 38, a. 1.

St. Thomas also observes that things such as baths, sleep,[204] or any other sensible consolation mitigate sorrow.

St. Thomas also notes that crying and groaning mitigate sorrow.

> Tears and groans naturally mitigate sorrow. And this is for a twofold reason. First, because a harmful thing afflicts more when enclosed interiorly, since the intention of the soul is multiplied around it, but when it is diffused to the exterior, then the intention of the soul is dispersed in a certain way to exterior things, and so the interior sorrow is diminished. And for this reason, when men who are sorrowful manifest their sorrow exteriorly either by tears or groaning, or even words, sorrow is mitigated. Secondly, an operation suitable to man according to his disposition is always delectable to him. Moreover tears and groans are certain operations suiting the sorrowed and pained. And therefore the delectables are caused in him. Since, therefore, every delight in some way mitigates sorrow or pain, as was said, it follows that sorrow is mitigated by wailing and groans.[205]

The first observation indicates that when something is kept within a person, the soul becomes more intent on the object. This may occur because the person thinks it over

---

[204]ST I-II, q. 38, a. 5. This is why people who are sad or depressed tend to sleep a lot. This is also why some people will go shopping when sad because of the delight in buying and possessing a new thing brings them a mitigation of the sorrow. This is also why some people drink excessively to deal with some sorrow since the pleasures arising from drinking mitigate the sorrow. However, the person must be clear that many things can mitigate sorrow but they do not take away the cause of the sorrow and therefore should not be employed as a way of solving their problems. Some things which cause delight but do not cause other problems may be useful to mitigate the sorrow for a while until the person can think more clearly. But those which cause other problems should be avoided.

[205]ST I-II, q. 38, a. 2: "lacrimae et gemitus naturaliter mitigant tristitiam. Et hoc duplici ratione. Primo quidem, quia omne nocivum interius clausum magis affligit, quia magis multiplicatur intentio animae circa ipsum, sed quando ad exteriora diffunditur, tunc animae intentio ad exteriora quodammodo disgregatur, et sic interior dolor minuitur. Et propter hoc, quando homines qui sunt in tristitiis, exterius suam tristitiam manifestant vel fletu aut gemitu, vel etiam verbo, mitigatur tristitia. Secundo, quia semper operatio conveniens homini secundum dispositionem in qua est, sibi est delectabilis. Fletus autem et gemitus sunt quaedam operationes convenientes tristato vel dolenti. Et ideo efficiuntur ei delectabiles. Cum igitur omnis delectatio aliqualiter mitiget tristitiam vel dolorem, ut dictum est, sequitur quod per planctum et gemitum tristitia mitigetur."

and over again[206] increasing the sorrow by thinking too much about it. Whereas if by some operation the pain or sorrow is expressed or exteriorized, then the sorrow or pain is mitigated, as the soul becomes less intent on it by it being, so to speak, borne out of the soul.

The second observation states that anytime one engages in an operation which is in congruity with or suited[207] to a disposition, there is delight or pleasure caused in the individual. Sometimes it is delight insofar as the operation is seen as the good of the person or the good of the disposition. So some who sorrow, when they sorrow, see that there is a congruity between their action and disposition, i.e. it can actually be seen as good. Pleasure, on the other hand, is something which accompanies motion and occurs when there is a well-conditioned faculty directed to a fine or good object, varying based on the faculty and its condition. Consequently, one can get a type of pleasure from sorrow. For a passion is a motion of an appetite and if the appetite (faculty) is well disposed toward the activity or motion of the passion, then when that object comes into contact with the well-disposed faculty, there is a certain pleasure that can arise from it. This is why one experiences a certain kind of pain when one is disposed toward being sad and someone cheers one up. At times, the faculty which is disposed toward sadness actually experiences an action contrary to it and so there is a kind of pain as a result of it. Often what happens is that the person, in experiencing the pain of the opposite motion, rejects it and prefers the pleasure gained from acting according to disposition. This is essential to understanding certain forms of depression, which are actually a strong attachment to the pleasure of acting according to the disposition. This also applies to other passions such as anger, fear and hate, because if the appetite is disposed toward them, there can be a kind of pleasure that is derived from engaging these passions. This makes it difficult to break people of them, not only because of disposition and habit, but because of the pleasure derived from being angry (which is different from delight) and fearing. St. Thomas' observation about stage plays, along with the observation of this note, is why horror films and the like are so successful even though they involve "evil" objects which normally do not give delight or pleasure. It can also be a sign that modern man's faculties are not disposed in the right way, otherwise, he would recognize these things for what they are, evil.

St. Thomas also notes that the compassion of friends in consoling mitigates suffering or sorrow for two reasons. The first is that sorrow is burdensome and when others have compassion for (i.e. suffer with) him, the burden is seen as carried by his friends and therefore lightened.[208] Secondly, when others have compassion, one sees he is loved and therefore he gets delight from considering the love of his friends for him

---

[206]Ibid., ad 3.

[207]Ibid., ad 1.

[208]ST I-II, q. 38, a. 3 and In Ethic. IX, l. 13, nn. 5 and 9.

which mitigates sorrow.[209]

Contemplation of the truth likewise mitigates sorrow. For contemplation of the truth brings delight; in fact, it is the highest form of delight. Since there is delight, it mitigates the sorrow.[210] However, a distinction is necessary regarding this observation, for sometimes when we know the truth of something, it brings us sorrow. Nevertheless, while contemplating a specific thing which is true may bring us sorrow, the contemplation of the nature of truth itself brings delight.[211] For example, while one may sorrow at learning that one's son has died at war, the contemplation of truth itself, which is a good, brings delight.[212] Consequently, delight from a superior part redounds into an inferior part of the soul and mitigates sorrow and even pain.[213]

There are six species of sorrow: three on the side of the object and three on the side of effect.[214] On the side of the object, the first is sorrow in the proper sense, i.e. sorrow arising out of the presence of evil to oneself. The second is mercy which is sorrow at the presence of evil of another, e.g. when we see someone suffering from starvation, we are moved by sorrow (mercy) to alleviate the person's hunger. The third is envy which occurs when the good of another is seen as one's own evil. On the side of effect, the first is called anxiety, which occurs when flight is taken away and there appears no refuge to which one can go to get away from the evil.[215] The second is acedia[216] which occurs when anxiety extends itself to the exterior members and results in sloth or slowness of movement. The last species of sorrow is what St. Thomas calls "amputare vocem" or loss of voice. This is a form of sorrow which is beyond anxiety

---

[209]ST I-II, q. 38, a. 3 and ibid., ad 2. Essentially speaking, the phantasm is altered and so the sorrow caused by the phantasm decreases.

[210]ST I-II, q. 38, a. 4.

[211]Ibid., ad 1.

[212]This is why engaging in studying can actually mitigate sorrow.

[213]ST I-II, q. 38, a. 4, ad 3. St. Thomas does not seem to offer much more than this observation, but it would seem that this could occur for two reasons. The first is that in his discussion on the beatific vision, he says that the activity of the higher faculties flows over into the lower faculties so that in the fulfillment of the higher faculties, the lower are also fulfilled in some way. The second is that when one contemplates the truth in the possible intellect, it is accompanied by certain images which are seen as good by the appetites and so the images cause delight.

[214]These six are delineated in ST I-II, q. 35, a 8.

[215]This is also called distress and anguish.

[216]The vice of acedia could include this species of sorrow. However, as a general rule, the vice of acedia or sloth is the result of hatred for spiritual goods.

and acedia and results in someone not even being able to talk.[217]

Connected to these but slightly different are the effects of sorrow itself.[218] The first effect of sorrow is that it takes away one's capacity to learn.[219] The common experience of man teaches us that it is hard to concentrate, to remember or to learn anything when we are sad. The second effect is called constriction[220] or heaviness (*aggravatio*)[221] which impedes one from considering his own motion, i.e. it keeps one from being able to move oneself. The third effect is that it debilitates operations[222] of the soul, e.g. operations or acts of the will. The last effect is that it causes more harm to the body than other passions.[223] St. Thomas observes that this is because it depresses the motions of life, i.e. vital operations, for one does not pursue the goods necessary for life, such as eating, etc.

Moreover, every passion causes a bodily change.[224] Now the other passions can actually aid life by moving the person to pursue the goods or avoid evils necessary for life. While sorrow may do that to a degree, as a general rule, it tends to depress operations of the soul and is therefore less likely to aid life. Another observation that should be made in connection to this is that there should be no surprise that suffering passion can cause not only temporary bodily (i.e. chemical and other) changes, but even permanent ones which may need to be corrected by chemical means. While the chemicals may not take away the cause, they can mitigate the effects so that the person can begin working to reverse the problems caused by the passions. Since the appetites can be moved by the will, it means that one can, through volitional acts, cause oneself to affect adversely the chemical operations in the body and in the brain. On the other hand, it would seem that unless there is some impediment, either chemical or otherwise, one could actually improve the chemical operations of the body and the brain by the volitional control over the appetites.

Finally, a few last observations should be made about the passion of sorrow.

---

[217]It would seem that the species of sorrow regarding the effects may, at times, merely be a matter of degree. Moreover, each one of these species may be seen as a genus in which further divisions may be made.

[218]The previous are species of sorrow, whereas the foregoing are effects of those species.

[219]ST I-II, q. 37, a. 1.

[220]ST I-II, q. 37, a. 2, ad 2.

[221]ST I-II, q. 37, a. 2.

[222]ST I-II, q. 37, a. 3.

[223]ST I-II, q. 37, a. 4.

[224]We may say that this bodily change is chemical or even electrochemical in some cases. This dimension of the nature of the bodily changes corresponding to each passion is best left to the subalternate science of psychiatry.

Sorrow contrary to reason is morally bad.[225] For instance, if one sorrows at the good of another, that is a sign there is something wrong with the person, i.e. if one sorrows at the wrong things, it is a sign that something is disordered. Sorrow that is in congruity with reason is morally good,[226] e.g. if we are sad because we have caused undue damage to another person's property, that is a good sign. It is good both because sometimes sorrow can purify us of other defects[227] and because it is a sign that the passion is subordinated to reason. Sorrow is sometimes useful as a way of motivating us to act contrary to evil[228] and to doing the good. At other times, if we experience sorrow with something that we love when we should not love it, that can help us to change our attachment or love for the thing. Lastly, it should never be assumed that bodily pain is the worst evil.[229] For since bodily goods are not the highest goods, bodily evils are not the worst evils.

G. Hope

With the six concupiscible passions having been delineated, it is now necessary to discuss the passions of the irascible appetite, the first of which is hope.[230] Hope is the irascible[231] passion which considers the good not yet obtained,[232] i.e. the future good,[233] for we do not have hope of something already possessed.[234] Unlike its contrary despair,[235] hope concerns the good which must be possible to obtain[236] but there is no hope in something which is impossible to obtain.[237] This makes hope different from desire, since desire is inclination toward some good not yet had, yet it does not

---

[225]ST I-II, q. 39, aa. 1 and 2.

[226]Ibid.

[227]This will be discussed in volume II.

[228]ST I-II, q. 39, a. 3.

[229]ST I-II, q. 39, a. 4.

[230]ST I-II, q. 25, a. 3.

[231]That is, pertaining to the irascible appetite: III Sent., d. 26, q. 1, a. 2; ST I-II, q.23, a. 2 and ibid., q. 40, a. 1, ad 3. Since hope is a motion of the irascible appetite, even animals can have hope. See III Sent., d. 26, q. 1, a. 1 and ST I-II, q. 40, a. 3.

[232]ST I-II, q. 23, a. 4,; ibid., q. 40, aa. 1 and 5 and ST I-II, q. 19, a. 11.

[233]III Sent., d. 26, q. 1, a. 1; ST I-II, q. 40, a. 1 and *De Spe*, q. 1.

[234]ST I-II, q. 40, a. 1.

[235]III Sent., d. 26, q. 1, a. 3; ST I-II, q. 23, a. 4 and ibid., q. 40, aa. 1 and 4.

[236]III Sent., d. 26, q. 1, aa. 2 and 3; ST I-II, q. 40, aa. 1, 4 and 5; *Comp. Theol.* II, c. 7 and *De Spe*, q. 1.

[237]ST I-II, q. 40, a. 1 and ibid., ad 3.

necessarily imply that it is possible. Yet, while hope presupposes [238] and is caused[239] by desire, hope, unlike desire, concerns that which is something arduous or difficult to obtain.[240] While desire may be for something arduous, it is not necessarily the case. Moreover, desire does not imply that the good is expected, as hope does,[241] i.e. hope looks forward to the obtainment of the good.

There are two kinds of hope, viz. hope in one's own capacities to come to the good and the hope in another's capacity to aid one in coming to the good.[242] When we have hope in our own capacities, it gives one power or strength to overcome the arduous to arrive at the good[243] and so it aids operation or action.[244] Yet, while hope gives one power or strength, anything that increases one's power is a cause of hope.[245]

Experience is the cause of hope in that one acquires some facility of doing something easily, i.e. through knowledge, habit, custom, etc.[246] Experience gives one a greater capacity to estimate whether something is possible and it rejects what is not possible.[247] Foolishness and inexperience can cause hope, not *per se*, but *per accidens* in that they remove the estimation that something is not possible.[248] Youth is a cause of hope since the future is ahead of the young, so they are more prone to hope;[249] also they lack a past which may have contained bad experiences. Since they do not have a bad past, they can envision good things and so their heart is "amplified."

Since the object of hope is the good, it is the cause of love or the increase of love.[250] For through hope one is moved to get a good object which is loved and so once the object is obtained, the passions of love and delight ensue from the union with the loved. Moreover, sometimes through hope, one comes to an object and begins to love

---

[238]ST I-II, q. 40, a. 1 and ibid., ad 3.

[239]ST I-II, q. 62, a. 4, ad 3.

[240]III Sent., d. 26, q. 1, aa. 1 and 2; ST I-II, q. 40, aa. 1; ibid., ad 2 and ibid., q. 40, a. 4; *Comp. Theol.* II, c. 7 and De Spe, q. 1.

[241]III Sent., d. 26, q. 1, a. 4.

[242]ST I-II, q. 40, a. 2, ad 1; ST II-II, q. 19, a. 1 and De Spe, q. 1.

[243]ST I-II, q. 42, a. 5, ad 1.

[244]ST I-II, q. 40, a. 8. Consequently hope implies access or approach (motion) to the good, while its opposite implies recession or withdrawal. See ST I-II, q. 40, a. 4.

[245]ST I-II, q. 40, a. 5.

[246]ST I-II, q. 40, a. 5.

[247]Ibid.

[248]Ibid., ad 3.

[249]ST I-II, q. 40, a. 6.

[250]ST I-II, q. 40, a. 7 and ibid., q. 62, a. 4, ad 3.

it or love it more, yet on the other hand, hope is caused by love first,[251] since through love one is moved to obtain some good. So one hopes that one can obtain the good.

H. Despair

The contrary of hope is despair,[252] which is a passion of the irascible appetite and which, like hope, concerns the good not yet obtained,[253] i.e. the future good. Yet, despair differs from hope because it concerns a good which is impossible to obtain.[254] This occurs because the object is "over excessive,"[255] i.e. it exceeds the faculty's capacity to obtain it.[256] Since the object is impossible to obtain, despair implies a recession or withdrawal from motion to the thing.[257]

Despair presupposes desire[258] in that one is moved to consider whether something is obtainable because it is desired and so despair is preceded by desire. Yet, despair shuns the good because of the difficulty in obtaining it.[259] Finally, despair is caused by fear,[260] since one sees some upcoming evil and he cannot avoid it.

I. Audacity

Audacity is a passion of the irascible appetite[261] whose contrary is fear.[262] Audacity has as its object some evil[263] and it is the passion which is aggressive toward imminent danger (evil) for the sake of victory over the danger,[264] yet includes within it

---

[251]Ibid.

[252]III Sent., d. 26, q. 1, a. 3; ST I-II, q. 23, a. 4; ibid., q. 40, a. 4; ibid., ad 3 and *De Spe*, q. 1.

[253]ST I-II, q. 23, a. 4.

[254]ST I-II, q. 40, a. 4 and ibid., ad 2.

[255]ST I-II, q. 40, a. 4, ad 2: "ex solo superexcessu boni."

[256]De Ver., q. 26, a. 4.

[257]ST I-II, q. 40, a. 4 and ibid., ad 2.

[258]ST I-II, q. 40, a. 4, ad 3.

[259]ST I-II, q. 41, a. 3.

[260]ST II-II, q. 129, a. 7.

[261]ST I-II, q. 40, proem. Since it is a passion of the irascible appetite, like the other passions it occurs with a bodily transmutation; see ST I-II, q. 45, a. 3.

[262]ST I-II, q. 45, aa. 1 and 3.

[263]ST I-II, q. 45, a. 4, ad 2.

[264]ST I-II, q. 45, a. 1.

the notion of security from the danger.[265] Following from hope[266] which contains the possibility of obtaining some good, the passion of audacity, which includes confidence in the aggression[267] and excludes fear,[268] moves one to pursue the "terrible" evil[269] in order to come to the good. While audacity follows on hope, which contains the apprehension of possible victory,[270] audacity does not always result when hope occurs, but only when the obtainment of the good requires the engagement of an evil which is vehement.[271] This is why sometimes audacity implies excess,[272] i.e. one goes to excess to obtain the good yet at the same time the good does not exceed the faculty or capacity to obtain it.[273]

Audacity can come from the fact that one does not have enemies, or cannot be hurt by any one, or it occurs when one does not see the danger.[274] Sometimes it is caused by bodily strength, experience in danger, the possession of a large amount of money, or through some power of another, e.g. a friend or a helper.[275] In other words, it comes from anything which appears to give one power or capacities to do something. Drunkenness causes audacity through a bodily change which affects our estimation of our greatness[276] or capacities. Those who are inexperienced are more audacious because they have less of a capacity, due to lack of knowledge to judge their own weakness or the present danger.[277] They do not have the capacity to judge themselves in light of or in comparison with the greatness of the danger. This also means those things which affect judgment can affect audacity, e.g. anger increases audacity,[278] since it affects one's judgment or even follows from judgment.

Since audacity is a passion coming from some sensitive apprehension, when there is little or no involvement of reason, it is quick or instantaneous and does not take

---

[265]Ibid., ad 3 and ST I-II, q. 45, a. 3.

[266]ST I-II, q. 45, a. 2; ibid., ad 1-3 and ST I-II, q. 45, a. 3.

[267]III Sent., d. 26, q. 1, a. 3.

[268]ST I-II, q. 45, aa. 3 and 4.

[269]ST I-II, q. 45, a. 2.

[270]III Sent., d. 26, q. 1, a. 3.

[271]ST I-II, q. 45, a. 2, ad 2.

[272]III Sent., d. 26, q. 1, a. 3.

[273]De Ver., q. 26, a. 4.

[274]ST I-II, q. 45, a. 3.

[275]Ibid. The last possibility is especially applicable to divine aid.

[276]Ibid., ad 1. This would also apply to certain kinds of drugs.

[277]Ibid., ad 2.

[278]ST I-II, q. 45, a. 4, ad 3.

counsel. The result is that it does not know all of the danger.[279] Age helps audacity by reducing the quickness of appetite and St. Thomas notes that experience can solve the problem of being too hasty.[280] Finally audacity can cause shaking (tremor)[281] and this is because it is the passion which requires quick or powerful movement and therefore disposes the body to it.

J. Fear

Fear is a passion of the irascible appetite[282] which concerns the evil not yet present (future).[283] Yet, the evil which fear concerns has a specific *ratio* or notion (perspective) about it. While audacity, which is its contrary,[284] concerns evil as not being able to harm, fear concerns the corruptive evil.[285] With fear, the evil is present in apprehension,[286] but the evil really pertains to something future.[287] Moreover, it does not concern evil *per se*,[288] but as difficult[289] and difficult in such a way that one cannot resist the evil.[290] Thus, the evil exceeds the power of the one that fears,[291] i.e. one fears because of the magnitude of the evil (object) or because of weakness on the side of the

---

[279]ST I-II, q. 45, a. 4.

[280]Ibid. This is because the cogitative power must make an association with the image to move the irascible appetite and it does this at times by means of going back into memory and therefore the more there is in memory, i.e. the more experience, the less likely the cogitative power is to assess the image quickly.

[281]ST I-II, q 45, a. 4, ad 1.

[282]ST I-II, q. 40, proem; ibid., q. 42, a. 3, ad 2 and In Ethic. III, l. 15, n. 2. Since it is a passion of the irascible appetite, it also occurs with a bodily transmutation. See ST I-II, q. 41, a. 1 and ibid., q. 44, a. 1.

[283]ST I-II, q. 23, a. 4; ibid., q. 41, aa. 1, 2 and 4; ibid., q. 42, a. 1; ibid., q. 42, a. 3, ad 2; ibid., q. 43, a. 1; ST II-II, q. 19, a. 11 and De Ver., q. 26, a. 24.

[284]ST I-II, q. 23, a. 4 and ibid., q. 45, a. 1.

[285]ST I-II, q. 41, a. 3 and ibid., q. 42, a. 2.

[286]That is it arises out of the phantasm of the future evil, see ST I-II, q. 42, aa. 2 and 4 and ibid., q. 44, a. 1.

[287]ST I-II, q. 41, a. 1, ad 2.

[288]ST I-II, q. 41, a. 2, ad 3; ibid., q. 42, a. 3 and ibid., ad 2.

[289]We do not fear everything in the future but only the arduous or that which is outside our power; see ST I-II, q. 42, a. 3, ad 2.

[290]ST I-II, q. 41, aa. 2 and 4 and ibid., q. 43, a. 1.

[291]ST I-II, q. 41, a. 4; ibid., q. 42, a. 3, ad 3; ibid. q, 42, a. 5; ibid., q. 43, a. 2 and In Ethic. III, l. 15, n. 2.

one fearing.[292]

There are two kinds of fear, viz. that which is of the sorrowful evil which is repugnant to nature[293] and that which pertains to the desire of appetite which is unnatural and so it is called unnatural fear.[294] Yet, since fear is of the corruptive evil, it implies flight or shunning the evil,[295] but flight follows fear as something consequent to it. Fear is caused by the possible privation of some good already had[296] or from suffering from some evil or harm.[297]

There are, according to St. Thomas, five species of fear and since the different kinds of fear are based on different objects,[298] then any further division regarding the different kinds of fear are divided within these five.[299] The first two concern the actions of the one who fears, while the other concerns exterior things. The first is what St. Thomas calls *segnities* or laziness. This kind of fear shuns or flees action because of the excessive amount of labor involved in performing the action.[300] For example, one may fear that his boss will ask him to perform some task, because of the excessive amount of labor or work involved. The next is called *verecundia* or shamefacedness and this is

---

[292]ST I-II, q. 42, a. 5.

[293]That is natural fear is that which arises from the natural desire to be or being. So something is feared because it either takes one out of existence or corrupts some good or aspect of one's nature. See ST I-II, q. 41, a. 3.

[294]ST I-II, q. 41, a. 3.

[295]See ST I-II, q. 41, a. 3 and ibid., q. 42, a. 1

[296]ST I-II, q. 42, a. 1.

[297]ST I-II, q. 41, a. 1; ibid., q. 42, a. 1 and ibid., q. 43, a. 2.

[298]ST I-II, q. 41, a. 4, ad 1.

[299]Modern discussions and labeling of fear can be useful if understood with respect to these five, so one does not have to reject the various distinctions regarding the types of fear in some modern psychological schools. Yet, one of the important reasons for delineating the different kinds of fear is to be sure that proper labels are actually given. For instance, "homophobia," which is often bandied about these days, is not, in most cases, a "fear" of homosexuals. Rather it pertains either to the passion of hate of homosexuals (even possibly volitional) or it refers to the passion of (or volition of) hatred of homosexual acts. Moreover, it is possible for a homosexual actually to suffer "homophobia," i.e. if one has the inclination towards homosexuality, one may fear being around others of the same proclivity lest the person engage in the disordered acts. It also is possible to hate the actions and orientation of homosexuality while still loving the person. Therefore, the modern news media and psychologists who lack the proper knowledge regarding the distinctions among the passions have often mislabeled people, which has only fueled the fire of public debate rather than dampening it.

[300]III Sent., d. 26, q. 1, a. 3 and ST I-II, q. 41, a. 4.

a type of fear arising out of a disgrace, which is a low estimation in the opinions of others.[301] This kind of fear is subdivided into that fear which occurs without one doing anything on one's own and that which is called shame, properly speaking, which occurs due to some act committed by oneself. For example, there is a distinction between being embarrassed because someone may see our nakedness without any fault of our own and the fear which is the shame due to some evil act which we have committed and people find out about it.[302]

The first of the next three, which deal with things exterior to the individual, is *admiratio* or amazement. This occurs when someone thinks of some great evil which results in a loss of the capacity to consider how to get out of it.[303] The second is stupor which is a kind of fear which occurs when we consider some unaccustomed evil occurrence and thus our consideration is great.[304] In other words, this is the fear that arises from the consideration of some future evil with which one is not used to dealing. As a result, the individual is moved to serious consideration since the imagination is unaccustomed to dealing with the object. The difference between the previous kind and this kind of fear is that the previous kind tends to result in a cessation of thought because of the magnitude of the evil, whereas this kind tends to get one engrossed in thought because one has never dealt with it before. As one gets engrossed in the thinking about the thing, one can lose contact with reality which is why it is called stupor. In both of these cases, the person can seem a bit dazed or distracted. The last and perhaps the most common type of fear is agony or anxiety. This is typified by the fact that the evil is unforeseen, i.e. one is unable to foresee if he is going to be harmed or not, since one is uncertain about what is to come. This is why people who suffer from arachnophobia get scared at the presence of a spider, because they cannot foresee if they are going to suffer some imagined harm. If, however, it is clear that they are going to suffer harm, then they suffer sorrow and not fear, e.g. a child who has been spanked in the past is told that he is going to be spanked and thus can suffer fear or sorrow. If he is not certain whether he is going to be spanked, or how, then he may have fear. If he knows exactly what is

---

[301]III Sent., d. 26, q. 1, a. 3; ST I-II, q. 41, a. 4; ST II-II, q. 144, aa. 1 and 2 and In Ethic. IV, l. 17, nn. 2-15. St. Thomas also refers to this as *timor ingloriationis* which is an apt description.

[302]Modern psychology has tried to do away with shame, but shame can be good insofar as it motivates one to correct one's conduct. Moreover, shamefacedness in general is not evil psychologically but points to a psychological mechanism by which we are moved to defend ourselves against a bad reputation or being thought of in a lowly fashion. The references in the previous footnote offer an insight into St. Thomas' clear understanding about the good of this kind of fear. It is possible for the fear to be bad, but only when it is not in accord with reason.

[303]III Sent., d. 26, q. 1, a. 3; ST I-II, q. 41, a. 4; and ibid., ad 4.

[304]III Sent., d. 26, q. 1, a. 3; ST I-II, q. 41, a. 4; and ibid., ad 4.

going to happen, then he suffers the passion of sorrow, flight, anger or possibly even despair. Many times people say they "hate" spiders, which really means that they do not like the presence of the evil of fear when they get around them. Once someone understands how and when spiders are dangerous, they are less likely to fear them since they have better knowledge of whether they should be feared or not.[305]

There is a further distinction with respect to fear, viz. proximate and remote (distant).[306] When something is temporally remote, because of the distance, we do not imagine it as future and thus it is not feared.[307] Things which tend to be perceived far in the future do not worry us because they are too remote. When St. Thomas says we do not consider them as future, he means that we do not consider them as coming any time soon. The evil must be proximate or imminent to cause fear,[308] e.g. some people, especially the young, tend not to fear death because it is too remote in the future. Yet, even if an evil is imminent, one can have fear with some hope of evasion of the evil.[309] What this seems to indicate is that if hope is complete, then it is unlikely that there is fear or at least very little of it. But fear tends to increase to the degree hope wanes, because hope wanes to the degree that the evil becomes less possible to avoid.

With hope, fear can be useful insofar as it can move one to counsel and in this sense fear can be good,[310] but if there is no hope, counsel never follows. Moreover, through fear, one can be moved to preserve oneself from evils as well as other fears.[311] For example, if one fears that an enemy may attack, one is moved to fortify his city in order not to suffer the evils which come from being besieged. One can also see that it is possible to have fear of fear[312] insofar as fear is seen as a future evil. A classic example in this regard is stage fright. Sometimes a person becomes fearful just thinking about the suffering he will endure due to stage fright.

Fear can be dealt with in various ways. First, since the imagination of man is within his rational and volitional control, he can, through a motion of the will, change

---

[305]Movies make use of this distinction from time to time. For example, they may have a man walking around snakes and he has no fear and then suddenly you will see a serious complexion come over his face because he realizes that there is a different and very dangerous kind of snake present. But if he can overcome the dangerous snake, he does not have fear since fear concerns that which the person cannot overcome.

[306]ST I-II, q. 42, a. 2.

[307]Ibid.

[308]See ST I-II, q. 43, a. 1 and ibid., q. 42, a. 2.

[309]Ibid.

[310]ST I-II, q. 42, a. 2, ad 1 and ibid., q. 44, a. 2.

[311]ST I-II, q. 42, a. 4, ad 1.

[312]ST I-II, q. 42, a. 4.

the phantasm which is causing the fear and thus he can will himself not to fear.[313] Connected to this is the fact that anything which removes the phantasm of future evil removes fear.[314] This is why at times people will distract themselves to get their mind off some impending evil. In addition, premeditation, i.e. thinking about the situation beforehand, can mitigate fear.[315] For example, sometimes if one knows that one is going to suffer stage fright, one can think about it by reasoning with oneself that there is no reason to be afraid since there will be no opportunity to embarrass oneself, etc. Moreover, one can take counsel so as to consider the circumstances in order to avoid certain evils and thus calm the fear. On the other hand, some circumstances can increase fear,[316] e.g. if one ponders how long he will have to stand up in front of a group of people, it makes the fear worse. Whereas if he thinks it will only last for a short time, that can make it better.[317] If the future thing feared is removed or does not come, that removes or remedies fear.[318] Security (from the future evil) implies perfect quieting of the soul from fear[319] and so if one can find those things which have the notion of security about them and imagine them as part of the situation, that can calm fear.

Further causes of fear regard sudden events or things, because one cannot foresee them and they make the one who fears weak.[320] Love is the cause of fear in that fear arises out of the consideration of losing something loved.[321] Hate is the cause of fear in that we hate the evil thing prior to fearing its onset[322] or if it is present, we fear

---

[313]Ibid.

[314]ST I-II, q. 42, a. 2. This mechanism applies to every passion.

[315]ST I-II, q. 42, a. 5.

[316]ST I-II, q. 42, a. 6.

[317]What this indicates is that the circumstances affect our image and in thinking about them, we can change the image for the better or worse. Then again, one must keep in mind reality, i.e. it is not good to rethink the situation in such a fashion as to try to calm the appetites down by lying to them. This violates the process of resolution which will be discussed below on how appetites are "taught."

[318]ST I-II, q. 42, a. 6, ad 1. This is essentially what the process of re-thinking the situation accomplishes, at least, cognitively, although not necessarily in reality.

[319]ST II-II, q. 129, a. 7.

[320]ST I-II, q. 42, 5 and ibid., ad 3. This fact coupled with the pleasure one derives from motions of the appetites as discussed above is why horror films, rides at amusement parks and things of this nature are so successful.

[321]ST I-II, q. 43, a. 1.

[322]Ibid., ad 2.

that we shall never avoid it or be rid of it.[323] Finally, one's material disposition[324] can be the cause of fear if one does not want some object[325] which may not be bad in itself but is contrary to one's disposition, e.g. if one has a lazy disposition, he may fear some person who makes him work.

The last thing to consider regarding fear is its effects. St. Thomas describes eight effects of fear. The first is contraction, i.e. a withdrawal of the person interiorly.[326] This is a natural reaction to some evil being present in that one wants to get away from it. With man, it means that the person may become introspective. The second is growing cold as a result of the bodily change brought on by the imagination.[327] The third is that the person becomes quiet or loses his voice.[328] This occurs because speaking is an outward motion, and since fear causes a contraction, one is less inclined to speak. Moreover, because of the effect of contraction, there is a contraction or loss of appetite,[329] which is the fourth effect. This is why people who are under pressure or fear something do not eat or engage in other bodily goods.[330]

The fifth effect of fear is that, as has been mentioned, under certain circumstances, it can move one to take counsel. Yet, a sixth effect of fear can actually be the impeding of taking good counsel:[331] if the fear is debilitating, then one may not possess the strength to take counsel. The seventh consequence of fear is a result of the first and second effects, i.e fear can cause a tremor or shaking which is an inability to

---

[323]Ibid., ad 1.

[324]Given the rationale, one's habits would also fulfill this reason.

[325]ST I-II, q. 43, aa. 1 and 2.

[326]ST I-II, q. 44, a. 1.

[327]Ibid., ad 1. Actually, this could refer to the various physiological/biochemical changes that occur due to fear.

[328]ST I-Ii, q. 44, a. 1 ad 2 and ibid., q. 44, a. 3, ad 3.

[329]ST I-II, q. 44, a. 1, ad 3.

[330]On the other hand, depressed people tend to eat because of the fact they are seeking some form of consolation so as to assuage their interior pain. People function differently regarding fear and depression, i.e. someone could eat when he fears or not eat while he is depressed. This occurs because of the fact that one who fears is suffering due to the presence of the imagined future evil. Consequently, he may eat to mitigate the passion of fear which is unpleasant. Contrariwise, some people who are depressed get a certain pleasure out of being depressed and so there may not be any drive to obtain the pleasures of bodily goods since they are already have some form of pleasure.

[331]ST I-II, q. 44, a. 2.

control one's exterior members.[332] The last effect of fear is that it impedes other operations,[333] such as the use of exterior motion as well as the interior faculties. This is why it is difficult to reason with those who are suffering from strong fear.[334]

K. Anger

The last passion is anger. Anger is a passion of the irascible appetite[335] which actually takes its name from this passion.[336] The object of anger is the evil already present,[337] and as such it has no contrary,[338] since the good already possessed pertains to the concupiscible passion of delight. Desire must be present for there to be anger[339] since anger contains a desire for vindication[340] and actually delights in the vindication[341] once had. Anger in seeking vindication must have hope for punishing a wrong doing[342] and seeks to harm or cause injury in order to put an end to the fight with the evil.[343] Anger is a complex passion which contains or is caused by hope and desire for vindication[344] and sorrow[345] at some wrong done. In this respect, anger always considers

---

[332]ST I-II, q. 44, a. 3. Connected to this is the loss of control of one's bowels (ibid., ad 1), legs and arms shaking, teeth tend to chatter, etc. (ibid., ad 3). Moreover, fear can actually cause the members to become more mobile which may or may not be connected to the aforesaid but it is why sometimes people who are afraid make quick jerky movements.

[333]ST I-II, q. 44, a. 4. Even though they may be more mobile, they have less control.

[334]This observation can be applied to any of the passions. Moreover, those who suffer strong fear may suffer a form of lethargy because they cannot fight the imagination which is being impeded and therefore cannot move.

[335]ST I-II, q. 40, proem. and ibid., q. 46, a. 3. Like the other passions, anger causes a bodily transmutation; see ST I-II, q. 48, a. 2.

[336]ST I-II, q. 46, a. 1, ad 1 and ST II-II, q. 158, a. 1. The name is derived from the Latin word for anger, viz. *ira*.

[337]ST I-II, q. 23, a. 4.

[338]ST I-II, q. 23, aa. 3 and 4.

[339]ST I-II, q. 46, a. 1.

[340]ST I-II, q, 46, aa. 1-4; ibid., q. 46, a. 6; ST II-II, q. 158, a. 4 and In Ethic. VII, l. 6, n. 2.

[341]ST I-II, q. 46, a. 2; ibid., q. 48, a. 1 and De Ver., q. 25, a. 2.

[342]ST I-II, q. 46, a. 1; ibid., q. 46, a. 6, ad 2 and ibid., q. 48, a. 2, ad 1.

[343]ST I-II, q. 46, aa. 2 and 4; ibid., q. 47, aa. 1 and 2 and *De Malo* q. 12, a. 1, ad 16.

[344]ST I-II, q. 46, a. 2 and ibid., q. 46, a. 3, ad 3.

[345]ST I-II, q. 46, a. 1.

two objects, viz. the good of vindication and the bad or harm of the one causing the sorrow[346] and therefore it contains within itself contraries.[347]

The vindication remedies the sorrow by causing the anger,[348] which moves one to obtain the good sought and subsequently the vindication quiets anger.[349] Hence, it ends with a cessation of motion,[350] i.e. it terminates in an act of the concupiscible appetite of delight or sorrow.[351] One can delight in the imagination of the vindication even though the sorrow is still present and the vindication has not yet occurred, but this is imperfect delight.[352] Yet, delight can remedy or quiet anger, not only in the vindication, but some other delight can remove the injustice from the imagination thereby mitigating anger, e.g. a wife may realize that her husband is angry with one of the children and so she prepares his favorite dinner so that the pleasures of the dinner will mitigate his anger. Moreover, delight can actually mitigate the anger with respect to the same object. Since anger is caused by the perception of some harm or injustice, if someone with whom we are angry does something that causes delight, then the anger is mitigated, since the object in the imagination under the *ratio* of harm is replaced with delight or the good.

Anger requires that the object be arduous,[353] yet the evil present is engaged because it does not exceed the faculties of the agent.[354] There are two sources of the motion of anger, viz. reason and imagination.[355] We have already seen that each passion is moved by the imagination. So anything that can affect the imagination, can cause anger. Anger can be caused by memory, i.e. by some injustice done in the past. Yet, anger caused by memory can diminish with time, when time causes the memory to fade or be lost altogether.[356] Reason can be the cause of anger, since like the other passions, anger obeys reason by means of the will, i.e. it is done with reason since an act of reason

---

[346]ST I-II, q. 46, aa. 2 and 3.

[347]ST I-II, q. 46, a. 1, ad 2.

[348]ST I-II, q. 48, a. 1.

[349]Ibid.

[350]ST I-II, q. 23, a. 3 and De Ver., q. 25, a. 2.

[351]De Ver., q. 25, a. 2.

[352]ST I-II, q. 48, a. 1.

[353]ST I-II, q. 46, a. 3.

[354]De Ver., q. 26, a. 4.

[355]ST I-II, q. 46, a. 7, ad 1.

[356]ST I-II, q. 48, a. 2, ad 2.

is required for anger.[357] Reason is able to cause anger because it announces the cause,[358] i.e. reason judges the injustice or harm and thereby moves the passion through the image. As a result, anger is more an act with reason than those passions of the concupiscible appetite,[359] since anger is not only caused by harm perceived[360] but according to the notion of the unjust or injustice.[361]

On the other hand, anger does not always obey reason, since anger in reaping the vindication does not always listen to the command of reason.[362] Even though reason may announce the injustice, the passion does not always listen when the vindication is being meted out. Anger can exceed the measure of justice judged due by reason[363] and so even though one may correctly judge the injustice, the passion may go beyond what justice requires. Consequently, anger can actually impede reason,[364] if it does not obey it when seeking vindication. When the harm exceeds justice, one perceives that and he is moved to sorrow.[365]

As mentioned, justice and injustice pertain to anger.[366] There are two logical possible causes of injustice, viz. oneself and others. Properly speaking, one cannot become angry with oneself,[367] since one cannot will oneself evil except under the notion of the good. At times, people become frustrated and it is said that they become frustrated or angry with themselves. However, this is actually their inability to act upon objects in the way they want. Hence, this is not anger since the thing or person does not cause one harm or injustice from his own actions but from his own inabilities. So when we get frustrated at not being able to do something or in doing something wrong, it is really only anger in a certain respect but not *per se*.

The second cause of injustice is others and anger is caused from someone (or

---

[357]ST I-II, q. 46, a. 4 and ibid., ad 3.

[358]ST I-II, q. 46, a. 5, ad 1.

[359]ST I-II, q. 46, a. 5.

[360]As such, it can be moved by the cogitative power.

[361]ST I-II, q. 47, a. 2.

[362]ST I-II, q. 46, a. 4, ad 3; ibid., q. 46, a. 5, ad 1; ibid., q. 46, a. 6 and In Ethic. VII, l. 6, a. 2.

[363]ST I-II, q. 46, a. 6, ad 2 and De Malo, q. 12, a. 1.

[364]ST I-II, q. 46, a. 4, ad 3 and ibid., q. 48, a. 3. Anger is also capable of impeding the use of reason in the same ways that the other passions are.

[365]ST I-II, q. 46, a. 6, ad 2.

[366]III Sent., d. 15, q. 2, a. 2, qu. 2, ad 3 and ST I-II, q. 46, a. 7.

[367]ST I-II, q. 46, a. 7, ad 2.

some thing) hurting or doing something unjust to us through action.[368] Since action is always of the singular, so is anger.[369] There are three ways in which an injustice can be committed by another against us.[370] The first is ignorance, i.e. someone commits some injustice against us due to their lack of knowledge. The second is when his action proceeds from passion and the third is when he does it by choice. Corresponding to these three ways are the three degrees of anger.[371] The highest degree of anger arises when the injustice is done by another through choice. The second is through passion and the last is when it proceeds from ignorance. The second and third ways cause less anger because passion and ignorance tend to reduce the voluntariness of the act and so we tend to realize that the person may not have full volition or choice. Consequently, it does not have the full notion of injustice.

Sometimes the quality of the individual causing the injustice can affect the degree of anger. Hence, the greater (more excellent) someone is the more he can be moved to anger by the injustice of those below him.[372] We tend to take greater offense when an inferior looks down on us or when he treats us unjustly than if someone who is superior to us treats us in the same way.[373] Yet, if there is some defect in the inferior, it can reduce the anger,[374] e.g. if he is intoxicated which moves him to audacity, then the superior is less likely to become angry since he knows the person is speaking under the influence of the alcohol. We cease being angry at the dead because they cannot cause harm anymore as well as the fact that by dying, the worst thing has happened to them.[375]

Other things can be the cause of anger or its increase. For instance, those with a choleric disposition are more inclined or prompt to act or be angry than those with other dispositions.[376] Yet, man in general or by nature is more inclined to concupiscibile objects than irascible, but the particular bodily disposition can affect that natural

---

[368]ST I-II, q. 46, a. 7, ad 3 and ibid., q. 47, a. 2. Actually, anger with respect to things is different from anger with people since things cannot cause injustice, but they can cause harm. On the other hand, a thing may be perceived as a sign of some injustice of another and so we become angry with the person by means of some thing.

[369]ST I-II, q. 46, a. 7, ad 3. This observation demonstrates the depth of Aquinas' insight into the nature of this passion. We do not become angry with people *in general*, but only with reference to particular and concrete acts.

[370]These three are delineated in ST I-II, q. 47, a. 2.

[371]These three are delineated in ibid and ibid., q. 47, a. 3, ad 2.

[372]ST I-II, q. 47, a. 3.

[373]ST I-II, q. 47, a. 4.

[374]Ibid.

[375]Ibid., ad 2.

[376]ST I-II, q. 46, a. 5.

inclination.[377] Being sick, weak or having other physical defects can make it easier for one to become angry due to the fact that one is more easily inclined to sorrow.[378] For example, when people are suffering some form of pain, they are more inclined to become angry at things which normally they would not.

Anger seeks to remove impediments to the thing loved and so anger can increase love.[379] Yet, since disdain and despite (contempt) accompany anger, we look down on those who do not seek our good[380] and if someone does not seek our good, then over time the anger we have toward someone can cause hate for them, particularly if the injustices persist. Like hate, anger tends to repel the injury or injustice by desire for vindication. Anger gives rise to great vehemence and impetuosity in action, for anger does not cause retraction, but pursuit.[381] Yet, if reason judges that the anger is inordinate, one becomes silent so as not to speak inordinately,[382] i.e. if the anger is inordinate, the person refrains from allowing the anger to cause him to pursue the injustice, so as not to sorrow later from going to extremes. Moreover, if anger impedes reason, it can impede reason's use of speech,[383] as when people become silent because they are very angry. These two observations about lack of motion either because reason refrains or the passion impedes reason's use also apply to the other members of the body.[384]

Conclusion

The discussion of this chapter has covered a great deal of territory. It has covered the appetites in general and in particular, i.e. the concupiscible and irascible appetites. It has covered the passions in general as motions of an appetite and it has covered those motions or passions in particular. The passions pertaining to the concupiscible part are love and its contrary hate, desire and its contrary flight, delight and its contrary sorrow. The passions pertaining to the irascible part are hope and its contrary despair, audacity and its contrary fear and anger. Consequently, man has eleven passions (not twelve since there is no contrary to anger).

The passions in man are very complex and yet the discussion of them here only

---

[377]Ibid.

[378]ST I-II, q. 47, a. 3.

[379]ST I-II, q. 48, a. 2.

[380]ST I-II, q. 47, a. 2.

[381]ST I-II, q. 48, a. 2.

[382]ST I-II, q. 48, a. 4.

[383]Ibid.

[384]Ibid., ad 3. St. Thomas observes in ibid., ad 3 that this can go so far as to cause even death.

begins to scratch the surface of their complexity. They have a great impact on the life of man and implications for psychology.[385] This is especially the case regarding their relationship to reason and will, as a passion is considered good or bad dependent on its relationship to reason and will. Consequently, the next consideration must be how reason, will and the appetites affect one another. It is perhaps one of the most important areas of consideration, as will become evident in the discussion of the causes of mental health and illness.[386]

[385]Clearly, further work is needed to be done. It may be possible to take some of the conclusions of modern psychology and the various distinctions among the different passions and use them in light of the foundation given here. This foundation is merely the general philosophical knowledge that is requisite to discuss the passions. Yet, it may be possible to arrive at some of the same conclusions regarding the passions that modern psychology has, e.g. regarding the different kinds of fear and anxiety. However, they must be able to be deduced from these general principles as well as others that are valid. One should not be too hasty to assume that the conclusions of modern psychology regarding a passion are correct considering the fact that its conclusions proceed from different and often erroneous principles.

[386]The appetites constitute the last of the faculties which play a role in mental health and illness. The reader may be aware of the fact that the subconscious or the unconscious was not covered. In the third volume, a more thorough treatment of the subconscious will be given. However, for now, suffice it to say that there is no faculty of the subconscious or unconscious. Everything that has been attributed to the subconscious is either incompatible with a sound philosophical anthropology or it is a misunderstanding or false conclusion drawn from certain observable things in man which can be explained by all of the other faculties.

Chapter 9: The Relationship of Reason and the Appetites

Man, due to his complex nature, lends himself to a complex understanding of his psychological constitution. At the heart of this issue is the relationship of the appetites to the intellect and will and how they affect each others' operations. Yet, since mental health is concerned about the intellect of man, it is essential to psychology to know how the appetites, reason and will affect one another. For that reason, we shall consider the relationship between the passions (appetites), reason and will in four different ways and how they act upon one another.

I. Antecedent and Consequent Passion

St. Thomas makes a very important distinction within the passions which has an effect on the science of mental health and illness. He notes that passions or appetites relate to the intellect and will antecedently or consequently, i.e. passions occur prior to intellection and volition and/or subsequent to intellection and volition.[1] The distinction between antecedent and consequent passion is key to understanding not only why man behaves the way he does, but how the emotions or passions are to be understood and addressed by the intellect and will.

For it is the common experience of man that we experience a discrepancy between what we will and think and the movement of the appetites.[2] In other words, it is the common experience of man that sometimes passions arise prior to our making a judgment regarding them. Moreover, at times, we experience a passion when we do not will to pursue the object of the passion. This is one of the things that marks the clear distinction between man and animals. Animals simply act according to their passions but man, on the other hand, can think and will independently of the passions. It is also the common experience of man that we can affect the subsequent appetite by what we think, e.g. someone may say something to us and it is only after we think about it a bit, that we realize we were insulted and as a result anger arises out of the judgment of reason which did not occur prior to thought or volition. Moreover, sometimes people actually will to be angry, even though the imagination did not move the appetite prior to volition.

This disparity between the passions and will the scholastics called the *lex fomitis*, i.e. the law of the flesh.[3] It is called the "tinders" because it is something which "inflames" on its own independently of the motion of the intellect and will. It is not a

---

[1]ST I-II, q. 24, a. 3, ad 1 and 3; ibid., q. 77, a. 6; ST II-II, q. 158, a. 1, ad 2; *De malo* q. 3, a. 11; ibid., q. 12, a. 1; De Ver., q. 26, aa. 6 and 7.

[2]ST I, q. 81, a. 3, ad 2.

[3]ST III, q. 27, a. 3.

real law, but it does have some aspects of a law, i.e. it is so by participation.[4] It is sometimes called a law because a law is an ordinance, i.e. an ordering and the law of the flesh indicates that the bodily passions have a life of their own independently of intellect and will.[5] This means that the intellect and will have a very specific relationship to the passions, as they have a life of their own and therefore must be approached with that realization. On the other hand, this distinction is absolutely necessary to ensure that psychologists understand that volition is distinct from and occurs independently of the passions. At times, the psychological community assumed that one merely acted out of passions like an animal.

II. Appetites and Passions as They Affect Judgment and Reason in General

Man is not moved to perform some action purely by the motive power of the appetites themselves, since man's primary faculty of action or motion is the will.[6] Man is not moved until the judgment of reason and volition occur.[7] Man awaits the judgment of intellect and will because the appetites are an insufficient motive power to move man.[8] The appetites are insufficient motive power because they lack sufficient act[9] in order to be able to move the intellect and will, which are the two highest powers of the

---

[4]ST I-II, q. 91, a. 6, ad 2. "Participation" indicates that something takes part in or has some aspect which is like the thing in which it participates. Hence, the law of the flesh is called so because, like physical laws, it acts certain ways given certain circumstances.

[5]The *lex fomitis* is a law in the sense that it comes from divine justice as a punishment for original and actual sin, see ST I-II, q. 92, a. 3, ad 1 and *Super epistula ad Romanos*, c. 7, l. 4. This topic will be discussed in detail in the second volume.

[6]Since animals do not have a will, their only motive powers, or powers which move them to perform some action, are the appetites alone, see ST I, q. 81, a. 3.

[7]Ibid.

[8]Ibid. By motion, one is talking about action which is above the mere instinctual or reactive, i.e. while the body can move on its own when presented with certain circumstances, e.g. a person's leg moves when hit with a rubber hammer as when a doctor checks one's reflexes, nevertheless, actions which are properly human must proceed from intellection and volition.

[9]This is based upon the principle of sufficient reason which states: the reason for the existence of a thing must be accountable either in itself or in another. Colloquially it is stated "you cannot give what you do not have." Since the appetites and passions are acts through a corporal organ, the body or material aspect of man does not have enough ontological act in order to move an immaterial faculty such as the intellect and will. This was likewise discussed in relation to the agent and possible intellects as well as the possible intellect's relation to the will in that the faculty which moves another faculty must be proportionate in act to the faculty which it moves.

soul. While the lower cannot move the higher, the higher can move the lower, and therefore the appetites do not move man while the intellect and will do. Yet, the appetites and passions can affect the intellect and will, not insofar as they act upon them directly, for they cannot move the intellect and will directly. Rather, they do so indirectly by acting upon other aspects or faculties of man and in so doing they can affect intellection and volition.

In numerous places, St. Thomas discusses the fact that the passions bind or impede the act of the intellect of judgment or the act of reason.[10] Passions can affect the operations of the intellect and will antecedently[11] and consequently. With respect to consequent appetite or passion, we have already seen that consequent passion can affect the operations of the intellect and will with respect to anger, insofar as the intellect may judge what is proportionate harm but the anger may affect the execution of that judgment because of the vehemence of the passion. In like manner, this can be said of the other passions, insofar as the other passions can impede the execution of what reason judges and will chooses, e.g. it is the common experience of all men that when they are confronted with something that brings delight, even though they may rationally judge that it must be put aside and choose to do so, the passion impedes the motions of the other faculties which the intellect and will move.

With respect to antecedent appetite, St. Thomas has a great deal to say. There are two ways to sort out everything he has to say. The first is to discuss the relation of antecedent passion to the intellect in general; the second is to consider specific ways in which antecedent passion relates to reason and will. With respect to the general ways in which antecedent passion affects the intellect, one may say that its relation is threefold. The first is when the antecedent passion, due to its vehemence, totally binds reason and thus one loses the use of reason.[12] Moreover, if the intellect and will are weak, i.e. suffer from vice, the amount of passion required to take away the use of reason does not need to be much. In fact, if the vice in the intellect and will is great, only a slight passion can cause reason and will to be affected. For example, someone who is very prone to desire, even when the passion or occurrence may be considered slight, the person's judgment is precipitated. A man who is prone to the passion of desire with regard to sex, finds that even something with the slightest sexual implication, binds his thought about sex for some time and he has a hard time changing his thoughts.

The second way is when the antecedent passion does not affect the operations

---

[10] II Sent., d. 5, q. 1, a. 2; ibid., d. 39, q. 3, a. 2, ad 5; SCG III, c. 108, n. 3; De Ver., q. 24, a. 8; ibid., q. 25, a. 1, ad 4; *De malo* q. 3, aa. 9 and 10; ibid., q. 12, a. 1; ibid., q. 8, a. 3, ad 15; ibid., q. 3, a. 11; De Ver., q. 26, a. 7, ad 3; ST I-II, q. 24, a. 3, ad 1; ST I-II, q 48, a. 4. The term "reason" refers to the intellect considered from the point of view of its capacity to engage in the process of reasoning, i.e. the third act of the possible intellect.

[11] *De malo*, q. 12, a. 1 and ST I-II, q. 77, a. 6.

[12] ST I-II, q. 10, a. 3; ibid., q. 77, a. 2 and *De malo*, q. 3, a. 10.

of intellect and will at all, either due to the sheer strength or virtue in the intellect and will or due to the lack of or slight amount of movement of the passion, which is insufficient to affect reason and will.[13] The third way is when the passion affects the intellect and will but not so as to take away the use of intellect completely.[14] This is, of course, by degree,[15] based upon the degree of vehemence of the passion and the amount of strength of the intellect and will. For example, with the passion of fear, if it is not so vehement as to take away the use of reason, it can actually move one to counsel or give one a capacity to counsel[16] so as to avoid the thing feared. Consequently, antecedent passion can be useful or harmful,[17] depending upon how it affects the operations of the intellect and will.[18] In one place,[19] St. Thomas observes that moderate sorrow can move one to learn because one wants to know how to avoid the sorrow.

Therefore, the question is *how* does antecedent passion bind the intellect and will. St. Thomas in his writings offers essentially a three-fold reason. The first is that when the sensitive powers, which the intellect and will depend on for their operations, are disturbed, the use of reason becomes bound.[20] St. Thomas observes in his commentary on Peter Lombard's *Sentences* that antecedent appetite or passion arises from inferior reason (the cogitative power) apprehending something as harmful or suitable prior to volition.[21] What this effectively means is that the cogitative power

---

[13]Continence is the virtue residing in the will by which one is able to refrain from unchaste acts regardless of the tumult of the appetites. This is the state in which those who have made a deep commitment to overcoming a vice find themselves. For example, the alcoholic who has finally made the commitment to overcome his alcoholism finds a certain strength in making the decision and depending on God for his strength to overcome the vice. Hence, when the moments come, by a clear intellectual grasp of the evil of his addiction and the will's commitment not to fall into the evil, the alcoholic can resist the appetite.

[14]ST I-II, q. 80, a. 3; ST II-II, q. 150, a. 4, ad 3.

[15]*De malo*, q. 3, a. 11.

[16]ST I-II, q. 44, a. 2, ad 2.

[17]See *De malo*, q. 12, a 1.

[18]The fact that passions can aid intellect and will not only in the execution of the some action by adding bodily strength from fear, for example, as well as impede reason is very important. Historically, there were those who held that all passions were evil. There are those who hold all passion is good, but the truth lies in the mean insofar as some passions are good and some are bad depending on their relationship to intellect and will. This subject shall be discussed below; however, one may read St. Thomas' discussion of this perennial problem in *De malo* q. 12, a. 1.

[19]ST I-II, q. 37, a. 1, and ibid., ad 2.

[20]ST I-II, q. 48, a. 3 and *De malo*, q. 3, a. 3, ad 9.

[21]II Sent., d. 24, q. 3, a. 1.

makes an assessment of some phantasm prior to intellection and volition and merges with the phantasm the aspect of good or harmful. The appetites, which are moved by the imagination, then incline to the object. The pivotal faculty is the imagination since it is the faculty which ultimately moves the appetites and whatever can affect the imagination can cause appetitive movements. Therefore, when something present in the five exterior senses is vehement, it makes its way into the imagination and only that which exerts more act over the imagination by its strength is able to override it.[22]

Furthermore, as the appetite is inclined toward the object in the imagination, the interior sensation or feeling which the passion causes is also merged with the image. While the cogitative power may move a specific passion by associating the *ratio* or perspective of the passion with the phantasm, the converse is also the case. As the object of the passion comes into the imagination, the passion arises and the sensation of the movement of the passions likewise becomes part of the phantasm. As a result, the cogitative power can make an assessment of the goodness or badness of the phantasm based upon whether the passion is pleasant or unpleasant. This assessment is then merged with the image. As the intellect converts back to the phantasm to make the judgment, the intellect sees the good or bad that the passion and cogitative power have placed in the phantasm. Since the intellect makes its judgment based upon the phantasm, if the phantasm is flawed or affected by passion, the intellect will have a hard time judging contrary to the information contained in the phantasm. The possible intellect can pass a judgment contrary to what is in the phantasm based only on its own intellective memory and/or habituation. Hence, someone who is swayed by passion may judge contrary to the phantasm as the conscience judges the action proposed in the phantasm as bad according to its intellective memory and so the judgment of the phantasm is based upon the intellective memory. This is why formation of conscience and intellective memory are so important. The possible intellect, if its formation is not strong, is likely to be affected by the phantasm since it depends on the phantasm for its judgment.

On another note, the other three interior powers can affect the imagination as well. The common sense faculty, if defective, can cause difficulties in the phantasm and therefore affect the operations of the intellect and will.[23] Moreover, the memory is able to re-introduce sensible species back into the imagination and thereby affect the judgment of intellect and will and, as was mentioned, if the cogitative power is badly affected it can cause antecedent passion by its assessments and associations.

Yet, this is not sufficient in itself, for even if the cogitative power and memory

---

[22]This would apply to everything from torture to things which cause vehement pleasure.

[23]For example, when the various exterior senses do not make their way into the imagination at the same time, this can lead to confusion and therefore fear or other negative passions.

affect the imagination, it would appear that the intellect and will could simply move the imagination and change the phantasm or move the cogitative power to disassociate some aspect of the phantasm from the remaining part of the phantasm. However, St. Thomas provides another aspect to the three-fold reason which helps to understand how this binds reason and will. He states that all of the powers are rooted in the soul, so that when the soul is intent on one passion, it draws the other faculties to its operation. Consequently, the one soul can have only one intention,[24] i.e. due to the nature of the soul, it can carry on primarily in the action of only one faculty at a time.[25] Connected to this is the fact that the intense action in one faculty can redound to other faculties,[26] as, for example, strong reason and will move the appetites and vice versa.

This effectively means that when there is a strong passion, the passion draws the soul to the operations of the appetite and so the phantasm which is moving the appetite remains in place. The intellect and will have a hard time moving the other faculties because they are caught up, due to the unity of the soul, in the one operation, now dominated by the strength of the appetite. From this we can derive the conclusion that anytime there is a strong passion, it weakens the intellect and will. When it becomes habituated, a weakness in the will occurs in direct relation to the strength of the vice in the appetite or other faculties. Moreover, since the intellect (and the will which is moved by the intellect) is dependent on the phantasm for the knowledge, it affects the operations of the intellect as it converts back to the phantasm in the act of judgment. Antecedent passion binds judgment by its strength and the soul cannot move to change the phantasm without difficulty.[27]

There are several connected conclusions and effects regarding this mechanism. The first is that passion binds, regarding the particular action or thing[28] under consideration, because the passions are about the particular. This means that universal considerations will be affected since the intellect has a hard time considering something universally since it is bound to the particular good or evil thing under consideration in the imagination. This results in a two-fold difficulty. The first is that, in the concrete particular situation, the person has a hard time thinking about more lofty or universal considerations as well as how universal principles apply in particular circumstances. The second is that over the course of time, when the appetites, intellect and will become

---

[24]ST I-II, q 37, a. 1 and ibid., ad 2; ibid., q. 77, aa. 1 and 2.

[25]De Ver., q. 25, a. 4. Here, by faculty we are talking about those faculties under rational control. Obviously the nutritive faculty and faculties outside volitional control, for example, carry on while reason acts.

[26]ST I-II, q. 77, a. 6 and De Ver., q. 25, a. 3.

[27]See ST I-II, q. 77, a. 1.

[28]II Sent., d. 39, q. 3, a. 2, ad 5; III Sent., d. 31, q. 1, a. 1; ST I-II, q. 58, a. 2; SCG III, c. 108, n. 3 and De malo, q. 3, aa. 8-10.

habituated in looking at the object the way the passion is moved toward it, the person's judgment begins to be affected about that particular thing, i.e. one cannot see it from a universal or outside that perspective.[29]

The next point, as we can see from the preceding, is that passions affect the intellect's ability to judge the truth of the matter due to loss of tranquility of mind which is necessary to judge truth.[30] Since the possible intellect must convert back to the phantasm in order to judge the truth of things, if the phantasm is affected by passion, one is unable to judge the truth of the matter. St. Thomas observes that this is because when one suffers passion, one is inclined to judge that something is greater or lesser than the truth of the matter. Passion impedes arriving at the truth due to impeding the rectitude of judgment.[31] In effect, reason judges based upon a phantasm which is not in congruity with reality. If the phantasm is affected by passion, the possible intellect can err by looking at the phantasm and judging that something is better than it is due to the pleasure or delight of the passion or worse than it is due to the unpleasantness of the passion, as in the case of fear, hatred or the like. At times, the phantasm may have a congruity with the truth as well as the assessment of the cogitative power. But when one takes counsel, one cannot think clearly due to the vehemence of the passion and so again one's judgment, which requires time to rework the phantasms to judge it properly, is impeded in the process of counsel, i.e. passion impedes counsel.[32]

This results in several conclusions. The first is that antecedent passion or appetite draws reason from its rectitude[33] which lies in truth, as truth is the good of the intellect. Passion makes something seem good or bad which is not really good or bad.[34]

---

[29]Modern society has provided a classic example of this. Culturally, in the past, fornication was looked down upon as a great moral and societal evil because of all the evil effects to the individual and society, one of which is the general erosion of morality within a society. As fornication and sexual licence became more pervasive, the society began finding it difficult to judge fornication as morally evil and today it has virtually no evil connotation at all. What started out as particular individual difficulties with respect to passions has affected, over the long haul, the universal judgment of society about the evil of fornication in general.

[30]*De malo*, q. 12, a. 1.

[31]ST I-II, q. 44, a. 2.

[32]ST I-II, q. 59, a. 2, ad 3.

[33]ST II-II, q. 158, a. 1, ad 2.

[34]ST I-II, q. 33, a. 3 and ibid., q. 77, a. 2, ad 2. Even if the antecedent passion comes across something which is bad and moves in that fashion, it still affects the judgment by not being able to re-work the phantasm to put it into perspective, i.e. only reason can judge truly how bad something is. Whereas passions tend to be disordered and even when they come across the truth regarding some aspect of the passion, they still affect judgment and consequently can be led away from the truth in subsequent deliberations. Moreover,

Next, antecedent passion impedes knowledge by inclining the soul toward the opposite,[35] i.e. one is inclined toward what is contrary to what he knows to be true, i.e. antecedent passion causes ignorance. Another difficulty is that, insofar as passion affects judgment, it affects syllogistic reasoning,[36] as syllogistic reasoning is the process by which one goes from judgment to judgment to arrive at a final judgment (conclusion.) This is why, as children and adults lead lives more dominated by the appetitive, it becomes difficult to teach them as they are impeded from reasoning syllogistically with facility because they are dominated by their passions.[37] In addition, physical pain and pleasure and interior pain and pleasure impede contemplation since it is necessary that the appetites be quiet[38] so that the soul can engage with facility in intellectual operations and so antecedent passion impedes learning.[39] In addition, passion impedes even knowing or remembering what one knew,[40] i.e. passion makes us forget. Another effect is that passion corrupts the estimation of prudence.[41] This comes from the fact that since prudence requires counsel, when counsel is compromised, so is prudence.

The last of the three-fold reasons why passions precipitate reason and will is, as St. Thomas observes, that passions cause bodily transmutations which impede reason.[42] This may be because of the chemical changes which are caused in relation to

---

sometimes passions indicate something is bad, but in certain circumstances only reason can assess whether the thing should be feared or just hated and if the passion hates something vehemently, it may not be moved to fear because it is binding reason. In other words, it may not get the *ratio* regarding the object of the appetite quite right, even though it does know it is evil or bad.

[35]ST I-II, q. 77, a. 2.

[36]ST I-II, q. 77, a. 2, ad 4.

[37]This can be seen from grade school all the way through college.

[38]ST I-II, q. 37, a. 1, ad 3.

[39]ST I-II, q. 37, a. 1. Two observations regarding this should be made. The first is that since the virtue of science resides in the possible intellect governing the second act of judgment, those who lead appetitive lives will be impeded in gaining knowledge or science. This makes one wonder if the modern advances in the empirical sciences are truly being advanced. The second is that parents and students should be advised that discipline and mortification directly contribute to learning as they quiet the passions. This topic will be seen in the discussion of this topic in volume II.

[40]ST I-II, q. 37, a. 1.

[41]Aristotle, *Ethics*, V: 6 (1140b13) and ST II-II, q. 53, a. 6.

[42]ST I-II, q. 33, a. 3 and ibid., q. 77, a. 2. This can be known in three ways. The first is the common experience of all men, e.g. when one finds oneself in a set of circumstances which cause a great deal of fear, one experiences the body shaking, etc. which indicates that there is some bodily effect from passion. The second reason is that

various passions. Nevertheless, the passion causes a dispositional change in the person which affects the operations of the interior senses and consequently reason. This indicates that when there is a bodily transmutation, reason is bound, i.e. it is not free in its action.[43] While some bodily changes do not affect reasoning, others do and it pertains to psychiatry and biochemistry to determine the differences between the two.[44] Furthermore, certain bodily transmutations cause a disturbing of the interior senses[45] or exterior senses and result in affecting the phantasm, e.g. when people are in a hot room, over the course of time the heat begins to affect them. They begin to recognize their suffering and so passion arises out of the judgment of the suffering and so they get angry since they cannot cool off. This also indicates that moods can affect the way people reason. "Mood" is another way of expressing material and appetitive disposition, e.g. when someone is in a bad mood, that is usually a sign that they are inclined or disposed toward anger or sorrow. This is also why people with some experience know that if they get out of a situation that makes them irritable (disposed toward anger), they will be disposed in another way or resume their normal disposition of cheerfulness (disposed toward the passion of love, delight and hope). Therefore, the general three-fold reason why passions affect judgment are the affecting of the phantasm, the unity of the operations of the soul and bodily transmutation.

III. Appetites and Passions as They Affect Volition

In the previous section, we have already seen some ways in which antecedent passion affects volition. To recall, the cogitative power assesses the phantasm and thereby moves the passions, captivating the faculties of the soul. Subsequently, the will has difficulty overriding the phantasm in the imagination, as the soul is intent on what the phantasm holds rather than something else.[46] As the intellect depends on the phantasm to make a judgment, and as the will is presented its object under the notion of

---

philosophically, we know that passions are an operation in a bodily organ, and therefore if there is an action in the faculty, there will be a bodily change. The last is that through modern science, it is known that certain physico-chemical changes occur when people experience different passions, e.g. adrenaline is released into the blood stream when fear occurs.

[43]ST I-II, q. 77, a. 2; *De malo* q. 3, aa. 9-10; ibid., q. 12, a. 3, ad 7 and ibid., q. 12, a. 4, ad 1.

[44]There are some bodily changes which are not caused by passions but can dispose one to passions, e.g. women as they age undergo chemical changes which can not only affect passions but the way of reasoning.

[45]ST I-II, q. 48, a. 3, ad 1.

[46]ST I-II, q. 77, a. 1.

the good which is the product of judgment, if judgment is compromised, so is volition.[47]

Antecedent passion is capable of a two-fold relationship with the will. If the object of the passion is the same as the object of the will, then there is volition *with* passion (*voluntas secundum passionem*). In this case, the passion does not impede the operation of the will but may actually excite[48] or move the will to willing its object.[49] Then there is passion which occurs contrary to the motion of the will; in this case, the object of the will is either the contrary of the object of the passion or it is a different object than that of the passion.[50]

Passions can, therefore, affect the volition. Regarding volition, one of the primary concerns is regarding the voluntary, i.e. whether the volition or an act of the will proceeds from the will as from an interior principle, i.e. whether it is free or not. Clearly, if passion can affect volition, then passion can cause something to be completely or partially voluntary (or involuntary).[51] The stronger the passion is, the more one will be impeded by it,[52] and consequently, the stronger the passion, the more voluntariness is compromised. As a result, while the motion of the will following upon passion[53] will be more intense, nevertheless it is not proper to the will.[54] It is not proper to the will because it is being moved by the passion (indirectly) and not from an interior principle. This means that antecedent passion can cause one to will something, but the culpability or merit of the act is reduced[55] because it is not free or as free.[56]

---

[47]ST I-II, q. 77, a. 1 and ibid., a 1.

[48]De Ver., q. 26, a. 6.

[49]Ibid., q. 26, a. 7.

[50]This state constitutes a suffering or evil for the person, as tranquility of the soul constitutes that all of the faculties come together in a single order toward one object. This contrariety is also the genesis of many mental illnesses.

[51]ST I-II, q. 77, a. 7.

[52]ST I-II, q. 44, a. 2, ad 2.

[53]That is assuming the object of the passion is the object of the will.

[54]ST I-II, q. 77, a. 6, ad 3.

[55]De *De malo*, q. 3, a. 11.

[56]This is true for the most part, however, there are virtues which can be gained which can help the individual act contrary to the passions and not completely compromise his voluntariness, e.g. continence which is the virtue in the will, helps one to will what is right despite the tumult of the appetites. Nevertheless, with continence there is still a reduction of the voluntariness, though not as much. Insofar as the will must act contrary to the passion, the soul is divided and consequently, the person is not totally carrying on in the motion of the will which indicates that it is not as voluntary as it could be. Something is completely voluntary when there is no impeding of the will on the side of passion and when the intellect is completely free to judge the object of volition. This topic was discussed in

Given the aforesaid, it can be seen that some modern psychologists have completely failed in their understanding of the passions. For some psychologists have actually encouraged people to lead a life according to antecedent appetite which results in a reduction of voluntariness of their directees' actions. Since it pertains to man to act according to his nature in order to be happy,[57] he is only truly happy when he is completely free and this comes not from leading a life according to passion but the absence of antecedent appetite affecting judgment and volition, so that the person is completely free. The lack of proper understanding of the faculties and their mutual relations has led some modern psychologists to cause considerable damage and it has resulted in directees spending long periods of their life with little relief from the psychological difficulties.[58]

IV. Appetites and Passions as They Affect Reason and Volition in Particular

There are several texts in which St. Thomas considers how the passions affect reason and these should be considered in detail as they reveal a penetrating understanding of the nature of man. The first passage for consideration is from the *Secunda Secundae* regarding the daughters of lust (*filiae luxuriae*) and the entire text is worthy of detailed consideration. The text begins as follows:

> When the inferior powers are vehemently affected by their objects, the consequence is that the superior powers are impeded and disordered in their acts. Through the vice of lust, moreover, the inferior appetite, viz. the concupiscible, vehemently intends its object, viz. the delectable, because of the vehemence of the delight. And therefore, the consequence is that by lust the superior powers are disordered the most, viz. reason and will.[59]

---

chapter seven.

[57]This will be known by virtue of the natural law and what constitutes man's final end which will be discussed in volume II.

[58]On a practical level, it leaves one a bit mystified as to why directees continue to go to these psychologists when it is evident that they have not been aiding them. It may be due to psychological factors or psychologists maintaining relationships of dependence of their directee on them which is completely contrary to the nature of voluntariness and therefore any sound psychology. Lastly, since prudence is compromised, directees are particularly vulnerable to manipulation.

[59]ST II-II, q. 153, a. 5: "quando inferiores potentiae vehementer afficiuntur ad sua obiecta, consequens est quod superiores vires impediantur et deordinentur in suis actibus. Per vitium autem luxuriae maxime appetitus inferior, scilicet concupiscibilis, vehementer intendit suo obiecto, scilicet delectabili, propter vehementiam delectationis. Et ideo

St. Thomas observes that the vice of lust impedes the use of reason and will the most. He also notes that lust causes disorder and this follows from the fact that carnal passion and vices, the more they extinguish or affect the judgment of reason, the further they pull someone from reason[60] or from acting rationally. They disorder reason by drawing it away from considering something freely. Insofar as they affect judgment and cause reason to judge falsely, they move the intellect to act contrary to right order. This follows from the fact that the intellect is ordered to knowing the truth and passion militates against that. Moreover, it disorders the will by inclining the individual toward pursuing the objects of the passions rather than that which is truly good. It causes disorder in the will by reducing its freedom by affecting the voluntariness of its actions as well as drawing the will to choose objects of passion rather than that which should be pursued as determined by right reason. Consequently, living life according to the passions leads to intellectual and volitional disorder.[61]

The above quote continues as follows:

> There are four acts of reason in acting. The first, indeed, is simple intelligence, which apprehends some end as good. And this act is impeded by lust, according to Daniel XIII:[62] "beauty has deceived you and concupiscence subverts your heart." And with respect to this is posited blindness of the intellect (*caecitas mentis*).[63]

Here, St. Thomas is noting that lust (or passion) blinds the intellect as to its capacity to judge simply what is good or what should be pursued. In general, the passions are said to cause blindness of the intellect and this is because the intellect cannot "see" clearly or freely that which it normally would through judgment, if the imagination were not "clouded" by passion. This defect of the intellect is a disorder which keeps the intellect from performing its proper function in arriving at the truth about the nature of ends regarding man. This is very important for the field of psychology in that the ends of human life, determined by man's nature, are not grasped properly and so the person ends

---

consequens est quod per luxuriam maxime superiores vires deordinentur, scilicet ratio et voluntas."

[60]ST II-II, q. 53, a. 6, ad 3.

[61]This also applies to passions in that passions become disordered by not following reason.

[62]Here St. Thomas is referring to the Book of Daniel in Scripture, i.e. Daniel 13: 56.

[63]ST II-II, q. 153, a. 5: "sunt autem rationis quatuor actus in agendis. Primo quidem, simplex intelligentia, quae apprehendit aliquem finem ut bonum. Et hic actus impeditur per luxuriam, secundum illud Dan. XIII, species decepit te, et concupiscentia subvertit cor tuum. Et quantum ad hoc, ponitur caecitas mentis."

up pursuing things which are contrary to his nature, which cause damage to him in various ways, such as psychologically, morally, spiritually and even physically. This first disorder is the first because all others flow from blindness of the intellect, i.e. the inability to know what is good, right and true.

Moreover, as one errs about the end of one's actions to be pursued, all other things in relationship to that end are affected.

> The second act is counsel which concerns those which are done for the sake of the end. And this also is impeded through the concupiscence of lust, hence Terentius says in Eunuch[64] speaking of libidinous love, which *in se* allows neither counsel nor moderation, you are not able to rule it by counsel. And with respect to this is posited precipitation, which imports a drawing away from counsel.[65]

Here, St Thomas observes that the second act the intellect engages in concerns those things which are for the sake of the end, viz. the means. Now since counsel is about the means, the passion of lust precipitates or destroys counsel[66] and so one is unable to "rule" insofar as to rule implies guiding something to an end. Since one lacks counsel, he is affected in his ability to discern the various means he could employ to arrive at his proper end. This is why many directees have difficulty in knowing how to free themselves from the mental illness or how to do those things which contribute to a person living a normal daily life. Their passions are destroying the ability to judge what to do.

The passage continues in relation to the means:

> The third act is the judgment of that which is to be done. And this impeded through lust, for it says in Daniel XIII:[67] "They turned to their senses out of the weakness of lust, that they might not recall just judgments." And with respect to this is posited inconsideration.[68]

---

[64]Act 1, Scene 1.

[65]ST II-II, q. 153, a. 5: "secundus actus est consilium de his quae sunt agenda propter finem. Et hoc etiam impeditur per concupiscentiam luxuriae, unde Terentius dicit, in Eunucho, loquens de amore libidinoso, quae res in se neque consilium neque modum habet ullum, eam consilio regere non potes. Et quantum ad hoc, ponitur praecipitatio, quae importat subtractionem consilii..."

[66]ST II-II, q. 53, a. 2 and ibid., q. 53, a. 3, ad 3.

[67]Daniel 13: 9.

[68]ST II-II, q. 153, a. 5: "tertius autem actus est iudicium de agendis. Et hoc etiam impeditur per luxuriam, dicitur enim Dan. XIII, de senibus luxuriosis, averterunt sensum suum, ut non recordarentur iudiciorum iustorum. Et quantum ad hoc, ponitur

In this section, St. Thomas observes that by leading a life according to passion (specifically lust), inconsideration is engendered. Now, as will be recalled from the decision-making process previously discussed, following the act of counsel, the intellect makes an act of judgment over which means is best. When the intellect is affected by passion, one does not consider the various means and tends to act hastily without consideration of what one is doing or is to do. Inconsideration[69] is a defect of and contrary[70] to right judgment which takes away synesis[71] and gnome.[72] Moreover, it causes one to lack caution and circumspection.[73] Inconsideration rejects and neglects to attend to those things which proceed from right reason.[74] Passion which causes inconsideration also destroys the ability of the intellect to know the particular as it pertains or falls under the universal.[75] In other words, it destroys one's ability to judge when a universal principle applies in a given situation, e.g. when a parent becomes angry, he fails to judge that his discipline of his child must ultimately be to correct the child's fault or error rather than to harm the child which anger seeks.[76]

---

inconsideratio."

[69]Inconsideration is sometimes called "thoughtlessness."

[70]ST II-II, q. 53, a. 4.

[71]Synesis is the virtue by which one judges about particular actions according to the common law or common occurrences. See ST I-II, q. 57, a. 6, ad 3; ST II-II, q. 48, a. 1 and ibid., q. 51, a. 3.

[72]ST II-II, q. 53, a. 2. Gnome is the virtue by which one judges about action when the common law does not apply or when something is not a common occurrence.

[73]ST II-II, q. 53, a. 2. Caution is the taking of proper care to consider the dangers involved in a course of action. Circumspection is the virtue by which one considers the various circumstances affecting a given action. Hence, someone who suffers passion does not take into consideration all of the dangers involved because he cannot judge properly. Moreover, he tends to be unable to look at his surroundings and judge them properly, e.g. someone who suffers from the passion of anger may forget his relation to someone he loves, such as when a wife who is angry with her husband says hurtful things to the husband because she is acting under the influence of the passion.

[74]ST II-II, q. 53, a. 4.

[75]ST I-II, q. 77, a. 2 and ibid., ad 1 and 2.

[76]As passion takes away one's ability to judge or know the particular in light of the universal in practical matters, it is safe to say that this also applies in speculative matters. In other words, when one reasons about matters pertaining merely to the truth and not for the sake of action, one's passions can cause one to judge something too hastily or without consideration or reflection, e.g. atheists, who do not *want* there to be a God on a practical level because it would require them to change their moral code or conduct, will often propose atheistic cosmologies without taking into consideration evidence to the contrary.

St. Thomas continues:

> The fourth act is the command of reason to act, which also is impeded by lust, insofar as, namely, man is impeded by the impulse of concupiscence and does not seek after that which he has decreed to be done. Hence, Terentius says in Eunuch[77] of a certain man who said that he would leave his mistress: "one false tear would undo this word."[78]

Here, St. Thomas observes that when someone suffers passion, the person is unable to carry out the command of reason, i.e. reason may have said "do this" but if one suffers from passion, he is unable to complete it. For example, if someone suffers from the passion of fear, he may command himself to run away from the danger but the fear may debilitate him from actually running. With respect to concupiscence, this is clearly seen as when one comes across something for which he has a strong passion of love; he may not be able to carry out the command of reason to resist it.

     This defect is called inconstancy in that one commands something but is unable to carry it out. Often it indicates a commanding of something to be done at one moment but then later changing one's mind or not carrying through due to the strength of the passion.[79] This defect indicates that one is unable to carry out the command but this also applies to the inability to carry out universal precepts in the particular. Even if one reasons or counsels rightly and makes the right judgment about what to do, if the passion is strong, it can cause the intellect to be inconstant in its command about carrying it out. Often what occurs is that someone knows that something is good or bad and judges it rightly in a given situation, but is unable to carry out what is necessary to fulfill the precept regarding the good or bad action. This often leads to justification in which reason is weak in fulfilling the precept and so one seeks to exculpate himself even to the point of rejecting the precept, if the passion is strong and the person is unable to

---

The import of this last observation is staggering if one reflects upon it. It means that entire nations, societies, and families can be drastically affected in the reasoning about truth and the good if their passions are disordered. In fact, it means that a society that is disordered at the level of the appetites is doomed to fail, since no society can exist without its foundation being based on the true and the good with respect to man.

    [77]Act 1, Scene 1.

    [78]ST II-II, q. 153, a. 5: "quartus autem actus est praeceptum rationis de agendo. Quod etiam impeditur per luxuriam, inquantum scilicet homo impeditur ex impetu concupiscentiae ne exequatur id quod decrevit esse faciendum. Unde Terentius dicit, in Eunucho, de quodam qui dicebat se recessurum ab amica, haec verba una falsa lacrimula restringet."

    [79]ST II-II, q. 53, a. 5, ad 2.

overcome it in the long haul. The reason passion causes inconstancy is because reason commands one thing, but then judges another subsequent to the command. Since the passion is affecting the judgment, the intellect changes or is unable to carry out the original command because judgment is affected.[80]

St. Thomas then delineates four more daughters or effects of lust (which can also be applied to other passions) which pertain to the will and he begins as follows:

> On the part of the will, a two-fold inordinate act follows of which one is about the appetite of the end, and with respect to this is posited self love, in which he inordinately desires to delight and by its opposite is posited hatred of God, insofar as, namely, he prohibits the desired delight.[81]

With respect to the will, there is the order the will has to the end and here St. Thomas indicates that disordered self-love arises from passion.[82] One can initially see that disordered self-love can be psychologically very damaging, e.g. if one loves oneself to the detriment of relations with others, one is not able to conduct oneself in society or in family life without hurting others, which indirectly harms oneself. Unfortunately, in this regard, some modern psychologists have failed to realize that self love is not always good and this point has to be clearly understood if one is ever to achieve mental health. Those who promote "self-esteem" in certain ways actually end up harming their directees because they do not know how the good of the individual is to be approached so that they might not suffer disordered self-love (pride). The second defect is hatred of God, since He prohibits the actions which the person desires to pursue. This can be

---

[80]See ST II-II, q. 53, a. 6, ad 1. While St. Thomas makes these observations in regard to lust, they can be, *mutatis mutandis,* applied to other passions. It should be dawning on the psychologist that life according to the passions is damaging to the directee and must be avoided. Means to reduce passion must be counseled so as to provide the directee with the ability to overcome his disorder.

[81]ST II-II, q. 153, a. 5: "ex parte autem voluntatis, consequitur duplex actus inordinatus. Quorum unus est appetitus finis. Et quantum ad hoc, ponitur amor sui, quantum scilicet ad delectationem quam inordinate appetit, et per oppositum ponitur odium dei, inquantum scilicet prohibet delectationem concupitam."

[82]What constitutes ordered self-love shall be discussed in volume II. It is only within the wider spiritual context that true self-love can be fully discussed. While a full discussion of this requires spiritual principles, we can say from knowledge of the Natural Law and from conclusions derived from natural theology (i.e. what we can know about God purely through the natural light of reason without appeal to revealed theology) that only true self-love will be that which is in congruity with man's real good which is consummate with the following and fulfilling of the Natural Law.

discussed in light of the Natural Law, which will be left for another time.[83]

Regarding the means, St Thomas observes the following:

> Another, moreover, is of the appetite of those which are to the end. And with respect to this is posited love (*affectus*) of the present age (life), in which, namely, someone wills to enjoy pleasure, and through its opposite is posited desperation of the future age (life), since he is exceedingly detained by carnal delights, he does not care to obtain spiritual [goods or delights] but he loathes them.[84]

When the person leads a life of the appetites, the appetites are bound to the goods pursuable in this life and so the person begins to love this life or physical goods above and beyond spiritual goods. Finally, he learns to detest spiritual goods because they are arduous or do not give the movements of the appetites that bodily goods do. However, the difficulty with this is that mental health is not a bodily good, even though it can depend on bodily goods. Consequently, if an individual or society pursues the life of the appetites, it will lead to a decline in the immaterial goods which are proper to the intellect (i.e. truth) and the will (the universal and real good and not necessarily the particular bodily good). Moreover, he will not pursue the goods of the soul but only bodily goods and so virtues and the like will decline as concupiscence, ignorance and error increase. Therefore, psychologists cannot counsel directees to live life according to the appetites as it will lead to mental illness. The particular ways the life of the appetites affects the intellect and will as well as the appetites themselves finds an initial discussion in St. Thomas. Obviously, a great deal more will have to be done to analyze fully all of the various effects and defects disordered appetites cause.

V. The Ability of the Intellect and Will to Effect and Affect Appetite

In previous chapters, it was seen that the intellect and will have a capacity to affect the appetites, e.g. with anger, at times, the appetite awaits the judgment of reason before it is moved. We have already discussed how the possible intellect and will can reformulate the phantasm; since the appetites are moved by the phantasm in the imagination, the intellect can affect the appetites by affecting the image in the

---

[83]In volume II, a discussion of the final end of man, his happiness and God will provide a way of understanding the profound damage regarding one's mental health and illness, resulting from living a life of appetites, in light of this defect of hatred of God.

[84]ST II-II, q. 153, a. 5: "alius autem est appetitus eorum quae sunt ad finem. Et quantum ad hoc, ponitur affectus praesentis saeculi, in quo scilicet aliquis vult frui voluptate, et per oppositum ponitur desperatio futuri saeculi, quia dum nimis detinetur carnalibus delectationibus, non curat pervenire ad spirituales, sed fastidit eas."

imagination. It pertains, therefore, to this part of the chapter to discuss further aspects of this relation.

St. Thomas says, and common experience clearly demonstrates, that we do not have despotic[85] control over the passions or appetites as we do over the members of our bodies,[86] such as the arms or legs. With certain parts of our bodies, we have despotic control, which means that merely by willing them to move or act, they do so, e.g. if one wants to walk, he simply commands the arms and legs to move, and one walks. If one wants to look at something, he simply commands his head to move or his eyes to move and they move.[87] There are other faculties which we have no control over, such as the process of digestion which occurs in the stomach or the beating of one's heart,[88] as one cannot command one's heart when to beat and when not to beat.

With respect to the appetites, we do not have despotic control because they have something proper to them,[89] i.e. they have their own proper motion.[90] The appetites have specific goods which they pursue and evils which they avoid which are different from those pursued by reason and will. Since the appetites pursue their own object, when presented with the object they are inclined in a way which is independent of the motion of reason and will. Moreover, the faculties over which we have despotic control have no specific object of their own, such as the hand which can have as its object any physical thing. So it does not have a specific object toward which it is ordered and it does not resist reason, unlike the appetites, by pursuing the specific object toward which they are inclined by nature.

Yet, the appetites do obey reason,[91] as we see in the case of anger and even with the other passions, but we do not have direct control over them, only indirect control by means of the phantasm. For that reason, we are said to have political and regal control

---

[85]By despotic is meant that the faculty would have no capacity to resist the command of reason and will; see ST I, q. 81, a. 3, ad 2.

[86]ST I, q. 81, a. 3, ad 2; ST I-II, q. 9, a. 2, ad 3; ibid., q. 17, a. 7; ibid, q. 56, a. 4, ad 3; ibid, q. 58, a. 2; and De Vir., q. 1, a. 4, ad 11.

[87]This occurs, of course, provided there is not some material indisposition which is affecting the normal operations of the locomotive and other faculties.

[88]There are isolated instances where the person has some voluntary control over these functions but as a rule, one does not.

[89]ST I, q. 81, a. 3, ad 2 and ST I-II, q. 17, a. 7.

[90]De Vir., q. 1, a. 4 and ibid., ad 11. What this essentially means is that since they have their own proper motion and motion is specified by its object, then the passions have their own proper good or evil as a cause of their motion.

[91]ST I, q. 81, a. 3; De Ver., q. 25, a. 4; ST I-II, q. 24, a. 3; ibid., q. 42, a. 4; ibid., q. 46, a. 4; *De malo* q. 10, a. 1, ad 1.

over the passions.[92] This means that we do not have absolute control over the passions, but they do obey reason and are controlled indirectly by means of the phantasm[93] which is a form of persuasion. Since the appetites have a life of their own, so to speak, we must persuade them by presenting them their object or by denying them their object or by presenting the opposite in order to persuade them to do what we want. This is why we are said to have political control. Just as a king who does not have despotic control over his subjects must convince them to act a certain way by presenting them with reasons to do what he wants, so must the intellect and will present in the imagination that which will move the appetite in the direction that we want. This is called regal control insofar as we are able to guide the appetites in their motions by means of the interior and exterior senses and even to take on habits of inclination by repeated persuasion, so that we are able to build virtue and vice in them. This means that the appetites are trainable so as to incline either according to the order of reason or will or against reason and will.

Even though the appetites have their own good and can fight against reason, yet insofar as they are trainable, St. Thomas observes that the appetites are *naturally* ordered to obeying reason.[94] In other words, it is not contrary to the nature of the appetites to be trained and moved by reason and will. Insofar as they are moved by the imagination, they are ordered toward being moved by reason and will which moves the imagination.[95]

With regard to regal and political control of the appetites, St Thomas makes different observations about consequent and antecedent appetite. With respect to antecedent appetite, he observes that it is outside of the command of reason.[96] This we know from common experience in that sometimes passions arise over which we have no control. However, there are things which can be done to control antecedent appetite. The first concerns things extrinsic to the individual, viz. by vigilance, one may foresee what moves the appetite and avoid that object to avoid motion of the passion or to embrace the object so as to move the passion.[97] Obviously, the object which moves our passion is not always under our control,[98] but sometimes it is and so in order to guide the appetite one must be vigilant regarding the objects which move it.

---

[92]ST I, q. 81, a. 3, ad 2; ST I-II, q. 9, a. 2, ad 3; ibid., q. 17, a. 7; De Vir., q. 1, a. 4, ad 11.

[93]De Ver., q. 25, a. 3. In ibid., q. 25, a. 4, and ibid., ad 4, St. Thomas observes that we move an appetite by proposing its object to it.

[94]ST I, q. 81, a. 3, ad 2; ST I-II, q. 56, a. 4 and In Ethic. I, l. 20 (242).

[95]This position of St. Thomas is important as it denies the position that the appetites should never be inhibited or adversely affected by reason and that reason should serve the appetites rather than exercise regal control over them.

[96]ST I-II, q. 17, a. 7.

[97]ST I-II, q. 17, a. 7.

[98]ST I-II, q. 17, a. 7, ad 3.

However, antecedent appetite can be controlled interiorly in different ways. The first is by confirming or denying the motion of the passions. We can confirm the passions by willing the continuance of the presence of the object which moves them or by willing the continuance of the image in the imagination. We can deny the antecedent appetite by taking away the image which moves them by changing to another image. Moreover, we can repress them[99] or we can reformulate the image so as to change the movement of the passions and train them. This essentially consists in affecting the antecedent appetite by determining the consequent appetite, i.e. we can affect the appetite which occurs prior to reason, by reason and will affecting the image and thus affecting the consequent passion.

Regarding this affecting the passions consequently, St. Thomas has many observations to make. We have already seen this with anger and this also applies to other appetites as well, that reason can instigate[100] them by modifying the image by determining the *ratio* through judgment or by how the object is viewed in the phantasm. While reason can instigate passions, it can also mitigate them, for by changing the phantasm we can mitigate the passion, i.e. quiet the passion. We can also mitigate passions by universal considerations,[101] for by considering universal things, the imagination comes under the dominance of reason and therefore the object of the appetite is not present, resulting in a quieting of the appetites. As a result, abstract thought and meditation[102] can mitigate the passions.

Moreover, we can pursue the opposite or contrary objects and that will mitigate the passions. Now there are two kinds of opposite or contrary objects, viz. that which moves another passion and that which is merely the contrary of a passion but does not move another passion. For instance, we can, in order to mitigate anger which arises out of an evil object, pursue some good or engage some good which will bring delight and cause a change in the passions. As a general mechanism, this can work for all the passions, i.e. pursue the object of a different passion so as to reduce the other passion. However, as reason can train the appetites, they learn when and when-not to move regarding a given object. So if we confirm antecedent passion, we train the appetite that antecedent motion is acceptable whereas if we deny the passion and work against it, we train the appetite that motion is not to occur, i.e. it is not to move in the presence of that object. Now this must be kept in mind when mitigating one passion by means of another so as not to cause the rise of the other passion outside the control of reason. However,

---

[99]De Ver., q. 25, a. 4. St. Thomas obverses that repression consists in reason and will not allowing the appetite to execute the acts in order to arrive at the object of the passion. For Aquinas, this does not have a negative connotation as it does in modern psychology. A full discussion of this will be given in a subsequent chapter.

[100]ST I, q. 81, a. 3.

[101]ST I, q. 81, a. 3.

[102]For example, prayer and reflection.

when reason exercises control and virtue is had in the appetites, even when one's appetite is moved, it becomes trained not to move until reason confirms or denies the object. Antecedent appetite, as it is mitigated and virtue is obtained, ceases moving antecedently and awaits the movement of reason and will.

Another means of mitigating passion, as mentioned, is the contrary of the passion which is not the object of another passion; that is, by mortification.[103] Mortification comes from the Latin words *mors* and *facere* which literally mean "to make dead." Mortification is particularly effective for passions regarding the good, viz. love and delight, since it denies the appetites their object and sometimes presents their opposite, i.e. pain. Mortification which can be taken up voluntarily provides a great deal of control over the passions.[104] By pain and difficulties, the appetites do not move and become quiet because their opposite object is present. As the appetites quiet repeatedly, they become habituated in the cessation of motion and as a result are less "alive." The mortification, if irrational, can cause a great deal of harm, but if it proceeds by right reason, it can quiet all of the appetites, not just those concerned with the good. It can quiet anger because anger arises out of the pursuit of one's own good or damage caused to one's own good. But if one does not have an inordinate love of one's own good, then one will not become angry. Moreover, by reason and will pursuing mortification, they become stronger and so they are able to exercise more control over the appetites.[105] One last way to mitigate passion is by moving the exterior powers to engage an activity so that the appetites will engage the activity and change their motion.[106]

While some psychologists have promoted a life dominated by passion, sensuality or leading a life according to the appetites, it is inherently repugnant to reason.[107] This follows from the fact that as passions dominate, reason becomes eclipsed

---

[103]Theological aspects of this will be taken up in volume II.

[104]Mortification has a natural occurrence independently of the voluntary engagement in it. When we pursue an object of an appetite excessively due to some vice, nature herself administers the mortification, e.g. if one eats excessively, nature brings about pain so as to cause the appetite for food to wane. Alcoholism is another example insofar as when one abuses alcohol, the hangover moves the person not to drink. It is only by disordered reason, will and appetites that one can be mortified by nature herself and yet reject it and continue in the abusive action.

[105]Appetites are like children in a sense. If a child recognizes that its parents are weak, the child will do whatever it pleases. But if the parents are strong and rational, the child will obey so as not to be punished. With appetites, if reason and will are weak, the passions begin to dominate and become strong. If reason and will are strong, the appetites tend to remain quiet as reason exercises more control over the imagination and other powers which affect them.

[106]De Ver., q. 25, a. 4.

[107]De Ver., q. 25, a. 4, ad 2.

by judgment being affected, i.e. one becomes intellectually blind, confused, etc. Consequently, leading a life according to the appetites is detrimental to reason and will, whereas leading a life according to reason is good for the whole person. The good of man consists in reason because reason knows the universal good and all of the particular goods contained under that universal good.[108] In other words, the appetites only incline to their own objects which move them and, consequently, they are unable to see or know the goods which pertain to the other faculties as well as the whole of man. Only reason can know all of the goods as well as the universal good for man. Therefore, while the concupiscible appetite might be moved to food, reason knows that if the person eats a certain type of food, it will kill him, e.g. with diabetics and sugar. The good of man consists in reason as its root[109] and therefore the life of man must follow reason and not appetite. As a result, the perfection of man will consist in reason's political and regal control of the passions by moderating them[110] according to what reason sees is truly good for the individual. Denial of this is due either to ignorance, malice or blindness caused by appetite.[111]

Consequently, those who say that passions are completely bad, fail to understand that only passions that are not under the rule of reason are bad, i.e. passions, when they are not moderated or under the rule of right reason, are actually bad[112] for the individual: alcoholism is a sufficient example to show this is the case. When passions cease being moderated by reason, they become irrational and therefore are bad for the individual since he begins to act and think irrationally by being under the influence of those passions. On the other hand, not all passions are bad. Some passion is good[113] when it is moderated by reason since it aids in the execution of acts of reason, e.g. motion of the irascible appetite as controlled by reason (called fortitude) can aid one in

---

[108]See *De malo* q. 8, a. 3.

[109]ST I-II, q. 24, aa. 3-4.

[110]ST I-II, q. 24, a. 3.

[111]This observation is made to bring to light to psychologists the sources of denial of the principle that reason must be the ruler of the whole man. It is often due to ignorance, since many psychologists do not understand the constitution of man, nor does their experience yield this understanding since their experience must be judged in light of objective principles which they do not know. Due to problems of a lack of resolution of the appetites (see below), some psychologists have seen damage caused by those who tried to control their appetites. This is because they did not know what they were doing. Malice can also be a factor, though rare. Sometimes psychologists are blinded by their own passions and the fact that to control a passion or do something to bring it under control often brings pain and sorrow which they are unwilling to endure.

[112]ST I-II, q. 24, aa. 2-4. By bad, we mean morally bad as well as naturally and psychologically bad.

[113]ST I-II, q. 24, aa. 2-4 and ibid., q. 59, a. 2.

battle. Moreover, not all antecedent passion is bad but only that which inclines one contrary to reason. This follows from the fact that sometimes antecedent passion can incline reason toward the good, if it has been properly trained (i.e. if virtue resides in the appetite), e.g. a starving man may be offered food by his enemy and yet the passion will incline the person to accept the food, even though it is from the enemy because humiliation by one's enemy is not as bad of an evil as starvation.[114]

Yet, antecedent appetite of any kind, while it may be good, is inherently imperfect. This follows from the fact that the primary agents of motion within man must be reason and will and when antecedent appetite occurs, the appetite has a life of its own and is not perfectly subordinated to reason. After attaining a state of virtue in which one has antecedent appetite which is always ordered to reason, perfect appetite moves only consequently, i.e. perfect appetite is consequent appetite. Insofar as it moves independently of reason, it is not completely under the control of reason and therefore possesses a capacity to act contrary to reason if presented its object. Moreover, insofar as there is antecedent passion, there is a reduction in the freedom of the individual and voluntariness of the action, as was previously seen. But man desires perfect freedom and perfect freedom is consonant only with consequent appetite which obeys reason.[115]

This eliminates several errors. There are those who say any passion is evil, but that simply is not true as was seen from the aforesaid. It also eliminates the error of those who say that passions are *always* good. While antecedent appetite may be good, even then it is imperfect. It can also be bad if it goes contrary to reason and will. In this respect, many psychologists have confused the genus of morals and the genus of nature, i.e. they have failed to see that while all appetites and passions, insofar as they are in act, are good,[116] they are not necessarily morally good since that requires a separate judgment about their order and relation to reason.[117]

St. Thomas makes further observations which are very important for the science of mental health. He observes that sometimes the amount of control we have over the passions can be affected by our material disposition.[118] This is well known to psychiatry

---

[114]Here we are prescinding from other moral considerations which may affect this form of action, i.e. it is assumed that no moral evil is being committed when one is accepting the food.

[115]In relation to this, see II Sent., d. 25, q. 1, a. 2, ad 7.

[116]In the genus of nature, all appetites and passions are good. St. Thomas observes this in ST I-II, q. 24, a. 4.

[117]The fundamental problem here is to fail to make the metaphysical distinctions between ontological, natural and moral goods and evils.

[118]ST I-II, q. 17, a. 7.

in that, if the material disposition is ill affected, it could bring out different passions.[119] However, even though one may have a material disposition which prompts one to antecedent appetite, one is still able not to act upon that antecedent appetite. Since one has free will, one does not have to allow the execution of the actions associated with the passion. Psychologists must be particularly careful not to exculpate the behavior of directees based on antecedent appetite unless the appetite is so strong and the intellect and will so weak that they are acting involuntarily.

While reason and will should maintain moderation over the passions, it must be clear that it is not merely the control of reason and will that is good, but *right* control of reason and will over the passions. In other words, the appetites can end up failing in rectitude if reason and will fail.[120] This can be understood in two ways. First, appetites can go awry if reason and will simply fail to exercise control. Second, appetites can also fail if reason and will incline them toward the wrong things, even though they maintain control over them. For example, a Nazi SS officer may be able to control his appetites greatly, but if he inclines his appetite toward anger so as to murder others, that is evil. The point is that one must not only exercise control by reason and will, but he must do so by directing the appetites to their right end.

The next observation regards the strength of the imagination. If the imagination or cogitative powers are weak, it may become difficult to control the passions,[121] as it may be difficult to control the imagination. This weakness can come from several sources. It could be from material indisposition. It could be from a simple lack of maintaining control over the imagination and cogitative power which results in them taking on a life of their own. It could be from the vehemence of some object in the exterior senses. Moreover, it could be from a strong cogitative power which associates the wrong things with the phantasm or from a strong imagination which is unable to be moved by the will.

The last aspect of control over the appetites has to do with specific observations St. Thomas makes regarding the will's relation to the appetites. The appetites obey the will as a motive power,[122] and this is for several reasons. The first is that the will can

---

[119]Mood changes by women going through menopause which causes many chemical changes is a common example. Because women are more complex chemically than men, as a general rule, they tend to have more difficulty subordinating certain appetites. While the difficulties women have due to their chemical complexities have often had a negative connotation, the fact that their complexity is associated with the process of giving life should help society to recognize that women are being called upon to endure more difficulties at this level for the sake of the good of society.

[120]*Comm. De anima* III, l. 15 (826).

[121]See ST I-II, q. 17, a. 7.

[122]ST I, q. 81, a. 3; ST I-II, q. 42, a. 4; ibid., q. 46, a. 4; De Ver., q. 25, a. 4 and *De malo*, q. 3, a. 11.

move the imagination and other faculties which affect the passions.[123] The next, as St. Thomas notes, is that the vehemence of the act of the will redounds to the lower appetites.[124] This indicates that the motion of the will affects the other powers by moving them according to the strength of its own motion. So if the motion of the will is strong, it redounds to the faculties that are moved by the motion of the will. This is why understanding the immaterial faculties and their effect on the lower faculties is so important. Moreover, since the soul can only carry on in one intention at a time, when the will moves intently or with strength toward some object, the rest of the faculties are bound to or carried along in the action. Just as it happens when the passions are strong, reason and will find themselves bound or inclined to carry on in the motion of the passion. In connection to the soul's unity of intention, the species of the motion of the will can thereby determine the species of motion of the passions, i.e. the object of the motion of the will determines the kind of motion of not only the will, but also of the other faculties of the soul. Even when someone has a passion in one direction, if the will's motion in another direction is strong, the passion will find it difficult to continue and the appetites will be inclined toward the object of the will. This capacity of the will

---

[123]If chemical changes are associated with the passions, not only bodily but cerebrally, it would follow that through acts of volition one can alter the chemical disposition of the body and brain. This, of course, would take place indirectly by moving the various faculties which would have a short term chemical effect. However, if it is repeated and/or vehement enough, it could cause long term or possibly permanent chemical changes in the body and brain. This can be for the good or the bad. As the life of the appetites dominate, it can cause chemical imbalances, whereas life led according to right reason can lead to chemical balance. Psychiatry has spent a great deal of energy trying to figure out how to control the chemical operations of the brain when people suffer mental disorders. While this is a necessary endeavor and should be continued, there should be some research devoted toward learning how to re-balance the chemical operations by volitional acts. With some disorders, it may not be possible, but there may be some mental disorders which have a chemical imbalance component that can be corrected chemically by volitional acts rather than by drugs. This is not to diminish the value of drugs which help to restore chemical balance to the brain and body, but that research should be sought to establish those disorders which require medication and those which can be corrected through volition. This would apply not only to those chemical imbalances caused by the passions but also those chemical imbalances caused by operations of the interior senses. In other words, merely thinking the right things could have a chemical effect on the brain whereas thinking the wrong things could cause biochemical disorders. Again, it would pertain to the empirical science of psychiatry to ascertain to which disorders this would apply, even though philosophically, it can be seen that through acts of volition it is possible to change the biochemical disposition of the body and brain.

[124]ST I-II, q. 24, a. 3, ad 1; ibid, q. 30, a. 1, ad 1.

to move the passions in these various ways[125] indicates the power over the appetites and passions the will can have. In fact, St. Thomas goes so far as to say that the will can move appetites spontaneously.[126] By this can be meant that the will can move the appetites at will, so to speak, but it can also mean that the will can move the appetites without any preceding passion or presence of object, e.g. one can decide to start thinking about one's wife and move the concupiscibile passion to love without her or any antecedent appetite being present.

From the aforesaid, it can be seen that passion in the lower part is a sign of the species and intensity of the motion of the will.[127] What this means is that one can get a read on the will (though not perfectly since there can be a disparity between appetite and will) by looking at the passions or motions of the lower faculties. This follows, again, from the principle of operation. While the will can be affected by reason which is bound by passion, since the will has the quality of freedom, it can choose not to incline itself toward the object of passion.[128] In fact, the will can even choose to move the intellect away from the object of the passion, move it to make a judgment contrary to what it has and then move it to reformulate the image, thereby changing the passion.

Lastly, one can choose to affect a passion so that he can act more promptly,[129] e.g. during war time, moving speeches engage the irascible appetite to make the men more prompt to fighting. Man is moved more easily and promptly by choice than by passion.[130] We tend to be more inclined to do something if we have chosen to do it than if we have passion, e.g. someone who fights a passion which is inclining him to something is less likely to do it than if he has made the choice to do it. We know this

---

[125]Above, will was often included in the way reason moves the appetites but this should be understood according to a different modality, i.e. the way reason moves the passions is different than the way the will moves them. Nevertheless, they are often mentioned together as a result of the fact that they act in unison as the intellect moves the will and together they move the other faculties, i.e. the intellect by command and guiding, the will as a motive power in its act of use.

[126]De Ver., q. 26, a. 7. It would seem that several things would need to be in place in order for the will to move the passion almost at whim, i.e. the appetite would have virtue, be materially disposed and one would have to have a strong will.

[127]De Ver., q. 26, a. 7 and ibid., ad 1. These references refer to the intensity of action; the author has added the aspect of species to this observation.

[128]De malo, q. 3, a. 10, ad 2. What is implied here, as was mentioned in the discussion of voluntariness, is that the amount of freedom can be by degree depending upon a variety of factors, already discussed. Consequently, if there remains voluntariness in the will and the appetite does not completely blind the intellect and precipitate judgment, etc., then the will can refuse to be inclined toward the object of the passion.

[129]ST I-II, q. 24, a. 3, ad 1.

[130]De Ver., q. 26, a. 7.

from common experience, e.g. we try to persuade someone to do something but if that does not work, then we try to move him through fear or some other passion, but in this case he is less likely to act than if he has made the choice to do so. This follows from the fact that the will is the primary motive faculty in man and choice being the act of the will has a greater effect on man's motion than motions from secondary motive faculties.

Conclusion

The relationship of reason and will to the passions is somewhat complex. But a thorough understanding of the passions, how they affect each other, the intellect and will and how they move the inferior potencies provides a good foundation for discerning the source of the various passions or other motions of the soul by psychologists. The passions have been largely enigmatic to modern psychology because it has failed to understand the nature of the soul and consequently the relation of the various potencies or powers of the soul and how they affect one other. But as the good for man consists in reason, it pertains therefore to discuss how the appetites and other powers can participate in reason and this is done by means of habits and virtues.

Chapter 10: Habits, Virtues and Vices

Modern psychology has spent some time discussing habits but very little has been said about virtues. But it is difficult to understand whether habits are good or bad without a coherent understanding of virtues and vices and so it is important that psychology address the issues of habits, virtues and vices so as to determine whether they are good psychologically.

I. Habits

A habit is a determinate species of quality,[1] i.e. a disposition in which the subject of the habit is disposed well or badly[2] toward a specific object or operation. A disposition implies an order of something having parts[3] which means that man, who has a complex nature, has many parts and a disposition determines how those parts relate to each other, e.g. an appetite disposed well to the operations of reason indicates that the two parts (appetite and reason) have some order or relation to each other. A disposition is something easily changed[4] and by habituation one can change one's disposition toward some object or action. Sometimes a quality is a disposition, sometimes it is counter-distinguished from a disposition,[5] i.e. some qualities cannot be changed[6] while others which can be easily changed are called dispositions.

Habit, on the other hand, implies a certain hardness (*diuturnitas*),[7] i.e. a habit

---

[1]ST I-II, q. 49, aa. 1-2. Here, the term quality refers to a metaphysical category or predicament. Without a basis in metaphysics, it is difficult for modern psychologists to analyze seriously the various faculties, qualities, dispositions, etc., and so it is impossible to formulate a method of counsel for directees when they really do not know what the various faculties, etc., are. Therefore, modern psychology must have within its intellectual formation a consideration of basic metaphysical tenets.

[2]Aristotle, *Metaphysics* IV, 20 (1022b10); *Nicomachean Ethics*, V (1105b25).

[3]ST I-II, q. 49, a. 1, ad 3; ibid., q. 49, a. 2, ad 1.

[4]ST I-II, q. 49, a. 2, ad 3.

[5]Ibid.

[6]For example, the intellect in man is, among the categories of Aristotle, a quality but one cannot change oneself to eliminate the quality of the intellect, i.e. become a being without a possible intellect. But one can change the disposition within the possible intellect through knowledge.

[7]ST I-II, q. 49, a. 2, ad 3.

199

is something difficult to change and common experience tells us this.[8] A habit also implies an ordering to action,[9] i.e. habits have a fundamental relationship or imply a relation to action. Moreover, since operation is the end of nature,[10] habit implies an ordering to the nature of the thing as to whether it suits that nature or not, e.g. man who has the faculty of speech may have bad habits, e.g. stuttering or something of this sort, and so that habit does not suit man because it does not suit his faculty of speech. Consequently, habits reside in powers as their subject,[11] i.e. they reside in the faculties which have the capacity to act. But not just any faculty is capable of having habits; if a faculty or power is determined to one action or one object, there cannot be habits,[12] e.g. the faculty of sight has as its object the visible only and so we cannot habituate the faculty of sight. Rather a habit occurs when a faculty or power can be disposed or related in many ways to one object or the one faculty can relate differently to many objects.[13] A single faculty is able to have many habits when many different objects can move the same power.[14] This is why people may have a disorder in a faculty with respect to one object but not to others, e.g. one can have a psychological (intellectual) disorder with respect to open spaces (agoraphobia) but not to closed spaces (claustrophobia).

---

[8]A habit is a disposition of the faculty which is hard to change which is different than an initial disposition of a faculty towards certain kinds of action, e.g. when someone is born, they have specific dispositions towards certain actions but those dispositions can be changed through the contacting of habits. For example, someone may have a natural disposition toward eating excessively, but the person can train their concupiscible appetite through habituation not to incline to eating excessively.

[9]ST I-II, q. 49, a.3.

[10]Ibid. What this means is that every created thing has two (metaphysical) acts, i.e. first act and second act. The first act is the act of existence in which a thing exists. But existence is not the full perfection of a thing, rather its operations or second acts in which it does something are its final perfection. This can easily be seen in the example of a car; the fact that the car exists is good but if it does not function, it is not perfect, only when it can perform its various functions or acts is it considered perfect. Moreover, a car is not designed to merely exist, rather the end of the vehicle, the reason for which it was made, is so that it can perform its second act which is to transport someone from point A to point B. Natural substances are the same way; a dog may exist, but if it cannot bark or walk it is not perfect and the nature of a dog is ordered toward being able to perform those actions and so the perfection or end of that nature is to perform those actions.

[11]ST I-II, q. 49, a. 3.

[12]ST I-II, q. 49, a. 4, ad 2.

[13]ST I-II, q. 49, a. 4 and ibid., ad 1 and 2.

[14]ST I-II, q. 54, a. 1.

No habit is principally in the body as a subject,[15] but it is principally in the soul and only secondarily in the body.[16] This follows from the fact that the faculty is rooted in the soul even though it operates through a bodily organ. Consequently, the habit is principally in the power in the soul[17] even though the body can be disposed and must be disposed[18] toward the operations of the soul and particularly of the specific habit. We also know that those sensitive powers which act out of instinct have no habits, but only those under the command of reason,[19] e.g. certain motor functions cannot be habituated while those under the command of reason can; if a doctor hits someone with a rubber hammer in the right location, the person's leg moves without volitional control and one cannot habituate reflex actions. However, one can habituate one's motor faculties regarding art, such as playing a piano, etc.[20] This means if habits occur only in those powers over which one has rational control, then animals, strictly speaking do not have habits. However, animals can participate in the reason of man insofar as man can train an animal[21] and thereby impose rational form on the operations of an animal.[22]

Habits cannot be in the exterior senses since they are determined in their actions.[23] St. Thomas observes in one place that the interior senses, since they are moved by reason, can be the subject of habits.[24] We know this through our own experience insofar as our memory has the habit of recalling certain things and our cogitative power has a tendency to associate certain things in certain ways because it is habituated that way. Habits can be in the appetites since they are able to be moved by reason. Moreover, habits are able to be in the will[25] since it is moved by reason and is capable

---

[15]ST I-II, q. 50, a. 1.

[16]Ibid. and ST I-II, q. 50, a. 2.

[17]Ibid.

[18]ST I-II, q. 50, a. 1.

[19]ST I-II, q. 50, a. 3.

[20]Strictly speaking there are not habits in the exterior members but in the powers which move them (ST I-II, 56, a. 3, ad 3) yet one can dispose one's exterior members toward the operations of those powers which move them.

[21]ST I-II, q. 50, a. 3, ad 2.

[22]Some might argue that an animal can contract habits on its own, e.g. a deer may get in the "habit" of following a certain path through the woods. This is true only insofar as God moves the animal through its nature and so if an animal gains a specific way of doing something independently of man it is through the intellect of God directing the thing through its nature.

[23]ST I-II, q. 50, a. 3, ad 3.

[24]Ibid.

[25]ST I-II, q. 50, a. 5.

of different dispositions to many different things. Finally, habits can be in the possible intellect as well.[26]

Everything that is moved (such as passive powers) is disposed by the act of the agent (the active powers)[27] and so the powers which are moved by reason, i.e. those which are capable of having habits, are disposed according to the act of the intellect. Since habits and their acts are distinguished by their objects,[28] the object of reason or the intellect which moves the various faculties will determine the species of the habit in that passive power. We know this through our own experience, e.g. a person can habituate his concupiscible appetite to liking chocolate by presenting it to the appetite as a good to be pursued and so the person can develop the habit of eating too much chocolate. Yet, the person may not have any difficulty eating other things in moderation. Moreover, because reason has presented the chocolate under the species of the good to the concupiscible appetite, that appetite gains a habit of inclining toward the chocolate or desiring it because it is informed by reason that it is good and so later when it thinks of good things it wants, it is inclined to seek chocolate since it is habituated that way.

This also brings to the fore the fact that habits are caused by repeated actions, i.e. it takes many acts to develop a habit.[29] This follows from the fact that the intellect (reason) cannot overcome the appetitive powers in single act, i.e. it cannot cause the quality of the habit in single act.[30] However, a habit can be augmented, decreased or corrupted due to the fact that the quality of habit can be received by the power according to degrees.[31] We know from common experience that sometimes we are more habituated with respect to one thing but not with respect to another, e.g. a person may notice that when he was younger his habit of eating excessively was stronger than when he was older. Smokers often find that in the beginning their habit was not as strong as it was subsequently.[32] The augmentation or diminuation of a habit is not by addition or

---

[26]ST I-II, q. 50, a. 4, and ibid., ad 1. This was initially discussed regarding intellectual memory but, as will be seen later on, there is a difference between habits in the sense of intellectual memory and habits with respect to intellectual virtues.

[27]ST I-II, q. 51, aa. 2 and 3.

[28]ST I-II, q. 54, aa. 1 and 2.

[29]ST I-II, q. 51, a. 2.

[30]ST I-II, q. 53, a. 3. With respect to the possible intellect, the habit of science is able to be caused from one act of reason even though this is not possible with the other powers (see ibid).

[31]ST I-II, q. 52, a. 1.

[32]Obviously some habits are easier to contract and maintain because of the habit's change of disposition in the body, e.g. in smoking, the intake of nicotine disposes the body more toward the habit of smoking. It should be observed, therefore, that those habits which have a chemical counterpart, the chemical counterpart is merely dispositional, even though

subtraction of the form of the habit, but a more or less perfect participation in the form of the habit.[33] What this means is that when one performs the same act and begins to build up the habit, one does not say one has "five" habits of fortitude, rather one says one has one habit of fortitude according to a certain degree.[34]

Obviously, this means that similar acts increase the habit, i.e. the species of the act corresponds to the species of habit which it increases.[35] Clearly, if one repeatedly strokes one's beard, one does not develop the habit of smoking but the habit of beard stroking. The augmentation and diminuation of a habit is based upon the acts which affect it. If the act is more intense than the habit, then there is an increase in the habit;[36] if the act is less intense than the habit, it decreases the habit; if the act is equal to the habit, then the habit is maintained; lack of use of the habit causes a decrease in the habit.[37] The diminuation and corruption[38] of a habit is caused by its contrary.[39] With respect to those habits of moral virtue, if one does not exercise acts to maintain or increase the moral virtues that pertain to the appetites, antecedent and inordinate passions will rise or come again.[40] From a psychological perspective, the aforesaid can greatly aid the directee in building, maintaining and diminishing habits. Finally, as can

---

it may be very strong. To actually have the habit, the bodily disposition is not enough, e.g. certain narcotics are known for their powerful qualities to draw one into habituation. Some dispose the body to such a degree that a single use can greatly incline the individual to the habit but the habit still requires repeated acts.

[33]ST I-II, q. 52, a. 2.

[34]In philosophy, this distinction is referred to as a difference between numeric increase (i.e. an increase of number of discrete units) and an increase of degree of participation of the form (i.e. the same form had more or less).

[35]ST I-II, q. 52, a. 3.

[36]These four are delineated in ST I-II, q. 52, a 3.

[37]See ST I-II, q. 53, a. 3.

[38]By corruption is meant the going out of existence of some thing.

[39]ST I-II, q. 53, a. 3. The contrary can be either the contrary object or the contrary act of the habit. With respect to the act, one can give the example of someone who has the habit of eating excessively: he can corrupt the habit of gluttony by fasting. With respect to the object, one can give the example of someone who fosters evil in the will by hating: he can foster good in the will (by loving). Acts are also determined by the object, e.g. throwing a baseball 90 feet over a plate can be a good pitch, but throwing a person over the plate may be bad. Both are acts of throwing but the objects which are thrown make the acts very different and, consequently, the same act with different objects can actually foster different habits. The same act with opposite objects can actually have opposing habits, e.g. speaking the truth and speaking the false have opposing habits to which they correspond.

[40]ST I-II, q. 53, a. 3.

be seen from the aforesaid, habits and their acts are distinguished according to their objects.[41]

Those habits which are gained through action are called acquired habits.[42] Acquired habits are different from what are sometimes called natural habits.[43] The first kind of natural habits are those that are natural according to the species, i.e. every person has them. These refer to the habits previously delineated with respect to the first principles of speculative reason. It also refers to the habits with respect to the first principles of practical reason.[44] The second kind are not really habits, even though, at times, they are referred to as habits and those are the natural habits of the individual. Strictly speaking, there are no natural habits of the individual, nor are there any initial habits in the appetitive faculties. However, one individual can have a better disposed body or organ toward a specific habit. Again, this is not a real habit but a disposition, e.g. those who have a better disposed brain are better disposed toward operations of the habit of science. Sometimes, people have a natural disposition toward affability but the actual habit of affability comes through acting according to the disposition. Most people act according to their bodily dispositions because it is easier. It is more arduous to act contrary to a bodily disposition, but this is necessary since not all bodily dispositions are toward good habits and so it is necessary to overcome the natural disposition and dispose the body to its contrary good habit.

Finally, St. Thomas makes some observations about intellectual habits which are important to the science of mental health. We have already seen some discussion with respect to intellectual memory, where the agent intellect causes the form in the possible intellect which causes a type of "habit." When the possible intellect understands the same object repeatedly, a habit is built up. St. Thomas observes that habits which are caused immediately by the agent intellect in the possible intellect are incorruptible *per se* and *per accidens*.[45] They are incorruptible *per se* in that the possible intellect is incorruptible since it is an immaterial accident and cannot suffer corruption like something material. Second, they are not corruptible *per accidens*, as when a habit is said to be corrupted in a faculty which operates through a corporal organ when the corporal organ is corrupted. Other habits in the possible intellect cannot be corrupted *per se* for the same reasons as just mentioned. However, they can be corrupted *per accidens*, i.e. by corrupting the interior senses upon which the exercise of the acts of the intellect depends, e.g. someone who suffers a stroke may not be able to

---

[41]ST I-II, q. 54, aa. 1 and 2.

[42]Acquired habits (virtues and vices) are often counter-distinguished from infused habits; these types of habits shall be discussed in volume II.

[43]The following topic is discussed in ST I-II, q. 51, a. 1.

[44]See the next chapter on the Natural Law.

[45]ST I-II, q. 53, a. 1.

exercise the habit of a particular science. Moreover, habits of the possible intellect can be corrupted by their opposite, viz. by contrary conclusions to that of science and by false reasoning which corrupts true opinion or science.[46] Hence, intellectual habits can be corrupted by judgment[47] and ratiocination.[48] Finally, intellectual habits can diminish when not used. St. Thomas affirms this

> . . . on the part of intellectual habits, insofar as a man is prompt to judging rightly of the imagined. Therefore, since man ceases the use of the intellectual habit, foreign images arise and sometimes lead him to the contrary; so that, unless he frequently uses the intellectual habit, in a certain way they are killed or compromised, the man is rendered less apt to judging rightly, and sometimes is totally disposed to the contrary.[49]

When a person does not use his intellectual habits, over the course of time, foreign images enter the imagination and the habits which are caused by judgment are diminished or corrupted by opposite judgments of the foreign phantasms. Consequently, it is necessary to use the intellectual habits frequently to maintain them.

II. Virtues and Vices in General

Sometimes the term habit can take on a negative connotation, but there are some habits that are good and there are some that are bad. Good habits are called

---

[46]Ibid.

[47]Ibid.

[48]This is extremely important for psychology. Someone can arrive at the truth but through false reasoning begin to develop bad habits in the intellect. Moreover, passion can corrupt judgment which in turn can corrupt the habits in the possible intellect.

[49]ST I-II, q. 53, a. 3: ". . . ex parte habituum intellectualium, secundum quos est homo promptus ad recte iudicandum de imaginatis. Cum igitur homo cessat ab usu intellectualis habitus, insurgunt imaginationes extraneae, et quandoque ad contrarium ducentes; ita quod, nisi per frequentem usum intellectualis habitus, quodammodo succidantur vel comprimantur, redditur homo minus aptus ad recte iudicandum, et quandoque totaliter disponitur ad contrarium."

virtues[50] and bad habits are called vices.[51] Since virtues and vices are habits, the preceding observations about habits also apply to virtues and vices. Because a virtue is a good habit, it implies a perfection[52] of the faculty [53] in which it resides.[54] Virtues (and vices) are operative habits[55] which help (or hinder) the faculty in its operations,

---

[50]ST I-II, q. 55, aa. 1 and 3 and In Ethic., II, l. 5 (305). Regarding the virtues, a reading of St. Thomas' two works *Quaestiones Disputatae de Virtutibus in Commune* and *Quaestiones Disputatae de Virtutibus Cardinalibus* is highly recommended. Many of the other observations made regarding virtues and vices as well as habits are also discussed in these two works but in somewhat greater detail than is afforded here.

[51]ST I-II, q. 55, a. 4.

[52]ST I-II, q. 55, a. 3.

[53]ST I-II, q. 56, a. 1.

[54]Virtues, which are good habits, have as their subject (i.e. that in which they exist) the various powers of the soul; see ST I-II, q. 56, a. 1. Again, they would reside in those faculties which are under the control of reason. Insofar as a virtue has as its subject the faculties of the soul which exist in the soul, they are accidents of accidents (see ST I-II, q. 56, a. 1, ad 3): "unum accidens dicitur esse in alio sicut in subiecto, non quia accidens per seipsum possit sustentare aliud accidens, sed quia unum accidens inhaeret substantiae mediante alio accidente, ut color corpori mediante superficie; unde superficies dicitur esse subiectum coloris. Et eo modo potentia animae dicitur esse subiectum virtutis." ["One accident is said to be in another as in a subject, not because an accident in itself is able to sustain another accident, but because one accident adheres to the substance mediating the other accident, as the color of the body mediating the surface; hence surfaces are said to be the subject of color. And in this way the power of the soul is said to be the subject of virtue."] One of the distinctions in scholastic philosophy which is helpful in understanding the nature of virtues as they reside in faculties is the distinction between the types of matter. The *materia ex qua* or "matter out of which" refers to the actual physical matter out of which something is made, e.g. a statue is made out of bronze; this type of matter does not apply to virtues. The *materia in qua* or the "matter in which" refers to that in which something resides, e.g. color has as it matter the substance of the man, so a man who has blond hair, the substance of the man or the hair is that matter in which the color of blond resides. Virtues have as their *materia in qua* the powers of the soul. The *materia circa quam* or the "matter about which" refers to the object or thing about which some faculty or virtue concerns itself. So the *materia circa quam* of the faculty of hearing is the "audible." Virtues are determined with respect to the *materia circa quam* and the faculty in which they reside, e.g. virtues in the concupiscible appetites deal with bodily goods. For a discussion of this distinction in relation to virtues, see ST I-II, q. 55, a 4.

[55]ST I-II, q. 55, a. 2. An operative habit is one which is ordered toward action and it is counter distinguished from an entitative habit. An entitative habit is one which can be increased through action but does not aid in the operations of the faculty, e.g. sanctifying grace is called an entitative habit because through action it can be increased or lost in the

which is why a virtue (or vice) is called a perfection (or imperfection). When a habit is a mode suited to the nature of the thing, then it has the notion of the good, i.e. it is a virtue.[56] Contrariwise, when a habit does not suit the nature of a thing, then it has the notion of the bad, i.e. it is a vice.[57]

The faculties in which virtues reside are either the will or in some faculty which is moved by the will.[58] This means that virtues are caused, strictly speaking, only voluntarily, i.e. virtues fall under the domain of the voluntary. Someone who does not know what he is doing does not build virtue. The reader may notice that above it was indicated that habits existed in faculties which were under the control of reason. If virtues are good habits, why then does St. Thomas say virtues are those over which one has *volitional* control? There is no real problem here in that one does not truly have volitional control over something unless one has rational control over it, for the will is moved by the intellect so if one has volitional control, one also has control by the intellect.[59] St. Thomas appears to emphasize that virtues come from volitional control to stress the fact that virtues are with respect to the good of the faculty, whereas habits are notionally indeterminate. Moreover, St. Thomas is likely stressing the volitional control to indicate that many of the virtues are in the domain of morality.[60]

The other powers which are under the volitional control are the possible intellect, the appetites and the passive intellect. St. Thomas observes that there are virtues in the possible intellect[61] but not, properly speaking, in the passive intellect or the four interior senses. He notes that Aristotle observes that there are habits in the passive intellect and Tullius says that there are virtues in the interior senses. However, St. Thomas explains that:

---

soul; yet it does not move the faculties to perform specific functions. The discussion of sanctifying grace shall be covered in volume II.

[56]ST I-II, q. 49, a. 2 and ibid., q. 49, a. 3.

[57]Ibid.

[58]ST I-II, q. 56, aa. 3 and 6.

[59]Here the issues of the distinctions of the acts of command in the intellect and use of the will are of prime importance. The intellect commands the act which builds up the virtue and in so doing moves the will to the act of use of the faculty which actually brings it about. The intellect must guide the action which brings about the virtue and this, again, is done through command.

[60]An act is said to be moral insofar as it proceeds from "deliberate will," i.e. it proceeds from intellectual judgment and freewill. While the topic of morality has not been discussed much in this text, the reader should be aware that once freewill is involved, one enters the domain of morality. Consequently, psychological matters have a relation to morality.

[61]ST I-II, q. 56, a. 3.

a virtue is a perfect habit which consists only in acting well; hence it is necessary that the virtue is in that power which is the final good of the act. Knowledge of the truth, moreover, is not consummated in the sensitive apprehensive powers, but in this way the powers are as if preparatory to the intellective knowledge. And therefore in this way, the virtues are not in these powers, by which the true is known, but more in the intellect or reason.[62]

While one can say there are habits in the four interior senses, they are not virtues properly so-called. The reason is that a virtue is capable of bringing about the final act of the power, but the acts of the interior senses are not complete in themselves insofar as they provide the data for abstraction and intellectual knowledge. Hence, the virtues are, properly speaking, in the possible intellect and not in the passive intellect. While we can say that the habits in the passive intellect are good, that good is always in reference to the operations of the possible intellect or the appetites and so they are not fully virtues.[63] On the other hand, the importance of good habits in the passive intellect is pivotal to mental health and illness.

The other faculties which are capable of virtues in the proper sense are the appetites, for virtues are in the appetites insofar as they participate in reason and not insofar as they are sensitive powers as such.[64] These powers participate in reason insofar as they are moved by reason, insofar as they receive formation or the formality of the object proposed by reason, or insofar as they obey reason.[65] Hence, an appetite is rational because reason imposes its form on the appetite[66] and insofar as the appetite does not obey reason or acts contrary to reason, it is irrational. Since reason can move the appetites by proposing its object, we can say that they are good insofar as they are disposed to be moved by reason, for a moved power is perfect or good insofar as it is

---

[62]ST I-II, q. 56, a. 5: "virtus enim est habitus perfectus, quo non contingit nisi bonum operari, unde oportet quod virtus sit in illa potentia quae est consummativa boni operis. Cognitio autem veri non consummatur in viribus sensitivis apprehensivis; sed huiusmodi vires sunt quasi praeparatoriae ad cognitionem intellectivam. Et ideo in huiusmodi viribus non sunt virtutes, quibus cognoscitur verum; sed magis in intellectu vel ratione."

[63]This will become clearer when the nature of mental health and illness are delineated. It is interesting to note that historically philosophy has named virtues pertaining to the possible intellect but not the passive intellect.

[64]ST I-II, q. 56, a. 4 and In Ethic I, l. 20 (nn. 239 and 242).

[65]Actually all three of these are the same; for insofar as the appetite obeys reason it receives the formality of the object proposed by reason and it is thereby informed or formed by reason.

[66]In Ethic., II, l. 1 (n. 249).

disposed toward the motion of the moving power and virtues are in the appetites as they are conformed to and moved by reason.[67]

It is important that the power which guides the individual and determines what is good, i.e. that which is to be pursued, is reason. For only reason knows both the universal good for the individual as well as the particular good in the concrete. Since reason knows all of the goods and the universal good to which the whole of the individual must be subordinated, only it knows the actions and objects which lead to it and therefore what should and should not be done. If one leads a life according to the appetites, the real good of the individual will be compromised since the appetites only know the good toward which they are ordered and not the universal good. But reason knows the universal good of the individual and, therefore, it knows if the good that pertains to the individual faculty should be pursued or not. Furthermore, reason knows the particular good in the concrete, insofar as it knows whether the good of the faculty should be pursued here and now. For instance, the concupiscible appetite may desire chocolate which contains sugar, but if the person is a diabetic, he ought not eat the chocolate. The fact that he should not eat the chocolate is known by reason and not the concupiscible appetite; so the particular good in the concrete is only fully or truly known by reason and, therefore, for the good of the individual and even for the good of the appetite itself, man must be guided by reason.[68]

Virtues in the appetites dispose one toward good action[69] which is very important since most people act according to their disposition. If one has disposed oneself toward the good by building virtues in one's appetites, it actually aids one in doing good. In maintaining psychological health, as in the moral life, it is important to build virtues so as to be able to act well. Those who suffer vice and give in to the prompting of vice make it more difficult to do the good and therefore make it difficult to lead a psychologically healthy life. Those who have encouraged directees to give into the appetites have, therefore, caused serious harm to their directees. While it will be difficult for the directees and, at times, seem almost impossible, psychologists must counsel their directees to build virtue so as to make the psychological life easier. Since vices dispose one toward bad action, a psychologist must never counsel the directee

---

[67]ST I-II, q. 56, a. 4 and In Ethic., II, l. 4 (n. 286).

[68]This is not to say that the appetites are bad in themselves or that they should be totally ignored. For instance, someone who is rather cerebral may ignore his appetite's desire for food and starve himself to death. If the appetites are ordered by right reason, they can actually lead to the good of the individual, for the good which the appetites pursue are real goods and so reason should take those real goods into consideration in the universal good of the individual. By nature, man will, thereby, not totally ignore the good of the appetites but he will reserve the judgment of whether the good is actually to be pursued according to the judgment of the truth and not the desire of the faculty *per se*.

[69]ST I-II, q. 56, a. 4.

toward action which will build up vice.

III. Virtues in Particular

As we have completed a cursory discussion of virtues and vices, it is now important to discuss very briefly the various virtues which affect mental health and illness.[70] As the faculties are in a hierarchy,[71] it would benefit the discussion to start with those which are the highest and proceed to those which are the lowest and, for that reason, we shall begin with the intellectual virtues and end with the moral virtues.[72]

A. The Intellectual Virtues

There are three intellectual virtues, viz. understanding, science and wisdom.[73] Intellectual virtues perfect the intellect in understanding or judging the true or truth.[74] The first intellectual virtue is *intellectus* or understanding. Understanding is the virtue[75] by which one considers self-evident principles[76] or grasps the principles immediately.[77] The second intellectual virtue is *scientia* or science, sometimes called knowledge. Here knowledge does not refer to its other meaning which is the known being in the knower. Rather it refers to the virtue by which one knows those things that are knowable in a specific genus.[78] It is the virtue by which one is able to judge those things which pertain to a specific genus, e.g. someone who has the science of biology (biology being the genus) is able to look at a cell and judge the things in the cell and thereby grasp the thing

---

[70]The vices will not be discussed at length as they are the negation or the opposite of the virtues. However, it would behoove the psychologist to have a detailed knowledge of the virtues and vices as delineated in the *Secunda Secundae* of the *Summa Theologiae* and the various *Quaestiones Disputatae* on the particular virtues.

[71]For the fact that the faculties are in hierarchy, see ST I, q. 77, a. 4.

[72]Here we are discussing those which are highest in the order of nature and therefore this tract will prescind from the discussion of the theological virtues which will be discussed in volume II.

[73]ST I-II, q. 57, a. 2.

[74]ST I-II, q. 57, aa. 1-2.

[75]The term "understanding" as the virtue should not be confused with the first act of the possible intellect in which one grasps the essence of a thing.

[76]These are the first principles, such as the principle of non-contradiction, the principle of identity, etc.

[77]ST I-II, q. 57, aa. 1-2. A self-evident principle is one in which once the terms are grasped, the truth of the proposition is immediately known as true.

[78]ST I-II, q. 57, a. 2.

judged. Another person is able to see the same cell, and if he does not have the science of biology, he is unable to see intellectually or judge the cell in the same way and therefore does not know the same things about the cell as someone with the virtue. Science proceeds by *inquisitio*[79] or inquiry, which is a formal method of proceeding by which one starts with first principles or things first known and proceeds to conclusions about those things known. Consequently, science helps one to judge, by means of drawing conclusions, the natures of things in a specific genus. One can conclude that there are as many sciences as there are genera of objects and so even if one has the virtue of *scientia* pertaining to one genus of things, he does not necessarily have the virtue with respect to other genera of things.[80]

The highest intellectual virtue is that which considers the highest causes of things.[81] As wisdom considers the highest causes, as well as causality itself, it pertains to the virtue of wisdom to judge and order all of the other sciences. This follows from the fact that one cannot have perfect and universal judgment about the things open to natural investigation through the other sciences without going back to the first causes.[82] Because wisdom considers the highest causes in the most universal fashion, only it can judge the other sciences as to what their subject matter should be as well as which method of inquiry is proper to it. This is why metaphysics, which is the study of being and causality in the most abstract way and which is a branch of philosophy, is the inquiry of the virtue of wisdom. Therefore, only those with metaphysical training are in a place to judge the other sciences as to their method of proceeding and as to their subject matter; for only they know the causes of things in a way proportionate to knowing whether a science is inquiring in a way proportionate to the thing studied. This is why it pertains to metaphysics to judge whether psychology and psychiatry are proceeding

---

[79]ST I-II, q. 57, a. 2. The process of inquiry also applies to wisdom but in a different way.

[80]This is very important because very often those who have doctorates in one field believe themselves to be competent to draw conclusions in another field, e.g. psychologists or medical doctors making statements about the science of morality or ethics, or those who study astrophysics making philosophical/metaphysical statements. Each aspect of the virtue of science which pertains to each genus must be studied separately. However, it should be noted that as the intellect becomes disposed to judge in a refined fashion by means of science in one field, it does make it easier to judge in genera which are closely related and therefore it makes it easier to expand one's knowledge when one already knows a great deal about a related field.

[81]ST I-II, q. 57, a. 2 and ST I-II, q. 66, a. 5. The highest form of wisdom is that which considers the highest cause of all, which shall be discussed in volume II.

[82]ST I-II, q. 57, a. 2.

in a way which is proportionate to their objects.[83] Moreover, the virtue of wisdom is also important as it is the virtue by which one orders one's life regarding actions; for only by the virtue of wisdom does one know the highest causes of things and therefore the hierarchy of things. Consequently, the more foolish[84] a society becomes, the less will its scientific inquiry and societal life proceed by wisdom, which directs things to their highest end.

B. The Moral Virtues

There are four moral virtues, viz. prudence, justice, fortitude and temperance. Prudence is defined as right reason concerning action.[85] Prudence is the virtue in which right reason is used to judge what should be done. There is a difference between doing (*agere*) and making (*facere*)[86] in that doing pertains to the actions which are primarily immanent to man, i.e. the effect of the action primarily pertains to some perfection or imperfection of the person. To make implies the effect of the action is transient since it terminates outside the agent and this is why "to make" refers to art. Art is the application of the action of a person for the bringing about of change in something exterior to the individual.[87] Consequently, art pertains to making, while prudence concerns action (doing)[88] and it therefore concerns the perfection of the individual, since the effect remains in the individual. Since to live well consists in acting well,[89] prudence is necessary to live well.

Prudence resides in the possible intellect but it is not listed as an intellectual virtue but a moral one because it guides or directs the other moral virtues.[90] Moreover, the matter or object (action) of prudence makes it a moral virtue rather than an

---

[83] As a science is defined as an organized body of knowledge of things through their causes, only metaphysics can say whether the method actually gets to the knowledge of the causes since only it has a perfect and universal grasp of the nature of causes and things which they cause.

[84] The opposite vice of wisdom is foolishness, see ST II-II, q. 46.

[85] ST I-II, q. 57, a. 2. In Quod., XIII, q. 15, a. un., St. Thomas uses this same definition for moral virtue in general and it may be used insofar as every moral virtue is the application of right reason to the matter of the virtue. However, it is more proper to prudence due to the subject in which the virtue of prudence adheres.

[86] ST I-II, q. 57, a. 2.

[87] Art here would encompass anything which produces some thing or product. Hence it would include everything from painting or sculpting to products of technology, etc.

[88] ST I-II, q. 57, a. 2.

[89] ST I-II, q. 57, a. 5.

[90] ST I-II, q. 58, a. 2, ad 1 and 3.

intellectual one.[91] Intellectual and moral virtues are distinguished[92] according to their matter and, as we have seen, the matter of prudence is action, while the matter of the intellectual virtues is truth. Consequently, the intellectual virtues perfect the cognitive faculties which know the truth whereas moral virtues perfect the appetitive faculties which concern action.[93] Yet virtues, which are habits, only perfect an appetitive power insofar as they fall under election,[94] i.e. free choice, for one does not develop a habit over those things which fall outside the voluntary. Moreover, since election concerns the means or action which helps one arrive at the end, the moral virtues have primarily to do with the means, even though they require rectitude regarding the end.[95] Prudence which pertains to actions concerns the means and for this reason, prudence is defined as the virtue by which one knows the means to attain the end.[96] This also means that prudence has a connection to three other virtues. While the act of prudence consists in commanding the right action,[97] before one can command the right action, other acts precede command and so prudence has a connection to other virtues which govern those acts which precede command. The first is the act of counsel which concerns the means and the virtue which governs the act of counsel is eubulia, which is the virtue of good counsel. Next regarding judgment of the means, there are two virtues which are necessary. The first is synesis which is the virtue which governs judgment about actions which fall under the common law,[98] e.g. the law that one ought not lie and so one can judge whether lying falls under that common law. The other virtue is gnome which helps one to judge whether actions should or should not be done based on the fact that

---

[91]ST I-II, q. 58, a. 3.

[92]St. Thomas discuss this in ST I-II, q. 58, a. 2.

[93]The appetites concern not only objects but action. The irascible appetite specifically concerns action in order to arrive at the good or avoid the evil. The concupiscible appetite has as its object the good but the object of the appetites require action in order to be obtained. Moreover, intellective appetite (will) moves the other faculties to action and so appetites concern action.

[94]ST I-II, q. 58, a. 1.

[95]Obviously, if one pursues the wrong things, he will perform actions which are bad and in the psychological sphere, if one does not pursue the right ends, it will cause damage to the various faculties, including the intellect and appetites.

[96]ST II-II, q. 47.

[97]ST II-II, q. 47, a. 8. St. Thomas observes that it is not enough to know the means to the end, to be truly prudent one must also command them. Obviously, we would say someone was foolish who knew the best thing to do but commanded something bad. Consequently, prudence governs the act of command of the intellect.

[98]The discussion of law shall be done in the subsequent chapter. These three virtues and their connection to prudence is discussed in ST I-II, q. 57, a. 6.

they do not fall under the common law.[99] These three virtues came up in the discussion in the previous chapter. Without these virtues, one has a hard time acting prudently. We also saw in the previous chapter that if one leads a life according to the appetites, it precipitates judgment. Therefore, without rectitude of the appetites one cannot act prudently[100] and so prudence requires that moral virtue exist in the appetites[101] so that they are ordered by reason rather than the appetites affecting the operations of reason.

On the other hand, one cannot develop moral virtue without prudence. Common experience bears this out: if one decides to eat to the point of causing health problems, one habituates the appetites in moral vice and so by commanding the imprudent actions of eating excessively, one cannot have a moderated concupiscible appetite. This requires that virtues in the appetites and prudence be built up concomitantly.

To complete the connections among the virtues, St. Thomas observes that one can possess moral virtues without intellectual virtues but not without prudence.[102] Many people do not have the opportunity to develop the intellectual virtues but all men engage in action and therefore they can develop moral virtue. It is the common experience of all men to know men of high virtue or noble character[103] who are not learned. On the other hand, one can have intellectual virtues without moral virtues[104] and this also is verified by the common experience of men, for all people have experienced a learned man who is not moral. However, on a practical level, it is difficult to maintain intellectual virtues without the moral. First, it is difficult because knowledge and judgment of universal principles can be corrupted through passion,[105] e.g. if one gives into the passions of the concupiscible appetites knowing this to be wrong, one ends up in contradiction. If the passion becomes habitual, then the person can begin to question the principle of non-contradiction. Furthermore, without proper moral discipline, one succumbs to the vice of *curiositas*,[106] which can detract one from pursuing the right knowledge. Moreover, as one pursues the objects of the appetites, the appetites become

---

[99]This is the virtue which helps with the difficult scenarios and the more this virtue is developed, the more one can act prudently in extraordinary circumstances.

[100]ST I-II, q. 57, a. 2.

[101]Ibid.

[102]ST I-II, q. 58, a. 6 and ibid., q. 61, a. 3, ad 1.

[103]This is why the discussion of character was of such prominence during the time Rudolf Allers was writing his works.

[104]Ibid.

[105]ST I-II, q. 58, a. 5.

[106]*Curiositas* is the vice in which one pursues useless and profane knowledge. The more one does that, the more the appetites resist pursuing the knowledge of right reason and the speculative intellect. See ST II-II, q. 167.

accustomed to having their objects and so they resist the imagination being used to pursue knowledge. This is why people who suffer concupiscence do not pursue the intellectual virtues and so time is spent seeking after the object of the appetites rather than those objects which perfect the intellect. Again, this is why if one's life is not governed by reason, one will not perfect all of one's faculties and will suffer imperfections in his faculties.

The second moral virtue resides in the will[107] and that is justice. Justice is the virtue by which one renders to another his due[108] and so justice has a fundamental reference to those things outside the individual, both persons and objects. All moral virtues about operations pertain in some way to the notion of justice,[109] even though they are distinguished according to their objects and faculties. This follows from the fact that those things of the irascible and concupiscible appetites pertain to other people and so moderation in those appetites pertains to justice in that those appetites are tempered according to the good of the other which must be rendered. Moreover, things other than people which pertain to the appetites will be treated according to what is due to them with respect to the individual, e.g. one will eat because it is necessary for human life, but one will not eat excessively because then one overvalues the good of the food and one does not use it in due fashion. Justice is a virtue of the will which means it is that virtue which perfects the will. Consequently, the person of good will is not only the person who renders others their due, thus maintaining right order among individuals, but good will also perfects the will's relation to other things. Consequently, a person of good will is not only the person who treats others well, but who leads a life in relation to other objects according to right reason.[110]

The third moral virtue resides in the irascible appetite[111] and is called fortitude.[112] Fortitude is the virtue by which one engages the arduous good.[113] This is of extreme importance for psychology, as many directees are weak and have disordered appetites and therefore are incapable or find it difficult to pursue the arduous good. However, psychologists must encourage the directee to engage the arduous good, i.e.

---

[107]ST II-II, q. 58, a.3

[108]ST II-II, q. 58, a. 11.

[109]ST I-II, q. 60, a. 4.

[110]Strictly speaking, things do not have rights and so justice is not rendered to them because they have no moral claim to the rights. However, to treat things in perspective often touches upon the relation one has to the Creator of the thing and so it can touch upon justice with respect to the Creator. For example, if we overvalue material things, it can detract from our relationship with God.

[111]ST I-II, q. 61, a. 2.

[112]Ibid.

[113]ST II-II, q. 123.

develop the virtue of fortitude, so that he can overcome the difficulties he has. Often this comes in the form of engaging the most difficult form of arduous good which is self, commonly called self-mastery, self-discipline and detachment from self.

The last moral virtue[114] is temperance[115] and it resides in the concupiscible appetite.[116] Temperance is the virtue which moderates the concupiscible appetite with respect to bodily goods.[117] All of these virtues are perfective of the faculty and therefore ought to be pursued. If they are not pursued, the problems discussed in the ninth chapter will also rise.[118] The various virtues are distinguished according to their objects,[119] but not all objects are equal. Intellectual virtues which have a higher object are higher than the moral virtues.[120] We have already seen that the intellectual virtues are in a hierarchy and this also applies to the moral virtues.[121]

IV. Other Observations about the Virtues

There is a certain aptitude in us by nature to have the virtues[122] and this is clear merely from the fact that we are capable of developing them by repeated actions.[123] Like habits, different people have different dispositions and so dispositions of the individual can aid in obtaining virtue but can also make it difficult.[124] Again, like habits, virtue is

---

[114]These four moral virtues are called cardinal virtues. They are subdivided into different virtues based on the different objects of the faculties.

[115]ST I-II, q. 61, a. 2.

[116]Ibid.

[117]ST I-II, q. 141.

[118]Actually, lack of these virtues can lead to mental illness.

[119]See ST I-II, q. 60, a. 5. This means that the various passions, which are differentiated by their objects, will also distinguish the various virtues, i.e. there are various virtues pertaining not only to the various faculties but to the various passions of those faculties.

[120]ST I-II, q. 66, a. 3. This follows simply from the fact that truth is greater than action; truth perfects the highest faculty, viz. the intellect, which is more universal and therefore greater than those faculties which pertain to particulars and action pertains to the particular.

[121]See ST I-II, q. 66, a. 1: The hierarchy of the moral virtues is first prudence, then justice, fortitude and temperance. This hierarchy is based upon the hierarchy of the faculties and their respective objects.

[122]ST I-II, q. 63, a. 1 and In Ethic. II, l. 1 (n. 249).

[123]ST I-II, q. 63, a. 2.

[124]ST I-II, q. 63, a. 1.

not complete in us by nature[125] but must be acquired. To have perfect virtue, one must have all of the virtues,[126] while to have imperfect virtue it is sufficient to have only one,[127] provided there are not connected virtues necessary for it. While the intellectual and moral virtues are not necessarily connected, in order that they be perfect, one must have them all, as the previous discussion has already proven. Also, if one does not have the intellectual virtues, one may err about the end to which the moral virtues guide the means.

As prudence is required for the other moral virtues and since something becomes a virtue as it is commanded by reason, then reason is the measure and rule of the rectitude of appetitive motion.[128] Hence, with respect to the other moral virtues, they consist in the adequation to measuring reason,[129] i.e. an appetite has moral virtue when it is in conformity with right reason. It pertains, therefore, to reason, to ensure that the appetites do not go to excess or defect in the pursuit of their objects and so moral virtue lies in the mean between excess and defect.[130] Yet, this mean is not with respect to the thing (*medium rei*) but with respect to the mean of reason (*medium rationis*)[131] and this is because the mean is with respect to the individual.[132] That is to say, moral virtues do not concern the average or mean of excess and defect of the thing itself to man in general, e.g. one does not say that two hamburgers are the mean with respect to man because for some men, two hamburgers are not enough to sustain them. Rather the mean is with respect to reason in that reason knows how much the individual ought to eat in order to sustain himself. Hence, what a man of small stature who does little physical exertion should eat is different from the amount appropriate to the man of large stature who does a lot of physical work. Hence, what is a mean for one individual is not necessarily the mean for another individual.[133] Since prudence comes through

---

[125]Ibid. and In Ethic. II, l. 1 (n. 249).

[126]ST I-II, q. 65, a 1.

[127]Ibid.

[128]ST I-II, q. 64, a. 1.

[129]ST I-II, q. 64, a. 1.

[130]ST I-II, q. 60, a. 4 and ibid., q. 64, a. 1.

[131]St I-II, q. 64, a. 2.

[132]Ibid.

[133]It should not be inferred that just because the mean is with respect to the individual that it is subjective. Sometimes it is called the relative mean, but the term relative does not mean relativistic. Rather it means that the mean has a relation to the individual. The mean is objective insofar as the person's constitution determines the mean for the individual and, in this sense, it is objective insofar as the intellect must conform itself to the reality of one's own constitution. It is not subjective in the sense of being subject to the caprice of choice of the will but is based on an objective intellectual judgment of the reality

experience,[134] reason must have some experience in order to know how much is a moderate amount for a specific individual. Hence, moral virtue pertains to that which reason can order and moderate;[135] if reason has no control over it, there is no virtue.[136]

Virtue is a principle of appetitive motion beginning in reason and it is also that by which appetites are moved by reason.[137] This indicates that virtue prompts the appetite to act reasonably and this is why virtues are so important for the science of mental health. Vice is also a habit which means that it is moved by reason and voluntary, but although it is moved by reason, it is contrary to reason.[138] It is contrary to reason because it pertains to reason to arrive at the truth about what is the mean in moral action with respect to the particular faculties. When reason commands something unreasonable, i.e. something contrary to virtue, it actually commands something contrary to its own nature which is to judge and command the truth.[139] Moreover, it is irrational because vice makes the other faculties resist the command of reason and the use of will. So when reason commands a vicious action, reason militates against itself insofar as reason loses some control over the faculty and therefore to command vice is irrational.

Finally, virtue is its own reward, for by obtaining moral virtues a person is perfected which is a cause of joy. Furthermore, insofar as one acts according to virtue, one is more free because the intellect and will are not bound by passion. Therefore, virtues aid in voluntariness and as man finds joy in freedom, then he will find joy and

---

of one's own constitution.

[134]ST II-II, q. 47, a. 3.

[135]ST I-II, q. 59, a. 4. This means that the faculties which can be moved by the intellect, viz. the will and appetites are implicated, see ST I-II, q. 59, aa. 4 and 5 and ibid., q. 60, a. 2.

[136]This also applies to intellectual virtue in that it also lies in the mean, see ST I-II, q. 64, a. 3. Essentially speaking, the intellectual virtues lie in the mean because the intellect when it judges something by excess or defect does not arrive at the truth. This was seen with respect to the passions which affect the phantasm which in turn causes reason to err in its judgment since it relies on the phantasm. This is why moral virtue which moderates the passion is important in arriving at the truth, not only of the practical intellect, but also of the speculative intellect.

[137]ST I-II, q. 59, a. 1.

[138]ST I-II, q. 59, a. 1 ad 2.

[139]This topic will be revisited in the discussion of the causes of mental illness. Moreover, anytime there is a vice, there is a concomitant weakness in the will in regard to the object of the vice. Also, there is a darkness in the intellect about that object, as reason has a hard time judging the vice properly.

happiness in leading a life according to moral virtue.[140]   Despite the general societal attitudes, life lived according to reason is a life of joy and happiness.[141]   Mentally ill people are not happy because they are fraught with internal division among their faculties or a lack of peace due to the dysfunction of some faculty. Virtue restores the order of the faculties and therefore it restores peace[142] and happiness to the individual; virtue, therefore, is essential for mental health.

---

[140]This was the position of Aristotle and Aquinas and will be discussed again in volume II.

[141]St. Thomas observes in ST I-II, q. 59, a. 3 that sorrow cannot be with virtue insofar as virtue is the cause, since virtue is a good or perfection and sorrow is not with respect to the good. However, sorrow can accompany virtue as when a man makes a choice based on truth which in turn causes him difficulties with others. Finally, virtue delights in its own (ibid.). Virtue is about the good, so someone who is virtuous will find virtue joyful. However, one should not be deluded into thinking that if one suffers from vice, obtaining virtue will be easy even though virtue is a good.

[142]St. Augustine's oft-repeated definition of peace is *tranquillitas ordinis*, i.e. the tranquility of order.

Chapter 11: The Natural Law and Conscience

Virtue is that quality ordered to operation which is suited to or in accordance with nature and vice is that which is not suitable or is contrary to nature. While some of what constitutes the nature of man and his faculties has been discussed, it pertains to this chapter to parse out further considerations of the nature of man as related to the necessity of following that nature in actions, which brings us to the subject of the natural law. The structure and nature of the natural law will be discussed in order to provide a more coherent understanding of the nature of man, so that psychologists can grasp more perfectly the nature of mental health and illness. In addition, the nature of conscience, so poorly understood by modern psychology, will be seen as connected to the natural law.

I. The Natural Law

A. Initial Observations

The very discussion of the natural law in the current academic context is quite daunting for several reasons. The first is that, in the ethical and moral community, there is a widespread dissension on the nature of the natural law, its application and every other aspect of it. Moreover, St. Thomas provides very little discussion of it; in fact, in the primary text of the *Prima Secundae* where it is treated, the discussion of the natural law constitutes only one question divided into five short articles and a few other brief passages.[1] Also, there are so many aspects and questions about the natural law that a single chapter seems almost inadequate to address all of the issues.[2] Finally, it is exceedingly difficult to discuss the natural law detached from a metaphysical treatment of natural theology or outside the context of St. Thomas' treatment of the natural law. St. Thomas places the issue of the natural law within the context of the overall

---

[1] In one respect, the amount of discussion St. Thomas provides seems almost insignificant compared to treatment of other topics. However, it appears that St. Thomas discussed the natural law to the degree that he viewed it necessary, which indicates that in the mind of the saint, everything necessary to adequately understand and treat the natural law is contained in his treatment of it. The author hopes that the reader will likewise accept this view, once the treatment in this chapter is given.

[2] This brings up the fact that, in the mind of the author, many of the questions about the natural law in the academic community are due to three fundamental problems: 1) a rejection of the foundation of the natural law in metaphysics; 2) the rejection of the Thomistic treatment of the natural law and 3) the Humean critique. All of these issues shall be addressed in various ways throughout this chapter, although it may not be to the satisfaction of certain segments of the academic community.

providential plan which includes grace. Therefore, without being able to show the connection of God to the natural law as understood through natural theology as well as the discussion of grace which aids man in fulfilling and understanding the natural law, the treatment will inevitability be inadequate. However, at a later time, the two aspects of the context will be provided for a fuller understanding of natural law and since our goal in this section of the book is to provide the subalternate principles from philosophy necessary to discuss psychological matters, we are left with the necessary, though unfortunate, circumstance of providing only a basic discussion of the natural law. We are driven to discuss it, even if it is inadequate, since the natural law, as the reader shall discover, is absolutely crucial in knowing those things necessary for the science of mental health.

B. The Nature of Law

Prior to discussing the natural law, one must have a firm grasp of the definition (nature) of law itself, for the natural law is a species within the genus of law. Since one must know the genus in order to have scientific knowledge of a species, we must first discuss the definition of law. St. Thomas provides a definition in the *Prima Secundae* which covers every aspect necessary for law: ". . . the definition of law is nothing other than a certain promulgated ordinance of reason for the common good by him who has care of the community."[3] A law is an ordinance of reason which indicates that it is a command of reason which structures, directs or orders future action. It is important to understand, therefore, that a law must be something which proceeds from reason and it is intended to supply order to a community by commanding certain things to be done and prohibiting others. Secondly, the intention of the law must be for the benefit of the community, i.e. it must be for the common good of all those to whom the law applies. Thirdly, it must be promulgated, for no legislator can expect the execution of a law without making the law known and this comes through a formal means or method of promulgation. Fourthly, it is done by him or those who have care of the community and this indicates that the person legislating must be a competent authority. Law binds the individual since it is an ordinance of reason and one ought not act contrary to reason.[4] Moreover, it binds since it is for the common good and one ought not to act contrary to the common good. Finally it is promulgated by someone who has the right to bind the citizens to the law since he occupies the office which has those rights.

---

[3]ST I-II, q. 90, a. 4: "definitio legis, quae nihil est aliud quam quaedam rationis ordinatio ad bonum commune, ab eo qui curam communitatis habet, promulgata."

[4]Here we are prescinding from the issue of irrational or immoral laws. Other aspects of law will likewise not be treated as time is not afforded here. It would behoove the reader to read questions 90-97 of the *Prima Secundae* to cover all the aspects of law.

C. Different Kinds of Law

There are three different kinds of law which St. Thomas delineates. The first is what is called the eternal law which constitutes the overall providential plan as it exists in the mind of God.[5] But since man does not have access to the mind of God, he cannot know the eternal law directly.[6] However, the mind and intentions of God can be known in a two-fold way through His effects.[7] The first is through the branch of metaphysics called natural theology by which one gains knowledge of the mind of God by means of His creation. The second is through the natural law which expresses the intention of God with respect to human nature. This reasoning is based on the principle of causality which states that the cause is somehow in the effect and so insofar as God causes man (as well as other things), we can know what God intended for man by the way He designed him. Analogously, we see this in the manufacturing of automobiles. Even if someone had never seen a man, but he did see an automobile, he could know a great deal about the intention of the maker. He would know that the maker intended for the car to transport a physical being which would guide the vehicle. He would also know by the various instruments and accessories certain aspects about man and his faculties, e.g. he would know by the existence of a radio that the being intended for someone with hearing to use it. Moreover, he would know that one should not put sugar in the gas tank since that would destroy the automobile's capacity to function; that would be outside the mind of the builder since there is no instrumentation for the sake of sugar. One could go on, but the same thing applies to man: God intended certain things regarding man and we know this by means of knowing man's nature and faculties.

The second kind of law, therefore, is "the natural law which is nothing other than the participation in the eternal law by a rational creature."[8] The eternal law is

---

[5]ST I-II, q. 91, aa. 1 and 2.

[6]Those in heaven can know the eternal law as shall be discussed in volume II.

[7]Here one must have a sound philosophical training in natural theology by which man is able to know the existence of God, His nature and attributes through the natural light of reason without any reference to revealed theology. It has always been assumed that one cannot talk about God without talking about revealed theology and this is the result of the intellectual poverty suffered by many Protestant sects due to the anti-intellectualism which dominated historically and still dominates certain segments of Protestantism today. The point is that one can discuss matters about God without reference to Tradition or Scripture. This is exceedingly important regarding the civil law which must be based on or with respect to the natural law. Unfortunately, with the advent of positivism in jurisprudence, civil laws have become divorced from natural law and as a result it has and will lead to or allow actions which cause mental illness.

[8]ST I-II, q. 91, a. 2: "unde patet quod lex naturalis nihil aliud est quam participatio legis aeternae in rationali creatura."

expressed in the effects of God and particularly in the natural law, which is the participation of men[9] in the eternal law of God. The natural law is the light of God given to man since the natural light of reason is that by which man is able to discern the good and the bad.[10] In other words, when God created man, He placed in him a light which gives him the capacity to grasp His intentions about man's own nature and thereby know what is right and wrong.[11] The last kind of law is civil law, sometimes called human law, which is enacted for the common good of men by other men who have the responsibility to do so.[12]

D. The Natural Law

St. Thomas' discussion of the natural law finds itself primarily in the *Prima Secundae* and in order to facilitate a grasp on the side of the reader of the mind of St. Thomas, the best approach seems to be to present the actual texts of St. Thomas and then to provide some commentary and explanation of them. St. Thomas begins the discussion by asking whether the natural law is a habit to which he responds:

> Something is able to be a habit in two ways. In one way, properly and essentially and so the natural law is not a habit. For it was said above that the natural law is something constituted by reason, just as a proposition is a certain work of reason. Moreover, it is not the same that he who acts and that by which he acts: for someone makes a suitable oration by the habit of grammar. Since therefore a habit is that by which one acts, it is not able to be that some law is a habit

---

[9]This also applies to angels.

[10]Ibid.

[11]Normally the discussion of right and wrong, good and bad, finds itself in the moral and ethical context. However, there are three different kinds of good and bad. The first is metaphysical in which one either exists or not, as existence is a good and non-existence is an evil. The second is physical good and evil, as when someone who lacks a limb suffers a physical evil but that is not a moral evil. The last is moral good and evil and that pertains to the rational creature which has the capacity to grasp God's intention about his own nature as well as to foresee the effects of his acts and assume responsibility by means of voluntary choice. Psychological good and evil pertains to the second and third kinds of good and evil.

[12]Other definitions are also given to the natural law but for the sake of brevity they shall not be discussed here since they merely express the same notion in different terms.

properly and essentially.[13]

The natural law is not a habit in the sense that it is something by which one acts like an operative habit. In the previous chapter, it was noted that virtues were operative habits because they inclined one to act a specific way and so they are that by which one acts, as they aid one to act well. So the natural law is not essentially or properly speaking a habit.

St. Thomas also notes that the natural law is something constituted by reason and by this he means that the formulation of the propositions of the natural law or the grasping of the natural law itself is something done by reason.[14] This follows from the fact that only a being endowed with reason is able to grasp the ordinance within himself toward certain ends[15] and the means to those ends, based upon knowledge of his own nature. No other faculty is capable of grasping the natural law. Moreover, this is why animals do not grasp the natural law but merely act according to their nature. Because they cannot formulate that toward which they should strive by reflecting upon their own nature, it is necessary that they be ordered as well as moved toward their ends from an exterior principle (viz. God), through their nature. Man however is different; he can grasp the ends of his nature, i.e. those things towards which his nature is fundamentally ordered. So when St. Thomas says that the natural law is something constituted by

---

[13]ST I-II, q. 94, a. 1: "aliquid potest dici esse habitus dupliciter. Uno modo, proprie et essentialiter, et sic lex naturalis non est habitus. Dictum est enim supra quod lex naturalis est aliquid per rationem constitutum, sicut etiam propositio est quoddam opus rationis. Non est autem idem quod quis agit, et quo quis agit, aliquis enim per habitum grammaticae agit orationem congruam. Cum igitur habitus sit quo quis agit, non potest esse quod lex aliqua sit habitus proprie et essentialiter."

[14]See ST I-II, q. 90, a. 1, ad. 2.

[15]In St. Thomas' commentary on the *Sentences* there is a lengthier discussion about "ends" of the genus and species of some thing. However, that discussion will not be afforded here for two reasons. The first is that the commentary in the *Sentences* is the earliest writing of St. Thomas and therefore tends to be less developed than the discussion in the *Summa*. Second, St. Thomas' discussion of ends in his commentary on the *Sentences* is more complex if considered in conjunction with his later writing. While most of what is stated in the commentary on the *Sentences* is in congruity with what is in the *Summa*, the approach and differences may appear at variance with each other and therefore, that will be left to a more scholarly discussion of the natural law than can be covered here. The discussion in the *Sentences* is found in IV Sent., d. 33, q. 1, a. 1 through IV Sent., d. 33, q. 2, a. 2.

reason, he does not mean that reason determines what the natural law will be.[16] Rather, he is indicating that in conforming his mind to the reality of his own nature, man sees that toward which his nature is ordered and is able to grasp and formulate that ordering.

St. Thomas continues his discussion of whether the natural law is a habit:

> In another way, a habit is able to be said of that which we hold by a habit, as faith is said of that which is held by faith. And in this way, since the precepts of the natural law are sometimes considered in act by reason, sometimes however they are in it habitually; only according to this way it is able to be said that the natural law is a habit. Just as indemonstrable principles in speculative matters are not the habit itself, but they are the principles of which it is a habit.[17]

The natural law is not a habit like other habits which can be increased, decreased or corrupted. However, it is a habit in the same fashion as the first principles of speculative reason are said to be in the intellect habitually. Just as the first principles of speculative reason govern the operation of the possible intellect regarding the considerations of truth, so the natural law governs the operation of the practical intellect. Right reason is reason as it is governed by the natural law.[18] Hence, when one deliberates about practical matters, the natural law governs the deliberation like the first principles of speculative reason. Just as the speculative intellect errs when it violates the first principles of speculative reason, so the practical intellect errs when it deviates from the natural law.

In relation to the issue of first principles, St. Thomas replies to an objection

---

[16]This statement must be understood in a specific sense. Since reason is the primary faculty which man must follow and considerations about the natural law take into account the fact that man has reason, reason is one of the things which determine the deliberations about the natural law. Moreover, man is bound to follow reason since reason grasps what is right and wrong and one must always do what is right. However, what this statement means is that reason must conform itself to the natural law and therefore reason is not free to judge as it pleases what is right and wrong. Moreover, it is not up to the will to decide what it wants to be right and wrong. Rather the will must conform itself to all of the precepts of the natural law in order to be good (I Sent., d. 48, q. 1, a. 3, ad 3).

[17]ST I-II, q. 94, a. 1: "Alio modo potest dici habitus id quod habitu tenetur, sicut dicitur fides id quod fide tenetur. Et hoc modo, quia praecepta legis naturalis quandoque considerantur in actu a ratione, quandoque autem sunt in ea habitualiter tantum, secundum hunc modum potest dici quod lex naturalis sit habitus. Sicut etiam principia indemonstrabilia in speculativis non sunt ipse habitus principiorum, sed sunt principia quorum est habitus."

[18]II Sent. d. 42, q. 2, a. 5: "The natural law is that according to which it is right reason" ("lex naturalis est secundum quam ratio recta est").

which makes an important clarification: "synderesis is called the law of our intellect insofar as it is a habit containing the precepts of the natural law which are the first principles of human works."[19] We saw in a previous chapter that synderesis is a natural habit by which we know the first precepts of the natural law and it relates to reason insofar as it is the understanding of the first principles used in the ratiocinating about practical conclusions and hence it moves prudence. The natural law insofar as it is an ordinance ordains or directs man and it guides the deliberations of reason about actions. The natural law contains precepts which are like the first principles of speculative reason which govern the speculative reason in its deliberations.

The next question, logically speaking, concerns these aforesaid principles of the natural law and St. Thomas addresses the question of whether there is one or whether there are many principles of the natural law:

> The precepts of the natural law in this way relate to practical reason as the first principles of demonstration relate to speculative reason; for both are certain self-evident principles. Moreover, something is said to be self-evident in two ways: in the first way, in itself and another way with respect to us. Whatever principle is said to be self-evident in itself is one which is predicated from the notion of the subject.[20]

Principles are self-evident either in themselves or with respect to us. A principle is self evident in itself when the predicate contains the very notion of the subject. This means that if one understands the terms involved, when the predicate is predicated of the subject, reason immediately grasps the proposition as true. For example, when the two terms man and rational are put together in the proposition: man is rational, if the two terms are grasped, one immediately knows that the proposition is true and thus it is self-evident in itself. Since the definition of man is "rational animal", when one states "man is rational" it is self-evident because the predicate contains the notion of the subject which is man (rational animal).

> Truly, certain propositions are self-evident only to the wise to those who understand what the terms of the proposition signify. . . In those

---

[19]ST I-II, q. 94, a. 1, ad 2: "synderesis dicitur lex intellectus nostri, inquantum est habitus continens praecepta legis naturalis, quae sunt prima principia operum humanorum."

[20]ST I-II, q. 94, a. 2: "praecepta legis naturae hoc modo se habent ad rationem practicam, sicut principia prima demonstrationum se habent ad rationem speculativam, utraque enim sunt quaedam principia per se nota. Dicitur autem aliquid per se notum dupliciter, uno modo, secundum se; alio modo, quoad nos. secundum se quidem quaelibet propositio dicitur per se nota, cuius praedicatum est de ratione subiecti..."

which fall under the apprehension of man, a certain order is found. For that which first falls into the apprehension is being, of which the understanding is included in everything whatsoever one understands. And therefore the first indemonstrable principle is that one cannot at the same time affirm or deny the same thing, which is founded upon the notion of being and non-being, and upon this principle all others are founded... Moreover, as being is the first thing which falls into the apprehension simply, so the good is the first which falls into the apprehension of practical reason, which is ordered to action; for all agents act for the sake of the end which has the notion of the good.[21]

This passage is quite loaded and deserves a great deal of reflection. St. Thomas begins by noting that certain self-evident principles are known only to the wise because only they understand the terms.[22] As we have seen, there is a great deal of philosophical knowledge required regarding the subalternate principles of psychology before one can even discuss what mental health and illness are. As many of the things regarding man are known only to the "wise," i.e. those who have adequate training and background, likewise many of the matters regarding the natural law will be known only to the wise.

The next thing St. Thomas observes is that among those things grasped by man there is a certain order, i.e. certain things are more fundamental or more foundational than others. He then gives the example of the principle of non-contradiction. He notes that the first thing that falls into the intellect is being and by this is meant that every thing

---

[21]ST I-II, q. 94, a. 2: "quaedam vero propositiones sunt per se notae solis sapientibus, qui terminos propositionum intelligunt quid significent... In his autem quae in apprehensione omnium cadunt, quidam ordo invenitur. Nam illud quod primo cadit in apprehensione, est ens, cuius intellectus includitur in omnibus quaecumque quis apprehendit. Et ideo primum principium indemonstrabile est quod non est simul affirmare et negare, quod fundatur supra rationem entis et non entis, et super hoc principio omnia alia fundantur... Sicut autem ens est primum quod cadit in apprehensione simpliciter, ita bonum est primum quod cadit in apprehensione practicae rationis, quae ordinatur ad opus, omne enim agens agit propter finem, qui habet rationem boni."

[22]This is why moral, ethical and psychological matters cannot be expected to be grasped by the average individual. Certain forms of rationalism as well as in the theological field in Protestantism have left people with the notion that they have the natural capacities within themselves to determine what is right and wrong. However, as shall be seen, the natural law, i.e. what constitutes the nature of man and therefore what they ought to do and not to do, is very complicated because it requires knowledge which the average individual does not possess. This means that in moral and psychological matters, short answers will rarely suffice and those who do not have the sufficient background cannot expect to be in a position to pass judgment on moral precepts as well as what constitues those things which contribute to mental health and illness.

which falls into apprehension is something that exists.[23] He then notes that from the notion of being and non-being is formulated the principle of non-contradiction upon which the other first principles of speculative reason are founded.

St. Thomas then does something of extreme importance. He notes that as the first thing that falls into the intellect is being simply, the first thing that falls into the practical intellect is the good. Here St. Thomas is implicating the convertibility of the transcendentals. He notes that the first thing that falls into the intellect is being simply and this indicates that the first of the transcendentals is being considered from the *ratio* or perspective of absoluteness or simply. In other words, the first transcendental is being and it is being looked at from the point of being *itself*, i.e. without any further qualification or perspective. He then provides the *ratio* for the transcendental of the good which is being which falls into practical reason, i.e. it is being looked at from the point of view of finality or end. As a being is constituted by an essence and existence,[24] then to know what is good for that being, one must look at the essence or being of the thing under the *ratio* of finality.[25] The convertibility of being and the good means that in order to know the natural law, in order to know what is good for a being, one must know the essence or nature of the thing.[26]

The issue of the transcendentals avoids the Humean critique which essentially states that one cannot get an "ought" from an "is," i.e. knowledge of what is good for a thing cannot be derived from its nature. The essence of the Humean critique consists in stating that one asserts in the conclusion what is not contained in the premises. The premise is the nature of the thing but then there is no other premise provided and one draws out what is good for the thing without the introduction of the notion of goodness; this argument is exemplified in the following incomplete syllogism:

---

[23]A great deal of discussion of this statement has been given by the metaphysical community but St. Thomas interpretes himself by noting that everything in the intellect is some thing or being.

[24]*De ente et essentia*, passim.

[25]Sometimes the *ratio* of the transcendental of the good is "desirability" but since the good is that which all things desire and the good is the end of some desiring faculty, then finality and desirability are correlative terms.

[26]The very term "natural law" contains this notion. For nature refers to the essence of a thing as it is a principle of activity (this will become important later on in the discussion of the role of faculties in the deliberation of the natural law) and law is defined as an ordinance of reason. Since an ordinance is the guiding of a thing toward some end, it means that the natural law is the ordinance or directing toward a finality contained in the nature of the thing. Hence, nature (essence-being) and law (ordinance to the good) contain the very foundational notion of the natural law, i.e. by the metaphysical knowledge of the essence of a thing, one is able to know that toward which it is ordered, i.e. what is good for it.

The intellect of man is structured toward grasping what is true.
_____
Therefore, it is good for the intellect of man to grasp what is true.

The major term of goodness is not provided in the syllogism. However, because Hume lacked a metaphysics (since there is nothing for him beyond the physical or knowable beyond the physical), he failed and others following his lead have failed to grasp the fact that this syllogism is enthymematic. What is to be supplied by the listener is the convertibility of being (nature) with the good. Hence the full syllogism would be:

The intellect of man is structured toward grasping what is true.
Being (of the intellect) and the good (of the intellect) are convertible.
_____
Therefore, the good of the intellect of man is to grasp the truth.

What is good for a thing is that which is in accordance with nature. For example, a car burns gas and it is good for the car to burn gas. The nature of the car is not designed to accept sugar in the gas tank, for it is bad for the car to pour sugar in the gas tank. Many have fallen prey to the Humean critique, but almost always it is due to a lack of understanding of the role of the transcendentals in the discussion of the natural law.

St. Thomas continues his discussion of the natural law:

And therefore the first principle in practical reason which is founded upon the good is: the good is that which all desire. This is, therefore, the first precept of the law, viz. that the good is to be done and sought, evil to be avoided. And upon this are founded all of the other precepts of the natural law, viz. that all those thing to be done or to be avoided pertain to the precepts of the natural law, which practical reason naturally apprehends to be human goods.[27]

Here St. Thomas observes that the first principle of practical reason is that the good is that which all desire. Now a desire is placed in a being for the sake of its fulfillment and perfection, for one does not desire that which is not a perfection or which is to one's determinent. Therefore, upon this first principle is based the first precept of the natural

_____

[27]ST I-II, q. 94, a. 2: "Et ideo primum principium in ratione practica est quod fundatur supra rationem boni, quae est, bonum est quod omnia appetunt. Hoc est ergo primum praeceptum legis, quod bonum est faciendum et prosequendum, et malum vitandum. Et super hoc fundantur omnia alia praecepta legis naturae, ut scilicet omnia illa facienda vel vitanda pertineant ad praecepta legis naturae, quae ratio practica naturaliter apprehendit esse bona humana."

law, which is that the good is to be done and pursued and the evil to be avoided.[28] This first precept is able to be grasped as true by all and is therefore self-evident, for all recognize by virtue of the fact that they have reason that the good is to be done and evil is to be avoided. St. Thomas then observes that all of the other precepts of the natural law, called the secondary precepts of the natural law, are founded upon this first precept. It means that every secondary precept is somehow derived from or is a further specification of the first precept.[29]

St. Thomas continues:

> Truly since the good has the notion of an end, evil has the contrary notion, whence it is that everything to which man has a natural inclination, reason naturally apprehends as good, and consequently as to be sought by action and their contrary as evil and to be avoided.[30]

Good and evil are contrary notions; the good is to be pursued since the good is the perfection or fulfillment of some thing and evil is to be avoided because it causes harm, is an imperfection or is bad for the thing. Now it is the common experience of men that we are inclined toward certain things and so St. Thomas notes that to which we have a natural inclination, i.e. that toward which we are inclined to pursue has the nature of the good and it is grasped by reason. For insofar as human nature is designed to pursue some thing, it is good for human nature. Here we see that the natural law is an ordinance placed in the nature of man to pursue certain goods for the perfection of that nature. Natural inclinations, i.e. inclinations which arise from human nature, and which are in congruity with human nature are good. For a natural inclination is incapable of being unnatural for that would imply contradiction; something is contrary to the nature of a thing insofar as it is unnatural and insofar as something is contrary to the nature of a thing, it is evil, for it is contrary to the natural inclinations of that nature. Hence, insofar as the natural law is an ordinance, it is an ordering of the natural inclinations of a thing toward that which is good for it.[31]

Here it is pivotal to understand what the term "nature" or "natural" means. There are several different meanings to the term nature: the first sometimes refers to something which is physical (this comes from the Greek term φυσις from which we get the word "physical"), e.g. when we say that it is "natural" for one's hair to grow. The

---

[28]Sometimes, the first precept is contracted to "do good and avoid evil."

[29]ST I-II, q. 94, a. 5 and IV Sent., d. 33, q. 1, a. 1.

[30]ST I-II, q. 94, a. 2: "Quia vero bonum habet rationem finis, malum autem rationem contrarii, inde est quod omnia illa ad quae homo habet naturalem inclinationem, ratio naturaliter apprehendit ut bona, et per consequens ut opere prosequenda, et contraria eorum ut mala et vitanda."

[31]See also ST II-II, q. 79, a. 2 ad 2 and Quod. XII, q. 7, a. 1.

second is when we refer to the sum total of all those things which we see in the physical universe, such as forests, animals, etc. when we say they are part of "nature." The third refers to the essence of a thing as it is a principle of motion which is the formal definition of the term "nature." This third meaning is what constitutes the meaning of the term "nature" in the concept of natural law. For the natural law indicates the fundamental ordinance placed in the essence of a thing toward specific ends and actions which achieve those ends. The essence determines the second acts of the thing, i.e. the essence of a thing determines what it can and cannot do, what it should and should not do insofar as something is in congruity with that nature or not. For example, the essence of a dog determines that it will bark, bite, etc., but not engage in rational discourse, because the essence of the dog is incapable of causing the accidents of intellect and faculties of speech. Hence, when one refers to natural inclinations, one is referring toward the ordering placed within the essence of a thing to specific kinds of secondary acts (i.e. the first act of essence determines the second acts of that thing).

The next meaning of the term "nature" are those things which usually occur in some nature although they are not natural to it in the sense that they are not something which is part of the essence or flows from the essence. There are two kinds of this type of "natural" occurrences, the first is physical or ontological, e.g. when we say that all men die. The second is something moral as when we say that all men lie, in which the action flows from deliberate reason and freewill. But this is not natural in the proper sense since it actually goes contrary to the nature of the faculties of intellect and speech. The last use of the term natural refers to a disposition that one may possess, e.g. when we say that it is "natural" for Mr. Doe to eat too much because of the fact that he has a sanguine disposition. So when certain acts are seen as in congruity with one's dispositions, it is said to be natural. However, this use of natural must not be confused with the third use because, at times, it can refer to the fourth use, viz. it is actually something contrary to the essence of man, e.g. when someone has a disposition towards drinking excessively.

This topic also necessitates the treating of another and that has to do with the two terms of "norm" and "average." Very often in psychology, particularly in statistical analysis, one notes that the "average" person does something and it is therefore labeled as "normal" for man to do it. However, the true norm is understood to be a law, determination or ordering in that which is proper to the nature of the thing, i.e. that which is commanded by the natural law. For what is natural to or the norm for a thing is that which is in accordance with its nature in the third sense above, not that which is due to the defects which occur in human nature, as is stated in the fourth sense of the term above. Consequently, psychologists cannot take as the "norm" that which the statistical average indicates nor what all men do, but rather that which is in congruity with man's nature.

The next thing St. Thomas does is to determine the categories of the natural inclinations:

Therefore, according to the order of natural inclinations is the order of the precepts of the natural law. For, firstly, the inclination of man is to the good according to nature, which he has in common with all substances, as namely every substance desires the conservation of its being according to its nature. And according to this inclination, it pertains to the natural law that the life of man may be preserved and the contrary impeded.[32]

The precepts of the natural law follow the order of natural inclinations and the first natural inclination found in all substances is the desire for the conservation or preservation of their being according to their respective nature.[33] This means not only that the thing desires to continue in existence but it desires to continue in its existence according to the mode of that existence, i.e. it desires to continue according to its essence. This means that man has a natural desire to continue to exist as well as to continue existing as a man.[34] In this category are all those matters pertaining to life, self-preservation both in existence as well as the preservation of health and bodily integrity. This means that in order for man to fulfill that natural desire, i.e. to act according to his nature, he must seek the integrity of his whole being. This also is why all men must respect the life and integrity of the being of other human beings; for if they do not, they go contrary to the law or ordinance placed in man.[35]

St. Thomas then lists the second natural inclination:

The second inclination in man is to something more specific, according to the nature which he has in common with other animals. And according to this, they are said to be of the natural law those "which nature teaches to all animals," such as the mixture of the

---

[32]ST I-II, q. 94, a. 2: "Secundum igitur ordinem inclinationum naturalium, est ordo praeceptorum legis naturae. Inest enim primo inclinatio homini ad bonum secundum naturam in qua communicat cum omnibus substantiis, prout scilicet quaelibet substantia appetit conservationem sui esse secundum suam naturam. Et secundum hanc inclinationem, pertinent ad legem naturalem ea per quae vita hominis conservatur, et contrarium impeditur."

[33]See also SCG III, c. 131, n. 3.

[34]In popular entertainment culture, there is an idea in vogue that eventually man will evolve out of being human into a higher state. This is not only against natural desire but it is also contrary to the philosophical notion that essences do not change.

[35]This is why men want to be men and to remain male and women want to be women and to remain female. The contrary desire to be the opposite sex is unnatural, i.e. contrary to the natural law.

masculine and feminine, education of children and the like.[36]

The second inclination in man pertains to all of those things which we have in common with animals, such as reproduction, eating, the upbringing of offspring, etc. It must be kept in mind that each nature is specific to each essence or species and therefore that toward which they are ordered will differ even though they are in the same category. For instance, what pertains to raising offspring for man is fundamentally different than what pertains to it with respect to cows. Hence, while this category of inclination is in common with animals, the *way* in which it is done differs from species to species and that specific nature teaches that species how it is to be done.[37] This is why it is not appropriate to raise children or treat them in the same way one would cattle, for example.[38]

Finally, the last category is given as follows:

> In the third way, an inclination is found in man to the good according to the nature of reason, which is proper to him; as man has the natural inclination to know the truth about God and to live in society. And according to this, those which consider this kind of inclination pertain to the natural law, for example that man avoid ignorance, that he does not offend others with which he ought to converse and other things of this kind.[39]

The third category is something specific to man alone who has reason. The natural law also inclines man to live in society and to get along with others. It inclines man toward pursuing the truth and to pursue the truth about God. All of these things are done in a way which requires reason and so this category which is proper to man, indicates that

---

[36]Ibid.: "Secundo inest homini inclinatio ad aliqua magis specialia, secundum naturam in qua communicat cum ceteris animalibus. Et secundum hoc, dicuntur ea esse de lege naturali quae natura omnia animalia docuit, ut est coniunctio maris et feminae, et educatio liberorum, et similia."

[37]Basic observation of different animals and how they raise their offspring indicates that the nature of the animals moves them to raise them in a fashion which brings about their good or perfection as it is done in accordance with their nature.

[38]See IV Sent., d. 33, q. 1, a. 1, ad 4.

[39]Ibid: "Tertio modo inest homini inclinatio ad bonum secundum naturam rationis, quae est sibi propria, sicut homo habet naturalem inclinationem ad hoc quod veritatem cognoscat de deo, et ad hoc quod in societate vivat. Et secundum hoc, ad legem naturalem pertinent ea quae ad huiusmodi inclinationem spectant, utpote quod homo ignorantiam vitet, quod alios non offendat cum quibus debet conversari, et cetera huiusmodi quae ad hoc spectant."

reason is the proper norm for man, i.e. what is in accord with reason is determinative of what should and should not be done according to the natural law.

Therefore, there are essentially three categories of natural inclination, viz. 1) that which is toward the conservation of his being; 2) that which is in common with all animals and 3) that which is proper to man alone who possesses reason. Therefore, in the most fundamental consideration of the natural law, one can consider whether some thing or course of action is proper to man by comparing it to these three categories. The first precept of the natural law was to do good and avoid evil, which is based upon the first principle of the natural law which was the good is that which all things desire. However, modern ethicians and moralists have labored under difficulties in determining exactly how one is to go from the first precepts of the natural law to the second, e.g. how does one go from "do good and avoid evil" to "thinking bad thoughts is evil or wrong?"

It is the opinion of this author that St. Thomas does answer this question, though not in a straightforward fashion. Initially, some acts which fall under secondary precepts can be judged based simply by comparing the action to the three categories, e.g. in the act of taking one's own life (suicide), one compares it to the natural inclination of conservation of one's being and one realizes that suicide vitiates against the conservation of one's being and is therefore contrary to the natural law. However, it is difficult to determine other secondary precepts which are not so straightforward regarding these three categories. While all secondary precepts are a specification of these three categories, how they fall under them, what the actual formulation and specification of the secondary precepts are, possesses some difficulty.

St. Thomas does address the issue, but it requires further considerations. The first thing St. Thomas does is make the following observation right after the preceding article:

> Every inclination of this kind of whichever part of human nature, e.g. the concupiscible and irascible, insofar as they are regulated by reason, they pertain to the natural law, and are reduced to one first principle, as was said. And according to this, there are many precepts of the natural law in themselves which, nevertheless, communicate in one root.[40]

Here, St. Thomas observes that all of the natural inclinations of man are rooted in the first precept of the natural law. However, what is of importance in the current context is the fact that he refers to the concupiscible and irascible inclinations or appetites. The

---

[40]ST I-II, q. 94, a. 2, ad 2: "omnes inclinationes quarumcumque partium humanae naturae, puta concupiscibilis et irascibilis, secundum quod regulantur ratione, pertinent ad legem naturalem, et reducuntur ad unum primum praeceptum, ut dictum est. Et secundum hoc, sunt multa praecepta legis naturae in seipsis, quae tamen communicant in una radice."

various secondary precepts of the natural law as governing the natural inclinations found in the various faculties are to be formulated by reason. Two things, therefore, are of importance; first the introduction of the fact that there are different inclinations in the various faculties which are part of the natural law and so one of the ways one begins the process of bridging the intellectual gap between the first and secondary precepts is to start with the fact that some of the inclinations find themselves in the various faculties.[41] The fact that the faculties are introduced to indicate that the secondary precepts may be determined according to the various faculties begins the process of making the first precept of the natural law more specified as found in the secondary precepts.

The second thing is the rooting of the natural law for man in reason itself and this is given further context in the following passage:

> Therefore, if we are speaking of actions of virtue insofar as they are virtuous, then all virtuous acts pertain to the natural law. For it was said that to the natural law pertains everything to which man is inclined by nature. Each is inclined naturally toward operation suitable according to its form as fire to heating. Hence, since the rational soul is the proper form of man, the natural inclination is in every man since he acts according to reason. And this is to act according to virtue. Hence according to this, all acts of virtue are of the natural law; for the reason proper to each one dictates that he act virtuously. But if we are speaking of the virtuous acts in themselves, namely, as they are considered in their proper species, thus not all virtuous acts are of the natural law. For many things become according to virtue which nature does not first incline but, through the inquiry of reason, man comes upon them as something useful to living well.[42]

---

[41]Not all the natural inclinations find themselves in the various faculties even though they may be executed by the various faculties, e.g. some of the natural inclinations found in the first category of inclinations are not tied to a specific faculty, such as the natural inclination of a thing to conserve its existence. There is no specific faculty which inclines one to self-preservation but that inclination is executed through other faculties, such as reason, the motive faculties, etc. Other inclinations come by means of a specific faculty and so the process of specification begins with the specific faculty.

[42]ST I-II, q. 94, a. 3: "Si igitur loquamur de actibus virtutum inquantum sunt virtuosi, sic omnes actus virtuosi pertinent ad legem naturae. Dictum est enim quod ad legem naturae pertinet omne illud ad quod homo inclinatur secundum suam naturam. Inclinatur autem unumquodque naturaliter ad operationem sibi convenientem secundum suam formam, sicut ignis ad calefaciendum. Unde cum anima rationalis sit propria forma hominis, naturalis inclinatio inest cuilibet homini ad hoc quod agat secundum rationem. Et hoc est agere secundum virtutem. Unde secundum hoc, omnes actus virtutum sunt de lege

St. Thomas observes that the natural law determines that one acts according to one's form or nature[43] and the essence or nature of man is a rational animal and so it pertains to man to act according to reason. Now reason sees the necessity of acting according to virtue and so the natural law specifies that man act virtuously when he acts. He notes that not every act of virtue is commanded by the natural law and this follows from the fact that some people are unable to perform certain acts, e.g. a poor man is unable to execute an act of liberality. Consequently, man must act according to reason which is according to virtue, so that while not every act of virtue is required by the natural law, whenever man acts, he must act according to virtue.

Another thing of importance that St. Thomas notes in the above passage is the fact that there are many virtues toward which nature does not first incline us, but which are known through reason. This provides two important notions. The first is that reason, again, must be the guiding principle in a person's life, for since the other faculties do not grasp the natural law – i.e. the perfection of the various faculties or the ends of the various faculties – reason, which can grasp them, must be followed. For example, the concupiscible appetite inclines towards its end of eating, but it does not know how much to eat for the sake of the perfection or good of the individual; that can only be grasped by reason. Hence, the natural law is not merely a following of impulses or the appetites, but a governing of the appetites and other faculties by reason, which is able to grasp the universal as well as the particular good. Therefore, the natural law commands that reason be the guiding principle of action.

The second thing of importance is that St. Thomas says that the natural law does not at first incline one to the various virtues. Now here one must understand what the term "first" means. While through the natural law – i.e. by nature – man is inclined toward his perfection which consists in the virtues, nevertheless the various faculties other than the intellect do not incline one toward virtue *per se*. Virtue is something grasped and commanded by reason which grasps the nature of man and his faculties and can therefore know what action will suit or build virtue in that faculty or nature. However, while the faculties provide the foundation for reason to grasp what is suited to them, the faculties themselves do not grasp it. This means that the faculties incline toward natural goods but the *mode* in which they incline may actually be bad for the faculty itself since it does not grasp what is virtuous. Hence, while the nature and the various faculties do incline one to virtue, this inclination is not the first inclination but

---

naturali, dictat enim hoc naturaliter unicuique propria ratio, ut virtuose agat. Sed si loquamur de actibus virtuosis secundum seipsos, prout scilicet in propriis speciebus considerantur, sic non omnes actus virtuosi sunt de lege naturae. Multa enim secundum virtutem fiunt, ad quae natura non primo inclinat; sed per rationis inquisitionem ea homines adinvenerunt, quasi utilia ad bene vivendum."

[43]This is the formulation of the principle of operation, i.e. act follows upon form or being.

a further inclination continued within the faculty and grasped by reason.[44]

To finish the discussion of how one goes from the primary to secondary precepts of the natural law, we can say that three things are to be taken into consideration. The first is the three categories of inclination; some actions are able to be judged to be good or bad based merely on the three categories without any further consideration, e.g. suicide is wrong because it goes contrary to self-preservation and therefore suicide is prohibited by the natural law. When reason judges a specific course of action in light of the three categories but requires further considerations to draw a conclusion about the goodness or badness of an action, then it can consider the various faculties, if any, to which the action relates. Each faculty has a specific nature[45] which determines its finalities. Not only is the nature of man designed a certain way, but within that design there are faculties which are part of the design and those faculties are structured in such a way as to incline the individual toward the good which is their perfection. To violate the structure of the faculties is to go contrary to the nature, since those faculties contain the inclinations of the nature of the thing.

Hence, the structure and nature of the faculties as grasped by reason guide reason in the deliberation about practical matters, i.e. about what is good or bad for the person. This involves a twofold consideration; the first is that the faculties tell reason what perfects them and what does not, both according to their intrinsic structure as well as in the order of virtue. Second, the very nature of the faculty tells reason whether there are any moral finalities toward which the faculty directs man. This consideration avoids the problem of physicalism which is the error which states that if a faculty is physically a certain way, then it must be that way. For example, if one were to assert that because there are no holes on the ear lobe it would be immoral to wear ear rings, one would fall prey to the error of physicalism. Some moralists hold that any discussion whatsoever of the natural law is a succumbing to physicalism. The truth, of course, lies in the mean; for insofar as reason is able to grasp the essence of a thing, its own essence as well as the nature and structure of the faculties, reason is also capable of knowing when a

---

[44]It is not clear whether this is the result of original sin or not. St. Thomas indicated earlier that each faculty has its own object which is not the same as reason's, which is why they tend to act independently of reason. This seems to be something outside the discussion of original sin. Moreover, the Church teaches that the praeternatural gifts kept the appetites perfectly subordinated to reason. Virtue performs that role as well. What we seem to be left with is that, while the faculties may contain within them the inclination to virtue grasped by reason, the actual ordering of the faculties is something which must be superadded to them either by a preternatural gift or by virtue or some other thing which keeps them ordered toward their intrinsic finality, which is the virtue proper to them.

[45]Here, of course, the term *nature* is being used analogically insofar as an accident is said to have a nature. For the consideration of the various ways in which words which are applied to the essence of a thing can also be applied to the accidents although analogically, see *De ente et essentia*, c. 6.

specific faculty contains a *moral* finality and when it does not, e.g. reason can grasp the nature of the faculty of speech and know that to tell a lie violates the nature of the faculty of speech,[46] but one can look at the ears and see that, while the ears are ordered toward hearing sound, hearing sound *per se* does not constitute a moral finality as such. Therefore, reason is able to grasp that some faculties contain an inherent moral finality and others do not.[47] Hence, one compares an action to the moral finality of the faculty to derive some of the secondary precepts of the natural law.

A third consideration in determining whether an action is good or not is whether it causes virtue or vice in the faculty to which the action relates. This will apply to the four faculties of the intellect, will and the two appetites and not to the other faculties except insofar as the use of those faculties leads to virtue or vice in these four faculties. So if the previous two considerations do not provide enough for concluding whether an action is good or bad, then whether a given action will provide a virtue or a vice will aid the consideration. Therefore, there is a sufficient explanation in St. Thomas' works to derive the secondary precepts, if one employs the three ways of deriving them.

St. Thomas continues his discussion of the natural law by asking whether the natural law is one in all men. His response is that the natural law, with respect to the first common principles, is the same in all both according to rectitude (i.e. what is right) and is known by all.[48] He goes on to note, however, that as to the particular conclusions, what is right is not the same for all nor known by all.[49] What St. Thomas has in mind is that while the precepts of the natural law are the same in all men, nevertheless concrete circumstances can impede the fulfilling of certain positive precepts of the natural law, e.g. the natural law commands virtue and one of the virtues is liberality. However, a poor man, due to his circumstances, cannot develop the virtue of liberality due to his poverty. Hence, while the natural law in general commands the development

---

[46]See ST II-II, q. 110.

[47]This inherent moral finality is grasped in two ways, the first is through the form or very nature of the faculty and the second is through the effects of the faculty. The method of using the nature of the faculties to determine whether something is good or bad is something which Aquinas does not mention explicitly except in the quote above. It is mentioned here at length because of the fact that it is used as a method by Aquinas throughout his writing and so even if he does not delineate it fully, his method indicates to us that it is to be used, e.g. see ibid. and ST II-II, q. 153, just to name two. As one reads his commentary on the *Sentences* as well as the *Prima Secundae* and *Secunda Secundae*, the use of this method by St. Thomas is absolutely clear. Hence, insofar as the faculties determine the mode or way in which a specific nature relates to various objects or goods, then they are to be used in the discussion of the natural law.

[48]See ST I-II, q. 94, a. 4.

[49]Ibid.

of liberality, a poor man is impeded in developing it. However, with respect to the negative precepts of the natural law, they bind everywhere and in all cases, e.g. one ought never commit murder.

St. Thomas then asks whether the natural law is mutable, to which he says that the natural law can be changed in two ways, i.e. by addition and subtraction.[50] The first is by addition as when something is added to the natural law for the sake of being useful to man, e.g. prior to the fall of Adam and Eve, the natural law did not command man to wear clothing. However, after the fall, due to man's inordinate inclinations, it was necessary to add to the natural law the requirement of wearing clothing. With respect to subtraction, since the essence of man does not change, then nothing can be subtracted from the natural law.

Finally, St. Thomas asks whether the natural law can be abolished or deleted from the heart of man. He responds by saying that to those precepts of the natural law which are the most common, the natural law is not able to be deleted from the heart of man. However, it is able to be deleted when reason is impeded in applying the natural law to the particular action due to some passion. Here St. Thomas indicates not so much that the natural law itself is deleted but that the man does not act according to the inclinations proper to the natural law due to passion. He then goes on to say that the natural law is able to be deleted from the heart of man as to the secondary precepts due to evil persuasions in which practical reason errs or due to depraved customs or corrupt habits.[51] When a person is persuaded contrary to the natural law, then the natural law is not operative. While it is still present insofar as the essence of man is present, the individual is not inclined according to the ends of the natural law due to the error. This also applies with respect to the passions and this is why when it comes to the discussion of topics such as sexuality, people are often blinded by their passions and so they judge erroneously about what is right and wrong.

Although the natural law is an ordinance by which man is guided to the good[52] and thereby aids man in doing the good,[53] if reason errs, the person is not guided toward the good by the natural law. This is why St. Thomas makes the following observation: "universal knowledge of the natural law, which is naturally present in man, sometimes directs man to the good, but not sufficiently since in applying the universal principles of the law to particular acts, it happens that man fails many times."[54] Man is prone to

---

[50]ST I-II, q. 94, a. 5.

[51]ST I-II, q. 94, a. 6.

[52]ST I, q. 113, a. 1, ad 1.

[53]SCG III, c. 117, n. 6.

[54]ST I, q. 113, a. 1, ad 1: "universalis cognitio naturalis legis, quae homini naturaliter adest, aliqualiter dirigit hominem ad bonum, sed non sufficienter, quia in applicando universalia principia iuris ad particularia opera, contingit hominem multipliciter

error given his current state and, as a result, the natural law is not sufficient always to incline man rightly. This is not due to any defect of the natural law but due to the defects within man which result in his inability to judge rightly concerning actions and to command and will what is right due to his defects.[55]

E. Observations in Connection to the Natural Law

One of the problems that has affected psychology's ability to discuss the natural law, right and wrong, etc., has been partly historical[56] and it has been partly due to the drawing of wrong conclusions from certain facts. Here we have in mind that fact that some directees when going to psychologists have had psychological problems because of their immoral living which goes contrary to the natural law. As a result, the psychologists have rightly diagnosed that the problem is connected to the directee's moral code. However, instead of counseling the directee to follow the natural law, modern psychology has caused a great deal of harm by counseling directees to ignore or act contrary to the natural law, which has lead to further problems and has not solved the original one(s). Psychologists must respect the natural law, seek to know it and direct those under their care toward following the natural law, for if they do not, they shall adversely affect their reason and lead them to mental illness, not away from it.

Another observation is that the natural law regulates the passions and actions in ourselves and others, which is why if people act in congruity with or against the natural law they can affect their own mental health as well as those of others. Moreover, if one conforms one's will to the natural law, it keeps the will from getting disordered and thereby does not move the intellect to disordered acts, which, in turn, make it disordered. Following the natural law maintains the faculties and perfects them, which can affect mental health by aiding the intellect in acting according to its own nature as

––––––––––––––––

deficere."

[55]Two observations are in order. The first is, again, that this is why what the average individual does is not necessarily the norm insofar as the average individual suffers defects which cloud his judgment. The second is that the formal analysis of moral matters and psychological matters must be left to the "wise," i.e. those who have a firm grasp on the nature of the natural law through formal inquiry and not left to the masses who tend often to be governed by disordered appetitive impulse rather than natural inclination.

[56]It simply is not possible to go into the motivations of the various psychologists who rejected these discussions in connection to psychology. However, current research is showing that it is often due to the type of lives the psychologists themselves led (e.g. see E. Michael Jones's text, *Degenerate Moderns*). Nevertheless, the subsequent psychologists, who accepted the statements rejecting these matters by the pioneers of modern psychology, have never seriously analyzed this issue, due in large part, no doubt, to the investigation into those matters to be considered unscientific or "pre-psychological."

well as by keeping the other faculties from disordering the intellect. Finally, the natural law regulates acts of reason and so one can never be led to mental illness if one follows the natural law, but not following the natural law can lead to mental illness.

II. The Conscience

Having completed a very brief discussion of the natural law which deals with right and wrong, we must now discuss the conscience, which is so poorly understood by modern psychology. The conscience is an act of the possible intellect, i.e. an act of judgment,[57] by which one applies one's knowledge of right and wrong to a specific course of action.[58] Contrary to the opinion of some, the conscience is not a power but an act.[59] If it will be recalled, freedom is primarily exercised through choice and there is an act of the intellect which precedes choice in the moral decision making process. Conscience is the act of the intellect by which judgment is applied to the object of election[60] as to whether the act is right or wrong, good or bad. The conscience is sometimes called the law of our intellect since it is the judgment of reason deduced from the natural law[61] as well as synderesis.[62] An act of synderesis[63] is an act by which the intellect applies the natural law to considered action. So as one considers a course of action or more than one course of action, the intellect makes a judgment about the action as to whether it is in accordance with the natural law by way of drawing a conclusion about the action.[64]

Since most people do not possess a firm grasp of the structure and nature of the natural law, it was necessary that a capacity to grasp the first principles of the natural law (synderesis) as well as a capacity to grasp the secondary precepts of the natural law be placed within reason itself. As man is able to see the finalities toward which his nature is ordered, he knows what he must and must not do. Hence, when conscience makes a

---

[57]II Sent., d. 24, q. 2, a. 4 ad 2; ibid., d. 39, q. 3, a. 3; ST I, q. 79, a. 3 and De Ver., q. 17, a. 1.

[58]ST I, q. 79, a. 13 and ST I-II, q. 19, a. 5.

[59]II Sent., d. 24, q. 2, a 4; ST I, q. 79, a. 13 and De Ver., q. 17, a. 1.

[60]De Ver., q. 17, a. 1, ad 4. By extension, conscience can be applied to any act of the intellect which precedes an act of the will which deals with whether the act is morally good or bad.

[61]De Ver., q. 17, a. 1, ad sed contra 1 and 2.

[62]De Ver., q. 17, a. 2, ad 4.

[63]The conscience depends on synderesis, see De Ver., q. 17, a. 1. St. Thomas observes in De Ver., q. 17, a. 1 ad sed contra 6 that synderesis is placed in us by God and so it guides the conscience in its acts.

[64]II Sent., d. 24, q. 2, a. 4. This is also why logic is important.

judgment, it applies the knowledge it has of what is right and wrong, what is suitable or unsuitable for man (i.e. by knowledge of the first principles of the natural law through synderesis and the secondary precepts of the natural law) and considers his actions in light of them. This is why moral formation is of absolute importance in the raising of children. But sound moral formation applies to adults as well and to society as a whole. Insofar as man is formed in what is truly right and wrong for his nature, this can determine the psychological health of that individual. For it is through the conscience that man acts according to his nature and since it is unnatural to suffer mental illness, one who follows his nature will never suffer mental illness.[65]

The acts of the conscience are of three kinds.[66] The first is that the conscience recognizes whether a current action under consideration should or should not be done and for this reason the conscience is said to bind or incite; for insofar as it judges what is right and wrong, one is bound and incited to follow the conscience; otherwise one will pay the price for not following the natural law. Since the natural law is a law, i.e. something binding, the conscience is that by which we are bound to the natural law through knowledge of it and the actions to which the natural law applies. The second kind of act of conscience is when we recognize what we should have or should not have done in the past and in this sense the conscience testifies, i.e. it testifies to the praise or guilt of the individual in following or not following the natural law. In this way, the conscience acts as a witness present to the individual regarding his past acts. The third kind of act of conscience is whether something was done well (good) or badly in the past and for this reason it is said to excuse, accuse or torment. If the individual has done something well or if it was done involuntarily, then the conscience excuses. If the individual has done something bad, then it accuses or torments the individual.

When the conscience torments the impious[67] or those who do the wrong thing, it is called the *vermis conscientiae* or the worm or vermin of the conscience, in which the conscience afflicts the soul.[68] This vermin of conscience is a stimulation of the conscience[69] or a stinging of the soul[70] in that it gnaws away at the interior soul.[71] In short, it is a punishment for doing what is wrong,[72] for inasmuch as the conscience is that by which we judge our actions in light of the natural law, if we break the law, we are punished. Since the natural law is something interior to the essence of man, that is, it is

---

[65]Here we are prescinding from those mental illnesses which are strictly biological.

[66]These three are delineated in ST I, q. 79, a. 13 and De Ver., q. 17, a. 1.

[67]SCG IV, c. 90, n. 9.

[68]IV Sent., d. 50, q. 2, a. 3b.

[69]De Pot., q. 5, a. 9, ad 13.

[70]*Catena Aurea in Marcum*, c. 9, l. 6.

[71]Quod., XII, q. 5, a. 3.

[72]*In Psalmos*, p. 49, n. 10.

"in" him, then when that law is violated, the punishment is also interior. This is why many directees who do not follow the natural law find themselves tortured interiorly. From this follows depression and confusion insofar as many are not clear as to what the source of the problem is. Moreover, as it gnaws away at the interior part of man, if it is not alleviated, it continues to torture the person and can lead to emotional and other psychological illnesses.

This is where modern psychology has caused a great deal of harm. Many schools of psychology think that the conscience is just a habituated way of thinking, but because the conscience is an act of the intellect which is governed by the natural law, it is something essential or natural to man and cannot be done away with. This is why psychologists have had very little success when it comes to matters of this kind because they counsel individuals contrary to their own nature, which can actually lead to more problems for their directees. Rather, the psychologists must query the conscience of the individual so as to find where the problem is and counsel the directee to stop acting contrary to his nature, as well as seek to have the conscience cleared. Moreover, the psychologist must urge the directee to form his conscience properly by conforming his conscience to the natural law.

The conscience can be cleared or cleaned in two ways: the first is through sacramental confession[73] and the second is by reversing in some fashion the bad act done.[74] For instance, if a person has treated his parents terribly or ignored his parents all his life and his conscience bothers him, he may develop the passion of hatred for authority over time. Consequently, the person becomes emotionally disturbed by not honoring his parents. In order to resolve this, the directee should be counseled to reconcile with his parents and begin honoring them, the conscience will then be cleared[75] and the individual will find peace of soul, i.e. the emotional life will quiet down since it does not have the object of trouble present to it any more.[76]

---

[73]This topic will be broached in the second volume at much greater length.

[74]De Ver., q. 17, a. 1, ad 3.

[75]This is true although the conscience is not cleaned or cleared entirely. Since the natural law is placed in the heart of man by God, it means that the person must also reconcile himself with God since he has violated God's (i.e. the natural) law.

[76]It should be noted that even when the person reconciles himself with the parents and this applies to all actions that are bad and even when he has reconciled himself to God, there persists in the individual other problems arising from doing what is wrong. The effects of evil acts cause tremendous damage to the appetitive, volitional and intellective state of the individual. They cause appetitive damage because the appetites become disordered by the bad acts commanded, e.g. when one engages in sexual acts outside the context of marriage, the appetites become attached to an object (i.e. a form of action) which is contrary to the natural law. The intellect becomes disordered because it has commanded something which is evil when it knew what was good. The intellect becomes disordered when the will

Furthermore, the will which is discordant with the conscience[77] is bad because it wills the bad object in the intellect. Insofar as it is discordant with the judgment of conscience, the will introduces disorder between the two faculties of intellect and will. Since what is in the intellect and will tend to flow over into the lower faculties, they become disordered as well.[78] Hence, one errs when he has chosen or elected something contrary to the judgment of conscience.[79]

Finally, the last consideration is with respect to the erroneous conscience since it is a fact of life that the conscience can err,[80] as the common experience of all men readily attests. The conscience can err in essentially two ways:[81] the first is with respect to what the natural law prohibits or allows, i.e. the conscience may err about the secondary precepts of the natural law. Hence when it reasons about what is to be done, it draws the wrong conclusion because it has the wrong principles (precepts) by which it judges. The second is in syllogizing or reasoning about what is to be done, i.e. it errs in applying the right principle or precept to the particular act. This is done in two ways, viz. in the actual reasoning process or in erring about the act to be done. For instance, one may know that adultery is wrong, but if one thinks that a woman is his wife when she is in fact not his wife, then he would erroneously draw the conclusion that it was permissible in this case to engage in the conjugal act with this woman.

The conscience, however, must always be followed,[82] even if it is erroneous.[83] Obviously the correct conscience always binds simply and unconditionally. However, even the erroneous conscience binds because a person does not know that he has an

---

dominates it rather than the will being moved by the intellect to the good, i.e. one does not act according to right reason. The will becomes disordered by willing the evil and thereby gains bad habits. Finally the will becomes disordered because it ceases submitting itself to the truth, i.e. to the intellect. So even if the conscience is cleared, there are other disorders that may need to be addressed.

[77]ST I-II, q. 19, a. 5.

[78]Since to will something the intellect has to formulate a phantasm, the bad form is made in the phantasm and the appetites are trained to the evil by means of the bad phantasm. Moreover, they are trained for what is bad by virtue of being presented with their object in a bad fashion or at an undue time, etc.

[79]De Ver., q. 17, a. 1, ad 4.

[80]II Sent., d. 39, q. 3, a. 2 and De Ver., q. 17, a. 2.

[81]See De Ver., q. 17, a. 2.

[82]De Ver., q. 17, a. 3. St. Thomas observes in ibid. that it is of divine precept that one must always follow one's conscience. Obviously one must always follow the natural law and so that act of the intellect by which knowledge of the natural law is applied must always be adhered to.

[83]II Sent., d. 39, q. 3, a. 3; De Ver., q. 17, a. 4 and Quod., III, q. 12, a. 2.

erroneous conscience at the moment in which he is considering whether the action is right or wrong, i.e. he does not know that he errs.[84] He only knows that he errs later after coming to knowledge of his error. Hence, even when he is erring, he thinks what he is doing is right and one must always do what one thinks is right. It should be noted, as it was previously, that when one acts contrary to the natural law, there are bad effects and this applies even to the erroneous conscience. Even if the conscience is not bad as a result of the evil done since it did not know it was evil, nevertheless, nature knows it, and disorders can arise because one is commanding actions which are, in fact, bad for the other faculties and so they can become disordered as a result.[85]

Conclusion

The very brief and basic treatment of the subalternated principles provided here should provide enough context to begin discussing mental health and illness itself. A psychologist should never content himself with the conviction that he knows enough to stop at this point. Knowledge of the subalternated principles should be filled out by a strong philosophical education and training prior to considering oneself adequately trained to treat psychological illness. Since the subalternated principles[86] have been adequately treated for our purposes, we now proceed to the third part in which we provide a consideration of mental health and illness *per se*.

---

[84]De Ver., q. 17, a. 4.

[85]This is why formation of the conscience is so important.

[86]That is the philosophical subalternated principles. Other principles shall be discussed in the second and third volumes.

Part III: The Philosophy of Mental Health and Illness

Chapter 12: The Nature of Mental Health and Illness

It is unfortunate that St. Thomas never did a formal treatise on mental health and illness and, no doubt, the reasons are primarily historical, in the sense that the issue of mental health and illness was simply not of great concern except in connection with the discussion of the sacraments. However, St. Thomas does make reference to them and although he does not go into a formal discussion about the nature of mental health and illness, his discussion is sufficient to derive at least some basic but essential notions about mental health and illness from his writings. After a short discussion of St. Thomas' treatment of mental illness, we can then proceed to a formal definition of mental health and illness and then make further distinctions as to the different categories or kinds of mental health and illness.

I. St. Thomas on Mental Health and Illness

There are many words which St. Thomas uses to refer to the mentally ill. The first of which is *amens,* coming from the two Latin words *ab mens* literally meaning from the mind or away from the mind but it is usually translated as mad or insane. He observes that the "amentes" suffer from a defect of reason,[1] i.e. they do not have use of reason.[2] He notes that someone who has a bad bodily disposition can be deprived of their use of reason and become insane.[3] Since they do not have use of reason, it also means that some of the "amentes" are entirely without judgment,[4] i.e. the act of judgment of the possible intellect is entirely impeded. Consequently, since they do not have the use of reason and since reason is that which proposes to the will its object, then the will is also affected. For this reason St. Thomas observes that the "amentes" do not have use of free will.

Another term that St. Thomas uses is *phrenetici,* who are those whose operations of the intellect are impeded[5] on the part of a bodily organ,[6] such as when someone has a lesion. Moreover, the phrenetic suffer from the imagination being

---

[1]ST II-II, q. 70, a. 3 and ibid., q. 88, a. 9.

[2]ST III, q. 68, a. 12, ad 1; ibid., q. 80, a. 9, ad 3 and In Ethic. I, l. 16, n. 11 (197).

[3]In SCG III, c. 85, n. 20, he notes that the celestial bodies can cause a bodily indisposition and cause one to be deprived of the use of reason. What is important is not so much the agency, but the fact that those who are ill disposed may be deprived of their use of reason.

[4]IV Sent., d. 9, q. 1, a. 5c.

[5]II Sent., d. 20, q. 2, a. 2, ad 3; III Sent., d. 15, q. 2, a. 3b; IV Sent., d. 33, q. 3, a. 1 and SCG III, c. 48, n. 8.

[6]SCG II, c. 73, n. 39 and ST I, q. 101, a. 2.

impeded in its proper operation[7] as well as they do not have use of their memory.[8] Since their imagination is impeded, the phrenetic do not have the use of reason[9] and so they are said to be *ex mente captis*, i.e. captive of mind.[10]

There are a few quotes of St. Thomas which can aid the discussion of the nature of mental health and illness and the first is from the fourth book of his commentary on the *Sentences*:

> Hence, we do not say that the phrenetic and others of captive mind,
> in which there is a flux of species of this kind to the organ of sensing,
> truly sense because of the victory of the imaginative power, but that
> it seems to them that they sense.[11]

Here St. Thomas is noting that the phrenetic and others whose minds are captive think they sense something because of the power of the imagination. The imagination is so strong that it affects what they think they sense. In this case, the imagination affects the judgment to such a degree that the person actually thinks he senses something when in fact he does not.

Another passage is in the *Prima Secundae*, which is as follows: "for judgment and the apprehension of reason is impeded because of the vehement and inordinate apprehension of the imagination and the judgment of the estimative power, as is clear in the mentally ill."[12] Here the "amentes" cannot exercise judgment or the apprehension of reason, i.e. reason is impeded in its proper operations, because of the vehemence and inordinate apprehension of the imagination. Since judgment depends on the imagination, then if the image in the imagination is too vehement, the person cannot exercise judgment on the phantasm. The reason this is the case is that when the imagination is held captive, the possible intellect is bound to (locked into) judging it the

---

[7]ST I, q. 84, a. 7; De Ver., q. 18, a. 8, ad 4; In Meta., IV, l. 14, n. 2 and *Super Ad Hebraeos*, c. 1, l. 1.

[8]SCG II, c. 73, n. 39. Another term St. Thomas uses for those whose memory is impeded but only the memory is the "lethargic," see SCG II, c. 73, a. 39 and ST I, q. 84, a. 7.

[9]ST I, q. 101, a. 2 and De Malo, q. 3, a. 4.

[10]IV Sent., d. 44, q. 2, a 1c; De Ver., q. 13, a. 1 and De Pot., q. 6, a. 5.

[11]IV Sent., d. 44, q. 2, a. 1c: "Unde non dicimus quod phrenetici et alii mente capti, in quibus propter victoriam imaginativae virtutis fit hujusmodi fluxus specierum ad organa sentiendi, vere sentiant, sed quod videtur eis quod sentiant."

[12]ST I-II, q. 77, a. 1: "Impeditur enim iudicium et apprehensio rationis propter vehementem et inordinatam apprehensionem imaginationis, et iudicium virtutis aestimativae, ut patet in amentibus."

way it is presented in the phantasm, rather than the possible intellect being able to make changes to the formalities or perspectives contained within the phantasm.[13] Furthermore, when the formality is very strong the intellect has a hard time not judging it that way unless the possible intellect itself is very strong.[14] Moreover, St. Thomas notes that if the estimative sense is too vehement, then again the person cannot exercise judgment. By estimative sense, we presume that St. Thomas means the cogitative power, so with the mentally ill, if the cogitative power associates something vehemently with a phantasm, the possible intellect is impeded in its judgment about the phantasm.

The next passage is likewise in his commentary on the *Sentences* and it is somewhat longer:

> Furor and concupiscence and phantasy are not in the demons properly but metaphorically speaking, since the sensitive part does not pertain to them, like those who are not angels. For every defect of the soul which occurs in us, is either from the phantasm so far as to knowledge, of which is falsity, according to the Philosopher, or from the irascible and concupiscible passions so far as to affection: And, therefore, the will of the demons by inordinately detesting or desiring something, is called furor and concupiscence; his disordered intellect is called phantasy. Moreover, this disordered intellect is from a depraved will: and therefore it is called perverted phantasy, since he is perverted who pertinaciously fights the truth. Irrationality and mental illness, furor and concupiscence import an obliqueness of the will from the right judgment of the intellect or reason; and ignorance not of speculation, but of election, insofar as every evil is ignorant.[15]

---

[13]In other words, the possible intellect cannot change the perspective given to the phantasm by some power or by the perceptive inherently contained in it from the sense data, e.g. the sense data in television often contains a formality or perspective within the very image conveyed in order to elicit a certain mood or judgment on the side of the watcher.

[14]This also applies to the will; even if the possible intellect judges it wrongly, if the will is rightly ordered and stronger than the imagination and possible intellect, then it can override the imagination and consequently order the possible intellect to judge a different phantasm in the imagination or even move the imagination to negate the current phantasm by imposing a negative formality on the phantasm by choice and thereby provide a different perspective of the intellect by which to judge.

[15]II Sent., d. 7, q. 2, a. 1, ad 1: "Furor et concupiscentia et phantasia non sunt in daemonibus proprie, sed metaphorice, cum pertineant ad sensitivam partem, quae non est in angelis. omnis enim defectus animae qui in nobis accidit, vel est ex phantasia quantum ad cognitionem, cujus proprium est falsitas, secundum philosophum, vel ex passionibus irascibilis et concupiscibilis quantum ad affectionem: et ideo voluntas daemonum inordinate

St. Thomas has said a great deal here in his comparison to demonic disorder and the mentally ill. The first is that the demons have a disordered intellect because of their depraved will. With respect to man, man is able to disorder his intellect by the will choosing to move the intellect to command what is false and to make judgments as true which the intellect knows are false. Moreover, in man, the intellect can arrive at falsity as a result of the passions which was seen previously. Hence, the intellect in man can become disordered or impeded in its operation as a result of disordered appetites.

II. A Formal Definition of Mental Health and Illness

From what St. Thomas has said, we can derive a formal definition of mental health. Since mental illness is the negation or the opposite of mental health, it is first necessary to give a formal definition of mental health and then a formal definition can be given of mental illness. The primary characteristic of the mentally ill, as St. Thomas discusses, is that they lack the use of reason and judgment and, on the other hand, the characteristic of mental health is the actual use of judgment[16] and reason. Since the mentally ill suffer from some defect of reason, then mental illness is something in the intellect itself. Therefore the actual definition of mental health and illness is contained in the very terms themselves. Mental health is a form of health (genus) of the mind or intellect (specific difference) and mental illness is an illness (genus) of the mind (specific difference). But the terms health and illness are primarily a reference to a quality of the body and so in their application to the intellect, they must be used analogically.

From the aforesaid, we can therefore give a more formal definition of mental health as the following: Mental health is a quality residing in the possible intellect which renders the faculty capable of acting according to its proper nature, i.e. rationally. Mental health is essentially a quality of the possible intellect just as bodily health is a quality of the body. Mental health is a quality[17] which gives the possible intellect the capacity to act according to its proper nature, i.e. mental health gives the intellect the capacity to exercise its three acts, particularly judgment and reasoning, which is a form of going from judgment to judgment. Now an operative quality in a faculty which aids

---

detestans et appetens aliquid, dicitur furor et concupiscentia; et intellectus suus deordinatus, dicitur phantasia. Haec autem deordinatio intellectus est ex prava voluntate: et ideo dicitur phantasia proterva, quia protervus est qui pertinaciter verum impugnat. irrationalitas autem et amentia, furor et concupiscentia important obliquitatem voluntatis a recto judicio intellectus vel rationis; et ignorantiam non speculationis, sed electionis, secundum quam omnis malus est ignorans."

[16]ST III, q. 68, a. 12.

[17]It may actually be the result of many qualities.

its action is called a virtue and so mental health is some kind of virtue.[18] The definition of mental illness is a defect or the lack of the quality of mental health and so its definition is: a lack of a due quality or a defect residing in the possible intellect which renders the faculty incapable of acting according to its proper nature, i.e. the intellect cannot act rationally. Here we see that mental illness is the lack of a due quality of the intellect and for that reason, it is a defect or an evil. This defect impedes or makes impossible the proper operations of the possible intellect leaving the person irrational. A lack of a due operative quality in a faculty which impedes its proper action is called a vice and so mental illness is some kind of vice.[19]

III. Further Specifications of Mental Health and Illness

Now mental health is possible only when the possible intellect is not being disordered by other faculties, viz. the will, interior senses and appetites.[20] St. Thomas makes a further distinction which helps us to see what mental health and illness are: "The furious and the mentally ill lack the use of reason *per accidens*, viz. because of some impediment of the corporal organ, not because of a defect of the rational soul, as with the brute animals."[21] From this observation we can make a distinction within the kinds of mental health and illness. There is a mental health and illness *per se* and a mental health and illness *per accidens*. Mental health *per se* is that quality of the possible intellect itself by which it acts according to its own nature; mental health *per accidens* is the bodily disposition or virtues and habits in the appetites and interior senses which make possible the exercising of the acts of the possible intellect according to its nature. Hence, the right habits in the interior senses and the virtues in the appetites aid the possible intellect in its operations. Moreover, mental health *per accidens* can be said of the will insofar as the will inclines itself toward rational forms, i.e. toward that which is truly good and therefore it will not cause disorders in the intellect.

Mental illness *per se* consists of a defect or defects in the possible intellect which makes it incapable of judging or reasoning *properly*. It is a disorder which makes one think contrary to rational principles. This occurs in those, for instance, who lie so habitually that the intellect becomes incapable of knowing the truth or judging the truth because of an interior defect. We can say this about any object of the intellect if the

---

[18]It is either a virtue or the conglomeration of "intellectual" virtues.

[19]It is either a vice or the connexus of intellectual vices.

[20]All exterior factors to the individual which cause mental illness do so by acting upon these faculties.

[21]ST III, q. 68, a. 12, a d 2: "furiosi vel amentes carent usu rationis per accidens, scilicet propter aliquod impedimentum organi corporalis, non autem propter defectum animae rationalis, sicut bruta animalia."

possible intellect is incapable of judging rightly about that object due to disorders introduced by other faculties or due to its own systematic erroneous judgment about an object. With mental illness *per se*, one performs acts of judgment, but they are disordered or contrary to rational principles, i.e. contrary to the very rational nature of the intellect.

Mental illness *per accidens* is when the possible intellect cannot exercise its proper function due to some extrinsic cause, e.g. the phrenetic are those who cannot exercise the use of reason or judgment because of problems in the phantasm or cogitative power. Hence, mental illness *per accidens* is either direct or indirect,[22] i.e. it is direct when the faculty has the capacity to render the possible intellect or to affect it directly and this would pertain to the interior sense of the imagination and the will. It is proximate indirect when the faculty affects the possible intellect by means of another faculty and this would pertain to the appetites and the other three interior senses which act upon the imagination. Now those things which cause mental illness *per accidens* by acting upon the three interior senses or appetites are called the remote indirect. They are remote indirect because they are further removed from those which affect it indirectly yet are proximate to the faculties which affect it directly. Here we have in mind the five exterior senses and those things which act upon them, e.g. environment, other people and things, etc. These things can be psychologically healthy or unhealthy depending upon their effect on the individual.

There are two last distinctions that must be made and that is with respect to objects and degrees of mental health or illness. Now in the common experience of man of those who suffer psychological difficulties, some have problems with some objects and not others, e.g. some cannot think rationally about open spaces because of the vehemence of fear while in all other aspects of the person's life there may not be any difficulties. Some have problems with one object, some with few, some with many and some are afraid or suffer psychological problems with respect to everything. Lastly, psychological illnesses are like bodily illnesses in that they vary according to degree, from slight to grave. Hence, some might have just a mild fear of heights which impedes their judgment slightly but which can be controlled through an act of the will while others cannot even function in any rational or volitional capacity when they are placed on a high location.[23] Lastly, there are a large number of different kinds of objects; each kind or category of object will be the basis of a different kind of mental health or

---

[22]This distinction would apply also to mental health, i.e. direct and indirect *per accidens* mental health.

[23]This distinction is important because how one overcomes a slight mental illness is different from one which is grave.

illness.[24]

Conclusion

With formal definitions of mental health and illness and the proper distinctions between them having been made, it is now possible to discuss how one loses and gains mental health and illness. Once it can be seen how one loses and gains mental health and illness, then methods of direction can be devised for the directee to procure and maintain mental health and to avoid mental illness. Furthermore, within the very discussion itself of how to avoid mental illness and gain mental health, psychologists as psychological directors will know how to avoid contracting the mental illnesses of their directees or other psychological illnesses associated with those of their directees.

---

[24]This is also true with mental health, in that mental health is often stronger in respect to some objects rather than others. Since mental health is a virtue and mental illness is a vice, then, like other virtues and vices, they determine how the faculty relates to its object. Those who have mental health relate well to the object whereas those who are mentally ill do not relate well to the object.

Chapter 13: Exterior Causes of Mental Health and Illness

Addressing the causes of mental health and illness shall complete this brief study of the philosophical aspects of the science of mental health and illness. It should not be assumed that if a cause is not listed here, it does not exist, for to discuss every conceivable cause of mental health and illness simply is not possible.[1] While the science of mental health and illness is a science, it is also an art and as an art it is practical and therefore is subject to a virtually infinite number of circumstances. Therefore, in this chapter, the categories of causes of mental health and some basic principles and observations about those categories shall be proffered in order to provide a clear direction to the science of psychology when it seeks to help those who suffer mental illness.

I. General Observations

From the previous chapter, it is clear that mental health *per se* is a quality in the possible intellect and mental illness *per accidens* exists in those faculties which have the capacity to affect operations of the possible intellect. Therefore, everything which aids the use of reason, i.e. whatever helps the possible intellect to act according to its proper nature, is a cause of mental health. This applies not only to those who are mentally ill and trying to gain mental health, but also it is true with respect to those who are already mentally healthy but wish to maintain their mental health. The converse is also true, viz. everything which detracts from the use of reason impedes the possible intellect in acting according to its proper nature and is a cause of mental illness. Those who are mentally healthy can lose their mental health when the possible intellect is impeded, though not always since how one reacts to those things which may cause *per accidens* mental illness can also lead to mental health. Those who are already mentally ill may find, through the various causes of mental illness, new mental illnesses or even become completely mentally ill.

Those who are mentally ill *per se* and *per accidens* to such a degree as to take them completely outside of contact with reality with no periods of lucidity are catastrophically mentally ill. It appears in these cases that two possible means of regaining mental health are able to be pursued. The first is through chemical means in which the imbalances in the brain or body are corrected through medications or proper diet. It may be the case, although research will have to be done to determine the truth of the matter, that various forms of stimuli can be the cause of bringing the person back into contact with his senses. This does not imply that the application of various

---

[1] On the other hand, if it is not listed here, a psychologist should not assume that it could still be a cause, e.g. the subconscious is not listed here and that is because it is not a real cause of mental illness. That topic shall be broached in volume III.

sensations to the individual has to be powerful or extreme, but that perhaps constant forms of sensations or particular kinds of sensation may actually cause physical changes in the brain to allow some periods or some degree of lucidity. As for those who are not catastrophically mentally ill, some ways of regaining mental health will be given in this chapter.

The categories of causes of mental health and illness are three in number, viz. (1) exterior causes, (2) ourselves and (3) angels and God.[2] It pertains therefore to this chapter to discuss these three causes.

II. Exterior Causes

The exterior causes are all those things which affect the senses and so this category includes anything that enters into a person's sensory experience. Yet, anything that enters into our sensory experience can actually lead either to mental health or illness. They can lead to mental illness if they are not judged properly by the possible intellect and if the possible intellect and will do not keep control over the lower faculties by means of properly forming the phantasms. If someone sees a spider and is scared because of antecedent appetite, through consequent appetite or through the reformulation of the phantasm, they can calm their fear if they judge properly about the spider. In fact, encountering nature can lead to mental health in two ways. The first is that if people judge rightly about the things of nature, then proper phantasms are stored in memory and the cogitative power is trained to associate properly and the passions are trained. Secondly, as this occurs repeatedly, good habits, i.e. virtues, are built up in the respective faculties which aid the person in the future to be able to approach various objects of nature in a healthy fashion. These observations apply to all of the categories of the exterior causes. Regardless of what happens to a person in human relations, contact with nature as well as with technology is dependent primarily on how the person reacts to it. If the possible intellect and will function correctly, these things can actually lead to mental health, regardless of how traumatic. On the other hand, all these things can lead to mental illness if right judgment is not obtained or bad will occurs.

The exterior causes are subdivided into three categories, viz. nature,[3] technology, and human relations. The things of nature include all those things which are

---

[2] Angels and God can be discussed based strictly on knowledge gained through the natural light of reason. However, since a full understanding of their causal action on our mental health is had only when knowledge of them is joined to what is known through revealed theology, they will be discussed in volume II. Also, even though God and angels are exterior causes, the treatment of them will not be done at this time.

[3] Here we are not using it in the sense of natural law, but in the second sense described in the chapter on natural law, viz. those things which comprise the physical universe.

not artificially produced by man and which do not encompass any relationship to human beings. This would include such things as forests, open fields, animals of various kinds, insects, etc. As a general rule, all natural objects are ordered toward aiding man's mental health. The reason this is the case is because man's intellect is fundamentally ordered toward knowing all things by knowing material things. The physical universe is fundamentally ordered toward man insofar as it is designed so that it is able to be known and used by man for his benefit. Moreover, man is ordered toward the physical universe in the sense that his knowledge and physical well-being is dependent upon it.[4] This also means that man can benefit psychologically from nature in three ways. The first is by being in contact with it. Those who are mentally ill often do not have much contact with anything other than the technological atmosphere and environment created by modern man. By putting someone in contact with nature, they are placed in the "natural" environment and so if they judge it properly, it can have a profound positive effect psychologically. Second, it also teaches man right order insofar as nature was designed for man and is there for his benefit. So provided he approaches it properly, he can learn his place in reality and therefore the truth known in the intellect and right judgments being made will contribute to virtues in the possible intellect which aid the act of judgment and therefore mental health. The third is that the natural world in being ordered and designed for man has a naturally good effect on man. For instance, those who go by a waterfall find the sound soothing to human nature, to the appetites in particular and it has a general calming effect on man. Different things in nature can be used to bring about different passions in man and so the appetites can be trained by being in contact with nature.

While natural objects have a naturally good effect on man psychologically, a particular individual can experience difficulties with nature due to prior experiences or contact with certain aspects of nature. These must be dealt with through contact with the thing of nature which causes problems with the aid of a psychologist to direct the person's experience of it. If that does not solve the problem, then the general means of direction by the psychologist as will be discussed with respect to the appetites, interior senses, possible intellect and will must be employed.

The second category of exterior causes is technology. Technology in itself is a good. As a good it can lead to mental health, however, it must be kept in its proper

---

[4]The providential plan of God is such that the universe was designed for man as he is the highest creation in the physical order and he has the capacity to change, manipulate and use it toward his benefit. While other creatures benefit from it as well, they only benefit from part of the physical universe, whereas man can benefit from all of it which is a sign that it was designed for man ultimately.

place. Technology or man's art over nature is a useful good[5] and is not an end in itself. This must be born in mind, otherwise if it is made into an end in itself, it can cause mental illness since it is a false understanding of the useful good or goods. For example, some people can suffer mental illness in relation to money[6] which is merely a useful good. Some people can suffer mental illness with respect to automobiles, especially if they have had a traumatic experience. Some people have an irrational fear of technological things because they lack knowledge about them,[7] e.g. some older people fear computers because they seem complicated or they do not understand how they function.

Technology can also lead to mental illness insofar as it is an artificial thing. This does not mean it is evil, but it means that as an artificial thing it can result in detaching people from reality. If people use technology too much, or if they know only technology and not natural things, then it can result in the intellect becoming detached from reality. For example, people who use computers a great deal and become engrossed in the cyber-life or in the computer to a great degree, do not develop social skills or they begin forgetting about the world outside of the computer. This applies to just about any form of technology. Furthermore, computers as well as other forms of

---

[5]There are three kinds of good, viz. the useful good, the honest good and the pleasurable good. The useful good is that which is a means for obtaining some other good. The honest good or the good simply speaking is that which is sought for its own sake and for no other reason. The pleasurable good is that which gives pleasure or delight.

[6]It should be noted that money is a particularly difficult useful good. Since money consists in the assignment of a value by reason to a specific physical thing which in itself is not necessarily valuable, money is a being of reason and not a real thing. While physical things are called money, they are, in fact, paper, metal or things of this sort. Money is a mental construct and this is clearly evidenced by the fact that in contemporary society, money is often merely an electronic number stored in a computer which is even further detached from a physical thing. Because money can provide a great deal to a person's capacities in life, it can often be the cause of mental difficulties as man can easily become attached to it because of what it can provide.

[7]Lack of knowledge of a thing is a powerful psychological force in man. Man tends to find knowledge comforting because he then knows the dangers involved regarding it and so he can avoid any danger with respect to it. Lack of knowledge leads to fear because a person fears being victimized or causing harm to himself or others because he does not understand the thing he is using. The solution is twofold to this kind of fear. The first is contact with the object under the guidance of someone who does know the object. This allows the person to allay the fear since he knows he will not cause problems or be victimized because he can depend on someone else's knowledge. The second is that the person must control the fear by keeping control over the phantasm. The more rational a person is, the less he tends to fear the unknown because he can keep things in perspective more readily.

technology give man a great deal of delight because they increase his power over nature. If man begins to think that he himself has become more powerful rather than the technology upon which he depends becoming more powerful, then it can lead to the false notion that man can manipulate reality at will. This results in a detachment from man's real condition in relation to nature. Moreover, as man becomes more and more attached to the power the technology has over nature, the person begins to develop expectations about nature itself or begins to view nature in a different fashion. The worst case scenario is when the person begins to fail to see himself as a part of nature, which is a form of detachment from reality. Accompanying this scenario is a detachment from the natural law and so man begins to manipulate himself in ways which are contrary to nature because he does not have a proper view of technology. Technology is a useful good and therefore it is similar to all of nature in the sense that it is there for man's benefit. Since it is there for man's benefit, man must use it only when it actually benefits him, otherwise it can lead to mental illness.

Technology can also lead to mental health, however, when it is used to affect the imagination in a positive fashion. People can suffer all of the problems mentioned in regard to computers and with respect to television. However, television is a profoundly useful tool because it is so human. What is meant by that is that television is a device by which the images in the imagination can be affected or caused. Hence, if someone has mental illness with respect to some specific object, watching television can often correct the phantasm or image in the memory or in the imagination. The reason this is the case is that the judgment or *ratio*, i.e. perspective about the object, can be delivered through the television by means of the image and sound. In this sense, televison is very closely approximated to the imagination. It functions in a very similar fashion and, so as a result, it has the capacity to become something which can greatly affect the appetites and emotions of man.

However, because television provides a constant stream of images, it is easy for a person to surrender volitional control of the imagination which is fed constant images and sound[8] by the television. This mechanism has a general pacifying effect, i.e. it makes the person passive. In order to watch television, there has to be a certain surrendering of the imagination to images provided by the television. Two observations are in order. The first is that this can be extremely dangerous in that one can just allow the television to do the thinking for him. Watching television should be more active in that the person should be passing judgments on what he is watching and when the television violates the truth, the person should recognize that, so that the television and programming is kept in proper perspective. Second, since it has a pacifying effect, it can lead to other problems, such as laziness, sloth, as well as allowing the programs on the

---

[8]As man is more drawn to sight than animals, this is why television is so powerful for man. Television is also very powerful because it uses the two highest sense faculties, viz. sight and hearing.

television to control and do one's thinking for oneself. Television is a good thing but like all good things its use must be moderated so as not to have too much control over the thinking of the individual.

The second thing is that television can cause mental health or illness. If the program gives the wrong images it can erode mental health by affecting how people judge the images. Since the images often contain a prepackaged perspective or judgment within them, if people are not judicious, they can begin causing the judgment to be determined without the full control of the individual. This medium is very powerful and so those in charge of it bear an awesome responsibility in its use.[9] Therefore, the television can cause mental illness if the person watching it is not careful. It can also cause mental health, however. If a psychologist can ascertain what the particular mental illness is of a patient, then he can prescribe the watching of certain programs which can help to calm the individual, or it can correct his judgment since the television images can contain a judgment contained in the image. It can also cause virtue, since the person can see the value of virtue and acts of virtue and so it can move the will to willing virtue. It can inform the patient of the truth which is the good of the intellect and therefore have a positive effect on the individual. Psychology would be greatly advanced on the practical level if proper programs were developed or used which could correct the judgment of the individual.

Other forms of technology can aid mental health as well. If technology is used properly and kept in perspective, it can aid man's judgment about himself and reality. It can also calm fears, etc. as when someone is fearful that they will not have food to eat; technology can be used to grow crops, harvest animals, etc. So the person can feel less fearful because they are less at the whim of physical forces. Moreover, they can provide delight in ways which can help depression, etc. Each of the passions can be affected by technology, if employed properly.

The last category of the world is human relations. This is perhaps one of the most complicated areas of psychology and as a result cannot be fully developed here. This category can be subdivided into: family, friends, those with whom one works, enemies, strangers and finally those to whom the interior forum is divulged. The subcategory of family has a profound effect on people and this is because of man's nature. For instance, in man's nature is placed a psychological mechanism in which children naturally look for guidance from their parents. It is natural to man to depend on, love and learn from one's parents since they are the most proximate relation children have, for there is no one naturally closer to a child than his parents. This means that

---

[9]Those who use it must conform themselves to the natural law and their programming must likewise be conformed to the natural law otherwise it can cause mental illness in those who watch it. It has become such a powerful force, that it can actually influence the course of a society's thinking to such great degree that it is almost more powerful than civil law.

parents have a profound psychological effect on children and this is a necessary part of man's nature. It is necessary because children are basically a *tabula rasa* when they are born and therefore they need a great deal of intellectual and moral formation.

With respect to parents, there are three considerations. The first is that one must keep in mind the principle of resemblance so that the mental health of the parents often begets the mental health of the child, though this is not always the case because a child does have free will and can therefore choose a path leading to mental illness. Next, the intellectual and moral formation given by the parents accounts for a large portion of the intellectual formation of children with the exception of schools that they might attend.[10] This means that the psychological impact parents have on children is astounding and parents must keep that in mind. Third, this psychological influence over the child can be there for good or ill. If the parents raise the children in a good psychological environment with all those things proper to human nature[11] and provided the child makes the right choices, he has a very good chance of reaching adulthood psychologically healthy. If parents exhibit a proper relationship among themselves the child learns stability emotionally and psychologically because of the stability within the relationship of the parents. The child also learns right order with respect to his place in life, i.e. he learns circumspection. If the family is rightly ordered, which is something largely dependent upon the parents, then the child learns the proper place of authority and his relationship to it. The child learns how to get along with other people by the

---

[10]This indicates that home schooling is actually more in congruity with the nature of man than private or public schools. The reason is that parents carry a natural authority in the mind of the child. This was placed there by God to ensure that the child would submit himself to the intellectual and moral formation by the parents; otherwise it would not be possible for the child to get a sound formation. Since home schooling keeps the authority structure more in congruity with man's nature, it allows the child to appropriate material more. When the child is sent to school, the natural authority of the parents is replaced by authority by proxy (*in loco parentis*), i.e. the child has to submit himself to the teacher, not because of any natural moral authority of the teacher but because the parents have given that authority to the teacher. Hence, home schooling is in more congruity with man's nature, provided the parents can give the child an adequate formation.

[11]This would include such things as a loving home life and a concern on the side of the parents for physical, intellectual and moral well-being of the child, which the child senses. This has a twofold impact. Since a child is naturally subordinate to the authority of the parents, the child needs affirmation as a subordinate, that the parents care about him, otherwise this natural subordination is short-circuited because the child must look elsewhere for its formation. The second is that the child is formed as to how one ought to treat a child and so the child will learn how to be a parent from his own parents unless factors exterior to the family have an impact on him.

adults training him to get along with his siblings.[12]

Negatively, parents can have bad, even devastating effects on their children. Instability in the relationship of the parents will inevitably affect the children, unless through judgment and will, they are able to keep a proper perspective: as a general rule, most children are unable to do this. For example, when parents fight, they teach their children to give in to anger which can lead to mental illness. Also, when they fight, they militate against the child's natural love for both parents and so the child can be greatly disturbed because two people he loves are fighting and willing bad things for each other.

If divorce occurs, the parents place the children in the worst possible scenario for several reasons. The first is that children become divided in their hearts over the parents, which naturally leads to interior conflict and mental illness.[13] Second, when parents divorce, it takes out of the children's lives one of the two people responsible for their formation. Children need both parents for a proper psychological formation[14] and the evidence supporting this proposition is mounting literally by the day. However, even a cursory consideration tells us that to expect one parent to raise the child places demands on the one parent which result in the parent's inability to tend to the psychological needs of the child effectively or completely. The fact of the matter is that a child needs the mother to be at home in order to direct it and comfort it in bad times and reward it in good times.[15] Secondly, children learn through the father working, what it means for a man to be providential for his family which is an integral part of masculine

---

[12]This indicates that, as a general rule, the larger the family the better, provided that other material and other psychological needs are met. It also means that single child family units are not ideal. However, parents who are unable to have more children can compensate by getting the child involved with friends and teaching him how to treat them. Moreover, they must moderate what they give the child so as not to raise the child's expectations about life too much.

[13]Psychologists who encourage people who are married to get a divorce do a great disservice not only to the parents but to the children. Often psychologists tell their directees that they should divorce for their own benefit. But divorce is contrary to the natural law and should never be done unless for the gravest of reasons, e.g. if the husband is beating the wife, or if the wife is engaging in gravely immoral behavior which is having a grave effect on the children.

[14]St. Thomas observes in ST II-II, q. 154, a. 2 and SCG III, c. 122 that man is a creature which, unlike some other animals, needs both parents for the proper upbringing of children.

[15]Since it is more natural for women to be able to empathize emotionally with children, it means that the natural order is such that women should be at home with the child and the father working to provide materially for the child. It also means that fornication is grave matter psychologically because it sets up a situation in which the child may be raised by one parent.

nature.

If divorce occurs and the child is left with the mother, the child is affected psychologically on two fronts. The first is that the child is affected negatively since the father is no longer providing for the family. Laws requiring child support and alimony help, but the child can still be left with the impression that he is materially abandoned. Second, in divorce in which the children are left with the mother, there is a natural sense of emotional and psychological abandonment. The father leaves the child and so there may be some sense of abandonment or even rejection since the child may feel as if the father was unwilling to stay in a difficult situation for his benefit. Since it pertains to masculine nature to protect the family, the child is left without a sense of protection and so the child may develop feelings of vulnerability. Anger can then arise because the child succumbs to fear which causes anger. Virtually every passion associated with evil can arise.

If the child is left with the father, then the child may not grow up emotionally secure or stable.[16] Part of feminine nature is to be able to direct children's emotions through emotional empathy. Women are more adept at this and it is a perfection which is absolutely necessary for the raising of children. Girls may not learn what it means to be a loving mother and boys will not learn to temper their emotions.[17] Moreover, in any divorce, the proper role of love and the necessity to develop the virtue of love by observing loving parents and imitating them in the family life is lost.

Outside the context of divorce, parents can affect the mental health of their children in a variety of ways. First, if the parents follow the natural law, they are more likely to raise mentally healthy children. This follows from the fact that the formation will be in accordance with the nature of the intellect and so the parents will be forming their children to act rationally. Conversely, the less the parents follow the natural law, the more likely the child is to end up becoming mentally ill.

Second, if the parents do not follow the natural law by not punishing the child when he acts contrary to the natural law or not rewarding him properly when he does something according to the natural law, then the child will be left to his own disorders and can therefore become mentally ill. In effect, parents must reward good behavior and punish bad behavior. Obviously, the punishment and rewards must likewise be governed by the natural law. If parents punish a child in such a way as to physically cause damage to the child, then this violates the natural law. Also, since it violates the natural law, the child naturally knows something is wrong and so he is likely to develop mental illness because the parents are supposed to protect him, but instead they are abusing him. On

---

[16]Conversely, boys left with their mother may not develop the proper virtues pertaining to the irascible appetites such as fortitude, etc., unless the mother uses other means to provide it.

[17]Femininity has a natural tempering affect on male passions with respect to the irascible appetite.

the other hand, parents must not assume that spanking a child is evil or bad for the child psychologically. The general principle is that if the punishment violates one of the three categories of natural inclination, then it is evil. Spanking the child causes physical pain but that is not the same as violating the conservation of his being. Moreover, parents must not violate the third category of natural inclination by mentally abusing the child.

Children also can be formed in mental illness if the parents violate the first principles. For example, if a parent teaches the child always to do what is right and to respect people by avoiding illicit sexual behavior and then the parent acts immorally in this regard, then the child is formed in contradiction. This is particularly problematic if the parents are strong authority figures, i.e. they insist on the child following the natural law but they do not. This can lead to *per se* mental illness if the child accepts the contradictory formation, since actions of the parents are also a type of formation. It can also lead to *per accidens* mental illness, e.g. if a child fully recognizes that the parent is telling him one thing and doing another, it can lead to psychological rebellion. The child may reject the authority of the parents and any other form of authority as hypocritical. The result may be that the child develops uncontrolled anger or some other disordered passion.

The converse is also the case, i.e. if the parent does not exercise his office properly by not forming the child at all, then the child naturally will become disordered. The reason this is the case is that the natural law in the child moves the child to recognize the authority of the parent and, if the parent never uses his authority, there arises a dissonance between the natural law inclination of respecting his parents and the parents never doing anything to elicit the respect.

Parents can likewise cause mental illness according to the principle of resemblance. What this essentially means is that if the parent is mentally ill, it can affect the children. Since children are naturally formed by their parents, if the parents are mentally ill, the child will learn that mental illness. Children are very astute and learn easily by imitation. Since this pertains to the third category of natural inclination of the natural law, children may learn these mental disorders without even reflecting on the fact that they are doing it. This is why the mental health of the parents is so important in the proper formation of the child.

There is, however, one thing that must be guarded against and that is the practice that was in vogue and still is to a degree in psychological circles and that is to blame all of one's problems on one's parents. While parents can cause problems, they are not the only source of psychological illness. Moreover, such an approach causes a great deal of psychological damage to the directee who should have a natural affection for his parents. By blaming the parents, the child becomes disordered in his relationship with the parents. Even though the parents are bad, they are to be honored.[18]

Spouses can have a great influence on each other as well and this is largely due to the emotional involvement often accompanying marriage. The principle of resemblance is important in marriage as spouses very often over the long haul become more like each other. Hence, if one spouse is psychologically ill, it will be difficult for the other spouse to maintain psychological health. In the very nature of man is to be found a certain psychology of marriage. It is natural for women to seek the approval of their husband and so if he is disapproving, that can lead to problems. Men naturally seek a wife who will raise good children and if the wife does not, it can cause problems between the spouses. Men can be tempered by women, which is a good thing since it can have a positive effect on the man as well society as a whole.[19] Women naturally look for a man who can provide for them and protect them[20] and when the husband fails in regard to one of these, it can cause psychological difficulties in the wife.

The next category is friends. Since friends are similar to family in that man tends to have affections for his friends; if those affections are violated then the person can be affected negatively. Here proper control and training of appetites will greatly affect the outcome of one's psychological health. If someone has been hurt in a previous experience, he should not commit the informal fallacy of hasty generalization and assume that no friends should be had or that certain people make bad friends, without giving individual people a chance.

The next category concerns those with whom one works. As a general rule, working environments are healthy to the degree that three things are observed, otherwise they can lead to mental difficulties. The first is that human nature is respected. Those who are expected to do things contrary to the natural law in order to keep their job can suffer psychological difficulties. The second is that the principle of subsidiarity and the

---

[18]This is required for people psychologically because without honor of parents who are the first authority in a person's life, the person loses respect for those in authority, for the institution of marriage as well as the instruction in motherhood and fatherhood.

[19]It can also be bad if the tempering is directed to the wrong things or done excessively.

[20]The feminist movement has actually been a case in which they proved these two aspects of feminine nature. Since women have insisted on working and building a career, they have had a bad influence on men psychologically who have become more feminized because they are no longer allowed to protect or provide for their wives which is an integral part of being male. Moreover women are less happy now that they work and this is slowly but surely being borne out in formal studies, even though it is common knowledge. Part of the problem is that the feminist movement has created an atmosphere in society where even the discussion of this topic is condemned. Lastly, women are becoming more masculinized because they are trying to acquire the traits proper to males by taking on the role of the male in the family and in society.

proper chain of command must be followed. This means that those in charge do not abuse their power and that employees respect the authority of those in charge. This also means that job descriptions are properly delineated and those in authority and those who work together respect the proper job descriptions and do not try to do things outside their job description, which may impinge upon others' jobs. The last is that those in authority reward good behavior and punish bad behavior. This principle, which is proper to any form of authority, requires that bad employees be not rewarded for their bad behavior. Employees that engage in bad behavior can cause psychological problems for those around them, especially those who may be prone to psychological instability. Finally, the employees and employers must work for the good of each other as well as the company to ensure a psychologically healthy atmosphere. This means that both the employees and employers must respect the natural law.

The next category of human relation is that of enemies. An enemy is defined as someone who wishes to do one harm. Enemies in life can be part of the family, former friends, those we work with and those we do not even know. Enemies invoke in us the negative passions and we must seek to keep a balance regarding our enemy. Willing what is best for our enemy[21] can go a long way toward helping one keep a proper perspective since it habituates the will in the good and therefore the will can positively influence the imagination and appetites.

The next category of human relations is strangers. Strangers are often the object of fear or even hate insofar as people dislike getting to know people and so they avoid strangers, which makes them an object of flight. Strangers can also be a source of fear in that we suspect that they can cause us harm. However, all dealings with strangers can lead to mental health, if we realize that man is by nature a social animal and that getting to know other people is actually a perfection on our part. Obviously, this does not mean that one should go around seeking strangers to get to know them, but in the normal everyday leading of life we inevitably come across strangers and how we take them can either be a cause of psychological difficulty or of aid for us.

This leads us to conclude this section with the observation that needs repeating. All of the things of the world can cause mental health or illness depending upon first and foremost our judgment of them. If we judge things of the world rightly, then we can achieve mental health. If we judge them wrongly, then it can lead to all sorts of problems. Right judgment can calm passions, train them, correct the cogitative power and memory and help the imagination. Moreover, right judgment can keep the will on track and this is very important when dealing with the world. This means that a good experience can lead to psychological health but it can also lead to psychological illness

---

[21]An enemy qua enemy is something which man naturally hates, i.e. we do not naturally will the good of an enemy. However, one can change one's perspective and view one's enemy as a human being needing help or a child of God, which helps one to will the good for him.

if we judge good experiences in a wrong way. For example, someone might have a good experience with a friend but then judge that he should always be around that friend. Thus he becomes fixated on being around the friend and might develop disordered passions with respect to the friend. Bad experiences can lead to psychological illness if we do not judge them properly, but they can also lead to psychological health if they are judged properly. For example, a child who acts up at the dinner table may be spanked.[22] This teaches the child that what he did was bad and so the child can judge that form of behavior as bad. For instance, if he lies at the dinner table and is spanked, the child learns that lying is wrong and so he will not lie in the future and therefore it can actually lead to his psychological health. Since children are often not easily reasoned with, they tend to learn through pleasure and pain and so the proper use of pain (a bad experience) can actually lead to mental health. Even the most traumatic experiences can have profoundly good effects if the person judges them rightly and wills the good. He will have to exercise great control over the passions and the cogitative power which react to the bad experience. We have all met people whose relative has died; they were in a car accident or who have undergone some other traumatic experience and it brought them to their senses and put them in contact with reality about the human condition. This then leads to reforming their lives and getting certain things which were psychologically bad out of their lives.

The last category of human relations pertains to those to whom the person divulges his interior life. They include people such as priests, ministers, rabbis,[23] psychologists and medical doctors.[24] The relation here is different from friendship because those who direct people's interior lives are viewed as authorities in some fashion. As for psychologists, normally someone with a mental difficulty goes to the psychologist and views him as an authority in one of two fashions. First, he sees him as someone with knowledge who has the capacity to instruct him or guide him to mental health based upon that knowledge. Secondly, sometimes the directee can place himself volitionally under the psychologist in a form of obedience, recognizing that he must do

---

[22]It is the unfortunate state of affairs that today people are unable to make the distinction between appropriate corporal punishment and abuse which has led many to say that all forms of corporal punishment are bad.

[23]The role of priests and other religious figures in psychological health and illness shall be covered at another time.

[24]Medical doctors, among which one could enumerate psychiatrists, shall not be discussed. Medical doctors do not *per se* deal with mental illness. Psychiatrists must accept the conclusions of a valid psychology and then those things which pertain directly to their field is their own proper place to develop. If someone divulges interior states to a psychiatrist, then the same principles would apply to the psychiatrists that applies to the psychologist.

what the psychologist says if he wants to recover his mental health.[25] Therefore, in the relationship the psychologist has with the directee, a few things must be respected. The first is that the relationship of psychologist to directee is ultimately about the good of the directee and not the empowerment of the psychologist. If a psychologist views the relationship as a form of empowerment because he can control people, it can lead to serious damage on the part of the directee.

The authority that the psychologist should have must be based on knowledge, i.e. by a sound and penetrating knowledge of what is covered here only in a basic and cursory fashion. He must conduct himself in such a fashion so as to inspire in the directee a confidence not only in his knowledge but in his good will to help the directee. This will lead the directee naturally to place himself under the guidance of the psychologist. This is important since it is necessary in the case of some mental illnesses that the directee submit under obedience regarding those things affecting his mental health. While some mental difficulties do not require submission of will and psychologists must be careful not to demand it when it is unnecessary, nevertheless some types of illnesses require it, especially those in which no volitional control is had by the directee over the thing causing the illness.

This also means that a psychologist must be sure not to develop a friendship in the proper sense with the directee but to maintain a proper professionalism with the directee. This safeguards against the problem of "familiarity breeds contempt." Furthermore, the relationship the psychologist has to the directee must be governed by the natural law and it is primarily the responsibility of the psychologist to ensure that the relationship follows the natural law.

The relationship of the psychologist with the directee, while being governed by good will and the natural law, must have the truth as the primary consideration. This means that the psychologist must not get emotionally involved but his giving of advice must be based upon the truth and objective psychological principles. When the directee has problems, the psychologist must learn prudence to know when the truth is to be revealed to the patient. He must learn that the expectations of the directee must be

---

[25]These two aspects of authority are also enjoyed by priests and religious leaders in their proper field. However, because the psychologist is entrusted with one's interior life it is often too easy for directees to treat their psychologist like a clergyman, i.e. looking at their psychologist as providing "salvation" for them. On the other hand, psychologists can get a clergy or God complex thinking that they have a capacity to solve all man's ills and that they can provide salvation to the human race if everyone would simply do as they say. Some famous writers in psychology have even expressed this, such as exhibited in B.F. Skinner's *Walden Two* (e.g. see chapter 33). The fundamental difference, of course, is that the finalities and means of the priesthood or clerical life are fundamentally different from that of psychology. Psychology uses natural means to obtain its end, viz. mental health. The finality of the priesthood is the salvation of one's soul, the remission of sins, etc. and it uses supernatural means to do so.

subject to the truth so that the real good of the directee is at the foremost of his mind.

Ignorance on the side of a psychologist can cause a great deal of harm to the directee. His lack of good will or the lack of having the good of the directee as primary can cause a great deal of harm. Also, any mental problems or even moral problems the psychologist has can have an adverse effect on the directee, which is why a psychologist must be a person of great integrity and character. The psychologist must be aware of the fact that he has the capacity to harm the directee as well as to help.[26]

---

[26]Because of the place a psychologist has in the relationship to the directee, it is very easy to abuse one's power. This is why the psychologist himself must be a man of virtue so that he does not abuse the power but through virtue uses the influence for the good of the directee.

Chapter 14: Interior Causes of Mental Health and Illness

All things which affect one's mental health are either within oneself or outside of oneself and the previous section has briefly dealt with those things outside of ourselves.[1] The causes which are within ourselves are numerous and they are more pivotal to our mental health than the exterior causes. For all the causes of mental health and illness which come from outside of ourselves have an effect on us only to the degree that we are disposed to them or to the degree that we allow them to affect us.

I. Physiological Causes

In the previous chapter, St. Thomas noted with respect to the phrenetici that their mental illness can be the result of bad bodily disposition. The physical causes of mental illness are the proper domain of psychiatry but it behooves our study to consider a few aspects of the physiological causes. Since all of the faculties which operate through a bodily organ depend upon the disposition of the body, then one's physical health has a direct bearing on mental health and illness. Psychiatry has discovered many cases in which the brain displays a bad chemical disposition or where there is some neurological defect which causes the person to suffer certain forms of *per accidens* mental illness.

However, a three-fold consideration must be given to these discoveries. The first is that the actual cause of the *per accidens* mental illness may not actually be the chemical imbalance or neurological problem but rather these physiological defects may be the result of actions of the agent. Here we are not referring merely to the ingestion of chemicals that may result in these physiological defects. As was clear from previous discussions, the possible intellect and will can actually cause chemical changes in the body through thought which affects the interior senses and appetites. Therefore, it is possible that the physiological defects are merely the effect of another cause which is deeper. Hence, when medication is administered, it may provide a chemical balance and help the patient, but the actual cause may be elsewhere and need to be addressed. In some forms of *per accidens* mental illness, it may happen that the person causes defects in the passive intellect or other faculties by his actions to such a degree that it may not be possible to correct the physiological imbalance through volitional actions. In these cases, it may be necessary to administer the proper medications first in order to begin solving the problem.

In other cases, it may merely be necessary to correct the person's acts of the possible intellect and will so that he can begin affecting the lower faculties which,

---

[1] While God, saints and angels which can affect us psychologically are outside of us, nevertheless they have an effect on the interior faculties. They shall be covered in the next volume.

provided they have a certain resilience, can bounce back and regain their proper disposition on their own. In the latter case, it may occur that the directee finds correcting the disposition exceedingly difficult or that he has a very hard time eliciting the acts from the intellect and will because of the material indisposition, even though theoretically the problem could be corrected merely by volitional acts. In these cases, it may be necessary to continue to give the medication until the person is capable of controlling the lower faculties volitionally. However, psychologists must be wary of calling on a psychiatrist to administer medication when it is unnecessary to do so. If the directee finds the situation difficult but manageable, then to proceed without medication is always preferable to relying on medication. The only time medication should be used is if the patient simply cannot control the lower faculties or when it is so difficult that no progress is capable of being made.

The second consideration is that there may be some *per accidens* mental illnesses which are strictly chemical and have no basis in volitional acts. In some of these cases, the only recourse would be medication or if the problem is neurological, some other form of treatment, if available. It may be necessary for some directees to tolerate certain dysfunctions of the lower faculties and to compensate for them by judgment of the intellect and choice of the will in order to move the intellect to make the proper judgments, if there is no treatment available to them.

The third consideration is that there may be cases which have as their source a physiological cause only but which can be corrected through elicited acts. In these cases, the person may have inherited or have some indisposition but he can correct it through volitional acts. Since disposition can be changed through volitional acts, there may be some forms of *per accidens* mental illness which can be corrected in this fashion. Psychologists should not be too quick to send someone to a psychiatrist for the dispensing of medications or other forms of treatment when the illness can be corrected through the natural psychological mechanisms in man. On the other hand, psychologists should not be too quick to rule out a physiological cause to *per accidens* mental illness. This requires an openness of mind so as to determine exactly what the cause is.[2]

The psychologist should keep in mind that *per accidens* mental illnesses can lead to *per se* mental illnesses, so if he discovers a *per se* mental illness, he should not be too quick to assume that the root cause is not physiological. Yet, not all *per se* mental illnesses have a physiological cause but can have other causes and so the psychologist should not be too quick to assume that a *per se* mental illness is caused by a physiological difficulty. It should also be kept in mind that certain environmental factors can cause stress and other emotions which can cause physiological problems.

Lastly, psychiatrists should remember what has been said here. Many

---

[2]This is why humility and other virtues are necessary for the psychologist. A psychologist who suffers from pride is bound to make bad judgments with respect to his own capacities to help his directees.

psychiatrists assume that all mental illnesses are from a physiological cause when they are not. This is why it is important for psychiatrists to realize that psychiatry is a subalternated science to psychology and it must accept the conclusions of the science of psychology as principles of its own science.[3] Even though it proceeds in a different fashion from psychology, it must accept the conclusions of psychology as principles of its own science. The ultimate goal of psychiatry is to provide the physical health for the proper operations of the soul, which acts through the body, and these are known through the philosophical science of psychology.

II. Interior Senses

The exterior senses are not the cause of mental health or illness in the proper sense. While it is true that things exterior to us which can aid or harm our mental health come through the senses, nevertheless, in themselves the senses do not have the capacity to cause mental illness or health.[4] This leads to the first set of faculties which must be addressed regarding their impact on mental health, i.e. the four interior senses. It has already been noted that *per accidens* mental illness is that which is predicated of the four interior senses and the appetites and so it is important to discuss, faculty by faculty, *per accidens* mental illness as well as the various causes of it.[5]

A. *Sensus Communis* or Common Sense Power

The common sense power, like the five exterior senses, is not a cause of mental illness. It can lead to mental illnesses if the individual who has a dysfunction of this faculty is not able to judge properly the data coming into the imagination from the common sense power. This is, strictly speaking, the only way that it can cause mental illness. Obviously, when the common sense power functions properly, it does contribute to mental health since it is providing the sense data accurately, even if the sense data itself, if not judged properly, can cause problems.

B. Memory

Since the memory through recall can introduce into the imagination a

---

[3]This means that psychiatrists should also be trained in a valid psychology.

[4]Through the virtue of custody of the eyes (and by extension custody of all of the senses), one is able to ensure that nothing harmful morally comes into the interior senses. This virtue can also be used to ensure that nothing psychologically damaging comes into the interior senses.

[5]*Per accidens* mental illnesses can also cause *per se* mental illnesses but that will be taken up in the next part of this chapter.

previously stored phantasm, it has the capacity to introduce into the imagination sensible species which can disturb the imagination. If the memory is very strong, it can lead to a disordering of the imagination by holding it captive to a specific memory, e.g. when someone has a traumatic experience, the memory can recall the experience repeatedly resulting in a disturbance of the various faculties. It can actually disorder the cogitative power by constantly recalling a specific memory so that the cogitative power begins to assess the species falsely or associate it with another species with which it should not be associated. The memory can also disorder the passions by what is remembered if it is remembered falsely or if the memory is unusually strong. One can also become disturbed if through the process of reminiscence one thinks one remembers something which is in fact false, e.g. as is the case among those who thought they had been sexually molested, even though they had not been, a psychologist "helped" them to remember their childhood experiences.[6]

Per accidens mental illness which affects the memory can be healed in a few ways. The first way is that when a memory that disturbs the individual is recalled, the cogitative power can be moved by the possible intellect and will to disassociate in the memory the thing causing the trouble. Sometimes it is necessary for the possible intellect to make an act of judgment about the memory and with an act of the will, reformulate the image or add to the image that which is curative of the thing remembered. Consequently, the memory will be re-stored and as a result, it will be cured. It may happen that one will have to perform this process repeatedly to habituate the various powers about the recalled memory as well as to habituate the memory itself regarding that specific memory. Conversely, one can cause damage to the memorative power by falsifying the sense species and moving the memory to store it in that fashion. Often when an experience is painful, people will remember it based upon the emotional pain involved rather than as it actually occurred because through an act of judgment or from the cogitative power, the person alters the phantasm so as to be in congruity with the pain rather than keeping the species whole or as it is. Hence, someone can begin causing problems for himself merely by the way he approaches certain experiences and this can have an effect on memory.

If a memory is bad as well as strong or persistent enough it can begin to affect the judgment of the possible intellect with respect to the object contained within the sensible species. For instance, if someone is tortured, memory may store the sensible species associated with the pain. Then when situations arise which are similar to the previous experience the person will recall the memory and the judgment can be

---

[6]This should be an indicator to psychologists that it is not a good idea to probe around in the past memories without due cause. Nor should there be a tendency to blame everything on one's childhood and as a result constantly probe the memory in the past. While past experiences may be the cause of mental illnesses, it should not be assumed they are the only cause.

precipitated. For example, if he is tortured in a musty building, that musty smell is associated or is part of the phantasm of the pain. When the person enters a building that is musty, he may experience fear since the memory will recall the sensible species of pain associated with the musty smell. As time goes on, the person experiences fear around musty things and the part of the species which is associated with the torture may be left behind due to the cogitative power's disassociation of the torture from the musty smell, even though the musty smell is still assessed by the cogitative power as harmful. The person eventually begins fearing musty things and then his judgment begins to be compromised about musty things. So when he gets around musty things, he begins to act irrationally. Therefore, how the memory stores things and how we think about them, which is likewise stored in memory, can have an impact on our mental health.

Sometimes memory can be healed by discussing it and merely flushing out the past memory. In some cases, memory can be cured if the thing which causes problems is experienced in a positive way. This results when the sensible species that was previously experienced in a bad way is stored in memory with the assessment of the cogitative power as good. Sometimes reminiscence can be used to heal the memory, if the reminiscence is carried out properly. It may happen that a memory is remembered as bad but incomplete and through reminiscence the person can correct the memory as he discovers that the memory is false or that it was not as bad as he remembered. It may be the case with those with false or incomplete memories that they need to depend on others who have a complete or true memory of a situation. Having contact with them or discussing the occurrence with them can be curative of the memory.

It should be noted that even though the memory may be healed, problems which have arisen in the other faculties may persist. It may happen that the other faculties are immediately quieted when the faculty in trouble is helped, but problems can persist in the other faculties due to habituation. This observation applies not only to memory but to all of the faculties and so the psychologist should not be surprised that, even after the cause of a mental illness is resolved, other problems persist. This is especially the case in the appetites since they are highly prone to habituation, particularly toward vice. However, since the cause is removed, the other faculties can be addressed and healed quickly since the cause is no longer present.

C. The Imagination

The imagination is a pivotal faculty with respect to *per se* and *per accidens* mental health. If one imagines the wrong things or things contrary to human nature, it can lead easily to physiological defects. It is a faculty which requires a great deal of training and control. The imagination is a power capable of habituation if in no other way than the fact that it can be habituated to be more susceptible to the movements of one power over another. For instance, those with strong possible intellects and wills very often can habituate the imagination to be submissive to their movements over the movements from the other faculties. This indicates that those who tend more toward a sensuous type of life will find keeping control of the imagination difficult and at times impossible if the possible intellect and will are very weak or suffer from vice. However, proper control of the imagination[7] is essential to maintaining mental health as well as to recovering mental health, if one is mentally ill.

Those whose imaginations break down will exhibit a distractedness. They will, at times, exhibit an inability to keep track of or judge time. They will also be disconnected from reality. If the imagination is not functioning correctly and since the possible intellect judges and concentrates on reality by means of the imagination, if the latter is disordered or not functioning properly, it can lead to a lack of connection to reality. On the other hand, if the imagination is very strong in itself but not susceptible to movement by the intellect and will, it can carry the individual off and the person becomes disconnected from reality. This form of *per accidens* mental illness can pose difficulties for the psychologist. If the imagination is too strong, the psychologist will find it difficult to counsel the directee because the directee will not be able to concentrate or listen to him.

Many times those with this condition also suffer from some kind of physiological defect. If the physiological defect can be treated, it may restore periods of lucidity or make it easier for the directee to begin working on gaining control over the imagination. Otherwise, the person will have to gain control over the faculty indirectly and this is done by using the external senses to try to bring the imagination out of its self absorption and into contact with reality.[8] Sometimes, the person may have an

---

[7]The virtue of custody of the mind is a virtue in which one has control over the imagination and possible intellect. It is an important virtue because by it one guards one's cognitive and appetitive faculties from sensible and intelligible species which can lead to mental illnesses. Normally this virtue has a strong moral connotation but it is pivotal to mental health as well.

[8]This is where television can both be damaging and beneficial. Sometimes television can actually cause the imagination to become difficult to control, e.g. those who watch television and then immediately afterward try to engage in intellectual discourse or prayer find the imagination hard to control because the imagination has been habituated in being controlled by the television. On the other hand, if someone simply cannot concentrate or be able to gain a control over the imagination, it may be the case that television can help. If the programming is such to aid the contact with reality, the televison can habituate the imagination to being controlled by an exterior agency and thus make it possible for it to slowly come under the control of the possible intellect and will. This is particularly the case if the imagination is very strong and this has not resulted from watching television. There are other forms of sensation which can also help, such as music and the like. Music is helpful because it moves the appetites and so the appetites can actually be used to hold the imagination so that it learns to be habituated and moved by exterior powers. Care must be taken, of course, because ultimately one wants intellectual and volition control of the imagination and not end up with a scenario in which the imagination listens to every other

imagination that is uncontrollable and so he becomes debilitated by being unable to do anything. In that case, it is primarily up to the psychologist to provide the means to aid the directee, often without much help from the directee. At times, the imagination may be virtually uncontrollable, but the person is able to maintain at least some presence of mind to be able to command certain things and thus begin affecting the imagination indirectly.

Since the imagination can affect so many powers, it can cause mental illnesses in many ways. If the imagination is not controlled it can cause disordered appetites; it can disorder the cogitative power; it can affect judgment and, consequently, the will. If the cogitative power is too strong, it can captivate the imagination and cause the imagination to be disordered, but the reverse is also the case. This is why what one imagines is very important since it can lead to mental illness. On the other hand, if the imagination is under the control of right reason, then reason can cure other faculties by means of the imagination. By using the imagination, it can quiet the appetites by providing the right phantasm for them so that they can be trained. If they are disturbed, the appetites can be changed and re-directed. Moreover, as was mentioned, the possible intellect can train the cogitative power by means of the imagination and so the imagination can be used to build good habits in the cogitative power. It has already been seen that the imagination can be used to heal memory.

This means that how the possible intellect and will control the image or phantasm in the imagination is crucial for mental health. Someone who has bad habits in the cogitative power (sometimes called fixations) can actually overcome them by reformulating the image so as to train the cogitative power not to associate something with a specific image. This brings us to the discussion of the reformulation of the image. Reformulating or the determination of the phantasm by means of the possible intellect and will means that mental health is often under the volitional control of the individual. Since one can disorder the various interior senses by what one chooses to think about, one can, in fact, cause one's own mental illness and conversely one can have volitional control over regaining and maintaining one's mental health.

This is why using the imagination for images that are 1) in congruity with the natural law, 2) true and 3) of the good, can actually lead to mental health. Those who entertain thoughts contrary to the natural law violate the finality of the interior senses and other faculties and this can lead to mental illness. Those who think about things in congruity with the natural law actually can aid their mental health. This is why even thoughts must be in congruity with the finality of man and his faculties[9] and these kinds

---

form of exterior agency other than the intellect and will. Since in man there is a certain disorder arising from original sin in which the lower faculties tend not to obey the higher, this must be kept in mind so that greater disorders do not arise from treatment.

[9]This is also why the Catholic Church and Christ Himself maintained that even thoughts of things contrary to the natural law were sins.

of thoughts must be counseled by the psychologist. The finality of the imagination is to provide the true sensible species so that the possible intellect can perform its functions and the will can move and guide the whole of man through it. The memory is designed to retain the truth and so its finality is the true sensible species and to force it to remember what is false is a violation of its finality. The appetites have their finalities and if one disorders them, it becomes hard to control any of the other faculties in man. The cogitative power is designed to perform its various functions according to the truth, which is why it is dangerous to think things contrary to the truth. Moreover, the cogitative power is designed to assess whether something is harmful or good according to the truth and so falsifying the image can disorder the cogitative power and violate its finality. The cogitative power is designed to assess something as being good for man which is truly good and when the possible intellect or will move the imagination and cause a false assessment by the cogitative power, this causes an unnatural state for the cogitative power and therefore it can become disordered, i.e. it leads to mental illness. Therefore, the finalities of man and his faculties must be respected in order for mental health to be obtained. When lower faculties are disordered by the command of reason and will, the conscience judges the actions wrongly. So the assessment of the cogitative power as well as the habituation in the appetites begin to be at variance with the conscience causing division within the soul which inevitably will lead to mental illness.

From time to time a directee can suffer from indeterminate phantasms in the imagination and the source of these can be one's experience, the memory, or even confusion as a result of the possible intellect and will's reformulating the image. However, the imagination can be used to clarify the phantasm. When the possible intellect and will begin the process of sorting out the phantasm, they may use exterior sense data in order to do so or they may be able to sort some of the phantasms out merely by judgment. This is particularly the case when there is conflicting data in the phantasm. Sometimes the possible intellect can add to the image to clarify it but care must be taken to ensure that what is added is in congruity with reality.

This is where the psychologist can be of great help or harm. He can be harmful if he does not help sort the phantasm out properly. He can, however, be very helpful if the phantasm is one which can be sorted out merely by the psychologist informing the directee of the truth. Moreover, the psychologist can help the directee to formulate the right phantasm in order to sort out the previous phantasm. This is the essential function of the psychologist, viz. to help the directee to form the right phantasms in order to correct the various faculties.[10]

---

[10]Aristotle observes that the essential function of a teacher is to provide the right phantasms for abstraction for the student. This also applies to the psychologist; in effect, the primary function of a psychologist is as a teacher, which is to help the directee formulate the right phantasm to gain mental health so that he judges properly and so that rationality may be restored. The psychologist is secondarily someone to whom obedience may need to

The reformulation of the image is a very powerful form of correction for the lower faculties and it can also be used to gain *per se* mental health. When the directee is counseled in such a fashion to reformulate the image according to the truth, then the possible intellect can judge it and begin to correct the vice in the possible intellect. As the will commands the truth to be considered, it becomes stronger. On the other hand, reformulating the image incorrectly can not only disorder the lower faculties, it can actually lead to *per se* mental illness, e.g. when one chooses to lie habitually, it can lead to a state in which the intellect is not capable of judging the truth properly because it has always been commanded to act contrary to its nature. Another case is when the will moves the intellect to contemplate things contrary to the natural law as good or as true. This is not formally a lie because a lie is something spoken, but a lie is based upon the fact that the intellect knows what is true but commands what is false. As the imagination is used to reformulate the image as something contrary to the natural law, it can lead to all sorts of disorders and mental illness.[11]

D. The Cogitative Power

A great deal has been said about the cogitative power but more needs to be said. Clearly if the cogitative power has been habituated in the wrong way, it can lead to mental illness. While the cogitative power may be habituated in the wrong way, not all bad habituations constitute *per accidens* mental illness with respect to the cogitative power. Rather, *per accidens* mental illness in the cogitative power is constituted by the cogitative power's inability to assess a given species correctly as well as not being able to assess it in other ways. This is commonly called fixation[12] in which the cogitative power always or for the most part and wrongly associates one thing with another and is unable to change the association. For example, if every time someone sees a member of the opposite gender and immediately thinks of engaging in the conjugal act and cannot think of anyone of the opposite gender without thinking of the conjugal act, then that person has a fixation. In this case, the cogitative power has been habituated to

---

be given in order to aid the will of the directee in moving the other faculties to what is right, but even the secondary function of a psychologist is contingent upon the first.

[11]An example of this would be someone who is considering the act of suicide which normally elicits fear in the appetites and harmful assessments by the cogitative power, etc. But if the lower powers are forced or persuaded it is good, the intellect becomes disordered and so one's mental health begins to be affected as the intellect begins to act irrationally, i.e. it is forced to act contrary to its nature. Eventually, if it becomes habitual, the person becomes mentally ill.

[12]Fixation may occur in one or more of the following faculties: the cogitative power, the will, the possible intellect and appetites. A fixation is constituted by the person's inability to draw one's faculties away from the given sensible or intelligible species.

associate the pleasures of reproduction always with the opposite gender and it is constituted as a fixation since it always and wrongly associates the conjugal act with the opposite gender. Since the conjugal act should only be engaged in by spouses under due circumstances, when a person desires it outside the marital context or associates conjugal relations outside that context, the cogitative power has associated wrongly.[13]

Fixations can be corrected by the normal method of training the cogitative power which has already been discussed somewhat. This method essentially consists in reformulating the image with the necessary sense data so as to train the cogitative power how to associate properly. Furthermore, the possible intellect and will can move the cogitative power directly to make the proper associations. At times, the cogitative power may be strong, as is usually the case with respect to fixations, which also means that there is a concomitant weakness in the possible intellect and will. Nevertheless, the possible intellect and will can gain indirect control over the cogitative power if it is too strong by changing the phantasm in the imagination rather than by trying to move the cogitative power directly. As time goes on, the cogitative power responds to the indirect movements of the will and there will come a point when it will begin to respond to the direct movement of the higher powers. Furthermore, use of the exterior senses to affect the phantasm can also aid the training of the cogitative power.[14]

Obviously, if the cogitative power can be trained for the good, it can also be trained for the bad and so one must be careful not to train the cogitative power in the wrong way through habituation. Often, along with the fixation, there is the tumult of the appetites since the association is accompanied by an assessment by the cogitative power of the good of the thing under consideration. Consequently, those who suffer fixations can often experience disordered appetites; at times, the disordered appetites can actually cause the habituation of the cogitative power by keeping the imagination captive and so the cogitative power is restricted in its association which causes the cogitative power to assess the image in the way the appetite reacts to it. This again is why vice in the appetites can lead to *per accidens* mental illness and it is also why virtue in the appetites can lead to *per accidens* mental health.

In a previous chapter, it was noted that one of the differences between the animal estimative sense and the human cogitative power is that the cogitative power is able to assess a phantasm impartially. In counseling the directee, psychologists must train the directee to consider impartially the phantasm which causes trouble. This will reduce passion in the appetites and give clarity to the judgment of the possible intellect.

---

[13]Since the drive for reproduction is so strong in man, it easily becomes the object of fixation, which is one of the reasons why it must be kept within the confines of marriage in order to protect it from becoming degraded.

[14]Television through its imagery can actually embody certain associations and make the sequence of scenes so that specific associations occur. In this sense, it can be a highly useful tool.

Sometimes this must be done by impersonal associations, e.g. if a woman develops a hatred for men because she has had many bad experiences with them, it may help her to consider situations relating to friends or family, in which women were treated well. After some time of reflection on this in a disinterested fashion, then it can be addressed personally by noting that perhaps it is the men she associates with that are the cause of the problem; or she could be asked to consider that, even though she has been treated badly by some men, not all men treat women poorly. In this process, the cogitative power is habituated with respect to one phantasm and then there is the association made to another phantasm, viz. oneself, and so the cogitative power can actually be corrected through associating different phantasms in an impartial fashion. Sometimes, when the mental disturbance is slight, the person may be able to command the cogitative power directly to consider it impartially.

Habituation of the cogitative power, then, is extremely important because the habituation often inclines the cogitative power to specific kinds of assessments. When the cogitative power becomes habituated in a specific fashion, it often leads to the habituation of the other faculties as well, such as the appetites and even the possible intellect and will. Since the cogitative power can move the appetites by its assessment of the harm or benefit of a specific sensible species, we know that it can actually train the appetites. In fact, the possible intellect and will can train the appetites by means of moving the cogitative power to make specific associations. In this sense, the cogitative power is extremely useful and important for mental health and illness, not only with respect to regaining mental health, but also in maintaining it. If someone is vigilant with respect to the cogitative power and moves it to the right assessments by making sure that its associations are in congruity with the truth and the natural law, then one can maintain mental health. On the other hand, if one does not maintain proper control over the cogitative power and if one moves it to make false associations, it can lead to mental illness. This means that environment and the like are not the only causes of fixation, i.e. *per accidens* mental illness. In fact, one cannot develop a fixation in the cogitative power without the will allowing it to be developed, unless there is some extremely strong sensible species and weakness in the will to keep the cogitative power from making the wrong association. This means that even if the person is not consciously aware of the fact that he is allowing his cogitative power to develop a *per accidens* mental illness, nevertheless, the will has at least not to stop the cogitative power. Even in those cases which are caused by environment or even training or formation by parents, etc., the *per accidens* mental disorders of this kind are within volitional control.

III. Appetites and Passions

There has already been a great deal of discussion about the appetites. It has also been discussed how they can be quieted by various means and so they shall not be covered again here. However, some basic observations should be made as well as further conclusions drawn. Clearly, the appetites can hold the soul captive and so it is important that they have virtue and be rightly ordered. It is also very important that all of those faculties which have the capacity to affect the appetites be rightly ordered. The appetites can be trained by the other faculties and this training can be to the detriment or the good of the person depending on whether that training or habituation has resulted in virtue or vice.

Since the appetite is moved by the presence of its object (ultimately present in the imagination), psychological effects can be had when people avoid the person, places and things which can disorder the appetites. On the other hand, it is important to be sure that the proper objects which can lead to virtue in the appetites come into the imagination. On occasion, an object which can cause disordered appetites does come into the imagination, but how this is handled is pivotal to mental health as well as the right order of the appetites.

There has been, in modern psychological circles, a great deal of discussion of repression. What is interesting is that modern psychology has not provided an adequate response to the issue of repression. The usual response is that one should never repress any thoughts or feelings, but with what has already been said, it is clear that such advice is harmful, to say the least. Psychologists have noted that when one represses a thought or passion, one has not solved the problem and that it will come back, often worse than it was before. In fact, repression can actually lead to mental illness because repression is usually accompanied by contradiction, e.g. the appetites may want a specific good while the possible intellect knows it is evil and so the person is left in a condition in which repression occurs but the appetites still desire their object or have a specific passion with respect to the object.

It should be noted that not all repression is bad, for a thought or passion which can cause us harm should be repressed. However, repression must accompany resolution, i.e. the resolving of the appetite through rightly ordered habituation. Resolution is the process in which an appetite or recurring thought (which often gives rise to appetite) receives a rational "answer" or correction to the passion which is disordered. This means that when an appetite has a passion which is at variance with right reason, reason answers or provides a rational phantasm which causes the appetite to cease in its disordered passion. Reason may also move the will or other cognitive faculties to accept the loss of its object as being ordered toward its own good.

It has already been mentioned that the appetites can be trained by reason, but repression is not a complete form of training. While in the normal process of taking away the phantasm the appetites are quieted somewhat, they still retain their disorder with respect to the object. Moreover, to have a phantasm and try to force a negative judgment on something that the person wants or a positive judgment on something the passions do not want does not solve the problem. In the reformulation of the image, the reason for why that object must not be sought in that way must be placed in the image. In so doing, the perspective which makes the object desired or feared will be separated out of the phantasm. In doing this, the faculties other than the appetites will also be trained in the process. If one merely represses the thought without resolution, the cognitive faculties will still associate or think about that object in that specific way. The various faculties must be trained by means of reformulating the image. When the image is reformulated, then the passions become quiet because their proper object is disassociated with the object at hand and so they cease movement and obey right reason. Since the appetites are ordered toward following right reason, they are fundamentally ordered toward the process of resolution.

An example of resolution may help to make the point clearer. If a man has an uncontrolled desire to possess another man's automobile, the passions of desire and delight in thinking about the car arise. But the man knows that theft is immoral and he does not have enough money to buy the car. As a result, a dissonance arises within the soul between the passions and the intellect and if the will is strong it will choose not to commit the evil of theft. As the man thinks about it, his desire becomes stronger and the appetites begin to move him to judge the theft as desirable and so the will says no and the dissonance in the soul arises. The repression makes the dissonance continue to get worse. Then one day he walks out of work and his own car, which he likes, is stolen and great sadness results. The appetites then see that stealing is an evil and so they stop desiring to steal the car. Moreover, as the man thinks about it, he begins to realize that he should be happy with what he has and all of this results from what he had taken from him. In this, the appetites see that what they have is sufficient or that to desire the other car is excessive and so the reasonable considerations of the man actually calm the appetites down and they begin to be rightly ordered. Then as the appetites begin to be rightly ordered, joy is experienced in the soul which gives more rational confirmation to the appetites being rightly ordered.

Often people have a problem with repression until their appetites get their object of repression and have a bad experience with it and then the appetites become quiet because of the bad experience. The bad experience changed the phantasm which was moving them and so the appetites began to become quiet and follow right reason. Ultimately resolution takes place when the phantasm is corrected. Many times people do not have the right phantasm but they may have the right judgment and this is where the repression can be damaging. Repression may be necessary at first in order for the person to gain some immediate control over the appetites but eventually the appetites must be trained by correcting the phantasm. This is why correcting memory is important, because a corrected memory does not keep recalling the phantasms which lead to repression. Getting the cogitative power rightly ordered ensures that it will assess the phantasm reasonably and therefore have an effect on the appetites. Resolution is an important capacity of the human cognitive and appetitive structure and it is necessary since man leads a dual life, i.e. material and immaterial. It is only when the immaterial provides the right ordering to the material that man is at peace. But it can only rightly order the material part by providing a rational structure to those things which move the material part.[15]

Another way in which one appetite can be corrected is by commanding a change in the phantasm which results in the movement of a different passion, e.g. if a person suffers from complacency which is a certain satisfaction in the concupiscible appetite – i.e. a certain level of delight with one's current state – one can begin to move the concupiscible appetite to desiring some other good. People who are lazy not only do not want to suffer the pain of engaging in activity, they often suffer from complacency in the concupiscible appetite. One of the ways to overcome laziness is to present the concupiscible appetite with some desirable good. This mechanism of using certain passions to overcome others must be used only with great caution. While moving the appetites to different passions trains the appetites to be submissive to the possible intellect and will, nevertheless, one can generate disordered passions or antecedent appetites which were not there beforehand. Moderation, i.e. virtue, can be used to move the appetites in this regard and virtue can be a guiding principle of moderating the appetites.

Another mechanism that is useful for getting control of the passions and rightly ordering them, which is somewhat different from repression but can be used in conjunction with the resolution of the appetites, is the process by which one changes the phantasm by distracting oneself with some other thing. For instance, if someone has road rage, he can often overcome it merely by changing his image to something he likes. By changing it to something he likes, he makes it easier to change the passion in the appetite since the appetite is getting something that is good for it. Again, resolution may be part of the picture, but this mechanism causes the appetites to calm down, especially if the person is thinking about something too much. Once the person has got his mind off the thing causing the disordered antecedent appetite, his thoughts will clear and then he can begin the process of rightly ordering the appetites. When people give in to the appetites or place reason at the service of appetites, there is an inherent disorder involved and this is why the appetite must be trained to serve reason or the higher powers.

However, the same mechanism, which can be used to resolve disordered passions, can be used to cause disordered passions. Since reason can persuade the

---

[15]This means that often in order to resolve a dissonance between faculties, the faculty that is disordered must be presented with something which it can see as good or as true, as in the case of the cognitive faculties, e.g. the cogitative power can be corrected by providing the perspective with the right phantasm by the possible intellect causing a specific formality in the phantasm. It may take the directee or even the psychologist some time to discover the right perspective to provide the directee. Other times, mere life experience can provide the right phantasm. With respect to the appetites, often they may desire something but when a bad perspective is joined to the phantasm because of some bad experience of the thing, the appetite learns that the thing is not unqualifiedly good or that it is good only under certain circumstances.

appetites through the imagination, if the intellect and will choose something which is disordered, it will have a disordering effect on the passions. Another phenomena that can occur is when reason learns to calm passions down in the case where the person chooses what is evil. In other words, if someone has properly ordered appetites, but later chooses to do something wrong, the passions may suffer sorrow as a result. If reason then calms the passions by directing him to some good that the person is gaining from it, then he can disorder the passions, even though he may experience a certain calm or satisfaction in the short term.

There are other things which can mitigate passion such as study, for the proper object of the appetite is absent when one studies and so the appetites remain calm. Study also increases the reason's power over the imagination and the cogitative power, thus making it stronger so as to be able to deal better later with matters pertaining to the appetites. Moreover, it makes the person more rational. It also makes it more possible to command acts of virtue based upon knowledge and the command that reason has over the lower faculties. As temperance and the various virtues into which it is subdivided and fortitude and the various virtues into which it is subdivided increase, the appetites make it more possible to act reasonably since they will move according to rational principles, as well as not encumber reason in its operations. Therefore, pursuit of virtue directly contributes to mental health.

In this way, the appetites, insofar as they are subjects of virtue, can actually aid the intellect in its operations. On another note, since exterior causes can often elicit certain passions or even help to calm others, exterior causes can be used to calm the passions and order the appetites, e.g. television has a tremendous capacity to elicit certain appetites by the images it presents. Therefore, television could actually be used to calm the passions and train the appetites. On the other hand, it can also be used to disorder the appetites and therefore have an erosive effect on mental health.

Antecedent passions are confirmed or denied by reason and will and so, through the commanding of consequent passion, the appetites are trained. Since antecedent passion can cause the loss of the use of reason, the various methods must be used to train the appetites so that they await the movement of reason and will, before they react to their proper objects. The more the appetites await the judgment of reason and the movement of will, the more this contributes to the use of reason and to mental health. However, the more one confirms disordered antecedent appetite, the more the use of reason is deteriorated. This indicates that when the antecedent passions are strong, the intellect and will are weakened and since the passions are moved by objects, the intellect becomes weak with respect to the particular object that is moving the appetite. This concomitant weakness of the intellect and will with respect to the strength of the passion and vice of the appetite is a sign that one can become mentally ill as a result of concupiscence,[16] i.e. disordered appetites. This is why one cannot lead a life governed by the appetites.

Therefore, objects which disorder the appetites should be avoided, especially if they are vehement. Some objects can cause either ordered passions or disordered passions depending on how one approaches them. Yet, objects which can vehemently act upon the appetites should be handled carefully because of their impact on the appetites. Since they can move the appetites strongly, they can also cause problems with respect to the use of reason and the stronger the object, the more it has the capacity to lead to mental illness. It is here where something should be said about appetites and the desire for sex. Sex is accompanied with such vehement pleasure that it must be handled with great care. This is why in the past there were all sorts of customs built up around sex to protect and to preserve its use in marriage only, where the effects can be properly channeled.

However, modern man has not observed restraint with respect to sex and it is no wonder that there is also a rise in mental illness. Sex is so vehement that it has a profound effect not only on the appetites but also on the imagination, the memory, the cogitative power, the intellect and the will. It is a very powerful force and so it must be handled with care, not only in the moral sphere but in the psychological sphere as well. When sex is properly ordered to the real good of the individual, which is done in congruity with the natural law, it can have a very good effect psychologically. It can strengthen the psychological bonds between spouses and when life is the product of the union, sex can be envisioned as a powerful creative force for the good. As a result, it can directly affect the psychological well-being of society.

However, if the sex is disordered by not following the natural law, i.e. failing to keep it between those of the opposite sex and within the confines of marriage, it can cause a tremendous amount of damage. When it occurs outside the context of marriage, it is contrary to the natural law and therefore has an inherent disordering effect on the appetites. Furthermore, because it is such a psychologically involved action, if there are no proper safeguards to protect the action and the people involved, which is precisely what marriage does, it can actually have a damaging effect on the intellect. For when such a great good is had and when someone reveals himself or herself to another, if there is no protection provided, the parties become vulnerable. When the relationship breaks up, the intellect is forced into a psychological dissonance from the fact that the person gave himself or herself exclusively on a physical, and in some cases psychological, level, but then they were completely rejected. The institution of marriage must contain the quality of indissolubility to ensure that when people give themselves exclusively, i.e. give intimate knowledge of themselves to others, that one of the persons in the marriage does not leave or reject his or her spouse by permanent separation. They may give

---

[16]ST I-II, q. 6, a. 7, ad 3; ibid., q. 10, a. 3; ibid., ad 2; ibid., q. 77, aa. 1 and 2 and ST II-II, q. 156, a. 1.

themselves to another "exclusively" but then later they separate which nullifies their exclusive giving. This contradiction can lead to mental illness. Moreover, if it is outside the marital bonds, people can use it as a way of gaining acceptance and go around seeking a fulfillment of a psychological (and moral) emptiness by engaging in the act repeatedly.

Moreover, the finality of the generative faculty is children,[17] and when sex is had outside of marriage, women can be forced into psychologically difficult situations if they suspect they are pregnant and there is not a stable atmosphere into which the child can be born. It can lead to abortion which is a serious psychologically damaging event.[18] While modern man has sought to minimize the importance of sex by saying it is not that big of a deal to have it outside the context of marriage, they have spent an enormous amount of energy pursuing it. Furthermore, all of the disorders that are arising because of extramarital sex are becoming ever more evident. Again, because the conjugal act is so emotionally (appetitively) involved, it must be placed within a structure or "institution," viz. marriage, in order to secure the psychological well-being of those involved.

This also means that for psychologists to instruct directees to perform actions like masturbation, or even to engage in extramarital sex or homosexual acts, is serious indeed. These acts have a grave impact on the formation of vice in the appetites as is clear from the fact that the more people do them, the less rational and volitional control they have. It means that they are actually counseling people to engage in acts which are contrary to the natural law and therefore disordering in a profound sense, given the vehemence or power of sex. Conjugal acts actually have a great capacity for psychological health but they also have a great capacity to destroy the use of reason and to take away voluntariness.

Passions can, therefore, incline someone to act contrary to the natural law and so the intellect is inclined to act contrary to its nature as well and this is why following the life of the passions can lead not only to the disorder of the interior senses and appetites themselves (i.e. *per accidens* mental illness), it can also lead to *per se* mental illness by destroying the use of reason, if the appetites get out of control. On the other

---

[17]See Paul VI, *Humanae Vitae*, passim and ST II-II, q. 154, a. 1.

[18]It simply is not possible to go into detail about all the psychological problems that abortion causes. However, it is the opinion of the author that abortion so violates the very nature of femininity, that the natural law intimates to every woman or almost every woman that ends her pregnancy, that it is seriously wrong. While this recognition may be *post factum,* or it may not become explicit in the mind of the woman, nevertheless, it militates against her very nature as a woman. Since the whole nature of femininity is to bear and raise children (that does not mean that is the only thing women can do), when a woman gravely contradicts it through abortion, the intellect which is ordered toward finalities of our faculties becomes gravely disordered because of the grave contradiction.

hand, the appetites, when they have virtue, can aid reason by inclining the person toward that which is in accord with reason, even though the use of reason may be diminished. For example, a man builds fortitude during war and it may happen that during a particular battle, the danger and fighting become particularly intense. The appetite by means of its previous habituation, i.e. the virtue, can incline the person to do what is right even though the intensity of the battle itself may make it difficult for him to think clearly.

While there has been a great deal of discussion about control of the appetites and training them properly, this training must also be accompanied by a continued awareness of the natural law. It is not enough that one has control over one's appetites; that control must be in accordance with the natural law. For insofar as it is in congruity with the natural law it is a virtue and can therefore aid a person in the future. But control of passions and directing them toward vice makes it more difficult to direct the passions properly in the future and lead a life according to reason.

Finally, leading life according to the appetites causes a disconnect from reality. The appetites, particularly when they are strong, only want their object. They are not interested in whether it is truly good for the person or not, they simply want their object. As a result, someone who leads his life according to the appetites will have a hard time keeping connected to reality. The possible intellect keeps connected to reality by means of the phantasm, but since the passion affects the image in the imagination and draws the intellect away from reality to the object of passion and binds the intellect to viewing the passion under the aspect of the good in the way the passions see it, it is hard for the person to judge according to the truth. Since the appetites merely want their object, they are not, properly speaking interested in the truth and so they must be guided by reason. One of the signs of the truth of this proposition is that those who have *per accidens* mental illness or even *per se* mental illness accompanied by *per accidens* mental illness caused by a passion – when they get around the object of the passion, lose circumspection, i.e. the virtue by which one keeps track of one's surroundings and circumstances. People will say and do things without thinking about their proper context. This means that perfecting oneself through virtue puts one into greater contact with reality. For this reason, if for no other, the appetites must be properly ordered by right reason. Many people are subject to their passions because of man's state in this life and so the development of virtue can aid people a great deal by helping them to act more according to reason and therefore reduce the opportunity to develop mental illness and increase the capacity to regain and maintain mental health.

In all of this, it can be seen that one of the tasks of the psychologist is to determine what the vices are that the directee may have. Then he must use his knowledge of human nature and the natural law and guide the directee toward pursuit of the opposite virtue. If one has pride, he must seek humility. If one is gluttonous or sexually out of control, he must pursue temperance. Whenever there is a vice in the appetites or a bad habit in the passive intellect, it means that there is a concomitant weakness in the possible intellect and will, which corresponds directly to the object of the vice of the lower faculties. Therefore, in order to strengthen the intellect or to bring it out of its mental illness, one must develop the virtue which will correct the faculty which has the vice. As the virtue is increased in the faculty, the weakness of the intellect and will which corresponds to that vice will begin to wane and strength (virtue) will be built in the possible intellect and will. By gaining the moral virtues, the passions will be kept in check and so the intellect will less likely be bound by it. Imitating the morally good man can aid one in developing virtues and if the psychologist is a virtuous man, it can greatly aid the directee since he will be guided by someone he can imitate.[19]

As one habituates the faculties well, it aids the person in dealing with difficult matters and so those difficulties will be less likely to lead to mental illness. Pursuing intellectual virtues can aid the person particularly if the object of their problem pertains to one of the sciences. If the person studies that science, then it will greatly help the person to see the object in perspective.[20]

IV. Possible Intellect

The agent intellect is never a cause, properly speaking, of either *per accidens* or *per se* mental illness. Since its function is merely to abstract, it performs its function always in the same way and so any defects in the concept which it produces must be the result of something in the phantasm, if this can be said. Since the maintenance of the phantasm in the imagination is the task of other faculties, then the agent intellect has no capacity to cause *per accidens* mental illness or *per se* mental illness.

We have already seen that the appetites and lower faculties can affect the judgment of the intellect and bind the intellect and its operations. In connection with this, St. Thomas makes the following observation: "Concupiscence does not totally bind reason like drunkenness, unless perhaps it is so much that it makes the man insane."[21]

---

[19]This is a delicate issue. Psychologists are often prone, due to human weakness, to the desire to be imitated. It is probably better if the psychologist suggests someone other than himself for the directee to imitate because he can point out the various virtues and virtuous acts the person performs in an impersonal manner. Whereas if it is himself, he is likely to exaggerate his virtue (lack of humility) and so he becomes less credible in the eyes of the directee.

[20]Since philosophy is the science which studies the essences of things, the study of good philosophy can always aid in gaining and maintaining mental health. On the other hand, bad philosophy can actually lead to mental illness as shall be seen shortly in the discussion of problems with the possible intellect since philosophy is a training of the possible intellect as well as the passive intellect.

[21]ST II-II, q. 150, a. 4, ad 3: "concupiscentia non totaliter ligat rationem, sicut ebrietas, nisi forte sit tanta quod faciat hominem insanire."

Elsewhere St. Thomas observes that love and anger can make one insane.[22] The basic mechanism is that when strong passions occur, they bind reason so that a person does not have use of reason. Now this insanity or mental illness may be temporary or a perduring state. As the person begins to lead a life in which reason is often or repeatedly bound or the person does not have use of reason with respect to a specific object, then the soul becomes habituated with respect to a specific object and so vice builds up in such a fashion that the person cannot encounter the object without loss of reason. This is *per accidens* mental illness if it is something in the passive intellect or from vehemence of the appetites. However, it can also be due to some vice or defect in the possible intellect itself in which, in the face of a some object, it simply cannot function, i.e. one cannot engage in acts of judgment or reason. If this occurs, then it is *per se* mental illness.

There has been in modern psychological circles the development of the theory of temporary states of insanity and these essentially consist in a temporary lack of the use of reason with respect to some specific object, e.g. if a man discovers his wife is being raped, the object presented to the intellect may move sorrow and/or anger against the rapist to such degree that the man does not have use of reason. However, it should be noted that this temporary insanity does not occur without some previous degree of defect in the possible intellect or other faculties.[23]

In some cases, it is also a perduring state in which any time a specific object comes into the passive intellect, one loses the use of reason. While temporary insanity may be more from a causal structure within the passive intellect or appetites, the perduring states are always within the possible intellect. The reason this is the case is that, with *per accidens* mental illness in which the problem is in the appetite or passive intellect, the person may still have some voluntariness and some use of reason. As a result, the person may experience profound fear but he can think clearly enough to be able to act. Consequently, there are two types of *per se* mental illness: that which is partial in which the use of reason remains though it is compromised; then there is that *per se* mental illness which usually has a *per accidens* mental illness counterpart[24] in which one simply has no use of reason with respect to a particular object.

This means that if the person engages in a life of the passions or does not have

---

[22]See ST I-II, q. 77, a. 7 and ST II-II, q. 175, a. 2, ad 2.

[23]What this means is that the person must have some degree in which he is leading a life of the appetites in order for the mechanism to function. Someone with perfectly ordered appetites and passive intellect is incapable of this kind of insanity. Moreover, those who have virtues in the various faculties will be inclined to act according to those virtues and so they will be less susceptible to temporary insanity. As society becomes more appetitive, the more temporary insanity will find itself in the society.

[24]That is, even when there is a defect in the possible intellect, there is usually some concomitant defect in the passive intellect or will, which relates to the *per se* mental illness.

proper control of the passive intellect or if there is something which causes problems in the passive intellect, he can, through repeated action, cause a vice in the possible intellect which is *per se* mental illness, since that vice makes the possible intellect completely weak in the face of the object. Hence, leading a life of the appetites can lead to *per se* mental illness. For this reason, it is necessary that one does not lead a life of the appetites and that one guides the appetites according to right reason.

As the *per se* mental illness may be with respect to a specific object, it has the capacity to spread to other objects and this may be the case for three reasons. The first is that as the cogitative power makes its associations and if there is mental illness, the cogitative power may begin associating the thing that causes mental illness and things which do not. For example, suppose someone was nearly hit by a red fire engine which led to a strong fear of red fire engines. As time progresses, that person may begin to fear other red things if they have some similarity to the red fire engine and later he begins to fear even things which have very little similarity to the red fire engine but nevertheless are red. As fear extends to the other things, the possible intellect loses its capacity to function properly with respect to them as well.

The second is that as the judgment is affected with respect to some object, the possible intellect may be affected in other judgments which are connected to the object which causes the problem. For instance, one may lead a life in accordance with the appetites. At first, the person may think that fornication is wrong, but as the person continues to commit fornication, the experiences begin to cause the judgment to begin to be affected and so one cannot act according to reason when presented with the object. But then as time goes on, one begins to think, since one's judgment is already affected about conjugal relations outside of marriage, that other forms of deviant sexuality are OK and one may even get to the point where one thinks that it is "natural" to engage in these deviant forms of sexuality.

The third cause is that as *per se* mental illness affects the possible intellect, it results in a general weakening of the intellect just as one vice in one faculty results in a general weakening of all aspects of the soul. As a result, the weakened intellect with respect to one object may find itself weakened in general or even weak with respect to other objects and so the mental illness can spread. This does not deny that people can compartmentalize their life psychologically, but more often than not, a problem in one area will spread to another.

We have seen that virtue is the good of the intellect. This is generally the case, insofar as any virtue is a perfection. Moreover, virtue in the intellect can actually aid one in avoiding mental illness since the virtue or strength in the intellect can be learned or transferred to other areas than that to which the virtue relates by means of judgment or association. Hence, just as vice in the intellect weakens the intellect, virtue strengthens it and so pursuit of the intellectual virtues, particularly prudence,[25] can aid in the maintenance and recovery of mental health.

We also saw that the truth is the good of the intellect. Since the intellect is designed or ordered toward knowing the truth, when it knows the truth, there is a completion or perfection of its nature. For this reason, knowing the truth aids mental health. As one seeks to conform one's intellect to reality, the intellect is perfected. Since the intellect is designed to know reality or conform itself to reality (which is truth), then it is good for the intellect to do so. Knowing the truth can actually heal mental illness in two ways. The first is that insofar as it is the good of the intellect it can counter mental illness which is evil for the intellect. Second, often simply by knowing the truth, that which causes the mental illness is dissipated. Sometimes it happens that one loses the use of reason because of falsity in the intellect.

For example, the actions of young children are not fully moral since they do not understand things fully. However, something may happen to them which does not affect the passions greatly, but their intellects are affected in their judgment of reality because of the occurrence. What this means is that children are very susceptible to intellectual formation and so they can easily be "deformed" intellectually. For instance, if a parent were to tell a child that lying was OK or that things which contradict each other can both be true, the child may take it on face value and the intellect is formed accordingly. As time goes on and the child acts according to that deformation, the actions militate more and more against the nature of the intellect and so the use of reason is eventually lost.[26]

Since truth is the rectitude of the intellect, then falsity is the deformation of the intellect. While not all falsity actually leads to mental illness, falsity itself has the capacity to lead the person to mental illness. The reason this is the case is that sometimes the various virtues or good dispositions a person may have may actually counter the falsity or keep the person in sufficient balance despite the falsity in the intellect. But if the person does not have good dispositions or virtue at least with respect to the object of falsity, then the person may be prone to mental illness with respect to that object.

---

[25]Since prudence is the virtue by which one knows the means to attain the end and since it concerns practical matters, prudence will aid in gaining and maintaining mental health which is affected by our actions. As one chooses the right things to do (means), he can arrive at the end of mental health.

[26]It should be noted that children are like adults and so this also applies to adults. However, children are more susceptible to intellectual deformation because of their lack of experience with reality. It should also be noted that sometimes children are told something is false and they may give notional assent, i.e. they may believe it. However, since the intellect is designed to function a certain way, it may not affect their reasoning since their intellect may be governed more by connatural principles rather than something told to them, especially if the child does not think what is told to them is that important.

As truth is the conformity of the intellect to reality, truth puts us in contact with reality. Now it has already been noted that those with mental illnesses are not in contact with reality, at least with respect to a particular object of the mental illness. But seeking the truth about the object of one's mental illness can actually lead to mental health. If the directee is troubled about some object, the first step to gaining mental stability with respect to that object is to recognize that he must not have the truth about it because otherwise he would not be so disturbed in the soul in the face of it. Such humility[27] can be the first step toward correcting the faculties which are not seeing the object properly, whether it is the appetites, the cogitative power or the possible intellect. The desire to conform oneself to the truth can greatly aid in advancing and even maintaining one's mental health.

From this we are to draw two conclusions. The first is that we must learn to conform ourselves to reality and not expect reality to conform itself to us. Very often people who end up mentally ill are those who refuse to suffer the process of conforming themselves to reality and since reality and what they want contradict each other and the intellect realizes this, eventually the contradiction leads to mental illness. We often meet mentally ill people who are unwilling to accept reality. On the other hand, some people are mentally ill and are willing to accept reality but their intellectual formation has, at some time, been deformed. In these cases, knowledge alone is sufficient to correct the mental illness (even though there may be some residual defects in other faculties other than the possible intellect).[28]

---

[27]Humility is often defined in different ways but the two main definitions are "willingness to live in accordance with the truth" which is a virtue in the irascible appetite by which the person's appetite submits to the truth of the intellect. The second is "not judging oneself greater than one is" and this is ordered toward our judgment of ourselves. However, both of these are the same thing merely looked at from different points of view. Both refer to the same virtue in the irascible appetite; it is just that one is with respect to judgment of the truth in general and the other the judgment of truth with respect to ourselves. Since we ourselves are part of the general objects of knowledge, we fall under the category of truth in general.

[28]Knowledge a person has of himself is of two kinds. The first is a particular form of knowledge of ourselves, i.e. when a particular person understands his own character or individual traits. The other is more systematic, i.e. philosophical knowledge of ourselves which sometimes can aid in regaining mental health. When someone is taught about the various faculties and their relations, that person can actually use that knowledge to know what to do when one of the faculties is not functioning properly, e.g. if someone knows that passion binds the intellect, then when passion arises, if he knows that changing the object in the phantasm can lead to a calming of the passions, then he can change his phantasm so that he can think clearly. On another level, formal philosophical studies should actually provide an avenue to mental health. It is ironic that many enter the field of psychology in order to seek a remedy for their own problems. However, engaging in formal philosophical

The next conclusion is that leading a life of the appetites means that one wants what the appetites want and not what the intellect knows as true. We have already discussed this in part, but it should be noted that following a life of the appetites takes us out of contact with reality. Since it is the place of the intellect to know reality and not the appetites, since they are not a knowing power but moved by a knowing power, if we follow the appetites, then we are not following the judgment of the possible intellect.[29] What this means is that when the appetites become disordered, their disorder is based on some falsity; otherwise they would not be disordered. As a result, when someone is under the sway of the passions, he is caught up in the fact that the appetites judge something to be good or to be done when in fact it may not be good. Hence, the appetites can actually draw the intellect away from judging rightly about reality and if the will desires the object of the appetite, it may actually move the intellect to ignore reality. This militates against the nature of the intellect which can lead to mental illness if there is not something helping the individual to maintain a balance. Hence, leading a life of the appetites is the first step to mental illness for those who have volitional control over their faculties.

The pursuit of the truth means that true knowledge is the good of the intellect and that sometimes mental illness can be corrected through knowledge. While it still requires choice on the part of the will to move the person to pursue the truth and conform himself to the truth, nevertheless, often a person falls into mental illness because he simply does not understand something properly. This is primarily in the act of judgment of the possible intellect but can be, secondarily, in the cogitative power's assessment of the thing. But if the possible intellect does not know the truth about something, then its judgment will be affected by the false association or assessment of the cogitative power. Once the person discovers the truth, then he can correct the cogitative power by formulating the right phantasm. Again, this is why intellectual formation is so important, particularly for children. For if a person receives the type of intellectual formation that can inherently lead to mental illness, then the child or adult is debilitated when it comes to maintaining mental health.

---

studies requires one to use one's intellect to think logically and systematically. Moreover, insofar as knowledge is a perfection of the intellect, then to gain philosophical knowledge perfects the intellect and so it can aid in regaining mental health or maintaining mental health. Very often people have problems because of the way they think about some thing and studying philosophy can correct how their intellect thinks about the thing. Moreover, the intellect can be strengthened through the arduous task of learning philosophy. Therefore, actually studying philosophical topics can aid mental health. On the other hand, it can also lead to mental illness if the philosophy is erroneous.

[29]Except in the case of those whose judgment of the possible intellect is that one ought always to follow one's passions either with respect to a specific object or with respect to all objects of the appetites.

This also means that when mental illness arises because of a defect of knowledge regarding oneself, it can often be corrected in two ways. The first is through a general knowledge of the nature of man, e.g. if someone thinks that he is completely evil and undesirable, he can often begin recovery by knowing the nature of the good and realizing that insofar as a thing exists, it is good and so he at least has the good of nature. From there, he can be taught how to pursue the good through virtue and good actions and so he can recover from his mental illness. The second is that when the psychologist can assess the directee properly, he can provide the necessary knowledge to the directee about himself so that the directee can begin conforming his intellect to the truth.[30] This will help him correct his judgment about himself and, in so doing, it can begin the process of recovery.

Mental health and illness are also affected by acts of judgment. Sometimes it takes a single act of judgment to send someone down the path of mental illness. On the other hand, it often takes one right judgment and a volitional choice to accept the other judgment in order to lead oneself back to mental health. Since mental illness is precisely the lack of the use of judgment, if a person can be directed to make the right judgment about the object, then he can regain his use of reason with respect to that object. This often means that the person must be led to the right judgment indirectly. Sometimes merely confronting him or merely presenting him with the right judgment can solve the

---

[30]Depression is an interesting illness. Depression has a root in two vices, the first is pride and the second is concupiscence, both of which are connected insofar as they reside in the concupiscible appetite. It is based in pride because people who are depressed are unwilling to conform themselves to the truth and insist that they know the truth about themselves or their situation. They are unwilling to submit themselves to the psychologist for direction. The second is that they actually derive a pleasure from the depression; this has been something completely absent from modern psychology's understanding of depression. In a previous chapter, it was noted that someone can derive pleasure from an action that is in congruity with a disposition even if the action concerns an object viewed as evil. This is why people have a hard time overcoming anger because there is pleasure derived from anger when it is in congruity with their disposition. The same holds true for depression. This means that there is a way to treat depression other than by mere chemicals. Sometimes depression can cause a chemical change and so treating it chemically can help. Sometimes it actually has a chemical origin and so using chemicals can help. But in all cases, depression (which is another name for the vice or bad habituation in the concupiscible appetite of sorrow) leads to or is also accompanied by the aforesaid mechanism. Therefore its solution is humility, to overcome the pride and move the directee to submit to the judgment of others; mortification, to overcome the attachment to pleasure, although this must be handled prudently so as not to give the directee another excuse for his sorrow; and pursuit of the truth through learning, i.e. the pursuit of knowledge. Inclining the directee to study results in the object of the sorrow being taken away and good objects (truths) taking its place. There are other means as well, but these three are particularly helpful.

problem but, in other cases, since his judgment is so impaired, it may be necessary to lead him to the right conclusion (judgment) indirectly. This can be done by discussing things that are connected to his false judgment and presenting the truth in a convincing manner. Then, as he gives assent to things that are connected, he can syllogistically or through induction, be led conclusively to the truth which contradicts his judgment. Now since the first principles are innate, even if a person violates them in one respect, if they are lucid at all, they will not violate them in every respect, otherwise they would be catastrophically mentally ill. If they are not, then the principles are operative at least in some respect and that respect must be found by the psychologist who can then lead the directee slowly to the eradication of falsity by means of showing the directee that his position is contradictory. Hence, judgment can be used to overcome *per se* mental illness.

It can also be used to correct the other faculties. Through an act of judgment and under the motion of the will, the image in the imagination can be altered to correct the lower faculties.[31] This means that through an act or acts of judgment, the person can correct *per accidens* mental illness if there is not a physiological cause. If there is a physiological cause and it is able to be corrected by the actions of the passive intellect under the motion of the possible intellect and will, then it does not prohibit correcting *per accidens* mental illness through action. If it is unable, then medication or some other form of treatment must be sought in order to correct the passive intellect or dispose it sufficiently enough to the point where the person can begin correcting it though actions.

Since science is a virtue which perfects the second act of the possible intellect of judgment, then pursuing scientific endeavors can lead to mental health. It was already noted that depression can be cured through pursuit of (abstract) knowledge. Since the virtue of science perfects the act of judgment, then pursuing science can aid mental health which consists in the use of reason or the use of judgment. On the other hand, someone who is exceedingly intelligent and very knowledgeable may find it difficult to maintain mental health. The reason for this is that someone who has scientific knowledge of something knows the truth about it. Now sometimes the truth is very ugly and painful and so the person may find in knowing the truth a cause of pain and so he may judge the truth wrongly or give in to sorrow and be led to mental illness, especially if the evil is overwhelming. Moreover, sometimes in knowing the truth, one realizes the

---

[31]Correct judgment can also be used to correct the will as well. But since the will is free to choose whether it will follow the truth or not, it is a much more complicated thing to correct a disordered will than the lower faculties. In this case, a person must make a conscious choice, if he desires to regain his mental health or even to maintain it to follow the truth wherever it leads regardless of the cost. Humility in the concupiscible appetite can aid the will since it will incline it to follow the truth. Thus, those who have a disordered will toward rejecting the truth should be moved to develop the virtue of humility. As the virtue of humility develops in the concupiscible appetite, the concomitant virtue or strength will grow in the will which relates to humility.

ugly truth about how contradictory man can be. As a result, the contradiction and knowledge of the truth, if not judged properly, can lead a person to mental illness because of the conflict. In effect, the more intelligent one is, the more he is able to grasp evil and so the more likely it is to affect him. The solution is not to encourage mediocrity in knowledge. Intelligence and knowledge are always a perfection. What needs to be done is to encourage virtue in the other faculties to aid the intellect in those difficult moments. In this respect, fortitude must be the hallmark of those of great intelligence as well as humility, which is a willingness to follow the truth. This will ensure that one will follow the truth, do what is right, regardless if it is arduous or not. Often those who are extremely intelligent suffer from delicate constitutions in the passive intellect, appetites or in general. This is why fortitude is the virtue which they must pursue.

As error in judgment can cause mental illness in the possible intellect, error can also flow over into the other faculties when the possible intellect moves the imagination by changing the phantasm. Error is the first cause of all mental illness of those who act voluntarily. The reason this is the case is that even traumatic experiences, i.e. exterior causes, cannot affect someone if he judges them rightly and through strength of the will maintains that right judgment. Even those with antecedent appetite and the wrong assessments of the cogitative power become mentally ill only after the possible intellect errs in judgment and confirms the lower faculties in their disorder. Otherwise, the possible intellect can deny them in their disorder and as a result they cannot continue to pursue the disorder if right judgment is had. The scholastic dictum that error lies in judgment provides a rich reflection on the source of mental illness.

Since the third act of the intellect which is ratiocination is the process of going from judgment to judgment, then if the judgment is erroneous, the reasoning process will likewise be erroneous. Now the lower faculties are moved by reason, i.e. the conclusions drawn by the possible intellect. The lower faculties which cooperate in the reasoning process by means of the phantasm can be led to the right conclusions by means of the reasoning process. This means that sometimes a mere judgment will not be sufficient to lead the lower faculties to proper order. However, since the lower faculties are fundamentally ordered toward obeying reason, then when they are presented with a reasonable object, they can be drawn to right order. Many people have experienced an antecedent appetite and once they think about it (changing the phantasm, etc.), they begin to realize that the thing desired or the thing causing anger is not really worth the emotional energy. Or they realize that the association by the cogitative power or the judgment of the possible intellect in the beginning was not correct. So once the person leads the lower faculties through the reasoning process carried out in the phantasm, the lower faculties follow the reasoning and therefore arrive at the right conclusion with the possible intellect. This orders the lower faculties to the truth, to what is reasonable and to following the cue of reason.

This means that the first principles can be taught to directees so that they can use them in their reasoning process. This can greatly aid their mental health. Even though the principles may be operative, we are able to act in accord with them more readily, if we know them explicitly. Furthermore, teaching the directee logic or encouraging him to use logical principles in his reasoning can greatly aid mental health and recovery. Since the lower faculties are designed to follow reason, then when reason acts according to its own nature, the lower faculties, as guided by the natural law, are inclined more toward following the reasoning process. If the reasoning process is flawed, the lower faculties can become disordered, whereas if the reasoning process is done according to the logical principles which are essentially the explication of the nature of the intellect and its proper acts, then the lower faculties will more readily respond.[32]

The use of logic and desire on the part of the directee to conform his intellect to reality is a powerful tool in fighting mental illness and in aiding mental health. Since logic is merely the art of right reasoning, it is the art in accordance with nature, i.e. the natural law as it governs the intellect. This is why choosing contrary to the natural law can cause so many disorders. Since the intellect is a mirror image of reality and it is ordered toward knowing reality, then to reject reality is contrary to the natural law and causes great disorders. This is why choosing something contrary to the natural law is so disordering because it goes contrary to the order of man's nature, part of which is his intellect. This is also why expecting reality to conform to us is contrary to the natural law.[33] Now those who want reality to conform to them are guilty of subjectivism, i.e. those who hold to a subjectivistic or relativistic view of truth are acting contrary to the natural law. This means that the proper conclusion of subjectivism and relativism is mental illness.

As psychology must encourage all men to follow the natural law, it also means that it must encourage people to follow the first principles, many of which are operative in the human intellect, as has been clearly seen. Knowledge and use of the principle of non-contradiction has already been seen as useful. The principle of sufficient reason, if taught to the directee, can help him not to react in an exaggerated fashion to the objects of his mental illness. In fact, it can teach him that certain things cannot cause his problems unless he allows them, since they are not a sufficient cause of his mental illness unless he allows them to be. Moreover, it can help him to realize whether things are

---

[32]Knowledge of informal fallacies can greatly aid the intellect in its approach to reality and it can keep its reasoning process from falling into error by making sure its premises are correct. This is why classes in logic often have a thorough treatment of informal fallacies so that the reasoning is not thrown off by the informal fallacies.

[33]Ironically, with the advent of technology, it has become more and more possible for man to manipulate reality to get it to conform to his own ideas. Provided his ideas are in conformity with reality, this can prove to be a great benefit to man. But since modern man is demonstrating that he is becoming more and more disordered, this manipulation is a sign that he is following the natural law less and less.

really to be feared or not based on whether they have the sufficient capacity to cause harm. The principle of operation is very important. If the directee can be taught the principle of operation in conjunction with the natural law, then encouraging him to follow the principle of operation in his own actions can greatly aid the intellect. The directee must also be encouraged to follow the connatural principles which will aid him in acting according to the structure of the intellect, which will aid mental health and recovery from mental illness.

To act contrary to these principles and to the natural law is to act irrationally. Since the natural law is structured for man to act according to reason, then to act contrary to the natural law is to act irrationally. Now since the intellect is a power capable of habituation, those who act contrary to the nature of the intellect, i.e. those who act irrationally, train the intellect to be irrational. Hence, not following the natural law leads to mental illness since mental illness occurs when one is irrational.

V. The Will

As perfect freedom consists in the intellect freely judging the truth and not being bound or encumbered in any way and the will moving from its own interior principle, since freedom is a perfection of man, then true freedom is also the goal of psychology. Psychology is not just about the right operations of the possible intellect. It is also about the right operations of those faculties which can affect the possible intellect, i.e. it is also about the appetites, the passive intellect and the will.

There has already been a discussion of the mechanism in which the intellect, when one chooses evil, judges what is right but is moved by the will to command what is false. Often, the will moves the intellect to reformulate the image so it can make a false judgment about the thing: to say that it is good so that the will can will it. This means that if one has a disordered will, it can lead to mental illness. The will in its relationship to the possible intellect is similar to the will in its relationship to the passive intellect. As the perfections and defects of the higher faculties can redound to the lower faculties, so the defects or disorder in the will can lead to disorder in the possible intellect. Since the will can move the possible intellect to perform acts contrary to the possible intellect's nature, it can cause disorders in the intellect.

This means that many mental illnesses are voluntary and this is the case in two ways. The first is implicitly, in the sense that the will does not explicitly will mental illness but moves the other faculties to perform actions which lead to mental illness. Another way is when the will by omission does not do something which will lead to mental health, e.g. when a passion arises, it chooses not to change the phantasm because it wants to relish the object of the passion. The second is explicitly, as when someone, though the historical occurrences are few, explicitly chooses to make himself mentally ill. After the initial choice, the intellect does not immediately become mentally ill but the will can move the various faculties and over the course of time bring about mental illness.

Ironically, just as the intellect can perform actions which lead to its own disorder, so the will becomes weak and less free as it becomes disordered. It has been shown that perfect freedom occurs both when the intellect judges clearly and the will moves strictly from an interior principle. But as the intellect becomes disordered, it cannot clearly judge things and so freedom is compromised. This means that the perfection of the will is twofold, the first is extrinsic in the sense that the will must choose the good of the other faculties for its own sake. The second is that it must choose the good as an inherent perfection of itself. This means that since the natural law commands what is perfective of each faculty, the natural law commands the act of the will of love which is willing the *good* (of another).

This willing of the good is not merely a selfish desire to obtain some good, since that is only partially perfective of the individual and can actually lead to imperfections when the desired good is not in accord with the natural law. The willing of the good of the other for one's own sake must be in congruity with the natural law. Moreover, in order for the will to be truly perfect and in a sense truly free, it must will the good of the other for the other persons's sake. Since both are goods perfective of the will, both are commanded by the natural law, because man, who has will, is the only animal which has the capacity to will something strictly for the sake of someone else and see it as his own good.

In psychology, this means that those who are mentally ill will often be characterized as not very loving except in the selfish sense and often not in congruity with the natural law. As a result, the psychologist must teach the directee what proper love is, i.e. what it means to love in congruity with the natural law.[34] Then he must encourage the directee to seek perfective love which is not only to love the true good of oneself but to love people for their own benefit. This can actually go a long way in helping to overcome mental illness, especially if the mental illness is related to specific people. By encouraging the directee to love others and to perform acts for their benefit, it can actually correct the judgment of the intellect about the other people and bring the judgment of the intellect into congruity with the natural law which is its good.

Moreover, by counseling the directee to have an authentic love for himself, he (i.e. the will) will be helped not to command actions which cause bad passions and vice. This will aid the directee in overcoming vice and developing virtue which helps the intellect. Next it will help him not to command what is false. Thus false phantasms, false memories from those phantasms and false associations in the cogitative power will not occur which will clearly aid mental health. Moreover, by commanding exterior actions which are based on authentic love, the directee will focus his attention on good things outside of himself and thus develop a good relationship to his exterior world, all of which are causes of mental health. As the attention is focused on the good outside of

---

[34]This will guard against things like encouraging directees to commit acts contrary to temperance or the sixth commandment, etc.

oneself, truth is built upon in the intellect as it seeks to conform itself to the good thing in reality; the passions will be subdued because they will see the true good and the imagination can be cured along with the cogitative power and memory. In all of this, it can be seen that love based on the real good puts one in contact with reality.

VI. Other Considerations

In psychology, one of things that psychologists must be aware of is the fact that most people act according to their material disposition. This is why alteration of the dispositions by means of acts of virtues and vice is so important. If one can change one's disposition to one more in congruity with virtue, then it becomes easier for the person to gain and maintain mental health. Dispositions are not necessarily bad but can actually aid growing in virtue as well. The psychologist must be aware of the different dispositions in order to counsel the directee when to act according to disposition and when not to act according to disposition.

As has been repeated several times, one must act according to the natural law, which means one must follow one's conscience at all times. This brings to the fore two very important aspects of the conscience. The first is that the conscience must be formed properly, otherwise it can lead to a great deal of psychological (as well as moral) damage. The role of parents in this matter, as well as a person's own responsibility to make sure that his conscience is properly formed is crucial. Psychologists must never explain away the conscience or advise the directee to act contrary to the conscience. As one acts according to one's conscience, if the conscience is properly formed, then one acts according to the natural law. As the natural law is a proper ordering of man then order will occur in the individual and peace will result.[35] When there is order in the soul a natural state of peacefulness, serenity or tranquility descends upon the soul.

This tranquility is the opposite of the nagging conscience (*vermis conscientiae*) which eats away at the soul. Since the higher faculties redound to the lower faculties, sorrow creeps into the concupiscible appetite. Other disorders can arise as the passions become disturbed and affect all of the other faculties. When a psychologist discovers that a directee has an erroneous conscience, the psychologist must correct the directee's intellectual formation so that the conscience can act according to the natural law. Furthermore, the psychologist must advise the directee to follow his conscience otherwise mental illness will continue or result.

This brings us to the second point about the conscience, viz. that it cannot be denied without serious problems arising. The psychologist must be sensitive to this. The dictates of conscience have not only moral repercussions but also psychological ones. It is not necessary to go into them all as they have been somewhat covered, but

---

[35]St. Augustine's famous definition of peace is "tranquillitas ordinis," i.e. the tranquility of order.

the importance and necessity of the conscience cannot be stressed too much. It is the judgment of the intellect that tells us what is right and wrong and if we do not follow it, we can cause psychological damage by not doing what is morally right.[36]

VII. Catastrophic Mental Illness

Mental illness can be slight or grave. It is slight if the person retains some use of reason even though habitually a specific object causes him problems. It is grave if the person has no use of reason or almost no use of reason in the face of the object. Now as was mentioned, one can have mental illness with respect to one thing, some things or all things. Mental illness in which one simply persists in a constant state of no use of reason is catastrophic.[37] It is not clear whether certain forms of sensation can be used

---

[36]There should be made a distinction between different senses of right and wrong. Sometimes something is right or wrong morally and this is because it is capable of being recognized only by he who has reason or intellect and it proceeds from deliberate will. However, there are other kinds of right and wrong which are not strictly moral. While moral rights and wrongs have a direct impact on psychological health, not all things which affect psychological health are necessarily moral. Some things which we do are right or wrong based upon their effect on our lower nature which may or may not be moral as such, e.g. writing and thinking about fictitious things can have an amoral dimension to them. For instance if one thinks about fictitious creatures and makes himself scared in the process without any intention of doing so, one does something which is psychologically bad but not necessarily morally bad. However, every intentional choice which affects our mental health is necessarily moral, for since one is a moral agent because he has reason and will, to compromise one's reason is always immoral. On the other hand, many people do things which are morally wrong even though their intention is not to do something evil, but there still is a psychological effect. Even if one does not want bad things to have their effects, they are actions, i.e. realities, nonetheless, and therefore their proper effects will flow from them whether we want them or not. At any rate, psychology must recognize that while its end is not to make people moral, a moral life is a necessary means to regaining and maintaining psychological health. The fact is that psychology, insofar as it touches upon the intellect and will, has an intrinsic connection to morality. It is not the place of psychology to dictate to moralists what is right and wrong, although at times it may be consulted to provide knowledge about the faculties or that particular aspect of man. Also it should not be assumed that morality is merely a matter of psychology.

[37]There should be made a distinction between those who are comatose or in a permanent vegetative state (PVS) and those who do not have the use of reason. Those who do not have the use of reason are consciously aware. While there have been some reports of those who are comatose having some awareness of their surroundings, it is unclear whether those in a PVS, as a general rule, are performing other functions proper to someone who is conscious.

to begin to have an effect on the passive intellect to gain moments of lucidity. However, those who are catastrophically mentally ill more than likely will need some form of psychiatric intervention in order to restore at least some functioning to the passive intellect. Once some use of reason is gained, then the psychologist can set about determining the various causes of the mental illness if there are any other than the physiological. If there are other causes than the physiological, then medication may have to be used for some time. Even if the problem or the cause is resolved, it may leave some physiological residual effects and so medication or other forms of treatment may have to be used until the person no longer suffers the physiological effects.

Those who are gravely mentally ill with respect to one object or more than one object but not catastrophically mentally ill must approach mental health indirectly. This was mentioned previously but some other observations are in order. The psychologist must use those things on which the person has a strong grasp in order to make the connections between those areas in which he is mentally lucid and those where he is not. As the psychologist guides the directee through the proper reasoning process, he can help the person slowly but surely to overcome the mental illness. Since those who are gravely mentally ill do not have the use of reason with respect to some particular object, one cannot use reason to help them with respect to that specific object. Rather, one must use those things over which he has lucidity and help the directee to reason to conclusions which can help to clear up the problem he does have. For example, if a woman is raped and loses her use of reason in the presence of non-family males, then her relationship and view of the family males can be used to help her see that not all males are rapists. The psychologist can affirm her relationship with her father and brothers and then discuss family relations in general and how they apply to different families, finally ending with a discussion of how some families are fine and others have problems, and so some males are OK and some are not. Then she can be shown slowly that most men are not rapists and so she does not need to be alarmed around men unless there is *due* cause for concern. She can then be taught what are the due signs for concern, how to protect herself and how to avoid males of this kind and so she begins to think more clearly about males. The point is that sometimes one must address the problem in an indirect but connected fashion.

With those who are slightly mentally ill, since they have some use of reason, it may be possible to use that reason to deal directly with the object of concern. With others, it may make it worse and experience will tell the psychologist when a person can and cannot use the direct approach. Since psychology is like medicine in that there is a scientific part and a practical part or a part of it which is an art, then the actual applications of the principles of psychology will come through the development of an art and not the application of scientific method. The indirect approach can be used with some directees but it should not be assumed that the one or the other method ought always be used. Rather prudence and experience will help one to know the signs when someone is open to the direct approach and when he is not.

Conclusion

The philosophy of man is very complex and psychology is even more complex. For the science of mental health not only takes into consideration the complex nature of man with all the various faculties and how they affect one another, it must also take into consideration all the various objects exterior to him to which the various faculties relate and how they can have a psychological impact on man. This book has been an initial look at these issues. It is in no way complete but the hope is that it has shown that the principles of Thomistic philosophy provide a solid foundation for the conclusions of this science. The conclusions reached in this text provide a start for those who practice in this field, but it is not enough.

The science of psychology is an important science for modern man. Perhaps one of the reasons it is more important to modern man than it was in the past is due to the fact that modern man is doing things which are more likely to lead to mental illness. Modern laws and social engineering based on bad psychology and a distorted view of man have done very little to aid mental health and, if anything, they have been the catalyst for mental illness. It is our hope that this small contribution to the science of psychology will provide a means for that science to gain a proper direction and foundation so that it can begin to have a consistently salutary effect on individuals and society as a whole.

Vol. 2: Sacred and Other Spiritual Causes

In honorem omnium sanctorum

Introduction to the Second Volume

The use of sacred means in aiding the mentally ill has been, by and large, limited to Protestants. Some Catholic psychologists will supplement their psychological work with sacred causes, or even use the sacred means for the most part. However, when psychology in the Catholic sphere was divorced from philosophy, the theological connection was lost. Since one's theological tenets are heavily influenced by one's cosmology and philosophy of man, one's philosophical outlook will have a direct impact on how one views spiritual realities. For example, if one adopts the position that man is strictly a material being and that God does not get involved in the affairs of men,[1] then the discussion of sacred causes is moot. Even if one holds that God does get involved in the life of man, yet one holds that man is strictly a material being, one's view of the operations of grace, the infused virtues and the gifts of the Holy Spirit will be drastically different from an authentic Catholic position. A truly Catholic psychology cannot be founded on any psychological approach which treats man from a purely materialist perspective, since the spiritual dimension of man is ultimately denied. Moreover, the empirical method by nature must exclude the consideration of sacred causes, since most sacred causes are by nature unmeasurable.[2]

However, since man has a natural inclination to know God,[3] empirical methods cannot adequately address those aspects of mental illness which have a connection to this natural inclination. Moreover, the Catholic faith teaches us about the involvement of the supernatural as well as the demonic in man's life. Therefore, before one can begin properly employing sacred causes to aid the process of regaining and maintaining mental health, it is necessary to delineate those causes clearly and determine how they affect the faculties of man. Yet, the proper relationship between the sciences of psychology and theology must be clearly delineated in order to avoid errors regarding the sacred causes. Errors in knowledge regarding the sacred causes lead to their misuse or abuse and so it is necessary to understand the sacred causes properly. We also know that there are other spiritual causes in the life of man which are not sacred (e.g. the demonic) which have a direct impact on the faculties of man and therefore his mental health.

The vast majority of Catholics, let alone Catholic psychologists, are fundamentally ignorant about the sacred and other spiritual causes. For this reason, it is the hope of the author of this text that Catholic psychologists will begin the process of learning the richness of the Catholic teaching on the sacred and other spiritual causes. With this volume, the author hopes to provide a beginning toward an authentic Catholic approach to these causes.

---

[1] This would be the Deist position.

[2] As was mentioned in the prior volume, psychiatry can have a legitimate scientific foundation provided it remains subalternated to philosophical psychology. In like manner, psychiatry need not take into consideration the sacred causes except by an admission that (a) they are there and can influence chemical and biological processes and that (b) if there is not an empirical explanation, one must remain open to a sacred or other spiritual cause.

[3] See prior volume, chap. 11.

Chapter 1: The Relationship of the Science of Theology to Psychology

The relationship of theology to the science of psychology and how the principles of theology affect the individual who leads a life in congruity with sound theological principle can only be understood when one has a clear grasp of the nature of the science of theology. However, due to modern historical conditions[1] and the influence of modern philosophy in the area of theology,[2] one must first understand what constitutes the science of theology. For this reason, this chapter will first look at the material and formal objects of theology as well as its method. Subsequently, the chapter will discuss the relation of theology to psychology. The remainder of this volume will examine how the various theological causes and influences affect mental health.

I. The Nature of the Theological Science

Every science is composed of a material object, a formal object and a method. The material object[3] is the subject or object of inquiry, i.e. it is the thing studied. The formal object is the *ratio* or perspective taken on the material object, e.g. one can look at a cell and study it from the point of view of chemical reactions (biochemistry), from the point of view of the nature of life itself (philosophy of animate nature sometimes called *De Anima*[4]) or even from the point of view of what materially makes up life (as in biology). Hence, it is possible for several sciences to study the same object from very different points of view. Lastly, there is the method which determines the *modus procedendi* or mode of proceeding in any science.[5]

The term theology comes from the Greek terms θεός and λόγος which means the science or study of God.[6] Insofar as theology is an organized body of knowledge of

---

[1]Here we have in mind the decay of organized religions and the direct, clear and volitional exclusion of the discussion of God from public fora. Also, we have in mind the clear moral and psychological decay within modern society.

[2]This observation requires a study of its own. To many Thomists, the various modern philosophical influences are well known. To the untrained eye, however, modern philosophical thought is practically "natural" to the way people think today, both in secular matters and in theology. Unfortunately, the discussion of this topic would be too protracted to be adequately addressed here.

[3]The use of the term "material object" does not mean that the object is necessarily material or physical. Rather, it is a consideration of the subject of inquiry prescinding from any other consideration, *ratio* or perspective.

[4]*De Anima* comes from the tract of Aristotle on the nature of life and historically the philosophy of animate nature was referred to according to these two terms.

[5]These three were discussed at greater length in volume I, chapter I.

[6]Garrigou-Lagrange, *De Revelatione*, vol. 1, p. 7; Tanquerey, *Synopsis Theologiae Dogmaticae*, vol. 1, p.1, and Parente, *Dictionary of Dogmatic Theology*, p. 282.

things known with certainty,[7] it is a true science.[8] But since theology is based upon God's knowledge, it is said to be a subalternated science since it receives its principles from another science.[9] Since theology is a science, it too has a material object, a formal object and a method.

A. Material Object

       Theology is the science of God[10] and so its material object *per se* and primarily is God.[11] The material object also includes created things under the aspect of their relation to God and so created things are part of the material object *per accidens* and secondarily.[12] It must be clear that theology is not about created things *per se* or essentially speaking but only insofar as they are seen in relation to God. As a result, theology is ultimately about God.[13] Since theology[14] considers God and all created things from the point of view of God, theology is wisdom (*sapientia*) since wisdom is the consideration of the highest causes of things and God is the highest cause of all.[15]

---

[7]See Tanquerey, op. cit., p. 2 and Ott, *Fundamentals of Catholic Dogma*, p. 1.

[8]Contrary to the modern understanding, theology is indeed a science since, as will be seen, it has the necessary constituents to be a science. Modern man usually conceives theology as merely matters of opinion.

[9]Essentially this means that the science upon which theology is based is the knowledge possessed by God and the blessed in heaven (*scientia Dei et beatorum*); see ST, I, q. 1, a. 2; Ott, loc. cit. and Garrigou-Lagrange, op. cit., p. 13. It is based on the knowledge (*scientia*) of God since He has revealed truths regarding Himself and the created order and it is also based upon the knowledge of the blessed (*scientia beatorum*) because through history, angels and saints have revealed certain things as messengers of God or under His divine inspiration.

[10]Ott, op. cit., p. 1; Attwater, *A Catholic Dictionary*, p. 520; *Catholic Encyclopedia Dictionary*, p. 945; C.E., vol. XIV, p. 580 and Garrigou-Lagrange, op. cit., p. 1.

[11]ST I, q. 1, passim; Ott, op. cit., p. 1; Tanquerey, op. cit., p. 2; C.E., vol. XIV, p. 580 and Garrigou-Lagrange, op. cit., p. 9.

[12]ST I, q. 1, passim; Ott, op. cit., p. 1; Tanquerey, op. cit., p. 2 and Garrigou-Lagrange, op. cit., p. 9.

[13]This is important to bear in mind since the current historical conditions have left people thinking that religion and theology are about man or themselves. This immanentism was warned against and condemned by Pope St. Pius X in *Pascendi Dominici Gregis*, passim.

[14]Since theology studies God and since theology studies the teachings revealed by God, St. Thomas calls theology the science of sacred doctrine (*sacra doctrina*); see ST I, q. 1, passim.

[15]ST I, q. 1, a. 6.

B. Formal Object

With respect to the formal object of theology, a distinction must be made. Man is capable of arriving at knowledge of God by the natural light of reason[16] and this is called natural theology. Natural theology is a philosophical science and is a branch of the broader study of metaphysics. However, natural theology only tells us what we can know about God through His effects, i.e. creation. Supernatural theology, sometimes called sacred theology or revealed theology, tells us things which can be known only by revelation and cannot be known through the natural light of reason. That does not mean that sacred theology does not include things that can be known through the natural light of reason. Rather, it differs from natural theology by its mode of knowing, viz. sacred theology knows things about God and creatures in relation to God by means of divine revelation.

For this reason, the formal object of sacred theology is from the perspective of what is accepted or known by faith from revelation.[17] There are two aspects to this which are of importance. The first is that one can only adequately understand revelation through the light of faith; for faith is the supernatural virtue infused in the intellect by which one gives assent to what is revealed.[18] As a result, faith is a necessary criterion to engage in the science of theology.[19] The second aspect is that the formal object is from the point of view of revelation. For this reason, revelation is pivotal in

---

[16]Vatican I, *Filius Dei*. See also ST I, q. 1, a 1; ibid., ad 2; Ott, op. cit., p. 1; Tanquerey, op. cit., p. 1-2; C.E., vol. XIV, p. 580 and Garrigou-Lagrange, op. cit., p. 1.

[17]ST I, q. 1, a 1; ibid., ad 2; ibid., q. 1, aa. 2 and 3; Ott, op. cit., p. 1; Tanquerey, op. cit., p. 1-2; C.E., vol. XIV, p. 580 and Garrigou-Lagrange, op. cit., p. 1.

[18]This will be discussed in a later chapter.

[19]The author is clearly aware that this statement might strike some as polemical. It is clear from modern exegesis that many theologians believe that in order to address the Scriptures "scientifically" one must "leave one's faith at the door," so to speak. They believe that faith adversely affects one's judgment about the Scriptures and so one cannot view them objectively. There are essentially two problems with this view. The first is the view of science that predominates in Scripture studies. It is clear that most Scripture scholars suffer from a rationalist mentality, holding that only the empirical sciences are real sciences. This issue has already been addressed elsewhere (see Vol. 1, Chap. 1). The second problem is with their view of what the Scriptures are. If the Scriptures are merely the product of human authors, their contention can stand. However, the Scriptures are divinely inspired, which means as an object of study they are not merely natural objects of study. Rather, they are supernatural objects of study. Now since the habit of science must be proportionate to the object, it is necessary to have faith (a supernatural virtue) in order to grasp truly the nature of that object, i.e. the Scriptures. Secondly, the formal object must be proportionate to the material object (see ibid.). Now since the Scriptures are a supernatural object, then the formal object of the science of theology must be from the point of view of faith which helps us to see them according to the divine light of revelation, as St. Thomas observes (see ST I, q. 1, a. 1).

understanding the proper object of theology, viz. God.

St. Thomas observes that the formal object of theology is from the point of view of deity.[20] St. Thomas thus calls attention to the fact that sacred theology concerns God in Himself, i.e. the interior life of the Blessed Trinity and the Incarnation. As a result, the natural light of reason will not suffice for this form of knowledge. Rather, we need a different science which can tell us about God in Himself. While St. Thomas observes that the formal object is from the point of view of deity, this is because we are not studying God through His effects, but what He is in Himself. This is why the formal object of deity and revelation are not at odds. For while one is seeking knowledge of God in Himself, he can only do that through the light of revelation and since revelation tells us about God in Himself, the two are not at odds.

C. Method

The method of sacred theology is essentially the same as the philosophical method, i.e. it proceeds by induction and deduction.[21] Theology procedes by induction since it draws from a variety of places in Scripture and comes to a conclusion about some doctrine, e.g. Tanquerey observes that the doctrine that the human nature in Christ is hypostatically joined to the divine nature is derived from a variety of places in Scripture.[22] Moreover, in the area of moral theology, much is based upon induction about the nature of man in its relation to divine justice.

Theology is also deductive since the articles of faith, i.e. the things revealed, constitute principles[23] from which we deduce other things contained within the articles of faith. We do not deduce to something contrary to the faith, "but to manifesting other things which are given in these doctrines."[24] St. Thomas observes, however, that this science is not different from other sciences in that theology does not prove its principles[25] like other sciences. This follows from the fact that the articles of faith are revealed and so they are accepted as principles from a higher science and therefore do not pertain to the science of theology to be demonstrated.

II. The Relation of Psychology to Theology

Since psychology is a branch of philosophy, how it relates to theology is contingent upon how philosophy relates to theology in general. Psychology relates in

---

[20]See ST I, q. 1, passim and Garrigou-Lagrange, op. cit., p. 9.

[21]Tanquerey, vol. 1, p. 4.

[22]Ibid.

[23]ST I, q. 1, a. 7.

[24]ST I, q. 1, a. 8, ad 2: "sed ad manifestandum aliqua alia quae traduntur in hac doctrina."

[25]ST I, q. 1, a. 8.

a specific way to theology which is proper to psychology itself. As to the general way psychology and philosophy relate to theology, there are several points to be made. The first is that philosophy is the "handmaid of theology," because it is able to aid theology in certain ways.[26] Traditionally this took the form of providing a scientific vocabulary which can be used in theology in order to gain further precision in the expression of theological concepts or doctrines. For example, the use of the term *substance* in philosophy greatly aided the definition of the doctrine of transubstantiation at the Council of Trent.[27] Since terms have specific meanings, the Church has always been very cautious in being sure that the perennial philosophy used by theologians is not inimical to the faith. Philosophy provides a means of developing rigorous scientific habits, i.e. intellectual virtues and so when one engages in the science of theology, one is habituated to the method and rigorous scientific thinking and will employ it in the science of theology. While the Church does not align herself with any specific philosophical system,[28] it has repeatedly encouraged the use of Thomistic philosophy as a way of avoiding error.[29]

While philosophy does help theology by being its handmaid, philosophy can also gain something from theology. Since theology is a science which reasons about the deposit of faith which is revealed by God, the teachings in the deposit of faith are more certain from the point of view of their cause which is God than the reasoning of men who are prone to err. For that reason, the teachings in theology can act as a corrective to philosophy regarding its conclusions. Since God is the author of all truth[30] and since He cannot contradict Himself, the truths of one science cannot contradict the truths of

---

[26]The Church's recognition of how theology and philosophy relate can be found in Leo XIII, *Aeterni Patris*, John Paul II, *Fides et Ratio* and in a number of other locations.

[27]See session 13.

[28]See John Paul II, *Fides et Ratio*, para. 49.

[29]The possible citations are numerous, but among others see: Leo XIII, *Aeterni Patris*, passim, but especially paras. 21, 25 and 33; Pope St. Pius X, *Pascendi Dominici Gregis*, para. 45; CIC/83 can. 252, §3 and Sacred Congregation For Catholic Education, *Ratio Fundamentalis*, paras. 79 and 86. It is not possible to discuss in detail the role of a perennial philosophy; since such a discussion is too involved, it will not be done at length here.

[30]De Ver., q.1, a. 8; ST I, q. 16, a. 5, ad 3; I Sent., d. 19, q. 5, a. 1; ibid., d. 19, q. 5, a. 2, ad 2; II Sent., d. 28, q. 5, ad 1; ibid., d. 37, q. 1, a. 2, ad 1 & 2 and Meta., l. 2, nn. 1956-1959.

another science.[31] Truth is one and so it cannot contradict itself.[32] Therefore, if theology tells us something which pertains to the domain of philosophy, theology can be used to ensure whether philosophy has reached the right conclusion or not. This is called the analogy of faith in which the teachings of faith can be used to check whether the conclusions in philosophy or any other science are correct. In the domain of psychology, this means that theology can be used to ensure that the conclusions regarding psychology are correct. Not all conclusions in psychology relate to theology, but some do. Even though one can employ the analogy of faith, the analogy of faith does not dictate the reasoning process itself within a given science, since each science is a science in its own right independent of theology and must proceed according to its own principles, which are not the same principles as that of theology.

Psychology can also benefit from theology in another way. While psychology's proper scientific method does not take theology into account, nevertheless, God revealed a great deal to man about his condition and the various causes of mental health and illness, which is the topic of this volume. Even though psychology proceeds by its own method and conclusions which are known through the natural light of reason, we can learn a great deal from God about our current state and how our actions affect our mental health. In fact, a full understanding of man is not complete without revelation. For man has a relation to God which affects him in the depths of his being, as we shall see, so that man only makes sense in the context of the divine. Moreover, the quality of our relationship with God has a direct connection to our mental health. We also have a relationship to the angelic. While it is possible to know that it is suitable that angels exist,[33] it is not possible to understand our relationship to them without revelation and the same holds true for those who have passed from this life.

While we can learn things from theology, strictly speaking, there is no theology of psychology. For psychology has its own proper formal and material object which is

---

[31]Vatican I, *Filius Dei*. This rests upon the principle of non-contradiction. Historically, there have been some philosophers who held to the two truth theory which asserts that the truths of theology can contradict the truths of philosophy and yet both are still true. This violates the principle of non-contradiction, without which rational discourse is simply not possible. Today this takes the form of people holding that it is acceptable to believe something even though it does not fit what is known through science.

[32]Truth is one since truth is convertible with the one, which is known through the science of metaphysics. However, without entering into the discussion of convertibility, it is easy to see that truth is one from the point of view of its nature. Since truth is the adequation of intellect and thing, truth exists in the intellect whenever it congrues with the thing, regardless of what that thing is. Therefore, since truth is always the same from the point of view of congruity itself, then truth is one. This does not deny that there are "truths" from the point of view of the truth in one's intellect regarding one thing which is ontologically distinct from the truth regarding another. But all truths are a congruity of intellect and thing.

[33]St. Thomas argues that the existence of angels can be known through the natural light of reason in SCG, l. II, cc. 91-101.

mental health, whereas theology has its own proper object of study, viz. God and creatures in relationship to God. Since psychology as such does not consider things in relation to God, there is no branch of theology called psychology. However, we can look to revelation and theology to provide knowledge about man's relation to God, angels, etc. and in an interdisciplinary way, we can arrive at a greater knowledge of the causes of mental health and illness. For example, those who are mentally ill can pray for the graces necessary for them to do those things which will help them attain mental health.

It must be clear, however, that while we will address those things which pertain to the domain of theology, they should not be seen as mere means to mental health. For example, while going to Confession aids mental health, it should not be done for that reason alone. For one ought to go to Confession to be forgiven of one's sins, to render justice to God, to be reconciled to Him, if one be in the state of mortal sin, etc. One goes to Confession in order to obtain grace to give God greater honor and glory, not merely for the sake of mental health. On the other hand, nothing forbids employing sacred means with a dual intention, viz. one natural and the other supernatural. For instance, one may go to Confession in order to alleviate mental difficulties but as long as one has the requisite supernatural sorrow for one's sins, that suffices. Yet, if supernatural things are sought for their own sake, the directee will find that the supernatural causes will be more effective. Also, if one seeks to be mentally healthy insofar as mental health is ordered toward one's spiritual welfare, that will be more rightly ordered and thereby have a greater influence on one's mental health. Any time a sacred means is employed, it must be sought in a manner that will not desecrate the means or give offense to God. Then and only then can the mental health be effected.

Since God and sacred things can actually affect mental health, psychologists can encourage their directees to employ them in their proper way. For example, sometimes someone will be doing something immoral which is affecting their mental health and their guilt before God may be bothering them or actually be the cause of the mental illness. As a result, the person should be encouraged to reconcile himself to God, which will remove the cause of the mental illness and then the directee can be counseled as to how to obtain and maintain his mental health.

Conclusion

The scope of this volume, therefore, is to discuss God and sacred things (studied in theology) as they affect mental health and to discuss other things studied in theology which can cause mental illness. Psychologists should be versed in theology to the degree necessary to guide directees for several reasons. First, in order to know if the cause of the mental illness is a theological one, e.g. the demonic, sin, etc. Second, the psychologist should be aware of the various theological means which affect mental health and illness so as to counsel the directee in what he should and should not do. Third, the psychologist must know whether the spiritual problems of the directee require a spiritual director in order to remove the causes of mental illness. For this reason, psychologists should have a working relationship with priests who are knowledgeable in psychology so that both priest and psychologist a) know what the directee needs and

b) what their proper competence is. Psychologists must not assume the role of a spiritual director, even though their field is closely related to theology. On the other hand, it is not the place of a priest, insofar as he is a priest, to do psychological counseling.[34] With the full knowledge of theology and psychology, both priest and psychologist together can be a powerful means of aiding those who are mentally ill.

---

[34]On occasion, a priest may be assigned the task of learning psychology by his superiors for the good of the Church. In this case, he can assume both roles of spiritual director and psychologist.

Chapter 2: Happiness

One of the characteristics that distinguishes the mentally ill and the mentally healthy is happiness. As a general rule, those who are mentally healthy possess some degree of happiness while those who suffer the affliction of mental illness lack some degree of happiness. While there are some mentally ill people who experience elation during their periods of mental illness, this is not true happiness because true happiness is based on something real, which will become clear as this chapter progresses. It pertains, therefore, to this chapter to discuss the nature of happiness for man. For if we can know what pertains to man's happiness, we can know those things which he should or should not do in order to attain happiness.

I. The Essence of Happiness

In the prior volume, it was shown that the natural law contains categories of natural inclination, i.e we are inclined by our very nature to pursue those things which are in accordance with our nature and we are not naturally inclined toward those things which will harm us. Now many natural inclinations are accompanied by desire for the end toward which we are inclined. It is for this reason that St. Thomas begins his treatise on happiness[1] with the question whether man acts for an end. For if our nature is to be fulfilled, if we are to follow the natural law and reach the ends for which our faculties are ordered, we must discuss whether man acts for an end and what that end is.

A. The End

In the *Prima Secundae*, St. Thomas begins the discussion by asking the question whether man acts for an end. He observes that man and irrational creatures differ based upon the fact that man acts through deliberate will whereas animals do not.[2] An action is essentially human, i.e. proper to man, because it proceeds from knowledge (intellection) and free will.[3] Man differs from animals because he knows what he is doing and he has the capacity to choose to do it or not, whereas animals tend toward their ends without fully understanding them nor do they act freely.[4] St. Thomas then

---

[1] St. Thomas did not actually write a treatise specifically on happiness. This is the name given to it among scholars, referring to the section in the *Summa Theologiae* which covers the topic, viz. ST I-II, qq.1-5.

[2] ST I-II, q. 1, a. 1. See also, ibid., q. 1, a. 2; ibid., q. 6, a. 1 and SCG III, c. 2.

[3] This was discussed in terms of the voluntary in vol. 1, chap. 7 of this work.

[4] The primary motive faculties in animals are their appetites. Since they only have a common sense power, imagination, memory and an estimative power, they only know the accidents of a thing and never understand the essence or nature of a thing. As a result, they are moved by the estimative power assessing that some object in the imagination is good.

observes that the object of the will is the good[5] and the end[6] and so it suits man who can know the end and freely choose to act for the sake of an end.

St. Thomas observes that when something tends to an end it does it in one of two ways. The first is when, as with man, the thing moves itself to the end and the other is when it is moved to its end by another, e.g. when an archer shoots an arrow towards a specific end.[7] The arrow is not moved from itself but by the archer. Man, on the other hand, moves himself and for this reason he is said to be the lord of his actions. A thing cannot be the lord of its action unless it does so knowingly and freely and so man moves himself toward the end which he apprehends.

The next logical question to be addressed is: whether there is an ultimate end toward which man is striving. St. Thomas remarks that there is a twofold order, viz. the order of intention and the order of execution.[8] The order of intention is the process by which the agent comes to knowledge of the end and intends or chooses to pursue the end. The order of execution is the actual process employed by the agent in order to arrive at the end, i.e. he performs certain actions in order to arrive at the end. Neither order can go on indefinitely, because if one never arrives at the thing which should be pursued in the order of intention, one will never do anything. On the other hand, the actions one performs cannot go on indefinitely, otherwise one will never reach one's end. Therefore there must be an ultimate end to man's actions.

It is impossible to have many ultimate ends for two reasons.[9] The first is that since each thing desires its own perfection, the ultimate end is seen as that which is the perfective or completive good, i.e. it perfects the one who reaches it. The second is that the ultimate end must totally fulfill every desire of man, otherwise he will seek something else. Then what he initially sought will not be the ultimate end since he will be seeking another thing. Therefore the ultimate end must fulfill every desire so that nothing else is desired. As every man is naturally ordered toward one ultimate end, so the human will is ordered toward one final end. Furthermore, every end which is sought in this life is done for the sake of the ultimate end.[10] Every good or end which is sought,

---

The image is changed by the assessment of the estimative power to being a good thing and so their appetites move toward it. They do not understand what they are doing, but are simply moved by these powers.

[5] See vol. 1, chapter 7.

[6] The good is an end insofar as the good is that which all things desire, i.e. the good is an end because it is seen as something which must be sought after. Since it must be sought after it comes at the end of some action which arrives at the end. For this reason, the good is called an end.

[7] ST I-II, q. 1, a. 2. See also ibid., q. 12, a. 5; SCG II, c. 23; ibid., III, c. 1, 2, 16 and 24; De Pot., q. 1, a. 5; ibid., q. 3, a 15 and In Meta, l. V, l. 16.

[8] ST I-II, q. 1, a. 4.

[9] There are actually three reasons. However, the third will not be discussed here for the sake of brevity. The three can be found in ST I-II, q. 1, a. 5.

[10] This discussion is found in ST I-II, q. 1, a. 6.

if it is not the ultimate end, is further ordered to another end, i.e. one seeks the particular goods or ends in this life as a means to a greater end[11] and, again, ends cannot go on indefinitely so there must be some ultimate end toward which even these ends are ordered.[12] Therefore, man is ordered to one ultimate end.[13] Since all men share in the same nature, all men enjoy the same ultimate end.[14]

St. Thomas completes the discussion of ends by asking whether the ultimate end for man suits other creatures. He says that the ultimate end of every creature is God[15] and so as to the end itself, the same end suits man and other creatures.[16] But Saint Thomas distinguishes between the ultimate end and the coming upon the ultimate end. While irrational creatures fulfill God's intention regarding them merely by doing what they do and achieving the end which they do by nature, they are not capable of actually reaching God Himself, but only those things which are in God's image, i.e. created goods. Therefore, man and irrational creatures differ in that man can actually reach his ultimate end, whereas other animals cannot.

B. The Ultimate End or That in which Beatitude Consists

Next St. Thomas shifts to the discussion of beatitude or happiness since

---

[11]This will become a little clearer in the discussion of whether man's happiness consists in created goods. Essentially speaking, all particular goods in this life are proximate ends to our final end.

[12]This follows from what was mentioned above. If one comes to an end and it does not completely fulfill one's desires, then one seeks another end so that any end which is not the ultimate end is sought on the way to the ultimate end. However, the end must be truly something toward which man is ordered by nature for it to be a means to the ultimate end and this is why ends in accordance with the natural law are so important.

[13]This essentially means that while man has various faculties ordered toward various things, these things are proximate ends which help us to move toward the ultimate end.

[14]For a further discussion of this see ST I-II, q. 1, a. 7 and In Ethic, l. I, l. 9.

[15]ST I-II, q. 1, a. 8.

[16]The Church teaches that creation was brought about for the glory of God (Vatican I, *Dei Filius*, can. 5 [Denz. 3025]) and so ultimately everything is about God. Moreover every creature, insofar as it pursues some good, pursues God implicitly. This follows from the fact that God is goodness itself (see ST I, q. 6, a. 3). So anything that pursues the good in any way is tending toward God. This follows from the metaphysical doctrine of participation, insofar as God is goodness itself and all created things participate in His goodness. What each thing pursues is goodness itself as seen in some particular good. For this discussion see SCG III, cc. 16-20.

"beatitude is the proper and perfect good of man."[17] St. Thomas asks several questions about whether beatitude can consist in riches,[18] honor,[19] fame[20] or power.[21] He says that none of the aforesaid four is able to be the ultimate end or that in which beatitude consists because[22] (1) in the possession of all of them one can suffer evil, and happiness excludes all evil. (2) happiness has to be self-sufficient and none of these are self-sufficient.[23] (3) happiness is the perfect good (since nothing else is sought) but even evil men can have the four aforesaid goods, so happiness cannot consist in those four, and (4) lastly, man is ordered toward happiness as from an interior principle and all of these are exterior causes, and therefore they cannot make man happy because happiness must fulfill that ordering interiorly since the order itself is interior.[24]

St. Thomas demonstrates also that happiness cannot consist in any bodily good because the body is ultimately there for the soul, i.e. it is for the operations of the soul. Therefore, bodily goods are for the sake of the soul, not the soul for the sake of the bodily goods.[25] The next possible goods are goods of the soul, to which St. Thomas makes a few important observations. He observes that all goods of the soul[26] are particular goods. Yet, the human will is ordered toward the good *in universali*.[27] That is to say that the object of the will is presented to it by the possible intellect and therefore it is at the universal level. Therefore the will is ordered to the universal good, not some particular good. Any particular good sought has to come under the notion of the universal good, i.e. as leading to it or as part of it in order for the will to be inclined toward it as the intellect presents the particular good universally. Hence, beatitude does

---

[17]ST I-II, q. 2, a. 4. In this he follows from Aristotle who observes that all men strive for happiness and that happiness is that which all men seek, see Aristotle, *Nicomachean Ethics*, l. 1, chap. 4 (1095a13-20). This will become clear in the discussion of beatitude. Essentially it means that all men by nature desire to be happy and when one is happy, he seeks nothing else and so it has the character of the final end. Or conversely, once one reaches one's final end, he must be happy, for it is that which fulfills all desires.

[18]ST I-II, q. 2, a. 1. See also SCG III, c. 30 and In Ethic., l. I, l. 5.

[19]ST I-II, q. 2, a. 2. See also SCG III, c. 28 and In Ethic., l. I, l. 5.

[20]ST I-II, q. 2, a. 3. See also SCG III, c. 29.

[21]ST I-II, q. 2, a. 4. See also SCG III, c. 31; In Matt., c. 5 and Comp. Theo., p. II, c. 9.

[22]These following four reasons can be found in ST I-II, q. 2, a. 4.

[23]If it is not self sufficient, it will require us to go outside of it for those things we need and so it will not be the final end.

[24]The interior ordering here is the Natural Law.

[25]ST I-II, q. 2, a. 5. We can also say that this is a valid argument for explaining why happiness does not consists in bodily pleasure. St. Thomas also addresses that in a separate question in ST I-II, q. 2, a. 6.

[26]For example, knowledge, virtue, etc.

[27]This argument is found in ST I-II, q. 2, a. 7.

not consist even in particular goods of the soul.

Next, he asks the question whether beatitude consists in any created good whatsoever.[28] He says that it is impossible that beatitude consist in any created good. For beatitude is the perfect good which totally quiets desire or appetite, otherwise, it will not be the ultimate end but some other thing. Now the object of the will is the universal good and so it is clear that the human will cannot be quieted except by the universal good. No created good is good universally (i.e. in every respect) for it does not contain all good. Only God is the universal good, i.e. the good which is good in every respect and in which every created good participates. Therefore, the ultimate end of man, i.e. his happiness, consists in God.

C. Beatitude Itself

When discussing beatitude, it is necessary to distinguish between the end or the object of beatitude and the possession of the object of beatitude.[29] We have seen that the object of beatitude is God Who is uncreated. But the *possession* of the object of beatitude is something created since it is something existing in the possessor. Therefore, as to the cause (object) of beatitude, it is something uncreated. As to the essence of beatitude, it is something created, viz. the possession of the object of beatitude.[30]

Beatitude must, likewise, consist in an action.[31] For everything intended is something which the possessor potentially has. But beatitude is the possession of the object and so the possessor is reduced from potency to act, i.e. the person goes from potentially having the object of beatitude to actually having the object of beatitude.[32] This actualization is done in some faculty which has the capacity to act and so beatitude must consist in some operation[33] of a faculty.[34] There are different faculties in man, so

---

[28]The question and answer to follow are found in ST I-II, q. 2, a. 8.

[29]See IV Sent., d. 49, q. 1, a. 2, qu. 1; ST I, q. 26, a. 3 and ST I-II, q. 3, a. 1.

[30]The argument is essentially saying that while God Who is uncreated is the object of beatitude or happiness, it requires a change or something caused in the possessor of beatitude to actually have the object of happiness. Therefore, the actual possession of the object of beatitude is something caused in the soul and that possession is something created or caused.

[31]In this St. Thomas is in accord with Aristotle, see *Nicomachean Ethics*, l. 1, chap. 7 (1098a5-17) l. X, chap. 6 (1176b1-8).

[32]This is Aristotle's definition of motion which St. Thomas uses.

[33]The term operation in English has the connotation of some process but in philosophy it is a technical term which can include motions or processes but it also means that actualization of some thing. That is, in created things there are substances and accidents. The substance is the first act of the thing and the accidents are the second act or actualization of the thing. Hence, the possession of some accident, i.e. the actualization of some accident is called second act. Second act is sometimes referred to as operation when it refers to something that the substance can do by means of the accident. Hence, the term

one must ascertain whether this pertains to a faculty which is of the sensitive part[35] or of the intellective part.[36] Beatitude cannot consist in an operation of the sensitive part since the object is uncreated,[37] therefore it must pertain to the intellective part.

At this point St. Thomas makes an important distinction. He says that there are two types of beatitude, viz. perfect and imperfect. In this life, the sensitive part can partake of imperfect beatitude insofar as the intellect needs the senses for its operation and since beatitude is something in the intellective part, the senses contribute to imperfect happiness.[38] In the next life, when man is resurrected, he will have perfect beatitude in the intellective part which will redound or flow over into the sensitive part so that all of the faculties are perfected.

Since beatitude is something in the intellective part, the precise location of the operation must be considered. He says that beatitude essentially consists in the intellect and not in the will.[39] For the will is moved when the object is present to it. The object of the will is presented to it by the intellect and so happiness cannot consist in an act of the will since the possession of the object of happiness is done in a prior act of the intellect. Hence, happiness, which is the possession of the object of beatitude, consists in an act of the intellect rather than the will.

Since beatitude consists in the possession of the object of beatitude which is God, St. Thomas observes that perfect beatitude or happiness consists in the vision of the divine essence.[40] Now the object of the intellect is the essence of a thing. If man knows the essence of some effect, he naturally desires to know the cause, not just *that* it is (*an sit*) but *what* it is (*quid sit*) and this is only done when he knows the essence of the thing. Therefore, since the intellect can know effects in the world, it desires to know the essence of the first and ultimate cause of the effects. So the perfection of the intellect, man's perfection, will be had when he has union with God as to an object. In effect, St. Thomas is saying that perfect beatitude is obtained when God (the object of possession) is immediately present to the intellect of man, i.e. God is not known through

---

operation does not necessarily imply motion but merely the actualization of some faculty or, to put it another way, the thing is said to be (to be in act) in the faculty.

[34]This is important because it means that man is not happy through his essence but through one of his accidents, i.e. through a faculty.

[35]This includes the passive intellect, the five exterior senses and the appetites.

[36]This includes the agent intellect, the possible intellect and will.

[37]What is unstated here is that all material things are created and since the sensitive part is ordered toward material things as their proper objects, it cannot be in the sensitive part. Since God is not material, happiness cannot pertain to the sensitive part.

[38]Imperfect happiness does not mean that one is sad. It means one is happy though not absolutely happy.

[39]See IV Sent., d. 49, q. 1, a. 1, qu. 2; ST I, q. 26, a. 2, ad 2; ST I-II, q. 3, a. 4; SCG III, c. 26; Quod., VIII, q. 9, a. 1.

[40]The following argument is found in ST I-II, q. 3, a. 8.

his effects, but known through an immediate intellectual vision of the divine essence. Hence, perfect beatitude consists in God being joined to the possible intellect.[41]

While the beatific vision consists in an immediate knowledge of God, the blessed[42] do not fully understand the divine essence. Since the human intellect is finite, it cannot fully understand the divine essence, even though the human intellect does know the divine essence. For this reason St. Thomas makes a distinction between different kinds of comprehension, viz. one kind of comprehension occurs when one fully understands the essence of a thing and in this case man does not have comprehension of God. The other kind of comprehension is knowledge of the essence of a thing in which one does not fully understand the essence of the thing and this is how we are said to know God.[43] So comprehension can be according to degrees, i.e. sometimes one person understands something better than another and in heaven one person is happier than another based upon the more perfect manner in which he apprehends the divine essence.[44]

St. Thomas then asks a series of questions which are important for our understanding of happiness. The first question is about whether we need some exterior goods for beatitude and he says that as to the essence of perfect beatitude, we do not. For the essence of perfect happiness or beatitude consists in the vision of the divine essence. Therefore, exterior goods are not necessary for the essence of perfect beatitude but as to imperfect beatitude, they are necessary. One cannot engage in contemplation nor exercise moral virtue without things exterior to the soul. Moreover, we do not need the perfection of the body, friends or a social life for the essence of perfect beatitude. However, St. Thomas says that while these things are not necessary for perfect beatitude, they do add accidentally to perfect beatitude[45] or a certain decorum to the perfect beatitude.[46] This distinction is important because many people mistakenly believe that happiness consists in the possession of some created thing in heaven.

Lastly, St. Thomas makes the point that man is able to come to perfect beatitude since his intellect by nature is capable of apprehending the perfect and

---

[41]See John 17: 3; Benedict XII, *Benedictus Deus* (Denz. 1000/530); Clement VI, *Super quibusdam* (Denz1067/570s); Council of Florence, *Laetentur caeli* (Denz. 1305/693); *Catechism of the Council of Trent*, p. 137; CCC 2548-50. Essentially this means that God's very essence is pressed onto the possible intellect.

[42]The blessed here refers to the *beati* in heaven, i.e. those who see God face to face.

[43]ST I-II, q. 4, a. 3.

[44]The degree of happiness in heaven is based upon the *lumen gloriae* which is a light infused into the created intellect by which it is raised to a level in which it is capable of sustaining the beatific vision. For a discussion of this, see ST I-II, q. 5, a. 2 and Ott, *Fundamentals of Catholic Dogma*, p. 479.

[45]ST I-II, q. 4, aa. 5-8

[46]ST I-II, q. 4, a. 6, ad 1.

universal good.[47]   Therefore there is a capacity on the side of man actually to be perfectly happy. However, this does not mean that he can attain perfect happiness on his own power. For to attain to the essence of God exceeds any natural power, for God is infinite and no created substance can attain to something actually infinite.[48] For this reason, divine aid is required to attain the vision of the divine essence,[49] which is the clear teaching of the Church.[50]

Once perfect happiness is had, i.e. once the beatific vision is attained, it cannot be lost. For to lose the beatific vision would be a punishment due to some blame. Rectitude of the will is required to attain to God,[51] and therefore we can never do anything in heaven to lose the beatific vision. Lastly, since we are not in heaven yet, there must be some action or actions which make it possible to reach our final end.[52] No end which is not yet possessed can be possessed without some action moving the person to the object. Hence, some action or actions are necessary in order to reach our ultimate end.[53]

II. Happiness and Psychology

Since God made man to be happy, man has a natural desire to be happy. This ordering toward happiness, since it is an ordering found in man's nature, is part of the natural law. In the prior volume, we saw that man and his faculties were ordered toward certain things and certain operations. Therefore, by seeking those actions and things which are in accord with our nature, we are able to reach an imperfect beatitude. This means that man can attain imperfect beatitude in this life by his own efforts.

Perfect beatitude, for St. Thomas, consists only in the beatific vision. Imperfect

---

[47]ST I-II, q. 5, a. 1.

[48]Ibid. There is a distinction between being potentially infinite and actually infinite. Man's intellect is potentially infinite insofar as it can know all things, but in itself it is not actually infinite. In this way, we can see that man is in potency to an infinite object but of itself the intellect cannot attain the divine essence since in itself the intellect is finite.

[49]Ibid. See also ibid., q. 62, a. 1; ibid., ad 1; III Sent., d. 27, q. 2, a. 2; IV Sent., d. 49, q. 2, a. 6; ST I-II, q. 12, a 4 and SCG III, c. 52 and 147.

[50]See footnote 41.

[51]See ST I-II, q. 4, a. 4. This is evident from the fact that in order to reach a truly good end, the will must be right, i.e. directed to that truly good end. God Who is the highest good is attained because the will is rightly ordered toward Him. If the will is not rightly ordered to God, it will seek some other end and therefore there will not be rectitude of the will.

[52]ST I-II, q. 5, a. 7.

[53]This actually contradicts the Lutheran notion that *sola fide* is the means to heaven. Even the trust which Martin Luther mentioned we must have (since faith is reduced to trust rather than a supernatural virtue – see below) – that trust itself is an action or a good work. While it is different from other good works, it itself is a good work.

beatitude, on the other hand, can be gained in this life in two ways. The first is through a life of moral virtue;[54] insofar as one leads a life of virtue, one gains a certain degree of happiness, since one is acting according to the Natural Law. The second way to attain imperfect beatitude is through contemplation,[55] which essentially consists of leading a life according to the intellectual virtues. The highest form of contemplation consists in wisdom,[56] which is the consideration of the ultimate causes of things.[57] Hence, the contemplation of God, i.e. thinking about God, constitutes the highest form of happiness in this life which we are capable of achieving on our own.[58] Since imperfect beatitude can be obtained through the contemplation of God in this life, the human intellect in its ordering toward God finds a fulfillment in contemplating God.

At this point a particular difficulty must be addressed regarding man's natural ordering. The difficulty lies in the problem of the relationship of man's natural ordering to God. Some will argue that man cannot have a natural ordering to a supernatural object because that ordering would be supernatural itself, and therefore not natural. Furthermore, no natural desire is in vain, for God does not create a nature which cannot reach its end through its nature.[59] But if man has a supernatural end, then he has a natural desire which is beyond his nature to fulfill. Therefore the principle that no desire is in vain is contradicted. The solution to this problem has been debated, fiercely at times, by Thomists and non-Thomists alike. However, the author tends to agree with a passage from St. Thomas which seems to solve much of the problem.

In the *Prima Secundae*, St. Thomas discusses the theological virtues and he makes the following observation:

---

[54]ST I-II, q. 3, a. 6; ibid., q. 5, aa. 5-6 and In Ethic., passim.

[55]ST I-II, q. 3, a. 5 and In Ethic., passim.

[56]In Ethic l. X, l. 13 and passim.

[57]This notion recurs throughout St. Thomas' writings; see I Sent., d. 1, q. 3a; ibid., d. 35, q. 1, a. 1, ad 5; SCG I, c. 94, n. 2; SCG II, c. 24, n. 4; ST I, q. 14, a 1, ad 2; ST I-II, q. 57, a. 2; ST II-II, q. 47, a. 2, ad 1 and In Meta, l. 1, passim.

[58]The difference between prayer and study consists in the end of each act. Prayer has as its end union with God Himself whereas study can have as its end the knowledge of God. While St. Thomas does not seem to say it, it would appear that prayer can grant a higher degree of happiness than study insofar as prayer is an action according the moral virtue of justice (see ST II-II, q. 83) as well as the employment of the virtue of wisdom. For prayer employs both the intellectual virtue by which one contemplates God, the ultimate cause, but it also includes the moral virtue of justice and therefore the moral and intellectual life converge in prayer. Prayer begets the highest form of happiness in this life since it partakes of both happiness begotten by the life of moral virtue and the happiness of the life of intellectual virtue. Regarding the difficulties people sometimes experience in prayer, see below.

[59]We see this, for example, in cows who can reach their ends of eating, reproducing, etc. by their own natural capacities.

Happiness or beatitude is twofold in man. One is proportionate to human nature, unto which man is able to arrive through the principles of his own nature. The other is a beatitude exceeding human nature to which man can arrive only by divine power according to a participation in divinity.... And since this kind of beatitude exceeds the proportion of human nature, the principles of human nature, from which he proceeds to acting according to his proportion, do not suffice to ordering man to the aforesaid beatitude. Hence it is necessary that man receive from God some other principles through which he may be so ordered just as through natural principles he is ordered to a connatural end, not nevertheless without divine aid. And principles of this kind are called theological virtues, since they have God as their object, insofar as through them we are rightly ordered to God.[60]

In this passage, what St. Thomas is saying is that perfect beatitude exceeds human nature's capacity to reach it and so additional principles must be added to man's nature so that he can reach his supernatural end. These principles are the theological virtues and here we see that St. Thomas is indicating that the natural ordering of the intellect to God is not enough; more is necessary. What is necessary is the ordering which arises out of the theological virtues. In the response to the third objection of this same question, St. Thomas deals with an objection which states that since man's intellect and will are ordered to God nothing else is required. His response is very revealing:

Reason and will are naturally ordered to God as [He] is the beginning and end of nature, nevertheless according to the proportion of nature. But to Him insofar as it is a supernatural object of beatitude, reason and will according to their nature are not ordered sufficiently.[61]

---

[60]ST I-II, q. 62, a. 1: "Est autem duplex hominis beatitudo sive felicitas... Una quidem proportionata humanae naturae, ad quam scilicet homo pervenire potest per principia suae naturae. Alia autem est beatitudo naturam hominis excedens, ad quam homo sola divina virtute pervenire potest, secundum quandam divinitatis participationem. ... Et quia huiusmodi beatitudo proportionem humanae naturae excedit, principia naturalia hominis, ex quibus procedit ad bene agendum secundum suam proportionem, non sufficiunt ad ordinandum hominem in beatitudinem praedictam. Unde oportet quod superaddantur homini divinitus aliqua principia, per quae ita ordinetur ad beatitudinem supernaturalem, sicut per principia naturalia ordinatur ad finem connaturalem, non tamen absque adiutorio divino. Et huiusmodi principia virtutes dicuntur theologicae, tum quia habent Deum pro obiecto, inquantum per eas recte ordinamur in Deum."

[61]Ibid., ad 3: "Ad Deum naturaliter ratio et voluntas ordinatur prout est naturae principium et finis, secundum tamen proportionem naturae. Sed ad ipsum secundum quod est obiectum beatitudinis supernaturalis, ratio et voluntas secundum suam naturam non

Man is naturally ordered to God but man cannot attain Him as an object of perfect beatitude by the principles of his own nature and so man is consigned, without divine aid, to seek God to the degree that he can. Presumably, St. Thomas has in mind the contemplation of God as an object of metaphysics or something of this sort. But since man is ordered to God and since man's will cannot be quieted without this supernatural object possessed in perfect beatitude, further principles must be added to human nature to direct it to the end. In the prior quote, St. Thomas said that the theological virtues order us to God *rightly*. Having an order to God at the natural level is not enough and the theological virtues order us *rightly* to God. In other words, knowing that man has a natural ordering to God does not tell him everything he needs to know in order to reach his end. He must have knowledge of the end and what we can reach by the natural light of reason about God is not enough to order us sufficiently to Him. Rather, the theological virtue of faith infused in the intellect accompanied by the deposit of faith further orders the human intellect by providing explicit[62] knowledge of the end (God) and means to the end (God). Secondly, hope encourages one actually to pursue God[63] and charity orders the will to God.[64] Hence, man has an ordering to God but one cannot reach Him, one cannot be rightly ordered to Him without addition principles (theological virtues) being added to our nature.

One other observation is germane to the discussion and that has to do with grace. St. Thomas discusses the Natural Law in the *Prima Secundae*, i.e. this ordering of man, right before the discussion of grace.[65] For Aquinas and for the Church, it is not really possible to fulfill the natural ordering in man, i.e. to follow perfectly the natural law without grace.[66] In effect, for St. Thomas and the Church, the discussion of man's

---

ordinantur sufficienter."

[62]By explicit here is meant knowledge beyond what we can know through the natural light of reason.

[63]This was Aristotle's dilemma. In the *Nicomachean Ethics* he has some indication that for man to contemplate the unmoved mover is what would seem to satisfy man, but he knows that man cannot reach this unmoved mover and so one is left without a sense of hope for man's real happiness. In fact, man is consigned to contemplate as much as possible, but it cannot be an ongoing affair because man must stop from time to time. In effect, man cannot be perfectly happy. The supernatural virtue of hope conjoined to faith helps one to see the attainment of God as a real possibility.

[64]It will be recalled that rectitude of the will is necessary to reach God and this is not completely possible without charity. For without faith one cannot know how to love God as an object of union and so faith points or directs one to God, but charity as a virtue governing the act of the will of love, moves one to union with God. Hence, one cannot bridge the gap between man and God without charity.

[65]See ST I-II, qq. 91-114.

[66]The Council of Trent teaches that one can fulfill the Ten Commandments (which are an explication of the Natural Law) by grace (see session VI, chap. 11) and canon two of that same session observes: If anyone says that divine grace through Jesus Christ is given for

ordering cannot be seen properly outside the context of God's aid in fulfilling the law. Therefore, to discuss man's ordering to God outside the context of grace tends to separate two things which are connected in the order of divine providence. It is clear that since God created man in the state of innocence (grace),[67] He had provided the means to attain the end to which He had ordered man in his nature. Once man fell, God immediately promises a savior to re-establish the order of grace,[68] i.e. God re-establishes the order of providence which He had intended for man. Therefore, the natural desire for perfect beatitude spoken of earlier must be seen in light of grace; the principle that God does not create a nature which cannot reach its end must not be applied to man, animals and stones univocally. For God intends to provide for man in a fundamentally different way than for creatures who lack intelligence.

On a psychological note, since God placed the ordering in man through the natural law, if we are to be happy, i.e. if we are to reach our ultimate end, we must follow the natural law. In effect, the ordering in the natural law is, at times, an ordering to proximate ends, i.e. particular goods; these particular goods must be seen as a means toward God. Psychologically, if man is seeking God, i.e. if he is performing actions which have their ordering to God, then those actions will lead him to happiness. Psychologists must recognize that ultimately their direction of directees might concern concrete actions viewed in light of the natural law, but the natural law ultimately orders us to God.[69] Therefore, in order to pursue psychological health, directees must be told that they must perform actions which have God as their end, either proximately or remotely. In the past, psychologists have viewed religion as an enemy of psychological health. The truth is just the opposite, i.e. perfect psychological health can only occur when the person strives for God. Conversely, psychologists sometimes tell directees that religion is bad and will lead them to fixations, which is not entirely true. While it is possible that a directee may not engage in religious practices properly and thereby be led to mental illness, true religious practices, if done properly, actually aid mental health. To encourage directees to reject religion is contrary to the natural law and therefore can actually lead directees to mental illness.[70] The intellect and other faculties are ordered to God; to deviate from this order is to disorder the faculties and therefore can be a cause of mental illness. Seeking God can actually begin the process of reordering the faculties and therefore begetting mental health.

Since St. Thomas and the Catholic Church hold that we cannot reach our

---

this only, that man may be able more easily to live justly and to merit eternal life, as if by free will without grace he is able to do both, though with hardship and difficulty, let him be anathema." The Council of Carthage condemns the proposition that we are able to fulfill the divine commandments (*mandata*) without grace (Denz. 227/105).

[67]See the next chapter.

[68]This is called the proto-evangelium and it refers to Genesis 3:15.

[69]This is evidenced by the fact that the third category of natural inclination of the Natural Law inclines man to seek knowledge of God.

[70]Atheism, therefore, is not a psychologically healthy philosophy.

ultimate end on our own, there is an ordering in man which needs God to find its fulfillment. For that reason, Christ came to earth to re-establish the order of grace which is the means to reaching our end.[71] But having the means is not enough. In order to arrive at an end, two things are necessary, viz. the means (and knowledge of the means) and the knowledge of the end. This is why there is a revelation, so that man may know his end, know the means to that end and actually possess the means to that end. Since God has revealed these matters to man, we can use the means revealed by God to fulfill our natural ordering. Furthermore, we can use those means to re-order our faculties and so the supernatural means are very important to psychology. God Who is a supernatural cause is more efficacious than we are in our actions. While man's actions can help to overcome his psychological illnesses, God is more efficacious in restoring the order in ourselves than we are.

Man was created by God and God preserves him in being.[72] So while man comes from God, he is ordered to return to God. This means that since God preserves man in being, there is an intimate relationship between God and man. Since God has ordered man back to Himself, this indicates that God wants the intimate relationship to be mutual. The relationship God has to man reaches to the depths of his soul because God keeps man's substance and accidents in being. Psychology cannot deny the need for man to reciprocate in this relationship. Religious practices such as prayer, ritual, etc. will have a profound psychological effect on man. So it is absolutely necessary to have the right religious actions so that we do not go contrary to the ordering placed in us by God.

In addition, since our final end is God and we are ordered toward having His eternal company interior to us, it means that our happiness consists in keeping God's company. Loneliness is the absence of companionship or the presence of another. In this life, we find that, at times, we are lonely even in the company of others and this is because there is something interior to us which recognizes that we are, in a sense, not really one with the other. In other words, we can have a psychological separation from a person who is right before our senses and this indicates that man's sense of loneliness is because there is lack of interior presence. Mere physical presence is not enough. Because one's intellect and will are ordered toward having an interior presence, if something or someone does not fulfill a person interiorly, that person will sense loneliness even when the other is physically present. As a result, exterior things can only fulfill a person to the degree that they become something interior to the person, which is done through knowledge. Companionship is essentially established through knowledge, which is an interior act. As we saw above, no created thing can perfectly fulfill man and so one can always have a sense of loneliness as long as he seeks created things. In fact, we often see people who are lonely, filling their lives with exterior things or people in order to find some interior satisfaction. This is a sign to the person that his

---

[71]Grace shall be discussed in a later chapter.

[72]See ST I-II, q. 104; De Ver., q. 5, a. 2, ad 6; De Pot., q. 5, a. 4 and Ott, *Fundamentals of Catholic Dogma*, p. 87.

fulfillment can only take place when he possesses an object interiorly which fulfills every aspect of himself and this is God alone. Loneliness is, therefore, the product of separation from God. On a psychological level, people who are lonely are those who are not pursuing God.[73] If God consumes a person's every thought, the person begins to approximate the eternal company of God which consists in an interior vision of God.[74] The person will begin to have an imperfect beatitude and loneliness will be averted. The point is that psychology must direct people toward the pursuit of God since He alone can perfect our interior natural inclinations and take away our true loneliness. While some people may not experience loneliness during this life by filling their senses and interiorizing the exterior experiences, nevertheless they always run the possibility of loneliness since created things are fleeting. Moreover, if they seek to fill themselves with creatures rather than God, they are seeking things which cannot perfectly fulfill them or make them happy, even if they think they will.

St. Thomas observed that we cannot reach God on our own power and so we need God's action to reach Him. Observance of the natural law disposes us to the action of God, for God would not order us to one thing through the natural law and then contradict that ordering in His supernatural action on man. In addition to following the natural law, we must also cooperate and do those things which God tells us to do so that He can actually bring us to Himself. Since this action of bringing us to God is something He does, we must be told by God what to do in order to cooperate with it. Only God can reveal to us the way to Him. Psychology must recognize that only God can instruct us in this way and for that reason, the Catholic Church teaches us that God has revealed to us those things necessary to reach Him. Leading life according to Catholic teaching is actually mentally healthy for man. No authentically Catholic practice is able to cause mental illness. Since God teaches the way to act according to His ordering to Himself, a disordered directee should be directed to lead a good Catholic life. This will aid the re-ordering of the intellect, which is ultimately an ordering to God.

---

[73]Here we are prescinding from those who have reached a certain level in the spiritual life where God will leave the person experiencing a certain abandonment in order to purify the person's intentions regarding his motivations in pursuing God. However, this does not occur until God recognizes that the person is spiritually and psychologically prepared for it.

[74]The definition of motion is the reduction of a thing from potency, insofar as it is potency, to act. An example of motion is getting a tan: the person goes from white which is potentially tan actually to being tan. But in the process of tanning the person begins to take on some of the tan or actuality of the tan by increments. This means that in motion the person takes on more of the actuality of the end as it moves closer to the end. In like manner, as we pursue God and do those things which lead to Him, as we think about Him and pray to Him, we begin to take on the actuality which is present in the beatific vision, not perfectly of course, but imperfectly. For that reason, as we take on more of the action of the beatific vision, we become happier. Imperfect beatitude in this life has its culmination in the action which most approximates the beatific vision and that is prayer. This will be discussed in a later chapter on prayer.

Catholics, or anyone else for that matter, who suffer mental illness should examine their lives to find out if anything they are doing is contrary to the teachings of the Church and therefore harmful to them psychologically. Even if they are not doing anything contrary to the teachings of the Church, they ought be sure that they are taking advantage of all of the means of grace available to them so that they can be aided in the fight back to mental health. This ordering to God means that man *needs* God. He not only needs God to keep him in being and to provide for him so that he has the necessities of life, but he needs God Himself for fulfillment. Our need for God is manifest in our natural desire for perfect beatitude and cuts to the depths of our very being because God is that toward which our very being is ordered. Therefore, while we may be able to deny our need for God and remain psychologically healthy for a while, as a society or as an individual, we will not be able to maintain our mental health for any given length of time when these needs are denied or rejected. Conscious rejection of the need for God goes contrary to the natural law and therefore will lead eventually to mental illness.

Therefore, a proper relation with God is an integral part of a mentally healthy individual. It is also a part of the science of mental health.[75] Psychological counseling depends heavily on the self-knowledge of the individual and self knowledge will never be complete without a proper understanding of one's relationship to God. While it is possible to engage in counseling which leaves God out of the picture explicitly, He must be implicitly included insofar as God is the cause of the order within the natural law. Provided directees are properly disposed, it is usually best that God play an explicit part in the counseling. The directee must be counseled to ask God to correct the faculties directly.[76] Moreover, the directee must do his part to dispose himself to the action of God, if He so chooses to correct the faculties directly.

Lastly, the directee must look to God's providence. This is why faith in revelation is so important. If God has created man with the ordering that He did, which we can know through the natural light of reason and if God has ordered man to Himself as we have discussed, then without revelation, man is left hanging. In other words, he knows that God is his end, but he will not know how to arrive at that end. It is for this reason that God's revelation, the Deposit of Faith, is a great comfort to those who are psychologically ill. It means that God has provided two avenues for them to overcome their psychological illness, viz. that which is strictly natural, as was discussed in the prior volume and that which is supernatural, which will be discussed in this volume. It also means that the directee can be assured that God is intimately involved in his life and that He is able to lead him away from his problems, if the directee will follow God on the path which He has revealed. Hence, God has provided knowledge of how we ought to lead our lives and so if the directee can lead his life according to authentic Catholic

---

[75]While we can know that we have a need for God through the natural light of reason, how that need is fulfilled is known only by revelation. In effect, while we can know our natural ordering to God, only a supernatural cause can accomplish our actually reaching Him. Therefore, while psychology as a natural science can know that we have a need for God, how that need is to be fulfilled can only be told to us by revealed theology.

[76]This will be discussed at further length in the context of actual grace.

teaching, he can be assured that God will provide for him, even if he does not overcome his mental illness, if it is caused by no fault of his own.

It must be stated that every form of mental illness which falls in the domain of the voluntary, because it is a disorder of the faculties, is in some way contrary to the natural law or even to some theological truth. We know this insofar as God designed the intellect and other faculties to function in specific ways and therefore to perform some action which disorders those faculties can never be seen as the Will of God. Moreover, man's psychological illnesses are actually an implicit denial of God's providence, i.e. God's taking care of man. This becomes clear after long reflection, but to demonstrate the point let us take the following example. Those who have an irrational fear of something are ultimately denying that God is taking care of them even in their darkest moments. They may also be exhibiting a disordered attachment to their physical well being, to something they own, or something of this sort which is contrary to Fear of the Lord.[77]

Lastly, something must be said about the principle of resemblance in this regard.[78] If the psychologist has ordered his life to God, he is more capable of begetting that proper order in the directee. To the degree that the psychologist orders his life to anything other than God, to that degree he cannot beget the proper order in his directee. Therefore, psychologists must accept and order themselves to God as their ultimate end and in so doing they will be more capable of helping those under their care.

Conclusion

Man is ordered toward God, in Whom happiness ultimately consists. Man can pursue imperfect happiness, which is a life in accord with moral, intellectual and theological virtues. But he is ultimately ordered toward perfect happiness, which is the beatific vision. Psychologists must counsel their directees to lead a life in accordance with the aforesaid virtues and according to Catholic teaching in order for them to have their faculties properly ordered. Catholics are in a better position to be able to help their directees and Catholic directees are much more able to take advantage of all of the spiritual means in order to regain mental health.

---

[77]Fear of the Lord is covered in chapter ten.

[78]The principle of resemblance was discussed in this work, vol. 1, chap. 6.

Chapter 3: Sin and the Effects of Sin

The discussion of sin in modern psychological texts is often relegated to a medievalism at best. Usually sin is treated as a theory which is inimical to mental health, i.e. belief in sin causes all sorts of phobias and other mental illnesses. The idea of sin, the argument goes, tends to make people suffer a sense of guilt which is unhealthy and so the psychologist is encouraged to eradicate the idea of sin from the "patient" so that he will no longer feel guilty and will therefore be mentally balanced and happy. The irony is that nothing could be further from the truth. The discussion of sin finds itself right in the middle of the whole question of mental health and illness in ways of which most psychologists are unaware. It is for this reason that the topic of sin will be discussed in this chapter.

I. The Nature of Sin in General

Sin is defined as a transgression of the law(s) of God,[1] i.e. any thought, word or deed against the law of God.[2] In the prior volume, it was observed that there was a natural law in man governing the deliberation about his actions and the actions themselves.[3] The natural law is derived from the eternal law which is the overall providential plan as it is in the mind of God.[4] Those who have achieved perfect beatitude see the divine essence and since the divine essence is not distinct from the divine intellect nor the divine ideas,[5] those who achieve perfect beatitude know the eternal law. In addition to the natural law, there are other laws which express some aspect of the eternal law, viz. divine positive law[6] and civil law.[7]

---

[1]C.E.D., p. 891.

[2]St. Augustine, *Contra Faustum*, l. XXII (PL 42, 418). It should be noted that most of the topics of this chapter can be found in *De Malo*.

[3]See vol. 1, chap. 11.

[4]Ibid.

[5]See ST I, q. 15 and De Ver., q. 3, a. 1.

[6]ST I-II, q. 91, a. 4. The divine positive laws are those laws which go above and beyond the natural law and therefore cannot be known through the natural light of reason. An example of a divine positive law is the precept of Christ to the Apostles, and therefore to the successors of the Apostles, "Going therefore, teach ye all nations; baptizing them. . . ." (Matt 28:19).

[7]ST I-II, q. 91, a. 4. For St. Thomas, since all authority on earth is ultimately derived from God, the civil laws also partake of the eternal law and therefore are binding in conscience, see ST I-II, q. 93, a. 3. The Church herself holds that all authority is ultimately derived from God, as can be seen throughout Scripture and the documents of the Church, but it can be seen especially in Leo XIII's *Libertas Praestantissimum*. Civil law is sometimes called human law which would also encompass canon law of the Roman Catholic

Since a law is an ordinance of reason, it indicates that it is an ordering by which God leads us to our ends. This is manifest in the discussion of the natural law. Divine positive laws must be followed insofar as they are a guidance or ordinance (direction) given to us by God to reach our final end, i.e. perfect beatitude. This means, therefore, that to commit sin, to transgress the natural, divine-positive or civil laws actually prevents one from reaching one's final end as well as the proximate ends of the faculties. Sins vitiate perfect and imperfect happiness and therefore sin ultimately is psychologically unhealthy.

Also, not to follow the divine law, i.e. to sin, which is a turning away from the light of reason and from the divine law,[8] is actually contrary to the nature of reason which is ordered toward God, and is therefore inimical to mental health and reasonable behavior. In effect, sin causes us to deviate from our course, i.e. going from where we are now to reaching our final end, which is God Himself, and for that reason, sin is a disordered act.[9] Lastly, a law is promulgated by him who has care of the common good and so sin is a deliberate rebellion against the authority of God.[10] The human intellect is designed, according to the natural law, to act according to the natural law and therefore there is something natural in man, i.e. in his intellect, which recognizes the authority of God and the necessity to obey His lawful commands, since they are ultimately there for the fulfillment of man's nature.[11] Insofar as right reason recognizes that God has promulgated the law and made man out of nothing,[12] right reason also recognizes that one is bound to follow the law in justice, i.e. one must obey God since it is due to Him that He be obeyed since He is the author of the law and our nature. Because God made us and preserves us in being, we have an obligation to act according to His intentions since we are His property, effectively speaking. This means that there is in man a natural inclination to obey God.[13] It is not man's place to determine what he should and should not do, but God's – and man naturally knows this. It is only through the darkness of sin that this element of the natural law is not able to be seen. Hence, it is psychologically healthy to desire to know God's commands and to desire to obey Him

---

Church.

[8]ST I-II, q. 86, a. 2.

[9]ST I-II, q. 87, a. 1.

[10]Attwater, *A Catholic Dictionary*, p. 490.

[11]The issue of rebellion against authority is quite important. The rejection of authority is actually contrary to the natural law and can have a profound impact on everything from the person's own interior life, to the family relations and to the common good of a society.

[12]Council of Lateran IV (Denz. 800/428); Council of Florence, *Cantate Domino* (Denz.1333/706) and Vatican I, *Dei Filius*, can. 5 (Denz. 3025/1805) of *De Deo rerum omnium creatore*. See also ST I, qq. 45-6 and SCG II, c. 16.

[13]In II Sent., d. 39, q. 3, a. 2, St. Thomas observes that to obey God is part of synderesis.

above one's own desires. Conversely, psychological illness can arise when we act contrary to His laws, i.e. sin can be the cause of mental illness.

We, therefore, come to the point where a proper discussion of the relationship between morality and psychology can now be given. For St. Thomas, a moral act is one that proceeds from deliberate will,[14] i.e. an act which is human or moral is one that is voluntary. In the discussion of the voluntary alone and the fact that many psychological illnesses fall in the domain of the voluntary, we also see that the discussion of morality falls within the domain of psychology. This also means that we must be subordinate to a moral code in order to be happy and mentally healthy. It is not our place to determine what is mentally healthy or not, based upon our view of what is moral. Rather, we must conform ourselves to God's moral code (laws) so that we can act according to the ordering placed in us by God and reach our ends.

While St. Thomas treats morality as pertaining to those acts which fall within the domain of the voluntary, most people associate morality with a set of rules or laws. Even in this case, morality finds itself in psychology. We have seen that God has promulgated in man a law by which he must live in order to be psychologically healthy. So even if one views morality in terms of laws, we are still bound by the moral code set out by God, not only in the natural law, but also in the divine positive law, since part of the natural law is to be obedient to God, not just in the natural law but unequivocally, i.e. in every command from God.[15]

Yet, for a Thomist, there is a clear connection between laws and the voluntary. For the voluntary is that which proceeds from deliberation, i.e. the intellect judges an action in light of moral principle or law and consequently judges whether an action is good or not. Then the will can accept that order or law as it relates to the action proposed or not. So even when one freely chooses, it is done either in accordance with or contrary to the laws of God. In light of this, we are able to see that the conscience is that which connects free will to the moral law.

II. The Nature of Original Sin

The Church has always made a distinction between original sin and actual sin,[16] sometimes called personal sin. Original sin is the sin which all men[17] inherit from our first parents,[18] viz. Adam and Eve. Actual sin or personal sin is that sin which we

---

[14]ST I-II, q.1, aa. 1 and 3 and De Malo q. 2, a. 5.

[15]It is for this reason that Christ said, man does not live by bread alone but by every word that comes from the mouth of God (see Matt. 17:4).

[16]The very existence of the two sacraments of Baptism and Penance demonstrates this distinction.

[17]The two exceptions are Christ Who had human nature and our Lady who was immaculately conceived (see Pius IX, *Ineffabilis Deus*).

[18]Council of Trent, session V (Denz. 1511-1531/788-790). See also ST I-II, q. 81, a. 3.

commit ourselves. Since both of these kinds of sin can affect us, it is necessary for us to discuss each in detail. We will cover original sin first, since it will help us to understand actual sin more fully.

Original sin, as inherited from our first parents, is communicated from parents to their children[19] by the passing on of human nature, i.e. by generation or propagation.[20] Since it is passed on to the children, it is not an actual sin of the person[21] who receives it. Rather, original sin consists in the non-passing on of grace[22] or the original justice[23] given to our first parents by God. St. Thomas, in this regard, makes the following observation:

> From this first original justice... there was a certain gift of grace given to the whole human race (nature) together in the first parents, which the first man lost through the first sin. Hence as that original justice would have been passed on to posterity together with the nature, so also the opposite disorder. But other actual sins of either the first parents or others do not corrupt nature so far as to what nature has; but only so far as that which belongs to the person, i.e. the proclivity to act. Hence other sins are not passed on.[24]

---

[19]Council of Trent, session V (Denz. 1513/790). See also ST I-II, q. 81, a. 1.

[20]Council of Trent, session V (Denz. 1511/788). See also ST I-II, q. 81, aa. 1 and 4 and Ott, *Fundamentals of Catholic Dogma*, p. 110. It should not be assumed that since it is passed on by generation or propagation that it is passed on through the semen of the father (see ST I-II, q. 81, a. 1 and ibid., ad 2-4) or ovum of the mother. Rather, it is passed on by the passing on of human nature.

[21]ST I-II, q. 81, a. 1.

[22]Council of Trent, session V (Denz. 1512/789). See also De Ver., q. 25, a. 6 and Ott, loc. cit.

[23]Council of Trent, loc. cit. See also ST I-II, q. 81, a. 2 and Ott, op. cit., p. 112. The term justice means several things in this regard. It comes from the Latin word *ius* which means right and so man was given certain things to which he could lay claim by virtue of this original state of grace. Moreover, it also means that man was right before God insofar as the soul was created and gave God due honor by reflecting His image not just in the nature of man but in the very participation in divine being. Hence, because man was participating in divine nature, he could merit things from God Who would give them to man in justice since justice is among equals and man was participating in the divine nature giving him a *certain* equality with God, i.e. by participation or derivatively and not by nature. He was also right before God insofar as the soul rendered to God what was due to Him insofar as the soul gave Him due honor and glory. When the soul loses sanctifying grace, it no longer gives Him the honor due to Him.

[24]ST I-II, q. 81, a. 2: "Et hoc modo iustitia originalis... erat quoddam donum gratiae toti humanae naturae divinitus collatum in primo parente. Quod quidem primus homo amisit per primum peccatum. Unde sicut illa originalis iustitia traducta fuisset in posteros simul

In this passage, St. Thomas is noting two things. The first is that God gave man an original state of justice or a state of grace and the first man lost it through sin. As a result, like other forms of inheritance, if the parents squander the inheritance, they do not have it to pass on. In this case, the first parents squandered the grace and state of justice and therefore could not pass it on to their children.

The second thing is that no personal sin is passed on in the passing on of original sin. The particular sins of the parents are not passed on to their children, e.g. the sin of lying is not passed on from parent to child. This does not deny that when parents sin, they give bad example to their children and so it is more likely that the children will develop the same vices. Nevertheless, the actual sins of the parents are not passed on.

Original sin is one in species, for it does not differ in kind from person to person even though it does differ in number, i.e. a number of human beings have it.[25] Hence, original sin is equal insofar as it is not received more or less as to the loss of the original gift of justice and grace.[26] Original sin resides in the soul alone, i.e. it is something in the soul.[27] What occurs in the flesh (body) is part of the punishment of original sin[28] and not original sin itself.

III. The Effects of Original Sin

The disorder which we see in the flesh and in the soul is the punishment due to original sin and in this regard St. Thomas makes a few observations. He notes that original sin is not an operative habit, as it is in the faculty inclining one to evil. Yet, he says:

> Habit is called a disposition of some nature which is composed of many things, as it relates well or badly to something and especially when such a disposition becomes as if natural, as is clear from sickness and health. And in this way original sin is a habit. For it is

---

cum natura, ita etiam inordinatio opposita. Sed alia peccata actualia vel primi parentis vel aliorum, non corrumpunt naturam quantum ad id quod naturae est; sed solum quantum ad id quod personae est, idest secundum pronitatem ad actum. Unde alia peccata non traducuntur."

[25]Council of Trent, session V (Denz. 1513/790). See also ST I-II, q. 82, a. 2. When we say that a number of human beings have original sin, we mean all human beings have original sin except those which the Church teaches us do not, i.e. our Lord and our Lady.

[26]ST I-II, q. 82, a. 4.

[27]ST I-II, q. 83, aa. 1 & 2. This essentially means that original sin is not something which we have, rather it is the lack of something which the soul ought to have, viz. original justice and grace.

[28]Council of Trent, session V (Denz. 1511/788).

a certain disordered disposition coming from the dissolution of the harmony in which the notion of original justice consisted, as also bodily sickness is a certain disorder insofar as the equality becomes dissolute in which consists the notion of health. Hence original sin is called the sickness (*languor*) of nature.[29]

Original sin unleashed a variety of natural disorders on man, many of which are bodily. Man has become disordered through original sin and this has profound implications for psychology. For example, the fact that man now suffers physical maladies means that any form of psychological illness which is strictly physiological has its origin in original sin, since sickness and death are the effects of original sin.[30]

Insofar as sickness is an effect of original sin, it also affects all of the powers of the soul which operate through a bodily organ. For insofar as the bodily organ can become ill disposed, the faculty will have difficulty performing its function. This can affect the cogitative power, the memory, the imagination, the appetites and any other power that acts through a bodily organ. Because of original sin, we are prone to disorder in our lower faculties.

This brings us to the discussion of the preternatural gifts which were lost at the Fall. The preternatural gifts which Adam and Eve possessed prior to the Fall were integrity, immortality and impassibility.[31] Since death is the result of sin, Adam and Eve were originally granted a gift prior to the Fall which would prevent them from dying and this is the preternatural gift of immortality. Moreover, since sickness and death are the result of sin, in the state of original justice, Adam and Eve could not get sick and this is the preternatural gift of impassibility.[32]

The preternatural gift of integrity consists of a lack of the disorder of the lower faculties to the higher faculties, i.e. in the beginning the lower faculties were completely

---

[29]ST I-II, q. 82, a. 1: "dicitur habitus dispositio alicuius naturae ex multis compositae, secundum quam bene se habet vel male ad aliquid, et praecipue cum talis dispositio versa fuerit quasi in naturam, ut patet de aegritudine et sanitate. Et hoc modo peccatum originale est habitus. Est enim quaedam inordinata dispositio proveniens ex dissolutione illius harmoniae in qua consistebat ratio originalis iustitiae, sicut etiam aegritudo corporalis est quaedam inordinata dispositio corporis, secundum quam solvitur aequalitas in qua consistit ratio sanitatis. Unde peccatum originale languor naturae dicitur."

[30]Council of Trent, session V (Denz. 1511 & 1512/788 & 789). See also Genesis 2:17; Romans 6: 23; CCC 405; II Sent., d. 30, q. 1, a. 1; III Sent., d. 16, q. 1, a. 1; IV Sent., d. 36, a. 1, ad 2; ST I-II, q. 83, a. 4; ST I-II, q. 85, aa. 5 and 6; ST II-II, q. 164, a. 1; SCG IV, c. 52; De Malo, q. 5, aa. 4 & 5 and Ott, *Fundamentals of Catholic Dogma*, p. 112.

[31]The preternatural gifts are discussed in ST I, q. 97.

[32]Impassibility includes the fact that a person could not suffer, in general as well as with respect to a particular bodily injury.

subordinate to the higher faculties.[33] Before Adam and Eve fell, their cogitative powers, imaginations, memories and appetites were perfectly subordinated to reason and will. This essentially meant that Adam and Eve did not have antecedent appetite or passion. Their appetites were perfectly subordinated to the dictates of reason and will and so they only had consequent passion.[34] As a result, Adam and Eve enjoyed perfect mental health. This follows from the fact that none of the lower powers would have impeded the operation of the higher powers. Moreover, their appetites would not have been disordered and therefore would not have drawn reason into error. In effect, none of their lower faculties on their own accord[35] could draw them into mental illness. The loss of the preternatural gifts by Adam and Eve has profound effects, with respect to mental health, on those to whom original sin was passed.

St. Thomas makes a number of observations regarding the disorders of original sin but the following is quite important for psychology. He observes that:

> So therefore the privation of original justice, through which the will was subject to God, is formal in original sin; however all other disorders of the powers of soul relate to original sin as something material. The disorders of the other powers of the soul are especially considered in regard to the fact that they are turned disordinately to a communicable good; which indeed the common name of this disorder is called concupiscence.[36]

St. Thomas observes in the article prior to this passage that the disorder of the powers of the soul is due to the fact that the will turned away from God. In effect, the punishment fits the crime. Since man was not ordered to God, man himself became

---

[33]The discussion of this effect of sin has already been alluded to above and will continue throughout the course of this chapter.

[34]St. Thomas observes, as was discussed in volume I, that the appetites have their own proper objects which differ from those of reason and will. As a result, the lower faculties have a capacity to go contrary to reason and will do so unless there is a preternatural gift to ensure that the motions of the lower faculties fall perfectly under reason and will. Hence, since man was created in a state of paradise (Council of Trent, session V [1511/788]), he needed something added to his soul to maintain the harmony between his powers.

[35]Obviously Satan tempted Eve through the senses and likewise Adam fell, at least by sense knowledge of the apple presented to him by Eve. Adam and Eve might not have fallen and so would not have developed any mental illnesses. Mental illness is connected to diabolic temptation, which will be discussed at a later chapter.

[36]ST I-II, q. 82, a. 3: "Sic ergo privatio originalis iustitiae, per quam voluntas subdebatur Deo, est formale in peccato originali, omnis autem alia inordinatio virium animae se habet in peccato originali sicut quiddam materiale. Inordinatio autem aliarum virium animae praecipue in hoc attenditur, quod inordinate convertuntur ad bonum commutabile, quae quidem inordinatio communi nomine potest dici concupiscentia."

disordered. Just as man, who is inferior, did not subject his will to God, Who is superior, so in man the inferior or lower powers do not obey the higher powers. Because of original sin, the will has become disordered and integrity was lost which meant that the faculties do not have the same harmonious relationship that they had before.[37]

St. Thomas also mentions that the will turns to the communicable good and here he means that whenever man sins (including original sin), there results a proclivity to turn toward created goods and turn away from God. After the Fall, even though man is ordered toward God as to his end, there is now a proclivity to evil, i.e. not to pursue created goods as means but as ends. Lastly, St. Thomas calls this concupiscence, insofar as we desire created goods rather than God.

We therefore come to a point where we can elucidate the four primary effects or wounds[38] of original sin. The first is sickness and death as we have already discussed.[39] The second is that the will has become prone to evil insofar as original sin inclines the will to actual sin[40] and it also means that the will is now weakened.[41] In other words, man finds it hard to will the good. For those who are mentally ill and can perform actions to overcome their mental illness, it will be more difficult to will this because of the weakness of the will arising from original sin.

The third effect of original sin is the disorder of the passions or appetites, sometimes called the *fomes peccati* or the tinders of sin or concupiscence.[42] This means, as St. Paul points out,[43] that the flesh wars against the spirit, i.e. the appetites do not want to obey reason[44] and they tend to go off on their own because the control of the spiritual

---

[37]The harmonious relationship of the faculties of intellect, will and appetites is recovered through virtue and so after the Fall man must develop his own virtues in order to maintain the proper order of his faculties. For that reason, psychologists must always encourage their directees to develop virtues as a way to safeguard against mental illness and as a way to get out of mental illness.

[38]See ST I-II, q. 85, a. 3.

[39]The order of listing is not according to ontological priority (i.e. according to what is most important). Insofar as we become subject to sickness and death and because men now commit evils, after the Fall man became subject to suffering, see CCC 405.

[40]ST I-II, q. 83, a. 3.

[41]Second Council of Arausicanum (sometimes called the Council of Orange [Denz. 383/186]).

[42]Council of Trent, session V, can. 5 (Denz. 1515/792). See also II Sent., d. 32, q. 1, a. 1 and ST I-II, q. 89. A. 5, ad 1. That the *fomes* is an effect of original sin, see De Malo q. 3, a. 6, ad 8 and Ad Romanos, c. 6, l. 2.

[43]Romans 7: 21-25.

[44]See ST I-II, q. 81, a. 3, ad 2 and Comp. Theol. I, c. 224.

faculties over the body has been debilitated.[45] The *fomes peccati* or *lex fomitis*,[46] as it is at times called, becomes a problem for man because it always instigates evil,[47] i.e it disposes one to the commission of sin[48] and for this reason we can say it works against synderesis.[49] The *fomes peccati* is an inclination of the sensitive appetites to that which is contrary to reason[50] and so all forms of sin can arise out of it.[51] Right reason is that which is in accord with divine and natural law[52] and so the *fomes peccati* inclines one to act contrary to right reason.[53] Insofar as the *fomes peccati* inclines one to violate the Natural Law, it can incline one to commit acts which degrade or erode mental health. As a result, the *fomes peccati* is a remote cause of mental illness.[54]

Furthermore, those under the punishment of the *fomes* will find it hard to overcome it, as St. Thomas refers to the *ligatio fomitis*,[55] i.e. the *fomes* tends to bind the lower faculties making it hard for the person to tame the lower faculties. Many of those whose mental illness is the product of sin[56] will find the correcting of the mental illness difficult because of the effect of the sin in disordering the lower faculties, i.e. in giving rise to the *fomes peccati*. Even if the mental illness is not caused by actual sin but only original sin, the person will have to grapple with the *fomes peccati*. Implicit in this is

---

[45]CCC 400.

[46]That is, the law of the flesh. It is not a real law but it has certain characteristics of a law, as St. Thomas observes in ST I-II, q. 91, a. 6.

[47]II Sent., d. 32, q. 1, a. 1; III Sent., d. 3, q. 1, a. 2a; IV Sent., d. 21, q. 1, a. 3a, ad 5; De Malo q. 3, a. 14, ad 8 and De Ver., q. 16, a. 1, ad 7.

[48]III Sent., d. 3, q. 1, a. 2a, ad 4.

[49]Mental illness as it arises from original and actual sin will be difficult to overcome because the law of the flesh is working against the person's discernment of the good and so it will affect prudence. Hence, it will be difficult for the person to know what to do in order to get out of his mental illness, not only in general but in the concrete circumstances.

[50]ST III, q. 15, a. 2.

[51]ST II-II, q. 119, a. 2, ad 1.

[52]See volume 1 of this work, chap. 11.

[53]In IV Sent., d. 3, q. 1, a. 3, qu. 1 and ibid., d, 43, q. 1, a. 4, qu. 2, ad 2, St. Thomas refers to the *incendium fomitis*. This refers to the fact that *fomes* tends to "burn," if you will, in the sense that concupiscence is said to burn within the person. This, no doubt, has a connection to St. Paul's observation in I Corinthians 20:9 where he says it is better to marry than to burn, i.e. it is better to get married where the desires of the flesh can have a proper outlet than to burn with concupiscence and commit all sorts of sin.

[54]St. Thomas says in IV Sent., d. 15, q. 1, a. 1c, ad 1 that the *fomes* is the remote cause of sin since the will is the proximate cause of sin. For that reason, the disordered will is the more proximate cause of mental illness than the *fomes*.

[55]III Sent., d. 3, q. 1, a. 2c, ad 1.

[56]See below for this discussion.

the fact that the *fomes* can be stronger in one person rather than in another. From this we can conclude that some people, insofar as they are more inclined according to the *fomes*, are more likely to fall into mental illness than those in whom the *fomes* is less strong. In this regard, the directee must be counseled to pursue virtue which lessens the disorder of the lower faculties and brings them more under the control of reason. As long as we are in this life, we are prone to the *fomes* arising and so it is necessary constantly to be maintaining and building virtue so that the *fomes* does not re-arise.[57]

The fourth effect of sin is the darkening of the intellect and there are several aspects to this effect. We saw in the first volume of this work that passions tend to blind the intellect and within that context, St. Thomas observes that the sins of lust tend to cause blindness of the intellect.[58] While this is particular to lust in some respects, blindness of the intellect is the result of any sin since intellectual blindness is the punishment for sin.[59] In the writings of St. Thomas, we see that the blindness of the intellect is twofold. The first is the blindness of the intellect due to the loss of the natural light of reason.[60] We saw above how the light of reason is impeded by the lower powers. As the lower powers are moved according to the disorder of sin, they become habituated to act contrary to reason and so they impede reason. Hence, the blindness of the intellect pertains to the loss of the natural light of reason. One cannot lose the light of reason completely, since as long as one has reason one can always use it. Nevertheless, the natural light of reason can be affected by sin and for St. Thomas this loss of the natural light of reason is a punishment due to sin.[61]

In connection with this, St. Thomas treats two problems that arise from sin which affect one's natural operations. The first is blindness of the intellect about which he says:

> Dullness is opposed to acuity. Something is called acute from the fact that it is penetrative. Hence also dullness is said of something which is obtuse, not having the ability to penetrate. The sense of corporal things is said through a certain similitude to penetrate the medium insofar as from something distant it perceives its object, or insofar as it is able to penetrate what is lesser or to perceive more deeply into the thing. Hence, among corporal things, something is said to be acute of sense which is able to perceive something sensible from the remote, either seeing or hearing or smelling and conversely it is said to have dulled senses which is not able to perceive unless it is a

---

[57]Mortification and prayer also reduce the *fomes*. For the discussion of mortification and prayer, see below.

[58]For a discussion of this point see vol. 1, chap. 9.

[59]De Malo, q. 5, a. 4; *In Hieremiam* c. 1, l. 7 and *Catena Aurea in Ioannem* c. 9, ll. 1, 3 and 4.

[60]*Super ad Hebraeos* c. 1, l. 2.

[61]See ST II-II, q. 15, a.1.

proximate and great sensible. . . . He, therefore, is said to be acute of sense with regard to intelligence who quickly apprehends the properties of a thing or also its effects, understanding the nature of the thing and insofar as it pertains to the least considerations of the conditions of the thing. He is said to be dull in intelligence who is not able to know the truth of a thing unless he is exposed to it a lot and then he is not able to attain to a perfect consideration of all those things which pertain to the notion of the thing.[62]

Someone has an acute intellect because they can easily penetrate the essence of the thing or its effects. Now someone is said to have a dulled intellect who cannot easily penetrate the essence of the thing or see the effects which arise from it quickly or at all.

St. Thomas goes on in the next article[63] to discuss the fact that lust and gluttony tend to focus the intellect and operations of the soul on the vehement pleasures which arise from their objects. As a result, man becomes greatly intent or applies himself to corporal things and so he is debilitated in those things which pertain to intelligence. In other words, as the mind becomes focused on some physical thing and sees it in a specific way, the intellect becomes focused on other things in the same way. For example with lust, the person becomes fixated or oriented toward venereal pleasure which lowers the mind by focusing on lower things. This results in the person's inability to consider spiritual things.[64] Consequently, the intellect, instead of pursuing knowledge which is not a corporal thing, becomes focused on physical things. When the intellect becomes focused on the physical thing from the point of view of the pleasure gained from it, then the intellect begins looking at other things from that point of view. This means that when someone sees another human being, he loses subtlety of mind in consideration of the man or the woman and only looks at him or her from the point of view of lust rather than in a fuller way. In this manner, his mind is said to be dulled because it cannot see the person or thing in a deeper or fuller manner.

---

[62]ST II-II, q. 15, a. 2: "hebes acuto opponitur. acutum autem dicitur aliquid ex hoc quod est penetrativum. Unde et hebes dicitur aliquid ex hoc quod est obtusum, penetrare non valens. Sensus autem corporalis per quandam similitudinem penetrare dicitur medium inquantum ex aliqua distantia suum obiectum percipit; vel inquantum potest quasi penetrando intima rei percipere. Unde in corporalibus dicitur aliquis esse acuti sensus qui potest percipere sensibile aliquod ex remotis, vel videndo vel audiendo vel olfaciendo; et e contrario dicitur sensu hebetari qui non percipit nisi ex propinquo et magna sensibilia. . . . Ille ergo dicitur esse acuti sensus circa intelligentiam qui statim ad apprehensionem proprietatis rei, vel etiam effectus, naturam rei comprehendit, et inquantum usque ad minimas conditiones rei considerandas pertingit. Ille autem dicitur esse hebes circa intelligentiam qui ad cognoscendam veritatem rei pertingere non potest nisi per multa ei exposita, et tunc etiam non potest pertingere ad perfecte considerandum omnia quae pertinent ad rei rationem."

[63]ST II-II, q. 15, a. 3.

[64]Ibid., q. 15, aa. 2 and 3. See also ST II-II, q. 148, a. 6.

These observations about gluttony and venereal pleasure can also be applied to any sin whatsoever. For in every sin, the action or thing desired is seen under the *ratio boni* and so that *ratio* in the intellect when willed moves the other powers according to that *ratio,* which falls over into the imagination and affects the cogitative power. Hence, when one sins, the cogitative power is trained to associate particular things in a sinful way. The next time the person encounters that thing, the cogitative power makes that association and it affects the person's ability to see the thing as it is. For example, when a person sees something not belonging to himself and decides to steal it, the cogitative power is trained to look at things not belonging to the person as possibly his, thus ignoring the order of justice. Hence, the sin of theft darkens the intellect in such a way that it prevents the intellect from seeing future things according to the order of justice.

A few conclusions can be drawn from this. The first is that every sin darkens the intellect, not only as to the specific sin (and so sin makes one blind to sin) but also to sin in general, insofar as the lower powers and the possible intellect itself are trained and habituated not to follow the Natural Law, i.e. reality. Hence, sin has an inherent stultifying effect. The second conclusion is that psychologists must tell people not to sin, especially in the area in which they are having troubles. Conversely, the opposite virtues to each vice can reverse the blindness of the intellect[65] and so psychologists must always counsel the opposite virtue.

Also, St. Thomas notes that the vehemence of venereal pleasure and pleasure associated with gluttony can dull the mind and the senses. We have already seen this in respect to the mind. As to the senses, the body tends to adjust itself to the actions and operations of the soul. This has been pointed out in the prior volume in regard to how our behavior can affect our bodily disposition. The senses also adjust themselves to the operations of the soul. As a result, sin can affect the acuity of the senses. We see this in venereal pleasure insofar as, if the pleasure is vehement, the senses adjust themselves to the vehemence. The next time the person seeks that same level of pleasure, he must do something more vehement to reach the same level of pleasure. Consequently, the dullness of the senses arising from sin can actually affect the image in the imagination and therefore affect the ability of the intellect to know. Virtuous actions, on the other hand, will actually heighten the senses and make them capable of providing more information and thereby leading to greater knowledge.

One of the effects of this conclusion is that when a person sins, he becomes blind to the sin and will find it hard to see (a) that he is sinning and (b) that the form of action is sinful. He will find it hard to see what is wrong with that form of action, even when it is explained to him. At times, a psychologist may find that certain directees do not have the ability to understand an explanation of their problem. This kind of directee must be told to follow the course of action laid out by the psychologist (i.e. one involving the building of virtue) and then as the directee begins doing the required

---

[65]ST II-II, q. 15, a. 2. Here St. Thomas refers to chastity and abstinence as restoring the clarity of mind of the intellect and this can also be extended to the other vices. This will be touched upon again in a somewhat different fashion in the chapter on mortification.

action, clarity of senses and mind will result and then the directee will be able to see why a particular sin was causing him problems.

St. Thomas also calls this blindness a kind of darkness of the intellect[66] arising from the darkness of sin.[67] Just as one cannot see when there is no light, so the intellect has a hard time knowing the truth when it is darkened by sin, not only regarding the supernatural things but also with regard to natural things. Hence, as a person or society becomes more and more sinful, it will become more foolish and unintelligent.

This brings us to the other aspect of the darkness of the intellect. The light in the intellect is of more than one kind. We have seen this in terms of the natural light of reason but St. Thomas also discusses the light of grace.

> Grace and virtues[68] are caused in the soul from the influence of the divine light, whose influence is impeded through sin, by which the soul turns from God. As clouds are placed between us and the sun, its radiance is taken away from us. Hence it is said in Isaiah 59: 2: our sin has divided us from our God. And so through penance sin is dismissed... in the first act of penance as to the offense, therefore, as the wind takes away the clouds the light of the sun is restored to us, so penance as removing something inhibiting, restores in us sanctifying grace and all the virtues.[69]

According to St. Thomas, there is a certain light that accompanies grace which is supperadded to the natural light of reason. This light of grace helps us to do the right thing as well as to see things intellectually. Sin results in the loss of the light of grace as well as wisdom[70] and so we may say that sin causes darkness of the intellect from the

---

[66]II Sent., d. 23, q. 2, a. 1, ad 3.

[67]*Super II ad Cor.*, c. 4, l. 2 and ST I-II, q. 109, a. 9.

[68]Here St. Thomas means the infused virtues.

[69]IV Sent., d. 14, q. 2, a. 2: "gratia et virtutes in anima causantur ex influentia divini luminis; quae quidem influentia impeditur per peccatum, quod animam a Deo avertit, sicut nubes interposita inter nos et solem, radium ejus a nobis prohibet. Unde dicitur isaiae 59, 2: peccata nostra diviserunt inter nos et Deum nostrum. Et quia per poenitentiam peccata dimittuntur...in primo poenitentiae actu quantum ad offensam; ideo sicut ventus auferens nubem, nobis lumen solis restituit, ita poenitentia tamquam removens prohibens, gratiam gratum facientem et omnes virtutes nobis restituit."

[70]IV Sent., d. 14, q. 2, a. 2; ST II-II, q. 15, a. 1; ST III, q. 1, a. 3, ad 1; *Super Evangelium Matthaei*, c. 12, l. 2 and *Super II ad Cor.*, c. 4, l. 2. Cf. De Ver., q. 18, a. 1, ad 1. Wisdom will be discussed latter. Essentially wisdom is the consideration of the highest causes of things and the gift of the Holy Spirit of Wisdom helps us to consider the things pertaining to God the way He sees them. Through sin we turn away from God, which means that we lose wisdom since we now consider the lower effects and not the highest causes. As a result, sin, again, has a stultifying effect insofar as foolishness is the opposite of wisdom.

loss of the grace.[71]

Elsewhere St. Thomas refers to this as sin obscuring God's face before us.[72] God, insofar as He is the cause of all things,[73] is the cause of our knowledge. But knowledge can proceed from grace. When we sin, grace is retracted, and so the divine light is also retracted. Psychologists must understand that if a directee does not lead a life according to grace, it will be more difficult to help the person than if he were leading a life according to grace and enjoyed God's light. Moreover, each time the directee sins, the divine light will be retracted and the person will find himself confused and having a hard time knowing what to do. On another note, psychologists must also recognize that grace can help them to be better psychologists. Since with grace comes the divine light, if the psychologist is leading a holy life, i.e. a life according to grace, the psychologist will find that he is more able to discern intellectually the difficulties and the solutions to them.

Another reason the intellect is darkened as a result of original sin and actual sin pertains to the discussion in the first volume. When someone acts contrary to the natural law, the will moves the possible intellect to judge the thing contrary to the way the intellect knows it to be. This means that violence is done to the intellect.[74] In consequence, the next time the intellect sees that same thing, it will be inclined to judge the thing contrary to the truth and that is a form of darkening of the intellect. The light of reason enables us to know the truth of things to a greater degree and for reason to be debilitated or inclined away from knowing the truth darkens the intellect. As the will moves the intellect in this way habitually, the intellect begins to be habituated and therefore formed, or perhaps more accurately, deformed. As we saw earlier in this chapter, this results in its looking at the object according to its habituation; eventually this leads the intellect to being unable to see (i.e. judge) the object rightly and at this point we have arrived at *per se* mental illness. Furthermore, the possible intellect is moved by the will to reformulate the image according to falsity or error. When this is done, the cogitative power is habituated since it sees the false subject and predicate as they are expressed into the imagination from the formality of that which is had in the possible intellect. Consequently, the cogitative power is then trained wrongly. Moreover, the will can move the cogitative power directly in this regard and thus further disorder the cogitative power. This leaves the possible intellect weakened because it depends on the phantasm for its judgment. If the cogitative power (and also imagination) is habituated in falsifying the phantasm, the person loses contact with reality and the intellect is darkened. Memory is also disordered and this has a later effect on the cogitative power when it performs associations. When the person experiences the object, the cogitative power re-associates based on what is in the imagination and memory. In the end, the person is simply not able to see the thing

---

[71]IV Sent., d. 18, a. 1, a. 2, ad 2.

[72]*In psalmos*, p. 37, n. 6.

[73]SCG II, c. 15.

[74]Violence against anything tends to weaken it.

differently, since the habituation of the cogitative power, memory, imagination and possible intellect results in the intellect not being able to see the thing as it is but according to falsity arising from the motions of the perverse will, i.e. because of the sin. Because the person cannot see it the way it is, his intellect is darkened. Moreover, the passions bind judgment, which means the intellect is further darkened by the passions, by not letting it perform its proper operation, since the intellect is now drawn into the object of the passion rather than being free to make proper judgments.

Adam and Eve caused severe damage to themselves in the one sin. This was not only because of the mechanism just explained but because they no longer had the preternatural gift of integrity and so their cogitative powers, memories, and imaginations no longer obeyed reason perfectly. The experience of going from perfect clarity of the mind to darkness must have been something traumatic for them. For us who labor under this punishment all of the time, it is not as bad experientially as to go from perfect clarity to profound darkness.[75]

This darkness of the intellect also leads to difficulties in coming to a knowledge of God and religious things.[76] Since original sin focuses our attention more on the communicable goods than the Incommunicable Good, it made man's flight to things beyond the material more difficult. With all of the disorder introduced into the various faculties, this also led to disorder in the relationship men and women have to each other.[77] In effect, it made common life more difficult. Another effect was that since Adam and Eve cooperated with Satan and followed his disorder rather than God's order, man is now under the domination of the diabolic.[78]

The last effect regarding the fall of Adam and Eve has to do with certain speculative matters. In informal discussion among certain theologians, there is some speculation that certain gifts, unfortunately called paranormal, which certain people have, were also lost by original sin. In other words, we find certain people who have the capacity to move objects (telekinesis) at will. According to a philosophical and theological analysis, one could hold that nothing prohibits (when considering the nature of the will itself) the will from having the ability to move objects outside the body. It would mean that the curtailing of the will's power to move things outside the body was a punishment arising from original sin. Given the fact that the will has more act than the potency in physical things, philosophically speaking, nothing in the will itself indicates that it does not have the power to move objects outside the body. However, by divine

---

[75]St. Thomas observes in De Ver., q.24, a. 9 that Adam and Eve also lost the infused virtues which restrained their lower powers, ordered their wills to God and fortified their intellects to contemplate the divine truths.

[76]Pius XII, *Humani Generis* (Denz. 3875/2305).

[77]CCC 400.

[78] Council of Florence, *Cantate Domino* (Denz. 1347/711 and 1349) and Council of Trent, session V (Denz. 1511/788), Session VI (Denz. 1521/793) and Session XIV(Denz. 1668/894). The ramifications of this can be fully seen in the chapter on the demonic influences in this volume.

punishment, the will was consigned to being able to move only the body as part of the punishment of weakening of the will.[79]

Other gifts are possessed by certain people which imply extreme intelligence in one area of knowledge, e.g. certain people with autism or certain forms of brain damage can perform intellectual acts in certain areas of knowledge simply beyond the common man. An example of this is the person who can multiply four-or-more-figure mathematical numbers virtually instantaneously. Other examples include those who can pick virtually any lock almost the minute they come in contact with it or those who can, on a single hearing of a musical piece, reproduce it perfectly on the same or another instrument. These gifts are sometimes considered "carry overs" from man's state prior to the Fall, insofar as Adam and Eve would have had these same capacities in all areas. In other words, Adam and Eve were created just a little lower than angels[80] and so their intelligence, by our standards, would have been extreme. With very little contact with a thing, they would virtually exhaust what there was to know about it and so it is likely that Adam and Eve, with heightened senses, imagination, cogitative powers and intellects, would have depended on reason less than we do.

Another example is the anecdotes of certain women being able to lift trucks when their child is under it, i.e. certain people under certain circumstances can experience accelerated motor function. Also, in people who lose one sense, another sense becomes heightened, e.g. in blind people who develop hearing and feeling skills which people who depend on sight more do not. This indicates that the senses are capable of providing far more information than we normally experience. Obviously, if this was the case with Adam and Eve, the darkening of the intellect, weakening of the will, etc. was both a severe punishment and a form of mercy on the part of God. It was punishment because now man is quite ignorant and prone to stupidity; the fact is that man now is not very intelligent in comparison to angels. On the other hand, it was a form of mercy because, given original sin, if man had disordered wills and yet retained these other capacities, it would have led to grave atrocities and evils, even worse than those which have been committed in the twentieth century. Man's technological advancement would have taken a few hundred years rather than thousands of years and it would have advanced farther than it is now. But because of the disorder in the will, men would have used that technology in ways unimaginable to us. They would have used the capacity of their wills to move things outside their bodies and their physical strength to kill each other. With heightened senses, physical suffering would have been more extreme and emotional pain and intellectual suffering would have been worse since human imaginations would have moved the appetites in a stronger fashion. Basically

---

[79]Unless the person can command things to move at will always or for the most part, one would not hold that this was a natural power but something demonic if they can move things only rarely or not for the most part. On another note, some have observed that when some things are moved by the will of a person or a demon, there is detectable change in the magnetic readings. This may merely indicate that the will causes these changes when it is acting upon things outside of itself.

[80]Psalm 8:6.

life would have been much worse.

IV. Actual Sin

Original sin is counter-distinguished from actual, sometimes called personal, sin, insofar as actual sin is the action which we perform ourselves. Original sin is not voluntary on our part insofar as we all receive it by means of receiving human nature. However, actual sin is voluntary since we choose to commit the sin. Voluntary acts are proper to ourselves[81] and so actual sin is proper to ourselves. Hence, sin is defined as "a free transgression of divine law,"[82] i.e. sin is any transgression against the laws of God, either divine positive law or the natural law.[83] This means the subject of sin is the will,[84] since it is the principle of acts[85] which are proper to man himself. Since God created us and preserves us in being and since He orders us to certain things and ultimately to Himself as our final end, then we, as dependent upon Him, owe Him our entire being. In fact, insofar as He preserves us in being, everything we have or are is His. This means that to sin is to go against God's will in His creating us. Since God has promulgated the natural and divine positive laws, we are bound to obey[86] them insofar as He is the cause of the will and thus we cannot go contrary to the ordering placed in the will and other faculties without offending God.[87] Therefore, sin is a form of disobedience to God.[88]

Sin is in the will as its subject and this means that sin is essentially immanent[89] since all moral actions are immanent.[90] When the possible intellect presents an object

---

[81]See vol. I, chap. 7 and ST I-II, q. 74, a. 1.

[82]Decree of Holy Office (Denz. 2291/1290) and CCC 1871.

[83]Both forms of law are promulgated by God.

[84]ST I-II, q. 74, a. 1 and De Malo q. 2, a. 3. Sin can also be said to be in the other faculties, not primarily or principally but secondarily insofar as the powers are moved by the will (see ST I-II, q. 74, a. 2 and De Malo q, 2., a. 2 and 3). When the will moves the powers according to something sinful, the will introduces the disorder of the sin into the other faculties. This should be clear from the prior volume and our discussion in this chapter. Moreover, passion can be sinful insofar as it is voluntary (see ST I-II, q. 74, a. 3).

[85]ST I-II, q. 74, aa. 1 and 2.

[86]Obedience is an act of the will in which one submits to the lawful command of another. The laws of God are commands insofar as we are bound to follow them, otherwise we will be punished, both in this life through the effects of sin (see below) and in the next life (see the conclusion of this volume).

[87]We offend God through sin because through sin we disorder His creation, both in ourselves and outside of ourselves.

[88]CCC 1871.

[89]ST I-II, q. 74, a. 1

[90]Ibid.

to the will, the will takes on the character of the object when it wills. The species of the act of the will is determined by the species of the object presented to the will, since actions are specified by the objects. By willing theft, one becomes a thief. By willing to lie, one becomes a liar.[91] This is important for psychology because people must psychologically appropriate their sins if they are ever going to overcome their sins and the effects of their sins. The classic example is the alcoholic. Until he admits to his sin (i.e. that he has a problem with abusing alcohol), he will never overcome his alcoholism. All sin is like this insofar as we will not overcome our sins or their effects until we own up to them and turn our wills away from them.

V. The Effects of Actual Sin

It should be observed from the outset that not every effect of sin can be addressed because there are simply too many of them. The categories of the effects of sin which we shall discuss here are numerous enough. Besides, the mere fact that each kind of sin brings its own specific effects makes it impossible to discuss them all. Nevertheless, a number of them can be and should be discussed so as to draw out the psychological ramifications of sin.

A. The Effects of Actual Sin in General

While sin does not take away the good of nature,[92] it does diminish the natural inclination to virtue.[93] As was discussed in the treatment of original sin, this diminishing of the natural inclination to virtue is also part of the effects of actual sin. Virtue can be found in four faculties and so the diminishing of the inclination to virtue likewise manifests itself in those four faculties, viz. the intellect, the will, the irascible appetite and the concupiscible appetite.[94] In addition, these faculties suffer further effects, all of which fall under the title of "wounds."

In every sin, the intellect or reason is left destitute of its ordering to truth which results in what is called the wound of ignorance.[95] This is clear from the first volume and the previous discussion and it is the common experience of man that sin leaves one ignorant. Just as original sin leaves us with a dullness of the intellect, so does actual

---

[91]The recent Holy Father, John Paul II, spent a great deal of his intellectual life explicating this topic and he has, in fact, prior to his becoming pope, actually written an entire text on this issue called *The Acting Person*. It is ironic that in an age of disassociation of people from their acts, God would give us a pope who declares and teaches clearly the opposite.

[92]ST I-II, q. 85, a. 1.

[93]Ibid.

[94]ST I-II, q. 85, a. 3.

[95]Ibid. and De Malo q. 2, a. 11.

sin.[96] Insofar as willing something contrary to the natural law leaves disorders in the possible intellect, the possible intellect becomes wounded. Like anything else that is wounded, the intellect is left weak and bereft of its vigor in its ability to know the truth. Clearly this is extremely important for psychology. It means that the average directee is going to suffer ignorance about his problem; even if it can be pointed out to him, it will be difficult for him to see it and the way out of it. For this reason, indirect means of counseling may be required for those whose mental illness is the result of sinfulness.

The next wound is that which pertains to the will, for the will is left destitute of its ordering to the good, i.e. each time a person sins, he increases his proclivity to evil.[97] This wound is called malice,[98] which is an inclination to will evil. The more one violates the laws of God, the more the will becomes fixated on evil. The next wound pertains to the irascible appetite and it is called the wound of weakness.[99] This wound leaves the irascible appetite hampered with regard to its ordering toward the arduous good.[100] The person becomes prone to cowardice and he loses his drive to do something which is right and at the same time difficult. Both this wound and the wound of malice cause the soul to lose strength to do the good and this makes it harder to act well.[101] Those directees committing sin, must be counseled to stop immediately; otherwise, they will continue down a path which will make it harder and harder for them to do what is necessary to correct their mental illness.

The last wound is that of concupiscence, which is the wound in the concupiscible appetite.[102] This wound leaves the concupiscible appetite destitute of its ordering to moderation with respect to delight and pleasure. Through sin, concupiscence or desire increases:[103] the more one sins, the more one's concupiscible appetite desires and seeks pleasure and delight. The more one sins, the more antecedent appetite will be insubordinate to reason and the stronger it will become, i.e. one will simply have more of it, not only as to the degree of its strength but also as to how often it occurs.

Aside from these four wounds there are other effects of sin. Sin is the *per se* cause of death[104] as sin merits the punishment of death.[105] Sin is also the *per accidens* cause of death, insofar as war and public strife are the effect of sin and injustice (which

---

[96]ST I-II, q. 85, a. 3. Each of the four wounds apply both to original sin and actual sin; see ibid.

[97]Ibid.

[98]Ibid.; ibid., ad 1 and De Malo q. 2., a. 11.

[99]ST I-II, q. 85, a. 3.

[100]Ibid.; ibid., ad 2 and De Malo, q. 2, a. 11.

[101]ST I-II, q. 85, a. 3.

[102]ST I-II, q. 85, a. 3 and De Malo q, 2., a. 11.

[103]ST I-II, q. 85, a. 3.

[104]ST I-II, q. 85, a. 5.

[105]Romans 6:23.

is also a sin).[106] Sin can be the cause of death in ourselves and others. It can be the cause of death in ourselves directly as when we try to commit suicide or do something which directly leads to our death, which is contrary to the first category of natural inclination of the Natural Law. Sin can also be the cause of our death indirectly, as when we engage in behavior which causes our death remotely, e.g. through AIDS which can remotely lead to one's death and which is caused by intravenous drug use, sodomy, etc.,[107] or in excessive eating which eventually leads to cardiac problems.[108] Grave harm can be caused to a directee if he is told that death and illness which are the result of sin are not the result of sin. This takes away from the person a motivation to follow the Natural Law, but it is also a denial of reality, which always runs the risk of causing more mental illness. In fact, many mental illnesses are the result of a denial of reality and to counsel the directee to deny reality is simply exacerbating the problem. In fact, just as physical illness can be caused by actual sin (e.g. an alcoholic can cause grave harm to his liver and therefore become sick), so also, as is clear from the entire discussion, actual sin can cause mental illness.

On another note, sin, since it resides in the will, leaves a stain on the soul[109] insofar as the soul lacks something that should be there, i.e. the right order of the will. Sin entails an unhealthy attachment to creatures[110] and many psychologists know the dangers of unhealthy attachments. People will become irrational and even mentally ill by their unhealthy attachment to some created good. Furthermore, sin engenders vice,[111] either intellectual (which includes mental illness) or moral, as in the case of the other faculties.

St. Thomas observes that whatever goes contrary to order deprives a person of that order;[112] this we have seen in relation to the will moving the intellect contrary to the order of the natural law and from the whole foregoing discussion. On one level, to be deprived of the order is merely a natural consequence, as was seen in the discussion of the relation of the will to moving the intellect contrary to its natural ordering. On

---

[106]Fulton Sheen has written an entire book on this called *Whence Come Wars*.

[107]While AIDS may be caused by these kinds of sin, not all cases of AIDS are the result of the sin of the person who commits the sin.

[108]Modern culture has tried to soft pedal this or deny it but common sense shows us that certain forms of behavior are medically dangerous. To deny it is tantamount to denying reality and it is usually driven by an agenda which wants to deny that certain acts are prohibited by the natural law. If a culture adopts this attitude, there is nothing psychologically to keep the culture from suffering death from the sin which it will engage in since there will be no inhibitions. While abortion and euthanasia are direct sins of a culture of death, other sins are also a sign of the culture of death.

[109]ST I-II, q. 85, a. 6.

[110]CCC 1472.

[111]CCC 1865. This is also treated in the prior volume.

[112]ST I-II, q. 87, a. 1.

another level, it is also a punishment and in this sense sin merits punishment.[113] St. Thomas observes that man participates in a threefold order, each of which can be perverted:

> Hence, according to a threefold order to which the human will is subject, man is able to be punished by a threefold penalty. For indeed first, human nature is subject to the order proper to reason; second, to the order exterior to man of governing, either spiritually or temporally, politically or domestically; third it is subject to the universal order of the divine government. Whichever of these orders is perverted through sin, he who sins, acts contrary to reason, contrary to human law and contrary to the divine law. Hence he incurs a threefold penalty, one from himself which is the remorse of conscience, the other from man and the third from God.[114]

Effectively speaking, every sin makes a person suffer in conscience by the remorse or sorrow of the conscience. We have already talked about the *vermis conscientiae* in the prior volume and this is the effect of sin. The fact is that many mental illnesses are the result of a nagging of conscience. Very often the person tries to bury the conscience in rationalizations or denial but the fact is that sin punishes a man mentally. For the recovery and maintenance of mental health, a clear conscience is absolutely necessary.

The second effect of sin is that man is often punished by other men, i.e. his relationship with other men is compromised. Mental illness can be caused by a rift in an important relationship due to sin. Sin separates us from others and makes our communal life difficult and as a result mental illness can arise not only from our sin affecting our relation to others, but sins of others affecting us.[115]

Lastly, we are deprived of the divine governance, which means that we are left to our own disorder. If man cannot be perfectly happy or even imperfectly happy without leading a life according to divine laws, i.e. divine governance, then those who sin are consigned to unhappiness, which is a sign of mental illness. As we are bereft of divine governance, we are left to our own sin and disorder. This means that sin is the

---

[113]Ibid.

[114]Ibid.: "Unde secundum tres ordines quibus subditur humana voluntas, triplici poena potest homo puniri. Primo quidem enim subditur humana natura ordini propriae rationis; secundo, ordini exterioris hominis gubernantis vel spiritualiter vel temporaliter, politice seu oeconomice; tertio, subditur universali ordini divini regiminis. Quilibet autem horum ordinum per peccatum pervertitur, dum ille qui peccat, agit et contra rationem, et contra legem humanam, et contra legem divinam. Unde triplicem poenam incurrit, unam quidem a seipso, quae est conscientiae remorsus, aliam vero ab homine, tertiam vero a Deo."

[115]This will be discussed toward the end of the chapter.

per accidens cause of other sin.[116] Insofar as we continue to deviate more and more from the law of God, through sin we become less subject to God's governance.[117] Since God created man and the universe for His glory and since they are His property, then for us to violate the order which He has created deserves punishment. Like all forms of punishment, it is not only penal but retributive, i.e. the person must pay back to the person against whom the injustice was committed. For that reason, every time sin occurs, we violate God's justice and we must therefore make retribution,[118] i.e. we must pay back or restore the glory due to God.

Since man is naturally inclined to justice, there is a therapeutic dimension to retributive justice with respect to God. We can regain and aid our mental health by paying back God what we owe since that is according to the right ordering of the faculties. Therefore, things such as prayer, mortification and other forms of meritorious action actually aid the person in regaining mental health.[119] We see this in some women who have had abortions and who go to Confession. Sometimes, women will know that God forgives them but they know that they have taken something from Him and the person they have killed which cannot be replaced. This desire to restore the transcendent order of justice (i.e. the order of justice to God) is so deep in the psychology of women (and men for that matter) that the post-abortive woman will often try to have a "replacement baby." It is also why women find a great deal of emotional mending when they pray for the aborted child[120] or pray for children who are in danger of being aborted. Moreover, re-ordering the faculties back to divine justice aids those who have committed sins and therefore is very good for the restoration of mental health.

The fact that satisfaction must be made[121] indicates that justice must be served even if mercy is granted. Even though we may be forgiven of a sin by God in Confession, the requirement to make restitution remains.[122] In other words, there is a

---

[116]ST I-II, q. 87, a. 2. Sin is not the *per se* cause of sin because only the will is the *per se* cause of sin. In other words, sin does not directly cause sin but only indirectly, e.g. through sin the will is left strongly inclined to sin and so the person is more likely to sin later.

[117]This ultimately means that we are happy, mentally healthy and living according to the way we were designed when we are subject to divine governance. This also means that the more we try to live and place ourselves volitionally under that divine governance, the happier we will be and the more healthy we will be mentally.

[118]ST I-II q. 87, a. 6.

[119]This will be discussed at greater length later.

[120]We shall prescind for now from the argument which deeply divides the theological community about the destination of the aborted as well as whether this practice in the end is really psychologically healthy.

[121]ST I-II, q. 87, a. 6.

[122]Ibid.

temporal punishment due to sin[123] and this temporal punishment includes not only paying God back by meritorious works for the sins which we have committed, but it also includes the disorder of the faculties and soul by the sin. Since man is naturally ordered to justice and rendering to God His due, it means that we must re-order ourselves as a matter of justice. If it is explained to the directee that he is paying back God what is due to Him and that this is a good work, this can aid the directee's understanding of himself in relation to God, thereby begetting order in his intellect.

B. The Effects of Mortal Sin

The Church has always made the distinction between mortal and venial sin[124] and St. Thomas has done a great deal to explicate the different effects of each. Mortal sin is a grievous offense against the laws of God.[125] Mortal sin differs from venial sin in that mortal sin is a turning away from God as one's ultimate end, i.e. from an incommunicable good to a created or communicable good[126] whereas venial sin does not represent a turning away from God as one's ultimate end.[127] In so doing, mortal sin irreparably perverts the order to God.[128] It is irreparable because once the soul has committed mortal sin, it cannot repair the damage on its own: it can only be repaired by divine power.[129] Mortal sin causes the loss of sanctifying grace in the soul[130] and so the soul cannot merit anything in justice from God[131] and this therefore makes it impossible for the soul to repair the order of justice.

Since the soul has turned away from God, it has lost an infinite good and therefore deserves an infinite punishment[132] and that infinite punishment is eternal

---

[123]CCC 1472. Temporal punishment is the punishment that remains even after forgiveness is granted and must be undergone either here in this life or in Purgatory.

[124]Council of Trent, session XIV (Denz. 1680/899) and CCC 1854.

[125]CCC 1854-1864.

[126]Council of Trent, session VI, can. 5 (Denz. 1525/797) and ST I-II, q. 87, a. 5.

[127]See below.

[128]St I-II, q. 87, a. 3 and ibid., q. 88, a. 1.

[129]ST I-II, q. 88, a. 1.

[130]Council of Trent, Session IV (Denz. 1544/808). See also CCC 1861. Traditionally, someone who has committed a mortal sin is said to be in the state of mortal sin, while he who has not committed mortal sin and has sanctifying grace in his soul is said to be in the state of grace.

[131]See Second Council of Orange (Denz. 388/191). Cf. Council of Trent, session VI, can. 32 (Denz. 1582/842). See also Davis, *Moral and Pastoral Theology*, vol. 1, p. 212. Not only can the soul not merit anything once it has committed mortal sin, it also loses the merit of its past acts done in the state of grace, see Davis, loc. cit.

[132]ST I-II, q. 87, a. 4.

damnation (the consignment of the soul to hell after death),[133] the loss of eternal beatitude,[134] the pain of loss and the pain of sense.[135] Even though the soul is given over to eternal punishment which includes the eternal company of Satan in the next life, in this life the person steps out of the order of God and is given over to the power of the devil.[136] This rupture of communion with God[137] excludes one from the reign or kingdom of God[138] and makes one an enemy of God,[139] since one is working against His order and will. As an enemy of God, one is subject to His just anger.[140] Mortal sin, like sin in general, causes guilt of conscience[141] and requires reparation.[142] Lastly, mortal sin results in the loss of the infused virtues and the Gifts of the Holy Spirit.[143]

Mortal sin has grave psychological consequences. Since the sin itself is grave, it means that mortal sin causes grave defects or disorders. Mortal sin has a greater capacity to cause all of the disorders of sin discussed so far in comparison to venial sin. Mortal sin is particularly dangerous because a person loses sanctifying grace, making it impossible to merit from God any graces which may help one regain mental health. A psychologist who allows or encourages action which is seriously sinful gravely harms

---

[133]Among others see Benedict XII, *Benedictus Deus* (Denz. 1002/531); Clement VI, *Super quibusdam* (Denz 1075); Council of Florence, *Laetentur caeli* (Denz. 1306) and CCC 1472.

[134]Council of Trent, Session XIV, can. 5 (Denz. 1705/915) and Leo X, *Exsurge Domine* (Denz. 1456/746).

[135]See Davis, loc. cit. The pain of loss is the sorrow which the damned experience as the result of the eternal separation from God. The pain of sense indicates that the damned also suffer physically (i.e. when they get their bodies back at the resurrection) and suffer other forms of torment.

[136]See Boniface VIII, *Unam Sanctam* (Denz. 870/468). This will be discussed towards the end of this volume.

[137]CCC 1440 and 1472.

[138]Innocent IV, *Sub Catholicae professione* (Denz. 835/453).

[139]Council of Trent, session XIV (Denz. 1680/899). This teaching of the Church helps one to realize that Christ was the perfect fulfillment of His own precept to love one's enemies. As long as we are in this life, even though we are an enemy of God, the effects of God's love are extended to us by virtue of our continued participation in His providence. After death, however, if we are enemies of God, the effects of love will be retracted and no longer extended to us.

[140]See Davis, loc. cit. While it is true that we are subject to His just anger, at times He chooses to extend His mercy for the sake of our redemption.

[141]Davis, *Moral and Pastoral Theology*, p. 211.

[142]Ibid., p. 212. What is implied here is that one, through the power of God, can regain sanctifying grace and then make reparation for the sin committed.

[143]ST II-II, q. 24, a. 12. Cf. ST I-II, q. 68, a. 5. See also Ott, *Fundamentals of Catholic Dogma*, p. 263.

his directee and opens the directee to even more disorders than he already has.

C. The Effects of Venial Sin

Venial sin is a slight offense against the laws of God.[144] It does not misdirect one away from God as the final end but only from the means to God.[145] Since the divine laws are an ordering, they concern the means to God as well as the ordering to God Himself, for the means themselves are either ordered to God or they are not. In this respect, St. Thomas says that venial sin does not cause us to turn away from God as our ultimate end but it is a failing on the side of the means, i.e. we are performing actions which will not lead us to God, though at the same time they do not take us away from Him as a final end.

Venial sin, however, can increase a habit or disposition which will lead to mortal sin[146] and so it is to be avoided by those seeking mental health. Since it can increase a bad habit, it means venial sin impedes the soul's progress in the exercise of virtues[147] and the practice of the moral good.[148] This also means that it weakens the supernatural virtue of charity and its exercise.[149] Since venial sin is about the means, it manifests a disordered affection for created goods.[150] Since it impedes the exercise of charity and the other virtues it causes tepidity of soul and so the person is less disposed toward the reception of grace.[151] Like all other sin, it is an injustice to God and so there is a temporal punishment due to venial sin.[152] Reparation is, therefore, due to God as a result of venial sin.

V. Further Effects of Actual Sin

A few other observations about actual sin are in order. In the prior volume, we discussed the effects of disordered action on the cogitative power, the memory, the imagination, the appetites, the will and the possible intellect. Since all voluntary acts contrary to divine laws are sins, any time man acts contrary to his nature, he will suffer the effects of sin in his faculties. While it was possible to conclude many things based purely in the natural light of reason about how voluntary acts contrary to the Natural Law are so disordering psychologically, we realize by the light of faith that there is

---

[144]CCC 1862.

[145]ST I-II, q. 87, a. 5 and ibid., q. 88, a. 1.

[146]CCC 1986 and ST I-II, q. 88, a. 3.

[147]CCC 1863.

[148]CCC 1863.

[149]Ibid. and Prummer, *Manuale Theologiae Moralis*, vol. 1, p. 273.

[150]CCC 1863.

[151]Prummer, loc. cit.

[152]CCC 1863 and ST I-II, q. 87, a. 5.

another level of consideration regarding the disorder man introduces into his life through violations of the natural and divine laws. We realize that voluntary acts against the Natural Law, i.e. sins, are seriously damaging in ways beyond what can be known through the natural light of reason. Psychologists must bear this in mind. No psychological theory which condones sin can ever be one that contributes to the mental health of individuals or a society.

Another psychological aspect of sin is the way it affects people other than the one performing the sinful action.[153] Our sin actually affects other people[154] in a variety of ways. Other people may be the object of sinful action or the sinful action we perform may have some disordering effect on them. For instance, when a spouse beats the other spouse, the sin does not affect the person only physiologically but psychologically as well. Rape is a clear example in this regard. Children often suffer the effects of their parents' sin, not only physiologically[155] but also psychologically. For example, children of alcoholics can suffer grave psychological harm. Therefore the doctrine on sin has a twofold benefit in counseling. The first is that it can be used as a way of explaining to the directee that he must avoid sin because it has various psychological disordering effects. Second, those who have suffered some injustice due to another person's sin, which may have led to some type of psychological difficulty, can see two things. The first is that God is not responsible for people's sin; people are responsible for their own sin and so the victim can always see God as a refuge even in the worst of situations. The second is that since sin weakens the will and disorders the appetites, etc., the person can easily see that the injustice committed against him is due to some disorder the perpetrator is suffering, either due to the sin of the perpetrator or from some psychological disorder which may or may not be caused by sin.[156]

Conclusion

Helping directees understand the various dimensions to sin can greatly aid their understanding of how to look at their relationships with other people and what to do in order to avoid becoming disordered or to work one's way out of a disorder. Clearly,

---

[153]CCC 1440.

[154]In ST I-II, q. 87, a. 7, St. Thomas observes how the sin can cause suffering in others.

[155]For example a child may suffer birth defects because of the mother's behavior during gestation.

[156]There is a distinction between objective and subjective sin. Subjective sin occurs when the action is voluntary, i.e. the person has sufficient knowledge and consent of the will. Objective sin occurs when the species of the action which one performs is by its nature sinful, but the person is not culpable for it. It should be noted that, while subjective sin is more disordering, someone can still suffer from the effects of objective sin, even if he has no intention of committing the sin. While objective sin causes fewer disorders, one should always be counseled to avoid the sin even if he is not culpable.

encouraging behavior which is sinful should never be seen as an option for a psychologist, for the psychological impact of sin is staggering: to encourage it is disastrous. Moreover, this chapter should settle in the mind of any reasonable Catholic[157] that morality and psychology are intimately connected. To ignore morality leaves one open to serious misdirection in one's own life and in the lives of others, as is the case with a psychologist who rejects the importance of morality. Lastly, not all mental illnesses are caused by actual sin. It is possible for the cogitative power to become disordered merely in a child's upbringing and so not all mental illnesses are caused by actual sin of either self or others. But had Adam and Eve not fallen, man never would have suffered mental illness. For this reason, we can rightly say that all mental illness is the result of sin, either original or actual.

---

[157] Actually one could argue that any reasonable person at all should be able to grasp this. For St. Thomas, sin is merely the transgression of the laws of God. We can know God's law by knowing the natural law and if we transgress the natural law, then we can know we are sinning, all by the natural light of reason. Theological training is not necessary to know that man sins.

Chapter 4: Infused Virtues

In the second chapter, it was noted that the ordering to God we have from human nature in itself does not suffice and so it is necessary to have another ordering by which man is directed to obtain the object of perfect beatitude.[1] St. Thomas says that this order given to man which goes beyond his nature consists in the theological virtues.[2] Each virtue is specified by its object and so the object of those theological virtues will be God since, as will be seen, each of the theological virtues considers God in some way. The theological virtues differ from the moral and intellectual virtues in that they concern different objects. Since the intellectual virtues consider the truth in relation to created things and the moral virtues concern action,[3] they differ from the theological virtues which have God as their object.[4] Therefore, since man can have virtues other than the intellectual and moral and since we have already seen that virtues have a direct bearing on mental health, then it pertains to this chapter to consider the theological and other infused virtues.

I. The Theological Virtues

A. Faith Itself

Faith is a theological virtue[5] and insofar as it is a virtue, faith is a good[6] habit.[7] Since each virtue is specified by its object and since God is the object of this virtue, St. Thomas observes that the formal object of faith is the first truth,[8] which is God Himself.[9] Virtues are distinguished according to their formalities or points of view, e.g. a woman can be the object of the virtue of temperance when looked at from the point of view of reproduction but she can also be the object of the virtue of justice insofar as one must render to her what is due to her. Hence, the same object materially can pertain to different virtues formally. Since God is the material object of each of the theological virtues, in order to distinguish the different theological virtues, it is necessary to look at God under different formalities.

God is looked at from the point of view of first truth insofar as man gives assent to what God reveals because it is God Who reveals.[10] Now God reveals not only

---

[1] This was also seen in ST I-II, q. 62, a. 1 and ibid., ad 3.

[2] ST I-II, q. 62, a. 1.

[3] See vol. 1, chap. 10.

[4] ST II-II, q. 23, a. 6.

[5] ST II-II, q. 4, a. 1; De ver., q. 14, a. 3.

[6] ST II-II, q. 4, a. 5.

[7] ST II-II, q. 4, a. 1.

[8] ST II-II, q. 1, a. 1 and De ver., q. 14, a. 8.

[9] ST II-II, q. 1, a. 1.

[10] Ibid.

Himself in revelation but also other things and so the material object is not merely God but other things which have an order to God.[11] Hence, faith includes certain things revealed about man, angels and the like, but these are viewed under the *ratio Dei*, i.e. from the perspective of God. One can say that the object of faith in one way is uncomplex as to the thing believed,[12] viz. God and all things in relation to God. It is because all things are viewed in relation to God that faith concerns an object which is simple, viz. God.[13] However, the object of faith on the side of the believer is complex since it is expressed through anunciables.[14] The anunciables are things to be believed which are distinguished according to articles[15] or symbols.[16]

Each virtue inclines us to act and so the virtue of faith inclines to the act of assent to that which is believed,[17] since to give assent is the act of faith.[18] Assent is an act of the intellect in which the intellect sees or adheres to some proposition as true.[19] So, we may define faith as a virtue (habit) residing in the possible intellect (the subject[20] of the habit or virtue) by which one gives assent (act of virtue)[21] to those things revealed by God (object of virtue sometimes called the deposit of faith). This definition of faith does not differ in substance from the two definitions which St. Thomas gives of faith. The first is *substantia sperandarum rerum argumentum non apparentium*[22] (the substance of things hoped for, the evidence of things unseen). In this definition, faith refers to the things in which one must believe, i.e. those things revealed by God and to

---

[11]Ibid.

[12]ST II-II, q. 1, a. 2.

[13]Faith is a single virtue because of the formality of the object of the virtue (i.e. God and the things pertaining to God) and so the perspective of God which is the first truth is the formality of the virtue. This one formality makes the virtue one or singular, see ST II-II, q. 4, a. 6.

[14]Ibid. An anunciable is something which has the capacity to be enunciated or spoken.

[15]ST II-II, q. 1, a. 6. St. Thomas calls these the *credibilia* or "believables," since they are things capable of being believed.

[16]ST II-II, q. 1, a. 9. The term symbol is used to refer to the fact that certain things which are to be believed are capable of being put into words which are a kind of symbol or other kinds of symbols which refer to the thing revealed.

[17]ST II-II, q. 1, a. 4.

[18]ST II-II, q. 2, a. 1.

[19]See Attwater, *A Catholic Dictionary*, p. 40.

[20]That faith is in the intellect as in a subject, see ST II-II, q. 4, a. 2 and De ver., q. 14, a. 4.

[21]This act of belief is in the second act of the intellect of judgment; see De ver., q. 14, a. 1.

[22]De ver., q. 14, a. 2.

this is given the phrase *the substance of things hoped for*, for God[23] and eternal beatitude are those things revealed and hoped for. The evidence (*argumentum*) of things not seen refers to two things, the first is to the faith which moves the intellect as if by argument,[24] if you will, to see the truth of what is revealed. The second refers to the things unseen, since eternal beatitude, God, etc., are things which are unseen.[25] The other definition of faith given by St. Thomas is: *habitus mentis, qua inchoatur vita eterna in nobis, faciens intellectum assentire non apparentibus* (a habit of the mind, by which eternal life is begun in us, making the intellect assent to things non-apparent). In this definition, the same elements in the other definition find themselves, viz. faith is a virtue or habit in the intellect by which we give assent to things that are non-apparent. But this definition also indicates that faith is the beginning of eternal life. Since faith is necessary to order us to God in a sufficient manner and since eternal beatitude consists in seeing God face to face, then faith is the beginning by which we start striving for perfect beatitude.

The act of the virtue of faith which is to give assent is given the name belief, i.e. one who gives assent to what God reveals is one who believes.[26] St. Thomas observes that with respect to faith and God there are three aspects. The first is that one believes God (*credere Deo*) and in this respect one believes what God has revealed because it is God Himself who reveals it. Since God is truth itself,[27] He is to be believed whenever He tells or reveals anything to us. In this respect, St. Thomas says that in order for man to come to the beatific vision, he must believe God as a disciple (*discipulus*) to the teaching master (*magister*).[28] We have to believe the veracity of God and since man cannot reach the beatific vision by his own natural capacities, he must believe God is telling him the way to eternal beatitude.

In the second respect, God is also the object of belief and so we say that we believe there is a God (*credere Deum*). In the third respect we say we believe in God as an end of our act of belief. In other words, we believe in God in the sense that through our belief we strive to attain God. In this respect, St. Thomas observes that belief in God refers to the motion of the will.[29] St. Thomas observes that while faith

---

[23]ST II-II, q. 4, a. 1.

[24]Here argument is used in the philosophical sense as "1. A reason or reasons for or against (a proposition, thesis, hypothesis, opinion, action, etc). 2. The process of finding, presenting or organizing reason for or against something." In effect, the virtue of faith makes the propositions or articles of faith believable since one can see the truth of the propositions by faith. For this reason, St. Thomas observes that the term *argumentum* indicates conviction which means that one holds firmly to the truth of the thing, or literally is overcome with (*cum vincere*) the truth of the proposition. See De ver., q. 14, a. 2.

[25]ST II-II, q. II-II, q. 1, a. 4 and De ver., q. 14, a. 2.

[26]See ST II-II, q. 4, a. 2.

[27]ST I, q. 16, a. 5; SCG I, c. 60-62; ibid., III, c. 51 and De ver., q. 1, a. 7.

[28]ST II-II, q. 2, a. 3.

[29]These three respects can be found in ST II-II, q. 2, a. 2.

makes it possible for the intellect to see the truth of the revealed propositions, there is not sufficient grounds for giving assent on the basis of the propositions alone. Rather, there must be a motion of the will to move the intellect to give assent to those things which the intellect sees as true through faith.[30] The motion of the will which moves the intellect to give assent to a supernatural object or proposition must likewise be supernatural. Since the theological virtues concern a supernatural object, only a supernatural act of the intellect is proportionate to that object. Faith is the theological or supernatural virtue which makes it possible for the intellect to perform this action. Now in order to move the intellect to a supernatural act, a supernatural motion of the will is required and for this reason St. Thomas observes that the will, in regard to moving the intellect to believe, is moved by grace.[31] We can see that faith is an act of the intellect presupposing an act of the will, since the will must move the intellect to give assent to the object of belief seen as true by faith.

Since the act of faith is an act of the intellect, then faith involves knowledge. The knowledge which pertains to faith concerns those things revealed by God. But a distinction must be made regarding the term knowledge. While it is true that those who believe what is revealed know what is revealed, nevertheless, there are some who know what is revealed and yet do not believe that it is true (they lack faith). "To know," for St. Thomas means that one knows the truth of a proposition through the natural light of reason, whereas "to believe" means that the proposition exceeds the capacity of the natural light of reason to know the truth of the proposition. Therefore, to believe and to know are mutually exclusive[32] as taken in this sense. When we talk about the knowledge of revelation as understanding it to be true, this is not to be understood in the same way as is knowledge in the proper sense, i.e. that proceeding by the natural light of reason.

However, this is not to deny that there are certain things that can be known by some but believed by others.[33] Here we have in mind that there are certain things which can be known about God through the natural light of reason, e.g. by following certain arguments,[34] one can come to *know* that God exists through the natural light of reason.[35] Moreover, many of his attributes can be known through the natural light of reason, e.g. one can know that God is omniscient.[36] However, some people simply do not have the

---

[30]ST II-II, q. 4, a. 1; ibid., q. 4, a. 2 and ibid., ad 2.

[31]ST II-II, q. 2, a. 9. The various distinctions within grace will be discussed at a later time.

[32]ST II-II, q. 1, a. 5 and ibid., q. 2, a. 4, ad 2

[33]ST I-II, q. 2, a. 4.

[34]St. Thomas gives four ways of proving God's existence in SCG I, c. 13, and in ST I, q. 2, a. 3, he gives five ways of proving God's existence, all from the natural light of reason.

[35]This is formally defined in Vatican I, *Filius Dei*, passim.

[36]SCG I, c. 50.

intellectual capacity or intellectual formation to follow the arguments laid down and so they may not come to knowledge of God's existence and attributes through the natural light of reason. Therefore, God's existence and attributes for such persons remain in the domain of faith. However, certain things cannot be known about God through the natural light of reason, e.g. that God is triune.[37] This indicates that for all people certain things about God remain in the domain of faith, while other things can be known through the natural light of reason.

Faith is more certain than the intellectual virtues on the side of the cause,[38] for the intellectual virtues have man as their cause whereas faith has God as its cause[39] and God is a more certain cause than humans. However, on the side of the subject, faith is not more certain than the intellectual virtues.[40] On the side of the cause of faith, we are more certain about the things of faith than we are of the things falling under the intellectual virtues. However, because of the disposition of our intellect[41] and because the objects of the intellectual virtues fall within the natural capacities of the human intellect, those things pertaining to the three intellectual virtues are more certain. Since certitude is taken on the side of the cause, faith is more certain simply speaking, whereas the intellectual virtues are more certain in a certain respect.[42]

Faith insofar as it is a virtue can be increased by performing actions in congruity with the virtue, as faith can be said to be greater in one than another on the part of the intellect (subject), as one has greater certitude or firmness (greater habit) than another.[43] However, faith is an infused virtue, thus the virtue cannot be begun by human capacities but is caused first by God. On the other hand, to reject one article of faith (heresy) causes the loss of the virtue.[44] Every habit is corrupted by the opposite action and so faith can be corrupted by a single action contrary to the virtue. Theological virtues are not like acquired virtues (moral or intellectual) in that the acquired virtues

---

[37]ST I, q. 32, a. 1.

[38]ST II-II, q. 4, a. 8.

[39]See below in the discussion of infused virtues.

[40]ST II-II, q. 4, a. 8.

[41]Ibid.

[42]Ibid.

[43]ST II-II, q. 5, a. 4. This indicates that faith can be greater in one individual than another based upon how much virtue one has. While faith cannot be greater in one individual than another according to the formal object which is God (see ibid.), it can be greater on the side of the material object, as articles of faith are taken more or less explicitly in one individual than another (see ibid.). What this means is that some people simply know more about the faith than others. In another way, faith can be greater in one individual than another on the side of the will, insofar as it moves the intellect with greater promptness, devotion or confidence (see ibid.).

[44]ST II-II, q. 5, a. 3.

are not lost through a single action to the contrary whereas the theological virtues are.[45]

Faith requires adherence to the infallible rule of the Church,[46] i.e. that to whom the teaching of revelation has been entrusted.[47] If one does not put one's rule in the Church, i.e. in the authority of that which has the right to teach (Magisterium), then the rule finds itself in the will, resulting in it becoming a matter of opinion.[48] Two things are required for faith:[49] 1) that it be proposed to man, which requires that man explicitly believes something and 2) assent by him to whom the faith is proposed. As to the first, God must reveal what is to be believed since faith concerns knowledge exceeding man. As to the second, assent has a twofold cause: 1) the first is exterior inducements, e.g. miracles, persuasions, etc. But none of these are sufficient causes since many see or hear the same thing and some believe and some do not, as was mentioned. The second is an interior cause in which God moves one by grace to give assent. In this respect God is the cause of faith insofar as it is a theological virtue, i.e. it is an infused virtue.[50]

B. The Psychological Ramifications of the Virtue of Faith

From the aforesaid, several psychological effects of faith can be addressed. The first is that faith, insofar as it is a virtue, is a perfection of the intellect. Therefore, contrary to modern psychological opinions, faith is not, in itself, harmful to one's psychological health. The second is that every mental illness is in some way contrary to the virtue of faith and its object (revelation). This has been mentioned before, but a more explicit treatment of it is in order. Faith looks at God and creation under the *ratio Dei*, i.e. faith helps one to see the created order as it is properly related to God its creator. Hence, faith helps us to understand certain things about creation which cannot be known through the natural light of reason, e.g. we know that God has explicit plans as part of His providential care for us as human beings. Therefore, certain phobias actually deny that God is taking care of the person who suffers the phobia. For instance, if one has a fear of the future, the tacit premise is that God will not take care of his needs in the future. Another example would be the case of the person who suffers from a desire to control excessively certain things in his life. This fixation denies that God is

---

[45]As will be seen this applies not only to faith but to hope and charity as well.

[46]ST II-II, q. 5, a. 1.

[47]The truth of this proposition will be discussed in a later chapter.

[48]ST II-II, q. 5, a. 1. See also ST II-II, q. 10, a. 2. Opinion differs from belief in that belief concerns whether one gives assent to the one and the same proposition or not, whereas opinion occurs when there are two contradictory positions and one can give assent to one or the other proposition. Concerning the difference between belief and opinion see De ver., q. 14, a. 1.

[49]The following comes from ST II-II, q. 6, a. 1.

[50]De ver., q. 14, a. 4. Infused virtues are counter-distinguished from acquired virtues based upon their cause. An acquired virtue has the person performing the action as its cause whereas infused virtues are those placed in the soul by God Who is their cause.

ultimately the author of history and so, try as we might, it is ultimately up to God to determine how and to what extent we will have control over anything.

Another aspect has to do with self-detachment. Now since faith tells us that the whole created order was created for God's glory, then we learn that creation is really about God and not us. Many fixations implicitly deny that reality is about God, e.g. the man who has a fixation on sex views the woman as something to satisfy himself rather than something created for God's glory. Also, every phobia stems from a) a lack of confidence in God to protect and take care of someone, i.e. it is a denial of providence; b) it is a manifestation of lack of detachment, as one is overly concerned about one's well being; c) it is a lack of a spirit of mortification, as it exhibits a lack of willingness to suffer some future evil. One could go on but the point is that when one looks at any created thing, about which any mental illness can be had, it can be seen that the thing is not looked at from the point of view of God or the faith.

All of the negative aspects mentioned above indicate one primary positive aspect, viz. the virtue of faith corrects our judgment. It corrects our judgment because it helps us to judge the world the way God sees it. Moreover, the images associated with various articles of faith provide an avenue of correction of the cogitative power, e.g. reading various descriptions of hell by the saints provides the cogitative power with the images which will actually aid one in detaching oneself from something to which one might have a fixation. The images of heaven provide the cogitative power with positive images which can aid one in overcoming sorrow. In effect, the various images associated with the doctrines of faith provide an avenue by which, if one meditates on the images, the various faculties are rightly ordered. For example, statues of the Holy Family help us to recognize the right order within families, how the various virtues are necessary to live rightly within a family, such as justice, charity, self denial by seeking the good of others over the good of self, etc. The doctrine of the saints provides ample examples of heroic Christian virtue which can incite one to develop the proper virtues and thereby ward off any possible mental illness in those areas.

The object of faith also helps us to correct our judgment about ourselves. Through the teachings of the faith we learn our proper relationship to God, family, friends and even enemies. Since relations can be prime material for mental health or illness issues, a proper faith helps our judgments of others to be rightly ordered. As our judgments are rightly ordered, this will redound to the imagination and the cogitative power, which will make associations in different ways than they would merely by natural habit. The images can be stored in memory so that in times of suffering or trial the person has something beneficial to occupy his imagination. He can see his suffering as ordered to something greater and can imagine or reflect upon it. All of the effects on the imagination and cogitative power will have an effect on the appetitive life as well. Since that which is higher redounds to that which is lower, no area of man's ontological make-up which relates to mental health is unaffected. Revelation provides a moral code by which a person can lead a life according to right reason and the natural law and, as a result, if we do what God tells us in revelation, since He knows how we are designed, since He designed us, we cannot but expect to achieve and preserve mental health by following His precepts and commandments. Moreover, since faith orders us toward the object of perfect beatitude (God), faith is the beginning of eternal beatitude and so we can actually begin the process of striving for happiness through faith.

One last word, however, is necessary regarding the virtue of faith. While faith itself is a perfection and those who act in accordance with that virtue can never adversely affect their mental health, it is possible that a man who has faith can actually act in ways not suited to that virtue and therefore adversely affect his mental health. At times, people will give assent to things which are actually contrary to the faith or not part of faith, which can lead to mental illness. This is why a clear knowledge of the faith is necessary on the side of the psychologist so that he can properly instruct the directee in the area of the faith which he does not properly understand. Moreover, since the teachings of faith command us to perform certain actions, if a directee does not understand the action to be performed, i.e. he does not know what to do or how to do it according to due circumstances, it can have an adverse effect. For example, the faith teaches us that God sometimes works by performing miracles and so some people will chase after any reported miracle. This manifests that the person does not understand that the certitude of his faith is caused not by miracles but by God and so it is not necessary to chase after apparitions or supernatural phenomena. Sometimes, people will presume that unless they receive some charismatic grace, there is something wrong with them. As will be seen later, charismatic graces have nothing to do with the holiness of the recipient and so a misunderstanding in the faith can lead to very serious problems.

On another note, since the faith teaches us that if someone leads a life according to that moral code taught by faith and later seriously violates it, this can lead to a dissonance in the soul: for example, women who believe that God is the author of life, as revelation teaches us, and yet they have abortions. The strength of their faith may actually lead to a more profound guilt and if that guilt is not rightly addressed, the dissonance between the virtue of faith and the evil done in the person can cause a greater mental illness than those who operate according to the natural light of reason and commit an evil act. This follows from the fact that the faith teaches more clearly the nature of evil and the punishment due to evil and so the person may be more disturbed than someone who knows nothing about the punishment due to sin. On the other hand, the faith can also provide a faster way out of certain mental illnesses. For instance, God's mercy and the teaching of the faith about human frailty and the fact that sorrow for sin brings about God's mercy, can have a tremendous healing effect on those who have done evil things. This leads us to the point made earlier, that no mental illness can come from the virtue of faith as such and that acting according to the virtue of faith actually helps to correct judgment.[51]

---

[51]This is true if for no other reason than faith is the further ordinance necessary to direct man to his final end. Hence, insofar as it is an ordinance, it gives an order and direction to one's life and therefore acts contrary to the disorder of mental illness.

C. The Virtue of Hope Itself

The theological virtue of hope like all theological virtues is an infused habit.[52] All habits which concern the good are virtues and so hope is a virtue[53] since it concerns or attains to God Himself.[54] The theological virtue of hope, like the passion of hope, concerns the future arduous good. The theological virtues concern God Himself and reaching God exceeds man's natural capacities.[55] Hope bears on two objects, the good to be obtained, viz. (1) eternal beatitude which is the proper and principal object of hope[56] or God Himself, in which eternal beatitude consists, and (2) the divine aid to be given.[57] Since hope concerns the attainment of an object completely exceeding man's natural capacities, man needs God's aid[58] to reach Him. Since by God's aid we can attain heaven, hope looks for or awaits the future good of eternal beatitude.[59] This essentially means that the person who has hope looks forward to the receiving of the divine good and actually waits for it. If one has no hope for the obtainment of an object, he does not wait for it or look to receive it.

Since hope is a virtue, it must reside in an operative accident or faculty. Since hope concerns God Himself and since God is not a body[60] and therefore not a material thing,[61] hope cannot be in the bodily senses or faculties since they do not transcend the physical.[62] Now this observation is important because many often seek some type of physical consolation regarding God or make their hope into something physical insofar as it pertains to some motion of the sensitive appetites. For example, people often imagine some created good which they will receive in heaven and so they misplace their hope in a created good rather than an uncreated good, as with those who think that heaven consists in never-ending sexual activity. It is also important insofar as some

---

[52]ST II-II, q. 17, a. 1.

[53]Ibid. and De spe, a. 1.

[54]ST II-II, q. 17, a. 1 and ibid., q. 17, a. 5.

[55]See chapter two.

[56]ST II-II, q. 17, a. 2 and De spe, a. 1. St. Thomas calls this the material object of hope, see De spe, a. 1.

[57]De spe, a. 1. St. Thomas calls this the formal object of hope, see ibid. St. Thomas observes that hope is caused by grace, see ST II-II, q. 17, a. 1, ad 2. Now this can be understood in two ways: 1) insofar as through grace God inclines us to Himself as our end and 2) insofar as the doctrine of grace provides the foundation for knowing that God's aid (grace itself) is not wanting.

[58]ST II-II, q. 17, aa. 1 and 2.

[59]De spe, a. 1, ad 2.

[60]See SCG I, c. 20.

[61]Ibid., c. 17.

[62]De spe, a. 2.

think that theological hope has to do with God giving them rewards in this life rather than Himself in the next. This is the problem with those who think that a sign of God's favor is the obtainment of money or some charismatic gift. These types believe that hope consists in God giving them these things rather than placing their hope in God Himself. This can have a profound psychological effect, especially when the person does not obtain the good that he thinks he should receive. From this arises a dissonance between thinking that God provides for and rewards the good and the non-reception of the expected rewards. He was good and did not receive what he thought he should have received. This cuts to the problem of how God's providence functions and it can affect everything from one's faith to one's mental stability. Here we have in mind Martin Luther who thought that the sign of God's favor was sensible consolations and since he received none, he tortured himself as to why. The moral of the story is that he was hoping in the wrong thing.

Since the theological virtue of hope cannot reside in the sensible faculties, it must reside in an immaterial faculty. Because hope concerns the good and not truth, it must reside in an appetitive power[63] and so hope resides in the will as in its subject.[64] In this respect, hope is a virtue which inclines the will to seek after and await the reward of God Himself. This virtue is necessary since it is not enough to have faith in God, i.e. to know He speaks the truth: we must actually have a virtue which moves us to seek Him. This is not to deny St. Thomas' observation that hope has a participative certitude in as much as hope participates in the certitude of faith. To put it another way, the certitude we have in hope comes from the certitude in faith. Hence, the more faith we have, the greater certitude regarding God's aid and therefore the more certain we are of attaining the beatific vision, i.e. the more hope we have.

Hope, in the proper sense of the theological virtue, is only in the *viatores* (wayfarers),[65] i.e. those who are in this life proceeding on the path to God. This follows from the fact that hope concerns an arduous future good, possible to obtain and we in this life can obtain God who is a possible future good that we could have. For this reason, in the proper sense, those in heaven do not have the virtue of hope any longer since the object is no longer possible to obtain in the future,[66] but is in fact present. However, in the broad sense, hope can be in those in heaven regarding us, for they can hope that we will reach heaven. But since hope concerns the attainment of beatitude which is proper to oneself, it is for this reason that hope in the proper sense is not in the blessed in heaven. Moreover, hope is not in the damned because a) it is contrary to their will[67] and b) they cannot attain eternal beatitude since their punishment is permanent.[68]

---

[63]ST II-II, q. 17, a. 6; ibid., q. 18, a. 2, and De spe, a. 2.

[64]ST II-II, q. 18, a. 1, and De spe, a. 2.

[65]De spe, a. 4.

[66]ST III-II, q. 18, a. 2 and De spe, a. 4.

[67]This will be discussed indirectly in the conclusion regarding hell.

[68]ST II-II, q. 18, a. 3 and De spe, a. 4.

In one place,[69] St. Thomas observes that it is vicious to hope in human aid, either of oneself or another human being, to reach eternal beatitude, since it is divine aid, not human aid, that is necessary. But in another place,[70] St. Thomas states that we hope principally and primarily in God to help us to obtain eternal beatitude and secondarily and instrumentally in man through which we are aided by any good which can help us to come to eternal beatitude. He gives the example of turning to Mary and the saints. Doing this is not the same thing as relying merely on human aid exclusively to help us get to heaven. Hence, in the latter case, one is hoping in God's aid by means of instrumental causation, whereas, in the former, one hopes in a merely finite thing, viz. man.

Lastly, along with St. Thomas we can say that it is not possible to hope too much in God.[71] But St. Thomas also notes[72] that one can hope falsely in divine aid by not adhering to the divine aid or by false opinion, e.g. presuming one is saved although one persists in sin. It is here that we see that hope is opposed by two vices, viz. presumption and despair.

Despair is the vice in which one estimates falsely about God's ability to save someone.[73] It implicitly rejects God's infinite power to move one to sorrow, to repent and to look to Him for help, and is a sin since it is disordered. Despair arises out of a sin which the person thinks is unforgivable.[74] This is often the case with women who have had abortions or with a person who commits a sin of which he did not think he was capable. He thinks the sin is so evil that even God cannot forgive him, but faith teaches us otherwise and thus helps to overcome despair. Despair also arises out of *acedia* or spiritual sloth, lust and love of venereal delights.[75] The person despairs because he does not think he can be lifted to a higher good, as in the case of lust or love of venereal delights. Moreover, with sloth, he simply does not think he can perform the actions necessary to cooperate with God's aid to reach heaven. Acedia is a certain sorrow at spiritual goods because they are arduous[76] and so the person despairs because it seems impossible to overcome the sloth or lust. In effect, acedia makes one sorrow at spiritual goods because they are seen as evil, i.e. they are seen as inhibiting complacency, either in the sensitive appetites or will, i.e. in merely being satisfied with lowly things. Spiritual goods often require suffering, pain or difficulty in order to obtain them and for this reason those with acedia or spiritual sloth simply lose hope in attaining God, which

---

[69]De spe, a. 1.

[70]ST II-II, q. 17, a. 4.

[71]De spe, a. 1, ad 1.

[72]Ibid.

[73]ST II-II, q. 20, a. 1.

[74]In the end there is only one sin that is unforgivable and that is the sin against the Holy Spirit, sometimes called final impenitence.

[75]ST II-II, q. 20, a. 4.

[76]Ibid.

requires effort.

Presumption, on the other hand, presumes on one's own ability, without divine aid, to reach eternal beatitude.[77] This is the sin of the Pelagians, other Gnostic sects and some Protestant sects. These types thought they could merit first grace[78] and get to heaven on their own. Presumption is caused directly by pride[79] which is the overestimation of one's good or excellence. One thinks himself more than merely human or he overestimates the good or excellence of human nature.[80] Presumption is also caused by inane glory since one desires a glory which is above what his natural powers are capable of reaching.[81]

D. The Psychological Effects of Hope

Some of the psychological effects of hope have just been mentioned but there are more. The theological virtue of hope can have effects on the lower faculties since the will moves the lower faculties in accordance with the virtue. The will can move the imagination according to the formality of hope and consequently affect the various appetites. For instance, hope can have a direct impact on the passion of fear, for fear is the passion which concerns a future evil which we cannot overcome. But hope moves us to seek God's aid in overcoming any obstacle that can affect our salvation and sometimes that obstacle is ourselves, others or even material things. Moreover, hope joined to faith helps us to realize that suffering in this life is not the worst of things and so we tend to fear less those things which can physically harm us. Hope moves us to place our happiness not in material goods or our physical well-being which could be lost, but in God, i.e. in our spiritual well-being. While one must always take reasonable care of one's body, this is done ultimately for the sake of God, and faith and hope helps us to see this. Hence, if a directee is suffering from fear, hope should be counseled, not just the passion of hope because the feared thing may be unavoidable, psychologically speaking, but hope in God's divine aid (providence).

Hope moves us to seek God as our end and so we will not seek created goods. As a result, this averts sorrow which arises because we do not get what we want. If what we want is God alone, our earthly life is seen as something to give God glory, rather than an end in itself after which we should seek. The directee who suffers sorrow can hope in God's ability to lead him to heaven where the problems of this life can no longer affect him. Moreover, since hope moves us to seek after God, what we do in this life has grave import and so directees, when counseled to hope, will not take a careless or overly fixated view of this life. In effect, hope provides us with a balanced view of this life.

---

[77]ST II-II, q. 21, a. 1.

[78]See chapter on grace.

[79]ST II-II, q. 21, a. 4.

[80]This is the sin of the modern age, thinking that men can save themselves, because of their infatuation with human nature.

[81]ST II-II, q. 21, a. 4.

Directees, who suffer mental illness and are greatly afflicted by it because they do not want to suffer, can hope in God's ability to overcome their mental illness. Even if they cannot do it on their own, God can help them, regardless of whether the illness is from an exterior or interior cause. Even if they have been afflicted with mental illness in this life, they can hope in God to bring them to Himself where there will be no more mental illness,[82] i.e. even if they do not overcome it in this life, if they do what is right, they will conquer it in the next life. Moreover, faith and hope help the directee to see that he should not ask God to take way his mental illness by using God as the means to a created end. Rather, since hope moves us to God Himself, the directee will see that he should overcome the mental illness and ask God to help him do so, so that he can give greater honor and glory to God, having been freed from the mental illness which may be an obstacle to reaching Him. Often mental illness becomes an obstacle to the person fulfilling his duties to God, e.g. he may not be able to pray, to do what is right, to aid his neighbor because of some mental illness. So it is important that the directee strive for the virtue of hope and make acts of hope in the will by which he tells God he trusts in His divine aid; this will have an effect on the lower faculties as well as possibly merit from God grace to cure the mental illness directly.

E. Charity Itself

Charity is a friendship between God and man.[83] Any friendship requires mutual love[84] and mutual love or benevolence[85] is founded on some communication.[86] With God, this communication and therefore friendship is the fact that God communicates

---

[82]This will be discussed later.

[83]ST II-II, q. 23, a. 1. Many of the references in the *Summa Theologiae* can also be found in *Quaestio Disputata de Caritate* with a greater depth of treatment than can be afforded here.

[84]ST II-II, q. 23, a. 1.

[85]Love is called benevolence insofar as one wills (volens) the good (bonum - bene) of the other.

[86]ST II-II, q.23, a. 1. Communication here does not necessarily mean talking or some other exchange of signs. Rather it means that there is something which is had in common which constitutes some kind of common life. For instance, it is not possible to have a friendship with someone on another planet circling a distant star since there is no basis of common life. Moreover, common life is not only as to proximity but of kind, e.g. it is not possible to have a friendship, in the proper sense, with a dog, since he does not share in the life of intellection and free will and so he cannot reciprocate intellective love which is the basis of true friendship. So man and dog do not share a common life as the dog's life is of a different order than ours. "Friendships," which we have with animals, are said analogically.

eternal beatitude to us.[87] Eternal beatitude is a good thing which God wills for us and which we will for ourselves and so it is the good of eternal beatitude upon which the friendship is based. Hence, the mutual love or mutual willing of the good between God and man is based upon eternal beatitude.

Yet, eternal beatitude is entirely beyond man's capacity to attain and so charity, by which one loves God, exceeds our natural powers. God must add some habitual form to our natural power which inclines[88] us and makes it possible for us to perform this supernatural act of love. Charity, therefore, is a virtue,[89] as it is an habitual form which God infuses in us so that we can love Him, as the divine good (*bonum divinum*) is the object of charity.[90]

Because charity concerns the divine good or God Himself, charity is higher than the moral and intellectual virtues.[91] Charity is higher than faith and hope because it attains to God Himself rather than being directed to our coming to God.[92] In effect, faith and hope move us to attaining to God, but since one of the effects of love is union, charity, which is love of God, involves our union to God. Charity, while being greater than the other virtues, nevertheless has a relation to the other virtues. If one considers virtues in relation to particular created goods, one can have the moral and intellectual virtues without charity.[93] However, if one considers the created goods as ordered to the ultimate end, viz. God, it is not possible to have true virtue without charity which orders one to the ultimate end.[94] Effectively this means that one cannot have true moral or intellectual virtue, i.e. one cannot be rightly ordered toward the objects of these virtues without them falling under the order to God, i.e. under the order of charity. Since charity orders the acts of all of the other virtues, charity gives form to the other virtues,[95] even to faith.[96] By "giving form" is meant that charity informs the other virtues by directing and guiding them and giving them a fuller significance and importance.

---

[87]ST II-II, q. 23, a. 1 and ibid., q. 23, a. 5. Eternal beatitude is founded upon or is possible because of sanctifying grace which is the created participation in divine nature. Hence, by sanctifying grace and eternal beatitude we can have a common life with God and therefore a friendship; see the chapter on grace.

[88]ST II-II, q. 23, a. 2.

[89]ST II-II, q. 23, a. 3.

[90]ST II-II, q. 23, a. 4.

[91]ST II-II, q. 4, a. 6.

[92]Ibid.

[93]ST II-II, q. 23, a. 7.

[94]This order is the effect of love, as love moves one to union with the beloved, it directs one to the beloved and so charity directs or orders us to God since by charity the soul is united to God (see ST II-II, q. 24, a. 4).

[95]ST II-II, q. 23, a. 8.

[96]ST II-II, q. 4, aa. 3 and 4.

Charity resides in the will as in its subject[97] since it concerns the good and the object of the will is the good. Since the object of charity is supernatural, only a supernatural virtue is proportionate to this object. Therefore, charity, being a supernatural virtue, exceeds our natural powers and so charity must be an infused virtue[98] since we cannot acquire it on our own.[99] The infusion of the virtue of charity is not based upon the condition of our nature (since it exceeds our nature) but upon the grace of the Holy Spirit.[100]

Since charity is a virtue, one must ask if it can be increased or decreased like the other virtues. St. Thomas observes that charity can be increased,[101] however, not by addition but by a greater participation in the form or virtue of charity.[102] This means that one does not have an increase numerically of the virtue of charity as if to say one has five charities as opposed to three charities. Rather, charity is had by degrees and so the more one has of the form of charity, the greater the virtue of charity.

Charity cannot be increased by any act whatsoever, however; but only by an act which renders us more prompt to acting to charity.[103] Hence, even if the action we are performing is good, it will not necessarily increase the virtue of charity, but only if it will make us more prompt in acting according to charity. While in the next life, the amount of charity we have is fixed, in this life charity can be increased indefinitely,[104] i.e. one can always increase the amount of charity he has. If it can be always increased, one can logically ask if charity can ever be perfect. To that, St. Thomas observes that perfection in charity can be understood in different ways. On the side of the thing loved, charity cannot be perfect because the object is infinite[105] and we cannot have infinite charity; only God can have infinite charity, i.e. by the love of His infinite Self. However, on the side of the one who loves, charity is only perfect in the next life where one is totally immersed in God. In this life, one can be said to be perfect in charity when one refers all his works and acts to God and foregoes other works and acts unless they are necessary. St. Thomas says this is not common to all who have charity. However, in another way, when man never thinks or wills anything contrary to divine love (charity), one can say this perfection is common to all who have charity.

---

[97]ST II-II, q. 24, a. 1.

[98]ST II-II, q. 24, a. 1.

[99]Effectively speaking, we cannot really love God in a proportionate way without charity.

[100]ST II-II, q. 24, a. 3. See the chapter on grace, particularly regarding the gratuity of grace.

[101]ST II-II, q. 24, a. 4.

[102]ST II-II, q. 24, a. 5.

[103]Ibid.

[104]ST II-II, q. 24, a. 7.

[105]The different ways charity can be said to be perfect are discussed in ST II-II, q. 24, a. 8.

This brings us to the question of the different levels of charity. Since charity can be had by degrees, St. Thomas observes that there are three grades of charity.[106] The first grade[107] consists of those who recede from sin and resist concupiscence and they are called the beginners (*incipientes*). Then there are those who intend principally to become proficient in the good. They intend to be strengthened by the augmentation of charity because they want to grow in their love for God; they are called the proficient (*proficientes*). The last grade of charity consists of those who principally intend to adhere to God and take fruition in Him. They desire to be dissolved in Christ, i.e. to lose themselves in God and they are called the perfect (*perfecti*).

Since charity is caused not by man but by God, it cannot be diminished by man's actions. Unlike acquired habits in which the virtue begins to diminish if there is a cessation of the act proper to that virtue, charity does not diminish if man ceases in acting.[108] Moreover, diminuation of charity is not caused by God since He does not cause defects.[109] Since charity cannot be diminished by either man or God, then charity does not diminish, rather it is totally corrupted. It is corrupted effectively by mortal sin which is its contrary.[110] For every mortal sin turns away from God and therefore ceases the union or love of God proper to charity. Every mortal sin corrupts charity meritoriously insofar as God retracts the causation of charity in the soul as a punishment.[111] As mentioned, charity is an order by which the person is directed to union with God through love. Mortal sin averts us from God to some created thing and is, therefore, contrary to the order of charity as such. Venial sin cannot diminish nor corrupt charity since venial sin does not avert one from God. However, venial sin can dispose one to mortal sin and so it must be avoided. On the other hand, the cupidity of venial sin is always diminished by charity,[112] for as one loves God and increases in the love of God, his desire to sin diminishes. Therefore, in this life, it is possible to lose charity through one mortal si,n[113] since through one mortal sin one can turn himself away

---

[106]These three grades of charity are also known as the three stages of the interior life. There are several works considering the three stages of the interior life; one of the best known being *The Stages of the Interior Life: Prelude to Eternal Life* by Reginald Garrigou-Lagrange. Many of the aspects in this volume will be touching upon various aspects of the spiritual life because mental health has a direct effect on the spiritual life. However, in order to understand the spiritual mechanism more perfectly and therefore be more capable of aiding their directees, psychologists should read the masters in that field, such as Garrigou-Lagrange, Ad. Tanquerey and Jordan Aumann.

[107]The treatment of the three grades of charity can be found in ST II-II, q. 24, a. 9.

[108]ST II-II, q. 24, a. 10.

[109]Ibid.

[110]Ibid.

[111]Ibid.

[112]ST II-II, q. 24, a. 10, ad 2.

[113]ST II-II, q. 24, a. 12.

from God. In the next life, i.e. in *patria* (heaven), one already has perfect union with God and therefore charity cannot be lost in heaven.[114]

Our Lord gave two precepts of charity[115] and so St. Thomas asks the question whether the object of charity consists in God alone. In regard to that he states the following:

> Since the species of an act is taken from its formal notion. . . the formality of loving one's neighbor is God; as we ought to love our neighbor as in God. Hence it is manifest that it is the same species of act by which God is loved and that by which one's neighbor is loved. And because of this, the habit of charity not only extends itself to the love of God, but also to the love of neighbor.[116]

Charity does not consist in love of God and love of neighbor simply, but the love of God and the love of neighbor *for the sake of God* (*propter Deum*). One's neighbor is not loved for his own sake but for the sake of God and God constitutes the formality, i.e. the perspective taken on one's neighbor. Hence, the virtue of charity is ultimately about God, even when one loves one's neighbor for the sake of God.

Charity does not, however, extend to irrational creatures since they cannot participate in the common life of eternal beatitude and so irrational creatures are not loved from charity in the proper sense.[117] However, we can love irrational creatures from charity insofar as we will them to be preserved for the honor of God and for the use of man to whom charity extends.[118]

The precept of charity to love our neighbor as our self[119] must likewise be understood in a certain way. With charity, one loves oneself under the notion of God or as referred to God.[120] Thus one is actually loving God when one loves oneself for His sake. This helps us to look past ourselves to God as something more lovable and to Whom we are directed. St. Thomas observes that one loves one's body as something created by God,[121] but not because of the infection of blame and corruption from the

---

[114]ST II-II, q. 12, a. 11.

[115]Matt. 22: 37; Mark 12: 30 and Luke 10: 27.

[116]ST II-II, q. 25, a. 1: "Cum autem species actus ex obiecto sumatur secundum formalem rationem ipsius. . . Ratio autem diligendi proximum Deus est, hoc enim debemus in proximo diligere, ut in Deo sit. unde manifestum est quod idem specie actus est quo diligitur Deus, et quo diligitur proximus. Et propter hoc habitus caritatis non solum se extendit ad dilectionem Dei, sed etiam ad dilectionem proximi."

[117]ST II-II, q. 25, a. 3.

[118]Ibid.

[119]See Matt. 22: 37; Mark 22: 30 and Luke 10: 27.

[120]ST II-II, q. 25, a. 4.

[121]ST II-II, q. 25, a. 5.

punishment due to sin. Rather, we must turn away from the disorder which occurs bodily[122] (*lex fomitis*) and not take delight in it. When we love God through charity, we are to take care of our bodies, not because they are an end in themselves but insofar as we love God to Whom we give glory by the reasonable care of our bodies.

St. Thomas also says that we ought to love sinners as they are capable of eternal beatitude but we must hate their sin since sin in itself merits hate.[123] Yet, what of evil people, ought they to love themselves? Evil people estimate themselves principally in terms of their bodily or sensitive nature, i.e. the exterior man. Hence, they do not know or love themselves truly. The good, on the other hand, love themselves truly since they judge themselves according to the interior man who seeks spiritual goods. Evil people do not seek the integrity of the interior man nor the spiritual goods and so evil people do not love themselves properly,[124] i.e. through charity.

Christ also commanded us to love our enemies,[125] but this is often misunderstood. We do not love our enemies insofar as they are enemies, because that is perverse and irrational.[126] It is perverse and irrational because we should not love that which seeks our harm. Rather, St. Thomas observes, we can love our enemies *in universali* (in general) insofar as we have an interior disposition to love them for the sake of God and so it is because they are viewed under the notion of God that we can love them. Yet, it is impossible to love all of our enemies in particular, since we do not have knowledge of all our enemies, yet we can retain a disposition of soul in which we would love them for God's sake, if we knew them.

Some exterior signs of charity must be exhibited or extended to all, e.g. praying for them and offering up our sufferings for their salvation[127] and this also applies to our enemies. However, as to particular persons, some signs or manifestations of love should or should not be extended to them. For example, while one ought to love our enemies *propter Deum,* it does not mean we must invite them into our houses where they may cause us harm. What is indicated here is that charity is not divorced from supernatural prudence, not only for our sake but also for the sake of our enemies or sinners. At times, the most charitable thing that can happen to a sinner is to be cut off from certain effects or manifestations of charity so that he comes to his senses about his sinful life. Extending certain effects of charity may confirm him in his sin and thereby do him harm. From this we understand that charity is not merely being nice, rather niceness is the effect of charity which is extended to people based on prudential judgment. This avoids a spirit of falsity which we find in certain people who are always nice, even when their niceness is out of place, unsuitable or even false. This is an important lesson for modern

---

[122]Ibid.

[123]ST II-II, q. 25, a. 6.

[124]ST II -II, q. 25, a. 7.

[125]Luke 6:27

[126]ST II-II, q. 25, a. 8.

[127]ST II-II, q. 25, a. 9.

Catholics, as they often think that charity is being nice and so public discourse is reduced to shallowness and simulation.[128] Often the niceties are governed by sensitive appetite rather than a true love of God, which seeks what will bring the person closer to God.

The order or hierarchy of charity is based upon two principles, i.e. the thing's relation to God[129] and its proximity to oneself. Since God is the cause of eternal beatitude, He is to be loved above all.[130] God is also the *ratio* under which we love the others[131] and therefore love of God is prior to love of neighbor. We must love God more than self because He is the good of all whereas we are only our particular good.[132] We must love ourselves spiritually more than our neighbor because one ought to love one's own spiritual good above the good of others since one's self is the basis for one's participation in beatitude.[133] In other words, charity is ordered to eternal beatitude and so the order of charity dictates that we love our own spiritual good above the good of others since we cannot attain our own eternal beatitude unless we love ourselves by means of charity. Also it is more natural to love our own spiritual good above our neighbor's and since charity never goes contrary to the order of nature, it is only fitting that charity would dictate that we love ourselves spiritually first.[134] In reality, we ought never undergo the evil of sin so that our neighbor can avoid it.[135] Yet, we ought to love our neighbor's spiritual good over our own bodily good since his spiritual good is a greater good than our bodily good.[136]

There are different kinds of neighbors: thus St. Thomas addresses which neighbors ought to be loved before the others. Among our neighbors, which one is to

---

[128]Simulation is the sin in which one performs some action in order to deceive, see ST II-II, q. 111.

[129]ST II-II, q. 26, a. 1.

[130]ST II-II, q. 26, a. 2.

[131]Ibid., ad 2.

[132]ST II-II, q. 26, a. 3. Essentially speaking, we may say that God is more lovable by nature than we are and therefore He deserves our love more than we do.

[133]ST II-II, q. 26, a. 4

[134]Modern theories of love argue that we cannot love others unless we love ourselves first. This is correct, assuming our love of self is rightly ordered. However, while many adopt this point of view, they do so based more on an intuitive observation from experience rather than by solid reasoning. The reason behind it is that love is the willing of a good of another. Love seeks the union of the lover with the loved. Now if the lover is evil or not good, then he cannot will union with the loved because it would be an evil for the loved and therefore it would imply contradiction. Hence, to love someone when you hate yourself implies contradiction.

[135]ST II-II, q. 26, a. 4

[136]ST II-II, q. 26, a. 5.

be loved is based upon the proximity of the neighbor to oneself.[137] Therefore, the first of those to be loved are those with whom we share blood relations, i.e. those closest to us are those who share consanguinity.[138] Among the consanguine, one ought to love one's son over one's father,[139] the father over the mother[140] and wife over parents.[141]

Having dealt with the virtue and its object, we now turn to the act of the virtue of charity and in regard to that St. Thomas says that the proper act of charity is love.[142] Charity not only includes benevolence (willing the good of another) but love, which seeks union with the Loved.[143] God is loved for His own sake and we can love God for the goods which He gives us.[144] Even the goods must be referred back to God, for if we stop at the goods He gives us, they become our end rather than God Himself and so we will not attain to the proper end of charity or that which is set out by the natural law. Hence, with respect to God, we must love the giver and only love the gift insofar as we see in it the goodness of God or God Himself, whom we seek. We must also realize that the gifts which God gives us are given in order to draw us closer to Him and so we must view them as a motivation to spur us on to closer union with Him. Whenever we have a love for a created thing, i.e. something God gives us, it takes up that much space in our heart. God is a jealous God[145] in that He wants nothing put before Him.[146] Essentially

---

[137]ST II-II, q. 26, aa. 6 and 7.

[138]ST II-II, q. 26, aa. 7 and 8. This is the basis for the dictum : "charity starts at home."

[139]ST II-II, q. 26, a . 9. This follows from the fact that while the father is more like God, nevertheless the son is, as it were, another self and so he is more proximate in that sense.

[140]ST II-II, q. 26, a. 10. St. Thomas observes in this article that *per se* the father is more like God than the mother and so he is more worthy of love than the mother. However, he also notes that one may end up loving one's mother more from a certain respect (*secundum quid*). Here we imagine that St. Thomas has in mind the fact that one might have a more natural affection for one's mother as well as the fact that the mother is the one that gestates the child and so there may be a closer bond on that level.

[141]ST II-II, q. 26, a. 11. In this article, St. Thomas points out that in one sense one would love one's parents over one's spouse since they are higher in the order of excellence than one's spouse. Yet, he observes that one's spouse is more conjoined to oneself than one's parents and therefore enjoys greater proximity. As a result, St. Thomas comments that one ought to have a more intense love for one's spouse while having more reverence for one's parents.

[142]ST II-II, q. 27, a. 1.

[143]ST II-II, q. 27, a. 2.

[144]ST II-II, q. 27, a. 3.

[145]Exodus 20: 3-5.

[146]Ibid. The fact that in Matt. 22: 37; Mark 12: 30 and Luke 10: 27 Our Lord said we are to love God with our whole heart indicates that we are to put nothing before Him.

this means that any created thing should not be loved for its own sake but *propter Deum*. In this way, God will take the full place in our heart which He wants. Finally, it is more meritorious in itself to love our neighbor than our enemy but it is more manifest of perfect charity to extend the love of God to things more remote, i.e. to our enemies.[147] While love of God is greater than love of neighbor,[148] nevertheless love of God alone is imperfect if it excludes our neighbor since our neighbor ought to be loved *sub ratione Dei* (under the notion of God). Therefore to love both God and neighbor is perfect.[149]

F. The Psychological Effects of Charity

From the aforesaid, some of the psychological effects of charity can be seen. While there are a number of psychological effects of charity, we will discuss seven of them here. The first has to do with right order. Since charity is a virtue which resides in the will by which one is moved by the Holy Spirit to love God, charity has an inherent ordering effect. Like the virtue of faith which gives right order to the intellect regarding the things of God and the created order, charity moves the will to act according to that right order. Since the will is that faculty by which we direct our lives[150] charity will aid the person to act according to right order. Once the soul is rightly ordered to God, i.e. once the ordering for which man's nature was made begins to be accomplished, there is a certain resonance in man's soul which tells him that things are right.[151]

This will have profound effects on the lower faculties as they will be moved and informed by charity,[152] which is the second psychological effect of charity. As the lower faculties are moved toward what is truly good, this will have a natural ordering effect on the lower faculties. Clearly the *ratio Dei* which governs charity will affect the imagination, not with respect to God but with respect to ourselves and to our neighbors. Charity will, therefore, have a quieting effect on our passions, e.g. if we are inclined toward anger because of some harm our neighbor has done to us, we will look at the

---

[147]ST II-II, q. 27, a. 6.

[148]ST II-II, q. 27, a. 8.

[149]Ibid. This is important as many of those following God whose passions are disordered often have a hard time loving their neighbor. They often feel justified because they love God and see some defect in their neighbor. However, this is a sign of imperfection for how can one love God and hate His image (man)? That would be analogous to a man who loved his wife but hated pictures of her.

[150]One can rightly argue that the intellect is the faculty by which we direct our lives and this would be correct. However, since we have free will, we can choose whether or not to follow that ordering known by the intellect. Ultimately, a person's life is not rightly ordered merely because he knows the right order but because he knows it and wills it. In this sense, the will is determinative of the direction of our lives.

[151]This will be discussed in the fruit of the Holy Spirit of peace.

[152]This entire discussion regarding the lower powers will become even clearer in the discussion on the fruits of the Holy Spirit.

person and love him for God's sake, thereby changing the image in the imagination regarding our neighbor from one who causes harm (and therefore one to whom we ought to harm) to one to whom we ought to do good. This will have a healing effect on the memory, as those who have harmed us in the past will be viewed in a rightly ordered fashion. Charity can also have a profound effect on the cogitative power insofar as the cogitative power will associate those things which bring about our own and our neighbor's spiritual good, rather than operating according to the mode of appetite.

The third effect of charity is that it perfects and rightly orders self-love. How many directees have problems because of disordered concern or love for self? This brings us directly to the issue of "self-esteem." Through charity and faith we realize that in comparison to God we are nothing. Very often the use of the term self-esteem is another name for the vice of pride. Humility is the virtue by which one does not judge oneself greater than one is, whereas pride is the vice by which one excessively judges one's own good. Many people have low self-esteem because they *ought* to have low self-esteem. If one is a grave sinner and if one's psychological problems are caused by these grave sins, one ought to have low self-esteem because it is rightly ordered, i.e. one is in truth lowly. To try to view oneself as worthy of that which one is not does not help one's self-esteem but makes oneself disordered and prideful.[153] Rather, the order of charity helps us to love and esteem ourselves because we are creatures of God. Hence, we learn that our real value is not in self but in God. There is a natural inclination in man to seek his good outside of himself and as long as one has false self-love, one will never seek the good outside of oneself, but within oneself. The problem is that we come up against our own nothingness, if we are truthful. If we think our real value is in self, then we are already deluded and disordered. True charity, on the other hand, helps one to love oneself for the sake of God, to will for oneself those things that are truly good for the interior man, and to help one to seek one's fulfillment in something greater than himself. For this reason, since charity rightly orders our self-love, it will have an inherently good psychological effect on us. Our psychological health is heavily affected by our view of self and so through faith and charity, that view will be properly ordered. Therefore, true self-esteem consists in loving oneself in relation to God.

The fourth effect of charity is that charity excludes mortal sin. We have already seen the negative effects of mortal sin and charity will help us to avoid those effects by helping us to avoid mortal sin. The fifth effect is that "charity covers a multitude of sins."[154] This passage can be understood in a number of different ways. However, in relation to psychological illness, we can see that through charity one will love God and not want to offend Him. As a result, one will avoid sin as well as be inclined away from sin by the very virtue of charity. The sixth psychological effect of charity is that it will rightly order all of the other virtues in the person and thereby affect them positively. It

---

[153]To try to cheer people up by telling them how wonderful they are when they are not is misplaced sentimentality. It has no foundation in reality nor in any sound psychological theory or practice.

[154]I Peter 4: 8.

helps us to avoid developing vices, as vices are disorders which are contrary to the order of charity.

Charity not only affects the person's interior life, but by rightly ordering the person, it has a natural tendency toward right order in one's relations with others. Hence, the seventh effect is that charity has an inherent capacity to effect good relations with others. This not only applies to the family where many psychological ills arise from lack of charity between family members, but also among friends, in the work place and in society in general. One of the signs of the lack of the presence of charity in the members of a society is the increased number of crimes,[155] laws,[156] and lack of cohesion among the members of the society.[157] In effect, a society can only become perfect through the virtue of charity. The above are by no means the only effects of charity but they do provide an initial understanding of the profoundly positive effects of the virtue of charity.[158]

II. The Infused Moral Virtues

A. The Infused Moral Virtues Themselves

The theological virtues are not the only infused virtues and so it is important to have an understanding of the other infused virtues in order to see the various aids God can provide which will have psychological effects. The infused moral virtues go by the same names as the acquired moral virtues, viz. prudence, justice, fortitude and temperance. However, infused virtues differ from acquired virtues in that acquired virtues have as their formality the rule of reason, whereas infused virtues have as their formality the rule of divine law.[159] In other words, infused virtues concern created things but from the point of view of how the divine law (revelation) regulates how we are to

---

[155]Christ said that the whole of the law (i.e. the 10 Commandments, of which the last seven deal with our neighbor) is summed up in the two precepts of charity, see Matt. 22: 40. If we love our neighbor for the sake of God, we will not be stealing from him, killing him, etc.

[156]As charity decreases, the following of the moral law begins to wane and so legislators will find it necessary to legislate a greater number of laws which are more coercive in order to protect the citizens from one another. Moreover, legislators will begin seeking to control the people as a desire for power increases, since they will not be performing their civil functions based on the love of neighbor but the disordered love of self.

[157]As the act of charity of love seeks union, so cohesion in a society will be greater through charity; lack of love proceeding from charity will cause a disintegration of the society and culture.

[158]It should be noted that since the order of charity is known by faith and since one loves God rightly or wrongly, then right faith is absolutely necessary for true charity. In fact, one of the signs of heresy is lack of charity.

[159]III Sent., d. 33, q. 1, a. 2d; ST I-II, q. 63, a. 4 and De vir., a. 10, ad 8.

relate to them, whereas acquired virtues take right reason as the rule by which created things are to be judged. This follows from the fact that, as the theological virtues concern God Himself, the infused moral virtues concern created things in relation to or as they are ordered to God.[160] Infused moral virtues move us to perform actions in relation to created things so that we will ultimately come to our final end. So we may say that the infused virtues help us to see created things as they truly are, i.e. as means for us to reach our ultimate end rather than as ends in themselves. Hence, the infused moral virtues help us to make use of created things so that we can reach God. Acquired moral virtues, on the other hand, help us to make right use of things as they pertain to this life.

Since the infused moral virtues order us to an end which is not in proportion to our nature, the infused moral virtues exceed our natural faculties' capacity to obtain them on their own. For this reason the infused moral virtues are caused directly by God.[161] Hence we cannot increase the infused moral virtues by means of our actions, but we can only do those things which dispose ourselves to God's increasing of the virtues[162] or perform acts which merit an increase in the virtues.[163] Even in the case of merit, the action which we perform is not causal, but makes us deserving of more virtue.

The infused moral virtues are actually necessary to reach our ultimate end,[164] for without them we would not relate properly to created things and thereby be diverted from God. This essentially means that the infused moral virtues order our intellect and will to the ultimate end (along with the theological virtues) as well as the inferior powers, viz. the irascible and the concupiscible appetites whose actions are ordainable to the ultimate end.[165] St. Thomas also states that the infused moral virtues prevail in that they make it such that the passions from the lower appetites are sensed, but in no way dominate[166] the soul. However, the infused moral virtues can be impeded in their acts by a contrary disposition[167] of the person in whom they reside.[168]

Insofar as these infused virtues ordain one to God, they cannot be had if charity is not had. For charity is that virtue infused in the will by God by which one is moved

---

[160]ST I-II, q. 63, a. 3, ad 2; ibid., q. 63, a. 4 and De vir., a. 10. See also De vir., a. 9, ad 7.

[161]ST I-II, q. 55, a. 4; De vir., a. 10, ad 7 and ibid., a. 11.

[162]That only God can increase the infused moral virtues is discussed in De vir., a. 11.

[163]De vir., a. 2, ad 18 and ibid., a. 10, ad 17.

[164]III Sent., d. 33, q. 1, a. 2c and ibid., ad 2.

[165]De vir., a. 10, ad 5.

[166]Ibid., ad 14.

[167]ST I-II, q. 65, a. 3, ad 2.

[168]While one may have the infused virtue of prudence, for example, some indisposition in the brain which would affect one's judgment may impede the act of the virtue of prudence.

to union with Him as to one's end. If one lacks charity, one will not be seeking God but will be pursuing created things for themselves. As a result, without charity, it is not possible to have the infused moral virtues.[169] Conversely, all of the infused moral virtues are infused with charity[170] since charity perfects how we deal with particular kinds of goods and actions. This follows from the fact that if one were given charity without the infused moral virtues, one would not relate properly to the created goods and thereby easily corrupt charity through mortal sin. For this reason, just as charity is lost through one mortal sin, so all of the infused moral virtues are lost through one mortal sin.[171] On the other hand, just as charity is not lost through venial sin, neither are the infused virtues lost through venial sin.[172] Furthermore, we have seen that without charity, one will lose the infused moral virtues and for this reason the infused moral virtues are connected not only by the infused virtue of prudence but by also charity.[173] Finally, given the aforesaid, we can say that only the infused moral virtues are perfect in relation to the acquired moral virtues, because they order man to the ultimate end, simply speaking, whereas the acquired moral virtues order one to the ultimate end only in a certain respect.[174] This follows from the fact that the acquired moral virtues have as their end the right use of things in this life and insofar as they are according to right reason, they are according to the divine law as it is manifest in the natural law. But in this case it is indirect, whereas with the infused moral virtues, they are ordered to the use of the things of this world directly as a means to God.

B. The Psychological Effects of the Infused Moral Virtues

Whatever good benefit can be said of the acquired moral virtues can also be said of the infused moral virtues.[175] Yet, the infused moral virtues help us to relate to objects in a more perfect way, i.e. they help us to relate to them as they truly are, viz. means to God. As all things in this life are means to God's glory and all things in this life can be used in some way to reach God, then we realize that man and all of his faculties, the lower ones included, were not ultimately meant to have created things as their final end, but God alone. As a result, the infused moral virtues help one to have a healthy relationship to and understanding of created things, even though created things

---

[169]ST I-II, q. 65, a. 2. In this article, St. Thomas observes that one can have the acquired moral virtues without charity but not the infused moral virtues.

[170]ST I-II, q. 65, a. 3.

[171]ST I-II, q. 73, a. 1, ad 2. Since charity is infused in the soul with sanctifying grace (see chapter on grace), the infused moral virtues are also had with grace, see IV Sent., d. 14, q. 1, a. 3b and De vir., a. 9, ad 18.

[172]ST I-II, q. 73, a. 1, ad 2.

[173]ST I-II, q. 63, a. 3.

[174]ST I-II, q. 65, a. 2.

[175]See prior volume, chap. 10.

have the capacity to cause a multitude of mental illnesses due to the defects arising from sin.

The infused moral virtues help to restrain the passions. In the prior volume, it was clearly drawn out how the passions can have an adverse effect on our mental health. The infused moral virtues help to reduce antecedent appetites by restraining the passions; they thereby have a direct effect on certain kinds of *per accidens* mental illness. Moreover, the infused moral virtues help keep us from being dominated by the passions. We saw in the prior volume how the soul can carry on in only one primary activity at a time and so when the passions dominate, we have a hard time changing our thoughts or thinking clearly. Infused moral virtues contribute directly to clarity of mind by reducing this effect in the soul. Furthermore, mental illnesses almost always are the result of the person not relating properly to some created thing,[176] and the infused moral virtues can help correct how a particularly affected faculty relates to that created object. Moreover, insofar as the infused moral virtues are in the soul and since the soul has a certain redundancy in the body, we can say that the infused moral virtues can positively affect bodily disposition, since they will incline the person to perform actions which are *secundum naturam* (according to nature) and which therefore have a positive effect on the body as it begins to conform itself to the operations of the soul in relation to these virtues.[177]

The infused virtue of prudence can have profound effects on directees in as much as it will direct them to judge intellectually the right thing to do in relation to the mental illness, particularly if the mental illness is arising from sin or is somehow impeding their advancement to God. Just as the acquired virtue of prudence directs and guides the other acquired virtues, so infused prudence will direct and guide the other infused virtues. Therefore, if a problem exists in the concupiscible or irascible appetite, the person will be enabled to know what to do to overcome the problem so as not to be impeded in the attainment or advancement toward God.

The infused virtue of justice in the will has two effects. The first is that it will help us to relate properly to God insofar as we will render what is due to Him. If a society manifests the fact that its members are not rendering to God what is due Him, we can rightly assume that they lack the infused virtue of justice. Since charity cannot be had without the infused moral virtues, we can also rightly say that society lacks charity.

Part of the virtue of justice is that of religion[178] and many psychologists have rightly noted that many people who suffer from mental illness have strange ideas and practices regarding God. Now the person with the infused virtue of faith, provided he is operating according to right faith, should not suffer these problems. Almost always such problems are a sign of some error regarding the object of faith. The infused virtue

---

[176]Here we are prescinding from the consideration of those mental illnesses which arise out of a biological cause.

[177]This is, incidentally, why virtuous and holy people at times tend to have a different bodily appearance.

[178]See ST II-II, q. 81.

of prudence can aid this insofar as the person will be inclined to judge what are the prudential practices in relation to God. Often people with mental problems do very imprudent things in their relation to God. This is one of the primary reasons God gives us infused prudence so that we can act rightly in relation to created things and thus serve Him rightly. Moreover, the infused virtue of religion, as it is part of the infused virtue of justice, will render God His *due*. In other words, mentally ill directees often do not render to God due or proper worship but render to Him some false kind of worship flowing from a distorted view of God, created things or themselves, i.e. flowing from the distortion of the mental illness. As a result, psychologists should encourage the person to dispose himself to the infused virtues as well as pray for the infused virtues, so that he can be rightly ordered regarding God.[179]

The other effect of justice is that it helps us to render to our neighbor what is due to him as a means toward reaching God. This will aid those relations that tend to cause psychological problems by helping the person to be rightly ordered regarding the person who causes injury and also it will help the person causing injury to stop and begin treating others rightly. Hence, infused justice can have a direct effect on the exterior causes of mental illness.

The infused virtue of fortitude can greatly aid in helping the mentally ill person find the strength to perform the actions to overcome his mental illness. This particularly applies if the mental illness arises from something sinful or something which could possibly impede his salvation. Therefore, regardless of what the person's problem is, he can always ask God for the fortitude to do what is right, as well as patiently bear the suffering of mental illness itself for the sake of His glory and for the merit of the grace of conversion or the curing of the mental illness itself. As fortitude has a tempering effect on the irascible appetite as a whole, the infused virtue of fortitude can aid greatly those suffering from anger. The infused fortitude will direct and guide the actions of the irascible appetite so that one does not go to excess regarding anger. Lastly, how many mental illnesses are caused by a person's lack of control over some aspect of the concupiscible appetite? The infused virtue of temperance can have an immediate effect of calming down the antecedent appetite, so that the person can think more clearly and not feel so weak in the face of the object that causes his problems.

Conclusion

The operations of the Holy Spirit on the soul are multitudinous and a full knowledge of them provides many avenues of avoiding mental illness and helping to overcome mental illness, particularly if the cause of the mental illness is actual sin. The various infused virtues can greatly aid the directee in his advancement towards mental health and for this reason psychologists should not keep from their directees the knowledge of the theological and infused moral virtues, or any other theological help for

---

[179]In connection to this, some directees end up mentally ill because of basic flaws in their understanding of the faith. As a result, a basic catechesis can sometimes solve the problem so that their faith is true.

that matter. It must be carefully borne in mind that we do not use these things to become mentally healthy, but we become mentally healthy by the right use of these things, so that we can reach God. Nevertheless, God has provided a great wealth of means to aid us in overcoming our problems and reaching Him. For this reason, we proceed to the next chapter where we will learn more about the divine aid which is available to us.

Chapter 5: Gifts of the Holy Spirit

Sometimes in a person's life, events unfold which leave him thinking that, in a given instance, he simply could not have done the right thing, given the unforeseen effects or the lack of time to reflect upon the situation in which he found himself. It is for this reason that God must aid man so that he can arrive at his final end without being diverted from it by unforeseen events or lack of reflection or understanding of how to proceed. For there are occasions in which man's natural capacities, acquired virtues and even theological and infused moral virtues do not suffice to lead him to his end. So God, Whose providence is not lacking, does not leave man without the aid to reach eternal beatitude and, consequently, God gives man the gifts of the Holy Spirit so that he may be led to his final end. The gifts of the Holy Spirit, as shall be seen, have a direct relation to mental health and so it is necessary to discuss them so that people may dispose themselves to the operations of the gifts.[1]

I. Gifts in General

The gifts are dispositions infused[2] by God into the soul of man by which he is disposed to be promptly moved by divine inspiration.[3] The gifts are higher perfections in which one is disposed to be moved by the divine,[4] i.e. it is God who moves us rather than ourselves and so the gifts are more eminent than the infused virtues.[5] The gifts are a higher perfection insofar as they have God as a motive cause rather than ourselves as is the case with the infused virtues. With the infused moral virtues and theological virtues, once God infuses them, we can bring about the acts which pertain to the virtues by the command of reason, whereas the gifts have the Holy Spirit as their motive cause[6] rather than reason. Effectively speaking, this means that even if we have the gifts, we cannot make use of them of our own accord but need God to move us through them.

The gifts, insofar as they are a disposition, are a certain habit by which man is perfected in promptly obeying the Holy Spirit.[7] Since they help us to live well, the gifts are virtues.[8] But the gifts differ from the infused theological and moral virtues in that they have God as the cause of their motion and so they are sometimes called the "divine

---

[1] Here we will prescind from the discussion of the less common gifts which do not depend upon one's state of grace, such as prophecy, speaking in tongues, etc.

[2] ST I-II, q. 68, a. 1. In this respect, they are like the infused moral and theological virtues.

[3] Ibid. In another place, St. Thomas says that the gifts help one to follow well the divine instinct, see ST I-II, q. 68, aa. 2 & 3.

[4] Ibid.

[5] III Sent., d. 34, q. 1, a. 1, ad 3.

[6] Aumann, *Spiritual Theology*, p. 92.

[7] ST I-II, q., 68, a. 3 and Aumann, *Spiritual Theology*, p. 91.

[8] III Sent., d. 34, q. 1, a. 1, ad 1.

virtues."[9] The gifts dispose all of the powers of the soul to divine action[10] and so the gifts extend to everything which is covered in the intellectual and moral virtues.[11] The gifts are primarily in the intellect or will but some have an effect on the lower powers such as the irascible and the concupiscible appetites.[12] The gifts are necessary for salvation insofar as they move us to the final end.[13] As was mentioned above, sometimes events occur about which it is beyond our capacity to know what to do. So that we do not fall into mortal sin, it is necessary that God guide us by His own motion. This why the term instinct is used, since we act based upon God's action on us rather than initiating the action on our own. Therefore, since God is a higher motive power, we can say that the gifts are to be preferred to the virtues.[14]

Lastly, since charity is that which orders us to God and effects our union with Him, none of the gifts can be had without charity.[15] This follows from the fact that if one did not have charity, he would be refusing to be obedient to God and since the gifts make the soul obedient to God, the gifts and lack of charity are mutually exclusive. Moreover, just as the moral virtues are connected through prudence, so the gifts of the Holy Spirit are connected through charity. This follows since all of the gifts have God as their end and charity is that by which we have union with our end.

---

[9]III Sent., d. 34, q. 1, a. 1, ad 6.

[10]ST I-II, q. 68, a. 8.

[11]ST I-II, q. 68, a. 4. For a discussion of the various ways in which the gifts differ from the virtues, see Aumann, *Spiritual Theology*, p. 92-3. Some of the differences will become clearer, if one keeps the discussion in the prior chapters in mind while reading about the various gifts.

[12]This statement is made with the understanding that it deals with a somewhat debated point. It appears that in the writing of St. Thomas, he seems to indicate that the gifts are in the intellect or will but he also mentions, as will be seen later, that they have an effect in the lower faculties. Some authors hold that certain gifts are both in the will and the lower faculties, but this does not seem to be very Thomistic, at least to our reading. Nowhere does St. Thomas say that one can have a single habit in two faculties; in fact, he states the opposite insofar as habits are distinguished based upon the faculty in which they reside. Therefore, even though, at times, St. Thomas talks as if the gift of Fear of the Lord, for example, is in the concupiscible appetite, it seems more accurate to say that it is in the will while also affecting the concupiscible appetite. As will be seen, this may be due to the nature of the gift but it may also be due to the principle of redundancy, which indicates that that which is higher redounds to that which is lower in the human soul and this will be seen in the discussion of Fear of the Lord and Fortitude.

[13]ST I-II, q. 68, a. 2.

[14]ST I-II, q. 68, a. 8.

[15]ST I-II, q. 68, a. 5.

II. The Gifts in Particular

A. The Gift of Fear of the Lord

The gift of Fear of the Lord is a gift infused into the will[16] by which one recedes from depraved delights and for this reason the gift of Fear of the Lord corresponds to temperance.[17] The gift of Fear of the Lord is not a passion of the irascible appetite, rather it is a fear in the will (intellective appetite). St. Thomas distinguishes between different kinds of fear in relation to the discussion of Fear of the Lord. The first is mundane or human fear which consists of turning away from God because of the evil the man has performed.[18] Since man turns away from God in this kind of fear, mundane fear is always evil.[19] It comes from the love of this world as our end[20] rather than God. So, as one pursues this world, he turns away from God, because God is seen as someone who stands in his way in relation to this world.

The second kind of fear is called servile fear in which one turns to God and adheres to Him out of fear of being punished.[21] Servile fear, insofar as it is concerned with oneself and one's own good is contrary to charity[22] which concerns God above all things. Servile fear has as its object punishment,[23] insofar as God can be feared as inflicting the evil of punishment[24] and so God can be said to be evil *secundum quid* or in a certain respect but not simply speaking or *in se*.[25] Moreover, one can suffer the evil of punishment, if he is separated from God,[26] which is the effect of one's sin. Since considering God's justice gives rise to fear,[27] servile fear sees that the punishment is evil and this in itself is good.[28]

The third kind of fear is filial fear or chaste fear which consists in a turning to God; it is a fear of the blame of sin insofar as one does not want to offend God.[29] Filial

---

[16]That the gift of Fear of the Lord is in the will, see Tanquerey, *The Spiritual Life*, n. 1335.

[17]ST I-II, q. 68, a. 4, ad 1 and III Sent., d. 34, q. 1, a. 2, ad 2.

[18]ST II-II, q. 19, a. 2.

[19]ST II-II, q. 19, a. 3.

[20]Ibid.

[21]ST II-II, q. 19, a. 2.

[22]ST II-II, q. 19, a. 4.

[23]Ibid.

[24]ST II-II, q. 19, a. 5, ad 2.

[25]ST II-II, q. 19, a. 1.

[26]Ibid.

[27]Ibid.

[28]ST II-II, q. 19, a, 4.

[29]ST II-II, q. 19, a. 2.

fear does not look to God as an active principle of blame, but as the end from which one can be separated by blame.[30] From this we see that the gift of Fear of the Lord refers to filial or chaste fear insofar as God moves us, not to self, but to Himself. Insofar as a thing is easily moved, it must first be a non-repugnant (non-fighting) subject and the gift of Fear of the Lord disposes man to being moved promptly by God.[31] Therefore, in the proper sense, the gift of Fear of the Lord is not servile fear and clearly it is not mundane fear. The last kind of fear is called initial fear in which one has a mixture of both servile fear and filial fear.[32]

As regards Fear of the Lord's relation to charity, St. Thomas observes that fear of punishment is included in one way with charity, as separation from God is a punishment and this fear pertains to chaste fear.[33] In another way it is contrary to charity, as one flees the punishment as contrary to one's own natural good or end.[34] Yet, in another way, it is distinguished from chaste fear in which separation from God is seen as bad for oneself, but one's own good is not the end and this pertains to filial fear.[35] From this we see that the more charity one has, the more one fears offending God[36] Whom one loves and therefore the more charity one has the more of the gift of Fear of the Lord one has. On the other hand, the more charity one has the less servile fear one will have, because one will be less concerned with self and more concerned with God. Hence, the more charity one has, the more one will turn away from created goods and turn toward God. The more charity one has, the more one flees depraved delights and this will have a tempering effect on the concupiscible appetite.

While turning from created things to God is an act of the will, nevertheless it has an effect in the concupiscible appetite by virtue of redundancy. As the will moves the imagination in light of charity, it will form phantasms which see the pursuit of unnatural and bad delights as something truly evil. In this respect, Fear of the Lord also affects the operations of the imagination as well as the cogitative power, which learns from the image formed in the imagination by reason and will and which is itself moved by reason and will to see the image as the love of charity sees it. This will likewise have an effect on memory, insofar as the past sins and desire for immoral delights will be assessed by the cogitative power as bad and the new image of the past sin as bad will be stored back in memory. This is one of the ways in which those are healed whose disordered living has left many pleasant but depraved images in the memory. Healing pertains not only to the evil that is inflicted upon us from outside but also that which we inflict upon ourselves, even though we did the evil in order to derive some pleasure from

---

[30]ST II-II, q. 19, a. 5, ad 2.

[31]ST II-II, q. 19, a. 9.

[32]ST II-II, q. 19, a. 2.

[33]ST II-II, q. 19, a. 6.

[34]Ibid.

[35]Ibid.

[36]ST II-II, q. 19, a. 10.

it. Hence, even past experiences stored in memory must be corrected and the gift of Fear of the Lord contributes to this.

Fear is the lowest of the gifts[37] and yet it is the beginning of the highest gift, viz. Wisdom, as Scripture says, Fear of the Lord is the beginning of Wisdom.[38] In regard to this, St. Thomas says that in one sense faith is the beginning of Wisdom as to the substance of Wisdom itself.[39] On the other hand, he says that when Wisdom becomes operative, its effect is Fear of the Lord, insofar as, in considering God, one seeks to avoid sin which pertains to Fear.[40] And so, in one sense, when we say that Fear is the beginning of Wisdom, we are speaking in terms of the operations of Wisdom. On the other hand, one cannot truly begin considering God for His own sake until one turns away from created things. For as long as our thoughts and desires are focused on created things, we will not see God as He truly is, i.e. we will judge Him in light of the world rather than the world in light of Him. From this perspective, Fear of the Lord is the beginning of Wisdom insofar as one cannot truly contemplate God who is the ultimate cause of things unless one turns away from the created world as one's end.[41]

From the aforesaid discussion, we can see that the gift of Fear of the Lord is an infused disposition in the will by which one turns away from created things toward God. Aumann defines the gift of Fear of the Lord as: "a supernatural habit by which the just soul, under the instinct of the Holy Spirit, acquires a special docility for subjecting itself completely to the divine will out of reverence for the excellency and majesty of God."[42] This definition does not differ substantially from the prior definition insofar as one who turns away from created things to God becomes docile to God's motion by looking to God as one's end rather than to created things. Hence, while the definitions differ, they are not exclusive of each other but merely look at the same thing from different points of view.

We have already seen some of the effects of fear. However, Aumann lists some

---

[37]ST II-II, q. 19, a. 9. In this article, St. Thomas observes that Fear is the first in the ascending order and last in the order of descending, which indicates that Fear is the least noble of the gifts.

[38]Ecclesiasticus 1:16.

[39]This statement can only be understood in light of the discussion which follows below. Nevertheless, we can say that Wisdom insofar as it is a consideration of God and all things in light of God can only truly be exercised with faith which gives us a supernatural knowledge of God. While the natural virtue of wisdom can do this to a degree, it cannot do it to the degree that faith and Wisdom can.

[40]ST II-II, q. 19, a. 8.

[41]It is for this reason that the gift of Fear of the Lord corresponds to the beatitude: "Blessed are the poor in spirit: for theirs is the kingdom of heaven" (Matthew 5:3). For if one is poor in spirit, i.e. one remains voluntarily detached from created things, then no created thing will separate him from God and so he will inherit heaven. See ST II-II, q. 19, a. 12.

[42]Aumann, *Spiritual Theology*, p. 262.

of the effects of fear which are worthy of note. The first is that Fear of the Lord gives one a lively sentiment of the grandeur and majesty of God, which leaves in the soul a profound adoration filled with reverence and humility.[43] Second, it gives one a great horror of sin and a lively sorrow for ever having committed sin.[44] Thirdly, the gift of Fear of the Lord inclines one toward an extreme vigilance to avoid the occasion of offending God.[45] Fourthly, it gives one perfect detachment from all created things.[46] As to the effects of Fear of the Lord as they relate to temperance, we see that Fear of the Lord gives one a vivid awareness of the sanctity and the purity of God.[47] Next it gives one a loss of interest in the pleasure afforded by creature attachments.[48] Third, it bestows on one a lofty degree of humility.[49] Lastly it gives one a profound appreciation for the beauty of the spiritual life of grace.[50]

The psychological ramifications of these effects cannot be fully appreciated without a fuller understanding of the spiritual mechanism which will be delineated as we go along. However, the fact that the gift of Fear of the Lord moves one to avoid sin means it also moves one to avoid those things which cause psychological damage. Moreover, it inclines one to detachment from the pleasures of created things and this is very important for the psychological life insofar as many psychological illnesses are due either to an irrational attachment to some created thing outside oneself or to an irrational or disordered attachment to self. As it bestows humility, it will incline one to live in accordance with the truth and not judge oneself to be greater than he is and so it will rightly order his judgment of himself as well as the assessment of self by the cogitative power.

While the gifts cannot be merited,[51] there are things which we can do to dispose ourselves to an increase of the gift of Fear of the Lord. With respect to all of the gifts, in order to increase them we can always employ the general means, viz. recollection,[52]

---

[43]Ibid., p. 264.

[44]Ibid.

[45]Ibid.

[46]Ibid.

[47]Ibid., p. 305.

[48]Ibid.

[49]Ibid.

[50]Ibid., p. 306.

[51]See ibid., p. 306. This essentially means that we cannot do anything directly to cause their increase.

[52]This consists of reflecting interiorly on God and spiritual matters.

purity of heart,[53] fidelity to grace[54] and frequent invocation of the Holy Spirit.[55] With respect to Fear of the Lord in particular, we can meditate frequently on the infinite grandeur and majesty of God.[56] We can accustom ourselves to converse with God with filial confidence filled with reverence.[57] We can meditate frequently on the infinite malice of sin and thus arouse a great horror for sin.[58] We can be meek and humble in dealing with our neighbor and beg frequently of the Holy Spirit a reverential fear of God.[59] We can cultivate a love of solitude,[60] recollection and faithful practice of mental prayer.[61] We can be vigilant in keeping custody of the senses[62] and making acts of love of God.[63] Finally, we can do all things for the salvation of souls and the glory of God.[64]

All of these things will have a positive effect psychologically. As the gift of Fear of the Lord increases, it will act contrary to the passions. Any *per accidens* mental illness which is rooted in the appetites will be affected by the gift. Moreover, it will rightly order one's will toward that which is truly good for man in accordance with the natural law, thereby helping one to avoid mental illness. Lastly, we must say, however, that the gift of Fear of the Lord can be impeded in its operation due to some indisposition in the soul.[65] This can be any vice or bodily disposition arising from vice.[66]

---

[53]This consists in never willing anything that will defile the purity of one's heart, i.e. one ought never will anything evil. Purity of heart does not refer merely to matters of the Sixth and Ninth Commandments but to anything which will lead one away from God.

[54]This essentially consists in cooperating with the graces that God sends to us. This will be discussed at greater length in the chapter on grace.

[55]Ibid., p. 265.

[56]Ibid.

[57]Ibid. Reverence consists in the honor and respect given to God as our Lord.

[58]Ibid.

[59]Ibid.

[60]Love of solitude is necessary insofar as through solitude we do not let the world or men disturb our interior recollection or attachment to God.

[61]Ibid., p. 306.

[62]Custody of the senses is the virtue by which one does not let anything into the senses which will draw one into sin. Its companion virtue, custody of the mind, is the virtue by which one does not let into the imagination anything sinful. Clearly custody of the mind can have a profound psychological effect insofar as we will also keep proper mental hygiene, i.e. we will not let things into our imagination that will cause us trouble.

[63]Ibid.

[64]Ibid.

[65]In ST I-II, q. 65, a. 3, ad 2, St. Thomas observes that infused moral habits can be impeded by some supervening extrinsic impediment and so an indisposition can impede its operations. Since the gifts of the Holy Spirit are habits in the sense that they are infused in us, by which the Holy Spirit moves us, then it would seem that the gifts as well can be

This essentially means that even mental illness can impede the operations of the Holy Spirit in one's life. While it is true that God can use any person for anything, regardless of their state, nevertheless, God likes to use the nature which He has created in a manner suited to it. As a result, if one has a mental illness it can actually impede the Fear of the Lord, as one will not be able to turn away from things in this life because of fixations or the like. Hence, while the gifts can help correct and perfect one's mental health, they can also be impeded by one's mental illness.

B. The Gift of Fortitude

The gift of Fortitude is an infused disposition in the soul by which one is able to sustain all dangers and difficulties which exceed human capacity.[67] This follows from the fact that the gift of Fortitude has for its measure an act of divine power and so one trusts in God's aid.[68] The gift of the Holy Spirit of Fortitude imparts a confidence not had merely by the virtues.[69] St. Thomas observes that sometimes it is not in man's power to come to the end of his work or to avoid evil or danger and sometimes he is even oppressed by the dangers and evils of life to the point of death. Fortitude is the gift of the Holy Spirit which leads man to eternal life which is the end of his good works and the avoiding of dangers. Therefore, man is given Fortitude and so he has a confidence, by which fear, its contrary, is excluded.[70]

Since Fortitude deals with avoiding dangers, Fortitude concerns the arduous. For it is truly arduous that one performs only works of virtue and leads a life only in accordance with virtue. This is commonly called the works of justice (*opera iustitiae*). For this reason, the gift of Fortitude corresponds to the beatitude:[71] "Blessed are they that hunger and thirst after justice: for they shall have their fill."[72] In effect, the gift of Fortitude is a habit of the soul by which the soul always acts in accordance with virtue and by which it is able to avoid dangers. While the gift of Fortitude is in the will,[73] so that the will may not vary from the course of virtue, nevertheless, because it deals with the arduous, Fortitude has an effect on the passions.[74] We know this to be the case since the passions can pull us away from leading the life of virtue. Consequently, this also

---

impeded due to some indisposition of the soul.

[66]Such as a high level of hormonal activity due to frequent illicit sexual conduct.

[67]III Sent., d. 34, q. 3, a. 1, qu. 2 and III Sent., d. 34, q. 1, a. 2.

[68]III Sent., d. 34, q. 3, a. 1, qu. 1 and ibid., ad 2.

[69]Aumann, *Spiritual Theology*, p. 312.

[70]ST II-II, q. 139, a. 1.

[71]ST I-II, q. 139, a. 2.

[72]Matthew 5:6.

[73]Tanquerey, *The Spiritual Life*, n. 1330 and Aumann, *Spiritual Theology*, p. 306.

[74]III Sent., d. 34, q. 3, a. 1, qu. 2, ad 2.

means that it has an effect on the irascible appetite. Since the gift of Fortitude helps one to reach eternal life and since it helps us to lead a life according to the virtues, we see it is necessary to have Fortitude in order to remain in the state of grace.[75] If we did not have Fortitude, we would be led into a life of passion and vice and thereby lose our state of grace. Given the aforesaid, Tanquerey defines the gift of Fortitude as "a gift which perfects the virtue of fortitude by imparting to the will an impulse and an energy which enable it to do great things joyfully and fearlessly despite all obstacles."[76]

The gift of Fortitude has other effects in addition to the aforementioned. The first is that the gift of Fortitude gives the soul relentless vigor in the practice of virtue.[77] It also overcomes all lukewarmness in the service of God. Thirdly, it makes the soul intrepid and valiant in every type of danger or against every kind of enemy. Fourthly, it enables souls to suffer with patience and joy. Lastly, it gives the soul the quality of heroism in great things and in small things.

There are ways of disposing ourselves for the increase of the gift of Fortitude, such as recognizing that our strength does not come from ourselves but from God and therefore we must humbly acknowledge our weakness(es).[78] We must take every opportunity to exercise fortitude in many of the circumstances of our lives.[79] Aumann observes that in addition to prayer, recollection and fidelity to grace we can do three things to dispose ourselves to an increase of Fortitude. The first is that we can accustom ourselves to the exact fulfillment of our duties in spite of any repugnance. Secondly, we should not ask God to remove our cross but only that He give us the strength to carry it. Lastly, we can voluntarily practice mortification faithfully.

Clearly, the psychological benefits of the gift of Fortitude are many. This gift will help one to do whatever is necessary in order to overcome his mental illness, especially if it is something that can impede his reaching eternal beatitude. Because mental illness is a vice either in the intellect or another faculty or both, it means that the intellect or other faculties are weak. Therefore, the directee must be encouraged to perform those actions which will overcome his weakness. This is obviously something arduous and so he should also do those things necessary to cultivate this gift.

The gift of Fortitude helps the person to carry his cross, i.e. it helps him to carry the burden of his mental illness, whether it is caused by himself or something over which he has no control. Hence, rather than the directee fleeing the problem by trying to avoid or get out from underneath the cross of mental illness, this gift will help him carry it

---

[75]Aumann, *Spiritual Theology*, p. 312.

[76]Tanquerey, *The Spiritual Life*, n. 1330. Aumann's definition is as follows (chapter 11): "A supernatural habit through which the Holy Spirit strengthens the soul for the practice of virtue, with invincible confidence of overcoming any dangers or difficulties that may arise."

[77]All of these effects of Fortitude can be found in Aumann, *Spiritual Theology*, p. 312f.

[78]Tanquerey, *The Spiritual Life*, n. 1333.

[79]Ibid., n. 1334.

valiantly. If he is able to overcome the mental illness, then by carrying the cross courageously, he will be able to overcome it more quickly because he will not avoid those things which are difficult yet helpful to him. If he cannot overcome it, because there are no means, then it will help him to continue living his daily life despite the cross which he has been given. Moreover, if he has no control over it and it is not due to any fault of his own, he will carry the mental illness as a means of mortification and self detachment.[80]

Psychologists should do all that they can to help their directee attain this gift and this means that the directee and the psychologist himself must be leading a life of virtue and grace. The psychologist through prayer and voluntary mortification can merit the change of disposition for the directee to receive the gift or to remove any impediments which might hinder the operation of the gift. The psychologist should inform the directee of the nature of this gift and the requirements in order to possess and cultivate it, so that this valuable means of overcoming his problem will not be lacking.

C. The Gift of Piety

The common or colloquial use of the term piety usually means devout and religious. While that is part of the gift of Piety it is not the same thing as piety in the broad sense. Rather, the gift of Piety has a very specific meaning. Piety is a gift of the Holy Spirit infused in the will[81] by which one has a filial love for God as Father, and a sentiment[82] of universal love for all men as brothers and children of the same Heavenly Father.[83] The very notion of the gift indicates that it is in the will insofar as it moves one to love God, not merely as Creator and Lord but as Father, i.e. in a familial and affectionate[84] sense.[85] For this reason, we see St Paul saying "you have received the spirit of adoption of sons, whereby we cry: Abba (Father)."[86] This gift has a two-fold aspect to it: on the one hand, it is that gift by which we exhibit a proper cult flowing

---

[80]The full import and value of this statement can only be understood in light of vicarious suffering which will be discussed in a later chapter.

[81]Aumann, *Spiritual Theology*, p. 293.

[82]By sentiment is not meant sentimental, in which the love is governed by passions. Rather, it means that the person loves God in an intimate sense in the will.

[83]Ibid.

[84]By affectionate, one does not mean governed by passion. Rather it means a desire for intimacy and close union with God. Since the gift is governed by the Holy Spirit and faith, it proceeds from right understanding as the principle of its loving and not from passion. However, it may involve consequent passion insofar as redundancy is concerned, i.e. what is in the will may flow over into the imagination and lower powers, but the passions are not the governing principle, rather they are governed by the right faith and love.

[85]ST II-II, q.121, a. 1.

[86]Romans 8:15.

from duty (*officium*) toward God.[87] Hence, it perfects the virtue of religion[88] (justice to God) by which we give due worship to God. This gift therefore makes our worship of God proceed from rightly ordered love rather than from disordered appetite. It draws us closer to God so that we do not perform our acts of religion as if from a distance from God, but recognize His intimate presence. The second aspect of this gift consists in seeing God as one's Father, and since all men share in the same nature, it recognizes all men as pertaining to God and as being the sons of God. Therefore, this gift approaches them through this familial love of God.[89] It is from this aspect of the gift which arises the cult of the saints.[90]

We can see therefore that this gift has several effects. The first is that it gives to us a filial respect and love toward God, our heavenly Father.[91] This avoids the problem often seen in modern Catholic circles in which people handle sacred things and talk about God in such a way as to lack proper respect. Filial does not mean familiar in the sense of approaching God without respect. The second effect is that it gives us a generous and tender knowledge that leads us to sacrifice self for God and His glory in order to please Him.[92] The third is an affectionate obedience which sees in the Commandments and God's counsels the wise and paternal expression of the divine will in our regard.[93] This aspect essentially means that we see the wisdom of the providential plan regarding ourselves since we know that God Who loves us as a Father would never abandon us or seek what is bad for us. This is important for psychology insofar as it helps us to recognize that when bad things happen to us, a) they are not from God and b) God allows them for the sake of our betterment, just as a father allows his son to do something difficult to make him strong. The fourth is that it enables us to adore the

---

[87]ST II-II, q. 121, a. 1.

[88]Tanquerey, *The Spiritual Life*, n. 1325 and Aumann, *Spiritual Theology*, p. 293. For a coverage of the virtue of religion, see ST II-II, q. 81.

[89]ST II-II, q. 121, a. 1, ad 3 and Aumann, *Spiritual Theology*, p. 293. It is because this gift approaches men as sons of God that patriotism takes on a higher significance than merely that which is accorded it through the infused virtue of piety or acquired virtue of justice. Patriotism, as it proceeds from the gift recognizes the common good for other men as something necessary for them to reach their salvation. So, in this sense, true patriotism seeks the salvation of the members of a given country as governed by the proximity of charity in relation to those with whom we live. In effect, this gift moves one to seek the good of country for the sake of the salvation of the souls of those in the country. It is for this reason that treason is not only a sin against justice, it is a sin against God as Father to the souls of those whom one places in jeopardy by virtue of one's treason.

[90]ST II-II, q. 121, a. 1, ad 3. The cult of the saints will be discussed in a later chapter.

[91]Tanquerey, *The Spiritual Life*, n. 1325 and Aumann, *Spiritual Theology*, p. 294.

[92]Tanquerey, *The Spiritual Life*, n. 1325.

[93]Ibid.

ineffable mystery of the divine paternity within the Trinity.[94] Fifth, it arouses a filial confidence in the heavenly Father.[95] Sixth, it causes us to see our neighbors as children of God and brothers in Jesus Christ.[96] Lastly, it moves us to love all those persons and things that are related to the Fatherhood of God and the Christian brotherhood.[97]

There are different ways to cultivate this gift. Again aside from recollection, prayer and fidelity to grace: 1) we can cultivate a spirit of being adopted children of God.[98] 2) We can cultivate a spirit of universal kinship toward all mankind.[99] 3) We can consider all things, even material things, as pertaining to the house of God.[100] 4) We should cultivate the spirit of complete abandonment to God.[101] 5) We can frequently meditate upon the texts of Scripture which portray the goodness and the paternal mercy of God towards men and particularly towards the just;[102] and lastly, 6) we can try to transform our ordinary actions into acts of religion by doing them in order to please God our Father.[103]

The psychological benefits of this gift are numerous. First, we can say that any mental problem a person has in regards to others can be helped by this gift, e.g. spouses will suffer marital difficulties because they have interiorly fostered an adversarial view towards each other, insofar as the other is seen as impeding them from what they want. In this respect, the gift of Piety helps one to recognize that the spouse is also a son or daughter of God and so one will naturally seek to avoid interior inclinations, which lead

---

[94]Aumann, *Spiritual Theology*, p. 294

[95]Ibid.

[96]Ibid.

[97]Ibid., p. 295. St. Thomas observes that this gift pertains to the following beatitudes: "Blessed are the meek: for they shall possess the land," "Blessed are they that hunger and thirst after justice: for they shall have their fill," and "Blessed are the merciful: for they shall obtain mercy," in III Sent., d. 34, q. 1, a. 4; ST I-II, q. 69, a. 3, ad 3 and ST II-II, q. 121, a. 2.

[98]Aumann, *Spiritual Theology*, p. 295. This means that we approach God with reverence and love but also love our neighbor for God's sake as the adopted sons of God.

[99]Ibid. This is important because it shifts the proper kinship of man from emotionalism to a true foundation in God as our mutual Father. Just as children out of respect for their parents will try to get along, so will those who have this gift try to have a respect for God by treating His other sons and daughters with justice.

[100]Ibid. By this aspect we can see that we ought not to be selfish and self absorbed, even in relation to things since they are ultimately for God and not ourselves.

[101]Ibid. Clearly, if He is all knowing and He has a Fatherly love for us, we can completely abandon ourselves to Him knowing that His providence in our regard will never be lacking.

[102]Tanquerey, *The Spiritual Life*, n. 1329. By the just is meant those in the state of grace.

[103]Ibid.

to the relationship being adversarial. This can also be said of those who neglect their spouse for any reason whatsoever, since the person will recognize the necessity of treating the spouse with the respect and solicitude due to a son or daughter of God. Psychologists should encourage those who suffer certain kinds of marital problems to cultivate the gift of Piety, of course, not only by doing those things just mentioned but also by staying in the state of grace. Here we see that spouses must recognize that when one of the spouses does not lead a life in accordance with grace, it can have an effect on the relationship, since the gifts and infused moral virtues will not be operative in their marriage.[104]

This gift can also help those who suffer some problem which causes them to perform acts which violate the order of justice regarding others, e.g. kleptomaniacs will see that the things they are stealing pertain to God and not themselves. They should not violate the order of justice regarding neighbor insofar as they both have the same Father in Heaven. In effect, this gift helps one to respect his neighbor and so one is less likely to steal. This gift can also avert problems of anger. Since this gift aids one in viewing one's neighbor as someone who must be respected because he is a son of God, then the person is less likely to view the other as someone to be harmed for the sake of vindication. Rather, the person's desire for vindication will be tempered, which means the person's conduct will proceed from meekness. Again, psychologists must look at the person's problem and view it in light of the supernatural mechanism of the spiritual life and this will help them to see which supernatural aids will benefit their directees. Thus the psychologist will dispose himself to the gifts in his own life and seek to foster the right dispositions for the gifts in his directees.

D. The Gift of Counsel

Counsel is a gift by which man is directed by God Who comprehends all in his counsel about particulars.[105] Since man cannot know all of the particulars which might affect the outcome of his action, God gives the gift of Counsel so that he might receive counsel from God[106] on what to do so as to arrive at his end. Because Counsel concerns particulars and since it aids man in doing the right thing, it corresponds to prudence as aiding and perfecting prudence.[107] This follows from the fact that, by Counsel, man's reason is perfected and aided insofar as it is regulated and moved by the Holy Spirit.[108] While prudence concerns three actions, viz. counsel, judgment and command, it differs from the gift of Counsel insofar as Counsel is God moving and aiding the intellect regarding the process of taking counsel. From this we see that Counsel is a gift of the

---

[104]This is one of the advantages of Catholic marriage and conversely a disadvantage of mixed marriages.

[105]ST II-II, q. 52, a. 1 and ibid., ad 2.

[106]Ibid.

[107]ST II-II, q. 52, a. 2.

[108]Ibid.

Holy Spirit which resides in the intellect and it concerns those things which are useful,[109] i.e. those things which will help us to attain our End. As the gift of Counsel aids man in the process of taking counsel, it is contrary to precipitation[110] and therefore it is contrary to disordered passions, gluttony or things of this sort,[111] which may affect our judgment about what to do.

Counsel guides us in all things ordered to eternal life, whether they are necessary for salvation or not.[112] Now God gives us counsel that we may be directed by God Himself to do the right thing.[113] Since God is omniscient,[114] man receives direction from Him, in relation to acting, as if taught through the certitude of the Holy Spirit above a human mode.[115] In effect, the gift of Counsel gives us certitude about what to do since God is that which moves us and He cannot fail in knowing what to do. Hence, the mode of certitude exceeds human reason.[116]

Given the aforesaid, Aumann defines Counsel as "a supernatural infused habit by which the Holy Spirit enables one to judge rightly in particular events what ought to be done in view of the supernatural ultimate end and personal sanctification."[117] In this we see that the gift of Counsel pertains to all of those things which help us not only reach our ultimate end, but also those things which are ordered to our ultimate end, viz. our sanctification. Tanquerey defines it as that which "perfects the virtue of prudence by making us judge promptly and rightly, as by a sort of supernatural intuition, what must be done, especially in difficult cases."[118] Tanquerey brings out the fact that Counsel aids us in difficult cases and this is clear from the nature of the gift, insofar as God can see particulars that we cannot and therefore can direct us when the situation becomes difficult to discern. In regard to the promptness mentioned by Tanquerey, Aumann remarks that "it is therefore evident that the gift of counsel is necessary in those cases in which an immediate judgment is required, but there is neither the ability nor the opportunity to make the decision under the virtue of prudence, which works always in

---

[109]Ibid.

[110]See Vol. I, chap. 9.

[111]See III Sent., d. 34, q. 1, a 2.

[112]ST II-II, q. 62, a. 4, ad 2.

[113]In ST I-II, q. 69, a. 3, ad 3. St. Thomas observes that counsel is ordered toward directing.

[114]ST I, q. 14 and SCG I, cc. 44-55

[115]III Sent., d. 34, q. 1, a. 2 and ibid., d. 35, q. 2, a. 4, qu. 1.

[116]St. Thomas observers that this gift corresponds to the fifth beatitude of "Blessed are the merciful: for they shall obtain mercy," not as to choosing mercy but as being guided by mercy. See III Sent., d. 34, q. 1, a. 4 and ST II-II, q. 52, a. 4.

[117]Aumann, *Spiritual Theology*, p. 279.

[118]Tanquerey, *The Spiritual Life*, n. 1321.

a human mode."[119] In effect, Counsel helps us discern the right thing to do when we may not have the time to sort things out or when it concerns things which are beyond our ability to know. Given this, it is clear that man's reason can fail and so this gift is necessary for salvation,[120] since there are certain situations which arise in a man's life about which he cannot know what to do and this ignorance may impede his reaching heaven.

From this we can see that Counsel has several effects. The first is that it preserves one from the danger of a false conscience[121] insofar as it will help one to judge the right thing to do. Second, it provides the solution to many difficult and unexpected situations and problems.[122] Third, it inspires superiors with the most apt means of governing others.[123] Lastly, it increases one's docility to legitimate superiors.[124] One will seek counsel and do as the superiors suggest since the superiors, in having this gift, will guide one in doing the right thing.

There are a number of ways to cultivate this gift. As always, recollection, prayer and cooperation with grace are necessary. Secondly, a profound humility[125] is necessary since one must recognize his ignorance so that he will be docile to the motion of God regarding what to do. Third, reflection and patience are necessary in order to realize that in some circumstances all human diligence is insufficient and to have confidence in God that in His time He will move the person with the knowledge of what to do.[126] Next, docility and obedience[127] are necessary for if we are not docile (i.e. willing to be led to the truth) or obedient, the Holy Spirit will not help us. Fifth, we must accustom ourselves to listen to God (Holy Spirit) and judge all things by His light, rather than allowing ourselves to be influenced by mere human considerations.[128] We cannot let human respect and human ways of thinking distract us from doing what God would have us do. Lastly, we must always act upon His promptings so that He will be more inclined to show us what to do in the future. Just as any person is more willing to suggest what to do to someone who shows that he is open to the suggestions given him, so the Holy Spirit will be more operative by the gift of Counsel if we are compliant.

There are several considerations regarding the directee in light of this gift. The first is that the directee must stop looking at his problem and what do to from the point

---

[119]Aumann, *Spiritual Theology*, p. 279.

[120]Ibid., and Tanquerey, *The Spiritual Life*, n. 1323.

[121]Aumann, loc. cit.

[122]Ibid.

[123]ibid. p. 280.

[124]Ibid.

[125]Ibid.

[126]Ibid.

[127]Ibid.

[128]Tanquerey, *The Spiritual Life*, n. 1324.

of view that is engendered by the problem. He must start looking to God to be led out of his problem. In this regard, directees should foster a habit of praying for the gift of Counsel as a means of disposing themselves to being led by God. Next, the directee must seek a psychologist who is holy and disposed towards the operations of the gifts so that he can have confidence in the counsels of the psychologist. Since mental illness is a disorder or bad habit in the intellect, the directee, as a rule, cannot expect to be guided by the Holy Spirit in his deliberations if the mental illness constitutes an impediment to the function of the gift of Counsel. This indicates that he should look outside of himself for the initial guidance on what to do. As the mental illness begins to be overcome, the intellect will become more suited to the operations of the Holy Spirit and so this gift will become more operative. The directee must eventually look to God, as the source of his knowledge of what to do and what not to do.

The psychologist must pray for this gift for reasons which are connected. The first is obvious, viz. so that he may give proper counsel and direction to directees. Since much of the psychological advice touches upon matters which can affect the person's reaching the ultimate end, the psychologist must be dependent on God's counsel so as never to lead the directee away from Him. Many times, psychologists have had a directee that posed problems which seemed difficult to figure or sort out. In this regard, if the psychologist is well disposed toward the operations of the gift, God will move him promptly to judge what is the right thing to do in less amount of time than would be achieved through mere human judgment. Lastly, since psychologists are in a position to affect the salvation of others by the advice they give, they must become dependent upon God so that they do not lead people astray, thereby jeopardizing their own salvation. Given this, it is clear that a psychologist must have humility in recognizing his limitations and pray ardently so that he will be disposed toward's God Counsel.

E. The Gift of Understanding

Man needs a light by which he can penetrate to what he cannot know through the natural light of reason and this light is given the name understanding (*intellectus*).[129] This should not be confused with the natural virtue of understanding by which one grasps the first principles of speculative reason, nor should it be confused with the act of understanding of the intellect by which one grasps the essence of a thing. Rather, the gift of Understanding relates first and principally to those things which fall under faith and also to all those things which are ordered to faith.[130] While the gift of Understanding extends to action (*operabilia*), it does not do so principally but insofar as by acting we are regulated by divine reason regarding those things considered and counseled, i.e. we consider things which become the rule (*regula*) for our actions.[131] In this respect, the gift of Understanding is contrary to ignorance of the faith, since it gives one knowledge of

---

[129]ST II-II, q. 8, a. 1.

[130]ST II-II, q. 8, a. 3.

[131]ST II-II, q. 8, a. 3, ad 2.

the things of faith. Just as *intellectus principiorum* helps one to grasp the truth of the first principles of speculative reason, so Understanding helps one to understand the first principles heard regarding the faith.[132] The gift of Understanding a) pertains to the speculative[133] and insofar as it pertains to the speculative, b) it pertains to a cognitive power,[134] i.e. it resides in the intellect and so the gift of Understanding disposes man's mind to be moved by the Holy Spirit[135] so that it has the capacity to penetrate intimately those things pertaining to the faith.[136] For this reason, Aumann defines the gift of Understanding as "a supernatural habit, infused in the soul with sanctifying grace, by which the human intellect, under the illuminating action of the Holy Spirit, is made apt for a penetrating intuition of revealed truths, and even for natural truths, so far as they are related to the supernatural end."[137]

While the gift of understanding helps one to penetrate the meaning of revealed truths, it does so in a divine way (*divino modo*),[138] since it is the Holy Spirit which moves the intellect by the gift. While the gift extends to all revealed truths,[139] when operative, it normally illuminates the mind of man so that he may know a certain supernatural truth.[140] Since it is God who moves one to understanding, this gift gives one certitude about the faith.[141] This certitude of the faith can be understood in two ways. The first is that Understanding gives one certitude about the doctrines of the faith and in this sense it enables one to see that despite the obscurity of the mysteries, they are credible, coherent among themselves and in accord with reason,[142] i.e. that they are true. The second is that it gives certitude to the act of faith by which one gives assent.

While Understanding principally pertains to the speculative insofar as it is

---

[132]III Sent., d. 34, q. 2, a. 2, qu. 1.

[133]ST II-II, q. 8, a. 6.

[134]Ibid.

[135]ST II-II, q. 8, a. 5.

[136]Ibid, a. 6.

[137]Aumann, *Spiritual Theology*, p. 251f. Tanquerey (*The Spiritual Life*, n. 1344) alternatively defines it as "a gift which, under the enlightening action of the Holy Spirit, gives us a deep insight into revealed truths, without however giving a comprehension of the mysteries themselves."

[138]Aumann, *Spiritual Theology*, p. 252 and Tanquerey, *The Spiritual Life*, n. 1344.

[139]Ibid.

[140]ST II-II, q. 8, a. 4. Because it gives us new knowledge of some teaching of the faith, St. Thomas says that Understanding pertains to the way of finding (*via inventionis*) insofar as we "find," as it were, a greater understanding about the truths of the faith. See III Sent., d. 34, q. 2, a. 2, qu. 3.

[141]III Sent., d. 34, q. 1, a. 5 and ST II-II, q. 8, a. 8.

[142]Tanquerey, *The Spiritual Life*, n. 1344.

ordered to supernatural knowledge of the faith,[143] it also pertains to the practical, not so far as to judgment (of the truth) but so far as to apprehension, that those things which are heard (*auditum*[144]) are grasped.[145] Therefore, it is not practical in the same way as Counsel is practical, since Counsel proceeds by judgment. Rather it gives us a right estimation about the end[146] (i.e. God) and therefore we recognize how various means will measure up to being able to arrive at that end. Therefore, of itself, Understanding is not practical except insofar as it provides us knowledge of truths which can govern our action.

St. Thomas observes that Understanding correlates to the sixth beatitude[147] of "Blessed are the pure of heart, for they shall see God."[148] Since sometimes pure of heart refers to purity from bad phantasms and error, the gift of Understanding acts contrary to thinking about God according to bodily phantasms and the perversity of heresy.[149] Essentially, Understanding keeps man from a) thinking about God in physical ways, i.e. in human terms or like created things and b) falling into error about the things of faith.

The gift of Understanding has several effects. The first is that it discloses the hidden meaning of Sacred Scriptures.[150] Next, it reveals the mysterious significance of symbols and figures[151] and so we are able to understand how different things in the Old Testament prefigure things in the New Testament. Third, it reveals spiritual realities under sensible appearances and as a result we are able to see the sublime realities in the ceremonies, etc., in the Church.[152] Fourth, it enables us to contemplate the effects that are contained in causes.[153] Fifth, it makes us see causes through their effects.[154] This

---

[143]ST II-II, q. 8, a. 6.

[144]The *auditum* is something proposed for belief and we come to know it through hearing.

[145]ST I-II, q. 68, a. 4 and ST II-II, q. 8, a. 6, ad 3.

[146]ST II-II, q. 8, a. 5.

[147]III Sent., d. 35, q. 2, a. 2, qu. 2 and ST II-II, q. 8, a. 7.

[148]Matthew 5:8.

[149]III Sent., d. 34, q. 1, a. 4 and ST II-II, q. 8, a. 7.

[150]Aumann, *Spiritual Theology*, p. 252. This line is loaded, to say the least. Since Understanding is founded on faith, then only if a person has right faith can he be enlightened through the gift of Understanding about the Scriptures. Second, given the general proclivity of the academic community to interpret Scripture in ways contrary to the faith, it makes one realize that they do not understand Scripture. Moreover, those who hold that one must put one's faith aside in order to study Scripture have short circuited from the very beginning the process of coming to a deep knowledge of the Scriptures through the gift of Understanding.

[151]Ibid., p. 253.

[152]Ibid.

[153]Ibid. Aumann joins to this effect the following observation: "This is particularly noticeable in contemplatives and in prayerful theologians. After long hours of meditation and study, everything is suddenly illuminated under an impulse of the Spirit. A word or a

essentially means that we are able to see God, the saints, demons, etc., operative in the things we see around us. Sixth, the gift confirms us in our faith.[155] Seventh, on a higher level, this gift helps us to contemplate God.[156] Eighth, it helps us to know a greater number of truths by aiding us to draw from revealed principles the theological conclusions contained therein.[157]

There are a number of ways to cultivate this gift. The first is to practice a vital faith with the help of ordinary grace.[158] This essentially means that one must practice one's faith and try to become holier. The second is to seek perfect purity of soul and body.[159] The third is that one should practice interior recollection.[160] The next is that one must have fidelity to grace[161] and this essentially means that one must cooperate with the grace that God sends one. The fifth is that one must invoke the Holy Spirit[162] so that one can obtain the graces to do the other things mentioned to cultivate this gift. Next, we can humbly implore God to infuse in us the divine light and make acts of faith.[163] Last, we can diligently study the faith so as to dispose our intellect towards the operations of the Holy Spirit in this regard.

The importance of this gift can be quickly grasped by any good Catholic psychologist insofar as many directees end up with mental illnesses because of a flawed understanding about some aspect of faith or about God. This flawed understanding moves them to perform actions which cause their mental illness. Those directees whose mental illness flows from bad theology should dispose themselves toward this gift by the means of cultivation as mentioned above. Psychologists who have directees with this problem should pray and do penance to merit the right disposition of mind for the directees so that God can move them by this gift and thereby avert the false thinking which is leading them to their mental illness. Psychologists should also be knowledgeable in the faith and dispose themselves for this gift so that when a directee asks questions about the faith, God can enlighten the psychologist to understand the truth in a way that will help the directee. Lastly, this gift enables the psychologist to recognize clearly which teaching of the faith the mental illness may contradict. In this

---

statement is then seen in all its depth and meaning."

[154]Ibid.

[155]Tanquerey, *The Spiritual Life*, n. 1346.

[156]Ibid.

[157]Ibid.

[158]Aumann, *Spiritual Theology*, p. 253.

[159]Ibid., p. 254. Purity here refers not merely to matters of the Sixth and Ninth Commandments but to all sin.

[160]Ibid.

[161]Ibid.

[162]Ibid.

[163]Tanquerey, *The Spiritual Life*, n. 1347.

respect, the psychologist will have a greater understanding of mental illness as contrasted with the penetrating understanding of the teachings of the faith gained by this gift. Moreover, since this gift gives us knowledge of what to do by knowing the end to which certain acts relate, this gift will give the psychologist a greater knowledge of the actions that the person can perform so as to remove the mental illness, as the illness may be an impediment to his salvation.

F. The Gift of Knowledge

The gift of Understanding differs from the gift of Knowledge in that the gift of Understanding concerns simple apprehension (of the truths of faith) whereas the gift of Knowledge concerns judgment.[164] To the gift of Knowledge pertains the right judgment of creatures,[165] i.e. it pertains to human or created things.[166] Since Knowledge concerns created things, it provides man with right knowledge about several things. The first is that our perfect good does not pertain to created things,[167] for we see that they cannot completely fulfill our desire for perfect beatitude. Next, since we are able to judge created things rightly, from Knowledge comes sorrow regarding our past errors.[168] In connection with this, the gift of Knowledge enables us to see our defects and the defects of mundane things.[169] Hence, "it enlightens us to the state of our soul," as Tanquerey points out, "as to its secret motions, their source, their motives, and the effects that may result therefrom."[170] From this we see that Knowledge enables us to know quickly and rightly (since it moves by divine instinct) what concerns our own sanctification and the sanctification of others.[171]

Third, Knowledge enables us to know that consolation is not to be had in this life but in the future life.[172] Hence, Knowledge enables us to see that this life is one of sorrow (*valles lacrimarum* – vale of tears). While those without this gift know that this life is difficult and fraught with sorrow, it seems so to them because this life does not always yield what they want from it. Whereas the gift of Knowledge enables us to know that created things cannot fulfill us, that they are fleeting, that man is affected by original sin which has affected the world, etc. In this respect, the gift of Knowledge is often

---

[164]ST II-II, q. 9, a. 1 and Aumann, *Spiritual Theology*, p. 255.

[165]III Sent., d. 35, q. 2, a. 3, qu. 1 and 2 and ST II-II, q. 9, a. 4.

[166]ST II-II, q. 8, a. 6; ibid., 9, a. 2 and Tanquerey, *The Spiritual Life*, n. 1341.

[167]III Sent., d. 35, q. 2, a. 3, qu.1 and 2 and ST II-II, q. 9, a 4.

[168]ST II-II, q. 9, a. 4. For this reason, the gift of Knowledge relates to the beatitude, "Blessed are they that mourn: for they shall be comforted" (Matthew 5:5).

[169]ST I-II, q. 69, a. 3, ad 3. Essentially, man sees that mundane things are fraught with problems in relation to man and so he sees that these things cannot be our end.

[170]Tanquerey, *The Spiritual Life*, n. 1341.

[171]Ibid.

[172]III Sent., d. 34, q. 1, a. 4.

accompanied with suffering insofar as one can see the evil in this world more clearly for what it truly is and so one suffers the evil of the world. On the other hand, the gift has a great psychological benefit, insofar as we see that things in this life should not be the center of our affections and so we are less likely to suffer the sorrow that accompanies the affections being placed in things which change or can be lost.

Since faith is a created thing,[173] the gift of Knowledge can extend to the things of faith[174] and in this sense Knowledge perfects faith.[175] Since Knowledge perfects faith, it enables us to discern what is to be believed and what is not to be believed.[176] Consequently, the gift of Knowledge enables one to overcome those who contradict the faith as well as enabling one to manifest the faith to others.[177] The gift of Knowledge principally concerns the speculative (i.e. it is not concerned with action but truth) and so Knowledge concerns the first truth which is God.[178] But it does not deal with God directly, rather it enables one to judge creatures in relation to God,[179] i.e. it tells us that created things come from God as their origin.[180] Secondarily, Knowledge extends to works insofar as through knowledge of those things which are to be believed, we are guided in our actions.[181]

The gift of Knowledge is a habit in the intellect[182] by which we are moved to judge rightly by the motion of the Holy Spirit; therefore, Knowledge gives us certitude in judgment.[183] From the aforesaid, we can see why Aumann defines it as "a supernatural habit through which the human intellect, under the action of the Holy Spirit, judges rightly concerning created things as related to eternal life and Christian perfection."[184] Since the Holy Spirit is the one that moves our judgment, we can say the gift of Knowledge helps us to see the created order the way God sees it, i.e. as it truly is and in a fuller fashion than is gained through human understanding and science.

---

[173]This can be understood in two ways. The first is in terms of the inherent meaning of the phrase, viz. that revelation and faith itself is something created by God. Only God Himself is uncreated. Secondly, that faith touches secondarily on things and so Knowledge can touch on faith which deals with created things.

[174]ST II-II, q. 9, a. 2, ad 1.

[175]Tanquerey, *The Spiritual Life*, n. 1340.

[176]ST II-II, q. 9, a. 2; ibid., ad 2 and ibid., q. 9, a. 3.

[177]ST II-II, q. 9, a. 1, ad 2.

[178]ST II-II, q. 9, a. 3 and Aumann, *Spiritual Theology*, p. 255.

[179]Tanquerey, *The Spiritual Life*, nn. 1339 and 1341.

[180]Ibid.

[181]III Sent., d. 35, q. 2, a. 3, qu. 2; ibid., ad 1; ST II-II, q. 9, a. 3 and Aumann, *Spiritual Theology*, p. 255.

[182]Ibid.

[183]ST II-II, q. 9, a. 2.

[184]Aumann, *Spiritual Theology*, p. 255.

In addition to the effects listed above, the gift of Knowledge causes several others. The first is it inspires us concerning the best method of conduct with our neighbor as regards eternal life.[185] Second, it detaches us from created things.[186] Third, it teaches us how to use created things in a holy way,[187] since we judge created things from the point of view of God or as God sees them. Fourth, it moves us to repentance and sorrow for our past errors,[188] i.e. it not only gives us knowledge of them but provides the knowledge which moves us to sorrow. Next, it helps us to make right use of created things.[189]

The ways of cultivating this gift are manifold. In addition to recollection, fidelity to grace, invocation of the Holy Spirit[190] and prayer, we can do the following. First, we can consider the vanity of created things[191] and this will dispose our intellect to this gift which helps us to see the vanity of created things. Next, we can accustom ourselves to refer all created things to God.[192] Third, we can oppose energetically the spirit of the world.[193] Fourth, we can see the hand of God in the government of the world and in all events of our life, whether prosperous or adverse.[194] Next, we can cultivate simplicity of heart[195] and we do this by not allowing our heart to become attached to created things and to God at the same time. Lastly, we can always look on creatures with the eyes of faith.[196]

Clearly, the psychological benefits of this gift are many. For this gift, along with other gifts which reside in the intellect, perfects the intellect itself through a habit (disposition). Therefore, of its very nature, this gift corrects mental illness. Moreover, since this gift allows us to see our state of soul and to judge ourselves in light of God, this gift has a natural tendency to undo selfishness, i.e. disordered concern for self. Since it helps one to see himself as he is, it will help him to know which disorders, whether psychological or spiritual, he may have, as well as their cause(s). Conversely, psychologists must cultivate this gift so as to be able to judge directees rightly and to see

---

[185]Ibid., p. 256.

[186]Ibid.

[187]Ibid.

[188]Ibid. The importance of this will be seen in the chapter on Confession.

[189]Tanquerey, *The Spiritual Life*, n. 1342.

[190]Aumann, *Spiritual Theology*, p. 257.

[191]Ibid.

[192]Ibid.

[193]Ibid. By this is meant that we will not follow the way of the world which sees as its end the enjoyment of created things. This gift helps us to keep our focus on God, even when dealing with created things.

[194]Ibid. As to those things that are adverse, see the chapter on purification.

[195]Ibid.

[196]Tanquerey, *The Spiritual Life*, n. 1343.

the best way to proceed in their counseling. This particularly holds true if the mental illness poses a threat to the salvation of the directee.

Because the gift of Knowledge helps us to see created things as they are, we will not become fixated on created things and, as created things ourselves, we will not become fixated on self. This in itself would cure most mental illnesses. Knowledge is opposed to ignorance and since many mental illnesses are caused by people doing things which disorder their faculties because they do not understand the psychological makeup of man, this gift will help them to know the nature of man. Consequently, it will give them an intuitive knowledge (perhaps not always explicit) about what man should be and do. This is seen in certain holy people who tend to know human nature rather well and know what suits man, even though they may not have a philosophical knowledge of man's nature.

One of the byproducts of knowledge is the clearing up of confusion. Confusion is the state which occurs when two contradictory things are melded together in such a way that the person cannot distinguish them properly. The gift of Knowledge gives us the right judgment about those things which can cause confusion, and so it contributes to clarity of mind. Those directees who suffer confusion about self, their state, or their relations with others or to created things should cultivate this gift so as to gain clarity of mind and thereby be able to do what is necessary to correct any disordered faculties they may have.

Since our intellect is ordered toward seeing God Face to face, when we refer all things to God, as this gift enables us to do, our intellect becomes rightly ordered. In this respect, directees who have certain kinds of fixations on self or things can dispose themselves to this gift, so that they are able to refer things to God rather than self and thereby effect right order in their intellect. This will enable them to make right use of things, countering many mental illnesses which involve the wrong use of things, e.g. drug and alcohol abuse, sexual addictions, violent behaviors, etc.

G. The Gift of Wisdom

Wisdom is the name for the gift of the Holy Spirit concerning knowledge of the highest cause simply speaking, i.e. God.[197] Since it concerns God, it pertains to Wisdom to have right judgment about God or divine things in themselves.[198] While the gift of Knowledge enables one to judge the world the way God sees it, the gift of Wisdom enables man to judge God the way He is in Himself. Since every gift has the Holy Spirit as its motive cause, this gift enables one to judge the things of God the way God sees them. Since Wisdom regulates judgment, it resides in the intellect as a subject as to the essence of Wisdom itself.[199] However, St. Thomas observes that Wisdom has charity

---

[197]ST II-II, q. 45, a. 1.

[198]Ibid. and ST II-II, q. 45, aa. 2 and 3.

[199]ST II-II, q. 45, a. 2.

as its cause,[200] which indicates that Wisdom is the effect of charity.[201] Wisdom presupposes faith,[202] for without faith a person would not have the right judgment which flows from the virtue of faith as it inclines one to give assent to the teachings about God, upon which our judgment of God in this life must be based.[203]

Wisdom judges rightly about divine things and divine rules (*regulae*) which comes through charity, so Wisdom presupposes charity.[204] This follows from the fact that Wisdom provides counsel insofar as by the divine, it judges human acts, thereby directing them by the divine rules (*regulae*).[205] Hence, Wisdom also concerns the practical.[206] St. Thomas notes that Wisdom is able to judge (*iudicium*) and order (*ordinare*) insofar as it acts according to the divine rules.[207] Since the intellect is moved by the Holy Spirit, the gift of Wisdom enables one to order and judge infallibly and rightly all things in relation to God.[208] Consequently, men have a certain similitude to God and for this reason they are called "sons of God."[209] Since the wise man (the man with the gift of Wisdom) knows how to order, he is prudent[210] and the teacher of others.[211] Since the wise man can direct or order things prudently, he knows that Wisdom is opposed to foolishness.[212] Hence, the wise also know how to remove

---

[200]ST II-II, q. 45, a. 2 and ibid., q. 45, a. 6, ad 2.

[201]These last two propositions are important since, for St. Thomas, Wisdom is in the intellect but it has as its cause the supernatural virtue of charity in the will. Some have actually proposed that Wisdom resides at once both in the will and in the intellect (See Tanquerey, *The Spiritual Life*, n. 1348); however, such an assertion lacks precision.

[202]ST II-II, q. 45, a. 1, ad 2.

[203]This assertion does not deny that one can make judgments about God from His effects (the created order) which are proper to the intellectual virtue of wisdom. What it indicates is that if man is going to make judgments about God beyond the natural order, he is going to need the supernatural light of faith and the gift of Wisdom.

[204]ST II-II, q. 45, a. 4

[205]ST II-II, q. 45, a. 3.

[206]Ibid.

[207]ST II-II, q. 45, a. 1.

[208]III Sent., d. 34, q. 1, a. 4. Since God is the motive cause and since He cannot fail, when He moves one through this gift, that motion cannot fail.

[209]Ibid.; ST II-II, q. 45, a. 6 and ibid., ad 1. For this reason, Wisdom pertains to the seventh beatitude "Blessed are the peacemakers: for they shall be called the children of God." See Matthew 5:9.

[210]It should be remembered that prudence governs the act of *precipere* or "to command," which involves guiding the lower powers. Hence, since the wise man orders, he can guide others.

[211]III Sent., d. 35, q. 2, a. 1 qu. 2.

[212]ST II-II, q. 46.

impediments to order and so they are called the peacemakers.[213] Since passions (and disorders in the lower faculties) disturb even those who are prudent, the wise man differs from the prudent man insofar as he is not disturbed.[214] As we have noted before, the gifts can be impeded in their operations and so one's appetites must not disturb one if this gift is to be operative.

While Wisdom has a practical side, nevertheless it is fundamentally ordered toward contemplating God.[215] Yet in order to do this, one must turn away from evil and created things and turn to God and for this reason, Fear of the Lord is the beginning of Wisdom.[216] Wisdom implies a certain eminence which suffices in regard to knowing, as in itself it has certitude of great and wonderful things (*magnis et mirabilibus*) which are unknown to others and so the wise are able to judge things others cannot.[217] Theology (*sacra doctrina* or sacred teaching) is called wisdom insofar as through theology, one can consider God. However, theology is a habit of mind (*scientia* or science) and so it is notionally different from the gift of Wisdom.[218]

---

[213]III Sent., d. 34, q. 1, a. 4. Since peace is defined by Augustine as *tranquillitas ordinis* (the tranquility of order), then those who know how to order or establish order, will be peacemakers. However, we may also say conversely that one cannot be a true peacemaker without being rightly ordered and this means one cannot be a true peacemaker without Wisdom. It is not enough to get people to stop fighting; one must establish a right order for the contention or strife to end. On a most profound level, this means that there cannot be perfect peace without governance coming from him who is wise, i.e. no one in charge of the common good can establish lasting and true peace without knowing man's order to God and this comes from the gift of Wisdom. In the context of modern political thought, since God is *de facto* excluded from the political arena, the politics of the day are doomed to foolishness. This will, inevitably, affect people's mental health.

[214]III Sent., d. 35, q. 2, a. 1, qu. 2.

[215]III Sent., d. 35, q. 2, a. 1, qu. 1, ad 1 and ST II-II, q. 45, a. 6, ad 3.

[216]ST II-II, q. 6, a. 3.

[217]III Sent., d. 35, q. 2, a. 1, qu. 1. In connection to this observation, St. Thomas links I Cor. 2:15: "Spiritualis iudicat omnia." From this it would seem to follow that the Holy Spirit cannot move the intellect regarding this gift unless one has a spiritual approach to things. Again, moving this into the domain of the secular, no nation can ever be governed by true wisdom unless its leaders are men with a spiritual approach to the created order. In the domain of psychology, no psychologist will be able to direct his directee rightly without a spiritual understanding and no directee will become perfectly rightly-ordered until he has a spiritual approach to his own life. Given this, we may say that atheists run a greater risk of mental disorder.

[218]ST I, q. 1, a. 6. Aumann (*Spiritual Theology*, p. 271) observes that Wisdom is superior to theology. Moreover, it can also be seen that the gift of Wisdom cannot be gained through theological studies since this gift is infused by God, not acquired by the habit of study; in connection to this see ST I, q. 1, a 6, ad 3. However, theological studies, if rightly carried out, dispose the intellect to this gift. On the other hand, if theological studies are mired down by heresy or take as their focus created things rather than God and created things

Wisdom cannot be in the intellect without charity or grace, i.e. mortal sin destroys Wisdom.[219] The logic in this statement can be seen in light of the nature of mortal sin: mortal sin consists in a turning away from God (an incommunicable good) toward a created or communicable good. Since Wisdom is ordered toward contemplation of God, mortal sin is ordered away from contemplation of God. Therefore, Wisdom is incompatible with mortal sin and cannot exist without sanctifying grace or charity. Conversely, Wisdom is in all of those who have grace, yet Wisdom is by grades and the higher grades of Wisdom are not in all of those who have grace.[220] Since Wisdom orders one toward the contemplation of God and by Wisdom, one sees that God is our final good, Wisdom perfects charity,[221] as one will love God more perfectly.

Given all of this, we can see that Wisdom is a gift of the Holy Spirit which is a habit (disposition) of the possible intellect by which man is moved to contemplate God, order all things to God and judge all things in light of God. For this reason we can say that Wisdom enables man to see God the way He sees Himself. Aumann[222] defines Wisdom as "a supernatural habit, inseparable from charity, by which we judge rightly concerning God and divine things through their ultimate and highest causes under a special instinct and movement of the Holy Spirit, who makes us taste these things by a certain connaturality." Tanquerey formulates the definition in a similar fashion: Wisdom is "a gift which perfects the virtue of charity by enabling us to discern God and divine things in their ultimate principles, and by giving us a relish for them."[223] In these latter two definitions, we see that Wisdom causes a divine delight that enables one to know something of the ineffable joy of eternal beatitude.[224] As the lover takes delight in the beloved and as Wisdom enables us to judge God, then that judgment of God moves the will to delight in God Who is the wise man's beloved. On the other hand, we may say that the foolish do not judge rightly about God and find judgments and discussion of God sorrowful or painful. One of the signs, therefore, of the foolish person, i.e. the person who judges God in a disordered way and by worldly standards, is the suffering of sorrow in relation to divine things.

Aside from the above mentioned effects, wisdom increases charity as well as perfects all of the other virtues.[225] "It renders Faith unshakable because of the quasi-

---

in relation to God, then those "studies" will actually create an indisposition to the gift of Wisdom.

[219]ST I-II, q. 68, a. 5, ad 1 and ST II-II, q. 45, a. 4.

[220]ST II-II, q. 45, a. 5.

[221]Aumann, *Spiritual Theology*, p. 271.

[222]Ibid., p. 270.

[223]Tanquerey, *The Spiritual Life*, n. 1349.

[224]Aumann, *Spiritual Theology*, p. 271.

[225]Tanquerey, *The Spiritual Life*, n. 1350.

experimental knowledge it gives us of the truths of revelation."[226] Next, Wisdom steadies hope and enables us to practice the moral virtues in their highest degree[227] and it makes the virtues truly divine.[228] Wisdom gives the saints a divine sense by which they judge all things.[229] Moreover, it makes the saints live the mysteries of faith in an entirely divine manner[230] and raises the virtue of charity to heroism.

The ways to cultivate this virtue are manifold. In addition to prayer, fidelity to grace and humility, one can cultivate this gift by seeing and evaluating all things from God's point of view.[231] We can combat the wisdom of the world, which is foolishness in the eyes of God.[232] This signifies that one must not judge things in a worldly fashion because in the end it is foolish and leads nowhere. Next, one can detach oneself from the things of this world, however good and useful.[233] Lastly, we can cultivate indifference to spiritual consolations.[234] This is important since some people end up with mental illness due to an over-attachment to spiritual consolations.

The psychological benefits of this gift can be seen in the effects and the nature of the gift. The very nature of the gift is perfective of the intellect and for that reason alone, psychologists and directees should seek it. Moreover, the gift of Wisdom rightly orders the intellect and since mental illness consists in an intellectual disorder, this gift will aid the mentally ill.[235] Since the gift of Wisdom enables the exercise of virtue and since mental illness consists in some kind of intellectual vice or has its cause in disorders and vices in the lower powers, the gift of Wisdom will aid mental health by enabling one to exercise virtues which will strengthen or restore mental health.

Since the gift of Wisdom enables one to see the uselessness of fixations on things of this world, the gift of Wisdom has a direct connection to all forms of fixation.[236] Since it gives one the ability to see the uselessness of fixations, the gift of

---

[226]Ibid.

[227]Ibid. Aumann, *Spiritual Theology*, p. 273.

[228]Ibid.

[229]Ibid., p. 272.

[230]Ibid., p. 272f.

[231]Ibid., p. 273.

[232]Ibid., p. 274.

[233]Ibid. See chapter on detachment.

[234]Ibid.

[235]On the other hand, it should again be noted that the operations of the Holy Spirit through this gift can be impeded by certain kinds of mental illness as well.

[236]Since fixation implies a disorder, one cannot have a fixation on God, properly speaking. However, it is possible that someone, who has problems, does not prudently conduct his life in relation to God, e.g. the person who cannot enter into any discussion without talking about God regardless of whether it is prudent or suitable to the situation. The wise man, whose sole desire and intellectual concern is God, knows when, where and how God is to be mentioned and served. Given the aforesaid, it must be concluded that

Wisdom begets clarity of mind and while Wisdom resides in the possible intellect, it will have an effect on the imagination and cogitative power. This is, of course, of extreme importance because the gift can direct and properly habituate the cogitative power, which in turn will affect the faculties to which it relates. The gift of Wisdom will have a direct impact on the sensitive appetites by presenting them with a phantasm which will cause a resolution in the appetites so that the appetites will not move antecedently or in a disordered way since they will be moved to follow reason alone. It is here that we see the depth of the notion that right reason must govern and direct all of the other faculties, not only for the reason mentioned in the prior volume, but also because, by the operation of Wisdom in the possible intellect (reason), all of the other powers will be rightly ordered.

The aforementioned also means that the wise man has rightly ordered phantasms which in turn rightly order his past memories and his judgment of them, both in the possible intellect and cogitative power. Since the gift of Wisdom coupled with the gift of Knowledge enables one to view the world from God's perspective, it will enable one to remain detached from created things so that they do not cause any mental harm. From this we can make a few observations about directees in relation to this gift. Directees must seek this gift so that they can judge rightly about those things causing them problems. This is particularly important from the point of view of those who suffer severe mental disorders as well as for those who have suffered some tragedy, e.g the death of a spouse, the rape of either oneself or a loved one or things of this kind. When a person can view these things from God's point of view, they can remain detached from them in a rightly ordered fashion. Rather than creating detachment characterized by suppression of intellectual activity or denial, this gift will enable one to see the situation rightly and thereby direct oneself interiorly and exteriorly in a fashion appropriate to the situation. Moreover, it will enable one to see the hand of God in all situations regardless of how dire they might be. This shift of focus enables one to keep a mental balance with regard to exterior things which can easily cause man who suffers from the effects of original sin to fall into mental disorders.

Lastly, this gift is absolutely essential for the good psychologist, for it will give him a way of judging his directee which will truly benefit him. It will aid him never to give advise which is contrary to the directee's advancement toward God and, contained under this notion, the psychologist will see that the directee's mental illness is an impediment toward perfect union with God. Since Wisdom moves charity and gives delight in it, the psychologist, animated by the charity moved by Wisdom, will have a strong desire to aid the directee in overcoming his problems.

---

directees whose religious practices are causing them mental illnesses are not engaging in rightly ordered religious practices. On the other hand, it must not be assumed that just because someone is engaging in religious practices or if God is the most important thing in his life, there is something mentally wrong with him.

Conclusion

Given the aforesaid, we see that the gifts of the Holy Spirit are necessary on the side of the directee and of the psychologist. They provide psychologists with the necessary habits by which God can be an active part in their counseling of directees on all levels. They will aid them in maintaining proper detachment from their directees (Fear of the Lord and Counsel) as well as giving them a true love for their profession as it is viewed in relation to God (Knowledge and Wisdom). The gifts will keep them from engaging in the profession for financial gain (Fear of the Lord and Piety). They will give them the strength to suffer (Fortitude) whatever is necessary to direct the directee according to prudence (Counsel). They will give them a true selflessness (Fear of the Lord) in relation to the directee so that the directee never suffers from the psychologist's own disordered personal concerns. In relation to directees, these gifts affect every faculty which has a capacity to cause mental illness or health. All of these gifts will enable the directee to relate rightly to those things which may cause him difficulty, whether they be from an interior cause or from an exterior cause. Finally, every psychologist must ascertain which gift the directee's problems contradict and counsel his directee in the means of cultivating the gift or gifts which will aid him. In so doing, the psychologist will help the directee to remove any impediments toward the operations of these gifts and thereby greatly aid the directee in the advancement of mental perfection.

Chapter 6: Fruits of the Holy Spirit

The richness of the spiritual life manifests the providence of God in our regard, that He desires that we partake of a life far exceeding what is visible. The depth and the height to which man is able to achieve by the grace of God is only revealed to and known by the person who turns away from the shallowness of the life of the flesh, i.e. the life of the appetites and who through diligence in study and prayer comes to the knowledge meant for those who share a life of intimacy with God. Clearly this is seen when considering the fruits of the Holy Spirit. As a person begins to achieve a level of virtue sanctified by the presence of God within the soul, manifestations of the work of God in the soul begin to flourish in a way noticeable to the person in whom God dwells. In the context of psychology, the fruits of the Holy Spirit place in relief a picture of man's mental health or illness and their causes, not yet seen in their fullness. While one can argue that such an observation can be said of what is discussed in any chapter in this three-volume series, and even more so of those to come, the fruits of the Holy Spirit gauge mental health and illness by providing a supernatural measurement by which we can judge the rectitude of man's faculties.

I. The Fruits in General

A fruit, according to the common use of the term, is produced by a plant and it implies perfection insofar as it is the last in the stage of a plant's growth.[1] Furthermore, the term fruit implies a certain sweetness.[2] For only that which is last and having delight is given the name fruit.[3] In all created things, operation is the second act of the agent and it is delightful if it suits the agent.[4] Therefore, in the man who possesses sanctifying grace (first act), the acts of the fruits of the Holy Spirit (second act) are delightful. "Acts of virtue sometimes are distasteful to us but once we grow accustomed to the practice of virtue, joy is had in virtue and the act of virtue."[5] Our operations or acts, insofar as they are certain effects of the Holy Spirit acting in us, have the notion of a fruit.[6] In man, a fruit of the Holy Spirit is any virtuous work in which man delights.[7]

---

[1] ST I-II, q. 70, a. 1.

[2] Ibid.

[3] Ibid.; ibid., ad 1; ibid., q. 70, a. 2; *Ad Galatas* V, l. 6 and Tanquerey, *The Spiritual Life*, nn. 1359-1360.

[4] ST I-II, q. 70, a. 1. First act is the act of existence of a thing, whereas second act refers to the operations that a thing performs.

[5] Tanquerey, *The Spiritual Life*, n. 1360.

[6] ST I-II, q. 70, a. 1 and ibid., ad 1.

[7] ST I-II, q. 70, a. 2; *Ad Galatas* V, l. 6 and Aumann, *Spiritual Theology*, p. 98.

When we perform certain actions arising from virtues,[8] whether infused or the Gifts of the Holy Spirit, in which we take delight, then these are called fruits.

Since the Holy Spirit is in us through grace,[9] through which we acquire the habits of virtue and by which we are made strong so that we can work (act) according to virtue – through the indwelling of the Holy Spirit or sanctifying grace we have the fruits.[10] Since a fruit proceeds from some seed or root, the distinction of the fruits are obtained according to the diverse processions of the Holy Spirit in us (branches, as it were). So we may say that when a soul responds faithfully to the actual graces which set in motion the virtues and gifts, the soul performs acts of virtue.[11]

In order to increase the fruits in ourselves we must observe three things. The first is that we must practice fidelity to grace, which consists in our always accepting the graces that come to us and acting according to them.[12] Second, we must do those things which remove any impediments to the operations of the virtues and the gifts.[13] Third, we must strive for excellence in grace, i.e. we become holy by growing in sanctifying grace. As the indwelling of the Holy Spirit grows by means of sanctifying grace and as the impediments are removed for the operations of the Holy Spirit, then the fruits of the Holy Spirit will flourish.[14]

The works of the flesh and sin are *praeter naturam* (aside from nature or contrary to nature) of those things which God has put in our nature.[15] In this sense, since the works of the flesh (disordered appetites) are contrary to reason, they are contrary to our nature. The Holy Spirit moves man through his mind, whereas the desires of the flesh move through sensitive appetites. This is an opposing motion to the motion of the Holy Spirit[16] and so the works of the flesh are contrary to the fruits.[17]

There are twelve fruits of the Holy Spirit[18] and they can be divided in several

------

[8]*Ad Galatas* V, l. 6; Tanquerey, *The Spiritual Life*, n. 1359 and Aumann, *Spiritual Theology*, p. 98

[9]See next chapter.

[10]*Ad Galatas* V, l. 6. St. Thomas refers here to Romans 6: 22 (Habetis fructum in sanctificationem – you will have fruit in sanctification).

[11]Tanquerey, *The Spiritual Life*, n. 1359.

[12]Just as a plant must accept the water and nutrients given by the gardener, so must we be faithful and accept the graces sent to us.

[13]Just as a gardener must prune a tree and uproot weeds, so we must remove any impediments or imperfections which impede the operations of the Holy Spirit.

[14]Just as a plant of the same species normally grows larger when the root or stock is larger, so we will have greater operations of the Holy Spirit when we increase His indwelling from which the fruits flow.

[15]*Ad Galatas* V, l. 6.

[16]ST I-II, q. 70, a. 4.

[17]Ibid. and *Ad Galatas* V, l. 6.

[18]See Galatians 5:22f and ST I-II, q. 70, a. 3.

ways. However, St. Thomas divides them according to three distinctions which give clarity to what the fruits are. (1) There are those fruits in which the soul of man is ordered within itself (*in se*). (2) There are those fruits in which the soul of man is ordered to that which is near (*iuxta*) the soul, and lastly, (3) there are those fruits in which the soul is ordered in its relation to that which is below (*infra*) the soul.

II. The Fruits in Particular

A. Charity (*Caritas*)

Charity is the first of those fruits in which the soul of man is ordered within itself.[19] The soul is well disposed in itself when it relates properly to good and evil[20] and the first disposition of the human soul to the good is through love, which is the first affection and the root of all affections.[21] Hence the first fruit is charity in which the Holy Spirit is particularly given as its proper simulation,[22] since the Holy Spirit is love.[23] Charity is also the first fruit because all other fruits flow from charity.[24] Through charity we have a close union to the spiritual by which one judges all other things.[25] This effectively means that through charity we are able to view things from a spiritual point of view. Since charity is the love of God and love of neighbor for the sake of God,[26] charity enables one to view all of the created order through the lens of God, if you will, and so through charity, we are able always to take a spiritual approach to life.

Charity is contrary to fornication which seeks to satisfy lust out of wedlock and as a result fornication is contrary to the person being wedded to God.[27] Since charity is that by which we have union with God and since God is our ultimate end, then only by avoiding fornication and the sins of the flesh is a person able to reach his ultimate end and be happy. As fornication and sins of the flesh arise in a person and society, charity is consequently extinguished. The proper effect of the death of charity is unhappiness, since the person or society lacking charity will not be directed toward God as to their ultimate end. Therefore, if the directee is to be happy, he cannot engage in fornication nor the sins of the flesh; even if a directee thinks that fornication is making him happy,

---

[19]ST I-II, q. 70, a. 3.

[20]Ibid.

[21]Ibid.

[22]See next chapter on grace.

[23]Ibid. That the Holy Spirit is the love expressed between God the Father and God the Son, see ST I, q. 37 (see also ST I, q. 20).

[24]*Ad Galatas* V, l. 6.

[25]III Sent., d. 34, q. 1, a. 5.

[26]See chapter on the infused and theological virtues for more thorough treatment of charity.

[27]ST I-II, q. 70, a. 4 and *Ad Galatas* V, l. 6.

he must be taught the true nature of his unhappiness.[28]

When considering this fruit psychologically, we can get an idea about what should be the proper state of the psychologist and the directee. If the psychologist is able to keep a proper spiritual perspective regarding the directee's problems, he is more likely to be able to direct the directee not only regarding the supernatural means but he is able to direct properly the natural means by spiritualizing them, that is by directing them under the spiritual lens.[29] To the degree that the psychologist lacks charity, to that degree he is unable to counsel the directee in right order. For this reason, we see, again, that the moral and spiritual state of the psychologist is critical in obtaining right advice. As to the directee, if he is not leading a life of charity but of the flesh, he will not have right order and he will not take delight in spiritual things or things of God since he will not take delight in loving God. On the other hand, the directee can be directed to practice charity and stay in the state of grace so that this fruit is operative in him, thereby enabling him to take a proper spiritual attitude toward his problems in particular and his life in general. Any activity which causes the loss of charity, i.e. anything that is mortally sinful, should be excluded from the directee's life. Here the sins of the flesh are seen as particularly damaging as they destroy the delight taken in a life of right order according to charity. Therefore, the natural law as well as the teaching of revelation must be counseled to the directee.

B. Joy (*Gaudium*)

Every lover takes joy in being joined to the beloved and so joy necessarily follows upon charity.[30] Since charity always has God present, joy follows.[31] We may also say that one takes joy in the good of charity and this joy is delightful, i.e. one takes delight in one's union with God. Since joy follows on charity, joy is the second of those fruits by which the soul is ordered in itself (with respect to the good).[32] Because the joy is taken in a supernatural object, the fruit of joy is greater that any joy than can be had from a purely natural thing.

---

[28]It is here that we come to see that the term "gay" is ineptly applied to homosexuals and their behavior. Since homosexual behavior is ordered toward the flesh, i.e. it is a sin of the flesh, by its very nature it is incompatible with charity and therefore can never make a person happy. This explains why, while many homosexuals will insist that they are happy, objective observations clearly reveal that they are not.

[29]By spiritualizing the problem, both the natural and the supernatural means are able to be employed and so the directee's recovery will be accelerated.

[30]ST I-II, q. 70, 3.

[31]Ibid. and III Sent., d. 34, q. 1, a. 5. God is always present when charity is present, since charity is present when sanctifying grace which is the indwelling of the Blessed Trinity is present. See the next chapter on grace.

[32]ST I-II, q. 70, a. 3.

St. Thomas observes that by uncleanness (*immunditia*)[33] we must understand whatever disturbances arise from fornication.[34] In the prior volume as well as in the chapter on sin in this volume, it was noted that violations of the divine positive law or the natural law lead to disorders in the soul. Clearly, then, we can see that when a person makes anything other than God his ultimate end, he will suffer disturbances, as this path is contrary to man's nature. Consequently, we may say that any action which causes mental illness, since it is contrary to nature, is also going to cause disturbance in the soul, perhaps at times imperceptible, but nevertheless there. Sometimes the disturbance is noticed after the person has been freed from the mental illness and only then does he notice the tranquility. St. Thomas then observes that these disturbances are opposed to the joy of tranquility.[35]

In regard to the directee, he must be counseled not to be worldly and to pursue God above all. In so doing, the joy which is a fruit of the Holy Spirit will arise in him. Otherwise, the directee will be consigned to suffer disturbances of the soul and never experience the spiritual joy proper to a life in God. Psychologists who, out of their own weakness or ignorance, allow directees to continue in sin are impeding this fruit in their directees. Given the aforesaid, joy can be a gauge of mental health and illness. As a person sinks into mental illness, there is not the right order in the faculties of the soul, which arises from charity, and as a result there is no joy. Thus, mental illness is manifested by a lack of spiritual joy, i.e. the lack of the fruit of the Holy Spirit of joy. However, as a person gains proficiency in the spiritual life, joy will naturally reveal the right order in the faculties and therefore the presence of mental health. However, we must also observe that lack of joy may not necessarily be a sign of mental illness; it is possible for a person to fall into mortal sin and not lose his psychological equilibrium. While his psychological equilibrium may not be perfect, nevertheless it will remain sufficient so as not to impede the right use of reason and therefore will not fall in the

---

[33]Notice should be taken from the etymology of the word *immunditia,* which is *in mundus,* literally meaning "in the world." So one is unclean because one becomes worldly or looks for his love in this world. Something is dirty because the dirt is in the wrong place, i.e. when dirt is in a field we do not say it is dirty, but when dirt is on one's shirt or in the house, we say it is dirty. In the same way, man is spiritually "dirty" or unclean when he allows the world to enter into his soul, where it does not belong.

[34]In the Old Testament, *fornicatio* did not refer necessarily to the conjugal act outside of wedlock. It had a broader meaning as well, insofar as it referred to idolatry. When the Jews worshiped pagan gods or broke the covenant with the true God they were said to have fornicated insofar as they had joined themselves to something other than God. In this sense, the covenant of the Old Testament was viewed like a marriage contract, so that if one made anything one's god other than Yahweh, one had "fornicated." Therefore, when St. Thomas says that we must see joy as opposed to fornication, we can take that both in the strict sense as a conjugal act outside marriage or as making anything other than God one's god.

[35]ST I-II, q. 70, a. 4 and *Ad Galatas* V, l. 6.

domain of mental illness.[36]

C. Peace (*Pax*)

The perfection of joy is peace and this is with respect to two things:[37] the first is with respect to the quiet from exterior troubles, for one cannot take joy in a thing perfectly if one is disturbed from the outside. When one's heart is made perfectly peaceful in one thing, i.e. when one's heart comes to rest in one thing alone, he is not able to be molested or disturbed, for he thinks of other things as nothing. As a result, as one's heart comes to rest in God alone through charity, then peace arises as the fruition of God, i.e. the fruit of the Holy Spirit of peace.[38] The second is that, as one rests in God alone through charity, there is a quieting or calming (*sedatio* in Latin) of the fluctuating desires. As one's desires come to rest in God alone, one desires nothing else. Therefore, one's appetites will not vacillate or fluctuate regarding other things and so peace takes over the soul.

Since peace is the tranquility which follows upon the joy arising from charity, peace is the third of those fruits by which the soul is ordered in itself (with respect to the good).[39] Moreover, since the fruit of the Holy Spirit of peace implies a coming to rest in God alone, idolatry, by reason of which war is being waged against the gospel of God, is opposed to peace.[40] Anything which goes contrary to the teachings of revelation, resulting in man committing idolatry by having something other than God as his good, goes contrary to peace. We can also say, therefore, that fornication or any of the sins of the flesh by their nature cause disturbances of the soul and therefore a lack of peace.[41]

In the context of psychology, we see that peace is a sign of mental health. For if one is rightly ordered, thereby indicating that reason is acting according to its nature and not being impeded or disturbed by lower powers in their inclination toward things other than God, then peace is a sign of mental health. On the other hand, lack of peace may be a sign of mental illness, for if the various faculties are not working in concert, reason will be impeded by the disturbance of the lower powers and as a result a lack of peace arises. But this peace is not merely a natural peace, although that is part of it. Rather, this is a peace that is supernatural, insofar as the faculties are not only ordered

---

[36]This conclusion must be seen in light of perfect mental health in heaven, which will be discussed in the conclusion to this volume.

[37]The sources of the following paragraph are III Sent., d. 34, q. 1, a. 5 and ST I-II, q . 70, a. 3.

[38]Peace is defined by St. Augustine (and accepted as such by St. Thomas) as the tranquility of order. When various parts within a society or a person are rightly ordered among themselves, then tranquility (lack of disturbance) arises.

[39]ST I-II, q. 70, a. 3.

[40]ST I-II, q. 70, a. 4.

[41]This is one of the reasons why one must have perfect detachment from any created good in order to reach God or have perfect peace.

within themselves but to God, which is a supernatural ordering. For that reason, supernatural peace, which is able to keep the faculties perfectly focused on one Object that perfectly satisfies, is greater than any peace that arises from tranquility in the soul which is simply due to a lack of natural disturbances. Nevertheless, both supernatural and natural peace are signs of mental health.

However, a lack of peace does not necessarily indicate disorder. For example, during a time of war, if the state is waging a war that is truly just, there will be peace arising from right conscience, even though exteriorly the state is fighting, even violently. It is here that we see the necessity of understanding the natural law and the divine positive law, for the men and the society that wage war for what is truly good are still rightly ordered within themselves, in relation to others and in relation to God. The exterior battles do not disturb their peace interiorly, for insofar as they are rightly ordered, they will see the war as something good and in congruity with their ordering to God and so interior peace will not be lost. However, if they wage an unjust war, it by nature causes unrest and lack of interior peace. On the other hand, we may also say that not waging war when it is rightly ordered is contrary to interior peace, as one seeks exterior peace at the expense of right interior order of conscience and man to God. Consequently, not fighting a war, whether it is with another nation, or in the form of small spiritual and natural battles that occur in our daily lives, can actually militate against mental health by deviating from the path of right reason which sees the battle as a necessary thing in the order of justice, either to man or to God.

D. Patience (*Patientia*)

Patience is the fourth of those fruits in which the soul is ordered in itself, yet it follows the prior three due to the fact that patience deals with evil rather than the good.[42] While peace keeps one from being disturbed by desires in relation to the good, patience keeps the soul from being disturbed by the imminence or presence of evil.[43] Patience is a constancy of soul in that the soul is not broken with respect to self.[44] When the act of patience occurs in the soul as a fruit of the Holy Spirit, the person remains constant and unbroken in his equanimity despite the evils which occur to him or outside

---

[42]ST I-II, q. 70, a. 3.

[43]Ibid. It should be noted that patience and long-suffering (the next fruit) are switched here as in comparison to their treatment in the *Secunda Secundae*; see ST II-II, q. 136. Patience in the *Secunda Secundae* deals with waiting for the good whereas long-suffering deals with enduring evils.

[44]III Sent., d. 34, q. 1, a. 5.

of him. Patience is contrary to witchcraft,[45] enmities,[46] contentions,[47] emulations,[48] animosity and dissensions,[49] since it makes one able to remain peaceful in the face of these evils.

Psychologically, as a person becomes holier and this fruit comes to act in one's soul, one can deal more effectively with those things which are likely to cause him harm. It helps him to keep his self-possession when he comes up against these evils. Those who are mentally ill normally do not maintain self-possession when they encounter evils, particularly when a specific evil is the cause of their problems. In this regard, the psychologist must counsel, among other things, the striving for holiness so that this fruit will have great fruition in the soul. Instead of the experience of these evils being unpleasant, one will have the delight of being self-possessed through patience. We see here how encouraging people to act out their anger or hatred, which is contrary to patience, is not healthy psychologically since it militates against their self-possession. By encouraging them to act out their anger, charity will be diminished and the fruit of patience will begin to wain. This is not only true with respect to the supernatural order in regard to the fruit of the Holy Spirit of patience, but it holds on a natural level as well. For as one acts according to the antecedent passion of anger or hatred, it merely increases the antecedent passion.[50] Psychologists must counsel holiness so that the directee will have patience in addressing his problems.

E. Long-Suffering (*Longanimitas*)

Long-suffering is the fifth of those fruits which order the soul in itself (with respect to evil) so that the soul is not disturbed by the delay of goods.[51] A lack of a good has the notion of an evil,[52] so long-suffering relates to evil insofar as one does not receive some good. Long-suffering also consists in the labor associated with some action or dealing with exterior difficulties[53] in relation to achieving the good. Effectively, long-suffering enables a person to endure hardships in order to arrive at some good which may be difficult to obtain and may be long in coming. Long-suffering

---

[45]See chapter on the demonic.

[46]Patience enables one to deal with people who are ill-willed and who do not seek our good but our harm.

[47]Patience makes us remain calm and self-possessed in the face of those who are disagreeing or arguing with us.

[48]Patience makes us keep self possession when others are trying to outdo us and thereby lessen what we do or belittle us.

[49]*Ad Galatas* V, l. 6.

[50]See the prior volume.

[51]ST I-II, q. 70, a. 3.

[52]Ibid.

[53]III Sent., d. 34, q. 1, a. 5.

is also contrary to witchcraft, enmities, contentions, emulations, animosity and dissensions, as long-suffering makes a person bear the evils inflicted on him by those with whom he dwells.[54]

Psychologically, long-suffering enables the directee to endure difficulties in order to achieve his mental health (a good) or something else which will aid his mental health. As the directee is counseled to become holier and strives for holiness, the fruit of the Holy Spirit of long-suffering will give him greater interior strength to endure whatever is necessary to achieve the good. It will give him the capacity to await the good and this is important since many directees suffer impatience regarding overcoming their mental illness or in dealing with the causes of the mental illness. Also, long-suffering makes them stay the course, so to speak, so that they will not stop doing those things necessary to achieve mental health despite the difficulties endured. For the psychologist, both long-suffering and patience are necessary, not only with respect to what should be counseled, but in their work. As a psychologist becomes holier and this fruit becomes present in his soul, he will be able to endure the difficulties which often occur in counseling those who are mentally ill.

F. Goodness (*Bonitas*)

Goodness is the first of the fruits in which the soul is ordered to that which is near it.[55] By the fruit of the Holy Spirit of goodness, the soul is well disposed to one's neighbor by willing to do good for him.[56] Goodness means that we want to do good things for those around us and this fruit is called rectitude and sweetness of the soul.[57] By this fruit the soul's right order toward one's neighbor becomes present and the good willed toward the person takes on a certain sweetness in two ways. The first way is with respect to self, as the person who possesses this fruit finds willing the good of his neighbor delightful. The second is that it makes one delightful to other people, since this fruit wills the good of the other which is manifested in the person's own actions. Because one wills to do good things to others, then this fruit helps us to forgive those who have done evil to us.[58]

The directee must be encouraged to seek holiness as it will make it easier to forgive those who may have harmed him, especially if he has developed a mental illness with respect to lack of forgiveness. Family and marital relations are smoothed out by this fruit. Any person who has developed a mental illness because of something that someone else has done to him can benefit from this fruit. For example, if a woman is

---

[54]ST I-II, q. 70, a. 4 and *Ad Galatas* V, l. 6.

[55]ST I-II, q. 70, a. 3.

[56]Ibid. and *Ad Galatas* V, l. 6.

[57]III Sent., d. 34, q. 1, a. 5 and *Ad Galatas* V, l. 6.

[58]ST I-II, q. 70, a. 4 and *Ad Galatas* V, l. 6. In this context, St. Thomas observes that goodness helps one to forgive those who have engaged in witchcraft, enmities, contentions, emulations, animosity and dissensions against us.

raped and if her degree of holiness is such that this fruit is operative, she will seek to forgive the person and do whatever is necessary for the person so that he will change his life. St. Maria Goretti forgave the man who stabbed her and offered it up for the salvation of his soul, which is a clear sign of the fruit as operative in the young saint's life. Again, psychologists must counsel the directee in holiness so that this fruit becomes operative. On the other hand, psychologists must be holy themselves so that they will the good for their directees. Few experienced counselors have not suffered something at the hands of one of their directees. Few counselors have never grown angry with their directees, which often leads to a desire to cut them off from counseling or something of this sort. But if a psychologist is holy, he will do what is necessary to help the directee through the operation of this fruit. Yet, it may also mean that insofar as the psychologist wills what is good for the directee through this fruit, then at times the psychologist may encourage the directee to seek the help of a more prudent or more qualified psychologist, i.e. the psychologist will put his own pride aside because he will want to do what is best for the directee.

G. Benignity or Kindness (*Benignitas*)

The second of those fruits which order the soul to those things near to it is benignity.[59] While the fruit of the Holy Spirit of goodness enacts good will on the side of the person who has it, benignity executes that good will or beneficence[60] through action. In other words, it is one thing to will something, it is another to do it and this fruit moves the person to do those things necessary for our neighbor's good rather than just will them. St. Thomas observes that the benign are those who do the good from the fervent fire of love for the doing of good for one's neighbor.[61] Through benignity, the person burns with a desire to do good for people and he comes to the aid of those in a state of need.[62] St. Thomas observes that benignity moves one to cure the evils of witchcraft, enmities, contentions, emulations, animosity and dissensions,[63] i.e. benignity moves one to eradicate evil by doing the good. In so doing, benignity makes the person communicate well with others.[64] "Communicate" does not necessarily refer only to the faculty of speech, although that is part of it. Rather, in the broader sense of this fruit, it involves living well with others. From this we see two more things. The first is that insofar as we do the good, we are ordering things toward the good or even God Himself, at least remotely. For this reason, benignity is sometimes called the spirit of wisdom,[65]

---

[59]ST I-II, q. 70, a. 3.

[60]Ibid.

[61]Ibid. and *Ad Galatas* V, 1. 6.

[62]*Ad Galatas* V, 1. 6.

[63]ST I-II, q. 70, a. 4.

[64]III Sent., d. 34, q. 1, a. 5.

[65]Wisdom 1:6.

as it pertains to wisdom to see and order things to God. Second, since it wills to do the good to others, benignity is contrary to envy insofar as envy is a vice in which one desires the good of another, not for the sake of the other but for one's own sake, so that the other may be deprived of that good.[66]

Psychologists must have this fruit as it will move them to do the right things for their directees. Moreover, they must counsel their directees to aspire to holiness so that doing good things for people becomes delightful. Many younger directees can become destructive for a variety of reasons, but one of the clear reasons for this is the lack of charity and consequently of this fruit. Married couples who suffer marital problems may find it difficult to do good things for their spouse and this fruit will facilitate a more peaceful marriage as each will be doing what is good for the other. This can also be applied to parents and children alike. This fruit is also contrary to anger insofar as anger seeks vindication by inflicting harm on the one causing the injustice. But this fruit enables one to do good things for the sake of those who harm us.

H. Meekness or Mildness (*Mansuetudo*)

The third fruit of the Holy Spirit, in which the soul is ordered toward that which is near it, is meekness.[67] Meekness is the fruit by which one endures with equanimity[68] evils which one's neighbor inflicts on him by inhibiting anger.[69] Meekness is the fruit in which one refrains from acts of anger or from going to extremes in one's reactions regarding those who harm us. Hence, by meekness one exercises proper self-restraint in the face of injury. Meekness is contrary to envy[70] since one refrains from harming those who are in possession of the good which is seen as an evil to oneself. Meekness is also contrary to homicide[71] insofar as homicide is an extreme in reactions.

Those directees who suffer anger, while they cannot gain this fruit directly, can seek holiness by which this effect will naturally overtake their soul and grant them meekness. While one should also strive for the virtue of meekness, this fruit actually makes one meek in action which has a calming effect on the soul. Directees who are inclined toward violence can strive for excellence in grace so that this fruit will result in the removal of those actions by which they harm people. Again, while other means and virtues should be sought, those who suffer from violence are rendered non-reactionary through this fruit. This fruit is a clear gauge of mental health or illness insofar as when a person is rightly ordered about how to react to people, then right

---

[66]See ST II-II, q. 36.

[67]ST I-II, q. 70, a. 3. A fuller treatment of the nature of the virtue of meekness and therefore the nature of the act of meekness can be seen in ST II-II, q. 157.

[68]III Sent., d. 34, q. 1, a. 5; ST I-II, q. 70, a 3 and *Ad Galatas* V, l. 6.

[69]ST I-II, q. 70, a. 3.

[70]ST I-II, q. 70, a. 4.

[71]*Ad Galatas* V, l. 6.

reason is dominant. On the other hand, if the person is reactionary in a way contrary to right reason,[72] it indicates a lack of this fruit and also the lack of mental health. Usually the mental illness is *per accidens* in the irascible appetite but it may also be a problem of how the intellect is viewing the manner in which people harm the person. A person, whose will is not rightly ordered (*per accidens* mental illness) or whose intellect views everything from the point of self (*per se* mental illness), is more likely to seek the harm of others and thereby lack this fruit.

This fruit is also necessary for psychologists because directees often do things which are capable of infuriating the psychologist. If a psychologist is holy, he will always be able to react with meekness or mildness and keep his own anger tempered. This fruit makes it possible for the psychologist to counsel the directee according to right reason, insofar as this fruit keeps the soul and mind of the psychologist viewing the directee according to God, i.e. from the perspective of what is best for the directee. Therefore, this fruit enables the counselor to give advice flowing from charity rather than anger.

I. Faith (*Fides*)

The fourth fruit of the Holy Spirit in which the soul is ordered to that which is near it is faith.[73] Faith in respect to the fruit can be taken in two ways. In the first way, the fruit is that by which we do not harm our neighbor either through fraud or deceit and in this sense faith is taken as fidelity.[74] Fidelity is in place when the person is loyal to the other; this fruit makes one loyal in the sense of always willing what is best for the person.[75] As one always seeks the good of the other, then this fruit makes one trustworthy, for one knows that the person in whom this fruit is operative will never do anything which is against his spiritual well-being. We can see how important this fruit is for psychologists. To the degree that this fruit is operative in the psychologist, he will always be someone upon whom the directee can depend to do truly what is right for him. This builds trust in the directee. This effectively means that a holy psychologist, all things being equal, is a more trustworthy psychologist. How often in the history of psychology have authors written things which they knew were questionable? How often have psychologists kept directees psychologically dependent on them so that they could continue to bilk the directees or their insurance companies? Even worse yet, there are psychologists who kept directees psychologically dependent in order to empower themselves (i.e. the psychologists). A holy psychologist is less likely to be fraudulent or deceitful and so he is inherently more trustworthy.

---

[72]This implies that certain reactions to things contrary to right reason are rightly ordered.

[73]ST I-II, q. 70, a. 3.

[74]Ibid.

[75]Since what is best is not always what one wants, this loyalty or fidelity is not the type which always seeks to placate the person.

One the other hand, this fruit also makes the directee trustworthy. This is one of the primary reasons that psychologists must encourage their directees to strive for holiness of life, so that the directee will be more trustworthy and less likely to deceive the psychologist. In the end, holiness makes the counseling more fruitful as the directee will be honest and the psychologist will direct him without deceit. The directee needs to know that he can trust the psychologist so that he can open himself up to the psychologist completely, in order that the wound of the mental illness will properly manifest itself so that it can be healed. Moreover, the directee needs to trust the psychologist so that if the psychologist is not capable, for whatever reason, to counsel the directee adequately, the psychologist will direct the directee to a psychologist who is able to address adequately his problems.

The second way this fruit is sometimes taken is as the faith in which one believes in God.[76] Man is ordered to that which is above himself and thereby man subjects his intellect and all that is his to God. Since this fruit subjects one intellectually to God, it grants certitude to faith.[77] This fruit is contrary to heresy[78] or sects in which one does not submit oneself intellectually to God or His Church.[79] The psychologist must have certitude about that which pertains to faith in order to know the proper spiritual mechanisms so that he does not lead directees astray by bad or inadequate theology. The directee needs confidence that the psychologist is orthodox and as the psychologist becomes holier, this certitude of faith will manifest itself in the actions and counseling of the psychologist. Yet, with a directee, this fruit gives him certitude of the faith so that he knows what he is to do in order to rightly order himself to God and within himself, thus affecting his mental health.[80]

J. Modesty (*Modestia*)

The first fruit which orders the soul about those things which are below it is modesty.[81] The fruit of the Holy Spirit of modesty disposes man well to exterior actions in which he observes due mode in what he says or does.[82] Modesty governs man's exterior actions so that he does what he ought, when he ought and how he ought. In the medieval period, the virtue of modesty was one that governed one's externals and this pertains not just to one's dress, as the modern sense of the term connotes, but to all forms of externals, from dress, to possessions, to what we say and do. Hence, for St. Thomas, it is a broader virtue than is sometimes taken today. However, since the fruit

---

[76]ST I-II, q. 70, a. 3.

[77]III Sent., d. 34, q. 1, a. 5; ST I-II, q. 70, a. 3, ad 3 and *Ad Galatas* V, l. 6.

[78]ST I-II, q. 70, a. 4.

[79]*Ad Galatas* V, l. 6.

[80]For more on faith, see the chapter on the theological virtues.

[81]ST I-II, q. 70, a. 3.

[82]Ibid. and *Ad Galatas* V, l. 6.

is an act and not a virtue, the fruit of the Holy Spirit of modesty makes one modest in speech, action and dress. For this reason it is contrary to drunkenness and revelings[83] by which we do not govern rightly our exterior comportment. Furthermore, it refrains from delight in riches and honors.[84] It refrains from dress which is inappropriate either by excess or defect. It protects from defect in those cases where one does not wear enough clothing to protect either oneself or others from lust. It refrains from excess, as when one wears too much makeup or excessively expensive clothing that is not suited to one's state in life or by moderating the use of jewelry, according to person[85] and time.

Modesty is necessary for the psychologist because it enables him to say at the appropriate time what he needs to say. Sometimes psychologists will feel inclined, like all people suffering from original sin, to say things which are out of place which is caused by appetite, e.g. when the directee does something silly or irritating. The fruit of modesty will keep the psychologist rightly governed in his externals and behavior. It will also aid him in keeping a professionalism in his comportment, as that is proper to his state.

With respect to the directee, the fruit of the Holy Spirit will move him to see that it is not necessary or at times appropriate to make social statements by the dress he wears, unless the social statements be appropriate and required.[86] It will aid women and men in wearing dress that will not draw others into passions of lust, thereby disturbing their peace of soul. True love of neighbor, i.e. charity, seeks the good of the neighbor and will inherently move one to moderate the dress so as not to elicit thoughts in the minds of others that are not appropriate. Directees who have a hard time controlling their speech, e.g. those "with a big mouth" or those who "can't seem to say the right thing at the right time," will find that as they grow in holiness these problems will begin to evaporate on their own. On the other hand, someone who does not moderate his speech or actions is opening himself up to mental illnesses since such activity will disorder reason. Moreover, this fruit moderates how parents, spouses and children will address and conduct themselves around each other.

We can begin to see why sins of sex are so damaging. Every sin against the Sixth Commandment results in someone doing or saying something that is not suited to time, person or place. This means that as a person commits sins against the Sixth Commandment, they will not only lose chastity, continence, and peace of soul as well as use of right reason, as seen in the last volume, but they will also lose the more subtle virtues, like circumspection and modesty (in dress and comportment). For as one engages in sins against the Sixth Commandment, one's exterior comportment is

---

[83]*Ad Galatas* V, l. 6.

[84]III Sent., d. 34, q. 1, a. 5.

[85]For example, the modern phenomena of men wearing female jewelry is contrary to this fruit and virtue.

[86]Given the current state of society, most young people do not know that their dress, which is designed to "make a statement," is actually contrary to the virtue and fruit of modesty.

inappropriate and subsequently this will flow over into externals, resulting in modesty being lost. This is why those with a problem with the Sixth Commandment often have a problem with wearing clothing that is inappropriate. As one indulges oneself in the pursuit of pleasure, selfishness consumes the individual, since that is what he is giving into. As a result, he will not want any inhibitions on his behavior or forms of expression (such as dress, etc.) since they will militate against this self-will and the desire to seek illicit pleasures.

K. Continence (*Continentia*)

The second fruit of the Holy Spirit ordering the soul to that which is below it is continence.[87] Since continence pertains to interior concupiscences or desires,[88] it can be taken in two ways. In one way, continence is taken as refraining from things that are licit.[89] In this respect, the continent man is one who uses licit things with due moderation and who practices self-denial even in regard to those things which are morally licit. In another way, continence is taken as suffering concupiscence but not being led into sin.[90] Continence is when the will remains steadfast in the truly good despite the tumult of the appetites. Someone who has continence may have the antecedent passion of desire in relation to sex but the will remains steadfast in what is right.[91] Given the aforesaid, continence is contrary to drunkenness and revelings[92] as well as lust.

Psychologically, this fruit is important in the area of chastity and for those mental illnesses that are related to lack of chastity. But it is also a necessary fruit regarding self restraint in general since the strength we gain from withholding ourselves from those things which are illicit, eventually affects other areas which are difficult in which restrain is required. In the first way that this fruit is understood, insofar as we refrain from things that are licit, this is important for directees who need to exercise restraint in things which are good but could cause them problems. For example, the alcoholic needs continence insofar as he needs to refrain from drinking alcohol even though drinking alcohol is morally permissible, generally speaking. Continence is also necessary for the psychologist insofar as the psychologist must be able to refrain himself when a) he has a directee who might cause the psychologist to become unduly emotional and b) in order to keep a proper focus even though the directee may be sexually attractive or when the topic discussed requires by its nature great interior restraint.

---

[87] ST I-II, q. 70, a. 3.

[88] Ibid.

[89] III Sent., d. 34, q. 1, a. 5; ST I-II, q. 70, a. 3 and *Ad Galatas* V, l. 6.

[90] ST I-II, q. 70, a. 3 and *Ad Galatas* V, l. 6. St Thomas observes in *Ad Galatas* V, l. 6 that the word continence implies that one holds oneself or contains oneself during battle.

[91] See ST II-II, q. 155 on the virtue of continence.

[92] ST I-II, q. 70, a. 4 and *Ad Galatas* V, l. 6.

L. Chastity (*Castitas*)

The last of the fruits of the Holy Spirit and the third of those fruits by which the soul is ordered to those things which are below it is chastity.[93] Chastity pertains to interior concupiscences[94] and for that reason it also may be taken in two ways. In the first way, chastity is taken as refraining from things that are illicit.[95] In another way, chastity can be taken for neither suffering concupiscence nor being led into it.[96] In other words, chastity is manifested when the concupiscible appetite does not move toward that which is illicit and as a result one is not led into sin, as well as in those cases where one simply lacks illicit desires. One of the fruits of the Holy Spirit is not to have illicit desires and to be moved only to that which is chaste. In this respect, chastity helps one to make right use of what is licit.[97] For this reason, chastity is contrary to fornication.[98]

It is not necessary to go into all of the psychological ramifications of this fruit. But given the current state of society, these have serious implications. Insofar as our society lacks chastity, it lacks this fruit of the Holy Spirit. This also means it lacks charity and therefore grace. This essentially means that as our society becomes more and more unchaste, its members will inevitably sink into mental illness, since the right use of the various goods and faculties will not be properly exercised. Apropos of what was said in the context of the prior volume, this will inescapably lead to more disorder in the interior faculties and therefore to more mental illness.

If a psychologist has a directee who is not making right use of the generative faculty, he must be told to stop immediately. He must be counseled to strive for holiness so that this fruit takes root and can keep his concupiscible appetite in order. Those whose mental problems stem from sexual disorders must, in addition to striving for the virtues of continence, chastity and modesty, strive for excellence in grace so that this fruit will be operative in the soul. When the directee finds the life of chastity distasteful and difficult, he can actively pursue holiness so that this fruit will make the chaste life rewarding. Many sexual fixations come from lack of holiness and so the more holy the directee is, the more likely he is to have mental health with regard to the things of the Sixth and Ninth Commandments.

As to the psychologist, he must be holy so that this fruit is clearly operative in him, particularly if he is counseling those of the opposite sex and even more so when he

---

[93]ST I-II, q. 70, a. 3.

[94]Ibid.

[95]III Sent., d. 34, q. 1, a. 5 and ST I-II, q. 70, a. 3. Hence, chastity deals with those things that are illicit whereas continence deals with those things that are licit.

[96]ST I-II, q. 70, a. 3 and *Ad Galatas* V, l. 6.

[97]*Ad Galatas* V, l. 6. This is an important point because those who are married and engage in the conjugal act according to due circumstances actually act according to this fruit. Chastity is not celibacy, i.e. the complete refraining from conjugal relations. Rather, chastity is the right use thereof, according to one's state in life.

[98]ST I-II, q.70, a. 4.

is counseling them in the areas of sexuality. The directee will sense whether the psychologist is chaste, not merely by an important and rightly ordered professionalism, but also by virtue of the fact that the psychologist's own appetites will not manifest themselves as disordered. The average person finds it difficult to hide his passions and the passion of lust is no exception. For this reason, the psychologists have to be of upright character and committed to holiness so that nothing impedes the operation of this fruit.

Conclusion

Throughout this chapter it has been rather clear that the fruits can indicate the degree of one's mental health or illness. If one has the fruits, that is a pretty good indication that he is mentally healthy. If he does not have holiness of life and therefore lacks these fruits, it is a sign that he may be mentally ill or at least it is a sign that he is open to becoming mentally ill. All of these fruits ensure the right order of the soul and the delight gained from the right order. For that reason, psychologists must encourage their directees to engage in those activities which will increase the indwelling of the Holy Spirit in them so that these fruits may be more and more present. The fruits of the Holy Spirit, in the end, make the execution of the lives of those who possess them rightly ordered.

Chapter 7: Grace

The richness of the teaching of the Catholic Church and her saints on the subject of grace constitutes one of the most fruitful reflections for psychologists and directees in all of the areas of psychology. Regrettably, the discussion of grace is virtually nonexistent in the psychological literature. Part of the explanation may lie in the fact that much of the discussion of the spiritual life and its relation to psychological health is encountered in Protestant psychological texts. Historically, the Protestants have not had a good grasp on the nature of grace and so it is often ignored. On the other hand, Catholic psychologists, having bought into the secular/modern view of psychology, tend to isolate the spiritual from the psychological, more often than not because many directees suffer from psychological problems arising from bad religious practices. The discussion of grace is left behind because many are ignorant about how influential and determinative of a person's life grace can be. For these reasons, grace must be treated so as to have an initial grasp[1] of how grace functions and its value for psychology.

I. The Essence of Grace

Grace, by the nature of its name, implies a gift that is gratuitously given and as a result does not imply anything which is due to an individual out of justice.[2] Grace in relation to God implies something supernatural in man coming from God[3] and so grace, being supernatural, is something beyond or above human nature. When God aids man in knowing, willing or doing something, this grace is not a quality but a motion in man[4] and so it differs from that grace which is a habit in the soul[5] not ordered toward action.[6] Grace is not an acquired virtue,[7] even though it is called a habit since it can be increased or lost through action,[8] but it is not an operative habit. Grace, being a habit, is an

---

[1]Dogmatic scholars may find this chapter disappointing since it will not constitute an in-depth discussion of grace. Many distinctions within the kinds of grace will not be presented since they take one more into the field of theology than is beneficial at this stage in the series on psychology. Moreover, this text will carefully avoid the debates which raged in certain areas on the nature of grace. Those more interested in a fuller knowledge of grace can, in addition to reading those passages from St. Thomas, read Garrigou-Lagrange's book *De Gratia*.

[2]II Sent., d. 26, q. 1 and ST I-II, q. 110, aa. 1 and 3.

[3]ST I-II, q. 110, a. 1 and Ott, *Fundamentals of Catholic Dogma*, p. 254.

[4]ST I-II, q. 110, a. 2.

[5]ST I-II, q. 110, a. 1, ad 3.

[6]De Ver., q. 27, a. 2 ad 7.

[7]ST I-II, q. 110, a. 3.

[8]See below.

accident[9] in the soul, i.e a quality[10] which permanently adheres or inheres in the soul.[11] Grace resides in the essence of the soul[12] and not in any of the faculties. For this reason, grace is not a virtue in the sense of a good operative habit inclining one to a specific kind of action.[13] Yet, grace is often called an entitative habit, since it is a being or an accident residing in the essence of the soul and it is counter-distinguished from an operative habit or virtue. Since sanctifying grace is not a virtue, it is not in the faculties of the soul.[14] Since grace is in the soul and since the soul is prior to the faculties, then grace is prior to the virtues as well as the powers of the soul.[15] St. Thomas observes, however, that as the powers or faculties flow from the essence of the soul, so from grace flows the infused virtues into the powers of the soul.[16]

Sanctifying grace is a participation in divine goodness.[17] Insofar as grace is a participation in the divine goodness, grace makes man pleasing to God.[18] Sanctifying

---

[9]II Sent., d. 26, q. 1, a. 2 and Ott, *Fundamentals of Catholic Dogma*, p. 255.

[10]II Sent., d. 26, q. 1, a. 4, ad 1 and De Ver, q. 27, a. 2, ad 7.

[11]Ott, *Fundamentals of Catholic Dogma*, p. 255.

[12]Council of Trent, Session VI (Denz. 1530/800; 1545/809; 1561/821); II Sent., d. 26, q. 1, a. 3; IV Sent., d. 4, q. 1, a. 3, qu. 3, ad 1; ST I-II, q. 110, a. 2, ad 2; ibid., q. 110, a. 4; De Ver., q. 27, a. 6 and Ott, *Fundamentals of Catholic Dogma*, p. 255.

[13]Here we are talking about sanctifying grace and not actual grace.

[14]ST I-II, q. 110, a. 4 and De Ver., q. 27, a. 6.

[15]ST I-II, q. 110, a. 4.

[16]ST I-II, q. 110, a. 4, ad 1. This essentially means that once grace is infused into the soul, those infused virtues and gifts which were discussed in prior chapters are likewise infused. From what has been seen from the prior chapters, the infusion of the virtues and gifts are necessary to protect the grace given to us by God. It would be pointless for God to infuse grace and then not give one any means of protecting it in the soul. St. Thomas also points out that the light of grace, which is the participation in divine nature (see below), is something other than the infused virtues which are derived from the light of grace and ordered to it; see ST I-II, q. 110, a. 3. See also Aumann, *Spiritual Theology*, p. 69.

[17]ST I-II, q. 110, a. 2, ad 2. St. Thomas notes that grace is more noble than the nature of the soul insofar as it is an expression or participation in divine goodness, yet it is not superior as to the mode of being of grace, see ibid. Since grace is a participation in divine goodness, it is greater than the soul which is merely natural and not supernatural. Yet, since grace is an accident, in this respect its mode of being is less than that of the soul, which is part of the substance of man.

[18]ST I-II, q. 110, a. 3; SCG III, c. 150, n. 2 and Aumann, *Spiritual Theology*, p. 73. Grace comes from the Latin word *gratia* or *gratum*, which means pleasing and so grace makes the soul pleasing to God.

grace is a created participation in divine nature[19] although it is distinct from God[20] and yet it constitutes a physical communion of man or the soul with God.[21] For this reason, Aumann says "sanctifying grace gives us a *physical, formal,*[22] *analogous*[23] *and accidental participation* in the divine nature."[24] Grace is also called the indwelling of the Holy Spirit and so it makes us a temple of the Holy Spirit.[25] Whenever one of the Persons of the Blessed Trinity is present, all are present by real concomitance;[26] then grace in addition to being called the indwelling of the Holy Spirit, is also called the indwelling of the Blessed Trinity.[27] All of this indicates that grace gives a certain spiritual being[28] since what is given is uncreated.[29] Therefore, we may define sanctifying grace as an entitative habit (a quality) residing in the essence of the soul by which one participates in divine nature, i.e. an indwelling of the Blessed Trinity.

Sanctifying grace is lost whenever a person commits mortal sin.[30] This follows from the fact that grace makes one a friend of God.[31] The Holy Spirit is the love of God

---

[19]2 Peter 1:4: "By whom he hath given us most great and precious promises: that by these you may be made partakers of the divine nature." See also De Ver., q. 27, a. 6 and Ott, *Fundamentals of Catholic Dogma*, p. 256. One may say that since grace is a participation in divine goodness and since divine goodness is not distinct from God's nature (see SCG I, cc. 27 and 38), then grace is a participation in the nature of God.

[20]Ott, *Fundamentals of Catholic Dogma*, p. 254. This is important because it indicates that man participates in divine nature; he does not become divine nature, i.e. there is not a hypostatic union of the two natures as there is in Christ.

[21]Ibid., p. 257 and Aumann, *Spiritual Theology*, p. 67f.

[22]By formal is meant that grace is an accidental form residing in the essence of the soul and so the participation is formal.

[23]Since grace is a participation in divine nature and distinct from God, then it is analogous to divine nature. Moreover, since it is an accident rather than the divine substance itself, it is analogous.

[24]Ibid., p. 68.

[25]Romans 5:5, 8:11; I Corinthians 6:19; 2 Corinthians 6:16 and Ott, *Fundamentals of Catholic Dogma*, p. 259.

[26]ST I, q. 42, a. 5.

[27]I Sent., d. 14, q. 3 and De Ver., q. 27, a. 3 ad 3.

[28]De Ver., q. 27, a. 6; ibid., ad 1, 3 and 4. This essentially means that man takes on a supernatural existence and so he operates on a supernatural level. For this reason grace not only makes the soul pleasing but renders one's work pleasing (see II Sent., d. 26, q. 1, a. 3, ad 2) and thereby becomes the foundation for supernatural merit (see below).

[29]II Sent., d. 26, q. 1, a. 1. While grace is a participation in divine nature and divine nature is uncreated, nevertheless, its existence in the soul is something created.

[30]Council of Trent, Session VI (Denz. 1544/808; 1573/833; 1577/837) and Ott, *Fundamentals of Catholic Dogma*, p. 263.

[31]Council of Trent, Session VI (Denz. 1528/799).

the Father and God the Son for each other; this means that grace is the love of God infused into our souls. Since mortal sin requires that one turn away from God, it constitutes a cessation on the side of the sinner of loving God and therefore the friendship, which is based on mutual love,[32] is broken on the side of man. As a result of the loss of the friendship, sanctifying grace is also lost.[33] With loss of grace comes the loss of the infused virtues,[34] save faith[35] and hope.[36] For since the infused virtues flow from the presence of sanctifying grace in the soul, once the grace is no longer present, the virtues are likewise lost.

Psychologically, the nature of sanctifying grace constitutes good material for a joyful meditation. Those directees whose problems are contrary to joy can meditate on grace, since by grace we participate in divine nature or goodness. Moreover, sanctifying grace provides a reference point for self-esteem. It was noted earlier that true self-esteem consists only in God and insofar as sanctifying grace is the indwelling of the blessed Trinity, the soul takes on a new worth and is thereby esteemed for the possession of grace. Conversely, the soul in the state of mortal sin (i.e. without sanctifying grace) is not one which should have too much esteem for itself except insofar as its nature is in the image of God. Directees must be encouraged to place their esteem in the grace given to them by God and this will move their esteem away from self to God, Who is the only true measure of what is worthy of esteem. The directee must be encouraged to remain in grace so that the infused virtues and gifts of the Holy Spirit remain present so that they can be operative in his life. Psychologists must also carefully guard their state of grace and never fall into mortal sin, as it will rob the soul of the infused virtues and gifts of the Holy Spirit, thereby depriving their counseling of any supernatural motivation. Moreover, the principle of resemblance is in effect here: like begets like. If counselors are not leading a life of grace, they are unlikely to be able to guide directees according to those aspects of the life of grace which touch upon mental health.

II. The Divisions of Grace

The term grace is not synonymous merely with sanctifying grace but extends to a variety of different distinctions within grace that are of importance. The first most

---

[32]ST I-II, q. 28, a. 2.

[33]We can also say that when one seriously offends God by mortal sin, one is unworthy of sanctifying grace and so rightly it is taken from the person. When a person commits a mortal sin, God ceases causing the grace in the soul of the person because his soul becomes unsuited to the grace because of the presence of serious sin in the will, which is in the soul.

[34]Ott, *Fundamentals of Catholic Dogma*, p. 263. See also Pope St. Pius V's condemnation of Michael Baius' propositions (Denz. 1931/1031)

[35]Council of Trent, Session VI (Denz 1578/838).

[36]Clement XI, condemnation of errors of Paschasius Quesnel (Denz. 2457/1407).

basic distinction within grace is between what is called *gratia gratum faciens* (grace making pleasing)[37] and *gratia gratis data* (grace gratuitously given).[38] GGF is that in which man is joined to God. GGD is a grace in which man cooperates with God so that he may lead others to God.

A. *Gratia Gratum Faciens*

GGF justifies the soul[39] before God and it makes one pleasing to God,[40] as we have seen. GGF is ordered toward meritorious acts[41] and makes us worthy of eternal life.[42] Since one is pleased (*gratum*) with another because he loves him,[43] so GGF causes God to love us.[44] GGF is distinguished between habitual grace and actual grace. Habitual grace is the sanctifying grace as it resides in the essence of the soul. Actual grace disposes the soul for the reception of the infused habits of sanctifying grace and the virtues.[45] Actual grace also actuates the infused habits thereby making them operative in the soul.[46] Actual grace also prevents the loss of infused habits.[47] Hence, actual grace constitutes an aid to man insofar as it is a motion in the soul placed there by God[48] so that he may either achieve sanctifying grace, the infused virtues or perform some meritorious act. For this reason actual grace is called divine aid. This indicates that actual graces can be of a variety of kinds and are given to the soul based upon one's need and God's Will.[49]

---

[37]Henceforth, GGF

[38]Henceforth, GGD. This distinction can be found in ST I-II, q. 111, a. 1 and De Ver., q. 27, a. 1.

[39]ST I-II, q. 111, a. 1 and ibid., ad 1.

[40]ST I-II, q. 111, a. 1, ad 1 and ibid., ad 3.

[41]ST I-II, q. 7, a. 7, ad 1.

[42]De Ver., q. 27, a. 1.

[43]SCG III, c. 150.

[44]Ibid., c. 151.

[45]Aumann, *Spiritual Theology*, p. 79.

[46]Ibid.

[47]Ibid.

[48]See above.

[49]Sometimes certain occurrences outside the soul will result in the soul coming to the knowledge of or being aided in doing something ordered toward his or the salvation of others. These are sometimes called actual graces but this is somewhat inaccurate. While it is true that certain exterior events are often arranged by God, these events are ordered toward the actual grace which God gives the soul to be able to be moved properly by the events. So in the strict sense, actual grace is properly in the soul, even though one can say by extension or analogously that certain exterior events are "graces."

Another distinction within GGF is what is called operating grace and cooperating grace. St. Thomas observes that there are two kinds of actions in us. The first occurs when the will is moved by God. This especially occurs when the will begins to will the good when it had previously willed evil and this grace is called *gratia operans* or operating grace,[50] since it is God operating in us. With respect to operating grace, St. Thomas says that an operation is attributed to the mover, not to the moved and so operating grace is attributed to God Who moves.[51] Habitual grace – insofar as it heals the soul – justifies the soul and makes it pleasing to God and so it is called operating grace[52] and for that reason operating grace makes us pleasing to God.[53]

The second kind of action in us occurs when the exterior act is commanded by the will and so the operation is attributed to the will. God assists in this act by strengthening the will interiorly so as to attain the act and by granting outwardly the capability of operating or performing the exterior act and this grace is called *gratia cooperans* or cooperating grace.[54] With respect to the effect in which our soul moves and is moved, the operation is attributed not just to God but also to the soul.[55] Effectively speaking, cooperating grace is the motion of the soul given to us by God with which we are capable of cooperating. When we cooperate with the motion of God and if we are in the state of grace, then we are able to merit that which the work deserves. For this reason, cooperating grace is a principle of meritorious actions which proceed from free will and so cooperating grace causes our work to be meritorious[56] and renders our work pleasing to God.[57]

Effectively speaking, if we cooperate with the actual graces sent to us by God, then we merit the reward that is proportionate and due to that work. It is here that we come into the discussion of fidelity or cooperation with grace. In the prior chapters, we saw that one of the ways to increase the operation of the gifts of the Holy Spirit in us had to do with our fidelity to grace. This essentially means that the infused virtues, sanctifying grace and the gifts of the Holy Spirit will increase in us when we cooperate with God. Any time any cooperating grace comes into the soul, the soul must cooperate with that actual grace. This manifests one's love for God as one wishes to comply with

---

[50]ST I-II, q. 111, a. 2 and De Ver., q. 27, a. 5, ad 1.

[51]ST I-II, q. 111, a. 2.

[52]Ibid.

[53]II Sent., d. 26, q. 1, a. 5.

[54]ST I-II, q.111, a. 2 and De Ver., a. 27, a. 5, ad 1. See also SCG III, c. 148.

[55]Council of Trent, Session VI (Dens. 1525/797); ST I-II, q. 111, a. 2 and Ott, *Fundamentals of Catholic Dogma*, p. 227.

[56]ST I-II, q. 111, a. 2.

[57]II Sent., d. 26, q. 1, a. 5. St. Thomas observes that operating grace and cooperating grace are the same but are distinguished according to diverse effects. Both are an operation of God, but one moves us without us (i.e. without our cooperation, which is one effect – *gratia operans*); the other moves us with us (another effect – *gratia cooperans*).

His work in oneself and this compliance also becomes the basis for future graces. Just as when we offer to help someone and they cooperate with us, we are more likely to help them in the future, so God is more likely to give us actual graces if we cooperate with Him whenever He sends them. Conversely, just as we tend to stop helping those who refuse our help, so God will be less likely to send a person grace if he does not cooperate with it. The point here is that the more we cooperate with God, the more He gives us.

Here we see the psychological ramification of grace. If God will move us to perform some work through actual grace, directees must always cooperate with God when He sends them this help. Since their desire is to overcome their mental illness, they must cooperate with God when He moves them to perform an action which will lessen the illness or the cause of the illness. Fidelity to grace is absolutely essential for a directee who depends on God and wishes to be aided by God to overcome his mental illness. Any actual grace rejected is a lost opportunity to improve one's mental health.[58]

Psychologists must also have a perfect submission or fidelity to grace since often God will move them by actual graces to perform some function which will aid the directee, e.g. when God moves the psychologist to pray or do mortification for the directee, or moves the psychologist to say something which will have a direct or even indirect impact on the psychological health of the directee. Psychologists who depend on self rather than on the grace of God will be less fit instruments of healing for directees than those who always cooperate with God.

Within the distinction of operating and cooperating grace, operating grace which precedes and affects a deliberate act of the will is called prevenient grace.[59] Sometimes the cooperating grace which accompanies or supports the deliberate act is called subsequent grace (*gratia subsequens*).[60] All of these distinctions indicate God's intimate involvement in our good works and in the saving of our soul so that we might achieve eternal life. It also means that God is intimately involved in our lives so that when someone cooperates with Him, he can overcome his psychological or spiritual difficulties. When a directee comes to a knowledge of how God's grace works in his life, this becomes for him a thing of great joy and consolation, since he sees that by God's grace he can sustain any difficulty, regardless of how much suffering is involved in it. Directees must be taught that if they cooperate with God, He can bring them out of any

---

[58]Here the presumption is that the actual grace touches upon the area of one's life which is affected by mental illness.

[59]Ott, *Fundamentals of Catholic Dogma*, p. 222. This grace is also sometimes called antecedent grace (*gratia antecedens*) since it is a grace which comes before our cooperation, exciting grace (*gratia excitans*) insofar as it excites us or moves us or calling grace (*gratia vocans*) insofar as God is said to call on us to do something.

[60]Ibid. Sometimes this grace is called aiding grace (*gratia adiuvans*) insofar as it aids one to perform the action or concomitant grace as it is a grace concomitant (*gratia concomitans*) with the act of the will. For a further discussion of prevenient grace see Council of Trent, Session VI (Denz. 1528/799); ST I-II, q. 111, a. 3; De Ver., q. 27, a. 5, ad 6 and Ott, *Fundamentals of Catholic Dogma*, p. 226.

psychological illness.

B. *Gratia Gratis Data*

As was mentioned above, grace gratuitously given (GGD) is a grace in which man cooperates with God so that he may lead others to God. GGD does not make one pleasing to God[61] since it is ordered toward leading others and not toward one's own sanctification or justification.[62] GGD is above the faculty of nature – i.e. man cannot achieve it on his own – and it is also above merit,[63] as man cannot merit GGDs. One cannot pray or perform some other work and receive this kind of grace. GGD is ordered toward the good of the Church,[64] since it is ordered toward exterior acts which manifest the faith.[65] Since man cannot move another man interiorly but only exteriorly by persuasion or teaching, GGD contains that which man needs so that he can instruct others about divine things.[66] We see, therefore, the GGDs are not meant for the use or benefit of the person to whom they are given, but they are given by God for the building up of the Church. While GGD is meant to prepare others for union with God, GGF begets that union and for this reason a GGF is greater than a GGD.[67]

St. Thomas observes that there are three things required to persuade or teach another.[68] The first is that man must have a full knowledge of divine things so that he may instruct others. This requires three things of its own and the first is that the principles of the science must be most certain to him who is to teach and with respect to this is the GGD of faith (*fides*). Faith here does not mean the theological virtue of faith but rather a supereminent certitude of faith.[69] The second is that the teacher must know the principal conclusions of the science and to this is posited "word of wisdom" (*sermo sapientiae*) by which one has knowledge of divine things. The third is that the teacher must have abundant examples and knowledge of the effects through which the causes are manifest and with respect to this is posited the word of knowledge (*sermo*

---

[61]ST I-II, q. 111, a. 1, ad 3.

[62]ST I-II, q. 111, a. 1.

[63]Ibid.

[64]ST I-II, q. 111, a. 5.

[65]ST III, q. 7, a. 7, ad 1.

[66]ST I-II, q. 111, a. 4.

[67]ST I-II, q. 111, a. 5.

[68]These three are explicated in ST I-II, q. 111, a. 4. All assertions made regarding these three are taken from this article unless otherwise noted.

[69]ST I-II, q. 111, a. 4, ad 2. The person who has this GGD has a certitude about the things of faith which exceeds normal faith.

scientiae), which is a knowledge of human things.[70]

The second thing required to persuade or teach others is that one must confirm one's teaching by "arguments"[71] in a way which is proper to divine power. The doctor does something which only God can do, viz. perform miracles with respect to man himself and, in this regard, is given the grace of healing (*gratia sanitatum*). If it is meant merely to manifest the divine power, it is called a work of power (*operatio virtutum*), e.g. when one makes the sun stand still or parts the sea. Another way confirmation occurs is when one manifests something only God can know and with respect to this is posited prophecy, in which one pronounces future contingents.[72] Moreover, when a person is able to know those things hidden in the hearts of men, which can only be known by God, this GGD is called discernment of spirits.

The third thing required to persuade or teach others is the possession of the faculty of speaking according to the idioms understood by others and this is called the "kinds of tongues" (*genera linguarum*).[73] The last kind of GGD St. Thomas lists is the interpretation of tongues (*interpretatio sermonum*) in which one is able to understand the meaning of that which is said by the gift of tongues.[74]

The discussion of GGDs comes with a warning, however. There are certain movements in Catholic and Protestant spheres which treat the GGDs as if they were GGFs. In other words, they think that the above charismata or charismatic gifts, as they are sometimes called, can actually be prayed for and merited, i.e. obtained by virtue of one's prayer. This is contrary to the very nature of the gratuitous gift and it manifests

---

[70]The GGDs of the word of wisdom and the word of knowledge indicates an abundance of knowledge of wisdom by which one is able to instruct others and overcome those who say things contrary to the faith; see ST I-II, q. 111, a. 4, ad 4.

[71]"Arguments" in Latin does not meant the same as it does in English. Argument in this case means proof or evidence.

[72]That is, one is able to predict the future. Here the true gift of prophecy, since it comes from God, is infallible provided the conditions under which the prophecy were given hold true. Often, people will claim the gift of prophecy but their lack of accuracy is hardly demonstrative of God's infallible knowledge. In fact, if a person predicts something and it does not come true, then they do not have the true gift of prophecy. Moreover, prophecy does not involve vague generalities which anyone could surmise but it normally includes detailed information.

[73]The full nature of the this gift is somewhat debated (see CE, vol. III, p. 590).

[74]This indicates that the person clearly understands what is said. It is not some "vague, subtle movement" of the "spirit" but a clear grasping of the meaning of what is said. The gift of tongues should never be exercised without the interpretation of tongues, see CE, vol. III, p. 590. Other authors discuss other GGDs such as Apostolate, which is a charism given to a member of the Church which is ordered specifically toward building up of the Church, such as was possessed by the Apostles. Another is government, which is a grace granted to those who have authority in the Church so that they may faithfully exercise their authority.

a lack of theological understanding. Moreover, the charismatic gifts often "displayed" at such meetings do not meet the requirements of a true GGD since what is said or done very often does not confirm the faith of others but actually leads an objective observer to wonder about the truth of the claim. In the case of true GGDs, the confirmation is clear.

The second warning that must accompany the treatment of the GGDs or charismatic gifts is that they do not indicate anything about the holiness of the person who receives them. Many in those movements who have a flawed understanding of these gifts tend to think that the bestowal of a charismatic gift manifests God's favor on them. This is contrary to the truth: it must be recalled that GGDs are not a sign of one's own grace or ordered to oneself but ordered toward bringing others to the faith or confirming them in the faith. Hence, the charismatic gifts do not necessarily reflect anything about the person who has them. This is actually an important point for psychologists insofar as people will often pray for something which is a GGD or something which is strictly gratuitous on the side of God and cannot be merited and then when they do not receive what they pray for, they become depressed. Sometimes people will even claim they have the GGDs when they do not, in order to make themselves appear important. Those with certain kinds of mental illness often claim they have these gifts, when it is clear that they do not.

Lastly, a word about the GGDs or charismatic graces should be addressed to those who seek after them. Aumann rightly points out that: "A person may also come under the power of the devil by reason of the habitual practice of evil or the uncontrolled desire to experience extraordinary phenomena or receive charismatic graces."[75] This observation is of extreme importance for psychology. While the discussion of the demonic will be taken up in a later chapter, this spiritual warning must be kept in mind. Some people who are mentally ill often become so by chasing after apparitions of our Lady or seeking out other manifestations of the miraculous. Often when they want the charismatic gifts badly enough, they will begin dissembling and acting as if they have them. This will open the door to the demonic as well as to mental illness which is based on lying. Sometimes people will desire supernatural phenomena so much that they begin imagining that they see supernatural things (e.g. like saints and demons appearing to them). This destabilizes the intellect as it divorces it from a grounding in reality, since the intellect is thus carried off into a fantasy land motived by disordered concupiscence (pride) and will.

The inordinate desire to receive charismatic graces may place one under the demonic because the person opens himself up to demonic deception. Often bound up with heavy appetitive overtones, many seeking and "displaying"charismatic gifts fail to recognize that even Satan can replicate certain things which appear as charismatic gifts. For instance, he can move one to speak foreign languages; he can make a person *appear* to heal someone who is ill, particularly if the cause of the illness is demonic. He can mimic apparitions to such a degree that often only the offices in the Church endowed with the true gift of discernment of spirits are able to sort it out. The point is that if one

---

[75]Aumann, *Spiritual Theology*, p. 411.

receives a charismatic gift, that is fine and one should use it for the good of the Church. However, certain kinds of these gifts are rare and it is better for people to practice solid Catholic devotions than pursue charismata.

III. The Cause of Grace

Because grace exceeds the natural, only God is the cause of grace.[76] As to habitual grace, a prior disposition is necessary in order to receive it,[77] since the soul must be prepared for the reception of the grace. Yet, with actual grace, no prior disposition is necessary,[78] since God can dispose us through actual grace. In fact, only God can prepare someone for grace by turning the person to Him or by directing him to Him.[79]

The motion of freewill by which one prepares for the reception of the gift of grace is an act of freewill moved by God and in this sense man is said to prepare himself,[80] i.e. by cooperating with God as He moves our will. If God ordains something, it comes about not coercively[81] but infallibly, since the intention of God cannot fail. So if God, Who moves, intends that the man whose heart He moves should attain grace, he will infallibly attain it.[82] From this we see that God is the first cause[83] of grace and man is a secondary cause[84] insofar as he cooperates with God in the attainment of grace.

---

[76]ST I-II, q. 112, a. 1 and De Ver., q. 27, a. 3. This does not deny our Lady's role as Mediatrix of all Graces insofar as she is the secondary and not the primary cause of grace.

[77]ST I-II, q. 112, a. 2.

[78]Ibid.

[79]ST I-II, q. 109, a. 6 and De Ver., q. 24, a. 15.

[80]ST I-II, q. 112, a. 2.

[81]See volume I, chap. 7.

[82]ST I-II, q. 112, a. 3. See also SCG III, c. 148.

[83]A primary cause is that cause to which the effect is primarily and principally ascribed and which can act without the secondary cause. In the case of grace, God is the first cause and we see this in relation to operating and cooperating grace.

[84]A secondary cause is that cause to which the effect is only secondarily and not principally ascribed and which acts only by virtue of the first cause. A secondary cause can do nothing on its own without the first cause moving it. The issue of grace and freewill has been one that has caused a great deal of debate, both within and outside the Catholic sphere. Nevertheless, it is important to recognize that in cooperating grace, one cannot properly understand it without a proper understanding of primary and secondary causality as well as contingent causality. In grace, one must first understand that God can act on us without our freewill with respect to operating grace and in this respect the first cause can act without the secondary cause. Yet, the first cause can also act by causing the secondary cause and in this respect the secondary cause acts by virtue of the first cause and here we see how this functions with cooperating grace. Yet, cooperating grace can be rejected since man must freely cooperate with it. In this respect, God can cause an act of the will contingently (i.e.

It is the common experience of Catholics that some people are holier than others and so one must account for the difference in degrees of holiness. On the side of GGF, it is not more or less, since GGFs join man to God and this essentially means that there is no mean between being joined to God and not being joined to God. However, on the part of the subject, grace is able to be received more or less.[85] In this respect, Ott makes the following comment about the teaching of the Council of Trent: "The Council of Trent, however, declared that the measure of the grace of justification received varies in the individual person who is justified, according to the measure of God's free distribution, and to the disposition and the cooperation of the recipient himself."[86] This basically means that one person can have more sanctifying grace than another and thereby be holier than another. Since sanctifying grace is an accident or quality residing in the essence of the soul, it is analogous to whiteness in the skin. One man can be whiter than another based upon the degree or amount of the formal quality of whiteness in the skin. Similarly, one person can have more sanctifying grace in his soul since the grace is a formal quality or accident which can be had by degrees based upon the disposition of the soul to the grace. Here we see the matter-form construct of grace, so to speak. Just as matter must be disposed to form and in some cases the amount of the form is based upon the disposition of the matter, so with grace the amount of grace is based upon the disposition of the soul. This disposition is based upon God's preparation of the soul and the soul's cooperation with that preparation; as St. Thomas observes in this respect, the reason for the diversity of levels of grace is from something on the part of the person preparing himself for grace. He who prepares himself more, receives more.[87] This essentially means that when man performs acts of cooperating with God's grace, the soul becomes more disposed toward the grace. This is why fidelity to grace is absolutely key to the advancement in the spiritual life, i.e. in becoming holy. We can now see what sanctified perfection consists in, viz. excellence in grace and the adornment of the soul with all of the virtues (both infused and natural) as well as the disposition of the soul to the operations of the gifts of the Holy Spirit. Yet it must be observed that the first reason for diversity in grace is not to be taken from the cooperation of the soul but from God, insofar as man's free will is prepared by God. The first cause of this diversity is taken on the part of God Who dispenses in diverse ways His grace so that, from diverse grades, the beauty and perfection of the Church

---

His causation does not determine the effect) in which the secondary agent determines the effect. So in the case of grace, God can move the person by cooperating grace and the person is still free to reject it or accept it. Without a proper philosophical understanding of primary and secondary causality as well as a proper understanding that the first cause can cause contingently and not necessarily, one cannot understand how cooperating grace is possible.

[85]ST I-II, q. 112, a. 4.

[86]Ott, *Fundamentals of Catholic Dogma*, p. 262 in reference to the Council of Trent, Session VI (Denz. 1528/799).

[87]ST I-II, q. 112, a. 4.

arises.[88] In effect, the amount of grace is first and foremost dependent upon God and how much He wants to dispense to a given soul and secondarily on the soul's cooperation with that grace.

Man can know he has sanctifying grace in three ways.[89] The first is by revelation, i.e. if God or a saint reveals to the person that he is in the state of grace, e.g. to our Lady by the angel Gabriel[90]. However, this is a special privilege and rarely given.[91] The second is if man were able to obtain the knowledge through himself with certainty and no one has this ability. The third is by conjecture through certain signs, e.g. delights or even sufferings from God, contempt for mundane things by the soul, or one's not being conscious of having committed any mortal sins since last Confession, etc.[92]

From the aforesaid, we see that God is intimately involved in man's life. While this was known from prior observations, we see that if a person leads a life of grace, God is even more involved in the person's life. Since God strengthens the will and enlightens the mind, we see that the more God gets involved in the life of the person, the more free he is. In other words, since freedom or voluntariness occurs with intellection and volition, then God, through the operations of grace, acts upon these two faculties in such a way that the person is actually freer than if God were not to do so. We see where the practical atheist's position is not well founded. He holds that he must get God and His "rules" out of his life to be truly free. The opposite is the case: the more God is involved, the more free we are.[93] On the psychological level, directees are often not that free in their actions; the very term "fixation" implies this, insofar as one is fixed rather than free with respect to a certain thing.

The directee can have hope that if he cooperates with God, he can be freed of his mental illness. God can and does give grace to those who dispose themselves and so the directee can be told that if he disposes himself to God, God can help his mental illness for the sake of making him a more fit instrument of God. Moreover, many approach God, in regards to mental illness, as if everything is dependent upon God. "If

---

[88]Council of Trent, Session VI (Denz. 1528/799) and ST I-II, q. 112, a. 4.

[89]These three can be found in ST I-II, q. 112, a. 5. These three are logical and not necessarily real, as will be seen from the paragraph.

[90]Luke 1:26.

[91]It is normally given to the soul for the sake of some reason in the divine economy of salvation or something of this sort.

[92]Here the certitude is merely a moral certitude and the degree of the certitude is based upon a variety of factors, some of which give a greater degree of certitude than others. Other signs will be mentioned later in the book.

[93]This also follows from the fact that antecedent appetites begin to wane as a person advances in holiness (see below) and so one is less bound by the appetites in one's life. This is why Christ said "I am come that they may have life, and may have it more abundantly" (John 10:10). We are more "alive" the freer we are, and so the more that grace and God are operative in our lives, the freer we are.

God wants me to be mentally healthy, He has to cause it." This is a form of resignation to one's mental illness and it denies one's own cooperation with God. Often God leads people slowly out of their problems so that they learn valuable lessons along the way and learn to develop virtues. While the directee must recognize that he can do nothing without God,[94] nevertheless with God he can overcome his mental illness.

IV. The Effects of Grace

There are virtually an infinite number of effects that can arise from God's grace, as He can help us in any situation and in any way. But we will only cover a few here. The first is that grace justifies the impious.[95] Justification has many meanings, all of which are connected to sanctifying grace. Justification is not a virtue[96] but a disposition in the soul by which it is subjected to God, i.e. there is no sin in the soul.[97] Hence, when one is justified, one goes from the state of sin (sometimes called the state of mortal sin) to the state of grace, or from the state of injustice to justice.[98] For this reason, grace causes the remission of sin or one could say in the remission of sin one is justified.[99]

In order to be justified as an adult,[100] there are four motions required.[101] (1) The first motion is the infusion of actual grace. (2) In order for the soul to be justified, it must accept the grace by free will[102] and by doing so one must move by freewill to God through faith. For justification of the impious there is required a motion of the mind by which one is converted to God and this first conversion is by faith, so faith is required for justification of the impious.[103] When man is justified, through free will he recedes

---

[94]John 15:5. This also follows metaphysically, insofar as being is not proper to any creature but only to God (Cf. SCG II, c. 15 and *De ente et essentia*, c. 5). Hence, if any being exists, whether it's an essential being or accidental being (motion or action), the secondary agent cannot act unless it acts by virtue of the first agent, viz. God.

[95]ST I-II, q. 113, a. 1 and De Ver., q. 28, a. 1.

[96]ST I-II, q. 113, a. 1. By noting that it is not a virtue, here it may be recognized that justification is not the same as the infused and acquired virtues of justice, which reside in the will.

[97]ST I-II, q. 113, a. 1.

[98]Ibid.

[99]See ST I-II, q. 113, a. 2 and De Ver., q. 28, aa. 2 and 7.

[100]It is possible for a child to be justified merely by Baptism before attaining the use of reason.

[101]These four can be found in ST I-II, q. 113, aa. 6 and 8.

[102]ST I-II, q. 113, a. 3 and De Ver., q. 28, a. 3.

[103]This issue is debated with respect to how much faith is required. Does one need a full knowledge of the Catholic faith, i.e. explicit faith, or only an implicit faith in which one would follow the right religion if one knew it.? St. Thomas argues that one needs to

from sin and approaches justice. Therefore one must have a tending to God. (3) But this can only be done when there is a motion of the will away from sin. In this respect, justice consists in rendering one his due. With respect to God, we render Him His due by turning to Him and turning away from violations of His law. (4) Lastly, there must be the remission of blame or sin and in this respect, the infusion of sanctifying grace causes the remission of mortal sin.[104] Here we say mortal sin insofar as one goes from the state of mortal sin to a state of (sanctifying) grace. However, grace can also cause the remission of venial sin as well.

While man can know things without grace, he can only know higher things from the light of grace.[105] Actual grace internally and directly enlightens the understanding;[106] from sanctifying grace flow the infused virtues, some of which affect the intellect in its operations. If a psychologist finds a directee who is not able to grasp something which he needs to know in order to overcome his mental illness, the psychologist can pray (assuming he is in the state of grace) and do penance so that he can merit the actual grace for the directee to see his problem. Grace has a direct effect on the intellect: while natural methods can and ought to be used to overcome the mental illness, the supernatural means of grace will more efficaciously enlighten the individual to perform those actions to avoid sin, which may be the cause of his mental illness.

We have also seen the next effect of grace which is to strengthen the will. While man can will and do the good without grace,[107] he cannot will or do the supernatural good without grace.[108] This follows from the fact that it is only by grace that man takes on a supernatural being and since act is proportionate to being, then only when he is in grace can man perform supernatural acts. St. Thomas observes that in the state of integrity (Adam and Eve before the Fall), man ordered all things to God and could love God above all.[109] However, after the Fall he could not do this[110] without grace. It is only through grace and charity that man can love God above all things.[111]

At this point, we see that it is through grace that one's actions are elevated to the level of the supernatural. Therefore, actions, which are normally merely natural, can

---

know God is the justifier in order to be justified (ST I-II, q. 113, a. 4, ad 3). Because the topic is so heavily debated, it will not be discussed here. However, one point should be noted: in order to have a motion of the will requires prior knowledge of some kind.

[104]In addition to ST I-II, q. 113, aa. 6 and 8, see also ST I-II, q. 110, a. 1, ad 3.

[105]ST I-II, q. 109, a. 1. This was discussed somewhat in the chapter on sin regarding the retraction of the divine light.

[106]Ott, *Fundamentals of Catholic Dogma*, p. 225.

[107]Council of Trent, Session VI (Denz. 1557/817).

[108]II Sent., d. 28, q. 1, a. 1; ST I-II, q. 109, a. 2 and Ott, *Fundamentals of Catholic Dogma*, p. 234.

[109]ST I-II, q. 109, a. 3.

[110]Ibid.

[111]Ibid.

take on a supernatural dimension by means of grace and charity. Hence, the taking care of a child, the loving of the child for the sake of God, the caring for one's spouse and all other naturally good acts take on a supernatural dimension. This is why there is a fundamental difference between the social worker who wants to help the poor but is not in the state of grace and the nun, who cares for the same poor in the same way but whose actions are supernatural, due to grace. In the case of the nun, her activity is ordered toward the glory of God and so the supernatural end has a proportionate means, viz. the supernatural action of taking care of the poor.[112] Here we see that when the directee does even natural things, if they are done in grace and ordered toward God, they take on a supernatural being. When the psychologist's work is ordered toward God and His glory by charity as well as grace, it takes on a supernatural meaning.

Man cannot fulfill the natural law without grace,[113] which means that "in the condition of fallen nature, it is morally impossible for man, without restoring grace (*gratia sanans*), to fulfill the entire moral law and to overcome all serious temptations for a considerable period of time."[114] Even in the state of grace, we need actual grace to do good always and to avoid evil.[115] Again, while it is possible to fulfill the commandments without grace, one cannot do it always or for one's entire life without grace. For psychologists this is important because directees must realize that they cannot always do what is right without God's grace. Therefore, grace strengthens the will so that man may always do what is right and so directees should be counseled to depend more on God than themselves in doing what is right in order to overcome their mental illness or to maintain mental health.

Through grace, man is elevated to a new dignity according to which the supernatural end of eternal life, which is perfect beatitude, suits him.[116] From sanctifying grace flows the theological virtue of charity since grace is given to him who has charity in order to incline him to the end which suits the sanctifying grace.[117] In other words, since grace makes us participate in divine nature, to reach God – which is the divine nature itself – suits the grace. There is a certain suitability between participating in divine nature and reaching divine nature itself, i.e. God through perfect beatitude.

Sometimes this is called the saving union, insofar as man is joined to God through sanctifying grace; then at the end of one's life, since God loves Himself,[118] He

---

[112]This will have more significance in the section on merit.

[113]ST I-II, q. 109, a. 4.

[114]Ott, *Fundamentals of Catholic Dogma*, p. 236. This comes from the Council of Trent which says in session VI that in order to avoid permanently all serious sin, i.e. to persevere to the end in justice, grace is required (Denz. 1541/ 806; 1572/832).

[115]ST I-II, q. 109, a. 9. See Ott, *Fundamentals of Catholic Dogma*, pp. 230 and 232.

[116]De Ver., q. 27, a. 2.

[117]Ibid.

[118]ST I, q. 19.

will not cut us off from Himself since He sees Himself in us through grace. Since grace is permanent and since the union is permanent,[119] then sanctifying grace constitutes the means of achieving perfect beatitude, i.e. God Himself. For this reason, sanctifying grace merits [120] and is necessary to reach eternal life,[121] and it gives man a claim to the inheritance of heaven.[122]

It is at this juncture that one sees the connection between the natural law, man's ultimate end and grace. The natural law orders us toward God as our ultimate end, but we cannot reach Him on our own. Since the ultimate end is a supernatural end, we need a supernatural means to attain that end and this is grace. The psychological implications of this are extensive. It means that, while one can obtain an imperfect beatitude through following the natural law on a natural level, one can actually have a greater happiness through grace. Through grace one finds a fulfillment of natural law, so that through grace nature finds its fulfillment. Moreover, with sanctifying grace are infused the moral virtues and since one can attain a level of imperfect happiness by leading a life according to the virtues, then grace directly contributes to imperfect happiness as well. Directees, if they wish to be happier, must lead a life of grace.

Like begets like: If psychologists want to be happier, they must lead a life of grace and this will have an impact on their directees. If a directee notices that a psychologist has a truer and deeper happiness than can be gained by leading a merely natural life, this will have a positive psychological impact on the directee. On one level, it will move the cogitative power of the directee to associate goodness of life and grace with joy and happiness. This will affect the person's judgment about what they should do, particularly if their mental illness arises from not following the natural law. In this respect, the psychologist becomes the example by which the directee can grasp the necessity of the supernatural life. While in modern psychological schools a certain artificiality regarding the professionalism sometimes keeps the directee in the dark about the character and psychological balance of the psychologist, in a more Thomistic or Catholic approach, the life of grace and its virtues in the psychologist become an example to the directee. This does not mean that the psychologist should lack a proper professionalism. Rather what it means is that his professionalism will be infused with a certain grace and naturalness. Since grace fulfills nature, the psychologist, while keeping a proper professionalism and distance, will manifest charity for the directee which will result in a more natural human demeanor as well as a distinctly supernatural appearance. Just as Aristotle says that in order to gain prudence one looks to the wise man to know how to act, so the directee will be able to look to the psychologist to see

---

[119]What is meant by "permanent" is that God always causes the grace in the soul, unless the soul commits a mortal sin. Outside that context, sanctifying grace is never lost.

[120]Council of Trent, Sessions VI (Denz. 1576/836; 1582/842); II Sent., d. 26, q. 1, a. 5 and Ott, *Fundamentals of Catholic Dogma*, p. 266.

[121]SCG III, c. 147.

[122]Titus 3:7; Council of Trent, Session VI (Denz. 1528/799) and Aumann, *Spiritual Theology*, p. 72.

what it means to be truly human, i.e. what it means for humanity to be infused with the life of grace. This in itself will provide a powerful image for the directee.

Another aspect of grace being the means to heaven has to do with the sufferings that many directees go through in this life. Since grace makes it possible to reach heaven in which we will have perfect beatitude,[123] even if the directee cannot overcome the mental illness in this life, or if the mental illness takes a long time to overcome, he can find consolation and hope in the fact that eventually, if he leads a life of grace, he will be freed from the mental illness in the next life.[124] While some might not find that prospect very encouraging, they will discover, as they lead a life of grace, that they will look forward to heaven more by means of the virtue of hope and this will aid them in courageously enduring their suffering. Grace sanctifies the soul,[125] i.e. it makes one holy. While holiness is by degrees, nevertheless anyone in the state of grace is holy. Grace bestows a certain decorum or beauty on the soul.[126] Sanctifying grace makes one a friend of God[127] and an adopted child of God.[128]

Lastly, Tanquerey makes a distinction which is important for psychology regarding the different kinds of graces.[129] He observes that those actual graces which are proper to the intellect and will are called interior graces. Yet, God also gives us exterior graces which are not in the intellect and will but in the senses and in the sensitive faculties. While Tanquerey discusses these graces in the context of how the exterior graces lead to interior graces by leaving an impression on the soul, through such exercises as reading of Scripture, listening to a sermon and things of this sort, nevertheless, we see that God can, by actual grace, act upon the senses and sensitive appetites. Those who lead a life of grace and strive for holiness and exercise true fidelity to grace find that as they advance in the spiritual life, the antecedent passions begin to wane.

The first reason this occurs is that with sanctifying grace come the infused

---

[123]See chapter two and the conclusion.

[124]On the fact that mental illness and perfect beatitude are mutually exclusive, see the conclusion.

[125]I Corinthians 6:11; Council of Trent, Session VI (Denz. 1528/799) and Ott, *Fundamentals of Catholic Dogma*, p.257.

[126]Catechism of the Council of Trent, II, 2, 49 and Ott, *Fundamentals of Catholic Dogma*, p. 257.

[127]Council of Trent, Session VI (Denz. 1528/799) and Ott, *Fundamentals of Catholic Dogma*, p. 258. Since grace makes one a friend of God, it is often said that mortal sin makes one an enemy of God because one is working against God and His divinely established order. We see why Christ was able to command one to love one's enemies, since God and some of the effects of His love extend to all men while in this life.

[128]I John 3: 1; Council of Trent, Session VI (Denz. 1521/793); Ott, *Fundamentals of Catholic Dogma*, p. 258 and Aumann, *Spiritual Theology*, pp. 69 and 71.

[129]This distinction and the following observations can be found in Tanquerey, *The Spiritual Life*, n. 124.

moral virtues which will have a tempering effect on the appetites. As the person becomes holier, this effect becomes more pronounced. As a result, a person will often find that as he does those things to advance in holiness, certain problems tend to evaporate on their own. In other words, directees, if they are advancing in holiness, will begin to notice a waning in their appetites and this is very important, given the conclusions of the first volume. Furthermore, actual grace is ordered toward the reception of and the preservation of sanctifying grace and this cannot be achieved without the appetites being arrested, since the appetites often lead people to sin. As a result, one of the actual graces God can bestow on a person is the calming of antecedent appetite. In psychology, therefore, if a person's mental illness has appetite as its cause, these actual graces should be sought from God. But in order to arrest the appetites, the cogitative power must also be corrected, otherwise the appetites will arise from assessments of the cogitative power. This would seem to imply that the correcting of the cogitative power through actual grace is part of either interior grace (strengthening of the mind) or exterior grace in some fashion.

Connected to this we see the importance of the grace of forgetfulness. Since the cogitative power makes its associations based upon those things stored in memory, God must also grant to the individual an actual grace by which certain memories are no longer associated with certain things. The psychological impact of this is profound. It means that those leading a life of grace are more likely to recover from traumatic experiences, in which the memory is imbued with sensible species, than would otherwise be the case. The grace of forgetfulness, however, seems to have a specific *modus operandi*. On the one hand, it causes the memory not to recall *specific* images or information about the past and so one can act calmly or rationally with respect to something that could cause, and may have caused, mental disturbances. On the other hand, this grace does not take away the ability to recall the specific sense species, but the person is not inclined to do so. In the spiritual life, this is important since the images of our past sins can be sources of temptations for us. In the psychological life, this is important since it will help us to calm the various faculties by not recalling images which can cause mental problems. Yet, this grace of forgetfulness is also accompanied by a distinct awareness of the ability to fall into the species of sin which correlates to the past sensible species. While the person is aware of his weakness in this area, he does not recall the specific images that relate to the sin and so he is able to advance in the spiritual life with due caution. Somewhat the same can be said for those advancing toward mental health. Since what is stored may not only be what we have done but what others have done, we can ask God for this grace to forget what other people have done, especially if it is a bad example leading us into difficulties. Moreover, this grace can help us not to recall the harm which people may have done to us and so this has a direct impact on the relations which we have with others, in our family life, in our places of work, etc. Given the aforesaid, we can see that God can correct any faculty by grace.

V. Merit

In his commentary on Peter Lombard's *Sentences*, St. Thomas observes that one of the effects of grace is merit.[130] Yet, how man is said to merit something from God must be understood correctly. For between God and man is an infinite distance which constitutes the greatest inequality. Yet, justice is between equals.[131] Since God and creatures are completely unequal, God owes no *mere* creature anything in justice. Because there is inequality, man cannot be just to God by absolute equality. Rather, as St. Thomas says, man can be just to God by a certain proportion and by this he means that man's merit with God only exists on the presupposition of the divine ordination so that man obtains from God, as a reward for his work, what God gave him the power to do.[132] In other words, man is incapable of rendering to an infinite being something infinite, because man is finite. Therefore, God must give man a power to do something and since it is God Who gives, then giving back has a certain proportion because of the thing given.

Since man moves by means of his free will, he can have a certain merit insofar as what is rendered to God is freely given. Eternal life is a good exceeding a natural capacity. Therefore no created nature is sufficient as a principle of a meritorious act in relation to eternal life unless some supernatural gift is added to man's nature and this is called grace.[133] Merit before God proceeds from freewill and grace.[134] Merit means "to be worthy of something in return for something done" or "a right to a reward" and so grace makes the act supernatural or worthy of something from God. On the other hand, sin is an impediment excluding one from eternal life since no one in the state of sin is able to merit eternal life, unless he be reconciled with God through grace.[135]

Among the kinds of grace, first grace is different from second grace. First grace is the grace one receives when one goes from the state of mortal sin to the state of grace, whereas second grace is the grace one receives after one is already in the state of grace. Man cannot merit first grace,[136] because the principle of merit, as was just mentioned, viz. grace, is lacking in the person in the state of mortal sin. Therefore, in the state of mortal sin, the person can merit nothing before God and if a person was in the state of grace but lapsed into the state of mortal sin, he cannot merit the reparation (i.e. to be put back into the state of grace).[137] However, once man is in the state of grace,

---

[130]II Sent., d. 26, q. 1, a. 5.

[131]ST I-II, q. 114, a. 1.

[132]Ibid.

[133]ST I-II, q. 114, a. 2.

[134]ST I-II, q. 114, a. 3 and Aumann, *Spiritual Theology*, p. 74.

[135]ST I-II, q. 114, a. 2.

[136]II Sent., d. 27, q. 1, a. 6 and ST I-II, q. 114, a. 5. This also follows from the Council of Trent, Session VI (Denz. 1529/799) which states that justification has God as the efficient cause.

[137]ST I-II, q. 109, a. 8 and ibid, q. 114, a. 7.

he is able to merit an increase of grace (second grace) for himself.[138]

One cannot merit first grace for another: only Christ is capable of that.[139] However, man can merit anything if it leads to his final end;[140] for this reason we can merit actual graces.[141] If temporal goods (i.e. non-spiritual goods) are considered as useful to virtuous works by which we are led to eternal life, directly and simply they fall under merit and the increase of grace. This applies to all those things which aid man in coming to beatitude after first grace.[142] However, if we consider the goods *in se* (i.e. in themselves) they are not able to be merited but only in a certain respect (*secundum quid*) and so they do not fall under merit simply but relatively, insofar as men are moved by God to do temporal works in which, with God's help, they can reach their purpose.[143]

The conditions for us to perform an act that is meritorious are based upon several things.[144] On the side of the meritorious work itself, the work must be morally good. Obviously an evil action does not deserve a supernatural merit. The action must be free from external coercion and internal necessity, i.e. the person must do it freely. Next, the action must be supernatural, i.e. accompanied and motived by actual grace and proceeding from a supernatural motive. On the side of the person meriting, in order that the action be meritorious for an increase in heavenly reward, the person must be in the wayfaring state, i.e. here on earth. Once one dies, one is unable to merit. The person must also be in the state of sanctifying grace, as the aforesaid clearly shows. Lastly, merit is dependent on the free ordinance of God.

Now the *degree* of our merit is based upon four things.[145] The first is the degree of sanctifying grace: the more sanctifying grace we have, the more meritorious are our actions. Therefore, the holier the psychologist, the more he can merit for his directees. The second is our degree of union with Our Lord. The closer we are to Him,[146] the more we can merit. The third is the purity of our intention or the perfection of the motive under which we act, e.g. if one seeks to merit the actual graces to overcome his mental illness so that he can advance more rapidly in the spiritual life, that is a more perfect motive than someone who simply does the meritorious act to be mentally healthy without any further intention of coming closer to God. The last thing upon which the degree of merit is based is the fervor or intensity of our actions.

---

[138]Council of Trent, Session VI (Denz. 1582/842); II Sent., d. 27, q. 1, a. 5 and ST I-II, q. 114, a. 8.

[139]ST I-II, q. 114, a. 6.

[140]ST I-II, q. 114, a. 10.

[141]Tanquerey, *The Spiritual Life*, n. 128.

[142]ST I-II, q. 114, a. 10.

[143]Ibid.

[144]All of these can be found in Ott, *Fundamentals of Catholic Dogma*, p. 265ff.

[145]These four can be found in Tanquerey, *The Spiritual Life*, nn. 237-243.

[146]This would indicate that the closer to God one is in prayer, i.e. the higher one ascends the levels of prayer, the closer one is to God.

As was observed, the psychologist, if he is in the state of grace and performs meritorious actions, can merit actual grace for his directee. A psychologist can merit an enlightening of mind and firmness of will which come from actual grace. He can merit the quieting of the appetites through actual grace. While it may take a lot of meritorious works to reach the degree of merit necessary for the actual grace to be bestowed, nevertheless, the psychologist should continue to perform meritorious works for his directee. In a sense, the psychologist should take "spiritual" responsibility for the directee insofar as he sees it as his obligation before God to do what he can on a spiritual level for the directee.[147] While this may not proceed from a relationship of justice between the psychologist and the directee, it does proceed from charity. Therefore, regardless of the problems of the directee, the psychologist can merit the actual grace which will help correct the problem. Even if the actual graces do not seem to be operative, the psychologist should not assume his meritorious works are for nought.

For those whose psychological problems are spiritual, the psychologists can aid the directee by meriting actual graces. In cases where the psychological illnesses are particularly severe and when natural intervention does not seem to work, the psychologist must resort to the supernatural. Since God can correct any natural evil, the psychologist through meritorious works of prayer and mortification can merit for the directee those graces necessary to correct the faculties.

On the side of the directee, he must always be sure to stay in the state of grace and perform actions which will merit the correction of his faculties and mental illness. All of the natural methods of overcoming mental illness, by means of sanctifying grace and a supernatural motive, i.e. by directing the actions to God, can not only have the proper natural effect, but even merit actual grace to help correct the problem. Therefore, if a directee remains in the state of grace and intentionally directs all his actions to God, the same natural action has both a natural and a supernatural effect. He can also perform meritorious actions which are not directly connected to his mental illness for the sake of his mental health as well.

Often, mental illness can be a trial for those in the directee's family. Yet, they can offer their sufferings and difficulties for the directee. Just as between husband and wife, when they find the personality defects of each other to be onerous they can offer their suffering up for the other in order to merit the actual grace for that very problem, so too can the family members of a directee offer up their dealings with the directee for his benefit. In fact, unless the nature of the mental illness is such that the person does not wish to reveal it to the family, directees should consider telling the family so that they can perform actions to merit the grace for the directee to overcome his problems. Even if the directee does not wish to reveal the nature of the problem, he can still ask the family to pray and do good works for him. This will increase charity within the family and also increase the eternal reward of those helping the directee.

The psychologist must ultimately view his work with all these things in mind.

---

[147]This does not mean that the psychologist becomes a spiritual director to the directee. The actual spiritual direction should be left to the priest.

He must view it as the work assigned to him by God for the natural and spiritual good of those he directs as well as being a means of meriting grace and a higher place in heaven. This gives the psychologist a supernatural motive in his work which may carry him even when the natural motives have waned. The directee must also realize that overcoming his mental illness, particularly if it is not self-inflicted, constitutes a means toward holiness as well as raising his level in heaven. In this respect, if he sees his mental illness through the eyes of supernatural merit, the burden will be easier to carry.

Chapter 8: Sacraments

When Our Lord promulgated the Sacraments of the New Law, He did so with a clear understanding that man comes to knowledge of spiritual realities by means of the senses. While in the prior volume it is clear that man comes to knowledge of the essences of material things by means of the senses, it is also true that we come to knowledge of spiritual realities by means of the senses.[1] The Roman catechism, commonly called the *Catechism of the Council of Trent*, defines a sacrament as a thing perceptible to the senses instituted by God which has the power of signifying and effecting sanctity and justice.[2] For this reason, a sacrament is sometimes defined as an outward sign instituted by God to give grace.[3]

Sacraments contain, therefore, three essential elements. The first is the external sign which we are able to see; we know when spiritual things occur or are present by the external signs. The external sign is composed of two essential parts, the thing (*res aut elementum*) and the word (*verbum*).[4] This refers to the fact that in every sacrament there is something which is acted upon by the agent confecting the sacrament. Hence, the thing acted upon in the sacrament of Baptism is the water poured on the head of the person being baptized. The word consists in that which the agent says or speaks when performing the action over the person receiving the sacrament. The word, in academic circles, is called the form whereas the thing is called the matter.[5] When the matter and form come together with the agent capable of confecting the sacrament and the right intention,[6] the sacrament is confected. This is why the Church teaches that the sign effects or causes the sacrament to be present. In effect, God Who is the primary agent, makes use of the person confecting, the matter, form and intention as secondary agents

---

[1]This is no better evidenced than in St. Thomas' fives ways of proving God's existence as seen in ST I, q. 2, a. 3. Each of the proofs begins in sensible reality and so by means of the senses, we are able to come to a knowledge of God's existence.

[2]*Catechism of the Council of Trent*, II, 1, 8. Here justice refers to the justice coming from sanctifying grace as delineated in the prior chapter.

[3]It is not possible to go into every aspect of all of the sacraments. Only those aspects necessary to have a proper understanding of the sacraments and which have a psychological effect will be discussed in this chapter.

[4]See Ott, *Fundamentals of Catholic Dogma*, p. 327.

[5]Hence, one sees that the essences of sacraments, like other physical realities, are constituted by the matter/form composite. The form makes the matter be a specific thing, e.g. the form of a dog, makes a particular amount of matter be a dog rather than a cat. Likewise, in sacraments, the form comes together with the matter to specify what it will be, e.g. if a priest pours water on a child's head but says "You are rather dirty and need a good washing," that is fundamentally different than if he uses the form for Baptism, "I baptize you in the name of the Father, and of the Son and of the Holy Spirit. Amen."

[6]Council of Trent, Session VII (Denz. 1611/854, cf. Denz. 793/424; 1262/672; 1310/695; 1462/752) and Ott, *Fundamentals of Catholic Dogma*, p. 343.

to bring about that sacrament.

The second element of every sacrament is the conferring of sanctifying grace.[7] The Council of Trent condemns the position that the sacraments do not confer the grace they signify[8] and so they confer grace on those who do not hinder the bestowal of grace.[9] Given the first and second elements of the sacraments, we see that the sacraments work *ex opere operato*[10] which means that they work by the very action that is performed. Every time the agent does what the Church intends (i.e he has the right intention), he is capable of confecting the sacrament[11] and he performs the work, the sacrament is confected. This is an important teaching since it gives one assurance that the sacrament has been confected.[12] Moreover, the fact that each sacrament has specific graces[13] which it confers is very important not only for one's spiritual life but also in the area of psychology.[14] St. Thomas observes that sacramental grace relates to grace commonly so called as species to genus[15] in which the sacraments infuse grace ordered toward specific effects necessary to lead a Christian life.[16]

The Church has adorned each of the sacraments with a ritual which disposes and prepares the soul for the reception of the sacrament. This disposition not only aids the person to be spiritually prepared to receive the sacrament worthily, with devotion and attention, but it also affects the person psychologically. As the liturgy unfolds in the

---

[7]See IV Sent., d. 1, q. 1, a. 4a; ibid., d. 18, q. 1, a. 3a, ad 1; ST I-II, a. 112, a.1, ad 2; ST III, q. 62, aa. 1 and 2; De Ver., q. 27, aa. 4 and 7; SCG IV, c. 57 and Quod. XII, q. 10.

[8]Council of Trent, Session VII (Denz. 1606/849; 1310/695). See also Ott, *Fundamentals of Catholic Dogma*, p. 328f.

[9]Ott, *Fundamentals of Catholic Dogma*, p. 328.

[10]Council of Trent, Session VII (Denz. 1608/851). See also Ott, *Fundamentals of Catholic Dogma*, p. 329f.

[11]The sacraments of Holy Orders can only be performed by a bishop. The sacraments of Confirmation can be performed by a bishop and by a priest duly authorized. The sacraments of Penance, Confession, Extreme Unction and the Holy Communion (here is meant the confection of the Sanctissimum) can only be confected by a priest or bishop. Anyone can confect the sacrament of Baptism under the right circumstances. Matrimony can be confected by a man and a woman capable of contracting the sacrament.

[12]Psychologically this is particularly important in sacraments like Penance, Extreme Unction, Holy Orders and Matrimony.

[13]That all of the sacraments confer grace see Council of Trent, Session VII (Denz. 1583/843a, cf Denz. 1606-1608/849-851).

[14]See below. Each sacrament has graces which aid various areas of one's psychological well being.

[15]ST III, q. 62, a. 2, ad 3.

[16]ST III, q. 62, a. 2. See also ST III, q. 62, a. 1; ibid., q. 64, a. 1 and De Ver., q. 27. That the sacraments confer specific graces is the common position of theologians, see Ott, *Fundamentals of Catholic Dogma*, p. 332f.

various sacramental rites, the person's intellectual judgment is directed toward God and certain truths contained and revealed through the sacramental action. This is stated in the phrase *lex orandi lex credendi* (the law of prayer is the law of belief). This essentially means that the prayers of the liturgy are conformed to the teachings of the Church. If one reverses the principle to *lex credendi lex orandi* (the law of believing is the law of prayer), then one realizes that what one believes determines how one prays. A logical connection exists between how we pray and what we believe.

From a psychological point of view, this principle as employed in the liturgy aids the person in many ways. It aids the Catholic in coming to a proper understanding of what the Church believes. If the liturgy is in conformity with the spiritual realities present as well as the teachings of the Church, then the liturgy aids the virtue of faith, whose psychological impact has already been discussed. It also provides sensible signs by which to direct the imagination and cogitative power in associating physical realities with spiritual ones according to a right order. Since man is designed to come to knowledge of spiritual realities by means of the senses, then in order for us not to err in judgment which can have an impact psychologically, man needs rituals by which his judgment can be directed rightly about spiritual matters. A religion which lacks these exterior signs will naturally degenerate into a state where one's own interior disposition becomes the principle of judgment about spiritual things, rather than objective reality which occurs when exterior sensible signs serve to direct the intellect in its judgment. Since the interior life is fraught with the problems generated by original sin giving man a proclivity to error, these exterior signs are essential for man not to become disordered in his relation to these spiritual realities and particularly to God. How one executes his rituals teaches those present how to relate to God. We have already talked about the critical relation of man to God and this relation can easily be upset if there are not external signs to direct and guide us.[17] Religious instruction comes not merely by formal teaching but also through the way in which religion is lived, part of which is a proper liturgy or ritual which teaches one a great deal about God and the spiritual life.

Moreover, a proper ritual causes a certain joy and interior peace insofar as there is a congruity between the infused virtue of faith and the liturgical actions commanded by the intellect or the liturgical action viewed by the intellect which are in congruity with that virtue. Peace is the tranquility of order in which among the parts there is proper relation and therefore peace is effected when the liturgy and the faith congrue. In effect, a proper liturgy will cause peace of soul which is clearly a desirable psychological effect.

On the other hand, rituals which are contrary to the supernatural virtue of faith create an interior dissonance or disagreement. This follows from the fact that the supernatural virtue of faith inclines the intellect to judge spiritual realities in one way while the ritual is treating them another, either in a contradictory fashion or in a way not suited to the spiritual realities. For example, if a priest were to treat our Lord in the Blessed Sacrament as if it were common bread, there would be a dissonance between the

---

[17]We see here how easy it would be to offend God and lose our proper relationship with Him and then suffer the psychological effects of the loss of that relationship.

virtue of faith which moves one to a profound reverence for God and the treatment of God under the appearances of bread and wine. For this reason, in order to ensure that no psychological harm is wrought by a ritual, three things are required. The first is that the ritual is consonant with the theological virtue of faith, i.e. it is orthodox. The second is that those things surrounding the ritual are likewise in congruity with the faith and the ritual itself, so that there is no dissonance in the various sensible species coming together in one phantasm. Lastly, the ritual must be performed in a manner proper to the ritual itself, i.e. according to the rubrics as prescribed by the competent authority and with due reverence and other virtues suited to this act of the virtue of religion.

Any dissonance in these three can cause a direct and bad psychological effect on those attending the ritual, particularly if the virtue of faith is strong in those in attendance or if in one of the three above, the thing or action is particularly dissonant with the virtue of faith. Therefore, it is necessary for the psychological health of men that God should establish a body of governance (i.e. the Magisterium) which has the right and duty to ensure that the rituals are properly executed and fit the sacred realities. If the members of the Magisterium do not fulfill these two aspects of their office, the psychological health of the members of the Catholic Church will begin to wane or will be weakened. Instead of religion causing psychological vigor, it will cause psychological weakness.[18]

On another note, if a religion is a false religion, then its rituals will likewise serve to weaken mental health or even beget mental illness. Since the intellect and will of man is ordered toward union with God, if any ritual deviates from the means to that union, then it will serve to beget intellectual and volitional disorder. This is not to say that someone cannot be a member of a false religion and maintain a certain mental balance, but it would have to depend heavily upon a strong personal character or constitution or a heavy dependence on a proper understanding of natural things. Means contain an implicit end[19] and so a different religion (means) implies a different end. The end toward which man's faculties are ordered will suffer various disorders because the finalities of those religions are not the same as the true finalities of man.

Psychology, therefore, must align itself only with that religion which is founded upon man's essence and the natures of things. Since God designed our nature, He also

---

[18]Obviously, one can see the importance of a Catholic culture insofar as it provides all of the sensible species to aid psychological health and direct the intellect to its proper end which is God.

[19]In formal discourse this is called the *finis operis* which is counter-distinguished from the *finis operantis*. The *finis operis* is the end of the work since each action is a movement toward something, i.e. some specific thing, e.g. swinging a baseball bat is ordered toward hitting a baseball. The *finis operantis* is the end for which the agent performs the action; the *finis operis* and the *finis operantis* may or may not coincide. Hence, it is possible for a person to have as a *finis operantis* the desire to have union with God but if he is ignorant about the nature of his action (i.e. his religion), the *finis operis* of the ritual may actually deviate from the end. This is why religious indifferentism and assuming all religions have the same end is dangerous.

designed His religion to fit that nature as well as the nature of things and the nature of man's relation to God. Any religion which goes contrary to human nature a) cannot be considered a true religion and b) will cause man psychological harm. But since man labors under ignorance and a proclivity to evil because of original sin, it is necessary for God to come to man to enlighten him. Man is not able to come to supernatural knowledge on his own and since the means to union with God are supernatural, likewise the knowledge of the means is supernatural. Therefore, God must come to man to reveal the means. Since without God we cannot know the means, then it is very easy to offend God and sever the relationship with Him if we employ a means or a religion of our own making. Thus, we see why revelation from God and His divinely-established means are necessary to attain union with Him. The sacraments are often called the ordinary means of sanctification and since the presence of sanctifying grace is the means to God, then we should consider the various ways these ordinary means aid mental health.

I. Baptism

There are seven sacraments[20] and the first is Baptism.[21] The matter of Baptism is water[22] as poured on the body.[23] The form of Baptism is the Trinitarian formula of "I baptize you in the Name of the Father, and of the Son and of the Holy Spirit."[24] Baptism consists in a "spiritual washing" away of original and actual sins by the conference of the grace of justification (sanctifying grace).[25] From this we see the first psychological effect. As we have seen throughout the course of the book, with sanctifying grace are infused the gifts of the Holy Spirit as well as the infused virtues, all of which have a psychological impact. For this reason alone, one should seek Baptism. On a developmental level, children who are baptized and whose circumstances provide a life in congruity with the virtues infused at Baptism are less likely to develop personality disorders because of the gifts and infused virtues. Also, they are more likely to be calm and less disordered from the effects of original sin.[26]

---

[20]Council of Trent, Session VII (Denz. 1601/844). Recently, in modern literature, the use of the term sacrament has been used to refer to things other than the customarily listed seven sacraments. However, the use of the term sacrament in modern parlance has taken on an analogical character and does not possess the same nature as these seven.

[21]Sometimes Baptism is referred to as anointing or christening but this is an accidental denomination and not an essential one. While at Baptism, the child is anointed with oil, this does not constitute the essence of the sacrament.

[22]Council of Trent, Session VII (Denz. 1615/858). See also Ott, *Fundamentals of Catholic Dogma*, p. 352. Sometimes the water is called the remote matter.

[23]Ott, *Fundamentals of Catholic Dogma*, p. 352. Sometimes the pouring of the water on the body is called the proximate matter.

[24]Ibid. p. 353.

[25]Council of Trent, Session VI (Denz. 1520/792.)

[26]Obviously bodily dispositions and circumstances can affect this.

Baptism, even if unworthily received, imprints on the soul of the recipient an indelible spiritual mark.[27] This sacramental character confers the power of performing acts of Christian worship by assimilating one to the High Priesthood of Jesus Christ.[28] The essence of the priesthood is to offer sacrifice[29] and by the reception of the indelible mark, one is able to offer one's suffering, prayers and good works as a sacrifice to God in order to merit something. While one must still be in the state of grace to merit, nevertheless, the indelible mark designates the soul as someone who can offer a sacrifice. On a psychological level, one becomes capable of offering sacrifice in order to merit the graces necessary to cure one's own mental illness or that of another.

Baptism also incorporates one into the Mystical Body of Christ by which one becomes a member of the Church.[30] Since the Church is both a spiritual and visible society, the membership in the Church is an incorporation into both a spiritual society and a visible society. As a member of a visible society, one is able to enjoy the goods which are proper to a society that is seeking holiness and right order, both of which aid mental health. As members of a spiritual society, we also know that the other members are able to pray and merit for us those graces necessary to obtain and maintain mental health.[31]

Moreover, in Baptism, if one is an adult, in order to receive the sacrament voluntarily which is necessary for validity,[32] one vows to lead a life in accordance with virtue, to avoid the allurements of the demonic and to die to the life of vice.[33] Clearly this will have a psychological impact; insofar as one fulfills his baptismal vows, he will lead a life which directly contributes to mental health. If one avoids vices, one is less likely to suffer mental illness. Parents must promise to raise the child in accordance with the theological virtue of faith[34] when their child is baptized which means that they will raise the child in a way that is suited to mental health. This is a future pledge not only

---

[27]Council of Trent, Session VII (Denz. 1609/852; 1624/867). It is because Baptism confers an indelible mark that it cannot be repeated. In fact, all sacraments that confer an indelible mark cannot be repeated. See also Ott, *Fundamentals of Catholic Dogma*, p. 355.

[28]Ott, *Fundamentals of Catholic Dogma*, p. 335. This priesthood is today commonly called the priesthood of the laity.

[29]Hebrews 5:1. This is actually the theme regarding the priesthood throughout the Old and New Testaments. See also ST III, q. 22.

[30]Ott, *Fundamentals of Catholic Dogma*, p. 355.

[31]As part of the invisible society, one enjoys the fruits of the prayers of the saints and angels which will be discussed in the chapter on devotion and prayer.

[32]Innocent III, *Maiores Ecclesiae Causas* (Denz. 781/411). Validity means that the sacrament actually occurs or is confected.

[33]ST III, q. 62, a. 2.

[34]Faith is infused with the baptism of children (ST III, q. 69, a. 6) and so the parents must promise to raise the child Catholic in order not to abuse the sacred virtue by its corruption through heresy or apostasy.

to the Church but to the child that they will provide the right circumstances for the child to grow in the virtue of faith and all other supernatural and natural virtues. Part of the rite of Baptism is the exorcism which provides images by which the person and the parents can further direct their lives away from those things which are likely to cause psychological (and spiritual) harm.

Since Baptism confers sacramental graces proper to itself, we can get an idea of what those graces are. Since we know that God gives the infused virtues and gifts of the Holy Spirit to us to protect our state of grace, the graces of Baptism will be directly ordered toward the preservation of the grace of justification infused during the Baptism. We also receive the graces to fulfill the baptismal vows which are ordered toward the preservation of this sanctifying grace. We receive the graces to lead a virtuous life which will directly affect our mental health. We will also receive the graces to exercise the priesthood of the laity for our own benefit and those of others. Psychologists can greatly aid their directees if they personally are faithful to their Baptismal graces and offer their prayers, sufferings and good works for their directees. While these sacramental graces are ordered toward the person who receives them, they can have a secondary effect on others.

Baptism provides the beginning of the life of grace, both sanctifying and actual. Our Baptism affects other people by the effects it has on both ourselves and them. Psychologists should be baptized for this reason and lead a life in accordance with their Baptismal promises. This also means that they must be leading a life according to the virtue of faith which will directly affect their counseling. Adult directees, if not baptized, if they are properly disposed, should seek Baptism since it will have an effect on their mental health. If they are baptized and suffer from mental illness, the psychologist must ensure that the person is faithfully fulfilling his Baptismal vows in order to ensure that the directee is on his way to recovery.

Another effect that Baptism can have is the mitigation of sorrow. For example, sometimes a child dies due to a miscarriage, an accident or illness. If the child is baptized, the parents of the child or the person being baptized can enjoy a certain consolation that at least the person or child is going to possess eternal beatitude. This is why teaching young people how to do an emergency Baptism – and under what circumstances it is permissible and even obligatory, as in the case of parents with a dying child – is so important. Many women who have had miscarriages and have performed emergency Baptism on the child who was dying during the miscarriage have received great consolation in knowing that their child is in heaven. The stronger a person's faith is, the more consolation this can bring.

II. Confession

Jesus Christ granted to men, by means of the sacramental priesthood, the power to forgive sins which are truly and immediately remitted.[35] This power to forgive sins,

---

[35]Council of Trent, Session XIV (Denz. 1709/919). See also Ott, *Fundamentals of Catholic Dogma*, p. 422.

given to the Church, extends to all sins without exception.[36] In order to be forgiven in the sacrament of Penance,[37] a person must have at least attrition,[38] although contrition is more perfect.[39]

The form of the sacrament of Penance consists in the words of absolution[40] and it is the absolution, along with the confession of the sins, the sorrow of the penitent and intention to do one's penance, which effects the forgiveness of sins. In other words, when the penitent confesses his sin with sorrow and has the intention of doing the penance assigned by the priest, then when the priest gives absolution,[41] the sins are forgiven. In order to receive absolution validly, the penitent must confess all mortal sins.[42] Even though it is not necessary to confess venial sins, it is useful insofar as one receives the sacramental graces ordered to the avoidance of those sins in the future. The sacrament of Penance is necessary for salvation for all of those who fall into mortal sin after Baptism.[43]

The principal effect of the sacrament of Penance is the reconciliation of the sinner with God.[44] The Council of Trent observes that this reconciliation with God

---

[36]Matthew 16:19; Council of Trent, session XIV (Denz. 1701/911). See also Ott, *Fundamentals of Catholic Dogma*, p. 422. This constitutes a great consolation for those whose mental illness may be the product of sin. Penitents can be assured that regardless of whatever sin they may have committed, God will forgive them in this sacrament.

[37]Ott, *Fundamentals of Catholic Dogma*, p. 430.

[38]Attrition, sometimes called imperfect contrition, is sorrow for one's sins which proceeds from a supernatural motive but not merely for the perfect love of God, e.g. if someone is sorry for their sins, not because it necessarily offends God but because they are afraid of being condemned to eternal punishment.

[39]Contrition is a sorrow for one's sins because of perfect love of God, i.e. one is sorry for having offended God Himself. For the distinction between the different kinds of contrition, see Council of Trent, Session XIV (Denz. 1677-8/898) and De Ver, q. 28, a. 8, ad 3.

[40]Council of Trent, Session XIV (Denz. 1673/896). See also Ott, *Fundamentals of Catholic Dogma*, p. 436.

[41]Council of Trent, Session XIV (Denz. 1709/919) and Ott, *Fundamentals of Catholic Dogma*, p. 436.

[42]Council of Trent, Session XIV (Denz. 1679/899; 1707/917) and Ott, *Fundamentals of Catholic Dogma*, p. 432.

[43]See Council of Trent, Session XIV (Denz. 1671/895) and Ott, *Fundamentals of Catholic Dogma*, p. 438.

[44]Council of Trent, Session XIV (Denz. 1674/ 896). See Ott, *Fundamentals of Catholic Dogma*, p. 437. This is why some after the Second Vatican Council "renamed" the sacrament of Penance "Reconciliation." While such a nomination is certainly true, it seems more fitting to name the sacrament, not after its principal effect, but after the nature of the sacrament. The term "penance" indicates that the person is converted or turned from his sin and turned toward God. Yet the term is broader than that insofar as penance is an act which

sometimes has the effect of begetting peace and serenity of conscience with a vehement spiritual consolation.[45] We see one of the first and most beneficial aspects of Confession, viz. that through the process of reconciliation, the person is able to gain a certain peace of soul. Peace is the tranquility of order and here the order is the relation between God our superior and us His subjects. When we are rightly subject to Him, there is a certain peace that arises from it. Through sin, one rejects this order and so, through the sacrament of penance, this order is restored. For those with a sensitive conscience, this restoration to grace and reconciliation to God can bring great tranquility.

This occurs in several ways. Since the conscience makes a judgment that the person has committed an evil, this redounds to one's self image, i.e. to the phantasm one has of oneself. From this arises appetitive sorrow (aside from the sorrow of the will which flowed from the judgment of conscience in the possible intellect). The cogitative power then associates the evil of the act with the person and this is stored in memory. Through Confession, the process is reversed. First, the conscience is cleared as one is no longer held accountable for the sin and so the *vermis conscientiae* is put to rest. Second, it re-orders the cogitative power because the sin can be somewhat disassociated from ourselves. Here we say somewhat, insofar as the cogitative power no longer views oneself under the aspect of sorrow, even though the cogitative power is capable of re-associating with ourselves some sinful action. It also helps to direct the cogitative power insofar as when one sins, the cogitative power will know from its past experience of Confession, where to look to seek mitigation of one's sorrow. This is important because by going to the sacrament of Penance regularly, the cogitative power is habituated in how to assess our sinful actions, i.e. it recognizes both that sin is bad but also once one has sinned, where he must go. Before one sins, the cogitative power will re-associate with the action the need for contrition and penance, the suffering from the sin, etc. and so it will be rightly ordered.

Hence, the sacrament of Penance mitigates sorrow and this is highly important for those who have committed sins and are now suffering the effects of those sins. Some of the effects of the sin can be mitigated directly by going to Confession and indirectly by the re-ordering of the faculties, which the sacrament causes. Often, people will

---

one performs to make up to God for the sins that one has committed. Since this world was created by God with the intention of manifesting His glory, each time we sin, we steal or take away from what is rightfully His, viz. glory as should be manifest in our good actions. Therefore, through the sacrament of Penance, one has sorrow for one's sins, his sins are absolved and then the priest assigns a penance to make up for the glory lost. Moreover, one can receive this sacrament without being in the state of mortal sin in which one must be reconciled with God. Venial sin does not sever the relationship with God and so one does not, properly speaking, need to be reconciled. This is why one does not have to confess venial sins, but it is still salutary and good for Catholics to do so, as will become clearer as the chapter progresses. Nevertheless, the term reconciliation tends to give some people the impression that one should only go to Confession to be reconciled, i.e. if one has mortal sin.

[45]Council of Trent, Session XIV (Denz. 1674/896).

commit a grevious sin, e.g. abortion, and even though they may be in a certain state of denial, the cogitative power has already associated with the self the evil of the sin. From this arises sorrow. As noted from the prior volume, the specific content or cause of the sorrow may be lost over time but the cogitative power continues in its habituated assessment of self toward sorrow. Over time, the person begins to become depressed, even though he is unaware that it comes from his sin. Even if it is not a grave sin but one which occurs often over the course of time, then the person's cogitative power begins to "accumulate," if you will, this bad assessment of oneself and so one's self-image begins to deteriorate. Obviously, if one is evil, this assessment is appropriate.

As the sorrow from the accumulated assessment of self begins to build and the specific reasons are forgotten or even if they are not forgotten, the person can enter into depression. We see, therefore, that there is a direct relation between sin and depression. Not all forms of depression are caused by sin, since there can be other causes. However, many suffer from depression not from a physiological cause but from their sin. Only frequent Confession can solve this form of depression. One Confession is not enough because they must begin to habituate the cogitative power to reassess themselves over the long haul and so they will slowly come out of their depression. While it is possible for God to give them the grace from a single Confession to overcome their depression, it is more likely that it will take some time to overcome the depression through frequent Confession.

Mistakes are often made in the spiritual life and in psychology by assuming that, if you do something once or a few times, the effect should be immediate. Clearly, given the fact that our powers are habituated by sin, as exampled in the above discussion of depression, and since acquired habits cannot be corrupted through a single action, then the habits which lead to depression likewise will not be overcome in a single action. People fail to realize how deeply sin wounds our spiritual and psychological nature and, just as a deep physical wound is not healed in a day, neither are our psychological "wounds" caused from sin. This applies not only to Confession but to the entire spiritual and psychological life. Quick fixes are rare and it is only when one has taken the time and done the work (i.e. performed the right actions repeatedly) that one begins to get a clarity of mind regarding those things which cause one's mental illness or the mental illness itself. Therefore, because someone does not see the effects of his psychological work immediately, he should not stop doing what is right.[46] Again, habits die hard and so it will take time and repeated action to get the desired effects. The more disordered someone is, the more work he will have to do to bring the faculties back into right working order due to the depth of the habituation. All too often, psychologists and beginners in the spiritual life abandon spiritual practices because they did not get the effect immediately or soon enough in their own judgment.

The sacrament of Penance also heals our imagination insofar as we now see

---

[46]It is analogous to the person who is out of shape physically. One cannot expect to be completely in shape by merely running once. Rather, physical conditioning requires repeated exercise for the body to come into shape. Likewise, in the spiritual life, we have to do things repeatedly to bring our soul "into shape," so to speak.

ourselves as having righted the wrong and having done the right thing. This helps us to improve our image of ourselves by recognizing that God is helping us through grace to perfect ourselves and to overcome our disorders. Second, it also helps us to recognize our ability to fall into the types of sins which we commit. This has a direct connection to what is called the grace of forgetfulness.[47] This grace works in a variety of different ways in different people according to their state in life but with respect to the penitent it has two primary effects. The first is that it helps the person not to recall the specific content of their sins. The images which we have of our past sins can cause us to fall into sin again, which will have further psychological effects; yet this grace helps us not to recall them. It seems that it works directly on the memory but it must also have an effect on the cogitative power insofar as it heals the association with certain kinds of acts or circumstances of our sins of the past. Since the function of the cogitative power is to go back into memory and associate with the phantasm in the imagination the sensible species which has been stored that is like or connected to the phantasm, then this grace breaks that association so that our past sins are not associated with the phantasm in the future. While this works antecedently, so that nothing comes into our imaginations that could cause us to sin or do harm to ourselves or others, it does not take away the person's ability to recall it voluntarily.

The second effect of the grace of forgetfulness is that it renders the person keenly aware of his ability to fall into this species of sin. For instance, if a person in the past had a number of enjoyable bouts with alcohol and had become an alcoholic, the grace of forgetfulness causes the cogitative power not to associate the past experiences with it, nor the memory to recall the specific times that he did it. But just like the fact that one can have an accumulative assessment of oneself as described above with regard to depression, the cogitative power can gain, by this grace and by our own custody of our imaginations, a capacity to assess the action as harmful, as well as easy for one to fall into, without digging up the specific sense species of our actions in memory. By this grace, the cogitative power performs this function under the impetus of God whereas by custody of the mind, it performs this function by habituation. The judgment of the possible intellect and the motion of the will removes the specific content and the negative judgment of the will redounds to the image. The cogitative power then learns that this action is bad and the cogitative power will disassociate from the image any specific sensible species. Hence, in the future, the cogitative power, once habituated, will not associate the specific image from memory, but it will give a negative assessment of the species of action which one has in the imagination.

This is one of the most important effects of this grace as well as the habit of custody of the mind and it leads us to another aspect of the cogitative power that is crucial for psychology. When the cogitative power is habituated in this fashion by custody of the mind, it is taught how to react to specific images or phantasms. As the cogitative power is habituated, it will actually begin to help one to maintain one's mental

---

[47]Some saints and authors call this the purification of memory.

health.[48] This follows from the fact that once it is habituated, it will react and assess the phantasm according to its habituation. This in turn will affect our judgment. For example, if a married man has a problem with adultery and he goes to Confession regularly and practices custody of the mind, over time the cogitative power will recognize that women who are not his wife should not be viewed sexually.

This normally occurs in the following way and it can be applied to anything that causes spiritual, moral and psychological harm. When a person recognizes that his cogitative power is not assessing a specific kind of image in accordance with virtue, he must start by practicing custody of the senses[49] and custody of the mind. Custody of mind is twofold and the control a person has over the imagination normally starts with the first and progresses to the second, as the habituation in the imagination grows. The first is that once an image which can cause harm comes into the person's imagination, he must switch it to something which he enjoys doing, which is morally licit and which will not cause psychological harm. So, in the case of the man with a problem with adultery, if he sees a woman who is not his wife and he notes that the cogitative power has made the assessment of good for sensible pleasure, he must switch his mind to something he likes, like fishing, or mechanical work, or something of this kind.[50] This first step normally occurs because the appetites will hold onto the image and so it is easier to switch to an image that the appetites like that is morally licit than to try and kick out the image altogether. As the man begins to make progress with chastity and custody of the mind,[51] he will begin to notice that the cogitative power is making the assessment less. As he gains greater control over the imagination, he can then begin the process of reformulating the image which causes him difficulty to a *ratio* or perspective that is in congruity with reality. In the case of the man with adultery problems, he can change the image of women he is around who are not his wife in such a way that he looks at them from the point of view of the salvation of their souls or as people worthy of respect and dignity. As time goes on, the cogitative power will begin to look at this image in that way which means he has gained psychological health in relation to that object.

This process avoids two problems. The first is it roots out the problem at the

---

[48]On the spiritual side of things, it helps one to maintain one's virtue and state of grace.

[49]Custody of the senses consists in never allowing into one's senses anything that will lead one into sin or cause one psychological harm.

[50]Some switch the mind to prayer which is better than merely switching the image to something we enjoy that is morally licit. Some people actually enjoy prayer even in the beginning stages and so these two are not mutually exclusive. However, normally, the appetites do not want to pray and so the use of prayer is often harder for those starting out and so the use of prayer normally occurs later in the first stage. It is always beneficial, once one has changed the image to something licit and is free of passion or temptation, to pray and thank our Lord and our Lady for the grace to overcome the problem.

[51]This can be applied to any object which causes mental illness.

level of imagination which affects judgment and then one's actions. The second is that this process redirects the faculties without falling into the problem of avoidance. One must avoid those persons, places and things which may cause psychological harm or cause one to fall into sin. This is based upon the truth, viz. the truth that one cannot relate properly to these things so that he must keep his distance so as not to cause himself further harm. As he begins to gain a certain amount of control over the problem and the mental illness or vice begins to wane, then he can reformulate the image more in congruity with reality and so he ceases having to avoid that which causes the image. Avoidance in the negative sense consists in not dealing with the thing as it is, whereas avoidance in the proper sense helps one in the initial stage as a recognition of truth, viz. the person has a problem with this. But it does not end in denying reality, as negative avoidance does, but ultimately ends up in a true understanding of the nature of the object which in the past caused trouble.

To return to the sacrament of Penance, we also realize that Confession, like the process explained above, helps one to appropriate one's sin or even one's mental illness. In other words, Confession helps one to own up to sin, recognize he has a problem with it, and therefore deal with it. Like the alcoholic who cannot address his problem until he admits he has one, so the sinner cannot address the sin until he appropriates it and recognizes that he has it as well as the problems which relate to the sin. Confession makes us own up to our sins so that we are more likely to begin working on them which will then have a direct psychological impact.

Moreover, by owning up to the sin, the intellect comes into conformity with the truth which will have a direct effect on the possible intellect. The truth is that by our sin we have committed evil, since sin is an evil. When we own up to it, we can be sorry for it since sin is an evil. The sensitive passion and motion of the will proper to the presence of evil is sorrow. Therefore, the faculties come into conformity with right reason and reality by sorrowing for the sin, which cannot occur until one appropriates one's sin. We see, now, why sorrow is necessary for God and the priest in Confession to absolve or forgive the sin. If one does not have sorrow, one's intellect is not conforming to the truth and the will is not following right order, which is to sorrow for the evil done. In effect, by not sorrowing for one's sin, one is not in contact with reality. Sin itself is a denial of reality or a stepping away from reality by the intellect and will, since one chooses something under the aspect of the good when in reality it is evil and harmful to oneself. God respects our free will and if we do not sorrow for our sin, then, in effect, we volitionally choose to keep our sin. God will not take our sin away from us unless we ask. But we will not ask unless we recognize our sin as evil and decide we do not want it as part of us. Moreover, if we want our sin, God cannot forgive us, because we continue offending Him by keeping our sin. It is only once we are sorry for our sins, that our faculties and soul are disposed toward God taking them away from us since we want them taken away. Again, God respects our freedom and He sees that once we are sorry for our sins, we suffer from them and then God's mercy will be extended to us.[52]

All of this orders the will back to God. Hence, confession has an inherent ordering effect on the faculties. Since man is ordered toward God for his happiness, then the man who frequents confession is more likely to be happy, since he is able to maintain that order and act in congruity with his last end. Just as a life of virtue begets imperfect happiness, so the life of frequent confession begets happiness since both a life of virtue and Confession lead us to God. Aristotle observes that in motion as one approaches the end of the motion, one takes on the nature of the end (e.g. as one begins to heat an object it begins to become increasingly hot as it approaches its optimal temperature) so, in confession and virtuous living, we begin to take on a resemblance of eternal life.

Going to frequent Confession begets a certain joy for two reasons. The first is what was just stated, viz. it begins to take on a certain resemblance of eternal life. Second, there will be a joy in fulfilling the natural and transcendent orders of justice. When we commit a sin, we violate God's right to perfect glory in His creation. Therefore, by going to Confession, one is able to reestablish the order of justice by having his sins forgiven and thereby increase in grace and give God greater glory. Moreover, we have an obligation in justice to ask God's forgiveness since we have offended Him. Part of the natural law is that man is ordered toward virtue, one of which is justice. Part of justice is retribution in which we pay back what we owe. This is a natural inclination and to frustrate it can lead to mental illness. By going to Confession, we re-establish the order of justice by paying back to God what is due to Him and thereby fulfill our natural inclination toward retributive justice.

Given all of the aforesaid, we can see that the sacrament of Penance or Confession is the sacrament of humility. By this is meant that this sacrament begets a great deal of humility, because one must not judge oneself greater than one is by appropriating one's sin. As one comes into conformity with the truth by willingly owning up to the truth about his sinfulness, one attains a certain humility which is sometimes defined as willingness to live in accordance with the truth. All virtues are rooted in humility insofar as without it one cannot attain the truth and therefore come to any virtue which helps our faculties to relate to their proper objects as they truly are. Since mental health consists in virtue, mental health requires humility and this sacrament directly contributes to humility.

We have already seen that, on an appetitive level, Confession aids *per accidens* mental health. However, confession also provides another appetitive benefit. By going

---

[52]Those who assert that God forgives everyone, even those not sorry for their sins, are not in contact with reality and are not aiding people. It essentially proposes that God acts irrationally, i.e. He gives us free will, we want our sin which is a deviation from Him and yet He still gives us Himself through His mercy. This is to imply contradiction since God would both give us free will and then deny our free will by forgiving our sins which the will desires to keep. Rather, God's mercy only extends to the contrite and to those who are ignorant and do not know what they are doing. The latter is the case when the sins are not truly voluntary.

to Confession and being able to confess one's sins to a priest, the sorrow from the sins which we commit is mitigated. As mentioned in the prior volume, when one tells a friend what saddens him, the friend is able to carry some of the burden and therefore the person suffering the sorrow experiences an alleviation of the sorrow. This is one of the reasons why going to a priest rather than merely confessing to God is more beneficial to our mental health. In fact, by confessing to a priest, one not only benefits from someone else carrying the burden, but one is also forced into an honest reckoning with oneself. It is too easy merely to ask God for forgiveness: because we do not see Him, this has less of a psychological impact than if we have to stand before someone who represents God and verbally formulate and confess our sins. As a result, by confessing to someone we can see, we are more humbled and sorry for our sins.

This brings us to a topic which is often misunderstood but needs to be addressed and that has to do with the distinction between real and emotional guilt. Real guilt is the judgment of the possible intellect, i.e. of conscience, that one has committed a sin. Emotional guilt is the guilt which we experience when the image in our imagination causes the passion of sorrow at something we have done. This distinction is very important for understanding how some mental illnesses occur. When one commits an evil, normally emotional and real guilt go hand in hand. So when one goes to Confession, each form of guilt tends to be alleviated. However, both forms of guilt can occur without the other, e.g. a person who is accustomed to leading a life according to the appetites, may commit a sin against the Sixth Commandment and because he is habituated that way, he does not feel any emotional guilt. However, he does know or is able to judge that he has done something wrong. On the other hand, it is possible for a person to have emotional guilt without real guilt. This often occurs in people who may have done something involuntarily or suffered some violence.

An example would be a woman who is raped. She may not have given any consent and was physically forced to undergo the rape. Since she did not give consent, there is no real guilt. But the cogitative power may have had a prior habituation in which it was trained to assess conjugal relations outside of marriage as evil. The result is that the woman emotionally feels guilty because the cogitative power associates the conjugal act with her and so guilt and sorrow arise even though there is no volitional consent. She may even think that she could have done something to prevent it and that may be the source of her emotional guilt, even if there was nothing she could have done. She can imagine her actions as different, which would have resulted in her not being in the presence of her attacker and so she thinks she could have done something. Obviously, if she has no means of knowing what is about to happen, she is not volitionally entering into the act. This kind of emotional guilt is remedied by viewing herself as unknowing before hand and as not having control over the situation and by viewing her attacker as being in control. In effect, she must disassociate herself from being the cause of the action.

Another example of emotional guilt when real guilt is not present is with respect to women who have had abortions. While the psychology of post-abortion women is complex and leads to a variety of different reactions in the women themselves, nevertheless, once a woman comes to the stage where she wants to be forgiven by God, Catholic women will often come to Confession. Their confessions are often fraught with deep self-sorrow or self-loathing, fear of what the priest might say, the sorrow of having committed the sin and fear of being punished eternally for it. When the priest gives absolution, women will often find that the fear of the priest dissipates, but fear of damnation, sorrow and self-loathing continue, due to the cogitative power's associating the act with themselves. Because they have truly committed the act and because it is irreversible since the child is dead, this emotional guilt often persists in women until death. By attending Mass faithfully and getting to confession frequently and leading a good life, women will often find the fear of damnation begin to wane because the cogitative power has recognized something good in the image they have of themselves. However, to be able to take away the emotional sorrow often requires a great deal. Women will often have "replacement" babies in order to make up for the child that they killed but they often find this does not solve the problem. The only way for the sorrow to be truly mitigated is by the woman fulfilling the transcendent order of justice. She is incapable of fulfilling the natural order of justice to the child, except perhaps by praying and offering up some kind of penance for the child.[53] In this way, the woman will begin

---

[53]This is said with a clear understanding that the status of unbaptized children who die is theologically debated. There are essentially five logical positions, some of which are in congruity with the faith and some that are not. There is that which states that all children who die unbaptized go to hell and such a position is reconcilable with Catholic teaching and Scripture. However, it does seem incongruous that God would create a child with free will and then damn the child without any responsibility on the part of the child. The second position is that of limbo in which those in limbo enjoy a natural happiness even though they are eternally separated from God. This position is favored by the Fathers of the Church and tradition, although some say it does not escape the prior incongruity of a child being consigned to something over which he had no choice. The third position states that children go straight to heaven, but this is contrary to Scripture and the teaching of the Church which states that no one can enter the kingdom of God without being baptized, albeit either by water, blood or desire. The fourth position holds that the faith of the parents suffices for the infusion of grace, but this position has arisen out of an erroneous understanding of the parental role in Baptism of water. The parents' faith is only a necessary condition for the child to be baptized since, by baptism, faith is infused into the child. If the child is not raised Catholic, the supernatural virtue of faith will be corrupted due to theological error in the child's upbringing. Since faith is supernatural and therefore sacred, to corrupt it is sacrilege. Therefore, the parents must have faith so that future sacrilege does not occur. However, even though it is a necessary condition to guarantee the right development of the knowledge in relation to the virtue of faith, the parent's faith or intention is not causal of the child's Baptism or the infusion of grace. The last position holds that God, at the moment of death, provides the child with sufficient knowledge in order for it to make a choice. In this case, the mother could pray for the child so that her prayers may merit some grace for the child which would incline him to make the right choice. Since God is outside of time, he can take the merits from an action which occurs to us in the future (though present to Himself from all eternity) and apply it in the past, since for God, past, present and future are one. Even if the status of the child is such that prayers cannot benefit the child, the prayers will not be wasted since they will go into the spiritual treasury of the Church.

to associate something good she has done for the child and so the cogitative power will begin, slowly, to change its perspective or *ratio* on the woman in this regard. Some women find some relief by helping others not to have abortions and go through the same trauma that they have and this aids the cogitative power by associating in the image something which she has done which is opposite to the abortion. A woman can also find some relief emotionally by doing penance and prayer to God in atonement for her sin of abortion and over the long haul this will provide some relief.

By confessing to a priest, the penitent is more assured of the forgiveness of the sins. Since the sacraments work *ex opere operato*, the penitent knows that if he is sorry for his sins and goes to Confession and receives absolution, there is a higher degree of certitude of the forgiveness. While confessing to a priest may be more humiliating, there is a certain relief once the confession occurs and the person has sense knowledge that he is forgiven by hearing the words of absolution. One of the objections of Protestants is that we do not need a priest. While the aforesaid should make it clear that God was wise in requiring confession of grave sins to a priest, nevertheless we can see that going straight to God does not give one the same assurance that his sins are forgiven and this is for two reasons. The first is that he does not have certitude whether God has granted the request of his prayer or not. But also, if one has committed mortal sin, he cannot merit grace and therefore the forgiveness of his sins by going directly to God, unless he has perfect contrition for his sins.[54] But because of the complexity of human motives arising from the objects of volition and the object of appetites as well as attachments to the pleasures in sin, etc. it is normally very difficult for one to have perfect contrition insofar as he is sorry because He loves God and sorrows at offending Him alone. More often than not, contrition is mixed, since we have other motives for seeking God's forgiveness, such as freedom from sin, freedom from the punishment of sin, the desire to be freed of the effects of sin, as in the case of directees and things of this sort. Therefore, by the sacrament of Penance the penitent has greater assurance that his sin is forgiven since only attrition is necessary – even though contrition is preferred – to have his sins absolved.

Moreover, through the sacrament of Penance, the penitent is aided more in leading a better life than if he merely goes to God to ask for forgiveness. Each sacrament begets sacramental graces, which, in the case of Confession, directly aid the penitent in avoiding the sins confessed in the future. This is crucial for directees whose psychological illness is caused by sin or whose psychological illness may dispose them to sin. One of the primary difficulties as a psychologist is that counsel can be given to the directee but very often the directee finds the fulfilling of what he is counseled, i.e. what he needs to do to overcome his problems, very difficult. Often directees simply lapse into past activities which beget or maintain their mental illness because of weakness of the will. But since grace strengthens the will, the sacramental graces of

---

[54]"The motive for perfect contrition is the perfect love of God, i.e. charity. It consists in this: that God is loved for His Own Sake above all" (Ott, *Fundamentals of Catholic Dogma*, p.427.) In other words, one has no other motive than purely the love of God and the sorrow at offending God Himself.

Confession will directly strengthen the will in relation to the actions which are sinful and may cause mental illness. This aspect of Confession cannot be stressed enough. Directees will often experience a certain strength after Confession to avoid the sin but as time goes on they find their strength weakening. This can be due to a variety of factors, but when the directee finds himself weakened, he must go back to Confession and confess his sins. Even if he has not committed the sin which is causing his mental illness, he can derive strength from the sacrament in regard to that sin by confessing it as a sin of his past life at the end of the confessing of his sins.[55] Therefore, when he reconfesses the sin from the past, the penitent receives grace again in order to avoid the sin in the future and to take away any effects which may remain from the past sins. Frequent confession of the sin which causes mental illness will eventually take away the mental illness presuming the penitent/directee is doing his part in not falling into the sin and confessing with true sorrow and sincerity. Directees who do not want to go to the sacrament of Penance must be told to continue to do so if for no other reason than the reception of the sacramental graces of Confession.

It is here that we see the value of general Confessions. General Confession can take two forms. The first is that one goes to Confession and tells the priest his sins since his last Confession plus anything else which may constitute sin but with which he is generally struggling. The second and more efficacious form is when the penitent confesses all of the sins of his past life. By confessing all of the sins of his past life, the penitent will gain the graces to stay out of the sins he has committed in the past as well as have some of the effects of those sins taken away. The directee should make a general Confession, on average, once every five years or more often at the discretion of a prudent priest in order to continue to gain the graces necessary to keep his mental illness at bay and to gain strength to overcome his mental illness. If a directee comes to a psychologist for the first time and has not made a general Confession in some time, he should be encouraged to do so in order to begin the process of healing the mental illness by submitting to God's action and grace.

Also, those who make general Confessions find the process purifying and it is also accompanied by a catharsis. All of the emotional build-up in relation to past sins and any residual appetitive attachments or reactions to sins will find a certain resolution by submitting the sins again to a confessor. Those who have committed grievous sins, particularly ones which they considered heinous or which have caused mental illness, will find great benefit from a general Confession. While the cathartic benefit is clear in

---

[55]"Those sins which are already forgiven directly by the Church's 'Power of the Keys' are a sufficient object of Confession. According to the declaration of Benedict XI, the repetition of Confession is an act of submission and therefore atonement. In this case the absolution, according to the teaching of theologians, results not only in the removal of any obstacles which remain as an effect of the sins already forgiven and which oppose the efficacy of grace (*reliquae peccatorum*), but also in the remission of the temporal punishments of sin which remain." -- Ott, *Fundamentals of Catholic Dogma*, p. 433. Cf. Benedictus XI, *Inter Cunctas Sollicitudines* (Denz. 880/470).

every Confession, it is particularly present in general Confessions.[56]

Forgiveness of one's sins also directly contributes to mental health, since by the forgiveness of sins the sorrow of the sin is released from the soul. This of course will have an effect on all of the various faculties which has already been discussed. This also applies to asking for forgiveness from those we offend through our sin, other than God. Part of sin is that we become a debtor to others. We have already seen this in relation to God but when we commit a sin against another person, we owe that person something because he has a right not to be sinned against. Therefore, by asking for forgiveness, the person can let go of any anxiety (which is another name for fear) about suffering at the hands of the other person. When we commit sins against others, they often seek retribution and by being forgiven, while we may be required to make some kind of retribution, we know that it will not be extracted from us at the hands of others. By asking for and receiving forgiveness we create an atmosphere among our relations that is more conducive to peace and therefore mental health. Often people in a family find their relations strained because of past offenses and this can even lead to mental illness among those with weaker psychological constitutions.

Often someone who is mentally ill has allowed his mental illness to cause offenses and difficulties within a family and so it is critical that he asks for forgiveness and asks others to pray and do penance for him to merit the graces for him to overcome his difficulties. In overcoming mental illness, the first thing that must be done is that exterior factors must be properly disposed so as not to continue to distract the person. If the family is hostile to the directee because of his mental illness, the family situation is another issue with which he must deal. Whereas, if the family comes together and forgives the person who has caused the family problems, an atmosphere of generosity can be created. The family will more likely put up with any antics which flow from the mental illness and use those antics as reminders to pray for the person and to offer up the suffering of those very antics for the person. The directee will know that the family is positively seeking his betterment, so he does not have to deal as much with the mess he has created exteriorly. This allows him to focus more on the interior battle for normalcy and can actually provide an exterior motivation to do what he needs to do in order to become mentally healthy, i.e. when he sees others acting in charity on his behalf.

Forgiving others also provides a great deal of psychological benefit. Forgiveness is the remitting or releasing from the debt of justice that one person owes to another because of some act which the person has committed against the other. For human beings, this has a profound impact. When we forgive someone, the possible intellect sees the good that can come from forgiving the person. Since we are all sinners, the possible intellect will judge and see the necessity of people practicing forgiveness for the sake of the common good. The will in letting go of the offense committed against him performs an act of detachment in which the good of vindication is let go. If we volitionally hold on to evils committed against us in order to seek vindication, it

---

[56]General Confession must be denied to the scrupulous because it will only aid and abet their problems.

will flow over into the lower faculties and cause disorders, such as anger, sorrow, fear of never getting revenge, the passion of despair when one feels that he cannot be vindicated and feels helpless. Forgiveness affects the cogitative power by disassociating with the image of the other person the desire for vindication. This will cause a decrease in anger and so we can begin to see that forgiveness can actually have a cathartic effect. Passions will quiet down and memory can be healed, since in the memory the harm caused to self will be forgotten in light of the good we have done to the individual by forgiving him.

Forgiveness must, however, be based in something real, i.e. we should forgive people when they are ignorant or sorry. If a person knowingly offends us and refuses to be sorry for it and continues offending, we should not extend our forgiveness exteriorly to them. We must always forgive them interiorly for our own benefit and because of Christ's precept, but sometimes the exterior effects of our forgiveness should not be extended for the benefit of the person committing the sins. If, however, we find that even though he does not want to be sorry for what he has done because of the blindness which his sinning against us has caused, we should forgive him because he displays practical ignorance. Since his judgment is blinded, we can forgive him for what he does because he does not fully understand what he is doing. On one level, we can forgive all human beings in this life[57] since we all suffer from blindness of the intellect due to original and actual sin. But caution must be taken that, for the well-being of a person, we do not extend the effects of our forgiveness until he has shown repentance. This is necessary; otherwise, the person may continue in offending people because he knows he can get away with it, since people will forgive him. Just as when God forgives us He does it for our benefit, so too must we do the same.

Two last issues remain in our brief discussion of the psychological benefits of Confession. The first has to do with why we undergo temptations. Penitents will often complain that they go to Confession, confess their sins and then sometime afterwards fall into the sins again after being tempted. Some will even complain that they cannot understand why God allows them to be tempted when He knows that they do not want to fall into sin anymore. There are a number of reasons why God allows us to suffer temptations but only a few will be discussed here.

The first reason is that, just as a person whose arm muscles are weak must work those arm muscles to become strong, so too we, when we have a weakness of the will (a vice), must perform acts opposite to the weakness in order to strengthen the will. Therefore, God allows us to be tempted by the sin which causes our downfall, not so that we may fall, but so that by saying no to the sin the vice or weakness may be overcome

---

[57]Forgiveness of those who have died is particularly important since it is able to put to rest all ill will and feelings towards those who have died. No greater vindication or justice can be levied against them than death and we know that God will extract justice from them. However, being mindful of our own capacities to be like them, in humility we should forgive them and pray for them so that they, if they be in heaven or purgatory, can pray for us. Many directees suffer from problems which arise out of not forgiving parents or others who have treated them badly.

by performing actions opposite in species to the vice. Hence, it is very difficult to grow in virtue unless we perform acts contrary to the vice and temptations are a normal part of growing morally, spiritually and psychologically strong.[58] Hence, it is not just a matter of corrupting a vice but developing a virtue.

The second reason is so that we will become more dependent on His grace and less dependent on ourselves. Since we are our own worst enemy in the sense that we are prone to doing the very things we know we should not, God wants us to become more dependent on Him. The third reason is so that we vanquish Satan who is often the source of the temptation. As will be discussed in a later chapter, we concede a certain amount of dominion over ourselves to Satan by acting in congruity with his temptations which are carried out in the flesh. Therefore, when Satan tempts us again, we are able to break his dominion over us.[59]

Temptations also remind the person of his weaknesses or even his mental illness. Without it being called to mind by temptation, it is too easy to be deluded that one has conquered the problem. We are also humbled by showing our need for God and what kind of a mess we can make out of ourselves. One of the signs that sin is deeply rooted in the soul is that it takes repeated actions to get it out. Temptations likewise cause us suffering if our will is rightly ordered and we desire to do the right thing. Since we have sinned and must pay back to God glory taken from Him, the temptations as a suffering become a means to atone for the sins of our past life, i.e. to fulfill the requirements of retributive justice by performing the meritorious action of rejecting the temptation. This is why saints would often say that their sufferings are the due punishment for the sins of their past life.

The point in all of this is that the directee should not be disturbed that temptations, which are in the area of his mental illness, may come. Rather, he must be properly directed by the psychologist to view them in a positive light, i.e. as a means to strengthen his intellect and will regarding the mental illness. As one overcomes temptations and sees things for what they really are, i.e. they cause us suffering and to be weak and vulnerable, the person will begin to get a clarity of mind from the very temptations. They will see that the mental illness is a true vice. Therefore, the directee should be counseled not to be troubled and not to assume something is wrong because he is tempted. Rather, temptations will come at periodic times according to the providential plan of God so that he may use them to overcome his problems. Each victory in the fight against temptations will build the person's confidence, rather than deluding himself that he has virtue in the absence of vice, i.e. in the absence of temptation and the thing which causes his fall.

The last aspect of Confession that must be addressed is the issue of those who

---

[58]We need grace to overcome temptations and so, since grace is gratuitous, we should not seek occasions of temptation on our own since we are not certain if God will provide the grace. However, when God Himself allows a temptation, we know He will provide the grace to overcome the temptation. For this reason, directees should be warned not to seek temptations out in order to become stronger.

[59]The psychological ramifications of this will be better grasped later in the book.

do not want to go to Confession at all. While we have already addressed those who might have intellectual objections, nevertheless there are all sorts of appetitive objections. Some are scared at what the priest will say. Assurance can be given to the directee that the priest is there to help and extend God's mercy and not to punish him. Some are scared of dealing with the very thing that is causing their mental illness. But they must be assured that God will give them the grace to endure the Confession in order to bring them into a state of grace and to deal with the problem. They can also be encouraged by discussing the benefits of Confession and how through the catharsis they will feel better (although this should not be stressed too much, since it can engender an attitude that one goes to Confession to feel better rather than to be reconciled with God and have his sins forgiven). Some do not like to go to Confession because they loathe the fact that they have to admit their sins. This is more common than may appear since often other reasons are given rather than the true reason which is pride. Some do not want to have to suffer their pride and self-respect. In nearly all cases, the fear of Confession is irrational.

While a great deal has been discussed regarding the directee, it is clear that psychologists must also confess regularly. Obviously, Confession will give them the grace to avoid sins which may compromise their own mental strength, which can be later affected by being around those who are mentally ill. As was warned against in the first volume, the principle of resemblance is in force. If the psychologist is mentally ill, he can affect his patients. Conversely, if the psychologist is mentally healthy and goes to Confession regularly, thereby enjoying the effects of frequent Confession, he can more readily testify to them. Also, it is not reasonable for a Catholic counselor to expect his directees to go to Confession or to listen to his advice when they know he does not heed his own advice. Many psychologists are mentally ill themselves and often go into psychology to learn about themselves. While psychology is not the place for the mentally ill to study any more than the sexually disordered should become priests, nevertheless, psychologists must recognize that due to original and actual sin, they suffer weakness, both psychological and spiritual, regarding which they need help.

III. Holy Communion

"The Eucharist is that Sacrament, in which Christ, under the forms of bread and wine, is truly present with His Body and Blood, in order to offer Himself in an unbloody manner to the Heavenly Father, and to give Himself to the faithful as nourishment for their souls."[60] This definition contains all of the essential elements of this sacrament. The Eucharist[61] is the Body, Blood,[62] Soul and Divinity of Christ,[63] i.e. the Whole of

---

[60]Ott, *Fundamentals of Catholic Dogma*, p. 370.

[61]This sacrament is also called the *Sanctissimum* (The Most Holy), the Blessed Sacrament and the Sacred Host. The term Eucharist in Greek means to thank or thanksgiving. In modern theological circles, the term Eucharist is often used so as to detract from the sacrificial aspects of the sacrament. However, the historical use of the term does not exclude but contains the sacrificial understanding and, in many cases, is the predominate

Christ[64] is really, truly and substantially[65] present. While the Eucharist is God, i.e. Christ, the accidents of the bread and wine remain, i.e. the appearances of bread and wine remain.[66] It is by the light of faith informed by the teachings of the Church, which has passed on the teachings of Christ on this Sacrament, that gives one assurance of the presence of Christ. The form of this Sacrament is by nature sacrificial insofar as the form indicates the sacrificing[67] of His Body and Blood in expiation for sins. Since the Eucharist is God, worship is due to Christ as present in the Eucharist.[68]

On a psychological level, this Sacrament is very important since it teaches man that things of the senses are there for us to come to knowledge of spiritual realities. When we see the accidents of the bread, by the supernatural virtue of faith we know that God is present. This helps man to direct his life of the senses to God by looking beyond the life of the senses to something deeper. Some might argue that such a doctrine is inimical to mental health since what one sees is not what the thing is. Yet it is through the supernatural virtue of faith that one recognizes the truth that even though It appears as bread and wine, It is still the Body, Blood, Soul and Divinity of Christ and faith also teaches us that the appearances of bread and wine are only appearances and so one is not backed into the intellectual contradiction of It being bread, wine *and* Christ. Since the substance of the bread and wine does not remain, It is not bread and wine.

On another level, God knows that man desires a physical "closeness" because

---

understanding of the term.

[62]That this sacrament contains the Body and Blood of Christ see Matthew 26: 26-28; Mark 14: 22-34; Luke 22:15-20; I Cor. 11: 23-25; John 6 and Council of Trent, Session XIII (Denz. 1651/883f). Cf. Fourth Lateran Council (Denz 802/430; 860/465).

[63]Council of Trent, Session XIII (Denz. 1651/883)

[64]Council of Trent, Session XIII (Denz. 1653/885). Cf. Council of Florence, *Decretum pro Armeniis* (Denz. 1320/698 – see also Denz. 1639/876) and Ott, *Fundamentals of Catholic Dogma*, p.385. This indicates that there is no aspect of Christ lacking to the Sanctissimum. It also means that the whole Christ is present under the sacred species of bread and the whole Christ is present under the sacred species of wine.

[65]"Substantially present" means that the substance of the bread is changed into the whole of Christ and therefore the substance of bread no longer exists.

[66]Council of Trent, Session XIII (Denz. 1652/884) The accidents include all those things perceived by the senses, such as size, weight shape, color, taste and smell.

[67]For a further discussion of the sacrificial aspects of this Sacrament see Ott, *Fundamentals of Catholic Dogma*, p. 402-412. The fact that God sacrifices Himself in the Calvary sacrifice and the fact that the Mass is the participation in the Calvary sacrifice, moves the directee to recognize to what lengths God is willing to go to save him. In meditating on the fact that Christ's Passion and Death involved so much suffering, the directee can be moved to sorrow for his sins, the psychological benefits of which we have already discussed.

[68]Council of Trent, Session XIII (Denz. 1656/888). See also Ott, *Fundamentals of Catholic Dogma*, p. 387.

of the nature of his body/soul composite. This is why it is not enough for someone merely to hear the beloved's voice, but he actually wants to see and to touch the beloved. This Sacrament has a twofold beneficial psychological effect in this regard. The first is that one can physically go to the local presence of the species of bread and wine,[69] and know that that which is contained under the appearance of bread and wine is God. As a result, there is a certain fulfillment in man in knowing that God is physically present. In this respect it is easier for man to direct his faculties to worshiping God Whom he knows is substantially present to him.[70] This presence can bring great consolation to the soul and for those who suffer mental illness, frequently adoring Our Lord either exposed in adoration or merely present in the tabernacle can greatly aid those who suffer from fear, sorrow and other negative psychological illnesses.

His presence in the Eucharist is a sign that God is providing for man, both because the Blessed Sacrament comes into presence at the Mass during the consecration and since the Mass participates in the Calvary sacrifice from which all grace and blessings flow. But it is also a form of providence in the form of Holy Communion. Holy Communion is the reception of this sacrament. The chief fruit of the Eucharist is

---

[69]This must be understood correctly so as not to fall into error. Since the whole Christ is contained in the Eucharist, it means that His accidents are also present, see ST III, q. 76. But since place is an accident, it means that the place of Christ's Body is not the same as the place of the bread and wine, since His Body is in Heaven and the bread and wine are present locally on earth. This is why the Church is very clear to point out that the substances of the Bread and Wine change and not the accidents, one of which is place. Therefore, it is not accurate to say that Christ is present locally under the bread and wine, but substantially.

[70]God's presence is of four kinds to man. The first is causally, since the principle of causal presence states that the cause is always present to the effect. In this respect God is everywhere as cause present to the effect. God, however, is not in a place, rather the effects (creation) are in a place and He is present causally, not locally, in this respect since God has no accidents, see I Sent., d. 8, q. 4, a. 3; ST I, q. 3, a. 6; SCG I, c. 23 and De Pot., q. 7, a. 4. The second is that God is present spiritually, as when He says, where two or more are gathered in His Name, He is in their midst (Matthew 18:20). By spiritually is meant that God listens to our prayers and is operative in the order of grace. The third is that God is present by means of sanctifying grace. This is His presence by analogy and by participation in His divine nature. The last is substantially present in the Eucharist. These are the forms in which God is present in some real way as opposed to God being present in mind only, e.g. when God is said to be present in the Scriptures, this is merely an implicit or mental presence, as we read them, even though He is causal of their original writing by means of inspiration. In the modern context, due to a lack of metaphysics, these various modes of presence have been blurred and often equated. However, such a blurring is neither Catholic nor helpful but actually harmful to people's faith and proper intellectual understanding. In effect, modern blurring of these presences is psychologically harmful to people because it leaves them in confusion.

an intrinsic union of the recipient with Christ.[71] Christ (God Himself) becomes food for the soul, preserves and increases our supernatural life.[72] Therefore, this sacrament provides for us spiritually and so man can be assured that God's providence for him is not wanting, just by gazing upon the sacred species, i.e. the Sacred Host which he receives in Holy Communion.

This sacrament, therefore, has its own sacramental graces that it begets. While in one sense it is the reception of substantial grace (i.e. God Himself Who is pleased with Himself), it also begets accidental grace in the soul. Hence, there is an increase in sanctifying grace which makes later acts more meritorious. For the directee, he must be encouraged to receive Holy Communion, daily if possible, to increase the amount of sanctifying grace in his soul so that all of the works which he does to merit the grace of overcoming his mental illness are more efficacious and more likely to be granted. By the frequent attendance at the Holy Sacrifice of the Mass and the frequent reception of Holy Communion, he can grow in holiness and the infused virtues and gifts of the Holy Spirit will ever more dominate his life.

For psychologists, frequent reception of Holy Communion will more likely beget a greater exercise of the gift of Counsel. It also means that the infused virtues will be more operative, one of which is prudence, which is absolutely indispensable for counseling.[73] Moreover, since it is incumbent on the psychologist to merit the graces for the directee to overcome his problems, frequent Holy Communion will make the psychologist's meritorious works more efficacious. In effect, frequent Holy Communion will make the psychologist's practice of psychology or counseling more efficacious.

Christ also pledged another effect of Holy Communion and that is heavenly bliss and the future resurrection of the body.[74] Since man is ordered toward perfect beatitude, this Sacrament becomes the means to that beatitude in two ways. One is the reception of the Sacrament in Holy Communion. The second is by virtue of the fact that only God saves, this Sacrament is God, therefore only this Sacrament can save. This also reveals itself by virtue of the fact that this Sacrament is at once God Who alone can bring man to perfect beatitude since it is beyond man's capacities, but that this sacrament is also the sacrifice by which the means to eternal beatitude (viz. grace) are restored. Since grace is the means to eternal beatitude, this Sacrament alone is that which can provide eternal life.

It is here that we begin to see the full psychological effects of being Catholic.

---

[71]See Ott, *Fundamentals of Catholic Dogma*, p. 394. How this is a union is open to discussion but will not be addressed here.

[72]Ott, *Fundamentals of Catholic Dogma*, p. 395. See also ST III, q. 79, a. 1.

[73]How this is the case will be seen in the third volume.

[74]John 6:55. See also Council of Trent, Session XIII (Denz. 1638/875) and Ott, *Fundamentals of Catholic Dogma*, p. 395. The psychological effects of the resurrection of the body will be discussed later.

For since God entrusted to the Catholic Church alone[75] the protection and administration of the sacraments and since this Sacrament is the means of salvation, being a Catholic provides one with the greatest means of salvation. Being Catholic, therefore, also provides one with the greatest means of grace, since by being a Catholic, one may receive Holy Communion according to the intention of God, which provides the greatest means to increase grace, upon which the supernatural curing of mental illness depends.

However, in order to receive Holy Communion worthily, one must be baptized[76] and be in the state of grace.[77] Directees must be encouraged to protect their state of grace so that they can approach Holy Communion. However, if a directee receives Holy Communion in the state of mortal sin, it is a sacrilege[78] and can therefore have the harmful effects of mortal sin. Priests and others who have encouraged the faithful to receive Holy Communion in the state of mortal sin, aside from the spiritual reality of offending God, have not added to the mental health of the faithful. When psychologists counsel the directee to receive Holy Communion, they should encourage the directee to make sure his conscience is clear of any mortal sin before receiving Our Lord in Holy Communion.

IV. Confirmation

The sacrament of Confirmation is that "Sacrament, in which, by the imposition of hands, unction and prayer, a baptized person is filled with the Holy Ghost for the inner strengthening of the supernatural life and the courageous outward confession of Faith."[79] Confirmation strengthens the individual in spiritual warfare[80] and enables him to lead a life in conformity with the Catholic faith more readily or easily, by being strengthened. In addition to strengthening the individual, there are several effects of Confirmation which aid one psychologically (as well as spiritually).

The first is that it confers an increase in sanctifying grace.[81] This alone can have a positive psychological effect. The next effect is that it perfects the grace of

---

[75]This follows from the mere fact that he entrusted the sacraments only to the Apostles.

[76]Council of Trent, Session XIII (Denz. 1661/933). Here we see one of the remote psychological benefits of being baptized, since one can receive Holy Communion and thereby increase grace, and merit actual graces to cure one's mental illness or maintain one's mental health. In this respect, we see that being Catholic is more conducive to mental health than any other religion. On the other hand, for a Catholic to reject his faith or act contrary to right Catholic thinking and worship is one of the quickest ways to lose mental health.

[77]Council of Trent, Session XIII (Denz. 1661/893).

[78]I Cor. 11:27-29. See also CCC 1385.

[79]Ott, *Fundamentals of Catholic Dogma*, p. 361.

[80]Regarding spiritual warfare, see chapter on the demonic.

[81]Council of Florence, *Decretum pro Armeniis* (Denz. 1311/695); CCC 1301; ST III, q. 72, a. 7 and Ott, *Fundamentals of Catholic Dogma*, p. 365f.

Baptism. We have already seen that the grace conferred at Baptism is ordered toward the living of the baptismal promises and so the grace of Confirmation perfects that grace and thereby makes it easier to lead a life according to the baptismal promises. Here we see that it has the psychological effect of aiding people so that they do not fall into sin which can cause psychological problems. Along with these last two effects and the fact that it confirms a person, i.e. strengthens him to lead the Christian life, psychologically this sacrament will give people strength in the face of what may cause mental illness. Hence, it can either aid someone who is mentally ill so that he has the strength not to do those things that may be causing his mental illness or it can strengthen someone so that he does not perform actions which will allow him to fall into mental illness.

Here we see the necessity of the directee being confirmed. If he has not been, he should be. This also applies to the psychologist as well. Yet, it also means that putting off Confirmation past puberty is problematic. Even though it is a sacrament of initiation[82] and some have argued therefore that it should be put off until one can make an adult decision to accept the faith, such an argument fails theologically. Since one has already received the Christian faith by virtue of Baptism, he is morally required in justice before God to fulfill the baptismal promises, even if they are made for him as a child, since he is not free to reject the Christian faith. Therefore, since he must adhere to the Christian faith, Confirmation should not be withheld to such a late date that the person will suffer ill effects and perhaps not be confirmed.[83] Moreover, it is entirely possible that a better decision can be made before puberty than after puberty. Since before puberty one can be taught the essentials of the faith, which is necessary to defend the faith, it seems more prudent to have Confirmation just before or at the time of puberty, so that the person is less swayed by the increase of passions and appetite which occurs during and after puberty. In fact, psychologically, if a person is confirmed before puberty, he is more likely to be able to govern the passions as he goes through puberty and his actions in relation to the passions since there is an increase of grace (and therefore the operations of the infused virtues, one of which is temperance) as well as the gifts of Holy Spirit. Spiritually and psychologically, it is better to confirm someone just before or at the time of puberty rather than later, such as eighteen or nineteen years of age. The argument that to receive it should be an adult choice does not suffice to withhold this sacrament from those who could benefit from it at the very time they may need it most.[84]

---

[82]CCC 1285.

[83]Pastorally, as a rule, fewer people are confirmed the longer it is delayed.

[84]Within the Catholic sphere, since in many dioceses this sacrament has been postponed to later ages, this may be why Catholic children have a harder time going through puberty than in the past. Granted the society in which they live has changed significantly; nevertheless human vices have not, since human nature has not, and therefore they should not put off Confirmation. Indeed, one could even say that since society has changed, it is all the more reason to give young people the strength to get through the adolescent years by confirming them.

The next effect of Confirmation is that it confers an indelible mark on the soul. St. Thomas observes that

> the character is a certain spiritual power ordered to some sacred actions....and therefore by the sacrament of Confirmation, spiritual power is given to man with respect to certain other sacred actions aside from those which are given to him in Baptism. For in Baptism, man receives the power with respect to those actions which pertain to his own salvation, as he lives according to himself; but in Confirmation man receives the power of acting with respect to those things which pertain to the spiritual battle against the enemies of the faith.[85]

Some refer to this effect of being able to perform actions in which one can fight to defend the faith as becoming a soldier for Christ. For psychology, directees in receiving Confirmation can more readily fight for the Catholic faith. Since often to regain psychological health one must act in a Catholic fashion which is counter-cultural, Confirmation will give the directee the strength to defend his actions and not to cower. Confirmation will also give the power to psychologists to defend the teachings of the faith to their colleagues and to their directees which can aid their mental health. Often directees have specious arguments against certain Catholic practices which aid them or in favor of some unchristian activity and so the psychologist will be aided by the indelible mark of Confirmation to defend the faith. This will aid the psychologist personally from not falling into worldly ways of thinking since often the spiritual battle is more interior than exterior.

The last effect in regards to the sacrament of Confirmation has already been mentioned, viz. the gifts of the Holy Spirit. A person may already possess them by virtue of being in the state of grace; nevertheless, by this sacrament, the gifts of the Holy Spirit become more operative and are infused according to a greater degree. Given the prior discussion on the gifts of the Holy Spirit, this is highly desirable psychologically.

V. Marriage

Matrimony is a sacrament[86] in which a man and woman, who are capable of marriage, associate in an undividable union by mutual agreement for the generation of offspring, and in which they receive grace for the fulfilment of the special duties of their

---

[85]ST III, q. 72, a. 5: "Character est quaedam spiritualis potestas ad aliquas sacras actiones ordinata... Et ideo per sacramentum confirmationis datur homini potestas spiritualis ad quasdam actiones alias sacras, praeter illas ad quas datur ei potestas in baptismo. Nam in baptismo accipit potestatem ad ea agenda quae ad propriam pertinent salutem, prout secundum seipsum vivit, sed in confirmatione accipit potestatem ad agendum ea quae pertinent ad pugnam spiritualem contra hostes fidei."

[86]Council of Trent, Session XXIV (Denz. 1801/971).

state.[87] From this definition we see that the essential properties of the sacrament of matrimony are unity (monogamy) and the indissolubility of the marriage bond.[88] On a psychological level, the indissolubility has a profound impact. Because of the nature of man's affections,[89] when someone who is close leaves permanently or even for a long period of time, sorrow arises because the loss of the presence of the individual is seen as an evil. Therefore, divorce by its nature leads to psychological suffering. While it is true that some are "happy" when they receive their divorce decree, nevertheless, the pain which one must suffer in order to sever the natural affections which lead to the divorce is psychologically difficult to sustain and often leads to mental illness, particularly in women whose natural affections are more readily given. Indissolubility provides a stability to one's affections insofar as they are not constantly shifting from person to person but become properly ordered toward one individual of the opposite sex.

The indissolubility is also necessary and even demanded by the natural law[90] – even though the sacramental bond is indissoluble once consummation occurs – for the sake of the proper upbringing of children and for the stability, both psychological and political, of a society. Emotional stability and proper spiritual, intellectual and psychological formation of children requires that the relationship between parents be stable. When divorce occurs, it leads to the splitting of emotional ties and causes interior dissonance in the child which disrupts the formation process on all levels.[91] This can also be said of those marrying insofar as it is not possible to advance spiritually when distracted by marriage instability.

Marriage is ordered toward the generation and rearing of children.[92] Since the natural law has ordered the generative faculty toward the begetting of children,[93] marriage provides the stable emotional, intellectual and spiritual atmosphere in which the child is able to reach adulthood as a healthy individual on all levels. No other way of rearing children has this inherent psychological and spiritual trajectory. Since children need both parents for a full intellectual, psychological and spiritual upbringing, marriage is necessary.

Society also needs marriage insofar as marriage provides a stability to family life or to the life of the children which is not had outside that context. Since the children are citizens and future leaders of a society, the society will become unstable if the state of marriage becomes unstable. The modern experiment in divorce and remarriage has

---

[87]See Ott, *Fundamentals of Catholic Dogma*, p. 460.

[88]Ott, *Fundamentals of Catholic Dogma*, p. 462.

[89]Affection may be defined as a voluntary (so it can be in the will) motion of the passion of love in the concupiscible appetite, normally expressed in ways that are both connatural to man and according to cultural convention.

[90]SCG III, c. 123.

[91]See volume I, chap. 13.

[92]See Ott, *Fundamentals of Catholic Dogma*, p. 462.

[93]Pius, XI, *Casti Connubii* and Paul VI, *Humanae Vitae*.

proven that lack of marriage stability erodes moral and intellectual standards within a culture.

However, the primary focus in this chapter on marriage is toward the spiritual aspects which contribute to psychological health. The first is that the sacrament of matrimony bestows sanctifying grace on the contracting parties.[94] Ample discussion of the benefits of grace have already been given. Yet, the grace from the sacrament of marriage is ordered toward the fulfillment of the duties of the state of marriage and gives the married parties supernatural strength for the fulfillment of their state.[95] Since people are affected by original sin, the mutual defects of the partners makes the married state difficult to sustain. The sacramental grace of marriage enables the couple to cope better with each other's defects and to fulfill the duties toward children and each other.[96]

Since marriages often suffer problems due to the defects of the spouses, the sacramental graces will have two functions. The first is that it will aid the two in overcoming the defects which adversely affect each other. Secondly, it will make it easier for the spouses to sustain each others defects. One of the primary means of overcoming a defect is by suffering.[97] The defects of each spouse, while they can be the occasion of the ruin of the marriage, also constitute one of the means for the other spouse to be purified of his or her own imperfections as well as a means to becoming holier, less self-absorbed, etc.

In this sense, marriage can actually contribute directly to mental health insofar as it provides the grace to suffer and be purified as well as the sacramental graces affecting the imperfection directly. Those who live together without the aid of the sacramental grace of marriage are less likely to be able psychologically to sustain grave or even minor defects of spouses. Those, who come to psychologists, who are living together and suffer psychological problems (the issues of conscience in that situation aside) may be actually causing their own problems by living with someone without the aid of grace. Sometimes nature can sustain people to a degree, but grace is more efficacious and therefore the married state is better than the non-married state for a man and woman living together.

Marriage is ordered toward the salvation of the souls of the two involved and therefore these sacramental graces of marriage will aid the two in helping each other save their souls. One of the ways this happens is by virtue of the fact that when a spouse sees the defect of the other spouse, grace will move the person not only to suffer the defect in a rightly ordered fashion which affects someone psychologically, but also to aid the spouses in overcoming that defect according to the means available. In other words, there are two ways, which spouses can aid each other in overcoming spiritual defects, which can have a profound psychological impact. The first is a natural means,

---

[94]Council of Trent, Session XXIV (Denz. 1801/971).

[95]Ott, *Fundamentals of Catholic Dogma*, p. 467. By state is meant the condition of being married.

[96]Such as fidelity, mutual help, etc.

[97]See next chapter.

such as counseling the spouse or doing things around the home which puts them at ease or makes them feel loved, etc. However, these means pale in comparison to the second means, viz. the supernatural means. When one spouse sees the defect of another spouse and offers his own prayers, sufferings and good works for that other spouse, then he can merit grace for the spouse which can heal the other spouse's problem. This is particularly important for psychologists to keep in mind when counseling directees who are married. They should involve the spouse in doing what he can spiritually in order to merit the graces for the other spouse's healing.

This brings to the fore one other aspect of the sacramental graces of matrimony, viz. the sacrament of matrimony can continually supply graces throughout the course of the marriage. Pius XI observes that husband and wife "will receive [actual graces] as often as they require it for the fulfillment of the duties of their station."[98] One spouse can always draw on the sacrament of matrimony to provide the actual graces to sustain the defects of the other spouse and to give him or her strength to provide the natural and spiritual aids in order to help the spouse. While this is effective on the spiritual level, it is also effective on the psychological level since many psychological illnesses result from spiritual problems. When a spouse notices a particular problem of his spouse, he should offer any suffering he incurs from his spouse's psychological problems specifically for the curing of the psychological problem. Moreover, he must consciously draw on the sacramental graces of marriage to perform the actions to merit the actual graces for their spouse.

Marriage is also ordered toward mutual help and the moral regulation of the sexual urge.[99] Since a large number of psychological problems come from immoral and improper sexual urges, fantasies, etc., marriage provides a clear means by which this drive can be regulated. Since the psychological health of a person or a society can implode if it violates the natural law,[100] and since conjugal relations outside the context of marriage are contrary to the natural law,[101] a society suffering from sexual license is bound to suffer an increase in psychological illness. For this reason, a society must protect the institution of marriage in order to direct properly the sexual force, in a way that is psychologically and spiritually healthy for the whole of society.[102]

---

[98]*Casti Connubii* (Denz. 3713/2237).

[99]Ott, *Fundamentals of Catholic Dogma*, p. 462. CIC/17 1013, par. 1.

[100]See prior volume.

[101]See SCG III, c. 122f. It is contrary to the third category of natural inclination insofar as fornication begets children who are not able to be brought up in a home in which both man and wife provide important formational contributions to both male and female children.

[102]This means that people wanting to marry must be regulated in how they approach marriage as well as being sure that everything is done to maintain chastity among the citizens of a nation. The Church herself has seen the necessity of regulating its own members in how and when they may contract marriage. Any priest who has been ordained for any length of time can give countless stories of how people ruined their lives by either not marrying and

VI. Holy Orders

Holy Orders is a sacrament in which spiritual power is transferred to one of the faithful by the imposition of hands and prayer of the bishop, together with grace to exercise this power in a manner pleasing to God.[103] Because of its historical significance in the Old Testament and in the New Testament, the priesthood is essentially ordered toward offering sacrifice for the priest's own sins and the sins of the people.[104] While the nature of the priesthood is first and foremost ordered to God, it is secondarily ordered toward aiding the people. In this respect, the priesthood becomes a means by which men save their souls and by which sacramental graces come into the world. Hence, we see that since Holy Orders is ordered toward grace, it will aid psychological health.

Because man comes to knowledge of spiritual realities by means of the senses, there is a desire[105] in man to have something sensible to which he can look in order to have certitude about what occurs spiritually. Since Holy Orders provides a sensible sign (the priest) who acts in the name of God, the priesthood provides a level of intellectual certainty about what occurs spiritually which cannot be gained otherwise. This means that the priesthood can provide a great deal of consolation, particularly to those struggling with sin, e.g when they go to Confession. The priesthood makes the Blessed Sacrament present which again provides great psychological aid.

---

living together or by not following the Church's laws on marriage and getting married outside the Church. What results later often includes psychological problems on the side of those involved in the ruinous affair. The laws of the Church regulating marriage ultimately protect everyone involved, from the parties contracting marriage to the Church and the whole of society. Those not wanting to follow the marriage laws of the Church are often governed by unbridled passions and disordered thinking arising from those passions.

[103]Ott, *Fundamentals of Catholic Dogma*, p. 450.

[104]Hebrews 5:1.

[105]This desire appears to be both something natural and something arising from original sin. On one level, man is ordered to coming to knowledge through his senses and so there is a natural inclination in man to seek sense knowledge in order to come to intellectual knowledge. On the other hand, the intellectual knowledge sometimes cannot be gained by sensible knowledge alone but must be pursued by means of reasoning. The problem arising from original sin is that man seeks sensible certitude in spiritual realities which often do not admit of physical certitude or which by their nature do not have a corresponding certitude in things of the senses, e.g. when a person desires to "see" his guardian angel, the person may desire this from a pious and even a natural motive, but it is misdirected insofar as there are certain things which we must take on the authority of God in this life and will be able to see only in the next. There are some spiritual realities which we can know with certitude in this life by means of faith or reason which cannot be known directly through things of the senses. Hence, if reason is rightly ordered, it will understand the different modes of knowing different realities and thereby not seek the knowledge of a reality in a mode that does not admit of it.

The priest, insofar as he is an *Alter Christus*,[106] is called to offer up his prayers, sufferings and good works on behalf of those under his pastoral care. Therefore, the sacramental graces of this sacrament have a direct effect on the priest, insofar as they make him holier, and indirectly on the people, insofar as the priest through these graces is able to merit more grace for those under him. In this respect, the priesthood constitutes a powerful means against mental illness.

On an intellectual, moral and spiritual level, the priest also possesses a certain spiritual authority which is very beneficial for mental illness. Directees will often anguish over whether a course of action is the right thing to do and then even if they do what they think is right they do not have the certitude that their course of action is pleasing to God. But since God granted authority[107] to the pope and bishops of the Church, who then concede some of that authority to the priest so that he may preach, sanctify and govern the faithful, the priest, bishops and pope stand as exercising authority granted by God Himself. Since the pope has personal infallibility in areas of faith and morals,[108] as well as the bishops in union with the pope at an ecumenical council,[109] those who submit themselves to this God-given authority can be assured that, if they follow the teachings of the Church, they know they are doing what is right. This provides a tremendous psychological freedom from having to be one's own moral authority. While most want to be their own "moral authority," what they really want is the "authority" to grant moral permissibility to their life of the appetites or something of this kind. But when a person wants to do what is right, he realizes that he is not fully capable of judging what is right on his own because of the profound blindness resulting from original and actual sin. Therefore, when he knows he can place himself under the authority granted by Christ Himself (God) to the heads of the Church, he is freed from having to carry the burden of devising his own moral system.

This also fits the natural inclination of man to learn from those outside of him. Just as children have a natural inclination to submit to the judgment of their parents in order to be properly formed intellectually, morally and spiritually, so in man is there a natural inclination to submit to God and derivatively to those to whom God grants authority to speak on His behalf, in order to reach the ultimate end. To reach the ultimate end requires supernatural knowledge since the object and the means to that object are beyond nature and natural knowledge. Therefore, if man is to reach perfect happiness, he must submit to someone who knows what perfect beatitude is and what the means are to it. Since this can only come from God, we must submit to God and to those who have received His authority to teach on His behalf. Again, this frees the individual

---

[106]*Alter Christus* means "other Christ." The priest is another Christ insofar as he offers the sacrifice of Calvary. Just as Jesus Christ offered Himself to God the Father in expiation for our sins, so the priest offers Christ to God the Father during the Holy Sacrifice of the Mass in expiation of our sins.

[107]Properly called jurisdiction.

[108]Vatican I, *Pastor Aeternus*.

[109]Vatican II, *Lumen Gentium*, par. 25.

from the lack of certitude about his own judgment regarding these matters since he does not have the capacity in himself to judge those matters perfectly since they are beyond him, just as the supernatural is beyond the natural.[110] Yet, the priest, while not having the same charism of office that the pope and bishops do, does have a charism proper to the priesthood in which he is able to direct those under his care.

VII. Extreme Unction

Extreme Unction is the sacrament in which one of the faithful, who is sick, by anointing with oil and the prayer of the priest, receives the grace of God for the supernatural salvation of his soul and often also for the natural healing of his body.[111]

> As Extreme Unction is a Sacrament of the living, it presupposes in general the remission of grievous sins. But if a person in mortal sin is seriously ill and can no longer receive the Sacrament of Penance, or if he erroneously believes that he is free from grievous sin, Extreme Unction eradicates the grievous sins *per accidens*, but still by reason of Christ's Institution. A necessary pre-condition of the forgiveness of sins is that the sinner has turned away from sin at least by an habitually continuing imperfect contrition.[112]

In effect, Extreme Unction prepares the person for a holy death, should it come from a serious sickness.[113] Any priest who has faithfully executed his office in regards to his obligations to the dying can testify to the profound psychological effect this sacrament has on all involved.

In those who are being anointed, the rites and sacrament of Extreme Unction

---

[110]Even those who still "claim the right" to determine religious and spiritual matters on their own must delude themselves by pride, judging themselves capable of knowing what can only be taught to man by God, both in the order of supernatural knowledge and in the order of supernatural virtues, viz. faith which is granted by God alone. Also as to the means, people assume they know the right thing to do religiously. However, the fact is that only God knows what pleases Him and, therefore, the only way we can come to knowledge of it is if He tells us and this we call revelation. It is analogous to someone who has never personally met another person to tell him what he likes and dislikes. Without people telling us in some way or another, we do not know what pleases them. In like manner, we do not know what pleases God unless He tells us. Right reason knows its own limits. Therefore if a person is acting according to right reason, he will know that he must submit to God's authority as granted to others, since they alone can tell us what we must do.

[111]Ott, *Fundamentals of Catholic Dogma*, p. 445.

[112]Ott, *Fundamentals of Catholic Dogma*, p. 448.

[113]By sick here is to be understood that the person is seriously ill, as the Council of Trent observes (Denz. 1698/910).

normally elicit one of two reactions.[114] There are those who are disturbed by the rite and this is normally because they have not been leading a good life. For them it means that it is the end of their time here on earth and they become disturbed because it means an end to the pursuit of those things to which they are attached in this world. Some even reject the sacrament in a last ditch psychological effort to avoid dealing with the fact that they are dying or could die. For some, the sacrament constitutes the visible sign at which they have final impenitence by refusing to receive the absolution of the priest and the conferral of grace of this sacrament.

Yet the other reaction tends to be one of profound consolation. If the person is leading a good Catholic life and has a strong faith in the teachings of the Church, seeing the priest on his deathbed constitutes a visible sign of great joy. While he still might have some fear of dying, by his faith, he knows that he is being prepared for death and should not fear his personal judgment before God. Among the truly faithful, this sacrament causes a mitigation of sorrow insofar as their imagination is filled with the signs of hope and their thoughts are directed to the joys of the afterlife. It also mitigates fear. Since man has a natural inclination to all of the virtues and he knows that in justice he must stand before God and account for the detraction from His glory in this world because of his sins, he knows that this sacrament will prepare his soul to be able to withstand that judgment. Because he is able to see his salvation being worked out before his eyes, this changes the image in his imagination to something with the perspective of joy and solace and so the sorrow and fear are mitigated. For some who have led morally corrupt lives, the vision of the priest before them moves them to sorrow for their sins and helps them to desire to be forgiven and anointed, since the priest is, at that moment, the visible sign of God's mercy.

For those who stand around the one being anointed, this sacrament also mitigates sorrow. Since death is an evil which they do not wish their loved one to endure, it causes them great sorrow. They also know that death is the final parting and so they will no longer see the person in this life. But when the priest anoints the one dying, those around them see the great mercy of God by seeing His priest prepare the dying person for death. By being anointed, they know the person is set right before God and therefore stands on the threshold of eternal life and bliss. They also know that God is actively working at that moment to save the person's soul through the hands of the priest. For those around the person dying, the vision of the priest changes the image in the imagination and thereby mitigates sorrow. Any good priest can testify to the fact that when this sacrament is administered, those anointed and those around the anointed will often show visible signs of peace. Even though the suffering continues, both in the dying and in those around the dying, there is a tranquility of order because man who is ordered to seeing God Face to face is seeing the final effects of that ordering.

Moreover, this sacrament confers grace which strengthens the person to die a holy death. It gives him the actual graces to ward off any last temptations and it gives

---

[114]There are other reactions, but these two tend to be predominant. Sometimes the person does not react at all. Sometimes they are incapable of reacting since they are unconscious.

him sanctifying grace so that the infused virtues and gifts of the Holy Spirit can be more operative. This sacrament helps one to have a psychologically healthy understanding of death, viz. that it is merely a passing to the next life. It is not the end in which one goes out of existence, which is contrary to our natural inclinations of conservation of our being. While our nature is being split, i.e. body and soul are being divided, nevertheless, the person knows that he will continue on. As the preface of the Holy Sacrifice of the Mass says, he knows that his life is changed not taken away.[115] The grace strengthens him and gives him courage since dying is perhaps the most difficult thing he will do.[116]

Yet, death for those who are unprepared constitutes one of the most psychologically disordering events of their lives. People often lose rational control, because they do not understand the nature of death and they have not prepared for it, nor are they being prepared for it. This is why it was often said in the past that Catholicism is the hardest to live but the easiest to die. When the clergy are conscientious about their obligations, they never let a soul die without the sacraments unless it cannot be helped. Catholics know that their religion provides for their death. Protestants have no such visible assurance.

Death either contributes to one's mental health or it erodes or takes it away. For some, death is a wake-up call, so to speak, and so the passions become subservient to reason which has to deal with reality: no one can escape death. Therefore, if the person is holy, the death moves the person to greater contrition for his sins and the sacrament of Extreme Unction gives him great hope. But to the person unprepared for death, it brings tremendous sorrow because he knows God's judgment will be harsh, if he believes in God; he knows not the destiny of his soul, if there is one, if he does not believe or doubts God's existence. Death can drive a person to irrationality because one is forced into a contradiction. One has a natural inclination to self-preservation, but the process of death brings about the dissolution of self. So one is driven mad by the prospect that reality and what one wants are in utter and complete contradiction. But for the faithful, death and Extreme Unction re-order the first category of natural inclination toward eternal life. The person is able to see that while he is dying now, he will continue to exist because he knows his soul is immortal and God has promised him the restoration of his body. In his imagination, he can see himself continuing on and so the instinct of self-preservation is directed toward being sorry for one's sins and seeking union with God.

To those who watch the dying, death provides the same reflection. The person is going; death is real; we may be next. Death either brings people to their senses, i.e. puts them in contact with reality, or it drives them away from it. To the virtuous person, death is a reminder and an incentive of the necessity to lead a good life, since one dies the way one lives. Whereas for the person who is not virtuous, death is an emotional

---

[115]The Latin is quite beautiful: *mutatur non tollitur*.

[116]It should be recalled that courage is the virtue which resides in the irascible appetite by which one is able to engage the arduous good and which concerns primarily the dangers of death, see ST II-II, q. 134, a. 4.

pain which has no natural mode of mitigation. Only supernatural faith can provide the mitigation of the sorrow in watching another person die. Supernatural faith moves the person to pray, offer up penance and do good works to merit grace for the person who is dying. In doing so, the sorrow is slightly mitigated because the person dying is now viewed under the *ratio* of goodness, i.e. one has done something good for the dying. But to the person without faith, death is irrational because it contradicts what seems to him to be the truth of the matter, viz. that man has a natural sense that he should live forever. The man without faith also is attached to the things of this world and does not embrace this world as a vale of tears in which suffering and penance are here for our benefit. Therefore, when a loved one to whom he is attached is taken, the person cannot view it under the rubric that the next life is better and the person dying, if dying a happy death,[117] will go to a better place. The person who has no faith does not look to the supernatural good of the one dying and therefore can only view his own suffering and pain and the suffering and pain of the one dying. Unless something mitigates this in some way, the person will become emotionally unstable.[118]

Lastly, Extreme Unction can heal, if it is to the spiritual advantage of the person.[119] While normally this occurs by healing the sickness which is causing death, some on occasion find that the healing also begets some psycho-physiological benefit, i.e. they are healed of the biological malady which is causing their mental illness. The mere fact of being healed brings joy and solace to the soul and so it has a psychological benefit on that level.

Conclusion

St. Thomas Aquinas observes that the sacraments are designed to relate to the various stages and aspects in human life: Baptism to birth, Confirmation to growth to physical perfection (adulthood), Holy Communion to food, Confession to restoration to health from sickness, the Sacrament of Marriage to the natural institution of marriage,[120] Holy Orders to the perfection of life by which one governs others and finally Extreme Unction to the restitution to perfect health through diet and exercise.[121] The sacramental life of a Catholic provides supernatural support in all areas of a person's life. Psychologically, the sacramental graces help the person to deal with life's changes,

---

[117]The term "happy death" means that the person dies peacefully and in the state of grace.

[118]Here we begin to see how attachments (e.g. to the one dying) are seriously dangerous not only to the spiritual life, but to psychological health as well. The issue of attachments will be addressed in the next chapter.

[119]Council of Trent, Session XIV (Denz. 1696/909). See also Ott, *Fundamentals of Catholic Dogma*, p. 449.

[120]Marriage is actually part of the natural law insofar as God – from the very design of masculinity, femininity and reason – requires marriage.

[121]ST III, q. 65, a. 1. See also IV Sent., d. 2, q. 1, a. 2 and SCG IV, c. 58.

stages and states. While the primary end of the sacraments is the sanctification and salvation of the soul of the one who receives them, undoubtedly the sacraments have a tremendous effect on mental health.

Chapter 9: Other Foundations of the Spiritual Life:
Prayer, Devotion, Detachment and Mortification

Throughout this volume, prayer has been mentioned numerous times and often in conjunction with the necessity to pray for the directee. In relation to merit, prayer plays a pivotal role, since by prayer one can merit the actual graces for the directee which aid him in overcoming his mental illness. Psychologically, then, prayer is one of the most important components of counseling and practice for the directee. Yet, prayer has many more psychological effects than have already been mentioned and it pertains to this chapter to address the various psychological benefits of prayer as well as the life of devotion, the doctrine of detachment and the practice of mortification.

I. The Necessity for Prayer

Prayer is an act of the virtue of religion,[1] which is a part of justice.[2] Since prayer falls under a virtue, it is required by the natural law, i.e. man has a natural inclination to prayer. While the effects of original sin have hindered the natural inclination somewhat, it is clear that man has this natural inclination. For example, in times of stress or extreme danger, people are often naturally inclined to pray to God for assistance to get out of the situation. Yet, prayer also has a direct connection to happiness. In the first chapter, it was noted that there are two kinds of happiness, one imperfect and the other perfect. Imperfect happiness is a happiness which occurs when the person leads a life in accordance with virtue and prayer, being an act of a virtue, will be a part of the happy life.

Yet, there is more. Prayer is one of the primary causes of imperfect happiness since prayer has a similitude to the beatific vision. As will be seen, prayer consists in raising the mind and heart to God and since perfect happiness consists in seeing God face to face through an intellectual vision, prayer will take on a similitude of the perfect happiness. Psychologically, those who are depressed can find great solace in prayer. While one should not pray for the consolations which come from prayer, nevertheless, prayer can directly aid depression. Even those who are not depressed can benefit from prayer since mental illness often causes the soul to be afflicted and so prayer can ease the affliction by causing imperfect happiness.

Since we have a natural inclination to prayer, directees will find that by not praying, their life will slowly lose the happiness that comes from this virtue. If one does not fulfill this natural inclination, he will not be truly happy. Psychologists must begin directees on a strong regimen of prayer, not only to merit the requisite graces, but to begin to lighten the burden of the affliction of the mental illness, as well as fulfill the natural law inclination to prayer.

---

[1] ST II-II, q. 83.

[2] In fact, the question on prayer in the above footnote is located in the *Secunda Secundae* section on justice.

II. The Nature of Prayer in General

Prayer is defined in various ways by the spiritual writers but they all tend toward common elements in a definition: "Prayer is the lifting up of our minds and hearts to God to adore Him, to thank Him for His benefits, to ask His forgiveness, and to beg of Him all the graces we need whether for soul or body."[3] The definition contains three essential elements. The first is that prayer consists in the raising the mind to God. By mind here is meant the whole of the intellect, including all of the parts of the passive intellect, but especially the imagination and the possible intellect. The person turns his thoughts to God or the contemplation of things under the notion of God. Just as charity is the love of God and love of neighbor for the sake of God, so prayer is the contemplation of God and created things from the point of view of God. We see here the close connection between charity and prayer. In fact, to exercise an act of charity requires an initial act of prayer insofar as one turns to God to love Him or looks to God by means of some created thing (e.g. a neighbor).[4] One can actually know the level of charity by the level of prayer. Directees who want to master charity to derive the ordering benefits of charity must engage in prayer. Psychologists must also pray in order to gain charity and be able to direct their entire practice toward God ultimately.

The second component of the definition of prayer is that it is a lifting of the will or heart to God. This aspect of the definition is important because it distinguishes the difference between studying things about God and prayer. In study, the finality (the intention of the will) is toward knowledge, whereas in prayer the finality of the will is union with God. This finality of God plays an important role regarding attaining heaven. Since we must perform actions to lead us to the beatific vision, prayer is an essential action since it is the actual process of moving the intellect and will toward its final end. This is why no one can be saved without praying,[5] since the means to attaining the

---

[3]*An Explanation of the Baltimore Catechism of the Christian Doctrine for the Use of Sunday-School Teachers and Advanced Classes*, n. 304 (p. 249). While this reference may not be a scholarly text, it does contain a clear definition of the essential elements, as will be seen shortly.

[4]While the initial act is a form of prayer, the subsequent act may not be a prayer in substance, i.e. one may be giving alms or something of this sort. However, Christ said to "pray always" (Luke 18:1), which means that there comes a stage in one's spiritual life where prayer is able to be constantly maintained by viewing everything under the rubric of God and so one can execute other acts while still in prayer. There is a danger for some to say "my work is my prayer", which may be true if it is constantly done as just mentioned. Yet, in most cases when that argument is used, people are not looking at their work from the point of view of God all the time, but merely using this argument as an excuse not to engage in the arduous task of formal prayer.

[5]Tanquerey observes in *The Spiritual Life* (n. 645 – emphasis his): "The necessity of prayer is based on the *necessity of actual grace*. It is a truth of faith that without such grace we are utterly incapable of obtaining salvation and still more of attaining perfection." Tanquerey in the same location also observes that prayer is the normal, efficacious and

beatific vision consists in moving the intellect to union with the divine species.

The last component of the definition contains four kinds of prayer, viz. adoration, thanksgiving, petition and contrition. We have already seen the benefits of contrition in the chapter on the sacraments. The other three, however, play an important role in psychology. Thanksgiving provides a positive direction of the will in recognizing and appreciating the good which God has bestowed on the person. The Latin for giving thanks is *gratias tibi ago*. The term *gratia* means pleasing and so giving thanks is an expression of being pleased with what is given and with the person who gives. This has a very important psychological benefit. Those who have mental illness often view the world under the perspective of the negativity of their mental illness. By giving thanks to God for one's life, the goods which He has bestowed on the person, one's family, etc., the burden of the illness can be lightened by appreciating God's goodness by thanking Him. This, in effect, turns the faculties toward something positive and can therefore ameliorate the mental illness.

God is also like us in that He appreciates the thanks when He does something good for us. Just as we are more inclined to give someone further gifts who appreciate what we give to them, so God grants even more to those who thank Him for what they have received. For the person with a mental illness, thanking God for what he does have can actually incline God to give him the grace to cure his mental illness as a further gift. St. Thomas observes that we have an obligation to return thanks to our benefactors as a part of the virtue of gratitude, which is part of the virtue of justice.[6] In this respect, God will reward the directee who thanks Him and fulfills his obligations in justice. Moreover, by performing acts of gratitude, the virtue is built up, thereby increasing one's imperfect happiness.

Adoration consists in "those acts of divine worship which are directed to God only, and of which the characteristics are recognition of his perfection and omnipotence and our own complete dependence on him (*latria*)."[7] By adoration one praises God in such a way that it is an action due to Him alone. This is important on the psychological level since it aids the directee's faculties to be ordered toward God in the right way. Indirectly it also aids the directee not to treat some created thing in a way that is not due

---

universal means to obtain grace.

[6]See ST II-II, q. 106.

[7]Attwater, *A Catholic Dictionary*, p. 10. Attwater also observes in that same definition that adoration can also be used in a different sense: "Veneration expressed for any person or thing worthy of, or thought worthy of, our reverence as rational creatures, e.g., a saint, a relic (*dulia, q.v.*), is sometimes called adoration but it is better to distinguish it by use of the word veneration thereof." In Latin the terms *latria* and *dulia* are used to distinguish these two forms of adoration. *Latria* is worship which is due to God alone since He alone is God as the definition makes clear. *Dulia*, on the other hand, constitutes a form of veneration or reverence for something because of its reference to God in some way. *Hyperdulia* is sometimes the word used in the veneration given to the Blessed Virgin Mary because of her excellence in grace which exceeds that of all other creatures combined. As a result, she is given a special kind of veneration.

to it. Some directees make gods out of themselves, e.g. one who has any kind of irrational fear ultimately considers himself the highest thing to be honored and protected. Whereas if one has a perfect subordination of one's mind and heart to God, one will always view something under the perspective of God. The *ratio* or perspective of self-preservation fades into the background and the will of God comes to the fore, thereby taking away from the image in the imagination the *ratio* which moves the irascible appetite to fear. Prayer will have a direct impact on changing the perspective of the directee and can therefore have an impact on any form of mental illness that falls within the domain of the voluntary.

We have already discussed "petition" informally over the course of the volume by noting that the directee and psychologist must make acts of petition to gain the graces to overcome the mental illness. The directee must be careful not to be "using God" to get some mere temporal good (mental health). Tanquerey notes that the proper object of prayer (which we can say is also the proper approach that the psychologists and directees must take to prayer and all spiritual aids regarding mental health) is God or a temporal good which leads to God.[8] The temporal goods should be prayed for but the intention of the directees and psychologists must be that the will of God in relation to the temporal good is to be done. If God so chooses not to give the temporal good, one must concede that God views the lack of that temporal good as better for the person.

Therefore, directees and psychologists must remain detached from mental health. It may be possible that God wishes to allow the directee to labor under the mental illness for some time in order to merit other graces for himself or for others which will be more spiritually beneficial. However, here we are talking about mental illness that falls in the domain of the involuntary. All of those mental illnesses which somehow fall under the voluntary, God wishes the person to overcome them since they stem from sin or spiritual imperfection. Yet, some mental illnesses are involuntary, such as those which come from genetic, chemical and other biological causes and so God may allow this to befall a directee for his spiritual betterment. The directee should pray to be freed from the mental illness and to obtain God's grace, but he must do so by approaching God in a spirit of piety[9] with a self detachment so that he is ultimately doing

---

[8]Tanquerey, *The Spiritual Life*, n. 649.

[9]By piety is meant from the point of view of the infused virtue of piety, in which the directee sees God as a loving and caring Father Who wishes what is best for him. If the directee turns to God in prayer with a spirit of piety, it avoids self-absorption and maintains a supernatural vision on self, prayer and mental health. Even if one has an intention to obtain some natural good, God sees the infused virtue of piety which includes a supernatural intention (since the perspective is from the supernatural infused virtue of piety) and therefore will be inclined to grant his request. While God wants us to turn to Him in prayer even for our natural needs, other sacred things cannot be used in the same way. They are fundamentally ordered toward supernatural ends, e.g. the gifts of the Holy Spirit and the Sacraments. However, nothing forbids the approach of these sacred things with a desire to obtain some natural good from them provided that one has a supernatural intention. So in the case of the sacraments, it is permissible to approach them with a natural intention,

it for God and not himself.[10] In this way, his prayer will be more efficacious.

Given the above, we can begin to see that in prayer, three things regarding the method of prayer are necessary for it to be efficacious, viz. (1) the proper dispositions on the side of the person praying, (2) the manner in which the prayer is done and (3) the object of prayer. We have already seen that the object of prayer must be God or some created thing as seen in relation to God. This is perhaps the key element in making sure the prayer is rightly ordered. Too often directees and psychologists will enter into prayer not with God as the end of the action, but themselves. Psychologists must not neglect to inform the directee of the proper manner of directing his prayer. If the psychologist is not able to do so, the directee should be sent to a priest who can train the directee in the proper method of prayer.

We have already talked about the four kinds of prayer and these divisions give us an initial understanding of the manner in which the prayer is to be done. *How* the prayer is done can be just as important as *that* it is done. We know this from our own experience in dealing with others: when they come to ask us for something, it is not merely that they ask but how they ask which often determines whether we will give them what they want. It is likewise with God. In the Old Testament, God laid out very strict rules on how he was to be worshiped[11] and this was to avoid offending Him by the *manner* in which we worship Him.[12] The directees and psychologists must recognize that they must pray in the proper manner in order to obtain what they want. Otherwise, God may not be pleased with how they pray or even offended and, as a result, the prayer will not obtain its effect.

Several things can be kept in mind regarding how to pray. Many directees are

---

provided all other conditions for their worthy reception are present, e.g. with the sacrament of Confession, a natural sorrow or intention does not suffice for absolution. But one can approach the sacrament of Confession with the intention of aiding one's mental health (natural intention) provided one has supernatural sorrow (which includes the supernatural sorrow for one's sins). While this is permissible, it is more efficacious to approach sacred items from a more strictly supernatural intention.

[10]In the experience of the author, this has become a serious problem among psychologists who use theological means. Most of them subordinate the supernatural goods, such as grace, infused virtues, gifts of the Holy Spirit, etc. to the person's mental health. This is, in the opinion of the author, why these means are often ineffective since they do not proceed from right intention and so they actually cause further psychological disorder by not ordering the faculties of will, intellect and passions in the right way.

[11]This is clear in the Pentateuch, e.g. Exodus 24-30.

[12]This is why orthodoxy or right faith is so essential for the psychologist and directee. Right faith will ensure that the prayer is done in the right way since a right faith will know how to approach God. Therefore, if the directee has rejected any aspect of the Church's teaching, he should be encouraged first and foremost to submit to the authority of the Church and correct his faith. When a directee chooses a counselor, he must never choose one who does not possess right faith since the psychologist can cause a great deal of damage by misdirecting the directee because of his error.

not in the habit of prayer and so they may not find praying easy. This is why they should be started out on vocal prayers which can be found in good Catholic manuals so that they find it easier to concentrate as well as know how to pray, which is exemplified in the prayers. Another is that directees often do not know what to say or how to say it and so formal prayers are normally better to use in the beginning. This also insures that they are praying for the right things with the right words. Prayers written by the saints and tested by the tradition of the Church provide excellent means for directees to get a proper direction in their prayer. Psychologists, unless the directees are somewhat spiritually advanced, should avoid encouraging them to do informal prayers initially since they often do not know how to do it properly and they can easily offend God.

Next, God likes prayers to be specific.[13] When someone asks us for help and does not specify what he wants, then we are left uncertain about his intention. Likewise with God, while He knows precisely what we need and want, nevertheless He wants us to make it specific for our own benefit. Since prayer is a means by which we come closer to God, He wants us to use prayers which name and ask for specific things so that we become more directed in the process. This will please God more and therefore be more efficacious since we dispose ourselves more perfectly to some specific spiritual good by asking for it by name. While God can answer generic prayers (e.g. "God help me to over come my mental illness"), He would prefer something more specific (e.g. "Lord help me to become detached from self so that I am less fearful in suffering some possible injury from strangers"). The psychologist can aid the directee by directing him to the proper formal prayers to say which will aid his specific problem.[14] Also, if the directee is sufficiently catechized and has a proper direction in his spiritual life, he can be inclined to the higher levels of prayer such as certain kinds of meditation in which the person himself chooses some particular thing. However, this should only be done if the directee knows what he is doing. His mental illness can often be exacerbated by fixating on his problem in the prayer rather than focusing on the particular good he needs which normally comes from a proper catechesis and direction by a priest and/or psychologist. If the psychologist has determined which particular faculties are disordered, he can encourage the directee to pray for those things which will affect those faculties directly and indirectly, as well as ask God to help to correct his faculties and give him the grace to perform the actions which will correct his faculties. In this respect, detailed knowledge of the mechanics of the spiritual life will greatly aid the psychologist in being able to counsel the directee in the right prayers to say. Psychologists should also ask the directee for what things he is praying and if the psychologist does not want to enter into the internal forum in this manner, the directee should be sent to a priest who can ensure that the things for which the directee is praying and the manner of prayer are rightly

---

[13]Gihr, *The Holy Sacrifice of the Mass*, p. 144.

[14]At some stage a manual of prayers for the mentally ill should be assembled. This would not only include all of the prayers which normally occur in good manuals of prayer, but specific prayers could be sought in the history of the saints to be added which would directly aid the various kinds of mental illness.

ordered.

The third condition regarding the method of prayer being efficacious is the proper dispositions on the side of the person praying. The first is humility.[15] As St. James says,[16] "God resisteth the proud and giveth grace to the humble."[17] The directee should be encouraged to foster the virtue of humility so that, when he prays, he may do it with the right dispositions. Second, the directee must pray with confidence.[18] If the directee prays in such a manner to indicate that he does not think his prayer will have any efficacy, God will think that the directee does not believe that He will provide whatever he needs. We know that God wishes what is best for us and so we must pray knowing that God will give us what we ask, if we are properly disposed. For this reason, the third requirement is the state of grace, since no prayer has any efficacy or merit without the directee being in the state of grace.

The directee must also pray with perseverance.[19] Sometimes the directee (or the psychologist) will think that his prayer has no merit in the eyes of God because he is praying all the time but not receiving what he asks. This may be due to the fact that the directee is asking for the wrong thing, in the wrong way or is not in the state of grace. Yet, it may also be the case that God wants a certain amount of prayer to be done in order to obtain the grace sought. Therefore, the directee must be sure never to cease in his prayer. This also applies to the psychologist, particularly in those cases where the prayer appears to be having no effect.

The directee must also pray devoutly and by this is meant that the directee must say his prayers with a strong love of God and a desire to have union with Him. Also, in order to be devout, he must say his prayers in a way that he seeks to be pleasing to God which flows from his love of God. Devout does not mean emotional or appetitive,[20] but that he has a strong attachment on the side of the will to God alone. Devotion will also ensure that the directee prays in a manner that shows respect, both interiorly and exteriorly. He will not take up bodily positions which indicate a carelessness regarding what he is doing.[21]

Lastly, the directee (and psychologist) must pray with attention.[22] If we do not pay any attention to God when we pray, we are in effect insulting Him, because we are

---

[15]Tanquerey, *The Spiritual Life*, n. 650.

[16]James 4:6.

[17]See also Genesis 18:27; Daniel 9:18 and Luke 18:13f.

[18]Tanquerey, *The Spiritual Life*, n. 650.

[19]*An Explanation of the Baltimore Catechism of the Christian Doctrine for the Use of Sunday-School Teachers and Advanced Classes*, n. 307 (p. 251).

[20]How the appetites hinder the ascent in prayer will be seen below.

[21]This is why the Church has always encouraged kneeling with hands folded in praying, if it can be maintained, since it bodily manifests our desire before God to be seen as taking our rightful place, i.e. a place of inferiority in relation to Him.

[22]Tanquerey, *The Spiritual Life*, n. 650.

saying to Him that lower things are more worthy of our attention. This is why Christ said, "this people honoureth me with their lips: but their heart is far from me."[23] Therefore, the directee must say the prayers with attention by trying to remain focused on God and the prayer.

Because many directees have disorders in the faculties which execute prayer, they will find praying attentively very difficult. Distractions constitute one of the primary reasons why many do not pray and so we should address the various ways of overcoming distractions. A distraction can be caused by a number of sources. The first is merely a lack of habituation on the side of the will and imagination by which one is able to keep control over the imagination. Sometimes this is called the virtue of custody of the mind.

Next is when the cogitative power, from some habituation or indisposition, associates with the image in the imagination something which changes the image and bears the imagination off, away from the control of the will. This is an important ability on the side of the cogitative power. Sometimes things will occur outside the individual and the cogitative power has to override the person's attention on the object in the imagination to bring the person into focus on some danger to be avoided or some good to be pursued. However, like all faculties, it has been affected by original and actual sin and can use this mechanism in an improper fashion or repeatedly and thus not allow the person to concentrate on what needs to be addressed.

This actually brings to the fore the question of concentration. The term "attention deficit syndrome" has been applied to just about anything, even when the person has a slight difficulty in concentrating. But naming it and understanding the problem are two different things. The first thing that must be addressed is attention, sometimes called concentration. The faculties of the imagination and cogitative power are always intent on something, i.e. they are always directed toward something that is in the imagination. Hence, the first component of concentration is order of the cogitative power to the phantasm in the imagination. When the cogitative power does not add to or take away anything in the imagination that is not directly connected to the image, then the cogitative power is said to be intent on the object and the first component of concentration is present.

The second component of concentration is subordination of the passions to the will by means of the object in the imagination. If the passions arise, the person cannot remain fixed on the particular image in the imagination since the passions will take control away from the will. The next component is the ability of the possible intellect to direct, by means of the will, what is in the imagination as well as to remain fixed on what remains alone in the possible intellect. Lastly, the will must be exercising control over the possible intellect, cogitative power and imagination. Therefore, concentration consists of the possible intellect and will maintaining direction over the cogitative power and imagination. If the will does not act upon the cogitative power or imagination, concentration will be taken over by the cogitative power (sometimes called day dreaming). At times, the will seeks to control the cogitative power and imagination but

---

[23]Matthew 15:8.

is unable to do so and this is when concentration is short or lost. Distractions in prayer occur because the cogitative power and imagination are (a) not properly disposed and (b) not habituated to remain under the control of the will and so they are quick to move out from underneath the control of the will.

Therefore, the methods of gaining better concentration are the same for overcoming lack of concentration, commonly called attention deficit syndrome.[24] The first method is to determine whether there is something that the person is doing to cause bad habituation on the side of the cogitative power and imagination. These two powers learn from the possible intellect and will how attentive they are to be to the possible intellect and will in the execution of acts. The cogitative power can cause motion of the lower faculties, including the faculty of locomotion and so, at times, it is necessary to allow the cogitative power to escape the control of the possible intellect and will and function on its own. This occurs in many circumstances in which a person reacts to a situation without reflecting, e.g. if a person is driving a car and a child darts out in front of the car, the person does not have time for the possible intellect and will to reflect on what to do. The cogitative power merely moves the lower faculties to swerve or brake without reflection.

This mechanism is necessary for our own survival since we must, at times, react without reflection in order to preserve ourselves from bodily harm. But since the cogitative power can be trained, it also means that how the cogitative power assesses what to do can be affected by moving the cogitative power according to habituation. For example, in playing the piano, when the person first starts learning, the possible intellect and will have to maintain judgmental control over the process since in the beginning only they understand the notation. But after the cogitative power is trained to associate specific sequences or notes with specific hand movements, the person can play the piano more smoothly than in the beginning when reflection takes time. As the person perfects his skills, the various faculties which execute this playing of the piano become more habituated and so the person does not have to think about it as much.[25]

During this process the possible intellect and will, from time to time, will reformulate the image to maintain the direction of the cogitative power. For example, as the person is playing the music on the piano, he will think ahead to what is coming so that when it does occur, the cogitative power knows what to associate and execute. But since the person does not have to reflect fully on each key that must be pressed, it is a sign that the cogitative power provides which keys to press based upon memory and habituation of the cogitative power itself.

What this means is that concentration can effectively be split. The person can

---

[24]In order to avoid allowing the modern psychological attitudes to dominate in the impressions of the reader, from here forward ADS or ADD (attention deficit disorder) will not be used.

[25]Another clear example is learning how to type. Once a person trains the cogitative power, they simply have to think of the word and move the cogitative power to execute it and the cogitative power makes the associations from prior habituation and memory on which keys to punch at the right time.

be thinking about one thing while the cogitative power executes something else that is connected to what the person is thinking. We find this occurring in speech in which the person does not have to think about the actual grammar or words at all times but merely formulates the image. He then moves the cogitative power to make the associations which formulate the grammar and say the words. At times, a person may have to stop and think about the right words, but as a rule, when he is talking, the cogitative power performs the lower functions so that the higher functions can be left to engage in higher matters. This is why, again, ideas (concepts) and images are distinct and pertain to distinct faculties, i.e. it makes it possible for a person to contemplate a concept while the lower faculties are guided by the image.

This has a direct impact on prayer. This mechanism makes it possible for a person to pray vocally while concentrating on the meaning of the words. It also makes it possible to engage in certain kinds of meditation, e.g in saying the Rosary, the possible intellect can consider the content of the mystery while the cogitative power either executes verbally the "Hail Mary" or subvocalizes the "Hail Mary."[26] However, it appears that this mechanism can only really occur when the cogitative power is submissive to the motion of the will over what is in the imagination and the cogitative power itself. When the person is distracted, the cogitative power may execute the verbalization of the prayers but the person may not be reflecting on the content of the prayer. While normally this split occurs to aid concentration while executing exterior acts, it can also occur in such a manner that the person is distracted, e.g. during a Rosary, one may be reciting the prayers but thinking about what is on his grocery list.

How is this possible? It becomes possible when in the process of learning how to pray or do any other activity in which this split concentration is necessary, the person moves the cogitative power to execute the exterior action while allowing himself to become distracted. In other words, the cogitative power will continue to execute what it has been told to do by the will even though what occurs in the imagination may not be connected to it directly since the cogitative power has learned that anything can float through the imagination while this act is still to be executed. This also is an important mechanism. This is how people can drive and yet be thinking of virtually any conceivable thing that is not connected to driving. It is a providential mechanism for man. However, it can also be to his detriment if he is not careful.

What this essentially means is that in relation to prayer, the cogitative power has to be trained not to affect what is in the imagination when it is executing the act of prayer as well as the imagination must be trained to come more perfectly under the control of the will. This normally comes through habituation and can only be achieved perfectly by habituation of the imagination to remain under the control of the will. Therefore, one of the primary means one overcomes distraction is by applying oneself by means of the will to governing the imagination. The person must exercise sheer will

---

[26]Subvocalization is what occurs when the actual word for the image is brought into the imagination but there is no external verbalization of the word. This mechanism often occurs when people are reading, i.e. they say the word interiorly even though it is not said exteriorly. Subvocalization can greatly aid comprehension.

power at times.

Yet, the imagination can be affected by the senses, so the person must strive for a life of exterior quiet so that the imagination is less habituated in being carried off by the senses. While this can sometimes lead to mental illness when a person prefers to imagine things that are unreal[27] rather than moving the imagination to conform itself to reality, nevertheless it is necessary in order to overcome distractions.[28] Exterior quiet is important and those who suffer from mental illness should try to lead a quieter life and they will find that the imagination is drawn less in different directions.

Effectively, this means that the imagination can be trained to allow itself to be controlled by different agencies. One can move the imagination to focus on exterior things more than interior things. One can train the imagination to listen to the will less and to exterior things more, e.g. in certain kinds of sports, less volitional control is needed and cogitative power control is needed more. On the other hand, one must be careful so that the imagination does not become dominated by these exterior agencies and thereby the person loses his ability to concentrate.[29] This is particularly the problem with television. Those who watch television will almost always suffer from distraction in many areas, particularly prayer.

Watching television trains the imagination and cogitative power to focus on the rapid succession of images[30] and so they are trained to direct themselves to something other than the will.[31] When they attempt to pray which requires the motion of the will, the cogitative power and imagination are not properly habituated and so they cannot be moved easily. Therefore, in order to overcome distraction, one must stop watching television or moderate its use.

Children who suffer from lack of concentration need two things in their lives to overcome the distractions.[32] First, all television, computers and video games must be taken away or exposure to them severely curtailed. This alone will have a profound

---

[27]This is one of the reasons why actors can undergo personality changes. Since they must act in such a way so as to keep the imagination focused on their character which they are portraying and their lines, unless the person keeps a proper perspective that he is acting as well as do things which can keep him in contact with reality, he can begin to lose contact with reality.

[28]This would apply not only to prayer but to study, work and any other activity in life that requires concentration.

[29]Tanquerey (*The Spiritual Life*, n. 655) observes that allowing oneself to become preoccupied can cause distractions.

[30]This would also apply to things such as video games and computers.

[31]This is quite important in the discussion of the demonic (see next chapter). When the demons tempt the person through causing something in the imagination and moving the cogitative power, if the will consents, the cogitative power and imagination are trained to listen to the exterior agent rather than the will. This is why custody of the mind is so key for the spiritual and psychological life.

[32]These two prescind from the possibility of the lack of distraction being biological.

tranquilizing effect on the child. Second, external discipline must be applied by those in authority, usually parents and teachers, to ensure that the child recognizes the seriousness and the necessity of remaining focused. This will move him to exert the will more over the lower faculties. As he does so repeatedly, he will find that distractions are less of a problem.

The same can be applied to directees. If they find themselves distracted, the psychologist should encourage the directee to stay away from television and any other device that causes a rapid succession of images and begin by structuring the person's life so that they can remain more focused. The rapid succession of images disposes the cogitative power and imagination toward rapidity of imagery and so when there is no rapidity of imagery, the person becomes distracted, bored and has a hard time remaining still or focused. This is why children who watch a great deal of televison find school boring and are unable to pay attention to what is taught, since teaching requires a slower series of images in order for the person to reflect on them and to make a judgment about them. School systems which are moving to computers as the main medium of education are making a mistake in the long run, since the children will not have properly disposed imaginations and cogitative powers to address those things which are slow paced.

Another way that the distractions can occur other than by external sensations and bad habituations is by bodily indisposition. If the directee's mental illness is biological, it may have an impact on his ability to pray. This is why he must do what he can to overcome his problem, so that it does not come between him and God. Sometimes, however, the body can be disposed toward prayer through mortification.[33] Sometimes one can overcome distractions by study, since studying habituates the imagination and cogitative power to remain under the control of reason and will. Another way to overcome distractions is by simply applying oneself repeatedly, so that any time the faculties wander off, the will can bring them back into focus. This is a necessary part of overcoming any distractions regardless of their cause.

One can also keep in the senses something which will aid the faculties in keeping their focus. Some spiritual writers suggest having a prayer book or images in view so that if one find himself distracted he can look at the prayer or image which will make it easier to direct the imagination since the imagination will now have the image in it by means of the senses. Lastly, one can pray to God to ask Him to move the faculties so that one can pray.

III. The Nine Levels of Prayer

Most people when beginning in the spiritual life, strive to stop sinning and once they stay out of mortal sin, they generally do not know the path to any higher level. The levels of prayer constitute the path by which one ascends to perfection and in the context of the science of psychology, the various levels have very significant benefits. For this reason, the various levels of prayer will be addressed.

The first two levels of prayer are those which all men are capable of engaging

---

[33]See below.

in regardless of their spiritual state. The first is vocal prayer: "By vocal prayer we mean any form of prayer expressed in words, whether written or spoken."[34] St. Thomas observes that there are three reasons why vocalization is added to prayers. The first is that vocal prayers incite interior devotion by which the mind is elevated to God since the exterior signs move the mind of man by apprehension and consequently devotion.[35] The vocalization helps the mind to apprehend better what is being considered. The second reason for vocalization is that we render to God to Whom we owe everything what is due to Him by using our whole being, viz. the soul and the body. The third is that the sentiments of the soul redound to the body. Given these three, if a directee suffers from distractions, vocalizing prayers may aid the process of praying. It may also aid the process of getting the appetites directed since they will be affected by what is apprehended.

In relation to vocal prayer, Aumann makes an important point:

> It should also be noted that vocal prayer as the public liturgical prayer of the people of God gives greater glory to God than does private prayer and has a greater efficacy because it is the prayer of the Christian community. Yet, considering the one who prays, the Christian most perfect in love is the one who prays most perfectly.[36]

This observation is important to dispel errors which have been in vogue for some time. While it is true that public liturgical prayer is more efficacious, it is not more efficacious by virtue of the nature of the prayer. It is more efficacious by the agency of the Church (which is accidental to the very nature of the prayer). Therefore, the tendency among some to argue that vocal prayer is the highest form of prayer because it is communal is false. As to the very nature of prayer, the transforming union is the highest. Psychologists must also be careful to avoid allowing the directee to contract the notion that unless he says the prayer publicly that somehow it is meaningless. On the other hand, some directees may labor under the mentality that public prayer is not good and this often flows from an appetitive revulsion to public prayer.

Yet, Aumann makes one more observation about vocal prayer which is important:

> The necessity of fervent recitation of vocal prayer cannot be emphasized too much, because vocal prayer is one type of prayer that can never be omitted completely, even when one arrives at the height of sanctity. The time comes in the practice of mental prayer when the inferior grades yield to the superior grades as one progresses in union

---

[34]Aumann, *Spiritual Theology*, p. 316f.

[35]ST II-II, q. 83, a.12. All three of these reasons are taken from the same article.

[36]Aumann, *Spiritual Theology*, p. 317.

with God, but this never occurs with vocal prayer. It is always beneficial, either to arouse devotion or to give expression to the intensity and fervor of one's love to God.[37]

Directees should be encouraged to engage in vocal prayer since it can help their mental illness.[38] While this is the case, they should not neglect the other forms of prayer. The second level of prayer is called meditation:[39]

Discursive meditation can be defined as a reasoned application of the mind to some supernatural truth in order to penetrate its meaning, love it, and carry it into practice with the assistance of grace. The distinguishing note of meditation is that it is a discursive type of prayer, and therefore attention is absolutely indispensable.[40]

Discursive prayer, sometimes called mental prayer, is a form of prayer in which one considers God, an attribute of God, an attribute of a saint or some other supernatural truth, by means of a phantasm in the imagination. The faculties are focused interiorly on the phantasm in the imagination and the possible intellect and will consider the truth from a variety of different points of view. In this form of prayer, the primary characteristic is that it is discursive.

This form of prayer aids mental health in several ways. The first is that by considering a supernatural truth, the proper objects of the appetites are not present. This is why when a person leads a life of the appetites, prayer is difficult because the appetites do not want to sit still while reason and will consider the object that is proper to them and not the appetites. For this reason, if a person persists in mental prayer, he will find that the appetites will eventually quiet since the object of the appetite is not present. Mental prayer, therefore, has an inherent mortifying effect. This is particularly useful for those whose mental illness stems from some disordered passion. If they persist in prayer, they will notice a drop in the passion, not only because of the mechanics of this form of prayer, but also because the grace gained by this form of prayer will have an ordering effect on the passions. In fact, this form of prayer can be used in petition to God for the graces to heal the mental illness.

Mental prayer also makes one more rational. By this is meant that as one prays more, the possible intellect, will and lower faculties become habituated in an ordered fashion. Since man has God as his final end, this as well as all other forms of prayer

---

[37]Ibid., p. 318.

[38]This would be the case unless the nature of the mental illness was disruptive to those around them. In this case, the directee should be encouraged to practice vocal prayer privately until the mental illness is cured.

[39]In some spiritual writers this is called contemplation. However, that term will be reserved for a different level of prayer. See Aumann, *Spiritual Theology*, p. 327.

[40]Ibid., p. 318.

order man to God. But it also makes man more rational because the lower faculties come under the command of reason more. Hence, those who pray often tend to find a certain clarity of intellectual vision arising from the practice of mental prayer. This follows from the fact that the passions affect the phantasm less, which results in clarity of vision.

This form of prayer is particularly useful in training the cogitative power. Since the possible intellect and will reformulate the image from various points of view, the cogitative power learns different ways of associating the various sensible species which come together in the newly formed image. As a result, as one prays more, the cogitative power associates those things in memory more which are ordained toward God or can be viewed from the point of view of God and therefore the person takes on a more supernatural outlook on his sensible life. The cogitative power learns to follow reason more since it is under the command of reason.[41] When prayer is done in this manner, the possible intellect and will move the cogitative power to associate various things from memory based upon past experience. For example, if someone considers God's goodness to man, the possible intellect and will move the cogitative power to go back in memory and associate all the times that God has been good to the person individually. This method of prayer is particularly helpful in all *per accidens* mental illnesses since it has an impact on those faculties. It also has the effect of making someone more "positive." If the meditation is carried out properly, the person orients his faculties toward supernatural truths which are goods. Those suffering from negative passions, such as anger, depression (sorrow) and the like, will find that this form of prayer will alleviate some of their difficulties.

There are a variety of methods of this form of prayer, e.g. the Ignatian, the Carmelite etc. However, they will not be addressed here. The psychologist should have a knowledge of the various methods to know which kinds of methods fit the various dispositions and difficulties of their directees, in order to know which one would suit the directee the best. The psychologist must resist the temptation to force the directee into the method which the psychologist himself uses, but base his judgment on what is best for the directee. The psychologist should be familiar with the various methods of prayer also in order to help the directee get a structured approach to his mental prayer. Normally, most directees do not have a habit of prayer and so they will find the process difficult due to bad habits or the mental illness itself as well as confusion since they may not know how to go about it. Once they become more advanced, this form of prayer can be followed in a less structured fashion since the faculties will be more disposed to entering into meditation more readily. A *traditional* method also will avoid directees getting involved in forms of meditation which are inimical to the spiritual/psychological life. There are many new forms of prayer available which can be dangerous and so the psychologist should counsel the directee to follow a traditional form.

The psychologist must also encourage the directee to take a gradual approach to developing the practice and habit of prayer. The directee must avoid hagiosthenia

---

[41]This should be seen in connection to the prior discussion in this chapter on the lower faculties as being moved by exterior agencies.

which is a Greek term meaning "tiredness of holy things." What can happen is that if the directee starts out trying to meditate two hours a day right away, he will find that his faculties are not properly habituated or disposed for that length of time. Therefore, in order to avoid hagiosthenia, he should strive for shorter periods, such as fifteen minutes a day. If he finds that he is inclined to do it longer, he can increase it gradually under the direction of the psychologist, or even better, under a spiritual director.[42] However, the psychologist should encourage the directee to work up to a proper amount of mental prayer each day, preferably thirty minutes to an hour each day. Hagiosthenia must also be avoided in matters such as the devotional life, mortification and things of this sort. The danger is always to try to do too much too quickly. As Christ said, "pray always."[43] But this is the goal (called the transforming union) and one should not presume one is more advanced than one is in the beginning stages. Just as a man who is sixty pounds overweight and out of shape does not attempt to run a marathon, so the beginners in the spiritual life must be conscious of their limits. If the psychologist allows the directee to go unchecked, hagiosthenia will kick in with the effect that the person becomes repulsed by spiritual things because of the ardor involved in attaining perfection. In this case, the directee will be worse off than when he started. Nevertheless, the psychologist should also encourage the directee to work on the habit of mental prayer.

The next level of prayer is described by Aumann in the following manner:

> Affective prayer may be defined as a type of prayer in which the operations of the will predominate over discursus of the intellect. There is no specific difference between affective prayer and meditation, as there is between meditation and contemplation; it is merely a simplified meditation in which love predominates. For this reason the transition to affective prayer is usually gradual and more or less easy, although this will vary with individuals.[44]

Affective prayer is important for psychology in several ways; however, a few admonitions must be given first. To enter into affective prayer, one should not try to force the entrance into it too quickly. Those who have attachments to sensible consolations will want to enter into this form of prayer too quickly. On the other hand, one should not try to stop oneself from entering it, i.e. there are some who think that any form of consolation is bad (Jansenists, for example) and so they will remain fixed in mental prayer. The transition from mental prayer to affective prayer should be natural.

The second admonition is given to warn psychologists of those who base their

---

[42]In fact, it may be best if the directee has a spiritual director (priest) working with the psychologist. That way there is no danger of mixing fora and the proper domains of psychology and theology will remain distinct. This would not apply, of course, if the psychologist were also a priest.

[43]Luke 18:1.

[44]Aumann, *Spiritual Theology*, p. 324.

spiritual life on consolations, whether sensible or spiritual.[45] Consolations and desolations must be viewed as means of attaining God. Having a consolation does not necessarily mean that one is spiritually advanced. On the contrary, it can mean that one is only beginning. Just as one must give a dog a snack in the initial stages of teaching him to do a trick and then later one can get him do to it without the snack, so God sometimes entices the soul by means of consolations. However, consolations cannot be the end of the spiritual life, because then a form of sacrilege occurs in which one uses a spiritual good for a worldly or profane use. One seeks spiritual goods to feel better or to experience the passion of delight. This can cause profound damage to one's spiritual life and it can actually lead to mental illness. Those who are grossly attached to consolations will often not experience them and so they are driven to depression or despair (or even madness) trying to attain the delights of the consolation. Consolations must be viewed as means. When God gives them to the soul, he must use them to propel himself higher in the spiritual life to gain greater union with God. Since God is the object of happiness and not the consolations, the consolations must be seen as a means of union with the Object of happiness.

Conversely, desolations should not be viewed as a lack of spiritual progress or lack of God's favor. While it is true that sin can cause dryness of soul, experiencing dryness or desolation is not always a sign of sin. Directees must be counseled on this. Desolation can actually be a sign of spiritual progress. As mentioned, just as we withhold the snack from the dog once he is able to do the trick without it, so God takes away consolations and leaves the soul desolate. If God always gave consolations, there would be a danger of the soul presuming that consolation must always accompany experience of God in this life. Desolation also serves another function. God will often leave the soul desolate in order to test the soul to see if it is continuing in the spiritual life because it loves God alone or whether there is some attachment to spiritual goods other than God. Since it is more arduous for us to do something when the faculties derive no delight, God wants to see if we are willing to do what is difficult in order to reach Him and please Him. Desolation also serves to teach us that, on our own, we are nothing. Through desolation we begin to see that we cannot find our fulfillment in ourselves and that God alone is the Object of happiness. For this reason, desolation can occur at any stage of prayer except the transforming union.

Consolations and desolations constitute a real danger for those who are mentally ill. Often directees are seeking some form of consolation due to the desolation of the mental illness. While mental illness may be a sign of sin and so the directee should not presume he is beyond consolations, nevertheless, he must accept the desolation as meaning what has been discussed. He can actually use the desolation of the mental illness as a form of mortification. On the other hand, consolations can also aid the directee. While he should not seek them and should learn to become detached from them, nevertheless the consolations when they come should be viewed as a means to advancing in holiness and aiding him in overcoming his mental illness.

---

[45]Sensible consolations are those given to the material faculties, whereas spiritual consolations normally occur in the intellect and will.

Affective prayer aids the psychological faculties in several ways. Affective prayer ordains the appetitive life toward charity, i.e. God. Affective prayer orders the cogitative power by teaching it that it should associate the good with God, not necessarily the pleasant life, but the good. Because of our sin, our experience of God is often painful, e.g. when one sees himself in relation to God's absolute goodness which sets in relief his absolute destitution. Yet, the cogitative power in all of this can be habituated to judge self negatively in the sense that what is best for self is not self but God. Moreover, the memory of the experience of affective prayer can spur the person on to pray more. It also helps to calm the faculties by making them more intent on the object of consideration. In this way, affective prayer begins a process of unifying the faculties in their operations which is more evidenced in the next level of prayer. Recognizing mental illness normally consists in the possible intellect recognizing some disorder and the lower faculties not following the command of reason. Hence, the faculties become disunified through mental illness whereas this form of prayer aids the unification. While that can be said also of all of the forms of prayer, it becomes more evident at this level in the life of the individual.

Affective prayer also moves the person to be more intense in the practice of the Christian virtues,[46] which we have clearly seen has a direct impact on mental illness. In fact, one may say that, since mental health is some quality or virtue, this level of prayer will move one to strive to overcome the mental illness more. Since mental illness ultimately makes it impossible for the faculties to be directed in a unified fashion to one Object alone in a rightly ordered fashion, mental illness ultimately blocks one from union with God. While it may be the case that morally the person may not be responsible and so he will still save his soul, nevertheless, rectitude of the faculties is required for the beatific vision.[47]

Affective prayer also increases the purity of intention of the individual. In effect, the person becomes less set on the things of this world and more on God and for this reason this form of prayer also increases charity. This is important for psychology since in many forms of mental illness the person's fixation on self or some other created good is the root of the mental illness. This form of prayer will aid in breaking these attachments. In addition, the person will become more detached from created things which can cause mental illness. In fact, we can say that every cause of mental illness is some created thing, either as a cause[48] or as an occasion[49] of the mental illness. This level of prayer also aids one in the faithful and exact fulfillment of the duties of one's state in life. This is important for those laboring under mental illness because they often cannot fulfill their duties in life because of the fixation caused by the mental illness. As

---

[46]The subsequent fruits of affective prayer can be found in Aumann, *Spiritual Theology*, p. 326.

[47]It is for this reason that the demons seek to cause mental illness in people. See next chapter.

[48]For example the demonic (see next chapter) or biological causes.

[49]For example when the person cannot control himself around alcohol.

they advance in prayer, they will find the execution of their duties easier.

The next level of prayer is called the prayer of simplicity:

> The prayer of simplicity was defined by Bossuet as a simple loving
> gaze upon some divine object, whether on God himself or one of his
> perfections, on Christ or on one of his mysteries, or on some other
> Christian truth. It is a form of ascetical prayer that is extremely
> simplified. The discursus formerly used in meditation has now been
> transformed into a simple intellectual gaze; the affections that were
> experienced in affective prayer have been unified into a simple loving
> attention to God. The prayer is ascetical, meaning that the soul is able
> to attain to this type of prayer by its own efforts with the help of
> ordinary grace, but often it is the transition point to mystical prayer.[50]

As in affective prayer, in this level of prayer the faculties are unified. Normally, those with mental illness will not reach this level since the faculties are normally disunified in the mental illness. However, this level of prayer will tend to remove any residual effects of the mental illness. This level can be reached on one's own effort with the aid of ordinary grace and it is normally viewed as a level of prayer in which a person passes from active to passive purgation. In this level of prayer, one will also experience in greater degree all of the effects of mental and affective prayer regarding the various faculties and the psychological effect on those faculties.

Those who reach this level of prayer should be seeing a spiritual director so that they can continue into the next level of prayer which is mystical contemplation. If a psychologist detects that one of his directees has reached mystical contemplation, the directee should be sent to a learned priest. Normally people at this level will not need a psychologist. Psychologists must be careful not to assume that those who pass over into the later five stages of prayer are mentally ill. There have been some psychologists in the past who tried to explain mystical phenomena in terms of mental illness and fixations. However, such explanations are based in profound ignorance, even though they are often touted as scientific.

We shall not cover the other levels of prayer since the psychological effects are more a matter of advanced psychology and do not pertain to an introduction in psychology. Normally, these levels of prayer cannot be discussed psychologically unless

---

[50]Aumann, *Spiritual Theology*, p. 329. Continuing on in that section Aumann observes: "The prayer of simplicity is thus the bridge between ascetical and mystical prayer. It is, as it were, the final disposition before the Holy Spirit begins to operate in the soul by means of his gifts. For that reason, one may frequently experience a blending of acquired and infused elements in the practice of the prayer of simplicity. If the soul is faithful, the infused elements will gradually be increased until they dominate the practice of prayer entirely. Thus, without any shock and almost insensibly, the soul proceeds gently from the ascetical practice of prayer to mystical contemplation. This is an indication of the unity of the spiritual life and of the fact that there is only one road to perfection."

someone has a great deal of theological background and philosophical background. Psychologists should normally have some idea of these last levels but anyone who is in these last levels should be sent immediately to a priest knowledgeable in the spiritual life.

IV. Devotion

Devotion is "a will to give oneself promptly to that which pertains to the service of God."[51] One has devotion when one desires to serve God promptly. Devotion in the colloquial use often indicates that the person is prompt in serving God in the various para-liturgical acts as well as someone who loves and seeks the intercession of the saints. Therefore, to discuss this aspect of the spiritual life which can greatly aid directees, we shall break the discussion into two parts. The first is a consideration of para-liturgical acts and the second is the devotion to saints and its benefits.

As to the first part, there are a wide variety of para-liturgical acts which can greatly aid a person's advancement in the spiritual life and overcome mental illness. One of the most important is the Rosary. The Rosary is a form of meditation in which one considers the various mysteries of Christ and our Lady. The Rosary is very efficacious on several levels. It is meritorious in the order of grace and therefore will aid the directee in that fashion. Countless stories are given by the saints about the efficacy of this prayer in rooting out mortal sin and sin in general and so any mental illness caused by sin can be greatly aided by the Rosary.[52]

Psychologists should form a habit of saying the Rosary themselves, perhaps even for their directees as a way of fulfilling their obligation to pray for the directees because of their state in life. The Rosary also affords all of the psychological benefits of both vocal and mental prayer, depending on the method of recitation. It forms an integral part of a proper devotion to our Lady.[53] Also, because it is normally said with a set of beads, the beads are a tangible means to stay focused since one does not have to concern oneself with counting the mysteries and Hail Marys.

Other para-liturgical acts have a great impact on the psychological life, e.g., saying the Stations of the Cross. This devotion aids in helping the person to see the love of God for him but also provides an example by God Himself on how to suffer. Those

---

[51]ST II-II, q. 82, a. 1: "voluntas quaedam prompte tradendi se ad ea quae pertinent ad Dei famulatum."

[52]One of the fifteen promises for those who daily recite the Rosary is "the Rosary shall be a powerful armor against hell, it will destroy vice, decrease sin, and defeat heresies." In this respect, since mental illness is a vice, it would appear that the Rosary may have a direct impact on mental illness. While it is still possible to become mentally ill (e.g. from a biological cause) even if one is saying the Rosary and staying out of sin, nevertheless it is unlikely that one who says the Rosary faithfully would fall into a mental illness which is in the domain of the voluntary.

[53]See below.

who are afflicted with mental illness can learn a great deal from Christ. Spending a holy hour in front of the Blessed Sacrament can greatly aid the directee on the level of grace and by focusing the faculties on something tangible. Making stops at stational churches or just making a visit to a church can help to focus the person and the faculties, as well as provide some quiet when there is tumult of the various faculties.

Litanies offer many points of meditation and can aid one in the life of prayer. They also provide virtues for which the directee should strive as can be evidenced in the litany of Loreto. The litany of humility provides several important things psychologically. In addition to grace and points of meditation, it also disposes the soul by the very meditation towards the practice of this virtue. It helps the directee and psychologist for that matter, to keep in contact with reality. It is very easy for the directee to get lost in what he wishes to be (freed from mental illness) rather than to be grounded in what he is. This litany also provides a certain meekness by tempering one's desire for one's own excellence. It can temper the passion of self-love. It can temper all of the other passions which flow from self-love, such as anger when one is injured. Humility can also mitigate sorrow when one views one's own good rather than humbly recognizing the need for suffering to become holy, as well as recognizing that one is not the center of attention. Prayer in general aids depression along with this litany since prayer draws one from considering self from the point of view of lacking some good (source of the depression). Prayer, when considering supernatural truths, takes away the object of depression from the imagination and so the passion of sorrow is lifted. The litany of humility also mitigates fear since fear is the passion which concerns some future evil which the person cannot avoid. Those suffering from various anxieties (fears) should pray the litany of humility and practice humility since it will take away from them the fear about suffering some harm since humility teaches us that we must ultimately suffer anything that God chooses to send us. It also will detach us from goods, about which, if we do not attain them, we have fear, since their future unattainability is viewed as an evil.

The number of devotions are large and so the psychologist must make sure that the various devotions which the directee employs are suited to the directee and his illness. Also, it is better to engage in a few devotions well than a large number poorly. The psychologist should also have a fairly decent knowledge about the various devotions. By having this knowledge, they are more able to recommend the various devotions which can aid particular directees and their problems.

The second part of the discussion has to do with devotion to various saints. However, prior to discussing saints, we should first note that devotion to the Sacred Heart of Jesus constitutes one of the most powerful forms of healing. Those who foster this devotion are granted the graces to make their hearts like Christ's Who said, "learn from Me, because I am meek, and humble of heart."[54] This devotion has a tempering effect on the passions and helps to reorient the person in a virtuous manner to God. Therefore, all psychologists and directees should work on this devotion.

Our Lady is also one who is indispensable to the psychologist and to the

---

[54]Matthew 11:29.

515

directee. St. Louis De Montfort makes the following observation about those who are truly devoted to our Lady:

> This devotion is a smooth way. It is the path which Jesus Christ opened up in coming to us and in which there is no obstruction to prevent us reaching him. It is quite true that we can attain to divine union by other roads, but these involve many more crosses and exceptional setbacks and many difficulties that we cannot easily overcome. We would have to pass through spiritual darkness, engage in struggles for which we are not prepared, endure bitter agonies, scale precipitous mountains, tread upon painful thorns, and cross frightful deserts. But when we take the path of Mary, we walk smoothly and calmly.[55]

A strong and rightly ordered devotion to our Lady can smooth out the path for directees in overcoming mental illness. In order to ensure that the devotion is rightly ordered, the directee should be encouraged to read St. Louis De Montfort's *True Devotion to the Blessed Virgin*. In it are contained the necessary directions to ensure that the devotion is rightly ordered. They should also be encouraged to make the total consecration to our Lady according to the mind of St. Louis since the total consecration can result in our Lady taking a more active control over the person's life and thereby guiding the directee by grace and natural means. Psychologists should also have a strong devotion in like manner to ensure that their practice takes advantage of the greatest source of grace among God's creatures, i.e. our Lady.

Devotion to our Lady can also help directees who have very specific problems. While it can help all directees, some have problems which can be greatly aided by our Lady in other ways. For instance, those who suffer from homosexuality can be taught through grace by our Lady what it means to be a male. She can also teach women what it means to be truly feminine. Those who are suffering from lesbianism normally have an aversion to our Lady precisely because of her rightly ordered femininity. However, they should be encouraged to develop a devotion to our Lady as well as to read about her and take her as an example. Those who suffer from problems arising from chastity can find great example as well as grace from our Lady. Those who are suffering from the trauma of abortion can help to reorient themselves as well as receive our Lady's graces by which their path to recovery can be smoothed. They can also learn from her the total self-giving that she gave to God in becoming the mother of God and thereby learn the nature of motherhood and the role of the feminine.[56]

Other saints can also help. Different saints are patrons of different persons and things and so devotion to the various saints can aid specific kinds of directees. For

---

[55]St. Louis De Montfort, *True Devotion to the Blessed Virgin*, para 152.

[56]This treatment, in no way, exhausts the large number of ways which our Lady can be an example.

example, those who are struggling with the difficulties of being a father and husband can foster a devotion to St. Joseph. Those who struggle with remaining chaste can pray to the various virgin saints throughout history, e.g. St. Maria Goretti. When the directees share the name of a particular saint, they should foster a devotion to that saint. This would likewise apply to those who have been confirmed; they should also foster a devotion to their confirmation saint. The psychologist should have a general knowledge of the various patron saints so as to make recommendations to the directee.

The last saint to consider, even though countless could be exampled, is the patron saint of the mentally ill, i.e. St. Dymphna. St. Dymphna, according to oral tradition,[57] was beheaded by her own father who wished to marry the saint after the death of her mother. There have been many cures of mental illness attributed to St. Dymphna[58] and it is unfortunate that devotion to her is not fostered among psychologists. Directees should be encouraged to foster a devotion to her. Psychologists should, likewise, foster a devotion to her, not because they are mentally ill (or at least they should not be) but because through her intercession she can help to heal those under their care. If possible, Catholic psychologists should ask the bishop to have a small shrine along with the Blessed Sacrament where counseling takes place. This way directees and psychologists can make visits to the Blessed Sacrament while also performing acts of devotion to St. Dymphna, should relics of the saint be available. The bishop could petition to have some sent to his diocese where he could place them in the shrine for the sake of devotion to the saint. Priests in charge of the social services where psychological counseling is done can offer Mass, with the permission of the bishop, on her feast day, May fifteenth. Directees can be encouraged to attend. Those in the families of directees can be encouraged to pray to the saint (and other saints as well) to intercede for those family members afflicted. We can surmise that St. Dymphna would have a particular care for those whose mental illnesses are the result of injuries inflicted by other family members.

V. Mortification

The term *mortification* comes from the two Latin words *mors* and *facere* which literally means *to make dead*. By mortification, the lower faculties are made "dead," so to speak. By mortification, the lower faculties cease having a life of their own independent of reason and will. This does not mean that one ceases having rightly ordered passions and things of this sort, but mortification reduces antecedent appetite[59] so that the lower faculties do not act independently of right reason. In this sense, one does not engage in mortification to die, but to live, since a lack of antecedent passion means a freer and more peaceful life.[60] Tanquerey defines mortification as "the struggle

---

[57]CE, vol. V, p. 221.

[58]See ibid.

[59]See below.

[60]See below.

against our evil inclinations in order to subject them to the will, and the will of God."[61] All actions which we do to subject our evil inclinations are a form of mortification. Mortification can go by different names, such as exercising self-control, self-discipline because it begets self-control, and discipline.

Mortification is necessary because of man's condition after the fall:

> what causes us to surrender to temptation is the love of pleasure or *the horror of hardship, the hardship of the struggle.* Mortification combats this twofold tendency, which is really but one; for by having us break with some few legitimate pleasures, it arms our will against those that are unlawful, thus giving us an easier victory over sensuality and the love of self.[62]

Man suffers from a "horror of suffering"[63] because his lower nature does not want to undergo pain and suffering in order to attain some good. Rather, it seeks pleasure and so one can be debilitated by this fear. For this reason, a person must develop a spirit of mortification in which he is willing to suffer in order to attain the good. Succumbing to this horror is one of the chief reasons for renouncing sanctity[64] and it is also one of the chief obstacles to overcoming mental illness. When the faculties become habituated in mental illness of any kind, the actions which are congruous with the disposition of the mental illness actually can have a certain pleasure associated with them. Contrariwise, actions which go contrary to the mental illness cause a certain pain and so directees must learn that the dictum, "no pain, no gain," has a certain truth in the context of their illness. They must work on the spirit of mortification so that they are not inhibited in doing the right things to obtain mental health.

To develop the spirit of mortification, several things must be done. First, the directee should take on some voluntary form of mortification. By foregoing licit pleasures, the person obtains a greater control when the time comes to forego illicit pleasures[65] or the pleasures which are associated with the things that cause his mental illness. The directee must also submit to the sufferings which God sends to him. Since God knows what is best, He will often send sufferings, trials and difficulties, which

---

[61]Tanquerey, *The Spiritual Life*, n. 754.

[62]Ibid., n. 763.

[63]This is the name that Aumann gives it in *Spiritual Theology*, p. 170.

[64]Aumann, *Spiritual Theology*, p. 170.

[65]See Tanquerey, *The Spiritual Life*, n. 768. Also in that same passage, Tanquerey observes that the directee must learn that pleasures are not an end but merely a means. Through the spirit of mortification the person is able to detach himself from pleasures as an end.

directly or indirectly will aid the directee in overcoming his mental illness.[66] Next, in order to engage in mortification, prudence and discretion are required.[67] Since those with mental illness often lack discretion and prudence in relation, at least, to the object(s) of their mental illness, they should rely on a spiritual director in conjunction with the psychologist to moderate and determine the kinds of mortification to be done by them. The directee must also begin developing a preference for suffering over pleasure.[68] By preference here is meant that the directee sees the necessity of being willing to suffer for the good over any inclination he might have to pleasure. Since mortification can beget a great many good effects as a means, more so than pleasure, then right reason sees that those who are in the wayfaring state must be willing to seek the more arduous path in order to attain the good.

Other observations about mortification have been mentioned throughout this volume. It has already been observed that mortification is a good work and so it can merit actual grace. Mortification can be done in order to merit the graces necessary to recoup or maintain one's psychological health.[69] Any form of suffering, either passive or active, can be used for mortification. One can use the things which one suffers involuntarily (i.e. passively) and offer them up for the graces necessary for mental health. This not only applies to the directee but also to the counselor and family of the directee who are able to offer their sufferings for him. Also one can take on active penances or mortifications in order to merit the graces necessary, such as fasting or doing things which one does not like to do but are necessary for one's state in life, e.g. cleaning the house, doing the dishes or things of this sort.

A directee can also offer up the suffering of the mental illness and humiliations which sometimes go along with the mental illness either for himself or for others. The notion of vicarious suffering has for all intents and purposes played virtually no role in the practice of modern psychology. Yet, vicarious suffering has a psychological benefit.

---

[66] Again, it should be noted that God sends these ultimately for the salvation of the soul and for its sanctification but since mental illness can impede the process of becoming holy, the sufferings that God sends will also aid mental health.

[67] See Tanquerey, *The Spiritual Life*, n. 769.

[68] Aumann, *Spiritual Theology*, p. 174.

[69] Maintaining one's psychological health can apply to two different kinds of individuals. It can apply to those who once lost their mental health and have recovered it. In this case, they may have to do more to maintain their mental health than those who have never lost their mental health. Then there are those who have never suffered any real form of mental illness and they do not have to do as much to maintain their mental health. However, even those who are mentally healthy can lose their mental health through voluntary action. They could also run the risk of losing it, even if they do nothing voluntary to lose it, if they are placed in a situation in which the average person would have a hard time maintaining a proper psychological balance, e.g. in a concentration camp where grave atrocities are occurring or things of this sort. In cases such as these, one must actively seek out those means which will maintain one's mental health.

As the person afflicted with mental illness offers up his suffering for those around him, he will change his view of himself to something more positive, i.e. he will view himself as a doer of good. This can aid depression or any other mental illness in which one sorrows at the mental illness, since one can see the mental illness as a means to something good.[70] While he must strive to overcome his mental illness since it can impede him in his advancement to sanctified perfection, nevertheless he can actually use the mental illness in perfecting charity.

Suffering and mortification can also have a purifying effect. When one suffers, one sorrows. The sorrow can be associated, if rightly directed, with the actions which aggravate the mental illness. As the person begins to see the action as sorrowful, he can find a motivation not to perform the actions. In fact, at times, people sorrow at the mental illness but want to remain attached to the actions which cause the mental illness. If the person can be encouraged to take a realistic approach toward his mental illness, he will see that the actions are only apparently good and not truly good and thereby he can lose his motivations to perform the actions. Sorrow can be used to purify the soul, i.e. to root out the mental illness.

Mortification also trains the cogitative power not to seek after the things of sense. Since an untrained or ill-trained cogitative power will assess something as good when it gives pleasure, mortification trains the cogitative power to assess as good something which actually leads to a rightly ordered end. In other words, the cogitative power (and thus the directee) learn that good comes through suffering and so it will not always associate good with the pleasures of sense.

Yet, even the senses themselves are purified in a way. Since the senses are a faculty operating through a bodily organ, they dispose themselves to the operations of the soul acting through the bodily organ. When a person engages in sensible pleasures, the bodily organ adjusts itself to the pleasure so that it can sustain that activity more. As a result, the more pleasure one seeks, the duller the senses become because they adjust themselves to a more vehement activity. On the other hand, as one engages in mortification, the senses begin to adjust themselves to be less sensitive to the pain and more sensitive to things that are not painful. As a result, those who engage in mortification or purification of the senses, find that their senses become heightened or more sensitive.

To return to the interior powers, the cogitative power will have a different sensible criterion upon which to base its assessment. As the body adjusts itself to suffering, the cogitative power judges the suffering in a lesser degree and so the person is less affected in his judgment about things that cause suffering. As a result, the mortification of the senses leads to a clarity of intellectual vision since the cogitative power is more apt to assess the sensible species, not based upon pleasure or pain, but upon what reason inclines it toward.

There must also be a mortification or a purification of the memory, which has already been somewhat discussed. However, the memory becomes purified or mortified

---

[70]Tanquerey in *The Spiritual Life* (n. 754) observes that "mortification is not an end in itself, but a means to an end."

when the person orders the suffering toward a good end. This has two effects on the memory. The first is that the cogitative power when it goes back into memory, normally associates what is good with the thing or what is bad if it is going to cause harm. But if the person suffers in a rightly ordered fashion, the cogitative power will not assess it as harmful and therefore not drag up anything in memory that might be seen as harmful. In this way, those who have suffered traumatic experiences can actually overcome various disorders by moderated mortification in accordance with right reason. Obviously caution and extreme prudence is required, since if the person does not understand the rationale behind the suffering, it can aggravate his problem. Yet, if the person through a rightly ordered mortification under the direction of a psychologist learns self-denial and is willing to suffer for the good, the traumatic experiences will be viewed in a lighter manner by the cogitative power and this will affect judgment.[71]

Mortification, since it requires the possible intellect and will to direct one's action, also begets mental health. If the suffering is directed toward a rightly ordered end, the possible intellect and will direct and guide the lower faculties to a good end. Sometimes in mental illness, the person has an attachment to some apparent good (i.e. it is not really good) and so when one engages in mortification which is directly contrary to the attachment of the lower faculties, they will resist reason somewhat. As reason continues to move the faculties to engage the object, the faculty is broken of its own inclination and comes under the direction of reason and will. In effect, mortification gives greater freedom in the end since one is not bound by the attachments of the lower

---

[71] In the spiritual life, the mortifying process on the senses is called the purification of the external senses and it constitutes part of the active purgative stage. The active purgative stage is what the person is able to accomplish in purifying and ordering the faculties on his own. But our defects are so deeply rooted in the soul that we cannot root them out on our own. In order to attain sanctified perfection, God Himself must take over and purify the soul completely. This later stage of purgation is called passive purgation. Purifying exterior senses, interior sense, possible intellect and will on our own is all part of the active purgation. It is required since the purgation and the level of prayer go hand in hand, i.e. one does not normally enter in to the passive purgative stage until one passes over into mystical contemplation, the fifth level of prayer. Also, as one actively purges his own faculties, concomitantly, the soul ascends the first four levels of prayer. This is necessary since the faculties have to be quieted by mortification (or God can do it by grace) in order to arrive at the prayer of simplicity in which the lower faculties do not drag the higher faculties off due to their disorders. Here we see how important psychological health is to attain the higher levels of prayer since disordered faculties can inhibit prayer. Since prayer is a similitude of the beatific vision as well as a means to the beatific vision, those who ascend the levels of prayer become happier as the prayer becomes more like the beatific vision. Those who are mentally ill will not be as happy since their mental illness often inhibits the activity of prayer. This is why psychology has such a grave import and psychologists must keep this in mind. It is also why the demons do everything they can to distract us during prayer since they do not want us ultimately to reach God or be happy. In the end, mortification is necessary, either in this life to ascend the heights of prayer or in the next, when, in purgatory, the imperfections are rooted out so that we can see God.

faculties. It will also beget peace since the lower faculties will fall under the order of the possible intellect and will and so there will be tranquility of order.

Yet, most psychologists suffer from the mentality that suffering is evil and that the goal of the psychologist is to minimize suffering. However, this is not necessarily the case. While the psychologist should not wish evil on anyone, he may be required at times to encourage the directee and his family to take on some form of mortification in order to overcome the directee's mental illness. Some forms of mental illness are directly aided by mortification, e.g. if one fasts one can actually reduce concupiscence[72] and conserve chastity.[73] This follows from the fact that the concupiscible appetite, while it is directed to two different categories of bodily goods, viz. food and reproduction, nevertheless, is a unitary faculty. If one moderates one's food intake, it can have an effect on the faculty in general and thereby reduce one's sexual drive.

Fasting also can reduce some eating disorders or vices.[74] If the eating disorder is based upon excessive eating, the person can reduce the inclination of the appetite by fasting. Just as the appetite is moved by the presence of the object, so the appetite retracts by the presence of its opposite. This applies to all forms of mortification. If there is some mental illness which is based on some appetitive attachment or if the person gets some pleasure out of the actions associated with the mental illness, the form of mortification which is contrary to the object moving the appetite should be employed. This will directly reduce the appetite and aid the process of healing the mental illness.

Suffering, if directed for the benefits of others, can help to keep one's perspective off of self. One of the problems with mental illness is that it often reduces the person to being self-absorbed. The suffering, if directed to the benefit of others, can bring the person out of himself and he will be less self-absorbed. Moreover, if the suffering is joined to the sufferings of Christ,[75] the sufferings can have a spiritual and psychological benefit. It is also the only way to make sense of suffering. Since the directee will often be confused and depressed about the mental illness, he may have a hard time making sense of his suffering. To make sense means to see the suffering as fitting into a rightly ordered world and life. But suffering can be rightly ordered when directed toward the good of others, as is the case with Christ. Suffering does benefit, not only the individual who suffers, but others, even if the cause of the suffering will never be overcome in this life. In this context, psychologists must be able and willing to counsel the directee to have a certain detachment from self so that if the mental illness is not cured, either temporarily or in the long term, the directee will understand that God allows it for his sanctification and the sanctification of others. In this way, the directee will see the suffering of the mental illness as a benefit, at least for others, and can therefore sustain it more easily. It will also help him to become self-detached. If the

---

[72]ST II-II, q. 147, passim.

[73]ST II-II, q. 147, a. 1.

[74]ST II-II, q. 147, a. 4.

[75]Since the passion and death of Christ constitute THE act upon which all merit hangs, nothing is meritorious unless it is joined to this act by intention.

mental illness is self-inflicted, however, he must be told to do everything to overcome the mental illness. If the mental illness is not self-inflicted, he should use it as an opportunity to grow in the virtue of self-detachment, the spirit of mortification, long-suffering, and charity toward others.

All of the aforesaid uses of mortification also affect mental health regarding the possible intellect. Since the possible intellect depends on the phantasm, the more those faculties which affect the phantasm are purified, the less likely they are to affect the phantasm which the possible intellect uses to judge. By commanding the acts of mortification to be performed, the intellect is strengthened by the habit of holding to the truth regardless of the tumult of the lower faculties. In connection to this, St. Thomas says that fasting (and we can say other forms of mortification) frees the mind to sublime contemplation.[76] This follows from the fact that the possible intellect by mortification ceases being trained or focused on material or created things (i.e. lowly things). For those suffering from mental problems such as depression, unrestrained anger and the like, the mortification will turn their mind to higher things and thus mitigate the anger or sorrow.

Mortification also strengthens the will since the will must move the lower faculties to the action of mortification even though they may resist it. As time goes on, the will becomes stronger and the lower faculties become more under the control of the will. Because mental illness is a vice or a connexus of vices and since every vice in a faculty other than the will also has a concomitant weakness in the will as relating to the object of the vice of the faculty, those with mental illness will find themselves weak in relation to the object of mental illness. Mortification done in direct opposition to the object of weakness will strengthen the will and give the person more power over the lower faculties.[77] On the other hand, directees who give into their passions will find that the passions weary and torture them. As St. John of the Cross rightly observes, the passions pull us this way and that and they are never satisfied.[78] The passions tire the soul out because the other faculties must always serve them unless they are brought under the control of reason and will through mortification and other means. As the directee gains more control over his passions and his mental illness begins to lift, if it is somehow connected to the passions, he will notice an increase in energy and peace of soul. In the soul is also a natural inclination to fulfill the requirements of retributive justice. If the mental illness of the directee is connected to sin, the directee will find some relief in conscience when he engages in some mortification for the sake of satisfying retributive justice.[79]

---

[76]ST II-II, q. 147, aa. 1 and 3.

[77]In modern parlance, we would say it will give the directee more power or control over his life. See Tanquerey, *The Spiritual Life*, n. 795.

[78]St. John of the Cross, *Ascent to Mt. Carmel*, Bk. I, c. 6.

[79]The fact that fasting (and we can say mortification) satisfies for sins, see ST II-II, q. 147, a. 1. It can also undo the effects of sin, which has been discussed in this chapter, see Garrigou-Lagrange, *The Three Ages of the Interior Life*, vol. I, chap. 20.

Mortification can cause difficulties for someone if the proper conditions under which it is performed are not observed. Sometimes it happens that a person feels under duress because he is giving up some good. The mortification during the time in which the person is in duress may actually aggravate the problem. This follows from the fact that the mortification is seen as another thing of sorrow. When the person is not in the state of duress, he can engage the mortification so that the duress will decrease.

It also happens that the person will engage in mortification but he really does not want to let loose of the object causing his problem. If this is the case, the directee must first be counseled to see the problem as it truly is and therefore have the motivation to overcome his problem. Once that occurs, the mortification will have its desired effect. Otherwise, it may make the directee's problems worse since he will be forced into contradiction, i.e. his heart is attached to the object of his problem and yet the mortification is militating against that object.

Psychologists must be careful when counseling mortification to ensure that the mortification is moderated according to the dispositions and physical conditions of the directee. If the directee is frail or has physiological problems that can be aggravated by the mortification, passive mortifications will have to be embraced rather than active ones. Also, the psychologist must ensure, if the directee is engaging in some form of mortification, once he experiences some good benefit from the mortification, he is not incited to go to extremes in the mortification.

VI. Detachment

One of the primary effects of mortification is detachment, sometimes called holy indifference. Detachment is an indifference, in the appetitive faculties, in relation to a created object. Detachment has as its finality perfect charity.[80] Detachment for the sensitive appetites consists in the cessation of all antecedent appetite. However, detachment is principally in the concupiscible appetite with respect to the passion of love. With perfect detachment in the concupiscible appetite, the appetite does not incline when its object comes into the imagination until reason indicates that it is to be pursued. Mortification causes detachment in relation to the passion of love by quieting the appetite through its opposite, i.e. pain.

Detachment is absolutely necessary to obtain perfect mental health in relation to any created good. This follows from the fact that if we are attached (have the passion of love) to some created good, the passion will always affect judgment.[81] Moreover, attachments indicate that the cogitative power is assessing the object according to the attachment, e.g. if one has an attachment to steak, whenever steak comes into the imagination, the cogitative power will be habituated by past passions of love for the steak and assess it as good. It can happen that some particular motions caused by attachments can fall under right reason, just as a passion is capable of inclining someone

---

[80]See below.

[81]See vol. I, chap. 9.

to do something morally right. However, the danger consists in making the passion (i.e. the attachment) the principle of judgment. Since the appetites are blind faculties, there are times when their objects come into the imagination and they ought not be pursued. Yet the person will struggle with the attachment. Just as any antecedent passion may be good but is inherently imperfect, so any attachment is inherently imperfect.

Detachment in the will consists in the will choosing to turn away from the object of attachment by letting loose of it or by not pursuing it. Just as when there is any vice in the concupiscible appetite there is a concomitant weakness in the will, so when there is an attachment in the concupiscible or irascible appetite, there is usually a concomitant attachment in the will. In the normal process of overcoming the attachments in the appetites, the first thing that must occur is a letting loose on the side of the will to holding or seeking the object of attachment. However, the will is normally the last to be purified of attachments since there can be volitional attachments without appetitive attachments, e.g. someone can have a volitional attachment to a conceptual approach to psychology even though he may not have any attachment in the sensitive appetite.

Once mortification, prayer and grace remove the attachments in the sensitive and intellective appetites, the person will undergo a certain confusion. This follows from the fact that through a life of attachments (passions) and vice, the principles of judgment were interior, i.e. they were based on one's attachments. For example, one would do something because of how one felt rather than the truth. This form of confusion can only be overcome by two things, viz. truth and charity. When a person has worked on overcoming a mental illness rooted in some attachment, they will find that they are a bit lost and do not know what to do once they are freed from the mental illness. It is in that moment that the person must direct his life based upon the truth of his state in life and seek to perform the actions of his state in life, e.g. a mother should spend more time taking care of the children. In the spiritual life, once one has undergone the process of removing all of the attachments, two virtues are necessary, viz. faith and charity. Faith is necessary since God strips the person even of the ways he thinks about God since those are inadequate.[82] So the person must proceed by faith, knowing that God will guide him and take care of him and that he must assent to the teachings of the Church to know what to do. Next, the motivation to continue moving down the path of perfection comes from charity in which at this stage the love of God has reached a sufficient level to keep the person moving.[83]

---

[82]When a person has been stripped of this, it is called the dark night of the soul and this is a necessary step so that the person can enter into the illuminative stage (which follows the purgative stage which has this effect) in which God directly enlightens the soul with the knowledge of supernatural things.

[83]Interesting cases of those having strokes have arisen in relation to these observations. Some stroke victims will have the neural network severed by which the body reports back to the brain the state of the body in which the passion or emotion is related. This results in the person having emotions but not being able to sense them and so, in effect, the cogitative power which used to assess the image based upon the passion no longer has

We see now the finality of detachment.

The reasons for the necessity of detachment from creatures for perfect union with God, as stated by St. John of the Cross, can be summarized in the following synthesis.

1. God is all, the necessary and absolute being, most pure act without the shadow of potency, who exists of himself and possesses the absolute plenitude of being. Compared with him, creatures are nothing; they are contingent beings that have more of potency than of act.

2. Two contraries cannot exist in the same subject because they mutually exclude each other. Therefore, light is incompatible with darkness and the All is incompatible with nothing.

3. If, then, creatures are nothing and darkness, and God is the All and light, it follows that the soul that wishes to be united with God must detach itself from creatures. Without this, union with God is impossible.

4. Hence it is necessary that the way and ascent to God should consist in mortifying the desires. Until these desires cease, the soul will not arrive at perfect union, although it may exercise many virtues, because it still does not perform those virtues with perfection, which requires that the soul be purged of every inordinate desire.

5. Some persons burden themselves with extraordinary penances and many other exercises and think that this or that will suffice for them to arrive at union with divine wisdom. If they would exert half the effort in mortifying their desires, they would advance more in one month through this practice than they would in many years by means of the other exercises. Just as it is necessary that one labor over the earth if it is to bear fruit, and without labor it will bear nothing but weeds, so also mortification of the appetites is necessary if there is to be any fruit or profit in the soul.[84]

Perfect detachment is necessary because one is not able to fulfill the precepts of charity

---

the information. This results in the possible intellect being presented with different phantasms and so the possible intellect becomes confused as to what to do since in the past it had based its judgment on the passions. Consequently, these types of individuals find no motivation in life because their motives (the passions) have been removed. The only way for these individuals to avoid becoming completely disillusioned and unmotivated in life is to begin the process of orienting their life through faith and charity, as is seen in those who go through the dark night of the senses and the dark night of the soul.

[84]Aumann, *Spiritual Theology*, p. 191f. These he summarizes from St. John of the Cross as seen in *The Ascent of Mount Carmel*, Book I, Chaps. 4-8.

without it.[85] Psychologically, since charity is the virtue which orders all of the other virtues toward their due end, it is not possible to have right order in the soul without charity, which is not possible without detachment. In fact, we can say that a vast majority of mental illnesses (mental vices) are due to a lack of detachment. For example, every phobia is rooted in an exaggerated attachment to self. Every fixation is rooted in some attachment to some created good. This means that every mental illness that is rooted in an attachment is inherently bad for the person spiritually. Therefore, it simply is not possible to separate a vast majority of mental health issues from spiritual issues. Every gift of the Holy Spirit is inhibited by attachments since the person seeks the thing to which he is attached rather than being free to be moved by God. Every infused virtue is inhibited by attachments. Charity is affected as we have seen and so is hope, since the person becomes fixated on created things and thereby does not seek after the Object of hope. As this becomes more pervasive in the soul, the person loses supernatural hope (and also natural hope). This is why many directees experience a sense of hopelessness and meaninglessness to their lives.

Therefore, psychologists must encourage detachment on the side of the directee. There are different objects of attachment. Some are created things outside the person, the other is the person himself. In fact, all attachments to creatures outside the person have a root in the person's desire to have that attachment fulfilled, i.e. the person is attached to self. This is why the spiritual writers are constantly encouraging self-denial.[86] It is only in denying ourselves our disordered attachments that we can actually seek what is best for ourselves, viz. God. Directees and psychologists must understand this if psychology is ever to get off the ground.[87] The directee can only begin the process of overcoming his mental illness if he is willing to put his attachments and pleasures aside and do what is arduous, which requires self denial. It is that simple. While attachments to certain things will appear reasonable and good to those who have

---

[85]See chapter on charity above.

[86]For example, Aumann observes in *Spiritual Theology* (p. 167): "Another precaution that must be taken in the struggle against sensuality is that of never going to the limit in regard to satisfactions that are permitted. This requires self-denial, and sometimes even in regard to lawful pleasures, especially if one is inclined to sensate satisfactions. With good reason does Clement of Alexandria say that those who do everything that is permitted will very readily do that which is not permitted. On the other hand, the mortification of one's tastes and desires will not damage one's health; rather it will usually benefit both body and soul. If we wish to keep ourselves far from sin and walk toward perfection in giant strides, it is necessary to reject a great number of sensate satisfactions."

[87]It is hard to imagine the current state of psychology. Many psychologists encourage their directees to commit sins in line with their attachments, e.g. some psychologists tell directees who feel guilty about sex just to give in to their vice causing their mental illness. So they encourage them to masturbate or engage in sodomy or things of this kind. They often argue that the directees have "hang-ups" about sex or any other object of attachment. Yet, by encouraging the attachment, the mental illness of the person increases, even if it is masked by not feeling guilty any more.

them, this is because they have habitually made the attachments their principles of judgment.

Conclusion

Therefore, psychologists must be detached from self in order to direct the directee with only the good of the directee in mind. No psychologist can properly counsel the directee unless he is detached from human respect and self, since counseling is often arduous and painful. Also, the detachment will help the psychologist keep a proper perspective and clarity of judgment about the directee without letting himself become attached or affected appetitively. Directees must clearly work on detachment. The psychologist must work on prayer to rightly order his own faculties and to direct the others to that right order. These main pillars of the spiritual life,[88] i.e. striving for detachment, prayer and devotion, constitute one of the primary means toward mental health for the directee and success in practice for the psychologist.

---

[88]There are other pillars of the spiritual life but they have been addressed in other places in this volume, e.g. the life of grace, the necessity to stop sinning, etc.

Chapter 10: Demonic Influences

> I greatly esteem those psychiatrists who are professionally competent and know the limitations of their science. They are honestly able to recognize when one of their patients exhibits symptoms that go beyond any known disease.[1]
>
> –Fr. Gabriel Amorth, Exorcist of the Diocese of Rome

It is the experience of this author that a vast majority of those in the psychological or psychiatric profession are not competent to judge whether a particular problem of a directee is actually mental illness, demonically influenced or both. Yet, a vast majority, due to their flawed empirical training, believe that they can clearly discern the signs of demonic influence. The irony is, of course, that their training has left them in a state of mind in which they categorically reject the possibility. As a result, any directee which might evidence signs of demonic afflictions is immediately labeled as mentally ill and even more so if the directee happens to think he is demonically influenced. Granted some are merely mentally ill and so the demonic influence is more imagined than real, but the existence of the demonic is likewise real[2] and so any psychologist who rejects outright the real possibility of mental illness stemming from a demonic cause lacks the scientific competence to be a psychologist.

Every science is an organized body of knowledge of things through their causes. If a person engages in the practice of a science refusing to consider possible causes, he is by that very fact unscientific. Now the demonic can cause changes to man and so for a psychologist to outright reject the consideration of the demonic as a cause is unscientific. This rationalistic scepticism which has pervaded every aspect of psychology does have an historical source but that will not be retraced here.[3] Rather, it should be noted that the existence of angels can be known from the natural light of reason[4] and the existence of bad angels is known through revelation and the teaching of the Church.[5]

One last observation about modern psychology and the demonic has to do with a more general observation which applies not just to those things pertaining to the demonic but in many other areas as well and that has to do with the issue of description or labeling. Modern psychology falsely presumes that it can rule out the demonic influence merely because it can (a) give a name to the aggregate of symptoms and (b) categorize the symptoms. Naming a disorder and labeling the symptoms is not the same

---

[1]Gabriel Amorth, *An Exorcist Tells His Story*, p. 61.

[2]See below.

[3]In the secular sphere, it began with "psychologists" such as Watson, e.g. see "Psychology as a Behavioralist Views It," p. 798, as found in *Classics in Psychology*. The desire to attain the certitude of the empirical sciences and enjoy their academic status is something evidenced in the very history of the modern psychological movement.

[4]SCG, II, c. 46.

[5]See below.

thing as knowledge of its cause. In modern psychology, what pertains to different kinds of demonic influence are given "scientific" names and therefore because they can label them, the modern psychologists think they know what they are. For example, "multiple personality disorder" is vaunted as a scientific achievement because they can label a set of symptoms, but at root they still have no idea as to the cause of "multiple personality disorder." Therein lies the danger; a label or name can be used when we are not certain of the cause, but once the cause is known, the name must be adjusted to fit the nature of the disorder. Yet, modern psychologists have already become set on the idea that a person manifesting different personalities is not demonically influenced. Almost always the causes they give are specious or violate the principle of sufficient reason, i.e. the cause named cannot sufficiently account for the behavior.[6]

The structure of this chapter is, therefore, first to discuss what angels and demons are. The second is to discuss why and how the demonic influences men. Next is a discussion of the ordinary and extraordinary ways in which demons influence men. What the directee and psychologist can do will also be discussed throughout the chapter.

I. Angelic Nature and the Demonic

Angels are pure spirits[7] who are endowed with intelligence[8] and free[9] will.[10]

---

[6]A superstition is sometimes defined as "an irrational belief arising from ignorance or fear." To deny the principle of sufficient reason or to assert conclusions which do not have sufficient reasons in the premises is irrational and requires belief to go from the premises to the conclusion. Modern psychology asserts conclusions about demonic influence which are not supported by the evidence. In this sense, the "belief" about the lack of demonic influence as well as many other aspects of their various psychological systems is nothing short of superstition, insofar as it is a form of irrational (contrary to first principles) belief based on ignorance. The unfortunate aspect of this issue is that modern psychologists dogmatically hold to their position, believing all the while that they are more knowledgeable than the rest.

[7]Fourth Lateran Council, *De fide catholica* (Denz. 800/428); First Vatican Council, *Dei filius* (Denz. 3002/1783); ST I, q. 50; SCG II, c. 46 and 49; *De substantiis separatis*, c. 18. See also Ephesians 6:12 insofar as we do not wage war with flesh and blood. See also Ott, *Fundamentals of Catholic Dogma*, p. 115f.

[8]ST I, q. 54-8 and SCG II, c. 46. Although angels are endowed with intelligence, Ott (*Fundamentals of Catholic Dogma*, p. 117) says: "The angels do not know the secrets of God (I Cor. 2:11), do not possess a knowledge of the heart (3 Kings 8:39) and have no certain foreknowledge of the free actions of the future (Is. 46:9f)." This is an important observation since it is one of the ways in which one knows whether the directee who claims to be receiving visions from God is, in fact, demonically deluded, i.e. whether he knows future contingents with certainty. Therefore anything the directee predicts that does not come true, even if he is able to predict things fairly well, is a sign that he is not receiving the vision from God, whose knowledge of future contingents is formally defined (see Ott, *Fundamentals of Catholic Dogma*, p. 41f). While angels can predict the future far better

Angels, therefore, do not have a body[11] but, like God, are purely spiritual. Because angels do not have a body or matter, they are not in a place, properly speaking,[12] nor are they in time.[13]

Created by God out of nothing,[14] they were first brought into existence in a state of innocence.[15] Those angels which sustained the test given to them by God[16] were then

---

than men, it is because of the superior intelligence and not because they are able to see future contingents, see ST I, q. 57, 4.

[9]This is implied by 2 Peter 2:4: "God spared not the angels that sinned." Angels could not sin unless they had free will. See also II Sent., d. 25, q. 1, a. 1; De Ver., q. 23, a.1; ibid., q. 24, a. 3; ST I, q. 59, a. 3; SCG II, c. 48 and De Malo, q. 16, a. 5.

[10]ST I, q. 59, a. 1; De Ver., 23, a. 1 and SCG II, c. 47. Also 2 Peter 2:11 states: "Whereas angels, who are greater in strength and power, bring not against themselves a railing judgment." Since angels have only one motive power, viz. the will, they have a stronger or more powerful will than man. This is why their influence, at times, can seem overpowering to directees.

[11]ST I, q. 50, a. 2; ibid., q. 51; I Sent., d. 8, q. 5, a. 2; II Sent., d. 3, q. 1, a. 1; De ente et essentia, c. 5; SCG II, c. 50f; Quod., XI, q. 4, a. 1; ibid., III, q. 8, a. un.; De substantiis separatis, c. 5 and 18.

[12]I Sent., d. 37, q. 3, a. 1; II Sent., d. 6, q. 1, a. 3; ST I, q. 52, a. 1; De pot., q. 3, a. 19, ad 2 and Quod., I, q. 3, a. 1. However, an angel can be said to be in a place "per applicationem igitur virtutis angelicae ad aliquem locum qualitercumque" ("by application, therefore, of the power of the angel to some place in some way." Angels are said to be in a place because through their wills they engage in an activity which acts upon a physical thing. Hence we say that our guardian angel is "here" because he performs some action on something in our presence or on our bodies.

[13]Since angels do not have a body, they cannot be in time since time is the measurement of motion of a physical thing. See I Sent., d. 37, q. 4, a. 3; Quod., IX, q. 4, a. 4; Quod., XI, q. 4, a. un. and ST I, q. 53, a. 3. Just as they can be said to be in a place insofar as they act through some physical thing, so can they be said to be in time, although not properly speaking, since their activity can be seen in the material thing which is in time.

[14]Fourth Lateran Council, De fide catholica (Denz. 800/428) and First Vatican Council, Dei filius (Denz. 3002/1783).

[15]That the angels were created in grace is a proposition which is sententia certa and not de fide. However, it does appear to be the common opinion of theologians (see Ott, Fundamentals of Catholic Dogma, p. 117f) and as Ott points out (ibid.), "Pope Pius V rejected the teaching of Baius that not grace but eternal bliss is the reward to the good angels for their naturally good works. D. 1003f [/1869] Jesus in the warning against scandal assures: 'Their angels in heaven always see the face of my Father, who is in heaven' (Mt. 18, 10). Cf. Tob. 12, 19. However, the indispensable precondition for the achievement of the immediate vision of God is the possession of sanctifying grace." See also II Sent., d. 4, a. 3 and ST I, q. 62.

[16]See Ott, Fundamentals of Catholic Dogma, p. 118.

given the beatific vision[17] and are now mediators for us who pray to them.[18] The angels that fell were created good by God and then became evil through their own fault.[19]

II. Angelic Nature and Demonic Influence

Demonic influence can be considered from two points of view, the first is concretely how they act upon man and the second is why they have dominion over man and how they gain it. As to the first, all of the spiritual writers tend to hold that the good and bad angels (demons) can act upon the body,[20] but the demons cannot act directly upon the soul or upon the higher faculties of the soul, i.e. the possible intellect and will. The good angels are said to be able to act upon the higher faculties of the soul insofar as an angel can strengthen the possible intellect[21] in order to move the possible intellect to a more perfect insight into the thing understood.[22] This enables the person being illuminated or strengthened in the intellect to see in the imagination what the image signifies[23] and therefore the angels can aid in our understanding of things. While they can strengthen the intellect, this is by acting upon it, not by the infusion of intellectual light, i.e. they cannot directly infuse the light of reason which is natural to us.[24] Morever, they cannot move us to draw conclusions, i.e. they cannot move the possible intellect to a specific conclusion,[25] even though they can aid the drawing of a conclusion by affecting the image in the imagination.[26] Angels cannot move man by infusing concepts directly in the possible intellect because it is contrary to our mode of knowing.[27] Therefore, they can only act upon the possible intellect by strengthening it which gives the possible intellect a greater capacity to understand, but that is the extent

---

[17]Matthew 18:10. See also ST I, q. 62, aa. 4-9.

[18]See prior chapter.

[19]Fourth Lateran Council, *De fide catholica* (Denz. 800/428). See also ST I, qq. 63f.

[20]Tanquerey, *The Spiritual Life,* n. 221.

[21]ST I, q. 111, a. 1; ibid., q. 111, a. 4 ad 4; Quod., IX, q. 4, a. 5 and De Ver., q. 11, a. 3.

[22]De Ver., q. 11, a. 3: "ad perfectius inspiciendum."

[23]ST I, q. 111, a. 3, ad 4.

[24]De Ver., q. 11, a. 3. Only God can infuse intellectual light; see ibid.

[25]Ibid.

[26]See below.

[27]De Malo, q. 16, a. 11. In other words, angels can mutually move each other to considering concepts because their mode of knowing does not depend on the phantasm in the imagination which is abstracted to give the concept. Man, on the other hand, must abstract and so angels act upon man in a manner in congruity with his mode of knowing, i.e. we gain concepts by abstraction.

to which they can act upon the possible intellect.

The angels cannot move or coerce the will of man directly,[28] but must move the will of man indirectly by affecting what occurs in the imagination.[29] Therefore, the demons are not the cause of sin,[30] except indirectly. The fact that the possible intellect and will cannot be acted upon directly by the demons is an indication that even if they tempt us, our fall into sin is our own fault. Directees, even if they are influenced by the demonic, should be counseled not to exculpate themselves because of the demonic influence, unless it is an extraordinary form of demonic influence in which they have no causal role. Moreover, they should not seek to claim demonic influence in order to exculpate themselves, which will be a strong temptation in order to avoid being responsible for their mental illness, be it caused by sin or voluntary action. They must realize that their state is ultimately their responsibility, unless it is due to chemical indisposition over which no medical treatment can be had or in the case of possession or things of this sort. Even if they did not cause it, they have the responsibility of cleaning it up, so to speak, if they find themselves in that state.

Since the demons can act upon the body, they can therefore affect those faculties which act through a bodily organ by affecting the bodily organ, viz. the cogitative power, the imagination, the memory, the common sense power, the senses and the appetites. To grasp clearly the psychological influence of the demonic, each one of these faculties must be treated in detail in order to understand how the demonic can affect the particular faculty. However, the mode of causation that the angels and demons use must first be addressed, since it determines which conclusions can be drawn in the area of psychology.

First, angels act upon the body by causing locomotion,[31] i.e. since the body is made up of parts (chemicals), they can affect the chemical arrangement within the body.[32] Yet, the movement of locomotion would also imply, within the brain, that they are able to cause certain electrical synaptic operations by moving the chemicals which make them possible and which cause the electrical occurrences.[33] This ability causes locomotion and, therefore, would make it possible for the angels to cause apparitional

---

[28]II Sent., D. 8, q. 5; ST I, q. 111, a. 2; ibid., q. 106, a. 2; ST I-II, q. 9, a. 6; ibid., q. 80, a. 1; SCG III, cc. 88 and 92; De Ver., q. 11, a. 3, ad 2 and ibid., 22, a. 9 and De Malo, q. 3, aa. 3 and 4.

[29]That is they move the passions which affect the image in the imagination, thereby affecting the judgment of the possible intellect which proposes to the will its object, see ST I, q. 111, a. 2, ad 3.

[30]De Malo q, 3, a. 3 and ST I-II, q. 80.

[31]ST I, q. 111, a. 3 and De Malo, q. 16, a. 11.

[32]St. Thomas often refers to this as a transmutation of the animal spirits and humors, which is another way of saying that the angels moves the various organs in the body by locomotion within the organs.

[33]This would also seem to be the mechanism behind why they can cause us to sense something, which is not truly present in the exterior senses. See below.

imaginings,[34] i.e. they can cause images in our imaginations and this is also why they are said to cause dreaming.[35] It should be remembered that this motion is not just in the interior senses (brain) but also in the passions and so they can cause a certain motion of the passions.[36] They can cause physical illness since they can move the matter within the body which would cause indispositions making one either susceptible to a certain illness (e.g. disposing the esophagus so that one has acid reflux) or in other organs by affecting the genes or other mechanisms responsible for cancer. We can suffer from many different kinds of ailments due to their influence.

In the psychological realm, the primary way the angels and demons affect man is by moving his imagination.[37] They do so by causing a motion in the imagination which begets a phantasm in the imagination.[38] St. Thomas observes that this occurs by the angels and demons forming an image in the imagination by moving the bodily organ.[39] Yet, they can only cause a phantasm which has something prior in memory, i.e. they must use prior sense data.[40] While they can form phantasms which we may have never seen before, nevertheless, they must use the data stored in memory to create a new image, somewhat in the same fashion as man who forms a new image by moving the various interior senses, e.g. when he has never seen a gold mountain but from the color of gold and the mountain which he has in memory, he is able to merge them together to form the image of a gold mountain.

The fact that the image data that they use is stored in memory is an extrapolation from the texts of St. Thomas. Since the data must be stored somewhere, normally this is to be understood as the data stored in memory since it is the only faculty that can store sense data.[41] This means that the angels and demons can use our past

---

[34]ST I, q. 111, a. 3.

[35]See below.

[36]See below.

[37]ST I, q. 111, a. 3.

[38]Ibid. and De Malo, q. 3, a. 4.

[39]De Ver., q. 11, a. 3 and De Malo, q. 16, a. 11.

[40]ST I, q. 111, a. 3 ad 2 and De Malo, q. 16, 11.

[41]This is derived from the phrase of St. Thomas in De Malo, q. 3, a. 4: "species interius conservatas quasi de quibusdam thesauris educunt ad principium sensitivum, ut res aliquas imaginentur." The term *conservatas* considered in relation to the fact that, in this same question in the De Malo, St. Thomas treats how the demons are able to persuade "solum per impressionem quamdam in vires sensitivas interiores aut exteriores" (only by a certain impression in the interior or exterior sensitive powers). Since reference is made to the interior sensitive powers and not just in the singular to refer to the imagination and since the term *conservatas* would appear to refer only to that power that has the capacity to conserve sensible species, viz. the memory, then it would appear that St. Thomas is saying the demons have the capacity to educe from the memory prior stored sensible species. St. Thomas refers to the memory as a treasury, see volume I, chap. 3 (B1). Cf. ST I, q. 111, a.

sense experience. As for the angels, it is a way to incite us to do the right thing by moving our memory to place something in the imagination which corresponds to joy or something of this sort when we experienced doing the right thing. Moreover, they can help us to remember what we have been taught so that we will be moved to do the right thing. This is why devotion to the guardian angels and to angels in general must be fostered by directees as well as psychologists. Since the psychologists are often unable to remember or associate the right things, the angels can move the memory of the psychologist to remember things which the directee has recalled or things which the psychologists know will aid the directee. As for the directee, the angels can assist in calling to mind those things which will aid him in overcoming his mental illness, e.g. he can remember something the psychologist has told him or some past experience which led to or helped get him out of his mental illness.

With respect to the demonic, our memory is a mine field,[42] so to speak. The demons can use our past experiences against us by moving the memory (i.e. by moving the bodily organ) to recall past sins so that they can be a form of temptation for us. This is why experienced spiritual writers often warned against sin because the remembrance of the sin can be used against us. For this reason, it was often said that it is easier for a man who has never had any sexual experience to maintain a celibate life than for the man who has had sexual experience. Two things must be done to block the demonic in this respect: (1) avoid sin as much as possible so that they do not have the sense data to use against the directee (or psychologist for that matter) and (2) do those things which will merit the grace of forgetfulness. St. Thomas is clear that the angels and demons cannot create sense data in our minds that is not there.[43]

While this is true with respect to sin and since sin can cause mental illness, the directees must be sure to avoid not only sinning themselves but viewing sins of others. By viewing the sins of others, e.g. watching someone commit fornication on TV or killing someone in a graphic fashion on TV, they provide the sense data for the demons to make suggestions to them by forming images in their imagination. In fact, the more programs one watches on TV, the more the demons can influence a person's actions since they have more data to use. Also, the more we see a thing, the more it becomes

---

3 ad 2 and De Malo, q. 16, 11.

[42]In De Malo, q. 3, a. 4, St. Thomas refers to the interior conserved species as a "treasury" (thesauris).

[43]The term used is *de nuda*. To understand this term one must understand between what is called a *tabula rasa* and *tabula nuda*. *Tabula rasa* is the term used by St. Thomas to refer to the fact that our intellect, while having a given structure and connatural knowledge as discussed in the prior volume, does not have any innate concepts, i.e. no conceptual knowledge is there. However, later philosophers describe Duns Scotus' position as the intellect not only has no concepts but not even connatural knowledge or a structure and therefore call it a *tabula nuda*. When the term *nuda* is applied to the demonic, it indicates that they cannot create sense data that was not there. St. Thomas gives the example that demons or angels cannot cause a blind man to imagine colors. See ST I, q. 111, a. 3; De Malo q. 3, a. 4 and ibid., q. 16, a. 11.

familiar and there is a natural mechanism in man by which he becomes comfortable with what is familiar.[44] The more we become familiar with the imagery of sin, the easier it is for the demons to coax us into sinning because we have lost our inhibitions with respect to the sin because we are comfortable with it.

Psychologically, we see this mechanism in women, who, when seeing something horrific, happen to have a natural inclination to cover the eyes or ears of their children so that they do not have to suffer the imagery that is there. But the mechanism's finality is beyond the desire to keep them from suffering emotionally; parents do not want their children to be "scarred," i.e. to have in their memory those things which can affect their psychological well-being by being remembered.

More conclusions can be drawn from this. For instance, the more violent the society becomes, the more the sense data will affect the mental stability of its members and the more they are able to be preyed upon by the demonic. Forms of media and entertainment must remain properly ordered so that people do not end up with imagery that can affect their passions (since the imagery in the imagination will disturb or excite the passions). Parents, for example, must be sure to keep their children from viewing shows which glorify sinful actions. Directees who have suffered something traumatic will be easier for the demonic to affect since the sense data of the trauma is available. For this reason, directees must consign the care of the body daily and devoutly to the care of their guardian angel so that the angel is given more dominion over the body and therefore is more capable of protecting it from demonic influence.

The data that is used from memory is moved into the imagination by the angel or demon to form sensible similitudes[45] to the thing that they wish us to understand. Because sensitive apprehension is designed to be moved,[46] demons are able to move it.[47] Since the angels and demons can act upon the imagination, several additional conclusions can be drawn from this. First, both good and bad angels are able to change the sensible species (i.e. the phantasm) in the imagination in order for us to understand what they want us to conceive in the possible intellect.[48] Moreover, they can cause dreams[49] and it is for this reason that the Church has always cautioned people about interpreting dreams. The modern psychological praxis of interpreting dreams may not reveal anything about the directee and a whole lot about demons and, for that reason as

---

[44]This is common human experience, both positively and negatively, i.e. we are comfortable around familiar surroundings and can become nervous, i.e. fearful or sorrowful around unfamiliar surroundings.

[45]ST I, q. 111, a. 1; ibid., q. 111, a. 3, ad 4 and Quod., IX, q. 4, a. 5.

[46]De Malo q. 16, a. 11, ad 3. This is also clear from the will moving the interior senses as can be seen in the prior volume.

[47]Ibid.

[48]De Malo, q. 16, a. 12.

[49]De Ver., q. 11, a. 3; De Malo, q. 3, a. 3, ad 9; ibid., q, 3, a. 4 and ibid., De Malo, q. 16, a. 11.

well as others, clear principles must be used when considering dreams,[50] so that one does not confuse what the source of the dream is.

Demons can also cause *per accidens* mental illness.[51] This stands to reason since they are able move the interior senses, they are able to cause them to dysfunction. Yet, they can only cause *per accidens* mental illness directly since they cannot operate on the higher faculties of the soul of the possible intellect and will. Yet, they can cause mental illness *per se* indirectly, by affecting the lower faculties and by the directee volitionally giving into what is proposed. Since they can affect the interior senses, they can also bind the use of reason,[52] since the possible intellect must convert back to the phantasm of which the demons have laid hold. Because they can move the imagination, they can also cause interior apparitions, i.e. they can make someone hallucinate.[53]

Angels can aid us in the opposite fashion by moving the imagination in a way that is conducive to the use of reason. While angels cannot move us to draw conclusions in the possible intellect, they can propose principles under sensible signs[54] in the imagination by which we judge and reason and thereby they can help us to learn, avoid sin and reason well. This means that angels can aid judgment. Conversely, demons are able to deceive us, not by moving the act of judgment, but by affecting the object of judgment in the imagination. They are able to present the image in such a way that one is likely to judge it falsely. In the prior volume, it was observed that truth is a mean between excess and defect and when the image in the imagination is affected by passion, it draws judgment to excess or defect by making it appear better than it is or worse than it is. In the same fashion, the demons are able to affect the image so that our judgment will be drawn to excess or defect.

The demons can also affect the common sense power since they can act upon the body and the common sense power acts through a bodily organ. Since time sequencing of the data entering the imagination is one of the functions of the common sense power, demons are able to cause the time sequencing to fail. They can also affect the function of distinguishing between sensible data within the five senses, i.e. they can affect how the common sense power, for example, is able to distinguish between white and hard. All of this indicates that the demons can cause confusion, not only through the common sense power but primarily by means of the imagination. On the other hand, God permitting, an angel can move the faculties which may be ill-disposed to a better disposition by moving the matter to a better arrangement and, as a result, cause clarity

---

[50]There will be a further discussion in the subsequent volume on the nature of dreaming.

[51]De Malo, q. 16, a. 11 and ST I, q. 111, a. 3 coupled with ibid., ad 2.

[52]De Malo, q. 3, a. 3 ad 9 and De Malo, q. 3, a. 4.

[53]An interior apparition is one occurring in the imagination. This occurrence does not happen without the permission of God.

[54]De Ver., q. 11, a. 3.

of mind.[55]

St. Thomas and the other writers do not seem to be clear about whether angels or demons can move the cogitative power. Yet, it would seem that they can.[56] Since they can act upon the body and since the cogitative power acts through a bodily organ, they should be able to affect it. If this is the case, the angels and demons can dispose the material component in the faculty of the cogitative power to perform the actions which it is normally capable of doing, i.e. association, assessment of good or harm and indifferent associations.

On the side of the demonic, they are capable of moving the cogitative power to going into memory and bringing out into the imagination an image corresponding to what they wish the person to do or think. They can, within that mechanism itself, pull out of memory the *ratio*s or perspectives upon sense data which is stored in memory which the cogitative power has done in the past. However, they can also move the cogitative power to associate what they want with the image. They can move the cogitative power to make assessments of good or harm and so they can affect our judgment about it, causing us, again, to think it is better or worse than it is. It would also mean that they can drag us through a series of particular reasonings in which they may start out with something harmless and then move slowly but surely to something harmful, by moving the cogitative power to make the series of particular reasonings. Those who practice vigilance and custody of the mind are aware that sometimes they will start out thinking something harmless and then suddenly there is a different perspective put on it. Sometimes people will let loose of their imagination due to fatigue or other factors and day dream, in which the imagination is left to itself. The demons can seize upon that opportunity to move the cogitative power and imagination to go through a series of logically connected images. The person may realize that what they were thinking was immoral or psychologically bad even though it was involuntary. Directees will often become confused because there is a series of images and so they think they had something to do with it. They mistakenly assume that demons only introduce a single image rather than being able to move one through images logically by using the natural structure of the cogitative power to perform particular reasonings. Conversely, the good angels can do the opposite. They can move the cogitative power to make the right associations so that we make the right judgments.

If the angels and demons can move the cogitative power to place a certain *ratio* in the image, they can indirectly move the appetites and cause passions. Yet, the appetites themselves operate through a bodily organ and as a result the demons and angels can move the passions.[57] In a complex fashion, they are able to draw out of memory into the imagination that which moves the passion. They then move the

---

[55]One begins to see that the spiritual warfare is clearly something carried out in the flesh of man.

[56]This assertion and the conclusions pertaining to the cogitative power must be understood as the opinion of the author.

[57]ST I, q. 111, a. 2

cogitative power or simply take out of memory the *ratio* pertaining to the specific passions. St. Thomas then observes that demons[58] cause a subtraction or apposition to the sensitive appetite to desiring or fleeing something by causing a bodily change. What this essentially means is that they can cause the sensitive appetite to intend or incline toward or away from something.[59] In effect, the demons can instigate antecedent passions, aid a passion by making it stronger or stifle a passion by subtracting or pulling on the bodily disposition which corresponds to the passion. This is why people who are obsessed will often have unnaturally strong passions. Conversely, the angels can also do the same but it would seem with some qualification.[60] It would seem that angels would normally not instigate antecedent passions but rather provide the imagination with the right image so that the consequent passions would be rightly ordered. Moreover, it is possible for an angel to weaken the passion by moving the material disposition of the body. If this is the case, a strong devotion to one's guardian angel should aid in the process of overcoming antecedent passion.

St. Thomas also says that demons know through experience[61] which passions a person is inclined towards and so they present in the imagination that which corresponds to the passions.[62] In the prior volume, the fact that the passions can bind judgment by the sense of the passion being merged with the image in the imagination was mentioned. Since the mechanism holds true, the demons are able to affect judgment by moving the passions.[63] This would also mean that they can affect reasoning as well and so when the demonic is involved, it is very easy to fall into error. This applies where the mode of influence either involves the passions or does not; if they affect the image in any way, they are able to affect the reasoning process.[64]

Angels, both good and bad, can also act upon the senses themselves,[65] since they operate through a bodily organ. For this reason St. Thomas observes that they can change the bodily organ and therefore change the perception of the sense.[66] In effect, they can change what we sense and so for angels, they can cause an apparition in the exterior senses (as well as interior). An important conclusion from this is that if someone reports seeing things, it should not automatically be assumed that the person is mentally ill. While they may be mentally ill or if they suffer from some material

---

[58]This would also seem to apply to the good angels in a positive sense.

[59]De Malo, q. 16, a. 11, ad 3.

[60]These qualifications are the opinion of the author.

[61]It is also probably the case since they know the particular disposition of the individual and so they will know to which passions he is disposed.

[62]De Malo, q. 3, a. 4.

[63]ST I, q. 111, a. 2, ad 3.

[64]Perhaps this is one of the reasons why man has a natural inclination not to listen to the arguments or "reasonings" of those dominated by their passions.

[65]ST, q. 111, a. 4.

[66]De Malo q, 16, a. 12, ad 2.

indisposition which causes hallucinations, nevertheless, since these occurrences can have several causes, one cause should not automatically be presumed in all cases. Such an approach would be inherently unscientific, since it would not strive to know all of the causes of a thing.

The angels, both good and bad, God permitting, can also offer the senses a sensible object formed from without, which occurs either by nature or by the action of the angel himself.[67] These exterior occurrences by angels are meant to direct the person in relation to their supernatural end, viz. God. But, on the side of the demons, it may be meant to have one or more effects, e.g. distracting one from his obligations or duties, causing despair in the person who will think that God is not protecting him, causing him to sin or things of this sort. It is possible that the demons do it for the purpose of causing mental illness in the person. These exterior occurrences are not necessarily something formed by the angel, as just mentioned; sometimes he can use exterior natural things to distract us, e.g. moving someone's imagination to telephone someone whom the demon wants to distract, moving someone to be irritated with another who has not done anything wrong, and other things of this kind. The fact that Satan can move others interiorly indicates that he can do so in order to distract not necessarily the person he is acting on but the person who is affected by the other person being acted on.

The angels and demons can also operate on non-moral faculties, such as the faculty of locomotion by which a person moves from place to place, e.g. some have experienced an angel acting upon their body in such a way as to cause them to perform specific functions in order to save their life, such as moving someone to swerve when driving his vehicle in order to avoid hitting someone. The angels and demons can also move the nutritive power,[68] e.g. by making someone feel hungry or by causing indigestion and things of this sort.

The last question to address in this section is how the demons can cause us to sin. Since the demons cannot act directly upon the will which is entirely immaterial, they can only induce us to sin by affecting the imagination and various other faculties which affect the imagination.[69] St. Thomas and the whole of Catholic tradition holds that the demons induce us to sin by a mode of persuasion.[70] This occurs by appearing sensibly,[71] e.g. the serpent in the Garden of Eden[72] or by the mode of persuasion by presenting something as good to the knowing power in man.[73] This can occur in two ways, the first is by illuminating the possible intellect. St. Thomas says that the demons

---

[67]ST I, q. 111, a. 4 and De Ver., q. 11, a. 3.

[68]ST I, q. 111, a. 4, ad 2.

[69]The section on the voluntary regarding coercion in the prior volume is helpful in understanding this section.

[70]De Malo q, 3, aa. 3 and 4.

[71]De Malo, q. 3, a. 4.

[72]Genesis 3.

[73]De Malo, q. 3, a. 4.

have the capacity to do this like the good angels, but they do not, since illumination is ordered toward knowing the truth and they want the person to be deceived.[74] Rather, they operate in the second way which is by acting upon the interior senses and passions by locomotion.[75] Therefore, the demons can be an indirect cause of sin, but only by acting exterior to us or by acting upon the interior senses and sensitive appetites in such a way as to make the sin appear good.

To further clarify what the demons can and cannot do, two long quotes from Jordan Aumann's *Spiritual Theology* are in order:

By reason of some contradiction involved or because they surpass the power of an angelic being, the devils *cannot* do the following:

1. Produce any kind of truly supernatural phenomenon because the supernatural by definition exceeds all natural created powers.

2. Create a substance because creation requires an infinite power, and no creature of any kind can be used even as an instrument of creation.

3. Raise a dead person to life, although they could produce the illusion of doing so.

4. Instantaneously cure wounds, fractures, lesions, etc., because this is something only the Creator can do.

5. Make truly prophetic predictions, since the devil does not by his own powers of intelligence know future contingencies, although he knows so many things in their causes that it may appear to human beings that what was predicted was a true prophecy.

6. Know the secrets of a person's mind and heart, since the devil does not by his own power have access to the human intellect and will. Because of his superior intelligence, however, he can conjecture much more easily and can know the temperament and character of individuals as well as the numerous circumstances of their life.

7. Produce in human beings extraordinary phenomena of the purely intellectual or volitional type because he does not have free access to the human intellect and will.[76]

---

[74]Ibid.

[75]Ibid.

[76]Aumann, *Spiritual Theology*, p. 420.

The second quote is the following:

> With God's permission the devil can do any of the following:
>
> 1. Produce corporeal or imaginative visions (but not intellectual visions).
>
> 2. Falsify ecstasy.
>
> 3. Produce rays of light in the body and sensible heat. (There have been examples of "diabolical incandescence.")
>
> 4. Cause sensible consolations and tenderness.[77]
>
> 5. Instantaneously cure sicknesses that have been caused by diabolical influence.
>
> 6. Produce the stigmata and all other kinds of bodily extraordinary phenomena, and any phenomena dealing with physical objects, such as crowns, rings, etc.
>
> 7. Simulate miracles and the phenomena of levitation, bilocation, and compenetration of bodies.
>
> 8. Cause persons or objects to disappear from sight by placing an obstacle in the line of vision or acting directly on the sense of sight; simulate locutions by means of sound waves or immediate action on the sense of hearing; cause a person to speak in tongues.[78]
>
> 9. Produce bodily incombustibility by interposing some medium, between the fire and the body of the individual.

III. Ordinary Diabolic Activity

We come, therefore, to more formal distinctions and the delineations of the different kinds of diabolic influence. Exorcists and spiritual writers make a distinction

---

[77]This is the reason why sensible consolations cannot be the foundation of the spiritual, moral or psychological life. There is also the danger of the demons giving one consolations for doing evil. This is one of the reasons why people find doing certain evil things pleasant.

[78]This is one of the reasons why Jordan Aumann observes that one can come under the influence of the devil by seeking charismatic graces; see below.

between what is called ordinary and extraordinary diabolic activity.[79] Ordinary diabolic activity consists essentially in two forms of activity by the demonic, viz. temptations and snares. Above we saw that the demons can use other people by moving or suggesting to them some course of action and for this reason Fr. Delaporte observes:

> External objects, and, above all, persons under his influence, the Devil makes use of as instruments to bring together a concurrence of circumstances which suddenly seize upon the unwary Christian, and cast him into the abyss. An obstinate hunter, Satan knows how to foresee and await.[80]

Because the devil goes about seeking someone "to devour,"[81] he knows that overcoming an adversary does not merely consist in waging war against the adversary himself but also using other people against him, even his friends and family, in order to move him to fall into sin or do something which causes others to sin. The demons understand complex causes to a much greater degree than we do and this is why we need the gifts of the Holy Spirit so that God can move us in those moments when our human reason fails. This is also why we need grace to enlighten us and strengthen our wills so that we are able to be aware of what the demons do and have the strength to fight against them.

In order to avoid snares, there are several means which the directee can employ. While Satan always desires to undermine our moral state by getting us to commit sin, he is also willing to use us unwittingly or involuntarily by getting us to commit objective sin in order to offend God.[82] For this reason, the directee must realize that the demons are willing to get the person to do things or place himself in circumstances which will aggravate his mental illness because Satan also likes natural disorders (i.e. in this case, mental illness). Therefore, what applies to avoiding snares in order to avoid sin or being victimized by demons for those trying to do good, also applies to those trying to overcome their mental illnesses.

Therefore, in order to avoid snares, the general means of avoiding the near occasion of sin must be observed, i.e. avoiding the persons, places and things which can cause one to sin or cause one to do something or affect one psychologically. Therefore, the directee must be willing to change his company and to disassociate with friends, perhaps temporarily if not permanently, if that is necessary to overcome his mental

---

[79]Amorth, *An Exorcist Tells His Story*, p. 32 and Aumann, *Spiritual Theology*, p. 404.

[80]Delaporte, *The Devil*, p. 126.

[81]I Peter 5:8f.

[82]Subjective sin is that which is done voluntarily, i.e. with sufficient reflection and knowledge and full consent of the will, whereas objective sin is a consideration of the action in itself, whether it is voluntary or not. While the demons prefer that we commit sin and offend God not only objectively but subjectively, they are willing to settle for us offending God even though we may not know or be able to do anything about it.

illness and not give the demonic an occasion for his fall. Places and things must also be avoided and sometimes this comes at a great price, e.g. if a person has a fixation rooted in lust, he may be required to sell his computer or cease surfing the internet if they occasion a fall for him. After he has overcome his mental illness, if he has attained sufficient virtue, then he can return to the use of these things while avoiding websites which led to his fall.

We can also pray and do penances and good works in order to merit the grace from God to be protected from the demons, for even Christ himself exhorted us to pray to God the Father so that we may be delivered from evil. Fostering a devotion to one's guardian angel so that he may guide the directee more efficaciously will aid in avoiding snares. We can also foster a devotion to our Lady and to St. Michael who have the capacity to subdue the demons and keep them at bay.

The other form of ordinary demonic activity is temptation. It must first be observed that no temptation or any ordinary or extraordinary diabolic activity can occur without the permission of God.[83] Since God knows our limitations and wishes what is best for us, He will never tempt us beyond our capacities since it would be to our ruin. Therefore, the directee should know that God will never tempt him beyond what he is capable to withstand and so even when temptations seem strong, he should not despair or give up. If his source of temptation is from the demonic, he should know that since they must have God's permission, the demons' power over men is not unlimited.[84]

Not every temptation is from the demonic, but some are from ourselves and from the world.[85] The directee should bear this in mind for two reasons. The first is that sometimes directees will use the demonic as an excuse for their falls. The second is that the reality of the situation indicates that not all temptations have their source in the demonic. However, the directee can always use the means to reject the demonic even if the temptations are not from the demonic. The demons are very intelligent and can move us in such a fashion that it only appears that the temptation is coming from the

---

[83]See Delaporte, *The Devil*, p. 127 and Szymanski, *A Notebook on the Devil and Exorcism*, p. 15.

[84]Szymanski, *A Notebook on the Devil and Exorcism*, p. 15. This can also be inferred from the fact that the angelic will is a stronger power than our will and if God allowed unrestricted warfare against man, man would be in a hopeless situation since the demonic will would always predominate since it is stronger. Moreover, its degree and how the temptation occurs must also be controlled by God since, again, He would not allow us to be tempted beyond our capacities.

[85]Aumann, *Spiritual Theology*, p. 157 and Delaporte, *The Devil*, p. 125. The Fathers of the Church and the spiritual tradition of the Church always referred to the sources of temptation as the world, the flesh and the devil. The flesh or concupiscence, as it is sometimes called, essentially consists in our attachments and habits as well as the mechanism of demonic movement of the body as described above.

flesh and so we are never certain if it is from them or not.[86] However, the means can be used in the event that it is from the demonic, so that if it is from the demonic, it will have its proper effect.

We saw above that the demons can use the cogitative power, the imagination, the memory, and our passions and so when we are tempted, they are able to use one, some or all of these in order to suggest to us some course of action which is sinful or, in the case of the directee, either sinful and/or harmful to his mental health. It should not be assumed that all movements of the demonic are directed to sin, i.e. that they act upon the faculties in order to get us to sin. At times, the demons merely suggest something to our imagination or make use of faculties so that we will err in judgment, which will have ramifications on others which in turn draws them into sin.

For instance, if a head of a corporation is affected by the demonic in his perception of the circumstances within his company, he may enact policies or do things which he thinks are prudent, but which are, in fact, harmful even though he cannot fully see the possible effects from his actions. In this sense, it is clear that the demonic can affect prudence since prudence requires the application of general principles in the concrete which requires the possible intellect to convert back to the phantasm to judge the particulars. Psychologists must be particularly aware of this. They themselves must take the means to ensure that the demonic influences them as little as possible, because their judgment about the prudential application of the general principles in the lives of directees can be directly affected. This is why virtue and particularly humility are necessary for the psychologist.[87]

In relation to temptations four areas will suffice to give an explication, viz. (1) the stages of temptations, (2) avoiding and remedies for temptations, (3) resisting temptations, and (4) why God allows temptations. As to the first, Tanquerey lists three stages of temptation:[88]

> According to the traditional doctrine, as expounded by St. Augustine there are three different phases in temptation: suggestion, pleasure and consent. a) Suggestion consists in the proposal of some evil. Our imagination or our mind represent to us in a more or less vivid manner the attraction of the forbidden fruit; at times this

---

[86]St. Thomas observes in ST I, q. 111, a. 1, ad 3 that not everyone that is illuminated by an angel knows it. While this applies to illumination, the same can be said of demonic influence. Since the demons can use our bodily dispositions towards specific vices, unless there is some indication, we are not certain that the movement is not merely the product of our dispositions rather than the demonic.

[87]Humility and the moral virtues will cause a dispositional change in the bodily organ, thereby making it more difficult for the demons to function. Moreover, prudence causes changes in memory, the functions of the cogitative power and imagination which also work against the demonic. See volume III on prudence.

[88]Tanquerey, *The Spiritual Life*, n. 906.

representation is most alluring, holds its ground tenaciously and becomes a sort of obsession. No matter how dangerous such a suggestion may be, it does not constitute a sin, provided that we have not provoked it ourselves, and do not consent to it. There is sin only when the will yields consent.

This stage of temptation consists in what was discussed prior, viz. that the demons move the faculties in such a way as to suggest something. Tanquerey continues:

> b) Pleasure follows the suggestion. Instinctively our lower tendencies are drawn towards the suggested evil and a certain pleasure is experienced. "Many a time happens," says St. Francis de Sales that the "inferior part of the soul takes pleasure in the temptation, without there having been consent, nay against the soul's superior part. This is the warfare which the Apostle St. Paul describes when he says his flesh wars against his spirit." This pleasure does not, as long as the will refuses to consent to it, constitute a sin; yet it is a danger, since the will finds itself thus solicited to yield consent.

Accompanying the suggestion can be pleasure in the sensitive appetites but this does not constitute consent and often directees will confuse the pleasure taken in the sensitive appetites with consent of the intellective appetite (the will). Moreover, since the demons can move the cogitative power which can perform a series of particular reasonings which modify the image through the process of reasoning, people will confuse "entertaining" the thought with this series of images. Like daydreaming in which the cogitative power goes off on its own, the demons can manipulate the cogitative power to cause this series of images. Some can confuse this as consent, which it is not. Lastly,

> c) If the will withholds acquiescence, combats the temptation, and repels it, it has scored a success and performed a highly meritorious act. If, on the contrary, the will delights in the pleasure, *willingly* enjoys it and consents to it, the sin is committed.

Since habits are voluntary, these temptations can only affect one's mental health if consent is given to them. The victory of overcoming the temptation can give hope to the directee. Therefore the directee should not view temptation as merely an affliction but a means to overcoming his difficulty.[89]

The second area regarding temptations that has an importance for psychology is the avoiding of the temptations. We must first avoid the persons, places and things which can cause us moral or psychological harm, as mentioned above.[90] This effectively

---

[89]More of this will be seen below.

[90]See also Tanquerey, *The Spiritual Life*, n. 912.

removes the "external matter," so to speak, which the demons can use to tempt us. The next is to be watchful[91] since it is easy to fall in an unguarded moment. While we should not be overly paranoid or fearful of possible temptations, nevertheless a calm and realistic vigilance will aid greatly. Just as soldiers must stand guard to keep their fellow soldiers who sleep from being overcome by the enemy, so the possible intellect and will must keep watch over the faculties by always remaining circumspect and ready to do battle. We must be vigilant because the devil never completely gives up on us[92] in the spiritual war except after death. As Aumann observes: "Sometimes the temptation does not immediately disappear, and the devil may attack again with great tenacity. One should not become discouraged at this. The insistence of the devil is one of the best proofs that the soul has not succumbed to the temptation."[93]

Yet vigilance is not enough; to vigilance must be added prayer,[94] by which God is placed on our side. Through prayer we can gain the grace of being protected from the devil and if God so chooses to allow us to be tempted, the grace will strengthen our will to remain steadfast. It is for this reason that Aumann notes that we need grace from God.[95] We must also "avoid that proud *presumption* that thrusts us into *the midst of dangers*, under the pretense that we are possessed of sufficient strength to triumph over them."[96] Without God, we cannot overcome the demons and so the directee must always foster a humility about his weakness in the areas of temptation, i.e. in the areas pertaining to mental illness. This humility will foster a filial dependence upon God Who is a greater source of strength than ourselves. It is also wise insofar as it keeps one rooted in reality about his own defect. Even after overcoming his mental illness, the directee must do everything he can to ensure that he does not fall into mental illness again, since he will always have the possibility to do so, if left to himself without God.

On the other hand, he must not fall prey to excessive fear about his propensity to fall.[97] If a directee is doing everything on his part and places himself at the mercy and power of God, he will not be tempted beyond his ability and God will provide for him. Entertaining these vain fears can actually perpetuate and aggravate the mental illness, since the object of fear, i.e. the object of mental illness, is before his mind continuing to habituate the mind. Therefore, vain fears must be avoided and ignored.

The directee should also be counseled to frequent the sacraments, particularly Confession and Holy Communion as well as employ the various sacramentals of the Church which aid in subverting the wiles of the demons.[98] Confession provides humility

---

[91]Ibid.

[92]Aumann, *Spiritual Theology*, p. 160.

[93]Ibid.

[94]Tanquerey, *The Spiritual Life*, n. 912.

[95]Aumann, *Spiritual Theology*, p. 160.

[96]Tanquerey, *The Spiritual Life*, n. 912.

[97]See ibid.

[98]Ibid., n. 224.

and sacramental graces. If the devil is tempting the directee in some area pertaining to his mental illness and if the directee is committing some sin which is the source of the mental illness, by receiving the sacramental graces of Confession, he will be strengthened in the area of sin and thereby it will have an indirect effect on the mental illness. Various sacramentals such as the scapular and St. Benedict medal can aid greatly in warding off the demonic. Use of holy water[99] and holy oils[100] can often help to keep the demons at bay and may also be used during temptations to bring them to an end.

The directee must also foster an utter contempt for the demonic. While the demons use those things which appear good to us in some way, we must always remember that they seek not just our moral ruin but our natural ruin, part of which is our mental health. The demons can deceive us by using the cogitative power to associate themselves with good things and so we must be very careful always to reformulate the image we have of them to one of vileness, evil and harm. In this way, the cogitative power will continue to work against them.

The next area of temptation which is important for psychology is resisting the temptations once they come. Some of the aforementioned remedies can also be used during temptations but there are other means which are important. Once temptations begin, the directee must be prompt in dealing with them; he must never let them linger. If he lets them linger, the demonic gain a greater foothold and it becomes more difficult to rout them out.[101] This also applies to those temptations which are not from the demonic, i.e. they must be dealt with swiftly. Since the lower faculties await the judgment of reason and the motion of the will, even though they may have initial motion from the presence of the object in the imagination, nevertheless, they refrain somewhat[102] until the will consents. If the will hesitates, the lower faculties perceive that it is permissible to continue in the object. From this can arise a stronger binding of reason since the faculties will incline more. Moreover, he must never give consent, because even if later he decides to overthrow the temptation, it will be harder since his reason and will will be bound by virtue of lower faculties holding the soul captive.

---

[99]The blessing of the holy water in the former *Rituale Romanum* is more commendable to those suffering from demonic temptations than that which is in the new *Book of Blessings,* since the old rite contains an exorcism of the salt and water which is more efficacious at warding off the demonic. Priests who are aiding psychologists should use this ritual, if possible, when supplying sacramentals and holy water, since more exorcisms are contained in the blessings.

[100]Here we have in mind specifically the blessing of holy oil, not that which is used in the administration of the sacraments, but that which is specifically ordered toward warding off temptations. This blessing appears in the *Rituale Romanum* under the title of *Benedictio Olei* (Titulus VIII, capita 19).

[101]Tanquerey, *The Spiritual Life*, n. 914.

[102]Unless they have been habituated always to give themselves fully to the object in question.

Next, he must act energetically[103] by not allowing regret or attachment to the object come in the way of his getting out from underneath the temptation. He must do so perseveringly, being willing to overthrow the temptation each and every time it comes into his mind.[104] He must make resolutions of will often so that each time a temptation comes into his imagination, he will reject it and if he makes these resolutions repeatedly, he will have a habituation in his will which will strengthen it so that when the time comes, it will be easier for him to reject the temptation. In psychology, this is of key importance. The directee must make resolutions of the will repeatedly, intending not to allow that which is causing his mental illness into his imagination. He must also fight humbly,[105] recognizing that he cannot do this alone and if he overcomes it, he must be careful to attribute it to God, our Lady, St. Michael or some particular saint he implores in the moment to aid him.

There are two other means of dealing with temptation which describe in an adverbial manner how one must do it: directly and indirectly.

> During temptation the conduct of the soul can be summarized in one important word: resist. It does not suffice merely to remain passive in the face of temptation; positive resistance is necessary. This resistance can be either direct or indirect. Direct resistance is that which faces up to the temptation itself and conquers it by doing the precise opposite from that which is suggested. For example, to begin to speak well of a person when we are tempted to criticize him, to give a generous alms when our selfishness would prompt us to refuse, to prolong our prayer when the devil suggests that we shorten it or abandon it altogether. Direct resistance can be used against any kind of temptation, except those against faith or purity, as we shall see now.
>
> Indirect resistance does not attack the temptation but withdraws from it by distracting the mind to some other object that is completely distinct. This is the type of resistance to be used in temptations against the faith or against purity, because in these cases a direct attack would very likely increase the intensity of the temptation itself. The best practice in these cases is a rapid but calm practice of a mental exercise that will absorb our internal faculties, especially the memory and imagination, and withdraw them from the object of the temptation. It is also helpful to have some hobby or pastime or activity that is interesting enough to absorb one's attention for the moment.[106]

---

[103]Tanquerey, *The Spiritual Life*, n. 915.

[104]Ibid., n. 916.

[105]Ibid., n. 917.

[106]Aumann, *Spiritual Theology*, p. 160f.

Indirect attacks are very useful for those matters pertaining to mental illness. If the directee can switch his thoughts, even for a short time, to something he enjoys to do which is morally licit and not connected to his mental illness or switch to praying, he will, over the course of time, find the temptations and passions associated with the temptations begin to wane. Once the object in the imagination is changed, any passions associated with the object will likewise change or dissipate. Moreover, the lower faculties learn that they are not to think about or become fixed on those objects. As time goes on, the directee will notice that when the object comes into the imagination, the passions and other faculties wait until the will gives consent because they will be habituated not to move right away. This is one of the first steps in the process of building virtue in relation to the mental illness.

Two more observations are in order. First, in the beginning, the appetite seeks or flees some object. As a result, it is normally easier to switch to something which appeases the appetite, i.e. something the appetites like. This teaches the appetites not to move as was mentioned, but it also teaches them that their objects of passion should be those proposed to them by reason and will. Appetites are willing to seek another object that fits the species of passion, e.g. if one is suffering from the desire of lust, he can switch it to desiring or engaging in the object of a hobby he enjoys, such as fishing, mechanical work or something of this kind. Later in his striving for virtue, it will become easier to switch the thoughts to something other than that which appeases the appetites because of the virtue slowly built up in the various faculties. This is why some directees find it easier to think about fishing than to pray. Even though prayer on a supernatural level is clearly more efficacious, nevertheless, grace builds on nature and so sometimes the natural means are easier, at least initially.

The next observation has to do with performing what is called a self exorcism. Christ showed us by His example when He said: "Get behind me, Satan."[107] When the directee experiences some temptation, whether it is from the devil or not, he can turn on the devil and say Christ's words or some similar words. Since we have a limited dominion over our bodies, we can exercise our rights to take control of them and kick the demonic out. Sometimes, if God permits, the directee will not be able to do this on his own, e.g. in cases of extraordinary diabolic activity. But in ordinary activity, this mechanism serves four functions.

The first is to attack the devil directly by throwing him out and taking back dominion over our faculties. The devil is a coward: if we have sanctifying grace in our souls, our attack has a supernatural efficacy, which the devil cannot resist. Second, this form of attack switches the imagination to attacking the devil which takes the image of temptation out of our minds. Third, it habituates the lower faculties to do the same. Those who employ this method will find that, over time, the lower faculties will become uncooperative with the demonic, particularly the cogitative power. If it associates the temptation with the rejection which the person does habitually, when the temptation comes and the person is not fully aware, the cogitative power will react against the

---

[107]Matthew 16:23.

temptation and, in effect, hold off and warn the person. When he comes to, so to speak, he realizes the cogitative power is resisting something and then he can affirm the association or assessment of the cogitative power by rejecting the temptation.

Finally, the last function it performs is to habituate the faculties even if Satan is not the one tempting. This will cause the demonic to stop attacking in this manner for fear of defeat. Just as one does not directly approach a dog that is viciously barking at him, so the demons will try some other approach.

We now come to the reason why God allows ordinary diabolic activity such as temptations and snares. It must be said outright that God Himself does not tempt us[108] but will allow us to be tempted for the sake of our spiritual good. God allows us to be tempted because He wants us to merit heaven.[109] We must show that we are worthy of eternal beatitude by being willing to undergo trials and show we are worthy of the reward of heaven. He also allows them for the sake of our purification.[110] When we reject a temptation, we become detached from the object of weakness that is being used to tempt us. In psychology, the self-denial through the temptation must be seen as a means to concretely attain detachment and self-denial. No mental illness can be overcome without self-denial and this is because once a mental illness becomes part of the directee, he is disposed toward that mental illness and will find some form of pleasure in it. To perform the actions contrary to it will be painful and this is one of the reasons God allows temptations: for the sake of being separated from the pleasure of his disorders. It is also a form of mortification, since it is a true suffering to fight against something one does not want.

Temptations also constitute a school of humility, so to speak, because they teach the directee to have a proper reckoning with the reality of his defects and to distrust himself in relation to those things to which the defects pertain. He is weak in his mental illness in relation to the object of his mental illness because mental illness is a vice and every vice is a weakness. Therefore, he must distrust himself because of his weakness. This distrust can cause some psychologists alarm but this stems from the fact that they do not understand that mental health consists in the ability to see reality for what it is and our weaknesses are part of that reality.

Moreover, through the temptation, one is able to turn away from the object of temptation and thereby become strong, i.e. to begin to build virtue in relation to the object. Virtue is a strength in relation to the object and so temptation gives one the opportunity to grow strong. Directees must recognize that temptations are allowed by God in order to make them stronger and so if temptations come often, it is merely God's way of telling the directee that he must continue to build virtue in that area. Sometimes directees will complain that they cannot understand why God allows them to be tempted with the possibility of a fall when He knows they are weak. Sometimes this is made in conjunction with the prayer for strength and they cannot understand why God has not

---

[108]Tanquerey, *The Spiritual Life*, n. 902.

[109]Ibid.

[110]Ibid., n. 903.

answered their prayers to make them strong or to overcome their mental illness. In fact, He has answered their prayers by the temptation, i.e. He has given them an opportunity to gain self mastery in the face of the object of their mental illness.

Because the proper office of the devil is to tempt,[111] through temptation we begin to see the true malice of the demonic. This aids the directee by making it easier for him to see that he must not give in to the object of mental illness, because the devil is using the object as a means of making him suffer through his mental illness. Therefore, as we turn from Satan and turn to God, we begin to hate the disorder in Satan (not his nature which is from God) as something for which perfect hate should be had, since he always and in all cases seeks our demise. It also moves us to perfect love of God because God always seeks our welfare and protects us from the demonic. This will re-orient the faculties in the person toward God and if it is coupled with charity, the faculties will be redirected and mental illness will be overcome.[112]

Temptations are also an opportunity of meriting, not only heaven, but additional grace which will aid the directee in the ways already delineated. Overcoming temptations is a means of humiliating Satan[113] and manifesting God's power and glory. In this, the directee can see that he is doing some good and so he is able to see the advantage to overcoming his mental illness, which becomes an incentive to take the various means to overcome the mental illness. It also moves one to prayer since we must depend on God and the benefits of prayer have already been discussed in the prior chapter. Lastly, temptations help the directee to see that he is disordered. The devil more than likely would not be prompting him in this way if the directee did not have some vice. While the demons can try us in various ways to discover our weaknesses, normally, they can look at our dispositions, read the vices which correspond to those dispositions and begin attacking. Therefore, temptations are a great source of self-knowledge. They tell the directee not only in what his mental vice consists but also the degree of his vice.

In all these things, the directee should not despair when temptations come, even if they come often. Psychologists must counsel the directee in the various reasons why temptations are allowed, especially in those aspects which show them as a means of overcoming his mental illness. Psychologists must also pray, do good works and offer up suffering for their directees so that they can sustain any temptation related to the mental illness. Clearly, the squeamishness that many psychologists have in counseling a directee about the involvement of the demonic in his mental illness is unjustified and unscientific. The psychologist must prudently read the directee to see if he is ready for the discussion of the demonic. At times, only the various means of temptations and why they are allowed can be discussed, prescinding from the discussion of the demonic involvement. However, to refuse to counsel the directee in the demonic as a matter of course rather than based upon prudence is tantamount to withholding medical treatment

---

[111]ST I, q. 114, a. 2.

[112]See the chapter on the infused virtues.

[113]Aumann, *Spiritual Theology*, p. 157.

to a dying man. This not only applies to ordinary diabolic activity but to the extraordinary diabolic activity as well. The avoidance of any discussion of the diabolic in cases where the diabolic may be present, because of some pseudo-scientific scepticism, is one of the most damaging effects of modern psychological practice today.

IV. Extraordinary Diabolic Influence

Extraordinary diabolic influence is that which goes above and beyond what is normal diabolic influence which all men must endure. Fr. Amorth provides clear distinctions regarding extraordinary diabolic influence which are helpful to the psychologist. Fr. Amorth distinguishes between six different forms, viz. external physical pain, demonic possession, diabolic oppression, diabolic obsession, diabolic infestation and diabolic subjugation.[114]

A. External Pain

External pain consists in demons acting physically on the flesh of the person in such a way as to cause pain and even, at times, bruising and lacerations. Historical examples of this kind of activity include St. Paul of the Cross, the Curé of Ars and St. (Padre) Pio. These forms of diabolic activity do not require an exorcist but merely prayers.[115] Some psychologists have been so crass as to suggest that this form of diabolic influence is merely the product of the mind of the directee. The principle of sufficient reason is clearly violated, since neither the intellect nor will have the capacities to cause these types of affliction.[116] These kinds of diabolic influences are sometimes accompanied by things outside the individual which the intellect and will of man do not have the ability to cause, e.g. voices being heard by others which do not originate from the individual suffering the infliction and things of this sort. If a psychologist comes across this kind of diabolic influence, it is scientific incompetence to assign a false or insufficient cause to the activity by saying it comes from the person afflicted. Psychologists should seek the advice of a learned priest who can come and discern the case since it goes beyond the competence of a psychologist to diagnose based upon the principles of his own science. He must remand the case to those who study a higher science, viz. theology and therefore to those who have the grace of office to judge such matters, viz. priests.

---

[114]Amorth, *An Exorcist Tells His Story*, p. 35-7.

[115]Amorth, *An Exorcist Tells His Story*, p. 33.

[116]One might argue that the praeternatural gifts could account for this. However, such a capacity would have to be there from birth and many of the cases of this kind of influence do not have any connection to some gift granted to a person by God at birth. Moreover, under normal conditions, the will is restricted not just to the body of the individual, but even to specific modes of operation on the body which do not permit this kind of activity.

B. Demonic Possession

The next form is demonic possession which consists in Satan or demons taking full possession of the body (and not the soul).[117] In these cases, the demons speak and act through the body of the possessed without the knowledge or consent of the victim, who is morally without guilt for the actions.[118] The signs of possession are many and so each psychologist should be familiar with them. Given this, each psychologist should read the proper literature written by knowledgeable exorcists who can give clear explanations of the signs. However, some signs are appropriate here to draw certain implications for the science of psychology. The *Rituale Romanum* gives several signs[119] which give an indication of diabolic possession:

> he [the exorcist] ought to ascertain the signs by which a person possessed can be distinguished from one who is suffering from melancholy or some other illness. Signs of possession are the following: ability to speak with some facility in a strange tongue or to understand it when spoken by another; the faculty of divulging future and hidden events; display of powers which are beyond the subject's age and natural condition; and various other indications which, when taken together as a whole, pile up the evidence.[120]

The basic signs of possession point to some agency which goes beyond the natural capacities of the individual, e.g. speaking in a foreign language or being able to understand it when the person has never heard or had access to the language. Psychologists often dismiss certain signs as irrelevant to the diagnosis precisely because their diagnosis cannot explain how the person can speak in foreign languages. Sometimes the person manifests capacities above and beyond their normal capacities, e.g. superhuman strength. While it must be conceded that super-motor activity is possible, e.g. in the cases where women have lifted trucks to save their children, nevertheless, when taken in conjunction with other signs, this sign can be a clear indicator.

Since it involves interpreting various signs, when a psychologist witnesses these

---

[117]Amorth, *An Exorcist Tells His Story*, p. 33 and *An Exorcist: More Stories*, p. 61

[118]Amorth, *An Exorcist Tells His Story*, p. 33.

[119]The fact that they are signs indicates that they do not give clear knowledge about the nature or actuality of the possession except to the learned and experienced, such as exorcists.

[120]The Roman Ritual, vol. II, p. 169, n. 3: "nota habeat ea signa, quibus obsessus dignoscitur ab iis, qui vel atra bile, vel morbo aliquo laborant. Signa autem obsidentis daemonis sunt: ignota lingua loqui pluribus verbis, vel loquentem. intelligere; distantia, et occulta patefacere; vires supra aetatis seu conditionis naturam ostendere; et id genus alia, quae cum plurima concurrunt, majora sunt indicia." Translation by Fr. Philip Weller.

signs in a directee, he should prudently investigate to see if the signs can have a natural explanation, e.g. if a person has studied a language, even though those around him may not know that he has studied the language. But if there is no natural explanation, the directee should be remanded to a knowledgeable priest or exorcist for evaluation.

Two extremes must be avoided. The first is to assume that possession and extraordinary diabolic activity never occurs and the other is a presumption that every strange activity is necessarily diabolic. This is why a psychologist must read the proper literature to be able to know when something is strictly natural and when it may be beyond his capacities to cure. Again, this is why psychologists must read the literature from credible exorcists to ensure that they are not becoming part of the directee's problem by not providing the right help at the right time. Those possessed (or even oppressed) will show an aversion toward sacred things, "often in conjunction with blasphemy."[121]

At this stage, we must consider certain kinds of possession which have been falsely labeled in the psychological community and therefore resulted in many directees not being helped. The first is what has become known as "multiple personality disorder." This label presumes a proper definition of personality, which psychology has yet truly to settle on, at least adequately. While the definition of personality may be debated, we can give at least basic observations about how personality is identifiable. The first is that personality comes from the word person which is defined as "an individual substance of rational nature."[122] A person is something which has intelligence and by intelligence is meant the ability to grasp concepts and not merely particular reason as is found in animals. While sometimes the term personality is applied to animals, in the strict sense, they do not have personalities since they are not persons. However, the term personality can be applied to them insofar as their material dispositions and particular species will determine the kinds of actions that they perform.

Yet, the term personality is properly applied to those who have immaterial intelligence and for this reason it should only be applied to God,[123] angels and men. In angels, their personality is dependent upon two things, viz. their nature[124] and their assigned task.[125] Each angel is given an assigned task to perform specific functions, e.g. guardian angels are assigned to protect specific individuals and so their personality is manifest in the activities which they choose to perform.

Man's personality, on the other hand, is more complex, for it is based on several factors. The first is human nature and by this is understood not just man's essence but the natural law, i.e. man is by nature inclined toward specific things. The

---

[121]Amorth, *An Exorcist: more Stories*, p. 61.

[122]See ST I, q. 29.

[123]How it is applied to God is different from how it is applied to men. For a treatment of the term person in relation to God, see ST I, q. 29, a. 3.

[124]Each angel is essentially different from another angel since each angel is its own species; see ST I, q. 50.

[125]See ST I, qq. 108-113.

next is bodily disposition which includes genetic differences along with environmental factors, such as diet, the amount of exercise and things of this kind which affect disposition, for people are inclined to different kinds of actions based upon disposition. This is why even children who do not exercise freewill will have clear personality traits. Some personality traits can also be picked up involuntarily insofar as the cogitative power may associate something of which the person is not fully aware and so the person will act based upon the cogitative power's assessments and associations. The last determinant of personality is the changes made to ourselves, i.e. the forming of habits and changing of dispositions based upon the free choices that we make and, in this case, free choice along with human nature are the primary determinations of personality of the person.

Because of the complexity of man's dispositions and the multitudinous choices he makes throughout life, people's personalities are often very complicated. Yet, this complication cannot explain certain aspects of possession. In other words, man has a *single* personality. Even if he is someone who acts in a variety of ways because he is mischievous or is a good actor, nevertheless, these are all part of a single personality. Possession is the only true form of multiple personality disorder, i.e. the demon who has one personality and the human who has another. Authentic multiple personalities, which are rare, are more than likely a form of possession insofar as the personality of the demon or demons[126] shows through in the human body. Demons can mimic any human personality because they know them all[127] and not all demonic activity is violent in nature. Therefore, just because someone exhibits a different personality which is placid, demonic influence should not be ruled out.[128]

Psychologists, when diagnosing whether a person might be possessed, i.e. if there is more than one personality, should be sure that the directee is not acting. It is possible that a directee could act as if he has multiple personalities and may even get to the point where he loses mental stability and is unable to distinguish within himself one from the other. But in this case, he still has one personality which is summed up in mental illness. But if the person is not an actor or if the person honestly does things involuntarily, it is unlikely that he suffers from the aforesaid and he is more than likely possessed. Yet, one of the determining factors to determine whether he has deluded himself or whether he is possessed is if, when he first started manifesting different "personalities," he had volitional control over the switching between "persona." If he

---

[126]In this case, if the number of demons possessing the person is more than one, the person can exhibit very different actions depending upon which demon is acting through the human.

[127]Angelic knowledge of man is exhausted instantaneously to the degree that each angel can know it. The result is that they fully understand every possible form of personality of man precluding certain aspects of free will and grace. That angels know an essence instantaneously, see ST I, q. 58.

[128]In cases of possible multiple personality, exorcists may have to perform an exorcism to discover whether the personality is actually coming from a demonic source.

did and he continued doing so and then over time he became deluded, it is likely that it has a natural cause. If it is something which appears suddenly, or which the person does not do voluntarily, even if from birth,[129] then it is more than likely possession. Such people should be taken to a trained exorcist for his evaluation.

Modern psychology must undergo a major revision about various mental illnesses and their causes. Some are clearly from a natural cause, as was described in the prior volume, but some are not. Fr. Amorth anecdotally shows why psychology must be, in the opinion of this author, revised:

> On April 24, 1988, Pope John Paul II beatified the Spanish Carmelite Father Francisco Palau. Father Palau is very interesting for our purposes because he devoted the last years of his life to those who were possessed by demons. He bought a hospice, in which he cared for the mentally ill. He exorcized all of them: those who were possessed were healed; those who were simply mentally ill remained ill.[130]

At some point, it will be necessary for psychologists and exorcists to discuss which mental illnesses are the result of demonic influences and which are not in order to provide guidelines for psychologists. Fr. Amorth rightly observes:

> Admittedly, it is difficult to distinguish between someone who is possessed and someone with psychological problems. However, an expert exorcist will be able to detect the difference more easily than a psychiatrist because the exorcist will keep his mind open to all possibilities and will be able to identify the distinguishing elements. The psychiatrist, in the majority of cases, does not believe in demonic possession; therefore he does not even consider it in his diagnostic process. . . . Here we touch a sensitive nerve: in difficult cases, the diagnosis requires cooperation between different fields of expertise, as we will demonstrate in our final analysis. Unfortunately, those who pay for the experts' errors are always those who are ill and who all too often end up ruined by medical mistakes.[131]

In order for psychology to have a true scientific footing and in order for it honestly to help others, the rationalistic scepticism must be put aside. An interdisciplinary effort

---

[129]For the fact that one can be possessed from birth see Szymanski, *A Notebook on the Devil and Exorcism*, p. 20.

[130]Amorth, *An Exorcist Tells His Story*, p. 61. Similar stories of exorcists exorcizing the "mentally ill" and curing them are recounted throughout Amorth's two books, *An Exorcist Tells his Story* and *An Exorcist: More Stories*.

[131]Ibid., p. 61f.

must be made to delineate clearly the possible causes of mental illness.

C. Diabolic Oppression

Diabolic oppression is manifest in symptoms from very serious to very mild illnesses: "There is no possession, loss of consciousness, or involuntary action and word."[132] Oppression affects one's health, employment and relationships and its symptoms include "unexplainable rages and a tendency to complete isolation."[133] Job (in the Book of Job) is a clear example of this kind of demonic influence. It can result in physical illness which cannot be cured by medical means. It can affect relationships, e.g. when unexplainably there is a "falling out" among family members. It can also affect people's employment, e.g. when they are fired suddenly and without reason.

D. Diabolic Obsession

The understanding of this form of demonic influence is particularly important for psychologists and psychiatrists:

> Symptoms include sudden attacks, at times ongoing, of obsessive thoughts, sometimes even rationally absurd, but of such nature that the victim is unable to free himself. Therefore the obsessed person lives in a perpetual state of prostration, desperation, and attempts at suicide. Almost always obsession influences dreams. Some people will say that this is evidence of mental illness, requiring the services of a psychiatrist or a psychologist. The same could be said of all other forms of demonic phenomena. Some symptoms, however, are so inconsistent with known illnesses that they point with certainty to their evil origins. Only an expert and well-trained eye can identify the crucial differences.[134]

---

[132]Amorth, *An Exorcist Tells His Story*, p. 33.

[133]Amorth, *An Exorcist Tells his Story*, p. 33f and *An Exorcist: More Stories*, p. 61. Amorth in *An Exorcist: More Stories* (P. 61) observes that this form of demonic influence can affect individuals as well as groups, even large ones.

[134]Amorth, *An Exorcist Tells his Story*, p. 34. Amorth describes this form of demonic activity in another place (*An Exorcist: More Stories*, p. 61) in the following manner: "*Diabolic obsession* causes an almost split personality. Our will remains free, but it is oppressed by obsessive thoughts. The victim experiences thoughts that may be rationally absurd but of such a nature that he is unable to free himself. The obsessed person lives in a perpetual state of prostration, with persistent temptations to suicide. We must be aware that the temptation to commit suicide is also present in *diabolic possession* and *diabolic oppression*."

From the point of view of an exorcist, or one may even say, from the point of view of reality, many mental illnesses are, in fact, a form of demonic influence. This has several implications for psychology and psychologists. The first is, again, that an interdisciplinary effort must be made to provide a fuller understanding of causes and categories of psychological illness. Second, it means that psychologists must be prudent, i.e they must make sure that the proper spiritual works are done in order to ensure that any possible demonic influence is abated.[135] Each psychologist must have the requisite knowledge to know when he is not capable of helping the directee or the extent to which he can help the directee. Modern psychology has been plagued by saviorism, in which it presumes it can rush in and save everyone from everything. Psychologists must know the limits of their science and themselves.

Certain forms of modern psychology will be inherently inadequate in relation to these kinds of causes. For instance, behaviorism which by its nature treats man no differently than an animal[136] denies the role of the immaterial. Therefore, in its efforts to "modify behavior," behaviorists will meet with failure since modification of the behavior does not solve the problem of demonic obsession nor any mental illness which has its root in the voluntary. Any psychology which takes its principal conclusions about mental health from a purely materialistic point of view will be inherently inadequate. Only a psychology rooted in Thomism will give an adequate response to people's mental difficulties, for only Thomism takes into consideration ALL of the possible causes as well as a proper delineation of man's ontological constitution and therefore can understand how the causes function.

With this form of diabolic activity, two approaches of the psychologist must be borne in mind. The first is that the psychologist must exhaust the natural possibilities and aids in counseling the directee in what to do. This does not imply that the psychologists have to go one by one through the various natural possibilities. It merely means that he must be knowledgeable of them and not find any natural possibility in his assessment of the directee. Further, he must ensure that the means that the directee and he, as a psychologist, can employ on the spiritual level are used.[137] If the obsession is one that can be broken merely by the prayers of someone in the state of grace, psychologists will note, in cases where this form of demonic influence is present, definite improvement. If after the various means are used and the directee has faithfully done his part, both on the spiritual and natural level, it may be prudent to send the directee to a priest or an exorcist.

---

[135]See below.

[136]Watson, loc. cit.

[137]See below.

E. Diabolic Infestation

Diabolic infestation occurs in things outside of man:

In this case, the malefic activity is directed toward places (houses, offices, stores, fields), objects (cars, pillows, mattresses, dolls) and animals, therefore it only indirectly affects man. As I mentioned in a previous chapter, Origen tells us that the early Christians resorted to exorcisms in these situations.[138]

Modern psychology, or more accurately, parapsychology, has misunderstood many phenomena. They often attribute this form of activity either to people or some "scientific" explanation which lacks sufficient reason or foundation. For instance, when objects move around a house, they will argue that it is because of a magnetic disturbance under the house moving the objects. Such an explanation might be reasonable if it were applied only to metallic substances, but in point of fact the psychologists apply it to anything, such as plastic, wood, etc. Sometimes they will argue that things are moving around because the people are disturbed. If that were the case, then these occurrences should follow the people outside the location where they occur, which often they do not.

Not too much will be said about these kinds of phenomena other than that directees should be counseled to ignore them. They should be told to contact a priest who can come and exorcize the house or thing which is affected. The priest will more than likely have to make an initial investigation to ensure that the exorcism is warranted so the directee should not be disturbed if the priest asks personal questions, particularly in order to ascertain the cause of the infestation. If the cause is the sin of the people living in the house, they must get to Confession and assure the priest that they will stop sinning in order that the demons do not return. Once this is done, the directee should be told to keep his mind off the activity and not to speak about it, which can glorify Satan by ingratiating the curious who seek knowledge of these phenomena.

Psychologists should not be too quick to accept or reject the recounting of these kinds of phenomena by a directee. Some will try to make up stories in order to draw a strange form of attention to themselves, so the counselor will have to address other problems in the directee. Yet, if the directee appears credible and the psychologist, in making a visit to the house, cannot find anything which would imply deception, the directee should be sent to a priest.[139]

---

[138]Amorth, *An Exorcist Tells his Story*, p. 34. See also Amorth, *An Exorcist: More Stories*, p. 61f.

[139]Amorth and other exorcists often lament the fact that many priests themselves suffer from the rationalistic scepticism which rejects any demonic activity. Often this is contracted while in the seminary in which "psychological" reasons are given and so anyone who complains about this or other forms of demonic activities is written off as mentally ill. Such an attitude is grave on the side of a priest and he will have to account for it before God since he has, as one of his tasks as a priest, to fight this kind of activity when occasion calls

F. Diabolic Subjugation or Dependence

This occurs when people voluntarily submit to or place themselves under Satan, e.g. by a blood pact with the devil or by a consecration to the devil.[140] If a psychologist discovers this in his directee, he must immediately counsel the breaking of the pact or subjugation. This is normally done through saying the words voluntarily which reject the pact and then he should get to Confession immediately. However, it may not end there. The demons will seek to take dominion over their "property" and so they will adversely affect the directee in the ways described above. The directee must be aware of this, so that when it occurs he can address it properly.

He must also engage in forms of mortification to break any residual bonds which the demons have over him which occur in the form of affecting his appetites and lower powers. He must also do prayer, penance and good works to make reparation for any evil that results or was the effect of this pact, e.g. within his family or among friends. He should also be sent to a priest to discuss any spiritual aspects of the case which must be addressed, at least for some time, to ensure that this does not happen again and that the directee knows what he must do on the spiritual level, to reverse not only the subjugation, but the effects of the subjugation.[141]

V. Ways of Falling Prey to Extraordinary Diabolic Activity

There are different categories of ways of falling prey to extraordinary demonic activity. The first is by God's permission;[142] in fact, no demonic activity can occur without God's permission. Since God is able to allow anyone to fall prey in this way, it should not be assumed that if one does fall prey, it is necessarily because of something he has done. As a result, falling prey to this kind of demonic activity is not a sign of someone's state of soul.[143]

The second way one can fall prey to extraordinary demonic activity is by being subject to an evil spell[144] or curse.[145] A curse or spell is "the intention of *harming others through demonic intervention*."[146] In these cases, the person, again, is not culpable for falling prey since it is done by another person using the demons. This is why things such

---

for it. The warning here is that psychologists should seek to be aware of the priests who are adequately trained and knowledgeable and open to these kinds of occurrences.

[140] Amorth, *An Exorcist Tells His Story*, p. 35 and *An Exorcist: More Stories*, p. 62.

[141] This advice will also apply to those who get involved in witchcraft.

[142] Amorth, *An Exorcist Tells His Story*, p. 56 and *An Exorcist: More Stories*, p. 62.

[143] Amorth, *An Exorcist: More Stories*, p. 62. Amorth observes that even saints have been possessed, see *An Exorcist Tells His Story*, p. 57.

[144] Amorth, *An Exorcist Tells His Story*, p. 57.

[145] Amorth, *An Exorcist: More Stories*, p. 62.

[146] Ibid. See also Amorth, *An Exorcist Tells His Story*, p. 57.

as witchcraft, sorcery, spells (malefice), bindings, evil eyes and maledictions are so dangerous.[147] This has become very problematic in the last forty years and particularly in the last ten years with the rise of witchcraft among teenagers and feminists.[148]

The third way of falling prey is by a grave and hardened state of sin.[149] Amorth gives the examples[150] of sexual perversions, violence, drug use, abortion,[151] homosexuality, living in irregular marriages, committing violent actions, superstitious practices,[152] direct invocation of the demonic,[153] and hypnotism[154] just to name a few.[155]

---

[147]These themes run throughout both of Amorth's texts in the prior footnote. See also Szymanski, *A Notebook on the Devil and Exorcism*, p. 19f.

[148]Some who get involved in witchcraft and magic often argue that there is a difference between white and black magic. Distinctions, however, must be made. Some make the distinction between white magic and black magic as follows: there is white magic which does not use the demonic but is an art form in which people temporarily deceive someone by playing a card trick or making someone disappear in a box when in fact he has not. Then there is the black magic in which one uses the intervention of the devil. This distinction is made by Szymanski, *A Notebook on the Devil and Exorcism*, p. 26, footnote 1. This is a legitimate distinction. However, sometimes this kind of magic is taken from the intention one has in performing it. So some call magic white when one uses the demons for a good intention and black magic when one uses the demonic influence for bad intentions. Such a distinction is false, since both use the demonic and can therefore be a source of problems. See Amorth, *An Exorcist Tells His Story*, p. 60.

[149]Amorth, *An Exorcist Tells His Story*, p. 58 and Amorth, *An Exorcist: More Stories*, p. 63. See also Aumann, *Spiritual Theology*, p. 411.

[150]These can be found in Amorth, *An Exorcist Tells His Story*, p. 58 and Amorth, *An Exorcist: More Stories*, p. 63.

[151]Amorth warns against the clear repercussions of this sin which are seen in exorcisms which often require long periods of time to liberate the soul. It is also the experience of this author that abortion constitutes not only an avenue for demonic activity, but also a short circuiting of the very female psychology. Since the nature of the feminine is to be able to bear children, the fact that a woman would go contrary to that strong and inherent natural inclination causes grave damage in self perception in which contradiction is the result, i.e. one views oneself as a woman which is to bear children and yet one aborts that which she bears.

[152]Examples of this are consulting fortune tellers, using Ouija boards, seeking cures from spiritualists, spiritism and seances. These are likewise listed in both of Amorth's books as well as Szymanski, *A Notebook on the Devil and Exorcism*, p. 19. Parents must be diligent in warning their children to avoid these things as well as being watchful since curiosity in the young often leads to getting involved in these.

[153] Szymanski, *A Notebook on the Devil and Exorcism*, p. 19.

[154]Ibid., p.19. "Recreational hypnotism" has become more frequent in modern years. People often do it as a form of entertainment rather than having some purpose to it in which strict guidelines are followed. The mechanism and guidelines for hypnotism will

Both Amorth and this author agree that, with the increase in abortions and collapse of married life, many more souls are being afflicted. Other cases which authors mention are balls (today called discotheques),[156] and modern forms of music.[157] Aumann remarks, in a quote already given, that "a person may also come under the power of the devil by reason of the habitual practice of evil or the uncontrolled desire to experience extraordinary mystical phenomena or receive charismatic graces."[158]

In these cases, the beginning part of the remedy is clear. One must have an authentic conversion of life and go to Confession regularly. All sexually perverted activity, homosexuality, violence, drug use, abortion, violent actions, and superstitious practices and direct invocation of the demonic must cease. Those living in irregular marriages must either get them regularized or repudiate the marriage. Parents must also keep watch over the kinds of music to which children listen. This applies not only to the Satanic forms but also those which affect the appetites by increasing antecedent appetite.[159]

Psychologists will often get directees who have become deluded or are under demonic influence because they specifically sought out mystical phenomena, as Aumann observes. The psychologist must address three aspects of this problem. First, the directee will often be beset by pride insofar as he wishes these things to happen to him so that he can have "bragging rights," so to speak. The psychologists must put him on a strict regimen to foster humility. Second, some suffer from the vice of *curiositas* and so they must be taught proper detachment from these things by seeking the virtue of diligence. Third, the directees must be taught that when they see things or when praeternatural phenomena occur to them, the demonic may be the cause and so they are to follow the advice of St. John of the Cross on these matters, viz. they are to ignore them. Since God can obtain from us anything and He needs us for nothing, if something which appears beyond the natural happens, we should normally ignore it. Moreover, since the devil can cause these things, one should ignore them and thereby take away from the demonic the ability to affect him.[160]

---

be delineated in the next volume.

[155]These activities not only cause demonic influence in the person doing them, but it can also cause them in others, e.g. many experience demonic infestations in their homes when warlocks or witches become active in their neighborhoods.

[156]Sutter, *Lucifer*, p. 27f; Amorth, *An Exorcist: More Stories*, p. 63.

[157]Amorth specifically refers to satanic rock music, *An Exorcist Tells His Story*, p. 58.

[158]Aumann, *Spiritual Theology*, p. 411.

[159]How music affects one psychologically will be addressed in the next volume.

[160]The opposite extreme must also be guarded against. Just because someone comes to a psychologist and talks of seeing things, we should not assume that they are demonic or assume that the person is mentally ill. Judgment should be suspended until sufficient knowledge can be gained to make a proper judgment.

Lastly, psychologists must be careful of two things. The first is that they do not seek the charismatic grace of healing because they can end up causing harm to themselves and to their directees. If God were to send it, that is His choice, but it should not be sought. If a psychologist were to receive this gift, he should be under a spiritual director to ensure its proper use. Psychologists must also warn directees about the dangers of pursuing charismatic gifts. The nature of these gifts have already been discussed in a prior chapter but the dangers are many, one of which is the ability to affect one's mental health by demonic influence.

VI. Broad Signs of the Demonic

There are some signs of the demonic not thus far listed but which are succinctly listed by Aumann:[161]

> 1. *Spirit of falsity*. The devil is the father of lies, but he cleverly conceals his deceit by half-truths and pseudo-mystical phenomena.

Normally, psychologists should take what the directee says at face value. But they must exercise due caution, stemming from the virtue of prudence, in recognizing that people lie. When the demons are involved, they will mix truth with lies in order to deceive the psychologist. Therefore, he must pay close attention to the directee in order to ensure the veracity of the directee by means of making sure that the information provided by him is coherent.[162] If a psychologist detects that the directee is not being truthful in what he says and it seems that there is some evil intent behind it, the psychologist should be aware that this is one of the signs of a demonic spirit. The remedy, if to the spirit of falsity is not joined more serious signs, is the ordinary means, viz. prayer, mortification and good works on both the side of the directee and the psychologist.

> 2. *Morbid curiosity*. This is characteristic of those who eagerly seek out the esoteric aspects of mystical phenomena or have a fascination for the occult or preternatural.

It is for this reason that "apparition" and miracle chasing[163] should be avoided. If a

---

[161]All fifteen quoted here are from Aumann, *Spiritual Theology*, p. 412.

[162]In philosophical parlance, coherent does not mean that one can understand it, necessarily. It means that the truth of two statements can be reconciled with each other.

[163]Apparition and miracle chasing consists in an uncontrolled desire to seek out reported apparitions of our Lady, saints, etc. not in order to give honor to them but merely due to a lack of faith. This does not include the desire to go to ecclesiastically approved sites of apparitions. The directee should be instructed to suspend his own judgment about these matters until the judgment of the Church is forthcoming. This is for two reasons. The first is that if the Church condemns some praeternatural phenomena as not being supernatural and

directee has this problem, he must begin working on the vice of *curiositas*. He should refrain the desire to see these matters by working on the virtue of diligence which directs one's activity toward something productive. The demonic can also incline one towards these things and since man has a natural desire to know,[164] when we see something we do not understand or which is out of the ordinary experience, we have a natural inclination to want to come to knowledge of it. However, this must be curbed since it can come from the demonic, though not always, and it can lead to other vices.

3. *Confusion, anxiety, and deep depression.*

This stems from the fact that the faculties in which these operations occur act through a bodily organ which the demonic can affect. The demonic can affect the phantasm (since it is a material thing) by putting conflicting data in the phantasm which results in judgment being confused. Also, anxiety is merely another word for fear and since fear is a passion of the concupiscible appetite, the demons can cause anxiety. Depression is a state of constant sorrow with few or no periods of relief. Since the demonic can by obsession afflict a person in this fashion, it can come from the demonic. If the depression does not seem to have any one thing to which the psychologist can attach a cause or if there is not a sufficient reason for the depression, it may be either chemical or demonic or both. Since the demons can move the chemical dispositions of the person, they can cause depression. If medicine is used because of the chemical indisposition and the depression dissipates, this is not a one hundred percent sign that it was merely physical.

4. *Obstinacy.* One of the surest signs of a diabolical spirit.

If the directee is simply not docile, i.e. not willing to be led and refuses to accept anything that is said, it may be a case of demonic influence. However, in many cases throughout the history of modern psychology, people of common sense refused to listen to the psychologist and immediately the directees were blamed. If a psychologist says something contrary to right reason or faith and the directee rejects it, the psychologist is to blame. However, if one is presenting a reasonable and sufficient explanation of his problems to a directee and he refuses to accept the truth or the means of overcoming his problem, the cause may be a diabolic spirit. The demons do not want the person to employ the means to overcome his mental illness (or moral depravity, which may also be causing his mental illness) and so they will move the person, both in the passions and in the imagination, to refuse to accept the proposal.

---

he is attached to the phenomena, his faith may be weakened. The second is that only the Church has the grace to discern these matters and so it is prudent to await the judgment of the Church.

[164]Aristotle, *Metaphysics*, Book I, chap. 1 (980a1).

5. *Constant indiscretion and a restless spirit.* Those who constantly
go to extremes, as in penitential exercises or apostolic activity, or
neglect their primary obligations to do some personally chosen work.

Virtue lies in the mean and the demons are always trying to get someone to go to excess or defect. From this arises an inclination to go to extremes in things like fasting and physical mortifications when the person is prepared neither for it nor has the physical constitution to sustain it. One of the goals of the demonic in this case is hagiosthenia, which is a certain tiredness or distaste for spiritual goods because of the pain or suffering endured in their pursuit. It differs from acedia[165] in that acedia results when a person has done nothing and wants to do nothing because of the ardor involved in the pursuit of spiritual goods. Hagiosthenia, on the other hand, is the distaste for these things arising from excessive pursuits of them when not conditioned to do so. Just as a person who is out of shape physically cannot get up and run a marathon and will quickly give up, so in the spiritual life if one is not properly conditioned through a gradual habituation in the virtues of prayer, mortification and self-denial, he will quickly develop distaste for the spiritual goods because they are difficult. The demons will try this tactic to get people ultimately separated from spiritual goods. Psychologists will also see this among directees, e.g. when a woman spends all her time praying at a church and doing volunteer work, while her obligations at home are neglected. The goal of the demon is to get the person to sin by not fulfilling the obligations of his state in life, which also affects other people.

6. *Spirit of pride and vanity.* Very anxious to publicize their gifts of
grace and mystical experiences.

When the first thing the directee wants to talk about is his "supernatural" experiences, two things can be assured. More than likely he does not have any or, if he does, they are from the demonic. When God touches a soul, it is deep in the soul and so the person retracts, so to speak, interiorly where the "touch" occurs. When truly supernatural things happen to people, they often do not want to talk about them; this is clearly evidenced in the lives of the saints.[166] Whereas when it comes from the demonic, the person is often gabby about the experience. Since pride is a vice in the irascible appetite,[167] the demons can move the appetite to the passion of pride and so strong pride is a sign of the demonic. In this case, Confession (the sacrament of humiliation) and acts of

---

[165]For a discussion of acedia, see ST II-II, qq. 20 and 35.

[166]For example, St. Theresa of Avila had to be compelled by her superiors to write her autobiography in which many mystical experiences are recounted.

[167]ST II-II, q. 162, a. 3.

humiliation[168] are to be prescribed. The devil hates humility and will flee anyone who is trying to obtain it.

7. *False humility*. This is the disguise for their pride and self-love.

Often directees will act in a self-deprecating fashion, only because their pride is driving them to seek out the recognition of others through human respect. False humility can be detected when the person refuses to recognize some personality trait which is good. Here we are not speaking of those who wish to refer the perfection to God because in this case they are willing to admit it is there but it must ultimately be referred to God.[169] Moreover, we are not talking about those who do not wish to talk about it because of a fear of pride. Rather we are talking about those who mimic humility but can be seen to be placing themselves in a position in which they can elicit people's praise, even though they are seemingly rejecting the praise. False humility is very dangerous. Since all virtues are founded upon humility, if a person falsifies humility, he cannot attain any other virtue. This is why the demons like it so much.

---

[168]In this case, humiliation can come by merely not talking about their gifts or graces since it teaches them that reality is about God and not themselves, so it is not their place to go around drawing attention to themselves by talking about their graces or gifts. The litany of humility by Cardinal Merry del Val is also particularly effective and directees should be counseled to recite it frequently. It is as follows: O Jesus! meek and humble of heart, hear me. From the desire of being esteemed, deliver me, Jesus. From the desire of being loved, deliver me, Jesus. From the desire of being extolled, deliver me, Jesus. From the desire of being honored, deliver me, Jesus. From the desire of being praised, deliver me, Jesus. From the desire of being preferred, deliver me, Jesus. From the desire of being consulted, deliver me, Jesus. From the desire of being approved, deliver me, Jesus. From the fear of being humiliated, deliver me, Jesus. From the fear of being despised, deliver me, Jesus. From the fear of suffering rebukes, deliver me, Jesus. From the fear of being calumniated, deliver me, Jesus. From the fear of being forgotten deliver me, Jesus. From the fear of being ridiculed, deliver me, Jesus. From the fear of being wronged, deliver me, Jesus. From the fear of being suspected, deliver me, Jesus. That others may be loved more than I, Jesus, grant me the grace to desire it. That others may be esteemed more than I, Jesus, grant me the grace to desire it. That in the opinion of the world, others may increase, and I may decrease, Jesus, grant me the grace to desire it. That others may be chosen and I set aside, Jesus, grant me the grace to desire it. That others may be praised and I unnoticed, Jesus, grant me the grace to desire it. That others may be preferred to me in everything, Jesus, grant me the grace to desire it. That others become holier than I, provided that I may become as holy as I should, Jesus, grant me the grace to desire it.

[169]Humility itself is the only perfection which cannot be recognized by any person (other than those confirmed in grace). For a discussion of this point see *Humility of Heart* by Bergamo.

8. *Despair, lack of confidence, and discouragement.* A chronic characteristic that alternates with presumption, vain security, and unfounded optimism.

These extremes indicate that the person is being moved this way and that. Bipolarism is often confused with this demonic activity. While not all forms of bipolarism are demonic in cause since they can have ourselves as a cause,[170] nevertheless, it should not be immediately presumed that it has a physical cause.

9. *Disobedience and hardness of heart.*

The demons disobeyed God and so they always incite others to disobey. If a psychologist notices this trait in the directee in such a manner that it is chronic (often coupled with obstinacy), he should pray, do penance and good works for the directee. This will either cause a reduction in the demonic influence or it will gain the grace for the person so that his will will be strengthened and he can be obedient.[171]

10. *Impatience in suffering and stubborn resentment.*

This characteristic should not be confused with the human spirit, i.e. that defect from a natural inclination and original sin in which we do not want to suffer for the sake of the good. The efforts involved in overcoming mental illness can be a tremendous suffering and psychologists should not be overly alarmed to see directees shrink from the arduous task of overcoming it. In fact, mental illness, because it causes dispositions, can be comfortable and so the directee must foster a spirit of mortification in order to overcome the pleasure of acting according to the disposition. This demonic sign is more of a hardened one in which the person refuses even to try to be patient or forgive those who have caused him harm. Christ counseled forgiveness precisely to break the demonic bonds over us and for man to be freed from the attachment to the injury caused by others.

11. *Uncontrolled passions and strong inclination to sensuality,* usually under the guise of mystical union.

The life of sensuality not only can disorder our faculties and cause mental illness but it can also be the opportunity for the demonic to gain and manifest control over us. Those who have unusually strong inclinations which seem to go above and beyond what is normally human may have some diabolic influence. The demons try to delude the person by moving him to concupiscence and then placing in his imagination the sensible

---

[170]Bipolarism is the result of violating the principle of non-contradiction. See volume III.

[171]Obedience is a virtue in the will; see ST II-II, qq. 104f.

species which will incline him to judge that somehow this is supernatural or mystical.

12. *Hypocrisy, simulation, and duplicity.*

Hypocrisy occurs when one says one thing and acts in an opposite fashion. This is a sign of the demonic since the demons are inclined, due to their malice of will, toward contradiction. Simulation[172] is a species of action in which one deceives by what one does. It is similar to lying in that in lying one says the false in order to deceive[173] whereas simulation occurs when one acts (not talks) in order to deceive. Because demons are constantly trying to deceive us, this is one of the signs of the demonic. Duplicity is from the demonic in that one acts and talks in a contradictory fashion. Duplicity differs from simple contradiction in that simple contradiction is due to some error in reason whereas duplicity is something chosen in the will. This is why the spiritual writers have always counseled simplicity of heart in order to avoid complex lives which can lead to acting in a contradictory fashion. If a psychologist recognizes that the directee is doing this knowingly and not out of weakness, it may be a sign of the demonic influence. He must be counseled to seek simplicity of life and an undivided heart in which he strives for an unwavering attachment to God (Who is Truth itself). Therefore charity must also be counseled.

13. *Excessive attachment to sensible consolations*, particularly in their practice of prayer.

Because the demons can act upon the concupiscible appetite and imagination in such a way to give one a sensible consolation, if a person has an attachment to sensible consolations, the demons can fool the person into thinking that the motion is from God. This is why certain aspects of the charismatic renewal are dangerous since it often has a tendency to make sensible consolations the mainstay of one's spiritual life. However, charismatics are not the only ones who suffer from this; a vast majority of Protestants and Catholics act in religious matters based upon how they feel interiorly. This has been one of the primary motivating causes of the heresy of modernism within the Catholic Church.

Those who suffer from this problem must be told that spiritual consolations are merely means to an end. Therefore, if the directee experiences consolations, he must use them to draw himself closer to God. However, he should not seek them. He should strive to make his adherence to God out of charity, which is the love of God, rather than the love of the consolation. Also, people who do this are less likely to engage in mortifications since they have an interiorly unpleasant effect. Directees who suffer from this should be told to engage in some form of penance, to use reason as illumined by

---

[172]See ST II-II, q. 111.

[173]See ST II-II, q. 110.

faith[174] as their guide in what to do and to practice self-denial so that they will stop looking to self as the principle of judgment in religious and psychological matters.

14. *Lack of deep devotion to Jesus and Mary.*

The demons hate God (Christ) and they hate our Lady who even now crushes their head.[175] Therefore, if the psychologist finds that the directee has hatred for Jesus and Mary, it can be a strong sign of the demonic influence.

15. *Scrupulous adherence to the letter of the law and fanatical zeal in promoting a cause.* This characteristic readily opens the door to diabolical influence in reformers and demagogues.

This statement is clear enough. The demons, again, will incite the person to extremes beyond where virtue lies,[176] since they do not want us to act in a prudent and virtuous fashion. Sometimes mental illnesses do not have a demonic cause but the psychologist should be open to the possibility that they do. One sign will often be found in conjunction with other signs and so if one finds an isolated case of one of these signs, he should not immediately conclude it is demonic. It usually takes some experience to discern when these signs are merely coming from a human spirit[177] and when they are coming from a demonic. Sometimes it will take a priest to be able to discern the matter since he has the grace of office which will aid him in that process. Psychologists, if they have no experience in these matters or have never diagnosed based upon the aforesaid signs (criteria), they should take counsel with a knowledgeable priest from time to time to ensure the accuracy of their diagnosis of the directee.

VII. Further Counsels Regarding the Demonic

There are times when the problems of a directee are more spiritual than

---

[174]Directees will often have false notions of faith. They must be counseled in its true nature so that their ideas of faith are not dominated by the idea that everything about God is pleasant *with respect to us*. While God in Himself is the most pleasant object, due to our imperfections, He can cause us great suffering, not out of an evil intention but for our own good. Just as an owl finds it painful to look at the noonday sun because his eyes are not properly disposed to it, so do we in our spiritual lives find true experiences of God often painful because we do not have perfect spiritual dispositions. Faith should not be coupled with emotional and sensible overtones.

[175]Genesis 3:15.

[176]Some virtues have no extreme, e.g. charity. Therefore, a psychologist must have a clear understanding of ALL of the virtues to ensure that they are not misdiagnosing an extreme, so to speak.

[177]See Aumann, *Spiritual Theology*, p. 413-415

psychological. In those cases, the psychologist should refer the directee to a knowledgeable priest who understands the spiritual mechanisms well and can thereby direct the person to overcome his problems. Psychologists should not assume the position of spiritual director, even though the temptation to do so will sometimes be great. If there are minor spiritual issues attached to the directee's main problem(s), the psychologist can be the primary director. If the problems, even the spiritual ones, clear up once the means the psychologist as a psychologist can use, there is no need to send the directee to a priest. At times, it may be advisable for the priest to make sure there are not other spiritual problems lurking about. The demonic will often tempt the psychologist to think that he can solve the person's problems, resulting in a blindness in his ability to see the true problems of the directee. Psychologists must be keenly aware of this and lead blameless and holy lives so that they are less likely to be influenced by the demonic.

St. Paul said, "where sin abounded, grace did more abound."[178] However, the converse, when understood properly, is also true: wherever good is done, be watchful, because the demons will seek to undermine the good work. Psychologists must recognize that their work is a good work, often rooted in the spiritual works of mercy. Therefore, they must be aware of and ask for God's and our Lady's protection of their work and those entrusted to their care, to keep the demonic at bay. Particular devotion to St. Michael and to one's own guardian angel is important for a psychologist.

There are other means of combating the demonic which both psychologist and directee can employ. Amorth talks about what is called self-liberation.[179] Since we have dominion over our bodies and especially if we are armed with sanctifying grace, we can perform what is basically a form of self-exorcism. This includes using Christ's words, "get behind me Satan"[180] and phrases to that effect. Whenever a person or directee is tempted, he should turn upon the demonic and reject its action upon him as has been discussed above. He must also turn to our Lady, St. Michael and his guardian angel in those moments to aid him. He must also never fail to thank them when the temptation passes so that in seeing the directee's gratitude, they will be all the more willing to aid him in the future. He must also throughout the day consign the care of his body to his guardian angel, St. Michael and our Lady so that they will watch over it and keep the demonic from acting upon it. This also is helpful for those who have demonically influenced dreams.

There is also a liberation by others who are not exorcists.[181] This includes everyone from priests who are not exorcists to holy laymen. This is important, because the psychologist must not only get the relatives and friends involved in praying for the

---

[178]Romans 5:20.

[179]Amorth, *An Exorcist: More Stories*, p. 99f (it is also touched upon now and again throughout the text).

[180]Matthew 16:23.

[181]Amorth, *An Exorcist: More Stories*, p. 101f. This is likewise discussed throughout the two texts of Amorth quoted in this chapter.

directee to merit the grace for his healing, they should also be encouraged to pray for the directee to secure his liberation, should the demonic be the source of the problem. Many exorcists testify to the efficacy of getting large numbers to pray for the liberation of those influenced by the demonic. While a psychological illness can be caused both by the demonic and our free choice and so the directee can be partly to blame, nevertheless, the friends and family should be counseled that there may be demonic influence and it may or may not be caused by the directee and so they should not judge him. Rather they should set about the task of offering up prayers, penances and good works to liberate the directee.

Lastly, there is the possibility of going to an exorcist. Amorth observes that this is not always necessary and that people should not burden the exorcists with those cases which can be liberated by the person himself or through the prayers of others.[182] In effect, sending a directee to an exorcist should only be done if the psychologist realizes that it is beyond his or others' capacities to deal with the directee.[183] Sometimes sending the directee to a priest without having to bother an exorcist will suffice.

In conclusion, psychologists must counsel the directee to take all of the ordinary means of sanctification to aid his liberation. Only when extraordinary means are necessary should he be sent to an exorcist. This leaves us with the conclusion that psychologists should not shy away from employing means to liberate directees from demonic influences. While prudence and moderation must be used, nevertheless, psychologists should not be deluded into thinking that it is not their place. God has brought the directee to the psychologist and the psychologist in the state of grace can merit grace for the directee. If the psychologist comes to knowledge of or suspects demonic influence, he has an obligation to take the ordinary means to help the directee. Failure to do so is a sin of omission.

While it is true that, until a psychologist is properly informed, he may want to wait a bit so that he does not cause greater problems, nevertheless once knowledgeable, he should not hesitate. To do so is against charity in relation to the directee. On the other hand, every psychologist has a grave obligation, due to the fact that mental illness can be caused by the demonic, to come to a sufficient knowledge about demonic influences. This requires going beyond what is covered here by reading texts of good exorcists. In order to make the most profit of their time and to avoid curiosity, psychologist should avoid, in the beginning, reading and viewing media which sensationalizes these matters. It can often confuse and even sow scepticism if the psychologist cannot judge the more extreme accounts and behavior of the demonic without a foundation in the principles behind their activity.

---

[182]Amorth *An Exorcist: More Stories*, p. 93.

[183]However, psychologists should be very reserved about judging their own abilities.

Conclusion

All of the sacred causes discussed in this volume have God as their finality. Other spiritual causes which are not sacred, e.g. the demonic, have as their finality a deviation from God. This final deviation from God is the eternal punishment of hell in which perfect mental illness is had. Those who die in the state of mortal sin enter hell[1] and, as a result, are permanently cut off from the Object of happiness.[2] The condemnation to hell also includes the eternal company of Satan[3] who is permanently bent on evil. Just as evil is irrational, so the eternal company of Satan will consist of an eternity around those who are irrational. Since hell consists in being permanently cut off from the good, rationality, which is a good, is absent from those who are in hell. For this reason hell is a place of perfect insanity.

Those who are in hell now (i.e. those who are in hell prior to the resurrection) suffer from perfect insanity, not only in the realm of *per se* mental illness but also *per accidens* mental illness. As to *per accidens* mental illness, the will is perfectly bent on evil and the person is not able to will the good. This means that the will moves the possible intellect always towards false judgment, except in those things pertaining to one's punishment. The possible intellect knows and cannot reject the rectitude of God's condemnation of the soul. It recognizes that the person is in hell and that it is fundamentally disordered. Yet, on matters pertaining to the truth, the possible intellect remains confused. This is for several reasons. The first is that all divine light has been retracted and only the dim natural light of reason remains. The second is that the natural law is still in place insofar as man has natural inclinations.[4] These natural inclinations along with the permanent disorder of the faculties to falsity and evil conflict the soul. Moreover, there is no freedom anymore since the will is permanently inclined toward the apparent good,[5] i.e. towards evil.

At the resurrection of the body, the physical faculties will be recouped and so the punishment of hell will extend to these faculties. In addition to the senses being tortured, the interior senses are likewise disordered, i.e *per accidens* mental illness in these faculties is complete except, again, to the extent that their right functioning is

---

[1]Athanasian Creed (Denz. 76/40). See also Ott, *Fundamentals of Catholic Dogma*, p. 479ff.

[2] That condemnation to hell is permanent, see the fourth Lateran council, *De fide catholica* (Denz. 801/429). See also Ott, *Fundamentals of Catholic Dogma*, p. 481f

[3]See the fourth Lateran council, *De fide catholica* (Denz. 801/429).

[4]These natural inclinations remain since human nature in hell is not changed. Some comments here are the author's own speculation.

[5]The will still has a natural inclination toward the universal good, but since the will has become permanently fixed on evil, the will becomes fixed on the good only under the appearance of the apparent good.

ordered toward punishment.[6] However, it would seem that outside that context, their disorder would afflict the soul. It would seem that the common sense power simply does not function rightly and so confusion in the imagination will occur since the sense data will not be properly timed.[7] Right timing would occur only to further torture the soul. The image in the imagination would be confused, not only from the common sense power, but because the cogitative power would not associate rightly, i.e. it would be subject to fixations on evil things. The memory would repeatedly draw up the evils of the person's life as well as the memories which would be placed there during the suffering in hell. In this respect, the suffering of hell is compounded, i.e. at least in memory.[8] The disorder in the imagination would consist in the person lacking any control over the imagination except when the person wishes to formulate some evil which compounds the suffering. Also, the appetites will be completely disordered in which the soul will vacillate between the negative passions of hate, flight,[9] sorrow, despair and anger.[10] These appetites will have a strength not experienced in this life since the resurrected body can sustain greater torture and motion since it is incorruptible. The limits of the body are extended and so the passion will be more vehement since they operate through a bodily organ. The passions will hold the imagination captive and the person will not experience any freedom regarding the passions. Judgment will be completely precipitated and the will will not have any choice but to follow the passions.

Mental illness, as we have described it in the prior volume and this one, is a precursor to eternal damnation. This does not mean that someone who is mentally ill will necessarily be damned, but that it is a manifestation of the reign of hell. Just as the demons can act upon our bodies in this life, so the damned in hell will suffer constant torture and humiliations by their attendant demons.[11] They can act, not only upon the lower psychological faculties, but upon the body as a whole. Hence, the person will not

---

[6]For example, one may experience a phantasm which is true in relation to the image of oneself but is done in order to torture the possible intellect (conscience) through judgment.

[7]Granted that time will come to an end, there is still a sequence of events in the aevum as is evidenced in the book of the Apocalypse.

[8]Conversely, the joy in heaven is compounded, at least in memory.

[9]One will experience this passion but it will never reach its goal.

[10]Anger will be experienced even though the desire for vindication will more than likely always be in vain. It may occur that if a soul is placed in charge of torturing other souls that there is some vindication on that level. However, the delight in the vindication would really be a malicious delight which in the end would make the person's experience of the delight mixed and unpleasant, since truly evil delights are always mixed with something unpleasant.

[11]It is not clear but likely that those humans that have a lower place in hell will have power over those who have a higher place (this follows since the hierarchy in hell is inverted). It may be the case that humans in hell can also torture other humans in this fashion.

have control over what the demons make him do. Again, hell is the place of perfect insanity. Here we see how aiding the mentally ill in this life so that they are not inhibited in pursuing the Object of perfect happiness is a profound spiritual work of mercy.

The Catholic faith also teaches us that those who die in the state of grace but are not perfect, must go to purgatory to be purged, (a) of any venial sins that they may have,[12] (b) any disorders in the faculties which they may have which are a result of the voluntary[13] and (c) of the temporal punishment due to sin.[14] Yet, since purgatory is designed to purge the soul of any imperfections so that it has perfect rectitude of will and disposition on the side of the intellect to see God Face to face, then purgatory directly aids mental health. On one level, at the particular judgment, God will communicate His knowledge of the person to him. This provides the person a perfect knowledge of what his defects are so that when he is in purgatory he desires to be freed from the problems which affect him. Hence, in purgatory, if there is any mental illness which is the result of the person's voluntary action, the mental illness will be purified from the soul. This is a great hope for those who struggle in this life. If they make sure that they die in the state of grace, even if they are unable to overcome their mental illness in this life, they know they will be freed from it in the next.

Heaven, the final end of man, is the place of perfect mental health. We saw in the first chapter that man's finality was set out, i.e. man is ordered toward the beatific vision. All spiritual means are ordered toward this end. In this respect, we see that God actively seeks the salvation of the soul and its perfect happiness. Psychologists must recognize that all of the spiritual means in this text lead to the ultimate end of man and that mental illness is a hindrance to that end.[15] Yet, the spiritual means have as their effect the begetting of mental health in some way. While this is not their primary effect, it is, nevertheless, an important one. The primary effect is to bring the person to God, i.e. to heaven where the beatific vision is enjoyed.

Prior to the resurrection, the possible intellect and will have perfect rectitude as was discussed in the chapter on happiness. In heaven, the person has perfect

---

[12] Ott, *Fundamentals of Catholic Dogma*, p. 482-485. This would also apply to mortal sins for which the person was not held culpable, e.g if someone goes to Confession in the state of mortal sin and confesses the sin with contrition and the priest fails to give absolution. The person is no longer held accountable for the sin (the priest is in this case).

[13] This is the punishment due to sin which is the result of the evil effects of sin.

[14] Ott, loc. cit. This is the retributive justice required to pay back to God for the detraction from His glory in the created order. One must do something to make up for that detraction.

[15] The layout of this text has a specific order. The first is the order of apprehension in which it is necessary to apprehend the end, i.e. the final end is delineated. Then the means to the end are discussed in the order of apprehension and execution. Finally, the fruit of the order of execution is discussed, i.e. the end which was first conceived. In the case of man, it is the ultimate end, i.e. the beatific vision.

beatitude which excludes any suffering that could arise from mental illness. Therefore, mental illness is incompatible with life in heaven. There cannot be any *per se* mental illness in heaven. There cannot be *per accidens* mental illness in heaven with regards to the will, since perfect rectitude of the will is required to enter heaven, i.e. to see God Face to face. This also means that the will in heaven enjoys the greatest amount of freedom. This follows from the fact that the possible intellect has perfect knowledge and the will has perfect rectitude and so no evil habits will inhibit the will.

After the resurrection, there will be perfect *per accidens* mental health in the lower faculties. All of the physical faculties will enjoy the attributes of the resurrected body.[16] These attributes render the lower faculties in a state where they perfectly adhere to the will of the person. Hence, those in heaven will have effective despotic control over the passions. The cogitative power will associate perfectly and without fixation. The memory will be purged and with each new experience in heaven the memories will be increased and so the appetitive delight in heaven will increase, at least accidentally.[17] The imagination will be perfectly under the control of reason and will. St. Thomas observes that the lower faculties participate in the beatific vision, not because they will see God, but because of the principle of redundancy which has been mentioned often in these two volumes. The formality of the beatific vision in the possible intellect will flow over into the lower faculties causing a form of appetitive delight incapable of being experienced in this life. The appetites, therefore, will also be perfectly ordered and only the positive passions will be experienced, at least this would seem to be the case. All of these considerations provide hope and joy to those who consider them and directees can be assured that, if they reach heaven, they will enjoy perfect mental health.

The science of psychology can learn a great deal from theology. Psychology can benefit from the knowledge of the sacred causes as well as from the sacred causes themselves. Theology also gives a proper finality to the science of psychology, i.e. God. In the end, mental health must be sought for the sake of God. If the directee can realize this and strive for God, the imperfect beatitude in this life will lighten the burden of his mental illness. Even if he never overcomes the mental illness in this life, his life will have a proper direction. He can be assured of eventual freedom from the mental illness if he dies in the state of grace and enjoy the hope that comes from that knowledge. Theology also gives a proper direction or finality to the psychologists' practice since they realize that, in the end, it is not about them or even the directees but about God. Their desire to help directees, if based in charity, will be to their eternal merit, whether they help to heal the directee's mental illness or not. By ordering their practice through charity, they will do the will of God and graciously accept what God gives them regarding the fruit of their labor. Whether they heal a directee or not will not be the deciding factor regarding their practice. Rather, whether they have done the will of God

---

[16] The attributes of the resurrected body are impassibility, subtility, agility and clarity. See Ott, *Fundamentals of Catholic Dogma*, p. 491f.

[17] It cannot increase essentially since the appetites insofar as they are created and material have a limit to their motion.

and moved the directee in the direction of God will be the factor upon which the success of their practice will be based. While normally it is the will of God that people do not suffer mental illness, sometimes God will allow the mental illness for the spiritual benefit of the directee. Yet, the psychologist will be properly detached in knowing that if he helps the directee to get to heaven, he will be freed from the mental illness. The psychologist should hope and work for that goal in this life, but the detachment and charity will reward the psychologist with peace, knowing that perfect mental health will come in the next, should the directee save his soul.

Vol. 3: Quodlibetal Issues and Practica

In honorem omnium angelorum

Part I:
Quodlibetal Issues

Chapter 1: Bodily Transmutations

In volume one,[1] it was observed that we can often change our bodily disposition by what we think and will. We are able to reformulate the image in our imagination and thereby affect passion, which in turn causes chemical and biological changes. Modern psychological and physiological studies are bearing this out more and more. In a study conducted by Ruben Gur, a professor of neuropsychology at the University of Pennsylvania, differences in the brain were noted in those who tell lies:

> Scans of the volunteers' brains during the deceptive periods revealed increased activity in multiple areas. The most significant was the anterior cingulate cortex – a small brain structure that looks like the two halves of an apple, some three inches behind the middle of the forehead. It is involved in such cognitive processes as paying attention, making judgments – and inhibiting a person's responses. Another active area was the left pre-motor cortex, which is a few inches inside the skull near the left ear. The area was partly activated because subjects had to respond to the computer by pressing a button. But the area also overlaps the prefrontal cortex, which is known to be involved in making inhibitory decisions.[2]

From a Thomistic point of view, lying is a volitional act since it includes an intention to deceive[3] which is something pertaining to the will. Moreover, in the process of lying the person first grasps the truth and their will moves the intellect to falsify the phantasm by reformulating the image. It is from this image that the words which constitute a lie are spoken. Since the intellect is ordered toward knowing the truth, which is part of the natural law, to lie is contrary to the natural law. The material component of the various faculties of man are designed to execute actions in accord with the natural law. When we act contrary to the natural law, there are some changes, or more accurately, some indispositions, which are caused in the lower faculties. This being the case, it would appear that every form of sin causes material indispositions in the body. In the future, as the studies become more extensive and are applied to different species of actions, it may be possible to verify that all sin causes some physiological damage. Obviously, this would be by degree, where some sins cause very little damage, while others cause great harm.

In a study conducted by Dr. Vincent Mathews of the University of Indiana Medical School in Indianapolis, a correlation between video violence and brain activity

---

[1]See volume one passim. (but especially chapter nine).

[2]See article written by Shakar Vedantam in the *Washington Post*, November 12, 2001, entitled, "Telling Lies Produces Changes in Brain, Researchers Find."

[3]See ST II-II, q. 110.

was noted:

> The researchers also found that among subgroups of the nonaggressive adolescents there were differences in brain function dependent upon the amount of previous violent media exposure. Control subjects with high violent media exposure had different brain activation patterns than control subjects with low violent media exposure. "There may actually be a difference in the way the brain responds depending on the amount of past violent media exposure through video games, movies and television," Dr. Mathews explained.[4]

Since exposing oneself to violent media is normally done within the domain of the voluntary, one can, by one's volitional acts, change the disposition of one's brain. From these two studies, we can see that this change in the material disposition of the brain and body may occur in two ways. The first is by what one commands volitionally, as in the case of lying, or in the case of reformulating the image, which causes passion. The second is by volitionally exposing the psychological faculties to sensory data, such as violent media, which then causes changes to the psychological faculties. We can see therefore that it is possible to change one's disposition directly by what one wills and indirectly by willing a thing which causes a later effect.

Would one develop the same physiological changes if one were involuntarily exposed to the same violent media (for example) or some other thing which has the capacity to cause changes? Aside from agents which work directly on one physiologically, such as medications and other chemicals, it is unlikely that exposure to those things which can cause such changes would have the same degree of effect on the psychological faculties. While it is probably the case that it would always have some degree of effect, nevertheless, since the cogitative power and lower faculties are aware of the confirmation of reason and will before they give themselves to something fully, it is unlikely that one who is involuntarily exposed to something would experience the same degree of effect.

Chapter 2: Music

St. Thomas observes that "musical instruments move the soul more to pleasure (delight) rather than form a good interior disposition."[5] This indicates two things. The first is that music does not form a good disposition. By this it would appear that St. Thomas means that the principal effect of music is not to cause a dispositional change

---

[4]Press release on December 2, 2002, by the Radiological Society of North America entitled "Violent Video Games Trigger Unusual Brain Activity in Aggressive Adolescents."

[5]ST II-II, q. 91, a. 2, ad 4: "musica instrumenta magis animum movent ad delectationem quam per ea formetur interius bona dispositio."

in the person. Although we do say that "music soothes the savage beast" which can mean that when one is disposed one way (e.g. to anger) it is possible to dispose the person in another way (e.g. towards the passion of love) through the pleasure of music. Today, with the capabilities of high powered amplification, music can be used to cause physiological changes in the body by the power of the vibrations acting upon the body. These vibrations can also cause pleasure independently of the auditory aspect of music.[6]

The second aspect of this quote is that music causes pleasure. Since music is something auditory, i.e. sensory, it enters into the imagination and causes pleasure. This pleasure may be of two kinds. The first is appetitive, insofar as the music moves the sensitive appetites.[7] Different kinds of music tend to elicit different kinds of appetites. Some music moves the concupiscible appetite to love, as when we see that some music moves people to be more amorous. Some music moves the irascible appetite, e.g. certain forms of military music incite the soldiers to fight harder. Horror movies make use of certain kinds of instruments and music to elicit the passion of fear in the audience. In fact, the modern movie industry is a testimony to the profound grasp man has of the ability of music to elicit any kind of passion. This artistic ability is a particularly strong psychological force when it accompanies the right kinds of images.[8]

Because music enters the imagination, it has the ability to affect not just the appetites but the cogitative power as well, particularly when the music evokes an emotional or appetitive reaction. As the person experiences the passion evoked by the music, the cogitative power associates that form of music with the pleasure of the passion. Hence, when someone listens to music often, the cogitative power becomes habituated to assessing the music in a positive fashion due to the pleasure. This positive assessment is then merged with the image and thereby affects the judgement of the possible intellect. It is for this reason that people will often say that a particular form of music is "good" even though it can be morally degenerate.[9] If the music is listened to enough and if it is disordered but still gives pleasure, it is possible for the music to habituate the possible intellect according to virtue or vice. In effect, music can cause *per se* mental health or illness. Music can also affect memory insofar as the experience of the music is stored in memory and music can leave either good or bad impressions of an experience based upon which passion the music elicited. Music, since it can affect judgment, can also affect volition and here we see that music can have a direct impact on the moral life of the individual. Because it can affect the faculties other than the

---

[6]In Schellenberg, Liechtenstein at a local church, there exists a bell tower in which the bell and tower are designed to create a resonance at the base of the tower. The effect of the design is that it can cause physical pleasure by the vibrations to the one standing next to it.

[7]*In Psalmos*, p. 32, n. 2: "item consonantiae musicae immutant hominis affectum."

[8]Images can affect how we judge the music and the music can affect how we judge and appetitively react to a particular image.

[9]How music affects morals will become clear throughout this chapter.

possible intellect, music can cause *per accidens* mental health and illness.[10]   In this sense, the use of music can cause (aid) mental health or destroy it.[11]

Because music affects the irascible and concupiscible appetites, teens and even adults can become attached to musical forms which elicit the emotions. For example, soft rock tends to affect the concupiscible appetite while hard rock or acid rock tends to elicit irascible passions. Because of the instability of the emotional life of teens due to the dispositional changes in the body arising from puberty, for the sake of the mental health of teens, music to which they listen should be regulated by their parents. When teens are allowed to listen to whatever form of music they want in the amount that they want, their mental health is affected thereby. This does not mean that they will be gravely affected, but they may.

Plato observes:

> But, as things are with us, music has given occasion to a general conceit of universal knowledge and contempt for law, and liberty has followed in their train. Fear was cast out by confidence in supposed knowledge, and the loss of it gave birth to impudence. For to be unconcerned for the judgment of one's betters in the assurance which comes of a reckless excess of liberty is nothing in the world but reprehensible impudence.[12]

Because music gives pleasure, if one gives oneself over to it without restraint, it tends to take on a life of its own. In other words, license regarding the pleasure of music leads to license in other areas of one's life. As a result, those who seek to restrict one's license are judged with contempt, e.g. those in authority and laws themselves. Parents will often find that a teenager who listens to music without restriction becomes difficult to handle and unruly. This is why Plato thought that music had to be regulated by the state, because it constituted such a powerful (psychological) force.

Implicit in this discussion is the fact that, since music has the ability to affect the appetites, it has the ability to corrupt the virtues of temperance and fortitude in an

---

[10] St Thomas observes (In Psalmos, p. 32, n. 2) that " Pythagoras, seeing that the young are made insane by the Phrygian sound, he changed the mode, so the soul of a mad adolescent is tempered to the state of peaceful mind, as Boethius says in the proemium to his music" (Unde Pythagoras videns quod juvenis insaniret ad sonum phrygium, mutari modum fecit; ita furentis adolescentis animum ad statum mentis pacatissimae temperavit, ut dicit boetius in proemio musicae suae.).

[11] The use of music in psychological warfare indicates that when the music is played at a high volume with specific kinds of melodies, it can have a destabilizing effect on the listener, especially when he does not exercise control over the music. Essentially, this indicates that the music affects the imagination and the cogitative power which in turn affects his judgment and volition.

[12] Plato, *Laws III* (701a and b).

individual. If a person does not listen to rightly ordered music or does not moderate his listening to music and the pleasure taken therein, it can corrupt temperance and make him intemperate. Likewise, since fortitude is a virtue lying in a mean between the excess of rashness and the defect of cowardice,[13] music which moves the irascible appetite excessively can corrupt fortitude. In like manner, if one listens to music for the sake of pleasure and does so without restraint, he will become attached to the pleasure and be unwilling to engage the arduous good which requires pain. As a consequence, one may become cowardly. Based on this analysis, it can even be said that license in the area of the pleasures of music can lead to effeminacy.[14] Effeminacy is a sorrow and an unwillingness to be separated from pleasure in order to pursue the arduous.[15] If males do not moderate the pleasures of music, they can become attached to them and thereby become effeminate.

Connected to the discussion of how music can corrupt virtues, we may say that music does not only have the capacity to corrupt temperance and fortitude but also prudence. This should be clear from the words of Plato above. However, since intemperance can affect one's judgment regarding what is prudent, if one is intemperate about the pleasures of music, this will lead to imprudence. Since prudence is an act of the possible intellect in which the universally known principles are applied in the concrete,[16] prudence requires rectitude of the phantasm by which the person is put into contact with the singular concrete circumstances. If intemperance (also affecting the assessment of the cogitative power) affects the phantasm, it will have the effect of drawing reason to excess and defect regarding its judgments. Therefore, prudence which requires coming to the knowledge of the mean in regard to actions will be corrupted by excesses in judgment.

If the pleasures of music can corrupt prudence, they can also corrupt the virtue of decorum. Decorum is the virtue by which one moderates one's externals.[17] Externals are of different kinds, including things such as dress, actions and possessions. Decorum is the virtue by which we moderate our dress in two ways. The first is to modesty[18] by which one takes due solicitude about not drawing others into sins of impurity. The second is more proper to decorum itself insofar as one's dress fits one's circumstances and one's state in life, e.g. decorum is the virtue which regulates doctors wearing a proper attire when practicing medicine or a priest wearing clerics when in public. But decorum also ensures that we do not go to excess in our dress, e.g. if a person were to wear very expensive clothing and jewelry to an informal dinner, his dress would not fit the circumstances. In this respect, the pleasure of music affects the judgment of the

---

[13]ST II-II, q. 123, a. 3.

[14]See Cole, *Music and Morals*, p. 25.

[15]See ST II-II, q. 138, a. 1.

[16]ST II-II, q. 47, a. 6.

[17]See ST II-II, q. 143, a. 1.

[18]See ST II-II, q. 168.

person and corrupts prudence regarding dress, i.e. it corrupts decorum. This is why those in the rock music scene tend towards immodesty in dress. It is also why some of the them tend toward piercing of body parts which are not suited by their nature to being pierced, e.g. the tongue. It is why they tend to "make a statement" by their dress as well. We also see the connection to Plato's observation that they will tend to reject authority and laws and their dress is often seen as a statement against the rules and customs of a society.

Decorum also moderates our external actions so that our actions fit the circumstances and our state in life. For instance, children who have not reached the age of reason and therefore are not yet capable of developing the virtues, tend to say things out of place which are often very embarrassing to the parents. In like manner, when one does not moderate the pleasures of music, it tends to affect one's exterior behavior. Since prudence is affected, the person will often judge based upon the pleasure of the moment rather than what right reason would dictate. Since a person can become habituated to judge according to pleasure by not moderating the pleasures of music, he will tend to act out according to the pleasures of the passions rather than according to reason. The manifestation of this problem is seen when teens and adults who listen to appetitive music without moderation tend to act erratically or irrationally. It is also manifest in their lack of reverence for elders, parents and authority figures in general. This is why there is a close connection between sex, drugs and rock and roll.[19] Each gives a form of pleasure and each constitutes something to which one can become addicted. While addiction to the pleasures of music may be less culturally unacceptable, nevertheless it does exhibit a lack of the virtue of temperance.

While appetitive pleasure is the first kind of pleasure which is caused by music, the second kind of pleasure which music gives is intellective pleasure. Beauty is that which is pleasing to a cognitive faculty.[20] In this respect, if music is truly beautiful, it is pleasing to the possible intellect. We must clearly distinguish between the pleasure that arises out of music which appeals to the sensitive appetites and the pleasure which the intellect obtains in the consideration of the harmony, clarity and perfection of the music. Beauty also draws one to contemplation.[21] When a beautiful woman walks into a room, the men there will tend to be drawn to look at her and watch her as she walks around the room. Conversely, an ugly woman tends not to draw the same consideration. When music is beautiful, it can draw one to contemplation, i.e. it tends to draw one toward an interior intellectual reflection.

If music is beautiful, it can enhance intellectual activity to which it is joined. Therefore music which moves the intellect to a consideration of the thing to which the music is joined can aid study and learning. St. Thomas says in the *Summa Theologiae:*

---

[19]Sometimes sex, drugs and rock and roll are done together at the same time in order for the person's experience of each to be enhanced.

[20]ST I-II, q. 27, a. 1, ad 3: "Ad vim cognoscitivam, ita quod bonum dicatur id quod simpliciter complacet appetitui; pulchrum autem dicatur id cuius ipsa apprehensio placet."

[21]Coffey, *Ontology*, p. 193ff.

> it is the same reason to the hearers, in which, although sometimes they may not understand what is sung, nevertheless they understand because (*propter quid*) it is sung, namely to the praise of God.[22]

A person may understand what is sung and the music enhances his understanding by joining music to the thing of consideration which provides more information about the thing considered. For example, if a person watches a sad scene in a movie, he knows it is something of sorrow, but when sorrowful music is joined to it, it increases his understanding of the evil or sorrow. Even if the person does not understand what is sung, e.g. a person may not understand the words of Latin in Gregorian chant, he can nevertheless recognize in the harmony and melody of the music, what the music is saying or how it is directing our consideration. For instance, the glory of God is reflected by a particular mode of Gregorian Chant or the seriousness of final judgment is reflected in the mode or tones of the *Dies Irae*. Conversely, if the music is too appetitive, i.e. it elicits emotions more than intellectual contemplation, or if the music lacks beauty,[23] it can detract from the consideration of the truth and from contemplation. Ugly music can distract one from study, learning and prayer.[24]

Modern studies are discovering that the playing of music can contribute to learning. Playing music increases intelligence by stimulating certain parts of the brain.[25] Other studies are finding that musical training increases math ability, i.e. it increases the person's ability to engage in spatial-temporal reasoning.[26] The Scholastics held that the study of music is a subalternated science (and art) to mathematics,[27] so they knew that learning music has a connection to intellectual formation.

Since music can draw us to contemplation or move our emotions, it constitutes a force by which people can be directed. St. Thomas observes:

> the affections of man are directed by instrumental and harmonious

---

[22]ST II-II, q. 91, a. 2, ad 5: "Et eadem est ratio de audientibus, in quibus, etsi aliquando non intelligant quae cantantur, intelligunt tamen propter quid cantantur, scilicet ad laudem Dei."

[23]While beautiful music can elicit emotions, generally speaking, it appears that music which lacks beauty tends to be more appetitive.

[24]Students are known to listen to appetitive forms of music while studying. This is often done to provide appetitive pleasure to the arduous task of studying. However, the pleasures of the music are not ordered toward the things studied and therefore tend to distract more than enhance studying.

[25]Jim Wilson, *Cognitive Chords*, as found on 10/1/03 on the website of *Popular Mechanics* at http://www.popularmechanics.com/science/research/2002/3/cognitive_chords/index.phtml.

[26]*fMRI Study of Correlation between Musical Training and Math Ability*, as found on 10/1/03 at http://www.irc.chmcc.org/Research_Areas/brain/fMRI/musicmathcorr.htm.

[27]See *In libros physicorum*, l. 1, c. 2, n. 4.

music in three ways: sometimes it establishes a certain rectitude and strength of the soul; sometimes one is drawn up into the heights; sometimes into sweetness and delight.[28]

The soul of the person is directed by music in three ways. The first is that it tends to strengthen the soul and directs it in the right thing. Plato says that the purpose of music is to take pleasure and pain in the right things.[29] Since music can affect judgment, it is clear that music can be used to direct people to the truth and to judge things rightly, not only in the speculative order but also in the practical order. Music can be used to move people to judge prudently[30] and if it can affect prudence, music can be used to develop virtue by moving people to perform acts of virtue. It is for this reason that Aristotle says that music forms character.[31] This forming of character can be done by directing the appetitive life of people to virtue. Music can also be used to portray character,[32] e.g. when we see a stern and evil man portrayed by low menacing tones. This also contributes to the building of character since people can be drawn to judge based upon virtue and vice rather than on the mere pleasure of the music.

Plato even says that music can be used to represent the masculine and the feminine.[33] If music is joined to the right kinds of imagery, it is possible for the music to directly contribute to the mental distinctions that people make about masculine and feminine character, both as to what is unsuited to those characters and what is suited to them.

> It will further be necessary to make a rough general distinction between two types of songs, those suited for females and those suited for males, and so we shall have to provide both with their appropriate scales and rhythms. ... Now it is perfectly possible to make the necessary regulations for both kinds of songs in both respects, but natural distinction of sex, which should therefore be our basis for discrimination. Accordingly, we shall pronounce the majestic and whatever tends to valor masculine, while it will be the tradition of our law and our theory alike that what makes rather for order and purity

---

[28]*In Psalmos*, p. 32, n. 2: "Affectus enim hominis per instrumenta et consonantias musicas dirigitur, quantum ad tria: quia quandoque instituitur in quadam rectitudine et animi firmitate: quandoque rapitur in celsitudinem: quandoque in dulcedinem et jucunditatem." See also ST II-II, q. 91, a. 2.

[29]Plato, *Laws II* (659d).

[30]In Job, c. 21.

[31]Aristotle, *Politics*, l. VIII, chap. 5 (1339a12-1340b19). We can say not only does it form character in a positive sense but as was seen above it can also form character in a negative sense.

[32]Aristotle, *Poetics*, chap. 1 (1447a27).

[33]Plato, *Laws II* (669c).

is peculiarly feminine.[34]

Since masculinity and femininity are accentuated by the stressing of different traits, music can contribute to the forming of masculine and feminine character. Previously, it was noted that listening to music without moderation regarding the pleasures of the music can lead to effeminacy. We see that this is the case with men. If men are forced to embrace or listen to forms of music which are more active on the concupiscible appetite than the irascible appetite and the intellect, it will have a feminizing effect on them. Not that they can never listen to such forms, but their listening must be more moderated and directed intellectually, so as not to have a feminizing effect on the men. Conversely, women who tend to listen to masculine music too much may take on characteristics proper only to men. Again, not that they cannot listen to them, but that they must be moderated and intellectually directed. Given normal, virtuous women and men, they will tend toward those forms of music in congruity with dispositions of their gender.

Yet, it should not be assumed that music is unmanly. Since it can form character by forming virtue, music can be manly. Virtue tends to temper the soul and moderate it, both with women and men. Plato observes that, if one never listens to music, it makes one hard and savage and yet, if one listens to music too much, it can make one soft and gentle.[35] The pleasures of music can have a tempering effect, not only on men but women. Yet, due solicitude must be taken to ensure that the pleasures of music neither make men effeminate nor cause lack of temperance in women.

We can begin to see why Plato said that it is false that the standard for good music is whether it causes pleasure.[36] Rather, music, which is part of the divine providential plan, is ordered toward the good of the soul, i.e. towards rectitude and strength of soul (virtue). The criteria for good music and bad music cannot be based purely upon the fact that a particular form causes pleasure. Such a position is nothing short of hedonism. Rather, good and bad music must be judged based on two distinct criteria. The first is its artistic merit, i.e. some music is more beautiful than others and some music is more capable of directing the appetitive life than others. The second is the moral character: those forms of music which tend to erode moral virtue, either because of their lyrics or because of their melody and musical quality constitute a danger to people's souls and their psychological health. Those forms of music which tend to build moral virtue are good insofar as their lyrics and musical style promote what is noble in man and in God's creation. Insofar as it contributes to moral virtue and even intellectual virtue, music aids psychological health.[37]

The second way in which music directs the soul, according to St. Thomas, is

---

[34]Plato, *Laws VII* (802e).

[35]Plato, *Republic III* (410c).

[36]Plato, *Laws II* (655d).

[37]It is possible to have morally bad lyrics with morally good harmony and vice versa. However, such music is inherently disordered.

that it draws one up into the heights. By this, St. Thomas means that it tends to lift the soul to the consideration of those things which are above him. In this respect, music can lift the soul away from earthly things to heaven.[38] Music incites one to devotion and in this respect is good for weak souls.[39] Music can be used to incite man to God[40] and so music can aid man's happiness by helping him advance towards his final end. Rightly ordered music can contribute to the building of the virtue of religion. Music of this kind is inherently beneficial psychologically. It can provide order to the soul, thereby bringing peace and directing one towards the object of perfect beatitude. On the other hand, we may say that music which tends to appetitive disorder detracts one from the final end and results in the person and society imbued with that form of music being drawn towards unhappiness, lack of peace (strife) and disorder.

Yet, because music can aid us in attaining our final end, we can see why St. Thomas says that the third way that music directs the soul is by sweetness and delight. This has already been seen with respect to the intellectual and appetitive pleasure given by music. Since music affects the various faculties of the soul, it has an ability to cause spiritual joy (by lifting one's mind and heart to the Object of joy which is God) and delight of the soul (by seeing the goodness of God as reflected in the perfections of the harmony of the music).[41]

Music, again, constitutes a powerful psychological force which can be used for the good or for the bad. Psychologists must be keenly aware of the kinds of music to which the directee is listening to ensure that the music is not contributing to his problem. Conversely, the psychologist may want to prescribe various forms of music to combat the particular psychological problem or vice the person is facing. In cases where the psychological problem arises out of or is exacerbated by both the kind and amount of music to which the directee listens, the psychologist may wish to tell the directee that he must remove all music or the forms of music causing his difficulty. This will have an immediate pacifying effect. Parents and psychologists may notice a drop in the disordered actions of the child. In effect, removing disordered music will restore basic decorum to the child or directee.

Psychologists must be aware of the psychological effects of the various forms of music so that they can make proper use of music in their practice. Directees must

---

[38]*In Psalmos*, p. 32, n. 2 and ST II-II, q. 91, a. 2. Given this, it would seem that certain kinds of music can contribute to the gift of the Holy Ghost of Fear of the Lord and even to Wisdom by disposing the soul to these gifts.

[39]ST II-II, q. 91, a. 2.

[40]*In Psalmos*, p. 32, n. 2.

[41]Pius XII, *Musicae Sacrae*, par. 4. Which music finds itself in religious ritual must not be based upon the pleasure it gives the congregation but upon whether it lifts the minds and souls of the congregation to God. It is very easy for musicians who are not properly refined or educated to assume that eliciting emotions from people is the same as causing a "religious experience." This is why pastors of souls must be very careful about the kinds of instruments and music allowed in church.

seek a proper detachment from music so as not to let the pleasures of music disorder them but have the proper ordering effect. Psychologists must also be aware of the fact that, because of human nature, we tend to take pleasure in those things that are according to our disposition. Therefore, when considering the psychological welfare of the directee, the psychologist will have to take into consideration the dispositions of the directee for two reasons. The first is to see whether certain kinds of music which may be prescribed may in fact act contrary to disposition and have a bad effect (it may also act contrary to disposition and have a good effect). The second is that they should not always allow directees to listen only to those forms of music which are according to their dispositions since it may aggravate their psychological problems, particularly if the psychological problems are in some way connected to their bodily disposition. Psychologists must also be aware that some people are more sensitive to music than others due to their dispositions.[42]

Lastly, regarding developmental psychology, since children tend to operate more on the level of the cogitative power and sensitive appetite rather than on the level of intellection and volition, psychologists and parents must be keenly aware of both the erosive and the ennobling effects of music in all of its forms. Parents must be judicious about the kinds of music to which their children listen and they must moderate the music both as to kind and amount to ensure that children develop proper character.

Chapter 3: Short and Long-Term Memory

Modern psychological as well as medical studies have discovered a distinction between, and some of the causes affecting, long-term and short-term memory. This is also manifested in those cases in which people suffer some form of head trauma and lose short-term memory but retain memories from their childhood or even adulthood. Deterioration in memory is caused by the passing of time which is the measurement of the change which causes the loss of memory[43] and so memory is affected by age. Yet memory can also be affected by pathological causes (such as Alzheimer's) which affect the material side of the faculty. Yet, both short-term and long-term memory can be affected by choices one makes, e.g. when one makes a choice, causing a rise in stress levels. The stress then causes physiological changes or has physiological effects which affect memory.

Memory can also be affected by passion[44] and, at times connected to this, memory can be affected by traumatic experiences. Often people will suffer amnesia when going through traumatic experiences. This mechanism can be physiological, insofar as stress levels or levels of passion, such as fear, etc., rise, causing biological and chemical changes which affect the memory. Yet, the physical mechanism of being unable to recall traumatic experiences or, in some cases, not only the traumatic

---

[42]Cole, *Music and Morals,* p. 13.

[43]See volume I, chapter 3 (II, 2, b).

[44]Ibid.

experience but also the time before and after the traumatic experience, appears to be from Divine Providence. The fact that memory lapses during traumatic experience actually reduce the stress and the trauma after the experience by not allowing strong images to be recalled from the imagination which could cause future problems for the individual. While the memory may store the information since at times it can be recalled via hypnosis,[45] the normal outcome is that the memory is not recalled. In the end, this mechanism contributes to the psychological health of the individual insofar as it reduces suffering the person would go through, by suppressing the imagery which can cause passions which would be difficult to control.

It is possible for a certain sorrow or frustration (anger) to arise due to the inability to recall something during that experience. However, the person should have a certain detachment from the experience and the memories. Reminiscence can be used to try to rebuild the memories, but due caution must be taken.[46] Sometimes memories will come back merely as one leads his life insofar as experiences can provide the sense data for the cogitative power to be able to make the associations and bring out the memory.

Chapter 4: Implicit Learning

One often notices that children will pick up the same mannerisms that the parents possess even though the parents do not "formally" teach the children those mannerisms by instructing them on how to engage in those mannerisms. In like manner, it is possible for children to pick up mental illnesses which are possessed by their parents. Common convention notices that spouses often become like each other in their mannerisms and actions.

There are several possible ways in which these mannerisms and mental illnesses can be received. The first is that the cogitative power is capable of learning without explicit teaching. When one's parents or spouse performs some actions according to a specific mannerism or as the result of mental illness, the memory stores those actions as a sensible species. Later a sensible species similar to the circumstances in which the parents or spouse performed that kind of action enters the imagination. The cogitative power then goes back into memory, sees the mannerism as associated with the sensible species and then brings that mannerism back into the imagination and merges it with the sensible species. The possible intellect then judges what to do based upon what is in the imagination and judges that the action is to be done according to the mannerisms of the parents. This is then proposed to the will and the will uses the lower faculties to execute the action. As the person frequently views the mannerisms or the actions pertaining to the mental illness of the spouse, the association of the cogitative power is trained toward that form of action. The cogitative power can learn these things without the person

---

[45]See chapter 8 on hypnosis.

[46]We have already warned about psychologists affecting the process of reminiscence in volume I, see chapter 3 (II, 2, c).

realizing it.[47]

Children can learn these things by watching them as they grow up and since children often do not know how to act on their own, they will tend to act according to the implicitly learned mannerisms of the parents. The actions of parents, whether virtuous or vicious, will have a formative effect on the passive intellect of the child and since the possible intellect depends on the passive intellect, it will affect the child's judgment, mental habits and even his choices. This is a good mechanism, however, insofar as the cogitative power can do a great deal of learning without the person being required to think about each step. Also, many things which children are not capable of doing on their own, they do see their parents doing. When it comes time for the child to do it, he will often have sufficient sense data in memory to be able to do what is necessary. This likewise applies to adults, particularly when learning physical actions or art. For instance, when an adult is taught how to use a keyboard on a computer, he often does not have to be taught much since he will have seen others using it prior to his own use. Learning how to play certain sports requires, aside from learning the rules of the sport, that one learn in this implicit manner by watching others engage in the sport. While refinement of the art or actions of the sport may require coaching, many of the actions associated with the sport are learned implicitly without the person ever thinking about it. This is why children can watch a game and then often run out and play it to a degree.

Another way in which children can pick up mental illnesses of parents is by someone inviting the demonic into the home. If a parent engages in some form of sinful action,[48] particularly the father who enjoys spiritual headship of the home,[49] the sinful action can invite the demonic into the home. The temptations which come from the demons to which the father or mother succumb can open the door to the demonic to affect those in the home. Hence, if the father has a severe chastity problem, the children may learn this explicitly, or implicitly as mentioned above or by means of the demonic in the home. Parents who have a spiritual authority over the home must be careful not to cede demonic influence into the home by their willingness to cooperate with the demons in sin.

Implicit learning has several implications. The first is that psychologists can take on the mannerisms or mental illnesses of their directees, if they are not careful and do not practice mental hygiene. This is done by sorting out the images in their imagination by means of judgment and will, so that the images are stored properly in their imaginations and the cogitative power is properly trained. Second, psychologists should not be surprised when the traits of mental illness are passed on within the home

---

[47]This will have much more significance in the discussion of the "subconscious" in chapter 6.

[48]This is particularly the case with witchcraft.

[49]See Ephesians 5:22f, Pope Pius XI, *Casti Connubii*, par. 26 and Leo XIII, *Arcanum divinae sapientiae*, par. 11, among others. All quotations from Scripture will be taken from the Douay Rheims.

to the directee. If the directee is a minor and the parents are unwilling to change their activities which are causing the implicit learning, not much can be done for the minor who will be around the activity most of the time. The parents must be willing to work on their own mental illnesses if they want the child to overcome his.

Psychologists should also not be surprised that women who were raised in abusive homes are attracted to abusive men. Since the child sees that husband/wife or boyfriend/girlfriend relationship in terms of abuse, the girl/boy will be attracted to those kinds of people. The cogitative power of the girl, when it views possible romantic involvement, does not know how to act on its own. As a result, the cogitative power assesses the image associated with romantic involvement based upon what is stored in memory regarding the parents. As a result, the natural inclinations toward romantic love will be skewed based upon what is stored in memory. This is also why women will go from abusive relationship to abusive relationship. Until they are taught differently (i.e. until their cogitative powers are trained differently) about the relationship of men and women, they will often not be able to break the cycle, since it is principally psychological.

A word of caution is due. There has been in vogue for some time now in American culture a practice of blaming one's parents for each and every problem that one has. While this may be legitimate in some cases for children prior to the use of reason, once the use of reason is obtained, the person becomes responsible (of course by degrees as one ages) for his own problems. Throughout this series, we have established that many mental illnesses fall within the domain of the voluntary. While children may not be as voluntary, once a person becomes an adult, it is up to him whether he will continue with the training of his parents, for good or ill. Therefore, a twenty year old cannot blame his parents for everything. Eventually he has to take responsibility for himself.

There are certain defects which we may have, caused either by original or actual sin or the training of our parents, which we are responsible for cleaning up. Even if someone else is to blame for some defect that we may have, it is our responsibility to clean it up, since the kind of person that we are is ultimately determined by our choices. We can choose to allow the defects of the parents to affect us or not. We can choose to accept the good training of our parents or not. At a certain point in a person's life, he becomes responsible for himself, whether or not he is a psychological mess. If he becomes aware of the defects his parents have bequeathed to him and he chooses to blame his parents and thereby do nothing about his own problems, he becomes responsible for the problems because he has allowed them to continue in himself under the ruse of blaming his parents. While overcoming the illness may not be easy, in the end, what he becomes is his own making. Likewise, if a child accepts the good training of his parents and builds virtue upon it, it is to his merit more so than the parents.

Chapter 5: Disconnected from Reality

The cogitative power has the ability to modify the sense species contained in the imagination by adding to the phantasm information from past experience as well as by assessing whether the phantasm is harmful or good. This ability of the cogitative power is necessary insofar as we could not learn, recognize things or people, gain prudence based on past experience, etc., without it. Yet, the cogitative power, if there is *per accidens* mental illness, can modify the sense species in such a way as to falsify the species and thereby make it impossible for the person to be in contact with reality. This is why habituation of the cogitative power is so important since, if there is any habit in the cogitative power which will assess or associate the wrong things with a phantasm, only judgment and volition can sort out the phantasm. But in many cases, the judgment follows the assessment and associations of the cogitative power. In a sense, when this occurs, people "live in their own reality," so to speak, since they are not in contact with reality.

This can be by degrees. For instance, someone who may suffer from the vice of lust will have an accompanying habit in the cogitative power which associates prior experiences with people of the opposite sex (the person remembers the pleasure or the experience of the past). At times, the person may not remember anything explicit about the past, but the cogitative power assesses the person of the opposite sex as good in the venereal sense and so the person suffering from lust will have phantasms that are not proportionate or adequated to those of the opposite sex. If judgment is habituated according to the vice, the phantasm will draw the possible intellect into a false judgment about the person. A life of the passions will cause this. The stronger the vice is, the stronger the passions will be. As a result, the more the cogitative power will be drawn into the assessments of those of the opposite sex according to the *ratio* or perspective of the vice of lust. Hence, the worse the vice, the more the phantasm will be assessed as good. Consequently, the more difficult it will be for the person to judge differently.[50] The stronger the vice, the less the person is able to remain in contact with reality. We may say that the cogitative power is able to modify the phantasm in a way which is not in congruity with reality.

However, we may go further and say that the cogitative power is actually able to alter the phantasm contrary to the sensed experience. That is to say that it is possible for the cogitative power to alter the image in the imagination based upon past experience or upon the dispositions of the passions. People often experience bad sensory events which, when they are in a good mood, do not seem as bad as when they are in a sorrowful mood. For example a boxer who may be angered by a foul during a boxing match which goes unpunished by the referee may be able to take more blows and fight with greater strength than one who may not be angered. After the fight, the boxer will indicate, even if it was a vicious boxing match, that from his perspective (after the anger) he did not notice the blows as much as he otherwise would have.

This ability of the cogitative power to modify the image has different parts. The cogitative power will be moved based upon the judgment, volition and the passion or the perspective placed in the imagination by the possible intellect and will. The cogitative power then associates and assesses based upon that perspective. But the

---

[50]The conclusions of chapter nine of volume one are particularly usefully to recall as to the influence of the passions over reason.

cogitative power can also disassociate insofar as it can divide the various sensible species in the phantasm from each other.[51] If the cogitative power has been trained or habituated in the past to divide specific kinds of sense species, when those sense species come into the imagination, one aspect of the sense species is divided out. In effect, the cogitative power alters the sense species based upon past sense experience.

This mechanism is necessary for man after the Fall. It is a mechanism which helps us to cope with difficult or bad situations by changing our perspective on the situation, thereby lifting some of the appetitive or intellectual burden from the situation. This makes suffering more tolerable. This mechanism is necessary for the day to day living of life which is often physically demanding and difficult. This mechanism is likewise necessary for passive and active mortification insofar as the person is able to look to the good effect that the mortification will bring about and thereby make the enduring of it easier. Since life can often be grueling and difficult, this mechanism is necessary to maintain mental health.

However, one must be careful with this mechanism, since it can also draw one out of contact with reality. This is why people, particularly children, who go through tragic or traumatic experiences, will sometimes escape into a "fantasy world." One will experience, by changing one's thoughts, that going through some traumatic experience like physical abuse does not seem to be as bad. The cogitative power learns that, when these traumatic experiences occur, the images should be modified or even switched to something different. Since the cogitative power can engage in a kind of reasoning process by which it modifies and changes the images,[52] it can draw one's attention away by changing to a completely different image. Those without adequate judgment (such as children prior to use of reason or before strong mental habits can be formed) are capable of slipping into a kind of dreaming to avoid the situation.

In one sense, this is not an explicit denial of reality even though the person may want to avoid the discussion of the traumatic experience. It may not be voluntary. Rather, it may be the effect of this mechanism drawing the person away from the traumatic experience by changing the phantasm as a form of flight. Since the cogitative power can assess something as harmful and also put the *ratio* of flight into it, the person may be involuntarily drawn out of contact with reality as a form of coping. As time progresses, the person may also do this as a form of seeking the security of pleasant phantasms. Those who engage in this due to some bad experience or even by choice may do so precisely because it is pleasant or it becomes easier for them to deal with a life which causes them great sorrow. Hence, for some, this disorder is chosen, though not explicitly. What is chosen is the avoidance of pain and the pleasantness of the escape. Those who wish to overcome this kind of difficulty can only do so by fostering a spirit of mortification, i.e. a willingness to suffer. They must also foster a detachment from the mental illness or disorder itself.

Once again it should be kept in mind that this mechanism can actually

---

[51]See volume one, chapter three (II, 4, a).

[52]See volume one, chapter three (II, 4, a).

contribute to mental health, if it is used to keep a proper perspective. For example, those who suffer are able, through this mechanism, to view the suffering or pain in a wider context, i.e. in the context of vicarious suffering, the short duration of this life, the possibilities of overcoming imperfections, etc. Often general principles in the possible intellect are unable to be applied in the particular due to suffering or passions. This mechanism helps one to keep a broader view of one's suffering or passions so that the general principles known to the possible intellect are able to be properly applied.

Thus, this mechanism can be good or bad, depending on whether judgment of reality is maintained or not. It is bad if it alters the sense species in such a way as to be contrary to the way things truly are. It is good if it alters the sense species in such a way as to provide a phantasm which is in more congruity with reality, not only of the amount of pain, suffering or passion, but to the broader context in which the possible intellect is able to see and apply general principles to the situation.

Every vice, every moral or spiritual defect is able to affect intellectual judgment in this manner. We can say that every vice has the ability to take one out of contact with reality. Every vice, therefore, is accompanied by a concomitant defect in the cogitative power. It appears that when the vice wanes, so does the bad habituation of the cogitative power. Hence, with each vice in the sensitive appetites, there is a concomitant *per accidens* mental illness in the passive intellect. But that does not mean that the person has a concomitant *per se* mental illness since judgment and volition, if not completely compromised, are able to overrule the operations of the cogitative power and reformulate the image properly.

When someone is overcoming mental illness, he often will not have the strength of will and judgment to be able to reformulate the image by judgment and volition. This is why one of the principal functions of a psychologist is to provide the right phantasm by which the judgment of the possible intellect of the directee can be corrected. In turn, the directee can reformulate his phantasms on his own later, thereby providing a way of overcoming his mental illness. As he does so, he will come into contact with reality and will experience a kind of clarity of mind in relation to his mental illness. The more he overcomes the vice, the more the bad habits in the cogitative power will be corrupted and therefore the more he will see reality clearly.

Chapter 6: The Unconscious or Subconscious

The existence of actions executed by human beings without reflection and without awareness of them has been known by philosophers for some time.[53] Modern theories of the unconscious (often called the subconscious), however, have some difficulties. In order to approach the discussion of unconscious acts, it is necessary first to discuss the modern theories and then give a Thomistic analysis and explanation.

---

[53]*Encyclopedia of Philosophy*, v. 8, p. 185f.

A. Initial Observations

The subconscious or unconscious is defined generally as: "1. Occurring or present without conscious perception, with only slight perception, or with peripheral attention to it. 2. imperfectly aware; not fully conscious."[54] Since conscious means to be aware,[55] subconscious or unconscious means that there is something which occurs in him causing acts. Knowledge regarding those things which occur unconsciously comes about by certain manifestations. These manifestations[56] are (1) sudden solutions of problems that perplex one for a long time; (2) problem solving and difficult mental constructive work done in sleep; (3) sudden brilliant ideas; (4) certain very strong likes and dislikes without any apparent reason; (5) the realization of strong desires;[57] (6) cases of hypermnesia;[58] (7) similar incidents of recall;[59] (8) peculiar phenomena of hysteria;[60] (9) post-hypnotic suggestion phenomena and (10) dual personalities.[61]

---

[54]Wuellner, *A Dictionary of Scholastic Philosophy*, p. 293. In the *Encyclopedia of Philosophy* (loc. cit), we read the following lines: "This is especially true of the twentieth-century conception of the 'unconscious,' the term being used here in a general sense for all those mental processes of which the individual is not aware while they occur."

[55]Deferrari defines "conscius" in *A Latin-English Dictionary of St. Thomas Aquinas* (p. 208): "(1) *knowing* or *conscious of something with another,* used with the gen., (2) *knowing something in one's self, conscious of,* with *sibi*." St. Thomas' use of the term indicates that the term "conscius" indicates knowledge, often closely connected to conscience or awareness of sin (e.g. see II Sent., d. 39, q. 3, a. 2, ad 4; IV Sent., d. 1, q. 3b; ST I-II, q. 42, a. 1; ibid., q. 112, a. 5; ST II-II, q. 60, a. 3 and De Ver., q. 17, a. 1, ad 2 and 3). For a very clear exposition of the basics of consciousness, see McInerny, *Philosophical Psychology*, p. 93-95. For further references regarding a more scholastic approach to conscius and consciousness see, among others, Brennan, *General Psychology*, p. 85; Brennan, *Thomistic Psychology*, p. 294-6; Maher, *Psychology*, p. 361-5 and Royce, *Man and His Nature*, p. 28f.

[56]The following manifestations are found in Duerk, *Psychology in Questions and Answers*, p. 173f.

[57]Duerk gives the example of telling one's subconscious mind to wake up at a certain time and one does so.

[58]See chapter 8 on hypnosis.

[59]Duerk gives the example of a fearful boy who after being hypnotized discovers the cause of the fear. He is brought out of the hypnosis, re-enacts the event and then is cured. See chapter 8 on hypnosis.

[60]For example, sleep walking.

[61]For an analysis of the issue of dual personalities, see volume II, chapter 10 and chapter infra on personality. All of the aforesaid effects can be explained by the cogitative power and other faculties.

B. Freud on the Unconscious[62]

> The developed form of Freud's theory of the unconscious may be summarized in the following way: (1) There are networks of ideas – attitudes, thoughts, feelings, objects imagined inside a person, and so on – that he cannot realize he possesses, because of the influence of other such networks, which he also cannot realize he possesses as long as he relies only on free association. (This is ordinarily described as "unconscious" conflict.) (2) These networks and their conflicts (a) influence the person's conscious ideas in all situations, reproducing the mutual relationships of networks, however difficult it may be to recognize them; and (b) in particular influence him at different times, so that childhood networks and conflicts influence adult ideas. (3) These networks are related in accordance with a large group of theoretical hypotheses, such as that of the Oedipus complex.[63]

For Freud, when a person represses something in the conscious state it soon develops into an unconscious resistance.[64]

> The Freudian unconscious is a pool of mainly repressed energies, distorted by frustration and exerting a stress on conscious reason and its shaping of the patterns of daily life. . . . The interpretations of dreams (which are symptoms and express wish fulfillment) and the process of free association can render accessible the regions of the unconscious producing the neurosis and can make possible a cure.[65]

For Freud, the unconscious exerts pressure on the conscious life which is known when the unconscious manifests itself in things like dreams, Freudian slips, psychosis and transference.[66] We can also gain access to the unconscious by means of hypnotism.[67] Repressed wishes in the unconscious strive to express themselves[68] and for that reason, the way to cure someone with a psychological illness is to get to the root of the repression. In other words, one employs hypnosis, free association and other psychoanalytic techniques in order to come to a knowledge of the repressed desire. The

---

[62]It should be noted that Freud rarely used the term subconscious. Normally he used the term unconscious.

[63]Edwards, *Encyclopedia of Philosophy*, v. 8, p. 190.

[64]Ibid., p. 191.

[65]Ibid., p. 187.

[66]Freud, *The Interpretation of Dreams*, p. 510.

[67]*Encyclopedia of Philosophy*, v. 8, p. 189.

[68]Freud, *The Interpretation of Dreams*, p. 510.

desire can then be made known to the patient, who stops repressing the unconscious desire and acts according to it. This allows the unconscious desire to be expressed and resolved and so the person is cured.

Freud made a distinction between what he calls the unconscious and preconscious. The unconscious is that which is incapable of consciousness. The preconscious is that which is capable of reaching consciousness.[69] For Freud the only way to gain access to the unconscious is through the preconscious, e.g. the psychologist may observe some symptom in a patient which he can make known to the patient. This symptom would be a manifestation of some repressed desire which the patient could recognize by free association or as it is manifest in dreams. The patient could then recognize this unconscious desire.

C. Those after Freud

Carl Jung did not agree exactly with Freud's theory of the unconscious or subconscious. Jung "strongly disagreed with Freud's emphasis on sex and the influence of early childhood on later personality. Jung believed that personality is governed by future goals, as well as past experiences."[70] Indeed, Freud's theory of the unconscious is heavily dominated by an emphasis on the sexual impulse and the dangers of repressing that sexual urge or drive. Yet, Jung also had a broader view of the unconscious in what he called the collective unconscious,

> the part of the unconscious composed of acquired traits and cultural patterns transmitted by heredity that is the foundation of the whole personality structure. It is universal, all men being essentially the same, is almost totally divorced from anything personal or individual, and is continuously accumulating memory traces as a result of man's repeated experiences over generations.[71]

For Jung, cultural patterns and acquired traits were explained by means of the collective unconscious which was passed on from generation to generation. These are things

---

[69]Ibid., p. 491 and 544. Wolman (*Dictionary of Behavioral Science*, p. 397) observes that "the preconscious includes all that one has in his mind but not on his mind at a particular moment. The mind of a newborn child is totally unconscious and only part of it ever becomes preconscious and conscious. The unconscious processes are 'primary processes;' and they are totally irrational, inaccessible to the conscious mind. Their existence can be inferred from dreams, amnesias, slips of the tongue and symptom formation. Some unconscious wishes are thrown back into the unconscious even before the individual becomes clearly aware of them; such a rejection of the unconscious wishes and impulses is called repression."

[70]Matheson, *Introductory Psychology*, p. 237.

[71]Wolman, *Dictionary of Behavioral Science*, p. 398.

which each person inherits and it explains why groups of people tend to behave the same when they have the same cultural background.

D. A Thomistic Analysis of the Unconscious

Since modern psychology has made use of the theories of the unconscious in its explanation of various psychological phenomena, it seems that a proper Thomistic analysis should be made of it to put the various theories of the unconscious in context as well to provide a deeper understanding of its nature. St. Thomas did hold that man performed actions of which he was unaware. In the *Summa Theologiae*, St. Thomas makes a distinction between what later theologians called the *actus hominis* (act of man) and the *actus humanae* (human act):

> Only those actions are called properly human, of which man is the lord. Man is the lord of his actions through reason and will, hence also free choice (*liberum arbitrium*) is called a faculty of the will and reason. Therefore those actions are properly called human, which proceed from deliberate will. Those other actions which suit man are able to be called acts of man; but are not properly human, since they are not of man insofar as he is man.[72]

There are some actions which man performs which do not proceed from reason and will. These actions man does without attention or unreflectedly:

> Actions which are done without attention are not from the intellect but from some sudden imagination or natural principle: as a disorder of the humors exciting an itch is the cause of scratching the beard, which is done without the attention of the intellect. And these tend toward

---

[72]ST I-II, q. 1, a. 1: "Unde illae solae actiones vocantur proprie humanae, quarum homo est dominus. Est autem homo dominus suorum actuum per rationem et voluntatem, unde et liberum arbitrium esse dicitur facultas voluntatis et rationis. Illae ergo actiones proprie humanae dicuntur, quae ex voluntate deliberata procedunt. Si quae autem aliae actiones homini conveniant, possunt dici quidem hominis actiones; sed non proprie humanae, cum non sint hominis inquantum est homo." While in this passage St. Thomas makes the distinction between *actus hominis* and *actus humanae*, in the general course of his writings, the terminology is different. Normally, St. Thomas uses the term *actus hominis* to refer to those which are proper to man, i.e. those proceeding from reason and will, e.g. see II Sent., d. 7, q. 2, a.1, ad 2; II Sent., d. 24, q. 1, a. 2, ad 1; SCG III, c. 140 and ST I, q. 94, a. 4, ad 4. This is merely pointed out so that the reader will not be confused when reading St. Thomas in different contexts.

some end, although it is aside the order of the intellect.[73]

Given the context of this chapter, this passage is rather loaded. First, St. Thomas is observing that there are some actions that are executed by man without the attention of the intellect and by this it is safe to interpret St. Thomas to mean that one does them unconsciously. He then indicates that the cause of these can be a disorder of the humors, to which we will give a fuller analysis later on, when we consider dispositions. But he observes two more things of import. The first is that the action is something which occurs in the imagination or which arises out of a natural principle. The second is that it does tend to some end (i.e. there is some finality to it) even though it is aside the order of the intellect, i.e. it is not done consciously or with the attention of the (possible) intellect. In other places, St. Thomas observes that these actions follow upon the apprehension of the imagination.[74]

Other writers in the Thomistic tradition likewise point out certain things which tend to be unconscious or subconscious. For example, Esser points out other areas where one tends to do things unconsciously:[75] (1) we sometimes have perceptions without attention, e.g. someone may not hear a clock chime or he may not see some thing in front of him. Upon later reflection, he remembers seeing it or hearing it. (2) We sense what are called the minimal sensibles (*minima sensibilia*), e.g. one may see a mountain covered with trees, but one does not perceive the individual trees. (3) Sometimes we have affections or appetites which arise spontaneously.[76]

A further Thomistic analysis is possible. We observed in a prior volume how the cogitative power is able to execute acts while the person is concentrating on something else.[77] This is a sign that we execute actions unconsciously. So, from the Thomistic point of view, unconscious acts do exist, but not in the way that Freud and others had imagined, as will become clear as we proceed. Second, if we take the above observation of St. Thomas that we perform actions because of some apprehension in the imagination, it would appear that unreflected acts are caused by something entering into the imagination, the cogitative power making some assessment of it and then executing an action which the cogitative power associates in memory with that action. So in the case of the man scratching his beard, he does it without reflecting.

---

[73]SCG III, l. III, c. 2, n. 9: "Actiones autem quae fiunt sine attentione, non sunt ab intellectu, sed ab aliqua subita imaginatione vel naturali principio: sicut inordinatio humoris pruritum excitantis est causa confricationis barbae, quae fit sine attentione intellectus. Et haec ad aliquem finem tendunt, licet praeter ordinem intellectus."

[74]St. Thomas often uses the example of scratching one's beard but from time to time he also uses the example of moving one's foot or arm (without reflection). For other examples of unreflected acts, see II Sent., d. 40, q. 1, a. 5; ST I-II, q. 18, a. 9 and De malo q. 2, a. 5 and ibid., ad 6.

[75]These three can be found in Esser, *Psychologia*, pp. 78-81.

[76]Antecedent appetite will be discussed below.

[77]Volume II, chapter 9.

However, the cogitative power executes the acts (1) based on past experience stored in memory which it associates with the image in the imagination and (2) based upon its habituation. In other words, it is possible to have some influence on unreflected acts depending on how the cogitative power is habituated and what we have in memory. Therefore, everything which affects memory or the cogitative power will have some effect on our unreflected or unconscious actions. In fact, all acts of the memory and the cogitative power are done unconsciously, even though the effects of those two powers are known consciously by affecting the image in the imagination.

Next, St. Thomas observes that there is finality to these unreflected acts but this finality is not the same as that which is ordered by reason. This is true insofar as the cogitative power apprehends something and then moves the motive powers and lower faculties to achieve some end, e.g. to eradicate the itch which in memory was seen to be done away with when it was scratched. But there is more to these finalities than just what is based upon past memory. The cogitative power can move the appetites and, at times, people will have a passion without being aware of it, e.g. when they get into a heated debate, they may be angry but they are so focused on the issue of the debate that they do not realize they are angry. This is because the cogitative power moves the appetites by its assessment of the phantasm in the imagination while reason carries on in a higher activity. The passion can also be moved by what is in the imagination without the assessment of the cogitative power. However, the former seems to be more the case because the cogitative power assesses the image as arduous while the person may not think that he is fighting for something. In either case, this allows us to execute bodily actions without having to think about the particular passion. Upon later reflection, the person realizes that he had the passion.

Moreover, each faculty has its proper object insofar as each faculty is ordered toward that object. This ordering in the faculties is accompanied by other natural inclinations in man which are not restricted to a particular faculty, e.g. reflex actions are a sign that man has natural law inclinations. Human beings are often unaware of the natural law inclination, even though they act according to it. This is something unconscious. Here is where Freud and others part company with Thomists. For Freud, these inclinations could not be frustrated without suffering psychological harm and were principally about sex. Whereas for the Thomist, man has three categories of natural inclination and it is not always necessary to fulfill certain natural inclinations, e.g. each person has a natural inclination toward marriage, which is part of the second and third categories of natural inclination. However, if a particular person does not marry and lives chastely, that does not necessarily constitute a case of repression. Moreover, there are some things which must be repressed for the sake of the person's psychological well-being.[78] Sexual inclinations, moreover, can be increased or decreased based upon virtue and vice and so to bring them to the point where one does not have any disordered sexual inclinations is a virtue, not a case of repression.

Another thing which people often do unreflectedly is to make judgments. As strange as that sounds, people have habits of judgment and will judge things in the

---

[78]See volume I, chapter 14 (III).

imagination according to their intellectual habits even though they are unaware of their habits of judgment. The activity of the agent intellect is an unconscious activity since we are unable to view (intellectually) the acts of the agent intellect. Yet we are aware that they occur, not by seeing them directly, but by the effects of the agent intellect, viz. concepts. From this we begin to see that the unconscious in a Thomistic sense is not a faculty but the activities of various faculties, habits, dispositions, natural inclinations, etc., which are not reflected upon. All of these things are there for the sake of man being able to execute acts of intellection and volition without having to think through the entire process as well as allowing him to remain focused on the task at hand.

Dispositions or one's temperament can also cause various faculties to act in certain ways.[79] People are often unaware that much of what they do is a result of their disposition. This is, more than likely, behind Jung's misinterpretation of the collective unconscious. The collective unconscious is due more to dispositions among peoples and races towards specific kinds of actions as well as habits of culture. It is not necessary to assign some part of the intellect called the unconscious the task of remembering past experiences of a given race or group of people. Furthermore, implicit learning plays a large role in the forming of cultural habits. This is largely a function of the cogitative power. Moreover, cultural habits are capable of being known and so they are not purely in the realm of the unconscious. We can also see that natural law inclinations would also form cultural habits and things of this sort and so it is not necessary to appeal to some "collective unconscious" to explain how groups of people tend to act the same way. Natural law inclinations, dispositions, culture and implicit learning suffice to explain Jung's "collective unconscious."

The distinction between unconscious and preconscious does have some validity, not insofar as they are separate parts of the mind or soul but insofar as they pertain to the ability to know the activities of various faculties, natural inclinations, etc. A vast majority of what occurs to man unconsciously can be known consciously. Moreover, one can exert rational control over most of the faculties which execute acts unconsciously. This control is not only direct, insofar as reason can move the cogitative power, the imagination, etc., but also indirect, insofar as reason forms habits in these powers and thereby affects their actions which are done aside from the command of reason. Since habits dispose and incline a faculty towards specific kinds of actions, one can affect those acts done unconsciously. Most of what pertains to the unconscious can be known with the exception of those things which reason is not able to know, e.g. permanently lost memories. But there are fewer of those things which cannot be known than things that can be known.[80]

Does free association tell us anything? Insofar as free association is a function of the cogitative power absent the control of reason, it can tell us something, such as the

---

[79]Regarding the temperaments, see the chapter in this volume on temperament.

[80]Here we are putting aside the sheer quantity of what a person permanently forgets in the course of his life and thinking more in the context of taking together all of the faculties of the soul and its natural law inclinations, dispositions, etc.

habituation of the cogitative power, etc. However, such free association, when interpreted outside the context of the persons' rational judgments and things of this sort, does not give a full understanding of the person's psychological state. Also, as will be seen with respect to dreaming, the cogitative power does not always act according to habituation, so it is possible that the person will associate things in free association that do not reflect the true state of the faculties of the soul. This appears to be more a product of human nature laboring under the effects of original sin.

In this context, we also see that the *lex fomitis* is largely misunderstood by modern psychologists. Disordered passions and desires are not natural to man but are the result of original and actual sin. To allow a person to stop repressing disordered passions and desires and to give expression to them can lead to serious psychological damage. For example, the disordered desire for sex (lust) which arises spontaneously is a manifestation, not just of habituation in the faculties, but also of the law of the flesh over which man lacks full control. While he can bring the flesh under the subjugation of reason by virtue, the *fomes* always have the ability to inflame, even in a man of virtue. In fact, God allows this in order for a person to perfect and maintain virtue by acting contrary to the inclinations of the flesh. This is an indication that we can shape those faculties which execute the activities unconsciously, but we cannot do so completely in this life.

There are also unconscious inclinations and activities which occur in the soul as a result of grace,[81] infused virtue and the Gifts of the Holy Ghost. Some spiritual writers do discuss what are called hidden motives and this can also be part of "unconscious" activity. Since sin and vice blind a person to the sin, he will often be motived by the vice of the sin without being aware of it.

It is also possible to habituate the various powers which execute acts unconsciously by what one senses externally. Events which leave a strong memory and emotional impact on the person can dispose him to act according to these impressions. Also, things such as television and movies can habituate the cogitative power by presenting the associations to the imagination. This, coupled with implicit learning, moves one to draw the conclusion that some unreflected activity can be a reflection of one's exposure to television. In fact, we can say that it is possible for the media to shape a culture "unconsciously" by determining the images presented on television and in other forms of media.

Therefore, given the aforesaid, it is not necessary to appeal to or assert the existence of some faculty or "part" of the mind called the subconscious or unconscious. Rather, all of the activities which the various psychologists ascribe to the "unconscious" can be explained by means of the various faculties as understood by St. Thomas. Taking the principle of economy into consideration,[82] it is not necessary to posit something beyond the Thomistic faculties to explain the unconscious activities we observe. What must also be avoided is the tendency to explain things in terms of the subconscious or

---

[81]See chapter 25 on inclinations of grace.

[82]Wuellner, *Summary of Scholastic Principles*, 291.

unconscious without having any way to verify them in observation. In the end, the Thomistic analysis makes more sense regarding these matters than the modern theories. As a last observation, very little time in psychology should be spent on analyzing and theorizing about the unconscious, since a more fruitful way to spend one's time is to study in detail the various faculties of the soul from a Thomistic point of view.

Chapter 7: Dreams

Modern psychology has spent a great deal of energy on dreams and interpretation.[83]   Also modern empirical studies have discovered many of the physiological aspects of dreaming. Since psychologists have given importance to dreaming and dream interpretation, it is necessary to discuss the psychological mechanism of dreaming, its causes as well as principles of interpretation.

A. The Nature of Dreaming

A dream is a series of images or phantasms in the imagination, sometimes accompanied by passions of the sensitive appetites experienced while sleeping. Dreaming is principally an activity of the imagination.[84] Yet, other faculties can be operative during dreaming. The cogitative power is able to move the dream along by a series of particular reasonings or associations.[85] It is also because of the activities of the cogitative power in viewing the image in the imagination and making associations, that, at times, people will experience problem-solving during dreams.[86] The connection or solution to some problem is remembered as being from the dream after the person is awake. It is because of the association of the cogitative power that there is often some coherence in a dream,[87] i.e. there may be a particular subject matter of the dream and the series of images are connected based on that subject matter or the subject matter becomes the basis for associating some other series of images in the dream. Yet, even though there is a certain coherence, there is often an incoherence[88] in the dreams in which the images do not seem truly connected and seem to have no correspondence to

---

[83]Freud wrote an entire tract entitled *The Interpretation of Dreams.*

[84]St. Thomas observes in IV Sent., d. 9, q. 1, a. 4a that dreams arise from the imagination. That dreams are a product of the imagination see also Maher, *Psychology: Empirical and Rational*, p. 176 and Reith, *An Introduction to Philosophical Psychology*, p. 104.

[85]Maher, *Psychology: Empirical and Rational*, p. 176f. Animals are able to dream since they have an imagination and an estimative sense.

[86]See *Dictionary of Behavioral Science*, p. 106. St. Thomas observes that we can apprehend something new in a dream, see ST II-II, q. 154, a. 5, ad 3.

[87]Maher, *Psychology: Empirical and Rational*, p. 176

[88]Duerk, *Psychology in Questions and Answers*, p. 179 and Maher, *Psychology: Empirical and Rational*, p. 176.

anything real. Dreams are often absurd[89] and are nothing more than "mental garbage," in the sense that the images are not only not real or unconnected but they are incapable of being real.[90]

During dreaming, the person is not capable of the use of reason[91] and will,[92] nor are reason and will in control of the lower faculties during dreaming.[93] This also means that there are no acts of judgment (comparison) or reflexion,[94] i.e. the possible intellect turning in on itself to know what it knows. Hence, there can be no acts of conscience[95] nor voluntariness during the dream itself.[96] For these reasons, dreams are not in the intellective part (i.e. the possible intellect and will) but in the sensitive part[97] (i.e. the interior senses and appetites).

Since the cogitative power is active during dreaming, so is memory, since the cogitative power makes use of memory to move the series of images in the imagination. Brennan holds that the common sense power can be operative during dreaming, at times when we recognize that it has performed the function of telling us whether something is real or not.[98] Perhaps this is the case, yet on the other hand there are times when the

---

[89]Maher, *Psychology: Empirical and Rational*, p. 177

[90]This is an important lesson insofar as coherence is something which comes either from reality (which is inherently coherent, structured and ordered) or reason (which by its nature is ordered toward the grasping of and the causing of order, coherence and structure).

[91]IV Sent., d. 9, q. 1, a. 4a and SCG III, c. 154, n. 16.

[92]Maher, *Psychology: Empirical and Rational*, p. 176f.

[93]Reith, *An Introduction to Philosophical Psychology*, p. 104. This is what distinguishes daydreaming from dreaming done during sleep. In daydreaming, reason and will can often start the imagination with some image pleasant to the dreamer and from time to time reason and will can guide the daydream. On the other hand, in dreaming done while asleep, the intellect and will cannot begin or guide the dreaming process except antecedently, as will be discussed in this chapter.

[94]Maher, *Psychology: Empirical and Rational*, p. 176.

[95]There are some who talk of some slight acts of conscience (see Esser, *Psychologia*, p. 101) but this is a misinterpretation of the association or assessment of the cogitative power regarding the image in the imagination. During the times when we are awake, we have acts of conscience which cause a formality in the image in relation to the particular action. This is stored in memory and then the cogitative power, during dreaming, is able to merge that memory with the image. This results in the person having the imaginative experience that this thing is "morally evil," which, in fact, is nothing other than the formality stored in memory from a prior act of influencing the imagination. This is also why people are able to have appetitive sorrow during dreaming and when they wake up, they misconstrue the appetitive sorrow or feeling of guilt with real guilt.

[96]IV Sent., d. 9, q. 1, a. 4a; ibid., ad 3 and 4 and ST II-II, q. 154, a. 5.

[97]De Ver., q. 18, a. 6, ad 14.

[98]Brennan, *Thomistic Psychology*, p. 125.

dream seems so real that the person thinks it is real during the dream[99] and this can even persist for some time after the dream until reason and the senses override the image in the imagination or the formality of being real in the phantasm in the imagination. But this false realness to the dream, as well as the incoherence and absurdity of the associations and images, leads us to conclude that it is possible to have false associations during dreaming.[100]

The external senses are bound during the process of dreaming.[101] In some dreams, the external senses are not able to introduce anything into the imagination. However, in other dreams, to a certain degree, they can introduce things into the imagination. We see this, for example, when someone is dreaming and something is said to him and he will respond, not always coherently, but in some manner. This incoherence may be due to the dreaming process itself or it may be the case that external sensations may not enter into the imagination unaltered,[102] e.g. one can touch the dreamer and he may imagine in the dream that he has been bitten by a bug.

Since dreaming occurs in the imagination and since the sensitive appetites are moved by the phantasm in the imagination, it is possible to experience passions during dreams. Since passions are moved by the formality in the image and since the images can be affected by the cogitative power, the cogitative power can effect passions during dreaming based upon its associations and assessments. The strength of the passion is based upon the phantasm.[103] The intensity of the dream is based upon the strength of the phantasm,[104] i.e. how clear or lucid it is to the dreamer, and the degree of the assessment of the cogitative power. The cogitative power can assess the goodness or badness of a phantasm by degrees and so it can affect the appetites by degrees.

B. The Causes of Dreams

While the imagination is the principal cause of dreaming and the other faculties, such as memory and the cogitative power, can affect the dream, there are other things which can cause or affect dreams. We have mentioned that external stimulus can affect

---

[99]Duerk, *Psychology in Questions and Answers*, p. 179.

[100]It is not clear what the actual cause of this is unless it is due to some physiological indisposition or is a natural physiological mechanism which is necessary for the well-being of the brain.

[101]De Ver., q. 12, a. 3, ad 2 and Reith, *An Introduction to Philosophical Psychology*, p. 104.

[102]Brennan, *Thomistic Psychology*, p. 217

[103]Esser, *Psychologia*, p. 101.

[104]Ibid. Esser indicates that the intensity of the dream is based upon the "vigilia" or vigilance. This would indicate that the more the person is aware of the dream, the more intense it is.

dreams.[105] Things which occur to us[106] or things which we do previously in the day can affect dreaming.[107] Prior intellectual and volitional acts can affect our dreams,[108] because they can affect the imagination and the cogitative power by how the possible intellect and will affect the image in the imagination throughout the day.[109]

It is here that we come upon the discussion by moral theologians and the scholastics regarding the issue of nocturnal emission or pollution.[110] This discussion is important to the area of psychology in order to see how we affect our dreams and how voluntary our dreams are. St. Thomas observes that pollution can be caused by our prior thoughts.[111] This is connected to the observation that dreams can be affected by what we think throughout the course of the day. Pollution can be caused by what we eat[112] insofar as it causes a dispositional change in us. For this reason we see that some dispositions are able to affect dreaming since they affect the disposition of the appetites, imagination, cogitative power and memory. Pollution and dreams can also be caused by demons.[113] Since the demons have a limited influence over our bodies,[114] they are able to affect one's bodily disposition, one's appetites, the imagination, the cogitative power and memory. If pollution occurs without any dreaming or imagination, it is a sign that it is from a purely bodily cause.[115] This bodily cause may be a bodily disposition or some weakness or inability to retain semen.[116] This principle can also apply to other aspects of bodily functions which occur involuntarily during sleep. The person should not assume that if there is no recall of a dream, that one must have been dreaming in

---

[105]Esser, *Psychologia*, p. 101; Brennan, *Thomistic Psychology*, p. 217 and Reith, *An Introduction to Philosophical Psychology*, p. 104.

[106]Esser, *Psychologia*, p. 101.

[107]Brennan observes that some hold that a majority of our dreams are drawn from events of the preceding day, see *Thomistic Psychology*, p. 217.

[108]IV Sent., d. 9, q. 1, a. 4a and 4b.

[109]In ST II-II, q. 95, a. 6, St. Thomas observes that our custom of thought and affection while awake can affect our dreams. This is a sign that dreaming can be affected by the habits in the cogitative power and appetites which we effect while awake.

[110]Pollution is a term used by moral theologians and scholastics to refer to the ejection of semen.

[111]IV Sent., d. 9, q. 1, a. 4b.

[112]Ibid. Some will notice that they dream if they eat too much before they go to bed or if they drink caffeinated beverages or things of this sort. However, due discretion must be taken regarding this observation. What affects one person may not affect another so it should not be assumed that everyone will be affected by the same things.

[113]IV Sent., d. 9, q. 1, a. 4b and ST II-II, q. 154, a. 5.

[114]See prior volume on demonic influences.

[115]IV Sent., d. 9, q. 1, a. 4b.

[116]Ibid. and ST II-II, q. 154, a. 5.

order to cause these things to occur.

St. Thomas and the moral theologians discuss the voluntariness of nocturnal emissions and we can apply those same principles to the voluntariness of what we dream, i.e. at times what we dream may have a connection to something voluntary. If we give consent to pollution before or after it occurs then it is voluntary.[117] In like manner, we may voluntarily do something which could affect our dreams and in this respect what occurs during the dream is voluntary, *not in itself but in its cause*. Likewise, when we accept or act upon some dream after it occurs, then the dream becomes voluntary, again not in itself, but in our acceptance of the dream. This is important because it indicates that while not all dreams are affected by what is voluntary, some are. Hence, we are indirectly responsible for any kind of dream which might be the effect of some prior sin, action, disposition, or vice (or even virtue) if it is voluntary. It is for this reason that St. Thomas observes that dreams can be a *sign* of blame or merit insofar as they are affected by our appetites or affections which may be good or bad.[118]

Leaving the discussion of pollution and returning to the causes of dreaming itself, we also see that dreams can be affected by different kinds of drugs (including alcohol) in different ways.[119] Dreams can also be caused by good angels,[120] since they too can affect our bodies. There are also cases in revelation where God has spoken to prophets and others in dreams.[121] Since God is the cause of everything that exists, He can cause us to dream.

Dreams can also cause a dispositional change in the person who dreams. While there may be no antecedent volitional cause of a dream, it is possible for the person to experience a disposition which has come from the dream and the passions which it causes. For instance, someone may have a very vivid dream which seems real in which his wife has spent his lifelong savings during the dream and he is angry. When he wakes up, he may have the disposition proper to the anger even though he may realize that it is not true because his wife is a frugal person. Since passions cause chemical changes in us, those chemical changes (i.e. dispositions) may persist after the dream. If the passion is bad, the person should not think about the dream, so that the dispositions of the passion will recede due to the cessation of the passion. Even if the passion is pleasant, the person should normally put it aside since passion can affect the judgment of reason unless he can make proper use of the disposition without it affecting reason and volition.

---

[117]IV Sent., d. 9, q. 1, a. 4b and ST II-II, q. 154, a. 5.

[118]IV Sent., d. 9, q. 1, a. 4b and ST II-II, q. 154, a. 5.

[119]See Reith, *An Introduction to Philosophical Psychology*, p. 104.

[120]ST II-II, q. 154, a. 5.

[121]ST I-II, q. 113, a. 3, ad 2; ST III, q. 7, a. 8, ad 1 and *De Sortibus*, passim. St. Thomas remarks in De Ver., q. 12, a. 3 that since the interior senses are freed from the exterior senses and since the interior senses are more quiet during dreaming, the interior senses are more disposed toward the impressions from God, the angels (both good and bad) and the saints.

C. Interpretation of Dreams

The interpretation of dreams has been something which has occurred throughout recorded history by philosophers and non-philosophers alike. Everyone from Plato and Aristotle to St. Thomas and Freud has devoted some discussion to the interpretation of dreams. It is, therefore, necessary to discuss the principles behind the interpretation of dreams, so as to avoid giving dreams more weight than one should or to giving them a wrong interpretation.

Historically, people have used dreams in two ways. The first is to use them as a means of predicting the future. The second is as a means of analyzing of one's psychological state. As to the first, using dreams as a means of predicting the future is part of what is called divination. St. Thomas observes that dreams can be seen in relation to the future in four ways. The first two are from a natural cause which is in the dreamer. The first of these causes is when the cause is in the dreamer when the dream moves him to do something.[122] In this case, the person has a dream and because of the dream, he does something, either by choice or by suggestion, i.e. the cogitative power associates something he experiences with what he dreamt and then that is merged with the image which affects his judgment and volition. Hence, he believes that his dream told the future because he followed the suggestion of the dream. The second of those causes in the dreamer is when there is a sign of the dream in the person. In this case, the person has some disposition prior to the dream, e.g. a sanguine disposition.[123] This disposition disposes him towards eating and so he dreams of eating sweets. The following day, he comes upon sweets and eats them due to the inclination of his disposition or even the dream. In this way, he believes that the dream predicted his eating of the sweets.

The third and the fourth means of divination by dreams are from an external cause. The third way is when some natural cause affects the dreams as well as the events which occur.[124] St. Thomas often gives the example of celestial bodies which act upon our bodies, disposing them to specific kinds of dreams.[125] These forms of causation can

---

[122]II Sent., d. 7, q. 2, a. 2, ad 6; ST II-II, q. 95, a. 6 and De Ver., q. 12, a. 3.

[123]See chapter on disposition.

[124]II Sent., d. 7, q. 2, a. 2, ad 6 and ST II-II, q. 95, a. 6. See also De Ver., q. 12, a. 3.

[125]This example should not be dismissed out of hand. It may be the case that those in the middle ages attributed greater agency to celestial bodies than we do today. However, modern statistical analysis at times seem to show a correlation between lunar phases and human behavior (e.g. see Al Lieber. "Human Aggression and the Lunar Synodic cycle." *Journal of Clinical Psychiatry.* 1978 May 39[5]:385-92). On the other hand, some statistical analysis does not see any correlation between lunar phases and human behavior (e.g. see G.B. Forbes and G.R. Lebo Jr. "Antisocial Behavior and Lunar Activity: A Failure to Validate the Lunacy Myth." *Psychological Reports,* June, 1977. 40 [3 Pt. 2]:1309-10). As a result, since the science is not clear, the possibility of celestial bodies affecting human

be received more or less based upon the efficacy of the exterior agent as well as the disposition of the dreamer. The fourth way of using dreams to predict the future is when an angel,[126] either good or bad, or God, provides information in the dream by which the person is able to know or predict the future.

Given these various ways of predicting the future, St. Thomas then provides the criteria for using dreams in this manner. These criteria are also the criteria for the interpretation of dreams in general: "Therefore it is to be considered what is the cause of the dreams; and whether the cause of the future event is able to be or whether one is able to know it."[127] When analyzing the causes of dreams, one must take into consideration the various causes of the dream and whether the cause can be known or not. In other words, we must look to those causes which we have discussed above.

When analyzing a dream, one must first assess whether the dream arises from a natural, supernatural (God) or preternatural cause (angels and demons). If the dream appears to be from God or a good angel (or saint), the principles of judgment shift to the domain of spiritual theology and the principles for proper discernment. In this particular case, if a psychologist has reasonable grounds for thinking a dream is from God, angel or saint,[128] he should refer the directee to a knowledgeable priest. The psychologist (unless he is a priest) should not assume it is his place to interpret this kind of dream.

If the dream suggests that it could be demonic, the psychologist must assess whether ordinary means will suffice to rid the directee of this kind of demonic influence.[129] However, the psychologist should not assume that a dream has a demonic cause without sufficient reason nor should they dismiss out of hand dreams being from the demonic. In the normal course of counseling, dreams will probably not be brought up unless the directee finds a particular dream disturbing or enjoyable. In the normal process of determining that a particular dream or dreams are from a demonic cause, one should not pay too much attention to the actual content unless it gives clear indication of being disordered and beyond natural causes. Some of the signs of demonic influence are that the dreams would be particularly vivid, having a profound coherence and clarity, often accompanied by brilliant colors. When it is from a demonic cause, the dream will seem outside the person's normal pattern of dreaming. Demons can also cause normal dreaming. In this case, one should first rule out any natural causes before assuming the dream is demonic. Demons can also cause nocturnal emissions and immoral dreams. Even though demons can cause dreams which have immoral content, these kinds of

---

behavior should not necessarily be denied.

[126]II Sent., d. 7, q. 2, a. 2, ad 6; ST II-II, q. 95, a. 6 and De Malo, q. 3, a. 4. See also De Ver., q. 12, a. 3.

[127]ST II-II, q. 95, a. 6: "est ergo considerandum quae sit causa somniorum; et an possit esse causa futurorum eventuum; vel ea possit cognoscere."

[128]This would be exceptionally rare.

[129]Here it would be good to know the principles of discerning demonic causes, as described in various spiritual writers as well as the chapter in the prior volume on the demonic.

dreams can also come from natural causes within ourselves, e.g. prior sin, vice and things of this sort. If a psychologist has reason to believe that the dreams are from a demonic cause, he should refer the directee to a priest who can apply these and other spiritual principles to determine whether they are truly demonic or not. The priest can also aid the directee by various spiritual means, if they are demonic.

It should be observed that, since demons are capable of affecting our dreams, when we have an immoral dream or one which seems to be from the demonic we should normally ignore it. The demons will often cause dreams to dispose us toward something immoral, to suggest something to us, or to dispose our cogitative power and other faculties towards vice. Moreover, there can be great danger in paying attention to demonically caused dreams since they can easily lead us to error. Thus, the demons will try to get us to succumb to the dream out of a vice of curiosity since the dreams will, at times, seem "wondrous" or "interesting." We should normally be in the habit of ignoring our dreams since they can be caused by the demonic and since they are often the result of mental "garbage," as we will see in relation to the natural causes.

When considering dreams, we can see that natural causes can give rise to dreams and their content. If dreams have a natural cause and they do not seem to disturb or affect the directee, the psychologist should not delve into them. He should normally leave them alone. It is only when the dreams disturb the directee that he can ask questions based on the natural causes. For instance, is he eating something before he goes to bed? Does he lack custody of the eyes and mind which causes him to see and imagine things which cause his dreams? What are his habits, virtues and vices? While the psychologist should not normally try to pin down any interpretation and meaning in the content of a particular dream; he should only ask questions to get to the cause, not the meaning of the dreams. Because we lack certitude about the causes of particular dreams, it is not really possible to have a scientific approach to dream interpretation. While there is a science of the physiology of dreams, we can never be certain of all of the causes. In the end, dream analysis admits of very little certitude and so as a general rule should be avoided.

Lastly, the psychologist at times will simply have to tell the directee that dreams are "mental garbage" and do not have any real significance. To delve into dreams without a sufficient reason is to run the risk of misinterpretation, both as to their meaning and their cause. Secondly, if a dream is mental garbage, it has no meaning other than the occurrence of a purely physiological mechanism which may be necessary to keep the brain properly disposed chemically and biologically. Furthermore, the psychologist's entering into the discussion of dreams without a sufficient reason and by attempting to ascertain the meaning of the dream beyond the signs or causes may be influenced more by the desires and mental habits of the psychologist than the directee.

Freud held that dreams expressed wish fulfillment.[130] This is true, to an extent. First, Freud did not discover anything new: St. Thomas already noted that a dream can be caused by proper acts of volition, affections and habits. Second, Freud exaggerated this aspect of his psychoanalysis, i.e. to take on more meaning than it had in reality as

---

[130]Freud, *Interpretation of Dreams*, p. 225-237,

he allowed wish fulfillment to dominate his diagnosis and theory as to the meanings of dreams.[131] Because the causes of dreams are varied and often uncertain, and because dreams are often just "mental garbage," as a general rule, psychologists should ignore them, not spend too much time on them and not formulate too many specific meanings to the dreams of their directees. If and only if they disturb the directee, should any time be given to them. They cannot give us certitude about the psychological state of the directee, since they can have a demonic cause and since they can be "mental garbage" or the cause cannot be known with certitude. The term GIGO[132] applies. If the psychologists tries to analyze something which is nothing more than mental garbage, his analysis will likewise be "mental garbage."

Chapter 8: Hypnotism

A. The Nature of Hypnosis

Hypnosis is defined as "an artificially induced sleep-like state characterized by increased suggestibility, decreased initiative and will to act on one's own, recollection of events not remembered in the normal state, and often amnesia for that which occurred while hypnotized."[133] This definition includes the essentials of hypnotism which has several characteristics. The first is that hypnotism is similar to sleep.[134] Some think that it is an artificial sleep but it is not.[135]

The principal characteristic of hypnosis is suggestibility insofar as the subject is susceptible to suggestions.[136] A Thomistic analysis would seem to yield the conclusion that hypnosis, due to the suggestibility, is principally a function of the cogitative power. Since it pertains to the cogitative power to associate or disassociate things in the image, hypnosis in which association or suggestion is made regarding

---

[131]Perhaps this is due to the fact that Freud himself had serious appetitive problems; see Jones, *Libido Dominandi*, passim. and Jones, *Degenerate Moderns*, chap. 8 (entitled "Sigmund and Minna and Carl and Sabina: The Birth of Psychoanalysis Out of the Personal Lives of Its Founders"). While it is conceded that this is an *ad hominem* argument, it is merely pointed out so that it can be seen that it is too easy for psychologists to impose their own personal psychological state on the directee.

[132]GIGO is a computer programing term for "garbage in, garbage out."

[133]Wolman, *Dictionary of Behavioral Science*, p. 181.

[134]Davis, *Moral and Pastoral Theology*, v. 2, p. 17 and Esser, *Psychologia*, p. 290. Some even refer to it as a form of hysteria although such a denomination seems inaccurate insofar as hypnosis is not a mental illness. The term hypnosis comes from the Greek term ὕπνος which means sleep (see Maher, *Psychology: Empirical and Rational*, p. 594).

[135]Duerk, *Psychology in Questions and Answers*, p. 197 and Esser, *Psychologia*, p. 291.

[136]Duerk, *Psychology in Questions and Answers*, p. 197 and Maher, *Psychology: Empirical and Rational*, p. 598.

various things, is a function of the cogitative power.[137] As the hypnotist introduces into the imagination those things which are associated, the cogitative power in this state then learns the connection. Upon later recall, the cogitative power then re-associates the suggestion with the image that contains the cue[138] given by the hypnotist. While it appears to be principally a function of the cogitative power, hypnosis would also require memory and imagination to be subordinated, in this state, to the hypnotist.

This brings us to the next characteristic of hypnosis which is an attention turned toward the hypnotist or a narrowing of attention to the hypnotist and nothing else, unless the hypnotist directs the subject's attention to something else.[139] Maher in his *Psychology* refers to this as fixation.[140] In a prior volume, we defined fixation in relation to the cogitative power.[141] Since attention is partly the function of the cogitative power,[142] this would also seem to fit the conclusion that hypnosis is principally a function of the cogitative power.

Hypnosis causes a memory to be stored in which the cogitative power is able to associate with some cue suggested by the hypnotist. This indicates that false memories can be planted by the hypnotist. In a prior volume, the same factors were present regarding the process of reminiscence.[143] Of course, the difference lies in the fact that in reminiscence, the activity is principally directed by the person who is doing the reminiscing. But it was noted that the psychologist had to be careful not to cause errors to be introduced into the reminiscence process. In like manner, due caution must be taken by the hypnotist not to plant false memories which could cause problems for the subject later.

Another characteristic is a certain obedience to the hypnotist.[144] However, the obedience is not absolute since there appears to be some indication that if the hypnotist suggests something gravely contrary to the conscience of the subject, it can bring the subject out of the hypnosis.[145] For this reason, since obedience is an act of the will, the hypnotist, strictly speaking, cannot rule the will.[146] However, it would be possible to affect the will indirectly by what is introduced into the imagination, since the possible

---

[137]Since animals have an estimative sense, which is their counterpart to the human cogitative power, animals have also been known to be hypnotized.

[138]A cue would be some sensible sign which the hypnotist would designate during the hypnosis. This sensible sign, once in the imagination, becomes the means for the cogitative power to make the association.

[139]Esser, *Psychologia*, p. 290.

[140]Maher, *Psychology: Empirical and Rational*, p. 598.

[141]Volume I, chapter 14 (II, D).

[142]Volume II, chapter 9 (II).

[143]Volume I, chapter 3 (II, 2, c).

[144]Esser, *Psychologia*, p. 291.

[145]See below.

[146]Maher, *Psychology: Empirical and Rational*, p. 600.

intellect must convert back to the image in the imagination to judge whether something is good in order to propose it to the will. Insofar as the hypnosis can affect the judgment of reason, it can affect the will. Voluntariness would be affected. If what is in the imagination is false and the person is unaware that it is false due to the suggestion (i.e. the association of the cogitative power), the voluntariness of the acts of the will and the actions suggested by the hypnotist would be reduced.

Yet, it is through the suggestion that the hypnotist can be said to command the subject.[147] Yet this command cannot be seen as despotic since the command rests upon suggestion. While those who are more susceptible to hypnosis and the suggestions made under hypnosis may be better subjects for the commands of the hypnotist, the command is still done by means of the suggestion.

These suggestions by the hypnotist can have, nevertheless, profound effects on the subject. The hypnotist, by means of suggestion, can cause the subject to hallucinate and to hear what has been suggested to him, even if it is not real.[148] There does seem to be a Thomistic explanation for these occurrences. In the normal process of coming to sensitive knowledge, the person senses something exterior to him. The sense species are then unified by the common sense power and expressed into the imagination. The cogitative power goes into the memory and merges with the image in the imagination the sense species stored in memory. In a prior chapter, we observed that the cogitative power, in the process, can actually modify the species in the imagination. This results in the person's experience not being in congruity with reality. All of this means that all experiences of something external to us are known by means of the image in the imagination. The possible intellect does not have direct access to the senses. This is why Thomists are known for being *moderate* realists. Hence, all knowledge and judgments about what we experience external to us come via the imagination. But hypnosis affects the imagination[149] by introducing into it the suggestion of the hypnotist. The person then thinks he hears or sees what is suggested because the image in the imagination is placed there by the hypnotist. In this respect, we can say that all hypnotic hallucinations are imaginative hallucinations.

The person hypnotized is also subject to the hypnotist for a time outside of the hypnosis.[150] This is a result of the fact that the hypnotist causes the cogitative power to associate something with the voice or cues given to the subject during hypnosis. Hence, post-hypnotic suggestions are not a product of hypnosis itself since the person is not, at the moment, hypnotized. Rather post-hypnotic suggestion is the result of the cogitative power and the residual association in the cogitative power regarding the cues or commands of the hypnotist.

---

[147]Esser, *Psychologia*, p. 291.

[148]Ibid.

[149]Maher, *Psychology: Empirical and Rational*, p. 594.

[150]Esser, *Psychologia*, p. 291.

Hypnosis can also be used to induce post-hypnotic amnesia.[151] While the will can move the memory to recall something directly, in the normal process of remembering, this is done by association of the cogitative power. While it might be the case that in hypnosis there is some mechanism which affects the memory directly, it is also possible that the hypnotist causes a disassociation to be placed in memory and as a result the cogitative power cannot associate the memory after hypnosis. If during the hypnosis the person is told something to remember but that he will not remember it until he receives a cue, the memory will come.[152] This would indicate that the cogitative power can be trained through hypnosis to associate in specific ways, i.e. it will not associate what the hypnotist has said until the proper cue is given. Then the cogitative power can go back into memory and associate what the hypnotist said based upon the cue. Modern studies, however, have not been able to demonstrate that there is a significant improvement in hypermnesia by means of hypnosis, even though the subjects of hypnosis believe there is.[153]

Autohypnotism can be brought about mostly by those who have been hypnotized before.[154] It would seem that the cogitative power is given the suggestion during hypnotism to enter into a state of hypnotism. There have been some instances where hypnotists have been able to produce preternatural phenomena through hypnotism. However, such phenomena are more akin to witchcraft. The person is placed in a hypnotic state in order to dispose him to a demonic activity. There have been cases where subjects are able to sense things which would not be possible in a normal state.[155] However, this could be explained in two ways. In one way, this could be preternatural in which one uses demonic means to heighten the senses or to provide sense knowledge where otherwise it would not be possible. The second explanation is that the cogitative power is able to focus more readily on the senses than is possible for the person under normal circumstances. Just as blind people develop hearing abilities which, normally, people may not have, in like manner, a suggestion could be made to the cogitative power which mimics a certain kind of an activity so that the person is not more perceptible to sensation as such (i.e. the senses themselves do not change) but one is more perceptible in the imagination.

The method of placing someone under hypnosis also suggests that what results is principally a function of the cogitative power in conjunction with memory and imagination.

---

[151]Maher, *Psychology: Empirical and Rational*, p. 600 and Kihlstrom, *Hypnosis, Memory and Amnesia* (as found at http://socrates.berkeley.edu/~kihlstrm/hypnosis_memory.htm on 10/17/03).

[152]Ibid.

[153]Ibid. Hypermnesia is an increased ability to remember. The article by Kihlstrom is particularly useful for those interested in understanding, in a variety of ways and contexts, how hypnosis affects memory recall.

[154]Duerk, *Psychology in Questions and Answers*, p. 197.

[155]Maher, *Psychology: Empirical and Rational*, p. 597.

The subject is requested to gaze fixedly at some object, such as a button, suspended at a little distance from his eyes and above his head; or to stare into the eyes of the operator; or to listen to a monotonous sound such as the ticking of a watch; or "passes" are made in front of his face and chest. After a time he often gradually falls into a drowsy or lethargic condition, like that preceding or following ordinary sleep.[156]

How this mechanism places one into a hypnotic state is not exactly understood. Perhaps in the future when further studies are done on the brain and its activity, the actual physical causal mechanism will be found. However, philosophically speaking, it would appear that this activity has some affect on the cogitative power. Since the person is required to stare at a fixed point or object, it would appear that this involves a voluntariness on the side of the subject or one may say at least there is no positive will to the contrary, i.e. the person allows it. The various motions made by the hypnotist appear to cause the cogitative power to come under the subjugation of the hypnotist. The person by placing his attention on the object fixes the cogitative power on the object and motion. The hypnotist normally speaks and so there is a link or an association made between the motion of the object and the voice of the hypnotist. As the person fixes the attention of the cogitative power on these two things, the cogitative power would then enter into a state in which the suggestions of the hypnotist are followed. Since the person moves the cogitative power to submit to the suggestions of the hypnotist, the cogitative power submits to the external agency of the hypnotist.

The motion would seem increasingly to draw the attention of the cogitative power as the motion continues. Our lower faculties, including the cogitative power, are normally attracted to motion. We see this when we involuntarily move our heads toward something which comes into our sight. As was observed in the prior volume, the cogitative power can execute the motion of the lower faculties and this would seem to be the case in the example of moving our heads involuntarily, i.e. it is essentially an activity of the cogitative power. The motion of the object during hypnotism draws the cogitative power's attention and that attention deepens as the motion progresses. The voice of the hypnotist directs the cogitative power by suggestion, in that the subject is told to watch the object and he continues to do so and listens to the hypnotist and follows his suggestions. Hence, it would appear that the motion causes a fixation of the attention of the cogitative power which increases or deepens as the person watches the repetitive motion. Each repetition of the motion causes the cogitative power to make a particular judgment. This causes a kind of training in which the cogitative power becomes fixed on the object.[157] As the cogitative power judges repeatedly, its attention

---

[156]Ibid., p. 595.

[157]Because this is a kind of training and may actually produce a habit in the cogitative power (see below), this may be why those who have been hypnotized are more easily hypnotized, since they already have the habit in the cogitative power.

becomes more fixed. The cogitative power likewise becomes fixed on those things associated with the motion and, in the case of hypnosis, it is the voice of the hypnotist. Hence, the attention of the cogitative power deepens and becomes fixed on the voice of hypnotist. As this state increases there comes a point where the cogitative power becomes subject to the suggestions of the hypnotist – commonly called hypnosis.[158]

B. Conditions for the Use of Hypnosis

Moralists as well as others give conditions for moral use of hypnosis and these conditions would also apply to the use of hypnosis by psychologists, not only because a psychologist should never do anything immoral, but also because of the psychological effects hypnosis has on the subject. The first condition for the use of hypnosis is that there must be a grave or proportionate reason for its use.[159] Hypnosis takes away use of reason,[160] since the subject is not able to have fullness of judgment because of the fixation of the cogitative power on the voice of the hypnotist. Moreover, the subject does not have full control of his other faculties while he is in hypnosis and so the subject is under the moral control of the hypnotist.[161] During hypnosis the person does not have the ability to deliberate and so there is no voluntariness to what the subject does during the hypnosis.[162] Even after the subject is out of hypnosis, due to post-hypnotic suggestion, the subject's knowledge is limited[163] due to the associations retained by the cogitative power. As a result, this can reduce the voluntariness after the hypnosis has passed. On the other hand, it can also enhance voluntariness if the hypnotic suggestion makes the right associations and/or confirms the associations which are rooted in reality. It must also be kept in mind that the subject can be responsible for what occurs during the hypnosis if he has prior knowledge of what is going to occur during hypnosis or if he is aware of the lack of moral character of the hypnotist.

Proportionate or grave causes for the use of hypnosis would be causes such as to cure drunkenness, masturbation or some other grave sin.[164] A psychologist may use it if there is some grave psychological illness which can be cured through hypnosis. However, if other treatments exist, for either the moral disorder or a psychological one,

---

[158]For the various levels of hypnosis and their characteristics, see Maher, *Psychology: Empirical and Rational*, p. 595 and Duerk, *Psychology in Questions and Answers*, p. 197.

[159]Davis, *Moral and Pastoral Theology*, v. 2, p. 18; Maher, *Psychology: Empirical and Rational*, p. 602 and Duerk, *Psychology in Questions and Answers*, p. 200.

[160]Davis, *Moral and Pastoral Theology*, v. 2, p. 17.

[161]Ibid., p. 18.

[162]Royce, *Man and His Nature*, p. 217.

[163]Ibid.

[164]Healy, *Medical Ethics*.

they are to be preferred.[165] Hypnosis may be used as an anesthetic,[166] provided that the subject is intolerant to other anesthetics or there is no anesthetic available.

The next condition for the licit use of hypnosis is that the hypnotist must have the consent of the subject.[167] This obviously follows from the fact that one surrenders one's moral faculties to the hypnotist. It is not morally permissible, without a grave reason, to trick the subject into being hypnotized, since it reduces the voluntariness of the subject because he does not "know"[168] he is being hypnotized. Since consent is required, the subject must have knowledge that he is hypnotized. However, grave reasons may require hypnosis under certain circumstances, e.g. if the subject poses a grave threat to himself or others.

The next condition is that due precautions must be taken.[169] Since hypnosis has the potential to cause serious psychological and moral harm to the individual, all reasonable precautions must be taken so that any possible harm is avoided. Among those precautions, we see that the hypnotist must avoid all scandal.[170] For instance, he must not hypnotize a subject under circumstances which could call into question his own character or the character of the subject. In connection to this, the hypnotist should not hypnotize any subject without the presence of a witness[171] whose good character is beyond question. The hypnotist must never suggest anything during the hypnosis that is contrary to moral uprightness.[172]

This brings us to the next condition for the licit use of hypnosis: the hypnotist must have a good character and be competent.[173] Hypnosis can cause serious damage to the psychological faculties and so the psychologist must be competent in his ability to hypnotize the subject, bring the subject out of the hypnosis, judge the suitability of the subject for hypnosis (both morally and psychologically) and make use of the hypnosis in such a fashion as not to cause psychological or moral ill effects. Since

---

[165]Ibid.

[166]Ibid.

[167]Ibid. and Davis, *Moral and Pastoral Theology*, v. 2, p. 18.

[168]Royce, *Man and His Nature*, p. 217.

[169]Davis, *Moral and Pastoral Theology*, v. 2, p. 18 and Healy, *Medical Ethics.*

[170]Davis, *Moral and Pastoral Theology*, v. 2, p. 18.

[171]Maher, *Psychology: Empirical and Rational*, p. 602.

[172]Royce *(Man and His Nature*, p. 216) observes: " Usually the suggestion to do something contrary to his moral principles will shock the subject out of the hypnotic state. For example, in hypnotic experimentis using a rubber dagger, an adult can be told to stab someone under the suggestion of hate. Given a real dagger, he will ordinarily wake up.... But if the person has weak moral convictions and is vulnerable to nonhypnotic persuasion or seduction anyway, he is understandably liable to act on immoral hypnotic suggestion." It is possible that the cogitative power when assessing the suggestion by the hypnotist assesses it negatively which thereby breaks the hypnosis.

[173]Maher, *Psychology: Empirical and Rational*, p. 602.

hypnosis can affect the moral life of the subject, the character of the hypnotist must be beyond question. Since hypnosis can cause serious problems to the body and soul of the subject in the hands of the untrained,[174] those without competence must be barred from engaging in hypnotism.

Another condition for the licit use of hypnosis is that the hypnotist is not permitted to seek effects which are preternatural or beyond what man is naturally capable of. Hypnosis is licit on the supposition that the effects of the hypnosis do not transcend natural causes.[175] Such a practice would lead to the possible involvement of the demonic. Also, the Church has condemned that form of hypnosis that is tainted with superstition or which leads to moral evil.[176]

Hypnosis may not be used for entertainment purposes or irrelevant scientific experimentation.[177] This should be evident from the prior discussion about the proportionate reasons for the licit use of hypnosis. However, physiologists and empirical scientists must be careful to use hypnosis only in experiments which are truly necessary.

The last condition which must be met is that hypnosis must not be used too often on the same subject and continued subjection to the hypnotist must be avoided. To hypnotize a subject too often or to continue to have him subject to the hypnotist is morally wrong because it is harmful to the mental faculties.[178] Maher observes that this can cause a hypnotic habit[179] which can render the subject excessively subservient to the hypnotist or others. It can also, by causing a hypnotic habit, be the source of greater fixations and more mental illnesses. "Prolonged use of hypnosis [can cause] great personal dependence of the patient on the therapist, inadvisable posthypnotic suggestion and, in obstetrics, disturbance of the normal mother-child relationship by too deep hypnosis."[180]

Psychologists may make use of hypnosis, therefore, provided these conditions are observed. However, in the normal course of counseling many directees, it is unlikely that other psychological means would be lacking. In the final analysis, hypnosis, while permissible under the above conditions, would be rarely used by a psychologist.

Chapter 9: More on Depression

Throughout the course of the past two volumes, various things were noted

---

[174]Ibid., p. 601.

[175]Davis, *Moral and Pastoral Theology*, v. 2., p. 18.

[176]Ibid and Maher, *Psychology: Empirical and Rational*, p. 602.

[177]O'Donnell, *Medicine and Christian Morality*, p. 104.

[178]Davis, *Moral and Pastoral Theology*, v. 2., p. 18.

[179]Maher, *Psychology: Empirical and Rational*, p. 601.

[180]O'Donnell, *Medicine and Christian Morality*, p. 105.

which mitigate the passion of sorrow.[181] Everything that mitigates the passion of sorrow does so in one of two ways. The first is by providing physical pleasure which affects the phantasm which in turn lessens the passion of sorrow. The second is by modifying the phantasm in cases where physical pleasure may not be a part of the modification of the phantasm, e.g. contemplation of the truth and speaking with others about the thing causing sorrow.

From this, one is able to see why those who suffer some kind of emotional pain or sorrow tend to engage in immoral activities which give sensible pleasure. For example, it is not uncommon for women who have had abortions to engage in all sorts of immoral and promiscuous activity in order to mitigate the sorrow from the abortion.[182] We also see that some people seek to engage in certain kinds of immoral activity in order to appease the intellective sorrow (i.e. in the will) or appetitive sorrow (i.e. when the intellective sorrow redounds to the image in the imagination causing appetitive sorrow). For instance, someone may do something immoral; his conscience tells him that he has done something bad and so in order to squelch the appetitive sorrow arising from the guilt, he engages in drinking or taking drugs.

However, caution must be taken since people must recognize that by engaging in forms of activity which mitigate sorrow they do not always take away the source of the appetitive sorrow. In these cases, the person must recognize that once the mitigation passes, the cause will persist and so will the sorrow. The following principle must be followed when advising directees about when to mitigate sorrow, viz. one should only seek to mitigate sorrow by things which do not take away the cause, when the cause has already been removed or is being removed. At times, the psychologist will need to get the mind of the directee off a problem not rooted in a rightly ordered cause of sorrow, e.g. if the person is struggling with feelings of anger (part of which is sorrow at the injury suffered) which are not rooted in reality. In this case, the person can seek to mitigate the sorrow by other means in order to get the sorrow out of the imagination so that the person can think clearly. But in cases where one must address the cause of the sorrow first before any appetitive mitigation should be sought, one must first deal with the cause of the sorrow. For instance, if a woman has an abortion and has not brought herself to contrition for the sin, she must first be sorry for the sin. Those who seek to mitigate the sorrow of the abortion without being sorry continue to conflict the intellect which knows the thing is sorrowful, even though the person has not appropriated the guilt of the sin. In this case, the person must first appropriate the guilt, be sorry for it and then the intellect will no longer have the dissonance. Then, the woman should get to Confession in order to seek sacramental absolution for the abortion. Subsequent to the absolution, she must do some form of penance to make up for the evil and that will mitigate the sorrow as her self-image is changed by doing the penance. In those cases

---

[181]Some of those mentioned were crying, groaning, taking baths, sensible consolations, speaking about the thing causing pain with another and contemplation of the truth.

[182]Reardon, *Aborted Women Silent No More*, passim.

in which the person may not be guilty of any wrongdoing, he must first determine the cause of the sorrow, come to some understanding of the cause and how to avoid it or to seek a spirit of mortification which will mitigate the sorrow.

Chapter 10: Brainwashing

Brainwashing is a process in which the habits of the cogitative power are stripped and the habits of judgment in the possible intellect are altered. This is done by repeated sensory experience which contains *ratio*s or perspectives in the image or sensory data. As this is done repeatedly, the cogitative power's habituation is changed to that which is in accord with the sensory data or image. The intellect's judgment is changed and new habits are developed in the possible intellect. The person does not lose his intellectual memory, rather the intellectual memory is altered by the repeated judgments to the contrary of what the person once thought. The degree of efficacy of a particular method of brainwashing is based upon (a) the degree and method of prepackaging the *ratio* in the sensory data to affect the cogitative power[183] and (b) the voluntariness of the person undergoing the brainwashing to submit to the agency of the brainwashing. When the intellect judges that the image is false and the will reformulates the image, this counteracts the brainwashing. However, due to lack of virtue, brainwashing cannot be resisted for long by most people. The less virtue a person has the less likely that he is able to resist the constant barrage of images.[184] To counteract brainwashing, one must employ a technique which reverses the associations of the cogitative power and re-establishes the prior associations. The judgments of the intellect will soon follow. Removal of the person from the source of brainwashing is the first requirement since it removes the source of the images in the imagination causing the difficulties. The psychological lesson that is to be learned from the process of brainwashing is that the cogitative power can be stripped of its habits and the habits of the possible intellect can be altered by constant and adverse phantasms.

Without entering into polemics about the matter, television and other forms of media must be used with great care so as not to be used to brainwash people. To use the media as a form of instruction in the truth does not fall under the notion of brainwashing since brainwashing by its nature has a negative connotation of being contrary to the will of the person being brainwashed. Education in the truth enhances voluntariness; brainwashing reduces voluntariness, since the person finds judging the truth of the matter more difficult due to the images in the imagination caused by the brainwasher. Therefore, it is not morally permissible for the media to be used to manipulate people's thinking against the truth. The use of brainwashing in all forms is immoral. This is why those people in charge of forms of media or other agencies capable of brainwashing must be of the highest moral character to ensure the right use of these media and

---

[183]These images are also stored in memory.

[184]Given this observation, one can also say that this applies to infused as well as acquired virtue. Grace can counteract any acts of brainwashing.

agencies.

Chapter 11: Prejudice

When analyzing the philosophical meaning of the term prejudice, we are not using the colloquial sense of the term even though there is a correlation. Prejudice in the colloquial sense means a partiality or a bias that prevents objective consideration of an issue or situation, often not based in reality. Prejudice, in the philosophical sense, means any activity of a cognitive faculty which occurs prior to judgment. This would include activities of the senses, the common sense power, the memory, the imagination and the cogitative power. All of these faculties engage in their activities prior to the judgment of the possible intellect. However, the activities of the cogitative power, memory and imagination are particularly important insofar as the reception of the image by the imagination and the preparation of the phantasm by the cogitative power and memory are necessary for any true understanding of the thing. For instance, if one encounters one's mother but the cogitative power does not associate prior memories with the image of one's mother in the imagination prior to judgment, one could not recognize one's mother. Since the habits of science cannot be employed in this life without phantasms,[185] then one cannot make use of intellectual memory without these activities occurring before judgment. We can say that the habits of the possible intellect and intellectual memory are also part of prejudice, since they exist in the intellect prior to any judgments and they affect judgment.

What this essentially means is that the assessments of the cogitative power of the image in the imagination and intellectual habits are necessary for our proper psychological functioning. "Prejudice," in this sense, is a necessary requisite for us to function as human beings or to engage in any true rational activity. Prejudice in the philosophical sense can then be defined as the assessment of the cogitative power based upon habits and what is contained in memory along with the habits of the possible intellect.

When analyzing whether a prejudice is good or bad, the standard is reality. If the habits in the cogitative power are good habits, they will provide a proper preparation of the phantasm so that when the concept is abstracted by the agent intellect, known by the possible intellect and judged by converting back to the phantasm, all will occur according to the truth, i.e. the intellect will be adequated to the thing. Right memory is also important regarding prejudice. If we also take into consideration intellectual habits, the prior right understanding and judgment of something causes a habit in the possible intellect which will incline it in the future to judge the thing rightly, i.e. according to the truth. All of these things are necessary in order for the prejudice to be rightly ordered and not to interfere with the ability of the intellect to judge objectively the truth regarding something. Since prudence is the application of general principles in the

---

[185]See volume one, chapter 4 (II C).

concrete,[186] which requires the intellect to convert back to a properly prepared phantasm to judge the individual thing, right prejudice is necessary for prudence.

Prejudice becomes false when any of those things which occur or exist prior to judgment are false. If the image is false, it can cause false judgment. If the cogitative power has been habituated in a false manner, the image will be prepared for abstraction by the merging of false memory (or the wrong memories) with the image. If one's intellectual habits are not good habits or if one's intellectual memory is false, judgment can also be compromised.

Given the aforesaid, not all prejudice is bad; in fact some of it is necessary. It becomes bad intellectually when prejudice affects judgment wrongly. It becomes bad morally only when evil action flows from false judgment due to the prejudice, or if the person volitionally habituates one of his faculties in error. Like many politically correct colloquial terms, a lack of distinction is harmful to the grasping of the truth.

Chapter 12: Self-Knowledge
"Know Thyself." – Plato[187]

A. Reflexion: The Basis of Self-knowledge

In volume one, a short discussion was offered regarding self-knowledge and at this time a more detailed study of self-knowledge is in order, since maintaining and recovering mental health is dependent upon self-knowledge. The basis of all self-knowledge is the ability to know oneself and the only way to know oneself is that one must be both the object of knowledge and the thing knowing at the same time. This ability of the intellect to know itself as an object and to know itself knowing is called reflexion. By reflexion the intellect reflex (or reflects) on itself.[188] Reflexion is an action in which the intellect turns in on itself to see itself.[189] This power of reflexion pertains to the possible intellect (through its act of judgment).[190] Material things are

---

[186]See part II of this volume.

[187]*Charmides* (164d).

[188]ST I, q. 76, a. 2, ad 4; ibid., q. 85, a. 2 and *In Libros de Anima* III, c. 8, n. 19.

[189]St. Thomas refers to this as a kind of forming a circle, see *In Aristotelis de Anima* I, c. 7, n.16. Dennis McInerny in *Philosophical Psychology* (p. 94) aptly describes this as "man is both the actor and an audience to himself."

[190]*De spiritualis creaturis*, un., a. 9, ad 6. In IV Sent., d. 49, q. 1, a. 1b, St. Thomas observes that a power can only know its act by reflexion.

unable to reflect on their own acts,[191] whereas immaterial powers are able to do so.[192]

By reflexion, the intellect can know a number of different things. The first is that the intellect can know its own act of understanding by seeing itself understand or, to put it another way, it can understand its act of understanding as well as how it understands.[193] It is for this reason that St. Thomas observes that we know ourselves to be intellectual.[194] Second, in seeing itself know something, the intellect knows itself.[195] Man's intellect differs from angelic intelligence insofar as the intellect must come to know some intelligible species before it can reflect on its knowing that intelligible species.[196] Third, the possible intellect comes to know the intelligible species itself through the act of reflexion.[197] This particular observation is important because it indicates that our first object of knowledge is not ourselves or our act of knowing. Rather our first object of knowledge is the essence of some material thing and then we are able to reflect on our knowledge of that. This is the foundation for saying that we do not know the concept of the thing (first). Rather we know the thing by means of the concept.[198]

Next, it is through an act of reflexion that we are able to know singulars by converting back to the phantasm.[199] It is here that we see that acts of reflexion differ.

---

[191]I Sent., d. 17, q. 1, a. 5, ad 3; III Sent., d. 23, q. 1, a. 2, ad 3; SCG II, c. 49, n. 8; ibid., IV, c. 11, n. 4 and ST I, q. 14, a. 2, ad 1. This is based upon the fact that no physical thing is able to bend back upon itself due to physical laws. Grenier observes (in *Cursus Philosophiae*, v. 1, p. 377 [n. 362f]) that the senses cannot know themselves. We may apply this to both the interior as well as the exterior senses.

[192]I Sent., d. 17, q. 1, a. 5, ad 3 and De Ver., q. 22, a. 12.

[193]De Pot., q. 7, a. 9: "et modum intelligit."

[194]SCG III, c. 46, n. 9.

[195]SCG IV, c. 11, n. 6. See also SCG II, c. 66, n. 5 and ST I, q. 87, a. 1.

[196]The intellect can only know itself when it is put in act by another intelligible species, see ST I, q. 87, passim and SCG II, c. 98, n. 2. In connection to this, St. Thomas observes that our knowledge first begins with the nature of some extrinsic material thing and then we can come to know ourselves by reflecting on that extrinsic thing, see SCG IV, c. 11, n. 5 and ST I, q., 87, a. 3. Sometimes that extrinsic thing is oneself; see below regarding knowledge of self as other.

[197]De Ver., q. 10, a. 9, ad 10 and *Questiones disputatae de Anima*, un., a. 2, ad 5. St. Thomas observes that since reason (possible intellect) can reflect on its own acts, it can order its own acts, see ST I-II, q. 17, a. 6.

[198]In volume one, we read that "unlike Descartes, Aquinas maintains that our first knowledge is of things extrinsic to ourselves and then we know ourselves subsequently." See SCG IV, c. 11, n. 5.

[199]ST I-II, q. 86, a. 1; ST II-II, q. 47, a. 3 ad 1; De Ver., q. 10, a. 5; ibid., ad 3; *In Libros de Anima* III, c. 8, n. 19; Gredt, *Elementa Philosophia*, v. 1, p. 441 (n. 556) and Grenier, *Cursus Philosophiae*, v. 1, p. 377 (n. 362f). The reference to ST II-II, q. 47, a. 3

Some acts of reflexion are those which merely remain in the possible intellect, e.g. when one knows oneself to understand some concept. But some acts of reflexion involve a turning of the possible intellect toward the phantasm and so it can know the individual. In this case, the possible intellect looks at both the concept in its own act of understanding and then converts back to the phantasm to "see"[200] the concept as pertaining to the particular. In this particular case, the phantasm which is in the intellect, from which the concept was abstracted by the agent intellect, is a particular similitude to the concept.[201] The possible intellect judges (or compares) through reflexion its concept in relation to the phantasm (singular).[202] In this respect, we do not know the singular or particular directly but only indirectly.[203] This specific kind of reflexion cannot be done without the cogitative power or the imagination.[204] Essentially, what this means is that the cogitative power must prepare the phantasm in the imagination for abstraction prior to the possible intellect's reflecting back on the phantasm. The preparation by the cogitative power is necessary in order to have a proper understanding of the thing understood, e.g. it would not be possible to relate the concept of "mother" to one's own particular mother without the cogitative power merging with the phantasm the prior sensitive memories of one's mother.[205]

The first kind of reflexion, in which one is able to know the intelligible species in the possible intellect, taken together with the second kind of reflexion, in which one converts back to the phantasm, is the basis for (a) knowing the existences of concrete things and (b) knowing the truth.[206] It is by this kind of reflexion that we know ourselves to be distinct from those things outside of us. We may even say it is the foundation for knowing that there are things outside of us, i.e. it is the foundation for us being in contact with reality and for knowing that our knowledge and reality are distinct.

---

ad 1 is of particular importance since it is by means of an act of reflexion on the phantasm that one has a knowledge of singulars that makes possible the application of universal precepts to singular concrete circumstances by an act of prudence.

[200]St. Thomas' famous word here is "respicit." See *De Trinitate*, p. 3, q. 5, a. 3.

[201]De Ver., q. 2, a. 6.

[202]Ibid. Reflexion is an act in which the same power turns on itself to know itself or its act. Since the passive intellect, agent intellect and possible intellect constitute a single power, when the possible intellect turns to the imagination (passive intellect) it is an act of reflexion.

[203]*Questiones Disputatae de Anima*, un., a. 2, ad sed contra 1.

[204]Ibid.

[205]See prior chapter on prejudice.

[206]De Ver., q. 10, a. 9 and In Meta., VI, c. 4, n. 14. It is here that we see the epistemological foundation for saying that knowledge of the existences of things is the foundation for knowledge of the truth.

B. Self-Knowledge

As mentioned, the basis of self-knowledge is the act of reflexion. But how we know ourselves is rather complicated. While only that which is subsistent knows itself,[207] nevertheless unlike God, we do not know ourselves essentially.[208] We, unlike God, do not know ourselves totally or perfectly.[209] Rather our knowledge of ourselves is rather poor but is able to be increased in a variety of ways.[210]

Since we do not know ourselves essentially, we know ourselves as an object of knowledge.[211] What this means is that we do not see our essence directly, but only know it and ourselves by means of an intelligible object or similitude (i.e. a concept) abstracted from the sensible species we have of ourselves.[212] Therefore, we do not see our souls directly but can only reason to knowledge of the soul (1) by means of our knowledge of ourselves gained through sensible species, (2) by reasoning regarding the intelligible species known in understanding and judgment and (3) by the immaterial acts we perform.[213] We know ourselves as "other",[214] which means that our knowledge of ourselves is distinct from ourselves, i.e. the intellect knows itself (and we can apply this

---

[207]ST I, q. 14, a. 2, ad 1. Only that which can bend back or reflect upon itself is subsistent since it is immaterial.

[208]SCG III, c. 46, nn. 2-6.

[209]III Sent., d. 14, q. 1, a. 2a, ad 2; ST I, q. 14, a. 3 and ibid., q. 87, a. 1. Cf. SCG I, c. 47, n. 2 and ibid., cc. 48-50. This observation applies not only to us in this life but in the next since to know ourselves totally would be to understand our relation to God perfectly. Perfect knowledge of a relation requires perfect knowledge of the terms; God is one of the terms of the relation and we cannot know Him perfectly. Therefore we cannot know ourselves perfectly. However, "perfectly" can be understood in two ways. In the first way, one has a fully exhaustive knowledge of a thing as we see in God in His knowledge of us and Himself. Human beings, due to the limitations of their faculties, cannot obtain this since it implies an infinite knowledge and our intellects are finite. The second is to know perfectly in the sense that one knows something to the degree that one is capable. In this sense, we will have a "perfect" knowledge of ourselves only at the beatific vision. The final judgment also contributes to self-knowledge, since God communicates His knowledge of us to us at that time. But it is only in seeing ourselves in God in the beatific vision that we will know ourselves to the degree that human understanding is capable.

[210]See below.

[211]III Sent., d. 23, q. 1, a. 2; ibid., ad 3; SCG II, c. 98, n. 2 and De Ver., q. 10, a. 8, ad sed contra 5.

[212]ST I, q. 87, a. 1. See also De Ver., q. 10, a. 8 and *Questiones Disputatae de Anima*, un., a. 17, ad 8.

[213]On a number of occasions, St. Thomas notes that there is a distinction between a scientific knowledge of human nature (and therefore ourselves) and what we know about ourselves through intellectual perception, see SCG III, c. 47, n. 10 and ST I, q. 87, a. 1.

[214]See III Sent., d. 23, q. 1, a. 2, ad 3.

to our knowledge of ourselves) as an object through reflexion.[215] As a result, even our knowledge of ourselves is mediate, not immediate.[216]

It is at this point that we must make the distinction between self-concept and self-image. The self-concept is that which is abstracted from our self-image and built up through complex judgments resulting in a complex self-concept. When we know ourselves through our self-concept, there is a distinction between the intellect knowing itself, since the intellect is present to itself,[217] and the formal content of the self-concept by which we know ourselves.

In our self-image, we know ourselves by means of sensibles,[218] e.g. one knows one's race, gender and a variety of other physical characteristics by means of the sensible species, i.e. man senses himself. This applies to what we know about ourselves not only through our exterior senses, e.g. by viewing ourselves in the mirror, but also through our interior senses, e.g. what we remember and imagine. Moreover, the sensations of passions are merged with our image and so we know our appetitive life.

St. Thomas observes that we also know a variety of other things about ourselves. He says that we can know our habits by the quality of the acts (or effects) that we perform which flow from those habits,[219] even though we cannot know the habits of the soul directly. In other words, if we look at the acts which we perform, we can know the habits from which they flow and so we can come to knowledge of the habits of our soul in this manner. St. Thomas also says that in order to know which habits we have, we must have a knowledge of what the various habits are.[220] A psychologist must have a knowledge of the habits in order to be able not only to know himself but also to know his directee by knowing the acts he performs and knowing from which habits those acts flow. Ignorance of the habits, virtues and vices contributes to ignorance of others and self. A psychologist must have the requisite knowledge of the virtues if he is to communicate that knowledge to the directee, so the directee can grasp the truth of the psychologist's diagnosis.

St. Thomas also observes that we know our acts of the will: "the act of the will is understood by the intellect, both insofar as someone perceives himself to will and

---

[215]De Ver., q. 10, a. 9, ad 10. This is simply another way of saying we do not know ourselves through our essence.

[216]ST I, q. 87, a. 1 and De Ver., q. 10, a. 8.

[217]ST I, q. 87, a. 1 and De Ver., q. 10, a. 8.

[218]SCG III, c. 47, n. 8. Maher in *Psychology: Empirical and Rational* describes the self-concept as a concrete perception of self combined with remembered experiences and actions of our past life, which includes an image of our bodily organism, dispositions, habits, character, hopes, regrets, resolutions and failures. While it must be conceded that each of these things is present in self-knowledge, nevertheless, his description tends to blur the distinction between self-image and self-concept and what pertains to each. Self-knowledge is twofold, viz. self-image and self-concept.

[219]SCG III, c. 47, n. 10; ST I, q., 87, a. 2 and De Ver., q. 10, aa. 9 and 10.

[220]De Ver., q. 10, aa. 9 and 10.

insofar as someone knows the nature of its act and consequently the nature of its principles, which is the habit or power."[221] The person knows that he wills something because he perceives himself to will it. This perception appears to be not only in the possible intellect,[222] but also in the lower faculties in which one sees the effects of what one wills. The person knows what he wills in three ways. The first is what St. Thomas mentions regarding the fact that one knows the principle from which the act proceeds, viz. the power or the habit. So by knowing the species of the habit, one knows what one wills. Second, one also knows what the possible intellect proposes to the will and so one knows the formal content of what one wills by reflecting on what one has in the possible intellect prior to an act of the will. Lastly, one knows what one wills by the species of the effects in the lower powers, e.g. the reformulated image, the passions caused by the image, and so on.

Before we proceed to the actual content of the self-image and concept, we must also realize that it is through the reflexion back to the phantasm that one knows the truth about oneself. Just as the truth is known by comparing what is in the possible intellect with what is in reality via the phantasm, so in self-knowledge we know the truth about ourselves by comparing the concept of ourselves to the image of ourselves. Since truth is the adequation of intellect and thing,[223] only when we have a true self-image which corresponds to who and what we really are can we attain to a true self-concept and thereby know the truth about ourselves. This means that true self-concept is dependent upon true self-image: we cannot have a proper and true understanding of ourselves without a true image. At times, one can have a true concept based on a true image and then later the image is falsified. Yet, one may still know the truth about oneself, since he knows the self-image is wrong based upon the true self-concept. If the false image persists, it will eventually affect our judgment of ourselves and thereby affect our self-concept.

Yet, true self-knowledge is among the most difficult things to achieve and we are highly prone to error when judging ourselves. While we can falsify our self-concept and image, we can also correct our self-image and concept through judgment. While we shall discuss how to achieve true self-image and concept in the next section of this chapter, on a general level, we can see that maintaining a true self-image and concept requires a variety of things. The first is that we must prune our self-image of those things which we know are false. We must reformulate our self-image based upon what we know is true of ourselves and this requires a certain strength of will (virtue, particularly justice and truthfulness). We must habituate the cogitative power to associate things in the right manner regarding ourselves. We must also purify our memory of false memories, particularly those regarding ourselves. We must also be very

---

[221]ST I, q. 87, a. 4: "actus voluntatis intelligitur ab intellectu, et inquantum aliquis percipit se velle; et inquantum aliquis cognoscit naturam huius actus, et per consequens naturam eius principii, quod est habitus vel potentia."

[222]This seems to be implied in ibid.

[223]See volume one, chapter five.

careful not to allow passions to affect our judgment of ourselves.[224] Lastly, we must have rectitude of the will, since the will can move the imagination and thereby affect our self-image, i.e. the will through sin can falsify our self-image. In fact, every sin falsifies self-image to one degree or another and so a life of virtue is required to attain true self-image and self-concept.

C. The Content of Self-knowledge

In order to judge our self-concept and image correctly, we need concrete principles and distinctions. While we have explained the general mechanism of self-knowledge, we must now discuss how we come to a concrete knowledge of ourselves, our traits, our personality, etc., by means of principled judgments. The first and perhaps primary understanding we have of ourselves is based upon our understanding of anthropology, i.e. the ontology of human nature. This includes everything contained in the first chapter of the first volume in this series. If any error arises in the understanding of the ontology of the person, it will affect the intellectual judgment about every other aspect of the person. We can know a lot about man's nature and therefore ourselves by comparing ourselves with inanimate things and animals.[225] The differences and similarities will provide us with some knowledge of our nature and our own personality traits.[226]

Next, we can know a great deal about ourselves and human nature by the actions which we perform. We become what we do,[227] and this is important for our self-image. It is often easy to disassociate our actions from ourselves by judgment of the possible intellect or disassociation by the cogitative power. This is particularly the case when what we do is evil.[228] Appropriation of one's sin is a necessary component of self-

---

[224]A review of chapter nine in the first volume would be particularly useful in regard to knowing how our passions can affect our judgment about ourselves.

[225]We not only know more about ourselves by comparing ourselves to animals, but as McInerny (*Philosophical Psychology*, p. 95) observes, we also know more about animals through self consciousness (or we may say self-knowledge).

[226]This is part of the rationale behind God's bringing the animals to Adam so that he may name them. God was showing Adam his differences from other animals as well as some things about himself (e.g. that he has dominion over the other animals). When Adam meets Eve, he then manifests true self-knowledge by observing that Eve was "bone of my bones, and flesh of my flesh" (Genesis 2:23).

[227]Pope John Paul II's book *The Acting Person* draws attention to the throughly Thomistic idea that the will or person becomes what he wills, since the species of the act of the will which is in the will is determined by what it wills, i.e. the object presented to the will in the possible intellect.

[228]Under the heading of evil, one can include those actions which lead to mental illness since they are evil on the level of nature as well as, at times, on the moral level.

knowledge.[229]

Moreover, our actions reveal not only certain aspects of human nature but they also reveal our habits, virtues, vices and other qualities (e.g. our disposition). If we look at the species of action which we perform, that will tell us something about the species of virtue, vice or habit, which we possess. Also, knowledge of the dispositions or temperaments can greatly aid in knowing what one is inclined toward. It can also give one a general knowledge of the personality traits of those who have the various dispositions.[230]

Our sin tells us something about our state of soul. St. Thomas says that sinners do not estimate themselves as they are,[231] i.e. sinners do not judge according to the interior man but the exterior man.[232] What he means by this is that sinners tend to judge themselves based on externals, such as beauty and physical traits (bodily size, shape, etc.), rather than on their spiritual well being. For this reason, St. Thomas says that sinners do not know themselves as they truly are, but as they *think* themselves to be.[233] In effect, sin blinds us because through sin the person becomes focused on some aspect of self which is not as important as his spiritual life. Our physical appearance, constitution and build do have a great impact on our self-image, because we are ordered toward knowing immaterial things by means of material things. However, in forming a proper image of ourselves, we must put away sinful actions which lead us away from our true nature as spiritual creatures ordered toward God as one's object of happiness and not toward happiness in created things. Fixation on material things is a sign of sin as well as mental illness.

We can also know a great deal about ourselves when we observe our reactions to what happens to us in the course of life. We can know what virtue we have by how we react to how people treat us, e.g. if we get excessively angry when someone injures us in some manner, that can indicate lack of the virtues of long suffering, patience and the spirit of mortification. It can also indicate to us that we have either a disposition toward anger or the vice of anger. How we react to things, such as animals and various possessions, tells us a great deal about ourselves. For instance, how we react and deal with things and people can tell us a great deal about our attachments (appetitive and intellective loves) to various things. A detailed knowledge of how passions function can aid us in looking at our reactions. For instance, if someone gets angry by some injury to some item he possesses, it can indicate an attachment (sensitive love) to that item. Knowledge of one's attachments provides a great deal of knowledge about one's inclinations, likes and dislikes. Sometimes we can simply do a general reflection on our appetitive life by remembering which passions or emotions tend to affect or dominate us. This will give us a knowledge of which antecedent appetites we must work on. It

---

[229]See volume two in the chapter on Confession.

[230]See chapter on dispositions.

[231]ST II-II, q. 25, a. 7.

[232]Ibid.

[233]Ibid.

will also give us a knowledge of the virtues and vices in our concupiscible and irascible appetites.

We can also look at how people react to us to come to a certain kind of self-knowledge. Maher observes that we have a dim consciousness of our position in the minds of other selves (people).[234] If we give due solicitude to how people react to what we do, it can indicate to us if we have a particular virtue, vice or personality trait. This requires, however, a knowledge of those around us and how they would be accustomed to reacting to various virtues, vices or traits. In knowing others around us, we can know that when they react, those reactions are based on their perceptions of us. Hence, if a vicious man reacts angrily to us this may not be a sign that we have done anything wrong, but that we have done something right or that we possess some virtue that he finds distasteful. On the other hand, if a virtuous man reacts negatively to something we do, this may be a sign that he perceives some defect or fault in our actions. While the more virtuous a man is the less likely his interior life will be manifested without moderation, nevertheless when we do things that are blatant or egregious, virtuous men normally will react in the appropriate manner.

Sometimes people will tell us our defects or virtues outright. The normal human reaction, due to man's state laboring under the effects of original and actual sin, is to reject negative comments outright and to accept positive ones warmly. However, therein lies the danger. Virtue is required in order to judge rightly about the person's comments. Virtue is required in the intellect and will in which one is habituated in leading a life according to the truth and always adhering to the truth. If one is prone to error, falsity and vice, one will react falsely to the comments of others, whether they are true or not. Humility is an absolute requisite in coming to self-knowledge. When people tell us something about ourselves, if we are not tempered in our self-judgment by humility, we will tend to go to excess or defect in our judgment about ourselves. Therefore, if we lack humility and someone says something positive about us, we will tend to allow that to affect our self-image and concept to a greater degree than we ought. If someone says something negative about us and we lack humility, we will tend not to focus on looking at whether what the person says is true or not. Rather, we will focus on the injury, since pride will incline our judgment to overestimate our goodness and therefore we will not see the truth of what the person says. As a result, we will not take the correction and so we will not correct or reformulate our image and concept of ourselves. We also need fortitude, since coming to self-knowledge and conquering self requires great self-discipline, self-control and self-denial; in a word, it is arduous.

Psychologists must be careful how they react to directees so as not to give them false impressions. Those who suffer from mental illness may not be able to make much use of this particular way[235] of coming to knowledge of self, since they often have very poor judgment of their relationships with others as well as people's reactions. Sometimes, the psychologist may even have to tell the directee to ignore how people

---

[234]Maher, *Psychology: Empirical and Rational*, p. 365.

[235]That is one can use the reactions of others.

react since it will distract him from his focus on becoming mentally healthy or people may not understand him properly so as to react to him properly.

We can also know something about ourselves by the defects which we observe in other people. Christ Himself said, "And why seest thou the mote that is in thy brother's eye; and seest not the beam that is in thy own eye?"[236] This indicates that we are often able to notice defects in those around us precisely because we have them ourselves. Virtuous people tend to be a bit oblivious to other people's defects. This is largely due to the fact that psychologically, their intellect, will and lower facilities are ordered toward the good because of their virtue. When they are around those who have some defect, they tend not to see it since they are focused not on defects but on the good and the true, whereas those who have defects tend to be focused on evil and falsity. As a result, their faculties are more attuned to finding them in their neighbor. However, a virtuous man can notice people's defects if he is trained or if he wills to do so. Yet, as a general rule, he does not will to do so and so he often does not observe them.

The moral to the story is that if we see some defect in someone else, we should use it as a means of examining ourselves to see if we have the same species of defect. If, in humility and truth, one does not see that he has the defect, he should take that moment as one in which God is allowing him to see the defect of the other in order to pray, do penance or something of this kind for him. Often virtuous people may see the defect of another because God reveals it to them. Yet, they should realize that they too could fall into that defect without the grace of God, even if they do not have that defect.

As a general rule, it is not good to dwell on the good aspects of ourselves. The reason for this is that passions of love and delight arise due to the consideration of the good. This will, in turn, affect our judgment of ourselves. Also, pride which judges our excellence to excess[237] will arise from too much consideration of our own good. This brings us to the topic of self-esteem, again. Throughout this series the concept of self-esteem has been criticized principally because psychologists have encouraged people to esteem themselves without any basis in reality. Yet, it was observed that self-esteem is true self-esteem only when the person sees himself in reference to God.[238] Reflections on self-knowledge, if done rightly, can adjust our self-esteem to be in accord with reality. When all good attributes, virtues and traits of the person are referred to God, then and only then is one's self-esteem rightly ordered. In effect, the only thing we ought to esteem is God and we esteem ourselves, not for our own sakes, but insofar as we are like God.[239] Also, we must be careful not to think about ourselves too much, since it can lead to a kind of self-absorption in which one becomes fixated on self due to the pleasure in thinking about the good of self.

Human respect can also affect our self-knowledge. Someone suffering from

---

[236]Matthew 7:3.

[237]ST II-II, q. 162, a. 3, ad 1.

[238]See volume two, chapter four.

[239]Esteem (and therefore self-esteem) essentially follows the order and conceptual outlook of charity.

human respect tends to respect the judgments of others over and above their true value.[240] As a result, our proper understanding of ourselves in relation to them is compromised by human respect, insofar as we do not see ourselves properly in relation to other people and so we do not know how much we should respect what they say or think about us.

Our relationships and friendships can tell us a great deal about ourselves. We can look at the types of friendship we tend to establish, e.g. are our friendships based on virtue or common vices? We can also know something about ourselves by discerning what we like about the people with whom we tend to be friends. This will indicate our likes and dislikes, dispositions, virtues and vices and so on. But our self-image and self-concept is not only affected by our friends whom we choose, but also by those with whom we have a relationship which is outside our control. Since the image of the person is often viewed in relationship to ourselves, this provides some content of knowledge about who we are, e.g. our family life (and how we relate to each person in the family) and those who attend schools with the various teachers and students with whom they relate. Those with whom we work (which often forms our image of the company for which we work) can also affect our self-image, not only because of the general image or impression we have of the company for which we work, but also because our actions in relation to that company tell us a great deal about ourselves.

We also know something about ourselves based upon our state in life. For example, we know something about ourselves if we are married (and based on the person to whom we are married) or if we are priests, religious or laymen. Part of our state is any position we might hold in relation to others, e.g. if we are the head of a state, company or association. One can know something about oneself if one is a head of a family (i.e. a father) or a mother or son or daughter. Our knowledge of our state taken in connection to our relationships, our place of living and surroundings and our place of origin makes us realize that man thinks of himself contextually.[241]

We also know something about ourselves by our acts of conscience. Since the conscience tells us whether what we have done in the past is good or bad, it says something about our moral character. Conscience is essentially an act of self-knowledge.[242] Frequent examinations of conscience are to be encouraged for the directee since this will provide him a great deal of knowledge about himself.[243] Since examination of conscience is sometimes difficult, it is often best to examine one's conscience with a concrete guide which contains the various sins and vices. This provides a means for the reflection of the directee to be more focused and concrete rather than to remain in generalities or impressions about himself.

The discussion of the examination of conscience brings us to the discussion of

---

[240]ST II-II, q. 63.

[241]McInerny, *Philosophical Psychology*, p. 95.

[242]Esser, *Psychologia*, p. 327.

[243]The only exception would be the directee who is scrupulous or prone to become scrupulous.

Confession and the supernatural means by which we can come to knowledge of ourselves. Frequent Confession provides self-knowledge for several reasons. The first is that one must appropriate one's sin and so one knows the truth about oneself.[244] Second, one must examine one's conscience which provides self-knowledge and, if done frequently, our knowledge of ourselves deepens and grows. Third, Confession tells us something about our virtue, since how we confess and with what virtues indicates the virtues themselves. For example, if someone confesses sincerely, truthfully, honestly and humbly, he has some insight into the state of his soul. Confession also provides grace which helps us to avoid sins in the future and so the grace will, at times, give us knowledge of our weaknesses in the areas pertaining to the sins confessed. Confession also provides an avenue of developing humility, which is a necessary virtue for self-knowledge. If one judges oneself greater than he is (pride), one will not know the truth about oneself since his judgment about himself will be false (excessive). If one is unwilling to live in accordance with the truth (pride again), one will not be able to know the truth about oneself because to accept the truth is often painful and arduous. Those unwilling to live according to the truth rarely are willing to suffer pain and the arduous to come to self-knowledge. Rather, they are normally people whose lives are governed more by appetite than truth.

Actual grace, since it enlightens the mind and strengthens the will,[245] can enlighten the person about himself. Through grace, God is able to teach us or to tell us about ourselves. This knowledge often is accompanied by a kind of certitude about the judgment of ourselves. In this regard, one of the most efficacious means of coming to knowledge of self is to ask the Holy Spirit to reveal one to oneself. Since God knows us perfectly, He is able to tell us the details of ourselves beyond any natural means of coming to knowledge of them. God also looks kindly on the soul who wishes to come to self-knowledge in order to eradicate any imperfection which might offend Him. Therefore, the directee should be encouraged, particularly when he is unable to see the truth about himself, to ask God to reveal his defects or the source of his mental illness, particularly if the mental illness has as its cause some sin or vice.

The religion to which we belong is perhaps among the most telling aspects of ourselves. Since religion determines the relationship we have with God and the mode of conduct in relation to God and created things, we can know a great deal about ourselves by the religion to which we give assent and the degree to which we live that religion. Part of this aspect of self-knowledge is that our religion can tell us whether we think religion is about us or about God. Whether we conform ourselves to a religion which is determined and established by God or whether we are part of a religion which places belief more in the hands of the believer, can tell us whether we are the type of individuals to conform ourselves to the truth or whether we want reality, religion and ultimately God to conform to us. This, in turn, will reveal to us the orientation of our

---

[244]As to the various aspects of Confession, see volume two in the chapter on Confession.

[245]See chapter in second volume on grace.

intellectual and appetitive life. If a religion is the true religion, it will inform us that reality is not about us but about God. A religion that focuses on the people rather than on God[246] will distort the order of reality and corrupt people's proper view of themselves. It simply is not possible to have true self-knowledge without true religion.[247]

This brings us to the topic of prayer. Prayer can provide a great deal of knowledge about ourselves. The way in which we engage in prayer reveals to us our attitude toward God. The finality of prayer also tells us what we think about our own finality. If the finality of our prayer is to get warm "fuzzy" feelings out of the prayer, the feelings are the finality, not God. Hence, how we react to sensible or spiritual consolation tells us a great deal about our appetitive life and the general orientation of our will. Another way the prayer provides self-knowledge is in regard to the matter of prayer. Some methods of prayer employ comparisons in which one contemplates some attribute of God in comparison to our failings, faults and perfections. Prayer can consider how the perfections found in ourselves have their source in God and how they are merely a participation in and an extrinsic manifestation of some perfection in God. By this comparison, we learn more about ourselves. Prayer also reflects our attitude toward God and our view of justice toward God: do we believe that we ought to pray[248] and sacrifice[249] to God or do we fail to pray? When we seek created goods over God, this reveals to us our intellectual understanding of happiness and the things we pursue. We can see, therefore, that the more we grow in knowledge of God, the more we know ourselves.[250] We realize that without a true knowledge of God, there is no objective standard by which to gauge and measure ourselves.[251]

Temptations provide an avenue of self-knowledge.[252] After we have gone through a temptation, we can reflect on how our various faculties reacted to the temptation, e.g. we can see what passions arose which will tell us about our antecedent appetites. We can see how our cogitative power assessed the temptation and what memories came to mind. We can observe how we judged the temptation which may tell us something about our intellectual habits. We can see how our will reacted and that will indicate whether our will is weak or whether the will manifested continence.

---

[246]By this we are not denying that in religion it is proper to care about people. Rather, it establishes that a true religion and true self-knowledge can only occur when the order of charity is properly established, followed and assented to. See volume two in the chapter on charity.

[247]This is true on several levels, however the most pronounced level is that each religion embodies a cosmology or world view which situates man within the world view. Hence, every religion determines man's knowledge of self in relation to God and the world.

[248]See ST II-II, q. 83.

[249]That we are all held to sacrifice: see ST II-II, q. 85, a. 1.

[250]Maturin, *Self Knowledge and Self Discipline*, p. 4.

[251]Ibid.

[252]Ibid., p. 37.

Moreover, we can look at the content of the temptation which will indicate to us one of two things. (1) God may be allowing us to be tempted in order to strengthen us. As a result, we can take the species of the temptation as a sign of to which species of weakness and to which faculties the weakness pertains as a form of learning something about ourselves. (2) There are times when a person does not have any particular weakness toward the temptations.[253] In these cases, the person should recognize that God is allowing the temptation either because He wants us to merit something for ourselves or someone else[254] or He wants us to atone for a particular sin which relates to the species of the temptation. Analysis of the temptation by the directee himself or by the psychologist can reveal a great deal about the state and habits of the various faculties.

In connection to temptation, we can do a form of self testing.[255] While temptations are allowed by God to test us, we can engage in testing ourselves. We should not do so by putting ourselves in the occasion of sin, for this is both sinful and unnecessary. If we know something is an occasion of sin, we already know the state of our faculties in relation to the object of temptation. However, if a psychologist detects that the directee's mental illness is connected to something not very apparent and provided no sin is involved, the psychologist can suggest a self testing and then discuss the results later with the directee. Self testing essentially consists in engaging some object or action to see the reaction of the various faculties in relation to the object. One must be careful in self testing so as not to aggravate the mental illness but to provide a true knowledge of the mental status of the directee. Caution must be observed also since sometimes self testing is not necessary and could be harmful. In those cases, psychologists are not morally permitted to ask the directee to engage in self testing.

Self-knowledge is a very complex thing. Our self-image and self-concept are very complicated but they do not necessarily defy analysis. On the other hand, we must be clear that the intellectual prowess of the directee or the person doing the analysis of himself does not guarantee self-knowledge.[256] Also, self analysis, even if carried out properly, does not necessarily lead to self-knowledge.[257] Sometimes vigilance is required to come to self-knowledge in which the person has to pay attention or keep his eye out for any signs that might reveal the state of his faculties to himself. Lastly, we must make a distinction between self-ignorance and self-deception. Self-ignorance is merely a lack of knowledge of ourselves which we all have to one degree or another and this can be overcome by the methods mentioned above as well as by consulting others who may be more able to gain an objective knowledge of us. Self-deception is when one volitionally alters his self-image or self-concept in order to suit some appetitive pleasure

---

[253]For example, Christ had no moral weaknesses and yet He was tempted.

[254]See volume two, chapter eight (II) for the various reasons why God allows temptations.

[255]Maturin, *Self Knowledge and Self Discipline*, p. 37-9.

[256]Ibid., p. 27.

[257]Ibid., p. 26f and p. 34.

or desire. In the end, it takes one away from reality in which his true self-knowledge consists. In this respect, self-knowledge is as heavily dependent on our ability to know ourselves as it is on our moral character.[258]

Chapter 13: Self-help

The term self-help usually designates a form of striving for some perfection, mental health or physical health in a way which does not require the aid of another. However, in order for a person to help himself, there are a few things required. The first is knowledge of one's defect. Often those who employ self-help do have some knowledge of their defect. However, their judgment of their defect may not arrive at the truth of the matter because they often judge to excess due to the passions involved. For instance, someone may recognize that he has some particular problem and the passion of sorrow arises which affects his judgment as to how bad the problem is, i.e. he thinks it is worse or better than it is.

The second thing which is necessary for self-help is knowledge of the perfection or thing for which one is striving. Many who do not understand their problems often seek advice in popular books, television shows and pop psychology. Sometimes these forms of media can aid people in knowing what to do, but more often than not these forms of media lack the depth necessary for the person truly to understand his problem. Also, when people turn to these forms of help in order to help themselves, they often do not have sufficient knowledge or intellectual principles to judge whether the suggestions really apply to their problem or are a true solution to their problem.

For this reason, when people suffer from minor psychological (or spiritual defects), these kinds of aids can be helpful if (1) what they assert about the problem, (2) the perfection and (3) the means to the perfection are true. However, major psychological difficulties as well as minor ones often require a second party for their diagnosis. This is necessary in order that the judgment of the one diagnosing is objective and more likely to discover the truth. If a psychologist is properly formed in psychology (such as that which is offered in these three volumes), he will be in a better place to know which possible psychological defects fit the symptoms of the directee.

This is not to say that popular books cannot help people. Rather, psychologists and directees should understand that there are definite advantages to seeking the counsel of a second party. Since knowledge of self is so complicated and prone to error, provided the psychologist is competent and the directee is forthcoming with the information necessary for the psychologist to diagnose properly, the directee stands a better chance of coming to true knowledge of his problem and the means to overcoming it.

On another note, we may observe that virtually every form of psychological healing, other than those which are spiritual or physiological in origin, are based on the principle of self-help. In other words, even when a directee goes to a psychologist, the

---

[258]Ibid., p. 30.

psychologist can only provide counsel and encouragement – nothing more. It is then up to the directee to employ the means counseled. He has to help himself. No one else can do it for him. Often directees expect the psychologist to heal them. Psychological healing is principally something done by the directee. Just as a doctor does not heal anyone properly speaking but merely provides the medicine, surgery, etc. by which one is healed, so with psychological problems, the psychologist can only provide the knowledge of the means by which the directee can be healed.[259] He can also encourage and pray for the directee.

However, grace builds on nature and so unless the directee is willing to cooperate with the grace as well as dispose himself as much as he can on the natural level (which is a form of self-help), then all the prayers and supernatural means will not help him. It is true that God can correct even natural problems by grace, but this too requires the cooperation of the directee insofar as the directee does not negate the work done in him by God. Given the aforesaid, in one sense, all of psychological healing rests on self-help. On the other hand, one can aid oneself more efficaciously by seeking the help and counsel of others.

Chapter 14: Predominant Fault

In spiritual theology, there is a doctrine which can prove to be very useful to the science of mental health, viz. the predominant fault. "The predominant fault is the defect in us that tends to prevail over the others, and thereby over our manner of feeling, judging, sympathizing, willing, and acting."[260] The predominant fault is some defect or vice in us which tends to dominate all of our other faults, i.e. it tends to be worse than all of our other faults. The predominant fault can also be the genesis of other faults, e.g. pride which can lead to anger. A proud person, when insulted, becomes angry because of the injury to himself. The predominant fault is also dangerous since it can compromise our good qualities.[261] When the psychologist analyzes the directee, he may come across a variety of problems or psychological defects in the directee. However, he must try to determine which one predominates in order to see whether that predominant fault is the cause of other psychological problems.

In order to recognize the predominant fault, one can take into consideration the various means of self-knowledge as delineated above. However, other means of zeroing in on one's predominant fault include asking oneself certain questions:

Toward what do my most ordinary preoccupations tend, in the morning when I awake, or when I am alone? Where do my thoughts

---

[259]This is something discovered in relation to alcoholics. Unless they arrive at the point where they admit their problem and are willing to do something about it, i.e. help themselves, no one else can help them.

[260]Garrigou-Lagrange, *The Three Stages of the Interior Life*, vol. 1, p. 314.

[261]Ibid., p. 315.

and desires go spontaneously? We should keep in mind that the predominant fault, which easily commands all our passions, takes on the appearance of a virtue and, if it is not opposed, it may lead to impenitence.[262]

The predominant fault often gives the directee a pleasure in thinking about the object of the fault. This is rooted in the observation made throughout this series that one gets a certain pleasure from experiencing something according to one's dispositions. We can know our predominant fault by observing that toward which we are easily and by disposition inclined.

> A second step in discerning the predominant fault, is to ask ourselves: what is generally the cause of my sadness and joy? What is the general motive of my actions, the ordinary origin of my sins, especially when it is not a question of accidental sin, but rather a succession of sins or a state of resistance to grace, notably when this resistence persists for several days and leads me to omit my exercises of piety?" Then we must seek sincerely to know the motive of the soul's refusal to return to the good.[263]

When transposing the consideration to the domain of psychology, the psychologist can ask the directee what are his predominant sins.[264] Sometimes, the psychologist simply has to ask the directee what actions does he perform that tend to exacerbate his problem or which he wishes he did not do. These actions constitute a sign of the problem. Asking the directee what his motives are can provide the psychologist with information regarding the voluntariness of the psychological defect. Knowing the motives can also provide knowledge of the finality of the psychological disorder. Once one knows the finality, he can know which faculties that finality could affect since certain finalities fall under some faculties and not others.

The directee can also ask himself:

> Have we not sought to excuse ourselves? Excuses come promptly, for the predominant fault easily excites all our

---

[262]Ibid., p. 316.

[263]Ibid., p. 317.

[264]Great caution is required here since the psychologist is entering into the internal forum. The directee has a right to refuse to discuss his particular sins or even his sins in general with the psychologist since his obligation to confess his sins only applies to the priest in the sacrament of Confession. However, since the psychological illness may manifest itself or be caused by sin, the directee may wish to divulge that information. Otherwise, the psychologist may not be able to help the directee. All of this points to the fact that the psychologist must be a man of irreproachable character.

passions... Morever, when the predominant fault has taken root in us, it experiences a particular repugnance to being unmasked and fought, because it wishes to reign in us. This condition sometimes reaches such a point that, when our neighbor accuses us of this fault, we reply that we have many bad habits, but truly not the one mentioned.[265]

The predominant fault causes a blindness in our ability to see it at times. But if the directee finds that when the fault is exposed he has a certain interior dissonance or appetitive revulsion toward the accusation, it probably is his predominant fault or, at least, a fault.

Knowledge of the predominant fault provides the psychologist with an ability to know the means to counsel the directee. Discovering the predominant fault by the psychologist as well as his informing the directee of the fault will cause an appetitive revulsion in the directee. The psychologist, therefore, should not be surprised when he finds appetitive resistance in the directee to his diagnosis.

Chapter 15: Temperaments or Dispositions

The term "temperament" is defined by authors in a variety of different ways. Wolman defines it as a predisposition of a person to emotional reactions.[266] Cunningham defines it as a regular psychological pattern of reacting to stimuli and social situations.[267] One of the best definitions is given by Jordan Aumann: "For our purposes we may define temperament as the pattern of inclination and reactions that proceed from the physiological constitution of the individual."[268] In our estimation, this definition contains the essential elements of temperament. The first element is that temperament indicates a pattern of inclination and reactions. This pattern is not merely emotional but also includes intellectual inclinations regarding patterns of judgment and things of this sort. The second component of temperament is that it is based upon the physiological constitution of the individual, i.e. it is based upon the material (or bodily) disposition of the person.[269] In this respect, any patterns of intellectual judgment that are tied to temperament would be those based upon the material disposition of the person. This material disposition affects everything from the operations of the passive intellect to the operations of the appetites.

In volume one of this work, it was noted that each faculty has its proper object and sometimes the faculty relates to its object well and sometimes it does not. A

---

[265]Ibid.

[266]Wolman, *Dictionary of Behavioral Science*, p. 371.

[267]Cunningham, *The Christian Life*, p. 119.

[268]Aumann, *Spiritual Theology*, p. 140.

[269]Brennan, *General Psychology*, p. 406 and Duerk, *Psychology in Questions and Answers*, p. 135.

disposition in a faculty occurs when the "matter is disposed to the reception of form"[270] or when "some agent is disposed to acting."[271] A disposition resides in the faculty and determines whether the faculty will act or be acted upon by its object well or poorly. The disposition affects the relationship the particular faculty has to its object. A disposition is the ability to effect or suffer something according to an innate readiness for certain kinds of activity. When a faculty is an active potency, if it is disposed well, then it acts well and with facility; if the faculty is disposed poorly, that type of action is difficult even though the faculty is able to perform it in a minimal sort of way. If the faculty is a passive potency and if it is disposed well, it will readily undergo the action proper to it; whereas if the faculty is disposed poorly, it will find the action difficult or painful.

The term "disposition" can refer to a habit insofar as a habit disposes the faculty toward a specific object well or poorly. Yet, Aquinas refers to a habit as a quality, because there is a difference between a habit and a disposition: "from which it is clear that the term habit implies a certain long duration; not however the term of disposition".[272] St. Thomas also observes that angels do not have dispositions since they are immaterial.[273] This follows from the fact that a disposition can only be had by that which has parts.[274] This arrangement of the parts determines how the faculty will function. Temperament, insofar as it is a disposition, principally refers to the arrangement of matter in the individual.[275]

---

[270]De Vir., q. 1, a. 1, ad 9: "materia disponitur ad formae receptionem."

[271]Ibid.: "aliquod agens disponitur ad agendum." See also IV Sent., d. 49, q. 3, a. 2. St. Thomas observes that through complexion, someone is more apt to concupiscence or anger, see SCG II, c. 63, n. 5; ST I-II, q. 46, a. 5 and ST II-II, q. 156, a. 1. By complexion, St. Thomas does not mean skin color or appearance as it is used in modern parlance. Rather, it refers to arrangement of the matter in the body.

[272]ST I-II, q. 49, 2, ad 3: "ex quo patet quod nomen habitus diuturnitatem quandam importat; non autem nomen dispositionis."

[273]Ibid., q. 50, a. 6: "habitus...qui sunt dispositiones ad esse naturale, non sunt in angelis, cum sint immateriales."

[274]ST I-II, q. 49, a. 4.

[275]This is the foundation for saying that personality is a broader category than temperament. See next chapter. Animals are said to have a personality, but of animals this is said only analogically since humans can change their personality and temperament by voluntary actions, whereas animals cannot since they do not have free will. When the term "personality" is used in relation to animals (and children prior to the use of reason) it refers to the temperament, i.e. bodily dispositions. Hence, when we say a child before the age of one or two has a personality, we are really referring to temperament which determines the actions of the material faculties. The same applies to animals. That animals can have temperaments, see ST I-II, q. 46, a. 5, ad 1. The consequence of this conclusion is that human psychology and animal psychology radically differ, since man has a personality and temperament whereas an animal only has a temperament, properly speaking. This is why a

Temperament is principally hereditary[276] or natural endowment[277] insofar as we inherit our bodily disposition from our parents, although environmental factors can also affect disposition or temperament. Esser draws our attention to the fact that temperament can differ according to peoples (*gentium* – e.g. the Italian disposition as compared to the German)[278] and age (e.g. adolescent dispositions as opposed to elderly dispositions).[279] In discussing the predominant defect, Garrigou Lagrange remarks that

---

profound grasp of analogy and the essence of man and animals is necessary, if any form of scientific comparison is to be made between the psychology of animals and the psychology of man.

[276]See Aumann, *Spiritual Theology*, p. 140.

[277]Cunningham, *The Christian Life*, p. 119.

[278]Esser, *Psychologia*, p. 351. This observation requires great intellectual precision in order to avoid a false racism. Since race is essentially a bodily disposition, it can be seen to pertain to two aspects of man. The first is that much of race pertains to non-operative qualities, e.g. the color of one's skin, general facial features associated with particular races, etc. Since these are non-operative, they fall outside the domain of the voluntary. Then there is that aspect of man which pertains to operative qualities, e.g. one's physiological disposition can affect the operation of the material faculties. Hence, the qualities of the material component of the faculty can affect its operation. In this respect, we see that certain races are inclined towards certain kinds of actions by disposition, e.g. Germans in general tend toward order and structure in their common life whereas the Italians tend toward a more relaxed approach regarding common life. However, in connection to this, several observations must be made in relation to the term "discrimination." The first is that discrimination based upon operative distinctions cannot be applied to non-operative qualities, e.g. one cannot discriminate against blacks (or whites for that matter, given the current academic milieu) in college admissions simply because of the color of their skin. However, if a doctor refuses to take someone's race into consideration when doing his examination of his patient's bodily health (and not his moral character), it is false discrimination. This follows from the fact that different races are prone to different kinds of medical conditions. To fail to take into consideration the race of a person when diagnosing certain illness is an injustice to the person since it can lead to an improper diagnosis which is contrary to what is due to him. The second observation is that while races may have different dispositions which constitute operative qualities in the body, these are not necessarily connected to moral character. Thirdly, while certain behavior may be observed among particular races, that is not necessarily a sign of disposition of that race. It can also be a sign of upbringing, the subculture of the members of that race, and things of this sort. Lastly, since each individual's disposition is proper to himself, only after one comes to a detailed knowledge of the person's moral character can one assess that his character is a result of his disposition. Therefore, even if every race has its generic disposition, that does not mean that each person in the race will have the operative dispositions of that race.

[279]Esser, *Psychologia*, p. 351.

It is a defect that has in each of us an intimate relation to our individual temperament. There are temperaments inclined to effeminacy, indolence, sloth, gluttony, and sensuality. Others are inclined especially to anger and pride. We do not all climb the same slope toward the summit of perfection: those who are effeminate by temperament must by prayer, grace, and virtue become strong; and those who are naturally strong, to the point of easily becoming severe, must by working at themselves and, by grace, become gentle. Before this progressive transformation of our temperament, the predominant defect in the soul often makes itself felt.[280]

The passage contains several important points. The first is that each person has a different temperament which inclines him to different virtues and vices.

Secondly, temperament, since it is a disposition, is changeable. Since the body disposes itself to the operations of the soul, the bodily disposition can be changed when one acts virtuously. This means that one's temperament can be changed. In relation to the discussion of the four temperaments, this means that perfection in temperament consists in not having any one of the four temperaments predominate. Sometimes people undergo changes of temperament due to voluntary actions, such as when they develop virtues and vices. Some people undergo a temperament change due to changes in their age, e.g. children when they go through puberty. Sometimes environmental factors can play a role, e.g. when people ingest various substances in the water which can change their bodily dispositions or when they change from a peaceful environment to a violent one, e.g. soldiers are noted for undergoing personality changes when they enter into fierce combat. This latter kind of change of disposition may be merely a reaction by the cogitative power in assessing the sense data and preparing the image in the imagination. However, if one remains in the environment for a long period of time, the difference in the appetitive and intellectual life will cause changes in the bodily disposition.

Thirdly, for psychology, this has great import. Most people develop their personalities and moral character according to their temperament. We have mentioned on several occasions that to act contrary to one's disposition causes pain. Due to the effects of original sin of weakness of the will and disordered appetites, most people do not act contrary to their disposition due to the arduousness involved. In a sense, they tend to take the "path of least resistance." Conversely, since to act according to disposition tends to give one a certain pleasure, there is a physiological incentive to act according to disposition. Some actions which are according to one's disposition can aid mental health; however, other actions performed according to one's disposition can incline one to mental illness. For instance, if one has a temperament which inclines one toward worrying, one can develop anxiety (fear) disorders. Psychology can make use of the knowledge of the different temperaments in order to give a diagnosis and to come to a better understanding of the directee. Since those with a certain temperament often

---

[280]Garrigou-Lagrange, *The Stages of the Interior Life*, vol. 1, p. 314.

have certain personality traits proper to the temperament, the directee can gain a greater knowledge of himself and other good and bad traits he may have by reflecting on his temperament and how he manifests it. The more a psychologist knows and has experience with people of various temperaments, the more he is able to understand the causes of mental illness which can arise out of the various temperaments.

Sometimes coming to knowledge of a temperament can be difficult and the more experience one has of the various temperaments and people who possess them, the more readily one can recognize them in oneself and others. Yet, some things can pose a difficulty in coming to knowledge of a person's true temperament. In other words, at times it is easy to misdiagnose a person's temperament due to a variety of factors. The first factor which can make the knowing of a person's temperament difficult is when a person is habitually given to sin,[281] e.g. when a sanguine person gives way to anger due to his environment. If one were to take him out of the environment, he would revert back to being peaceful and calm. However, certain circumstances will incline him quickly to anger which can be misinterpreted as a choleric temperament. If he maintains the anger, his temperament will change to being choleric.

Another factor which can affect one's reading of a person's temperament is how far advanced the person is in the spiritual life. The more perfect a person is, the less any one of the temperaments predominate.[282] Hence, as one grows in virtue, the material dispositions in the faculties arrange to accommodate the virtue. As a result, one is less prone to anger, if one were choleric or to sensuality, if one were sanguine. Temperament or disposition is by degree and so, as one becomes more perfected, the less predominate a temperament is and so the less noticeable it is.

It is also difficult to determine a person's temperament if the person has a mixed temperament.[283] This occurs when the person has two different temperaments, one which predominates and the other which is more recessive.[284] Most people have a predominant *and* a recessive temperament. Since temperaments are had by degree, it is possible that a person can have a strong or weak predominant temperament and the same can be said of the recessive temperament.

A. The Sanguine Disposition

Traditionally, the depositions are broken into four kinds, viz. the sanguine, the choleric, melancholic and the phlegmatic. Sanguine people react quickly and strongly but not permanently and the reaction tends to last for a short period of time.[285] Sanguine people tend to be light hearted (since they are not inclined to sorrow), imaginative,

---

[281]Hock, *The Four Temperaments*, p. 11.

[282]See ibid.

[283]Ibid.

[284]Aumann, *Spiritual Theology*, p. 140.

[285]Ibid; Cunningham, *The Christian Life*, p. 120; Hock, *The Four Temperaments*, p. 11.

vivacious[286] and joyful.[287] For these reasons, we can say that the sanguine disposition is one in which the positive passions of the concupiscible appetite predominate, viz. love, desire and delight. Sanguine people, because of their general positive outlook, tend to be optimistic.[288] From this we may say that sanguine people tend to be prone to the passion of hope.

The positive traits of the sanguine disposition are many. Sanguine people tend to be friendly or affable,[289] pleasant, agreeable (*iucundus*)[290] and more loving.[291] Sanguine people tend to be compassionate toward those who suffer.[292] They are also described as docile,[293] candid,[294] sincere[295] and spontaneous.[296] They tend to be cheerful[297] and have a contagious enthusiasm.[298] The sanguine disposition tends to react vehemently to injuries but quickly forgets or recovers from offenses and tends not to hold any rancor[299] or be obdurate in evil.[300] Given the aforesaid, it is easy to see that sanguine people tend to be extroverts.[301]

The negative traits of the sanguine disposition tend to be superficiality,[302] instability[303] and inconstancy.[304] Those with this disposition tend to be hasty in

---

[286]Maher, *Psychology: Empirical and Rational*, p. 393.

[287]Duerk, *Psychology in Questions and Answers*, p. 135.

[288]Cunningham, *The Christian Life*, p. 120; Aumann, *Spiritual Theology*, p. 141 and Hock, *The Four Temperaments*, p. 28.

[289]Cunningham, *The Christian Life,* p. 120 and Aumann, *Spiritual Theology*, p. 141.

[290]*Sententia Libri Ethicorum*, l. III, c. 12, n. 1.

[291]ST I-II, q. 48, 2. ad 1.

[292]Cunningham, *The Christian Life,* p. 120 and Aumann, *Spiritual Theology*, p. 141.

[293]Cunningham, *The Christian Life,* p. 120

[294]Ibid.

[295]Aumann, *Spiritual Theology*, p. 141.

[296]Ibid.

[297]Cunningham, *The Christian Life,* p. 120 and Aumann, *Spiritual Theology*, p. 141

[298]Aumann, *Spiritual Theology*, p. 141

[299]Cunningham, *The Christian Life,* p. 120 and Aumann, *Spiritual Theology*, p. 141.

[300]Hock, *The Four Temperaments*, p. 32.

[301]Ibid., p. 31.

[302]Cunningham, *The Christian Life,* p. 120 and Aumann, *Spiritual Theology*, p. 141.

[303]Cunningham, *The Christian Life,* p. 120.

[304]Aumann, *Spiritual Theology*, p. 141.

judgment[305] and they tend to dislike reflection and the contemplative life.[306] They tend to be loquacious[307] and dislike loneliness.[308] They are prone to vanity,[309] they enjoy flattery[310] and tend toward envy.[311] Their predominant faults tend to center around sensuality[312] and so they are prone to lust and gluttony.[313] Sanguine people tend to be ready to undertake anything but are quickly discouraged.[314] Lastly, they tend to rely on feelings in matters of religion.

When a psychologist discovers that a directee has a mental illness which is connected to the tendencies of the sanguine disposition, he should encourage him to develop certain things in accord with his disposition. Sanguine people should be encouraged to develop obedience[315] since they are docile by nature. They should be encouraged to develop their cheerfulness and candor.[316]

Yet, they should be encouraged to develop certain virtues contrary to their disposition, e.g. temperance, modesty and chastity.[317] This will curb their sensuality and moderate their good qualities so that they do not become exaggerated. They should be encouraged to develop detachment, since this will also curb their sensuality as well as vanity, envy and the like.[318] They should be encouraged to develop the virtue of silence which will aid them in being detached from the pleasures that arise from

---

[305]Ibid.

[306]Cunningham, *The Christian Life*, p. 120.

[307]Ibid.

[308]Ibid.

[309]Ibid.

[310]Ibid.

[311]Ibid. This is rooted in the concupiscible appetite's passion of desire.

[312]Cunningham, *The Christian Life*, p. 120 and Aumann, *Spiritual Theology*, p. 141. This is due to a tendency to have an inordinate love of pleasure, see Hock, *The Four Temperaments*, p. 30.

[313]Aumann, *Spiritual Theology*, p. 142.

[314]Duerk, *Psychology in Questions and Answers*, p. 135. This is a sign of their disposition toward the passion of hope, but also of their concomitant inconstancy.

[315]Cunningham, *The Christian Life*, p. 120.

[316]Ibid.

[317]Ibid.

[318]Sanguine people often tend toward the vice of human respect and this will aid in curbing that as well.

loquaciousness.[319] They should get into the practice of prayer and reflection[320] which will help them to overcome the tendency to hasty judgment and lack of circumspection and will moderate their extroversion so that it does not become exaggerated. The sanguine person, because he is prone to sensuality, must practice daily mortification of the senses, custody of the eyes, ears, tongue and sense of touch and guard against overindulging in exquisite foods and drinks.[321] Because he is prone to please others and to be friendly, he must see to it that he is not influenced by bad company and does not accept bad counsel and direction.[322] If a psychologist finds that a directee's mental illness stems from his sanguine disposition, he should counsel the directee to adopt a regimen for his daily life[323] so that it becomes more structured and less prone to the inconstancy of a life guided by the appetites.

Psychologists in dealing with sanguine directees must observe several points.[324] The directees should be taught to engage consistently in self-denial. They must be counseled to persevere at their work and observance of order must be continually encouraged. The psychologist should allow the directee's positive traits to be exercised, yet he will counsel moderation regarding them.

B. The Choleric Disposition

The choleric person is quick to react and his reaction remains a long time.[325] He is liable to strong passions[326] and the choleric disposition is hallmarked by its proneness to anger.[327] The choleric disposition is prone to despair[328] and this would follow insofar as anger often gives way to despair. The choleric temperament is noted

---

[319]When speech is performed in accord with disposition, it gives a pleasure to the person speaking. This is why those who suffer from loquaciousness tend not to be of evil will but are inclined mainly by self-absorption.

[320]Aumann, *Spiritual Theology*, p. 141.

[321]Hock, *The Four Temperaments*, p. 33.

[322]Ibid.

[323]Ibid.

[324]These points are enumerated as pertaining to the education of sanguine children, but they can be applied, *mutatis mutandis*, to the counseling of directees with a sanguine disposition. Similar observations will be made with reference to the other temperaments throughout the chapter.

[325]ST I-II, q. 46, a. 5; ST II-II, q. 156, a. 1, ad 2; Aumann, *Spiritual Theology*, p. 143; Cunningham, *The Christian Life,* p. 120 and Duerk, *Psychology in Questions and Answers*, p. 136.

[326]Maher, *Psychology: Empirical and Rational*, p. 393.

[327]SCG III, c. 85, n. 19; De Ver., q. 5, a. 10, ad 7 and ibid., q. 22, a. 9, ad 2. See also SCG II, c. 63, n. 1 and ST I-II, q. 46, a. 5.

[328]Duerk, *Psychology in Questions and Answers*, p. 136.

for the predominance of the passions of the irascible appetite and this is how it is distinguished from the sanguine disposition in which the positive passions of the concupiscible appetite predominate. Choleric people tend to react favorably to reason and high ideals.[329] They are practical rather than theoretical which means they are more inclined to work than to think; inactivity is repugnant to them.[330]

The positive traits of those with the choleric temperament are a keen intellect with great powers of concentration and endurance.[331] They tend to have high ideals[332] and a strong will.[333] They tend to be constant[334] and generous.[335] All of these positive traits tend to make them capable leaders.[336] The negative traits of the choleric temperament are a certain stubbornness (obstinacy)[337] and impatience.[338] Those with this disposition tend to be proud[339] which is why they are also very sensitive to humiliations.[340] Choleric people tend to be domineering[341] and are characterized by a certain hardness.[342]

> The choleric despises his fellow man. To his mind others are ignorant, weak, unskilled, slow, at least when compared to himself.

---

[329]Cunningham, *The Christian Life*, p. 120. We noted in the first volume that the irascible appetite is closer to reason insofar as its object is often proposed by reason. Those who are prone more to irascible passions would thereby be more prone to follow the lead of reason as compared to those prone to passions of the concupiscible appetite.

[330]Aumann, *Spiritual Theology*, p. 143.

[331]Aumann, *Spiritual Theology*, p. 143; Cunningham, *The Christian Life*, p. 120 and Hock, *The Four Temperaments*, p. 16.

[332]Cunningham, *The Christian Life*, p. 120.

[333]Aumann, *Spiritual Theology*, p. 143 and Cunningham, *The Christian Life*, p. 120.

[334]Aumann, *Spiritual Theology*, p. 143.

[335]Aumann, *Spiritual Theology*, p. 143 and Cunningham, *The Christian Life*, p. 120.

[336]Aumann, *Spiritual Theology*, p. 144 and Cunningham, *The Christian Life*, p. 120.

[337]Aumann, *Spiritual Theology*, p. 144 and Cunningham, *The Christian Life*, p. 120.

[338]Aumann, *Spiritual Theology*, p. 144.

[339]Aumann, *Spiritual Theology*, p. 144; Cunningham, *The Christian Life*, p. 120 and Maher, *Psychology: Empirical and Rational*, p. 393.

[340]Cunningham, *The Christian Life*, p. 120.

[341]Cunningham, *The Christian Life*, p. 120 and Hock, *The Four Temperaments*, p. 19.

[342]Aumann, *Spiritual Theology*, p. 144.

He shows his contempt of his neighbor by despising, mocking belittling remarks about others and by his proud behavior toward those around him, especially toward his subjects.[343]

Because of his pride and self-will, even though he is often noble and magnanimous, he often falls into lower vices such as deceit and hypocrisy.[344] Those of choleric disposition tend to lack compassion and sympathy for their fellow man.[345]

Psychologists should encourage the choleric to develop the virtues of fortitude[346] and magnanimity,[347] which are according to his disposition. Contrary to his disposition, he should be encouraged to develop humility[348] which will temper his inclination to pride and anger. He should be encouraged to develop the virtue of meekness,[349] which is the virtue opposite of anger. He should develop the virtues of kindness[350] and charity, which will temper his inclinations to being domineering, his despising others and his hardness.

The psychologist should also encourage the choleric directee to moderate and direct his goals according to the order of charity. This will provide direction to his desire for high ideals, his nobility and his practical side. The choleric must be encouraged to depend on God and humbly beg Him for assistance[351] in overcoming his mental illness. He will be able to overcome his mental illness when he depends on God rather than only himself. He will also make greater progress when he humbles himself to ask his fellow man for help and direction.[352] His tendency is to forge ahead on his own, but he lacks the intellectual direction necessary to do so. The fact that he has a mental illness, more often than not, will be caused by his own actions (imprudence) and therefore he must ask others to help him. The choleric directee must be encouraged, again, according to the order of charity, not to consider himself but others. The choleric person will be prone to mental illnesses that are rooted in solipsism and he must be turned outward. But this turning must be properly directed. The psychologist should put him on a strong regimen of humility, including frequent and daily recitation of the

---

[343]Hock, *The Four Temperaments*, p. 19.

[344]Ibid.

[345]Ibid., p. 21.

[346]Cunningham, *The Christian Life*, p. 120.

[347]Aumann, *Spiritual Theology*, p. 143 and Cunningham, *The Christian Life*, p. 120.

[348]Cunningham, *The Christian Life*, p. 120.

[349]Ibid.

[350]Ibid.

[351]Hock, *The Four Temperaments*, p. 23f.

[352]Ibid., p. 24. This would particularly apply in the case of asking the psychologist for help and if there is a spiritual cause to his mental illness, he must be willing to ask a priest as well as others to help him.

litany of humility, reading books on humility and fostering an acceptance of humiliations. He should seek to develop a strong devotion to the Sacred Heart of Jesus as a means of obtaining humility and meekness.

The choleric is likely to make the lives of those around him bitter and difficult.[353] Therefore, the psychologist should encourage him to meditate on the sufferings of others, particularly those he is causing. He should encourage the directee to meditate on the sufferings of Christ and how He bore them patiently and without acrimony. The psychologist must always maintain calm around the person who is choleric[354] since being angry with someone who is choleric only exacerbates the anger of the choleric. Psychologists who are choleric must be on guard so that they do not become angry with directees and they must be realistic about the ability of the directees whom God sends them, as to what they can accomplish.

C. The Melancholic Disposition

The predominant inclination of the melancholic disposition is toward sorrow.[355] In contrast to the sanguine disposition which is inclined toward the positive passions of the concupiscible appetite, the melancholic disposition is inclined toward the negative passions of the concupiscible appetite, viz. sorrow, hatred[356] and flight. Because of their sorrow they tend to be very pessimistic.[357] St Thomas says that those with a melancholic temperament desire delights in order to expel sorrow.[358] Modern authors hold that melancholics react slowly but permanently to what they experience.[359] Because they are disposed to being moved permanently, they tend not to forget easily.[360] They do have

---

[353]Ibid., p. 25.

[354]Ibid.

[355]Aumann, *Spiritual Theology*, p. 143; Maher, *Psychology: Empirical and Rational*, p. 393 and Duerk, *Psychology in Questions and Answers*, p. 136. See also SCG II, c. 63, n. 1 and *Sententia Libri Ethicorum*, l. III, l. 12, n. 1.

[356]This aspect of their personality is a bit complex since their hatred is more ordered toward sorrow than anger. As the chapter progresses, the likes and dislikes (hatreds and loves) will be delineated more clearly.

[357]Aumann, *Spiritual Theology*, p. 143 and Cunningham, *The Christian Life*, p. 120.

[358]ST I-II, q. 32, a. 7, ad 2. Throughout this series, we have noted the various things which mitigate sorrow. It is not clear if St. Thomas would hold that the melancholic tend to seek out these means of mitigation, or if this is a general psychological observation he is making about their temperament.

[359]Aumann, *Spiritual Theology*, p. 142 and Cunningham, *The Christian Life*, p. 120. St. Thomas says that the melancholic are greatly moved by phantasms (see *De Memoria et Reminiscentia*, l. VIII, n. 4 and *Super ad Hebraeos*, c. 1, n. 1.).

[360]Aumann, *Spiritual Theology*, p. 142.

a tenderness and generosity for their friends[361] but often do not feel at home in a crowd.[362] They tend to be passive and not vivacious, quick, or progressive.[363]

The positive traits of the melancholic types are that they are contemplative (pensive)[364] or inclined toward reflection, piety and the interior life.[365] Melancholics tend to be sympathetic[366] and companionate.[367] Aumann observes that they are long suffering[368] while Hock and Cunningham observe that they have a fear of suffering and a dread of interior exertion and self-denial.[369] These are not necessarily mutually exclusive insofar as one can have a certain dread or fear of suffering, but while suffering, one can endure the suffering well and for long periods of time.

The negative traits of those who have a melancholic disposition are that they tend to surrender easily[370] and are overly serious.[371] They tend to be too reserved except with close friends,[372] since they find it difficult to reveal themselves.[373] They are inclined to be irresolute and dreamy[374] and they tend to concentrate excessively on themselves.[375] They are also suspicious,[376] perhaps due to their negative outlook. They tend toward

---

[361]Duerk, *Psychology in Questions and Answers*, p. 135.

[362]Hock, *The Four Temperaments*, p. 35.

[363]Hock, *The Four Temperaments*, p. 36.

[364]Cunningham, *The Christian Life,* p. 120 and Duerk, *Psychology in Questions and Answers*, p. 135.

[365]Aumann, *Spiritual Theology*, p. 141 and Hock, *The Four Temperaments*, p. 35.

[366]Cunningham, *The Christian Life,* p. 120.

[367]Aumann, *Spiritual Theology*, p. 141.

[368]Ibid., p. 142.

[369]Hock, *The Four Temperaments*, p. 36 and Cunningham, *The Christian Life,* p. 120.

[370]Cunningham, *The Christian Life,* p. 120. By surrender easily here does not mean in relation to suffering necessarily; rather they tend to give up on projects or lose hope too quickly.

[371]Ibid.

[372]ibid.

[373]Aumann, *Spiritual Theology*, p. 143.

[374]Cunningham, *The Christian Life,* p. 120. Hock (*The Four Temperaments*, p. 37) observes that the melancholic person is irresolute "on account of too many considerations and too much fear of difficulties and of the possibility that his plans or works may fail." He also says that "the melancholic can hardly reach a decision."

[375]Aumann, *Spiritual Theology*, p. 143.

[376]Cunningham, *The Christian Life,* p. 120; Duerk, *Psychology in Questions and Answers*, p. 135 and Maher, *Psychology: Empirical and Rational*, p. 393.

scruples,[377] despondency and pusillanimity.[378] Hock observes that

> the pride of the melancholic has its very peculiar side. He does not
> seek honor or recognition; on the contrary, he is loathe to appear in
> public and to be praised. But he is very much afraid of disgrace and
> humiliation. He often displays great reserve and thereby gives the
> impression of modesty and humility; in reality he retires only because
> he is afraid of being put to shame. He allows others to be preferred to
> him, even if they are less qualified and capable than himself for the
> particular work, position, or office, but at the same time he feels
> slighted because he is being ignored and his talents are not
> appreciated. The melancholic person, if he really wishes to become
> perfect, must pay very close attention to these feelings of resentment
> and excessive sensitiveness in the face of even small humiliations.[379]

Not only from the nature of his pride but in general, personalities which arise from melancholy tend to be complex – unlike the sanguine person whose concupiscence tends to make him less complex due to his focus on bodily goods and pleasures. Given the aforesaid, we can see the predominant faults found among the melancholic are sorrow,[380] fear, aversion, despondency[381] and despair.[382]

When a psychologist finds that his directee has a melancholic disposition, he should encourage him to develop certain virtues in accord with his disposition. Among them are a spirit of prayer,[383] since he is inclined toward the interior life. He should encourage the directee to develop detachment and a spirit of mercy.[384] There are also virtues which the psychologist should encourage the melancholic directee to develop contrary to his disposition. He should encourage him to develop a joyous attitude[385] which will come principally by keeping custody of the mind in which he does not allow depressing and sad thoughts into his imagination. He should work on fortitude,[386] which will help him to be more sociable and steadfast in his resolve. He should develop

---

[377]Aumann, *Spiritual Theology*, p. 143 and Cunningham, *The Christian Life*, p. 120.

[378]Hock, *The Four Temperaments*, p. 36.

[379]Hock, *The Four Temperaments*, p. 38.

[380]Cunningham, *The Christian Life*, p. 120 and Duerk, *Psychology in Questions and Answers*, p. 135.

[381]Cunningham, *The Christian Life*, p. 120.

[382]Hock, *The Four Temperaments*, p. 40.

[383]Cunningham, *The Christian Life*, p. 120.

[384]Ibid.

[385]Ibid.

[386]Ibid.

charity and hope.[387]

When counseling melancholic people, the psychologist should keep the following in mind.[388] The psychologist must have a sympathetic understanding of the melancholic. His temperament and his personality are often complex and difficult to discern for those who do not understand the peculiarities of the melancholic temperament. The psychologist must have a good knowledge of the melancholic temperament and how it manifests itself in different people, otherwise he will be prone to making mistakes in his diagnosis of the directee. The psychologist must also gain the confidence of the melancholic directee. This is not at all easy and is usually only able to be accomplished by giving him a good example in everything and by manifesting an unselfish and sincere concern for his well-being. The psychologist must be encouraging and not rude, harsh or hard since these reactions prevent the directee from placing his confidence in the psychologist. The psychologist should encourage him to be busy about psychologically beneficial activities, such as work and hobbies in order to keep his mind off of his sorrow. Melancholic people tend to be very sensitive and so the psychologist must be careful not to weaken their nerves since melancholic people are prone to nervous breakdowns.[389] The psychologist must take special care to be kind and friendly. Special care must be observed in verbally chastising the melancholic, otherwise obstinacy and excessive reserve may result. Remonstration on the side of the psychologist, at times necessary, must be given with caution and great kindness and with no appearance of injustice or ill will.

D. The Phlegmatic Disposition

The phlegmatic temperament is hallmarked by its placidity,[390] tranquility[391] and quiet.[392] Those who have the phlegmatic temperament react slowly and not

---

[387]Ibid.

[388]The following points are adapted from Hock, *The Four Temperaments*, p. 44f. Many of these points can be applied, again, *mutatis mutandis*, to those suffering from depression.

[389]A nervous breakdown is a psychological state in which the possible intellect and will can no longer exercise rational control, due to the onslaught of uncontrolled passions and circumstances of life. The breakdown is a loss of self-possession which occurs when the possible intellect and will can no longer handle the vehemence and continuity of disorder and evil in the person's life.

[390]Cunningham, *The Christian Life*, p. 120.

[391]Maher, *Psychology: Empirical and Rational*, p. 393.

[392]Duerk, *Psychology in Questions and Answers*, p. 135.

permanently[393] to their experiences and they are devoid of strong passions.[394] Fr. Aumann gives a good description of phlegmatics:

> The good characteristics of phlegmatic persons are that they work slowly[395] but assiduously;[396] they are not easily irritated by insults, misfortunes, or sickness;[397] they usually remain tranquil, discreet, and sober; they have a great deal of common sense and mental balance. They do not possess the inflammable passions of the sanguine temperament, the deep passions of the melancholic temperament, or the ardent passions of the choleric temperament. In their speech they are orderly, clear, positive, and measured, rather than florid and picturesque. They are more suited to scientific work which involves long and patient research and minute investigation than to original productions. They have good hearts, but they seem to be cold.[398] They would sacrifice to the point of heroism if it were necessary,[399] but they lack enthusiasm and spontaneity because they are reserved and somewhat indolent by nature. They are prudent, sensible, reflective, and work with a measured pace. They attain their goals without fanfare or violence because they usually avoid difficulties rather than attacking them. Physically phlegmatics are usually of robust build, slow in movements, and possessing an amiable face.[400]

From the aforesaid, we can see why phlegmatics are considered passive.[401] St. Thomas

---

[393]Aumann, *Spiritual Theology*, p. 145 and Cunningham, *The Christian Life*, p. 120.

[394]Aumann, *Spiritual Theology*, p. 143; Duerk, *Psychology in Questions and Answers*, p. 135 and Maher, *Psychology: Empirical and Rational*, p. 393.

[395]See also *Sententia Libri Ethicorum*, l. III, l. 12, n. 1; Cunningham, *The Christian Life*, p. 120 and Maher, *Psychology: Empirical and Rational*, p. 393. Because they tend to work slowly, Cunningham in *The Christian Life* (p. 120) observes that they need constant goading and surveillance.

[396]See also Cunningham, *The Christian Life*, p. 120.

[397]See also Hock, *The Four Temperaments*, p. 46.

[398]See also ibid.

[399]Although they are in general incapable of great acts, whether good or evil; see Maher, *Psychology: Empirical and Rational*, p. 393. See also Aumann, *Spiritual Theology*, p. 145.

[400]Aumann, *Spiritual Theology*, p. 145.

[401]Cunningham, *The Christian Life*, p. 120.

observes that they can be inconstant.[402] Phlegmatics tend to demand little and they get along with others due to a lack of convictions.[403] They tend to be inclined toward ease and comfort[404] and they tend to be unambitious, procrastinators and disinterested.[405] The predominant faults of phlegmatics are dullness and sloth.[406]

Those of phlegmatic temperament should develop the virtues of patience, affability and perseverance[407] which are according to their disposition. Contrary to their disposition they should develop zeal and temperance.[408] They can overcome the negative tendencies of their disposition by deep convictions.[409] Psychologists must often prudently confront phlegmatics in order to motivate them to overcome their mental illness and the negative aspects of their temperament

The more a psychologist knows about the various temperaments and dispositions, the more he will understand human nature and human psychology. Lack of knowledge of the four temperaments makes one unsuited to psychological counseling and exhibits an ignorance of one of the basic components of personality and character.

Chapter 16: Personality

The term "personality" is often used today and its definition through philosophical and psychological history has changed. The issue of personality is important since it includes the notion of character, as we shall see shortly. Sometimes the terms "personality" and "character" are considered by some authors as coterminous, having the same meaning even though different words are used. However, as Rudolf Allers has rightly pointed out, character is an important factor regarding one's mental

---

[402]ST II-II, q. 156, a. 1, ad 2. Perhaps this is due to a low level of motivation on the side of the passions. Cunningham in *The Christian Life* (p. 120.) observes that they are unreliable. Perhaps this is connected to their inconstancy.

[403]Cunningham, *The Christian Life,* p. 120.

[404]Ibid. and Hock, *The Four Temperaments,* p. 46. Hock also observes that they are inclined toward eating and drinking.

[405]Cunningham, *The Christian Life,* p. 120.

[406]Ibid. The description of the phlegmatic temperament tells us something about man in the state of original sin. Man in the state of original sin tends to follow his appetites and in the absence of appetite he tends to do nothing. This is why once the appetites are conquered in the spiritual life a different motivation is necessary. Charity and hope motivate the soul to continue its efforts and work toward perfection and charity can only become dominate as the passions wane.

[407]Ibid.

[408]Ibid. The zeal will motivate them and the temperance will make them detached from the pleasures of complacency and sloth.

[409]Aumann, *Spiritual Theology,* p. 145.

health and one's mental resilience.[410]   Modern psychology has begun a practice of classifying different personality characteristics through an empirical approach with such inventories as MMPI and the like.   In order to know whether such a practice is scientifically valid, we must first establish what personality and character are.[411]

When looking closely at some modern philosophical psychologists as well as philosophers, one tends to derive a somewhat similar definition of personality. Wuellner gives five definitions of personality, each worth reviewing for the sake of providing important philosophical principles regarding personality:[412]

> n. 1. *technical scholastic sense*. the subsistence proper to a person; that perfection whereby an intellectual nature is unshared by the being of another; that form, mode of being, relation, etc., that explains (in different theories) why rational substance is complete as a person.

This is the usage of the term *personalitas* which one often sees in St. Thomas' writings. It is a metaphysical term which indicates the subsistence proper to that which has a rational nature. The term in Aquinas' writings often appears in relation to discussions of the individual Persons in the Trinity.   The term also implies a certain incommunicability in which one substance cannot become one in substance or share its existence with another. This does apply to human persons, insofar as a person is defined as an individual substance of rational nature. Individuality indicates two metaphysical aspects; (1) the substance cannot be divided and still remain a person[413] and (2) the substance is distinct in being from other substances. Each person, by virtue of this metaphysical analysis, is unique.[414] This is why the third definition of personality is: "personal identity; personal individuality with its total set of traits and differences from other persons." There is a direct connection between the ontology of the kind of person and the kind of personalities which that person can have. It is human nature itself which

---

[410]Allers, *The Psychology of Character*, passim.

[411]The validity of empirical testing of personality will be addressed in the second part of this volume. For now, what personality is will be established.

[412]All five of these are taken from Wuellner, *A Dictionary of Scholastic Philosophy*, p. 227.

[413]In this respect the term "supposit" is often used.

[414]The basis for the uniqueness of persons differs based upon the kind of person one is. In God, the differences are based upon opposition of relation. In angels, it is based upon degree of existence of substance as related to degree of intellectual power (accidents). In human beings, the uniqueness is based principally on the individuation of matter but also upon the variations of accidents as will be seen in the discussion of the nature of personality. This is why the second definition of personality is: "the property or fact of being a person, or of being *this* person" (emphasis mine).

sets the limits on the kinds of personalities we can have[415] even though the degrees of various accidents (characteristics and traits) can vary infinitely.[416]

The next three entries of Wuellner complete a basic definition of personality:

> 3. personal identity; personal individuality with its total set of traits and differences from other persons. 4. the sum total of the actualities (perfections) and potencies of a given person; hence, one's physical, mental, and emotional traits, habits, qualities, and their external expression. 5. the psychophysical abilities and unique patterns of behavior whereby a person gives his own special exterior expression of himself when associating with other persons.

These three definitions include several important points. The first is that personal identity and personality are connected. Identification has epistemological implications insofar as it indicates that the particular characteristics the person has make him distinguishable from others and knowable as an individual.

The fourth and fifth definitions are the operative psychological definitions. Both express the same notion but from different points of view. The fourth definition is an ontological definition whereas the fifth definition is a psychological one. But since psychology is a philosophical science, the fourth undergirds or gives proper understanding to the contents of the fifth. Therefore the fourth is a scientific definition and will be used for the purposes of our considerations here, even though the fifth would be more often operative in most psychologists' minds.

From the fourth definition, the nature of personality can be unpacked. The definition includes two kinds of elements, viz. those over which we have no volitional control and those over which we do have volitional control. Among those over which we do not have volitional control, we find physical traits or more properly physical accidents, such as bodily build, facial features and structure, hair and eye color. Our perception of someone's personality is often affected by his physical accidents (the way he appears). For example, a man with sharp slanted eyebrows and eyes close together tends to have a "meaner" look to him than someone with big wide open eyes and normal eyebrows. They can exhibit the same habits but our perception in one case will be different than another. People will often interpret the action of someone who is beautiful or innocent "looking" in a better light than someone who has a mean look to him.

---

[415]This is based upon the principle of operation (*agere sequitur esse*), since first act (nature) determines second act (operations or accidents).

[416]This is based upon the notion that quantity by magnitude is infinitely divisible while discrete quantity is not. Human accidents exist in the human substance according to quantity of magnitude. Good angels likewise have personalities based upon the magnitude of their intellects and the task which they are assigned by God, which directs their choices of will always fixed in the good. Demons have personalities based upon the magnitude of their intellects, the negation of the task assigned to them by God, the tasks assigned to them by Satan and their choices of will, which are directed always to the evil.

One's appearance not only affects others' perception of the person, but it also affects one's perception of oneself.[417] This self-perception which is part of self-knowledge can affect personality development. A tall, handsome man with commanding features may find it easier to develop leadership skills because of people's perception of him and, consequently, their behavior toward him than a short dumpy fellow with plain simple features. Even though the short man may have greater virtue to lead, he may find that others are not inclined to follow his lead due to their perception of his "personality" via his physical accidents. A person of average intelligence often develops a concept of how others perceive him and he will often conform his own character development according to the concept, whether for good or ill.

Those aspects of personality which fall under volitional control, when taken together, we call "character."[418]

> **Character, *n.*** the habitual moral virtues and vices of a person, founded on his dispositions and together distinguishing his moral personality; integration of a person's nature and nurture in his habits and the expression of these in his living.[419]

Character is the sum total of one's virtues and vices.[420] It is founded on one's disposition; however, one can change one's disposition by means of voluntary action. Character is manifest in one's exterior actions. In this respect, character both determines our personality but also determines our exterior actions or manifestation of personality.[421]

In the perception of personality, the exterior actions are the means by which the person's character is known and consequently one's personality. Personality is one of the means by which we know the interior life of the person and his psychological state. Since one's interior life tends to determine one's behavior insofar as one's character (moral habits) inclines to act, the state of the various faculties can be known to some

---

[417]This is particularly the case with the inseparable accident of gender.

[418]See Brennan, *Thomistic Psychology,* p. 292f.

[419]Wuellner, *A Dictionary of Scholastic Philosophy*, p. 49.

[420]Aumann (*Spiritual Theology*, p. 146) expresses it this way: "Character can be understood in an ethical or a psychological sense. Ethically, it comprises the pattern of habits cultivated by an individual in accordance with his or her accepted principles and values. Psychologically, it is the organized totality of the tendencies and predispositions of an individual, grouped around and directed by a predominant tendency. Our interest is in the ethical aspect of character, which is largely influenced by education, environment, and, above all, by one's personal effort. The formation of character and the development to maturity as a person will depend ultimately on the cultivation and perfection of the virtues."

[421]See Brennan, *General Psychology,* p. 405.

degree.[422] Given all of the above, we may say that personality is the sum total of the accidents of a person.

The various moral virtues are had by degree and, therefore, even in addition to disposition, a person's moral virtue will affect his patterns of action. A personality has a uniqueness based upon the various combinations of accidents,[423] both non-moral and moral. These combinations make the person recognizable as an individual and constitutes his uniqueness. However, uniqueness or individuality in one's personality ought not be founded on vice. Vice tends to make one's personality singular and what is meant by that is that vice orders one's faculties towards created goods. These created goods are finite and not infinite. Since vice is a habit contrary to right reason, a vice moves one towards communicable particular goods. Virtue, on the other hand, is that which is in accord with right reason. Right reason is a universal power and moves the other powers to the good insofar as the particular good falls under the good in general.[424] As one develops virtues, the lower faculties participate in reason, which directs the lower powers to be moved by reason alone. This leaves the lower faculties directed to the good in general. Right reason is that which is ordered to God as to its final end. God is the universal good and so as the various faculties of the soul become more directed toward the universal good (*summum bonum*), they begin to take on characteristics of the universal good.

Virtue, therefore, has a universalizing effect on the faculties and a person's personality. What this means is that vice fixates a person on single things, whereas virtue directs the person to all things as they ought. The person with perfect virtue does not have predominant habits which make the person's personality singular or unique. Those with vices or bad habits have "oddities" or "quirks" regarding their personality. Those with a "singular" personality find that they fit into certain circumstances and not others, e.g. they feel comfortable around their own, so if they are rich they feel uncomfortable around the poor. Virtue, however, tends to universalize the personality by making the person's exterior actions always fit the object or person with which they deal. A singular personality does not always relate to some object or person in the way that one should, due to his various habits and his relationship to those objects. Those with a universal personality can appeal to all people, regardless of who they are. This

---

[422]This is why in the process of coming to knowledge of a possible future spouse, those courting should seek to know the person's moral character above all, since it will determine how the two will live life together. Those courting should strive for a knowledge of the virtues and live virtuously themselves so that each can be a good spouse by aiding the other spouse to lead a good life. Moral virtue and knowledge of the virtues will help those courting to judge more objectively the true character and personality of their possible future spouses.

[423]That personality belongs to the order of accidents, see Royce, *Man and His Nature*, p. 268.

[424]Sometimes this is called "participation in reason."

is the rationale behind St. Paul's statement of being all things to all people[425] and Guardini's observation that Christ did not have a personality like we have.[426] Vice is an evil or a lack of a due good in some faculty and so we say that vice is a potency. All created substances have their individuality based upon some form of potency[427] and so as the creatures become more actual, they take on the characteristics of God Who is universal being itself. In like manner, as the faculties are actualized by virtue, the person begins to take on a more universal personality which is not characterized by any one of the particular temperaments or vices. However, since man is not the universal being (God), he will always have some features which will distinguish him from others, even if they are supernatural, such as particular graces, degrees of supernatural virtue, charismatic gifts, etc.

These observations have a psychological import. Since mental illness is a vice, mental illness will have a particularizing effect on the person. This means that his personality will begin to be conformed to his predominant vice or mental illness. All the other faculties will be directed to the end of the vice which gives his personality singularity insofar as he is ordered toward or fixated on some particular created good dominating his mental habits. These will be expressed and seen in his actions. This is why mental illness is so dangerous to the spiritual life, since it deviates one from the good in general to be fixated on some created good.[428] Mental health, since it indicates the right functioning of reason as well as the absence of *per accidens* mental illness in the other faculties but their proper following of right reason, by nature makes one's personality universal. Those who are mentally healthy can fit in anywhere with anyone, whereas those suffering some form of mental illness find that others have a hard time being around them and they do not fit in. Mental health universalizes a personality; mental illness makes the personality singular and therefore appealing only to certain other personalities.

The various causes of different personalities have varying ability to affect personality building or change. Since the principal part of personality is character,

---

[425]I Cor. 9:22: "I became all things to all men, that I might save all."

[426]Guardini, *The Humanity of Christ*, passim (it is a general theme throughout the text). Since Christ's human nature was joined to the universal good itself, this universality flows over and is expressed through the human nature. This is why we never read in the Gospels any actions which would manifest personality characteristics in Christ. Moreover, since Christ's soul was filled with infused and natural virtue, it became the perfect medium through which the divine universality could shine.

[427]In angels, their individuality is based upon the potency of their essence whereas in man and all lower creatures it is based upon matter which is a certain potency.

[428]What is implicit in this statement is that it is not possible to have a fixation on God since, if one's faculties are consumed by God, one has achieved the end for which his faculties are designed and so one is mentally healthy. Fixation is not the proper word for the soul being consumed in God, rather perfect charity (since charity directs all of the other virtues), holy constancy or sanctified perfection would be proper designations.

personality has as its principal cause volitional acts and the virtues and vices flowing from those acts as its cause. People can actually change their personality by the free choices they make. Another factor which affects one's personality is one's inheritance, viz. one's disposition and bodily constitution. While certain aspects of the bodily constitution can never be changed, they still affect one's personality by affecting one's self-perception, as we have already mentioned. This in turn can affect the development of various virtues. In the chapter on disposition, we observed that most people act according to disposition and so most people's personality is heavily influenced by the disposition or temperament. However, one's temperament can be changed; one ought to strive for a disposition in which one temperament does not predominate.[429]

Not all habits are moral; some are intellectual. Therefore, our intellectual habits can affect our personality. It logically follows that one's education or intellectual formation has a direct bearing on one's personality. Personality is also affected by one's circumstances in life, sometimes called environment.[430]

> The environmental factors are almost too numerous to mention, and they exert an especially strong influence on the individual during the formative years. The influence of example on children is too obvious to be denied. While the most forceful environmental influences are to be found in the lives of other human beings, such commonplace things as nutrition, climate, neighborhood environment, and home life also exert a subtle but definite influence. Here again, the effects are not immediately evident in a growing child, but environment during youth is responsible, to a large extent, for those attitudes and evaluations that are most deeply rooted in the personality.[431]

Children are more susceptible to their circumstances than adults because children do not have the same use of reason by which they are able to analyze exterior factors. Children, until the age of puberty, tend to function more at the level of the cogitative power than at the level of judgment of the possible intellect. As a result, they are more susceptible to training when younger, which means that circumstances affect them more than

---

[429]This will normally be achieved merely by attaining all of the virtues.

[430]The term "circumstance" is a better term than environment in the psychological sphere since the term circumstance implies a relation which environment does not. The term environment tends to emphasize something independent of the person, whereas circumstance tends to see one's surroundings as in relation to the person. Circumstance comes from the two Latin words *circa* and *stare* which mean to stand around and so this implies a relation by its very etymology. No doubt the term environment has taken greater root in the psychological community because of the extrinsicizing that has occurred in the methodology of empirical psychology. Since modern psychologists think that one cannot know the interior life or the acts of consciousness of the person at all, one must focus on exterior things or behavior.

[431]Aumann, *Spiritual Theology*, p. 146.

adults.[432] Culture, as an environmental factor, will have a direct impact on the development of personalities. This is why in various nations or regions, people will tend to certain kinds of personality traits since they are more socially acceptable, preferred or dominant.

Another cause of variety in one's personality are demonic influences. Depending on the will of God, some people will simply be tempted to certain species of sin more than others. While the demons often tempt us according to our disposition and so the demonic influence may be indistinguishable from the person's inclinations according to his disposition, the demons can also tempt people in ways which would seem out of character. Sometimes the demons will do this to "test" the individual to see what he is willing to do. Someone who has strong demonic temptations will often suffer a strained personality, having conflicting elements in their personality.

The last area of causes of personality development and types is those coming from the supernatural order. The infused moral and theological virtues will have a direct impact on the character of a person which will affect his personality. There are also specific graces given to some people and not to others. These graces will affect the development of virtue as well as choices and exterior actions which manifest one's personality. We see this in those who have a more "supernatural" personality, while others have a more "mundane" personality. Here we see the connection between one's religion and personality. Different religions will affect psychological and character formation. Since Catholicism possesses the various supernatural means for salvation, these means will have a more universalizing effect than other religions.[433]

We come now to the final consideration of this chapter, viz. multiple personalities. Throughout this series on psychology, multiple personalities as a concept has been criticized. We can now give a more comprehensive analysis of what is called multiple personality disorder. A clear description of modern psychology's concept of multiple personalities is given in the *Dictionary of Behavioral Science*:

> An extreme form of dissociative reaction to stress in which two or more separate personalities exist. The person may shift from one personality to another which is often very different from the other. Each personality has no memory of the other's thoughts and actions. One of the personalities may function unconsciously and be aware of the conscious personality but it manifests itself early indirectly as in

---

[432]Issues relating to these topics will be brought up in the chapter on education, part of which will discuss developmental psychology.

[433]One's attention is drawn to the fact that the very term *Catholic* means universal. Some religions will not have a universal appeal to all personalities types due to the nature of the religion. Catholicism, by its very nature, transcends personality, cultural and national types. For those of good will, Catholicism will have an inherent attractiveness to every personality type. For a further discussion of personality and character, see McInerny, *Philosophical Psychology*, pp. 246f.

automatic writing.[434]

This definition includes three elements in relation to our discussion. The first is that multiple personality is an extreme form of disassociation. The second is that two or more personalities exist in the same person. The third is that each personality has no memory of the other's thoughts and actions, yet there are cases in which one personality may function unconsciously while being aware of the conscious personality.

Two of these three elements are problematic, metaphysically speaking. The second element, viz. multiple personalities, is of its very nature metaphysically impossible. Since personality is the sum total of all of the accidents and since all of the accidents reside in one person, regardless of how contradictory one's actions may appear, they still constitute one personality. In *Man and His Nature* by James Royce, we read:

> A hysterical case of multiple personality, then, is simply two sets of accidents inhering in one substance. The person is the same, but the psychological personality may change, as first one and then another set of habituation associations and emotions is operating.[435]

While Royce indicates that the psychological personality may change, what is important to recognize is that the accidents which make up personality may be arranged in disparate groups. These two or more groups together constitute the total personality. For instance, in one person, it is possible to have a group of accidents which revolve around the vice of anger and a set of accidents that revolve around the virtue of love, so that in a single person one views at one time a very angry person and at another time very amorous person.[436]

Some have described these differing sets of accidents as multiple characters rather than multiple personalities:

> Subject to this reservation, we will now turn our attention to those remarkable cases described as multiple personality, splitting of personality, *état second*, etc. As will be made clear later on, they should properly be called cases of multiple character, for the misuse of the term " personality " in this way, as already stated, is an offence against clarity of ideas and purity of speech. The assumption that there are multiple persons in one and the same individual is inadmissible, at least as long as it remains a question of human entities; we will disregard the phenomena of demoniacal

---

[434]Wolman, *Dictionary of Behavioral Science*, p. 276.

[435]P. 268.

[436]See Allers, *The Psychology of Character*, p. 16.

possession.[437]

In this passage, two things are of import. The first is that to use the term "multiple personalities" is at root a misnomer. Since personality is the conglomeration of accidents in a person and since persons are indivisible, it is not possible to have more than one person and therefore more than one personality co-existing in the same substance.[438] Therefore, strictly speaking, one cannot have multiple personalities.

However, it is possible to have what *appears* to be multiple characters. As mentioned, it is possible to have in a single person vacillations in behavior based upon different virtues and vices. We see this often in people who are "diagnosed" by modern psychology with bi-polar disorder. It is possible that the cogitative power can be habituated to prepare a phantasm one way based upon one kind of exterior sensation or phantasm while preparing the phantasms in a completely different way with a different set of external sensations or phantasms. In this way the passions can swing wildly, if the person suffers from vice. The possible intellect can then become habituated in its judgment regarding these phantasms and passions. This will affect all of the other psychological faculties. However, even the term "multiple characters" is not accurate, technically speaking. If character is defined as the habitual moral virtues and vices of a person, these two different sets of vices and all the accidents which go along with them constitute a single character. While the external manifestations of the two or more aspects of the person's character or personality will appear to the observer as two distinct persons or characters, this occurs simply due to the fact that the observer does not see the two sets of accidents as residing in the same metaphysical person but considers them as conceptually distinct.

Allers ends the passage quoted above by indicating that he will disregard the issue of demonic possession. To enter into this discussion, we may read the following passage from Brennan:

> This adoption of several different rôles by one and the same individual is compared by Lindworsky to the *dramatis personae* where many parts are taken by one actor; but with this difference, of course, that whereas the actor can at any moment become aware of his off-stage life, the subject of multiple personalities cannot retrace his pathway back to a normal existence, but is condemned to face the world with the particular personal or social ego which his presently evolved mental constellations have imposed upon him. It should be carefully noted, however, that even with the most extreme cases of

---

[437]Ibid.

[438]Boethius' famous metaphysical definition of person must be kept clearly in mind: an *individual* substance of rational nature. A person as such cannot be divided without it ceasing to be a person. Also, it is not possible to have two persons in the same entity since that would constitute two substances in the same non-distinct metaphysical entity which is metaphysically absurd.

schizophrenia, there is no scientific evidence for suspecting the essentially unalterable identity of the pure or substantial ego.[439]

The person who suffers what modern psychology calls multiple personalities cannot make his way back to normal existence. In effect, the various manifestations of different virtues, vices and characters, do not enjoy the same continuity in the consciousness in the individual. Those whose character is split in the sense of having very different vices and virtues are aware of the various times in which they vacillate, e.g. in those who are "diagnosed" with what modern psychology calls bipolarism. Drastic changes in personality can be seen when people undergo some physical trauma, e.g. a blow to the head or severe stroke. But the subsequent personality does not coexist with the prior personality in the person.

Demonic possession can occur in different ways depending on the degree and kind of possession. In some cases of demonic possession, the person possessed may remember some of the things which occur outside his control, while in other cases the person is completely unaware of what the demons are doing with his body. In those cases of *manifestation of multiple personalities* in which the conscious identity does not persist in the person, this may be the result of demonic possession. Since the personality of the demon is manifested during possession in the outward actions of the person who is possessed,[440] there will be a veritably different personality than when the person is not possessed since there are different "personae" being manifested. In some cases of possession, when the person is aware of what the demons are doing, the person will indicate later that he had no control over it. In cases in which the possession is of such a kind that the demonic activity comes and goes, the person will appear to vacillate between the various personae. In cases where the demonic possession is strong and the demon retains total control over the person until the exorcism is complete, there may or may not be a manifestation of different personae. If the demon wishes to deceive the exorcist (or psychologist for that matter), he may move the body of the person to manifest very different personalities. It is very easy to become deceived when the personalities appear very harmless or even benign. It is a common misconception that when demons possess someone, they always manifest that possession in very cruel and evil ways. Demons can possess or even obsess a person in ways that make him appear kind, gentle and sweet. This is done to deceive others for the sake of some evil end which may not be known. If there are many demons who possess the body of the person, the various personalities of the demons can come out. This can also be in combination. One demon may be vicious and cruel, clearly manifesting evil, while another may manifest a benign or harmless character. Authentic cases of "multiple personality disorder" are truly rare; in such cases, the psychologist should refer the directee to an exorcist who can determine if the manifestations have a demonic cause.

---

[439]Brennan, *General Psychology*, p. 425.

[440]Except in the cases of deception. See infra this paragraph.

Chapter 17: Psychological Wounds

The term "wound" is used from time to time in modern parlance and in some psychological circles. It tends to be used in the same manner in both arenas. A close analysis of what constitutes a psychological wound and its healing can provide a greater understanding of how man is designed to function. The term wound is an analogical usage from a physical reality, viz. any break in the skin or an organ caused by violence or surgical incision. Sometimes it is also taken for a casualty of military personnel resulting from combat. Both, in a sense, have an analogical significance in psychology.

A philosophical analysis of the notion of a wound yields the following characteristics. (1) A wound is something which is inflicted by oneself or another, so there is some agency causing the wound. (2) A wound causes some harm to something good, i.e. there is something good which undergoes some type of damaging action. (3) When a wound occurs psychologically, there is some evil caused or associated with the good. That is to say that something which is viewed as good has some evil now associated with it, e.g. the person may view himself as good but someone embarrasses him publically and so the evil of embarrassment is associated with the person. In this case, the wound is something affecting the cogitative power. (4) A wound is something which normally causes pain. (5) A wound requires a healing process. (6) Only that which is physically capable of healing can heal. Likewise, in the psychological realm, only those with the proper psychological tools and resilience can heal. (7) The healing process regarding the wound can be accelerated by medicine.

When we analyze the notion of a wound, there are several components that occur psychologically. The first is that when the person is wounded, the perception of the injury remains, either actually or potentially. It remains actually when it is present in the imagination or in the possible intellect. It remains potentially when the habit of association in the cogitative power is built up by maintaining the phantasm of the wound in the imagination. This habituates the cogitative power. Even if the person does not think about the injury for a long period of time, when the phantasm reoccurs in the imagination, the cogitative power will re-associate the injury in memory. Also, since a wound is something which causes pain, the will and the concupiscible appetite will be habituated in sorrow at the presence of the image or concept of the injury and so the person with the wound will experience sorrow in the will or the sensitive passion of sorrow. Therefore, a psychological wound is complex, involving the cogitative power, the possible intellect (particularly in judgment and reasoning), the will and the concupiscible appetite. When a person is physically abused, unless the judgment of the possible intellect modifies the image or the cogitative power modifies the image based upon past habituation, a psychological wound will occur in relation to the image of the thing or person causing the psychological wound.

It is possible after some healing of the wound still to have the emotional wound while not having the volitional wound. Much like the distinction between emotional and real guilt, a wound can heal intellectually (e.g. if someone forgives the person) while the cogitative power still retains the association of the person, event or thing with the pain, sorrow and injury. A physical wound often debilitates the whole person, e.g. a person shot in the leg during war time often cannot function as a soldier fully, if at all. In like manner, a psychological wound tends to debilitate the person psychologically. This comes from the fact that sorrow or any strong passion tends to captivate the soul.[441]

"Time heals all wounds." This is true, not only physically, but psychologically. However, St. Thomas' observation about time causing forgetfulness should be recalled. It is not time that causes the forgetfulness *per se* but only *per accidens* insofar as time is the measurement of change which causes the forgetfulness. In like manner, time heals psychological wounds, not *per se* but *per accidens*. It heals the wounds because over time, the person recalls the image less often, which causes the wound and the phantasm to fade from memory. Since there is not a recurring remembrance of the wound, the habit of association in the cogitative power begins to be corrupted. Some habits are corrupted if not used and the habit in the cogitative power falls under this causation. Also, as time tends to put a psychological "distance" between the person and the wounding event, the evil seems less imminent and therefore there will be less passion of sorrow.

Man in the state of original sin has an inclination arising from *lex fomitis* to focus on the negative and to take delight in the negative. The directee must fight this inclination by moderating the appetites and other faculties through virtue. Some of the virtues which aid in overcoming wounds are humility, meekness, fortitude, longsuffering and patience. Sometimes the virtue of knowledge, particularly of human nature, can put the cause of the wound in perspective, e.g. if the wound is caused by some person that is close to the directee. The directee should be aware of the fact that by fighting against the inclinations of the various faculties which are affected by the psychological wound, he will suffer. However, this suffering is only temporary in comparison to the suffering that will endure if the directee does not fight against the inclination in the faculties arising from the law of the flesh. If the directee does not fight against the bad inclinations, he will allow the wound to consume him and it can drive him to various mental illnesses. By not fighting against the inclination, he allows the injustice or injury to continue and the wound will not heal. In effect, he creates his own misery.

Often those who suffer some psychological wound will lack emotional or appetitive stability because the sorrow of the wound will cause many other passions. Sorrow causes anger and since the wound is something which persists, the person suffering from a wound will find it difficult not to hold on to the anger arising from the sorrow. This will cause the person to develop those habits associated with anger. The sorrow itself, since it persists, will incline the person to mull over the phantasms that are associated with the anger. The principal function of the cogitative power is to associate with the phantasm in the imagination the images stored in memory. The person who is in the habit of sorrow (such as someone with a psychological wound) will find that the sorrow itself will be merged with the phantasm in the imagination. In turn, the cogitative power will associate those images most vivid in relation to sorrow. This explains why

---

[441]This was part of the theme of chapter nine of volume one.

those with depression or wounds often cannot get the images out of the imagination.[442] Those suffering from wounds must also be careful not to give in to the subtle form of delight or pleasure that arises when we experience passions according to our disposition. Over time a wound will dispose the person to the passion of sorrow from which this pleasure can arise. Those who suffer wounds are prone to the passion of despair since the sorrow will seem unmitigated.

They will also be prone to the passion of hatred since the sorrow will constantly remind them of the evil that they have suffered which will move them to hate the thing which causes the injury.[443] The wound can also be increased by desire insofar as sorrow can cause desire since the person who sorrows desires to be released from the evil that he suffers. Those who suffer wounds sometimes find themselves being inclined away from anything that requires social interaction. Since sorrow causes flight, those who are wounded will often seek refuge in isolation and quiet. As the wound "festers" (habituates the various faculties of the soul), the person will find that social interaction will cause pain, not just with the person causing the wound, but with all people. Since we are inclined as human beings toward social interaction by virtue of the third category of inclination of the natural law, we receive a certain pleasure by fulfilling that inclination. As a result, this pleasure acts contrary to the pleasure received by the passion of sorrow in relation to the person's disposition of that passion. Since the passion of delight moves one contrary to sorrow, it will cause the wounded person suffering or pain since he will be robbed of the pleasure of the passion of sorrow. This is often why those who sorrow find it painful to try to be cheerful. Since human nature is weak because of original sin, human beings have a hard time fighting their passions and dispositions. Sorrow can also cause the passion of fear, since the person can fear future suffering from the wound itself as well as fear of being wounded again. Those who have been wounded will often find themselves subject to many phobias (habits of fear).

All of this indicates that the person with the wound can suffer many psychological ills and will often undergo swings of passions (mood swings). While not all swings in the passions are a sign of a wound, since they can be caused merely by chemical imbalances or physiological defects, nevertheless, constant mood swings in someone who does not have the disposition or characteristics of mood swings could be

---

[442]This mechanism applies to all of the passions since they all affect the imagination. One particular passion that manifests this most clearly is the passion of lust (love). When the hormonal levels rise and the concupiscible appetite becomes disposed toward venereal pleasure and bodily changes occur, the sensation of which finds its way into the imagination. The cogitative power associates the images with the disposition or passion. Once the image associated with the phantasms is merged by the cogitative power, this, in turn, increases the passion since the appetites are moved by the presence of their object. Again, the same applies to all of the other passions.

[443]This is important to keep in mind, particularly in relationships. A single injury can, over time, separate the affections of one individual from another, particularly when the relationship is very close and therefore injury is more keenly felt, e.g. in marriage.

exhibiting the suffering of some wound. Wounds have a great capacity to affect our judgment, which in turn can affect our spiritual life by drawing our attention to the wound rather than God.

In volume one on the chapter on the passions, we discussed the various things which can mitigate sorrow. These things can also help to heal the psychological wound. But caution must be observed since, like all things that cause pleasure or delight, these things which mitigate sorrow can themselves become the occasion of developing bad habits. Since the person finds some relief of soul from these things which mitigate sorrow, it is very easy to become habituated in them. Those who have been wounded are prone to sobbing uncontrollably, e.g. after they have developed a strong habit of crying,[444] or they may develop alcoholic tendencies since the alcohol dulls the pain of the psychological wound by affecting one's phantasms. It was mentioned that sometimes those who suffer wounds become reclusive. But it is also possible for someone suffering a wound to be compulsively social, since this can provide pleasure which mitigates the sorrow.

Those who have suffered wounds may often become abusive of others and this is for two reasons. The first is that since wounds can cause anger, when the person abuses others, either verbally, emotional or even physically, he gets the delight arising from vindication. In this respect, a person can become abusive as a means to mitigate his sorrow. But this is psychologically misdirected since the vindication often moves the person to recognize that he is inflicting pain on others. This can cause him additional sorrow added to the sorrow of the original wound. This can exacerbate the wound, moving him to seek mitigation as well as causing further wounds in himself. Misery loves company. Psychological wounds will often drive people to make the lives of others difficult. There is a practice in some psychological circles in which the person who has been wounded is allowed to take out his anger (frustration) on the person who caused the wound. While some will find mitigation for the sorrow, it does not heal the wound, but tends to make it worse, as we have just seen. Therefore, psychologists, as a rule, must avoid this kind of practice.

We also see from the aforesaid how wounds often corrupt prudence. Since wounds can cause a turbulent life of the passions, our phantasms become affected. This affects the habits of the cogitative power which in turn affect the phantasms. Prudence requires that the possible intellect by means of judgment apply the universal precept in the concrete by converting back to the phantasm to see whether the concrete circumstances fit the precept. Those who have been wounded will often think that in meting out anger they are "teaching others a lesson" or something of this sort, but in fact their prudential judgments have been compromised.

The healing of a wound requires a healing of each of the faculties involved in the wound. It requires a healing or purification of the memory.[445] In addition to praying

---

[444]See chapter on obsessive compulsive.

[445]See volume two, chapter on sacraments, under Confession, and part II of this volume, under memory.

for the grace of forgetfulness, the person can work on trying not to think about the injury. This will allow the habituation of the memory regarding the phantasm of the injury to begin to wane. Not thinking about the injury will also begin to train the cogitative power not to associate the injury and bring it into the imagination frequently. The possible intellect must correct its habit of judgment regarding the injury by consideration of various truths, such as the frailty of human nature laboring under original sin, which is the basis of forgiveness. The fact that without the grace of God the directee himself could have been the cause of the injury or even worse injuries is fruitful reflection to correct judgment. Reflection on how the directee himself has caused injuries to others can help him to see the injury he suffers in context. Trying to view the injury from the point of view of vicarious suffering as well as meditating on the injuries Christ suffered, Who was in no way deserving of them, helps one to see how little one's suffering is compared to Christ's.

Self wounds can be particularly difficult for the person to overcome, since the cause of the offense and the one offended are one and the same. Self wounds occur when we do something evil which either directly or indirectly causes our psychological impairment. It can directly cause one's psychological impairment when the person knows that engaging in the activity will worsen his psychological illnesses, e.g. the alcoholic who drinks knowing it is going to continue causing him problems. Self wounds can be indirectly caused, e.g. when a person seeks after some good while being blind to or ignoring the evil that will be inflicted on him as a result, e.g. women who have abortions knowing that it is seriously wrong. This kind of wound often tends to be deeper and harder to overcome. Since punishment and vindication are the proper actions in relation to evil action and evils inflicted, those who cause their own wounds will often be self abusive. Just as one gets a delight from vindication of evils of others, one will get a certain delight in abusing himself.

Recent psychiatric studies show that suffering abuse can cause harm to the brain.[446] Of course, we have occasionally drawn attention to the fact that the body adjusts itself to the operations of the soul. When a person is abused, the body begins to be damaged since it is not designed for that kind of operation. This is important for those suffering wounds to keep in mind. For their own benefit, they must let go of those things causing the wound so that they do not suffer physiological damage.

Healing a wound can be a complex and difficult process. Yet, to understand it properly, we need to discuss how each of the faculties must be addressed. Since a wound is something which is remembered, i.e. it is something in memory, the first thing that must happen is purification of memory. We have already talked about this in other places, but we should bear in mind that the principal means of purifying memory in the case of a wound is by practicing custody of the mind. As one keeps the phantasms of the wound out of one's mind, it lessens the repetition of the storing of the memory and therefore will weaken the memory. This is not a matter of denying reality. On the contrary, it is a recognition of the reality that one cannot handle this wound without keeping it out of one's mind. Custody of the mind will also habituate the cogitative

---

[446]Any cursory web search will produce studies in this regard.

power not to bring that image out of the memory or associate that image with those who have caused the wound.

Here, an explanation is in order. Some would hold that it is a denial of reality to act as if the person causing the wound did nothing. This is not the case. What first must be established is a custody over the faculties causing the wound to continue and fester. This requires keeping the injury out of one's mind. It may require, provided duties and circumstances in life will permit, a withdrawal from the one causing the problem, not to punish the one who caused the injury but to let the directee get his mind off the cause of the wound so that associations of the cogitative power do not continue. Then the person must work on forgiving the person by means of understanding, which will reformulate the image of the injury and the one causing the injury in congruity with reality, which we will discuss below. This must be joined with detachment of self (which likewise will be discussed below). These things done in conjunction will cause a healing of the wound.

Detachment is a key to (a) overcoming wounds and (b) avoiding being wounded. A wound is an injury which persists in something which is good. If we are detached from the good of self, then when it is injured, we take less offense at it. Since detachment is a lack of that habit of the passion of love in relation to created things and since sorrow arises out of love, those who are detached will not suffer sorrow when they are offended. Only someone who suffers from attachments is capable of being wounded. Further, the degree to which one can be wounded is in direct proportion to how attached one is to the thing which is injured, whether self or something in relation to self.

Detachment also helps the person to be able to embrace vicarious suffering. We have already discussed vicarious suffering elsewhere, but a reflection on it in the current context is helpful. Since vicarious suffering helps to give rationality and direction to one's suffering, one can see the good in the suffering, not in itself, of course, but insofar as through it one can gain many spiritual things for self and others. If those who are detached, and even those who are not, take Christ as their example in suffering, they will be able to make sense of the wound and overcome it much more rapidly since they can direct the suffering toward a rational end which will aid them psychologically. To this end, a strong devotion to the Sacred Heart, which was "bruised for our offenses,"[447] helps us to join our suffering to Christ, to see how He suffered so that we could emulate His example and gain the graces for ourselves and even for the person who caused the wound in order to overcome our trials and defects. Developing a spirit of mortification is indispensable, both in overcoming a wound and not suffering a wound when injuries are inflicted.

Detachment will give a stability to a person's emotional life which can be turbulent when the person is wounded. Since all passions rise out of love, if one is detached, no other passion will arise since sorrow will not arise from an evil inflicted on the good loved. One must work on detachment from the vindication of anger and the pleasures arising from pursuing the objects of the passions which give us pleasure due to our dispositions. Detachment is a habit or a conglomeration of habits in various

---

[447]Litany of the Sacred Heart.

faculties (e.g. the concupiscible and irascible appetites, the will and the cogitative power which associates according to attachments). Therefore it takes time to develop. Those who are wounded will find it difficult to develop those habits, but they should not get discouraged by the difficulties, nor should they get discouraged if they do not see results right away. As they work on detachment, over the course of time they will find that the wound will fade (or be healed, we may say analogically).

Forgiveness also directly affects the wound. Here, the reader is directed to review the discussion of forgiveness in the second volume. Forgiveness is an action in which the person lets go of the injury. If the person causing the injury or wound is sorry, the directee can be moved to forgive the person since the directee sees that the person sorrows at the injury caused. The sorrow of the injury is lessened since the person sees that the other suffers for what he has done. Yet, even if the person is not sorry for inflicting the injury, the directee can be moved to forgive the person, since that is what Christ would have him do. Yet, Christ does not have us do things without rational motive. We forgive others because, if we do not, the wound continues to fester in our souls. Hence, we forgive others so that we may benefit from it. Those who do not forgive perpetuate the suffering from the injury, whereas those who forgive, turn away from suffering the evil of the infliction by not holding on to it. Moreover, we can always remember that in forgiving another, we recognize that it is not our place to extract vengeance. We can forgive people or suffer the evils which they direct toward us because we know that in the end justice will be served because of the General Judgment. We can also forgive people because we know that people are not functioning the way God had intended because of original and actual sin. We can forgive people because we know that without God's grace we could be worse than the one inflicting the injury. Through forgiveness, we detach ourselves from appetitively and intellectually holding on to the injury. In this respect, forgiveness removes the cause of the wound so that it can heal over time. The person must foster the virtue of mercy by which he is inclined to forgive people of the debts they owe him. Anytime anyone injures us injustly, he becomes our debtor because what he owed us, i.e. right treatment, was not rendered. But it is only through a habit of forgiveness that one can overcome the cause of the wound (the injury). Frequent meditation on Christ's words will help a great deal, such as "forgive us our debts, as we also forgive our debtors."[448] Also, "judge not, that you may not be judged."[449] The directee can never be certain of the interior motives of those who caused the injury. This meditation and the meditation on mercy and reflection on how the directee could be the cause of the injury without the grace of God can mitigate the sorrow of the wound.

Self inflicted wounds also require the person to forgive himself. By this is meant that he must let go of the fact that he has done something either to himself or to another which is evil. He must accept that without grace and even with grace but by free choice, all of us are capable of the worst of crimes. He must do all of the things

---

[448]Matthew 6:12.

[449]Matthew 7:1.

mentioned in this chapter to correct his faculties in relation to himself rather than to others.

The directee who has suffered a wound can also take consolation in Christ's words, "Behold, I make all things new."[450] Those who suffer injury feel "used" and degraded. But through humility and a strong devotion to the Sacred Heart and a striving for holiness, the wounded person will experience a certain newness or refreshment. Lastly, in heaven, everyone has let go of past injuries. If one wants to have a taste of heaven in this life, he must forgive those who trespass against him as Our Lord taught us in the Our Father. Hell is full of those who brood over past injuries and those who brood over past injuries make their own version of hell in this life.

Chapter 18: Subtlety of Judgment

Precision and subtlety in judgment is affected by appetitive attachments to the various truths, propositions and terms which reason uses to ratiocinate.[451] Reason is affected in its judgment when there are appetitive attachments to the images which correspond to different truths. This is because the appetitive reaction to the particular true or false proposition, or in the term or terms in the proposition is merged with the image in the imagination and thereby affects judgment which converts back to the phantasm to judge the truth of the proposition or term. This is why human beings tend to judge to excess or defect some proposition or term. This affects the reasoning process because the appetitive imagery in the imagination affects the judgment of reason; reason will judge a term as distributed when it is not, because the passion merged in the image draws reason to judge to excess. Also, the passions may blind the judgment of reason, causing reason not to see that a term is distributed. It can even affect the grasping of the terms, which affects reasoning.

The cogitative power is affected in that the passions affect its assessment of the images relating to the terms in the syllogisms. Sometimes passion affects the judgment of the terms even when reason is not syllogizing and the person does not grasp the true nature of the thing to which the term relates. Reason can be so affected so as to not be able to see that a particular term corresponds to some real thing. The cogitative power relies on memory in order to prepare the phantasm. If prior passion is associated with a phantasm, the cogitative power will assess and prepare the phantasm based upon this prior passion, even when the person is not experiencing that passion at the moment. For example, if a person has experienced great sorrow in the presence of a friend and years later in a discussion with a third party the friend is discussed, the cogitative power will merge a negative assessment with the phantasm. Passion does not necessarily have to arise when the negative assessment is made but judgment will still be affected because of the negative assessment in the phantasm. Past judgments confirm the assessment of

---

[450]Apocalypse 21:5.

[451]Review of chapter nine of volume one will aid the reading of this chapter if one's memory of that chapter has waned.

the cogitative power which is habituated in that assessment. The memory of the confirmation of judgment is stored and will later affect the judgment of the individual. Therefore, prior judgments, passions and habits of the cogitative power will affect the subtlety of the person's judgment even when there is no current passion. These prior passions, judgments and habits will affect intellectual precision and will block the individual's ability to grasp the truth and connections between terms.[452]

Virtue, by moderating the passions, will also affect the assessment of the cogitative power and the judgment of reason. Since truth lies in a mean between judging excessively and not enough (by defect), moral virtue will directly contribute to the grasping of truth and the connections of terms by moderating the passions which will affect the phantasm. When the sensible species proper to the passions are lacking from the phantasm, the intellect is more likely to see the truth correctly since the passion will not make the object under consideration greater or less than it is by good or bad passions. The striving for moral virtue will also purify memory by the storing of the images affected by virtue. Mortification, prayer, fasting and abstinence (all of which are virtues) will have a direct impact on the clarity of the phantasms which affect judgment. They will also fix the will in the good (convertible with the true) and so the will will not falsify the phantasm. All of these things lead to an ability on the part of the intellect to see the more subtle aspects of terms and propositions and thereby gives a person a grasp of the truths which are more difficult to see as true.[453] This is clearly manifest in the fact that some people are able to grasp the truths regarding modesty and the virtue of decorum whereas those prone to passions tend to see the crude and immodest life as acceptable. But these conclusions extend beyond morality and the moral virtues and touch upon all aspects of scientific endeavor, since science is a virtue perfecting judgment. Those in education must strive for moral virtue in order to have clarity of mind regarding the areas that they study.

The converse is also the case, however. If a person or society engages in a life of the passions, the intellect will be blinded to the more subtle truths. As the vices associated with the passions deepen, the person or society begins to experience a "dumbing down" effect, even though they will be blind to the fact that this is happening. The more virtuous a society is, all things being equal, the more it will be capable of intellectual achievement in all of the sciences. This is even more true in the cases of the "subtle" sciences, i.e. philosophy (particularly metaphysics and epistemology) and theology.

In the realm of psychology, this truth has a threefold application. The first is that those engaging in research regarding psychology will advance more rapidly when they are virtuous. The virtues will give them a clarity of mind by which they are able

---

[452]This is sometimes called insight.

[453]This is manifest in the lives of St. Augustine and St. Thomas. St. Augustine did not begin to achieve the heights of intellectual insight regarding the truths of the faith until he mastered chastity. St. Thomas was given a supernatural gift of chastity. In both cases, chastity leads to clarity of intellectual vision.

to grasp the more subtle things regarding human nature and psychology. The second application is regarding the psychologist. The more virtuous the psychologist, is the more he is able to detect the subtle aspects of the states of directees' faculties and their psychological conditions. Since prudence requires conversion to the phantasm to judge, the virtuous person will have clear phantasms and thereby be able to know what prudence dictates in particular cases. This is not only because the psychologist will grasp the principles of psychology better, but he will have a clear grasp of the circumstances of the directee's life and so the psychologist will be able to apply the principles to the circumstances of the directee by judgment more readily and accurately. The third application is for directees. If they suffer a blindness regarding their condition, it is because of passion, the way the cogitative power is preparing their phantasms and/or their judgment, all of which are affected by virtue and vice. Mental illness itself is a vice, which is why the person cannot grasp what to do. The directee must be encouraged to obtain the virtue which is opposite the vice so that he will enjoy a clarity of mind about the subject. Those who suffer some vice do not often see why it is wrong until they obtain the opposite virtue. Then a clarity of mind results from the virtue regarding the mental illness or vice and they are able to grasp intellectually what is disordered about the mental illness.

Chapter 19: Intellectual Deprivation

In chapter nine of the second volume in the section on detachment, it was observed that mortification, prayer and grace remove the attachments in the sensitive and intellective appetites and the person will undergo a certain confusion. This follows from the fact that through a life of attachments (passions) and vice, the principles of judgment were interior, i.e. they were based on one's attachments. For example, one would do something because of how one felt rather than according to the truth. When a person has worked on overcoming a mental illness rooted in some attachment, he will find that he is a bit lost. It was noted that some stroke victims have the neural network severed in which the body reports back to the brain the state of the body in which the passion or emotion is related. This results in the person having emotions but not being able to sense them and so the cogitative power which used to assess the image based upon the passion no longer has the information. This results in the possible intellect being presented with different phantasms than before and so the possible intellect becomes confused as to what to do, since in the past, it had based its judgment on the passions.

These observations fall within the domain of what is called deprivation. While there may not be sense deprivation, there can be intellectual deprivation. People will often have the same experience when, for example, someone dies, when someone leaves one's life, or when one overcomes a drug addiction or things of this sort. A fuller explanation is in order at this time. The person will have no motivation because there are no passions. But there is a certain intellectual deprivation that occurs in the aforementioned examples. This deprivation is caused in three ways. The first is that the phantasms in relation to the things which are no longer extant (such as in death or someone leaving us) are often (1) no longer present and/or (2) have changed. For example, after a loved one has passed away, the survivor no longer sees the other person and so there are no phantasms of the person, except in memory. The phantasms of the person have also changed, e.g. when someone dies, the imagery of their death is part of the phantasm in memory. Phantasms of things to which the person relates have changed. When someone dies or leaves, he is no longer present in his house, in his favorite chair and things of this sort. As a result, these objects which relate to the person now lack their former relation since the person has passed away or left. This changes one's view of those objects and so "things just don't seem the same." It can also affect self-perception when one's relationship to the person or thing is strong, because it changes our perception of self, of which the accident of relation is a part.

The next aspect of intellectual deprivation concerns the cogitative power. Since the cogitative power is habituated regarding the things that are stripped from us, once they are gone, the cogitative power undergoes a change in relation to those things. This can happen in three ways. First, when the cogitative power is habituated in associating the thing which has been stripped from us with ourselves or some other thing, it will continue to incline to do so because of habit. Second, the thing which the cogitative power used to take into consideration is no longer present (e.g. when a man's wife dies, he is used to conducting his life taking her into consideration). This leaves the cogitative power at a loss regarding its habituation since it now does not have the phantasm or the phantasm of the thing has been changed to such a degree that the cogitative power can no longer associate other things which relate to it. Hence, the person will be a bit confused; he does not know what to do because the cogitative power no longer has the phantasms by which it made associations. The third aspect of intellectual deprivation concerns the judgment of reason. Reason depends heavily on the phantasm and habits in reason exist in relation to certain phantasms. When the phantasms change, reason may lack the habits by which to judge the change of phantasms because reason is used to judging different phantasms. This also adds to the confusion.

The remedy for intellectual deprivation has somewhat been addressed in the second volume of this work in the place cited. Charity and truth can keep the person motived, so that his life does not stagnate and this suffices for the intellectual appetite.[454] The principal way in which the intellect overcomes the deprivation is through supplying the intellect with phantasms which are not related to the person as such, so that it can become accustomed to the lack of the thing to which it was habituated or attached. Other phantasms which keep the mind occupied can help greatly, such as work, physical activities, hobbies and the like. This will give the appetitive faculties a redirection and provide phantasms for the intellect which will keep it occupied. As the intellect is focused on other phantasms, the habits in the material faculties (i.e. cogitative power, sensitive appetites, etc.) will begin to wane regarding their inclination toward the missing thing. In this respect, time is a key element.

Another way is to reformulate the image in a way which is rightly ordered. For

---

[454]It would also suffice for all of the other faculties but only in cases of those more spiritually advanced.

example, if someone were to lose a loved one, he could set about praying for him or pray to him for his help. He could view him as needing help because he is in purgatory and if he died in the state of grace as being able to provide intercession. One can consider the person's happiness in heaven and things of this sort which will help to change the image and train the cogitative power so that it does not experience the deprivation or lack of phantasms.

All of this comes with a warning, however. The suggestions of reformulating the image and activity must not detract from reality. If a person has accepted the loss of the thing to which he was attached, these suggestions will be helpful. They will also be helpful for those who are not quite ready, but in time will be ready to accept the truth. But they cannot be employed interminably as a way of avoiding reality because this is contrary to mental health.

Chapter 20: Laughter

A sense of humor and ability to laugh is one of the hallmarks of mental health. Conversely, an inability to laugh or disordered laughter may be a sign of mental illness. Laughter can play a minor role in diagnosing mental illness as well as a minor role in recovering from certain kinds of mental illness. St. Thomas observes, with most of the philosophical tradition, that laughter is something proper to man.[455] Laughter is proper to human nature because it requires two elements. The first is an ability to grasp something which is incongruous. We laugh because we perceive some incongruity in the thing or person about whom we laugh, e.g. G.K. Chesterton often gave the example of laughing at a well dressed man who appears dignified chasing his hat as it is blown down the street. The second element is that one must have the proper bodily organs to laugh. Angels see incongruities but they do not laugh because they do not have bodies.

Yet, animals which have bodies also do not laugh, since they do not have reason by which they are able to grasp the incongruous. Obviously, we see animals that perform actions which appear to us as laughing, however, a further analysis helps us to realize that this is not a true form of laughter. Some animals simply make the sounds which appear to us as laughing, e.g. certain birds, hyenas and the like. Other animals, such as chimpanzees, do appear to laugh at things which we laugh at and so we read into their behavior those things which are proper to man. In the case of animals higher in the hierarchy of animals (i.e. those with more powerful passive intellects), their laughter does correspond to certain kinds of events. However, these animals do not perceive the incongruous, because that requires grasping the nature of a thing and then judging that some thing in that nature (such as an accident) or something external to that nature does not fit that nature. Hence, to grasp what is laughable requires acts of judgment, which animals lack. Animals, however, make laughing sounds as an expression of visual and

---

[455]St. Thomas observes this throughout his corpus but one can see it in I Sent., d. 8, q. 1, a. 1, ad 1; III Sent., d. 20, q. 1, a. 1c; ST I, q. 3, a. 4, ST I-II, q. 51, a. 1; ST III, q. 16, a. 5; De Pot., q. 10, a. 4, ad 7; *De fallaciis*, passim and *In libros posteriorum analyticorum*, passim.

auditory pleasure which is not ordered toward the fulfillment of those faculties ordered toward bodily goods. In other words, animals "laugh," not because they grasp the incongruous, but because they experience an appetitive pleasure which is not associated with a bodily good as such. For the animal, this is purely at the level of the estimative sense and passions in contrast to human beings whose laughter proceeds from reason.

From this we see that animals do not laugh in the proper sense, but laughter as it is ascribed to them is an analogical predication, i.e. it is analogical because the difference is that they do not have reason and cannot grasp incongruity. The thing which is the same is that they engage in bodily gesticulating which in human beings is understood as laughter. Since God and angels do not have bodies they cannot be said to laugh, but they can be said to grasp the incongruity, which indicates that they can have a sense of humor. From this we see that laughter proceeds from the principles of our nature,[456] those two principles being animality and rationality.[457] Laughter, being proper to man, is not his nature itself but a proper and inseparable[458] accident[459] (risibility).

Like animals, we tend to laugh at things which are pleasing to us.[460] For this reason laughter is a sign of joy,[461] since when we are joyous we are disposed to pleasure and therefore are more likely to laugh. Yet, laughter also increases joy[462] insofar as it gives us pleasure. In this respect, laughter is good therapy for those in a state of depression, even though most who are depressed will suffer some pain from the laughter. When we laugh at times when we think we should be sorrowing, the laughter causes sorrow or pain since we see the laughter does not suit us.[463] The laughter is contrary to our disposition which is present because of the apprehension of reason. Because laughter causes us pleasure, and because what pleases us is often based upon bodily disposition, then taste in what is humorous is based upon our bodily disposition, since the bodily disposition determines what gives the person pleasure. Likewise, one's virtues and vices will determine what pleases us in two ways. (1) Since the body adjusts itself to the operations of the soul and when one has a virtue or vice, there is a concomitant bodily disposition in relation to that virtue or vice, virtue or vice will determine what we can take pleasure in regarding humor. (2) Something humorous is grasped at the level of reason and so both the intellect and will can be pleased with what is humorous. This is why at times someone can take delight intellectually in something humorous while maintaining a proper restraint from the manifestation of that delight

---

[456]ST I, q. 3, a. 4; ST III, q. 24, a. 2, ad 2 and De Anima, q. 12, a. 7.

[457]Of course, the classical definition of man is a rational animal.

[458]*De principiis naturae*, c. 2.

[459]ST I, q. 3, a. 6.

[460]In Job, c. 9.

[461]In Job, cc. 3, 8 & 29.

[462]ST I-II, q. 38, a. 2, ad 2.

[463]Ibid., ad 3.

(laughter).[464] Taste in humor is based upon disposition, virtue and vice.

One of the signs of mental health is the ability to grasp something as humorous and to be able, at least, to take intellectual delight in it. We are precluding those of lower intelligence who, as a result, have a harder time grasping what is incongruous. These persons are not mentally ill but merely slow in grasping what is humorous. Whereas the mentally ill will either find no humor in anything, since they cannot grasp reality (incongruity) for what it is, or they will find humorous those things which are not truly humorous.

For this reason, what is pleasing to us, both intellectually and bodily, ought to follow right order and that right order is based upon the order of right reason. Right reason is that which is in accord with the natural law and so properly-ordered humor is found only in those things which do not violate the natural law. To reformulate this, we can say that we ought not to laugh at anything which is contrary to the natural law (sin). We ought to laugh only at those things which are truly laughable, i.e. only those things in which the pleasure is in accord with the natural law and therefore laughter ought to be in accord with virtue. Hence, since virtues and vices are distinguished according to their objects, morally good and bad laughter (as well as mentally healthy and unhealthy laughter) is based upon the object of laughter, the end of the agent laughing and the circumstances in which one laughs.

Uncontrolled laughter is a sign of immoderation and a lack of refraining of the soul[465] and St. Thomas says that it is a venial sin.[466] This particular lack of refraining is called hilarity.[467] To laugh at inappropriate times and things takes away from one's own excellence or glory,[468] i.e. it lowers us and is therefore contrary to the virtue of magnanimity.[469] Yet, to laugh when one ought suits one's own excellence and glory and so laughter itself when done according to virtue is not contrary to magnanimity. Right reason abstains from laughter (and the pleasure of laughter) when necessary.[470] To refrain from inept signs of joy and laughter pertains to the virtues of humility,[471] modesty,[472] decorum and honesty.[473] Abstention from disordered laughter is listed as a

---

[464]God and angels can take delight in the humorous in this way.

[465]See *Sententia libri ethicorum*, IV, l. 16.

[466]ST I-II, q. 88, a. 2.

[467]St. Thomas calls hilarity a sign of lack of restraint in ST II-II, q. 148, a. 6.

[468]See ST II-II, q. 146, a. 1, ad 4.

[469]Regarding the virtue of magnanimity, see ST II-II, q.129.

[470]ST II-II, q. 146, a. 1, ad 4.

[471]ST II-II, q. 161, a. 6 and ibid., q. 162, a. 4, ad 4.

[472]When one laughs at things which are not suited to one's state, or circumstances, or it is against purity and modesty, it becomes a sin against modesty. For a treatment on modesty and decorum, see ST II-II, qq. 169f.

[473]*Sententia libri ethicorum*, IV, l. 16, n. 3.

good act along with fasting and kneeling,[474] since it seeks to moderate the soul's attachment to the pleasures of laughter through abstinence.

Foolishness is connected to hilarity[475] since foolishness is a vice opposite to wisdom,[476] which ennobles the spirit and turns the soul upward rather than downward to pleasure which foolishness seeks. Moreover, to incite laughter in others which does not suit our circumstances is contrary to virtue,[477] since to do so seeks to move people to something contrary to right reason. Vanity moves one to inordinate laughter[478] and this would appear to be the case when one laughs in order to be pleasing to others, which vanity seeks. Derision uses laughter as a means to carry off the honor and glory of another[479] and is done to cause shame to another.[480] Derision seeks to harm one's neighbor[481] and so St. Thomas lists it among the sins against justice.[482]

From the aforesaid, we can see that rightly ordered laughter can cause mental health and disordered laugher can cause mental illness. Disordered laughter can cause mental illness since it affects the cogitative power's habits of association by the pleasure in the imagination. The cogitative power associates the pleasures of laughter either to excess or in the wrong manner with things which should not be laughed at. This takes the person out of contact with reality if the laughter becomes too excessive. Disordered laughter also affects the passions by disposing them to immoderate pleasures of laughter. It affects judgment by affecting the phantasm which in turn habituates the possible intellect. Like pleasures of other kinds, unless moderated they can cause blindness to the possible intellect because of the habits caused in the possible intellect and the effect they have on the phantasms. Disordered laughter can cause weakness of the will if there is a vice in the lower appetites (i.e. the vice of hilarity). We also know that those who suffer from mental illness often laugh immoderately and at unsuitable things. On the other hand, some people, who are mentally ill, laugh at nothing, which is a sign that they do not grasp reality for what it is or have some other vice or disorder which prevents the laughter or which prevents the person from taking pleasure in the laughter.

Yet, laughter in accord with right reason can cause mental health in a variety of ways. Rightly ordered laughter affirms the intellectual judgment in the truth, i.e. when there is a true incongruity which suits being laughed at, then laughter strengthens

---

[474]*Catena Aurea in Matthaeum*, c. 23, l. 7.

[475]ST II-II, q. 148, a. 6.

[476]See ST II-II, q. 46.

[477]ST II-II, q. 72, a. 2, ad 1.

[478]*Catena Aurea in Matthaeum*, c. 12, l. 11.

[479]ST III, q. 46, a. 5.

[480]ST II-II, q. 75, a. 1 and *Contra doctrinam retrahentium*.

[481]Ibid.

[482]ST II-II, q. 75 finds itself within the tract on justice in the *Secunda Secundae*. Also within that question one can see the degrees of gravity of the sin of derision and under what circumstances it suits one to laugh at another in a derisive fashion.

the intellect. Rightly ordered laughter also affirms and builds the right kinds of phantasms which in turn build the right kind of habits of association in the cogitative power. Rightly ordered laughter can help heal memory when the laughter is associated with some painful event in the past at which one should laugh. When the laughter is moderated and according to right reason, it can aid the person in bringing his appetites under control and directing them in a way which is in accord with virtue; rightly ordered laughter can build virtue in these lower faculties.

Psychologists have noted other benefits regarding laughter. The first is that it can improve relationships. This follows from the fact that the pleasure we take in laughing with other people (or even at other people) is associated with the person and therefore affects the association of the cogitative power with the person. This in turn affects judgment and volition in that the person is more inclined to love the other because of the pleasure of the person's company. This is often why women like men who have a sense of humor and seek to find that sense of humor in men they are courting. Howard Bennet observes that

> Wender recently reviewed the importance of humor in family medicine. He sees humor as a means to narrowing interpersonal gaps, communicating caring, and relieving anxiety associated with medical care. Patients also use humor to express frustration with their health and with the medical establishment. ...Some patients do not appreciate humor, and it can be counter productive to use it in their presence.[483]

The importance of this in psychology is that the psychologist should have a sense of humor and the prudence of knowing when to use humor to lighten the spirits of the person he is counseling. Prudence is based on circumstances so a psychologist should have a proper knowledge of different people, the general circumstances in which people find themselves, and what sorts of humor are appropriate and when. The psychologist himself must be a man of virtue so that he can easily determine those times when laughter is unsuited to the circumstances.

Humor can aid in education and learning,[484] which should be implicit in the observations made above regarding how laughter affects our faculties. When a psychologist needs to drive home a point to a directee who may have a hard time understanding what is being taught, the psychologist can prepare the directee a bit by humor or use humor as a means to teach. Obviously, care and moderation must be taken because the directee must also recognize that the psychologist has to maintain a certain proper seriousness, particularly about the directee's condition.

---

[483]Howard Bennet, *Humor in Medicine*. This article is good from the standpoint of providing a summary of the various health benefits of laughter, including immunological benefits and the like, but they will not be discussed here since they pertain more to medicine than to psychology.

[484]A. Ziv., *Teaching and Learning with Humor: Experiment and Replication.*, J. Exp Educ, 1988, 57: 5-15.

Chapter 21: Involuntary Vices

Throughout this series of volumes, various kinds of habits have been discussed. It was observed that someone can increase (or perfect) or decrease the inclination of some of his faculties towards certain objects by the actions he performs. When a disposition or quality is increased or decreased by action, it is called a habit. A habit is an inclination towards a specific form of action and it aids the faculty in acting well or poorly in a given action. Habits correspond to a specific object as well. The faculty, therefore, resides in the soul, but the faculty can have a natural disposition towards its operation with respect to a specific object.

From these observations we can deduce several conclusions. The strength of the habit determines how strongly the person is inclined to perform a given action, sometimes called the "force" of the habit.[485] It is entirely possible that the habit would become so strong that the person loses his ability to control it, even though the habit was developed voluntarily. When a bad habit becomes very strong, the person feels "forced" to perform the action corresponding to the vice. This uncontrolled habit is what modern psychology calls "obsessive compulsive disorder."

However, modern psychology was not the first to discover this nor is its nomination of it as descriptive as that which is contained in the philosophical/moral tradition. In modern psychology, obsessive compulsion is explained principally in terms of how the person feels in relation to compulsive action as is exemplified in the following definition:

> **Compulsion**: 1. The state in which the person feels forced to behave against his own conscious wishes and judgment. 2. The force which compels a person to action against his own will or forcing a person to act in this way.[486]

Sometimes obsessive compulsion is explained in terms of effects, as the name denominates, viz. that the person has obsessive thoughts[487] and is driven to act from these thoughts.[488] Yet, these definitions are descriptive definitions and not causal or essential definitions. The scholastic tradition, on the other hand, has provided an essential nomination whose definition is not only essential but provides a causal

---

[485]Davis, *Moral and Pastoral Theology*, vol. 1, p. 32.

[486]Wolman, *Dictionary of Behavioral Science*, p. 71.

[487]In ibid., p. 260, we read, "**Obsession** An idea or impulse which persistently preoccupies an individual even though the individual prefers to be rid of it."

[488]In ibid. we also read, "**Obsessive compulsive behavior**: behavior characterized by repetitive, irrational thoughts called obsessions and actions called compulsions." See also definition of "obsessive compulsive neurosis", ibid., p. 253.

understanding of this mental illness.[489]

In the scholastic tradition, a habit is acquired by degrees and it is possible for a habit to become so strong that the person loses voluntariness over the habit in relation to a specific kind of object. Habits can be so strong so as to block the voluntariness of an action:[490]

> Many other aspects of these obstacles have been brought to light with the advance of medical sciences, inasmuch as it has studied and analyzed various neuroses. These may be considered as habitual obstacles to free acts. These diseases add their own momentum, as it were, to the motions of the sensitive appetites; at other times, they prevent the full and free advertence of the intellect. Accordingly, the will is diverted from the pursuit of the true good, and consequently these sufferers are less responsible.[491]

What Davis is essentially pointing out is that neurosis and obsessive compulsions (we may say in most cases) are simply involuntary vices (bad habits), which is a true essential nomination. It is essential because the two terms of *involuntary* and *vice* provide the essential meaning to understand these kinds of actions people undergo or perform.

The first point is that this disorder is a vice or bad habit, since it is repeated action in relation to a specific object. St. Thomas says that vices render a person weak[492] in relation to a specific object and this is why the person with this kind of vice "feels" like they have no control over it. In chapter nine of the first volume, a discussion was developed regarding the passions and how they bind reason. Since vices are either rooted in the appetites or affect the appetites, these involuntary habits or vices have the same effect as the passions to which they relate. Therefore, those who have these involuntary habits suffer (1) from all of the effects discussed in relation to the daughters of lust, e.g. precipitation of judgment and blindness of intellect. Those who have these vices will often not be aware of them because of intellectual blindness. Sometimes they will be aware of them, but these vices will still affect their judgment. This follows from the fact that the habits incline the various faculties which affect judgment, viz. the passions, cogitative power, imagination and memory. Since they are affected in this manner, those suffering from involuntary vices will suffer a corruption of prudence and will not know how to act in relation to the object of the vice. They will also suffer inconstancy when trying to overcome the vice.

(2) Since involuntary habits affect the person the same way as the passions,

---

[489]Again, this is why scholastic terminology should be adopted and employed rather than the modern terminology.

[490]McHugh and Callan, *Moral Theology*, vol. I, p. 19 (n. 40) and ibid., p. 22 (n. 53).

[491]Davis, *Moral and Pastoral Theology*, vol. 1, p. 30.

[492]ST I-II, q. 71, a. 1, ad 3.

those contracting these vices will suffer a loss of volitional control.[493] (3) When the inclination towards these actions in relation to the involuntary vice arise, due to either thought or disposition, the person will find it almost impossible to combat them. This flows from the fact that like the passions, once these thoughts arise, the habit will bind the soul so that it cannot engage in other operations, due to the unitary nature of the soul and its faculties. (4) Involuntary vices cause bodily dispositions and when the thoughts arise in relation to those dispositions, the person is affected by the bodily transmutations. The disposition can both be caused by and be the cause of the images associated with these vices which are in the imagination. Since the cogitative power assesses what is sensed and associates what is sensed (as present in the imagination) with what is in memory, when a person feels a certain way because of his disposition, the cogitative power will bring up the thoughts associated with that disposition. This is an important mechanism in relation to addictions (as will be seen in a subsequent chapter).

Yet, the obsessive thoughts do not necessarily need the bodily dispositions in another faculty, other than the cogitative power to be constantly present to the mind. If a person constantly thinks about something and views everything in reality under the *ratio* of that object of thought, the cogitative power is habituated to think of everything in those terms. For example, those who have a fixation on sex often develop a habit of mind in which every single object of their experience is related to sex or sexual pleasure.[494] Some directees cannot imagine anything or anyone without first thinking about sex. Those who suffer from these involuntary vices, because they constantly think of everyone and everything under the rubric of their fixation, cannot imagine someone else not having this problem.[495]

Therefore, those who suffer from involuntary vices will suffer all of the disorders in the various faculties which contribute to the involuntary thoughts and

---

[493]Here it would behoove the reader to re-familiarize himself with chapter nine, since many of the observations made in this chapter will depend on a detailed knowledge of that chapter. The more the reader understands chapter nine of volume one, the more he will grasp how involuntary vices affect the person psychologically.

[494]One must wonder if this is not the problem with the members of the mainstream entertainment industry, since in the average watching of five to ten minutes of television, it is rare not to see something regarding sex, either in the advertisements or the programing itself. The coupling of the Watsonian method of advertising (see Jones, *Libido Dominandi*, passim.) with the Freudian and other psychologists' fixation on sexual matters has left modern entertainment in a morally, spiritually and psychologically deplorable state.

[495]This is often why the average person on the street who is the product of our modern sexually-fixated society cannot imagine a priest who is truly celibate and is not preoccupied with sexual matters. In fact, in psychology circles themselves, there is a general attitude that not to be fixated on sex is disordered.

actions of this disorder, i.e. the memory,[496] imagination,[497] cogitative power,[498] possible intellect,[499] will[500] and appetites. Therefore, we can see that the contracting of involuntary vices as well as the vices themselves are contrary to the order of reason.[501] Since habits are principles of action,[502] the person will find himself performing these actions involuntarily for two reasons. The first is because of the inclination of the vice itself. The second is because of the mechanism described earlier regarding the cogitative power's ability to execute motions independently of reason and will. Moreover, since the person will "feel" like he has no control over it and since the inclination from the vice is strong, he will find it almost, if not entirely, impossible to keep himself from performing the action.

St. Thomas observes that when a person develops a habit, a certain pleasure arises out of the habit.[503] As a person begins developing a virtue or a vice, at first there may not be much pleasure in it at all; in fact, it may even be painful. But as the person progresses in the virtue or regresses in the vice, he will get more pleasure from the respective habit. Again, this will become more important regarding addictions discussed in the subsequent chapter. However, in relation to the subject of this chapter, many will find overcoming involuntary vices difficult, because they get pleasure out of the vice. If the object of vice itself also gives pleasure to the faculty due to the nature of the object itself (e.g. in food or sex) the vice will be even more difficult to break. The person will have to overcome the attachment not only to the pleasure of the object itself but also to the pleasure coming from the disposition and/or habit in the faculty. Also, since different people have different dispositions, some people will be more prone to developing some involuntary habits than others, e.g. those who are sanguine will be more likely to develop involuntary vices in relation to food than those who suffer from a melancholic disposition. While some melancholic people will develop a strong attachment to food because it gives consolation in the face of their sorrow, generally,

---

[496]The memory is affected because the images and associations pertaining to the object of the vice are stored in memory.

[497]The imagination is habituated to be under the control of faculties other than reason and will, due to the "force" of the habit which affects the various faculties which affect the imagination.

[498]The cogitative power is habituated in the associations of the vice.

[499]The judgment and reasoning of the possible intellect is affected by the images in the imagination arising from these vices as well as the intellectual habits (vices) which are fostered from constantly thinking and judging about the object of the vice in this manner.

[500]The will is weakened (voluntariness is reduced) and habits in the will can develop in relation to the object of the vice.

[501]ST I-II, q. 71, a. 2.

[502]Brennan, *Thomistic Psychology*, p. 393 in reference to pp. 267-268. This is one of the reasons why they are called operative habits.

[503]See, among others, De Vir., q. 1, a. 1.

they will not be inclined to do so.

Yet, modern psychology is so crass at times as to lump virtue in with vice. In other words, since a virtue inclines one toward a good action and since psychology often mistakes what is good for what is bad, many psychologists have lumped virtuous people and their actions in with "obsessive compulsive behavior." Yet, involuntary habits and virtues are direct contraries, since involuntary habits or vices as well as vices in general reduce one's voluntariness or take voluntariness away by weakening the various faculties, particularly the will and the faculty to which the object of the vice directly relates, e.g. the concupiscible appetite in relation to the vice of lust. A virtue actually strengthens the faculty (since virtue comes from the Latin word *vis* which means power) and makes the person more capable of voluntary action. In other words, a virtue gives the person a greater ability to choose to perform the action or not to perform the action. The fact that the virtuous person will always or for the most part follow the inclination of virtue does not mean he suffers from an involuntary vice but rather that there is the virtue of constancy in the will in relation to the object of the virtue.

It was also observed in the second volume that sometimes the demonic can cause obsessive thoughts. These can likewise lead to actions and so it is possible that a modern psychologist would diagnosis a person as having obsessive compulsive disorder when, in fact, the person may be under demonic influence. While it should be clear from this chapter that one can develop an involuntary vice on one's own without the demonic, the demonic can cause obsessive behavior by its effects on the material faculties. Moreover, certain forms of possession can be misconstrued as "obsessive compulsive" and this is why for a psychologist to diagnose directees properly he needs some working knowledge of the demonic and how demons can hide themselves behind what appears to be mental illness.

To overcome involuntary vices, the directee should make use of the indirect means of overcoming his mental illness as previously discussed. Moreover, all of the means in discussing fixation throughout these volumes can be employed. He must work on custody of the eyes and custody of the mind to keep the object of his vice out of his imagination. This alone will calm the affected faculties so that he can exercise more direct control over them. He can work on the virtue opposite the vice, which will slowly help him to gain voluntary control over the faculties in relation to the object of the vice.

Chapter 22: Addiction

In the prior chapter, two points were mentioned regarding addiction. The first was that the cogitative power interprets or assesses the feeling arising from a disposition to the addiction with the drug pertaining to that addiction. In the normal course of contracting an addiction voluntarily, i.e. by choices and volitional actions, the person has the image of the drug and the pleasures arising from that drug in his imagination. The cogitative power then associates the pleasures of the drug with the drug itself. Depending on the strength of the drug or the ability of the drug to form addictions, the person will experience a shorter or longer period in which the cogitative power makes the association regarding the desire for the drug[504] with the specific drug. If a person is drugged and experiences the addictive effects of the drug but does not know the object pertaining to that desire or craving, the cogitative power will not make the association between the drug and the craving.

It is possible for a person to develop a physical addiction or what is sometimes called a dependency on a drug without contracting any concomitant habits which go along with the normal contracting of that addiction. Most people who suffer from addictions do so by developing concomitant habits with the addiction. This is why children who are addicted without understanding why do not seek after the drug, but simply suffer the effects of withdrawal. If the child or person is old enough, he may know he craves something, but he does not know what he craves.

While the addiction, in those who develop the habits associated with the addiction may be considered as merely the material disposition of the body corresponding to the habits, that does not seem to be entirely the case. Since the habits in relation to the drug are sometimes in faculties other than the faculty affected by the drug itself, the disposition of the faculty and the addiction may be distinct. For example, someone may have an addiction to a drug which principally affects the brain, but it also gives him pleasure. As a result, from repeated action, the brain becomes dependent on the drug while the concupiscible appetite develops an unnatural vice or habit in relation to the drug which has a separate disposition from the brain which is addicted. This seems to follow, since the science of addiction has advanced greatly in the last few decades in which addiction is traced back to the mesocortical limbi or subcortical brain stem system,[505] a part of the brain sometimes called the addiction center of the brain. In the brain, there are receptors which are affected by the drug which causes the addiction, yet the concupiscible appetite is not only in the brain.[506]

The second thing which was discussed in the prior chapter was that an involuntary vice which has as its object something which gives pleasure of itself and not merely according to the disposition of the faculty of the vice makes it hard to overcome the vice. In relation to addictions, we see, therefore, that there are two components to the common addiction, viz. the vice, possibly even an involuntary vice, and the physical

---

[504]In modern parlance this is called a craving, but a craving is merely a bodily desire for some specific object.

[505]Abrams, *Brain Addiction Disorders*.

[506]Brain mapping, which has provided detailed knowledge of the various areas of activity associated with various functions of the brain, indicates that the passive intellect, while in the brain, does not utilize the entire brain. The brain seems to perform more functions than those of the passive intellect. Yet this would not affect any aspect of Thomistic psychology already delineated since Thomists have always known that activities of the passive intellect are localized and no Thomists, to the knowledge of the author, have ever held that the passive intellect takes up the entire brain. Modern brain studies, while properly the domain of the empirical sciences, can provide material for philosophical analysis, as we have done here. This will be discussed at greater length in part II of this volume.

dependence (craving). Therefore to overcome an addiction, one must break not only the physical dependence but also the vices or bad habits connected to the addiction. The development of some drugs has shown great promise in aiding addicts overcome their addiction. Yet, even in the cases of patients who undergo these chemical treatments, they still suffer from the concomitant vices. Aside from the use of chemical means to overcome the addiction, the normal process of breaking the dependency is done by the brain itself but only after going through withdrawals that are proper to each drug. By the Providence of God, the brain has a mechanism to overcome the dependency on its own provided no more of the drug is introduced into the brain.

Therefore, to overcome the average addiction, the person must do several key things. He must, obviously, stop using the drug, which will, over the course of time, break the dependency. But in order to cope with the vices, he must therefore do those things necessary to break them. Actions contrary to his vices must be performed. He must exercise custody of the mind and custody of the eyes to keep the images of the drug and the experiences of the drug out of his imagination. He must avoid the persons, places and things which will cause him to fall into the drug use again.

There has arisen a practice in the psychological and psychiatric community to call things addictions which are not truly addictions. Addictions, in the proper sense, are hallmarked by two components, the physical dependence on a chemical not naturally produced by the body and the concomitant vices. While it is true that the brain produces many "addictive" drugs on its own, it is designed, assuming it is functioning properly, to moderate these on its own and these drugs are often necessary for the brain's proper functioning. But an addiction to external chemicals is different since neither the brain nor the person moderates these drugs. The person who uses in moderation a drug which could be addictive cannot be said to have an addiction since there will be no concomitant vices nor will there be cravings for the drug. Once the cravings begin, one has begun to enter into the domain of an addiction. The fact that people engage in activities which stimulate the brain's production of highly addictive chemicals does not of itself constitute an addiction in the proper sense, but it would be more accurate to say that they contract a bad habit (vice), even if there are some chemicals produced by the brain by the activities of the vice. While some call these addictions, they are not properly so called.

Some are said to have an "addictive personality." This is true only of those who develop addictions since personality is something which falls in the domain of the voluntary. However, the term "addictive personality" should not be predicated of those who have not voluntarily developed addictions, since it would be more accurate to say that those people who could easily develop addictions have an "addictive disposition." It is possible for someone to have an addictive disposition, either by inheritance or by development.

Chapter 23: Control

Involuntary vices essentially reduce someone to "being out of control," at least in relation to the area of his vice. One characteristic of those who lack self-control over some area of their life is a tendency to seek to control others. The psychological mechanism behind this appears to be the fact that it is rooted in appetite and the appetites, in those who lack self-control, lack virtue. When a person's appetites lack virtue, the person tends to follow the appetites where they lead since, without virtue, the appetites will have strong antecedent passions which will affect the person's judgment. When a person does not have self-control, the appetites do not want to be inhibited from their objects, either from an internal source or from an external source. As to the internal, the person who lacks virtue in his appetites will experience rebellion when reason tries to control the appetites, but the appetites will also make him suffer. In other words, if the appetites are denied their object by some internal inhibition, e.g. from reason or will, the appetites become afflicted with sorrow since the absence of their object is viewed as the presence of an evil from which sorrow arises. Therefore, the person will be afflicted interiorly.

Exteriorly, the appetites move the person to subordinate all things to the appetites, i.e. the appetites affect and subordinate reason and will and seek to move the other faculties (via the imagination which affects judgment and volition) to their ends. Since these appetites normally seek exterior objects, they seek to subordinate external means to provide them with their object. This also entails removing any obstacles toward the obtainment of the object. Other people can be an obstacle to the attainment of the object of the appetite. This results in reason judging or the cogitative power assessing other people as being an obstacle to the object of the appetite. In order to remove people from being an obstacle to the object of their appetite or to use people themselves as the object of their appetite (e.g. in venereal pleasure), some people seek to control others to subordinate them to their appetites.

Trying to control others, apart from controlling those seeking to cause harm to others, is irrational. It is irrational because it is rooted not in reason, which recognizes each person as a free individual, but in appetite which is not subordinated to reason, i.e. it is not virtuous. Those who are virtuous are detached from the objects of their appetites and therefore do not feel the need to control others to obtain those objects, again because they are not attached or subordinated to those objects. The more virtuous a person is, the less he seeks to control others, unless duty require it for the sake of the common good or to protect others from harm.

Chapter 24: Relativism and Subjectivism

Modern life is fraught with relativism and subjectivism on all levels and this has caused serious problems for psychology. Since the human intellect is designed to come to knowledge of things by means of the senses, the human faculties are essentially oriented outwards. Subjectivism causes psychological damage because it trains the various faculties to act contrary to their nature, i.e. it orders them towards the self rather than towards those things which are outside of man. Subjectivism does not lead to happiness since happiness for man is eudaemonistic rather than solipsistic. Psychological counseling techniques which do not provide a proper direction to the directee but which only listen to him "without prejudice" contribute to the directee's unhappiness. Regardless of what the directee wants, the psychologist is not merely a pacifier, only listening to the directee so that he may feel better by getting things off his chest, so to speak. Also, those who argue that one should not be judgmental as a psychologist are irrational. The entire counseling endeavor is ordered toward judging the state of the faculties in order to arrive at a means to counter the disorder of the faculties. While subjectivism may be appetitively appeasing (principally to those whose appetites are not rightly ordered), it has no capacity to produce mental health.

Relativism holds that truth is relative and it directly militates against the good of the intellect. Since the intellect is ordered toward the truth, which is the conformity of the intellect and thing, the intellect either conforms or it does not. Since the principle of the excluded middle applies to whether one conforms or not, all truth is absolute, because it conforms to the thing. If the intellect does not conform to the thing, one does not have the truth. If one has part of the truth, one still does not have the truth as such, since truth conforms not by degree, but as the thing is. Hence, relativism militates against mental health by weakening the intellect. The intellect is weakened because the person does not seek to conform himself to reality but seeks to judge everything in terms of self or some other invalid criteria.

Relativism and subjectivism affect the possible intellect by developing habits in the possible intellect which incline the judgment of reason away from things as they are. Since truth is the good of the intellect, relativism and subjectivism militate against mental health. They disorder the will since the will is ordered toward the good in general, not the apparent good. But in the case of relativism and subjectivism, the intellect does not discern between apparent and real goods and therefore the will which is moved by the possible intellect does not choose based upon the truth. Subjectivism and relativism actually reduce the voluntariness of the action of the will since the will needs knowledge (truth) presented by the possible intellect in order to be able truly to choose.

The cogitative power becomes disordered by the reformulations of the possible intellect and will according to false judgments of the possible intellect regarding the truth, since relativism and subjectivism have disordered this judgment. These images get stored in memory which affect later deliberations. Moreover, the passions become vicious because they are moved by what the individual wants rather than by what is truly good for him. The final trajectory of subjectivism and relativism is away from the truth in which man's moral, spiritual and psychological good consists. The trajectory is toward vice, sin, ignorance (since he does not know the truth), mental illness and ultimately unhappiness, since happiness is something had in accord with virtue. Therefore, psychology must abandon all relativism or subjectivism, both in its theory and in its practice.

Chapter 25: Inclinations of Grace

In the prior volume, it was noted that the two principal effects of actual grace are to enlighten the mind and the strengthen the will.[507] When the mind is enlightened, it can set up an inclination by which the intellect is moved to judge or reason in a specific manner. Likewise, when the will is strengthened, there may be established in the will an inclination toward willing a specific good. Other graces can likewise set up inclinations which are specific to that type of grace. For example, those who receive the grace of a vocation to the priesthood or the religious life will often describe inclinations associated with the grace. While these inclinations must be carefully distinguished from inclinations arising from appetite, they are there, nonetheless. For instance, when a man has a vocation, he will often have a desire to offer the Holy Sacrifice of the Mass or to hear confessions. He may even have a desire for celibacy. These inclinations have often been misunderstood by psychologists. There have been occasions when young men have had strong graces inclining them toward religious life. While they have the ability to see that marriage is a good, they may have no desire for the married life but actually find an interior peace in silence, solitude and chastity. The interior peace is the effect of the grace. Since peace is the tranquility of order,[508] when the person with a vocation comes to the place where that vocation is fulfilled, there is a peace which results. There is a congruity or tranquility between the desires caused in the will of the person by the grace and the presence of the object toward which that grace is inclining the person. This harmony between the two causes a certain peace.

However, it has happened in the past and will continue to happen, that those who receive these graces, but do not fulfill the desires arising from the inclinations of grace will be unhappy and go through life enduring a kind of subtle suffering. For example, there are occasions when seminarians have had vocations to the priesthood or religious life and have chosen marriage instead. While the Church has always said this is not sinful, to do so may create a certain lack of peace in the soul. Most of them are not happy in their marriages since the desires arising from the inclinations of grace of the vocation cause a discord with their chosen state in life. This should not be diagnosed as some type of mental illness. Even more so, if a seminarian has no desire for marriage, and in some rare cases where the grace of chastity is very strong, no desire for conjugal relations, this should not be diagnosed as a psychological illness. While in some cases, these inclinations have been diagnosed as mental illness because they are supernatural rather than natural, this manifests even more clearly the necessity of faith on the side of the psychologist to understand the difference between a mental illness where there is a loss of a natural desire and one which arises from grace.

These inclinations also find themselves in what are called "graces of state." For example, a priest who has received the sacrament of Holy Orders also receives certain graces which incline him toward the fulfillment of his office as priest, i.e. to offer Mass, hear confessions, etc. When the priest fails to fulfill the obligations of his state, he will often enter into a kind of depression or state of sorrow or unhappiness. This is the result of the lack of fulfillment of the desire of the inclinations of the graces of state. On the

---

[507]See volume two, chapter seven (III).

[508]St. Augustine, *The City of God*, Book XIX, chapter 13.

other hand, when a priest fulfills his obligations, there is great peace and happiness.

All of this means that when God establishes inclinations in the faculties of the soul which has these specific kinds of graces, the person should act according to them. Otherwise, emotional and psychological problems can arise. Psychologists who have directees manifesting these kinds of graces should place the directees under the care of solid spiritual directors who can sort out the natural and supernatural inclinations and guide the directees to their fulfillment.

Chapter 26: Misdiagnosis of Supernatural Activities

In the prior chapter, we discussed inclinations of grace which, at times, may seem mysterious to those who do not have the Faith. These inclinations of grace and other supernatural activities in the life of people are often subject to misdiagnosis by psychologists not familiar with these supernatural activities. The problem is likewise complicated by the fact that some supernatural activities may resemble psychological problems. But psychological problems and supernatural activities differ, not only as to the causes and the effects, but as to their very essence, for mental illnesses are contrary to the mental health of an individual, whereas supernatural activity always builds on the nature of the intellect itself.

For example, the dark night of the soul as described by St. John of the Cross could easily be misinterpreted as "clinical depression" accompanied by "obsessive compulsive disorder." In the case of the dark night of the soul, the person enters into what the spiritual writers call passive purgation which is an activity of God on the soul by which the soul is purified of its spiritual defects. This activity leaves the soul exceptionally arid and without consolation. The soul also finds no joy in the things of the world and often undergoes tremendous suffering and confusion due to the fact that God is in the process of stripping from the soul the habits of mind by which the person judges the world and God by created standards. Since the soul is habituated into thinking of God and the world in created terms and this is taken from him, the soul will seem confused. God is seeking to habituate the soul to think according to the light of faith which is supernatural, rather than by natural principles and standards. Hence, since the person views everything from the point of view of the light of faith, it would seem that the person is "obsessed" when, in fact, the person is being perfected and purified.

This singular focus on God is not a fixation, for it should be recalled that a fixation was defined as "the cogitative power always or for the most part and *wrongly* associates one thing with another and is unable to change the association."[509] While the cogitative power may be always or for the most part associating things according to the divine order, this is not done wrongly since God is the cause of all things[510] and the

---

[509]Volume one, p. 283f. Emphasis does not appear in the original sentence.

[510]ST I, q. 45.

cogitative power was created for His glory.[511] Therefore, it is right that the soul should seek to see everything from the point of view of God. However, modern psychologists, who tend to dismiss God altogether in relation to diagnosis of psychological health and illness, are more than likely to misdiagnosis this activity of God.

Moreover, St. John observes that in this state the soul will sometimes be given consolations during this period to lighten the burden of the dark night, but only for brief periods. The soul then is plunged back into the darkness. This is done by God when He recognizes the soul needs some reprieve since God knows the soul's spiritual limits. This change from darkness to consolation back to darkness can easily be misinterpreted as "bipolar disorder."

Only through the eyes of faith is a psychologist going to be able truly to recognize the cause of supernatural activities in the concrete. While someone could be trained without faith to know the criteria and perhaps see the difference, faith gives one an ability to see the supernatural cause as supernatural. There should be a certain resonance in the psychologist when he sees the person going through the dark night, since the supernatural cause in the person going through the dark night would cause some kind of "complacentia" or vision of fittingness in the person of faith. In other words, the person of faith would recognize that those going through these stages are undergoing a supernatural activity, not a mental illness.

Some people will mimic supernatural activities due to mental illness and this is why the psychologist must not only have faith but he must have an knowledge of the general spiritual mechanisms, their essences, causes and effects. For example, the dark night is a state of soul in which God (cause) is purging the soul of its imperfections (essence). It is accompanied by the fulfillment of the one's state in life, prayer, and other supernatural phenomena (the effects), whereas depression suppresses the faculties and their functioning so the person has a tendency toward lethargy rather than a desire to fulfill his state in life. Depression has a natural cause (either psychological or biological) and it differs in essence.

In order to distinguish the two, a psychologist must have a proper understanding of spiritual life, its various stages and the various supernatural activities of God and the various effects they produce on the soul. Here we return to the issue of the nature of a "science." Since a science is an organized body of knowledge of things through their causes, it is only by a knowledge of supernatural causes that a psychologist can be considered to be a true "scientist" in relation to mental health. Moreover, since the science determines one's practice in psychology, just as it does in the medical field, how one understands human nature and the spiritual life will affect one's practice. Normally, a psychologist should have a working knowledge of the various supernatural activities of God and other spiritual causes. However, if he does not, he should work in tandem with a priest who knows the differences between supernatural and natural activities and who can easily recognize the differences. In any case, a psychologist in this state is more likely to commit errors since he will not know whether something is

---

[511]To recognize God as a cause in everything and therefore to refer all things back to God is merely to see the truth, i.e. to conform one's intellect to reality.

natural, preternatural or supernatural.

Chapter 27: Inattentional Blindness

A common scene in the daily lives of married women is the one in which the wife goes to her husband who is watching television to tell him something. As she speaks to him, her voice does not register with him. It appears as if he only sees and hears the television. One would begin to think that it has something to do with the husband becoming tone deaf to the pitch of his wife's voice over the course of time since usually at the beginning of marriage this is less of a problem than in the later stages of marriage. But this experience and observation that sometimes people hear us but they are not "listening" indicates that there is some psychological mechanism which accounts for this.

> The term inattentional blindness entered the psychology lexicon in 1998 when psychologists Arien Mack, PhD, of the New School for Social Research, and the late Irvin Rock, PhD, of the University of California, Berkeley, published a book, "Inattentional Blindness," describing a series of experiments on the phenomenon.[512]

Inattentional blindness, sometimes called "functional blindness,"[513] is a condition in which one is paying attention to one thing and fails to see another thing even though it is in the field of sensation. Inattentional blindness occurs when a person is looking at something but does not "see" it. Many experiments have been done on this psychological mechanism by modern psychologists and the existence of the mechanism is verifiable both in the common experience of human beings and in laboratory experiments.

This mechanism has several aspects to it. Mack observes that when presented with two pictures in which dots are evenly spaced in one picture and closely and unevenly spaced in another, "the grouping of elements in a scene on the basis of their closeness is not a function of proximity on the retina, but on their *perceived* proximity."[514] Mack observes that this indicates that "grouping cannot occur automatically at the lowest level of perceptual processing, and this leaves open the possibility that it might fail to occur without attention."[515] What this indicates is that perception is not something done at the level of sense but at a higher level. In the Thomistic understanding of the faculties, this would indicate that this kind of perception is something done by the interior rather than the exterior senses. Mack observes that "the parsing of the visual array into objects was not dictated simply by the presence of

---

[512]Carpenter, *Sights Unseen.*

[513]Mack, *Inattentional Blindness.*

[514]Ibid.

[515]Ibid.

the image on the retina, and therefore must be the result of activities carried out by the perceptual system."[516] To be more precise, this function of distinguishing sensory objects is something initially[517] done at the level of the common sense power.

In the first volume, we observed that the proper function of the common sense power is to unify the various sense species from the five senses and so the common sense power is the medium between the five exterior senses and the other interior sensitive powers, i.e. it is that which lies between exterior sensation and the other three interior senses as well as the other sensitive powers such as the appetites. Since the common sense power lies between the various powers and since it is the proper function of the common sense power to unify the five exterior sense species, the common sense power has the function of expressing that unified species into the imagination and memory. Here we see that in the context of this chapter, the common sense power does two things. The first is that, in unifying the various sense species, it gives "form" to them. What this means is that the exterior senses merely report what they "see,[518] hear,[519] etc.," but things such as three dimensions are not found at the level of the senses. This is something which is put together by the common sense power because we have two eyes. Binocular vision gives the common sense power the ability to put the two sense species from the two eyes together and create a three dimensional image along with all of the other sense data about the image. The second thing the common sense power does in the current context is that it provides perception at the lowest level. In other words, the recognition of the visual array discussed above regarding the dots is done by the common sense power.

In the first volume, we saw that St. Thomas sometimes notes the second thing the common sense power does, viz. the common sense power has the power of judgment and this refers to the common sense power's capacity to discern or distinguish among the various types of sensation. In other words, it pertains to the common sense power to distinguish, e.g. between white and sweet, i.e. between the species proper to one sense faculty and that proper to another. This also means that when one discerns some sense data proper to a specific sense, one does so through the common sense power. When one discerns the fact that a thing is hot and sharp, it is done through the common sense power as well as when one discerns that something is warm and blue. Although the five exterior senses cannot judge their species in comparison to the species of other exterior senses, the common sense power, which is the terminus of the five senses, does have this capacity since all five senses lie before it. As the common sense power has the power to unify and distinguish the various five senses, if something is wrong with the common sense power, then its function will break down, e.g. St. Thomas makes the

---

[516]Ibid.

[517]Why it is "initial" will be seen as the chapter progresses. The common sense power does not fully explain every aspect of this psychological mechanism.

[518]Each eye reports only two-dimensional information.

[519]Even hearing is three dimensional since a person can locate sounds around him based upon how the sounds hit the two ears differently.

observation that, when we think we see double, it is the result of a bad disposition in the common sense power resulting in its inability to unify the species. Yet, we may further say that the better disposed the common sense power is, the more it is able to make these distinctions with greater acuity. All of this indicates that the common sense power can be used to segment out certain things to which we do not want to pay attention while focusing on others. Hence, inattentional blindness with respect to exterior sense data begins and is performed through the common sense power.[520] Another indication that this is something done at the level of the common sense power, at least initially, is that humans can tune themselves to specific perceptual dimensions, such as brightness, shape, color, etc.[521] Since the common sense power forms the perceptual dimensions, it has the capacity to distinguish between them even within the same sense species, as has been mentioned.

Yet, the psychologists indicate other aspects connected to this initial activity of the common sense power. Carpenter observes something called "change blindness,"[522] which occurs when we see something but we do not observe the changes in what we see, e.g. a magician tells us to pay attention to a card and while we are doing that he makes a change to something right in our field of vision but we do not "see" it. This is important because this indicates that some forms of inattentional blindness are not due just to the common sense power, but also to memory and the cogitative power. In order to judge the change, two things must occur. The first is that the common sense power must put the sequential sense species which the person experiences into memory. Second, the prior and posterior sense species must be compared to see the difference and this is something which would be done, at least initially, by the cogitative power in its process of preparing the phantasm for abstraction.[523] This is also supported by the fact that some psychologists make reference to what is called "inattentional amnesia."[524] In fact, it is because of these different occurrences coming together in various cases of inattentional blindness that has led psychologists to debate precisely where the inattentional blindness is to be assigned. However, from what has already been said and from what will follow, it will be shown that there are three kinds of inattentional blindness, viz. sensitive, imaginative (or cogitative) and intellectual. Sensitive or sensory inattentional blindness is the process carried out at the level of the common sense power. But as we have seen with change blindness, inattentional blindness can

---

[520]It is interesting to note that Mack (ibid.) discusses how there is also auditory deafness and tactile insensitivity. This is a clear indication that this function is performed by the common sense power.

[521]Carpenter, *Sights Unseen*.

[522]This kind of blindness is generally noted by the psychologists who discuss inattentional blindness unless they are focusing on some specific aspect of this psychological mechanism which takes them outside the discussion of change blindness.

[523]"Initially" is said here because it could also be done by the possible intellect through judgment.

[524]See Carpenter, *Sights Unseen*.

also be something carried out by the cogitative power in relation to the different phantasms stored in memory.[525]

Inattentional amnesia is what some psychologists say is occurring since the differences in the sense species are not recalled or remembered. However, the distinction of the three kinds of "blindness" provides a clearer understanding of the different functioning of the different faculties which produce different kinds of blindness. The fact that there is also an imaginative blindness is based upon the fact the human beings, while focusing on one thing, can be distracted by motion. "Results showed that observers were to react faster to the objects falling closer to and in the attended region rather than objects in the unattended region."[526] This indicates that human beings are by instinct drawn to pay attention to motion. While the quote above indicates that the closer the motion, the more attention is paid to it, this again is based upon instinct. Since self-defense requires us to pay attention to motion coming towards us and the closer the object of motion, the greater its ability to cause harm, instinct moves us to pay attention to motion occurring closer to us. Mack observes that:

> early experiments revealed that a colored spot that is seen about 75%
> of the time when it is presented parafoveally in a quadrant of the cross
> may be seen only 15% of the time if it is presented at fixation when
> the cross is located parafoveally.[527]

What this indicates is that the common sense power is by instinct designed to pay attention to things which come into our parafoveal vision, since objects heading toward us have the ability to harm us. The common sense power then issues this parafoveal species into the imagination, where it is assessed by the cogitative power. Yet, it is possible to train the cogitative power to ignore those things which occur in parafoveal vision.

Herrell arrives at the following conclusion from his experiments:

> The results show a main effect for the type of music, with a 75% of
> the participants that hear the techno music will have a decrease in the
> attentional blindness, without looking at gender. Classification of the
> participant will not influence the amount of inattentional blindness.
> With the addition of a certain rhythm (i.e. the techno music), male
> participant's inattentional blindness will see an increase versus the

---

[525]Intellectual inattentional blindness will be discussed below, even thought it has already been discussed throughout this series under different names.

[526]Herrell, *A Research Proposal: Inattentional Blindness: Can Auditory Distractor Make a Difference?*

[527]Mack, *Inattentional Blindness.*

female participants.[528]

This finding indicates two things which can be concluded independently of the empirical research. The first is that auditory cues can enhance[529] or decrease inattentional blindness. Again, the common sense power can distinguish between sight and hearing but when something comes into the hearing, there is an instinct which inclines the common sense power to introduce the possibly dangerous or important sense data into the imagination for the cogitative power's assessment. The second thing that is indicated by this passage is that men and women function differently at this level. While the explanation of it at this time would take the discussion too far afield, what is indicated here is that material disposition of the organ can affect the degree and function of the common sense power and the interior senses which affect inattentional blindness.[530]

Yet, one thing which has not been mentioned is the fact that humans can volitionally move the passive intellect to block the phantasms from the common sense power. When a person is paying close attention to or trying to discern something in the imagination, there is a blocking of the images from the common sense power entering into the imagination. This is why when someone is engaging in abstract thought, he is inattentive to his senses. St. Thomas does not appear to mention to which faculty this function pertains. However, a cursory analysis would seem to indicate that it is a function of the common sense power under the motion of some other faculty. In many cases that faculty would be the will. However, in people with mental illness in which they are completely cut off from reality, it does not appear to come from the will since it does not appear volitional. However, this inattention to the senses could be a function of the cogitative power. Since the cogitative power can modify the sense species as the sense species comes into the imagination and it would also be possible for the cogitative power to prepare the phantasms for abstraction, this process would require the cogitative power to have the ability to block sensible species coming in through common sense power unrelated to the phantasms being prepared for abstraction.

It would appear that the cogitative power can block the sense species coming into the imagination. The cogitative power also appears to have the ability on its own to move the common sense power. We notice that when a thought spontaneously comes into our minds prior to judgment and volition, we find ourselves abstracted from our senses for a short period of time. Part of this could be the fact that the soul can only carry on predominantly in one activity at a time, and so when the imagination is captive,

---

[528]Herrell, *A Research Proposal: Inattentional Blindness: Can Auditory Distractor Make a Difference?*

[529]Herrell indicates in ibid. that people are normally more likely to recognize an object when there was an auditory distractor or "cue."

[530]Women's inattentional blindness appears to be more imaginative due to the higher activity of the appetites in the life of women connected to child bearing. Men's inattentional blindness tends to be sensory and in some way connected to the cogitative power.

the other faculties, one of which is the common sense power, do not engage their activities. On the other hand, we observe in animals (and also in ourselves – particularly when the object of consideration pertains to our passions – but it is easier to observe in animals) that they can remain fixed on one sense object while tuning out other objects. For example, when a cat is pursuing a mouse, the cat will remain focused on the mouse and block out all other sense data unless, as was mentioned above, the common sense power overrides the concentration due to some object which could pose a threat to the cat. But this would indicate that the estimative sense of the cat is moving the common sense power of the cat to focus on the visual species of the mouse. In like manner, human beings are sometimes involuntarily distracted by something they see and the cogitative power moves the common sense power to focus on it so that the cogitative power can consider the thing in the phantasm coming from the senses through the common sense power. All of this can be done without volitional activity or activity of the possible intellect. This often happens with things that move and "catch our eye," so to speak. This activity is trainable, since the cogitative power is capable of being habituated.

Yet, when a person is unaware as to what is before his senses while the consideration of a phantasm in the imagination occurs, this is not necessarily something disordered unless it becomes so uncontrollable as to be a sign of mental illness or physical difficulties in the passive intellect. When this inattentional blindess to the senses occurs in a rightly ordered way, it is a necessary mechanism for the sake of concentration and for the sake of learning. It is also necessary for self-knowledge since self-knowledge is something based upon self-image and self-concept, the understanding of which is done by the possible intellect and imagination and not by the senses, at least in the actual act of self-knowledge. While we may use the senses to gather information about ourselves or even about other things, when we perform a reflexive act, it is done with sensory inattention.

The more intelligent a person is, the more likely he is to suffer from inattentional blindness. This follows from the fact that the better disposed the material faculty is to an operation, the more it is able to perform that operation. Since intelligence is based upon the disposition of the passive intellect, a more intelligent person is able to suffer from imaginative and sensitive inattentional blindness. On the other hand, an intelligent person is more likely to develop intellectual habits which may affect the inattentional blindness. Since the cogitative power and memory are the subject of habits, the more intelligent a person is, the more he can train the cogitative power to observe differences and the more his memory will take note of them. Yet, because of his intelligence, it is possible for him to develop habits which do not make him more perspicacious and therefore more prone to inattentional blindness.

This brings us to other aspects of man's psychological constitution which can affect inattentional blindness. It was observed that the cogitative power can change the image in the imagination and divide out parts of the sensible species which it is trained to divide out; or by mere assessment the cogitative power may divide out of the phantasm something which the cogitative power assesses as not suited to the direction of the preparation of the phantasm for abstraction. This means that imaginative inattentional blindness can be caused by the cogitative power, both in a good sense and in a bad sense. In a bad sense, if the habits in the cogitative power are not rightly ordered, the phantasms can be falsely or poorly prepared by the cogitative power. In those with *per accidens* mental illness, imaginative inattentional blindness can cause them not to see things that they should see. This is often why those with this kind of mental illness may be shown something which is plain to everyone else but which is not plain to the person with the mental illness. For example, if a person has a problem of abusing his spouse, the cogitative power can be trained to segment out of the phantasm her suffering, which will affect his judgment.

In a good sense, imaginative inattentional blindness can help the person grow in virtue and mental health by training the cogitative power to divide out of the phantasms those things which can lead to mental illness. Moreover, sensitive and imaginative inattentional blindness is a necessary mechanism for man's survival and mental health. While not every inattentional blindness is good for him, the mechanism itself makes it possible for man to survive in certain kinds of situations, e.g. during war, a man cannot be distracted by what is going on around him.[531] He must remain focused on his tasks so that he and others are not killed. Moreover, inattentional blindness has a "flip side," so to speak. While modern psychologists are focusing on the fact that we are not consciously aware of certain things during this period of blindness, they have not mentioned the fact that focused attention contributes to learning. In other words, when we are trying to concentrate deeply on some object to understand it better, we cannot be distracted by things which do not pertain to the object of consideration. Focused attention, which conversely means being blind to other things, is necessary for our learning, our survival and our day to day functioning at work, driving, play, etc.

Yet, inattentional blindness can make or break *per se* mental health or illness. Since the blindness affects the image as prepared by the cogitative power, the possible intellect is affected in its judgment regarding that phantasm. If a person has *per accidens* mental illness,[532] which causes imaginative inattentional blindness, it will eventually affect the habits in the possible intellect and will. These habits in the possible intellect will incline the intellect to judge in specific ways leading to intellectual inattentional blindness, i.e. the person will not be able to see the truth about certain things. The entire discussion of the passions and how they affect volition and intellection is germane to the discussion of inattentional blindness.[533] This is also why

---

[531]Man can also focus on one sense while being inattentionally blind to other senses. This is why driving under certain circumstances while listening to a cell phone can be dangerous since one will be inattentionally blind to visual data which are crucial for driving.

[532]For example, a person who has a fixation on something suffers inattentional blindness to other things. All fixations are accompanied by at least one of the three kinds of inattentional blindness.

[533]One of the most notable kinds of inattentional blindness is seen in those who are unable to see that they have a particular sin or vice. This is due to the fact that they are fixated on the good of the object of the sin and therefore do not see the evil of the object as

people who are mentally ill are not in contact with reality, because the inattentional blindness focuses them on something other than reality and so they are unable to see reality for what it is. The more severe the mental illness, the more inattentional blindness the person will suffer. Therefore, a proper attention and focus, determined and specified by moral, intellectual and infused virtue, is necessary to overcome mental illness and to maintain mental health as well as simply to function as a human being.[534]

Chapter 28: Developmental and Educational Psychology

Little can be said about this topic without entering into an entire discussion that would fill a volume on its own. However, for the sake of providing some insight into educational and developmental psychology, a short discussion is in order. To begin the discussion, a short discursus on the voluntary is necessary. In the first volume, it was observed that for an act of the will to be voluntary there must be two things, i.e. full (perfect) knowledge regarding the thing proposed and the motion of the will itself to the object. In order for one to do something fully voluntarily, one must have a perfect grasp of what one is willing. The involuntary occurs when full knowledge is absent, i.e. when ignorance occurs in the intellect, the voluntariness is diminished. Since the will is moved only by the possible intellect, only that which affects the possible intellect can affect the voluntariness of an act of the will, other than the will itself. It was also observed that passions do not cause the involuntary *per se*. However, insofar as the passions affect knowledge in the intellect, they can affect the voluntary. Consequently, things such as fear, concupiscence, weakness, illness, bodily violence and the like, diminish the judgment of reason and thereby cause the involuntary. The voluntary can be affected by degree. St. Thomas observes that when someone is completely ignorant of what he is doing, the act of the will is totally involuntary. He also discusses how ignorance diminishes the voluntary and so the voluntariness of an action can either be complete or incomplete depending upon one's knowledge. This leads to the conclusion that some actions are completely voluntary while other actions are mixed since they are a mix of the voluntary and the involuntary as a result of and to the degree of the ignorance.

---

becoming part of them through volition. Conversely, virtue would help to overcome this kind of intellectual inattentional blindness.

[534]In theology, inattentional blindness actually has a place as well. For instance, those in heaven, who see God, see Him Who is the cause of all things; therefore, materially they see the end of the world, all people's sins, etc. But by divine action, those in heaven undergo an inattentional blindness in which they cannot formally see these things. Like the people who undergo lab experiments who say they did not see something when in fact they saw it materially but not formally or intellectually, so those in heaven see all that God causes materially but do not know certain things formally. This is why they do not "know" when the end of the world is and why they do not "see" some people's sin. After the resurrection, all unintentional blindness will come to an end. This is, of course, a reasoned theological opinion of the author.

Ignorance can be of different kinds.[535] There is a kind of ignorance which St. Thomas discusses which is quite important:

> But about the proper object, [the intellect] has two acts, viz. simple understanding [simplicem intuitum],[536] and deliberation, insofar as, of the proper object, it consults the eternal notions. According to the simple understanding, it is able to have some inordinate motion about the divine, e.g. when someone immediately suffers a motion of infidelity. And although infidelity according to its genus is a mortal sin, nevertheless, the sudden motion of infidelity is a venial sin. Since the mortal sin is not except that it is contrary to the law of God, something pertaining to fidelity is able to occur [in the intellect] suddenly under some other notion, before consultation regarding it is able to be taken or he is able to consult the eternal notion, i.e. the law of God; e.g. when someone suddenly apprehends the resurrection of the dead as impossible according to nature, and he errs in apprehending before he has the time to deliberate what is given to us to be believed according to divine law.[537]

What this passage essentially means is that it is possible for a person to have simple apprehension and even judgment about some concept in the possible intellect, before the possible intellect is able to make a judgment about whether it is morally right or wrong. Hence, sometimes something is involuntary even when the possible intellect can engage in considerations about the object, because the judgment about whether it is morally right or wrong according to the divine laws is not yet made.

---

[535]Here in this case, the different kinds of ignorance are not in reference to the voluntary, involuntary and non-voluntary distinction, or even between antecedent and concomitant ignorance.

[536]Deferrari in *A Latin-English Dictionary of St. Thomas Aquinas* (p. 560) translates this as "simple view." Here it has been translated as simple understanding and it should not be confused with the first act of the intellect. Rather it refers to acts of the intellect which can include judgment.

[537]ST I-II, q. 74, a. 10: "Sed circa proprium obiectum habet duos actus, scilicet simplicem intuitum; et deliberationem, secundum quod etiam de proprio obiecto consulit rationes aeternas. Secundum autem simplicem intuitum, potest aliquem inordinatum motum habere circa divina, puta cum quis patitur subitum infidelitatis motum. Et quamvis infidelitas secundum suum genus sit peccatum mortale, tamen subitus motus infidelitatis est peccatum veniale. Quia peccatum mortale non est nisi sit contra legem dei, potest autem aliquid eorum quae pertinent ad fidem, subito rationi occurrere sub quadam alia ratione, antequam super hoc consulatur, vel consuli possit, ratio aeterna, idest lex dei; puta cum quis resurrectionem mortuorum subito apprehendit ut impossibilem secundum naturam, et simul apprehendendo renititur, antequam tempus habeat deliberandi quod hoc est nobis traditum ut credendum secundum legem divinam."

In the context of psychology, we see that when referring to the intellect we are able to engage in two different kinds of involuntary acts. First, it is possible for a person to have an image in the imagination and the cogitative power sets about through practical syllogisms, causing motion in the image in the imagination. Also, when we dream, often how active the cogitative power is and how vivid the dreams are is based upon the disposition of the passive intellect at the time of sleep. Second, we are able to engage in judgments of the possible intellect without having full judgment about whether something is morally right or wrong. In fact, sometimes these two are connected, i.e. passion in the imagination can block a person's judgment about the moral rightness and wrongness of something, because the possible intellect is engrossed in a consideration of the object under the *ratio* of the passion and is not provided anything in the imagination to consider it according to divine laws.[538]

In the context of developmental psychology, this means that the degree of deliberation, i.e. the acts of the possible and passive intellect are determined, all things being equal,[539] by the development of the disposition of the passive intellect corresponding to age. In order to grasp this fully, it would be best to consider generally the various stages children go through. It is the common experience of man that children from the time of birth to about two years of age,[540] do not engage in actions which clearly manifest judgment. Most of the things which children do between those ages constitute functions on the level of the cogitative power alone. Generally speaking, the cogitative power is not developed enough to prepare the phantasm for abstraction and judgment. Even language skills at this age do not manifest judgment but only association of the cogitative power.[541]

From the ages of about two or three to about four or five, the cogitative power begins to develop in such a way as to provide basic phantasms for abstraction and judgment. But these phantasms are only prepared in the lowest degree, so that the

---

[538]It may also be the case that the person's habits are not sufficient to incline the intellect to make the moral judgment or the person may not receive the grace initially to make the judgment. These instances are important to indicate to the person the status of the faculties of the soul as to their inclinations, the degree of their inclinations and their habits since all of these will influence the course of these kinds of acts of the possible and passive intellect.

[539]It is possible that grace and environmental factors can affect the degree of intellectual activity in which a child can engage.

[540]Age demarcations vary greatly, depending on the particular child's physiological and intellectual development and dispositions.

[541]This is why primates can be taught some language skills which do not require abstraction and judgment, since their highly developed estimative senses can engage in the association of sounds with things or even interior emotional states. But this clearly does not reflect abstract thinking or judgment but merely association. One clear sign of this is that they are normally taught language centered around concrete things, not abstract things, such as beauty or truth. No ape, regardless of how advanced, would ever be able to engage in a conversation about the nature of truth.

activities of the possible intellect are restricted to non-moral, non-reflexive and therefore non-contemplative judgments. At the next stage which begins from about four or five, depending on the child, he enters into a stage in which the phantasms are prepared sufficiently enough to make basic judgments about what is morally right and wrong. But because the cogitative power is not developed to the highest degree, the child cannot make finer distinctions in the moral life, e.g. children at this age are generally not able to make judgments (because the phantasm preparation by the cogitative power is not fully developed yet) in order to know when something is mortally sinful or not. Parents can tell the child that a particular kind of sin causes one to go to hell or is a mortal sin, but the child does not sufficiently grasp it for the possible intellect to be fully deliberate. From about the ages of ten to fourteen, depending on the child, puberty begins. One of the principle effects of puberty is to dispose the possible intellect to full deliberation about truth and what is morally right and wrong.[542] This is why it is not until children go through puberty that a fuller grasp of relations at the familial or societal level occurs and why children before puberty do not take a personal and intellectual interest in things such as politics.

From the time the child enters into puberty to the time of adulthood, all things are judged in a deeper fashion and perhaps even differently based upon the new kinds of phantasms. Accompanying this intellectual development, according to God's providential plan, there is also the development of the child physiologically, sexually and emotionally. The new emotional life is not only based upon the fact that the child is physiologically more developed but is also due to the more highly prepared phantasms. Normally, if the intellectual maturation process is carried out properly and not blocked by societal or parental defects, such as withholding children from difficulties (suffering)[543] and responsibility,[544] the judgmental development should occur sufficiently within two to three years allowing for proper emotional and moral stability of the child to engage in a vast majority of adult activities. This emotional stability is ultimately based upon the development of intellectual, moral and theological virtues.

Educationally, therefore, how a child is taught is based upon the degree of his ability to form phantasms. Infants, from the age of birth to two years old, generally cannot make judgments. Therefore, how they are trained is based upon the functions in which the cogitative power can engage. Before the age of about one year of age, the cogitative power is not developed enough to begin the process which is used from about

---

[542]These age demarcations can be applied, *mutatis mutandis* to those who suffer developmental defects. Those suffering from various levels of mental retardation will be able to engage in varying levels of intellectual activity based upon the degree of development or, more metaphysically stated, more disposed passive intellects.

[543]Although one does not make the child suffer needlessly, one should also not keep the child from engaging difficulties or sufferings such as hard work and the like, for the child to gain a proper grasp of reality.

[544]If appropriate responsibilities are withheld from the child, he will develop habits which hinder his ability to act responsibly.

one to two years of age, viz. training by pleasure and pain.[545] The cogitative power, at this stage, assesses things based upon pleasure and pain and so that is how the child must be trained. The pleasure affirms the cogitative power in its assessment, thereby training[546] the cogitative power to assess positively in those matters pertaining to pleasure. The pain trains the cogitative power to assess something negatively which should be assessed negatively.[547] Teaching consists largely in preparing the phantasms for the student, i.e. the one who is learning. In the case of infants, the phantasms must be prepared most concretely, i.e. sensorially with a stress on the sense of touch.

From the ages of about two to four, the child is progressively able to make associations but the training by reward (pleasure) and punishment (pain) is the foundation for the training of the child's conduct. However, the verbal dimension is able to dominate more during this stage since linguistic development rapidly advances. Until the child reaches the stage of between four and six, when he is able to make basic moral judgments, reasoning with the child is fruitless because the child cannot understand the abstract notions sufficiently well to be able to understand and make the connections between what he is being told and what he is to do. During this stage, teaching can take on a more verbal approach but tactile teaching is still necessary. Visual abilities will also increase during this stage, which is why visual training, such as block shapes and the like, can be used to train the child. Color discrimination, while done by the cogitative power in the infant stage, is grasped more by the child at this stage. Therefore education at this stage should include a more sensory-based approach.

In the stage from about four or six to ten or fourteen, the principal differences have to do with how the child can be taught. Since the cogitative power has reached a stage where it can prepare the phantasms well enough for moral judgments, low level abstract notions can be introduced to the child at this time, progressing to greater

---

[545]A normal parent will begin to detect when the child is able to make the associations of pain with avoidance. For some children, they may be able to make these associations as early as nine or ten months, other children may take up to a year.

[546]Since the child cannot engage in the voluntary, habits cannot be developed at this stage. It is analogous to training an animal.

[547]Two observations are in order. The first is that morally, the punishment (pain) that is inflicted must always be ordered toward the child's physical, psychological, moral and spiritual well-being. Excessive punishments (abuse) or punishments which are not rooted in reason are immoral since they can cause harm to the child. The second is that rightly ordered punishments are actually necessary for the cogitative power's proper development. If the cogitative power is not trained in this way, the child can be affected for life, if that kind of training persists, because the child will not grasp the painful or negative aspects of reality properly and thereby will end up irresponsible in his conduct, because he will not grasp the painful realities of immoral conduct. Moreover, God himself teaches us through Scripture that parents must discipline their child so that he does not end up in hell; see Proverbs 23:13-14. As much as modern psychology might like to think that we should never punish a child, reality and God tell us otherwise.

complexity based upon the individual child's intelligence.[548] Thus more verbal and visual approaches may be taken,[549] yet the verbalizations and visualizations must be presented more concretely than can occur after puberty. It is during this stage that the child can begin to develop habits. Since habits fall within the domain of the voluntary, and it is at the beginning of this stage that the voluntary begins to occur, since moral judgments by the possible intellect begin to be made, the child can then begin to develop habits. While these habits will be of lesser degree than after puberty due to the degree of voluntariness at this stage, these initial habits are quite important, since they often determine the trajectory of the child's entire life.

During this stage, the child's intellectual formation is a combination of development of habits and training of the cogitative power. Many of the things the children learn at this stage are still grasped by association and not fully by intellectual judgment. Therefore, their training is more of a mix of training and development of intellectual habit. After puberty when full deliberation can occur, the habits are able to be more fully developed and the cogitative power can be more habituated rather than trained. After puberty when full deliberation can occur and judgment is deepened and more reflexive acts are capable of being engaged in, more abstract presentation of notions and concepts can occur.[550]

In the context of mental health, we see that children from the age of birth to two years cannot truly be said to develop mental illness, although two things can occur to them to cause them psychological difficulties. (1) If their upbringing is normal (i.e. is according with rational principles), they simply will not develop mental illness. However, they can be trained to associate the wrong things at this stage in their development which can affect the next stage of their development. While this training is not mental illness in the proper sense, since they cannot develop habits, it can be considered a mental deformation. (2) There are some rare occasions when a child is demonically influenced so that from the age of one or so he manifests very irrational behavior. Material maladies and deformities put aside, if a psychologist notices this in a child, he should refer the child to a priest for his judgment about the possibility of

---

[548]It should be recalled at this time that intelligence is based upon the material disposition of the passive intellect, which will vary from child to child.

[549]Since the senses are in a hierarchy, the dependence of a child on the various senses begins with the lower senses and moves toward the higher senses as the child develops.

[550]This is why things such as logic and basic philosophical notions can begin to be taught to children after about fourteen years of age. Before then, children may learn certain aspects of logic but it is more by association than by judgment of the possible intellect. Again, each child will vary based upon the development of the disposition of the passive intellect.

demonic influence.[551]

For children between the ages of two and about four or six, since some judgment can take place but voluntariness is lacking, there is still not an ability to develop mental illness in the proper sense. However, because the cogitative power is more developed, it is more susceptible to things such as implicit learning and false associations. Therefore, parents have an obligation to keep out of the child's experience anything which could cause false associations in the cogitative power. Bad conduct arising from these false associations will progressively become harder to break the more the child is exposed to the thing causing the disorder.

Once a child reaches the age of about four to six, i.e. when the cogitative power can prepare the phantasm well enough to know something is morally right or wrong, the voluntary begins to take place. This is the stage when mental illness can begin to be realized, although normally, the mental illness will not be grave unless the experience of the child entails grave disorders. However, at this stage, it is important for parents to teach their children right conduct so that they develop proper moral and mental habits. Conversely, children at this stage can overcome their mental difficulties by right instruction, encouragement by parents and others as well as by performing actions contrary to the vice of the mental habit.[552] At this level, while the child can develop *per se* mental illness, it is more likely that his mental illnesses would be a *per accidens* mental illness. This is due in large part to the fact that his voluntariness is less and his ability to perform reflexive intellectual acts which can affect the possible intellect is less.

Once a child goes through puberty, he becomes susceptible to all forms of mental illness in their varying degrees. It is crucial at this stage, since the possible intellect is able to make deeper (more voluntary) moral judgments and the person is able to engage in more reflexive actions, that the education or moral formation is done more in order to help him to develop to be his own man or, in the case of girls, to become her own woman. In other words, the reflexive dimension of their development requires that they appropriate their formation which is not able to be done fully at the earlier stages. This ability to engage more deeply in reflexive actions explains why this stage is important since it is the stage in which the child will either appropriate or reject his moral and educational formation. Since acceptance of the moral and educational formation can determine the child's conduct (since what is in the will is first in the intellect), this acceptance or rejection can affect psychological development, i.e. the

---

[551]This observation applies to every stage in development insofar as the demonic can cause an influx of bad phantasms causing the child's psychological and moral development to be corrupted.

[552]Incidentally, day cares can pose serious problems to the mental health of children. During this stage when habits are being formed, without the proper moral formation, children will pose a greater risk of performing actions which will develop habits in their intellects which will affect their mental health. Since most day care facilities do not encompass proper moral formation of the children and proper vigilance in this regard to ensure the child's conduct is proper, the child is more likely to suffer psychological problems as he gets older.

development of intellectual virtues or vices. Prior habituation aids greatly in inclining the young adult to accepting or acting according to his prior formation. The more the prior formation begets good habits (rightly ordered thinking), the more likely that the child will accept that formation. However, since the child has freewill, it is also at this time that the child will be able to accept or reject that formation. It is possible for a parent to raise their child perfectly and yet the child may still reject that formation.

Prior to puberty, parents must keep out of their child's experience those things which affect his mental health because he is not fully deliberate. Little by little he can be taught to avoid these things. But when the child goes through puberty, the educational dimension must change to one of helping the child to avoid on his own the things which can affect his mental, moral and spiritual downfall. Parents who treat their child who has gone through puberty in a controlling manner (except when necessary for the sake of the child or for others) can affect negatively the proper development of the child to stand on his own, i.e. to develop virtue. If he does something only because his parents make him, his action is less voluntary and therefore he does not develop the habits by which he can stand on his own.[553] The parents must help him to develop the habits on his own through responsibility so that he can become his own man or, in the case of a girl, her own woman.[554]

---

[553]This does not include the child who does what his parents ask out of a proper development of the virtue of piety and a desire to fulfill the fourth commandment.

[554]These observations apply in the context of marriage as well. If a husband tries to control his wife, she will not develop proper virtues. If she tries to control her husband like a son, the husband will find it difficult to develop proper virtue in relation to her.

Part II:
Practica

Chapter 1: Prudence

The fact that psychologists diagnose directees and then counsel them to perform certain actions means that the principal function of the psychologist is to guide the directee in actions[1] which will help overcome his psychological problem. The virtue that regulates action which has as its predominant effect something(s) interior to the individual is *not* the virtue of science as modern psychology has purported. Rather the virtue that regulates actions is prudence. Moreover, the very act of counseling which is an action of the psychologist is an act of prudence requiring his own interior act of counsel before he suggests to the directee any course of action. Counsel is an act of the virtue of prudence. Therefore, the principal virtue governing the practical application of the scientific knowledge about human nature as laboring under the defects of original sin in the concrete circumstances of the lives of directees is the virtue of prudence. This is the virtue that every psychologist must master before he counsels any directee. It is also the very virtue which is lacking in a directee who continues to perform actions which manifest mental illness. Therefore, in order to have a better grasp of the practice of psychology, (1) it is necessary to discuss prudence in great detail. (2) It is necessary to discuss the criteria for diagnosis and (3) a more detailed analysis of the act of counseling itself by the psychologists will be examined. (4) Finally, a few questions on the use of empirical sciences in psychology will be considered.

A. Prudence in General

St. Thomas defines prudence in two different ways but the two definitions convey the same meaning, viz. "the application of right reason to action"[2] and "right reason of action."[3] Prudence is a virtue in the practical intellect as in a subject.[4] Because it resides in reason, prudence perfects reason[5] as to its operations in relation to practical matters.[6] Since prudence deals with actions, i.e. practical matters, prudence helps the person to know what is to be done.[7] In relation to the psychologist this is

---

[1]Actions here is taken in the moral sense, i.e. they may be exterior acts (such as throwing a baseball) or interior acts (such as thinking and willing).

[2]ST II-II, q. 47, a. 4 and 8: "applicatio rectae rationis ad opus."

[3]ST I-II, q. 57, a. 5, De Vir., q. 5, a. 1, ad 3 and In Ethic. VI, l. 7 (n. 1196): "recta ratio agibilium."

[4]ST I-II, q. 56, a. 2, ad 4; ibid., a. 3; ST II-II, q. 47, aa. 2 and 5 and De Vir., q. 1, a. 6.

[5]ST I-II, q. 61, a. 2.

[6]St. Thomas observes in III Sent., d. 33, q. 1, a. 1b that prudence makes right reason.

[7]ST II-II, q. 47, a. 1, ad 2.

716

important because it helps the psychologist to know what both he and the directee should do. For the directee, prudence helps him to know what is to be done to overcome his mental illness. St. Thomas says that prudence helps one to reason well so that he may live a whole life well.[8] Prudence does not just help the person in a particular case to know what should be done, but it also helps the person to know how a particular action affects his whole life.

In relation to actions, as we saw in the first volume, there are two things: the end (*finis*) and the means to the end (*ea quae sunt ad finem*). Prudence has a specific kind of relationship to the end and the means. As to the end, prudence orders the means to the end;[9] if it is acquired prudence, it is a natural end; if it is infused prudence, it is a supernatural end. The ends of prudence are pre-established, by being either naturally known or known through science, hence prudence does not establish the ends.[10] Thus, the ends of human nature are pre-established by human nature[11] or, we may say by, the natural law. Man is naturally inclined to specific ends which differ from the ends of cows, bats and other animals, which was seen in the discussion of the three categories of natural inclination. Hence, man cannot choose his ends because they are predetermined by nature, e.g. man is ordered, whether he likes it or not, to the end of marriage. But man can freely intend to order a means to that end or not; in other words, man has the capacity to choose the means which will help him achieve that end.

These ends may be naturally known,[12] e.g. most people know that man is ordered toward marriage, living in common and things of this sort. But some ends are only known through science (philosophy and theology) and by this is meant that only after a formal study of human nature and the natural law is someone able to know with certitude whether something is an end or not for man. Here we see why psychological practice depends on one's view of man. If one thinks that man can be treated just like an animal, ignoring reason and free will, as in many materialist conceptions of man, the psychologist will treat his directee in a manner consistent with training an animal. He will employ empirical means while disregarding the true ends to which man is ordered, which can only be known through the philosophical and theological sciences. In effect, one's conception of man determines one's prudential judgments.[13] Moreover, since man

---

[8]Ibid., q. 47, a. 2, ad 1 and ibid., q. 47, a. 13. In ST I-II, q. 57, a 5, St. Thomas notes interestingly that prudence helps one to act well and *to be good* and this is important since the directee wants the evil of his mental illness to be removed and for him to be "well."

[9]ST II-II, q. 47, a. 1, ad 2; ibid., q, 47, aa. 2 and 5.

[10]ST II-II, q. 47, a. 6.

[11]III Sent., d. 33, q. 2, a. 3 and ST II-II, q. 47, a. 15.

[12]Synderesis is the connatural habit (ST II-II, q. 47, a. 5, ad 3) which establishes the ends which determine prudential reasoning (ibid., ad 1). For a fuller discussion of synderesis and its affect on practical reasoning see volume one, chapter six (III,C). Synderesis affects the major premise of the practical syllogism, see below.

[13]This will become even more manifest in the discussion of the application of universals to particulars.

is designed and structured in a specific way, only a philosophical psychology which takes into consideration theological teachings about man will ever be able to "fix" man; that is, only a philosophical psychology can direct man through prudential reasonings regarding which actions will help overcome the mental illness of the directee. This is perhaps the key issue regarding the practice of psychology, viz. how one's scientific understanding of man and his ends determines which means the psychologist will employ. Since the end determines the means, as we saw in volume one in the decision-making process, one's view of man determines one's counseling.

Since we can choose to direct means to specific ends, prudence helps one to relate by conforming to right ends,[14] i.e. prudence helps one to direct his life to the right ends for his life. Hence, if a person is not prudent, he will not direct his actions or conform himself to the right ends of human nature. This is precisely the problem with those who are mentally ill: they direct their actions to ends which do not suit human nature or they use unsuitable means to a good end. In both cases, mental illness can be the result. In fact, St. Thomas observes that any malice (vicious habit) corrupts right estimation of the end.[15] In effect, those who have misdirected the means to the wrong ends or even the right ends, do not have proper understanding of the end. If we translate this more philosophically, it signifies that those who are mentally ill do not have a right estimation about human nature, which is ordered to specific ends. Since mental illness is a vice, it affects one's judgment about human nature and its ends, causing one to engage in destructive behavior. Reiteration of the point is necessary: psychological counseling is about prudence insofar as the psychologist must have prudence to guide the actions of the directee to achieve the right end of human nature called mental health. This is why it is absolutely crucial that a psychologist have a right conception of human nature and its ends, achieved only through a detailed philosophical formation.

As to the means, St. Thomas has a great deal to say. The means has two components to it, viz. the object or the action and the circumstances surrounding the action. With respect to the action, St. Thomas observes that prudence helps establish the mean (*medium*) with respect to the means (*ea quae sunt ad finem*).[16] Virtue lies in the mean;[17] this indicates that the person does not go to excess or defect in his actions, so that his actions will not exceed or fall short of the end which he is trying to achieve. Prudence helps one to judge whether a given course of action will go to excess or defect in relation to the end, e.g. in order to be physically healthy, prudence helps one to know that eating half a hamburger may not be enough but that five hamburgers is too much. Therefore, prudence would judge that two hamburgers for a large grown man is a good mean. Those who are mentally ill (because of their mental illness) judge to excess or defect in relation to the means, which is why their actions cause them so much psychological damage. For this reason, St. Thomas says that prudence helps reason to

---

[14]III Sent., d. 33, q. 1, a. 1b.

[15]In Ethic., VI, l. 4 (n. 1170).

[16]III Sent., d. 33, q. 2, a. 3 and II-II, q. 47, a. 7.

[17]See volume one, chapter ten (IV).

relate suitably to the means (*ea quae sunt ad finem*).[18]

In relation to the circumstances surrounding the action, the fundamentals of prudence become clearer. Prudence helps one to judge rightly, i.e. to know circumstances which are singulars.[19] Circumstances which surround an action take the consideration of the action from an abstract affair to one in which the person must consider concretely how the action relates to the given circumstances. This is why St. Thomas says that even though nature inclines us to some end that is predetermined, the actions in relation to the end are diversified according to persons and affairs,[20] or we may say according to circumstances.

In relation to psychology, we must say that the process of counseling requires knowledge of the circumstances of the directee in order to know whether a given course of action, i.e. a counseled means, will suit the directee or not. Directees, because of their mental illness, will more than likely have a difficult time judging their circumstances, especially if their mental illness is from an exterior cause. The psychologist must have a good knowledge of the directee relative to the circumstances of his life, which might affect the course of counseling. But this requires that the psychologist himself be prudent so that he can judge the circumstances rightly.

Since prudence helps the person to know the action *to be taken*, prudence deals with future outcomes to specific kinds of actions. Hence to know the future from knowledge of the present or past pertains to prudence.[21] Since the future is contingent, because the possible outcomes of one's actions can vary, prudence deals with contingents.[22] Prudence helps one to read the circumstances based upon past experience to see the possible (contingent) outcomes of the course of action.

Since prudence requires knowledge of human nature and of circumstances, it requires knowledge of universals and particulars.[23] Prudence applies the universal principles and knowledge known by the possible intellect about man and his ends to the concrete, particular and singular in which he must act.[24] For example, a person may know the universal principle that eating excessively is bad for one's health. But when

---

[18]ST I-II, q. 57, a. 5.

[19]That prudence helps one to know the singulars, see II-II, q. 47, a. 3. Regarding singulars and their role in psychology, see Richard Cross' article "Can Catholics Counsel?"

[20]See ST II-II, q. 47, a. 5.

[21]ST II-II, q. 47, a. 1. Since it deals with the future, prudence must pertain to reason (possible intellect) since the passive intellect can only know the present or past (through memory), see ibid.

[22]III Sent., d. 33, q. 2, a. 2a; ST I-II, q. 57, a. 5, ad 3 and ST II-II, q. 49, a. 1. Also, circumstances are contingents because they could be otherwise than they are in a particular case, since God can change history to modify the circumstances in which one finds oneself.

[23]In ethic., VI, l. 6 (n. 1194). In ST II-II, q. 47, a. 3, St. Thomas notes that prudence knows the universal principles of reason and singulars about which actions are concerned.

[24]ST II-II, q. 47, a. 3, ad 1 and ibid., q. 47, a. 6.

he is sitting at the dinner table and a large amount of food is placed before him, he must apply the universal principle in the concrete. How hungry is he? How much does his body require so that he does not become weak and ill? Based upon past experience, he then judges how much he should eat so that he does not eat excessively.

This general principle is applied in the concrete by the possible intellect converting back to the phantasm to judge how much he should eat.[25] So that he can properly apply the universal principle, i.e. judge the universal principle's applicability to the phantasm, the phantasm must be properly prepared. For this reason, prudence requires rectitude of appetite about the end for which the person is striving.[26] Obviously, if the concupiscible and irascible appetites suffer from vice, their disordered passions will affect the phantasm and thereby affect prudential judgment.[27] This is why a psychologist *must* be a man of preeminent virtue so that his appetites are moderated by virtue and do not affect his judgment about the directee, the actions to be taken and the circumstances. As to the directee, since most mental illness is accompanied by disordered appetite, he will find it very difficult to apply universal knowledge in the concrete due to his disordered phantasms.[28] This is why he must depend upon the prudential judgment of the psychologist in order to know, at least in the beginning, what to do when various circumstances arise.

Yet, one also needs rectitude of the rational appetite, viz. the will.[29] If a person is ill-willed, even if he knows the proper universal principles, he will not apply them concretely since he does not want to do so. Moreover, he will affect the phantasms by the disorder of his will redounding to the imagination which will affect his prudential judgment. This is why a virtuous psychologist will be a better psychologist and a well-intentioned directee more likely to choose mental health.

Prudence is perfected not by the exterior senses but by the interior senses, one of which is memory.[30] Through experience of past events, one learns about the possible outcomes of future events. Here we see two essential criteria for prudence; the first is experience, not just any kind of experience, but the right kind of experience. If one is always around others who make wrong decisions and one never learns the proper outcome for which one should strive, he will not have the right experiences by which he can judge properly. Experience is what is stored in memory, so the right memories are necessary for prudence. This is why when some past event has psychologically destabilized the directee, the memory must be purified so that the preparation of the

---

[25]The possible intellect must convert back to the phantasm since that is where the singular is known.

[26]In Ethic., VI, l. 4 (n. 1173).

[27]See chapter nine of volume one.

[28]His phantasms are disordered by the mental illness itself.

[29]ST I-II, q. 56, a. 2, ad 3 and ibid., q. 56, a. 3.

[30]ST II-II, q. 47, a. 3, ad 2.

phantasms can be done properly.[31] Since memories are required, young people do not have prudence,[32] as a general rule, because they lack experience (memories) by which to judge what to do. Those children who have been baptized and are in the state of grace (the same applies to the mentally ill) have infused prudence. However, even though they have the habit, they cannot act according to prudence[33] due to lack of memory or, in the case of the mentally ill, due to the obstacle of false or bad memories in relation to the object of mental illness. St. Thomas observes that there is no prudence in sinners[34] and the same would apply to the mentally ill, not because they may be sinning or because they have some moral vice, but because their intellectual vice of mental illness prevents them from judging properly. Prudence is normally[35] in the elderly;[36] because of the process of aging they are more materially disposed toward clearer phantasms and they lack the motions of the passions. The elderly also have more experience and therefore more memories from which to draw on. In fact, those who are inexperienced will often be overwhelmed by circumstances, since there can be an infinite number of circumstances and experience is necessary to know which circumstances affect the given course of action and which do not. Through experience, the infinite number of possible singulars are reduced to a finite number, since the person knows what happens in most cases.[37]

Yet, in order to be prudent, the phantasm has to be properly prepared by the cogitative power. Prudence perfects particular reason (cogitative power) to the right estimation of singular operable intentions.[38] While prudence is in the possible intellect as in a subject, nevertheless as one acts prudently and has rightly ordered experience, the cogitative power is trained to discern which experiences (sense data about singulars) fit the phantasms that are present in the imagination. In this way, the cogitative power prepares the phantasm for a proper prudential judgment. All of the discussion on *per accidens* mental illness pertaining to the passive intellect comes to bear on this very process. If the cogitative power has bad habits, the phantasms simply will not be prepared properly and the person will have a hard time applying the universals known in the possible intellect to the concrete circumstances known through the phantasm. This is why a psychologist should never be mentally ill, since his cogitative power could not prepare his phantasms in the right way to be able to make prudential judgments in order

---

[31]This topic will be discussed at greater length in relation to the virtue of memory below.

[32]That acquired prudence is not in the young, see ST II-II, q. 47, a. 14, ad 3.

[33]See ibid.

[34]See ST II-II, q. 47, a. 13.

[35]The presumption here is that the older person has tried to lead a virtuous life. This is not always the case.

[36]ST II-II, q. 47, a. 15, ad 2.

[37]ST II-II, q. 47, a. 3, ad 2.

[38]In Ethic., VI, l. 9 (n. 1215).

to counsel the directee. Moreover, if he is an immoral man with vices, his phantasms will not be prepared in an indifferent way in relation to the directee but will be affected by the appetitive movements and the assessments of harm and goodness of the cogitative power. In a word, he will not think clearly. As to the directee, before he will begin to be able to operate prudentially on his own in relation to the object of his mental illness, he must follow the prudential judgments of the psychologist, perform the actions which will beget the proper habits in the various psychological faculties and, after time, his cogitative power will be able to sort out the memories and prepare the phantasms properly. This is why, when people perform the actions of virtue over the course of time, they experience a kind of clarity of mind. But as long as the bad habits exist in the psychological faculties, directees simply will have a hard time being prudent in relation to the object(s) of their mental illness.

Yet, prudence is not merely a single judgment, but often requires several acts of reason, both of universal as well as particular reason. What this means is that several actions may occur on different levels. The cogitative power (particular reason) may go through a series of particular syllogistic-like actions in order to prepare the phantasm. Moreover, the possible intellect may have to make several judgments, directing particular reason in its preparation of the phantasm. Then, over the course of the process, the possible intellect judges as to what is to be done in a particular case. This process is called "taking counsel," which is the fifth step in the decision-making process.

Counsel makes use of what is called the "practical syllogism." A practical syllogism is one in which, like any other kind of syllogism, there are three propositions, viz. two premises and a conclusion. In a practical syllogism, however, the conclusion is not a universal but a particular. The major premise is a universal proposition about moral action, e.g. all excessive eating is immoral and should not be done. The minor premise, then, particularizes the syllogism by introducing the circumstances, e.g. eating these five hamburgers is eating to excess. The conclusion has two qualities about it. The first is that the conclusion, like the minor premise, is particular or singular. The second is that the conclusion takes the form of a command, i.e. one should not or one should do this, or more simply put, "do this." As in the case of our example, the syllogism would be as follows:

All excessive eating should not be done.
Eating these five hamburgers is eating to excess.
Therefore, do not eat these five hamburgers.

Sometimes the practical syllogism may conclude in permissibility. In the process of taking counsel, several forms of action may be proposed in a given set of circumstances in which the practical syllogism may be performed for each species of actions proposed. Reason then draws the conclusion about what is permissible to be done, but then it pertains to the act of judgment in the decision-making process to judge which is the best means or counseled action. Choice then specifies or determines what one will do. Command then follows after choice using the counsel as a guiding principle in how the action is executed.

In order to syllogize about actions, one must be virtuous, otherwise one will err regarding the principles of demonstration, i.e. particulars as known in the interior senses. If one is affected by passion or vice, the distribution of the middle terms may not be seen by reason, e.g. if one has the vice of gluttony, five hamburgers may not be judged as excessive (minor premise) and so one will not think that the major applies to the minor by the distributed term "excessive." The person will then think it is permissible or even a good thing to eat the five hamburgers.

We can see here that error in the reasoning process occurs in those who are mentally ill. They may be in error about the general principle, e.g. if they have always been taught that eating excessively is good, they may not know gluttony is immoral. Implicit learning can have a great impact on the formulation of these general principles as well as their applicability to the particular circumstances. The person laboring under a mental illness may also easily err concerning the judgment of the circumstances and therefore will not see terms in the syllogism as distributed or they may even think they are distributed when in fact they are not. For example, if a person knows that dieting is good for someone who is overweight, but he is a very thin, frail man who needs to eat more in order to sustain his health – if he thinks that he should diet, he does not read the circumstances properly (*who* being the circumstance he does not understand). Hence, he thinks that dieting is good in this case because he does not judge himself properly.[39]

If a person knows the right thing to do but does not do it, we would not say he is prudent. For this reason, prudence deals with three acts in the decision-making process. First, prudence affects the act of counsel in which one judges in order to find the means to attain the end.[40] The second act is judgment,[41] which determines the best means. The third act of the decision-making process which prudence affects is command. Command consists in applying counsel and judgment to action.[42] The prudent man is the man who acts prudently, not just the one who counsels well. In fact, we may say that command is the principal action of the virtue of prudence since one cannot be prudent without commanding what is prudent. For this reason, St. Thomas says that prudence is *bene praeceptiva*,[43] which we may translate as "commands well"; the person who is prudent is the person who commands well. This is important for the directee and for the psychologist. While the psychologist must take his own interior counsel to discern the proper action the directee should take, he must command what he *interiorly* counsels which has as its object the exterior act of counseling the directee.[44]

---

[39]This is the problem with people who suffer from certain eating disorders.

[40]ST I-II, q. 57, a. 6 and ST II-II, q. 47, a. 8.

[41]ST I-II, q. 57, a. 6.

[42]Ibid. and ST II-II, q 47, a. 8. In III Sent., d. 33, q, 2, a. 2a and In Ethic., VI, l. 4 (n. 1164), St. Thomas observes that the proper matter of prudence is counselable actions.

[43]ST I-II, q. 57, a. 6; ST II-II, q. 51, a. 2; ibid., 51, a. 3, ad 3; In Ethic., VI, l. 9 (n. 1240) and De Vir., q. 5, a. 1.

[44]This line may need some explanation. Every human act has some object upon which it acts. In the case of counsel, the object about which the act of counsel concerns itself is a proposed exterior action.

Even if the psychologist knows what the directee should do, it does not help the directee unless the psychologist actually *exteriorly* counsels the directee to do it. The psychologist must command himself to counsel the directee. As to the directee, he will suffer all kinds of difficulties in each of the three acts of counsel, which will unfold as this chapter progresses. But the good news is that even if the directee cannot take very good counsel, if he follows and does what the prudent psychologist tells him to do, he can do the right thing and develop prudence. The directee has to make a choice at a certain stage. Either he must choose to follow his own counsel, which is why he is mentally ill to begin with or he must choose to follow the direction of the psychologist. Therefore, the first step toward prudence for the directee in relation to the object of his mental illness is to take counsel that he should follow the psychologist's direction; in a sense, counsel is the directee's first act of prudence in relation to the psychologist.

From all of this we see, therefore, that acquired prudence is gained through action.[45] Since prudence directs actions and since all of the other moral virtues are obtained, increased or decreased through action, prudence is the cause of the other moral virtues.[46] There is a redundancy of prudence to the other virtues[47] because prudence directs the other virtues.[48] One cannot be temperate, for example, without being prudent. St. Thomas makes the following observation:

> prudence not only directs the moral virtues in choosing those which are to the end [means], but also in determining the end. Moreover, the end of each moral virtue is to attain the mean of its proper matter, which indeed the mean is determined according to the right reason of prudence.[49]

Even though the end of human nature is that, for example, we eat food, prudence must set the amount (*medium aut finis*) of the food so that one does not eat too much or too little (*ea quae sunt ad finem*). It is up to prudence to establish the mean for the other moral virtues and so one cannot have any of the other moral virtues without prudence.[50] In the context of psychology, with any mental illness that might be caused by a lack of a moral virtue (i.e. one has an immoral vice), it is necessary to overcome that vice, and so one must start with prudence. The disorders in the cogitative power, memory and

---

[45]ST II-II, q. 47, a. 14, ad 3.

[46]De Vir., q. 1, a. 6.

[47]ST I-II, q. 61, a. 4.

[48]Ibid. and III Sent., d. 33, q. 2, a. 5. See also De Vir., q. 1, a. 6.

[49]ST I-II, q. 66, a. 3, ad 3: "prudentia non solum dirigit virtutes morales in eligendo ea quae sunt ad finem, sed etiam in praestituendo finem. Est autem finis uniuscuiusque virtutis moralis attingere medium in propria materia, quod quidem medium determinatur secundum rectam rationem prudentiae."

[50]St. Thomas says in III Sent., d. 33, q. 2, a. 1c, ad 2 that prudence guides all moral matters.

other faculties other than the possible intellect will begin to be affected as the person acts prudently. We saw above how the passive intellect affects the judgment of prudence. Yet, through judgment and a motion of the will, the "prudential" phantasms formulated by the possible intellect in the imagination will begin the process of correcting those faculties.

On the other hand, prudence requires the other moral virtues.[51] This follows from our previous discussion where it was mentioned that if the appetites, both intellective and sensitive, lack virtue, their disordered passions and motions (as in the case of the will) will affect the phantasm in the imagination and thereby affect the judgment of prudence. Therefore, the more just, fortitudinous and temperant one is, the more prudent one can be because he will have clearer phantasms. The question must then be asked: which comes first, prudence or the other moral virtues? It appears to be a vicious circle: one cannot have prudence without the other moral virtues and yet one cannot have the other moral virtues without prudence.[52] The answer lies in learning prudence from someone else. In other words, one should look to the wise and prudent man and by imitation or by his counsel on what to do in order to build virtue. Here we see the wisdom of someone with mental illness (if he does not know what to do to overcome his mental illness) going to a psychologist who can direct him. Ultimately, this is why the term "directee" is chosen, so that the person being counseled can be directed in his actions so that he can attain the virtues necessary to overcome his mental illness. This is also why the term "patient" should not apply to someone being directed by a psychologist, since the psychologist must counsel the actions which the directee must perform. Therefore it is not a passive activity on the side of the directee like the term patient implies.[53] In fact, psychologists should be wary of the directee who comes into his office expecting the psychologist "to make him well." All the psychologist can do is direct the directee; he cannot make him well. Only the directee, who can perform the actions necessary to overcome his mental illness, can make himself well by following the exterior direction.

B. The Integral Parts of Prudence

Prudence is a cardinal virtue[54] and can be subdivided into the subjective parts of prudence. Prudence also has potential parts, i.e. virtues which are annexed to prudence because of the nature of their matter but which are not part of prudence *per se*.[55] Yet, prudence has integral parts, i.e. other virtues without which prudence could not

---

[51]De Vir., q. 5, a. 2.

[52]This dilemma was noted by Aristotle and the subsequent solution was also offered by him as is seen in his *Nicomachean Ethics*.

[53]Obviously, those being attended to by a psychiatrist could legitimately be called patients.

[54]III Sent., d. 33, q. 2, a. 1c; De Vir., q. 1, a 12, ad 26 and ibid., q. 5, a. 1.

[55]The potential parts shall be discussed in the next section of this chapter.

exist. To get a better grasp on the practical aspect of psychology, it is important to understand the integral parts of prudence and how they affect the psychologist in his counseling and the directee in the living of his life.

1. Memory (*Memoria*)

The first integral part of prudence is memory. We have already discussed memory somewhat, in relation to the faculty and the actual memories that one has. This integral part of prudence is the *virtue* of memory.[56] The virtue of memory is a cognitive integral part[57] of prudence, in which one has knowledge of the past,[58] since knowledge of the past is taken as proof of what could happen in the future.[59] As mentioned, experience is required to acquire memories[60] and prudence requires many memories.[61] The more memories one has, the more prudent one can be, since he will have more particulars[62] from which to consider possible future outcomes of circumstances and actions.

Through a good habit of memory, i.e. by remembering the right things, we are less likely to suffer wonder (*admiratio*) and therefore we will be less bound in our action when something unaccustomed arises.[63] By willing to remember we can better order our considerations of prudential matters.[64] When we meditate on what we remember, thereby building the habit of memory, we are more able to know quickly what to do from what we remember.[65]

In order to develop the good habit of memory, several things must occur. We must, by acts of the will, move the memory to recall things which pertain to practical matters under consideration. If we do this often, the habit becomes refined and we can also develop phantasms stored in our memory into more useful phantasms. This occurs when reason places formalities and adds and removes things from the phantasm stored in memory, making the phantasm fuller and richer. Second, the cogitative power must be habituated to knowing which memories to recall. Having a well-disposed faculty of memory is not enough. One needs to have the right habits, both in the faculty of

---

[56]That memory is an integral part, see I-II, q. 57, a. 6, ad 4 and II-II, q. 48, a. 1.

[57]Ibid.

[58]Ibid.

[59]ST II-II, q. 49, a. 1, ad 3.

[60]III Sent., d. 33, q. 3, a. 1a and ST II-II, q. 49, a. 1. See also Aristotle's *Metaphysics* (980b29).

[61]ST II-II, q. 49, a. 1.

[62]See ibid., ad 1.

[63]Ibid., ad 2.

[64]Ibid.

[65]Ibid.

memory and in the cogitative power so that the right phantasms are prepared for the judgment of the possible intellect. This training of the cogitative power is also done through considerations of our experiences and past memories. For example, suppose someone who has a drinking problem is perplexed as to why his past experiences were so bad. If by a proper consideration, he remembers that he always has problems whenever he drinks, the next time he is around alcohol he may avoid it, knowing the problems he has had in relation to it.

The next thing required for a proper habit of memory is due solicitude. Memory helps one to take due solicitude since the experiences are impressed upon memory.[66] When we have a proper habit of memory, our memory will bring to mind those things which will move us to take due care and concern of those things which we ought. In fact, we often see the opposite: when someone forgets about the chicken he put in the oven, he will not do the "prudent" thing and remove the chicken from the oven when it is done cooking. Instead the chicken burns and only upon smelling the smoke does he remove it. Conversely, if a person gets in the habit of remembering things which he knows he should, the habit will aid him at the times when he needs to know those things necessary for prudential action.

A proper habit of memory is required so that we take due solicitude. Some people simply do not take due care to remember things that they should. A person must have a habit by which he intentionally consigns to memory those things important for prudent living. When a person is in the habit of remembering important experiences, he recalls those memories automatically without thinking. Yet, there are other people who do not seem to learn from their experiences and this is because they do not consign to memory those things they should. If a person gets into a habit of remembering his experiences, he will be more capable of directing his life properly.

Due solicitude requires that the person knows when he should give his concern to some thing.[67] We should not have solicitude about things which are irrelevant or when it is not a suitable time for considering them. Solicitude implies a certain study which one employs to come to knowledge of something.[68] We tend to give greater study when there is fear of failing[69] and those who seek to be prudent must give due care to their consideration of those things which can affect their future actions. St. Thomas delineates four things which can make solicitude illicit regarding temporal matters:

> First, we must not constitute our end in them,[70] nor serve God for the
> sake of the necessities of food and clothes. . . . Secondly, we must not

---

[66]ST II-II, q. 49, a. 1, ad 2. In this passage, Saint Thomas observes that the experiences are pressed upon the soul, but here we would understand that to mean memory, either sensitive or intellective.

[67]See ST II-II, q. 57, a. 7.

[68]ST II-II, q. 55, a. 6.

[69]Ibid.

[70]See ibid.

be so solicitous about temporal matters, as to despair of divine aid....[71] Thirdly, the solicitude must not be presumptuous, as when man is confident to be able to procure the necessities of life without God's help. . . . Fourth, man busies himself about the time of solicitude when he is solicitous now of something which does not pertain to the care of the present time but to the care of the future.[72]

In another place, St. Thomas gives an additional reason why solicitude may be illicit: "solicitude for temporal things is able to be illicit because of the excessive study which is given to procuring temporal goods since man ought to serve more principally spiritual things."[73] Contained in these passages we see that our primary concern must be about spiritual matters and only secondarily about temporal matters. Yet due solicitude is required on our part even for temporal matters (such as mental health), but it must be moderated by the understanding of when solicitude regarding temporal matters is illicit.

The directee must get into the habit of taking due solicitude to remember those things which will help him act prudently. Because of the blindness that mental illness can bring in relation to the object of mental illness, the directee will often find that he will not be in the habit of remembering the bad things that happen to him due to the actions which aggravate the mental illness. When a person suffers passion or becomes fixated on something, the lower faculties will often prohibit the remembering of crucial experiences so that the directee cannot act prudently. When he is counseled by the psychologist, the association of the counsel with his problem aids the directee to remember what to do. As he gets in the habit of remembering his past experience and what the psychologist has told him, his memory and cogitative power will be habituated in the right way.

For the psychologist, this means that in relation to the directee, he must take due care to remember what the directee conveys to him. The modern practice of taking notes is to be commended, not as an absolute, but only as a general rule. Taking notes can help the psychologist to consider the directee's communications with the

---

[71] See ibid.

[72] ST I-II, q.108, a. 3, ad 5: "Primo quidem, ut in eis finem non constituamus, neque Deo serviamus propter necessaria victus et vestitus. . . . Secundo, ut non sic sollicitemur de temporalibus, cum desperatione divini auxilii. . . . Tertio, ne sit sollicitudo praesumptuosa, ut scilicet homo confidat se necessaria vitae per suam sollicitudinem posse procurare, absque divino auxilio. . . . Quarto, per hoc quod homo sollicitudinis tempus praeoccupat, quia scilicet de hoc sollicitus est nunc, quod non pertinet ad curam praesentis temporis, sed ad curam futuri."

[73] ST II-II, q. 55, a. 6: ". . . Potest esse temporalium sollicitudo illicita propter superfluum studium quod apponitur ad temporalia procuranda, propter quod homo a spiritualibus, quibus principalius inservire debet, retrahitur"

psychologist and thereby aid him in discerning what the directee should do.[74] Taking notes also aids the psychologist in keeping better track of his different directees, especially if he has a busy schedule. A quick review of past meetings before each session can prevent confusion about the different directees and their problems.

Yet, this should not be a hard and fast rule. There may be circumstances or matters which are discussed that should not be put in writing in order to safeguard the reputation and psychological well being of the directee. For example, if during a meeting a directee begins to reveal something very personal which could have a grave impact on the counseling done by the psychologist, it may be inopportune or inappropriate for him to sit by indifferently and take notes. Rather he should stop and listen to the directee for two reasons. (1) It aids the directee in the revealing of something deeply personal because the psychologist is manifesting his concern by looking at the directee instead of the pen and paper. (2) A great deal of information (particular sense data) is gained by the psychologist by looking at the directee. The mode of expression of the directee reveals a great deal about the interior state of the directee in relation to the information being expressed. As a general rule, psychologists should never do any counseling without first having seen the directee for a few sessions so as to get a read on the directee which can only come through seeing him. He can give some counseling over the phone or via mail, only after having established some history with the directee. The psychologist needs a proper phantasm of the directee which comes through direct sensory experience in order to know how serious the directee is, how deep the problems may be, whether the directee is being duplicitous or hiding things, etc. Speech can often mask the interior state of a person when physical signs manifest in his body and expression do not. The psychologist should be in the habit of committing these to memory so that he can employ proper prudence, which requires knowledge of the singulars in order to act prudently.

The habit or virtue of memory has three opposites. First, when a person does not remember things that he should, he suffers from the vice of forgetfulness. While forgetfulness can be from a purely physiological cause, it can also be volitional. Those who lead a life of the passions tend to suffer from precipitation and inconsideration, manifesting a lack of judgment and counsel which require remembering. Hence, those who lead a life of the passions will slowly fall into a vice of forgetfulness. Since remembering takes a certain amount of "psychological energy," those who lead a life of the passions will tend to find the virtue of memory distasteful since it requires them to overcome the complacency of the passions in not remembering. This vice affects all considerations of prudence and that is why the virtue of memory is an integral part of prudence.[75]

---

[74]Mere concerns of litigation should not drive this practice but an honest concern for remembering what is necessary, so that the psychologist can make prudential judgments regarding the directee.

[75]This may appear to be contrary to the grace of forgetfulness. The grace of forgetfulness, while allowing the person to forget the specific content of past memories, leaves the person aware of the fact that he can fall into a specific species of sin. Therefore,

In past centuries, generations were more habituated in remembering, not only in their education but in their daily lives, since survival often depended on remembering ways of surviving. In the modern context, this does not seem to be the case for several reasons. The first is that modern culture has set up conditions in which "the idiot is protected from himself." Since modern culture allows for irresponsible behavior and does not require people to suffer from the bad consequences of their behavior, modern culture teaches people that memory is not important: no matter what happens, you will not be held responsible for it. Therefore, there is no point in remembering if (a) it is going to require energy and (b) you do not to have to pay the consequences for your actions. The second seems to be the advent of modern forms of communication, particularly television. As one watches television, since the sense data coming from the television often does not have any correspondence to reality or have any connection to the person's own experience, the lower faculties are habituated in enjoying the image and then disregarding it. Rarely is there anything on television which is necessary for people's prudential living. Third, the general availability of low cost books and computers which can access information quickly, there is less incentive on the side of someone reading or learning to commit things to memory when they can be easily accessed. In the medieval period, a scholar may have had access to a major historical work only once in his life and so he needed a highly habituated memory to be able to commit vast portions of reading to memory quickly and accurately, without repetition. One has to wonder if the decline of memory training due to all three of these has resulted in a decline of prudence simply because people are not inclined to remember information that is to their intellectual, moral, spiritual and psychological advantage.

The second opposite to the virtue of memory is when a person remembers the wrong things. A virtue is a good habit which means that the virtue of memory will move a person to remember the right things at the right time. Yet, psychological trauma and lack of the virtue of memory can be responsible for someone having images in his mind that do not suit the object under consideration. In fact, every fixation has as one of its components the vice of remembering the wrong things. A great deal has been said throughout the course of these volumes about how this can be undone, so that aspect of this vice will not be considered here. Yet, it should be noted that psychologists should counsel their directees, among other things, to remember things in a specific way and to consider and remember them often. When the time comes for the person to depend on his memory for the right information, the memory will be habituated to recall the right sense data. We have also talked about purification of memory which can also directly contribute to overcoming this vice.

One method which some psychologists use to overcome this vice is by leading the directee through a past traumatic experience in order to reformulate the image so that it can be stored back in memory. By going through the traumatic experience, the psychologist can help the directee by separating out of the phantasm those things which are false or harmful. He can then merge with the image a *ratio* or perspective which can

---

the virtue of memory and the grace of forgetfulness are not opposed insofar as the grace of forgetfulness still leaves intact the memory of his ability to fall into a kind of sin.

give the directee a different understanding of the phantasm (experience). The cogitative power and memory can be trained by the directee's considering the experience under that aspect and slowly but surely the virtue of memory will be built up so that the directee remembers rightly. After the phantasm is corrected, the effects on the other powers will wane through the volitional work of the directee. Great care must be taken in this regard so that the psychologist be competent[76] and very prudent in the process.

The third opposite to the virtue of memory is the vice of negligence. We have already mentioned it somewhat above, but it should be observed that this vice occurs when someone volitionally forgets or fails to remember things that he knows he should. This vice arises because of a lack of due solicitude and consideration of experiences. Essentially speaking, a person is going to be prudent when he is thoughtful and prone to contemplation. If a person finds these distasteful, he will be prone to forgetting things because he will not consider them. As the person brings the images of his experience to his imagination often, the memory and cogitative power are habituated to remember those things under the formality that reason places on them during consideration or contemplation of them. One who is negligent in remembering is bound to lapse into imprudence.

2. Understanding (*Intellectus*)

Understanding is a cognitive[77] integral part[78] of prudence and is sometimes known as intelligence (*intelligentia*).[79] It is not to be misunderstood as the intellectual virtue of understanding, the connatural habit *intellectus principiorum*, nor the first act of the possible intellect of understanding. Rather, this is a practical virtue which gives a person knowledge of the present, either contingent or necessary.[80] This virtue gives one the ability to grasp the current state of affairs as they are. It gives the person knowledge not just of universal principles in general, but of which universal principles apply in a given case.[81] For this reason, St. Thomas says that understanding gives one a right estimation of a particular end[82] and this means that, in a particular situation, the person grasps (understands) the nature of the situation and knows which end is to be achieved

---

[76]By competent is meant that the psychologist must have a proper psychological training which is imbued with a proper philosophical and theological understanding of man and his faculties. Error in this regard can lead to more mental illness on the side of the directee.

[77]ST II-II, q. 48, a. 1.

[78]Ibid. and ST I-II, q. 57, a. 6, ad 4.

[79]ST II-II, q. 48, a. 1 and ST I-II, q. 57, a. 6, ad 4.

[80]III Sent., d. 33, q. 3, a. 1a and ST II-II, q. 48, a. 1

[81]See III Sent., d. 33, q. 3, a. 1a, ad 1 and Prummer, *Manuale Theologiae Moralis*, vol. 1, p. 458.

[82]ST II-II, q. 49, a. 2, ad 1 and ibid., a. 3.

given the circumstances. He knows this end by applying universal knowledge to the concrete situation through understanding. The whole process of prudence is derived from understanding.[83]

Yet, St. Thomas makes an interesting observation which affects the application of the universal principles. He says that understanding helps one to judge not the proper sensibles, but the interior sense of the particular.[84] What this means is that the person grasps the end to be achieved based upon what the interior senses tell the person. This is very important because, since virtue lies in the mean relative to the individual, the person only knows what he should strive for (the particular end) when he judges it in light of both his exterior experience and his interior state. For example, if an alcoholic judges not on what his interior senses tell him but upon the consideration of alcohol in itself which is good, he will not judge based upon his past negative experience retained by his memory and assessed and prepared for abstraction by the cogitative power. Understanding gives the person the ability to look at the situation, judge himself interiorly based upon his own personal past experience and then know for what end he must strive. This judgment then acts as a principle which determines the subsequent ratiocinative process of reason regarding what is to be done, i.e. it is the principle which determines the process of counsel.

This virtue is often lacking in the mentally ill, since they are unable even to know the end for which they should strive. They find themselves in a situation where "they don't even know where to begin" as far as what to do and where to go. When a psychologist has a good grasp of the circumstances in which a directee lives and the directee's problems, he can tell the directee that when he is in certain situations, he should perform a specific act of virtue. For example, a general principle is "avoid all occasions of sin", which can even be formulated as "avoid all occasions of mental illness." Normally, when a person encounters a situation which is in an occasion of sin or one which aggravates his mental illness, he should immediately excuse himself and leave the situation. However, those who are mentally ill are often conflicted and they cannot grasp the circumstances clearly enough to know they should flee the situation. Therefore, the psychologist can help the directee to apply the principles in the concrete by telling him, "whenever you are in a room alone with alcohol, get up, immediately leave the room, and occupy yourself with something to get your mind off of it" or something of this sort. In this case, the end is set before him of separating himself from the occasion of his fall. When the occasion happens, the directee can rely on the prior judgment of his psychologist to do the right thing.

This virtue tends to come more naturally to some rather than others. Some people find it very easy to gasp the principles and easily apply them. If a child is trained with general principles when he is young and properly disciplined by his parents, he will find the development of this virtue easier as he gets older. However, if his parents are inconsistent with discipline or if their formation of him by rewards and punishments is

---

[83]ST II-II, q. 49, a. 2.

[84]Ibid., ad 3.

irrational, the child will find the application of principles in the concrete difficult.

3. Docility (*Docilitas*)

Docility is a cognitive,[85] integral part[86] of prudence in which one acquires knowledge by learning from another.[87] One man cannot know all of the particulars which a person can encounter in life. So he needs to be taught by others, especially the elderly who have a healthy understanding about the ends of acts.[88] Essentially, this virtue makes one receptive to learning[89] from others. Those who can learn from the good acts and the mistakes of others as well as from the general knowledge of others are more likely to act prudently. This is because they can store the other person's counsel in memory and use it when appropriate circumstances arise. The aptitude to docility is from nature, but its completion is from human study, in which the person applies himself to the great documents and texts, frequently, reverently and with care, not neglecting them out of ignorance nor despising them because of pride.[90] If a person is not willing to learn from the great and prudent writers of the past, he is unlikely to be able to achieve a more developed virtue of prudence. While the common man can watch others, avoid pitfalls by following their example and even from time to time ask another's counsel, greatness of prudence requires a thorough knowledge of universal principles as well as how those principles have been applied throughout history. Knowledge of those of a single lifetime is not as great as knowledge accumulated by great authors over centuries. Man is able to be more prudent when he relies on the wisdom of the ages, rather than on mere contemporary wisdom.[91]

Docility requires a certain discernment of judgment since one must choose wisely those from whom one takes counsel. This may be difficult, but one of the ways one does so is by observing other men and how they conduct their lives. If a particular man seems virtuous and prudent, docility should be more readily given to him than someone who is not prudent. There is a false docility among those who, knowing their sin or mental illness, will choose to take counsel from someone whom they know will confirm them in their disorder. Psychologists must be careful of directees who are "counselor shopping" in order to find a counselor who will make them feel good about themselves, despite their disorder, rather than one who will provide true prudential counseling.

Docility is a *sine qua non* of effective counseling. If a directee is obstinate and

---

[85]ST II-II, q. 48, a 1.

[86]Ibid. and ST I-II, q. 57, a. 6, ad 4. See also ST II-II, q. 49, a. 3.

[87]ST II-II, q. 48, a. 1.

[88]ST II-II, q. 49, a. 3.

[89]Ibid.

[90]Ibid., ad 2.

[91]This is why tradition is so important.

unwilling to take counsel from the psychologist,[92] he should immediately dismiss the directee, unless the psychologist realizes that a certain amount of time will be necessary in order to win the trust of the directee. However, the psychologist must be careful not to assume this from false motives, such as financial gain. If the psychologist recognizes obstinacy in the directee, he should inform the directee to seek the counsel of someone to whom he can listen and trust. The psychologist does not do the directee any favors by confirming him in his obstinacy by going through the counseling process while nothing is truly accomplished. The directee is only able to advance when he is docile. But docility is a virtue lying in a mean as well and the psychologist must be aware that there are obstinate directees as well as the blindly obedient. The psychologist needs to make sure that the directee understands that he needs direction, while at the same time desiring to take the counsel, obtain the virtue, overcome his mental illness and be able to act upon his own without the constant intervention and counsel of the psychologist.

On the side of the psychologist, docility is needed in two ways. The first is that the psychologist must learn about man, his psychological constitution and the practice of psychology from others. He must be willing to consult books of great psychological writers in order to learn what is necessary to be a good psychologist. A proud psychologist is a dangerous psychologist, because he often is overconfident of his own abilities and therefore will assume he understands human behavior better than he, in fact, does. The second way in which a psychologist must be docile is that he must be willing to go to other psychologists for advice regarding particular directees. While there may be times when he should simply refer the directee to a psychologist more capable in a given area, there may be circumstances in which that may not be prudent, e.g. if he has a directee who finds him trustworthy while fearing and distrusting others. In this case, the psychologist should have the humility to know his limitations and the docility to seek the advice of someone more knowledgeable than himself. Pride and obstinacy are the hallmark of many modern psychologists, especially if they have any success, regardless of how little. Even the best of psychologists should know that there are times they are simply going to have to seek the advice of others.

Obviously, the training of new psychologists requires a great deal of docility on the side of the student. Not only does the student need the universal principles and knowledge of man's psychological constitution, but he needs great docility to learn from other psychologists' past experience in dealing with the mentally ill. Application of the universal principles in the concrete requires some experience. While some students will have a greater aptitude (the virtue of understanding as explained above), they will still need concrete advice and direction in the beginning stages of counseling. A proud student should not be permitted to continue in any reputable psychological school since he will pose a danger to future directees.

---

[92]Here we are prescinding from those whose obstinacy is from a demonic cause. In this case, the psychologist should refer the directee to a priest.

4. Shrewdness (*Solertia*)

Shrewdness[93] is a cognitive, integral part[94] of prudence, sometimes called *eustochia*. Shrewdness is a skill or quickness of mind in discovering something, especially the principle of a thing.[95] Eustochia is "the capability or virtue of good conjecure[96] or guessing in practical things."[97] Shrewdness is a quickness[98] at finding[99] or conjecturing about the means to the end.[100] St. Thomas observes that it is a kind of subtlety or ease of conjecturing the means[101] and it depends more on a natural genius than from custom.[102] Prummer defines shrewdness as "a prompt conjecture about the congruent means to some intended end to be obtained or shrewdness is a certain perspicacity quickly apprehending the means, which happens from natural aptitude or also from exercise."[103] Prummer goes on in the same location to observe that shrewdness is by degrees, since it is based upon a natural gift even though it can be developed through exercise. Essentially, this means that some people are simply quicker at knowing which means will lead to a given end in a particular set of circumstances, either by natural ability or by habit (exercise).

Some directees will have an ability to know quickly what to do once the end of mental health has been properly explained to them. Others will find themselves with virtually no ability to know what to do. Those with less shrewdness will require more counseling about concrete circumstances and how to deal with them. As to psychologists, no one should be a psychologist without some degree of shrewdness. If he is not able to find the means quickly and easily, the directee will perceive this and lose confidence in the psychologist. There may be some circumstances which will pose

---

[93]The term solertia does not seem to have a good English counterpart since shrewdness sometimes has a negative connotation. However, the use of the term shrewdness here does not imply anything negative but, quite the contrary, it is a positive designation. Deferrari, in *A Latin-English Dictionary of St. Thomas* (p. 979), translates solertia as shrewdness, skill and quickness of mind.

[94]ST II-II, q. 48, a. 1.

[95]See Deferrari, loc. cit.

[96]III Sent., d. 33, q. 3, a. 1d; ST II-II, q. 48, a. 1 and ibid., q. 49, a. 4.

[97]Deferrari, *A Latin-English Dictionary of St. Thomas*, p. 363.

[98]III Sent., d. 33, q. 3, a. 1d; ST II-II, q. 49, a. 4 and ibid., ad 4.

[99]ST II-II, q. 48, a.1 and ibid., q. 49, a. 4.

[100]ST II-II, q. 48, a.1 and ibid., q. 49, a. 4. See also In Ethic., VI, l. 8 (n. 1219).

[101]*In Libros Posteriororum Analyticorum*, I, l. 44, n. 12.

[102]III Sent., d. 33, q. 3, a. 1d.

[103]Prummer, *Manuale Theologiae Moralis*, vol. 1, p. 458: "est prompta coniectura circa media congruentia ad aliquem finem intentum obtinendum, seu sollertia est quaedam perspicacitas velociter apprehendendi medium, quae contingit ex naturali aptitudine et etiam ex exercitio."

some difficulty for finding the means and it may take the psychologist some time to discern the means, even if he is exceptionally shrewd. Yet, those without shrewdness simply will not be prudent, because they will be forced to make judgments about what to do before they can really find the means to the end. This opens the door for greater error on the side of the psychologist which can cause great damage to the directee. When a psychologist is shrewd, he should be sufficiently circumspect and reflective so that he is not too hasty in thinking that the means he arrives at quickly may be the best. The more shrewd a man is, the quicker he will come to the right means, but due to human ability to err, he should always have a certain self-reflection on the matter to make sure that his response proceeds from true discernment of the principles and circumstances involved rather than from appetite or something of this sort.

5. Reason (*Ratio*)

Reason or reasoning is a cognitive[104] integral part[105] of prudence in which one proceeds from the knowledge he has to other knowledge or judgments.[106] Sometimes called good reasoning,[107] reason is the ability to apply universals to particulars well.[108] In the discussion of the practical syllogism, we discussed how the universal is applied in the concrete by the recognition of the middle term and its proper distribution. Reason, the integral part of prudence, aids the person in being able to do precisely that.

Some people have a good ability to grasp universal principles, such as "retributive justice demands that one pay back what one has stolen." But as to the actual application in the concrete, they may have great difficulties, e.g. moral theologians indicate that one does not have to pay back the person from whom one has taken money, if there is some grave harm that would come to the person who has stolen the property. But those who lack the integral part of prudence of reason will find that they have a hard time applying the principles of retributive justice because they have a hard time seeing the principles embodied in the circumstances. As a result, they may cause themselves harm by giving money back to their boss, for example, and then they are fired because of it.

Directees will experience this very problem. Their difficulty is due to the fact that they will lack clear or rightly ordered phantasms due to the influence of their mental illness on the phantasm itself. Fixation does not allow for an ease or subtlety of judgment because the phantasm is held bound by the faculties affected by the fixation, such as the imagination and cogitative power. Even when the psychologist gives the directee the universal principles, he will not always apply them well without some experience or practice. Going through different kinds of scenarios with the directee so

---

[104]ST II-II, q. 48, a. 1.

[105]Ibid. and ST II-II, q. 49, a. 5.

[106]ST II-II, q. 48, a. 1.

[107]ST II-II, q. 49, a. 5.

[108]Ibid., ad 2.

that he can see how the principles are applied will be helpful. The psychologist can present a scenario related to the directee's mental illness[109] and then ask him to suggest a course of action. The psychologist can then help the directee to judge if the course of action is good or bad. This helps to develop some habit of mind so that when the directee encounters circumstances similar to the scenario, he can apply the principles. As the directee begins to overcome his mental illness, the phantasms will clear up and his ability to apply the principles will be more easily accomplished.

Those of lesser intelligence will have a more difficult time with this integral part of prudence due to their slowness of mind. Since they will have less of the integral part of understanding which will help them to grasp the circumstances, they will have greater difficulty applying principles. On the other hand, because they are of lesser intelligence, their mental illness will be less voluntary and therefore less ingrained or habituated.[110] The counterpart to this proposition is that those who are more intelligent will have a greater ability to have and develop the integral part of reason, but they will also have more severe mental illnesses which are not from a material cause. Since their mental illness can be more severe because it will be more voluntary, they have a greater ability to corrupt this integral part. Therefore, their blindness may be more severe. However, once they are able to see how to apply the principles in the concrete and to reason well, i.e. as they begin to develop this integral part of prudence, they may advance more rapidly, provided they do not overanalyze the circumstances. Those who are more intelligent may be more prone to analyzing the circumstances excessively which will affect the integral parts of understanding and reason.

Reason is also a *sine qua non* for being a psychologist. No person who has difficulty in applying universals in the concrete through practical syllogisms should ever be allowed to practice psychology since the difficulty will have a direct bearing on his counseling. Schools of psychology should dismiss students who suffer from a lack of this integral part as a matter of charity to the student and to his possible future directees. As a psychologist ages and gains more experience in counseling, this aspect of prudence will grow since he will have a greater number of experiences from which he can see how the principles applied and worked under different circumstances in the past. From time to time, even if a psychologist is shrewd and can reason well, he will need to consult other psychologists about the application of the principles in concrete cases. This allows for the pooling of a greater number of experiences, since different psychologists will have slightly different experiences and therefore have a greater knowledge regarding the application of one principle as opposed to others. As has been mentioned throughout this series in relation to how the life of the appetites affects the phantasms, the more virtuous and mentally healthy the psychologist, the more he will reason well and therefore the more prudent will be his counseling. All of this discussion should indicate

---

[109]This is true unless the presentation of the scenario itself will aggravate the mental illness.

[110]This would hold true in cases other than those in which the mental illness may be caused by some grave material defect.

that some psychologists will simply be more successful at counseling since they will have greater prudence depending, on their degree of possession of the various integral parts of prudence.

6. Foresight (*Providentia*)

Foresight is a preceptive,[111] integral part[112] of prudence by which one applies knowledge to action[113] by ordering action to a suitable end.[114] Foresight implies distance,[115] i.e. the person with foresight is able to see how a given action will achieve a future end. St. Thomas says that foresight is a more principal part than the other parts, since all the parts of prudence are necessary so that one can order the means to the end which is seen by foresight.[116] St. Thomas says that the name of prudence comes from providence or foresight (*prudentia/providentia*)[117] and foresight occurs when something future is seen by the person before it is done[118] or before it happens and he is able to foresee any obstacles so that they may be removed.[119] It is a kind of prescience or foreknowledge in which a person can read the circumstances and know what would happen if various actions should be tried in those particular circumstances.

The difference between shrewdness and foresight is that shrewdness is a quickness at the process of conjecturing, whereas foresight is the ability to foresee through the conjecturing what will happen. So one is the quickness of mind while the other is the actual "vision" into the future. Prummer observes that foresight is taken in two ways, viz. (1) for the ordination of the means to the end and (2) for the consideration of future events.[120] The ordination of the means to the end is why this part is a preceptive part of prudence rather than a mere cognitive part of prudence, even though it does require a knowledge or ability to see intellectually what outcomes will come from the various causes and circumstances in a given case. It is preceptive because foresight commands or orders the means toward a future end.

Directees may not have good foresight since it requires a reading of the circumstances, i.e. the particulars which are known through the phantasm. Since the mentally ill frequently have disordered phantasms, they will have a difficult time making

---

[111]ST II-II, q. 48, a. 1.

[112]Ibid. and ST I-II, q. 57, a. 6, ad 4.

[113]ST II-II, q. 48, a. 1.

[114]Ibid.

[115]ST II-II, q. 49, a. 6.

[116]Ibid., ad 1.

[117]Ibid.

[118]III Sent., d. 33, q. 3, a. 1a.

[119]III Sent., d. 33, q. 3, a. 1b.

[120]Prummer, *Manuale Theologiae Moralis*, vol. 1, p. 459.

judgments which manifest foresight. Again, as the psychologist helps the directee to act properly, the phantasms will clear and then foresight will be more able to operate. Going through scenarios may also help this form of a difficulty if a psychologist recognizes it in his directee. As for psychologists, again, this is a *sine qua non* in order to give counseling; since counseling requires giving instructions about what the directee is to do, if a psychologist has a hard time seeing future events arising from given courses of action, he will misguide the directee.

St. Thomas says that foresight is impeded in three ways.[121]

> In one way on the part of the way of finding, which sometimes seems good but is not. Caution removes this impediment, of which it is to discern from the virtues the preference of the species of virtue to vice.

Foresight can be affected when something appears good to a person that is not. If a person develops a preference for virtue and keeps that in his mind when considering what should be done, he will judge what should be done based upon whether it will attain virtue or whether the proposed course of action proceeds from vice.

> In another way, from the very order to the end; either the way is not of itself apt to the end, or it is impeded by something extrinsic so that it is not able to lead to the end; and this pertains to circumspection, which is caution of contrary vices by which prudence especially is impeded.

Sometimes foresight is impeded by something extrinsic to the agent. If a person is incircumspect, he does not keep track of those things outside of him or around him and so his proposed action will not take into account external impediments. Sometimes, the very means by its nature will not achieve the end.[122]

> In a third way, on the part of the very man tending to the end, who is not able to find suitable ways to the intended end: hence it is

---

[121]III Sent., d. 33, q. 3, a. 1b: "Uno modo ex parte ipsius viae inveniendae, quae quandoque videtur bona, et non est; et hoc impedimentum cautio aufert, cujus est ex virtutibus vitia virtutum speciem praeferentia discernere. Alio modo ex ordine ipsius in finem, ne scilicet via quae de se apta est ad finem, aliquo extrinseco impediatur ne in finem ducere possit; et hoc ad circumspectionem pertinet, quae est cautela vitiorum contrariorum, quibus praecipue prudentia impeditur. Tertio modo ex parte ipsius hominis tendentis in finem, qui vias accommodas ad finem intentum invenire non potest: unde oportet quod per doctrinam ab aliis accipiat. Quia oportet principia operabilia vel a se habere prudentem, vel ab alio faciliter accipere. Qui autem neutrum habet, hic inutilis est vir."

[122]How these first two ways affect psychology will be seen more readily once caution and circumspection have been addressed. See below.

necessary that he receives through teaching from others. Since it is necessary regarding the operative principles that either he has prudence from himself or he easily receives it from another. He who has neither, is a useless man.[123]

In this case, a man's very own lack of the operative principles affects his ability to be prudent so he must get them from another. In psychology, docility aids the directee in obtaining foresight by going to the psychologist who can give him the operative principles and therefore the ability to apply them in the future. Without operative principles, or to put it another way, unless a man is a principled man, he simply will not be prudent. A man may not be principled for two reasons. Either he simply does not know the principles, which is the case with most directees who do not know the psychological constitution of man[124] or he is unwilling or unable to apply the principles in the concrete. If a person has no principles, he will not have foresight because he will not know what is going to happen or if he knows what will happen, he may not know whether it is good or bad for him morally or psychologically. If he lacks the ability to apply the principles in the concrete, i.e. he lacks the integral part of reason, he will not have foresight because he will not know if certain principles or actions will produce certain future events by the application of the principles in the concrete. All of this tells us that while foresight is the more principal part of prudence, foresight itself depends on the other principal parts for its operation.

7. Circumspection (*Circumspectio*)

Circumspection is a preceptive,[125] integral part[126] of prudence in which one applies knowledge to action.[127] Knowledge here concerns the circumstances[128] of the action and so circumspection compares the end which one wants to achieve and the

---

[123]St. Thomas then goes on to discuss how docility is necessary for the person in this situation.

[124]If a person follows the moral code of the Catholic Church which embodies a following and developing of all of the virtues, the person is more likely to be prudent and not have mental illness. The moral code of the Catholic Church is founded upon and takes into full consideration the ontological structure of man and its proper operation.

[125]ST II-II, q. 48, a. 1. It is not completely clear why this is a preceptive part rather than a cognitive part, other than the possibility that prudence requires that the person execute the action when the circumstances are right; see infra this paragraph. The fact that the person must command the action in due circumstances may be why it is a preceptive integral part rather than merely a cognitive integral part.

[126]Ibid.

[127]Ibid.

[128]Ibid.

circumstances in which one finds oneself to see if the end fits the circumstances.[129] For example, a child might need disciplining, but the public place in which a parent finds himself indicates that this is not the place where it should be done.

In the prior volumes, we observed several things in relation to circumspection. First, it was noted that passions affect circumspection.[130] Since passions affect the phantasm, they affect the judgment of the singular (circumstances as represented in the phantasm). Second, it was noted that if a child is raised with right order within the family (proper circumstances for psychological health), he will learn circumspection.[131] This essentially means that a rightly ordered environment aids the child in judgment of singulars which will have an appreciable effect on his prudence. Having parents who are virtuous (also a circumstance of the child) will directly affect the child's judgment. In the context of psychology, this means that the directee's environment will have a direct impact on his phantasms and therefore prudence. If anything in his environment is vicious or disordered, it has the capacity to affect the directee. Thus, the office and surroundings in which the directee is counseled by the psychologist will have a great impact on the perception and prudence of the directee, since they affect his phantasms of the circumstances and the psychologist himself.[132]

Third, it was noted that those with mental illness will lack circumspection.[133] Fourth, it was observed that those who lose chastity will lose the more subtle virtues such as circumspection.[134] The subtlety of the virtue of circumspection is based upon the fact that passion and mental illness draw one into an interior consideration of one's appetitive state. In other words, a person, through passion or mental illness, is taken out of his contact with reality, of which the circumstances are a part. For this reason, highly developed circumspection is a sign of mental health and/or virtue. This is why throughout this series, there has been constant encouragement to understand the link between morality and psychology. Without a proper moral life, the directees will not be prudent and therefore they simply will not know the proper courses of action by which to overcome their mental illness. If a virtuous person has something traumatic

---

[129]ST II-II, q. 49, a. 7 and ibid., ad 3.

[130]See volume one, chapter nine (IV).

[131]See volume one, chapter thirteen (II).

[132]There have been some details given throughout this series, but suffice it to say, when designing an office, all of the moral, intellectual and theological virtues should be taken into consideration. Pictures which represent the various virtuous actions, Gifts of the Holy Spirit, etc. should find a place there. The office should not be too "sterile" but should be a place which positively affects the perception of the directee, not only about the psychologist, but the entire staff of the office as well as the directee himself. Emotionalism as manifest in color schemes and pictures should be avoided, general speaking. It may be the case that different office styles will be necessary, based upon different kinds of directees, e.g. children, rape victims, etc.

[133]See volume one, chapter fourteen.

[134]See volume two, chapter six (IIJ).

happen to him, while the trauma may cause a kind of interior retraction in which the person becomes introspective, nevertheless, he can use his virtues to overcome this and keep his psychological faculties rightly ordered. Since virtues are a strength, he can use the strength from the virtues to help him to command the actions necessary to overcome his problem as well as to see reality (circumspection) for what it is.

8. Caution (*Cautio*)

Caution is a preceptive,[135] integral part[136] of prudence by which one applies knowledge to action[137] in order to avoid impediments[138] and evils.[139] Caution differs from providence because caution deals with evils and their avoidance, whereas providence deals with the good, i.e. achieving the end. St. Thomas says that caution is an adjunct to contrition[140] and by this he means that when a person is sorry for his sin, he will be cautious in the future so that he can avoid the sin and not be sorry for more sin.

In a similar manner in the context of psychology, if the directee suffers from his mental illness and he recognizes his suffering, he can use that to be cautious and therefore more prudent. From time to time we have mentioned things such as custody of the mind and custody of the eyes. These are virtues developed from prudential caution. The person knows that if he fails to keep custody of the mind, he will easily fall into sin or the action or circumstances which could cause his mental illness to be aggravated. The Church has always taught her children that they must avoid the occasion of sin. The same applies in psychology, *mutatis mutandis*, with the directee in his avoidance of those things which can cause or aggravate his mental illness. Caution is necessary, therefore, for the directee to overcome his mental illness.

The psychologist must also have caution in several ways. He must have caution when first dealing with a directee so that his actions are measured and moderated so as not to give the wrong impressions to the directee. Next, he must practice caution regarding certain kinds of directees, e.g. a male psychologist has to practice great caution with women who suffer from sexual problems or trauma. The psychologist himself will have some weakness unless he is morally perfect, which is exceptionally rare among humans in general and even rarer among psychologists. Therefore, he must be cautious in relation to his own weaknesses, even if they are not mental illnesses. This may require him to be cautious around some directees or even to decline to take a specific directee if he realizes the directee could pose some problem for him, due to his

---

[135]ST II-II, q. 48, a. 1.

[136]Ibid. and ST I-II, q. 57, a. 6, ad 4.

[137]ST II-II, q. 48, a. 1.

[138]Ibid. and *Super Ephesios*, c. 5, l. 6.

[139]ST II-II, q. 49, a. 8.

[140]IV Sent., d. 17, q. 2, a. 2d.

weaknesses or due to his own personal history.

Caution is a virtue or action lying in a mean. The danger is in the extremes: when the directee or the psychologist are not cautious enough or when they are too cautious. If the directee is not cautious enough, he will find himself in circumstances which could aggravate his mental illness or at least impede his progress toward becoming mentally healthy. If the psychologist is not cautious enough, it can lead to everything from contracting mental illness himself to litigation. As for the excess, if the directee is too cautious, he will not engage in actions which could be helpful to him in overcoming his mental illness. The psychologist must help him to find the mean. If the psychologist is too cautious, he will find that his practice will not be as successful, because he has to have sufficient daring in confronting or helping directees or he may not be inclined to take directees whom he could very well help, even though he would have to exercise a moderated caution.

C. Potential Parts of Prudence
1. Good Counsel (*Eubulia*)

Potential parts of a virtue are those parts which do not fall directly under the virtue, but which are connected to the virtue by the matter about which they are concerned. The first subjective part[141] is the virtue of good counsel[142] or euboulia.[143] Euboulia, as the virtue of good counsel, is a certain inquisition[144] or finding of the means.[145] Through the virtue of euboulia, one is able to find a suitable means according to due time and other circumstances.[146] The difference between prudence and euboulia is that euboulia is about the process of taking counsel, whereas prudence is principally about commanding (preceptive) the right action.[147] All of the integral parts of prudence affect counsel but are not counsel itself. Despite the distinction between euboulia or good counsel and prudence, euboulia is ordered toward prudence.[148] A further

---

[141]ST II-II, q. 48, a. 1.

[142]III Sent., d. 34, q. 1, a. 2; ibid., d. 35, q. 2, a. 4a; ST I, q. 22, a. 1 ad 1; ST I-II, q. 51, a. 1 and De Vir., q. 5, a. 1.

[143]For the sake of grammatical clarity, the term *euboulia* will be used instead of good counsel.

[144]In Ethic., VI, l. 8 (n. 1218).

[145]ST II-II, q. 47, a. 15, ad 1. The term for "means" is *ea quae sunt ad finem* which indicates that the means is not just the action which helps one attain the ends but also the circumstances which are also used to attain the end. For a lengthy discussion of this, see the author's two-part article, "The Morality of the Exterior Act" as found in the *Angelicum* (LXXVI [1999], pp. 183-220 and LXXVI [1999], pp. 267-410).

[146]III Sent., d. 33, q. 3, a. 1c.

[147]See ST II-II, q. 51, a. 2.

[148]Ibid.

distinction is in order since above it was noted that there are three acts of prudence, viz. counsel, judgment and command. Counsel here is the act of counsel not the virtue. The integral parts of prudence affect counsel but are not the virtues of counsel. Rather counsel is a separate virtue since prudence is more preceptive, i.e. more ordered toward commanding (executing action) than the discursive process of coming to know what should be done.

There are four conditions for euboulia.[149] The first is that it must be about the good. Since euboulia is a virtue and virtue is always about the good, the virtue of good counsel must always concern the good and not evil. Once evil enters the process of counsel as real means, it ceases being an act of euboulia.[150] Directees must realize that their counsel about what to do must be about what is morally upright and mentally healthy; otherwise they will not take good counsel. For psychologists, the virtue of counsel is necessary for them to be a good psychologist. While they may have the acquired virtue of euboulia, the infused virtue of euboulia is more efficacious at finding the right means and about having a means ordered toward the supernatural end of man. The same applies to the virtue of prudence. Since prudence is about commanding the right actions, the psychologist must have at least the acquired virtue of euboulia but preferably the infused virtue of euboulia. Again, this is why the moral character of the psychologist has a direct bearing on his counseling of directees, since it affects the interior process of taking counsel in the psychologist himself.

The second condition for euboulia is that it must proceed from a true syllogism to arrive at the means to the end. It was noted above that the integral parts of prudence and prudence itself deal with drawing a practical conclusion from a universal premise and a particular premise. A false syllogism will not follow logical rules and is therefore contrary to right reason. If it is contrary to right reason, it cannot be part of the virtue of good counsel which lies in the practical intellect as a subject. While it is true that sometimes people will stumble upon the right or even prudent thing to do from bad reasoning, nevertheless the bad reasoning itself is not a good form of counsel. Since many directees suffer from problems which affect the integral part of prudence of reason, they will be affected in their process of taking counsel for the same reasons. Likewise, all observations made about psychologists in relation to those integral parts which would affect the judgment of prudence will likewise affect the process of taking counsel.

The third condition for euboulia to be present is that euboulia attends to that which is useful to the end to which a man ought to strive and according to a due mode and time. What this essentially means is that the virtue of good counsel considers (1)

---

[149]These are taken from In Ethic., VI, l. 8 (nn. 1228-1233).

[150]This is why St. Thomas observes that euboulia is not found in sinners, since every sin is against good counsel; see ST II-II, q. 51, a. 1, ad 3. By sinners here is meant those in the state of mortal sin. While the natural virtue of euboulia may be in sinners, even if at times it is not employed, the infused virtue of euboulia is not since one must be in the state of grace to have any of the infused virtues. That euboulia may be infused, see ibid., ad 1.

whether the action suits the end, (2) whether the circumstances fit the action and (3) whether the circumstances fit the end. Due mode and time are circumstances and so euboulia makes use of circumspection in order to reason properly about the means.

The fourth condition for euboulia is that it must be directed to the good of the whole human life. It is not enough for the action to be good here and now without any reference to it being good for the person's whole life. A certain context must be kept intellectually to make sure that what the person may do in the concrete circumstances fits into a perspective which takes into account the effect this action will have on the person's entire life. It is not enough to satisfy oneself here and now, but one must look to see how this will affect one's whole life which means how it will affect the achievement of his final end. Committing a mortal sin might help one save his home, but if the person dies before he gets to confession, the action was exceptionally imprudent.[151]

Obviously, a psychologist must excel at this virtue, taking into consideration all four conditions. A psychologist who placates the directee or solves short-term problems but aggravates things in the long run is not very prudent. The psychologist must excel at this virtue since this virtue along with prudence is the very foundation of his practice.

2. Synesis

Synesis[152] is a potential part[153] of prudence in which one judges those things which fall under and are according to the common law.[154] There are certain things which happen to a person that, when a person contemplates a course of action, he realizes that the judgment of the means falls under normal precepts, e.g. if he drives off in another man's automobile he knows that it falls under the precept of "though shalt not steal." Synesis judges the means and not the end.[155] There are three acts related to prudence, viz. counsel, judgment (of the means) and command.[156] The act of counsel is affected by the integral parts of prudence as well as the virtue of counsel. The act of judgment of the means[157] is affected by the integral parts of prudence as well as by the virtue of

---

[151]It would be imprudent based purely on the fact that it offends God.

[152]There is no English correlating term to synesis. Most moralists simply use the term directly in English without any modification.

[153]ST II-II, q. 48, a. 1.

[154]III Sent., d. 33, q. 3, a. 1c, ad 3; ST I-II, q. 57, a. 6, ad 3; ST II-II, q. 48, a. 1; ibid., q. 51, a. 4 and ibid., ad 4. See also III Sent., d. 35, q. 2, a. 4b, ad 3.

[155]ST II-II, q. 51, a. 3, ad 1.

[156]These are three acts of the intellect which deal with the means regarding the decision-making process as delineated in volume one, chapter seven.

[157]It should be recalled in volume one that judgment of the means is a different act of the intellect in the decision-making process than judgment of the end.

synesis when the action falls under the common law.

St. Thomas notes that synesis helps one to grasp things as they are[158] and gives one a right judgment about the means.[159] For this reason, Deferrari defines synesis as "the virtue of common sense in practical affairs, i.e. the habit of judging rightly about the practical individual cases according to the customary rules of life."[160] We have noted that those who are mentally ill do not have contact with reality. For that reason they cannot be expected to judge according to synesis in relation to the object or objects of their mental illness. This is why counsel is needed from the psychologist, and later follow up meetings may be necessary, to see if the directee has judged rightly based upon the counsel of the psychologist in the living of the directee's life. If the directee did not judge rightly, the psychologist can help him to see what would have been the better course of action so that the directee can learn what to do in the future. For the psychologist, he should have the ability to judge according to common laws and principles, and if he cannot, he should not be counseling others.

3. Gnome

Gnome[161] is a potential part in relation to prudence and it is the virtue which judges of those things which recede from the common law.[162] Deferrari defines it as an "aptitude[163] or ability to judge rightly over the extraordinary things of life."[164] Sometimes it happens to a person that the circumstances in which he finds himself are out of the ordinary and not common and so the virtue of gnome helps him to judge what to do according to "higher principles."[165] In *Prima Secundae*, St. Thomas indicates that the higher principles are the natural law itself.[166] This means that in order to exercise the virtue of gnome, a person has to have knowledge not just of general precepts, such as "thou shalt not steal" but about the very structure of human nature and the application of the natural law in concrete circumstances. If a man has a knowledge of the three

---

[158]ST II-II, q. 51, a. 3, ad 1.

[159]ST I, q. 22, a. 1, ad 1. See also ST II-II, q. 60, a. 1, ad 1.

[160]Deferrari in *A Latin-English Dictionary of St. Thomas*, p. 1026. In the same entry in Deferrari, he observes that synesis is better than euboulia since the right judgment about the best means is better than taking counsel about all of the possible means.

[161]Like synesis, there is no English correlating term to gnome. Most moralists simply use the term directly in English without any modification.

[162]ST I-II, q. 57, a. 6, ad 3; ST II-II, q. 51, a. 4 and ST II-II, q. 80, a. 1, ad 4. See also De Vir., q. 5, a. 1.

[163]Gnome implies a certain perspicacity of judgment, see ST II-II, q. 51, a. 4 and ibid., ad 3.

[164]Deferrari in *A Latin-English Dictionary of St. Thomas*, p. 443.

[165]ST II-II, q. 51, a. 4.

[166]ST I-II, q. 57, a. 6, ad 3.

categories of natural inclination and what falls under each category, he will have the ability to know what should be done in extraordinary circumstances. On the other hand, some who are very bright may have a decent grasp of human nature (and therefore what suits it, i.e. the natural law) and know what to do in extraordinary circumstances.

While most of what a psychologist will deal with falls under the common law or common principles, there are times when directees will reveal circumstances or interior states which are out of the ordinary. Formal training in a Thomistic psychology will greatly aid the psychologist in acting according to the virtue of gnome. Yet, the psychologist needs a certain intelligence to be able to develop this virtue so that he can make use of it when necessary. If the psychologist has not developed this virtue very highly or would prefer not to counsel directees with extraordinary circumstances or problems, he should refer the directee to someone who is known for being able to discern and counsel difficult and extraordinary cases.

D. Vices contrary to Prudence

In order to get a more rounded view of prudence and its application in the work of a psychologist, it would behoove the discussion to consider vices into which people fall which are contrary to prudence. Since most directees suffer from imprudence and its associated vices, this is not a fruitless endeavor. Moreover, it will set the virtues in greater relief so that the subsequent chapters on counseling and diagnosis can be more easily grasped.

1. Precipitation

Imprudence has four species, viz. precipitation, inconsideration, inconstancy and negligence.[167] The first species of imprudence is precipitation and some discussion has already been afforded in volume one, chapter nine. It was observed that counsel is about the means. The passion of lust precipitates or destroys counsel[168] and so one is unable to "rule," insofar as to rule implies guiding something to an end. When someone lacks counsel, he is affected in his ability to discern the various means he could employ to arrive at his proper end. In the first volume, it was observed that this is why many directees have difficulty in knowing how to free themselves from the mental illness or how to do those things which contribute to a person's living a normal daily life. Their passions are destroying their ability to judge what to do.

Precipitation, then, is a defect of counsel[169] in which one does not take adequate counsel or the act of counsel fails due to passion clouding the judgment of reason. Precipitation is a failing in one or more of the following areas.[170] It is a failing in

---

[167]Prummer, *Manuale Theologiae Moralis*, vol. 1, p. 460.

[168]ST II-II, q. 53, aa. 2 and 6 and ibid., q. 53, a. 3, ad 3.

[169]ST II-II, q. 53, aa. 2 and 5.

[170]See ST II-II, q. 53, a. 2.

docility when the person's judgment is affected in such a way that he does not take counsel from another when he should. Sometimes precipitation is caused by passions other than lust, e.g. fear, as when a directee, due to shame about his problem, fears discussing it with the psychologist. The psychologist must encourage the directee to be "transparent," i.e. to be completely open and bring his problems to the psychologist. If the directee is unwilling to take counsel, for whatever reason, he is like the person who has a wound but will not let the doctor examine him in order that he may be healed. As for the psychologist, he must likewise have a certain docility in two respects. First, he must be willing to take counsel with other trained personnel. If he has pride or some other vice, precipitation will cause him not to take counsel and he will be prone to jumping to conclusions about the directee. Second, the psychologist must also *listen* to the directee. Docility plays a role here insofar as the psychologist must be willing to following the directee's explanation of his problem in order for the psychologist to know the truth about his problem. Sometimes psychologists will have some success with one form of counseling and so the psychologist counsels every directee in that form of counseling whether he needs it or not because the psychologist does not listen to the directee to be able to take proper counsel about what to advise the directee to do.

Precipitation may also be due to a failure in memory. Sometimes passions bind the various faculties and so the faculty of memory and the cogitative power cannot recall those things which would affect one's judgment. For instance, an alcoholic would be precipitous if, when he saw a bottle of wine, he immediately began trying to open it without remembering the bad experiences he has had when he has gotten drunk. This is why directees will often be imprudent because they will not take counsel due to the fixation which prevents them from remembering those things necessary to help them to think a situation through. The psychologist must keep track of what the directee has told him as well as his past experience, so that through a proper act of memory, he can recall what is necessary to discern what the directee should do.

Precipitation may also be due to a failure in reason. Since the soul is held bound by passions, fixations and the like, the directee will not be able to make the acts of ratiocination in order to recognize what he should do. He simply will not reason well. Someone who is precipitous lacks one of the virtues or integral parts of prudence: reason, memory or docility. This is why sometimes the psychologist must slow the directee down, get his mind off the object of mental illness and lead the directee through proper acts of intellectual consideration in order for the directee to build memory, docility and reason. Above, we talked about the practical syllogism and how without the integral part of prudence of reason, one could not arrive at a proper conclusion, i.e. knowledge of what to do. Those who suffer from the vice of precipitation will find the reasoning process difficult and they will often draw the wrong conclusions because their judgment is affected by their mental illness. As for the psychologist, he will find that if he is mentally ill himself or if he suffers from disordered passions, he will not be able to reason well about the directee and what he should do.

In order to overcome the vice of precipitation, one must discern where the failing lies. Does it lie in a lack of memory, docility, reasoning or a combination thereof? He can begin working on trying to remember things from the past when he comes into contact with the object of his mental illness. He can slow down and reason rather than hastily jumping to conclusions about what he should do. He can begin doing all of those things which affect the appetites and the various faculties as has been suggested throughout this series in relation to his particular difficulty.

St. Thomas' discussion of precipitation helps us to see how the counseling process must proceed, but also how it can go awry:

> The grades of the means, through which it is necessary to descend ordinately, are memory of the past, understanding of the present, quickness in considering future events, reason in conferring one with another, docility through which someone acquiesces to the opinion of a superior (*maior*), through which grade someone ordinately descends through right counsel. If someone is carried off to acting by the impetus of the will or passion, passing through these grades, there will be precipitation. Since, therefore, disordered counsel pertains to imprudence, it is manifest that the vice of precipitation is contained under imprudence.[171]

In order for a person to act prudently, there has to be a specific series of steps taken through the counseling process, otherwise the person will end up acting imprudently and this applies both to the directee and the psychologist.

2. Inconsideration

Inconsideration was likewise discussed in the same aforementioned volume. It was noted that lust causes inconsideration. In the decision making process, following the act of counsel, the intellect makes an act of judgment over which means is best. When the intellect is affected by passion, one does not consider the various means and tends to act hastily without consideration of what one is doing or is to do. Inconsideration, sometimes called thoughtlessness, is a defect of and contrary to right judgment which takes away synesis and gnome. In other words, the person is not able to discern matters in regard to whether they be according to the common law or are extraordinary. Inconsideration causes one to lack caution and circumspection. Inconsideration rejects and neglects to attend to those things which proceed from right reason. Passion which causes inconsideration also destroys the ability of the intellect to know the particular as it pertains to or falls under the universal. It destroys one's ability to judge when a universal principle applies in a given set of circumstances.

---

[171]ST II-II, q. 53, a. 3: "Gradus autem medii, per quos oportet ordinate descendere, sunt memoria praeteritorum, intelligentia praesentium, solertia in considerandis futuris eventibus, ratiocinatio conferens unum alteri, docilitas, per quam aliquis acquiescit sententiis maiorum, per quos quidem gradus aliquis ordinate descendit recte consiliando. Si quis autem feratur ad agendum per impetum voluntatis vel passionis, pertransitis huiusmodi gradibus, erit praecipitatio. Sum ergo inordinatio consilii ad imprudentiam pertineat, manifestum est quod vitium praecipitationis sub imprudentia continetur."

All of these observations apply, *mutatis mutandis* to mental illness, which we have noted throughout this chapter. Even if they manage to take counsel, directees will often be affected in their judgment about what is the best thing to do. The vice of inconsideration makes it difficult for the directee to apply universal principles in the concrete. Thoughtlessness and hastiness of judgment have to be rectified which can only be done when the directee strives to be more reflective, less passionate and less fixated on the object of his mental illness. We also see why, if a psychologist is not mentally healthy and not a virtuous man, his counseling of directees will pose difficulties. His interior process of counsel will be affected by his own mental problems and vices, making him a bit hasty in his judgments. He will not give due consideration to circumstances or the particularities of the directee's situation and his application of general psychological principles will be done poorly at best.

3. Inconstancy

In the first volume in relation to inconstancy, it was observed that when someone suffers passion, he is unable to carry out the command of reason.[172] For example, in a time of war, a soldier may properly counsel and judge what should be done in a given battle and decide to do it, but then fear can take over and he does not command himself to do what he has chosen and thought should be done. This defect is called inconstancy in that one commands something[173] but is unable to carry it out.[174] Often it indicates a commanding of something to be done at one moment, but then later changing one's mind or not carrying through due to the strength of the passion.[175] This defect indicates that one is unable to carry out universal precepts in the particular. Even if one reasons or counsels rightly and makes the right judgment about what to do, if the passion is strong, it can cause the intellect to be inconstant in its command about carrying out the chosen action. Often what occurs is that someone knows that something is good or bad, judging it rightly in a given situation, but is unable to carry out what is necessary to fulfill the precept regarding the good or bad action. In the first volume, we also noted that this often leads to justification in which reason is weak in fulfilling the precept and so one seeks to exculpate himself even to the point of rejecting the precept. Passion causes inconstancy because reason commands one thing, but then judges another subsequent to the command. Since the passion is affecting the judgment, the intellect changes or is unable to carry out the original command.

These observations would also apply to those laboring under various forms of

---

[172]Inconstancy is when one fails to command that which he has counseled and judged; see ST II-II, q. 53, a 5.

[173]This is why St. Thomas says it is contrary to the preceptive aspect of prudence; see ST II-II, q. 53, a. 2.

[174]St. Thomas notes that inconstancy implies a certain recession from an infinite proposed good; see ST II-II, q. 53, a. 5.

[175]ST II-II, q. 53, a. 5, ad 2.

mental illness. St. Thomas says that one recedes from a prior proposed good because something disordered pleases him.[176] This applies not only to passions but also to mental illness. On occasion, we have mentioned that there is a mechanism by which one derives a certain pleasure when something arises according to his disposition. This is why many directees are inconstant. Sometimes they cannot face the object of their mental illness and they shrink from suffering. On the other hand, in those cases where the mental illness involves fear and flight (in modern circles called avoidance) the person gets a pleasure from the complicity of not facing the object, i.e. pleasure arises out of the security of being away from the object.

Inconstancy is one reason why psychologists must have a certain fatherly dimension to them.[177] In addition to counseling the directee properly, they must be able to encourage the directee to face his difficulties and to do the right thing. In fact, sometimes the directee is able to be constant, even when he has inclinations from the vice of inconstancy, because he is able to rely psychologically on the fortitude of the psychologist. Since we have confidence either in ourselves or in others who can help us, preserve us from danger and fortify us, the directee will often do the right thing because the psychologist stands by him. Even if the psychologist is not physically present, the directee can remember the psychologist's counsel and his encouragement. Sometimes the directee will do the right thing because it is less painful than having to face his psychologist with the weight of failure on his shoulders.

Since it pertains to reason to command, inconstancy is a defect of reason[178] and it pertains to imprudence.[179] Since it pertains to a defect of reason, inconstancy pertains to defects in some of the cognitive parts of prudence. Inconstancy can arise due to improvidence,[180] e.g. a young man gets the courage up to ask his girlfriend to marry him, but when he arrives to ask her, he finds that she is in a discussion with her parents who are insisting she not get married at this time. As a result, he backs away from asking her because of fear of rejection due to the unforeseen circumstance of her parents discouraging her.

Inconstancy can arise out of a defect of understanding (*defectus intelligentiae*). Understanding is the integral part by which the person grasps the present situation and if he fails to grasp it, he may not command something to be done because he will change his mind once he realizes that his counseled and chosen means will not work. Inconstancy can arise out of a defect of shrewdness (*solertia*). Sometimes the person is

---

[176]ST II-II, q. 53, a. 5.

[177]The dynamics of gender in counseling have direct import. However, because of the complexity of that issue, it will not be addressed here, since it would require much too lengthy of an explanation.

[178]ST II-II, q. 53, a. 5.

[179]Ibid.

[180]The discussion of theses defects can be seen in ST II-II, q. 53, a. 2. While the names of the defects are given here, the defects are opposed to the obvious integral parts as named above. These defects in relation to inconstancy also apply to the vice of negligence.

not quick enough to grasp the means which will really achieve the end, choosing instead a different means which later he recognizes will not work. Since inconstancy arises out of defects in the cognitive parts of prudence, the psychologist should not be surprised when the directee is inconstant, not out of any moral weakness as such, which can also occur, but out of an inability of reason to function properly due to the mental illness.

4. Negligence

Negligence is the last of the four species of imprudence and it implies a defect of due solicitude.[181] Negligence consists in a defect of an interior act which pertains to election[182] and the effect of negligence is omission.[183] Negligence occurs when someone does not choose to command an act which he should and so negligence, while pertaining to choice, is also about the act of commanding.[184] Negligence manifests a defect in which a person lacks a prompt will[185] to do what is right. Above, it was noted that the third opposite to the virtue of memory is the vice of negligence, which occurs when someone chooses not to remember, when he should do so. So negligence can include not only failing to command exterior acts, but also failing to command oneself to remember.

A directee may simply choose not to do the right thing out of the vice of negligence. The psychologist must encourage him to do the right thing and if he refuses, then the psychologist should indicate to the directee that he cannot continue as his directee unless he is willing to do what is necessary to overcome his mental illness. The psychologist must also be careful not to be negligent. Sometimes a psychologist is negligent, since to do the right thing for the directee would require a certain amount of suffering and self-denial. Sometimes a psychologist may be negligent in order to dismiss the directee quickly and not really deal with his problems. Both need a promptness of will if they are going to achieve mental health for the directee.

5. Carnal Prudence

Prudence is the virtue by which one commands a good means to a good end. But sometimes people enter into deliberation about means which are not morally good. Carnal prudence is a vice in which the good of the flesh is seen as the end of one's life,[186] and so one sets about deliberating on the means to satisfy the flesh. Carnal

---

[181]ST II-II, q. 54, a. 1. In ibid., a. 2, St. Thomas says that negligence is opposed to solicitude.

[182]ST II-II, q. 54, a. 2.

[183]Ibid.

[184]Ibid.

[185]Ibid.

[186]ST II-II, q. 55, a. 1.

prudence disorders a man with respect to his final end;[187] for carnal prudence does not order man's actions to God, Who is man's true final end, but to some created good, more often than, not the good of the flesh.

> The flesh is for the sake of the soul as matter is for the sake of form and the instrument for the sake of the principal agent. And therefore one licitly loves the flesh as ordered toward the good of the soul as an end. If, however, the ultimate end is constituted in the very flesh, the love will be disordered and illicit. And in this way carnal prudence is ordered toward love of the flesh.[188]

One employs carnal prudence when he directs his means to the flesh as if it were the final end of his life, i.e. if he thinks his happiness consists in the flesh or some created good. Prummer observes that carnal prudence is one in which "a suitable means is deliberated unto living according to the flesh or according to corrupt human nature, or even that which has the flesh as the ultimate end."[189] St. Paul observed that true prudence is subject to the law of God whereas carnal prudence cannot please God,[190] because it employs immoral means to attain its end.

Those who suffer from mental illness will often fall into carnal prudence because their mental illness becomes so encompassing that they are unable to deliberate about means which are not ordered toward some created good in a disordered way. Those who are mentally ill are often mentally ill because they are employing immoral actions to attain some delight or to avoid some evil and as a result their psychological faculties are affected thereby. Directees must be counseled to take a more spiritual approach to their mental illness, which is why the sacred and other spiritual causes have to be known by the psychologist, so he can counsel the directee to pursue spiritual as well as natural means that are truly good to overcome his problems.[191]

Psychological "therapies" which employ immoral means to an end can never attain true mental health, since mental health is that which is in congruity with the natural

---

[187]Ibid.

[188]Ibid., ad 2: "Caro est propter animam sicut materia propter formam et instrumentum propter principale agens. Et ideo sic licite diligitur caro ut ordinetur ad bonum animae sicut ad finem. Si autem in ipso bono carnis constituatur ultimus finis, erit inordinata et illicita dilectio. Et hoc modo ad amorem carnis ordinatur prudentia carnis."

[189]Prummer, *Manuale Theologiae Moralis*, vol. 1, p. 461: "excogitat media idonea ad vivendum secundum carnem seu secundum corruptam naturam humanam, vel etiam quae habet bona carnis ut ultimatum finem vitae."

[190]Romans 8:6-8.

[191]For example, the teaching of detachment is helpful because one can have a perfect attachment to God and not to the created object of his mental illness. Use of Confession and the like are means which can often break the directee from looking at his problem from a purely natural point of view.

law. Immoral means are never in congruity with the natural law.[192] Yet, it can be cogently argued that modern psychology in its methods and views about man has been a trip down carnal prudence lane. Some of the "fathers" of modern psychology had serious moral problems and their counseling techniques engendered those very disorders.[193] The fact that many modern psychological counseling techniques involve encouraging the "patient" to give in to his sexual desires and begin expressing them, as well as the counseling of out and out sexual immorality such as masturbation, homosexual relations[194] and the like, manifests that the "prudence" in many modern psychological schools is nothing short of carnal prudence. Moreover, the fact that modern psychology is often bereft of any sound understanding of philosophical and theological anthropology and engages in counseling without a clear understanding of human nature is often motivated by carnal prudence, such as the desire to fulfill the counselor's feelings of helping people, and simply listening to the directee, without suggesting any true course of action or without confronting the directee in charitable and prudent ways, in order to make the directee feel better.

Some psychologists are driven by human respect and pride which are the works of the flesh. Sound theological teaching has often been discouraged among modern psychologists and the open anti-theism among some of the founding "fathers" of the psychology is a sign that they will not counsel means for the directee to reach his true final end (God), but rather some carnal end. Also, the fact that empiricism has dominated modern psychology binds its methodology to carnal prudence. That many employing the empirical approach deny or ignore anything above and beyond the physical means that all methodology and counseling will not be ordered toward the proper functioning of the spiritual faculties of the soul and will not fall under an ordering of the actions of the directee to God and His precepts. Hence, it is at this point that the crossroads of modern psychology can be clearly evaluated. When in history modern psychologists deviated from the path of rational psychology to pursue a purely empiricistic approach to man and his psychological well-being, they manifested and continue to manifest the dominance of carnal prudence in modern psychology.

---

[192]For instance, some counselors using reparative therapy to help homosexuals overcome their sexual disorder will encourage them to entertain impure thoughts about women to aid the change to a heterosexual orientation. However, entertaining impure thoughts develops the vice of lack of custody of the mind and is contrary to the natural and divine positive laws. Therefore, it should be strictly forbidden and must not be used.

[193]E. Michael Jones' works, such as *Degenerate Moderns* and *Libido Dominandi,* have cogently argued this point.

[194]The very fact that homosexuality was removed from the DSM IV is a clear sign of carnal prudence governing modern psychology.

6. Craftiness (*Astutia*)

Craftiness, sometimes called cunning, slyness or subtlety,[195] is the vice which inclines one to come to an end, either good or bad, by not using true or good means, i.e. means which are simulated[196] or apparent.[197] Craftiness is like solicitude because care is taken when considering the means but not in a true way.[198] Craftiness is executed through guile and fraud and is against the Christian virtue of simplicity.[199]

Many directees will be astute in the sense that they may be intelligent and able to deliberate about ways of fulfilling the inclinations of their mental illness. But the directee must be taught not to use illicit means. In their practice, psychologists must realize that ends do not justify the means[200] and, therefore, they must be sure to use only good means (morally and psychologically good) to achieve the end of mental health for their directees. Mental health achieved by illicit means is not true mental health since it involves some falsity in the means and will therefore have some bad psychological effects on the directee.

7. Guile (*Dolus*)

As mentioned, guile is the vice by which craftiness is executed.[201] Deception is principally done by words and so guile is mostly attributed to speech[202] although it can

---

[195]Deferrari in *A Latin-English Dictionary of St. Thomas* (p. 97). The term "astuteness" in English is avoided, since in English this term normally has a positive connotation in which the person has an acute intelligence.

[196]Simulation is the sin in which one does something in order to deceive someone else. Like lying which is the saying of the false in order to deceive (see ST II-II, q. 110), simulation is when one *does* (not necessarily says) something in order to deceive, e.g. if someone asks a question and one gives a gesture which deceives the person, like pointing in the wrong direction or something of this sort, then one commits simulation. For a discussion of the sin of simulation, see ST II-II, q. 111.

[197]ST II-II, q. 55, a. 3; ibid., ad 2; and ST II-II, q. 111, q. 3, ad 2. Here the term "apparent" indicates that it is a means that appears good but is, in fact, morally bad.

[198]See ST II-II, q. 55, a. 3.

[199]Prummer, *Manuale Theologiae Moralis*, vol. 1, p. 461f.

[200]This is based upon the Pseudo-Dionysian principal of the integral good, which states: "Bonum est ex integra causa, malum ex quocumque defectu." (The good is from an integral cause, evil from any defect whatsoever.) If in a moral act any of the fonts of the act are bad (the object, the end or the circumstances), the whole action becomes bad in the process. Therefore, the moral principle that the ends do not justify the means is based upon the metaphysical principle of the integral good. This is one of the reasons why ethics cannot be separated from metaphysics.

[201]ST II-II, q. 55, a. 4.

[202]Ibid., ad 2.

also be by deeds. Guile is the vice in which the person is deceptive through words which are the means by which he achieves his end. Some directees will suffer from guile, not necessarily out of malice but out of a certain compulsion arising from their mental illness. Psychologists may even observe guile in their directees who seek to manipulate the psychologist in order to get out of him what they want. The virtue of veracity[203] is essential for the directee, but also the virtue of simplicity. This means that the directee cannot be duplicitous, but must be straightforward and have a certain transparency before the psychologist. Once guile enters the picture, the directee ceases being docile because he is not really trying to arrive at the truth, since this requires him to be honest and straightforward with the psychologist.

The vice of guile is not always restricted to the psychologist in relation to the directee. If the mental illness is known by the directee's family or those around him, he may resort to craftiness and guile in order to continue in his mental illness, e.g. if the end is to achieve better family relations, he may be more crafty in hiding his true feelings, intentions or actions in order to avoid "getting caught." Again, simplicity, the virtue by which the person manifests himself as he is and does not use bad means to attain a good end or does not appear one way when he is truly another, is the virtue for which the directee must strive. He needs to do so in order that others may help him and so that his psychological faculties can be rightly ordered.

H. Fraud (*Fraus*)

Fraud is the vice in which one is deceptive more by deeds than by words. The execution of *astutia* by deeds[204] is more proper to fraud than guile, which is by words and deeds but more principally words. The same observations apply to fraud as to guile. Psychologists will note that some directees, especially those inclined toward loquaciousness, will be inclined toward guile more than fraud, while other directees will be inclined more toward fraud.

Conclusion

Since psychology, in its practice, must be about the virtue of prudence, a clear discussion of prudence has been necessary. It should be clear from this chapter that the principal virtue which the psychologist must employ in his practice is prudence. But prudence cannot be separated from the universal principles of human ontology. In order to counsel properly, therefore, the psychologist must first know the universal principles of human nature and all of the categories of causes of mental health and illness.[205] Second, the psychologist must know which moral or practical virtue helps him to apply

---

[203]Regarding the nature of the virtue of veracity, see ST II-II, q. 109.

[204]ST II-II, q. 55, a. 4. See also Prummer, *Manuale Theologiae Moralis*, vol. 1, p. 462.

[205]This was discussed in volumes one, two and part of this volume.

the universal principles in the concrete, viz. prudence. Now it is necessary to discuss two stages in the process of counseling, viz. diagnosis which is the cognitive aspect of knowing what to tell the directee and the counseling itself, which is the preceptive aspect of counseling.

Chapter 2: Diagnosis

When diagnosing or trying to discover the particular problem or problems of a directee, there are some general principles to keep in mind. While it simply is not possible to explore every aspect of diagnosis, particularly of the specific mental illnesses, a general outline can be delineated regarding the categories necessary to keep in mind in order to make a proper diagnosis. The finality of the diagnosis is to acquire particular knowledge of the directee and his circumstances so that a prudential course of action can be counseled by the psychologist. When diagnosing, the psychologist may not follow these logical steps which will be laid out through this chapter. In fact, in most cases, he will not do so, since he should be sufficiently proficient at diagnosing most mental illnesses or difficulties quickly. However, the steps are laid out here systematically for the sake of a proper treatment as well as to provide an outline for the psychologist if he discovers a particularly difficult case to diagnose.

A. First Distinction - General Categories of People Seeking Advice

When a person enters the office of a psychologist or talks to him outside of his office, there are three possibilities about what the person is seeking. The first is that the person may be seeking knowledge about psychology itself in order to know how to avoid certain mental illnesses, i.e. he is seeking preventative advice. For example, if a soldier is going to war, he may want to know what he can do in order to reduce the psychological stress of war or to avoid certain mental illnesses. In these cases, the information does not address any particular problem of the person since he is simply seeking information. However it may happen that he has slight mental difficulties but they are not too serious and he is not interested in counseling as such but just to know how not to aggravate the difficulties when he goes to war.

The second kind of individual the psychologist will encounter as a professional are those seeking advice about the mental illness of third parties. In this case, the psychologist must listen to the problem and then diagnose as best he can without seeing the person. He should not insist on seeing the person with the mental difficulties since there may be legitimate reasons as to why those seeking advice for the third party do not want to divulge the person's name or identity. In cases where the third party might pose a physical threat to others or to the common good, the psychologist should encourage those seeking advice, if they cannot handle the problem themselves, to make sure they bring the third party either to someone who can help him or to the authorities, not only for the sake of those whom he might hurt, but also for his own benefit.

Diagnosing a third party without seeing him brings to the fore the problem of diagnosing someone through the eyes and perspective of those asking advice. Questions can be asked to clear up certain difficulties in arriving at sufficient information. However, as a general rule, the psychologist should stick to general principles and avoid giving concrete counseling without actually seeing the person. This is for two reasons. The first is that the problem may be more in the people asking for advice about the third party than in the third party himself. Second, the principle of proximity applies. The principle of proximity states that one should not give counseling to someone who is not proximate to him. Proximity or actually being able to see the person and talk to him directly, provides a great deal of information that cannot be gained through talking to someone over the phone or by correspondence. Since diagnosing often requires seeing the person so that the psychologist can observe the expressions of the directee which will reveal certain states of the various faculties, the psychologist should insist on not giving concrete advice without first seeing the directee to know if his advice fits the directee. In prudence, it was discussed that one must know the circumstances in order to know if the action fits the circumstances. The circumstances in this case are the particularities of the directee. Therefore, the psychologist, as a rule, should not give advice to a directee unless he sees him face to face.

Yet, this rule does not apply everywhere and in all cases. Some psychological work may involve dealing with people in distress or people in situations where they are holding others captive and the psychologist will have to talk the person down from the situation without too much knowledge of the person or being able to see him. But these are not the normal counseling situations which require that proximity play a role. Also, once the psychologist knows the directee well by past counseling or in his personal life, it may be possible to give some guidance by correspondence or by telephone, provided that the directee is not asking the psychologist to analyze the circumstances in which the directee finds himself without the psychologist actually knowing the circumstances. If the circumstances are not germane to the discussion, counseling can be given in this case. The third kind of person the psychologist will encounter is one who has a mental illness or illnesses and needs counseling himself.

B. Second Distinction - The General Categories of Causes of Mental Illness

When diagnosing the directee, one must distinguish the possible mental illness into one of the three categories of causes, viz. physical, psychological and preternatural. If the psychologist determines in discussing the problems with the directee or in observing his actions that the problems he is manifesting are preternatural (demonic), he should simply refer the directee to a competent priest and providing the priest with the reasons why he thinks the problem is preternatural. At times, the psychologist may discover supernatural occurrences in the directee or in his circumstances and likewise he should send the directee to a competent priest. Psychologists must have a sufficiently open mind regarding the causes if they are going to arrive at the proper cause. While most of the problems they will encounter will be of a psychological nature, psychologists should not assume that all problems or occurrences in the directee's life are simply natural. On the other hand, due caution has to be taken in diagnosing something to be preternatural or supernatural since some directees may mimic or falsely represent their mental illnesses in order to be judged differently than they truly are. These considerations should manifest why having the theological virtue of faith will greatly aid in making these distinctions in diagnosis.

If the psychologist determines that the problems are physiological in nature, he should direct him to competent medical personnel who will be able to diagnose the problem properly. When they diagnose the problem, they will divide it into chemical, biological, etc. or they may determine that there is no biological factor involved and so the directee should be returned to the psychologist for further diagnosis. The psychiatrists or medical personnel may determine that the problem is physiological but that the problem can be addressed by things such as diet or change of conduct. In the case of diet, they can give the guidance to the directee without any further assistance from the psychologist, unless the dietary restrictions may have some form of psychological impact on the directee other than curing his mental illness or unless they believe that diet plus counseling should be done together. If the problem can be solved by simple conduct, since volitional acts can affect the material disposition of lower faculties, they should refer the directee back to the psychologist or to a psychologist who specializes in the field which pertains to the physiological imbalance. If the problem is determined as principally or strictly psychological, or if the psychologist has certain knowledge that a particular mental illness, while being physiological in nature, is correctable by change in conduct and volition acts, he should proceed to a consideration of the distinctions within mental illnesses themselves and their causes.

C. Third Distinction - Mental Illnesses from an Exterior Cause

When considering exterior causes, one must look to the circumstances in which the directee finds himself. Those circumstances will provide the psychologist with the information necessary in order to counsel a course of action so that the directee can reach mental health (the end). The discussion of prudence in the prior chapter should indicate two aspects of the circumstances that must be considered. The first is the circumstances themselves as in reality and the second is the circumstances insofar as they personally affect the directee, since the same set of circumstances can affect two different people differently. Prudence has to base its judgment on the interior senses of the directee since the effect of the circumstances on the interior senses determines the prudential judgment and course of action for the directee. If a directee is ignoring the circumstances which are affecting him psychologically,[1] he will not be able to come to terms with them. While it is true that sometimes one must turn away from the circumstances through custody of the eyes or custody of the mind, this is not a form of ignoring the circumstances. In fact, it is the exact opposite. The person recognizes the circumstances, judges that they could cause harm and then turns from them to keep them from harming his psychological faculties.

In order to get a better grasp on the circumstances, each category of circumstances shall be discussed in detail and a short discussion of the very nature of

---

[1] This reminds one of Aristotle's line: "Of all of these [circumstances], no one ignores them except the insane." See Aristotle, *Ethics*, I. 3 (1111a7): "" ἐ ὐ ὐ ὐ ἰς ἇ ἁ ´ ἡ ό ς." In relation to this observation, see also In Ethic., III, 1. 3 [417].

circumstances will be provided.[2] This is not without its difficulties due to the fact that there is not always agreement among authors about what the various circumstances are, which is explained by different interpretations of the texts of Saint Thomas. So it will be helpful to sort out the various views in order to have a clearer idea of what they are. St. Thomas defines what he means by circumstances in a multitude of places but they convey the same meaning, viz. something "is called a circumstance which stands around the act, is extrinsic to it, [and is] considered outside the substance of the act."[3] A circumstance is something that plays a role in action or conduct but does not pertain to the substance of the act. This is because it is not considered part of it, i.e. it is considered outside the substance of the act as an accident[4] of it.[5] Although a circumstance is something standing outside the substance of the moral act, it should be noted that it is part of the moral act. In other words, like an accident in natural things, it does not differentiate the substance or essence of the thing, but is a modification of the substance. By "modification" is clearly meant that it does not change the essence of the act but somehow affects the act's morality. In the context of psychology, we may say that the circumstances affect the individual's perception of his concrete situation, which in turn affects how he acts in the context of those circumstances. So his action must be analyzed as something distinct from the circumstances to see if what he is doing fits his circumstances as well as to see if he has the right perception of his circumstances. His conduct will flow from his mental health or illness, which affects his perception of the circumstances.

There are basically three ways circumstances affect a human act's morality and we may say three ways in which they relate to consideration of the conduct of the directee and his perceptions.

> A circumstance is related in three ways to an act of sin. For sometimes it neither varies the species nor aggravates it, as to hit a man dressed in white or red clothes. Sometimes, indeed, it constitutes the species of the sin, either when the act, to which the circumstance relates, is from its genus indifferent, as when someone lifts a straw from the earth in contempt of another, or when [the act] is good from its genus, as when someone gives alms for the sake of human praise, or when [the act] is bad in its genus and it adds to it some other species of evil from the circumstance, as when someone steals a sacred thing. Sometimes, indeed, it aggravates the sin, not, however,

---

[2]The section which follows is taken in large part from the author's unpublished doctoral dissertation entitled *The Morality of the Exterior Act in the Writings of St. Thomas Aquinas.*

[3]De Malo, q. 2, a. 6: "dicitur autem circumstantia quod circumstat actum, quasi extrinsecus extra actus substantiam consideratum."

[4]See ST I-II, q. 7, a. 1.

[5]See also ibid., q. 7, aa. 2-3 and ibid., q. 18, a. 3, ad 1 and 2.

constituting the species of sin, as when someone steals much.[6]

The first way a circumstance relates to the act is that it does not affect its morality, i.e. the goodness or badness of the act, in any way whatsoever. St. Thomas gives the example of hitting a man in white or red clothes, for it is irrelevant if the man is wearing red or white clothes.

In the context of psychology, this indicates that some circumstances of the directee will not have any import whatsoever. A prudent psychologist will be able to determine quickly which circumstances are important in themselves and which are not, as well as which circumstances are affecting the directee and which are not. This is why prudence is so important for the psychologist, as mentioned in the prior chapter. He must be able to assess circumstances, which requires prudential judgment. Without prudence, he will err in judging the relevant circumstances. Moreover, he must have a certain quickness of mind to be able to read the circumstances quickly without laboring over them too much. Those circumstances which have no import are called indifferent circumstances.[7]

It is very common for the directee to feel the need to present many circumstances in order that the psychologist or counselor might understand his problem, even though many of the things are not necessary for his understanding *per se*. This inclination can combine with other qualities of the directee to produce an onslaught of information. The directee may not feel that the psychologist understands him without all of this information. The directee can then fall prey to a distrust of the given counsel and reject it, based on the feeling that the counsel lacked sufficient understanding.

Moreover, there may exist a certain inclination on the side of the directee to be heard, which can easily dominate him, since he receives comfort from the psychologist who listens to what the directee thinks is important. Thus, discretion is important on the part of the psychologist. In the beginning sessions, the psychologist should normally listen more for the directee's sake as well as out of prudence. After the directee feels that the psychologist or counselor understands him, he can help the directee to recognize what things are essential for his understanding and what things are not. In later meetings, the psychologist will need less information from the directee since he already has some context and understanding of the directee. The psychologist should be sure

---

[6]De Malo q. 2, a. 7: "circumstantia tripliciter se habet ad actum peccati. Quandoque enim neque variat speciem neque aggravat, sicut percutere hominem indutum veste alba vel rubea. Quandoque vero speciem peccati constituit, sive actus cui advenit circumstantia ex suo genere indifferens sit, sicut cum aliquis levat festucam de terra in contemptu alterius, sive sit bonus ex genere, sicut cum aliquis dat eleemosynam propter laudem humanam, sive sit malus ex genere et addatur sibi alias species malitiae ex circumstantia, sicut cum aliquis furatur rem sacram. Aliquando vero aggravat quidem peccatum, non tamen constituit peccati speciem, sicut cum aliquis furatur multum."

[7]An initial distinction must be made between what is important morally and what is important psychologically. While most circumstances are important psychology *because* they are important morally, this will not always be the case.

not to allow the directee to give too much information or dominate the discussion.

Another practical problem that is related to circumstances is that the directee will not alert the psychologist as to the point that he is making. The directee may then add more and more circumstantial information to provide the context for understanding his problem. This makes it very difficult for the psychologist to keep everything straight in his own mind since he does not grasp the point of the directee. The "story" may lead in a direction that is quite different than the intended point. Taking notes in these circumstances is critical since the psychologist will be able to review what he wrote in light of the point, once it is revealed. In certain cases, the psychologist may want to use a more direct approach in which he tells the directee to provide him with a topic sentence or his basic point. The psychologist may want to explain to the directee that this is necessary for him to process the information about the circumstances with his point clearly in mind.

The second way the circumstance relates to the moral act is by constituting the species of sin. In the context of psychology, this would be translated from the domain of the moral from constituting the species of the sin to the circumstances which constitute the cause of the mental illness. A psychologist must be able to read whether given circumstances in the life of the directee are causing his mental illness, e.g. a directee may suffer from some mental illness because of his treatment by his parents or the existence of mental illness in the parents themselves.

Finally, a circumstance can aggravate or diminish the goodness or the badness of an act. For instance, if a man were to steal five dollars, that would not be as bad as if he stole a hundred dollars. The species is theft but the amount stolen made it worse in the case of the theft of a hundred dollars. In psychology, this would indicate that some circumstances may not cause the mental illness of the directee but they do aggravate the mental illness or pose occasions for problems for the directee. On the other hand, some circumstances will actually diminish the mental vice of the directee by affecting his perceptions and his subsequent volitional acts. The psychologist and directee must be careful to choose those circumstances of the directee over which he has control so that he can affect his mental health positively.

As to the actual circumstances themselves, we find in the writings of Saint Thomas various listings of the circumstances given by the various authors; but he himself, in his work on *De Malo,* lists seven, viz. who, what, where, by what aid, why, how and when.[8]

1. Who (*Quis*)

The circumstance of "who" (*quis*) refers to the "principle agent"[9] or the one

---

[8] De Malo q. 2, a. 6.

[9] Ibid.: "ex parte agentis principalis, cum consideramus quis fecerit." See also *In Ethic.*, III, c. 4 and ST I-II, q. 7, a. 3.

performing the act, i.e. something attributed to the person.[10] Secondary authors have referred to it as a special quality of the person performing the act[11] and this seems to indicate what Aquinas has in mind. For example, for an unmarried man to fornicate is bad, but if the unmarried man is a cleric, it is worse because he violates the vow of chastity. In this case, the particular state of the man augments the gravity of the act.

In the ambit of psychology, the quality of the directee will play a two-fold role. The first is in relation to his mental illness which is a quality in the directee. The mental illness itself is a circumstance of his conduct. The second is that there may be some particular quality of the directee which has affected his mental health. If the directee accidentally runs over a small child who is no relation to the directee, his psychological trauma is likely to be less, particularly if he is mentally healthy, than if the directee is the child's mother or father. The psychological effect on the directee will be much more drastic and in a different way than on a complete stranger. Sometimes this circumstance is as simple as the quality of the person in relation to someone else, which is connected to the accident of relation but which affects the relation itself. This the psychologist must keep in mind since some directees are affected in their relationships with others because of the quality they may have in themselves, e.g. how a daughter relates to her mother is different from how she relates to her father. Therefore, the psychologist should get a correct read on who the directee is.

Here we see why it is important to know the directee's situation in life and his past history. Even if the history does not relate directly to the psychological problem, a person's past history is carried along with him in memory as a quality of the person. Moral and spiritual uprightness are qualities of the person. Particular roles in life that have been given them or that they have assumed are qualities of the person, such as being a father, a husband, a head of a corporation, etc. Therefore, the psychologist must know the circumstance of "who" in relation to the directee.

2. In What Way or How (*Quomodo vel Qualiter*)

The circumstance of *quomodo* or *qualiter* is sometimes referred to as "how," "in which way" or "in what way." There is essentially no difference between these three ways of referring to this circumstance.[12] This circumstance almost always refers to the way in which the action is performed.[13] However, Aquinas is more specific in his commentary on the *Sentences,* where he says that "since way (*modus*) means measure, everything which pertains to measure either by way of continuous or discrete quantity,

---

[10]IV Sent. d. 16, q. 3, a. 1b: "ex eo quod est attributum personae."

[11]See Fanfani, *De Actibus Humanis*, p. 120; Prummer, *Manuale Theologiae Moralis*, p. 72 and Noldin, *Summa Theologiae Moralis*, p. 73.

[12] The only time Saint Thomas refers to this circumstance as "how" (i.e. *qualiter*) is when he is commenting on Aristotle's *Ethics*. See In Ethic., III, c. 3.

[13]See De Malo, q. 2, a. 6 and ST I-II, q. 7, a. 3.

is meant in 'in what way.'"[14] He assigns this circumstance the job of measuring the quantity of the act. This is what makes it different from *circa quid*,[15] viz. that *quomodo* measures the quality[16] or quantity of the act; whereas *circa quid* measures the quality or quantity of the object or the matter of the exterior act. Moreover, *circa quid* and the circumstance of *quomodo* are different kinds of measuring from another type of measuring alluded to in the moral act, i.e. when and where. *Circa quid* and *quomodo* refer to the measurement of the thing and the act respectively, while the others refers to time and location which are different forms of measuring a given act.

An example of the circumstance of *quomodo* or *how* can be seen in St. Thomas' discussion regarding the question on self-defense.[17] In that article, Aquinas maintained that a due proportion was necessary regarding the "amount" or "quantity" of force taken by the agent and the end for which he sought, i.e. his own well-being. Consequently, when one considers the morality of the act of self-defense, it will be good or bad depending on the quantity or measure of the act itself in relation to its object. So if slapping a man lightly suffices to render him incapacitated, that quantity of force is preferred to killing him.

In the ambit of psychology, how a directee performs his actions tells the psychologist almost as much as the action itself. Since the cause is always in some way in the effect, the various psychological faculties will affect how the exterior action is executed by the directee. Since execution of the action requires intellectual judgment which is founded upon the actions of the interior senses and sensitive appetites, these things will directly affect the directee's execution of certain actions. This is why, again, proximity is so important since it provides knowledge of the circumstance *how* the directee is explaining himself. This is not only in the qualities of the words and the words themselves chosen, but also the body posture and gesticulation. As is sometimes said, it is not so much in *what* people say but in *how* they say it.

This circumstance also provides the psychologist with a great deal of knowledge about the directee when the psychologist observes the reactions of the directee in relation to the object of mental illness. Since the habits of the various psychological faculties will incline the directee to judge and assess and emote in relation to the object in a specific way, those can be known by the psychologist.

3. By What Aid (*Quibus Auxiliis*)

This circumstance is sometimes translated as "means" and although it is part

---

[14]IV Sent., d. 16, q. 3, a. 1b, ad 6: "cum modus mensuram importet, omnia quae ad mensuram pertinent vel per modum quantitatis continuae vel discretae, importantur in quomodo."

[15]Regarding the circumstance of *circa quid*, see below.

[16]See IV Sent., d. 16, q. 3, a. 1b: "quomodo quantum ad qualitatem actus."

[17]See ST II-II, q. 64, a. 7.

of the means, i.e. that which is for the end or the *ea quae sunt ad finem*,[18] it is not the totality of the means. Rather, the means would include the act itself along with all those persons, places and things which helped or entered into the moral act. In other words, the means is the object of election which is the exterior act and all its circumstances. However, in reference to this circumstance, it is better rendered literally, i.e. "by what aid," in order to distinguish it from the means in the sense delineated in the previous chapter.

"By what aid" is a circumstance of the act which is referred to as the instrumental cause or agent of the act.[19] There are, then, two efficient causes of the moral act, viz. the person performing the act and the instruments or "aids" used to obtain the end. For example, a man may decide to kill someone, so he chooses between one of two aids, either a gun to shoot the individual in the back of the head or a slow acting, very painful poison. While killing the other person is seriously wrong, it is even worse when the person drags it out by using something very painful like the aforesaid poison.

In psychology, the import of this circumstance reveals the principles of judgment of the directee. What means he chooses can indicate the state of certain faculties. It can reveal the associations he makes between certain kinds of objects and actions and the various tools or means he can use to obtain his end, so it can reveal the habituation of his cogitative power. Knowledge of this circumstance by the psychologist can indicate to him the state of the passions of the directee, how they are affecting his judgment and what virtues and vices are in the sensitive appetites. For example, if he tends to choose means which hurt people more, this may indicate the degree of his anger. It can also reveal the habits in the possible intellect which affect his judgment about the means to be employed and it can indicate the state of his will, i.e. what the habits are in his will.

4. Where (*Ubi*)

The circumstance of "where" is very easy to explicate, much like the circumstance of "who." "Where" indicates a measure of the act and refers to the location or place in which the act takes place.[20] An example of this would be a married couple who perform the conjugal act in public. While the essence of the act is good, the location is bad, and for this reason the circumstance of "where" renders the act bad.

Another aspect of the circumstance of *where* is not in the manner in which the directee acts, but the manner or quality of action of other people in relation to the directee, since the other people are part of the directee's circumstance of *where*. The psychologist can learn a great deal about how the directee is reacting and whether he is

---

[18]See prior chapter.

[19]See De Malo, q. 2, a. 6; In Ethic. III, c. 4; IV Sent. d. 16, q. 3, a. 1b and ST I-II, q. 7, a. 3.

[20]See De Malo, q. 2, a. 6; In Ethic., III, c. 4; IV Sent., d. 16, q. 3, a. 1b and ST I-II, q. 7, a. 3.

reacting rationally or according to a mental illness based upon whether the reaction fits his circumstances. If people are treating him in a way that warrants the reaction he is having, this can actually be a sign of mental health rather than illness.

This brings us to a case where two circumstances converge,[21] viz. *who* and *where*. One of the qualities of the directee (*who*) is also connected to where, i.e. those to whom he is related and with whom he lives. How much the psychologist should know about the relationships the directee has and their qualities depends on the nature of the mental illness. Some mental illnesses will require detailed knowledge of the relationships he has, e.g. if he suffers from some mental illness which makes him more reclusive such as certain forms of depression. Other mental illnesses will have very little, if any, connection to the relationships which he has since the relationships may not have any connection to the mental illness.

Mental illness is connected to relationships in three ways. The first is that some mental illnesses affect the relationship, i.e. from the directee to those around him, e.g. someone who suffers from extreme problems of anger will vent his anger on others, even though the extreme anger is not caused by these others. The second is when the relationship he has with others is itself the exterior cause of the mental illness, even though others may not be affected by his mental illness. This happens with some directees who tend to suffer silently and try to deal with their problems and not affect other people. The third way in which mental illness and relationships are connected is when the directee affects others and is affected by others, i.e. there exists a mutual causal structure between the mental illness of the directee and others. With children, the predominance of the causes falls upon others rather than the children. Most children, aside from those with material indispositions or who are affected preternaturally, will simply develop somewhat normally having only slight difficulties. This is rooted in the fact that their ability to judge is not yet sufficiently developed in order to develop severe mental illnesses, as was discussed in part one. Yet, they can be affected by others to such a degree that they can develop severe mental illnesses even though they themselves may not affect others as much. While there are times when the mental illness of a child disrupts the family life, aside from cases in which a child with problems is adopted by another family, most children with disruptive mental problems live within a disordered family life. With adults, the connection between mental illness and others will have a predominance normally in one term of the relation, i.e. either the predominant problem is on the side of the others with whom the directee relates or it is more predominate on the side of the directee himself. There are some rare cases in which the directee is both the cause of problems with other people and the people are equally the cause of the directee's mental illness.

When a psychologist can determine the qualities of the relations in which the directee finds himself, the psychologist can discover where the problems or possible causes of the mental illness lie, whether they lie in the relations or not, and then proceed to counsel the directee in two ways. First, if the cause is on the side of others with whom

---

[21]See discussion below regarding when one category of circumstance is also another.

he has relations, he can counsel the directee on how to deal with other people. Second, if it is on the side of the directee, he can work on getting the directee to obtain a proper self-knowledge so that he can recognize his problem and address it.

It is a fact of life that we tend to take personal interest in those whom we counsel, i.e. we want to see them succeed and we want to protect them from harm. However, the psychologist must be sufficiently detached and have sufficient virtue so that he can arrive at the truth regarding the relationships the directee has with others. Only through a lack of antecedent passion can the psychologist see things clearly. If a psychologist's passions and personal interests affect his judgment, he will be more likely to place the blame where it ought not be placed. If he likes the directee and wants him to succeed, he may be more inclined to blame others, when the real problem is with the directee. On the other hand, if he finds the directee annoying and cannot control his judgment in the face of the annoyance, he may have the tendency to blame the directee for things which are not his fault. Clear phantasms are necessary to find the mean where truth lies in relationships which are the cause of the mental illness. This should be a motivation to the psychologist to be detached, not just from the directee, but from the psychologist's own desire for success in relation to helping the directee.

Another aspect of the circumstance of *where* has to do with what has become known in modern psychology as "environment." In order to avoid adopting the exaggerated role environment has taken in relation to issues of psychology and among certain schools of psychology, it would be better to stick to the more ontologically and gnoseologically precise term of "circumstances"[22] or even "where." We have discussed this before, but the surroundings of the directee can affect the assessment of the cogitative power and therefore judgment and mental health. Modern studies, for example, have shown that certain colors can elicit different moods, so the color of one's room at home and things of this sort can affect the person. Behaviorism has wrongly concluded that environment determines everything, but as we have seen, one does have free choice and so one can choose to allow certain colors or one's surroundings in general to affect him or not. With children, surroundings are more important because children are more governed by the assessments of the cogitative power than others. In a society noted for sin,[23] immaturity[24] and mental illness, surroundings are very important. Yet, even in a mentally healthy culture, surroundings are very important because they affect people's judgment. In fact, culture itself is a form of surroundings *where* people are located and therefore it affects them psychologically.[25] For the psychologist to ascertain the circumstances or the surroundings of the directee, i.e. where

---

[22]One may even say the *accidents* of the directee, since circumstances are like accidents.

[23]Surroundings can be the occasion of sin for people.

[24]The immature are those who have not obtained the habit of living their life according to reason, but according to the assessment of the cogitative power and passion.

[25]This is why those in charge of the common good have a grave obligation to keep sin and other things which could affect people's mental health out of the public arena.

he lives, the people with whom he relates, i.e. all of his external accidents, is important in determining the prudential judgment of what the directee should do and therefore the counseling given by the psychologist. We have already discussed some of this in the first volume in relation to exterior causes and since these are virtually infinite, psychology should suffice in determining the categories of these exterior causes so that general principles can be developed in relation to these exterior categories. It is not possible to take into consideration every possible kind of exterior circumstance in which a person may find himself, since they are virtually infinite. Once general principles are known by the psychologist, he will be able to apply those principles in sorting out which circumstances are relevant and which general principles apply in dealing with the particular circumstances.

5. When (*Quando*)

Much like "where" and "who," "when" is very easily explicated and almost self-evident. "When" refers to the time in which the act was performed. [26] An example would be a man who decides to go for a walk at 11:00 PM knowing that there is a curfew at that time. The act of walking is morally indifferent, but the fact that he went for a walk at a prohibited time makes the act bad.

There are some directees who will do repeated actions at certain times each day because of their mental illness. On the other hand, if someone is in a routine in which he does something every day at the same time, it should not be presumed that he has a fixation since it may be the effect of good habit. Sometimes directees will not know *when* to do something and this is rooted in their inability to judge prudently due to confused or uninformed phantasms. Often, learning when to do something is rooted in knowing the nature of the action and the other circumstances which fit that form of action and then when the circumstances come together that suit the action, the directee will know it is time to perform the action. If there is a lack of knowledge or a mental illness which affects knowledge of the action or of the other circumstances, the directee will say things when they are not suited or are out of place. When he does this, the psychologist can ask more about the other circumstances, the nature of the action or even the qualities of the directee to determine where the source of misjudgment lies.

6. Why (*Cur*)

The circumstance of "why" refers to the reason the act was done. Because the end is the reason why the act is done, it would follow that the end is what is referred to with respect to the circumstance of "why."[27] However, there are two ends in human action, viz. the proximate and the remote, and this is why Saint Thomas makes the

---

[26]See De Malo, q. 2, a. 6; In Ethic., III, c. 4; IV Sent., d. 16, q. 3, a. 1b and ST I-II, q. 7, a. 3.

[27]See ST I-II, q. 7, aa. 3 and 4.

following distinction:

> The end is two-fold: the proximate and the remote. The proximate
> end of the act is the same as the object and receives its species from
> it. However, from the remote end it does not have a species; but the
> order to such an end is a circumstance of the act.[28]

The proximate end refers to the object of the moral act or the exterior act from which the interior act of the will of election has its species. Whereas, the circumstance of "why" refers to the remote end which does not pertain to the substance of the act. For instance, the substance of the act in the act of theft for the sake of giving alms is the act of theft, i.e. the act of theft is the proximate end of the will because that is what the person is seeking to do, i.e. to commit theft. Whereas the giving of alms, the reason the theft was committed, does not pertain to the substance of the act but is the circumstance of "why," i.e. the remote end. Moreover, the remote end or the reason why the act was performed pertains to the object of intention, for the end chosen in intention is the cause of the whole act and of the subsequent deliberation about the means in the decision-making process. Therefore, the circumstance of "why" refers to that which is willed in the act of intention. Sometimes the terms *proximate end* and *remote end* refer to the object of intention but in different ways. Sometimes a person may have as his intention to steal a car in order to sell it to get the money. To obtain the money would be a proximate end to stealing the car since that is the first thing the person wants to obtain. But the remote end, i.e. the further reason why he steals, is because he wants to amass wealth so that he can retire young and so a youthful retirement is his remote end.

In the realm of psychology, the circumstance of *why* is highly important. It is the circumstance that reveals the intention or motive of the directee in performing the acts which lead to his mental health or illness. The psychologist can come to a great deal of knowledge about the directee when he knows why he is doing certain things which are exacerbating his mental illness. The act of the will reveals the states of the faculties, not only of the will in which may be *per accidens* mental illness, but also, what is willed is always known first. Therefore, the psychologist can sometimes get to knowledge of the states of the faculties prior to the will when he knows the intention of the directee. Perhaps his appetites have affected his judgment and spurred him on to making these choices. Perhaps prior habituation in the memory, imagination, cogitative power or in the possible intellect have inclined him to judge that he should do something for the reason he has done it. The circumstance of why also reveals how the directee perceives not only his interior states but also exterior circumstances, for often his motives are connected to exterior circumstances or interior states rather than being truly free in which he is not bound by those things.

---

[28]De Malo q. 2, a. 4, ad 9: "duplex est finis: proximus et remotus. Finis proximus actus idem est quod obiectum, et ab hoc recipit speciem. Ex fine autem remoto non habet speciem; sed ordo ad talem finem est circumstantia actus." See also ibid., q. 2, a. 7, ad 8 (versus finem).

Also, the psychologist should seek to be aware of any remote ends to the directee's actions. While a directee may reveal his proximate end for doing certain things, even for gaining mental health, nevertheless his remote end may not be so noble or good. For example, if a directee seeks to become mentally healthy (which is his proximate end), but he does it as a matter of human respect for his parents or even the psychologist, this is not a good reason. The psychologist can sometimes make good use of a bad remote end, but extreme care has to be taken so that no guile or deception occurs on the side of the psychologist in doing so and that no use of illicit means occurs. Sometimes setting up proximate and remote ends for the directee to achieve can motivate the directee to continue to strive for mental health. If he can achieve some proximate end, the directee can be encouraged to seek after some remote end which is more perfect, e.g. if he can try to stay away from some specific thing which is affecting his mental health and start with that, once he achieves that, the psychologist or the directee may judge that the directee is ready to seek to purify his faculties in relation to his mental illness because he has achieved this small goal.

7. What (*Quid*) and About What (*Circa Quid*)

This particular circumstance has become somewhat misunderstood in the recent discussion of it in the moral sphere. For the sake of psychology, it is important that these two circumstances be distinguished so that their psychological implications can be drawn out. For some have claimed that the circumstance of "what" actually refers to the object of the exterior act.[29] Another interpretation mistakes this circumstance for the exterior act itself.[30] It is not certain how this circumstance came to be mistaken for the object of the exterior act and the exterior act itself. But there may be two possible sources of the confusion; the first is that some want to say that the exterior act is actually accidental to the interior act of the will and therefore it can be considered a circumstance to the interior act of the will. The second source may be Saint Thomas himself, because at times he refers to this circumstance in such a way that it may appear that he is not making a distinction between the exterior act and this circumstance. [31] In order to

---

[29]For example, Bernard Häring claims this in his work *The Law of Christ*, (p. 291): "*Quid* (what): this does not really mean a circumstance, but rather the very object of the action. But since a highly diversified and variable relationship exists above all between object and agent, the 'quid' (what) can also be listed among the circumstances under a certain aspect."

[30]Nelson, in *The Priority of Prudence* (p. 42), states: "The relevant circumstances, according to the account Thomas adopts, are really a set of questions one asks about the act: "who, what, where, by what aids, why, how, and when" (q. 7, a. 3). The answers to questions about *who* did the act, *what* act was done, *where* was it done, and so forth, determine the act's moral species. In that respect, the two most important circumstances are *why* and *what was done*, the former because it specifies the end, which is the will's "object and motive," and the latter because it specifies the substance of the act."

[31]For instance see ST I-II, q. 7, a. 3.

respond to the two possible sources of this error, it will be necessary, first to consider the relation of the interior act to the exterior act and, secondly, to delineate clearly this circumstance in order to have a clear idea of what Saint Thomas has in mind regarding it.

Regarding the relationship of the exterior act to the interior act, the following quote from St. Thomas is important:

> And similarly, in the act of the will, the end is the reason for willing that which is to the end; hence the end is desirable even without that which is to the end. . . . The act of the will is related formally to the exterior act, and the exterior act is related not accidentally but materially to such sin.[32]

In this quote, Aquinas says that the exterior act is not related accidentally to the interior act but materially. But he does say elsewhere[33] that the exterior act does not add to the essential goodness or badness of the interior act. Rather, the exterior act only adds an accidental goodness to the interior act. From this, some have drawn the conclusion that the exterior act is accidentally related to the interior act. But this is not so.

In the questions which deal with the problem of the relation of the interior act to the exterior act,[34] Saint Thomas is very careful never to say that the exterior act itself *relates* accidentally to the interior act. Rather, what he does in these questions is first make a distinction between the order of apprehension[35] and the order of execution.[36] He then observes that, in the order of apprehension, the exterior act is the object of apprehension and therefore is the object of volition. That is why he says that it relates materially and not accidentally to the act of the will, i.e. the exterior act is ordered essentially to the interior act of the will. He then notes that when one is talking about the goodness and the badness of acts in the order of execution, the essential moral goodness[37] has already been determined, because the will has already willed the exterior act as its object. Therefore, the exterior act in the order of execution (it is still the object of the will regarding command and use) *adds* an accidental goodness to the interior act of the will. The distinction is brought out by the phraseology, i.e. the exterior act both

---

[32]De Malo q. 2, a. 2, ad 5: "Et similiter in actu voluntatis finis est ratio volendi id quod est ad finem; unde finis est appetibilis etiam sine eo quod est ad finem. . . . Actus voluntatis se habet ut formale ad actum exteriorem, et actus exterior se habet non accidentaliter sed materialiter ad tale peccatum."

[33]For example, see II Sent., d. 40, q. 1, a. 3.

[34]That is, ibid.; De Malo q. 2, aa. 2 & 3; ST I-II, q. 20, aa. 3 & 4.

[35]The order of apprehension is the process by which the person comes to know the proposed course of action that he may carry out.

[36]The order of execution is the actual process by which one executes or performs the action grasped and chosen in the order of apprehension.

[37]Or we may even say the psychological goodness.

in the order of apprehension and the order of execution *relates* in an essential manner to the interior act, while it only *adds* goodness to the interior act of the will as executed. The reason this is the case is that the exterior act as apprehended remains the object of the interior acts of the will all the way through the act of the will of use. But the exterior act, as executed independently of the will, adds only an accidental goodness (qua executed) to the essential goodness (i.e. that goodness coming from the exterior act as apprehended) of the interior act of the will. Therefore, the first source of the possible mistake about assigning the exterior act to the accident of "what" cannot be seen as valid since the exterior act relates materially (i.e. essentially) to the interior act of the will and not accidentally.

The second source of the confusion has to do with the Thomistic texts themselves. The first thing that is necessary to do in this case is to consider Saint Thomas' distinction between *circa quid* and *quid*. He says that "in 'what' is included not only the effect, but even the object, such that both 'what' and 'about what' are understood."[38] Aquinas divides this circumstance into two parts, viz. the effect of the act and something pertaining to the object. Regarding that which is the effect of the act, he says:

> . . . On the part of that which is *quid*: for that someone pouring water
> on someone, washes him, is not the circumstance of washing; but that
> in the washing, he cools or warms him, heals or hurts him, this is the
> circumstance.[39]

He gives an example of what he means by *quid*, viz. "what" refers not to the washing, for that pertains to the substance of the act, but to the effect which is warming or cooling the person.

In the quote above in reference to the distinction between "what" and "about what," it may have appeared that he is saying that the object of the moral act is a circumstance, but this cannot be the case, as has already been discussed. However, Aquinas explains himself in the response to an objection[40] which says that *circa quid* is not a circumstance because the object is not a circumstance. His response is as follows:

> that condition of the cause from which the substance of the act
> depends, is not called a circumstance; but some other adjunct
> condition. As in the object, it is not called a circumstance of
> theft that it is belongs to another, for this pertains to the

---

[38]De Malo q. 2, a. 6: "in quid includatur non solum effectus, sed etiam obiectum, ut intelligatur et quod et circa quid."

[39]ST I-II, q. 7, a. 3, ad 3: ". . . ex parte eius quod est quid, nam quod aliquis perfundens aliquem aqua, abluat ipsum, non est circumstantia ablutionis; sed quod abluendo infrigidet vel calefaciat, et sanet vel noceat, hoc est circumstantia."

[40]ST I-II, q. 7, a. 3, obi. 3.

substance of theft; but that it is great or small.[41]

In the response, he makes the point that the circumstance which pertains to the object, viz. *circa quid*, does not refer to the object itself; rather it refers to something about the object which is circumstantial; e.g. that the thing taken is a lot or a little. He gives the same line of argumentation in the *De Malo* where he states that the circumstance does not give the species but refers to the quantity of the object.[42] The logic of this stands on the fact that sometimes in the object there is something which is moral[43], but does not differentiate what kind of act one is doing, yet does aggravate or diminish its goodness or badness. For instance, the act of theft of five dollars is not as bad as the act of theft of a hundred dollars. Both have the same species, viz. theft, but one is worse due to the quantity stolen. Moreover, this circumstance does not seem to pertain merely to the quantity of the object but can also seem to refer to a particular quality of the object. For example, in the *De Malo*,[44] Aquinas refers to the division of the act into its various aspects and causes, and on the part of the material cause to which the circumstance of *circa quid* refers, he gives the example of one hitting one's father or a stranger. It would, then, appear that this circumstance can also refer to a quality about the object. Therefore, *quid* refers to the effect and *circa quid* refers to a quality or quantity of the object, but not the object itself.

In the domain of psychology, these distinctions have some importance. There are directees who think that what they do exteriorly is not important; it is how they feel or what is "inside" that is important. Therefore, they do not see a problem with continuing a course of action that is destructive to themselves or others, because they feel they have chosen something that is acceptable. This is a sign of mental illness insofar as they are disconnected from reality and are not able to judge their actions objectively.

Moreover, many directees refuse to accept the effects of the actions which are causing their mental illness, i.e. the circumstance of *what* is not accepted as a cause of their problems. Sometimes the effect of the action is the mental illness itself. This is often noted in directees who, being attached to their object of mental illness, refuse to correct their activity because of some pleasure or joy they get out of the object of mental illness. Even if they want to correct the mental illness, they may not be able intellectually to grasp the effect their actions are having on them. Sometimes the effect of their actions is on something exterior to them which, once known by them, affects

---

[41]Ibid., ad 3: "illa conditio causae ex qua substantia actus dependet, non dicitur circumstantia; sed aliqua conditio adiuncta. sicut in obiecto non dicitur circumstantia furti quod sit alienum, hoc enim pertinet ad substantiam furti; sed quod sit magnum vel parvum."

[42]See De Malo, q. 2, a. 7, obi. 7 and obi. 8 and their corresponding responses ad 7 and ad 8.

[43]One may also say important psychologically, even if it does not affect the morality of an act.

[44]De Malo, q. 2, a. 6.

their mental health. For example, a woman who has an abortion might know it is wrong and she might even know it is killing an innocent human being, but her judgment is affected by some other consideration, such as placating her boyfriend who does not want to be a father.[45] After she goes through with the abortion, the reality of the effects of her action (the death of the child and herself becoming a killer) is recognized. The change in judgment is the result of the change in the phantasm, viz. the pressure from the boyfriend is no longer part of her experience so the effect it had on the phantasm is no longer present. Moreover, the association by the cogitative power and by judgment of the possible intellect with her self-knowledge of her abortive action becomes fixed. This will affect her self-knowledge and thereby torture her, especially if she has a sensitive conscience. In like manner, some alcoholics, being in a state of denial because the pleasures of alcohol affect their judgment, deny that the evil effects that they are causing others are real or very serious. Once they get a kind of clarity of mind from abstaining from alcohol for a while and admit their own problem, they are able to grasp the reality of the effects of their actions. Again, this is caused by a change in the phantasms; what was contained in the prior phantasm is no longer contained in the subsequent phantasm and so the possible intellect is not affected in its judgment. This too can affect people psychologically. This indicates that there are some psychological illnesses which can be from a complex cause or causes. Sometimes people's mental illness is from one cause, while the effects of their mental illness also cause them further mental distress or mental illness.

In relation to the circumstance of *about what*, some directees will have fixations on the qualities of certain objects which do not merit any consideration, e.g. it may be the case that a particular directee had a very good experience with an object of a particular color. As a result, he seeks objects of that color. He gets a pleasure from obtaining objects of this color, since he desires them based upon the cogitative power's assessment that objects of this color give one pleasure.

Sometimes the quality of the object indicates the very psychological illness itself, e.g. in the case of homosexuality. The fact that someone seeks to have conjugal relations or romantic involvement with a member of the same gender is a mental illness, since it is a connexus of problems in which the person judges as suitable something which is contrary to reality, i.e. it is contrary to the natural law. Therefore, the very object or quality of the object of the person's fixation can tell the psychologist the mental illness itself.

An observation is in order with respect to commensurate circumstances. This refers to the fact that sometimes it happens that one circumstance is actually another. For instance, it may happen that the circumstance of *where* is also the circumstance of *by what aid*. For example, a man may know that a particular location will aid him in committing his crime. Hence, he uses the location, or the location is a "means" by which he is able to commit his crime. Sometimes the circumstance of *who* has a connection to *where* as in the case of family relations.

---

[45]Examples of these types of occurrences and how they affect women psychologically is demonstrated in Reardon's book, *Aborted Women Silent No More*.

An analysis of circumstances may require that the psychologist leave his office and see the circumstances of the directee first hand. Sometimes the directee may not have a proper grasp of his circumstances, due to his judgment being affected because of the phantasms arising from his perception of his circumstances. Sometimes the directee may not know enough to be able to indicate to the psychologist which circumstances are a problem. Therefore, in these cases, the psychologist will need to go to the places where he thinks the directee might be having problems to get a grasp of the nature of the directee's circumstances.

D. Fourth Distinction - Mental Illnesses from an Interior Cause

Throughout this series, we have discussed the various interior causes of mental health and illness, therefore a full explanation would only serve to be redundant. However, some basic observations concerning this subject should be in order. Since mental health is some kind of mental virtue or a lack of mental vice and mental illness is some kind of mental vice, the psychologist should be knowledgeable of all of the kinds of virtues and vices of each and every faculty which affect the possible intellect as well as the virtues and vices of the possible intellect itself. He should also have a general knowledge of how the various psychological faculties can be affected by indisposition and the general categories of the general indispositions.[46] Therefore, he should have a knowledge of the different kinds of virtues, vices and material indispositions which affect (1) the sensitive appetites, (2) the common sense power, (3) imagination, (4) the memory, (5) the cogitative power, (6) the possible intellect and (7) the will. The full diagnosis of the psychologist consists in knowing the various causes and so knowledge of the exterior causes, while being part of the diagnosis, is only part of it. The psychologist must come to a knowledge of the state of the interior faculties as manifest in the actions and discussion he has with the directee. Therefore, the diagnosis will consist in locating which specific vices are causing the problem and in which faculty or faculties. To this end, simply talking with the directee, as well as other observations made in this series about how the psychologist can get to know the directee, would be pertinent.

Also, making use of a particular examen may be useful. A particular examen, much like its counterpart in the spiritual life, would contain the various vices or actions a directee could be performing. The directee can read over the examen and let the psychologist know what applies to him or what does not and to what degree. The directee can indicate what he thinks either in written or oral form.[47] This is similar to finding his predominant fault, as is done in the spiritual life. By use of a particular examen, the directee can help the psychologist determine which is the predominant vice

---

[46] A detailed knowledge would be more proper to a medical doctor or a psychiatrist. When a psychologist is uncertain whether something might be from a material indisposition, he should consult a competent medical doctor or psychiatrist.

[47] As to personality inventories, see the chapter on empirical considerations.

or disorder in his faculties. While this observation may seem too general, for the psychologist who knows how the faculties function and the various vices these faculties can have, what we have delineated here suffices for an introduction to psychology. For a more advanced study or knowledge of these matters, more would obviously be necessary.[48]

---

[48]This is, in fact, one of the primary projects that needs to be developed, viz. a detailed book containing all of the virtues, vices and indispositions of the various faculties for the sake of aiding the psychologist in diagnosing those whose difficulties require a more detailed consideration.

Chapter 3: Counseling

The basics of diagnosis, which, in the order of psychological counseling, we may say is the order of apprehension is the order by which one comes to precise knowledge of the problems of the directee. In the order of execution, i.e. in the process of counseling and aiding the directee, the psychologist must be able to counsel well. In this chapter, we shall discuss three areas which affect good counseling. The first is the nature of counseling itself; the second is the qualities which are necessary to be a good psychologist; the third is the qualities of the directee to be a good directee and to have hope of success of overcoming his mental illness. We have already noted that in the diagnosis stage, if the directee is found to have preternatural occurrences in his life or if his problems are strictly physical, he should be sent to competent individuals, such as a priest or a psychiatrist (or some medical professional) for help. This chapter deals strictly with those things which pertain to problems which are only psychological or require psychological counseling, as in the case of someone who not only needs medical or psychiatric help but also requires concomitant or subsequent counseling.

A. Counseling Itself

The object or finality of psychological counseling is mental health. Mental health consists in virtues in the various faculties, particularly the possible intellect. Therefore, the nature of true psychological counseling is virtue counseling, which we may say is the proper nomination of the counseling which this series is proposing. There has been a variety of practical observations made throughout this series on how to obtain the virtues pertaining to mental health so they will not be repeated here. However, from the chapter on prudence, it is clear that the act of counseling for a psychologist is an act of prudence insofar as he counsels the directee in actions which will lead to mental health and which will overcome or remove his mental illness. The proper finality of the virtue of prudence is to act well and to attain virtue, either that of prudence itself or other virtues. Since prudence is directive of the other cardinal virtues and since action is required to overcome mental vice, prudence moves the psychologist to counsel the virtues which are opposite to the mental vice. Since the mental vices or illnesses can be either in the possible intellect or the faculties which move or affect the possible intellect, psychology will also be concerned about attaining the virtues in those faculties insofar as they affect mental health. Diagnosis determines the mental vice: counseling prescribes the action to obtain the opposite mental virtue or mental health.

Not only should the psychologist seek to counsel the right actions to the directee according to prudence given his interior states and exterior circumstances so the directee can obtain mental health, he must also teach and counsel the directee on how to maintain that mental health once it is obtained. This is sometimes called *mental hygiene*. The ultimate goal of the psychologist is to provide the means for the directee to be self-sufficient without depending or relying on the psychologist. While this may not necessarily produce monetary success, that should not be the goal or aim of the psychologist.[1] Self-sufficiency comes through knowledge and virtue on the side of the directee. The virtue gives him the strength to depend on himself or on God and knowledge gives him the ability to know what to do. If the directee does not become self-sufficient, it is a sign that either the counseling is not right, the intentions of the psychologist are not right or the directee is not employing the proper means counseled by the psychologist.

Knowledge on the side of the directee should be two-fold. He should have at least some theoretical knowledge, i.e. principles by which he can judge what he is to do. This may require speculative as well as practical principles. Depending on the directee, the psychologist may find it advantageous to teach him some of the human ontology so that he knows the faculties, the vices in those faculties that he is suffering and how to deal with those faculties and vices. Sometimes the directee, once he knows how man functions, may gain a better self-concept and understanding and can therefore be more practical. The psychologist should avoid too much detail or surpassing the intellectual capabilities of the directee in providing this knowledge. The psychologist may need to explain to the directee the various faculties and their functions and how the vices in the various faculties are affecting his mental health. On the other hand, it may be easier to provide the directee with reading materials which explain the ontology and are at his level so that he can read and refer back to the materials. He would also be able to take it at his own pace.

The theoretical knowledge is not enough. The directee needs practical knowledge which comes through prudence and all of its integral parts. This is why it may be necessary for the directee to depend on the psychologist in the earlier stages for judgment about what to do, even if he knows the human ontology. The directee needs to develop prudence in relation to the object of his mental illness and since he will have a hard time judging what to do because of the affected phantasm, the psychologist, in the beginning, will have to help him out. It was observed that synesis is the virtue by which one knows those things which fall under the common law. Some directees will have problems that deal with common, every day issues and so it will be easier to guide them and get them on their feet psychologically than in cases where common laws and principles do not apply. In those cases where the problems of the directee and the judgment of his circumstances and actions require going to higher principles, the psychologist will have to rely on the virtue of gnome. In these cases, the directees will probably have to depend more on the psychologist for a greater length of time than in common cases.

As to obtaining and maintaining mental health, the directee must be counseled to practice custody of the mind and custody of the senses (eyes) in relation to the object of mental illness. Just as there are stages of diagnosis, there are different stages of

---

[1]The amount a psychologist charges has to be moderated. What some psychologists charge, particularly when they do not counsel anything of value which really helps the life of the directee, is unconscionable. While the psychologist has a right to make a decent, perhaps even a good living, he should not impoverish the directee in the process. As was earlier noted, he should not bilk the directee.

psychological counseling. The stages of psychological counseling are distinguished based upon the degree of mental illness of the directee and the degree of success he has had in following the counseling of the psychologist. In the beginning stages, the directee must be diagnosed and then given initial counseling to avoid those persons, places and things, if possible, which can aggravate his mental illness. The psychologist must give to the directee the basic counseling and knowledge of the problem and how to overcome it. In a subsequent stage, the psychologist helps the directee to continue to strive for mental health by helping him to perfect his knowledge of how to overcome any falls that he may have had in relation to the object(s) of mental illness. There comes a final stage where the psychologist and directee recognize that no more counseling may be necessary as long as the directee follows the regimen or counseling provided by the psychologist. At this stage, the door should be left open for the directee to come back should further problems arise.

As for the falls, the psychologist can recommend doing a particular examen at the end of each day to see how the directee is doing. This is commendable unless the nature of the mental illness as such requires a certain distance from the phantasms pertaining to the object of mental illness in order for the directee to begin overcoming the problem. Once he has gained a certain degree of virtue, he may be able to address the object more directly. When the consideration of the falls in relation to the mental illness are helpful, the psychologist can counsel the directee to consider how he did each day. When he falls, he should get back up. He should not be discouraged, but use each fall as an opportunity to strengthen his resolve and to gain knowledge for avoiding those kinds of falls in the future. When the psychologist meets with the directee, he can discuss the falls to measure the progress of the directee so that he can know when it is time for the directee to stand on his own without his aid.

Counseling should be done at regular intervals depending on the nature of the mental illness and the progress of the directee. The intervals in the beginning may need to be shorter than toward the end of the counseling. The psychologist should not allow long intervals in the beginning since the directee may be adversely affected when he is just starting out in gaining virtue. Frequent meetings will help to shape the prudence of the directee. As the directee progresses, the psychologist can lengthen the time between meetings as a sign to the directee that he needs to work on standing on his own more and that he needs the psychologist less. The directee should be assured that this is a good sign. If the directee has feelings of abandonment, the psychologist must address them directly so that the directee knows that the ultimate goal is to be entirely independent of the psychologist.

If a directee skips a meeting for a legitimate reason, the psychologist should not be disturbed. If, however, the directee skips one or more meetings, it may be a sign that either he lacks confidence in the psychologist or he fears addressing his problems. Good characteristics in the psychologist can aid the directee in placing his confidence in the psychologist and incline him to be open without fear in taking his problem to the psychologist.

Relationships of the directee can be used to the advantage of the psychologist and the directee alike. The psychologist should realize that encouragement and support on the side of those around the directee will have a direct impact on his progress. The support should be of two kinds, viz. natural and supernatural. Natural support is when the family encourages and supports the directee. They should not coddle the directee nor condone bad conduct but should support and encourage good conduct. The family and other relations can take an active interest, when it best suits the directee in the judgment of the psychologist, by helping minimize any exterior causes which might affect the directee. They can also engage in activities with the directee which will help him to develop the proper virtues and overcome his mental illness. However, relations must be counseled against overzealousness in this regard. On the other hand, the psychologist may have a directee whose relations are not interested in helping him, for either legitimate or illegitimate reasons. The psychologist must work around these things which may require more counseling to help the directee to deal with the lack of support. The relations can also support the directee supernaturally through prayers, sufferings and good works offered to God for the sake of the directee. The supernatural means are far more efficacious than the natural and the directee will advance much more rapidly if the family and friends can provide true supernatural support.

On a psychological level, support of friends and family helps to shape the self-image and self-concept of the directee and it also helps him to form phantasms in relation to the object of mental illness. Proper support from the relations helps the memory, since the directee can rely on the strength of those around him when he is weak and he will remember their support. If his mental illness has some connection to his relations, he will find that their support will help to cure or modify his phantasms in relation to them. This will help memory and the associations of the cogitative power and in turn affect his judgment and volition.

This psychological impact of relations pertains to the psychologist as well. The quality of the relationship the directee has with the psychologist can make or break the reception and following of counsel on the part of the directee. The psychologist must be careful to follow all proprieties and proper ethical standards in relation to the directee. On the other hand, he must have the qualities necessary for the directee to be able to approach him. The phantasm of the psychologist in the mind of the directee will affect the directee's perception of the counsel given. This is why the psychologist should have a rightly ordered and moderated concern about the directee's judgment of him. This must be based on virtue and has its finality only in helping the directee, rather than any concern on the side of the psychologist regarding human respect. It is a professional concern, for if the directee does not trust the psychologist or find him approachable and the psychologist becomes aware of this, either the psychologist must make adjustments to the directee or he should send the directee to someone whom he thinks the directee will find more approachable.

The psychologist should be the one to determine the times of meetings, taking into consideration the schedule of the directee and the nature of his mental illness. Some mental illnesses require a greater adaptation of schedule on the side of the psychologist, while others may require more frequent meetings. The reason the psychologist must be the one to determine these matters is that the psychologist must avoid allowing the directee to "get in the driver's seat" of the psychologist/directee relationship. While the psychologist must have all due care and concern for the directee, part of that care and concern is a recognition that some directees desire to control the psychologist and his life. This may be for a variety of reasons, but it is not good for the directee to think that he should control the situation. While the directee has every right to determine the control over his own life and the psychologist must respect that, that does not translate into allowing the directee to control the times, places and manner of meeting.

This indicates that the psychologist should be somewhat of a fatherly figure.[2] The father is the head of his household and so the psychologist should be the one directing the meeting. He should not allow the directee to control the content of the meetings either, since his mental illness will often drive him to fixate on the object of his mental illness. Since the object or end of counseling is the mental health of the directee, the psychologist should avoid unnecessary talk about things which are not germane to the mental illness. This does not mean that there are not cases in which small talk is appropriate. In fact, for some directees, in the beginning stages and throughout their counseling, small talk can take the mind of the directee off his problems, if that is suitable. Small talk can establish a trust in the psychologist on the part of the directee. Since we have a natural inclination to trust those with whom we agree since we perceive that they know the truth and will more than likely act according to it, the directee and psychologist can engage in small talk from time to time (but not all of the time nor most of the time) in order to build the trust of the directee in the psychologist as well as helping the directee to establish that the psychologist himself is normal and approachable.

Great caution must be taken when counseling another psychologist's directee. This should be done only when it is necessary, otherwise the directee should be encouraged to wait until he can talk to his own psychologist. When it is in fact necessary, it is best if the psychologist has some knowledge of the directee beforehand so as not to suggest courses of action which may be contrary to the counseling of his regular psychologist. It should normally be presumed that one who counsels the directee regularly has a greater grasp of the directee's circumstances and his interior state and therefore is more capable. But there may be instances where a directee has been counseled by a psychologist to do something which is objectively harmful to the directee or is objectively sinful. In this case, another psychologist may have to intervene but should normally do so with the directee's psychologist first. If the psychologist persists, a course of action may be necessary to get the directee away from the psychologist who is counseling things that are clearly and objectively harmful or sinful.

Some mental illnesses have their root in sin. For these cases, the psychologist should be aware of good priests to whom he can send the directee in order to go to confession and get pastoral and spiritual counseling regarding the sin. If the problem is strictly a matter of sin, the psychologist can simply refer the directee to the priest. If

---

[2]In the case of small children, female psychologists may be more successful since they can assume a motherly relationship with the directee. This, of course, depends on the nature of the mental illness for there may be some mental illnesses for which a more fatherly role would be more suitable for children. Also, due respect on the side of female psychologists must be given to the parents of the child, so as not to supplant the role of the child's true mother since that is not psychologically healthy.

the sin is only part of the problem and there are true psychological problems in addition to the sin, a joint effort of priest and psychologist will be necessary to help the directee overcome his problems. Even if the mental illness is not connected to sin, nothing forbids the psychologist to encourage the directee to pursue a strong spiritual life and to lead an active Catholic life. We have already delineated the advantages of this in the prior volume.

The psychologist can also encourage the directee to place images in his places of living and work which counter the disordered phantasms and bad mental habits. The frequent viewing of the images will help to affect the various faculties such as memory, the cogitative power, imagination and the possible intellect. This practice has an analogy in the Catholic tradition of decorating one's home with images of our Lord, our Lady, the saints and other Catholic images in order to lift one's mind and heart to God. In like manner, by using these various images or even written sayings placed in strategic locations, the directee can help himself to redirect and focus his attention on those things which will be mentally healthy.

Most directees will need to be counseled that they should not take consolations or pleasurable experiences in relation to their mental life as the principle of judgment of their progress or their mental health. Since many of them will have psychological difficulties in which the thinking about the object of their mental illness gives them a certain pleasure due to their disposition, they should be counseled not to consider whether something gives them a pleasant experience, but whether it is true and good for them mentally. They must also be counseled not to assume that desolations or feelings of sorrow are a sign that something is wrong. In the beginning stages of overcoming their mental illness, how they feel cannot be the principle of judgment about their progress and whether they are doing the right thing. They must get into the habit of following (right) reason and its dictates as informed by good counseling, rather than how they feel.

Lastly, we might suggest that in the process of counseling, one should eliminate predominant vices or faults first. In the diagnosis phase, the psychologist should come to knowledge of the particular problems of the directee and which are more prior in the order of their disordering effects. The psychologist should have the directee begin working on the predominant mental vice and later work on the less severe and damaging. This may take some time, but the psychologist may find that many of the lesser faults or vices are rooted in the predominant mental illness or mental vice. Once he removes that vice, the others will quickly fade, sometimes on their own.

B. The Qualities of a Good Psychologist

We have already mentioned throughout this series the various qualities which the psychologist must have. Among them are humility, faith, holiness of life, knowledge and prudence. But there are a few which have not been mentioned which should be addressed at this time. The psychologist should be a teacher of sorts insofar as he must teach the directee the nature of his problem and instruct him on how to overcome it. He must instruct the directee not only by what he says, but the psychologist must manifest that teaching in his own life. Because psychological counseling rests heavily on the instructional component, we see why the term "directee" is more suited, again, than the term "patient" which implies a manipulation or control. Rather, the directee must be willing to listen to what the psychologist will teach him, otherwise the counseling will have no effect.

The psychologist must be a man of kindness, but his kindness must flow from virtue and charity, not sentimentalism. If his kindness is not rooted in virtue or charity, it will tend to be duplicitous since he will be kind at times when it is not suited or when true prudence dictates that the effects of kindness not be extended to a particular directee. From this he will fall into a kind of simulation[3] or guile in which his actions are false. While being kind, he must not be soft and infortitudinous, but he must be able to be firm in a fatherly kind of way. The firmness should manifest good will and be rightly ordered. He should be frank so that the directee realizes that the psychologist is honest and does not hide things from him. His frankness should not degenerate into rudeness but should be a manifestation of the virtue of truthfulness[4] and lack of human respect.

The psychologist must not only be a man of knowledge and prudence but a man of intelligence. Lack of intelligence should be a sign that he ought not be a psychologist, since intelligence coupled with virtue is required to direct the minds of others. To do so is a grave responsibility and should only be taken on by those who have adequate intelligence. This intelligence should not be imagined by the psychologist but real as judged by those who train him for counseling. Ignorance and lack of intelligence would pose grave dangers to those who might be directed under him. Psychologists should be men of sound judgment, which is connected to prudence.

The psychologist should have fortitude so that he does not yield to the desires of the directee. He must be willing to tell a directee and others who affect the psychological health of the directee those things which may hurt their feelings but nevertheless are necessary. While one should not unnecessarily hurt the feelings of others, this should not keep the psychologist from saying things that are necessary for the psychological health of the directee, even if he thinks it could upset people emotionally. Since mental health, not the passions or emotions, are the primary concern of the psychologist, he must have a rightly ordered understanding and ability to direct the emotional life of others and, when necessary, contradict it for their psychological well being. All of this boils down to the fact that the psychologist should have the ability to give fraternal correction to his directee and others.[5]

The psychologist should also have the ability to console the directee when it will truly aid him. Prudence dictates that there are times when the directee should not be coddled but there are other times when, in order to direct the emotional life of the directee rightly, the psychologist will need to console him. Great care must be taken,

---

[3]Regarding the sin of simulation, see ST II-II, q. 111.

[4]Regarding the virtue of truthfulness, see ST II-II, q. 109.

[5]Fraternal correction is a work of charity, sometimes called admonishing the sinner. See ST II-II, q. 33.

however, so that the directee does not become emotionally dependent on the psychologist; a good psychologist will be aware of this possibility, particularly with vulnerable women. While he must have the ability to console, he must not be sentimental or affectionate with his directee since it does not suit their relationship. While these things have a place in family life, they do not in the professional life of a psychologist. The psychologist should not appear cold but should have an approachable personality and disposition. If he is a man of virtue, the virtue will have a universalizing effect on him so that he is not emotional, yet he will possess the virtues of benevolence and benignity. Virtue and concern for the directee will make him the kind of man who puts others at ease, which is necessary for the directee to be able to open himself up to the psychologist.

The psychologist should have the ability to encourage the directee at the right times. He should be a man of zeal, insofar as he should have a real desire to help those who are psychologically ill for their sake and not for his own. He should have a certain disinterestedness, however, in their progress, i.e. he should desire to see them progress for God's sake and for the sake of the directees and not for his own sake. This disinterestedness is a form of detachment from self, since if he is self-interested he will impede the mental health of the directee, since his counseling will be about himself rather than the directee. Lastly, the psychologist should be a man of self-knowledge and self-possession. He should have self-knowledge so as to know his moral, physical, psychological and spiritual limits in relation to different kinds of directees. He should be self-possessed so as to be able to control himself in those circumstances where he knows he has reached his limits, so that he can guide the directee to a psychologist who is able to address the specific difficulties of the directee.

C. The Qualities of a Good Directee

We have likewise postulated certain attributes which are necessary for the directee, such as humility, docility, etc. But there are a few more that should be observed so as to provide a better knowledge of the directees who are most likely to succeed in overcoming their mental illness. The directee must have a resolve or a resolution of will to overcome his mental illness. He must say to himself that he will do whatever it takes to obtain mental health. Since mental health is that which is in accord with virtue, this statement comes with the recognition that he will never sin in order to obtain mental health since the two are mutually contradictory. He must be willing to employ the means determined by the psychologist. His resolve in doing what he must will establish a constancy in his conduct. Those directees that are inconstant will have great difficulties and suffer frequent setbacks. The directee must strive for integrity which is the quality of soul in which one has not done nor does not allow himself to do anything contrary to virtue. Constancy and a striving for integrity are the ways out of mental illness.

The directee should be cooperative and respectful to the psychologist. Disdain, contempt or disrespect for the psychologist will block the judgment of the directee regarding the suggested counsel by the psychologist. In other words, without respect, the directee will disregard and ignore what the psychologist suggests. Trust and openness are necessary and these are connected to docility. If the directee does not trust the psychologist, the psychologist should refer the directee to someone he can trust. Because of the pleasure and attachments that many directees develop to the the mental illness itself or the object of their mental illness, many directees will not be open or willing to reveal themselves, because it will be painful to be separated from the object of their pleasure. They will suffer a fear of being open, not only because they may fear suffering or being wounded, but because the very opening up goes contrary to the inclination of the soul to enclose itself around the object of mental illness in order to hold onto its interior possession of the object of mental illness.

The directee should be sincere and benevolent, i.e. of good will. His resolution should give him a certain perseverance so that all of these things come together to manifest a clear intent to correct his problem. Many directees are simply "looking for an ear." This is a way of saying that many directees will be looking for someone with whom they can discuss their problems in order to further the attention and fixation on the problem rather than to correct it. This is why the psychologist must maintain control of the counseling process and if he detects this in his directee, he should keep a control over the direction of the discussion. This control should have as its finality not to continue to placate the directee in his mental illness, but to lead him out of it.

Chapter 4: The Role of the Empirical

A. General Observations

The last consideration to be given to the practical aspects of psychology is the precise role of the empirical sciences in relation to the science of psychology. Throughout the course of this series some of the data provided by the empirical sciences has been used. The method of its use is two-fold. First, the empirical sciences may conclude things pertaining to the material aspects of the faculties and still remain legitimate conclusions. However, if conclusions are drawn by an empirical science as to the philosophical significance of the finding, such conclusions are outside the scope of the empirical science and will be a violation of its proper methodology, often resulting in basic errors. Therefore, when a psychologist makes use of the data (premises) or the conclusions of an empirical science, he does so *as a philosopher*. He must employ a proper philosophical methodology in order to draw valid conclusions about the nature of man's faculties and how they function.[1] The data or legitimate conclusions from an empirical science become the premises in the deduction, and in some cases induction, in the philosophical method. However, the philosophical method must be employed since the faculties, mental health and illness and some of the influences on the faculties cannot be empirically tested or examined. Rather, they can only be adequately addressed by the philosophical method.

The second aspect of the use of data and conclusions from the empirical sciences is that psychology can make legitimate use of them, provided the psychologist realizes that the data and conclusions from the empirical sciences are limited in scope and do not provide a full understanding as to the causes and influences affecting mental health and illness. Psychologists must be careful not to conform the psychological science to the empirical sciences, when the reverse process is actually the case. The empirical sciences can only have a full understanding of the significance of their findings based upon a philosophical analysis as to how these findings fit in the overall scheme of psychology. As was mentioned in the first volume, psychiatry (and we may say some of the other empirical sciences) are legitimate in their study of man as long as the empirical scientists realize that the true meaning of their findings will only have full understanding in the science of psychology. For example, empirical scientists may discover the various chemicals involved in the passion of fear, but that does not entirely explain the nature and significance of fear. Only an understanding of the irascible appetite which is a composite faculty including a material and an immaterial element provides a full understanding of the nature of fear.

These observations will prevent psychologists from falling into two errors. The first is to think that empirical sciences have greater certitude than the philosophical and, as a result, to be tempted to conform the philosophical understanding of man and his faculties to the empirical sciences. These cannot give a complete picture of man since they do not take into consideration the immaterial aspects of man and his faculties. This

---

[1]The first chapter of the first volume in this series should be reviewed as to the proper methodologies that distinguish the philosophical from the empirical sciences.

was the temptation, often fallen into, by those psychologists of the last century who were trying to bridge the gap between a Thomistic understanding of man and the current empirical science of the day.[2] While their work is still important and useful in many aspects, there was a tendency to drop certain philosophically known truths in order to make the rapprochement between the orders of the sciences possible. In the end, this debilitated the psychological science. Rather, philosophical psychology must maintain its proper philosophical groundings in the truths which are known by reason. Upon turning to the empirical sciences, the philosophical science can gain a greater understanding of its own conclusions, e.g. when it is known that action causes material dispositions, the precise understanding of the dispositions (chemical and biological arrangement of the matter of the faculty) will be known in the empirical science. But this knowledge in the empirical science does not change the essential understanding of the philosophical psychology. If the empirical sciences proceed according to a proper methodology, with honesty and a desire to know the truth, their conclusions, remaining strictly in their own fields, will provide support for knowledge and conclusions in relation to philosophical psychology. It is only when the two spheres keep a proper distinction in methodology that the two can properly advance and the two can properly coexist harmoniously and with mutual help.

Not only do the empirical sciences aid philosophy, but philosophy will aid the empirical sciences by a certain "analogy of knowledge." Similar to the notion of the analogy of faith in which faith guides the philosophical sciences in knowing whether their conclusions are true or not, even though they are distinct sciences, so can the knowledge known about the nature of man in philosophy provide a proper understanding in the empirical sciences as to whether some of its conclusions are right or wrong. For instance, philosophical psychology will indicate what is proper behavior for a mentally healthy person. The empirical sciences can then set about determining the material dispositions that are proper to mental health. Another example would be that virtue has a concomitant disposition in the material side of the faculty. The empirical science, in having a knowledge of the virtues gained from philosophical psychology or ethics, can then set about determining the proper disposition to each virtue. In fact, in a certain sense, it is the philosophical sciences that provide a direction to the empirical. The empirical sciences can study all sorts of dispositions but they will never fully understand which dispositions are right for man and which are not. They may notice that some dispositions are good physiologically, but even that does not suffice when knowing whether the disposition is good in relation to mental health, virtue or things of this kind. While we have discussed how the material dispositions deteriorate due to vice, nevertheless, a full understanding of the proper dispositions and functioning of man is simply not known except by philosophy.[3]

---

[2]Examples would be, Rudolf Allers and Michael Maher.

[3]We may say even further, given the scope of these three volumes, that a full understanding would only be known by philosophy as informed by faith, as is evidenced in the second volume.

The second error that will be avoided in having a proper understanding of the relationship between the empirical and the psychological sciences is the tendency of some, since the time of Rene Descartes[4] and August Comte,[5] to think that the empirical are more noble sciences. Because of the nature of the objects studied in the philosophical sciences, some of which are immaterial, they are more noble sciences than the empirical. Philosophical psychology is a more noble science than empirical sciences which treat man because philosophical psychology deals with things that are immaterial and therefore are by nature more noble than the material. Knowing that philosophical psychology is a more noble science and has a fuller understanding of man will keep philosophical psychologists from failing to keep the proper divisions and methods of the sciences clear in their own minds and in practice.

Given the above observations, we can say that if the proper distinctions of the sciences and their methodologies are rigorously observed, nothing would forbid the empirical and the philosophical sciences from working together to increase our knowledge of man. It may be even possible for one man to engage in both sciences provided that he realizes that they are distinct sciences, and that when acting and reasoning as an empirical scientist, he is engaging in a different method and science than when he is reasoning and making observations as a philosopher.

B. Empirical Psychological Testing

We must, given the aforesaid, address certain forms of psychological and personality testing which proceed by an empirical methodology. We must say that such testing such as the MMPI and the like fail in their scope to take into consideration two components which invalidate the nature of the testing. The first is that the nature of the questions which they ask depend upon the veracity of the testee. While there is a veracity factor figured into the test, this does not prohibit someone of intelligence answering in a consistent manner yet falsely and thereby fooling the veracity factor. Even if the testee desires to be truthful, due to psychological conditions he may not be able to answer truthfully. In other words, it is entirely possible for a testee to answer all of the questions as truthfully as possible, but because of misassociations in the cogitative power or blindness in the possible intellect, he may not be able to see that the answers he gives are in fact false. This is a common problem experienced by all men who are blind to the very vices that they have. This is the lesson in Christ's observation to take out the beam in one's own eye before removing the mote in one's neighbor's.[6] It is too

---

[4]Descartes in his *Discourse on Method* inverted the order of the sciences based on a mathematical certitude (while ignoring metaphysical certitude which is more certain) rather than on the nobility of the nature of the material object of the science.

[5]Comte in his work entitled *Introduction to Positive Philosophy* associated the metaphysical and religious with an immature understanding of things and rooted all mature thought in positive sciences.

[6]Matthew 7:3.

easy given the human psychological structure and the effects of original and actual sin to be blind to one's own interior state. In fact, in mental illness, one is often blind to the very cause of the mental illness. Most directees simply do not know the cause. If they did know the cause and the nature of their problems and their disorders and therefore would be able to answer truthfully, they would have no need of a psychologist but only someone to encourage them to stop doing the things which cause their problems.

The second component which is lacking in the composition of the MMPI and like empirical testing procedures is that they fail to understand that certain psychological and personality factors are not open to empirical investigation because they are not empirical by nature. Virtue, vice, mental habits, the influence of the demonic, grace and the gifts of the Holy Ghost are not capable of empirical measurement. Therefore, since personality is more complex than material disposition, personality is not fully open to empirical measurement and investigation. If personality were identical to material disposition, such as in an animal, empirical testing would suffice. But since man is also immaterial in his nature and in his faculties, empirical testing is not a proportionate methodology to personality (material object of study). The fact that man has an immaterial component to his nature and the fact that the questions cannot fully and accurately reflect the interior state of the directee is proof that this form of testing simply will not be accurate, even though it often provides a false impression that it is. Some psychologists are so convinced of the ability of the MMPI and other forms of testing to provide knowledge of the state of the psychological faculties, that they actually will tell the directee that they now know what his personality is, even though the directee, when hearing the psychologist recount the results, finds the results completely incongruous with his interior state. Such experience will often be had by those experiencing supernatural influences in their lives. This also is why psychological analysis of this kind is folly in relation to the lives of saints.

Moreover, these psychological tests often admit of interpretation on the side of the psychologists. In other words, the yes and no questions will provide a series of numbers or statistics but their actual meaning is not always clear and therefore requires an interpretation on the side of the psychologist. His interpretation will be affected by his understanding of man's ontology, his own virtues and vices, his appetites which affect his judgment and so on. In this respect, the conclusions of the psychologist, since they are based on forms of induction from the data, can hardly be considered to be certain and therefore enjoy the same degree of certitude as true empirical research.

Moreover, many of the empirical tests, since they rely on statistical analysis, require yes or no answers or even in those that are more sophisticated, they require the person to determine the degree of something which he perceives in himself. First, virtues, vices, habits and the like are by degree (magnitude) and not discrete units which can be empirically measured.[7] Therefore there will always be a tendency towards inaccuracy based upon that very fact. Second, there is the problem of the person judging his own interior state, assigning a number or a yes or no to the question when his own

---

[7]Regarding the metaphysical distinction between discrete quantity and magnitude, see Aristotle's, *Metaphysics* (L. V, chap. 13).

judgment is often erroneous, especially when he is mentally ill. Some interior states or psychological states do not admit of a yes or no response to their existence because, again, they are by degree and may admit of admixture of their opposites, e.g. the question asked of women, "Do you like men?" The answer could be yes and no or even, "I like some men a lot and some men only a little", or even, "I hate men who are vicious and I love men who are virtuous." The question, however, does not admit of the variety of degrees and different perspectives of the individual. Even though other questions in the test may try to reveal this, it still requires a judgment or interpretation on the side of the testee that may not be apparent or may be falsely interpreted on the side of the psychologist. All of these considerations show that testing of psychological states, other than those that are strictly physical, is not truly scientific nor empirical. Asserting otherwise is based on ignorance, philosophical error, bad will or perhaps even all of the above.

However, nothing would prohibit the devising of a questionnaire which would include various psychological states, virtues, vices, habits, dispositions, forms of behavior, etc., to which the directee could respond to the best of his ability. This questionnaire could provide a point of reference for the psychologist and could be discussed in detail with the directee to get a better understanding of his problems. The questionnaire would not include yes or no questions but would have to be phrased in such a manner as to provide more of an essay-type format for the answer, which would allow the directee to express himself more fully rather than to be pigeon-holed, so to speak, by a constricted question when the true answer may not be yes or no.

C. Statistics

Does human behavior admit of statistical analysis? The answer is more complex than the question. Some behavior does admit of statistical counting (e.g. how many days of work you missed this year), while others do not. Again, since statistics require discrete units and much of behavior is also by degree which does not admit of discrete units since it is a magnitude, some human behavior does not admit of statistical analysis. For example, if one were to assert the statistic that seventy-five percent of all women strongly support a particular political candidate, the term "strongly" admits of degrees and therefore is not truly measurable empirically. Ironically, however, it appears that virtually every aspect of human conduct seems to be open to statistical analysis, except the success rates of psychologists.

Conclusion

The outline of a philosophical psychology presented in this series provides a basis for those seeking a Thomistic foundation for a rational psychology. It is not an advanced treatment of psychology which would include a detailed analysis of each mental vice and its causes. However, our hope in providing this series is to supply the intellectual foundation for future work in this area. It is not our expectation that this would be the final word but merely the beginning of establishment of the science of mental health on a course which will eventually provide greater success in the counseling of the mentally ill and in helping those who are mentally healthy to maintain their mental health. It is also our hope that those wishing to know more about Thomistic psychology and who wish to do a more advanced study would turn to St. Thomas' own writings: "Ite ad Thomam."

Bibliography

Abrams, Michael. *Brain Addiction Disorders.* Quest Publishing Company, Inc. 1999. As found at http://www.addictionrecov.org/paradigm/P_PR_S99/abrams.htm. (2 Dec. 2004).

Allers, Rudolf. *The Psychology of Character.* Sheed and Ward. London. 1931.

Amorth, Gabriel. *An Exorcist Tells His Story.* Ignatius Press. San Francisco. 1999.

--------------------. *An Exorcist: More Stories.* Ignatius Press. San Francisco. 2002.

Aristotle, *The Basic Works of Aristotle.* Richard McKeon, ed. Random House. New York. 1941.

Attwater, Donald. *A Catholic Dictionary.* The MacMillan Company, New York, 1941.

Augustine, *The City of God.* Penguin Books. New York. 1972.

Aumann, Jordan. *Spiritual Theology.* Christian Classics, Inc. Westminster, Maryland. 1987.

Baum, Robert. *Logic.* Holt, Rinehart and Winston. New York.1981.

Bennet, Howard. "Humor in Medicine." *Southern Medical Journal.* 2003.

Bergamo, Cajetan Mary da. *Humility of Heart.* TAN Books and Publishers, Inc. Rockford, Illinois. 1978.

Bourke, Vernon. *Ethics: A Text Book in Moral Philosophy.* Macmillan Co. New York. 1963.

Brennan, Robert. *General Psychology; An Interpretation of the Science of Mind Based on Thomas Aquinas.* The Macmillan Company. New York. 1938.

--------------------. *Thomistic Psychology; A Philosophic Analysis of the Nature of Man.* The Macmillan Company. New York. 1941.

Canons and Decrees of the Council of Trent. trans. By Rev. H.J. Schroeder, O.P. B. Herder Book Co., St. Louis. 1930.

Carpenter, Siri. "Sights Unseen." *Monitor on Psychology*, vol. 32, no. 4, April 2001.

Catechism of the Council of Trent. TAN Books and Publishers, Inc. Rockford, Illinois. 1982.

Catechismus Catholicae Ecclesiae. Libreria Editrice Vaticana. 1997.

The Catholic Encyclopedia. The Gilmary Society. New York. 1929.

The Catholic Encyclopedia Dictionary. The Gilmary Society. New York. 1941.

Coffey, Peter, *Ontology, or the Theory of Being; an Introduction to General Metaphysics.* P. Smith. New York. 1938.

Cole, Basil. *Music and Morals: A Theological Appraisal of the Moral and Psychological Effects of Music.* Alba House. New York. 1993.

Comte, Auguste. *Introduction to Positive Philosophy.* Hackett Publishing Company., Inc. Indianapolis. 1988.

Congregation for Catholic Education, *Ratio Fundamentalis,* 1980 (no particular edition cited).

Cross, Richard, "Can Catholics Council? The Loss of Prudence in Modern Humanist Psychology". Taken from a lecture to the faculty and students of Christendom College on October 22, 1993.

Cunningham, Francis. *The Christian Life.* Priory Press. Dubuque, Iowa. 1959.

Davis, Henry. *Moral and Pastoral Theology.* Sheed & Ward. New York. 1943.

Deferrari, Roy, J., ed. *A Latin-English Dictionary of St. Thomas Aquinas.* St. Paul

Editions. Boston. 1986.

Father Delaporta. *The Devil*. TAN Books and Publishers, Inc. Rockford, Illinois. 1982.

De Montfort, Louis. *True Devotion to the Blessed Virgin*. Montfort Publications. Bay Shore, New York. 1975.

Denzinger, Henricus and Adulfus Schönmetzer. *Enchiridion Symbolorum: Definitionum et Declarationum de Rebus Fidei et Morum.* Herder. Friburg. 1976.

Descartes, Rene. *Discourse on Method.* Trans. by Donald A. Cress. Bobbs-Merrill. Indianapolis. 1984.

Duerk, Hilarion. *Psychology in Questions and Answers*. P. J. Kenedy and Sons. New York. 1936.

Edwards, Paul, ed. *The Encyclopedia of Philosophy*. MacMillan Publishing Co., Inc., and The Free Press. New York. 1972.

Esser, Gerard. *Psychologia; in Usum Scholarum.* Typis Domus missionum ad St. Mariam. Techny, Illinois. 1931.

Fanfani, P. Ludovicus J., O.P. *Manuale Theorico-Practicum Theologiae Moralis ad Mentem D. Thomae.* Libreria "Ferrari." Roma. 1950.

Forbes, G.B., G.R. Lebo, Jr. "Antisocial Behavior and Lunar Activity: A Failure to Validate the Lunacy Myth." *Psychological Reports.* June, 1977.

Frued, Sigmund. *The Basic Writings of Sigmund Freud; Translated and Edited, with an Introduction, by Dr. A. A. Brill.* The Modern Library. New York. 1938.

Garrigou-Lagrange, Reginald. *The Three Stages of the Interior Life: Prelude of Eternal Life*. TAN Books and Publishers, Inc. Rockford, Illinois. 1989.

----------------------------------. *De Gratia* (no particular edition cited).

Gihr, Nicolas. *The Holy Sacrifice of the Mass; Dogmatically, Liturgically and Ascetically Explained.* B. Herder Book Co. St. Louis, Missouri. 1935.

Gredt, Josephus. *Elementa Philosophiae Aristotelico-Thomisticae.* Herder and Co. Friburgi Brisgoviae. 1937.

Grenier, Henri. *Cursus Philosophiae*, Le Séminaire de Québec. Quebeci. 1953.

Guardini, Romano. *The Humanity of Christ: Contributions to a Psychology of Jesus.* Pantheon Books, New York. 1964.

Häring, Bernard. *The Law of Christ: Moral Theology for Priests and Laity*. Vol. 1. Trans. by Edwin G. Kaiser, Newman Press. Westminister, Maryland. 1964.

Healy, Edwin. *Medical Ethics*. Loyola University Press. 1956. Excerpts from this text were taken from http://www.ewtn.com/library/DOCTRINE/HYPNOTSM.TXT. (2 Dec. 2004).

Herrell, Leah. "A Research Proposal: Inattentional Blindness: Can Auditory Distractor Make a Difference?" http://hubel.sfasu.edu/courseinfo/SL02/lh2noisetask.htm. (2 Dec. 2004).

Hock, Conrad. *The Four Temperaments*. Bruce Publishing Co. Milwaukee. 1934.

Holy Bible. Douay Rheims Version. TAN Books and Publishers, Inc. Rockford, Illinois. 1989.

Image Research Center. *fMRI Study of Correlation between Musical Training and Math Ability*. http://www.irc.chmcc.org/Research_Areas/brain/fMRI/musicmathcorr.htm. (1 Oct. 2003.)

John of the Cross. *Ascent of Mount Carmel* as found in *The Collected Works of St. John of the Cross*. ICS Publications. Washington, D.C. 1979.

John Paul II. *Codex iuris canonici.* 1983.

---------------. *The Acting Person.* Trans. by Andrzej Potocki. D. Reidel Publishing Co. Boston. 1979.

---------------. *Veritatis Splendor. Acta Apostolicae Sedis.* Vol. 85 (1993).

Jones, E. Michael. *Degenerate Moderns: Modernity as Rationalized Sexual Misbehavior.* Ignatius Press. San Francisco. 1993.

---------------------. *Libido Dominandi: Sexual Liberation and Political Control.* St. Augustine's Press. South Bend, Indiana. 2000.

Kihlstrom, John. F. *Hypnosis, Memory and Amnesia.* http://socrates.berkeley.edu/~kihlstrm/hypnosis_memory.htm. 17 Oct. 2003. (Updated version of a paper presented at the 75th annual meeting of the Association for Research in Nervous and Mental Disease, "Biological and Psychological Perspectives on Memory and Memory Disorders", New York, December 1995.)

Kinkead, Thomas. *An Explanation of the Baltimore Catechism of the Christian Doctrine for the Use of Sunday-School Teachers and Advanced Classes.* TAN Books and Publishers, Inc. Rockford, Illinois. 1988.

Lieber, Al. "Human Aggression and the Lunar Synodic Cycle." *Journal of Clinical Psychiatry.* 39[5], May 1978.

Leo XIII. *Aeterni Patris.* Rome. 1879.

-----------. *Arcanum divinae sapientiae.* Rome. 1922.

Mack, Arien. "Inattentional Blindness." *Psyche.* 5(3), May 1999.

Maher, Michael. *Psychology: Empirical and Rational.* Longmans, Green, and Co. New York. 1910.

Matheson, *Introductory Psychology: the Modern View.* Dryden Press. Hinsdale, Illinois. 1982.

Maturin, B.W. *Self Knowledge and Self Discipline.* Longmans, Green and Co. New York. 1917.

McInerny, Dennis. *Philosophical Psychology.* Alcuin Press. Elmhurst, Pennsylvania. 1999.

McHugh, John and Charles Callan. *Moral Theology; a Complete Course Based on St. Thomas Aquinas and the Best Modern Authorities.* J. F. Wagner, Inc. New York. 1929.

Nelson, Daniel Mark. *The Priority of Prudence. Virtue and Natural Law in Thomas Aquinas and the Implications for Modern Ethics.* Pennsylvania State University, University Park, Pennsylvania. 1992.

Noldin, H., S.J., *Summa Theologiae Moralis: De Principiis.* Vol. 1. Oeniponte, Innsbruck. 1956.

O'Donnell, Thomas. *Medicine and Christian Morality.* Alba House. Staten Island, New York. 1991.

Ott, Ludwig. *Fundamentals of Catholic Dogma.* TAN Books and Publishers, Inc. Rockford, Illinois. 1974.

Parente, Pietro. *Dictionary of Dogmatic Theology.* Bruce Publishing Company. Milwaukee, 1951.

Paul IV. "Humanae Vitae." in *Acta Apostolicae Sedis.* Vol. 60 (1968).

BIBLIOGRAPHY

Pius IX. *Ineffabilis Deus*. Rome. 1854.

Pius X. *Pascendi Dominici Gregis*. Rome. 1907.

Pius XI. *Casti Connubii*. Rome. 1930.

Pius XII. *Musicae Sacrae*. Rome. 1955.

Plato, *The Collected Dialogues.* Pantheon Books. New York. 1966.

Prummer, O.P. Dominicus. *Manuale Theologiae Moralis*. Herder & Co. Friburgus. 1931.

Radiological Society of North America. Press release entitled, "Violent Video Games Trigger Unusual Brain Activity in Aggressive Adolescents." December 2, 2002.

Reardon, David. *Aborted Women Silent No More*. Loyola University Press. Chicago. 1987.

Regis, L.M., O.P. *Epistemology*. The Macmillan Company. New York. 1959.

Reith, Herman. *An Introduction to Philosophical Psychology*. Prentice-Hall. Englewood Cliffs, New Jersey. 1956.

Ripperger, Chad. "The Morality of the Exterior Act" as found in *Angelicum*. LXXVI (1999).

--------------------. "The Species and Unity of the Moral Act" as found in *The Thomist*. 59, 1, January, 1995.

Rituale Romanum. Benzinger Brothers. Chicago. 1947.

Royce, James E. *Man and His Nature; a Philosophical Psychology*. McGraw-Hill. New York. 1961.

Sheen, Fulton. *Whence Come Wars*.

Shipley, Thorn, ed. *Classics in Psychology*. Philosophical Library, Inc. New York. 1961.

Skinner, B.F. *Walden Two*. (No particular edition cited.)

Sutter, Abbé Paul. *Lucifer: or the True Story of the Famous Diabolic Possession in Alsace*. Bouch Printing Works, Ltd., London, 1922.

Szymanski, Dominic. *A Notebook on the Devil and Exorcism: An Exorcist and Other Authorities Tell the Truth about the Devil*. Franciscan Marytown Press. Kenosha, Wisconsin. 1974.

Tanquerey, Adolphe. *The Spiritual Life*. The Newman Press. Westminster, Maryland. 1930.

Theresa of Avila. *The Book of Her Life,* as found in *Collected Works*. Vol. I. ICS Publications. Washington, D.C. 1987.

Thomas Aquinas. *Thomae Aquinatis Opera Omnia*. Iussu Impensaque Leonis XIII, edita. Roma: ex Typographia Polyglotta et al. 1882.

---------------------. *Summa Contra Gentiles*. trans. Anton Pegis. University of Notre Dame Press. 1975.

Vatican Council II: The Conciliar and Post Conciliar Documents. Austin Flannery, ed. Liturgical Press. Collegeville, Minnesota.1975.

Vedantam, Shakar. "Telling Lies Produces Changes in Brain, Researchers Find." As found in the *Washington Post*. November 12, 2001.

Watson, John. "Psychology as a Behavioralist Views It" as found in *Classics in Psychology*. Thorne Shipley, ed. Philosphical Library, Inc. New York. 1961.

Weller, Philip. *The Roman Ritual*. Bruce Publishing Company. Milwaukee. 1952.

BIBLIOGRAPHY

Wilson, Jim. "Cognitive Cords." *Popular Mechanics.*
http://www.popularmechanics.com/science/research/2002/3/cognitive_chord
s/index.phtml. (1 Oct. 2003).

Wolman, Benjamin. *Dictionary of Behavioral Science.* Van Nostrand Reinhold Co. New
York. 1973.

Wuellner, Bernard J. *A Dictionary of Scholastic Philosophy.* Bruce Publishing Co.
Milwaukee. 1966.

------------------------. *Summary of Scholastic Principles.* Loyola University Press.
Chicago. 1956.

Ziv, A. "Teaching and Learning with Humor: Experiment and Replication." *Journal of
Experential Education.* 1988.

Diagram of the Ontological Structure of Man

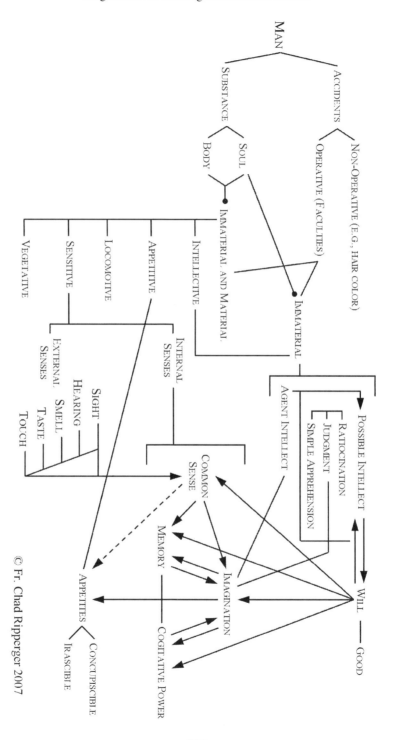

© Fr. Chad Ripperger 2007

Brief Lexicon

A

Abstraction: the process by which one proceeds from particulars to universals; to separate a part from the whole; an operation performed by the agent intellect in which it draws out the essence or concept latent in the phantasm, i.e. an operation in which the agent intellect makes explicit to the possible intellect the essence implicit in the phantasm in the passive intellect.

Accident: that which does not exist of itself but in another as in a subject; refers to the last nine of the ten categories of Aristotle.

Accident, Inseparable: an accident which once received cannot be removed; e.g. gender.

Accident, Proper: an accident which always accompanies a given substance; whenever a given substance exists, the accident is likewise present; an accident which is essential to a thing, e.g. the intellect in man.

Act: in ontology, it refers to the existence of a thing.

Act, First: the form of a thing, in the sense of its essence or integrity; the faculty or principle of operation, e.g. the intellect or will; counter-distinguished from second act.

Act, Second: the operation of some nature (i.e. that which is in first act); the operation of some faculty; counter-distinguished from first act.

Agent: in ethics, it refers to he who acts; in ontology, it refers to that which causes.

Agere Sequitur Esse: Act (or operation) follows being; as a thing is so it acts; the mode of being determines the mode of operation; everything acts according to its nature in act.

Analogy: the use of two or more terms in which their meaning is partly the same and partly different; predication common to several inferiors of a name, which is accepted in different senses, in such a manner, nevertheless, that some principle warrants its common applicability.

Anthropology, Philosophical: the philosophical science which has man as its object of study.

Appetite: an active tendency or faculty which inclines toward a given object or end; the conscious striving for an end known either spiritually or sensorially.

Apprehension, Simple: the first act of the intellect by which one grasps the essence of a thing; sometimes called understanding.

Argument: a course of reasoning aimed at demonstrating the truth or falsity of something; sometimes used as a synonym of syllogism.

Attribute: that quality which benefits a thing in a peculiar and original manner, so that, if other things share in it, it befits that thing above all and for the most part; a perfection naturally needed or present in a thing; some thing which belongs to or is predicable of a thing which is not accidental but essentially belongs to the thing; sometimes refers to the proper accident of a thing which does not enter into its definition.

B

Being: (1) a thing which exists; (2) the act of existence.

Body: the material element in a composite living thing.

C

Categories: the predicates of a proposition; the modes of being that may be asserted in predication, which are substance, quantity, quality, relation, place, time, habit, disposition, action and passion.

Cause: that upon which something depends for its existence or for its coming to be.

Choice: an act of the will in which the means are selected.

Change: the process by which one thing becomes another; a transition from one form of existence to another.

Circumstances: those which are said to stand around a thing and are not essential to it.

Composite: a being which is made up of more than one part or element.

Composition: a form of the second act of the intellect (judgment) in which two things are placed together, i.e. one thing is affirmed of another; counter-distinguished from division.

Comprehension: Understanding; when counter-distinguished from apprehension it refers to an exhaustive understanding of a given essence, whereas apprehension refers to the presence of the thing known to the intellect without an exhaustive understanding of the essence of the thing.

Concept: the essence of a thing as it exists in the mind of the knower.

Conclusion: a statement which is inferred from two premises.

Connatural: that which belongs to a nature and exists in it from its beginning; innate; not acquired; present by natural endowment.

Conscience: a form of the second act of the intellect in which the moral goodness or badness of an act is judged; sometimes incorrectly referred to as a faculty.

Conscious: a state referring to sensitive or intellective awareness.

Corruption: the going out of existence of a thing; in a substantial change, the one substance that goes out of existence is said to corrupt; counter-distinguished from generation.

D

Deduction: a form of logical reasoning in which the conclusion necessarily follows from the premises; a form of argumentation in which one proceeds from the general to the particular.

Definition: the formulation of the essence of a thing.

Disposition: the ability to effect or suffer something; the innate readiness of something for certain kinds of activity; the order or arrangement of that which has parts.

Distinction of Reason or Mental Distinction: a distinction in the mind of the knower which is not really distinct in the thing, i.e. in reality.

Division: a form of the second act of the intellect (judgment) in which two things are separated, i.e. one thing is denied or negated of another; counter-distinguished from composition.

E

Effect: that which depends upon something for its existence or for its coming to be.

Empiricism: a philosophical system or epistemology which asserts that man only has sense knowledge of reality; a philosophical system which envisions or treats man as something strictly material.

End: that toward which something aims; that toward which something is ordered or directed.

Enthymeme: a logical argument in which one or more of the premises or the conclusion is missing.

Epistemology: the philosophical science which studies how man knows.

Equivocal: the use of a term which has two or more meanings.

Essence: what a thing is; that by which a thing is what it is.

Ethics: the philosophical science which studies human action from the point of view of its moral goodness or badness.

Evil: a lack of a due good or perfection.

Existence: the actuality of a thing; the perfection by means of which something is an existent; that by which something is.

F

Faculty: a potentiality or power of the soul by which it acts; a proper accident flowing from the essence of the soul by which it acts.

First Philosophy: a branch of metaphysics which studies the first principles or causes of things.

Form, Substantial: the constitutive element of a substance which is the principle or source of its activity and which determines it to a definite species or class; that which makes matter into a certain kind of being, e.g. the form of dogness makes this matter be a dog; the intelligible structure, characters constituting a substance or species of substances, as distinguished from the matter in which these characters are embodied.

Formal Object: the point of view taken; the second element of every science which corresponds to the second act of the intellect.

Fortitude: willingness to fall into battle; the moral virtue, residing in the irascible appetite, which concerns the arduous good; the gift of the Holy Spirit, residing in the irascible appetite, which aids one in the spiritual battle that he may attain heaven.

Freedom: As to the will: the intrinsic capacity of the will for self-determination; as to man's external acts: the state or quality of not being forced or determined by something external insofar as it is joined to a definite internal faculty of self-determination.

G

Generation: the coming into existence of a thing; in a substantial change, the one substance that comes into existence is said to be generated; counter-distinguished from corruption.

Genus: that part of the essence of anything which belongs also to other things differing from it in species; a class of objects possessing an identical character and consisting of two or more sub-classes or species; counter-distinguished from species.

Good: that which is desirable; that toward which all things aim; a transcendental, i.e. being as seen from the point of an appetitive power; the true or real good is that which contains all the necessary perfections due to it; the apparent good is that which is good only under a certain aspect.

H

Habit: A habit is a quality in a faculty which inclines the faculty towards a specific form of action.

Hylomorphism (or Hylemorphism): the doctrine that all physical things are composed of matter and form.

I

Imagination: the interior sense which maintains the presence of the phantasm in the passive intellect and which allows the combination of previous sense experience with the present phantasm.

Immanent: a form of action which remains with or in the agent; counter-distinguished from transient.

Induction: a form of philosophical reasoning in which the conclusion does not necessarily follow from the premises, the certainty of the conclusion is based upon the amount of support provided by the premises; a form of argumentation in which one proceeds from the particular to the general.

Inference: in logic, the procedure by which one derives the conclusion from the premises.

Intellect: the faculty by which a spiritual substance knows.

Intellect, Agent: an immaterial part of the intellect of man which abstracts the essence of a thing from a given phantasm.

Intellect, Passive: the material part of the intellect of man, which includes the common sense power, memory, imagination and the cogitative power (the brain).

Intellect, Possible: the immaterial part of the faculty in man by which he knows; this faculty performs three acts: (1) simple apprehension, (2) judgment and (3) ratiocination.

Intention: in the broad sense, any act of the will directed toward some thing; in the strict sense, the act of the will concerning a possibly obtainable end.

J

Judgment: the second act of the possible intellect which produces a proposition.

Justice: to give someone his due; the moral virtue, residing in the will, which concerns what is due to another.

K

Knowledge: the possession of the thing known by the knower.

L

Law: a promulgated ordinance of reason with respect to the common good, by he who has care of the community (ST I-II, 90, 4 - quaedam rationis ordinatio ad bonum commune, ab eo qui curam communitatis habet, promulgata).

Law, Eternal: the concept or notion of the divine wisdom insofar as it is directive of all acts and motions (ST I-II, 93, 1 - ratio divinae sapientiae, secundum quod est directiva omnium actuum et motionum).

Law, Natural: the expression or participation in the eternal law by a rational creature; the sum total of the ethical precepts implanted by God in the rational nature of man.

Logic: the philosophical science and art of right reasoning.

Love: willing the good of another; the act of the will by which one desires the good of another, either for one's own sake or for the sake of the other.

M

Man: rational animal; an embodied rational soul.

Man, Philosophy of: see anthropology, philosophical.

Matter: that out of which something is made; the passive element in change; the substrate of substantial change.

Method: the *modus procedendi* or way of proceeding in a given science.

Memory: the interior sense which stores and retrieves sense knowledge or data.

Metaphysics: a philosophical science which studies being and its attributes; metaphysics is broken into three branches: (1) first philosophy, (2) ontology (sometimes called metaphysics in the more restrictive sense) and (3) natural theology.

Motion: the reduction of a thing from potency, insofar as it is in potency, to act.

N

Nature:the essence of a thing as it is a principle of motion or action.

Necessary: that which cannot be otherwise.

Non Sequitur: a conclusion which does not follow from its premises.

O

Object: a thing - "res" in Latin; a being; that about which some action or faculty concerns itself.

Ontology: the branch of metaphysics which studies being qua being.

Operation: see second act.

P

Passion: the condition of a thing (or faculty) as acted upon by other things; sometimes refers to the appetites.

Perfection: the state of being complete; a state in which a thing possesses all the goods proper to it.

Person: an individual substance of rational nature.

Phantasm: an image residing in the imagination.

Philosophy: love of wisdom; the science which studies the essences of things.

Place: the boundary of the containing body at which it is in contact with the contained body; the innermost motionless boundary of a thing; one of the ten categories.

Potency: that which is capable of being actualized; sometimes used in the same sense as faculty.

Power: see faculty.

Power, Cogitative: the interior sense which has the power of association and prepares the phantasm for abstraction; proper only to man and counter-distinguished from the estimative power in animals.

Power, Estimative: the power in the intellect of an animal which has the capacity to make associations; the counterpart to the cogitative power in man – however, an estimative power of an animal does not prepare the phantasm for abstraction since there is no immaterial part to the intellect of an animal.

Predicaments: see categories.

Premise: a statement or proposition used in support of a conclusion.

Premise, Major: the premise in a syllogism which contains the major term, i.e. the predicate term.

Premise, Minor: the premise in a syllogism which contains the minor term, i.e. the subject term.

Principle: that from which any thing in any way proceeds; the starting point of being, change or thought.

Principle, First: a principle which does not proceed from a prior principle in its own series.

Principle, Logical: a truth from which other truths proceed, i.e. a principle of knowledge; a logical principle may be expressed in (a) an ontological formula, then a general truth or a definition is expressed in terms of being; (b) a logical formula, then a general truth or proposition is expressed in terms of thought or speech (that is, of affirmation, negation, or predication). The philosophical principles of thought in scholasticism are usually principles about real beings.

Principle, Ontological: a being from which another proceeds.

Principle, Practical: a principle concerned with activity, whether doing or making.

Principle, Real: see principle, ontological.

Principle, Self-Evident: a principle which is immediately known, i.e. one which is seen to be true without reasoning or deduction from other principles.

Priority: when one thing is before another, in the order of being, time, causality or thought.

Privation: the condition of a substance that lacks a certain quality which it is capable of possessing and normally does possess.

Property: a characteristic feature of a thing; an accident essential to and common to all members of a class or species; an attribute that does not form part of the essence of its subject but necessarily results from that essence as a formal effect; a characteristic trait or attribute of a class of things.

Proposition: an assertion which affirms or denies something; the product of the second act of the intellect, viz. judgment.

Prudence: the moral virtue by which practical reason rightly judges the means.

Q

Quality: that by virtue of which a thing is such and such; one of the ten categories.
Quantity: how much; the magnitude of a thing; the amount; one of the ten categories.

R

Ratiocination: the third act of the intellect in which one goes from judgment to judgment; sometimes called reasoning.
Rationalism: a philosophical system in which the criterion of truth is not sensory but intellectual and deductive, i.e. the criterion for truth is reason and not reality.
Realism: the epistemological position which holds that man can have true intellectual knowledge of things.
Realism, Moderate: a form of realism which holds that we can have true intellectual knowledge by means of the senses.
Realism, Radical: a form of realism which does not distinguish between reality and the thing known.
Reason: the intellectual principle in man by which man knows; the intellect.
Reasoning: see ratiocination.
Relation: the reference of one thing to another; those things are called relative which, being said to be either *of* something else or *related* to something else, are explained by reference to that other thing; one of the ten categories.
Relation, Causal: a real relation between two things which exists by virtue of the fact that one of the things causes the existence of the other.
Relation of Reason: a relation between two things which only exists in the mind of the knower and not in the things themselves.
Relation, Real: a relation which actually exists in reality between two things.

S

Science: an organized body of knowledge; knowledge of something through its causes; the intellectual virtue, residing in the intellect, by which one judges rightly (i.e. it directs the second act of the intellect of judgment) about the things of this world; the gift of the Holy Spirit, residing in the intellect, by which we judge the things of this world the way God judges them.
Science, Subalternated: a science which receives its principles from a higher science.
Self-Evident: that which is immediately known; what is self-evident is prior to and not capable of proof.
Sense, Common: the interior sense which unifies the sense data from the five exterior senses into a single phantasm and expresses it into the imagination; the epistemological acceptance of the fact that the senses put man in contact with reality and that man can derive true intellectual knowledge from sense knowledge; the underlying principle in moderate realism.
Senses, Exterior: touch, taste, smell, hearing and sight.
Senses, Interior: the sub-faculties of the passive intellect, viz. common sense, memory, imagination and the cogitative power.

Simple: that which is not composed of parts.

Sign: an intelligible referent to another thing.

Significance: the intelligible content of a sign.

Soul: the substantial form of the body; the formal element in a living composite being.

Species: the subdivision of a genus constituted by the specific difference; common nature or essence; counter-distinguished from genus.

Subject: in the ontological order, that upon which accidental determinations depend for existence, or that in which forms are received; in the logical order, that of which something is predicated.

Substance: that which exists of itself and not in another as in a subject.

Syllogism: a logical argument in which a conclusion is inferred from a major premise and a minor premise.

Synderesis: the habit by which one judges rightly concerning the first principles of practical reason.

T

Temperance: the moral virtue residing in the concupiscible appetite by which one attains moderation with respect to bodily goods.

Theology, Natural: the branch of metaphysics which has as its object of study God, his attributes, separated substances (angels) and creation as they can be known by the natural light of reason by means of created effects.

Theology, Revealed: the sacred science, which by the light of faith, studies the deposit of faith, i.e. that which has been revealed by God.

Time: the measurement of motion; one of the ten categories.

Transcendentals: being or being under a certain aspect, i.e. being, one, true, the good and the beautiful; that which overflows or applies to all of the categories and therefore applies to every thing.

Transient: a form of action which does not remain with or in the agent; a form of action in which the motion passes from the agent to the patient; counter-distinguished from immanent.

Truth: the adequation of the intellect and thing ("adaequatio intellectus et rei"); the congruity between what is in the intellect or mind of the knower and the thing known as it exists in reality.

U

Understanding: the capacity to grasp the essence of the thing; the first act of the possible intellect; the intellectual virtue which aids one in grasping the essence of things; the gift of the Holy Spirit, residing in the possible intellect, by which we intuitively grasp the things pertaining to faith.

Univocal: the use of two or more terms in which their meanings are the same, for instance the word "animal" can be applied with the same meaning to a dog and a cat.

V

Virtue: a good habit; that which makes the faculty act well and perfects the faculty; the capacity to do something.
Violence: motion contrary to the nature of a thing.

W

Will: rational appetite; an elicited appetite which follows upon intellectual cognition, i.e. the good as apprehended by the intellect; the immaterial faculty of intellective desire.
Wisdom: the consideration of the ultimate causes of things; the intellectual virtue, residing in the possible intellect, aiding the third act of the intellect, by which we consider the ultimate causes of things; the gift of the Holy Spirit, residing in the possible intellect, which aids us in the consideration of God, His attributes and the things of this world as they are in relation to God.